"TR—OUTDOORSMAN AND CONSERVATIONIST"
Bob Scriver—1988

A limited edition (250 numbered copies) bronze offered by the Boone and Crockett Club as one of its special Centennial Year Commemoratives. Details may be obtained from the Club's office.

Records of
North American
Big Game

A BOOK OF THE BOONE AND CROCKETT CLUB
CONTAINING TABULATIONS OF OUTSTANDING NORTH AMERICAN
BIG GAME TROPHIES, COMPILED FROM DATA IN
THE CLUB'S BIG GAME RECORDS ARCHIVES.

EDITED BY WM. H. NESBITT AND
JACK RENEAU

NINTH EDITION
1988
THE BOONE AND CROCKETT CLUB
DUMFRIES, VIRGINIA

Records of North American Big Game

Library of Congress Catalog Card Number: 88-072182
ISBN Number: 0-940864-13-4
Published November 1988

Published in the United States of America
by the
Boone and Crockett Club
P.O. Box 547
Dumfries, VA 22026

This Centennial Edition of the all-time
records book is dedicated to the far-sighted
individuals who 100 years ago first conceived
of the Boone and Crockett Club at a dinner
called by Theodore Roosevelt.

Theodore Roosevelt, founder
J. Coleman Drayton
George Bird Grinnell
Col. James E. Jones
Thomas Paton
John P. Pierrepont
Archibald Rogers
E. P. Rogers
Elliott Roosevelt
J. West Roosevelt
Rutherford Stuyvesant

Members of the Boone and Crockett Club met with the President Ronald Reagan on February 29, 1988 to commemorate the 100th Anniversary of the Club's first formal meeting, held on February 29, 1888. Present were (1-r) Club President Dr. James H. Duke, Jr.; Wesley M. Dixon, Jr.; Club Treasurer Sherman Gray; Club Secretary John P. Poston; Club Conservation Committee Chairman George C. Hixon; President Reagan; William I. Spencer; Richard P. Carlsberg; Guido R. Rahr, Jr.; Howard W. Pollock; and Lowell E. Baier.

Foreword

One hundred years ago, a small group of concerned, far-sighted men, led by Theodore Roosevelt, founded the Boone and Crockett Club in an effort to counter existing forces that otherwise would have decimated much of the existing North American wildlife and vast areas of priceless, beautiful American landscape. These men were successful in establishing what is now the oldest conservation organization in America. Through the process of legislation, they were able to secure for posterity the awesome beauty of the then fledgling Yellowstone Park, and subsequently they exerted necessary initiative to establish the entire national park system. Through their efforts, the commercial hunting of wildlife became illegal, and the American bison was saved. It was because of the foresight, wisdom, and commitment of these men that we enjoy today many of the especially beautiful forests, streams, mountains, and prairies of America, and the wildlife that flourishes in many areas where it otherwise would have been lost.

As the decades have passed, the Boone and Crockett Club membership has taken the leadership in many significant conservation programs, with a recent example being the successful effort to save the Florida Key deer. At a later date, some of the members of the Boone and Crockett Club initiated a movement to prevent the construction of a dam across the Yukon River. Had this proposed project been completed, a vast area of wildlife habitat would have been lost, as would entire historic herds of migrating caribou. Of even greater significance, had this land mass and its indigenous wildlife not been saved, an entire culture of native Americans would have had their traditional way of life destroyed.

More than a half-century ago, members of the Boone and Crockett Club conceived a scientific, demographic reference book of North American big game. It was from this embryonic concept that the Club's records book was born. Through the efforts of a few dedicated members, and with the assistance of many interested and qualified friends, the highly refined techniques for scoring each of the species of North American big game has been derived. The refinement process continues until this date. It should be emphasized

that this book is an important scientific reference, primarily containing a quantitative data base for the occurrence of the larger examples of each of the species, in specific geographical areas, and a compendium of related information. With each edition of the records book, significant new information is added. It is noteworthy that, contrary to the opinions of some, the number, and especially the size, of measured specimens continues to increase. This fact verifies the value of modern wildlife management programs that include selective hunting.

This edition of the records book, published in the Club's Centennial year, is unique in several respects. It symbolizes the completion of 100 years of conservation service, as detailed in the concise history of the work and achievements of the Club that is included in this edition. It also symbolizes the beginning of a second century of conservation. The problems and issues that impact the wildlife and habitat of North America are as great today as they were at the time of the founding of the Boone and Crockett Club; however, the problems are different. It is incumbent upon all of us to join together to contribute in whatever way possible to ensure the greatest long-term potential for nurturing and growth of these invaluable resources. We, of the Boone and Crockett Club, pledge the commitment of our resources and energy to that end. Let us together move into the new century with determination, vision, and enthusiasm.

Dr. James H. Duke, Jr.
President
Boone and Crockett Club

Contents

CONTENTS

Illustrations

ILLUSTRATIONS

RECORDS OF
NORTH AMERICAN
BIG GAME

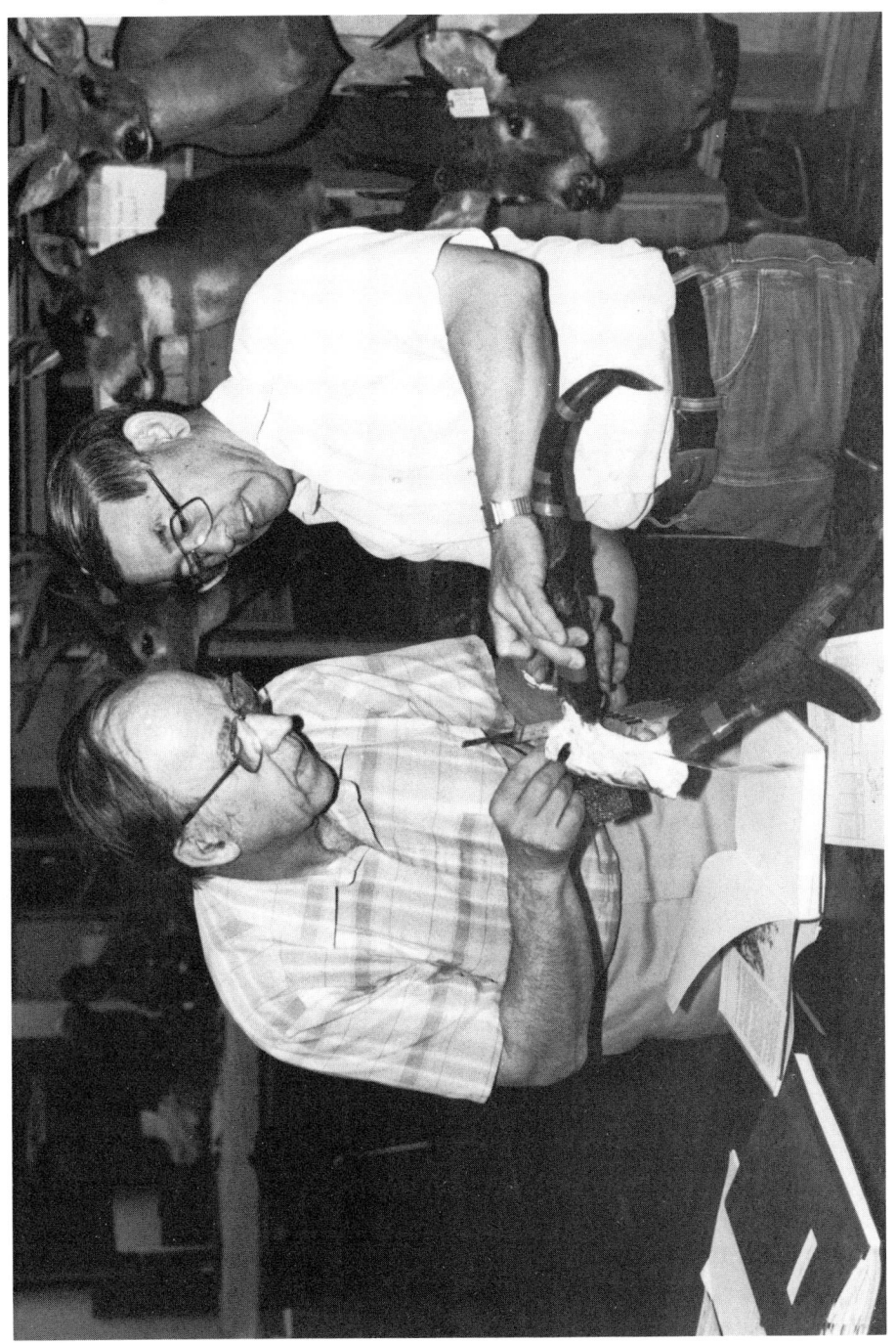

Dr. Philip L. Wright (l) and George K. Tsukamoto measure the new World's Record pronghorn taken by Michael J. O'Haco, Jr., in Arizona. Dr. Wright served as a Consultant to the 19th Awards Judges Panel (1986) and George Tsukamoto was Chairman of the Judges Panel.

Reflections on 40 Years of Trophy Measuring

Dr. Philip L. Wright

In this chapter I have attempted to describe the history of the big-game records keeping program as observed by one who has been involved continuously for over 40 years, first as a museum curator, then an Official Measurer, then a member of the Records Committee for 17 years, with nine of these years as Chairman, and finally for the past two years as the Emeritus Chairman. I have tried not to duplicate what I have written in the 8th edition of the Records Book (1981) or the 18th and 19th Awards books, nor to repeat extensively what others have written in the previous editions of the records books. I have been aided materially by my fellow Club and Committee member, George W. Johnson, whose involvement goes back to 1932, and whose files are remarkably complete and fully available to me.

My involvement with the records keeping began with the receipt in 1947 of the 32-page booklet entitled "North American Big Game Competitions." It was published by the Records Committee chaired by Dr. Harold Anthony. This carefully prepared and attractively printed brochure announced the first competition to be conducted after the end of the year 1947. It was widely circulated to natural history museums, fish and game departments, taxidermists, well-known big-game guides, and interested big-game hunters. It reproduced the then simple score charts and described the Club's interest in fair chase and the preservation of big-game hunting. The Club conducted three successive competitions for 1947-49, and the rankings for these trophies were all based upon simple measurements of length of the longer antler or horn or the greatest length of the skull. There were no "final scores," based on adding and subtracting various measurements, as there are in today's system.

We entered two cougar skulls from the University of Montana (then known as Montana State University) Zoological Museum and received the 2nd and 3rd awards at the 1949 competition. The medals were directed to the hunters who had taken the big cougars and had then generously donated the skulls to our museum.

During this period, Sam Webb was actively working as Chairman of a special Club committee to devise a scoring system, making it sufficiently broad to become generally accepted as the single proper method of evaluating all of the desirable qualities of native North American big game trophies, with the system to be called the Official Scoring System. This story is told in detail by Mr. Webb in earlier editions of this book, and it represents the most significant accomplishment of the records-keeping programs. The other

1

main partners in this effort were Grancel Fitz and Dr. James L. Clark, each of whom had established his own trophy scoring system. By the time of the 1950 competition, the new Official Scoring System, which had been widely circulated and then approved by the Club, was in effect. That competition designated new World's Records in several classes and clearly established the validity of the new scoring system. In 1951, Sam Webb took over the chairmanship of the Records Committee. This was appropriate, as he had worked diligently to get the new system approved. The previous Chairman was Dr. Harold Anthony, who was the Curator of Mammals at the American Museum of Natural History and an active promoter of the records-keeping program during his years as Chairman.

Webb's account describes the earliest efforts of the Club to start a records program. It gives major credit to Prentiss Gray, who edited the Club's first records book in 1932. Later, after Mr. Gray's untimely death in 1935, Alfred Ely edited the second edition in 1939. Mr. Gray had the cooperation of Rowland Ward of London, who had been recording North American trophies taken largely by British sportsmen, and a sizable number of the trophies shown in both the first and second editions were located in Great Britain. A number of these trophies ended up in the British Museum of Natural History in London. Efforts were made to see that these trophies were re-scored after the Official Scoring system went into effect, but there was little interest shown by the museum curators. I made two trips to the British Museum to do exactly that. I was able to locate only two Yukon trophies taken by Frederick C. Selous, the celebrated English hunter, in 1904. But upon re-measuring, they were found to be below the minimum entry score. The storage area of the museum suffered some bomb damage during World War II, and some of these trophies were destroyed or moved to other storage. Undoubtedly there are several outstanding American trophies taken in the early part of the century or late 1800's that are still housed in that museum, but it would take a concerted effort to identify and score these trophies. The species involved are primarily moose, elk, and caribou.

During the earlier days of the records program, the Records Committee relied heavily on mammalogists in natural history museums to check the scores of entered trophies. In 1951, Sam Webb recognized the need for naming qualified and interested people to become Official Measurers, with a letter of request to some 70 persons that was dated 17 April 1951. Some of these persons accepted the appointment and continued to measure and record trophies throughout their active lives. The newly-appointed Official Measurers were urged to use great care in measuring trophies. They were also encouraged to actively search out suitable heads for entry, and especially to find and re-measure those trophies listed in the 1939 book that had been scored by the old system. The only specific detail mentioned in that letter was a caution about not following the lower edge of the horn in taking the basal circumference of sheep horns. (This still remains a problem today, with overzealous hunters being prone to take this measurement incorrectly.) There was no program for training the Official Measurers in a formal way.

Of that original group, only George Johnson, Ed McGuire, and I remain active in scoring trophies. Johnson's service to the Committee dates back to 1932, when he entered a Coues' deer taken by his grandfather in Arizona before the turn of the century. He entered additional trophies during those early years, and he later established a successful whitetail

trophy program in Virginia. George also served on the Safari Club's records committee for a time, and he actually authored the scoring system used today by that organization. Unfortunately, through some quirk of fate, George did not join the Boone and Crockett Club until 1984, over 50 years after his initial efforts in trophy scoring.

After 1951, efforts were made to expand the numbers of Official Measurers, and almost anyone interested who volunteered was designated as a Measurer. This was necessary because many parts of the country did not have any measurers available. It was in the summer of 1954 that, on request of the Montana Fish and Game Department, I conducted a one-day measuring school at the University of Montana's Biological Station at Flathead Lake. All four "students" were approved by Mr. Webb and they became Official Measurers. I conducted other such schools in later years. Dr. Rusten, during his term as Chairman of the Committee, conducted programs for those interested in learning about measuring techniques at the North American Wildlife Conferences.

In 1973, when the National Rifle Association and the Club agreed to jointly sponsor the records-keeping program, a professionally trained wildlife biologist, Harold Nesbitt, was employed to conduct the program. During the prior 10-year period, when the files were housed at the Carnegie Museum, two secretaries (Mrs. Walter Toerge and, later, Mrs. Dorothy Petrovsky) maintained the files. They were supervised over most of that period by Dr. Rusten, who was working full-time as a practicing physician in the Minneapolis-St. Paul area. Dr. Rusten traveled periodically to Pittsburgh at his own expense to review entries and take care of other Committee duties. This continued devotion and great effort by Dr. Rusten was greatly appreciated by those who knew and understood it, and it has been unsurpassed in the history of the Club.

When Nesbitt took over, he sensed that the quality of scoring by the volunteer Official Measurers varied greatly and that a formal system of training new measurers was necessary. To do this, he instituted a four to five-day school at which prospective new measurers were confronted with examples of each kind of native North American big game trophy and were taught to score them under direct supervision. Many of these schools have now been conducted by Nesbitt (recent ones by Jack Reneau, Director of Big Game Records). Since 1975, prospective measurers have had to complete this course in order to be designated Official Measurers. It is not possible to fully train a competent measurer in such a short period, but the workshop is a necessary prerequisite to experience.

Mr. Reneau now spends a good deal of his time in scrutinizing the ever-increasing numbers of entries before acceptance. The submission of at least three photos, which had always been requested in the past, became a required part of a completed entry at the same time that the measurer schools were begun. With these, Reneau carefully scrutinizes each entry, studying the score chart to see, for example, if in antlered trophies the proper points have been designated as normal or abnormal. He finds it necessary to send the Committee Chairman a number of score charts with unresolved problems. If the Chairman feels uncertain about how to score the trophy, the problem may be referred to the entire Committee. The annual meetings of the Records Committee, held in December, always have a number of such problems to be decided by a vote of the Committee.

Currently, all of the data submitted for each trophy are computerized so that it is possible

Pictured here at an early big-game "Competition" Judging of the Boone and Crockett Club are Dr. Elmer M. Rusten (l) and Frank Cook. Dr. Rusten served as Records of North American Big Game Committee Chairman for several years, and Frank Cook has been present at all such judging activities for the past several decades.

to look at printouts that contain many more data than are listed in the records book(s). All of the early score sheets have now been computerized, and this has resulted in the detection of numerous errors in earlier entries. Thus, if trophies appear in this volume with a different score than was shown in an earlier edition, this will usually be the reason for the change.

The first 11 Big Game Competitions were conducted at the American Museum of Natural History in New York City. They were transferred to the Carnegie Museum in Pittsburgh in 1963, with the next three sited there. Since then, the programs have been conducted in widely-separated areas of the continent in an effort to involve big game hunters and all others interested in our native big game animals. Awards programs have been located at Atlanta (1974), Denver (1979), Kansas City (1980), Dallas (1983), and Las Vegas (1986). Fifty-nine men have served as judges for the competitions (later Awards), and they have been invited both from within the Club membership and from among the more active Official Measurers. About half of the judges have come from within Club membership. Judges from Canada and from widely-separated areas of the U.S. have always been included. Customarily, no one serves as a judge more than three times. But the Committee, realizing the need for continuity in its programs, started in 1968 to invite some previous judges with long service, intense interest, and great devotion to the program, to serve as Consultants to the Judges Panel. Of these, Frank Cook of Alaska needs special recognition, as he has been present either as a judge or a consultant at every Awards program since 1966. His recollection of previous decisions, and his mature judgment, have been eagerly sought by the Judges Panels.

When Sam Webb assumed chairmanship of the Records Committee in 1951 from Harold Anthony, Betty Fitz (Grancel's wife) was named Secretary of the Committee and the files were moved to the Fitz apartment at 5 Tudor City Place, New York. Betty carried on this function admirably until the office was transferred to the Carnegie Museum in Pittsburgh in 1963. Until his death in 1963, Grancel Fitz was available to answer detailed questions from measurers. I have several such responses from Grancel, which I have used many times since in making rulings about difficult decisions in scoring. Fitz had, by far, the greatest experience of anyone with the scoring system, and I had no problem with any of the decisions he made for me or others. After the Official System was approved, Fitz and his close friend Sam Webb scored many of the largest known trophies, including several World's Records that still stand today.

Initially, trophies with split skulls that had an Official Measurer's estimate of the spread were accepted by the Committee. As the programs became more competitive, this practice was disallowed. In a booklet carefully prepared for the Official Measurers in 1967, Dr. Elmer Rusten, then Chairman of the Committee, spelled out several other matters that would disqualify trophies for entry. In recent Awards programs the judges have resorted to x-rays to determine if mounted antlered trophies had split skulls, and trophies so found have been disqualified.

During the early years of the program, trophies could be scored for submission prior to the end of the 60-day drying period, with the understanding that the score would be checked again after the 60 days had elapsed. This is, of course, no longer allowed.

During Dr. Rusten's period as Chairman, the Committee decreed that cougars taken in states or provinces where there were bounties on them would not be accepted for entry. Today, perhaps spurred by this action, bounties for cougars are virtually non-existent, and cougars are recognized as game animals throughout their range, as well as being highly valued as trophy animals.

A great deal of effort has been made to insure that the trophies submitted are fairly and adequately scored. The policy that the Judges Panel scores are final has been rigidly followed. The judging sessions, held several weeks in advance of the Awards banquet, are highly organized. The Chairman of the panel has copies of all the original entry sheets for the invited trophies in advance. Thus he and the consultants have the opportunity to study possible scoring problems and to point them out to the judges. Routinely, two teams of judges score each trophy independently. If the scores are not identical, the panel Chairman, or one of the consultants, attempts to resolve the difference. Sometimes several hours are spent in resolving a vexing problem of interpretation of trophy quality. Today, new World's Records are designated only by these panels. As one who has been involved with all of the last seven Awards programs, dating back to 1971, I can state that none of the World's Records designated during that period ever had any questionable quality.

Although a good number of trophies invited to the Final Awards are scored higher by the judges, the majority are scored the same as, or below, the entry score. Part of this is that trophies continue to shrink after they are killed, and this shrinkage may continue for months or years. The Committee is concerned with the problem of shrinkage and has considered it many times. The 60-day drying period prior to official measurement was established many years ago as an arbitrary allowance for the major shrinkage in a fresh trophy. It would be ideal if a panel could review each entry score, compare it with the judges' score, and then let the initial measurement stand if they thought the trophy had been properly scored in the first place. In the interest of objectivity, however, the Committee has ruled in recent years that such a procedure would involve varying levels of guesswork, and they have emphatically rejected this possibility. When hunters have complained about the loss of score due to shrinkage, I have used the example that Theodore Roosevelt's cougar, which stood as the World's Record for many years, was not officially scored until more than 50 years after it was killed!

Because there is such intense interest in the precise standing of each entry, the entry scores of trophies that have been invited to be sent to the Final Awards Judging and are *not* sent are shown with an asterisk. Although the initial score, as taken by the Official Measurer, is allowed to stand in the majority of entries, those very large trophies ranking in the top ten of their category must either be Panel scored or verified by two additional scorings before they take their final place in the all-time listing. Eventually, asterisked trophies neither sent to the panel nor so rescored will be dropped from the all-time records book listings.

In recent Awards programs, much effort has gone into consideration for the Sagamore Hill Award. Club officers have felt that not only should this award be made only for an exceptional trophy (in most cases a new World's Record), but it should also be a case where the hunt was conducted under the best of sporting conditions. Careful review of the

hunters' account of his hunt, discussion with the guide and/or with hunting partners, and perhaps with the supervisory game biologist in the area of the hunt, as well as lengthy phone calls with the hunter, have been preliminary steps in making this award.

The principle of fair chase in hunting big game animals was part of Roosevelt's thinking in establishing the Club. The initial Club by-laws, approved in 1888, prohibited unfair chase by members of the Club. Trapping of cougars or bears, shooting of animals while they were swimming, and "crusting" of moose (hunting from snowshoes) were and still are grounds for expulsion from the Club. Initially, "calling" of moose was forbidden. In one of the early Club books, Roosevelt admonished one of his writers for describing hunting of caribou with the help of snowshoes.

With the great emphasis on fair chase within the ranks of the Club throughout its history, it is surprising that a Fair Chase Statement was not required of hunters entering trophies until 1963. Those in charge had always assumed that the entered trophies were taken in fair chase, but hunters were required to sign a sworn statement to that effect for trophies entered in the 11th Competition of 1962-63. The Records Committee had actually been considering a "Fair Chase Statement" since the late 1950's, as hunters and guides began to use airplanes to spot game in Alaska and other areas. Some flagrant incidents of such "air-spotting", followed by landing nearby to kill the animals, were the catalyst for the first formal "Fair Chase Statement. That signaled the curtailment of trophy hunting of polar bears by that method and encouraged laws preventing air spotting in Alaska and other states and provinces. At the same time (1963), the Committee imposed the restriction that the direct use of motorized vehicles in taking a trophy was to be regarded as Unfair Chase. More recently, the Committee imposed the requirement that trophy animals could not be taken by use of electronic communications (including "walkie-talkies") or from within an escape-proof enclosure. This last definition was primarily directed toward commercial shooting preserves where non-native animals are released to be shot be clients.

During the first years of the records keeping, bison were actually shot with special permission on federal wildlife refuges or purchased alive and later dispatched. There are many times the number of bison alive today, and many more opportunities for hunters to shoot them, than in the late 1940's. Currently, bison must be classified by the state or province as a game animal, a hunting license must be purchased, and the animals cannot be restricted by an escape-proof fence, in order to be eligible for entry. Beyond these requirements, bison taken in the lower 48 states are not eligible for awards, since the Committee believes that bison hunting in these areas is generally not as sporting a proposition as hunting for the other big game species.

A great deal more could be offered here in this review, but the important theme has been brought out above. From a simple desire by Sam Webb, Grancel Fitz, James L. Clark, Prentiss Gray, Alfred Ely, and many others to record and honor exceptional trophies of sport hunting, the world's best-recognized trophy records system for North America has evolved. From the start, great emphasis on Fair Chase has enhanced the program's integrity and helped encourage good sportsmanship afield. It has thus been a most worthwhile endeavor, one that I and all my fellow measurers, Club members, and big game hunters have enjoyed greatly.

21st Awards Minimum Entry Scores (1989–1991)

Category	Awards Records Book	All-Time Records Book
black bear	20	21
grizzly bear	23	24
Alaska brown bear	26	28
polar bear*	27	27
jaguar*	14–8/16	14–8/16
cougar	14–8/16	15
Atlantic walrus*	95	95
Pacific walrus*	100	100
American elk (typical antlers)	360	375
American elk (non-typical antlers)	385	385
Roosevelt's elk	275	290
mule deer (typical antlers)	185	195
mule deer (non-typical antlers)	225	240
Columbia blacktail deer	120	130
Sitka blacktail deer	100	108
whitetail deer (typical antlers)	160	170
whitetail deer (non-typical antlers)	185	195
Coues' whitetail deer (typical antlers)	100	110
Coues' whitetail deer (non-typical antlers)	105	120
Canada moose	185	195
Alaska-Yukon moose	210	224
Wyoming (Shiras) moose	140	155
mountain caribou	360	390
woodland caribou	265	295
barren ground caribou	375	400
Central Canada barren ground caribou	330	345
Quebec-Labrador caribou	365	375
pronghorn	80	82
bison**	115	115
Rocky Mountain goat	47	50
muskox	105	105
bighorn sheep	175	180
desert sheep	165	168
Dall's sheep	165	170
Stone's sheep	165	170

* Must be taken and/or possessed in full compliance with Marine Mammals Act, Endangered Species Act and/or other Federal/State laws.

** From lower 48 states, eligible only if recognized by state as game animal, with a hunting season and license specified.

Current Conditions of Trophy Entry

Jack Reneau
Director of Big Game Records
Boone and Crockett Club

After you've had an opportunity to digest the trophy listings elsewhere in this book, you may recall a trophy or two that you or a favorite hunting companion may have taken that you feel may be of sufficient trophy quality to make the Awards and/or all-time records book. You may then ask yourself, "How do I determine if my trophy makes the records book?", and, "How do I enter my trophy in the Boone and Crockett Club records book if it does make the minimum score recognized by the Club?"

There is a very regimented chain of events and requirements that must be adhered to by each trophy owner entering a trophy in the Awards Programs. The more closely these requirements are followed, the shorter the time to get a trophy accepted in the records archives. We could simply list these requirements and let everyone figure out exactly what they mean, but I would prefer to discuss each entry requirement in detail so that you can avoid many of the pitfalls that lengthen the time it takes to process each trophy.

Before we get too deep into this discussion, I should point out that all trophies must dry under normal atmospheric conditions for 60 days before they can be officially measured. This doesn't necessarily mean 60 days from the date of kill. For example, trophies that have been frozen for any length of time and/or boiled must dry 60 days *after* they are removed from the freezer or boiling water before they can be officially scored, *regardless* of how long they dried before being frozen or boiled.

After the 60-day drying period has elapsed, you should then make a rough measurement of your trophy using the score charts and scoring information at the back of this book. If you need more detailed scoring information, you should obtain a copy of the official measuring manual, *Measuring and Scoring North American Big Game Trophies*, available from the Club and many book and sporting goods stores.

If you determine that your trophy is near or exceeds the minimum entry score, you should contact the Club office for a list of measurers nearest you. (There are currently 650 Official Measurers scattered throughout North America.)

You should then contact one of the measurers to arrange a time and place of mutual convenience to have your trophy scored. Official Measurers are volunteers who generously donate their time to score trophies. Thus, arrangements to have a trophy scored will need to be made at the measurer's convenience.

If your trophy meets or exceeds the applicable minimum score shown on the list that accompanies this chapter, the Official Measurer should give you the original, signed and dated score chart, along with other necessary entry information, to send to the records

office. If your trophy comes up short of the minimum score for entry in the all-time records book, *Records of North American Big Game*, do not panic or despair. Your trophy could still exceed the minimum scores set for the Awards records books.

Beginning with the 18th Awards, the Club began publication of triennial Awards program records books. Entry into these books is allowed at the Awards book minimum score, lower than required for the all-time records book. For example, 170 is the minimum score for entering a typical whitetail deer in the all-time records book. The minimum score for entering a typical whitetail deer in the Awards records book is 160 points. Thus, your trophy may be eligible for a one-time listing in the Awards book, even though it scores too low for listing in the all-time records book. Lower minimum entry scores for the Awards records books are shown on the accompanying list.

Except for the lower minimum entry scores, trophy entry requirements for the Awards records book are the same as for entry in the all-time records book.

Obviously, the first item needed to enter a trophy is a *current version*, *original* score chart, signed and dated by an Official Measurer of the Boone and Crockett Club. It's surprising how many entries are received in the records office that do not comply with this most basic requirement. The records office frequently receives photocopies (not acceptable) of score charts. On other occasions, the records office has received entries submitted on score charts that have been out-of-date for many years.

The information box of the lower portion of the score chart should be completed in full, including the location of kill, the name of the hunter(s), owner(s), and the guide, as well as the addresses of the current owner and the guide.

Insofar as the location of kill is concerned, we simply need the county or a geographic location (e.g. river, mountain, etc.) where the trophy was taken or found. All trophies from the lower 48 states are listed in the records books by county, while all trophies from Canada, Alaska, and Mexico are listed by geographic location.

The second entry requirement is the $25 (U.S. funds) registration fee. If the registration fee is absent from the entry materials, or if the incorrect amount is tendered, the trophy owner is notified that the entry fee is needed and processing is held up until the correct amount is received.

Thirdly, each entry must be accompanied by clearly-focused photographs. Black-and-white or color photos will suffice, but slides are *not* acceptable. All bear and cat entries must be accompanied by photos of the front, left side, right side, and top of the clean, dried skull. All other entries must be accompanied with photos of the front, left side and right side of the trophy showing the rack or horns in good detail. The photos can be of either the mounted or unmounted trophy. Side photos should be taken at right angles to the trophy.

Besides adding valuable information to each trophy's file that could not be obtained in any other way, the photos enable us to verify the scoring procedure used for each entry by comparing the photographs to the score chart.

The fourth item that must be submitted with each hunter-taken trophy is a signed Fair Chase Statement, with the hunter's signature notarized. The correct Fair Chase Statement is on the back of all *current* score charts.

The fifth item needed for hunter-taken trophies is a completed Hunter, Guide and Hunt Information (HGH) form, *even* if the services of a guide or outfitter were not employed for the hunt. The hunter simply needs to complete the parts of the HGH form that apply to his or her particular trophy. The HGH form is available from Official Measurers or from the records office.

Finally, a copy of the appropriate hunting license (and tag if applicable) must accompany each hunter-taken trophy. If a copy of the license is no longer available, the trophy owner can submit a statement from an appropriate official of the Game and Fish Department verifying that the license (and tag) was in the possession of the hunter at the time the trophy was taken. If the Department no longer has records at its disposal to verify the license purchase, the records office will accept a statement from Game and Fish Department personnel stating this fact. The Records Committee may then, at its discretion, waive the hunting license copy requirement.

The last three items listed above (Fair Chase Statement; HGH form; and hunting license) are only required for hunter-taken trophies. Obviously, trophy owners submitting trophies that were "picked up", or are of unknown origin, or were taken by a deceased hunter, are not required to submit these items.

In addition to all of the items previously mentioned, there are several other items requested, but not required, to complete entry into the records archives. If available, we would like to obtain a good-quality field photo of each owner with his (or her) trophy shortly after the animal was killed. Such photographs are regularly used in various Boone and Crockett Club publications, including the *Boone and Crockett Club Associates Newsletter*.

We would also like to obtain the age, and method of aging, of each entry if age was determined by a competent authority. We also want the rack or tusk weights (in pounds and ounces) for caribou, elk, moose, and walrus. Details for providing this information are given on the back of each HGH form mentioned above.

The age data will be useful in managing big-game populations in the future for trophy animals, as well as supporting the theory of trophy hunting. The rack and tusk weights can be used to make comparisons between certain North American big-game species and their counterparts in other parts of the world.

Trophies submitted to the records office that are postmarked before December 31, 1988, are eligible for entry in the Boone and Crockett Club's 20th Awards. The 20th Awards entry period includes all trophies accepted during the years 1986-1988. All trophies postmarked after that date will be eligible for entry in the Boone and Crockett Club's 21st Awards (1989-1991) which closes December 31, 1991.

All trophies accepted during the 20th Awards will be listed in *Boone and Crockett Club's 20th Big Game Awards*, which will be published during 1989; all trophies accepted during the 21st Awards will be listed in *Boone and Crockett Club's 21st Big Game Awards*, which will be published during 1992. Trophies accepted in either the 20th or 21st Awards that exceed the all-time minimum entry scores shown on the accompanying list will then be listed in the 10th edition of *Records of North American Big Game*, which will be published sometime after 1991.

Once the records office has received all required items for a particular trophy, it is accepted for listing in the all-time and/or Awards records books. Each accepted trophy is recognized by a handsome certificate, suitable for framing.

If you, or anyone you know, is planning on entering a trophy, please be sure to follow the procedures outlined above. It will ensure that your trophy is processed with minimum delay.

There are some changes in trophy scoring procedure and also in minimum entry score for one category that need to be noted by sportsmen as the 21st awards entry period (1989-1991) gets under way.

Beginning 1 January 1989, the definition of a point for all deer and elk is as follows: "To be counted a point, a projection must be at least one-inch long, with the length exceeding width at one-inch or more of length". Note that this is a slightly different definition of a point than has been used in the past. The original definition of a point in the deer categories stated that the entire *length* of the point had to exceed the width of its base. There is no change in the actual scoring of a point, it is measured from tip to base.

Since the beginning of the records keeping system, excessive inside spread (greater than longer main beam) results in the trophy receiving credit for inside spread only of the amount equal to the length of the longer main beam, and with an additional penalty assessed for the difference between length of the longer main beam and the inside spread. Thus, there was in effect a "double penalty" as the trophy was "losing" the difference between the longer antler beam and the inside spread total, and then was penalized this same amount. After long and careful review of this situation, it has been decided that the penalty portion of this measuring procedure will be dropped. Inside spread will still be limited to the length of the longer antler, but no longer will the difference between the measured inside spread and the longer antler beam (where spread exceeds beam length) be assessed as a penalty. There is no change in the method of taking the inside spread measurement.

As those who follow the records books closely will know, minimum scores have not been raised in any category since 1968. However, beginning 1 January 1989 the minimum score for muskox will be raised to 105 for both the Awards and all-time records books. This is a result of an extensive review of the trophy entries and minimum scores in all categories, with the determination that the minimum score has been set too low for today's muskox hunting. This is the only category in which minimum score is being raised for the 21st Awards entry period.

Finally, for the 21st and later Awards entry periods, the lower entry scores required for the Awards records books (one-time listing, only for that entry period and records) have been extended to include pickup, unknown origin, and older hunter-taken trophies, *so long* as the trophy has *not* been previously entered in an entry period or published in a records book. This will enable proper recognition of fine trophies that fall short of the all-time records book minimums.

Stories Behind the New World's Records

WM. H. NESBITT
EXECUTIVE DIRECTOR
BOONE AND CROCKETT CLUB

This 9th edition of the all-time records book recognizes nine new World's Records. It also recognizes, for the first time, 45 additional top-10 trophies in their respective categories. The reader is referred to the 18th and 19th Awards records books for further details and the hunting stories for the trophies discussed here.

The 1981 edition recognized a new World's Record pronghorn, scoring 93, taken by Edwin L. Wetzler in Yavapai County, Arizona in 1975. Wetzler's trophy became the World's Record with the disqualification of the long-standing pronghorn record, the H. M. Beck trophy. The Beck trophy was disqualified due to the discovery of modifications that had been made to its horn structure (see 1981 records book for this story). With the establishment of Wetzler's trophy as the World's Record, an old myth about a superior race of pronghorn, as represented by the Beck trophy that was some 10 points better than the next closest trophy, was put to rest. But, the closeness of Wetzler's trophy to other high-ranking pronghorns suggested that there might still be other larger pronghorns out there; and indeed there were. The 19th Awards saw the invitation of Michael J. O'Haco's trophy, taken in Coconino County, Arizona in 1985. After Judges panel measurement, O'Haco's trophy was officially scored as 93-4/8 and recognized as the new World's Record. In further recognition of the outstanding trophy quality of this pronghorn, and the Fair Chase hunt conducted by O'Haco to obtain it, this trophy was given the coveted Sagamore Hill Award medal at the 19th Awards of 1986. An interesting footnote here is the fact that there was another potential World's Record pronghorn, entry-scored at better than the then-World's Record score, that was withdrawn from the Awards (and therefore from listing in this records book) by its owner. It would have been interesting to see where it would have placed after the Judges Panel decision.

The Canada moose category has been very stable at the top for quite some time. In fact, the exceptional Canada moose taken in 1914 by Silas Witherbee at Bear Lake, Quebec, stood as the World's Record for the category since the current records keeping system was begun in 1950. Therefore, the Judges' eyes and ears certainly perked up when they were notified that for the 18th Awards, there were two Canada moose that each had been entry-scored at better than Witherbee's long-standing record. And, after the Judges had made their decision, both trophies were still at final scores ahead of Witherbee's moose. So, there is now a new World's Record and a new Number 2 for the category, with Witherbee's moose being Number 3. For Michael Laub, a childhood dream of a "real" big game hunt

13

B&C Photograph by Wm. H. Nesbitt

The 18th Awards (Dallas, Texas: 1983) Judges Panel and new World's Record cougar skull, non-typical whitetail, and Columbia blacktail deer. From left to right: Steve Kubasek; George K. Tsukamoto; Dr. Philip L. Wright; Dean Murphy, Chairman of Judges Panel; Dr. Glen C. Sanderson; Ed Williamson; Glenn A. St. Charles; and Frank Cook (not present for photograph were F. Lane Howard and Dr. Robert E. Speegle).

came true in October 1980, when he hunted the Grayling River of British Columbia. There, he was lucky enough to find and kill an exceptional moose that scores 242 points and is now the World's Record. For Albertoni Ferruccio of Switzerland, it was a long trip to Teslin River, British Columbia. But, it was more than worth all the travel time and discomfort when his hunt resulted in an exceptional moose that the Judges measured at 240-2/8 points, now the all-time Number 2 for the category. Mr. Ferruccio made the long trip from Switzerland to be at the Awards program, and there he made many friends and also swapped a few hunting tales with fellow hunters.

The Canada moose category provides an excellent illustration of a new policy put into effect with this edition. In previous editions, those trophies that were invited to a Final Awards Judging and were not sent were shown with asterisks but were given a ranking in category based upon their entry score. Beginning with this edition, this practice has been modified so that the asterisk is still shown, but since the entry score is subject to the Judges Panel measurement (or additional verifying measurements by Official Measurers), these trophies are now shown at the end of the category listing and are unranked. This is the only fair way to deal with this situation, since it is obviously unfair to continue listing them in a ranked sequence with other trophies whose final scores have indeed been verified by the Judges Panel as required. In this case, there were a half-dozen trophies at the top of the list for the 1981 edition that are now shown at the end of the list, resulting in a noticeable "shakeup" at the top of the list. This same phenomenon can be seen in a number of other categories and will not be referred to further in this article. The reader can ascertain these changes for himself or herself.

In Columbia blacktail deer, the 1981 book showed Clark D. Griffith's trophy, taken near Elk City, Oregon in 1962 and scoring 170-6/8, as the World's Record. The 18th Awards brought Lester Miller's exceptional trophy to the Judges Panel, where it was determined to have a proper final score of 182-2/8, thus qualifying as the new World's Record for the category. Taken in Lewis County, Washington, it actually predated the Griffith trophy by a decade, having been killed in October of 1953. Miller's story is a fine one of persistence and hunting skill, and he still tells it with verve and vigor after these many years.

Throughout North America, there is no more popular or widespread big game animal than the whitetail. And, almost everywhere the whitetail is found, there are slightly unusual specimens that qualify for measurement and potential listing in the non-typical category. The long-standing record for the category came from near Brady, Texas in 1892, with a score of 286. It is on display at the Lone Star Brewing Company, which owns it. The 18th Awards contained a most pleasant surprise, a monstrous non-typical whitetail deer entry from the Missouri Department of Conservation. It was a deer that had reverted in owner-ship to the state after being found dead. Once the measuring questions about its massive antlers had been decided, the Judges found it to have a correct final score of 333-7/8, some 50 points above the long-standing World's Record and thus easily the new World's Record. Little did anyone suspect that the next entry period would bring yet another monster to the Judges Panel, one that at entry measurement would surpass the 333-7/8 final score for the Missouri whitetail. Dick Idol is well known to trophy antler collectors, and his "Hole-In-

The-Horn" buck was widely ballyhooed as a new World's Record, based upon the entry measurement, which did indeed exceed the Missouri whitetail's score. But, a mass of antler material required special interpretation and could easily swing the final score by a considerable number of points. After long and spirited discussion, the Judges Panel found that Idol's deer was deserving of a final score of 328-2/8, again almost 50 points above the Lone Star buck but still behind Missouri's exceptional buck. Thus, this edition recognizes two non-typical whitetails that both displace the long-standing World's Record for the category.

The World's Record grizzly bear of the 1981 edition was a pickup by James G. Shelton in Bella Coola Valley, British Columbia in 1970. A huge grizzly was taken on Dean River, B.C. by Roger J. Pentecost in 1982 and entered in the 19th Awards. The Final Judging found it to have a correct final score of 27-2/16, putting it in a tie for the World's Record with Shelton's pickup. Thus, Pentecost's grizzly becomes the largest hunter-taken trophy for the category. And, there is a fine hunting story of how Pentecost found and killed his trophy bear.

In the cougar category, a big tom taken at Tatlayoko Lake, British Columbia, in 1979 by Douglas E. Schuk, and owned by Charles M. Travers, was found to have a correct final Judges Panel score of 16-4/16. This was 4/16 inch above the previous World's Record of 16 taken by Garth Roberts in 1964 in Garfield County, Utah, and thus another World's Record.

The 18th Awards provided the first recognition for the newly-established category of Roosevelt's elk. With a heavier body and shorter, but thicker, antlers, Roosevelt's elk could not readily compete in the long-established American elk category. With the establishment of the new category, a number of fine trophies were recognized. The new World's Record was a trophy scoring 356 and taken in Clatsop County, Oregon in November, 1959 by Pravomil (Milo) L. Raichl. An emigre to the U.S. from Czechoslovakia, Raichl had learned hunting skills in his youth as a forester and game warden. In America, he enjoyed the cool quiet of the rain forest and found his trophy on a hunt that involved a little help from Diana, the goddess of the hunt. Following the end of the 18th Awards, a minor modification of the scoring technique for Roosevelt's elk was approved and put into effect for the 19th Awards entry period. With the new guidelines, an older trophy was recognized as the new World's Record, with a score of 384-3/8. This trophy was taken in Clatsop County, Oregon, in 1949 by hunter Robert Sharp. Sharp's story is an interesting one in which his trophy was lost and then found and brought into the records keeping program by Harold E. Stepp of Alaska, who owns the trophy today. Both men were at the 19th Awards program, and they added much to the general activities with their individual accounts of association with this exceptional trophy.

The new category of Central Canada barren ground caribou was created for the 19th Awards entry period. At the Final Awards Judging, the scores were extremely close between the top two entries. A pickup from Rendez-vous Lake, Northwest Territories by Tom W. Barry was judged the new World's Record at a score of 408-6/8. It was barely ahead of the trophy killed by Raymond H. Bonar at Courageous Lake, N.W.T., in 1985 at a score of 408-2/8.

Another new category for the 19th Awards was Sitka blacktail deer. For a number of years, it was well known that the Sitka blacktail deer of the Alaska islands never grew antlers large enough for entry in the Columbia blacktail deer category. At the 19th Awards, the World's Record was recognized for Sitka blacktail deer, with a score 123-4/8 as taken at Uganik Bay, Alaska, by Donna D. Braendel in 1983. As with any new category, the top 10 trophies entered were invited to the Final Awards Judging. An amazing seven were there, creating quite an impressive display and an excellent cross-section of what future Sitka blacktail deer hunters can expect to see under ideal conditions.

There are a number of other exceptional trophies listed in this edition for the first time, as can be noted when reviewing the top few of each category. In closing this review, let's mention just a few of the more spectacular ones.

The black bear category shows a tie for Second Place, at a score of 22-8/16, between Cal Parson's trophy and Fred Peters' big bear. Parsons killed his trophy near Porcupine Plain, Saskatchewan in 1977, while Fred Peters hunted Gila County, Arizona in 1985 to find his bear. Close behind these two exceptional trophies is the pickup trophy from Sevier County, Utah that scores just 1/16 inch less (22-7/16). It is owned by the Utah Division of Wildlife Resources and was found dead in 1982.

In grizzly bear, Harry Leggett, Jr.'s exceptional bear scores 26-13/16 and ranks as Number 3 for the category. It was taken along Wakeman River, British Columbia in 1980.

In typical whitetail deer, two trophies moved into the top 10 as a result of the 19th Awards period. Steve Jansen's trophy, score 204-2/8, from Beaverdam Creek, Alberta in 1967, became the all-time Number 4, while Peter J. Swistun's big buck, scoring 200-2/8 from Whitkow, Saskatchewan in 1983, became the all-time Number 6 for the category. Considering the widespread interest in whitetail hunting, and the great numbers taken, it is amazing that the trophy quality in the upper portion of the ranking continues to be so high. It's an excellent reflection of the outstanding programs of wildlife management being carried out by the individual states and provinces.

Interestingly, the non-typical whitetail category also showed two new entries to the top 10. Doug Klinger hunted near Hardisty, Alberta in 1976 to take his huge non-typical that scores 277–5/8 and now is the all-time Number 5. Richard A. Pauli hunted on his farm in Peoria County, Illinois in 1983 to find his big buck that scores 267-3/8 and now ranks as Number 10 all-time for the category.

In the Coues' typical whitetail deer category, Kim J. Poulin's buck, scoring 130-4/8 and taken in Pima County, Arizona in 1981, now ranks as the all-time Number 4. In Coues' non-typical whitetail deer, there is also a new Number 4, as taken by Oscar C. Truex in 1983 in Pima County, Arizona. Truex's trophy scores 143-6/8 points.

In the Canada moose category, a large bull from Island Lake, Manitoba was taken by an Indian in 1980 and later came into the ownership of Jack E. Dunn. Scored at 223-5/8, it ranks as the all-time Number 8 for the category.

David B. Parent killed a big moose in 1982 near Granite Mountain, Alaska. Later it came into the possession of Earl D. Hahn, who entered it in the 19th Awards program, where it was officially scored at 249-1/8. It now ranks as the all-time Number 6 for the category.

B&C Photograph by Wm. H. Nesbitt

The 19th Awards (Las Vegas, Nev.: 1986) Judges Panel and new World's Record pronghorn and all-time No. 2 non-typical whitetail and desert sheep. From left to right: (kneeling) C. Randall Byers; Glenn A. St. Charles; George K. Tsukamoto, Chairman of Judges Panel; Frank E. Bertoia; Horace G. Gore; Thomas A. Cavin; (standing) Frank Cook; Charles E. Wilson, Jr.; Walter H. White; John G. Stelfox; Mike Wickersham; Murff F. Bledsoe, III; David G. Boland; and Dr. Philip L. Wright.

In the Wyoming moose category, Aldon Hale's trophy scores 200-3/8 points. Taken in Lincoln County, Wyoming in 1981, it now ranks as the all-time Number 3.

In mountain caribou, there is a new all-time Number 4 and Number 5. John A. Kolar hunted Mountain River, N.W.T. in 1984 to take his trophy that scores 444. Jay L. Brasher hunted the Spatsizi Plateau, B.C. in 1984 to take his trophy that scores 442-7/8.

Gordon J. Birgbauer Jr. hunted Rocky Pond, Newfoundland in 1984 to find his big woodland caribou. The Judges Panel scored it 347; it now ranks as the all-time Number 10 for the category.

In the Quebec-Labrador caribou category, exactly half of the top 10 are new in this edition. Part of this is due to the shifting of asterisked trophies to the end of the list, while the other reason is simply exceptional trophy quality being harvested today. The new all-time Number 2 was taken at Tunulic River, Quebec by James A. DeLuca in 1983, and it scores 464-4/8. The new Number 3 scores 460-6/8 and was taken in 1978 at Ungava Bay, Quebec by Lynn D. McLaud. The new Number 4 was also taken at Ungava Bay, Quebec. It was killed by Don Tomberlin in 1985, and it scores 439-1/8. Don L. Corley was the lucky hunter for the new Number 6 that was taken at Mistinibi Lake, Quebec in 1983 with a final score of 434-7/8. Charles E. Wilson Jr. hunted Mistinibi Lake in 1980 to take his big caribou that scores 429-2/8 and ranks as the all-time Number 9 for the category. DeLuca's trophy is worthy of one additional mention. It is an example of the alternate route of additional verifying measurements being submitted to move an asterisked trophy into its proper location in the rankings, in lieu of coming before a Judges Panel.

In the pronghorn category, Joseph P. Fornara hunted in Yavapai County, Arizona in 1984 to find his prize that scores 90-4/8 and ranks as all-time Number 8.

In the muskox category, half of the top 10 trophies are new in this edition. The all-time Number 2, scoring just one point less that the World's Record at a score of 121, was picked up by John G. Stelfox in 1983 along the Ellice River, N.W.T. Neal Wortley now owns the trophy taken by Joe Scotti in 1983 at Thirty Mile Lake, N.W.T. This big bull scores 112-4/8 and ranks as all-time Number 6. A three-way tie exists for Number 8 at a score of 110-4/8. Adam Ovilek killed his bull at Holman Island, N.W.T. in 1981, and later transferred ownership to Roger Britton. William Phillippe hunted Holman Island in 1982 to take his prize. David V. Collis killed his bull in 1985 at Banks Island, N.W.T.

A surprising four of the top 10 in desert sheep are new in this edition. This is surprising because generally it is very hard to get an exceptional desert sheep these days. Greg Koons was in Pima County, Arizona in 1982 when he picked up the new all-time Number 2 for the category, with a score of 201-3/8. Javier Lopez del Bosque hunted Baja California, Mexico in 1979 to find his big ram that scores 192-5/8 and ranks as all-time Number 4. Claude Bourguignon hunted Baja California, Mexico in 1982 to find his ram that scores 191-2/8 and is the all-time Number 7. Carl A. Mattias Sr. hunted Pima County, Arizona in 1982 to find his prize that scores 187-7/8 and ranks as the all-time Number 10.

Well, that's the end of our quick review of the "cream of the crop" of this edition. These trophies certainly furnish an emphatic "yes" to the question, "Are the *really* big ones still out there?" Better start making plans for next hunting season now!

The previous eight editions of the Boone and Crockett Club's big-game records books. Clockwise from 12 o'clock are: 1939, 1952, 1958, 1964, 1971, 1977, and 1981 editions. The 1932 edition is shown in the middle. The 1952 book is the first to be based upon the scoring system adopted in 1950 and used today.

Books of the Boone and Crockett Club

This list is provided as a reference to regular edition titles published by the Boone and Crockett Club since its inception. Titles now out-of-print are indicated by "(OP)" following the citation; those that have been reprinted by the Club and are now available are shown by "(OP/R:1988)" with the numerals indicating reprint year. Where printing numbers are known, they are given for possible collectors' reference. This list repeats information from similar lists in earlier editions of the records books.

I.   All-Time North American Big Game Records Books

1. *Records of North American Big Game*. 1932. Prentiss N. Gray, ed. New York: Derrydale Press. x + 178 pages. (500 copies) (OP/R:1988)
2. *North American Big Game*. 1939. Alfred Ely, Harold E. Anthony, and R.R.M. Carpenter, eds. New York: Scribner's. xxiv + 533 pages. (3,000 copies) (OP)
3. *Records of North American Big Game*. 1952. Samuel B. Webb, Grancel Fitz, and Milford Baker, eds. New York: Scribner's. xiv + 174 pages. (3,500 copies) (OP)
4. *Records of North American Big Game*. 1958. Samuel B. Webb, Grancel Fitz, and Milford Baker, eds. New York: Henry Holt and Co. xvi + 264 pages. (6,500 copies) (OP)
5. *Records of North American Big Game*. 1964. Milford Baker, ed. New York: Holt, Rhinehart and Winston. xviii + 398 pages. (10,500 copies) (OP)
6. *North American Big Game*. 1971. Robert C. Alberts, ed. Pittsburgh, Pa.: The Boone and Crockett Club. xx + 403 pages. (17,300 copies) (OP)
7. *North American Big Game*. 1977. Wm. H. Nesbitt and Jack S. Parker, eds. Washington, D.C.: The National Rifle Association and the Boone and Crockett Club. xvi + 367 pages. (10,500 copies, 1977; 5650 copies, 1978 second print) (OP)
8. *Records of North American Big Game*. 1981. Wm. H. Nesbitt and Philip L. Wright, eds. Alexandria, Va.: The Boone and Crockett Club. xii + 409 pages. (15,000 copies, 1981; 10,000 copies, 1984 second print)
9. *Records of North American Big Game*. 1988. Wm. H. Nesbitt and Jack Reneau, eds. Dumfries, Va.: The Boone and Crockett Club. xiv + 498 pages. (15,000 copies)

II. Awards Entry Period/Special Records Books

1. *Boone and Crockett Club's 18th Big Game Awards*, 1984. Wm. H. Nesbitt, ed. Alexandria, Va.: The Boone and Crockett Club. xiv + 306 pages. (10,000 copies)

21

2. *Measuring and Scoring North American Big Game Trophies*. 1985. Wm. H. Nesbitt and Philip L. Wright, eds. Alexandria, Va.: The Boone and Crockett Club. 176 pages, paperback. (10,000 copies)

3. *Boone and Crockett Club's 19th Big Game Awards*. 1986. Wm. H. Nesbitt and Jack Reneau, eds. Dumfries, Va.: The Boone and Crockett Club. xvi + 410 pages. (7,500 copies)

4. *Records of North American Whitetail Deer*. 1987. Wm. H. Nesbitt and Jack Reneau, eds. Dumfries, Va.: The Boone and Crockett Club. x + 246 pages, paperback. (10,000 copies)

III. General Hunting/Conservation Books

1. *American Big Game Hunting*. 1893. Theodore Roosevelt and George B. Grinnell, eds. New York: Forest and Stream Publishing Co. 345 pages. (OP/R:1984)

2. *Hunting in Many Lands*. 1895. Theodore Roosevelt and George B. Grinnell, eds. New York: Forest and Stream Publishing Co. 447 pages. (OP/R:1986)

3. *Trail and Camp Fire*. 1897. Theodore Roosevelt and George B. Grinnell, eds. New York: Forest and Stream Publishing Co. 355 pages. (OP/R:1988)

4. *American Big Game In Its Haunts*. 1904. George B. Grinnell, ed. New York: Forest and Stream Publishing Co. 497 pages. (OP)

5. *Hunting at High Altitudes*. 1913. George B. Grinnell, ed. New York: Harper and Brothers. 511 pages. (OP)

6. *Hunting and Conservation*. 1925. George B. Grinnell and Charles Sheldon, eds. New Haven, Conn.: Yale University Press. xvi + 548 pages. (OP)

7. *Hunting Trails on Three Continents*. 1933. George B. Grinnell, Kermit Roosevelt, W. Redmond Cross, and Prentiss N. Gray, eds. New York: Derrydale Press and Windward House. (Split printing with Derrydale producing 250 copies) xiv + 302 pages. (OP)

8. *American Game Mammals and Birds: A Catalogue of Books, 1582 to 1925*. John C. Phillips, ed. New York: Houghton Mifflin Co. viii + 639 pages. (OP)

9. *Crusade for Wildlife*. 1961. James B. Trefethen. Harrisburg, Pa.: Stackpole Co. and the Boone and Crockett Club. 377 pages. (OP)

10. *An American Crusade for Wildlife* 1975. James B. Trefethen. New York: Winchester Press and the Boone and Crockett Club. (Note: the original hardback was reprinted as a paperback by the Club in 1982 and later years.) xii + 409 pages. (OP)

11. *The Wild Sheep in Modern North America*. 1975. James B. Trefethen, ed. New York: Winchester Press and the Boone and Crockett Club. xv + 302 pages, paperback.

12. *The Black Bear in Modern North America*. 1979. Dale L. Burk, ed. Clinton, N.J.: Amwell Press and the Boone and Crockett Club. 301 pages, paperback.

Centennial Celebration Held in Dallas, Texas

The Boone and Crockett Club celebrated its Centennial Year during 1987–88. This combination period was chosen since the Club was originally formed during a similar period one hundred years earlier. The Boone and Crockett Club was organized at a dinner hosted by Theodore Roosevelt in December of 1887. Then, the first formal meeting of the Club was held at Pinauds Restaurant in New York City on February 29, 1888.

With a century of solid, well-described accomplishments in the fields of hunting and conservation, it was obviously necessary to hold a proper celebration during the Centennial Year to recognize the Club and its achievements. The planning for the Centennial Celebration got under way several years in advance of the actual event, and after due consideration of several sites, Dallas, Texas was selected as the location. A major reason for the selection of Dallas was the opportunity to schedule the Centennial Celebration during the same period of time as the annual "Hunters Extravaganza" of the Dallas Safari Club. The Boone and Crockett Club and the Dallas Safari Club share a significant number of members and certainly share common interests and goals. The Dallas Safari Club was quite eager to help celebrate the Boone and Crockett Club's Centennial and agreed readily to the scheduling of concurrent sessions, which would allow members of both groups to enjoy the activities of both events. The dates for the Boone and Crockett Club activities were set as Thursday, March 17 through Saturday, March 19, 1988. The location for all events was the Hyatt Regency Hotel, DFW.

The Centennial Celebration activities got under way with a welcoming cocktail party on Thursday night that gave everyone a chance to meet and visit. This was followed on Friday with several sessions to offer insight into the activities and history of the Club. These sessions included a talk by Stephen S. Adams, Chairman of the Ranch Committee, on the current operation and goals of the Theodore Roosevelt Memorial Ranch, the Club's centerpiece project for the Centennial Year. A film festival was held that was obviously very popular, featuring films on various outdoor subjects, including "TR" and nature. The special sessions were continued on Saturday, with talks by Walter H. White, Chairman of the Records of North American Big Game Committee, and Wm. H. Nesbitt, Executive Director of the Club. White discussed the current records keeping for native North American big game and its future objectives, while Nesbitt presented an illustrated history of the Club and its accomplishments.

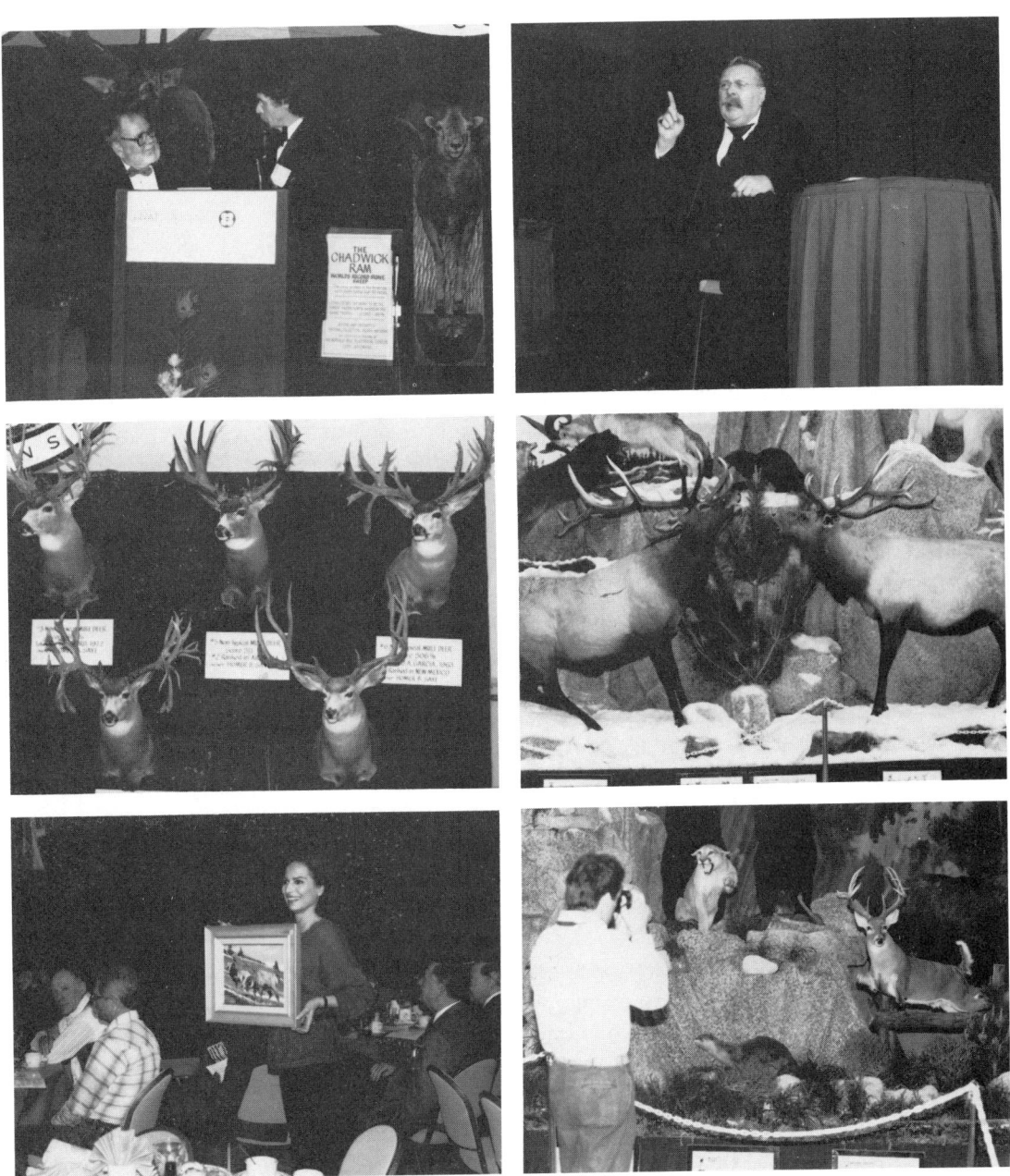

B&C Photograph by Jack Reneau

Scenes from the 1988 Centennial Celebration. Clockwise from upper left. Warren Landwermeyer, President of Dallas Safari Club and Dr. James H. "Red" Duke, Jr., Boone and Crockett Club President. Joseph P. Earley recreated Theodore Roosevelt to the delight of those assembled. The next two photographs show some of Don Corley's outstanding trophy collection that was on display. The Centennial Celebration Auction included some beautiful wildlife art. The displays included some of Homer Saye's outstanding mule deer antler collection.

The Centennial Celebration activities in Dallas were culminated on Saturday night by a President's Cocktail Party, hosted by Club President Dr. James H. "Red" Duke, Jr. This party followed the Dallas Safari Club Hunters Extravaganza closing banquet and auction. At the cocktail party, President Duke presented special appreciation plaques to the donors of auctioned items, and all who were present enjoyed a "birthday cake" that commemorated the Club's first century of achievement.

There were certainly some memorable highlights of the Centennial Celebration activities. The Dallas Safari Club had chosen the theme of the "Year of the Elk" and had illustrated this theme with some magnificent displays of elk and other fine trophies. As a jointly-sponsored display, Don Corley's entire collection of all 28 species of native North American big game animals was put on display. To show all of these trophies in a single display is a monumental task, but the result spectacular. Tommy Caruthers, who was in charge of all exhibits for the events, designed a special display, a 24-foot-high artificial "mountain" that well emulated the real thing. The trophies were arranged on the "mountain" roughly at the levels at which they would be found, from the wet meadows of the flatland to the peaks of the mountain. Naturally, those present called it "Tommy's mountain," and it was one of the highlights of the entire concurrent events. Sincere thanks go to Don Corley for making his collection available, and to Tommy Caruthers for his ingenuity and dedication that made this spectacular display possible.

Among the other outstanding trophies on display were the Chadwick Stone's sheep, the World's Record for the category and acclaimed by many folks as the finest specimen of North American big game ever taken; the Harry Swank Dall's sheep, the World's Record; and the E. C. Haase Rocky Mountain goat, the World's Record for the category. An excellent collection of top-ranking mule deer, owned by Homer Saye, was also on display, along with numerous other outstanding trophies. It was truly a visual feast for those who appreciate beautiful game animals.

Another very memorable part of the activities was the special "Lunch with the President" on Saturday that preceded the Club's fundraising auction. Well-known actor Joseph P. Earley was engaged to recreate his role as Theodore Roosevelt, one that has earned him considerable fame and placed him in movies and television films about the great conservation president. Mr. Earley, who is familiar with the Club and its accomplishments, threw himself into the task with enthusiasm, developing a very fine review of Roosevelt's life, with emphasis on TR's role in founding the Boone and Crockett Club and helping guide it during its early days. (Theodore Roosevelt served as the first President of the Club and was a vital part of its activities until his untimely death.) Earley's performance left many people speechless. All felt that they had experienced a most unique recreation of one of the most important figures in hunting and conservation.

The fundraising auction came off in remarkably fine style, due to the hard work of a number of people under the direction of Steven C. Christenson, who served as Chairman of the Centennial Celebration Committee. His helpers included Charles K. Maretzky, Jr., Don L. Corley, Dr. Robert E. Speegle, and Robert Kubick. Corley, Speegle, and Kubick deserve special credit for assembling the outstanding group of hunts that were offered. This

was a true "once-in-a-lifetime" auction of hunts, appropriate for the once-in-a-lifetime Centennial of the Club. Without the efforts of those mentioned above, and a whole lot of other folks, it simply would not have been possible to create such a successful event.

In addition to hunts, the auction included outstanding wildlife art from four of the best-known names in wildlife art today, assembled by Alfred E. King of King Galleries. Artists Ken Carlson, Michael Coleman, Guy Coheleach, and Bob Kuhn each prepared an original oil painting and also donated a remarqued print. And, a specially-bound set of all of the books of the Boone and Crockett Club, assembled with the help of Ludo Wurfbain of Worldwide Hunting Books, was also offered at auction. It was, as you might guess, a "one-of-a-kind" set with matching calf-leather bindings and special inscription pages.

A beautiful bronze of Theodore Roosevelt on horseback, No. 1 of a limited edition casting being offered by the Club (see color frontis of this book for photo of bronze), was also auctioned. The bronze is by well-known western artist Bob Scriver, who has faithfully created Roosevelt on one of his favorite horses, decked out in the garb he favored above all else: buckskins. The bronze project was conceived and carried out by Lowell E. Baier, who also put together the very popular film festival at the Celebration. He deserves a great deal of thanks from all those present who enjoyed the fruits of his labors

A final, major Centennial Year project of the Club that was not quite finished in time for Dallas, but was near completion as this book went to press, is a special edition of fine Ruger rifles commemorating the Centennial of the Club. Through the fine cooperation of Bill Ruger, these guns will be carefully selected and appropriately identified with the Club's medallion and engraving as being part of the special Centennial issue.

The donation of hunts and other items was quite essential to a fundraising auction that was sponsored by the Club on Saturday. A significant amount of money was raised by the auction to help further the Club's conservation projects. We are pleased to list here the donors of items that made this auction such a success.

It was with some sadness that persons departed the Centennial Celebration, knowing that they would not again participate in such a unique event. But, all those who were fortunate enough to be in attendance have a wealth of memories of a very special event, that both celebrated a century of achievement and marked the beginning of a second century of service by the oldest continuing hunting and conservation organization in North America, the Boone and Crockett Club.

Donors of Hunts to B & C Centennial Celebration Auction

Myles Bradford
Dalziel Hunting, Ltd.
Dease Lake, B.C.
Canada moose hunt

Lynn and Penny Castle
Denali Park, Alaska
barren ground caribou hunt

Mike Young
Hells Kitchen Guide Service
Salem, Utah
cougar hunt

Marvin and Warner Glenn
Douglas, Arizona
Coues' whitetail deer hunt

Randy Haecker
R. R. Haecker Outfitter, Inc.
Jackson, Wyoming
American elk hunt

Keith N. Johnson
Anchorage, Alaska
Alaska brown bear hunt

Bud and Mike Branham
Adventure Unlimited
Hurricane, Utah
black bear hunt

Terry Cook
Guided Arctic Expeditions
Inuvik, N.W.T.
muskox hunt

Rick Furniss
Rick Furniss Outfitting
Whitehorse, Yukon
Alaska-Yukon moose hunt

Bubba Glosson
High Sierra Outfitters
Kempner, Texas
pronghorn hunt

Hank Hankerd
Hank Hankerd, Ltd.
Wasilla, Alaska
grizzly bear hunt

Archie Lang
Turnagain Holding, Ltd.
Watson Lake, Yukon
Stone's sheep hunt

Gary Moore
G. F. Moore Outfitters, Ltd.
Dawson Creek, B.C.
Rocky Mountain goat hunt

Joe Peddle
Shenandithit Camps, Ltd.
Corner Brook, Newfoundland
woodland caribou hunt

Jim Schaafsma
Arrow Five Outfitters
Klamath Falls, Oregon
Columbia blacktail deer hunt

Red Sorenson
Red Sorenson and Sons Outfitting
Victoria, B.C.
mountain caribou hunt

Ridge W. Taylor
Jackson, Wyoming
mule deer hunt

Fred Webb and Sammy Cantafio
Webb Qaivvik, Ltd.
Lansdale, Pennsylvania
Central Canada barren ground caribou hunt

Les Nelson
Duck Mountain Outfitters
Minitonas, Manitoba
whitetail deer hunt

Steven Perrins and Buckey Winkley
Kodiak Safaris
Anchorage, Alaska
Sitka blacktail deer hunt

Stan Simpson
Ram Head Outfitters, Ltd.
Warburg, Alberta
Dall's sheep hunt

Honorable Mike Sullivan,
Governor of Wyoming, and
Wyoming Dept. of Game and Fish
Governor's Permit for Wyoming moose

Fred Webb
Webb Qaivvik, Ltd.
Lansdale, Pennsylvania
Quebec-Labrador caribou hunt

Boone and Crockett Club Conservation Stamp Prints

In recent years, conservation stamps have become quite popular, using the format and size popularized by the familiar "Duck Stamp Prints." Several organizations have broadened the approach from just waterfowl to other game birds. The Boone and Crockett Club went a step beyond this with its decision to offer a Conservation Stamp Print series based upon the big-game animals of North America.

No organization could be more appropriate to offer a Conservation Stamp Print series of native North American big game animals than the Boone and Crockett Club, long recognized for its records book for such animals. And, the revenues from this program are used for the Club's annual Grants-In-Aid for wildlife research, as well as other conservation programs. It was decided to offer 1,887 prints in recognition of the founding year of the Club, 1887.

The Boone and Crockett Club Conservation Stamp Print program was begun in 1982 with the selection of artist Bob Kuhn, who chose to paint the most popular big game animal of North America, the whitetail deer. For 1983, the artist was Guy Coheleach, who painted a beautiful barren ground caribou group. For 1984, Ken Carlson depicted a magnificent American elk bull bugling. Michael Coleman was selected to do the 1985 Stamp Print, and he chose as his subject an Alaska brown bear in a typical Kodiak Island setting. For 1986, Ken Carlson depicted bighorn sheep in a Rocky Mountain setting that will start any sheep hunter's heart thumping faster. For the special Centennial Year Stamp Print of 1987-88, Bob Kuhn rendered a memorable American bison scene that directly evokes feelings of days long-gone, appropriate for remembering the many achievements of the Club during this first century.

It is anticipated that all 26 species of North American big game will be depicted in this series. It is a very unique series, not paralleled by the offerings of other conservation organizations in their stamp print offerings. It is likely to be a worthwhile collectible, appreciating in value over the years, due both to the uniqueness of the offering and to the high esteem in which the wildlife artists chosen for the work are held.

We are pleased to present, in the following pages, the six Conservation Stamp Prints that have been offered to date. For further information on the series and ordering information, write directly to the Club office or contact local art galleries.

"1982 BOONE AND CROCKETT CLUB CONSERVATION STAMP PRINT"

Bob Kuhn

"1983 BOONE AND CROCKETT CLUB CONSERVATION STAMP PRINT"

Guy Coheleach

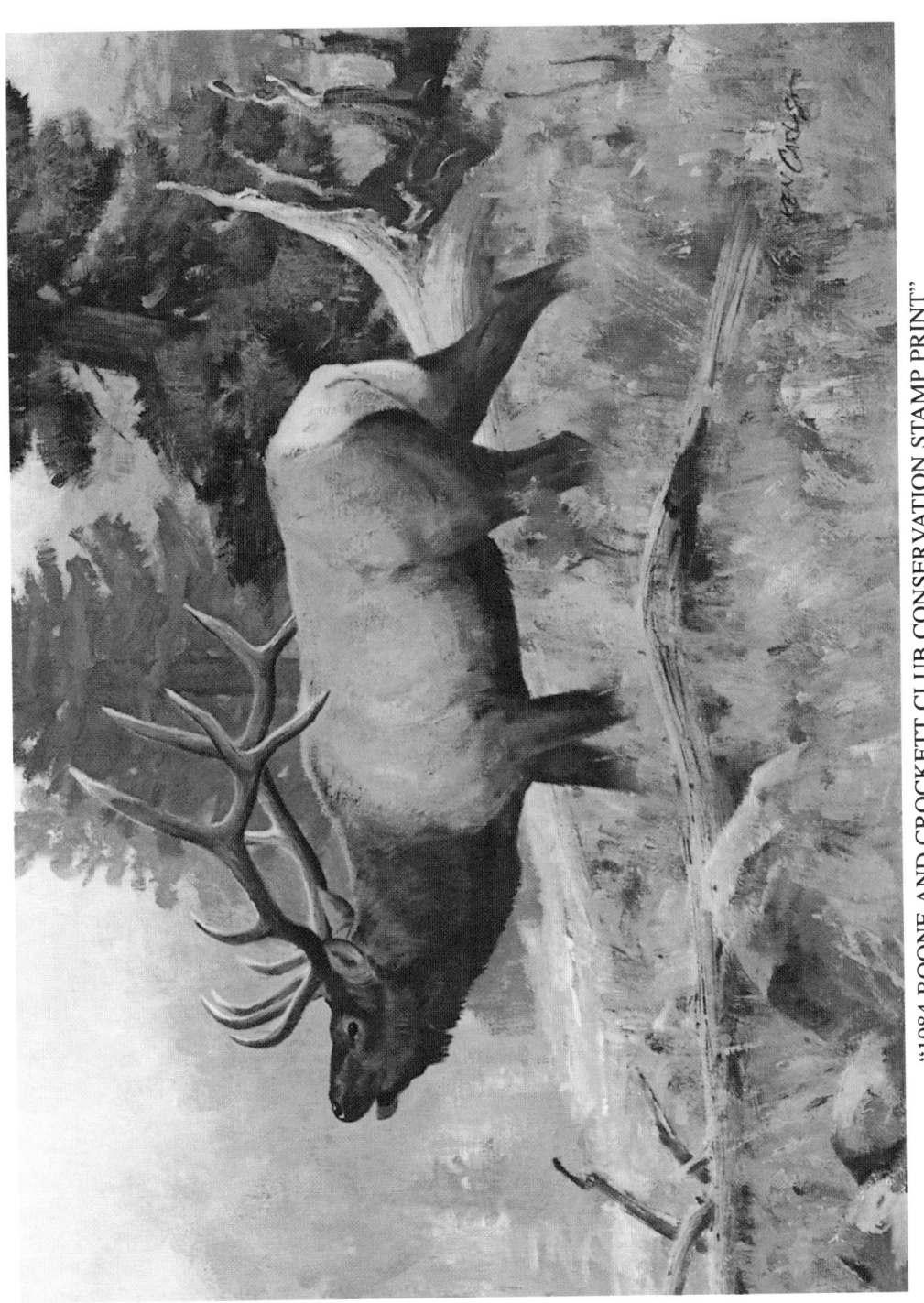

"1984 BOONE AND CROCKETT CLUB CONSERVATION STAMP PRINT"

Ken Carlson

"1985 BOONE AND CROCKETT CLUB CONSERVATION STAMP PRINT"

Michael Coleman

"1986 BOONE AND CROCKETT CLUB CONSERVATION STAMP PRINT"

Ken Carlson

"1987–88 BOONE AND CROCKETT CLUB CONSERVATION STAMP PRINT"

Bob Kuhn

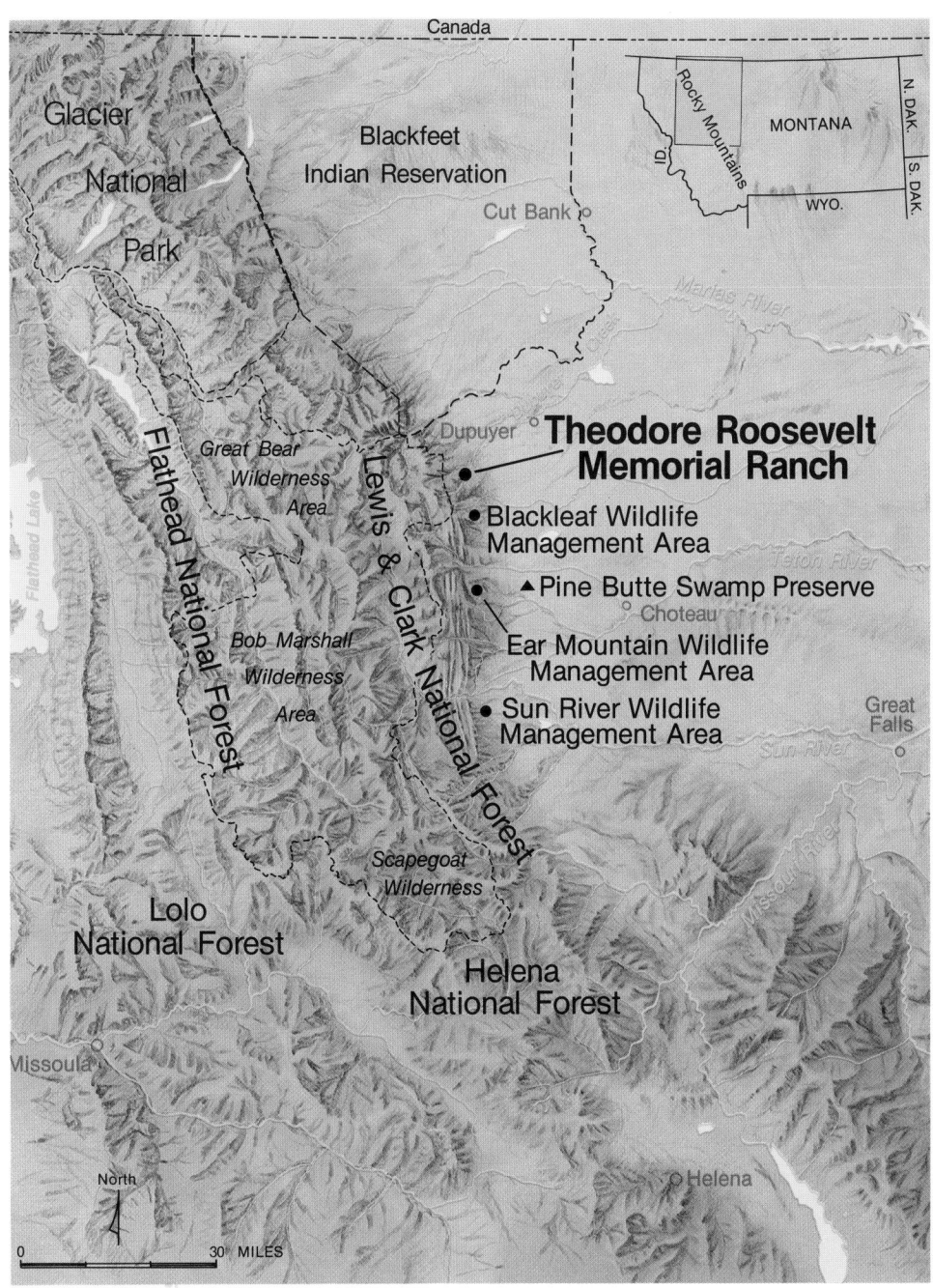

The Theodore Roosevelt Memorial Ranch is located southwest of Dupuyer, Montana, on the East Slope of the Rocky Mountains, closely adjacent to other important wildlife habitat and management areas.

The New Western Frontier

WILLIAM L. SEARLE, PRESIDENT
THE BOONE AND CROCKETT CLUB FOUNDATION

Once our great western lands seemed limitless. There was ample room for the deer and growing crops, for grizzlies and herds of cattle, for buffalo and hunters. Today, the wild Rocky Mountain west is shrinking, as land uses and conflicts intensify. Wildlife must share the rangelands with livestock, causing strains for both. Conservation of some wild species causes trouble for the profitable management of ranches. To complicate matters, timber, gas, and oil production is crowding in. Consequently, ways must be found to make wildlife and economic values more compatible. That is "The New Western Frontier."

To celebrate its 100th year, the Boone and Crockett Club has acquired a 6,000-acre ranch on the East slope of the Rocky Mountains, just west of Dupuyer, Montana. The Club has named the ranch for its founder, Theodore Roosevelt. The Theodore Roosevelt Memorial Ranch is dedicated to finding ways to manage the inherent conflicts between the conservation of wildlife and man's use and development of land.

The Boone and Crockett Club established the Boone and Crockett Club Foundation to manage the TRM Ranch and its various programs. Working in collaboration with the University of Montana, the Foundation is mounting a program to provide graduate-level research students a controlled outdoor environment in which to study, devise, and demonstrate wildlife range and livestock management techniques.

One of the nation's most pressing environmental and conservation problems, and one with high potential for controversy, is in the western rangelands where wildlife and livestock must competitively share land and forage, thus posing a threat to each other in the long term.

Conservationists, with good reason, press for the preservation of threatened species and respect for our great national wildlife heritage. Ranchers and farmers, with equal reason and right, seek to protect their livestock and crops from invasion of wildlife that could threaten them. On this their economic survival obviously depends.

In a simple sense, then, with wildlife habitat throughout the West shrinking from increased and conflicting land use, a pressing and mounting need emerges to find ways to make wildlife, ranching, and agricultural values and needs more compatible. Therein lies the great opportunity of the New Western Frontier. Among the things that must be done are these:

1. Wildlife habitat must be maintained and improved on both private and public lands. Without suitable habitat, many wildlife species inevitably will decrease in number or disappear.

2. Research is needed—hard, practical, and realistic studies to develop techniques and methods for reducing competition between the demands of wildlife and those of agriculture, especially ranching as carried out today.
3. The information must be provided to ranchers, environmentalists, hunters, and the general public, to demonstrate the new methods and techniques that are found for dealing with this critical problem of great importance to the West and the nation as a whole.

Accordingly, the TRM Ranch research program will address four important objectives in fulfilling its fundamental purpose of searching for solutions to the wildlife/livestock competitive relationship:

1. It will expand the critical area of wildlife habitat.
2. It will mount a program of applied research to find new methods and techniques for benefiting wildlife, range conditions, and ranching.
3. It will undertake a program of education and public information on wildlife/ranch matters.
4. It will continue to function as an operating ranch.

The TRM Ranch was purchased with the full support of the Montana Department of Fish, Wildlife and Parks. The Department considers the TRM Ranch to be an important ecological area, strategically located to serve wildlife in coordination with other key conservation properties. It is part of the land area that comprises the northern Rocky Mountains, the Lewis and Clark National Forest, the Bob Marshall, Great Bear, and Scapegoat Wilderness areas, and also Glacier National Park.

On the TRM Ranch, at least seasonally, can be found all the species of wildlife that once occurred in pre-settlement days of the region, with the single exception of the bison. Its brushy riparian areas are the principal paths for grizzlies traveling to and from the mountains. The ranch accommodates a rich diversity of other wildlife, including the black bear, cougar, elk, mountain goat, bighorn sheep, mule and whitetail deer, wolf, golden eagle, barred owl, peregrine falcon, merlin falcon, and many less obvious, but equally important, species.

The applied research program is the central focus of the whole project. It is the core of the major Boone and Crockett Club investment in seeking to meet this critical challenge. The research program will be carried out by, and in cooperation with, the University of Montana Wildlife Biology Program. By formal agreement, the Boone and Crockett Club Foundation is setting up a $900,000 endowment within the University to underwrite a Boone and Crockett Club Professorship that will directly carry out the research program and direct the activities of graduate students in their own research programs at the Ranch. Under this agreement, the TRM Ranch facilities are to be available to professors and post-doctoral and graduate students from colleges and universities nationwide.

The TRM Ranch offers a unique opportunity for practical, "hands-on" research to delineate better ways to manage the interface of livestock and wildlife on ranching and other

agricultural areas. It should certainly help to remove some misconceptions and animosities that have long plagued the relationship between stockmen and wildlife managers.

The basic research is already under way at the TRM Ranch. Exclosures are in place (to exclude grazing of both domestic and wild animals and thus provide a "control" by which to gauge experimental conditions) and basic transects of the vegetation are being set up so that seasonal and annual changes in the vegetation, as related to livestock numbers and wildlife on the area, can be properly recorded. These will be the first small steps toward the basic understanding required to properly carry out the more complex research programs of the future.

The TRM Ranch will continue to function as an operating cattle ranch, alongside and complementary to its research activities. It is considered essential to do so in order that the techniques developed through the research programs will have a greater credibility with the ranching community, a factor that cannot be discounted in developing and maintaining wildlife habitat along the Rocky Mountain front and elsewhere. Without this practical backdrop, it would be hard to envision ready acceptance of results by ranchers and other agricultural area managers, whose very livelihood can depend upon such decisions. It is just for this important task that the TRM Ranch is being developed and will show its great worth in future years.

The Theodore Roosevelt Memorial Ranch is the major Centennial Year project of the Club, large in scale and importance to wildlife and wildlife habitat of the future. If you would like to be a part of this grand beginning of the second century of the Boone and Crockett Club, write to the Boone and Crockett Club office for details. It is a project large enough to offer a challenge to all those who love our native wildlife and want to help ensure that it will be there for the enjoyment of future generations.

The Theodore Roosevelt Memorial Ranch is excellent big-game habitat, with particular importance as a wintering area for elk and mule deer, and spring and summer range for the grizzly bear and many other animals.

Boone and Crockett Club Grants-In-Aid Program

GEORGE C. HIXON
CHAIRMAN
CONSERVATION COMMITTEE

A little-known aspect of the Boone and Crockett Club is its Grants-In-Aid Program for wildlife research. For the past eight years, during my tenure as Chairman of the Conservation Committee, the Club has made annual grants that total over $200,000. Each year the Club has made grants that are generally in the $1,000 to $5,000 range, totaling about $25,000 to $40,000 per year. While grants are usually made to researchers in the field of big-game management, the Club has also made grants for the study of coyotes, bobcats, wolverines, and the endangered ocelot. In addition, we have been long-time supporters of the Shooting Sports program of the National 4-H Clubs and of the Northern Wild Sheep and Goat Council.

We consider these grants to be very important to achievement of the Club's goals and objectives. They obviously result in summary findings that are useful for wildlife management program development and/or further studies. In addition, they directly aid the academic development of wildlife researchers and managers. It is important to aid these individuals in their development, as they will help influence public opinion, policy, and general attitudes toward wildlife, hunting, and conservation in tomorrow's world.

A list of some of the wildlife researchers aided by the Grants-In-Aid program during earlier years underscores the program's importance in support of career development. Dr. David Mech, perhaps the foremost wolf researcher of today, was a graduate student on the long-term Isle Royale wolf/moose studies that have been supported since their beginning. His later wolf/deer studies in Minnesota were also funded by the program. Dr. Lynn Rogers received support for his vital studies of the black bear in Minnesota, with results helping elevate the black bear's status in that state to a valued game animal. It was considered a vermin animal, without protection, prior to the study, and therefore was not managed or protected by the usual wildlife programs of the state. Dr. Maurice Hornocker received funding for his classic studies of the cougar in Idaho. Here, the situation was quite similar to that of the black bear study of Lynn Rogers. Little was known of the cougar, due to its secretive habits, and the public opinion of it was negative, with the assumption that mountain lions were directly detrimental to deer and elk populations, as well as posing a threat to domestic livestock. Hornocker's results helped bring out the true facts of the importance of the cougar to the ecosystem by helping "trim" game populations of old, sick, and infirm animals. His studies have received wide publicity, both in magazines and in several TV specials. His later studies of the importance of the wolverine to the northern forest ecosystem were also funded by the Grants-In-Aid program.

One of the most unusual and valuable projects funded by the program was a movie about the

ecological havoc caused by feral (wild and free-ranging) burros in southwestern National Parks. With funding from several sources, and produced by the Sierra Club, this film demonstrates in graphic detail just how devastating these wild descendents of the faithful donkeys of the early-day prospector can be. As you will likely recall, this was a very emotional issue several years ago, with several "Animal Friends" groups opposing any reasonable control programs for the burros, in spite of the easily demonstrated problems caused by burros to the daily life of desert sheep and other native wildlife. Unfortunately, feral burros can be started at almost any time by simply releasing tame animals into the wild. It is not so easy to re-establish desert sheep when they have been extirpated from an area. This film helped to get the problem across in a factual way to administrators and the public, although the problem is not yet totally solved.

Each year the Club reviews a sizeable number of requests for funding, of which we are generally able to aid three to six projects. This selection process involves a detailed review of each request by the entire Conservation Committee. The selection is often agonizing, for we are unable to help many of those researchers with quite valid projects because of our budget restraints. However, I believe that over the years the Club has made excellent use of its conservation dollars. With such noted wildlife researchers and administrators as Durwood Allen, Dan Poole, Jim Teer, Wendell Swank, and Phil Wright serving on the Conservation Committee, we are not lacking in first-class scientific advice in choosing projects for funding.

In 1986 the Boone and Crockett Club purchased a large cattle ranch near the town of Dupuyer, Montana, and named it the Theodore Roosevelt Memorial Ranch in honor of our founder. The ranch has excellent wintering grounds for mule deer and elk. Grizzly bears are often seen on the ranch and in the adjacent Forest Service lands. A major purpose of the ranch is to provide a study area to observe the interactions of cattle ranching and big game management. Working closely with various departments of the University of Montana, the Club has, over the past two years, initiated the necessary baseline studies for this important work. This naturally has consumed a great portion of the yearly funds normally available for the Grants-In-Aid Program. However, as the baseline studies are completed, we expect this trend to slow down so that in the future, full Grants-In-Aid funding will be available for grant purposes.

Qualified researchers or graduate students who would like to apply for the Grants-In-Aid Program can obtain the necessary application by writing or calling the Club office. Note that applications *must* be completed and in the hands of the Conservation Committee Chairman by November of each year, as the Committee meets in early December to review the applications. Applications received at other times of the year will be held for consideration the following December. Projects approved for funding will receive the grant early in the following year.

Following, you will find a list of projects the Club has sponsored over the past eight years. Some of these, such as the Isle Royale moose/wolf studies, have been ongoing projects for many years. Others have only been funded for a single year. (For a fine review of the Grants-In-Aid Program prior to the 1980's, see Fred Pullman's chapter in the 8th edition of the all-time records book, 1981.) As can be noted from this list, there is a considerable diversity in the subjects addressed by funded projects, but they do have a common characteristic of expanding needed knowledge or suggesting practical solutions to current or future problems of wildlife and its habitat.

Boone and Crockett Club Grants-In-Aid Recipients During the 1980's

Donald J. Bedunah and Russel Offerdahl
University of Montana "Plant Communities of the Theodore Roosevelt Memorial Ranch."

Robert A. Gagliuso
Oregon State University "Habitat Alterations and Human Disturbance: Their Impact on Mountain Lions in Southwestern Oregon."

Audry E. Goldsmith
University of California (Berkeley) "History and Research on the Reintroduction of Pronghorn in California."

John T. Hogg
Wildlife-Wildlands Institute "The Conservation of Genetic Resources in Bighorn Sheep."

Lynn R. Irby
Montana State University "Management of Bighorns in the Upper Yellowstone River Valley."

Donald A. Jenni
University of Montana "Bighorn Sheep Social Behavior and Ecology."

Gary M. Koehler
University of Idaho "Demography of a Low Productivity Bobcat Population."

Thomas E. Kucera
University of California (Berkeley) "Ecology and Productivity of Two Eastern Sierra Deer Herds."

Les Marcum and Gary Olson
University of Montana "Movement Patterns and Habitat Use of Bull Elk that Winter on the Theodore Roosevelt Memorial Ranch."

Mark Masteller
Colorado State University "Dominance, Spacing Mechanisms, and Population Regulation in Mountain Goats."

Bruce McLellan
Canadian Border Grizzly Project "Aspects of the Behavior of Grizzly Bears in Response to Hydrocarbon Exploration and the Presence of Humans."

John Richard Medcraft
Iowa State University "Wildlife and Surface Mine Reclamation in Northeastern Wyoming."

Gary D. Miller
University of New Mexico "Ecology of Desert Bighorn Sheep in Western Arizona."

National 4-H Council
Washington, D.C. "4-H Shooting Sports Program."

Northern Wild Sheep and Goat Council "Sponsorship of International Meeting."

Rolf O. Peterson
Michigan Technological University "Isle Royale Wolf and Moose Studies."

Lorraine Triest Rudd
University of Wyoming "Winter Relationships of Moose to Oil and Gas Development in Western Wyoming."

Michael E. Tewes
Texas A & I University "Recovery of the Endangered Ocelot in Texas."

Boone and Crockett Club Associates Program

From its beginning, the Boone and Crockett Club has been a very small organization in terms of membership, although its achievements have been of major proportions. The key to its success has probably been this small membership, allowing for in-depth discussion of issues, followed by quick action as needed. But, its limited membership (limited by its bylaws to a maximum of 150 regular members) does mean that many persons who agree with its aims and objectives cannot hope to be a part of its membership. For that main reason, the Boone and Crockett Club Associates Program was created in 1986. It offers the opportunity for anyone who agrees with the Club's aims and objectives to help support the Club and its work by being a part of the Associates Program.

The Associates Program is open to all individuals who agree with the Club's rules of Fair Chase and its emphasis on sportsmanship while afield. Enrollment in the program is yearly, or for multiple years, and specific benefits include a quarterly newsletter that is the publication of record for the Club. It is in the pages of the newsletter that changes in trophy entry requirements, changes in scoring techniques, the Club's stand on particular issues, and other hunting and conservation news items are brought before the Club members, Associates, and the Club's Official Measurers for the big game records keeping. The Official Measurers receive the newsletter as a courtesy, since it is used as a medium of information exchange between the Club and measurers on subjects directly and indirectly related to trophy measurement and the entry of trophies.

A significant benefit of the Associates Program is the 20% discount offered on books, the Club's Conservation Stamp Prints, and other products that are offered from time to time by the Club. (In fact, the 20% discount on two copies of this very book that you are reading would pay for a year's subscription to the Associates Newsletter, at the time this book went to press.)

Other features of the Associates Program include the opportunity for Associates to register their better trophies for recognition in the pages of the newsletter, and also to submit hunting stories for consideration of publication in the newsletter. Associates will also receive priority in invitations to the Final Awards Banquet and other activities that recognize the outstanding trophies entered in each Awards. And, special recognition items are offered to allow Associates to enjoy their affiliation with the Boone and Crockett Club to its fullest.

If the Boone and Crockett Club Associates Program sounds like something you would enjoy, write to the Club office for a brochure and application blank for the program.

B&C Photograph by Jack Reneau

Shown at the entrance to the TRM Ranch in 1985, shortly after its purchase by the Boone and Crockett Club, are Club members: (l to r, kneeling) Judge F. Anderson; Wendell G. Swank; (standing) Wm. H. Nesbitt; Harold W. "Buck" Julien; Arthur C. Popham, Jr.; George C. Hixon; Ronald A. Bishop (deceased); C. R. Palmer; Howard W. Pollock; John H. Batten; William I. Spencer; Bayard D. Rea; Edward G. Zern; Alfred Ely, Jr.; John M. LeBolt; Sherman Gray; William L. Searle, Jr.; H. Norden van Horne; D. Lee Bassett; and William C. MacCarty III.

Trail Blazers In Conservation
The Boone and Crockett Club's First Century

GEORGE B. WARD AND RICHARD E. McCABE

The story of the Boone and Crockett Club is one of sportsmen dedicated individually and collectively to the art and traditions of the hunt and to the "preservation" of game animals. It is a chronicle of high-caliber hunting, politics, programs, and people. It is the very track of the conservation movement in North America. It is a 100-year history of accomplishment.

The Club had its formal beginning in New York City, on a December evening in 1887. Eleven men, each a sportsman and energetic and influential person, gathered at a dinner party called by one of their number and heard a proposal to form a fellowship chartered to enhance camaraderie through their mutual interest in hunting and wildlife. But the proposal had an even broader objective, to address and work to resolve nationwide problems that jeopardized game animal populations. The dinner guests heartily endorsed the idea, and a brief constitution was drafted.

The real genesis of the Boone and Crockett Club, however, evolved much earlier and in places other than metropolitan New York. And the actual catalyst was not the camaraderie of an elegant meal. The seeds of the Club were germinated, in fact, long before vanguards of European civilization first crossed the great ocean to discover and explore America.

Panorama

The process of time and forces of nature had molded a fertile and diverse New World landscape that was a unique trove of mineral and living resources. It was a wild land of awesome proportion, yet equally unbounded opportunity.

Those who followed the explorers and endured to settle sought to capitalize on what the wilderness produced or represented. To some it was material wealth, to others personal freedom, and to still others colonial supremacy. To all, the land was an arena of competition, competition against other interests and competition with the environment.

For many decades, the newcomers clung tenaciously to the fringes of the New World, grasping eagerly at the resources found there, but prohibited by inadequate technology, by politics, and by the land itself from penetrating far into the uncertain but alluring interior.

English, French, Spanish, Dutch, Russians, Portuguese, and others approached the continent from different compass points and motives. The Spaniards fanned out across the South and Southwest; Russians probed the Pacific Northwest; Frenchmen laid claim to the

47

northland and uncharted center; the English and Dutch struggled for handholds along the Atlantic coast. Then, for two centuries, these national interests bartered, bullied, and battled in contests for imperial sovereignty and the spoils thereof. Ultimately, the power that prevailed was that of the colonists, whose spirit of self-determination fostered a new nation "conceived in liberty."

As the United States was fledged and then expanded, it became in reality, and in the eyes of the world, *the* land of opportunity. It also became a melting pot of nationalities and cultures. Through enterprise, ingenuity, tenacity, and sheer numbers, the new Americans surged across the continent in pursuit of better livelihoods and bigger dreams. Emboldened by governmental sanction of manifest destiny, and bolstered by the long-ingrained Judeo-Christian ethic that both urged and justified man's dominion over nature, the pioneers wrested homesteads from the wilderness.

The "taming" of the United States from 1700 to 1900 was a remarkable phenomenon. Not only was the country populated from coast to coast; the movement west took place in tandem with a spate of mechanical inventions and discoveries that lifted the young nation to a new social and industrial plane. The principles of democracy and free enterprise in the U.S. opened a floodgate of enthusiasm, ideas, and industry. It was, as one writer suggested, the "Second American Revolution," a period when, for the first time in non-primitive society, individual well-being was constrained only by the limits of initiative, perseverance, and luck.

That two-century period has been viewed quite differently by various historians, who do all agree that it was unprecedented. Some say that it was a time when Americans capitalized on the cornucopia of opportunities available to them, though some people certainly did better than others. It was human nature, and the very object of democracy, to take advantage of myriad brass rings that the land and its resources availed. Other historians have recorded the time as a period of frenzied exploitation, with wanton disregard for the long-term well-being of the land and society.

Whatever the case, the United States was settled and solidified as a world power. The principal consequence of this emergence through opportunism or exploitation was a loss of some of the very resources that attracted and sustained the first colonists. Pristine America's vast virgin forests were cut, prairies were plowed, and wetlands were filled or drained. Minerals were rapaciously siphoned or sifted from streambeds and hillsides. Topsoils were leached of nutrients or allowed to erode at rates far exceeding replacement. Beaver, deer, bison, elk, wolves, bear, passenger pigeons, pronghorn, wild turkey, bighorn sheep, plumed birds, and other wildlife were killed to extinction or nearly so for subsistence, market, or as imagined obstacles to "progress." Domestic livestock displaced wild ungulates on pasture lands circumscribed by barbed wire. "Soddies" and log cabins replaced wicki-ups and hogans. Train tracks and telegraph lines dissected the landscape, pragmatically reducing the country in time and space. The breechloading rifle, steam engine, cotton gin, and other mechanical marvels of the age efficiently chiseled away further at the vestiges of wilderness. Such corollaries of unbridled liberty provided the sparks of conscience and foresight that were to ignite as the Boone and Crockett Club.

By the late 1800's, it was clear, at least to a few people, that the effects of America's

rapid growth and prosperity were accomplished at a great expense of natural resources. That expense was less a matter of utilization than one of non-management. Wildlife, for example, was depleted by such intense and unregulated killing that some animals were reduced in number and distribution to an extent that recovery was both uncertain and, for some species, unlikely.

To say that wildlife numbers were reduced by the last decade of the 1800's is a considerable understatement. Beaver had once been common throughout the country and the mainstay of a lucrative fur trade industry. By 1887, they had been eliminated in nearly all states east of the Mississippi River and were very rare in the western states. Bison may have numbered as many as 40 million in 1800. By 1887, there were fewer than 5,000 in the U.S. The white-tailed deer population in the U.S. at the time of colonization was no less than 24 million. By 1887, no more than 500,000 remained. In pre-Columbian America, wild turkey likely exceeded 15 million. By 1887, the turkey was extirpated from most of its original range and probably numbered fewer than 400,000. The western plains may have supported 10 million pronghorn in the early 1800's. By 1887, fewer than 25,000 pronghorn could be found. Elk also numbered 10 million when European civilization first arrived at America's doorstep. By 1887, fewer than 150,000 elk survived. It is believed that 3–5 *billion* passenger pigeons flew the country's spacious skies during the colonial era. By 1887, perhaps a few million remained and the population was in a rapid tailspin that would end 27 years later when the last passenger pigeon died in a zoological park in Cincinnati.

Gone completely were Audubon's bighorn sheep, Eastern and Merriam's elk, heath hen, great auk, and Carolina parakeet, to name a few.

As sportsmen, the Club founders were very aware of what the plight of wildlife meant in terms of future hunting prospects. As Americans, they saw clearly what it represented in broader resource terms to the national health. As businessmen, industrialists, journalists, and politicians, they recognized that it lay with them, and others of like vision, to attempt "so far as possible" to relieve and correct the situation.

At the time, the term "conservation" had not been applied, or even considered with regard to natural resources. In fact, to that time, the concept of conservation was contrary to the pace and scope of America's maturity as an economic, social, and military force. The losses of wildlife, particularly evident in the few decades following the Civil War, were the first convincing evidence that the country's resource wealth was subject to the law of diminishing returns and, without mechanisms to halt the momentum of exploitation, could be tapped out.

To be sure, the Club's founders were not the only ones to recognize the seriousness of the wildlife predicament. Beginning in the mid–1800's, a number of other prominent citizens had warned against the indiscriminate "slaughter of wild creatures." But the Club founders were among the first to pledge to do more than hand-wringing.

Touchstones

One of the first orders of business was a name for the new fraternity. The founders decided on Boone and Crockett--two illustrious names from the country's frontier past,

FOREST AND STREAM.

A WEEKLY JOURNAL OF THE ROD AND GUN.

TERMS, $4 A YEAR. 10 CTS. A COPY. } SIX MONTHS, $2.

NEW YORK, FEBRUARY 16, 1888.

{ VOL. XXX.—No. 4. NOS. 39 & 40 PARK ROW, NEW YORK.

CORRESPONDENCE.

THE FOREST AND STREAM is the recognized medium of entertainment, instruction and information between American sportsmen. Communications on the subject to which its pages are devoted are respectfully invited. Anonymous communications will not be regarded. No name will be published except with writer's consent. The Editors are not responsible for the views of correspondents.

ADVERTISEMENTS.

Only advertisements of an approved character inserted. Inside pages, nonpareil type, 30 cents per line. Special rates for three, six, and twelve months. Seven words to the line, twelve lines to one inch. Advertisements should be sent in by Saturday previous to issue in which they are to be inserted. Transient advertisements must invariably be accompanied by the money or they will not be inserted. Reading notices $1.00 per line.

SUBSCRIPTIONS

May begin at any time. Subscription price, $4 per year; $2 for six months; to a club of three annual subscribers, three copies for $10; five copies for $16. Remit by express money-order, regi ered letter, money-order, or draft, payable to the Forest and Stream Publishing Company. The paper may be obtained of the newsdealers throughout the United States, Canadas and Great Britain. For sale by Davies & Co., No. 1 Finch Lane, Cornhill, London. General subscription agents for Great Britain, Messrs. Davies & Co., and Messrs. Sampson Low, Marston, Searles and Rivington, 188 Fleet street, London, Eng. Foreign subscription price, $5 per year; $2.50 for six months. Address all communications,

Forest and Stream Publishing Co.

Nos. 39 AND 40 PARK ROW. NEW YORK CITY.

CONTENTS.

with a rich opportunity. It already has a proud history and it should remain for many years to come the practice ground of thousands, each one inspired by the story of the struggles which have been had in small arm work on that memorable range. Turned into pasture lots, cut up into a struggling town site, the range with its story of a decade and a half of endeavor and triumph will become a mere tradition. This is worth something, and this cannot be put into the bond of transfer against the modest reservation which the directors demand.

SNAP SHOTS.

A T a dinner given recently in New York by a well-known gentleman who is interested in big-game shooting in the West, it was proposed to form a club which should bear the title of the Boone and Crockett Club. Only persons who have killed one or more varieties of North American large game with the rifle are to be eligible to membership, and the name, embracing as it does those of two of the best known American rifle shots, sufficiently indicates the character of the organization. It is essentially a club of American riflemen who use the arm for hunting. The suggestion made by their host was warmly welcomed by the gentlemen present, and a few names were suggested of persons who might be glad to become members of such an association. The members of the club, so far as it is developed, are all persons of high social standing, and it would seem that an organization of this description, composed of men of intelligence and education, might wield a great influence for good in matters relating to game protection. It would be premature at present to speak of the possibilities of such a club, but as matters develop in regard to it, the public will be kept advised upon the subject.

The price paid for these buffalo has not been made public, but that the figure was high may be inferred from the fact that on more than one occasion Mr. Jones has refused $500 apiece for buffalo.

In the Massachusetts Senate the Committee on Agriculture have been directed to consider "the expediency of providing by law for the offering of bounties for the destroying of injurious birds and other animals, including English sparrows, crows, hawks, foxes and woodchucks, which are destructive to farm crops." The committee may profitably familiarize themselves with the course of Pennsylvania. The law there giving a bounty for hawks and owls was repealed last year, because competent naturalists proved to the satisfaction of the Legislature that those birds were useful instead of injurious, and that laws to promote their wholesale systematic destruction did not partake of the rankest folly. If hawks and owls are useful allies of agriculture in Pennsylvania they cannot be injurious in Massachusetts.

We observe that Capt. Chas. A. Bramble, of Fredericton, N. B., has recently returned to his home, closely followed by a Dutch blessing from Mr. Wm. C. Harris, who is the editor of a paper printed in this city. It is understood that Capt. Bramble offered to sell the fishing rights of the Renous River to Mr. Harris, and Mr. Harris's intimate friends, Messrs. Fred. D. Storey and E. Hartzig; and that when Mr. Harris failed to take his share, the entire interest was assumed by the others; hence these tears. It would be a mistake for Capt. Bramble or any of his numerous friends to take Harris seriously; he is only playing the part of a man who says naughty things when a fish gets away; and however much such objurgations may assuage the fisherman's chagrin, they do not affect the fish one iota.

Club founding member and life-long conservationist George Bird Grinnell announced the formation of the Boone and Crockett Club in his magazine, Forest and Stream, in the February 16, 1888 issue. Interestingly, the first *formal* meeting of the Club had not been held at that time (it was February 29, 1888), indicating Grinnell's optimism for success of the new organization. (Magazine copy courtesy of William B. Ruger.)

names that are synonymous with America's pioneering vitality and with rugged individualism, the very personification of the soul of Nimrod, the hunter. Daniel Boone was born in 1735 in Bucks County, Pennsylvania. Limited in formal education, Boone's adventurous nature led him to acquire exceptional skills in woodcraft at a young age. Even at a time when self-reliance and courage were commonplace virtues among the people of settlement communities, Boone was distinguished for his uncommon boldness and enterprise.

At age 34, Daniel Boone, in the company of five others, pressed into the wilds of what is now the State of Kentucky. At a site along the Kentucky River, he constructed a fort (Boonesboro) and soon settled his family and 30 volunteers there.

Boone's proficiency in carving a settlement from the wilderness, provisioning it by trapping and hunting, and defending it from almost continual siege by Indians, became legendary. He was once captured by Indians and taken to Old Chillocothe on the Miami River, where he was adopted by a Shawnee chief. Boone subsequently escaped after learning of an impending Indian raid on Boonesboro, returning to the settlement in time to warn its inhabitants and help in repelling the attack.

Boone remained in Kentucky until 1795, playing a prominent role in the history of the territory until its admission to statehood in 1791. When the state was surveyed, his land claims were disputed. So, Boone moved to Missouri, then a Spanish province, where he had been awarded a grant of 8,000 acres. With the Louisiana Purchase, Boone again lost his holdings, but Congress awarded him a parcel of 850 acres.

A popular notion about Daniel Boone is that he moved westward from Kentucky to find "elbow room"—solitude and distance from advancing civilization. While in fact a man contemptuous of urban surroundings and the trappings of regimented life, Boone was never in retreat from civilization. His pathfindings were usually undertaken as an agent of settlement. The wilderness he explored he intended to civilize. Nevertheless, his pluck and woodsmanship were the stuff of tales and folklore. Boone himself was amused, and sometimes annoyed, by his celebrity status.

Whatever the true measure of Daniel Boone's motivations, character, and skills, he came to symbolize that mythical cadre of leatherstocking frontiersmen who bridged the time and place between wildland and civilization.

Toward the end of his life in 1820, Boone recognized and lamented the unnecessary loss and retreat of wildlife. Yet, he continued to be lured to the hunt as late as his 82nd year of life.

Boone's junior by about 50 years, but his equal in fame, was Davy Crockett. Born in Tennessee, Crockett, like Boone, was wilderness educated. His ambition, shrewdness, wit, hunting expertise, and marksmanship made him legendary. He fought with General Andrew Jackson against Creek Indians, and he was elected three times to Congress, where his eccentricity of manner and backwoods dress added to his renown and public mystique.

Shortly after retiring from Congress, Crockett further ennobled himself to the public and to history by taking up arms with Texas in its fight for independence. A casualty of the Mexican army's sacking of the Alamo in 1836, Davy Crockett--woodsman, hunter, scout, Indian fighter, politician, and soldier--added the mantle of hero.

Both Boone and Crockett were the archetypal American buckskinned hunter, full of grit,

A young Theodore Roosevelt in the hunting garb he favored above all other, buckskins. He is shown here with a favorite Winchester big-game rifle. The photograph was obviously taken in a studio, with "props" to simulate an outdoor setting, a practice popular at that time.

determination, and savvy afield. They symbolize still the restlessness and sense of adventure that lie deep and indelibly within the breast of every true hunter. And for the past 100 years, their names have been linked in the title of an organization that is widely and correctly associated with conservation of America's natural resources, and with the best traditions of sport hunting.

THE GREENHORN

The real catalyst for formation of the Boone and Crockett Club was the loss of America's wildlife, combined with the alarming realization that, without some sort of intervention in the processes of decline, animal populations could not and would not recover. But as is the case in the origin of most organizations or institutions of any merit, the initiative of formation befell one individual.

The Boone and Crockett Club was the inspiration of an energetic, 29-year-old New York State assemblyman, smitten by the thrill of the hunt and frontier lore. Host of the December 1887 dinner party at which the idea for the Club was proposed and embraced, Theodore Roosevelt approached the Club's founding with the same bullish enthusiasm that he eventually employed in campaigns for the military, hunting in the West and abroad, establishing a cattle-ranching operation, combating corruption in New York's political machinery, and successfully bidding for the presidency of the United States.

Most Americans today likely perceive that Theodore Roosevelt was a westerner, a man whose daring-do as a Rough Rider, whose "High Noon" attitude toward criminals, and whose manner and affectations (at least in the public's eye and memory) were pure cowboy. In truth, Roosevelt came from a privileged eastern, urban background. His image as a man of the frontier was one he acquired and nurtured.

Contrary to the robust stature he enjoyed in adulthood, Roosevelt led a sickly, asthmatic youth. His family's wherewithal gave him opportunity as he grew to become involved in athletics and strenuous trips in the out-of-doors, particularly to hunt. Such "manly" activity, besides bolstering Roosevelt's frame and general health, imbued him with competitive drive and sense of accomplishment.

It may be fairly surmised that his exposure to wild things and wild places during those formative years, when physical well-being and discipline were his ostensive goals, gave Theodore Roosevelt an appreciation for the beauty and invigorating qualities of nature. But, there were other factors that contributed to what became a lifelong passion for wilderness and wildlife.

Roosevelt's parents approved of and encouraged his active youth, including the traditions of hunting and the sporting life. And there was Robert Barnwell Roosevelt, Theodore's uncle. "Uncle Rob" was a flamboyant character whose vocational and avocational careers young Theodore was to mirror in many respects. Robert Roosevelt was an attorney, reformer, congressman, author, and sportsman. He drafted legislation creating the U.S. Fisheries Commission, and he wrote three books that reflected his deep interest in hunting and fishing. He was also keenly aware of the need to protect game populations from overhunting and wanton waste. Theodore, therefore, was benefactor of a rich familial heritage of outdoor opportunity, experience, and perception.

Another certain influence on the young Roosevelt was his appetite for reading. Above all, he enjoyed literature that dealt with natural history. "I can no more explain," he wrote in later years, "why I like 'natural history' than why I like California canned peaches. . . . All I can say is that almost as soon as I began to read at all I began to read about the natural history of beasts and birds." Roosevelt's fascination with the mysteries of animal life was not an unusual preoccupation. But his devotion to study of the natural world at a young age, and for a lifetime, was quite remarkable, particularly at the time. And when not absorbed with reading about natural history, Roosevelt fell under the spell of adventure literature, including every type of prose, from western "dime" novels to the more sophisticated works of James Fenimore Cooper. Such fiction surely helped romanticize that reader's vision of the landscape and its wildlife, adding to their intrigue and allure.

By the time Theodore Roosevelt was ready to attend college, he sought to become what he termed an "outdoor naturalist." His inspirations were such men as John James Audubon, Alexander Wilson, Spencer Fullerton Baird, and Elliot Coues, patriarchs then of the budding science of natural history in the U.S. But Roosevelt found that natural history at Harvard University (which he attended from 1876 to graduation in 1880) was too sedentary. Though he appreciated the work done in the laboratory, he felt that science was too wrapped up in "minutiae."

What ultimately catalyzed Theodore Roosevelt's enamorment with wildlife and wildlands was a series of hunting trips in the early 1880's to the Great Plains. On those occasions, he was awed by the imposing size, beauty, and power of big game he found, and by the grandeur of their environment. It was as if Roosevelt's life till then--the rigors of athletics, the study of life forms and their mannerisms, the hunting trips to the Adirondacks, Maine, and the Midwest--was all preparatory to his confrontation with the West.

The full story of Theodore Roosevelt's early adventures in the West are chronicled in a number of books he wrote, most notably *Hunting Trips of a Ranchman*. Portions are recounted here because certain events kindled in Roosevelt the sensitivity and responsibility for wild living resources that prompted and became the very foundation of the Boone and Crockett Club.

Lord of the Plains

Theodore Roosevelt's first trip West, to the Dakota Territory in 1883, was motivated by the prospect of establishing a cattle ranching operation and also for reasons of health. There is little doubt that Roosevelt's quest to experience for himself the adventures of this wild land of which he read so much and yearned to see was a considerable encouragement. Central to that quest was the American bison.

Widely reported to congregate in moving herds miles (and days) long, bison (or buffalo, as commonly called) represented the continent's astonishing wealth of wildlife. Stories of bison abundance, ferocity, and importance to the irascible and feared Plains Indians placed the animal in near-mythical regard by eastern readers. It was a beast to be seen to be believed and, for the sportsman/hunter, to be reckoned with.

Following the Civil War and up to the time of Roosevelt's trip, the immense herds of bison were ruthlessly exploited, primarily for hides, but to some extent for meat and as a

means of subjugating the last of the hostile Indians. With the bison's range invaded and fragmented by railroads that provided efficient access to markets in the East, and with the advent of the Sharps carbine rifle and other breechloading firepower, the Great Bison Hunt of the post-Civil War era was carnage. In less time than the natural life of a bison, entire herds numbering millions of animals were eliminated. Year round, the hide hunters followed the nomadic animals, leaving a wake of rotting carcasses.

In time, in very short time, America's bison population (of perhaps 40–60 million) dwindled in number, size, and distribution. At first, their disappearance was credited to altered movement. When it began to be apparent in the late 1870's that the animals were not just missing, but truly gone, the loss was viewed with ambivalence. Fashion and textile manufacturing developments no longer necessitated the bulky hides. Livestock on open grasslands became a new and lucrative industry. The Indian was disfranchised, to the relief of new waves of homesteaders, ranchers, and other opportunists. Bison bones were a valued commodity for fertilizer. So, even to those few people who witnessed the change, what did it matter? Conservation? The uniquely American concept of more and better elsewhere was more than a notion; it was a fixation. And the bison, if not native American Indian culture, was its foremost victim.

In 1883, the bison was still the perceived "lord of the plains," and a source of drama and test for Theodore Roosevelt. The plains and badlands of the Dakota Territory were refuge to the beleaguered and sole-surviving "northern herd" of bison.

Roosevelt arrived in the 3 a.m. darkness of a November morning in the town of Little Missouri (now Medora), in far westcentral North Dakota. After securing lodging, his first order of business was to locate a hunting guide. He found one in Joe Ferris, who reluctantly agreed to hire on with the "dude" in wire-rim spectacles, who seemed overanxious to get on with a hunt to "shoot buffalo while there were still buffalo left to shoot."

On the morning they were to begin the hunt, a cold rain was turning the badlands into a quagmire of gumbo mud, but Roosevelt insisted that they get underway. They left camp (Gregor Lang's ranch near Pretty Buttes) at 6 a.m. and wandered for hours through rugged terrain and unimproved weather, with no sign of bison.

That night, exhausted by the day's futility, Ferris collapsed in his buffalo robe at Gregor Lang's, while his charge stayed up into early morning hours discussing with Lang everything from reform politics to the cattle business.

Early the next morning, 24-year-old Roosevelt was ready to start hunting again, even though the rains continued. Joe Ferris saw that little but discomfort was to be gained by chasing about in such conditions, but he developed a grudging admiration for the obsessed tenderfoot. So, as the week progressed and the rain persisted, they stumbled about the badlands by day in search of bison. By night, Roosevelt discussed politics and cattle with Lang, while Ferris slept soundly in his buffalo robe.

At that point in time, the late-night discussions on cattle were proving to be more productive than the hunting. The irony was that at the same time Roosevelt was seeking a bison as an initiation into the fading wilderness, he was laying groundwork for his participation in cattle ranching--the type of operation that was a definite factor in hastening the bison's extirpation and in closing the frontier.

Photograph Courtesy of Montana State Historical Society

One of the last bison killed in Montana from the original herds that once blanketed the western plains. This bull was killed in 1882, near the cattle camp of Potts and Harrison, near Townsend, Montana.

Even when the weather finally broke, the men knew that their chance of shooting a bison was slim. The great Sioux hunts of that and the previous year, 40 miles east of the badlands, had virtually eliminated the remnant northern herd, leaving only a few scattered and elusive animals. Nevertheless, the two hunters' spirits were buoyed by the clearing skies. "I never saw anyone so enthused in my life," wrote Ferris. "He was so eager to shoot his first buffalo that it somehow got into my blood; and I wanted to see him kill his first one as badly as he wanted to kill it."

On the prairies east of the Little Missouri River, their luck improved. There, Roosevelt finally saw his first bison, an old bull that rushed out of a coulee and disappeared over a steep bank. There was no time to fire. Although the men pursued the animal for miles, they never saw it again.

Later that same afternoon, they sighted three bison in the distance on an open plain. Roosevelt and Ferris picketed the horses and began a half-mile stalk on hands and knees through cactus and rock. When within less than 200 yards, Roosevelt raised up and fired at one of the bison. Dust flew from its hide, indicating a hit, but the tough, resilient bull galloped off with the other two. Roosevelt and Ferris returned to their horses and trailed the shaggy beasts, catching an occasional glimpse of them in the distance. Just after sunset, they saw that their quarry had paused in a distant hollow. The hunters decided to rush them.

In the light of a full moon, Roosevelt whipped his weary mount forward after the fleeing bison but could get no closer than 60 or 70 yards. Ferris, on a stronger horse, suddenly sped ahead and caused the wounded bison to swerve in Roosevelt's direction. As his floundering horse struggled across the broken ground in the near darkness, Roosevelt urged it to within 20 feet of the lumbering bull. Poor visibility and the lurching of the horse sent his first shot astray. He drove his mount closer, but the bull suddenly turned and charged. The terrified horse lashed its head about, slamming Roosevelt's rifle back against the hunter's forehead. A deep cut poured blood into Roosevelt's eyes, but he immediately rode again at the bison which was then charging Ferris's horse. Ferris swerved out of the way, jumped off his horse and fired at the bull escaping into the darkness. Roosevelt's horse was spent, so the excited hunter dismounted and, for a while, attempted to follow the bison on foot.

There was no hope of returning to Lang's ranch for the night. In fact, the two men were not sure where they were. It was dark and they had no water and very little food in the midst of a region whose forbidding terrain was most aptly named. With no wood available either for a fire or to hitch the horses, Roosevelt and Ferris tied their horses' bridle reins to their saddles, which they had removed to use for pillows in an attempt to get some rest.

The horses, and their riders, were nervous despite their exhaustion. They were in a region infested by horse thieves and by Indians who refused to abide by reservation boundaries. About midnight, the horses stampeded at some uncertain fright, dragging the saddles from under the hunters and across the plains.

After tracking down their horses, the two men once again wrapped themselves in their blankets, only to be awakened an hour or so later by a chilling and torrential downpour. It was at this point that Roosevelt exclaimed in earnest, "By Godfrey, but this is fun!"

For the next several days, they continued to hunt in the cold rain, once seeing a few bison. A shot by the myopic Roosevelt only frightened the animals off. As Joe Ferris put it years later, "Bad luck followed us like a yellow dog follows a drunkard." On their return to camp, they encountered rattlesnakes, stumbled over a steep bluff on their horses, were thrown from their mounts, and became mired in quicksand. By the time they reached Lang's, Ferris was completely taken with his strange, Pollyannaish companion. "I never saw anyone so more sure than ever that he wanted to shoot a bison, invest in cattle, and become a rancher."

In a matter of days, Roosevelt had written out a check for the princely sum of $14,000 for purchase of a partnership and holdings of Chimney Butte Ranch, a cattle ranching operation. Fittingly, the very day after realizing his goal of becoming a rancher, Theodore Roosevelt finally got his bison.

In mid-December, Roosevelt and Joe Ferris had just crossed the Montana line, near the upper waters of the Little Cannonball River, when their mounts spooked and turned toward a nearby coulee. Sure that the horses had scented bear or bison, Roosevelt dismounted and crawled up the coulee, where he saw hoofprints. A moment later, he spotted "a grand bison bull." The bison was walking along, unaware of danger and grazing as it went. When Roosevelt rose up, the bull tossed its head and tail as if to run. But before it moved, Roosevelt fired a bullet behind the animal's shoulder. The wounded bull bounded up and over the opposite side of the coulee, as Roosevelt fired two more bullets into its flank. The hunter feared that this prime bull, too, would escape, but it was found in the next coulee, dead.

Killing his first bison after such a grueling hunt was a great symbolic moment for Roosevelt. His recounting of the event, in *Hunting Trips of a Ranchman*, portrays the experience in all of its "wretched" detail, but is rather matter-of-fact in describing his kill. Joe Ferris, however, recalled a much different reaction by the tenderfoot, including an uninhibited "Indian war-dance" around the fallen bull.

". . . the very toil I had been obliged to go through," Roosevelt wrote later, "made me feel all the prouder of it."

When Roosevelt returned to New York that winter, he took along the bison head and hide, symbols of his pride in his accomplishment and the animal. He had been in the badlands all of three weeks, but he returned, by fate, a novice rancher and, by design, a westerner.

Back in New York, his eastern world soon began crumbling about him with the near-simultaneous deaths of his mother and his wife. Political problems soon plagued him as well. In despair and disgust, Roosevelt returned to the badlands several times during the next two years, for wilderness hunting, to tend his growing cattle interests, and perhaps as an escape from personal turmoil to a new, or at least broader, identity.

Buckskins

When Theodore Roosevelt returned to the Dakota Territory in June 1884, ranching involved a sizable portion of his wealth (he had acquired the Elkhorn ranch, 42 miles up the Little Missouri from his initial holdings), but hunting was still foremost on his mind.

"There are two things I want to do," he told his friend. "I want to get an antelope, and I want to get a buckskin suit."

Roosevelt's guided bison hunt of 1883 was his initiation to the land, its charms, endless vistas, and adversities. His 1884 hunt for pronghorn was more a test of self, being ". . . off entirely alone, with my horse and my rifle, on the prairie. I wanted to see if I could not do perfectly well without a guide and I succeeded beyond my expectations."

In the course of the five-day excursion, which, as usual, included sleeping in a wet blanket on the ground, Roosevelt, by his own admission, made some fine shots on pronghorn. He was invigorated by the hunting and enjoyed making careful observations of the native flora and fauna. "I felt as absolutely free as a man could feel," he rejoiced in a letter to his sister. He also succeeded in securing and wearing buckskins, the traditional frontiersman garb. And although photographs he had taken of himself in his fringed leather raiment (which were published in his first book) provided gist for laughs among some of his contemporaries, they also soon came to exemplify the man's persona. His reasons for donning buckskin, however, went much deeper than mere publicity; he was wearing what he considered "the most picturesque and distinctly national dress ever worn in America. It was the dress in which Daniel Boone was clad when he first passed through the trackless forests of the Alleghanies . . . it was the dress worn by grim old Davy Crockett when he fell at the Alamo."

Wilderness Fermentations

In 1884 and 1886, Theodore Roosevelt further steeped himself in the western experience by making extended hunting trips into areas both remote and pristine. His venture to Wyoming's Big Horn Mountains in the fall of 1884, and his trip to the Coeur d'Alenes of Montana in 1886, were hunts that brought him intimate, even mystical, contact with the wilderness. Characterizing the impact on Roosevelt of these two experiences, it might be said that, whereas his earlier western hunts were concerted attempts to make himself part of the western wilderness, the later trips made wilderness intuitively part of him. It is a distinction clear only to those for whom wilderness is more than a place.

The trip to the Big Horns in northcentral Wyoming, some 235 miles from the Elkhorn Ranch, was, for Roosevelt, a true pioneering adventure. Neither he nor his hunting partner (Bill Merrifield) had previously visited those rugged mountains with their dense forests and grassy parklands. An important aspect of this trip was Roosevelt's desire to hunt elk, ". . . as noble and lordly game as is to be found in the Western world," and the grizzly bear, ". . . king of the game beasts of temperate North America, because the most dangerous. . . ."

His first acquaintance with either animal was on the return to camp one evening when he came across a huge pawprint. "It gave me rather an eerie feeling in the silent, lonely woods, to see for the first time the unmistakable proofs that I was in the home of the mighty lord of the wilderness." Roosevelt never located that grizzly, but he had his confrontation several days later as he and Merrifield hunted a mountain forest whose sounds suggested "the sad and everlasting unrest of the wilderness."

That morning, the two hunters found that a grizzly had eaten at the carcass of an elk.

Tracks were nearby and the hunters suspected that the bear might be bedding in the vicinity. Following tracks, Merrifield passed by a tangle of fallen logs. He suddenly sank to one knee and turned back to Roosevelt, ". . . his face fairly aflame with excitement." Roosevelt was walking past Merrifield, his rifle at the ready, when the grizzly raised up among some stunted spruce. He was a "monstrous fellow," some nine feet tall, weighing about 1,200 pounds. When he saw the hunters, the bear dropped down onto all fours, the hair on his neck and shoulders bristling. Roosevelt quickly aimed and fired. The great bear began to rise again, then fell on its side.

If killing the grizzly was a triumph of the hunter's nerve and a symbol of competence, the bull elk Roosevelt pursued and killed evoked a powerful inspirational response that went beyond mere romanticism. "No sportsman can ever feel much keener pleasure and self-satisfaction than when, after a successful stalk and good shot, he walks up to a grand elk lying dead in the cool shade of the evergreens, and looks at the massive and yet finely molded form, and at the mighty antlers which are to serve in the future as the trophy and proof of his successful skill. Still-hunting the elk on the mountains is as noble a kind of sport as can well be imagined; there is nothing more pleasant and enjoyable, and at the same time it demands that the hunter shall bring into play many manly qualities. There have been few days of my hunting life that were so full of unalloyed happiness as were those spent on the Big Horn range. From morning till night I was on foot, in cool, bracing air, now moving silently through the vast, melancholy pine forests, now treading the brink of high, rocky precipices, always amid the most grand and beautiful scenery. . . ."

Roosevelt's 1886 hunting trip for mountain goat to the northern spur of the Coeur d'Alene Mountains in Montana proved equally invigorating. On that successful hunt for one of the most inaccessible of all North American big game animals, and in what Roosevelt called "the heart of the vast wooded wilderness," the hunter, no longer a tenderfoot, saw signs that he was following in the footsteps "of that adventurous and now fast vanishing folk, the American frontiersman."

On several occasions during that hunt, he observed the faint ax scars of a trapper's blaze, causing him to reflect that "The trapper and the miner were the pioneers of the mountains, as the hunter and the cowboy have been the pioneers of the plains; they are all of the same type, these sinewy men of the border, fearless and self-reliant, who are ever driven restlessly onward through the wilderness. . . ."

Insight and Incite

In winter 1886, an intensive blizzard from the north raged over the Dakota grasslands. Icy "northers" filled gullies and gulches with snow and the carcasses of unprotected livestock. Among the casualties was more than 60 percent of the Elkhorn Ranch stock: with them went Theodore Roosevelt's ranching career.

The dollars lost in Roosevelt's cattle business were irrevocable; the experience and insight he gained as a result of the investment became cornerstones of his private and political crusades for wildlife and other natural resources.

As a rancher, Roosevelt was witness to the consequences of poor land-use practices. He saw gullies carved where fire, clear-cutting, and overgrazing eliminated protective cover

from shallow topsoil. And he watched the force and devastation of flooding to which these abuses contributed.

As a hunter, he was exposed to the fetid litter of market hunters, and he observed senseless killing by transient "sports." He saw bears, wolves, eagles, and mountain lions trapped, shot, and poisoned as real or perceived threats to sheep and cattle. So, too, did he view the killing of wild ungulates—elk, deer, mountain sheep, and pronghorn—because of presumed competition with livestock for prairie forage.

As a sportsman, Roosevelt was repelled by the wasting of the land and its living resources. As a political figure of good connection, reasonable clout, and great ambition, he was compelled to act.

That action, characteristic of others he would take in his celebrated political life, was well-conceived, timely, and decisive. Theodore Roosevelt's December 1887 dinner meeting was a critical first step in halting the momentum of destruction of America's wildlife.

TAKING AIM

The men who joined with Theodore Roosevelt in founding the Boone and Crockett Club represented an American aristocracy of sorts. Writers, scientists, explorers, military leaders, industrialists, and political figures, they shared an enthusiasm for big game hunting and each had traveled extensively in the West. Those in attendance at Roosevelt's December 1887 meeting were George Bird Grinnell, E. P. Rogers, Archibald Rogers, J. Coleman Drayton, Thomas Paton, Colonel James E. Jones, Rutherford Stuyvesant, John J. Pierpont, Roosevelt's brother Elliot, and his cousin J. West Roosevelt. They were the nucleus of the new club.

In a series of Club meetings that followed Roosevelt's dinner party, the thrust, direction, and organization of the Club were formulated and refined. Club members would identify major prolems facing wildlife and wildlife habitat. They would form committees of knowledgeable individuals to study these problems; then, they would communicate with public officials to recommend appropriate action and legislation. The Club would invite "experts" on matters of concern, particularly those relating to diminishing wildlands and wildlife, to acquaint the membership with the causes and scope of the problems. It would then invite politicians and other influential persons to Club dinners and social activities where they too could be enlightened and persuaded to support necessary measures to bring about constructive change. And the Club would restrict its membership of "American hunting riflemen" to no more than 100 (now 150) regular members and "such associate (now called professional)and honorary members as may be elected."

The chartered criterion for Club membership was having "killed with the rifle in fair chase, by still-hunting or otherwise at least one of the various kinds of American large game" (this included bear, bison, mountain sheep, caribou, cougar, musk-ox, mountain goat, elk, wolf, pronghorn, moose, and deer). An unwritten criterion, it appears, was that prospective members be of such position and means as to effect favorably the Club's immediate advocacy and its long-term mission, the preservation of wildlife.

The early membership rosters feature some of America's foremost figures in a variety of endeavors. Included as regular or associate members were the likes of historian Francis

Photograph Courtesy of Montana State Historical Society

Elk killed in velvet in Yellowstone by Frederick Bottler in 1875. During the spring of 1875, Bottler and his brother, Philip, reportedly killed about 2,000 elk in the vicinity of Mammoth Hot Springs. Such wanton killings of wildlife eventually helped bring about needed protection for Yellowstone as a National Park, as well as spurring development of game laws.

Parkman, novelist Owen Wister, U.S. Army major generals William Tecumseh Sherman and Philip H. Sheridan, artist Albert Bierstadt, U.S. Senator George G. Vest, Secretary of the Interior Carl Schurz, and geologists Clarence King and Raphael Pumpelly. In terms of the sphere of influence, knowledge, and capability, the Club's roll was elite. To newcomers, outsiders, and adversaries, it could also be intimidating. Theodore Roosevelt's son Archibald, who spent some of his formative years in the White House during his father's presidency and so was no stranger to the high and the mighty, commented in his later years that when he joined the Club in the 1920's, he and other young members were truly in awe of the prominent older members. Archibald recalled that those distinguished senior members responded to the young members' deference by generally ignoring them.

Yellowstone Preserve

That the Boone and Crockett Club was more than an excuse for its membership to share brandy, cigars, and hunting tales was evident from the start. At the Club's first formal meetings, the members initiated action to save Yellowstone National Park (the nation's first national park) from poachers, speculators, and other interests that threatened the Park's pristine condition. "Resolved that a committee of 5 be appointed by the chair to promote useful & proper legislation toward the enlargement & better Government of the Yellowstone Natl Park." A single resolution, in a single sentence, but it marked the beginning of the Boone and Crockett Club's conservation crusade.

Among the "committee of 5" was George Bird Grinnell. If Theodore Roosevelt was the heart and soul of the Boone and Crockett Club, Grinnell was its brain and backbone. In correspondence in 1926, Charles Sheldon wrote to a fellow Club member: "The Boone and Crockett Club has been *George Bird Grinnell* from its founding--all its books, its works, its soundness have been due to his unflagging work and interest and knowledge."

Author, publisher, ethnologist, naturalist, and sportsman, Grinnell was editor of the national magazine *Forest and Stream*. For a number of years before the advent of the Boone and Crockett Club, Grinnell used the magazine to espouse "conservation" causes. In fact, the modern connotation of conservation is thought by some historical researchers to have originated with Grinnell, in 1884.

Grinnell first visited the West in 1870, accompanying Yale University paleontologist Othniel C. Marsh on a geological expedition. In 1874, Grinnell was a civilian member of General George Armstrong Custer's "survey" expedition into the Black Hills. A year later, he was with Captain William Ludlow's U.S. Army Corps of Engineers' reconnaissance of the Yellowstone region.

In the course of his western travels, Grinnell became acquainted with a number of the notable frontier personalities of the day, including Charley Reynolds, "Buffalo Bill" Cody, and Frank and Luther North. From them, and through his eyewitness and insight, Grinnell gained understanding and deep appreciation for the grandeur and bounty of the western landscape, and he developed an equally profound concern for the protection of those values and vitality in the face of unrestrained national growth and expansion. He wrote in 1890: "Almost within the life of *Forest and Stream* [founded in 1873] we have seen the wave of settlement roll from this side of the Missouri on to the West, until it broke against the

mountains of the main range and then dividing into streams, creep by canyon, pass and river valley, up onto the arid plateau of the central region. As the crest of this wave advanced it blotted out the buffalo, the antelope, the elk and the deer. While it is, perhaps, not true to say that the days of big-game hunting in the Western country are over, it is a fact that large game now exists only in isolated localities, and that such localities are so surrounded by settlements that the game cannot get away; its migration to wilder regions is no longer possible."

Yellowstone National Park symbolized to Grinnell the collision of civilization and wilderness. The consequence he saw of that instance was not merely a process of taming and incorporation, but an act of ecological violence and compromise of human as well as natural values. Yellowstone became his cause.

In great measure because of George Bird Grinnell's forceful involvement in the Yellowstone Park issue long before the Boone and Crockett Club was formed, the matter helped to marshal enthusiasm for creation of the Club and then to serve as impetus and bond for the organization during its formative years. In fact, it was in the midst of the Yellowstone controversy that the Club's leading forces were first brought together.

On July 2, 1885, *Forest and Stream* printed a review by Grinnell of Theodore Roosevelt's book *Hunting Trips of a Ranchman*. It was a generally positive critique and complimented the author's fresh style. However, Grinnell also pointed out some shortcomings in the narrative, which were attributed to the author's somewhat limited experience as a rancher and westerner. Roosevelt, concerned about the apparent condescension of some of Grinnell's words, went to Grinnell's office to face his critic. That meeting prompted a long and fruitful friendship between the two men. With the younger Roosevelt, Grinnell shared his understanding and perspectives on the serious and fragile stature of America's wildlife. In Roosevelt, Grinnell found an aggressive and politically mobile ally for his conservation crusade.

Indeed, Yellowstone National Park was threatened from its very beginning (March 1872) when President Ulysses S. Grant signed the Organic Act that created it as the first national park, ". . . a pleasuring ground for the people." It was "set aside" to protect the area's wondrous features and unique phenomena: spewing geysers, bubbling cauldrons of colored mud, exotic mineral structures, and awesome scenery. Concern for Yellowstone's forests and wildlife came later.

In 1872, Yellowstone Park was distant and remote from the civilizing hubs of the young nation. By the end of 1883, however, the Northern Pacific Railway brought the world to Yellowstone's northern entrance. Many of the first visitors were the merely curious. Others came to exploit. The Park's minerals, timber, and wildlife, particularly big game, were vulnerable to the freebooters. Although the U.S. Secretary of the Interior was authorized to regulate the Park, he was not given practicable means to enforce protective regulations. With the arrival of the railroad and its myriad and diversely motivated passengers in 1883, the Secretary of War was empowered to send U.S. Army troops to enforce the Park regulations. This came about at the urging of General Philip Sheridan (later a Club Associate Member), who visited the Park in 1882 and saw that its management was untenable. Sheridan's call for military involvement was strongly and widely supported in a three-page

article in the January 1883 issue of Grinnell's *Forest and Stream* magazine.

Still, it was three years before a contingent of the U.S. First Cavalry, under Captain Moses Harris, arrived to impose order and restraint. As the new Park superintendent, Harris pursued his mandate vigorously, but even so, his authority was too tightly circumscribed and transparent. Profiteering sawyers hacked away at the Park's forests; market hunters easily poached Yellowstone's wintering herds of bison, elk, and pronghorn; souvenir seekers and commercial vendors vandalized the resplendent mineral deposits; sightseers wantonly defaced the Park's geysers and rock formations; and neophyte campers' unattended fires charred vast tracts of the landscape. Yet, in most cases, offenders could only be expelled from the Park. No serious legal steps were available to impose sufficient punishment, even for grievous damage, to serve as a deterrent for unlawful acts. Regulation enforcers could do little more than verbally chastise and temporarily expel the few violators they were able to track down in the expansive Park.

General Sheridan made several other significant contributions to the process of protecting the Park. First, he put forth the idea that the Park should be expanded significantly (by 3,344 square miles), primarily to create an additional preserve for game animals. Secondly (and most important) he interested U.S. Senator George Vest of Missouri (also, later, a Club Associate Member) in the Park's cause.

Over the next several years, Vest put forth bills in Congress to expand the Park, give Park rules and regulations the force of law, limit concessionaire privileges and monopolies, and provide for a fully salaried staff (with deputy marshal authority) to manage the Park. Although most of Vest's proposed legislation failed to get full support of or action in the House of Representatives, the Senator was able to prevent commercial enterprises from securing monopolies that, under the guise of Park management, maintenance, or improvement, threatened to deplete the Park's presumably protected resources. Vest did succeed in attaching a rider on the Sundry Civil Appropriations Bill for fiscal year 1884, which permitted the detailing of troops to the Park to prevent unlawful trespassing and other violations.

Among those who lobbied and otherwise sought to override constraints on exploitation of the Park resources and prospects was the Northern Pacific Railroad. For nearly a decade since its spidery line of tracks had been laid across the northern plains to the Park boundary, railroad officials had attempted to gain a right-of-way through the Park, but they were repeatedly denied. In 1892, they sought to achieve their goal deviously. The railroad lobby prompted a bill in Congress to return part of Yellowstone National Park to the public domain. The "Segregation Bill," as it was called, would have withdrawn more than 600 square miles from the Park, including some of its most critical big game habitat. Once that area was withdrawn from Park status, the railway company then could apply, under the Railroad Act of 1862, to acquire the land, or a significant portion of it, at no cost to construct a railway that would be financed by government loans. (From 1852 to 1890, the federal and state governments granted more than 116 million acres to western railroads and advanced them $64 million in bonds.) In 1852, there were 5 miles of rail west of the Mississippi River; by 1890, rail lines wended over more than 72,000 miles in the West.

Boone and Crockett Club members, and Grinnell's *Forest and Stream*, had long opposed

This photograph of writer Emerson Hough on skis illustrated just how easy it was for poachers to closely approach elk in Yellowstone on heavy snow. Hough's articles in Forest and Stream magazine were vital to the generation of public support for park status for the Yellowstone region.

66

giving railroads a right-of-way through Yellowstone National Park, and Northern Pacific's new strategy was resisted as well. A pamphlet by Grinnell concerning the Park and its crises was distributed to newspapers nationwide in an attempt to inform the American people and stir public protest. Despite the concern and efforts of the Club and its members, the Segregation Bill passed the Senate in February 1893. It failed in the House, however, when Grinnell's *Forest and Stream* printed a telegram from railroad lobbyist P. J. Barr to Montana democrats that asked them to exert pressure on the Speaker of the House. Grinnell's revelation of the railroaders' pork barrel shenanigans, and a stinging editorial, ended (at least temporarily) the Segregation Bill's chances of passing.

Public awareness of the Park depredations and Northern Pacific's encroachment scheme was enhanced, and public opinion was galvanized, by a sequence of events beginning the next year. In October of 1893, Park superintendent George S. Anderson noted that bison were concentrated in the Park's Pelican Creek area. He cautioned his skilled civilian scout, Felix Burgess, that the herd might attract the attention of poachers and that Burgess should carefully patrol the area.

The following March, while scouting on skis in deep snow in that area, Burgess and a trooper discovered the heads of six freshly killed bison. Moving on, the two men heard shots. From the top of a slope covered with lodgepole pines, they caught sight of someone bending over a fallen bison. Burgess recognized the man as Ed Howell, a notorious poacher, busily removing the bison's head and hide. Howell's rifle was propped against another nearby carcass. Armed only with a 38 caliber service revolver, Burgess was separated from Howell by a 400-yard wide snowfield. Howell was well-known for his criminal activity and propensity for violence. He was also much better armed than Burgess, but Burgess seized the opportunity to capture the poacher literally red-handed. Skiing down the slope as quickly and quietly as possible, he actually was able to "get the drop" on an astounded Howell.

The telling of this dramatic incident in *Forest and Stream* was a national sensation that focused public attention and outcry on the serious plight of Yellowstone's wildlife. Grinnell had sent a reporter, Emerson Hough, to Yellowstone for the winter. And as luck would have it, Hough and famed western photographer F. Jay Haynes were able to record, in word and photo images, this vivid scene and others that dramatically documented the jeopardy of the Park's wintering herds of big game.

Forest and Stream made clear in its coverage of the story that the government had been grossly negligent in not providing any legal or administrative means to punish criminal activity within the Park. Superintendent Anderson could confiscate the heads and hides, burn Howell's camp and supplies, and take away his weapons. But, in Anderson's own words, "There is no law governing this park except the military regulations. There is no punishment that can be inflicted on this low-down fellow."

Grinnell's editorial volleys that accompanied and followed Hough's expose urged form and substance to the public outrage. "We suggest that every leader who is interested in the Park or in natural history, or in things pertaining to America, should write to his Senator or Representative, asking them to take a personal interest in the protection of the Park."

Conservation historian James B. Trefethen detailed what then occurred. "The national

press picked up the cry, and the [public] response was overwhelming. Petitions and individual letters by the hundreds poured into Congress--from sportsmen and nature lovers, from people who had visited the park, and from people who hoped to visit it. The American people *for the first time* [author's emphasis] had begun to realize that they owned a national park, and they were determined to keep it."

A week after Hough's article was printed in *Forest and Stream*, U.S. Congressman John F. Lacey of Iowa (a Boone and Crockett Club member) introduced legislation much like the bills Senator Vest had repeatedly brought to the Senate. With the firestorm of publicity generated by coverage of the Howell case, Lacey's "Act to Protect the Birds and Animals in Yellowstone National Park" moved swiftly through legislative channels and was signed into law by President Grover Cleveland on May 7, 1894. The persistent vigilance of the Boone and Crockett Club and, in particular, charter member George Bird Grinnell, had paid off handsomely.

The Yellowstone Park Protection Act (the "Lacey Act of 1894") finally gave Park administrators some real power and authority. The law saw to it that a representative of the United States Circuit Court was established in the Park itself, with U.S. marshals on hand to arrest those who violated park regulations. No birds, fish, or mammals could be taken from the Park. Penalties for killing game, or removing timber or mineral deposits, included substantial fines and jail sentences of up to two years. The best symbol of changes brought about by the Lacey Act was a jail built in the Park, to incarcerate those who violated regulations.

Interestingly, Ed Howell was not prosecuted for his poaching, because his violation clearly was *ex post facto*. Nevertheless, the incident served notice that subsequent criminality in the Park would not be taken lightly.

The long-range significance of the Lacey Act of 1894, which certainly owed its promulgation to Boone and Crockett Club members, was that it firmly established the legal precedent, policy, and overall administrative structure that would govern Yellowstone and all subsequent U.S. national parks. As Trefethen noted, the Act was the benchmark for laws and policies the National Park Service has used to administer national parks and preserves since that agency's inception in 1916.

But for the unflagging devotion of Boone and Crockett Club members such as Sheridan, Vest, Grinnell, Lacey, and others, there would be no Yellowstone Park as we know it today. Of the Yellowstone Park Protection Act, Grinnell wrote in 1910, "It may fairly be said that since then [1894] that great reservation has never been exposed to any special dangers."

Land of the Walled-in Lakes

During the Boone and Crockett Club's early years, its members appear to have spoken with a single voice for conservation. That voice belonged to George Bird Grinnell. His causes became the Club's, and it is reasonable to say that his medium (*Forest and Stream* magazine), became a forum for the Club. So capable and far-sighted was Grinnell that other Club members, including Theodore Roosevelt, eagerly lined up behind him, or at his side, to do battle for the protection of wilderness, wildlife, and hunting.

Grinnell was the consummate outdoor journalist of his era, reporting and proselytizing as befit the tenor of the time. With Roosevelt, he wrote portions of and co-edited the first

books in the Boone and Crockett Club series. In his magazine he produced articles that helped popularize hunting as a legitimate sport. He championed the need for wildlife protection, and he used straightforward propaganda to counter those who rallied and railed against the newfangled notion of conservation—his cause, and the Boone and Crockett Club's cause.

Of special interest to Grinnell was a region of northwestern Montana, known to certain Indians as the "Land of the Walled-in Lakes." As of the last decades of the nineteenth century, few people except Indians had ever ventured far or long into the rugged region. Adventurers such as Lewis and Clark, fur trappers, government surveyors, and a few others knew of the area, but they knew very little.

In the early 1880's, Professor Raphael Pumpelly, one of the first associate members of the Boone and Crockett Club, broached the region's vast interior. He was greatly inspired by the majestic landscape and its wildlife. Pumpelly's description captured Grinnell's imagination, which was further incited by writings about the region by J. W. Schultz, a hunter and adopted Indian. Schultz portrayed the Land of the Walled-in Lakes as a sportsman's Eden.

During the autumn of 1885, Grinnell first ventured to the region. There, he explored and hunted with Blackfeet Indian friends and found that "Appekunny" Schultz had not exaggerated its grandeur and wildlife abundance.

It should be recognized that Grinnell, in addition to his other credits, was an outstanding ethnologist. From his experiences, observations, and associations among the Indians, he ultimately produced two classic studies of Indian life and culture, one dealing with the Blackfeet and the other with the Cheyenne. Perhaps as much as any non-Indian before or since, he saw or sensed the kinship tie of the American Indian to the land and its living resources. He obviously was attuned to things wild and primitive. As such, he was quickly, convincingly, and inextricably attracted to the Land of the Walled-in Lakes. He also saw that the forces that besieged Yellowstone soon would threaten even the distant paradise of northwestern Montana. During years of hunting and exploring in this region, Grinnell discovered and named scores of natural sites. Mountains, glaciers, lakes, and passes not surprisingly bear the names of his Indian friends, buckskin hunting companions, and Boone and Crockett Club comrades.

The early 1890's brought the Great Northern Railroad to northwestern Montana. With the "firehorse" came the inevitability of change. Grinnell was adamant in his objection to altering the pristine qualities of the Land of the Walled-in Lakes, and with the Boone and Crockett Club behind him, sought to have the area preserved.

While touring the West in 1896, Gifford Pinchot and Henry S. Graves of the U.S. Forest Commission (both of whom would eventually become Chief Foresters of the United States *and* members of the Boone and Crockett Club) inspected the region at Grinnell's suggestion. Guided by an Indian, the two men traversed ground that Grinnell had walked, and they reacted to its beauty and wildness as Grinnell surely knew they would. On this trip, Pinchot even killed a bighorn ram that would help qualify him for regular membership in the Club. The tour bore fruit when the Commission recommended that a forest reserve be established in the area surrounding the St. Mary Lakes. President William McKinley ac-

Photograph by Sherman Gray

This commemorative plaque was erected by the Boone and Crockett Club in September 1987 as part of its centennial year activities. It recognizes the discovery of Grinnell Glacier and other accomplishments of long-time Club member George Bird Grinnell. (Grinnell discovered the glacier in 1887.)

cepted the recommendation, creating the Flathead Forest Preserve.

Grinnell was pleased, but he still wanted the Land of the Walled-in Lakes preserved as a national park. In 1895, Canada had created Waterton Lakes National Park to the north. It was Grinnell's goal to establish a U.S. equivalent. Just as he had interested Pinchot and Graves in the area, Grinnell now saw the need to involve others who could help. He sought out Senator Thomas B. Carter of Montana, an important figure on relevant Senate committees. The two developed a strong friendship, and Grinnell nominated the Senator for associate membership in the Club. Like so many friends and acquaintances of Grinnell, Carter's enthusiasm increased through his association with Grinnell and other Club members, and also as his knowledge grew concerning this special corner of his home state. In 1910, Carter introduced legislation in the Senate that led to the creation of Glacier National Park. With the stroke of President William Howard Taft's pen on May 11, 1910, the Park was born, and the vision and persistence of George Bird Grinnell was again rewarded.

It is particularly fitting that Glacier National Park, George Bird Grinnell's Land of the Walled-in Lakes, features a mountain and a glacial lake bearing the name of the man who conceived and engineered protection of the region's natural character for as long as the chance of time allows.

Forest Fortunes

Just after the turn of the century, an aging hunter who had wandered the West when it was truly wilderness lamented its passing in the pages of *Forest and Stream*: "Where Beaver Bill and the Flatheads fought the Crees," he wrote, "government engineers are building an immense dam to store water for an irrigating canal. The wild Indians, the buffalo and other game have disappeared, and busy ranchers till the soil where the old time trappers made their camps. It is well that they are in their graves, those adventurous old plainsmen, for there is no longer any place for them to roam."

Members of the Boone and Crockett Club, including its founders, knew all too well the truth of the old hunter's requiem. Roosevelt, Grinnell, and their compatriots often wrote similar sentiment—sometimes wistful, sometimes bitter, but usually with a glimmer of hope. For decades, Americans had bemoaned the vanished frontier, the disappearance of wildlife, the death of the mountain man, the Indians throttled and subjugated, the last ride of the cowboy. To most, the era of the trailblazer and teeming, free-roaming herds of wildlife was over, relegated to fading, romantic memory and to history books.

Members of the Boone and Crockett Club, though sometimes pessimistic about the prospects of recovery, were not disposed toward melancholy. Where others saw hopelessness, they saw opportunity. Where others found respite in rancorous finger-pointing, they were moved to action. It is clear from the biographies of individual members of the Club that these were realists, but realists who achieved their social rank and influence by countering the impossible with vision and tenacity. Together in the Boone and Crockett Club, invigorated by the insight and enthusiasm of the fellowship, they saw the decimation of America's wildlife and wildlands not as a swan song, but as a challenge.

One thing the Club's members realized was that protecting one national park and creating another represented only the beginning of a lengthy, complex process of recovery. As the

Yellowstone struggle made obvious, such investments, without proper safeguards and means of administration, could be undermined or gradually eroded at the whim of conflicting interests. Likewise, merely setting aside a national park here or there was not enough to ensure "the preservation of the large game of this country," as called for in the Boone and Crockett Club by-laws. The American forests, both inside and outside of national parks, were, in Theodore Roosevelt's words, "great nurseries for wild game," and they needed specific kinds of protection.

The Club's early interest in protecting America's forests is indicated by the fact that former Secretary of the U.S. Department of the Interior Carl Schurz, one of the first and most outspoken proponents of land reform, including management, was made an associate member of the Club in its first few months of existence. This early concern about forests, as wildlife habitat and timber reserves and for watershed protection, was intensified by the Club's efforts to save Yellowstone Park during the years 1887 to 1894. In fact, George Bird Grinnell noted in 1910 that the Club members' work on behalf of Yellowstone led directly to "the impulse to attempt to preserve western forests generally." They realized that the devastating abuses of Yellowstone, caused by market hunters, lumbermen, tourists and others, would be repeated elsewhere and, possibly eventually, everywhere. The kind of protection and administration brought to the Park through the Lacey Act of 1894 needed to be spread to other areas, particularly to the nation's forests.

Schurz, an immigrant political refugee from Germany, rose to political influence as minister to Spain during Abraham Lincoln's administration and as a U.S. Senator from Missouri from 1869 to 1875. He had developed an interest in forestry during his youth in Germany, where silviculture was a well-advanced art. As Secretary of the Interior under Rutherford B. Hayes, Schurz was one of the first public officials to recognize the important interrelationships among natural resources, and the first to advocate the need for a system of national forest reserves with a federal forestry agency. He also departed from the tradition of the time by selecting his staff on the basis of merit rather than political favor. This established a level and precedent of professionalism to the administration of federal natural resource programs.

Historian James Trefethen wrote that when Schurz took office in 1877, ". . . the western public lands were being systematically looted by timber thieves, ravaged by wild fire, and appropriated through fraud by lumber companies and livestock owners." Knowing of the value of forests as wildlife habitat, for retarding soil erosion and maintaining water supplies, Schurz attempted to plug loopholes in homestead and pre-emption laws that permitted widespread abuse of forested land claims by "cut-and-run" profiteers.

Schurz also promoted forest reserves and watershed protection by the reseeding and reforestation of cut-over and burned-over areas. He urged military protection of public land to prevent timber theft and fire, and to eliminate the slaughter of wildlife. The abuse, overuse, and misuse of public land resources he called "murder of our future prosperity."

At the time, Americans remained bent on maximizing individual wealth, all too often at the expense of the nation's fast-draining cornucopia of renewable and mineral resources. With few exceptions, Schurz's exhortations and pleas were ignored. He wrote later, "I found myself standing almost solitary and alone. Deaf was Congress, and deaf the people

seemed to be."

Among the few who shared Schurz's foresight were the American Association for the Advancement of Science and the American Forestry Association. As early as 1876, the two organizations cooperated to introduce bills before Congress to protect forested lands in upper watersheds of the nation's largest rivers. Those efforts also came to naught, since championing conservation at the time (as Carl Schurz learned) was still counter to the national economic tenor.

When the Boone and Crockett Club came into being during the next decade, a new force was added to the muffled hue and cry for reform.

Ironically, the Club was able to help bring about timely protection for the forests in 1891, three years before passage of the Lacey Act brought protection to Yellowstone. This occurred because the Lacey bill precipitated a rancorous tug-of-war involving many powerful interests, whereas "An Act to Repeal Timber Culture Laws and for other purposes" was created (or, more exactly, connived) with far less visibility. In fact, the crucial portion of the bill, authorizing the President to establish forest reserves by Executive Order, was "buried" as the last of 24 sections. It went virtually unnoticed until President Benjamin Harrison signed into law the Sundry Civil Service Appropriation Act of 1891, and the President began to exercise the power its subsequent enactment gave him. The section reads: "That the President of the United States may, from time to time, set apart and reserve in any State or Territory having public lands bearing forests, any part of the public lands, wholly or in part covered with timber or undergrowth whether of commercial value or not, as public reservations, and the President shall, by public proclamation declare the establishment of such reservations and the limits thereof."

Less than a month after the Act was signed into law, President Harrison set aside more than a million acres in the Yellowstone National Park Timberland Reserve, on the eastern and southern borders of the Park.

The Boone and Crockett Club played a major role behind the scenes in this successful effort to protect national forest land. In what became its standard method of operation, the Club, through formal and informal associations, was able to seek out knowledgeable and influential people who could steer the Club's conservation agenda. In 1887, the year the Club was founded, member William Hallett Phillips, a Supreme Court lawyer, directed his attention to then-Secretary of the Interior Lucius Q. C. Lamar, and succeeded in interesting Lamar and a small nucleus of Congressmen in the issue of forests.

In 1889, when John W. Noble was appointed Secretary of the Interior under President Harrison, Phillips and his congressional allies, plus other Club members including Arnold Hague of the U.S. Geological Survey, worked on cultivating Noble's support for forest protection. This attention clearly had a positive impact. Acting on a suggestion put forth in part by Hague, Secretary Noble insisted that the all-important Section 24, providing for the establishment of forest reserves, be tacked onto the bill. Noble then persuaded the President to sign the bill, and also induced him to set aside the first forest reserves, including the vast Yellowstone Reserve. The size and shape of this enormous reserve were defined by Club member Hague, who worked in close counsel with Noble. Eventually, through the influence of Noble (later an associate Club member), President Harrison would

set aside more than 13 million acres of forest reserves. In this oblique fashion, the national forest system was born.

Creation of forest reserves, however, like the authorization that established Yellowstone National Park, meant little if they could not be effectively regulated and protected. Echoing the view of former Interior Secretary (and then associate Club member) Schurz, the Boone and Crockett Club's answer to this dilemma was for the government to provide the kind of military protection that had been sent to Yellowstone National Park in the mid–1880's. Predictably, many westerners were adamantly opposed to the "withdrawal" of what they considered to be their forests. It seemed that an insoluble sticking point had been reached between the people who supported set-aside protection of forest reserves (including many easterners and members of the American Forestry Association and the Boone and Crockett Club) and the westerners and others who felt that the forests should be freely exploited for timber, wildlife, and minerals.

What ultimately and paradoxically saved the early reserves from the maelstrom of political in-fighting and outrage in the West was that the Act did not contain provision for enforcement. Those voicing discontent knew very well that without some sort of enabling legislation, the Act was a paper tiger; they could ignore the law and exploitation could continue with impunity. In time, anger turned to grumbling, grumbling turned to murmurs, and murmurs turned to apathy.

As western wrath diminished and died, the Boone and Crockett Club, in its usual manner, continued stumping for protection of the reserves by lining up influential supporters and registering its position on the matter with the populace. In an 1893 *Forest and Stream* article, Theodore Roosevelt and George Bird Grinnell wrote: "We now have these forest reservations, refuges where the timber and its wild denizens should be safe from destruction. What are we going to do with them? The mere formal declaration that they have been set aside will contribute little toward their safety. It will prevent the settlement of the regions, but will . . . preserve neither the timber nor the game on them. The various national parks are watched and patrolled by Federal troops. . . . The forest reservations are absolutely unprotected—they are still without government and without guards. This should not be. If it is worthwhile to establish these reservations, it is worthwhile to protect them. A general law providing for the adequate guarding of all such national possessions should be enacted by Congress . . . supplemented by laws of the states in which the reservations lie. The timber and game ought to be made the absolute property of the government, and it should constitute a punishable offense to appropriate such property within the limits of the reservations."

As the situation developed (or more accurately, as the force of law languished), there proved to be a middle ground between complete protection and outright exploitation. It was, as Carl Schurz had pointed out years before (and continued to in the intervening years), that forest reserves, like most other public land, could be managed for sustained productvity of multiple resource benefits. With judicious and proper management, forests could be maintained as wildlife habitat, sources of timber, and watershed protection.

With the effects of natural resource exploitation beginning to show in the late 1800's, and with a burgeoning, urbanizing society with growing demands for a steady stream of

products from the nation's soils, forests, and waters, conservation began to be viewed as a sound course, rather than as an obstruction to free enterprise and individual prosperity. Pricking the American conscience at every opportunity was George Bird Grinnell from his *Forest and Stream* soapbox.

It was during this period of ferment that Gifford Pinchot came onto the national scene. A forester who had studied in Europe, Pinchot had first applied his training in 1891 to the management of forest land on a 7,000-acre private estate in North Carolina. He demonstrated there that, as in Europe, a forest could be managed for wildlife and other values without loss of commercial timber productivity.

In 1896, Hoke Smith, Secretary of the Interior under President Grover Cleveland, requested the President of the National Academy of Science to put together an advisory group of scientists to assess and make recommendations on the nation's forests. Among the seven selected to the National Forestry Commission were Arnold Hague of the U.S. Geological Survey and young Pinchot, the only member of the elite group with practical forest management experience. Hague, with whom Pinchot traveled extensively on Commission business and developed a close friendship, was a member of the Boone and Crockett Club.

Pinchot's work with the National Forest Commission led him to conclude that America's forest resources could, and should, be managed by trained foresters rather than merely protected by the military or otherwise. Such management would have three important consequences: protection of the forests and their values as wildlife habitat and for watershed protection; sustained, profitable use of wood products; and, garnering the gradual support of those who resented the exclusion of loggers, miners, and hunters from reserves, especially in the West. In this controversial position, Pinchot was supported by Hague.

The Commission, though divided on the degree and manner of protecting forest reserves, produced a final report in 1896 that supported the principle of creating such reserves. It contributed to President Cleveland's decision, in the final weeks of his administration, to place more than 20 million additional acres in reserves.

Many westerners, unaware of the Commission and its report, were again outraged by the seemingly covert and unilateral set-aside. They moved swiftly through legislative channels not only to nullify President Cleveland's actions, but also to restore all forest reserves to the public domain. A bill to that effect passed in the Senate the day it was introduced.

Pinchot had feared but anticipated the reaction. He and Hague hurriedly sought out Congressman Lacey, with whom they drafted countering legislation authorizing the Interior Secretary "to make sales of timber on any forest reservation now or hereafter proclaimed, for mining or domestic purposes, under such regulations as he may prescribe, and to make all needful rules and regulations in furtherance of the purposes of such reserves, for the management and protection of same."

Congress discarded the Senate-passed westerners' bill, adopting a version of the Lacey proposal. Even though President Cleveland surprisingly let the entire bill die, the immediate threat to the forest reserve system had been circumvented.

When William McKinley assumed the U.S. presidency, the westerners renewed their attack. Again, Pinchot and Hague parried. They enlisted the support of Hague's boss, Dr.

Photograph Courtesy of Wildlife Management Institute

A sight modern sport hunters would have trouble believing. A carload of fine American elk carcasses awaiting shipment to meat markets in the East. Shot by market hunters before such activity was outlawed, the pile includes some *fine* antlers that would be trophies then or today.

Charles D. Walcott, Director of the U.S. Geological Survey. Walcott had considerable clout with a number of western congressmen and was able to convince them, as James Trefethen noted, "that the forest reserves, properly managed, could be a tremendous asset to the West."

While Pinchot, Hague, and Walcott were buoyed by support of the American Forestry Association and pressed the good fight on Capitol Hill, the Boone and Crockett Club went into the western states with petitions, supporting forest reserves as ". . . necessary for the preservation of the timber and to secure the continuous and equitable flow of streams and the prevention of floods and water famine. Ranching and stock raising are both at stake when the water supply is threatened. We are informed that legislation will be proposed for the full development of all the resources of the reserves. This is the proper method of relief."

On June 4, 1897, after western interests had been given assurances that they would not be "locked out" of the forest reserves, President McKinley signed into law the new Civil Service Appropriation Act, which directed the Interior Secretary "to regulate their [the reserves'] occupancy and use and to preserve the forests therein from destruction."

Rendezvous

As the forest reserves and Yellowstone and Glacier National Parks scenarios illustrate, the Boone and Crockett Club was a cadre of sportsmen who were activists for conservation on their own, but who also were strongly motivated and able to band together propitiously from their divergent paths to rally timely enthusiasm, information, political savvy, and sense of mission from the fellowship of the Club. That was how the Club began in 1887, and how it continued into the 20th century.

On a snowy December evening in 1984, a century to the year after Yellowstone National Park received protection under the Lacey Act, Boone and Crockett Club members gathered at the boyhood home of their Club's founder, Theodore Roosevelt, in New York City. On that occasion, long-time Club member and officer John W. Hanes, Jr. cogently observed, "The Club has some remarkable members who have achieved remarkable things for conservation. All of them would tell you that whatever they have achieved owes something, often a great deal, to the tradition of the Club and the men who founded it. They were the prime movers. We only do our best to live up to the standards that they set."

FIREBRANDS AND FIREDRAKES

The hard-fought successes of the Boone and Crockett Club during its first decades were victories for conservation. They seem now to have been the stuff of common sense, but at the time the struggles were waged, conservation was unique to the American psyche. To temper the aggressive, free-wheeling opportunism that the country's resource wealth permitted for 300 years required more than a gradual shift of national attitudes and ethics. Restraint had to be imposed before the limits of natural resources were reached. To suggest restraint, much less to impose it, required foresight, compromise, ingenuity, sacrifice, and no small measure of courage. Personal reputations, careers, and fortunes were at stake, and these are what the Boone and Crockett Club members risked repeatedly in the cause

of a greater good.

To be sure, the motivations of the Boone and Crockett Club were not entirely altruistic. Its members were hunters, and threats to their coveted sport were correctly seen as real, serious, chronically imminent, and multifaceted. At the time, the legality of hunting was not at question. However, the feasibility of hunting opportunity then and for the future, by diminution of game and the resources on which wildlife depended, certainly was. The revolutionary paradigm that what was good for wildlife was good for people gained recognition, acceptance, and momentum through the efforts of the Boone and Crockett Club.

As previously indicated, most of the conservation investments were not investments under the aegis of the Club. They were actions by individual members inspired and encouraged by Club affiliation. The Boone and Crockett Club was, in effect, in the proverbial shadows as a brain trust and ready reservoir of political sway. At no time was this more evident than when Theodore Roosevelt, first President of the Boone and Crockett Club, became the 26th President of the United States.

New Growth

Roosevelt had reluctantly been drafted as William McKinley's Vice-Presidential running mate. Less than a year after their election in 1900, McKinley was tragically assassinated and Roosevelt assumed the nation's highest office. He reached out immediately to his friend, advisor, and fellow Boone and Crockett Club member Gifford Pinchot to help draft his inaugural message to Congress.

Two years before, after successfully engineering protection of the federal forest reserve system, Pinchot had been appointed Chief of the U.S. Department of Agriculture's small and ineffectual Forestry Division. He sought immediately to effect multiple-use management of the forest reserves. It was first necessary to wrest authority of the reserves from Interior and place it with Agriculture. Solidly behind Pinchot in this quest were the Secretary of Agriculture (James Wilson), the American Forestry Association, the newly formed Society of American Foresters, and (of course) the Boone and Crockett Club.

Roosevelt, too, was in favor of the transfer, and he encouraged legislation to that end. Soon after taking office, the President met with Pinchot, C. Hart Merriam (Chief of the Biological Survey), Merriam's assistant T.S. Palmer, and Congressman Lacey, who was Chairman of the House Committee on Public Lands. From that meeting of highly placed government officials, who not coincidentally were members of the Boone and Crockett Club, came a bill that promised to accomplish the transfer and "authorize game and fish protection in forest reserves, and for other purposes." It met defeat, however, when an amendment was added that would have essentially given control of the federal reserves to state governors.

Forces behind the original bill's purpose regrouped, mobilized support, and waited for a new opportunity. In the meanwhile, Pinchot was building up the Forestry Division and molding it into a competent, professional agency.

Opportunity came after the American Forestry Conference of 1905. The conference was sponsored by the American Forestry Association, and most major forest resource interests were represented, including mining, livestock ranching, timber, railroads, farming, and

recreation. The call for placing the forest reserves in the Agriculture Department was loud and clear, and a bill with that charge raced through Congress less than a month after the Conference convened. President Roosevelt wasted no time signing the Transfer Act into law. Its enactment, wrote James Trefethen, ". . . made possible the establishment of the U.S. Forest Service, and 86 million acres of forest reserves--now national forests--were for the first time placed under control of men qualified to manage them." It was a trenchant victory for Boone and Crockett Club cronies Roosevelt and Pinchot, and for the cause of conservation.

By the time Theodore Roosevelt left the White House in 1909, the U.S. Forest Service was well-established and charged with stewardship of nearly 150 million acres of national forests.

Another highly significant contribution of President Roosevelt to the nation's wildlife habitat base was his enthusiastic endorsement and implementation of the Reclamation Act of 1902. This act would ultimately affect more than one-third of the nation's landscape.

During the late 1800's, much of the West was considered the "Great American Desert." This vast, arid region was valued almost exclusively for mining and for raising livestock, but not by many. The key to ranching (or any occupation in the region), or merely traveling through it, was water. By whatever means possible, stockmen garnered all available water rights, effectively barring competition from other ventures. They considered the open range, public land, to be theirs.

While cattle ranching in the West was reaching its zenith in the 1870's and 1880's, Major John Wesley Powell of the U.S. Geological Survey was exploring and analyzing the arid lands. He reported in 1878 that, in fact, most of the soils of the Great American Desert were fertile and could be made productive. Powell urged the federal government to construct dams and irrigation channels, at locations he had carefully identified, on all major watercourses west of the 98th Meridian.

Powell's advocacy of water redistribution infuriated the western cattlemen and miners. They did not mind the idea of more readily accessible water; they did object, however, to the notion of sharing it with others, especially with homesteaders who might want to fence, plow, and stay. For a time, western politicians were able to stall the matter.

Roosevelt, who had a deserved reputation as a monopoly fighter, liked what he saw in Powell's report and later writings. When he became President, he used his considerable influence to push through the bill that he would sign into law as the Reclamation Act of 1902.

When Theodore Roosevelt left office seven years later, 30 reservoir projects were under way, with the capacity of irrigating 3 million acres. The new water supplies created habitat attractive to nearly all western wildlife. They stimulated the nation's economy, and they provided homes and communities for citizens who husbanded the land.

The vestige of the Old West that Theodore Roosevelt had visited in the Dakotas during the 1880's was gone altogether when he became U.S. President a score of years later. As President, he gave new life, literally and figuratively, to the region of the world he venerated most and that had been his inspiration for founding the Boone and Crockett Club.

Game Trails

At the core of the Boone and Crockett Club involvement in wildland protection and management was the urgency of conserving wildlife, especially big game. The ultimate goal of sustained yields of game animals meant first reversing the animal populations' precipitous declines. Club members knew that to reverse the trends of extirpation of virtually all big game populations, and before safeguards could be effective, the public had to admit to the prospective irrevocability of its own impact on wildlife numbers and habitat.

To that end, the Club initiated efforts to create a permanent exhibit dedicated to America's wildlife, a zoological park in New York City. About 1890, Club Secretary Madison Grant proposed the idea of such a park as a showpiece of big game and the principles of game preservation advocated by the Club.

Grant shared the popular and pervasive view that America's big game populations would likely continue to decline to extinction. The park, he reasoned, would be a last refuge and, at the same time, a site for "scientific investigations, publications, lectures, and animal act exhibitions." Despite such pessimism, Grant perceived that a zoological park could be a means for the Boone and Crockett Club to carry out its seemingly impossible mission to preserve the dwindling "stocks" of game. The natural-setting display of big game animals was intended, in Grant's words, "to preserve to future generations some remnant of the heritage which was our fathers', and which, to a great extent, still is ours, though so few of us have learned to estimate it at its true value."

Theodore Roosevelt (then President of the Boone and Crockett Club) brought the matter before the Club membership, which promptly established a committee chaired by Grant to investigate the idea.

Grant's committee found that bills proposing zoos in New York City had been floundering in the State Assembly for several years because of certain politicos, who viewed the matter as an elitist land grab, and pet store owners who perceived it as a threat to their businesses. The Club contacted State Assemblyman Andrew H. Green, who had previously introduced these bills. Green agreed that if the Boone and Crockett Club would support his bill, he would give the Club control of the zoological society created by the legislation. Assemblyman W. W. Niles, Jr., who represented the district where the park tentatively would be located, agreed to fight for the bill if the Club would organize the New York Zoological Society. An agreement was struck, and Club members Madison Grant and C. Grant LaFarge were therefore among the Society's original incorporators.

The bill passed. On May 7, 1895, the New York Zoological Society came into existence, with a large contingent of the Boone and Crockett Club membership on its board and as members. The southern end of Bronx Park had been found to have the size and landscape necessary for the park, and a 261-acre tract was granted to the Zoological Society by New York City.

What made this zoological park different from others was not only its size, but the concept behind its creation. It was designed to contain entire herds of North America's large quadrupeds (not merely a few individuals), and they were to live in a habitat approximating their natural surroundings. Club members also set up, in the early years of the next

century, the National Collection of Heads and Horns at the park to commemorate ". . . the passing of the big game of the continent." (See 1981 edition of *Records of North American Big Game* for complete history of NCHH.)

Quite obviously, the efforts of the Boone and Crockett Club were not single-focused. The zoological park issue overlapped the Club's work to protect Yellowstone National Park, to establish Glacier National Park, and to secure and properly administer the nation's forest reserves (discussed earlier).

National parks and forests, the Club had argued from the outset, should serve as refuges for wildlife, as well as for the conservation of their other intrinsic and considerable resource values. In *American Big-Game Hunting* (1893; the Boone and Crockett Club's first book), editors Grinnell and Roosevelt included a chapter on "Our Forest Reservations." In it was written one of the Club's foremost aims--that the forests, if properly protected, would serve as wildlife reservoirs, ". . . the nurseries and breeding grounds of game and the large wild animals which are elsewhere inevitably exterminated by the march of settlement." Therein, though somewhat obscurely, lies the seed of the National Wildlife Refuge System.

The Boone and Crockett Club's position, that portions of forest reserves should be set aside as game refuges, came to fruition with the Yellowstone Park Protection Act; but, the protection of that act, and its enforcement, applied only to Yellowstone. Encouraged by that success, the Club continued to agitate, privately and publicly, for an effective system of game refuges.

In 1901, the Club appointed a committee to pursue the idea of creating game refuges throughout the entire United States. Alden Sampson, Chairman of the committee, was made a game reserve expert under Roosevelt's Secretary of Agriculture. In this position, he traveled extensively to the forest reserves to examine the prospect of establishing federal game refuges within them. His committee's report in 1902 emphasized the need for such refuges.

While Sampson and his committee were studying the game refuge question, the Boone and Crockett Club was sponsoring a private study of the Black Mesa Forest Reserve in Arizona, one of the first privately funded scientific wildlife research efforts in the U.S. Edward W. Nelson (a future Chief of the U.S. Bureau of Biological Survey) completed the study and recommended that select parts of the Black Mesa Forest Reserve be made into refuges for pronghorn and mule deer.

Based on the conclusions of the Sampson committee and the Nelson study, Senator George C. Perkins of California, a member of the Club, introduced a bill in 1903 that authorized the President to establish game refuges in public forest reserves. This bill also provided that anyone killing or capturing animals within such a refuge would be fined or imprisoned. Perkins's bill passed the Senate, but not the House of Representatives.

Despite such occasional setbacks, the Club and its members continued to stump for wildlife protection. In March 1903, President Roosevelt signed an order creating the first officially designated wildlife refuge in the United States, Pelican Island National Wildlife Refuge in Florida, to protect brown pelicans from plume hunters. Several years later, Roosevelt established the Wichita Forest Reserve in Oklahoma (later known as the Wichita

Photograph Courtesy of Denver Public Library

The results of months of market hunting for the American bison, or "buffalo," as it was popularly known. Shown here are 40,000 bison hides awaiting shipment from the Wright and Roth corral, Dodge City, Kansas. Photograph taken about 1874.

Mountains Wildlife Refuge). And in 1908, the central symbol of wildlife destruction, the American bison, was protected by a designated sanctuary, the National Bison Range in Montana. The wildlife refuge system, a goal of the Boone and Crockett Club for years, had become a reality.

In the tug of war against time and the forces of unreserved free enterprise, those seeking to retain and perhaps even rebuild the remaining vestiges of America's wildlife heritage had finally gotten a foothold. But without some means of placing in check the slaughter of game animals for commercial markets, it was a tenuous grip indeed. Virtually unregulated subsistence and sport hunting contributed to the extraordinary decline of the nation's wild-life following the Civil War, but they paled by comparison to the ravages wrought by market gunners. From the mountains of Wyoming to the prairies of Kansas, to the marshes of the Dakotas, to the woodlots of Michigan, to the bottomland forests of Arkansas, to the swamps of Florida, to the coastal wetlands of New Jersey, to the waters of Chesapeake Bay, and wherever else game was relatively bountiful, market gunners plied their efficient, usually lucrative, and always devastating trade. The consequent decline of wildlife merely made the animals' hides, meat, feathers, and other salable parts in greater demand.

If the killing of game for fun and profit could not be controlled, the successful efforts of the Boone and Crockett Club and a few other organizations and individuals to preserve and protect wildlife habitats would clearly amount to little more than symbolic gestures. Boone and Crockett Club members, however, were not the type to find satisfaction in gestures, symbolic or otherwise.

On the matter of market gunning, the Club's stance was again typified and voiced by George Bird Grinnell. In 1894 he wrote in *Forest and Stream*: "The game supply which makes possible the general indulgence in field sports is of incalculable advantage to indi-viduals and the nation; but a game supply which makes possible the traffic in game as a luxury has no such importance. If this is granted, public policy demands that the traffic in game be abolished. . . . We suggest this declaration, *The sale of game should be forbidden at all seasons*, as a plank in the platform of that vast body of men . . . interested in preserving the game of the continent. . . ."

At the time, there were some state laws that forbade the taking of game during certain times and in certain ways, or that set a limit on the bag. But such laws, highly variable even among the states that had them, were full of loopholes and impossible to enforce.

In 1897, Congressman Lacey was approached by advocates of a federal law to ban the sale of wildlife products. The primary thrust for this law had come from the American Ornithologists Union, which had long been opposed to the killing of birds for plumes with which to adorn women's hats. Plumed hats were highly fashionable in the late 1800's, and raids on coastal rookeries and nesting colonies took a frightful toll on such bird populations as herons, egrets, ibises, terns, and others.

George Bird Grinnell was a charter member of the AOU and a close friend of Lacey. On July 1, 1897, Lacey introduced a bill intended to make the interstate transport of wildlife products taken in violation of state law a federal offense. It also would make the possessors of wildlife or wildlife products subject to pertinent laws in the state to which the item had been transported.

Lobbying against the bill were, of course, the milliners, market gunners, restaurateurs, railroaders, and others who gained from the trade in wildlife. Lacey's bill was defeated.

For the next several years, the bird protectionists (principally the AOU and state Audubon societies) undauntedly mustered the support of fish and game protective associations, scientific groups, local bird clubs, the League of American Sportsmen, and the Boone and Crockett Club. The ground swell of support for Lacey's reintroduced bill in 1900 helped push it through Congress. The Game and Wild Birds Preservation and Disposition Act (Lacey Act of 1900) became law on May 25, 1900. The new law prohibited interstate shipment of illegally killed wildlife, and it placed severe limitations on the importation of exotic wildlife.

The Lacey Act of 1900 is considered by many to be the legal cornerstone of fish and wildlife conservation in the United States. It soon made the marketing of most poached or otherwise unlawfully taken or transported wildlife too risky and expensive, giving the beleaguered animal populations some respite from punt guns, repeating rifles, and mesh nets. It also expanded the scope and breadth of responsibility of the Bureau of Biological Survey, the forerunner of the U.S. Fish and Wildlife Service and formerly a small and benign bureaucracy that was more curatorial than governmental. That the man who sponsored the law, and whose name still is popularly associated with it, was a Boone Crockett Club member is no surprise.

By itself, the Lacey Act of 1900 was no panacea for the deplorable state of wildlife populations. Its effectiveness hinged on adequate state conservation laws. But where such laws existed, they generally were weak and unenforceable. A crusader for more realistic and practical state game protective laws was T. Gilbert Pearson. A biologist, Pearson's initial mission was to protect non-game birds from year-round gunning in North Carolina. His was not a popular stance, but his perseverance and persuasiveness paid off. In 1903, almost single-handedly, Pearson successfully lobbied for a bill that he drafted himself. Pearson's bill was a model state game law that provided protection for most non-game species and imposed a $10 license fee on non-resident hunters. The license revenue was earmarked for game law enforcement.

Pearson's achievement in North Carolina gained him national attention among the conservation/sportsmen's organizations. In 1904, he was asked to head up the new National Association of Audubon Societies for the Protection of Wild Birds and Animals. It was incorporated in New York City, to serve as the parent organization of the then-loose network of state and local Audubon societies. In time, it became the National Audubon Society. Pearson's tireless leadership brought the association to prominence and influence in national conservation affairs. Until his death in 1943, Pearson was one of America's foremost fighters for conservation reform. He was also a member of the Boone and Crockett Club.

Raising Dust

In 1900, the Territory of Alaska was a disconnected and distant appendage of the United States, having been purchased from Russia in 1867 for $7.2 million (about 2 cents per acre). Though huge (586,400 square miles), remote, and, for the most part, pristine, Alas-

ka's lands and wildlife were nonetheless in jeopardy.

Until it was learned that some of Alaska's stream beds flashed gold, few Americans considered the territory anything more than a national embarrassment, "Seward's icebox." The Klondike gold rush of 1897 caused an immediate reappraisal of "the great frozen wasteland of the North." It also prompted a sudden influx of neophyte prospectors and dreamers willing to risk all on the chance of sifting a fortune from the Yukon's inhospitable landscape.

Before then, from the mid–1870's until the turn of the century, future Club members Henry P. Allen, Edward William Nelson, Charles H. Townsend, George Bird Grinnell, Joseph Grinnell, and others took part in scientific expeditions and explorations of Alaska that gave them a great familiarity and appreciation of the land, its people, and its wildlife. Once the pandemonium of the gold rush got under way, it became quite apparent to the Boone and Crockett Club that the fortune seekers posed a distinct threat to the territory's big-game populations. The cost of provisions shipped from the states was exorbitant. The logical alternative to grossly inflated food prices was local sources--Alaska's wildlife. Professional gunners abounded and invariably did a highly profitable business in the absence of legal constraints. The meat of moose, caribou, mountain sheep, and bear found a ready market, while the animals' hides and other parts were used or exported for further profit.

Though it was noticeable to all that Alaska's big game could not indefinitely endure the lawless carnage, few cared. Certainly the gunners and miners did not object. And most Americans in the states were too removed in both distance and perspective to be concerned; not so the Boone and Crockett Club.

In 1901, the Club's Executive Committee urged the passage of laws to protect Alaska's wild game. Club members Grant and Lacey worked on a bill that was greatly influenced by information provided by fellow Club members with intimate knowledge of the Alaskan environment. The bill became law on June 7, 1902, with President Roosevelt's signature. It proved to be a landmark piece of legislation, the first in a series of Alaska game laws defined and defended by the Boone and Crockett Club that became models for game laws elsewhere.

The 1902 Alaska Game Law prohibited the killing of wild animals and birds for commercial purposes. It established hunting seasons, and it allowed the Secretary of Agriculture to create additional regulations or modify those set up by the law. For species seemingly threatened with extinction, the statute permitted the Secretary to restrict hunting to the point of prohibition for five years. Certain exceptions were made for Alaska's native people, and for others working or traveling in the wilderness, who were allowed to kill game for personal use only. Hides, meat, and trophy heads could be shipped out of Alaska only by special permits available to legitimate scientists and sportsmen.

The validity of the new law was quickly challenged. On February 8, 1904, Senator William P. Dillingham of Vermont introduced a bill in Congress that not only would have repealed the game law, but also would have removed protection from certain previously protected species (bear, mountain goat, and mountain sheep). The bill was proposed after Dillingham completed a two-month trip to Alaska, during which Alaskans had convinced

Photograph Courtesy of Alaska Natural History Association

Mount Denali, Alaska. Charles Sheldon, Boone and Crockett Club member and well-known explorer of Alaska, led the long fight to get necessary legislation passed to preserve the mountain and its surrounding as a part of the National Park System. Originally called Mount McKinley by white explorers, the mountain is known today by its Indian name, Denali.

him that the game law was leading to disaster. The Senator returned to Washington, D.C. convinced that bears were running rampant, that local citizens were doing without food they previously acquired by hunting, and that natives were denied a subsistence diet because the game was, in effect, reserved for wealthy, non-resident sportsmen.

Boone and Crockett Club members Grant and Hornaday, and other conservationists including George Oliver Shields of the Camp Fire Club, immediately began a campaign to educate Dillingham about the true nature of Alaska's wildlife situation. Through numerous letters from Club members and others, and directly from his fellow senators, Dillingham learned that the situation was not at all what he had been hoodwinked into believing. For example, in a joint letter, Club President W. Austin Wadsworth and Club Secretary Grant wrote to Dillingham: "It is scarcely credible that the Senate of the United States, having before it the destruction of the buffalo and other large mammals in the West, which today is a standing reproach to the civilization of our country, would deliberately remove from the statute books all protection for the game animals in the one locality [Alaska] where they still exist in anything like their former numbers."

In response to the fusillade of fact and well-reasoned opinion, Dillingham withdrew his bill and the matter ended there. In 1908, Congressman W. E. Humphrey of Washington State, a Boone and Crockett Club member, introduced a new Alaska game law that improved on the 1902 statute.

Denali

Not everyone who ventured north at the turn of the century was drawn there by the sirens of precious metal. Among those who were not was a New Englander by birth, a Yale-educated engineer by vocation, and a hunter by choice. His name was Charles Sheldon.

While living and working in Mexico between 1898 and 1902, Charles Sheldon had hunted desert bighorn sheep and had become deeply interested in the scientific study of wild sheep. He retired from the business world in 1903 at the age of 36 and set off in sporting and scientific pursuit of bighorns. His searches carried him from the deserts of Mexico to the icy mountains of interior Alaska. Sheldon was truly a pioneer. He studied an animal about which little was known, and he explored regions that seldom, if ever, had been visited by modern man.

In 1903, while planning a hunting trip to Alaska, Sheldon became acquainted and friends with Edward W. Nelson, Chief of the U.S. Bureau of Biological Survey (and a Boone and Crockett Club member). Sheldon and Nelson found in each other kindred spirits. They were individuals for whom hunting and natural history were life's breath. Through Nelson, Sheldon soon became a Boone and Crockett Club member, one whom Theodore Roosevelt came to regard as the very best kind, a hunter/naturalist like himself whose knowledge, convictions, and initiative would reap great rewards for wildlife, hunting, and conservation.

Sheldon's 1906 travels up the Tanana River, toward the majestic peaks of the Alaska range, were one of the first expeditions to that region. Approaching Mt. McKinley, Shel-

don was awe-struck by the towering, snow-clad mountain. He preferred to call the rocky colossus, reverently, by its Indian name *Denali*--the High One. Equally as stunning to Sheldon as the area's natural beauty were its game populations. From July 1907 to June 1908, Sheldon stayed to hunt, explore, collect, and live an extreme adventure.

When he left in 1908, Sheldon took not only the idea for a national park, but maps delineating boundaries around a proposed park area of more than 2,000 square miles. His fellow Boone and Crockett Club members were very excited about the project, but nearly a decade would pass before Sheldon's brainchild would gain the attention and political momentum necessary for congressional consideration.

In the years immediately following 1908, Alaska experienced steady development. Population centers such as Fairbanks were soon springing up within 100 miles of Denali. Explorers, prospectors, adventurers, market gunners, and (in 1915) the Alaska Railway began to penetrate the area that Sheldon hoped would someday be a park. It was the approach of the railroad toward Denali that spurred the Boone and Crockett Club to action. Its game committee, chaired by Sheldon, and the Club's Executive Committee strongly endorsed the idea of a national park in the Mt. McKinley area. Other interested organizations and individuals were enlisted to generate public support for the idea. Edward Nelson of the Biological Survey, a Club member and Sheldon's mentor, supported the proposal. The same was true of Stephen T. Mather, then in charge of national parks. The Club also found a legislative champion in James Wickersham, U.S. Delegate of the Alaska Territory.

On the very day that he became a member of the Boone and Crockett Club, Stephen Mather wrote to Charles Sheldon, enthusiastically inviting him to visit Mather and his colleagues to discuss Sheldon's proposal for a new national park. Consequently, and soon thereafter, Mather became involved in the campaign, using his position and influence to bring into the drama other notable conservation figures who could effectively work for the park's creation. These included Belmore Browne of the Camp Fire Club and John B. Burnham of the American Game Protective Association (and also a Boone and Crockett Club member).

In drafting legislation to create the park, the name "Denali," Sheldon's choice, was shelved. Otherwise, the bill was almost entirely based on Sheldon's mapping and knowledge of the area, and his vision of what ought to be. Delegate Wickersham introduced the bill in April 1916 into the House of Representatives. Within days, Senator Key Pittman of Nevada sponsored its version in the Senate.

Once the bills were introduced, the Boone and Crockett Club moved to consolidate favorable public and political opinion on the matter. The Club also helped publish and distribute a timely defense of Mt. McKinley National Park.

Despite some political maneuvering and skirmishing, the bill was passed by both the House and Senate in early 1917. Charles Sheldon himself took the legislation to the White House and watched as President Wilson signed it into law. It was appropriate that the man who had lived with Denali, and had conceived its preservation as a national park, should be present when the mere motion of a pen culminated what for him had been a dream, a cause, and a gift for perpetuity.

TRIUMPHS AND TRAGEDIES: BETWEEN THE WARS

The death of Theodore Roosevelt in 1919 did not spell the end for the Boone and Crockett Club. But times indeed were changing; the land and society were not what they had been even a few decades before the Club was founded.

The years between World War I and World War II, the 1920's and 1930's, were a time of tragedy and triumph. America had propelled itself to a position of international power. Its people were leaving the farm for oil fields and urban industry, for new opportunities and the promise of a better life. With population growth and technological innovation, coupled with increased mobility and leisure time, the human pressure on public land intensified. A fairly simple social equation of more people, more transportation, more time, and more money led to heightened demand for outdoor recreation, including hunting and fishing, that put new strains on America's lands and wildlife.

While some wildlife populations remained depressed from the "Exploitation Era" of the late 1800's, and others, because of destroyed, diminished, or damaged habitat, were recovering slowly, a few species rebounded and thrived too much under the near-total protection. Reduction of hunting pressure and continued elimination of predators caused some animals, particularly certain big game, to expand rapidly beyond the biological carrying capacity of their habitats. "Managing" wildlife then was mostly guesswork. And though in many cases guesswork was better than nothing, there were instances, serious instances, where it backfired.

The Lesson of the Kaibab

One example of this problem was in the Grand Canyon National Game Preserve of the Kaibab Plateau in northern Arizona. When President Theodore Roosevelt created this preserve in 1906, it provided protection for a population of a few thousand mule deer. By the 1920's, however, elimination of hunting and such natural predators as mountain lions and wolves, plus a reduction of cattle and sheep grazing, had allowed the unmolested deer to erupt to enormous numbers. The numerous deer began to destroy the preserve's vegetation, just as too many livestock in a fenced pasture can quickly reduce it to hardpan and dust. The inevitable result on the Kaibab Plateau was the destruction of deer habitat, and the death by starvation of thousands of deer. Out of this tragedy—the result of man's good intentions—grew a new understanding of how land and wildlife must be managed.

Conservationists to that time assumed that restoring and maintaining big game involved a straightforward solution: creating national parks, forests, and game refuges. The Kaibab Plateau tragedy and other similar events clearly showed the solution was not quite so simple. Blanket protection for some species just doesn't work. The grim lesson of the Kaibab Plateau and elsewhere was that people need not only to provide sanctuary for wildlife, but to manage space and other habitat components. To do otherwise in an increasingly artificial environment is to court disaster. Being well-intentioned is not enough.

The Boone and Crockett Club followed the Kaibab situation with great interest and concern. Since the Club's beginning, its members had always been willing to learn,

The "father" of the science of modern wildlife management, Aldo Leopold. Trained as a forester, Leopold applied his unique grasp of ecological principles and common sense to the task of stewardship for wildlife with the outstanding result that we enjoy today in management of much of our wild areas.

change, and adapt to dynamic conditions and as improved knowledge called for new strategies and policies. Very frequently, Boone and Crockett Club members were on the cutting edge of change.

One such member was Aldo Leopold, now widely recognized as the "father" of modern wildlife management. The Kaibab Plateau situation helped Leopold frame his cardinal ideas about the need for flexible scientific management of natural resources. He came to realize the intricate and often critical interrelationships in the environment, and the need for ecological balance. Leopold was a scientist and a philosopher, but he wasn't a dreamer. He knew and considered in his teaching the predominant role of the human animal in compromising and controlling the natural environment.

Aldo Leopold's studies and his writings remain the foundation of ecological awareness in the U.S. and much of the rest of the world. His work, more than that of anyone else, gave direction and credibility to the unique blend of art and science that is wildlife management today. Leopold's land ethic was in part (1) that the role of *Homo sapiens* changes "from conqueror of the land-community to plain member and citizen of it," (2) that "conservation is a state of harmony between men and land," and (3) that "a thing is right when it tends to preserve the integrity, stability, and beauty of the biotic community." Leopold's land ethic can be termed the principal tenet of modern conservation. His insight and foresight, if not awakened by the Kaibab Plateau fiasco, certainly gained focus from that tragedy and from constructive intellectual and social exchanges with his fellow members of the Boone and Crockett Club.

Plenary Agenda

In 1924, the Boone and Crockett Club was involved in a national recreation conference. This was an important step toward dealing with the growing pressures on national parks, forests, and wildlife preserves. The kind of intelligent and flexible management that Leopold called for was a discussion topic at this conference, which proved to be a milestone in the conservation movement.

Earlier, the Club had forcefully asserted that a far-reaching, coordinated policy needed to be adopted, one that would allow the nation to manage and utilize its great public natural resources intelligently. The Club suggested that the President of the United States should see to it that a policy be adopted that would codify how the American people could most effectively manage and regulate their public lands for maximum enjoyment and use. As a direct result of the Club's publication of these ideas in a widely distributed leaflet, plus the influence of several Club members on President Calvin Coolidge, a conference was called by Coolidge to establish a National Recreation Policy.

The President's Conference on Outdoor Recreation first met in May 1924. It continued to meet annually until 1929. From the beginning, the conference focused on a broad range of topics, including "every interest in the out-of-doors from lawn tennis and the study of wild flowers to white water canoeing and moose hunting." But more important than the range of interests was the underlying theme that the nation needed to develop a coordinated approach on the federal, state, and local levels to regulate public lands and manage the animals that lived on them.

The conference was promoted by the Boone and Crockett Club, and Club member Theodore Roosevelt, Jr., served as its Executive Chairman. Club members Charles Sheldon, John M. Phillips, T. Gilbert Pearson, and John C. Merriam chaired conference committees. These committees were served by many other Club members, including John Burnham, William B. Mershon, Frederic C. Walcott, C. H. Townsend, Vernon Bailey, Frank M. Chapman, T. S. Palmer, and Barrington Moore. When the conference was established as a permanent organization, a number of Boone and Crockett Club members served on its Executive Committee and advisory council. These included Chauncey J. Hamlin (Executive Chairman), George E. Scott, George Shiras III, and others.

Hundreds of delegates from conservation organizations and wildlife agencies attended the first conference in 1924. In resolution after resolution, the delegates called for changes that would streamline conservation efforts and wildlife programs to handle the growing demands on public land. In general, the President's Conference on Outdoor Recreation set the agenda for a broad-based approach to the many concerns and problems of America's natural resources. The list of resolutions passed reveals the enormous breadth and depth of this ground-breaking meeting: citizenship values; federal land policy; state parks and forests; survey and classification of recreation resources; plants and flowers; birds; game and fur-bearing animals; fish; pollution and drainage; international relationships; financial encouragement of outdoor recreation; value of outdoor recreation to industrial workers; municipal parks and playgrounds; educational programs; and, outdoor recreational needs of children. The significance of each resolution topic was stated, and ways were proposed to deal most effectively with the subject or issue.

The Executive Committee of the conference concluded that a paramount need was "close cooperation of such private agencies and Government agencies, federal, state, county and municipal." With coordinated efforts, it would be possible eventually "to evolve a National plan for outdoor recreation in which each agency, public and private, will have and play its part, to the end that our country will be a happier, pleasanter and healthier place in which to live."

In creating this conference, the Boone and Crockett Club had an enormous impact on the visibility and direction of the conservation movement. The conference was, in one historian's opinion, "the greatest single contribution of the Boone and Crockett Club to the nation."

Dry Winds

In the late 1920's and the 1930's, as the conservation movement was enjoying its early successes and gathering support, strength, and sophistication for further gains, nature finally collected on a national debt of sorts.

For decades, homesteaders, farmers, ranchers, and others in the West and Midwest had caused or permitted the nation's topsoil to be frittered away. Clear-cutting forests, overgrazing grasslands, burning, draining or filling wetlands, poor row-cropping practices, and more contributed to the exposure of soil to the erosive forces of wind and water. The situation was a disaster waiting to happen.

At risk in the agricultural belt was not only the national economy but a wildlife resource

dear to nearly all Americans—waterfowl. In the absence of bison herds and flocks of passenger pigeons, the continental population of ducks, geese, and swans was always a tangible measure of resource wealth and, by the spectacle of migration, an index and harbinger of seasonal rhythms.

Even though most of the nation's waterfowl actually came from nesting grounds in Canada and Alaska, so that habitat protection was not of apparent urgency, there was still reason for concern for the species in the U.S. long before the 1920's and '30's. Among the first to express such concern and press for preventative action was the Boone and Crockett Club. In the 1880's and 1890's, Grinnell's *Forest and Stream* called for curbs on spring shooting (which decimated or at least disturbed breeding waterfowl), and for restrictions on market hunting. The Lacey Act of 1900 helped stop interstate commerce in game and reduce the take of waterfowl by market gunners.

In late 1904, George Shiras III, a Congressman from Pennsylvania and a Boone and Crockett Club member, began work on draft legislation that he entitled, "A Bill to Protect the Migratory Birds of the United States." It proposed that since state laws were ineffective in protecting birds such as waterfowl that migrated across state lines, the federal government should have "custody" over such animals and regulate the hunting of them. Shiras's bill never came to a vote. But, over the next decade, as waterfowl populations declined, his concept of federal authority over management of migratory birds gained currency.

In 1911, the American Game Protective and Propagation Association was founded by sportsmen and leaders of the Sporting Arms and Ammunitions Manufacturing Industry. Not surprisingly it included some Boone and Crockett Club members. The Association was chartered as a non-profit organization to work nationally with wildlife resource decision makers, administrators, educators, managers, and other private concerns to restore, protect, and enhance America's dwindling wildlife. A small, mobile, and aggressive organization that supported its involvement in resource issues and legislation with the best available scientific information, the Association became an immediate influence on the national conservation scene. From the outset, it was committed to the idea that the recovery of waterfowl and other migratory birds depended on federal jurisdiction. The Shiras bill, dormant for nearly a decade, became the special cause of the Association's President, John Bird Burnham. Burnham was formerly New York State's Chief game warden and, before that, a staff member of Grinnell's *Forest and Stream*. Eventually, he was also a Boone and Crockett Club member.

Burnham, with the help of others, campaigned vigorously to enlist the support of sportsmen's clubs and organizations to convince congressional nay-sayers and fence-sitters that proper protection for migratory waterfowl could be done only by federal administration. The campaign was not without difficulties. A number of people, including Congressman Lacey, had concerns about the constitutionality of such legislation. They reasoned that the vesting of regulatory authority with the federal government might well be a violation of states' rights.

In September 1912, Burnham met with William S. Haskell (also of the American Game Protective and Propagation Association), William T. Hornaday, Madison Grant and Henry Fairfield Osborn of the New York Zoological Society, T. Gilbert Pearson of the National

Photograph Courtesy of Wildlife Management Institute

A very large bag of waterfowl in the days prior to game laws and bag limits. This photograph was taken near Devil's Lake, North Dakota at an unknown date.

Association of Audubon Societies, Edmund and Julius Seymour of the Camp Fire Club, and George Bird Grinnell and Charles Stewart Davison of the Boone and Crockett Club. All were supporters of the "Shiras bills," redrafted and introduced in Congress by Congressman John W. Weeks of Massachusetts. (All but Haskell and the Seymours were then, or soon to be, Boone and Crockett Club members.) The conveners decided that the bill had little chance unless it was broadened. They chose to rewrite a bill similar to Weeks' that had been introduced by Senator George P. McLean of Connecticut. It was expanded to include all migratory birds. The import of the revised draft legislation (the Weeks-McLean Bill) was the inclusion of migratory insectivorous birds. Though the significance of these birds relative to protection of agricultural crops was somewhat overblown, it served to tilt favorably the "farm vote." Important influence for the measure also came from such individuals as industrialist Henry Ford, a strong advocate of songbird protection.

Still in doubt was the question of the bill's constitutionality. In fact, Senator Elihu Root of New York (a long-time Boone and Crockett Club member) prepared to oppose its passage, even though he was a staunch supporter of the concept of protecting wildlife, because he believed the bill to be unconstitutional. As a former Secretary of State and Nobel Peace Prize winner, Root was a legislator of considerable clout. His opposition could prove fatal. So, some of his Boone and Crockett Club comrades advised him that the bill would not be unconstitutional if it was enacted to fulfill the terms of an international treaty. Root therefore introduced a resolution to make the protection of migratory birds the subject of such a treaty, and the resolution was passed in 1913.

The new draft, appended as a rider to the Agricultural Appropriations Bill, was passed by Congress in March 1913, and unwittingly signed into law by President William Howard Taft. In the harried days before he departed office, Taft signed the Agricultural Appropriations Bill without knowing of the rider. He had earlier warned Congress he would veto any bill appended with riders dealing with basic legislation. Furthermore, he agreed with those who saw the matter as fundamentally unconstitutional. When Taft later learned that he had signed the Weeks-McLean Bill into law, he admitted that had he known that it was part of the Appropriations package, he would have used his veto power.

Therefore, by the luck of timeliness and presidential oversight, the Weeks-McLean Migratory Bird Act went into effect, outlawing springtime gunning and granting the Secretary of Agriculture the power to set hunting seasons.

Not until 1916, however, did the international treaty condition of the Act come to pass. In that year, through the efforts in particular of Boone and Crockett Club members Burnham, Palmer, and Nelson in their professional capacities, "The Treaty Between the United States and Great Britain for the Protection of Migratory Birds in the United States and Canada" was signed and ratified. It was not until 1918 that the U.S. House of Representatives passed an enabling act that, with President Woodrow Wilson's signature, made the treaty operative.

All during the years of political maneuvering to see Shiras's 1904 concept through to law, Boone and Crockett Club members (especially those on the Club's game preservation committee) were working for the cause in league with other sportsmen's organizations. The eventual success of that work, patience, and cooperation accorded federal authorities

95

the right to regulate the hunting of migratory birds. With the treaty in effect on both sides of the U.S./Canada border, North America's migratory birds were under the full protection of the treaty. The Bureau of Biological Survey was assigned the monumental task of devising regulations for the U.S. to ensure the survival of waterfowl. This task included spring shooting and market gunning restrictions, protection of endangered species, closed seasons, bag limits, and much more.

Within two years of promulgation of the treaty's enabling act, the continent's waterfowl populations showed clear signs of recovery. Then, slowly at first, disaster struck. It came in the form of cloudless skies and sunshine. Drought gripped the agricultural regions of North America beginning in the late 1920's, not fully releasing until the late 1930's.

The agricultural regions coincided with the continent's primary duck-breeding range, including the prairie provinces of Canada and the prairie pothole portions of North and South Dakota, Minnesota, Iowa, Nebraska, Colorado, and Montana. Without water and stable, fertile soils, the region could not support the vegetation needed by waterfowl for nesting success and survival.

The drought produced a shortage of grain, especially wheat, and farmers, hoping to maximize productivity, plowed up or plowed to the edges of dried-up or drawn-down potholes. Seldom did this help the farmers during the unrelenting dry period, and it certainly never helped waterfowl. The loss of habitat over such a large area, for such an extended time, caused puddle duck population numbers to plummet. With fewer "puddlers" in the migration, diving ducks were shot in numbers disproportionate to their usual numerical occurrence in autumn flights.

By the authority it vested in federal agencies to tighten hunter bag limits, the 1916 Treaty was able to prevent hunting pressure that otherwise might have snuffed out some duck species, or at least some populations, altogether. But even the best of regulations could not bring rain or rectify past land abuses that gave drought the force of fire. The problem was rather simple; its resolution was not.

Respite and Refuges

Boone and Crockett Club members were among the first to grasp the seriousness and broad implications of the "Dirty Thirties" drought, and they were among the first to attempt to deal with them.

A primary solution was the creation of a system of sanctuaries or refuges that could preserve waterfowl habitat along the birds' migrational corridors, where they bred and raised their young, and where they wintered. As wetland habitat gave way to farms, towns, and other developments, waterfowl populations would continue to shrink to dangerous levels. Refuges could provide permanent wetland habitat, and perhaps areas of public hunting opportunity, if population numbers increased and could be sustained at huntable levels.

The Club had supported this idea long before the crisis years of the 1920's and 1930's, but it was not until then that widespread backing developed. Bills to create game refuges and public shooting areas were promoted in the early 1920's. An important new idea that surfaced in connection with these bills was the concept of having hunters purchase a duck

stamp, with the proceeds being used to buy land for and also administer wildlife refuges.

Public hunting on refuges became a controversial issue that threatened to scuttle the entire effort. Anti-hunting forces felt that the game refuges were merely a way of concentrating ducks for the sporting pleasure of hunters. One of the leaders of this contingent, ironically, was a hunter and Boone and Crockett Club member, William Hornaday. Because of Hornaday's charismatic personality, outspokenness, and his aggressive campaign, bills promoting the creation of refuges/shooting grounds were defeated regularly between 1925 and 1929. Hornaday was especially opposed to hunting with pump and semiautomatic firearms, and to the discretionary authority of the Secretary of Agriculture and the Bureau of Biological Survey in setting waterfowl hunting season dates and bag limits. In February of 1929, a federal refuge system was finally established under the Norbeck-Anderssen Migratory Bird Conservation Act, but the public hunting provision was omitted to aid its passage into law.

As a result of the debate over the fate of waterfowl, and the acrimony created by anti-hunting forces, conservationists became concerned about the need to educate sportsmen concerning the broad, national problems of waterfowl conservation. This concern of Boone and Crockett Club members Lewis R. Morris, Charles Sheldon, George Bird Grinnell, and John C. Phillips, along with other sportsmen, led to the founding in 1927 of the American Wild Fowlers. The AWF was dedicated to supporting the concept of game refuges, helping the Bureau of Biological Survey scientifically assess the problems of waterfowl, and countering the well-organized anti-hunting forces. Until 1931, when this Boone and Crockett Club-based organization closed its doors, American Wild Fowlers played a vital role in the conceptualizing, drafting, and passage of the Norbeck-Anderssen bill. It also organized successful opposition to legislation proposed in 1930 that would have taken regulatory authority over migratory game bird bag limits and seasons out of the hands of the Bureau of Biological Survey, with its scientifically trained staff, and put it into the hands of congressmen with little or no knowledge of wildlife. In addition, American Wild Fowlers funded scientific studies and worked closely with biologists such as Frederick C. Lincoln. Lincoln's studies had revealed that North America's waterfowl largely follow four separate flyways (Pacific, Central, Mississippi, and Atlantic) in their semiannual migrations between the northern breeding/nesting grounds and their southern wintering areas.

After nearly five years of effective work in behalf of the continent's nearly exhausted duck populations, American Wild Fowlers was disbanded. The leaders, mostly Boone and Crockett members, foresaw the need instead for a large citizen/sportsman organization that could generate the resources and support to carry on necessary work for waterfowl. The organization's files were turned over to a new group formed the year before and known as More Game Birds in America Foundation. In 1937, that foundation was reorganized and renamed Ducks Unlimited.

The Migratory Bird Hunting Stamp Act, which became law on March 16, 1934, was another major waterfowl conservation effort that had a significant Boone and Crockett Club connection. These federal "duck stamps," required of all U.S. waterfowl hunters 16 years of age and older, generate revenues earmarked for the purchase, development, and management of waterfowl refuges. Since the first stamp was designed by Boone and Crockett

Photograph Courtesy of Wildlife Management Institute

J. N. "Ding" Darling, cartoonist, activist, and conservationist. Under his direct guidance, the "Duck Stamp" Act and other progressive legislation gave a firm base for the successful management programs of today. Other accomplishments included proposal of the National Wildlife Federation, which he headed in its early years.

Club member Jay N. ("Ding") Darling in 1936, nearly 100 million stamps have been sold, with almost $300 million in proceeds going toward acquisition of approximately 2.5 million acres of habitat.

Frederic C. Walcott, Senator from Connecticut and a Boone and Crockett Club member since 1905, was responsible for establishing a Senate Special Committee on the Conservation of Wildlife Resources. He served as its Chairman, helping steer the Duck Stamp bill successfully through his committee. Walcott was also one of the founders of the American Game Protective and Propagation Association, that evolved into the American Wildlife Institute and, in 1946, became the current Wildlife Management Institute. WMI has proved to be a major force for conservation, with long-standing, strong ties to the Boone and Crockett Club.

Ding Darling, a talented newspaperman and Pulitzer Prize-winning cartoonist, also proved to have a talent for tough and intelligent administrative work as Chief of the Bureau of Biological Survey (later the U.S. Fish and Wildlife Service). He began in March 1934, under the Franklin Delano Roosevelt administration. A frequent critic of New Deal policies, Darling nevertheless was appointed to the post by President Roosevelt and was given a free rein in administering the Bureau. He brought to the task enormous energy, ingenuity, and enthusiasm. These qualities rubbed onto his staff, then beset by the depressing problems attendant to the on-going drought.

Darling wasted no time in stepping up efforts to protect waterfowl. He strengthened the federal conservation warden staff and its resources in order to strike hard and often at the outlaw gunners and duck "bootleggers" who were operating along the Mid-Atlantic coast, in parts of California, and in bottomlands of the Mississippi, Missouri, and Illinois rivers. Darling also made effective use of the duck stamp to plan and establish a system of refuges along waterfowl's primary migrational corridors. He also instituted radically stringent hunting regulations to reduce hunter harvest of the drought-depleted populations.

Another extremely valuable and enduring innovation by Darling was the formation of the Cooperative Wildlife Research Unit Program. A wildlife science research and training program at state land-grant colleges and universities, the "Co-op Units" were funded and administered jointly by the Bureau, the wildlife agency of the state in which the Unit was established, and the American Wildlife Institute. Darling's intent was to create well-distributed, self-sustaining centers where research could be undertaken on regional as well as national subjects, and where intensive, graduate-level training in biological sciences could provide and maintain a pool of highly competent wildlife administrators, educators, researchers, and managers. In this wholly successful endeavor, Darling was strongly supported from the outset by fellow Boone and Crockett Club member Aldo Leopold.

In 1935, at the first North American Wildlife Conference (called by President Roosevelt at the behest of Darling, and sponsored by the American Wildlife Institute), the indomitable Ding proposed that the tens of thousands of sportsmen and hundreds of conservation clubs nationwide should unite as a single federation in order to address issues and other matters of common interest and concern most effectively. Darling's inspiration and the prototype for a "General Wildlife Federation" was a well-organized coalition of sportsmen's clubs in Indiana. The person who engineered the Indiana organization was C. R.

("Pink") Gutermuth, who, in the years ahead, would gain considerable and deserved fame on the national conservation stage. "Ding" and "Pink" were to join forces on many occasions to effect gains for wildlife. Gutermuth also would join Darling as a member of the Boone and Crockett Club.

Another state in which sportsmen were well-organized, and a further clear example to Darling that his concept was sound and feasible, was New York. There the organizer was Karl T. Frederick, and Frederick, too, was destined for Boone and Crockett Club membership.

Less than six months after Darling's persuasive call for a general federation, 29 states had mobilized or were in the process of mobilizing their conservation/sportsmen's clubs under a federation umbrella. Fifteen other states already had some form of coalition. Ten months after his call, Darling resigned from the Bureau of Biological Survey he so effectively served for 18 months, to become the first president of the organization he had proposed, the National Wildlife Federation. It has since become the world's largest citizen-membership conservation organization and an important voice in natural resource matters at the state, national, and even international levels.

Darling's hand-picked successor at the Bureau was Ira N. Gabrielson, also a Boone and Crockett Club member. "Gabe" would become the first head of the U.S. Fish and Wildlife Service, the successor to the Bureau of Biological Survey.

A Firm Foundation

By the late 1930's, when moisture began to revitalize the drought-stricken heartland and the nation began to recover from the epidemic of economic depression, the building blocks of an effective wildlife conservation program were at hand. In large measure through the leadership of the Boone and Crockett Club, and the independent efforts of its regular and professional (then associate) members, there were laws to protect wildlife from overkill; refuges and other habitat preserves managed in the best interest of natural resources; and a fledgling academic/research program to bring the management of wildlife under the cloak of science.

Still needed, however, was a mechanism to finance wildlife programs, particularly at the state level. A steady source of funding was essential to aid the recovery and stabilization of wildlife populations, to enhance wildlife habitat, and to continue refinement of on-the-ground management to sustain wildlife benefits for the public. At the time, state appropriations for wildlife conservation were regularly raided or diverted for state programs wholly unrelated to wildlife management. But just where the additional dollars would come from, and how their flow could be maintained, were perplexing and pressing questions.

As early as 1925, an idea had surfaced in a committee of the International Association of Game, Fish and Conservation Commissioners (now the International Association of Fish and Wildlife Agencies), that was reviewing and making recommendations on a bill that eventually became the Migratory Bird Conservation Act of 1929. On the committee of five were John Burnham, President of the American Game Protective Association, and T. Gilbert Pearson, President of the National Association of Audubon Societies. Both (as noted earlier) were Boone and Crockett Club members. The idea was to direct an existing 10-

percent federal excise tax on sporting arms and ammunition to finance wetland acquisition.

A bill to that effect was put before the U.S. House of Representatives' Ways and Means Committee and rejected. In fact, the tax was repealed soon thereafter. In 1929, it was reinstated by President Hoover to help recovery from the era's economic depression. In 1937, the excise-tax-for-wildlife idea was revived. The necessary legislation called for an excise tax on sporting rifles, shotguns, and ammunition to be collected by the U.S. Treasury and then credited to the U.S. Bureau of Biological Survey. The receipts would then be allocated to state agencies, on the basis of the size of each state and its number of licensed hunters. The states would contribute $1 for each $3 received from the federal funds, with the state's matching dollars coming from hunting license sales. The total funds produced would be earmarked for wildlife conservation.

The Federal Aid in Wildlife Restoration Act (better known as "Pittman-Robertson" or just "P-R") was signed into law by President Roosevelt in September 1937. The law was amended later to safeguard state hunting license receipts against diversion from the program's matching funds: the states must invest all hunting license monies in the program, or lose eligibility for any of the federally collected and administered excise tax receipts. Later, federal excise tax receipts on handguns and archery equipment were added to the program account.

The P-R Act has come to be widely regarded as the nation's "premier conservation effort." The roughly $2 billion (including state contributions) that the law has generated for wildlife management programs since its enactment represents the mortar for the building blocks of conservation that the Boone and Crockett Club and others had assembled prior to the Act. Club members laid the conceptual groundwork for the law, provided the legislative channel, and helped generate broad public and political support.

Tribulations and Trophies: The Postwar Period

World War II put wildlife conservation in the United States on a back burner, as the nation's resources, manpower, and attention were diverted to foreign battlefields. Except for reduced hunting pressure on many species recovering from the drought years, gains for wildlife during that time were few. The losses also were few, since counter-conservation activities also were redirected or idled by the war effort.

The triumph of the war for the U.S. and its allies was both costly and sobering. The jubilation that greeted the returning troops was as much a manifestation of relief as it was a celebration of victory. After five long years, Americans could get back to the business of building better lives and a more prosperous country.

The Boone and Crockett Club was much changed when the war ended. Though its numbers remained essentially the same and its purpose was unchanged, the Club had new faces and new priorities. Gone were the founders; gone or inactive were leaders of the Club's tumultuous early years; gone were the men who had been the front line of conservation from the time that the word had meaning. In their stead was a new cadre of sportsmen equally dedicated to the honorable sport of hunting and to the pre-emptory course of conservation. But rather than being alone in the quest for more wildlands and wildlife, and for reasonable treatment of both, Club members found themselves in company with many

A NATIONAL REFUGE HAS SAVED THE KEY DEER

THE LAST OF THE "TOY" DEER OF THE FLORIDA KEYS

IN MIDWINTER OF 1934 the above cartoon was hastily drawn by "Ding" to call attention to the unsportsmanlike hunting methods which were decimating the remaining Florida Key Deer. After the war, the regional office of the U. S. Fish and Wildlife Service in Atlanta reported with increased alarm that an estimated 26 Key Deer remained. In June 1952 the Boone and Crockett Club of New York hired a full-time warden to protect the remaining Key Deer. The National Wildlife Federation contributed towards continued warden service and in 1957 Congress authorized the establishment of the NATIONAL KEY DEER REFUGE. Since 1958 the North American Wildlife Foundation spearheaded a drive for funds to acquire the necessary lands for the establishment of this inviolate refuge. The Boone and Crockett Club, the Wilderness Club of Philadelphia, and public spirited individuals have pledged additional sums which will make possible the preservation of the smallest species of North American Deer. Present estimated Key Deer population—over 200. Thanks for your help.

Mission Accomplished
Ding Darling

J. N. "Ding" Darling's cartoon of the plight of the tiny Key deer summarized the situation and helped bring public pressure to bear so that a federal refuge could be created to protect the deer and their habitat. Notice the hand-signed note: "Mission Accomplished Ding Darling"

other individuals and organizations awakened to the cause of wise use of natural resources.

Paradoxically, many of the organizations that moved to the forefront of the national conservation movement owed their beginning directly or indirectly to Boone and Crockett Club initiatives. In many cases, if not most, the heads of those organizations were Club members.

Though in the limelight even less so than before, the postwar Boone and Crockett Club continued its important work, true always to its founding constitution. Under the presidency of Archibald B. Roosevelt, son of Theodore Roosevelt, the Club re-energized itself in the aftermath of the great war.

Key Deer and Key People

In 1934, while touring prospective sites for possible waterfowl refuges, Boone and Crockett Club member and Chief of the Bureau of Biological Survey Ding Darling cruised in a commercial launch through the Florida Keys. There he observed an uninhabited islet smoldering from fires set by Cuban fishermen to drive deer into the water. The fishermen clubbed or shot the swimming deer for food. It was a common practice, the astonished Darling learned. It was highly destructive, both of the deer and the Keys' mangrove vegetation.

Then and there, Darling penned a caricature of the lawlessness. The cartoon, "The Last of the 'Toy Deer' of the Florida Keys," featured gunners and their dogs annihilating the Keys' diminutive whitetails that had been chased to open water. It was widely published, and it was the first salvo in a long struggle to save the Key deer and its habitat.

Ding Darling's dramatic artwork helped to bring about legal protection for the deer, but Key residents simply ignored the regulations. By 1950, the Key deer population probably was much less than 100 and its survival was much in doubt.

In 1951, the Florida Wildlife Federation, National Wildlife Federation, National Audubon Society, and Wildlife Management Institute pressed for a bill in Congress to create a federal Key deer refuge. At odds were Florida land developers. When the bill was put to question, it failed to pass by a single vote.

With the deer still in jeopardy, the conservationists regrouped to prepare new legislation for the next legislative session. It was clear, however, that until such time that the Keys could be safeguarded by state or federal authorities, some stopgap security was needed. National Wildlife Federation Executive Director Richard Borden, also Chairman of the Boone and Crockett Club's Conservation Committee, approached Pink Gutermuth with a proposal to establish a fund to protect the victimized Key deer. Gutermuth, Vice-President of the Wildlife Management Institute, Secretary of the North American Wildlife Foundation, and a Boone and Crockett Club member, readily agreed to put up $5,000 from the Institute for that purpose. Noting the urgency of the matter, given the precarious status of the "toy" deer population, the Boone and Crockett Club authorized a sum of up to $5,000 to hire and equip a warden.

Jack C. Watson, a biologist, was hired by the Boone and Crockett Club to investigate the Key deer and its habitat and to patrol the proposed refuge area to prevent poaching. Watson threw himself into the multiple tasks and, with support of state and federal wildlife

agencies, was able to report within a year that the deer were increasing.

Although real estate developers were able to block the passage of another Key deer refuge bill in 1952, the Boone and Crockett Club continued to provide protection in lieu of a permanent refuge. At Richard Borden's urging, the National Wildlife Federation assumed the cost of the project for a year until the federal government authorized the leasing of lands in 1954 for a refuge.

Even though the Key deer were recovering under the Boone and Crockett Club's watchful eye, Pink Gutermuth knew that nothing less than a permanent refuge would solve their problems. He encouraged the North American Wildlife Foundation to help finance initial portions of a Key deer refuge. Gutermuth traveled to Big Pine Key to choose a refuge headquarters site, which would be the opening wedge in the fight to create an even larger refuge. Through his contacts with Radford R. Crane of the Raymond E. and Elben F. Crane Foundation, an initial tract of nearly 20 acres on Big Pine Key was deeded to the North American Wildlife Foundation in 1955, for transfer to the U.S. Fish and Wildlife Service for the proposed refuge headquarters.

The acquisition, though not nearly what was needed to protect Key deer, served notice to Congress that the refuge idea was more than the whim of local do-gooders looking to dip into the national treasury. It showed that the idea of a Key deer refuge was the serious and determined intent of national conservation groups.

A bill authorizing establishment of the National Key Deer Refuge and acquisition of an additional 1,000 acres of land for the refuge was signed into law by President Dwight D. Eisenhower in August 1957. However, no funds were appropriated for purchasing the extra acreage needed. Again, Pink Gutermuth turned to the Crane Foundation. He also obtained $10,000 commitments from both The Wilderness Club of Philadelphia and the Boone and Crockett Club. Lands were purchased in the name of the North American Wildlife Foundation and transferred to the U.S. Fish and Wildlife Service.

In this manner, another refuge was added to the system of federal wildlife preserves dotting the U.S. landscape at strategic locations. The National Key Deer Refuge was unique in that its establishment was brought about almost exclusively by private interests, and it not only saved a wildlife population but an entire subspecies. At every turn in the complicated process of creating the refuge was the Boone and Crockett Club, either directly or, in usual fashion, indirectly by the good work of its members.

Measuring Up

In the mid-1930's, when Ding Darling was focusing attention on the Key deer of Florida, the Boone and Crockett Club became involved in keeping records of North America's native big game. By the time the Key deer refuge had become a heated issue (after World War II), so too was the Club's trophy records keeping.

For hundreds if not thousands of years, hunters have kept, preserved, and displayed in one form or another a part of their big game quarry. Often the horns or antlers are saved, or the hide, teeth, hooves, or claws. Before the widespread availability of paintings and other wall decorations, mounted animal heads, horns, or antlers were quite fashionable, as were hides "in the hair" for rugs and furniture coverings. But even then, the saving and

collecting of animal parts had more than a pure utilitarian origin.

Most, but not all, hunters retain a part of their successfully taken quarry for reasons that can only be understood by other hunters. It is, in part, a means of preserving the spirit and vitality of the animal. It is, in part, a symbol of the grand contest between man and the environment as represented by the animal. It is at least a tribute to the hunter's skill, to luck, to the experience of the chase, and to the animal.

In a sense, every game animal hunted and killed under legal rules and the ethical code of Fair Chase is a trophy, regardless of its age, sex, or size. However, trophy also may refer to the tangible evidence of a hunter's capability. It is not unusual for people to assess the relative size of such evidence, not only as indicative of the animal's fitness and unique-ness, but also as testimony to the hunting skills and selectivity of the hunter. Trophy antlers and horns are as much a measure of the challenge of the hunt as they are a measure of the quarry.

Not until the late 1800's were North American big game trophies systematically collected and displayed. In fact, one of the first attempts anywhere in the world to record big game trophies was by Rowland Ward, Ltd., of London, England, in 1892. Compared with the more systematic measuring and listing of later years, Ward's catalog was a somewhat hap-hazard attempt. Three years later, at the First Annual Sportsmen's Exposition in New York City, Boone and Crockett Club members Roosevelt, Grinnell, and Archibald Rogers judged displays of big game that included many heads taken by Roosevelt and his fellow Club members. In the first decade of the new century, the Club furthered its interest in heads and horns with the development of the National Collection of Heads and Horns (NCHH), under the curatorship of William Hornaday.

In 1929, seven years after the construction of the NCHH building at the New York Zoological Park, Boone and Crockett Club member Prentiss N. Gray determined that the Club should examine and catalog the best available trophies of North American big game. As the Chairman of a Club committee appointed to carry out this task, Gray began the cataloging with the National Collection of Heads and Horns. He also took in all trophies that could be located in public and private collections. Using a simple scale evaluation, Gray's committee began its enormous chore.

Any system of ranking trophies is potentially controversial. Gray was well-aware that no one dimension of an antler, horn, or skull could determine the best physical specimen. A system had to be devised that would coordinate a number of different measurements in a manner that would eventually be acceptable to all knowledgeable sportsmen.

In 1932, after three years of measuring, the Boone and Crockett Club published 500 copies of *Records of North American Big Game*. This volume included the accumulated record measurements and was illustrated by Club member and renowned wildlife painter Carl Rungius. It quickly sold out. Within two years, the Remington Arms Company re-printed the records with the measurement forms used so that readers could see how trophies were compared. The public response was excellent.

With new trophies being measured continually, the Boone and Crockett Club decided to issue a sequel to the 1932 volume. An expanded edition, *North American Big Game*, appeared in 1939. It included comprehensive lists of North America's big game trophies

B&C Photograph by Wm. H. Nesbitt

The Boone and Crockett Club's first big-game records book for native big game. It was published in 1932 by Derrydale Press. With only 500 copies printed, and featuring top-quality paper and materials, it is eagerly sought by collectors today and a fine copy commands a price several hundred times its original price of $10.

and worthwhile articles on conservation subjects. A major article emphasized that the trophy hunter is motivated by the challenge of pursuing an animal of superior quality, and that to take such an animal requires the hunter to be intimately familiar with the animal's physiology, behavior, and habitat. The article stressed that the trophy hunter is a strong advocate of conservation, and that, in modern times, trophy animals are produced only under circumstances of careful management. The article pointed out that detailed records of trophies are of interest to scientists who can use the data to identify trends in big game populations. The size of big game trophies (skulls, horns, and antlers) being the result of a complex set of physiological and environmental variables (genetics, nutrition, age, habitat, etc.) trophy production is an indicator of habitat quality and animal population size and well-being.

Controversy was another by-product of the Boone and Crockett Club's popular records keeping activity. Inevitably, some people disagreed with the measuring standards and felt that certain World's Record trophies were not deserving of that status. The appearance of the Club's 1932 record book stirred up the controversy. So, Prentiss Gray attempted to clear the air by requesting James L. Clark, a professional taxidermist who did work for the American Museum of Natural History, to come up with an improved and equitable system of measurement.

In 1935, Clark's new system was copyrighted and Clark began an annual North American big game trophy competition at his taxidermy studio. When the Boone and Crockett Club undertook preparation of its 1939 record book, the editorial committee asked M. Grancel Fitz to write a chapter on trophy-rating systems. Fitz commented favorably on Clark's composite scoring system, but noted certain problems and suggested potential alterations. Clark was disturbed by the challenge to his system. He was further piqued that the refined method Fitz advocated was well-received among sportsmen, including the Boone and Crockett Club, which adopted it unofficially. Clark's system naturally had its proponents also; the result was a serious conflict.

Samuel B. Webb, a noted big game hunter and later a Club member, had long held an interest in the comparison of trophies. It was his hope to bring about a compromise among then current points of view that would result in a scoring system acceptable to all sportsmen and scientists. After World War II, he approached the Club about putting together a universal system of measurement for each native big game species. He was spurred on in this area by the success of the Club's "competitions" for big game, held yearly beginning with 1947. In these competitions, a Judges Panel decided the top trophies. Obviously, an acceptable scoring system was needed to produce uniform results. Webb had discussed the issue with Clark and Fitz, as well as Harold E. Anthony, a director of the American Museum of Natural History and Chairman of the Club's Records Committee. In 1949, Boone and Crockett Club President Archibald Roosevelt asked Webb to form a committee to address the complicated problem and increasingly sensitive conflict. The Club also agreed that, when and if Webb's committee devised a universal system, the Club would adopt it to score all available trophies and publish a new records book with the results. Webb's committee consisted of Clark, Fitz, Anthony, Milford Baker, and Fredrick K. Barbour. All were Club members except Webb and Fitz.

The committee spent two years developing a scoring system that included elements of both the Clark and Fitz methods. When the charts explaining and illustrating the system were completed, they were sent for review to hundreds of knowledgeable individuals, including hunters, zoologists, state conservation officials, and hunting guides. The comments and suggestions of the respondents were considered and, in some cases, incorporated into the final system. Webb and Fitz then tested the new system by measuring hundreds of trophies to see how well it determined and differentiated overall trophy characteristics and quality. Its work completed, the committee turned the system's charts over to the Club, which officially adopted the new system at the 1950 annual meeting. The Club then began to remeasure all known trophies. Webb and Fitz personally applied the new system to several important collections, including the National Collection of Heads and Horns and the Smithsonian Institution collection.

The new official scoring system had a significant impact on the listing of World's Record trophies. Besides expanding and refining the measurement criteria, the new system, for the first time, divided some trophy categories, such as whitetail deer, into typical and non-typical classes. It also went beyond a single measurement, such as the length of the longer antler, to a comprehensive assessment and a final score for ranking within category that was based on length, spread, circumferences, symmetry, and other factors. The Club's widespread remeasuring of trophy collections, and the application of the official system to candidate trophies, created a new set of records that was published in the Club's third records book, released in 1952. Included were ranked lists of trophies with selected measurements, reproductions of the score charts, and photographs of the World's Record trophies. The new system was received with acclaim. It quickly became the accepted standard of measurement for native North American big game. The system has been fine-tuned over the years, but it remains essentially intact today.

As previously mentioned, the Club began a series of big game competitions in 1947. They were initiated to encourage hunters to submit their trophies for measurement, to ensure that the Club's records books are as accurate and up-to-date as possible. The competitions also were intended as a means of urging participants to be more selective in their hunting. It was required that records book trophies be hunted under scrupulous conditions of "Fair Chase," as defined by the Club. The "competitions" begun in 1947 were conducted annually from 1947–1951. The next seven were conducted at two-year intervals, and since 1970 they have been on a three-year basis. Since 1973 they have been called "Awards" programs rather than "Competitions."

From the Club's inception, the concept of "Fair Chase" was of paramount importance to the Club. An article of the Club's Bylaws noted: "The term 'fair chase' shall not be held to include killing bear, wolf or cougar in traps, nor 'fire-hunting' nor 'crusting' moose, elk or deer in deep snow, nor killing game from a boat, while it is swimming in the water." The particular significance of the Club's position was that at the time (1888), the practices it condemned were not only legal in most areas, but popular and widespread. The Boone and Crockett Club's members espoused and practiced restraint was an ethical example that other sportsmen would embrace as an essential condition of modern hunting.

In more recent years, as airplanes, radios, motorized vehicles, and escape-proof fencing

came into usage in ways that encouraged hunters to disadvantage the quarry's escape mechanisms, the Club formalized these into the current Fair Chase Statement required of all hunters entering trophies into the records keeping. A good example is the tenet dealing with air spotting of game, followed by landing in its vicinity to shoot it. The Club made this practice "Unfair Chase" in 1963 (therefore automatically rejecting any trophies so taken from entry into the records keeping) *prior* to actions by Alaska, Canada, and other states and provinces. Today, air spotting on the same day as a kill is universally banned, a tribute to the Club's leadership in hunting ethics.

Medals and certificates were awarded to the highest-scoring trophies entered in each Awards period (formerly "competitions"). The Sagamore Hill Medal, established by the Roosevelt family in honor and memory of Boone and Crockett Club notables Theodore Roosevelt, Theodore Roosevelt, Jr., and Kermit Roosevelt, has been (and may be) awarded by the Judges Panel for special recognition of a truly superior entry taken under notable Fair Chase conditions.

For the trophy recognition program of 1973 (and later), the "competition" was renamed "Awards program," to emphasize trophy excellence rather than competition among hunters taking the trophies. The year 1973 was an especially memorable one for the Club, for it was the start of nearly a decade of cooperative big-game records keeping with the National Rifle Association of America. The jointly sponsored program was known as "The North American Big Game Awards Program" (NABGAP), and it became a unique side bar to the Boone and Crockett Club's history.

The "Nabgap" Years

High Expectations and Soul Searching

The records keeping for trophy big game became a project jointly sponsored and administered by the Boone and Crockett Club and the National Rifle Association on June 30, 1973. It is fair to say that the union would not have been made except for the unusual circumstance of the NRA's hierarchy at the time. Both Maxwell E. Rich, NRA's Executive Vice President, and John E. Rhea, its President, were Boone and Crockett Club members. At that same time, a number of Club members felt that big game records keeping was contrary to the best interests of wildlife, conservation, and the Club itself. W. Douglas Burden, an avid environmentalist, big game hunter, and member of the Club since 1920, suggested in 1974 that the Club should divorce itself from trophy big game records keeping and the awards program. He felt that the Boone and Crockett Club could be true to its heritage only if it would disown trophy "competitions." Burden also contended that the emphasis on trophies was causing hunters to seek out the finest male specimens of big game, thereby removing those prime animals from their populations' breeding stock and, in essence, diluting the species' gene pool. He also expressed the opinion that some gunners and guides, anxious to be listed in the prestigious records books, were lying, abandoning Fair Chase principles and cheating in other ways in attempts to take records book trophies. Conservation, Burden felt, was being compromised by competition and commercialism, all unwittingly endorsed by the Club's sponsorship and promotion of its programs.

The

National Rifle Association of America

and The

Boone and Crockett Club

In consideration of common goals

To conserve North American wildlife resources;

To establish high ethical standards for all participants in the sport of hunting;

To foster the rules and principles of fair chase;

To recognize outstanding achievements by sportsmen in taking select trophy game animals; and

To promote public understanding and appreciation of the ancient and noble sport of hunting in relation to the wise use of our natural resources, the

National Rifle Association of America and the Boone and Crockett Club agree to join together in support and sponsorship of

North American Big Game Trophy Programs

For the Boone and Crockett Club

For the National Rifle Association

June 30, 1973

The "North American Big Game Awards Program" (NABGAP) was created with the signing of this agreement between the Boone and Crockett Club and the National Rifle Association of America in June of 1973. The co-sponsored program lasted through the end of 1980, when the Club then assumed full responsibility for all phases of the records keeping.

He and some other Club members opined that recording trophies served no useful scientific purpose other than to illustrate the range of antlers or horns an animal can develop. Furthermore, in a letter to Frederick Pullman (Chairman of the Club's Conservation Committee) Burden expressed his sentiment that the Club should divorce itself completely from the National Rifle Association. Other members agreed, asserting that the affiliation with the hard-right, pro-gun NRA disenfranchised the Club with non-hunting conservationists who otherwise supported the Club's total program.

The records keeping rift within the Boone and Crockett Club was crystallized by agitation from external sources. In October 1974, *Defenders of Wildlife* magazine ran a feature article entitled "The Bigger the Horns the Higher the Price." It took the Boone and Crockett Club to task for lending credibility to trophy competition which, the author felt, led to harmful and destructive hunting practices. Of even more import (due to the credibility of both magazine and author) James K. Morgan's article in *Audubon Magazine*, "Slamming the Ram into Oblivion," took trophy hunting to task for a supposed degradation of gene pool values and disruption of the social hierarchy of sheep by removing the largest ram as a "trophy." The article's title alluded to a common hunting term, "Grand Slam," accorded to the feat of taking by sport hunting all four of the native sheep (bighorn, desert, Stone's, and Dall's) of North America. Interestingly, the Boone and Crockett Club's records keeping has *no* such distinction or category, and the term is not used in the Club's records book(s) depiction of trophies.

Even though the Boone and Crockett Club had always incorporated and actively stressed the concept and principles of Fair Chase in all of its programs, and attempted at every opportunity to assure compliance with its lofty ethical standards, there was no escaping the fact that there were gunners who pursued trophy animals at any cost merely for personal fame and gain. Nor, as the records' sanctioning body, was the Boone and Crockett Club immune to criticism, however partial and uninformed, for the illegal and unethical actions of a very few notorious trophy seekers.

The matter was a bitter pill for members of the Club. It was a sad, fretful, and unfortunate irony that their organization, founded as a fellowship of hunters dedicated to Fair Chase and perhaps the most influential advocacy sportsmen's group ever for the conservation and wise use of big game, found itself in defense of programs undertaken to enrich the traditions, values, and opportunities of hunting. The matter also was quite divisive.

Actually, concern within the Club over its trophy hunting/records keeping role had existed long before member Burden pointedly registered his objections. The embers of discontent were fanned to flame by the agreement with the National Rifle Association in 1973.

The Boone and Crockett Club signed the cosponsorship agreement with NRA in a concerted attempt to reach more hunters about the Club's records and Awards program. NRA's membership base of a million members (and increasing steadily at the time), plus its media outreach to the public, offered great promise for the Club's conservation forum. NRA could easily underwrite the costly administrative expenses associated with maintaining the records in proper fashion. At the same time, involvement with NRA might, in the words of Club Records Committee Chairman (and life-member of the NRA) Jack S. Parker, ". . . help off-set some of the unfavorable press received [by the NRA] on the anti-gun front—

indicating an organization with broader sportsman's interests."

Some members of the Boone and Crockett Club vigorously opposed the joint effort with the NRA, and several Club members resigned when the Club went forward with the arrangement. These members felt that NRA's preoccupation with gun legislation had narrowed its concerns to the point that it had little interest in or concern for conservation and the issues of ethical hunting. They feared that the highly controversial NRA would tarnish the Club's image and draw attention away from the Club's conservation record.

The resignation of some Club members over the joint effort with NRA, and the feeling of other members that emphasis on trophy records keeping was detrimental to the Boone and Crockett Club's conservation efforts, compounded the factionalism within the Club. To air and settle these differences, the Club in 1974 formed an *ad hoc* committee on future direction, with Frederick Pullman as Chairman. W. Douglas Burden's communications regarding the Club's direction and programs provided a focus for opinion and debate. His desire to end the Club's participation in records keeping was strongly supported by some and denounced with equal ardor by others. Many meetings and discussions were held, and numerous letters were circulated among Club members.

Pullman's *ad hoc* committee met formally on November 25 and December 3 of 1974, to hear extended argument from opposing sides of the issues. Out of the meetings came a new statement of purpose for the Boone and Crockett Club. At the end of the December 3 meeting, Club President John Rhea asked each committee member if he could accept the draft statement as a reasonable expression of the Boone and Crockett Club's current purposes and functions. Each committee member agreed to the essence of the statement, although there were minor disagreements about wording. The committee unanimously passed the statement of purpose and an addendum concerning the implementation of the statement. These documents were presented to the Executive Committee on December 4, 1974. The statement of purpose read: "It is the policy of the Boone and Crockett Club to promote the guardianship and provident management of big game and associated wildlife in North America and to maintain the highest standards of fair chase and sportsmanship in all aspects of big game hunting, in order that this resource of all the people may survive and prosper in its natural habitats. Consistent with this objective, the Club supports the use and enjoyment of our wildlife heritage to the fullest extent by this and future generations of mankind."

Besides the Pullman committee documents, an accompanying report was presented to the Executive Committee. The latter emphasized that, out of all the debate and discussion, one opinion was clear: the Boone and Crockett Club was unequivocally an association of big game hunters and that it placed itself in the role of representing big game hunters of North America. The report further noted that, since its inception, the Club had attempted to make clear that North American big game animals were not an inexhaustible food resource. They were "animals which should be treated with respect for their value for sport and recreation." Implicit was the reasoning that, because of the value placed on game animals, it was only natural that the Club had long been interested in the comparative quality of trophies. And such interest naturally led to keeping records and ultimately to publishing records books and conducting awards ceremonies. "Accordingly, this is what

we are known for," the report continued. "It is unfortunate and essentially our own fault, that we are not known for our extensive conservation activities, even within our own membership."

This remarkable admission was the result of considerable soul-searching on the part of many Club members, who reached the conclusion that preoccupation with trophy records keeping had been a factor in some Club members' lack of knowledge or interest in the critical conservation issues of the day. The new statement of purpose was an attempt to bring the Club's conservation work back to a central position with the entire membership, not just a dedicated few.

Rededication to Principles

The *ad hoc* committee's report was not remiss, however, in emphasizing that, for the previous 12 years, the Club had been supporting numerous wildlife studies in its continued effort to contribute to conservation. Research projects funded wholly or in part by the Club included Adolph Murie's study of wolf predation on Dall's sheep in Alaska; long-term studies of wolf/moose relationships on Isle Royale (Michigan), directed by Durward L. Allen; Lyle Sowls' studies of desert bighorn sheep and wild burros; a study of the significant economic and ecological impacts of the proposed (and subsequently defeated) Ramparts Dam in Alaska; and Maurice Hornocker's studies of the mountain lion. The report brought these studies and others to the Executive Committee's attention to emphasize that, indeed, the Club continued to move on many conservation fronts.

The report to the Executive Committee also specifically addressed the controversial points raised by Burden and others, including the suggestion that the Club should discontinue its records keeping and awards program. The majority opinion of the *ad hoc* committee was that the records provided the Club "with the strongest means of communicating with American hunters." Hunters who otherwise might hear little or nothing about "Fair Chase," or the ethics of sportsmanship and conservation, were reached by the Boone and Crockett Club through the popular records books and Awards programs. The report noted that when the Club made a public statement that it would no longer accept for the Awards programs records of mountain lions taken from states where they were bountied, the action strongly influenced legislation that provided game status protection for cougars. Also, by excluding polar bears from the Awards programs, the Club had influenced protective regulations for polar bears in Alaska and Canada. And in a meeting on the morning the Executive Committee received the *ad hoc* committee's report, the Club had agreed that the threatened grizzlies of the lower 48 states would not be accepted for Awards. The Club's position on such matters would be widely circulated, and it would serve as notice of wildlife conservation priority to many of the nation's sportsmen and others.

The Club members realized, of course, that if its records keeping program was discontinued, such an action would not dissuade hunters from seeking trophy animals. They realized, too, the strong likelihood that another organization or faction would quickly assume administration of the records keeping if the Boone and Crockett Club defaulted. And there could be no assurance that such a group would emphasize Fair Chase hunting. The membership, fully cognizant of the pitfalls and vulnerability to criticism that the records

program exposed the Club, was equally aware that abandoning the program meant the loss of a significant and successful conservation forum.

Throughout its existence, the Boone and Crockett Club had never skirted thorny issues, and the internal matter of whether or not to continue the records and Awards program was just such a situation. Pullman's *ad hoc* committee duly recommended that the Club continue its stewardship of North American big game records, but that measures be taken to strengthen assurance that trophy animals were hunted legally, ethically, and with all possible sportsmanship--in sum, by Fair Chase.

The Club's Executive Committee accepted this recommendation and thereupon made changes in the trophy acceptance procedures. So there would be no misunderstanding of the conditions of the hunt, participating hunters would henceforth be required to have their signature of the Fair Chase Statement (on the back of each score chart) notarized by a Notary Public.

By itself, the requirement of a certified and notarized Fair Chase hunting statement is not fail-safe insurance against violation. However, in tacit combination with the Boone and Crockett Club's reputation and traditions, and with its judicious, unbiased, and professional handling of the records and Awards programs, the statement has come to mean more than a mere statement of not having hunted unethically or illegally; it is a pledge of honor. And honor among hunters of Fair Chase is sacrosanct.

And Some New Directions

At the same time that the Executive Committee was reviewing the troubled status of the records and Awards programs, the Club committed itself to doing more for big game management than simply funding research. It decided to initiate projects of its own, and the first was a workshop, cosponsored with the Wildlife Management Institute and the National Audubon Society, on the management biology of North American wild sheep. This workshop was a direct response to the inflammatory charges of the *Audubon Magazine* article, "Slamming the Ram Into Oblivion." In fact, although a great many studies had been carried out on sheep, there was no central source of information either to support or to refute many of Morgan's allegations in the article. James K. Morgan was a qualified biologist working for the BLM on wild sheep. *Audubon Magazine* had always been a most respected publication, stretching all the way back to the days of its first editor, George Bird Grinnell. The issues raised could not be ignored. The workshop might or might not answer all of them, but it would surely sum the available knowledge so that either current management programs would be vindicated or suggestions for needed change would be promulgated. The final result of the three-day meeting in 1974 of the continent's leading wild sheep biologists was the book, *The Wild Sheep in Modern North America*, that pulled together and synthesized the known accumulation of information available for current and improved management of the wild sheep of the continent. While not totally satisfying critics of sheep hunting, it laid to rest the wild suppositions of dire threat to the stability of sheep populations posed by modern sport hunting. It also suggested important new topics for needed sheep research.

In 1977, in conjunction with the Campfire Club of America, the Boone and Crockett

Club sponsored another workshop, much like the wild sheep workshop of 1974. This time the subject was the North American black bear. As had been the case with the sheep workshop, there was a good deal of data and research on black bears, but no core reference to answer troubling questions regarding state or local populations of black bears and their long-term management needs. In some states with black bears, they were not classified as game animals and little was known about them. The workshop would, at the least, draw all such current knowledge together so that it could be used by all those needing such reference. The published results of that meeting, *The Black Bear in Modern North America*, is an authoritative reference on black bear ecology and management for the continent. The Club considered other topics for possible future workshops, but decided not to stage such unless (as in the case of the two workshops held) there was a compelling need.

A Marriage Grown Cold

The Boone and Crockett Club's commitment to an expanded conservation program, and its dedication to maintaining, upgrading, and safeguarding its big game records keeping and Awards programs, still left unresolved the matter of its affiliation with the National Rifle Association. The intended symbiosis of the two organizations' alliance on the records and Awards programs did not materialize. For the most part, this was due to the intense political struggles within NRA during the mid- and late 1970's, struggles that led to a change of command. The relationship between the Club and NRA had been arranged in the first place by Club members Parker, Rhea, Robert Ferguson, Pink Gutermuth (then NRA President-elect), and General Maxwell E. Rich, NRA's Executive Vice-President. The change of command was both bloody and distinct.

At the NRA Annual Members Meeting at Cincinnati, Ohio in 1977, a carefully orchestrated overthrow of the Executive Vice-President and his control was carried out by a group of NRA members convinced that Rich's strong push of NRA into a broader stance (proposed move of the NRA headquarters to Colorado Springs for alliance with the Olympic Training Center there and other organizations; the "outreach" encouraged to conservation issues and groups; and even the records keeping with the Club) put in jeopardy NRA's long-time work on gun issues as *the* central focus of NRA energy. Whether the successful overthrow of Rich and his administration was really what rank-and-file NRA members wanted is still debated. But, no one debated the position of Harlon B. Carter, who was put into office as Executive Vice-President of NRA by the revolt. Carter quickly squashed the move west and firmly re-established NRA's only mission as gun rights, both in the use and also the freedom to possess and use, as guaranteed by the Second Amendment of the Constitution.

Carter made his stand on conservation issues quickly known to NRA staff dealing with hunting, conservation, and the relationship with the Club. "There are at least 35 organizations dealing with conservation issues; there is only one that is protecting your gun rights— that's the NRA." Under this dramatic reversal of climate, not surprisingly, support for the records keeping withered within the NRA. Gutermuth was held in disfavor, and Max Rich was gone from the scene. The new NRA hierarchy offered only minimal staff support for administering the complex big game records keeping and Awards programs. As a result,

cooperation between the Club and NRA was often strained and progressed to a breaking point. In 1980, Club President Parker oversaw an agreement to dissolve the relationship. That accomplished, the Club relocated and regeared itself again to sole administration of the big game records and Awards programs. Friction within the Club over the relationship began to dissolve immediately, as the Club again was able to chart its own course.

The "North American Big Game Awards Program" (as the cooperative program between the Club and NRA was called) thus lasted less than a decade. That it continued as long as it did was largely due to the efforts of Wm. Harold Nesbitt.

Nesbitt was hired in September, 1973 by the NRA as Assistant Manager of the Hunting and Conservation Department. Making the cooperative big game records keeping success-ful was his priority assignment. The program and NRA/Club relationship prospered under his influence. Under the Club's tenure, Official Measurers were appointed by recommen-dation of currently appointed measurers, a system open to problems of misinformation being taught and further garbled. Also, the likelihood was remote that measurers would have the time and trophies to train new measurers to score all possible categories. Nesbitt, therefore, soon devised a workshop approach to measurer training. The results were ob-vious and significant in reducing visible errors on completed score charts and at the Awards Final Judging, held after each three-year period of trophy entry.

Nesbitt also strengthened other aspects of trophy entry requirements. Clear photos of the trophy became a requirement, so that he and his staff could review the measurements of the score chart against the photos, identifying errors and improper application of the scor-ing system. He also wrote a manual for training Official Measurers that was later expanded into the book, *Measuring and Scoring North American Big Game Trophies*.

As an NRA employee, Nesbitt was an outspoken and effective voice for the positive effects of selective trophy hunting and the values of the records keeping in broadening NRA's appeal to hunters in general. But the partnership was a two-way commitment that NRA found to be very different from its straight-line command chain, top to bottom. Making NRA live up to its commitment, in terms of staff support and financing, became increasingly difficult. The "end" was reached at the NRA Annual Meetings of 1980 (held at Kansas City, Missouri).

At the NRA's Annual Meetings, the 17th North American Big Game Awards program was also held. The Boone and Crockett Club scheduled an Executive Committee meeting, as they always did at the Awards program. They requested Harlon B. Carter, Executive Vice-President of NRA, to address the Club's concerns, specifically Carter's refusal to allow William J. "Jack" Reneau (a former NRA staff member working directly with the records keeping who had left NRA for the U.S. Forest Service) to be replaced to get staff support up to proper level. Carter's response was belligerent. He reminded the Club mem-bers present that he was charged with running the entire NRA and he could not be "pushed" into hiring folks. The encounter left Club members present with a disturbing feeling of low NRA priority for the program. Interestingly, Carter was himself a Club member, having joined in 1978, and was well aware of the concerns on both sides of the agreement and its fulfillment.

The Club met privately and formulated an ultimatum letter to Carter. Either the NRA

would honor the agreement in all aspects, including proper staff support, or the Club would ask for dissolution of the agreement. Carter responded that terminating the relationship seemed in the best interests of all. Consequently, by official agreement and simply as a matter of business, on January 1, 1981 the Boone and Crockett Club again assumed full responsibility for and control of the records keeping program. For both parties, the severance came with relief and little, if any, ill-feeling.

Harold Nesbitt agreed to leave NRA and become Administrative Director (later Executive Director) of the Club. The Club office was set up in nearby Alexandria, Virginia, and the transfer of files and materials was accomplished by the deadline of January 1, 1981. (The office was moved to Dumfries, Virginia in 1986.)

Interestingly, Jack Reneau, whose departure from NRA staff was the catalyst for the eventual dissolution of the co-sponsorship agreement, today works for the Club as Director of Big Game Records.

With the establishment of a professionally-staffed Club office, the Club also became more aggressive in merchandising and promoting its messages, books, and other services. With Nesbitt steering the course, the Club has become its own publisher, greatly increasing net income to be used for conservation and funding the big game records keeping. No longer would the Club feel the need for a cooperative partner to assure continuation of the big game records keeping at a proper professional level.

CENTURY MARKS

The Boone and Crockett Club's involvement in national conservation affairs did not end, by any means, with its efforts toward passage of the all-important Federal Aid in Wildlife Restoration (Pittman-Robertson) Act in 1937, coincident with the 50-year "golden" anniversary of the Club. In fact, during the Club's second half-century, its members were at least doubly active in the formulation, enactment, and implementation of natural resource legislation.

From 1887 to 1937, conservation had grown from less than zero, inasmuch as notions of resource limitations and restraints were not merely unregarded or disregarded, they were popularly dismissed as heretical twaddle. During that time, to bring about any form of conservation, its few proponents had to overcome the momentum of exploitation as well as ignorance in government, industry, agriculture, and the general public. Consequently, each legislative gain for conservation, however small, narrow or short-lived, was a remarkable victory. And for most of that time span, conservation was the business of providing protection and refuges for wildlife, particularly game species.

From 1937 to 1987, conservation evolved not only as a science, but as a national imperative. And it expanded, inevitably and necessarily, to include the natural resources stressed by human population growth and expansion. These were all natural resources, including air, water, soil, minerals, flora, and, of course, wildlife, both game and non-game.

This transition was as equally belabored as during the first 50 years, for reasons of complexity of resource issues and their reciprocal relationships, and also the sheer "workload" to bring resource utilization and demand in balance with supply. Conservation further matured from a concept of moderation to one of sacrifice. This was no less stressfully

Several Boone and Crockett Club members are shown here at a meeting with U.S. President John F. Kennedy in May 1963. From left: Fairfield Osborn; Carl W. Buchheister; Stewart L. Udall, Secretary of the Interior (fourth from left); Daniel A. Poole; Ira N. Gabrielson (partially hidden behind the President); and C.R. "Pink" Gutermuth.

acknowledged and accepted by society than had been the notions of restraint by the prior generation. In fact, acknowledgment and acceptance by society, not only that the nation's resource wealth was limited but that society's lifestyle and traditional institutional operations were the culprits of scarcity, came grudgingly. Not until the late 1960's and early 1970's was the public fully convinced that the Judeo-Christian ethic--man's dominion--and equating pell-mell growth with progress were, at least, mistakes or, at most, elaborate hoaxes.

To bring about change, new strategies were required, along with renewed dedication and new legislation. As was the case when Theodore Roosevelt, George Bird Grinnell, Gifford Pinchot, John Bird Burnham, T. Gilbert Pearson, Charles Sheldon, T. S. Palmer, Frank Chapman, C. Hart Merriam, and others first raised hue and cry over the rapid, wanton decimation of wildlife, there were many in later decades whose reaction to environmental crises was to proclaim doom and/or seek relief in name-calling and finger-pointing. Others, however, rose above the choruses of lip service and accusation, to activate constructive measures to reverse the nation's fast track to an empty cupboard. Most of these individuals were conservationists of long-standing, well before environmentalism became a national buzz-word, cause celebre, and perceived crisis. Nearly all were sportsmen, and many were members of the Boone and Crockett Club.

The continuum of conservation leadership in the U.S. has always been strongly represented by the Boone and Crockett Club membership, through their vocational affiliations, Club fellowship, and personal investments. The proof is that there has not been, from 1937 to 1987 and since, a single piece of national legislation, policy, or program on natural resource conservation that has not involved contribution and direct participation by one or more members of the Boone and Crockett Club. The names of many of the nation's most influential conservationists are found on the Club's roll. Aldo Leopold, Ira Gabrielson, Ding Darling, Pink Gutermuth, Frederic Walcott, John Phillips, Olaus Murie, Henry Stimson, Clarence Cottam, Stephen Mather, Henry Graves, Clarence King, William Beebe, George Shiras III, Alexander Wetmore, and many others, now deceased, carried on the Boone and Crockett Club founders' activism for improved management of wildlife and related natural resources. Carrying that torch now are Club members Daniel Poole, Durward Allen, Elvis Stahr, Philip Wright, Wendell Swank, Lee Talbot, Russell Train, Sherman Gray, Keith Hay, James "Red" Duke, William Spencer, Patrick Noonan, Ian McTaggart Cowan, Lloyd Swift, James Timmerman, Joseph Linduska, Maurice Hornocker, John Gottschalk, S. Dillon Ripley, Nathaniel Reed, James Teer, Jack Berryman, Lynn Greenwalt, George Harrison and many, many others.

As throughout the Boone and Crockett Club's history, not all members are front-line "players" on the national wildlife conservation scene. Most, in fact, are not. But each contributes, through ideas, enthusiasm, dollars, and otherwise, to the Club's constitutional objectives. The foremost common denominator among the biologists, scientists, educators, administrators, business executives, and communicators who comprise the Club's Regular, Honorary and Professional membership is that they all are sportsmen, in the truest, finest sense and tradition of the term. They also are individuals for whom Fair Chase and the opportunity to hunt in wild places are more than mere heritage, they are personal, sacred

obligations. That is the essence of Boone and Crockett members and of the Boone and Crockett Club itself, the nation's oldest, continuing national conservation organization.

In 1986, the Boone and Crockett Club initiated an "Associates Program" to accommodate a growing interest among non-members in the Club's activities. Hunters and others who share the Club's principles of sportsmanship and conservation have thus been allowed to be a part of the organization as Associates. As such, they are kept abreast of Club programs and opportunities and are able, through that affiliation, to form a bond for responsible hunting and for wildlife. In this manner, too, the Club has been able to expand its outreach and to invite others to be part of its heralded tradition, services, and challenges. To adopt the program, however, the Boone and Crockett Club reclassified its elected Associate Members, past and present, as Professional Members, who remain an integral and vital component of the fraternity.

The New Frontier

In the early 1980's, the Boone and Crockett Club sought a significant project to commemorate its approaching centennial anniversary. Such a project would need to serve as testimony to the Club's full century of involvement in the conservation of wildlife resources, as a tribute to its distinguished membership past, and as a living legacy for the future.

In 1984, the Club chose to purchase the Triple Divide Ranch (to be renamed the Theodore Roosevelt Memorial Ranch) and launched an ambitious campaign to underwrite the acquisition. That decision and effort were especially timely, for the Rocky Mountains' East Front is under increasing pressure from development. The Front was and is being meticulously probed for energy reserves. With such exploration come roads, facilities, and other uses that, if improperly planned and implemented, can seriously compromise the region's natural character, amenities, and values.

On the ranch are found, at least seasonally, virtually all the wildlife species (except bison) that occurred there in the pre-settlement, wild West. There are black bear, elk, mule and white-tailed deer, mountain lion, mountain goat, wolf, bighorn sheep, coyote, golden eagle, barred owl, peregrine, prairie and merlin falcons, goshawk, red-tailed hawk, grouse, and many other less obvious species. Even the threatened grizzly bear traverses the ranch seasonally.

To effect a complicated series of arrangements necessary to acquire the ranch, the Club established the Boone and Crockett Club Foundation, which also would serve to manage the property. With the cooperation and assistance of The Nature Conservancy, the transaction was completed in mid–1985, and the Theodore Roosevelt Memorial Ranch became a reality.

According to William Searle, President of the Boone and Crockett Club Foundation, the ranch "is dedicated to finding ways to manage the inherent conflicts between the conservation of wildlife and man's use and development of land." The opportunity that the ranch represents to strike chords of compatibility between wildlife, ranching, and agricultural values was dubbed "The New Western Frontier" by the Foundation. And to realize The

New Western Frontier, four objectives were set forth: (1) expand the region's chain of critical and unique wildlife habitat; (2) implement a program of applied research to find new methods and techniques to benefit wildlife, range conditions, and ranching, in concert; (3) undertake a program of education and public information on wildlife/ranching matters; and (4) continue to function as an operating ranch.

The first objective is part of a larger plan to acquire land along the Rockies' East Front for dedicated wildlife habitat. In conjunction with the State of Montana and The Nature Conservancy, the Club and its Foundation hope that the Theodore Roosevelt Memorial Ranch can serve to encourage the purchase of other lands to enhance wildlife habitat in general and, in particular, the critical winter range of big game and other species.

The second objective, an applied research program, is the central feature of the Club's investment. It is underway, in cooperation with the Montana Wildlife Biology Program at the University of Montana (Missoula). The Boone and Crockett Club Foundation, by formal agreement, has established an endowment to underwrite a professorship with additional support for student training and graduate-level and post-doctoral research at the Ranch. The agreement calls for the Ranch facilities to be made available to educators and graduate and postdoctoral students from colleges and universities throughout North America. This important program is designed for "hands-on" research in both laboratory and field conditions, to delve into new, practical opportunities to manage ranchlands economically and compatibly with wildlife.

Education and public information, the third objective, is an important aspect of the Foundation's agreement with the University of Montana. It is essential that practical information resulting from the research program be developed and widely disseminated to ranchers in Montana and throughout the West as well as to other interested parties. In addition to the purpose of informing ranchers and others of prospects for improved range management for livestock *and* wildlife, the informational/educational outreach will help resolve long-standing misconceptions and animosities that have plagued the relationship between stockmen and conservationists.

Also, the Ranch will serve as an "outdoor laboratory," where visitors can see for themselves the effects and multiple benefits of the research programs and the applications of new land-management techniques.

The Theodore Roosevelt Memorial Ranch will fully continue its ranch operation, alongside and complementary to its research and educational programs. This fourth objective is necessary to help subsidize the total program and to lend credibility to its research outputs.

The Ranch carries the name of the Boone and Crockett Club's founder and first President, but it truly is a memorial to each and every Club member since the organization began, and to the vision and ideals that have forged their association. The Ranch is a fitting capstone to the Club's first century of accomplishment in the restoration, conservation, and sound management of wildlife resources. It is, in a broader sense, affirmation of the Boone and Crockett Club's continuing commitment to wild animals, to wild places, to hunters, and to all others who use and enjoy America's out-of-doors.

Photographs Courtesy of George B. Ward and Richard E. McCabe

George B. Ward (left) and Richard E. McCabe

George B. Ward describes himself as a lifelong sportsman. He is the Assistant to the Director of the Texas State Historical Association and is the Managing Editor of the Southwest Historical Quarterly. Prior to this position, he was on the faculty of Bowling Green University, Bowling Green, Ohio. His dissertation at the University of Texas, Austin (1980) was titled, "Bloodbrothers in the Wilderness: The Sport Hunter and the Buckskin Hunter in the Preservation of the American Wilderness Experience." He is the author of "Boone and Crockett: National Collection of Heads and Horns", a brochure published by the Buffalo Bill Historical Center to mark the opening of the display of the Boone and Crockett Club's NCHH there. He has published on a wide range of western and popular culture topics. He lives with his family in Austin, Texas.

Richard E. McCabe is Secretary and Director of Publications of the Wildlife Management Institute in Washington, D.C. Prior to joining WMI in 1977, he was on the faculty of the University of Wisconsin/Madison. He completed undergraduate studies in English at Wartburg College, Waverly, Iowa, and graduate studies (agricultural journalism/wildlife ecology/mass communications) at the University of Wisconsin, Madison. He has edited, designed, and produced a number of award-winning books, and he has contributed to a wide variety of other books and publications on natural science and natural history topics. His particular area of interest is North American ethnozoology. Currently a resident of Annapolis, Maryland, he is an avid retriever dog handler and hunter of upland game birds and waterfowl. He has taken mule deer, whitetail, elk, and pronghorn, and will hunt moose and caribou in Alaska in the fall of 1988.

Geographic Boundaries for Trophy Entry

Geographic boundaries are of considerable importance in the records keeping. The records keeping is set up only for native North American big game animals. For such purposes, the southern boundary is defined as the south boundary of Mexico. The northern limit for trophies that may inhabit the offshore waters, such as polar bear and walrus, is the limit of the continent and associated waters held by the U.S. or Canada. Continental limits and associated waters define the east and west boundaries for all categories.

In addition to the broad geographic boundaries described above, carefully described geographic boundaries are necessary in certain categories that closely resemble each other, due to the fact that they are set up to recognize sub-species. Examples include Wyoming and Canada moose, Columbia and Sitka blacktail deer, and others. For these cases, specific boundary descriptions are spelled out for the smaller category to prevent specimens of the larger being erroneously entered and thus receiving undue recognition.

Categories for which such boundaries are spelled out include: grizzly and brown bear; American and Roosevelt's elk; mule, Columbia, and Sitka blacktail deer; whitetail and Coues' deer; Canada, Alaska-Yukon, and Wyoming moose; barren ground, Central Canada barren ground, mountain, woodland, and Quebec-Labrador caribou; bighorn, desert, Dall's, and Stone's sheep; and Atlantic and Pacific walrus.

In addition, special considerations are also spelled out for certain other animals. For example, bison exist today as wild, free-ranging herds in their original setting only in Alaska and Canada. Bison from the lower 48 states are, in many cases, semi-domesticated ad regulated as domestic livestock. Thus, hunter-taken trophies from the lower 48 states are acceptable only for the records book(s), not for consideration of the usual place awards, and only if they were taken in a state that recognizes bison as wild and free-ranging (and which requires a hunting license and/or big game tag for such hunting).

Detailed description of the applicable geographic boundaries is given in the trophy data section for the affected categories. Hunters are encouraged to read and understand such boundaries before taking, or even planning, hunting trips in order to avoid possible disappointment.

Tabulations of Recorded Trophies

The trophy data shown herein have been taken from score charts in the Records Archives of the Boone and Crockett Club. Trophies listed are those that continue to meet minimum score and other stated requirements of trophy entry for the program, through the 19th Awards entry period (1983–1985). The final scores and rank shown are official, except for trophies shown with an asterisk. The asterisk is assigned to trophies whose entry scores are subject to certification by an Awards Panel of Judges. The asterisk can be removed (except in the case of a potential World's Record) by the submitting of two additional, independent scorings by Official Measurers of the Boone and Crockett Club. The Records Committee of the Club will review the three scorings available (original plus two additional) and determine which, if any, will be accepted in lieu of the judges panel measurement. When the score has been accepted as final by the Records Committee, the asterisk will be removed in future editions of the all-time records book, *Records of North American Big Game*, and other publications. In the case of a potential World's Record trophy, the trophy *must* come before a Judges Panel at the end of an entry period. Only a Judges Panel can certify a World's Record and finalize its score.

Asterisked trophies are shown at the end of the listings for their category. They are *not* ranked, as their final score is subject to revision by a Judges Panel or by the submission of additional, official scorings, as described above.

Significant changes may be noted in the scores and rankings in certain categories as the result of an intensive review and verification of data in the Records Archives carried-out prior to preparation of this edition. Note that "PR" preceding date of kill indicates "prior to" the date shown for kill.

The scientific and vernacular names, and the sequence of presentation, follows that suggested in the Revised Checklist of North American Mammals North of Mexico, 1979 (J. Knox Jones, *et al*; Texas Tech University, December 14, 1979.)

Photograph by E. P. Haddon, U. S. Fish & Wildlife Service

BLACK BEAR

Black Bear

Ursus americanus americanus and related subspecies

Minimum Score 21

Score	Greatest Length of Skull Without Lower Jaw	Greatest Width of Skull	Sex	Locality Killed	By Whom Killed	Owner	Date Killed	Rank
23 10/16	14 12/16	8 14/16	U	San Pete Co., Utah	Picked Up	A. R. Lund & M. Daniels	1975	1
22 8/16	14 6/16	8 6/16	M	Porcupine Plains, Sask.	Calvin Parsons	Calvin Parsons	1977	2
22 8/16	14 1/16	8 7/16	M	Gila Co., Ariz.	John F. Peters	John F. Peters	1985	2
22 7/16	13 11/16	8 12/16	M	Sevier Co., Utah	Picked Up	Utah Div. of Wildl. Resc.	1982	4
22 6/16	13 11/16	8 1/16	M	San Pete Co., Utah	R. W. Peterson & R. S. Hardy	Rex W. Peterson	1970	5
22 6/16	14 3/16	8 3/16	M	Gila Co., Ariz.	Roy A. Stewart	Roy A. Stewart	1978	5
22 4/16	13 9/16	8 1/16	M	Apache Co., Ariz.	R. R. Barney & H. E. Booher	Richard R. Barney	1968	7
22 4/16	14 1/16	8 3/16	M	Ft. Apache Res., Ariz.	Jimmie C. James	Jimmie C. James	1971	7
22 3/16	13 13/16	8 5/16	M	Graham Co., Ariz.	Peter C. Knagge	Peter C. Knagge	1982	9
22 1/16	13 11/16	8 6/16	M	Uintah Co., Utah	Hal Mecham	Hal Mecham	1975	10
22 1/16	13 13/16	8 4/16	M	Arran, Sask.	Harry Kushniryk	Harry Kushniryk	1981	10
22	13 6/16	8 10/16	M	Hahns Peak, Colo.	W. L. Cave	W. L. Cave	1964	12
22	13 8/16	8 6/16	M	Graham Co., Ariz.	Thomas E. Klepfer	Thomas E. Klepfer	1972	12
22	13 12/16	8 4/16	M	Garfield Co., Colo.	Joseph R. Maynard	Joseph R. Maynard	1977	12
21 15/16	13 6/16	8 12/16	M	Land O' Lakes, Wisc.	Ed Strobel	Ed Strobel	1953	15
21 15/16	13 13/16	8 2/16	M	Swan River, Man.	Jim E. Russell	Jim E. Russell	1973	15
21 15/16	13 5/16	8 10/16	M	Lincoln Co., Wyo.	C. William Redshaw	C. William Redshaw	1976	15
21 14/16	13 11/16	8 3/16	M	Smithers, B.C.	Indian	Jack Adams	1975	18
21 14/16	13 10/16	8 4/16	M	Lincoln Co., Wisc.	Robert P. Faufau	Robert P. Faufau	1981	18
21 14/16	13 12/16	8 2/16	M	Hirsch Creek, B.C.	Cecil W. Brown	Cecil W. Brown	1984	18
21 11/16	13 6/16	8 6/16	M	Ft. Apache Res., Ariz.	G. Boyd, P. Ellsworth & G. Brewer	Greg Boyd	1964	21
21 13/16	13 7/16	8 6/16	M	Tatlanika River, Alaska	Barry W. Campbell	Barry W. Campbell	1966	21
21 13/16	13 6/16	8 6/16	M	Ft. Apache Res., Ariz.	Gary W. Sholl	Gary W. Sholl	1969	21
21 13/16	13 6/16	8 4/16	M	Graham Co., Ariz.	Bruce Liddy	Bruce Liddy	1976	21
21 13/16	13 7/16	8 7/16	M	Carbon Co., Pa.	Robert F. Kulp	Robert F. Kulp	1983	21
21 13/16	13 6/16	8 6/16	M	Big River, Sask.	William Dear	William Dear	1985	21
21 12/16	13 9/16	8 6/16	M	Delta Co., Colo.	Quincy Hines	Quincy Hines	1967	27
21 12/16	13 8/16	8 6/16	M	Bayfield Co., Wisc.	Byron Bird, Jr.	Byron Bird, Jr.	1976	27
21 12/16	13 6/16	8 4/16	M	Gila Co., Ariz.	Mike Lisk	Mike Lisk	1984	27
21 12/16	13 10/16	8 2/16	M	Garfield Co., Utah	Clint Mecham	Clint Mecham	1985	27

127

BLACK BEAR—*Continued*

Ursus americanus americanus and related subspecies

Score	Greatest Length of Skull Without Lower Jaw	Greatest Width of Skull	Sex	Locality Killed	By Whom Killed	Owner	Date Killed	Rank
21 11/16	13 9/16	8 6/16	U	Mendocino Co., Calif.	E. J. Vamm	Univ. Calif. Museum	1928	31
21 11/16	13 9/16	8 5/16	M	Gila Co., Ariz.	Clay Warden	Milo Warden	1975	31
21 11/16	13 5/16	8 6/16	M	Menominee Co., Mich.	Ray Bray	Andy Bray	1984	31
21 10/16	13	8 10/16	M	Mendocino Co., Calif.	Andy Bowman	Univ. Calif. Museum	1930	34
21 10/16	13 9/16	8 5/16	M	Lake Co., Oreg.	Martin V. Pernoll	Marvin V. Pernoll	1967	34
21 10/16	13	8 10/16	M	Custer Co., Idaho	Robert L. Caskey	Robert L. Caskey	1967	34
21 10/16	13 4/16	8 6/16	M	Grande Cache, Alta.	Laurier Adam	Laurier Adam	1984	34
21 10/16	13 8/16	8 2/16	M	Gila Co., Ariz.	Harold W. Mosser	Harold W. Mosser	1985	34
21 9/16	13 4/16	8 5/16	M	Garfield Co., Colo.	Robert C. Maurer	Robert C. Maurer	1955	39
21 9/16	13 3/16	8 6/16	M	Collbran, Colo.	O. K. Clifton	O. K. Clifton	1957	39
21 9/16	13 9/16	8 3/16	M	Williams Fork River, Colo.	C. Stehle & J. Grove	Clyde Stehle	1958	39
21 9/16	13 5/16	8 3/16	M	Vilas Co., Wisc.	Wisc. Dept. Nat. Resc.	Neal Long Taxidermy	1959	39
21 9/16	13 4/16	8 5/16	M	Mesa Co., Colo.	Hartle V. Morris	Hartle V. Morris	1962	39
21 9/16	13 5/16	8 4/16	M	Clinton Co., Pa.	Donald Sorgen	Donald Sorgen	1968	39
21 9/16	13 2/16	8 2/16	M	Vilas Co., Wisc.	John J. Volkmann	John J. Volkmann	1973	39
21 9/16	13 2/16	8 7/16	M	Ouray Co., Colo.	Thomas C. Middleton	Thomas C. Middleton	1978	39
21 9/16	13 6/16	8 3/16	M	Catron Co., N.M.	Sam Ray	Sam Ray	1983	39
21 9/16	13 6/16	8 3/16	M	Zeballos, B.C.	Gary M. Biggar	Gary M. Biggar	1983	39
21 8/16	13 6/16	8 6/16	M	Gallatin River, Wyo.	J. P. V. Evans	U. S. Natl. Museum	1914	49
21 8/16	13 9/16	7 15/16	M	Bayfield Co., Wisc.	Earl B. Johnson	Earl B. Johnson	1953	49
21 8/16	13 8/16	8 3/16	M	Forest Co., Wisc.	Richard Ruthven	Wisc. Buck & Bear Club	1968	49
21 8/16	13 9/16	8 3/16	M	Chiriacuahua Butte, Ariz.	W. O. Morrison	W. O. Morrison	1969	49
21 8/16	13 9/16	8 5/16	M	Lincoln Co., Wyo.	Charles R. Nixon	Charles R. Nixon	1973	49
21 8/16	13 7/16	8 4/16	M	Ventura Co., Calif.	James B. Wade	James B. Wade	1977	49
21 8/16	13 4/16	8 1/16	M	Augusta Co., Va.	Joseph R. Lam	Joseph R. Lam	1977	49
21 8/16	13 5/16	8 7/16	M	Apache Co., Ariz.	Joseph H. Lyman	John F. Peters	1978	49
21 8/16	13 5/16	8 5/16	M	Garfield Co., Colo.	Robert W. Jackson	Robert W. Jackson	1980	49
21 8/16	13 5/16	8 3/16	M	Bonneville Co., Idaho	George R. Adams	George R. Adams	1982	49
21 8/16	12 14/16	8 10/16	M	Harrison Hot Springs, B.C.	Domenico Abbinante	Domenico Abbinante	1982	49
21 8/16	13	8 6/16	M	Pike Co., Pa.	Paul D. Longenbach	Paul D. Longenbach	1983	49
21 8/16	13 6/16	8 2/16	M	Gila Co., Ariz.	Rick Corven	R. Corven & R. Gifford	1983	49
21 8/16	13 6/16	8 2/16	M	Marshall Co., Minn.	James E. Kelley	J. & B. Zimpel	1984	49

128

21 7/16	13 7/16	8 5/16	M	Mariposa Co., Calif.	Bert Palmberg	Bert Palmberg	1957	63
21 7/16	13 7/16	8 5/16	U	Wales Is., Alaska	Picked Up	L. R. Hall	1962	63
21 7/16	13 7/16	8 5/16	M	Megal Mt., Nfld.	Ben Hillicoss	Ben Hillicoss	1963	63
21 7/16	13 7/16	8	M	Albemarle Co., Va.	Grover F. Sites	Grover F. Sites	1964	63
21 6/16	13 7/16	8 5/16	M	Pierce Co., Wash.	T. Johnson & B. Paque	Tracy Johnson	1968	63
21 6/16	13 6/16	8 5/16	U	McKean Co., Pa.	Picked Up	Pa. Game Commission	1969	63
21 6/16	13 6/16	8 5/16	M	Douglas Co., Wisc.	Kenneth J. Burton	Kenneth J. Burton	1972	63
21 6/16	13	8 7/16	M	Nordegg, Alta.	Leo F. Hermary	Leo F. Hermary	1977	63
21 6/16	13 12/16	7 11/16	M	Sevier Co., Utah	Milton L. Robb	Milton L. Robb	1980	63
21 6/16	13 4/16	8 5/16	M	Pierceland, Sask.	Bryce Burgess	Bryce Burgess	1980	63
21 6/16	13 4/16	8 3/16	M	Iron Co., Wisc.	Gary G. Johnson	Gary G. Johnson	1982	63
21 6/16	13 10/16	7 13/16	M	Flat Lake, Alta.	Dale T. Loosemore	Dale T. Loosemore	1983	63
21 6/16	13 11/16	7 12/16	M	Peesane, Sask.	Peter Janzen	Peter Janzen	1984	63
21 6/16	13 3/16	8 4/16	M	Cholmondeley Sound, Alaska	Philip A. Indovina	Philip A. Indovina	1984	63
21 6/16	13 3/16	8 3/16	M	Gila Co., Ariz.	D. Highly Falkner	D. Highly Falkner	1984	63
21 6/16	13 3/16	8 4/16	M	Fox Creek, Alta.	William Hellebrand	William Hellebrand	1985	63
21 6/16	13 3/16	8 5/16	M	Prince of Wales Is.., Alaska	Picked Up	Robert Kase	PR1954	79
21 6/16	13 13/16	7 9/16	M	Sandpoint, Idaho	Ronald Lee Book	Ronald Lee Book	1969	79
21 6/16	13 5/16	8 1/16	M	Reserve, N.M.	C. J. McElroy	C. J. McElroy	1970	79
21 6/16	12 12/16	8 10/16	M	Franklin Co., N.Y.	James Donner	James Donner	1970	79
21 6/16	13 11/16	7 11/16	M	Pike Co., Pa.	Robert Loux	Robert Loux	1971	79
21 6/16	13 10/16	7 12/16	M	Carbon Co., Utah	R. Peterson & R. S. Hardy	Rex Peterson	1975	79
21 6/16	13 6/16	8	M	Bayfield Co., Wisc.	Larry L. Frye	Larry L. Frye	1975	79
21 6/16	13	8 6/16	M	Humboldt Co., Calif.	Dean Earley	Dean Earley	1977	79
21 6/16	12 13/16	8 6/16	M	Pitken Co., Colo.	Chris Green	Chris Green	1980	79
21 6/16	13 4/16	8 4/16	M	Thorne Bay, Alaska	Tod L. Reichert	Tod L. Reichert	1985	79
21 5/16	13 6/16	8 4/16	M	Colorado	E. T. Seton	U.S. Natl. Museum	1897	89
21 5/16	13 7/16	7 15/16	M	Yarmouth Co., N.S.	John L. Bastey	John L. Bastey	1945	89
21 5/16	12 15/16	8 6/16	U	Centre Co., Pa.	Picked Up	Wayne B. Harpster	1946	89
21 5/16	13 6/16	8 2/16	M	Rockbridge Co., Va.	Richard L. Merchant	Richard L. Merchant	1953	89
21 5/16	13	8 6/16	M	Buffalo Park, Colo.	John L. Howard	John L. Howard	1958	89
21 5/16	13 5/16	8 3/16	M	Olympic Pen., Wash.	Lauren A. Johnson	Lauren A. Johnson	1960	89
21 5/16	13 3/16	8 6/16	M	Cynthia, Alta.	Bert Klineburger	Bert Klineburger	1963	89
21 5/16	12 15/16	8 3/16	M	Mendocino Co., Calif.	R. LeVoir	R. LeVoir	1968	89
21 5/16	13 6/16	8	M	Vilas Co., Wisc.	Gene H. Whitney	Gene H. Whitney	1971	89
21 5/16	13 5/16	8	M	Lincoln Co., Wyo.	Michael G. Duwe	Michael G. Duwe	1972	89
21 5/16	13 4/16	8 1/16	M	Gila Co., Ariz.	Gregg G. Fisher	Gregg G. Fisher	1975	89
21 5/16	13 7/16	7 14/16	M	Langlade Co., Wisc.	Larry S. Behrends	Larry S. Behrends	1976	89
21 5/16	13 11/16	7 9/16	M	Cochise Co., Ariz.	Michael Steliga	Michael Steliga	1981	89
21 4/16	13 3/16	8 1/16	M	Los Angeles Co., Calif.	Unknown	Univ. Calif. Museum	1928	102
21 4/16	13 6/16	7 14/16	U	Shoshone River, Wyo.	Picked Up	Anselmo Lewis	1952	102
21 4/16	13 6/16	7 12/16	M	Ann Arbor, Mich.	Loren L. Lutz	Loren L. Lutz	1956	102
21 4/16	13 2/16	7 12/16	M		Albert Erickson	Albert Erickson	1957	102

Black Bear—*Continued*
Ursus americanus americanus and related subspecies

Score	Greatest Length of Skull Without Lower Jaw	Greatest Width of Skull	Sex	Locality Killed	By Whom Killed	Owner	Date Killed	Rank
21 2/16	13 2/16	8 6/16	M	Arizona	Paul B. Reynolds	Paul B. Reynolds	1965	102
21 2/16	13 6/16	7 11/16	M	Olympic Pen., Wash.	Bert Klineburger	Bert Klineburger	1967	102
21 2/16	12 11/16	8 6/16	M	Sawyer Co., Wisc.	Ted Roberts	Ted Roberts	1968	102
21 2/16	12 12/16	8 6/16	M	Curry Co., Oreg.	Joe W. Latimer	Joe W. Latimer	1968	102
21 2/16	13 1/16	8 3/16	M	Hudson Bay, Sask.	Neil Southam	Neil Southam	1969	102
21 2/16	13 1/16	8 6/16	M	Williams, Ariz.	James E. Coy	James E. Coy	1970	102
21 2/16	13 6/16	7 14/16	M	Snowmass, Colo.	Ronald D. Vincent	Ronald D. Vincent	1974	102
21 2/16	13 7/16	7 13/16	M	Pinal Co., Ariz.	Bruce R. Gifford	Bruce R. Gifford	1980	102
21 2/16	13 7/16	7 13/16	M	Tehama Co., Calif.	Jim Cox	Jim Cox	1980	102
21 2/16	13 4/16	8 2/16	M	Sawyer Co., Wisc.	Harvey W. Klein	Harvey W. Klein	1982	102
21 2/16	13 4/16	8 2/16	M	Khyex River, B.C.	Edward Dickens	Edward Dickens	1982	102
21 3/16	13 6/16	7 13/16	U	Queen Charlotte Is., B.C.	C. de Blois Green	Univ. Calif. Museum	1911	117
21 3/16	13 8/16	7 11/16	M	Alberta	James C. Wynne	James C. Wynne	1966	117
21 3/16	13 2/16	8 1/16	M	Bayfield Co., Wisc.	G. Michaels	Gerald M. Weber	1966	117
21 3/16	12 15/16	8 6/16	M	Alberta	F. A. Stromstedt	Univ. of Calgary	1967	117
21 3/16	13	8 3/16	M	Thurston Co., Wash.	Hugh M. Oliver	Hugh M. Oliver	1969	117
21 3/16	12 15/16	8 6/16	M	Eagle Co., Colo.	Charles T. Coffman	Charles T. Coffman	1971	117
21 3/16	13 4/16	7 15/16	M	Ashland Co., Wisc.	Herman Straubel	Herman Straubel	1972	117
21 3/16	13 1/16	8 2/16	M	Stonecliffe, Ont.	Robert M. Weir	Robert M. Weir	1974	117
21 3/16	12 13/16	8 6/16	M	Madison Co., Mont.	Gerald D. Morgan	Gerald D. Morgan	1974	117
21 3/16	13 1/16	8 6/16	M	Oneida Co., Wisc.	Fred C. Hageny	Fred C. Hageny	1975	117
21 3/16	13 4/16	7 15/16	M	Gila Co., Ariz.	Kae L. Brockermeyer	Kae L. Brockermeyer	1977	117
21 3/16	13 3/16	8	M	Clinton Co., Pa.	Orwin W. Srock	Orwin W. Srock	1981	117
21 3/16	12 5/16	8 4/16	M	Carbon Co., Wyo.	Hugh D. Beavers, Jr.	Hugh D. Beavers, Jr.	1981	117
21 3/16	13 1/16	8 2/16	M	Neck Lake, Alaska	F. A. Lonsway, Jr.	F. A. Lonsway, Jr.	1983	117
21 3/16	12 11/16	8 6/16	M	Yolo Co., Calif.	Walter D. Foster	Walter D. Foster	1983	117
21 2/16	13	8 2/16	M	Kuiu Is., Alaska	L. W. Potter	L. W. Potter	1951	132
21 2/16	12 12/16	8 6/16	M	Essex Co., N.Y.	William R. Waddell	N.Y. Cons. Dept.	1955	132
21 2/16	13 6/16	7 12/16	M	Lincoln Co., Wyo.	R. Langford & W. R. Ryan	Ralph Langford	1955	132
21 2/16	13 3/16	7 15/16	M	Los Angeles Co., Calif.	Leo J. Reihsen	Leo J. Reihsen	1961	132
21 2/16	13 4/16	8	M	Mammoth Mt., Calif.	Clarke Merrill	Clarke Merrill	1963	132
21 2/16	13 12/16	7 9/16	M	Chinitna Bay, Alaska	Basil C. Bradbury	Basil C. Bradbury	1964	132

21 9/16	13 5/16	7 13/16	M	Shasta Co., Calif.	Ivan L. Marx	Ivan L. Marx	1965	132
21 9/16	12 12/16	8 6/16	M	Collbran, Colo.	R. R. Lyons & H. V. Morris	Raymond R. Lyons	1965	132
21 9/16	12 15/16	8 3/16	M	Chelan Co., Wash.	Virgil R. Bedient	Virgil R. Bedient	1965	132
21 9/16	13	8 6/16	M	Mesa Co., Colo.	Waldemar R. Kuenzel, Jr.	Waldemar R. Kuenzel, Jr.	1966	132
21 9/16	12 14/16	8 4/16	M	Raven Lake, B.C.	Robert G. Wardian	Robert G. Wardian	1967	132
21 9/16	13	8 6/16	U	Trinity Co., Calif.	Picked Up	Robert E. Frost	1967	132
21 9/16	12 9/16	8 6/16	M	Montrose Co., Colo.	Earl L. Markley	Earl L. Markley	1970	132
21 9/16	14 1/16	7 7/16	M	Sublette Co., Wyo.	A. Jack Welch	A. Jack Welch	1971	132
21 9/16	13 7/16	7 11/16	U	Clam Lake, Wisc.	Picked Up	M. Reynolds & J. Olson	PR1971	132
21 9/16	13 6/16	7 12/16	M	Gila Co., Ariz.	Daniel J. Urban	Daniel J. Urban	1972	132
21 9/16	13 5/16	8	M	Lake Co., Calif.	David C. Sharp	David C. Sharp	1972	132
21 9/16	13 4/16	7 14/16	M	Gunnison Co., Colo.	Dick Cooper	Dick Cooper	1977	132
21 9/16	13 5/16	8 6/16	M	Gila Co., Ariz.	Robert E. Barnes	Robert E. Barnes	1978	132
21 9/16	13 5/16	8 6/16	M	Lodgepole, Alta.	Jim H. Van Manen	Jim H. Van Manen	1979	132
21 9/16	13	8 3/16	M	Ethelbert, Man.	Paul A. Bormes	Paul A. Bormes	1979	132
21 9/16	13 5/16	8	M	Preeceville, Sask.	David S. Hodgin	David S. Hodgin	1982	132
21 9/16	13 8/16	7 9/16	M	Graham Island, B.C.	Roger Britton	Roger Britton	1982	132
21 9/16	13	8 6/16	M	Goose River, Alta.	T. Barker & R. Mompere	Thomas Barker	1983	132
21 9/16	13 5/16	8 3/16	M	Terra Nova River, Nfld.	James A. Young	James A. Young	1984	132
21 9/16	12 12/16	7 15/16	M	Hudson Bay, Sask.	Neil Southam	Neil Southam	1984	132
21 9/16	13 5/16	8 6/16	M	Marquette Co., Mich.	Gerald J. Isetts, Sr.	Gerald J. Isetts, Sr.	1984	132
21 9/16	13 5/16	7 14/16	M	Indian Lake, La.	B. V. Lilly	U. S. Natl. Museum	1904	159
21 9/16	13 7/16	7 14/16	M	Coahuila, Mexico	B. V. Lilly	U. S. Natl. Museum	1906	159
21 9/16	13 7/16	7 9/16	U	Santa Barbara Co., Calif.	Charles Tant	Univ. Calif. Museum	1940	159
21 9/16	12 12/16	7 15/16	M	Columbia Co., Wash.	Glenn Ford	Fred Van Arsdol	1954	159
21 9/16	13 7/16	8 6/16	M	Paonia, Colo.	William O. Good	William O. Good	1960	159
21 9/16	12 9/16	7 15/16	M	Mt. Gentry, Ariz.	Cliff Edwards	Cliff Edwards	1960	159
21 9/16	13 5/16	8 6/16	M	Steamboat Springs, Colo.	Norman Garwood	Norman Garwood	1964	159
21 9/16	13	7 14/16	M	Peace River, Alta.	Don W. Caldwell	Don W. Caldwell	1965	159
21 9/16	13 5/16	7 15/16	M	Gila Co., Ariz.	George L. Massingill	George L. Massingill	1971	159
21 9/16	13	8 6/16	M	Price Co., Wisc.	J. Valiga & J. Hanson	Joseph Valiga	1971	159
21 9/16	13 5/16	7 14/16	M	Iron Co., Wisc.	Gerald Brauer	Gerald Brauer	1972	159
21 9/16	12 13/16	8 4/16	M	San Carlos Indian Res., Ariz.	Michael D. Gunnett	Michael D. Gunnett	1973	159
21 9/16	13 9/16	7 11/16	M	Hubbard Co., Minn.	Dean J. Como	Dean J. Como	1974	159
21 9/16	12 15/16	8 6/16	M	Logan Lake, B.C.	Norman W. Dougan	Norman W. Dougan	1978	159
21 9/16	13 5/16	7 14/16	M	Graham Island, B.C.	Roger Britton	Roger Britton	1978	159
21 9/16	12 15/16	8 6/16	M	Greenlee Co., Ariz.	Michael W. Goodyear	Michael W. Goodyear	1979	159
21 9/16	13 10/16	7 7/16	M	Graham Island, B.C.	Roger Britton	Roger Britton	1980	159
21 9/16	12 15/16	8 6/16	M	Teller Co., Colo.	Samuel T. Harrelson, Jr.	Samuel T. Harrelson, Jr.	1982	159
21 9/16	13 5/16	8	M	Spirit River, Alta.	John Dobish	John Dobish	1982	159
21 9/16	12 13/16	8 6/16	M	Apache Co., Ariz.	William J. Morris	William J. Morris	1985	159
21	12 15/16	8 6/16	U	Queen Charlotte Is., B.C.	Unknown	Douglas McIntyre	PR1959	179
21	12 9/16	8 6/16	M	Vancouver, B.C.	Elmer E. Kurrus, Jr.	Elmer E. Kurrus, Jr.	1964	179

BLACK BEAR—Continued

Ursus americanus and related subspecies

Score	Greatest Length of Skull Without Lower Jaw	Greatest Width of Skull	Sex	Locality Killed	By Whom Killed	Owner	Date Killed	Rank
21	13	8	M	Hamilton Co., N.Y.	James McIntyre	N.Y. Cons. Dept.	1965	179
21	12 12/16	8 4/16	M	Collbran, Colo.	Cecil E. Alumbaugh, Jr.	Cecil E. Alumbaugh, Jr.	1967	179
21	12 11/16	8 5/16	M	Oconto Co., Wisc.	Calvin E. Schindel	Calvin E. Schindel	1968	179
21	13 2/16	7 14/16	M	Overflowing River, Man.	Victor Kostiniuk	Victor Kostiniuk	1971	179
21	12 15/16	8 4/16	M	Garfield Co., Colo.	J. D. Liles	J. D. Liles	1974	179
21	13 3/16	7 14/16	M	St. Louis Co., Minn.	Robert J. Manteuffel	Robert J. Manteuffel	1977	179
21	13 4/16	7 12/16	M	Wasatch Co., Utah	Picked Up	Utah Div. of Wildl. Resc.	1980	179
21	13	8	M	Routt Co., Colo.	Jerome W. Keyes, Jr.	Jerome W. Keyes, Jr.	1980	179
21	12 12/16	8 4/16	M	Bradford Co., Pa.	Ray B. Moyer	Ray B. Moyer	1981	179
21	13 3/16	7 14/16	M	Coconino Co., Ariz.	Michael P. Whelan	Michael P. Whelan	1981	179
21	13 4/16	7 15/16	M	Hamilton Co., N.Y.	Marshall E. Conklin	Marshall E. Conklin	1981	179
21	12 7/16	8 6/16	M	Fremont Co., Wyo.	Timothy B. Hill	Timothy B. Hill	1981	179
21	13 3/16	7 13/16	M	Langlade Co., Wisc.	Michael Steliga	Michael Steliga	1982	179
21	13	8	M	Ft. Assiniboine, Alta.	George Plashka	George Plashka	1982	179
21	12 14/16	8 2/16	M	Macon Co., N.C.	C. Rick Jones	C. Rick Jones	1983	179
21	13 3/16	7 13/16	M	Wild Goose, Ont.	William G. Tellijohn	William G. Tellijohn	1985	179
21	12 10/16	8 6/16	M	Echouani Lake, Que.	Collins F. Kellogg	Collins F. Kellogg	1985	179
21	13	8	M	Cholmondely Sound, Alaska	Gerry D. Downey	Gerry D. Downey	1985	179
22 9/16*	13 11/16	8 11/16	M	Lycoming Co., Pa.	John C. Whyne	John C. Whyne	1983	
22 6/16*	13 12/16	8 6/16	M	San Carlos Indian Res., Ariz.	Joseph A. Waite	Joseph A. Waite	1975	
22*	13 14/16	8 2/16	M	McKenzie Inlet, Alaska	Fred J. Hoppe	Fred J. Hoppe	1981	
21 13/16*	13 13/16	8	M	White Fox, Sask.	Picked Up	Douglas E. Miller	1974	

*Final Score subject to revision by additional verifying measurements

132

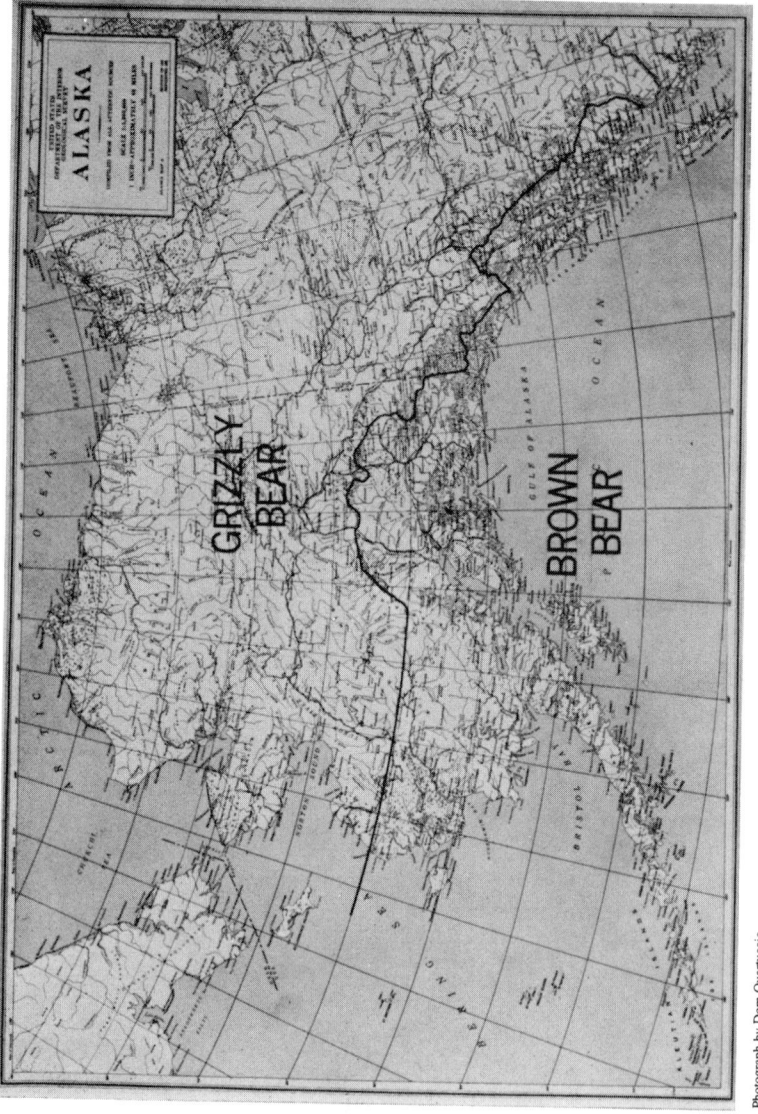

This map shows the line of demarcation between Alaska brown and grizzly bears, as drawn by the Boone and Crockett Club for records keeping purposes.

GRIZZLY BEAR

Boundaries of the Alaska Brown Bear and Grizzly Bear

A line of separation between the larger growing coastal brown bear and the smaller interior grizzly has been developed such that west and south of this line (to and including Unimak Island) bear trophies are recorded as Alaska brown bear. North and east of this line, bear trophies are recorded as grizzly bear. The boundary line description is as follows: Starting at Pearse Canal and following the Canadian-Alaskan boundary northwesterly to Mt. St. Elias on the 141° meridian; thence north along the Canadian-Alaskan boundary to Mt. Natazhat; thence west along the divide of the Wrangell Range to Mt. Jarvis at the western end of the Wrangell Range; thence north along the divide of the Mentasta Range to Mentasta Pass; thence in a general westerly direction along the divide of the Alaska Range to Houston Pass; thence westerly following the 62nd parallel of latitude to the Bering Sea.

Grizzly Bear
Ursus arctos horribilis

Minimum Score 24

Score	Greatest Length of Skull Without Lower Jaw	Greatest Width of Skull	Sex	Locality Killed	By Whom Killed	Owner	Date Killed	Rank
27 7/16	17 5/16	9 12/16	U	Bella Coola Valley, B.C.	Picked Up	James G. Shelton	1970	1
27 1/16	16 14/16	10 6/16	M	Dean River, B.C.	Roger J. Pentecost	Roger J. Pentecost	1982	1
26 13/16	16 1/16	10 6/16	M	Wakeman River, B.C.	Harry Leggett, Jr.	Harry Leggett, Jr.	1980	3
26 10/16	16 6/16	10	M	Rivers Inlet, B.C.	F. Nygaard	Univ. of B.C.	1954	4
26 10/16	17	9 9/16	M	Lonesome Lake, B.C.	J. Turner	Douglas Kenefick	1965	4
26 8/16	16 1/16	10 5/16	M	Ungalik River, Alaska	Stanley F. Smith	S. Smith & G. Fait	1983	6
26 8/16	16 9/16	9 14/16	M	Yanert Glacier, Alaska	Xavier T. Riedmiller	Xavier T. Riedmiller	1970	7
26 6/16	16 5/16	10	M	Bella Coola, B.C.	Walter C. Shutts	Walter C. Shutts	1957	8
26 6/16	16 13/16	9 9/16	M	Farewell Lake, Alaska	John C. Schwietert	John C. Schwietert	1968	8
26 6/16	16 8/16	9 14/16	M	Seaskinnish Creek, B.C.	Paddy H. S. Wong	Fred Y. C. Wong	1982	8
26 6/16	16 5/16	10 6/16	M	Cluculz Creek, B.C.	Thomas C. Roberson	Thomas C. Roberson	1983	8
26 6/16	16 10/16	9 11/16	M	Slave Lake, Alta.	B. Twin & D. Auger	R. W. H. Eben-Ebenau	1953	12
26 6/16	16 5/16	10	M	Knights Inlet, B.C.	Thomas N. Bernard	Thomas N. Bernard	1967	12
26 5/16	16 5/16	9 9/16	M	Swan Hills, Alta.	Wilfred Hartfelder	Wilfred Hartfelder	1974	12
26 4/16	16 9/16	9 9/16	U	Elliott Hwy., Alaska	Unknown	Alaska Dept. Fish & Game	1967	15
26 4/16	16 12/16	9 8/16	M	Tashenshini River, B.C.	William G. Underhill	William G. Underhill	1970	15
26 4/16	16 5/16	9 1/16	M	Ferry, Alaska	Jamie C. Smyth	Jamie C. Smyth	1973	15
26 4/16	16 1/16	10 3/16	M	Nulato Hills, Alaska	Randy A. Tarnowski	Randy A. Tarnowski	1978	15
26 4/16	17	9 4/16	M	Kakwa River, Alta.	Klaus Wernsdorf	Klaus Wernsdorf	1979	15
26 3/16	17	9 3/16	M	Tatla Lake, B.C.	Robert L. Tuma	Robert L. Tuma	1971	20
26 3/16	16 1/16	10 4/16	M	Buckland River, Alaska	Bill McDavid	Bill McDavid	1977	20
26 3/16	16 12/16	9 7/16	M	Bear Lake, B.C.	DeVern Gardner	DeVern Gardner	1984	20
26 2/16	16 10/16	9 8/16	M	Nechako River, B.C.	R. J. Nielson	R. J. Nielsen	1971	23
26 2/16	16	10 2/16	M	Kantishna River, Alaska	Theodore B. Kelly, Jr.	Theodore B. Kelly, Jr.	1972	23
26 2/16	16 1/16	9 13/16	U	Kwatna Bay, Alaska	J. G. Bartlett	J. G. Bartlett	1976	23
26 1/16	16 1/16	10	M	Smiths Inlet, B.C.	Donald M. Swarthout	Donald M. Swarthout	1963	26
26	16	10	U	Lake Minchumina, Alaska	Val J. Blackburn	Val J. Blackburn	1956	27
26	17	9	M	Bella Coola, B.C.	J. Harstad	John Lesowski	1959	27
26	16 1/16	9 15/16	M	Tweedsmuir Park, B.C.	Michael R. Caspersen	Michael R. Caspersen	1969	27
26	16 8/16	9 8/16	M	Kobuk River, Alaska	Charlie Horner	Charlie Horner	1971	27

Score	Greatest Length of Skull Without Lower Jaw	Greatest Width of Skull	Sex	Locality Killed	By Whom Killed	Owner	Date Killed	Rank
25 15/16	15 12/16	10 3/16	M	Rapids Roadhouse, Alaska	H. Herring	H. Herring	1964	31
25 15/16	16 3/16	9 3/16	M	Bella Coola, B.C.	Bernard J. Meinerz	Bernard J. Meinerz	1968	31
25 15/16	16 3/16	9 3/16	M	Klinaklini River, B.C.	Jerry Stubblefield	Jerry Stubblefield	1970	31
25 15/16	16	9 5/16	M	Iskut River, B.C.	Fritz A. Nachant	Fritz A. Nachant	1980	31
25 14/16	16	9 4/16	M	Telkwa River, B.C.	Matt Helstrom	Lowell A. Davison	1957	35
25 14/16	16 3/16	9 5/16	M	Owikeno Lake, B.C.	Alexander M. Peterson	Alexander M. Peterson	1959	35
25 14/16	16	9 4/16	M	Christmas Mt., Alaska	Mark E. Gilson	Mark E. Gilson	1980	35
25 14/16	16 2/16	9 2/16	M	Muskeg River, Alta.	Dale B. Kolberg	Dale B. Kolberg	1981	35
25 14/16	16 3/16	9 3/16	M	Gardner Canal, B.C.	Steven B. Garland	Steven B. Garland	1984	40
25 13/16	15 15/16	9 14/16	M	Wood River, Alaska	Horace Black	Horace Black	1963	40
25 13/16	16 3/16	9 3/16	M	Bella Coola, B.C.	Roger L. Adams	Roger L. Adams	1965	40
25 13/16	16 3/16	9 3/16	M	Spatsizi River, B.C.	Howard W. Gambrell	Howard W. Gambrell	1985	43
25 13/16	15 13/16	9 15/16	M	Alaska Range, Alaska	Elmer R. Schlachter	Elmer R. Schlachter	1971	43
25 12/16	16 6/16	9 9/16	M	Kwatna River, B.C.	Robert C. Riggs	Robert C. Riggs	1981	43
25 12/16	16	9 12/16	M	Hanna Ridge, B.C.	Dale T. Dean	Dale T. Dean	1984	43
25 11/16	16	9 12/16	M	Bond Sound, B.C.	William Kemp, Jr.	William Kemp, Jr.	1985	47
25 11/16	16 3/16	9 3/16	M	Owikeno Lake, B.C.	W. W. Meeker	W. W. Meeker	1959	47
25 11/16	15 11/16	10	M	Tatshenshini River, B.C.	Robert E. Miller	Robert E. Miller	1974	47
25 11/16	16 3/16	9 6/16	M	Kimsquit River, B.C.	Norman E. Kinsey	Norman E. Kinsey	1977	47
25 11/16	15 11/16	10	M	Meziadin Lake, B.C.	J. D. Jensen & R. S. Curtis	Jae Dea Jensen	1979	47
25 11/16	16 1/16	9 6/16	M	Bralorne, B.C.	Bert Klineburger	Bert Klineburger	1956	51
25 9/16	16 3/16	9 7/16	M	Dease River, B.C.	Herb Klein	Herb Klein	1960	51
25 9/16	16 2/16	9 8/16	U	Eagle Creek, Wyo.	Picked Up	L. L. Lutz & H. Sanford	1961	51
25 9/16	16	9 10/16	M	Brooks Range, Alaska	John H. Epp	John H. Epp	1965	51
25 9/16	15 9/16	10 4/16	M	Nabesna River, Alaska	Jack A. Shane, Sr.	Jack A. Shane, Sr.	1966	51
25 9/16	16 2/16	9 8/16	M	Kuskokwim River, Alaska	George Panagos	George Panagos	1968	51
25 9/16	15 15/16	9 11/16	M	Tok River, Alaska	Robert S. Thompson	Robert S. Thompson	1974	51
25 9/16	16	9 10/16	M	Machmell River, B.C.	Herbert J. Wenk	Herbert J. Wenk	1975	51
25 9/16	15 14/16	9 12/16	M	Sheslay River, B.C.	John Welsh	John Welsh	1983	51
25 9/16	16	9 6/16	M	Missouri Breaks, Mont.	E. S. Cameron	U. S. Natl. Museum	1890	60
25 9/16	16 4/16	9 6/16	M	Klinaklini River, B.C.	Grancel Fitz	Mrs. Grancel Fitz	1953	60

				Locality	Hunter	Date	Owner	Rank
25⁹/₁₆	16	9⁹/₁₆	M	Kitseguecla Mts., B.C.	Jack Adams	1975	Jack Adams	60
25⁹/₁₆	16³/₁₆	9⁹/₁₆	M	Carpenter Lake, B.C.	Jim Sprangers	1982	Jim Sprangers	60
25⁸/₁₆	16²/₁₆	9⁹/₁₆	M	Owikeno Lake, B.C.	J. C. Russell	1957	J. C. Russell	64
25⁸/₁₆	16	9⁹/₁₆	M	Maxan Lake, B.C.	Alfred E. Matthew	1967	Alfred E. Matthew	64
25⁸/₁₆	16	9⁹/₁₆	M	Cassiar Mts., B.C.	Arlow Lothe	1969	Arlow Lothe	64
25⁸/₁₆	15¹⁵/₁₆	9⁹/₁₆	M	Wakeman Sound, B.C.	Dennis King	1969	Dennis King	64
25⁸/₁₆	15¹²/₁₆	9¹²/₁₆	M	McKinley River, Alaska	John R. Cardis	1970	John R. Cardis	64
25⁸/₁₆	16	9⁹/₁₆	M	Big River, Alaska	George Engel	1976	George Engel	64
25⁸/₁₆	16³/₁₆	9⁵/₁₆	M	Prince Rupert, B.C.	Murray B. Wilson	1979	Murray B. Wilson	64
25⁸/₁₆	16⁶/₁₆	9	M	King Salmon Creek, B.C.	John K. Fritze	1980	John K. Fritze	64
25⁸/₁₆	15¹²/₁₆	9¹²/₁₆	M	Kuskokwim River, Alaska	Bernard V. Davis	1983	Bernard V. Davis	64
25⁷/₁₆	15¹²/₁₆	9¹¹/₁₆	M	Upper Boulder River, Mont.	Ted Johnston	1934	E. C. Cates	73
25⁷/₁₆	16	9⁷/₁₆	M	Tweedsmuir Park, B.C.	Lloyd B. Walker	1950	Lloyd B. Walker	73
25⁷/₁₆	15¹³/₁₆	9⁹/₁₆	M	Clearwater River, Alta.	Jack Allen	1957	Jack Allen	73
25⁷/₁₆	15⁵/₁₆	10⁵/₁₆	M	Zohini Creek, B.C.	Paul R. Beebe	1967	Paul R. Beebe	73
25⁷/₁₆	16⁶/₁₆	8³/₁₆	M	Nordegg, Alta.	Charles W. Matter	1974	Charles W. Matter	73
25⁷/₁₆	15¹⁴/₁₆	9⁶/₁₆	M	Kitlope River, B.C.	Darryl W. Hodson	1975	Darryl W. Hodson	73
25⁷/₁₆	15⁵/₁₆	10³/₁₆	M	Lakelse River, B.C.	William J. Harvey, Jr.	1979	William J. Harvey, Jr.	73
25⁷/₁₆	15¹⁴/₁₆	9⁹/₁₆	M	Toad River, B.C.	Paul E. Robey	1981	Paul E. Robey	73
25⁷/₁₆	16²/₁₆	9¹⁴/₁₆	M	Andreafsky River, Alaska	John C. Bruno	1981	John C. Bruno	73
25⁷/₁₆	15¹³/₁₆	9¹³/₁₆	M	Wedeene River, B.C.	Stuart Haslett	1983	Stuart Haslett	73
25⁵/₁₆	16⁶/₁₆	9	M	Slave Lake, Alta.	R. W. H. Eben-Ebenau	1944	R. W. H. Eben-Ebenau	83
25⁵/₁₆	16¹/₁₆	9⁵/₁₆	M	Kleena Kleene, B.C.	A. W. Travis	1961	A. W. Travis	83
25⁵/₁₆	15⁵/₁₆	9¹³/₁₆	M	Northway, Alaska	James A. Johnson	1964	James A. Johnson	83
25⁵/₁₆	16	9⁶/₁₆	M	Mussel Inlet, B.C.	Victor W. Budd	1967	Victor W. Budd	83
25⁵/₁₆	15¹⁰/₁₆	9¹²/₁₆	M	Edson, Alta.	Jack Armstrong	1967	Jack Armstrong	83
25⁵/₁₆	15³/₁₆	10³/₁₆	M	Brooks Range, Alaska	Rusty Pickus	1979	Rusty Pickus	83
25⁵/₁₆	15⁴/₁₆	10⁴/₁₆	M	Kuskokwim River, Alaska	Michael T. Carlucci	1981	Michael T. Carlucci	83
25⁵/₁₆	15¹²/₁₆	9¹⁰/₁₆	M	Bond Sound, B.C.	James H. Garner	1982	James H. Garner	83
25⁵/₁₆	15¹³/₁₆	9⁸/₁₆	M	Anahim Lake, B.C.	Ace Demers	1951	Ace Demers	91
25⁵/₁₆	15¹⁴/₁₆	9⁷/₁₆	M	Kwatna River, B.C.	Walter W. Butcher	1954	Walter W. Butcher	91
25⁵/₁₆	15¹/₁₆	10⁴/₁₆	M	Granite Lake, Yukon	Jim Papst	1969	Jim Papst	91
25⁵/₁₆	16⁴/₁₆	9¹³/₁₆	M	Kobuk River, Alaska	Hugh H. Chatham, Jr.	1971	Hugh H. Chatham, Jr.	91
25⁵/₁₆	16¹/₁₆	9⁹/₁₆	M	Eutsuk Lake, B.C.	W. R. Macfarlane	1974	W. R. Macfarlane	91
25⁵/₁₆	15⁷/₁₆	9⁹/₁₆	M	Brooks Range, Alaska	Warren K. Parker	1979	Warren K. Parker	91
25⁵/₁₆	16	9⁶/₁₆	M	Skowquiltz River, B.C.	Robert C. McEntee	1981	Robert C. McEntee	91
25⁵/₁₆	15⁹/₁₆	9¹⁴/₁₆	M	Scoop Lake, B.C.	Darrell A. Farr	1981	Dwight E. Farr	91
25⁴/₁₆	16³/₁₆	9⁶/₁₆	M	Tonzona River, Alaska	George G. Houser	1985	George G. Houser	91
25⁴/₁₆	15⁵/₁₆	9¹¹/₁₆	M	Anahim Lake, B.C.	C. D. Carrington	1957	Univ. Calif. Museum	91
25⁴/₁₆	16³/₁₆	9¹/₁₆	M	Salmon River, B.C.	Al Rand	1964	Al Rand	100
25⁴/₁₆	16³/₁₆	9¹²/₁₆	M	Cascade Inlet, B.C.	Walter A. Frame	1964	Walter A. Frame	100
25⁴/₁₆	15⁴/₁₆	9	M	Yanert River, Alaska	Herbert A. Biss	1965	Herbert A. Biss	100

GRIZZLY BEAR—Continued
Ursus arctos horribilis

Score	Greatest Length of Skull Without Lower Jaw	Greatest Width of Skull	Sex	Locality Killed	By Whom Killed	Owner	Date Killed	Rank
25 5/16	15 15/16	9 15/16	M	Anahim Lake, B.C.	Bernard Nofziger	Bernard Nofziger	1970	100
25 5/16	15 13/16	9 7/16	M	Kynoch Inlet, B.C.	P. J. Kennedy	W. G. Hawes	1971	100
25 5/16	15 15/16	9 5/16	M	Berland River, Alta.	Donald Brockman	Donald Brockman	1978	100
25 5/16	15 12/16	9 8/16	M	Alaska Range, Alaska	David L. Kulzer	David L. Kulzer	1979	100
25 5/16	15 10/16	9 10/16	M	Gisasa River, Alaska	Billy R. Deligans, Jr.	Billy R. Deligans, Jr.	1985	100
25 3/16	15 7/16	9 12/16	M	Bella Coola, B.C.	Umberto Benedet	Umberto Benedet	1957	109
25 3/16	16 4/16	8 15/16	M	Wrangell Mts., Alaska	Peter W. Bading	Peter W. Bading	1963	109
25 3/16	15 9/16	9 9/16	M	Teller, Alaska	Harry Armitage	Harry Armitage	1965	109
25 3/16	15 11/16	10 2/16	M	Motase Lake, B.C.	Joel Franzoia	Joel Franzoia	1970	109
25 3/16	15 9/16	9 11/16	U	McClinchy River, B.C.	Picked Up	Bernie Gano	PR1974	109
25 3/16	16 2/16	9 1/16	M	Bella Coola, B.C.	Richard K. Miller	Richard K. Miller	1975	109
25 3/16	15 6/16	9 13/16	M	American River, Alaska	John M. Griffith, Jr.	John M. Griffith, Jr.	1977	109
25 3/16	15 6/16	9 14/16	M	Andreafsky River, Alaska	James P. Barkman	James P. Barkman	1980	109
25 3/16	15 9/16	9 10/16	M	Kingcome River, B.C.	Graydon A. Peat	Graydon A. Peat	1983	109
25 3/16	15 14/16	9 6/16	M	Yellowstone River, Wyo.	Bill Nymeyer	Jack H. White	1960	118
25 2/16	16 2/16	9	M	Lignite, Alaska	Leonard Spencer	Leonard Spencer	1963	118
25 2/16	16 2/16	9	M	Mentasta Mts., Alaska	Basil C. Bradbury	Basil C. Bradbury	1965	118
25 2/16	15 13/16	9 5/16	M	Kotzebue, Alaska	F. W. Hatterscheidt	F. W. Hatterscheidt	1968	118
25 2/16	16	9 4/16	M	Bella Coola, B.C.	Howard Morrisey	Howard Morrisey	1971	118
25 2/16	15 8/16	9 9/16	M	Butedale, B.C.	Walter R. Peters	Walter R. Peters	1974	118
25 2/16	15 6/16	9 12/16	M	McGrath, Alaska	Curtis C. Classen	Curtis C. Classen	1974	118
25 2/16	15 12/16	9 6/16	M	Parsnip River, B.C.	Graham Markland	Graham Markland	1977	118
25 2/16	16	9 5/16	M	Cluculz Creek, B.C.	Ed Roberson	Ed Roberson	1978	118
25 2/16	15 6/16	9 12/16	M	Beaver Creek, Alaska	Picked Up	Abram Walter	1979	118
25 2/16	15 9/16	9 8/16	M	Blue Ridge, Alta.	Thomas E. Deacon	Thomas E. Deacon	1983	118
25 1/16	15 11/16	9 6/16	M	Teton Co., Wyo.	C. C. Craven	Jackson Hole Museum	1938	129
25 1/16	15 13/16	9 4/16	M	Knight Inlet, B.C.	Frederic N. Dodge	Frederic N. Dodge	1954	129
25 1/16	15 14/16	9 3/16	M	Bella Coola, B.C.	L. Rowe Davidson	L. Rowe Davidson	1958	129
25 1/16	15 10/16	9 7/16	M	Caribou Flats, B.C.	Edward Escott	Edward Escott	1962	129
25 1/16	15 11/16	9 9/16	M	Yanert River, Alaska	E. G. Brust, Jr.	E. G. Brust, Jr.	1964	129
25 1/16	16 3/16	8 14/16	M	Selby River, Alaska	Kenneth T. Alt	Kenneth T. Alt	1965	129

Score			Sex	Locality	By Whom Killed	Owner	Date	Rank
25 1/16	15 8/16	9 9/16	M	Bob Quinn Lake, B.C.	Dave Miscavish	Dave Miscavish	1971	129
25 1/16	15 2/16	9 1/16	M	Pikmiktalik River, Alaska	Donald B. Huffines	Donald B. Huffines	1984	129
25	16 3/16	8 13/16	M	Lewistown, Mont.	Mildred Connor	U. S. Natl. Museum	1888	137
25	16	9	M	Atnarko River, B.C.	David Maytag	H. J. Borden	1959	137
25	15 9/16	9 7/16	M	Nabesna River, Alaska	Marven Henriksen	Marven Henriksen	1964	137
25	15	10	M	Kotzebue, Alaska	Glen E. Park	Glen E. Park	1965	137
25	15 11/16	9 5/16	M	Yellowstone Natl. Park, Wyo.	Picked Up	Picked Up	PR1965	137
25	15 4/16	9 12/16	M	Hart Peaks, B.C.	T. T. Stroup	T. T. Stroup	1966	137
25	15 3/16	9 13/16	M	Mt. Hayes, Alaska	Benjamin H. Robson	Benjamin H. Robson	1968	137
25	15 4/16	9 12/16	M	Noomst Creek, B.C.	James G. Shelton	James G. Shelton	1970	137
25	15 10/16	9 9/16	M	Tacu River, B.C.	W. N. Olson	W. N. Olson	1971	137
25	15 8/16	9 8/16	M	Stikine River, B.C.	Donald R. McClure, Sr.	Donald R. McClure, Sr.	1971	137
25	15 13/16	9 3/16	U	Hinton, Alta.	Oliver Hannula	Oliver Hannula	1972	137
25	15 15/16	9 1/16	M	Whitecourt, Alta.	Sid Wheeler	Sid Wheeler	1974	137
25	15 8/16	9 8/16	M	Richland Co., Mont.	Picked Up	Jack Stewart	1976	137
25	14 14/16	10 2/16	M	Fortymile River, Alaska	James B. DeMoss	James B. DeMoss	1980	137
25	16 1/16	8 15/16	M	Owikeno Lake, B.C.	Robert K. Fisher	Robert K. Fisher	1981	137
25	15 13/16	9 13/16	M	Bella Coola River, B.C.	James G. Shelton	James G. Shelton	1983	137
25	15 6/16	9 10/16	M	Koyuk River, Alaska	John Macaluso	John Macaluso	1985	137
24 15/16	15 6/16	9 5/16	M	Taseko Lake, B.C.	A. Cecil Henry	A. Cecil Henry	1956	154
24 15/16	15 4/16	9 1/16	M	Teller, Alaska	Jack D. Putnam	Jack D. Putnam	1965	154
24 15/16	15 7/16	9 5/16	M	Dudidontu River, B.C.	Bob Loewenstein	Bob Loewenstein	1965	154
24 15/16	15 4/16	9 11/16	M	Ootsa Lake, B.C.	J. Block & D. Vantine	John Block	1965	154
24 15/16	15 10/16	9 5/16	M	Lakelse River, B.C.	Victor Lepp	Victor Lepp	1968	154
24 15/16	15 12/16	9 3/16	M	Wrangell Mts., Alaska	James E. Saxton	James E. Saxton	1977	154
24 15/16	15 13/16	9 5/16	M	Nusatsum River, B.C.	Picked Up	Randy Svisdahl	1980	154
24 15/16	15 6/16	8 12/16	M	Tonzona River, Alaska	Wayne J. Pensenstadler	Wayne J. Pensenstadler	1982	154
24 14/16	16 2/16	9 5/16	M	Atnarko, B.C.	F. N. Bard	Chicago Nat. Hist. Mus.	1938	162
24 14/16	15 12/16	9 5/16	M	Chilcotin, B.C.	R. J. Pop & J. Beban	R. J. Pop	1954	162
24 14/16	15 6/16	9 7/16	M	Atnarko River, B.C.	Carl Molander	Carl Molander	1957	162
24 14/16	15 7/16	9 3/16	M	Chisana, Alaska	Larry Folger	Larry Folger	1957	162
24 14/16	15 13/16	9 5/16	M	Meziadin Lake, B.C.	Larry T. Spangler	Larry T. Spangler	1962	162
24 14/16	15 13/16	9 5/16	M	Alaska Range, Alaska	Jack Williamson	Jack Williamson	1963	162
24 14/16	15 6/16	9 9/16	M	Brooks Range, Alaska	E. Wayne Gilley	E. Wayne Gilley	1963	162
24 14/16	16 3/16	8 11/16	M	Taku River, B.C.	Robert J. Lacy	Robert J. Lacy	1964	162
24 14/16	15 2/16	9 1/16	M	Shishmiref, Alaska	James Harrower	James Harrower	1964	162
24 14/16	16 3/16	8 11/16	M	Knights Inlet, B.C.	Levon Bender	Levon Bender	1965	162
24 14/16	15 6/16	9 8/16	M	Cassiar Mts., B.C.	H. Kenneth Seiferd	H. Kenneth Seiferd	1966	162
24 14/16	15 7/16	9 7/16	M	Brooks Range, Alaska	W. F. Krebill	W. F. Krebill	1966	162
24 14/16	15 6/16	9 7/16	M	McGregor Mts., B.C.	Edward Johnson	Edward Johnson	1967	162
24 14/16	15 6/16	9 5/16	M	McGregor River, B.C.	C. C. Carpenter	C. C. Carpenter	1968	162
24 14/16	15 12/16	9 7/16	M	Telkwa River, B.C.	Richard Pohlschneider	Richard Pohlschneider	1969	162

GRIZZLY BEAR—Continued
Ursus arctos horribilis

Score	Greatest Length of Skull Without Lower Jaw	Greatest Width of Skull	Sex	Locality Killed	By Whom Killed	Owner	Date Killed	Rank
24 14/16	15 6/16	9 8/16	M	Seaskinnish Creek, B.C.	Thomas D. J. Fulkco	Thomas D. J. Fulkco	1977	162
24 14/16	15 3/16	9 11/16	M	Klutina River, Alaska	Robert M. Decker	Robert M. Decker	1979	162
24 14/16	15 10/16	9 4/16	M	Andreafsky River, Alaska	James W. Latreille	James W. Latreille	1980	162
24 14/16	15 8/16	9 6/16	M	Tatla Lake, B.C.	Donald L. Gardner	Donald L. Gardner	1980	162
24 14/16	15 15/16	8 15/16	M	Barney Creek, B.C.	Roy Pattison	Roy Pattison	1984	162
24 13/16	15 7/16	9 6/16	M	Chisana River, Alaska	Larry Folger	Larry Folger	1957	182
24 13/16	15 9/16	9 4/16	M	Livengood, Alaska	Ada Holst	Ada Holst	1961	182
24 13/16	15 3/16	9 9/16	M	Tatla Lake, B.C.	R. D. Brooks	R. D. Brooks	1962	182
24 13/16	15 5/16	9 6/16	M	Tonzona River, Alaska	Francis Kernan	Francis Kernan	1964	182
24 13/16	15 4/16	9 4/16	M	Clarence Lake, Alaska	E. A. Munroe	E. A. Munroe	1964	182
24 13/16	15 12/16	9 1/16	M	Warden Creek, Alta.	Harvey R. Cook	Harvey R. Cook	1964	182
24 13/16	15 12/16	9 1/16	M	Chetwynd, B.C.	William E. Dugger	William E. Dugger	1964	182
24 13/16	15 6/16	9 2/16	M	Slim Lake, B.C.	Freda Stalder	Freda Stalder	1968	182
24 13/16	15 4/16	9 6/16	M	Noatak River, Alaska	John E. Batson	John E. Batson	1970	182
24 13/16	15 11/16	9 6/16	M	Telkwa Range, B.C.	Jack Adams	Jack Adams	1978	182
24 13/16	15 11/16	9 2/16	M	Kilbella River, B.C.	Larry Sawchuk	Larry Sawchuk	1984	182
24 13/16	15 14/16	8 14/16	M	Burnt Trail Creek, B.C.	Tom Housh	Tom Housh	1985	182
24 12/16	15 8/16	8 15/16	M	Spanish Lake, B.C.	Bill Niemi	Bill Niemi	1953	194
24 12/16	15 8/16	9 4/16	M	Sheep Creek, Alta	R. V. Broadbent	R. V. Broadbent	1963	194
24 12/16	15	9 6/16	M	Brooks Range, Alaska	Lewis A. Meyers	Lewis A. Meyers	1964	194
24 12/16	15 10/16	9 12/16	M	Terminus Mtn., B.C.	Herb Klein	Herb Klein	1965	194
24 12/16	15 8/16	9 6/16	M	Kitimat, B.C.	Hans Lackner	Hans Lackner	1969	194
24 12/16	15 3/16	9 4/16	M	Burrage Creek, B.C.	Jack Worthy	Jack Worthy	1970	194
24 12/16	15 15/16	8 13/16	M	Toklat River, Alaska	George P. Mann	George P. Mann	1971	194
24 12/16	15 8/16	9 3/16	M	Bella Coola, B.C.	Joe M. Colvin	Joe M. Colvin	1973	194
24 12/16	15 4/16	9 8/16	M	Alaska Range, Alaska	Earl K. Edstrom	Earl K. Edstrom	1976	194
24 12/16	15 8/16	9 4/16	M	Wigwam River, B.C.	Ray S. Koontz	Ray S. Koontz	1977	194
24 12/16	15	9 12/16	M	Turnagain River, B.C.	Arthur E. Crawford	Arthur E. Crawford	1980	194
24 11/16	15 4/16	9 7/16	M	Tok River, Alaska	Lewis B. Wyman	Lewis B. Wyman	1965	205
24 11/16	15 7/16	9 6/16	M	Stevens Lake, B.C.	R. L. Hambrick	R. L. Hambrick	1965	205
24 11/16	15 7/16	9 11/16	M	MacMillan Plateau, Yukon	Paul Yeager	Paul Yeager	1967	205

24 11/16	15 14/16	8 13/16	U	Lesser Slave Lake, Alta.	Picked Up	James Erickson	1967	205
24 11/16	15 6/16	9 7/16	M	Alaska Range, Alaska	Tony Caputo	Tony Caputo	1967	205
24 11/16	15 8/16	9 3/16	M	Butte Inlet, B.C.	Thomas M. Utigard	Thomas M. Utigard	1970	205
24 11/16	15	9 11/16	M	Toklat River, Alaska	Timothy A. Sanderson	Timothy A. Sanderson	1976	205
24 11/16	15 6/16	9 6/16	M	Kuzitrin River, Alaska	H. Doak Neal	H. Doak Neal	1976	205
24 11/16	15 3/16	9 8/16	M	Toad River, B.C.	Bruce H. Morrill	Bruce H. Morrill	1980	205
24 9/16	15 6/16	9 6/16	M	Kwatna Bay, B.C.	Norm Roettger	Norm Roettger	1982	205
24 9/16	15 4/16	9 5/16	M	Point Hope, Alaska	Richard K. Siller	Richard K. Siller	1965	215
24 9/16	15 8/16	9 2/16	M	Camp Island Lake, B.C.	Harold L. Jones	Harold L. Jones	1965	215
24 9/16	15 6/16	9 5/16	M	Brooks Range, Alaska	T. W. Bohannan	T. W. Bohannan	1968	215
24 9/16	15 11/16	8 15/16	M	Seymour Inlet, B.C.	Tim Fischer	Tim Fischer	1969	215
24 9/16	15 6/16	9 6/16	M	Wiseman, Alaska	David L. Howard	David L. Howard	1970	215
24 9/16	15 6/16	9 6/16	M	Toklat River, Alaska	Gary Miller	Gary Miller	1972	215
24 9/16	15 6/16	9 6/16	M	Mosley Creek, B.C.	Charles Harvey	Charles Harvey	1976	215
24 9/16	15 4/16	9 6/16	M	Alaska Range, Alaska	Victor Geibel	Victor Geibel	1978	215
24 9/16	15 6/16	9 6/16	M	Toklat River, Alaska	Howard W. Neice	Howard W. Neice	1981	215
24 9/16	14 12/16	9 14/16	M	John River, Alaska	Rick J. Schikora	Rick J. Schikora	1982	215
24 9/16	15 3/16	9 7/16	M	Pilgrim River, Alaska	Karen J. Chadwick	Karen J. Chadwick	1982	215
24 9/16	15 6/16	9 3/16	M	Whiteswan Lake, B.C.	A. C. Gilbert	A. C. Gilbert	1937	215
24 6/16	15 13/16	8 12/16	M	Tatla Lake, B.C.	D. McDermott	D. McDermott	1954	226
24 6/16	15 13/16	9 5/16	U	Bella Coola, B.C.	William P. Mastrangel	William P. Mastrangel	1956	226
24 6/16	15 6/16	9 6/16	M	Atnarko River, B.C.	Martin Anderson	Martin Anderson	1957	226
24 6/16	15 6/16	9 2/16	M	Owikeno Lake, B.C.	Norman W. Garwood	Norman W. Garwood	1960	226
24 6/16	15 7/16	9 6/16	M	Hulahula River, Alaska	Richard Sjoden	Richard Sjoden	1963	226
24 6/16	15 4/16	9 6/16	M	Ray Mts., Alaska	Mario Grassi	Mario Grassi	1965	226
24 6/16	16 6/16	8 8/16	M	Anahim Lake, B.C.	M. V. Nearing	M. V. Nearing	1966	226
24 6/16	15 6/16	9 4/16	M	Tok River, Alaska	John W. Waller	John W. Waller	1968	226
24 6/16	15 6/16	9 3/16	M	Meziadin Lake, B.C.	Teuvo Pahti	Teuvo Pahti	1968	226
24 6/16	15 1/16	9 8/16	M	Cape Lisburne, Alaska	Gerrit N. Vandenberg	Gerrit N. Vandenberg	1969	226
24 6/16	15 6/16	9	M	Kispiox River, B.C.	W.J. Love	W. J. Love	1971	226
24 6/16	16	8 6/16	M	Graham River, B.C.	Edward F. Lundberg	Edward F. Lundberg	1976	226
24 6/16	14 15/16	9 10/16	M	Yanert River, Alaska	Robert J. Barham	Robert J. Barham	1977	226
24 6/16	15	9 6/16	M	Quesnel Lake, B.C.	Thomas E. Phillippe, Sr.	Thomas E. Phillippe, Sr.	1978	226
24 6/16	15 13/16	8 12/16	M	Chuckwalla River, B.C.	George B. Morris	George B. Morris	1979	226
24 6/16	15 7/16	9 3/16	M	Motase Peak, B.C.	Roger L. Pock	Roger L. Pock	1984	226
24 8/16	14 11/16	9 13/16	M	Mt. McKinley, Alaska	Howard W. Pollock	Howard W. Pollock	1953	243
24 8/16	15 2/16	9 6/16	M	Cassiar Mts., B.C.	Elgin T. Gates	Elgin T. Gates	1953	243
24 8/16	15	9 6/16	M	Bella Coola, B.C.	James A. Perry	H. J. Borden	1959	243
24 8/16	15 6/16	9 6/16	M	Big Delta, Alaska	Harold E. Hogan	Harold E. Hogan	1961	243
24 8/16	14 15/16	9 6/16	M	Tatla Lake, B.C.	Harold A. Cowman	Harold A. Cowman	1964	243
24 8/16	15 13/16	8 11/16	M	Kleena Kleene River, B.C.	Martin J. Durkan	Martin J. Durkan	1966	243
24 8/16	15 2/16	9 6/16	M	Kotzebue, Alaska	C. J. McElroy	C. J. McElroy	1968	243

GRIZZLY BEAR—Continued
Ursus arctos horribilis

Score	Greatest Length of Skull Without Lower Jaw	Greatest Width of Skull	Sex	Locality Killed	By Whom Killed	Owner	Date Killed	Rank
$24\frac{6}{16}$	$15\frac{1}{16}$	$9\frac{9}{16}$	M	Brooks Range, Alaska	Jerry N. Martin	Jerry N. Martin	1968	243
$24\frac{6}{16}$	$15\frac{2}{16}$	$9\frac{6}{16}$	M	Tweedsmuir Park, B.C.	Tom & Clara Ritter	Tom & Clara Ritter	1969	243
$24\frac{6}{16}$	$15\frac{2}{16}$	$9\frac{7}{16}$	M	Brooks Range, Alaska	Rick Reakoff	Rick Reakoff	1969	243
$24\frac{6}{16}$	$14\frac{11}{16}$	$9\frac{13}{16}$	M	Lakelse River, B.C.	Kolbjorn Eide	Kolbjorn Eide	1970	243
$24\frac{6}{16}$	$15\frac{6}{16}$	$9\frac{2}{16}$	M	Coast Range, B.C.	L. D. Hirzel & J. Petersen	Laverne D. Hirzel	1971	243
$24\frac{6}{16}$	$14\frac{14}{16}$	$9\frac{10}{16}$	M	Miner Lake, B.C.	Dwight E. Farr, Jr.	Dwight E. Farr, Jr.	1971	243
$24\frac{6}{16}$	$14\frac{12}{16}$	$9\frac{12}{16}$	M	Stikine River, B.C.	Fred P. Grob	Fred P. Grob	1973	243
$24\frac{6}{16}$	$15\frac{5}{16}$	$9\frac{3}{16}$	M	Tonzona River, B.C.	Jill L. Nunley	Jill L. Nunley	1974	243
$24\frac{6}{16}$	$15\frac{5}{16}$	$9\frac{3}{16}$	M	Colville River, Alaska	Richard A. McClellan	Richard A. McClellan	1974	243
$24\frac{6}{16}$	$14\frac{13}{16}$	$9\frac{1}{16}$	M	Ogilvie Mts., Yukon	Vearl Fowler	Vearl Fowler	1976	243
$24\frac{6}{16}$	$15\frac{2}{16}$	$9\frac{6}{16}$	M	Brooks Range, Alaska	Calvin Danzig	Calvin Danzig	1977	243
$24\frac{6}{16}$	$15\frac{6}{16}$	$8\frac{15}{16}$	M	Table River, B.C.	George W. Morris	George W. Morris	1978	243
$24\frac{6}{16}$	$15\frac{7}{16}$	$9\frac{1}{16}$	M	Kugururok River, Alaska	Bruce A. Moe	Bruce A. Moe	1978	243
$24\frac{6}{16}$	$15\frac{5}{16}$	$9\frac{6}{16}$	M	Fraser River, B.C.	Paul F. Bays, Sr.	Paul F. Bays, Sr.	1978	243
$24\frac{6}{16}$	15	$9\frac{6}{16}$	M	Terminus Mt., B.C.	William E. Greehey	William E. Greehey	1982	243
$24\frac{6}{16}$	$15\frac{1}{16}$	$9\frac{7}{16}$	M	Koyuk, Alaska	K. James Malady III	K. James Malady III	1985	243
$24\frac{5}{16}$	15	$9\frac{7}{16}$	M	Cold Fish Lake, B.C.	William E. Goudey	William E. Goudey	1956	266
$24\frac{5}{16}$	$15\frac{8}{16}$	$8\frac{15}{16}$	M	Dease River, B.C.	John Caputo	John Caputo	1958	266
$24\frac{5}{16}$	$15\frac{6}{16}$	$9\frac{1}{16}$	M	Brooks Range, Alaska	Bobbie J. Cavnar	Bobbie J. Cavnar	1966	266
$24\frac{5}{16}$	$15\frac{5}{16}$	$9\frac{2}{16}$	M	McClaren Glacier, Alaska	Gordon S. Pleiss	Gordon S. Pleiss	1967	266
$24\frac{5}{16}$	$15\frac{7}{16}$	9	M	Brooks Range, Alaska	Don Elder	Don Elder	1968	266
$24\frac{5}{16}$	$15\frac{4}{16}$	$9\frac{3}{16}$	M	Ocena Falls, B.C.	Richard D. Dimick	Richard D. Dimick	1969	266
$24\frac{5}{16}$	$15\frac{2}{16}$	$9\frac{5}{16}$	M	Colville River, Alaska	Alfonso I. Casso	Alfonso I. Casso	1970	266
$24\frac{5}{16}$	$15\frac{5}{16}$	$9\frac{1}{16}$	M	Grande Cache, Alta.	Laurier Adam	Laurier Adam	1976	266
$24\frac{5}{16}$	$15\frac{8}{16}$	$8\frac{15}{16}$	M	Kelly Creek, B.C.	Rick H. Jackson	Rick H. Jackson	1980	266
$24\frac{5}{16}$	$15\frac{5}{16}$	$9\frac{2}{16}$	M	Alaska Hwy. Mile 175, B.C.	Kerry Q. Gronewold	Kerry Q. Gronewold	1984	266
$24\frac{4}{16}$	15	$9\frac{6}{16}$	M	Alaska Range, Alaska	Selmer Torrison	Selmer Torrison	1958	276
$24\frac{4}{16}$	$15\frac{2}{16}$	$9\frac{6}{16}$	M	Alaska Range, Alaska	Hank Kramer	Hank Kramer	1964	276
$24\frac{4}{16}$	$14\frac{10}{16}$	$9\frac{12}{16}$	M	Yanert River, Alaska	P. W. LaHaye	P. W. LaHaye	1965	276
$24\frac{4}{16}$	$15\frac{5}{16}$	$9\frac{1}{16}$	M	Alaska Range, Alaska	Alberto Pipia	Alberto Pipia	1966	276
$24\frac{4}{16}$	$14\frac{15}{16}$	$9\frac{7}{16}$	M	Brooks Range, Alaska	Paul H. Magee	Paul H. Magee	1967	276

				Locality				
24 9/16	15 6/16	9	M	Atlin, B.C.	Jack E. Carpenter	Jack E. Carpenter	1967	276
24 6/16	14 12/16	9 10/16	M	Prince George, B.C.	Wayne H. Laursen	Wayne H. Laursen	1969	276
24 6/16	15	9 6/16	M	Colville River, Alaska	E. H. Borchers, Jr.	E. H. Borchers, Jr.	1970	276
24 6/16	15 3/16	8 14/16	M	Wrangell Mts., Alaska	Victor W. Bullard	Victor W. Bullard	1971	276
24 6/16	14 14/16	9 8/16	M	Ogilvie Mts., Yukon	Philip R. Murphy	Philip R. Murphy	1972	276
24 6/16	15 6/16	9 6/16	M	Cassiar Mts., B.C.	Monte Hofstrand	Monte Hofstrand	1975	276
24 6/16	14 11/16	9 11/16	M	Kelly River, Alaska	J. B. Goodman & E. Remsing	James B. Goodman	1976	276
24 6/16	15	9 6/16	M	Alaska Range, Alaska	Steve Casey	Larry W. Casey	1977	276
24 6/16	15 10/16	9 6/16	M	Murray River, B.C.	Carl Kortmeyer	Carl Kortmeyer	1980	276
24 6/16	15 6/16	8 12/16	M	Clyak River, B.C.	Marvin Opp	Marvin Opp	1983	276
24 6/16	15 3/16	9 6/16	M	Nalbeelah Creek, B.C.	Wayne Moon	Wayne Moon	1983	276
24 6/16	15 6/16	9 6/16	M	Tagagawik River, Alaska	Roland L. Quimby	Roland L. Quimby	1983	276
24 6/16	15 6/16	9 6/16	M	Knight Inlet, B.C.	Norman W. Dougan	Norman W. Dougan	1984	276
24 6/16	15 6/16	8 15/16	M	Bear Berry, Alta.	Phil Temple	Phil Temple	1958	294
24 6/16	14 6/16	8 12/16	M	Kitimat, B.C.	Ewald Kirschner	Ewald Kirschner	1958	294
24 3/16	15 3/16	9 5/16	M	Blackstone River, Alta.	Wilhelm Eichenauer	Wilhelm Eichenauer	1963	294
24 6/16	15 7/16	9 6/16	M	Nabesna River, Alaska	C. W. Houle	C. W. Houle	1965	294
24 6/16	15 6/16	8 14/16	M	Cassiar Mts., B.C.	Henry E. High	Henry E. High	1965	294
24 6/16	15 6/16	9 6/16	M	Teller, Alaska	Bill Glunt	Bill Glunt	1965	294
24 6/16	15 6/16	9 6/16	M	Tetachuck Lake, B.C.	Torben Dahl	Torben Dahl	1966	294
24 6/16	14 10/16	9 11/16	M	Brooks Range, Alaska	Robert L. Cohen	Robert L. Cohen	1967	294
24 6/16	16	8 5/16	M	Edson, Alta.	Otto Braaz	Otto Braaz	1969	294
24 6/16	14 14/16	9 6/16	M	Toba Inlet, B.C.	Jack C. Glover	Jack C. Glover	1970	294
24 6/16	15 7/16	8 14/16	M	Graham River, B.C.	William J. Fogarty, Jr.	William J. Fogarty, Jr.	1978	294
24 6/16	15 7/16	8 14/16	M	Chatsquot Creek, B.C.	Roger J. Ahern	Roger J. Ahern	1978	294
24 6/16	14 15/16	9 6/16	M	Selwyn Creek, Yukon	Rod G. Hardie	Rod G. Hardie	1979	294
24 6/16	15 6/16	8 15/16	M	Cranberry River, B.C.	Fred Y. C. Wong	Albert Wong	1982	294
24 6/16	15 6/16	9 6/16	M	Dease Lake, B.C.	G. C. F. Dalziel	G. C. F. Dalziel	1956	308
24 6/16	15 10/16	8 12/16	M	South Hay River, Alta.	Bert Shearer	Bert Shearer	1957	308
24 6/16	14 13/16	8 10/16	M	Selkirk Mt., B.C.	Eli Paulson	Eli Paulson	1957	308
24 6/16	14 6/16	9 7/16	M	Kotzebue, Alaska	Don D. Giles	Don D. Giles	1965	308
24 6/16	15 6/16	9 6/16	M	Kuskokwim River, Alaska	Edward W. Williams	Edward W. Williams	1967	308
24 6/16	14 6/16	9 6/16	M	Brooks Range, Alaska	Stanley Blazovich	Stanley Blazovich	1970	308
24 6/16	15 6/16	9 6/16	M	Bella Coola, B.C.	Howard Creason	Howard Creason	1971	308
24 6/16	15 7/16	9 6/16	M	Sheep Creek, Alta.	Rolly Balzer	Rolly Balzer	1972	308
24 6/16	14 9/16	8 13/16	M	Nilkitkwa River, B.C.	Roger Britton	Roger Britton	1976	308
24 6/16	15 6/16	9 6/16	M	Trout Lake, B.C.	Paul L. Reese	Paul L. Reese	1982	308
24 3/16	15 3/16	9	M	Nabesna, Alaska	Ernest B. Schur	Ernest B. Schur	1958	318
24 3/16	15 8/16	9 6/16	M	Gardiner, Mont.	Marguerite McDonald	Marguerite McDonald	1964	318
24 3/16	14 4/16	8 11/16	M	Moose Creek, B.C.	R. Angell	R. Angell	1964	318
24 3/16	15 2/16	9 6/16	M	Toba Inlet, B.C.	Kenneth L. Wagner, Jr.	Kenneth L. Wagner, Jr.	1968	318
24 3/16	14 14/16	9 5/16	M	Likely, B.C.	Louis Tremblay	Louis Tremblay	1970	318

GRIZZLY BEAR—*Continued*
Ursus arctos horribilis

Score	Greatest Length of Skull Without Lower Jaw	Greatest Width of Skull	Sex	Locality Killed	By Whom Killed	Owner	Date Killed	Rank
24 4/16	15 1/8	9 2/16	M	Alaska Range, Alaska	Gilbert L. Shelton	Gilbert L. Shelton	1975	318
24 4/16	14 3/8	9 4/16	M	Tetlin Indian Res., Alaska	Robert B. Rhyne	Robert B. Rhyne	1976	318
24 4/16	15 2/16	9 1/16	M	Parsnip River, B.C.	Richard O. A. Gunther	Richard O. A. Gunther	1976	318
24 4/16	15 6/16	8 13/16	M	Big River, Alaska	Dale G. Moffat	Dale G. Moffat	1977	318
24 4/16	14 13/16	9 6/16	M	Kuskokwim River, Alaska	Roger J. Ahern	Roger J. Ahern	1977	318
24 4/16	15 5/8	8 11/16	M	Nusatsum River, B.C.	Randy Svisdahl	Randy Svisdahl	1983	318
24 4/16	15	9 3/16	M	White Creek, Alaska	J. H. Harvey & V. Landt	John H. Harvey, Jr.	1985	318
24 3/16	15 3/16	8 15/16	M	Chisana River, Alaska	Larry Folger	Larry Folger	1961	330
24 3/16	14 15/16	9 3/16	M	McDonnell Lake, B.C.	W. C. Gardiner	W. C. Gardiner	1966	330
24 3/16	15 2/16	9	M	Dawson City, Yukon	Donald R. Hull	Ray C. Dillman	1971	330
24 3/16	15 6/16	8 8/16	M	Bella Coola, B.C.	Hugh M. Klein	Hugh M. Klein	1972	330
24 3/16	15	9 2/16	M	Sikanni Chief River, B.C.	Dale E. Mirr	Dale E. Mirr	1973	330
24 3/16	15 2/16	8 14/16	M	Quintette Mt., B.C.	Dennis J. Brady	Dennis J. Brady	1977	330
24 3/16	15 5/16	9 1/16	M	Chatanika River, Alaska	Robert L. Nelson	Robert L. Nelson	1981	330
24 3/16	15 5/16	8 8/16	M	Koeye River, B.C.	William H. Dunstan IV	William H. Dunstan IV	1983	330
24 3/16	15 5/16	8 8/16	M	Kuskokwim River, Alaska	Anthony J. Bianchi	Anthony J. Bianchi	1984	330
24 2/16	15 9/16	8 7/16	M	Lake Owikeno, B.C.	R. C. Bentzen	R. C. Bentzen	1960	339
24 2/16	15 9/16	8 14/16	M	Flathead Co., Mont.	T. H. Soldowski	T. H. Soldowski	1963	339
24 2/16	15 3/16	9 5/16	M	Brooks Range, Alaska	Ted Schlaepfer	Ted Schlaepfer	1964	339
24 2/16	14 13/16	9 3/16	M	Nabesna River, Alaska	F. C. Hibben	F. C. Hibben	1967	339
24 2/16	14 14/16	9 2/16	M	Quesnel, B.C.	Larry Chaves	Larry Chaves	1968	339
24 2/16	14 5/16	9 8/16	M	Toklat River, Alaska	Ronald Lauretti	Ronald Lauretti	1971	339
24 2/16	14 9/16	9 2/16	M	Gataga River, B.C.	James E. Carson	James E. Carson	1977	339
24 2/16	14 15/16	8 15/16	M	Tatlatui Lake, B.C.	Paul S. Burke, Jr.	Paul S. Burke, Jr.	1978	339
24 2/16	15 5/16	9 3/16	M	Sukunka River, B.C.	Albert R. Heikel, Jr.	Albert R. Heikel, Jr.	1979	339
24 2/16	14 14/16	9 1/16	M	King Salmon River, B.C.	Phil Forte	Phil Forte	1981	339
24 2/16	15	9	M	Noatak River, Alaska	Stephen P. Connell	Stephen P. Connell	1984	339
24 2/16	15 5/16	9 6/16	M	Pine River, B.C.	Brian R. Goates	Brian R. Goates	1985	339
24	14 11/16	9 6/16	M	Bella Coola, B.C.	Wynn Beebe	Wynn Beebe	1960	351
24	15 5/16	8 11/16	M	Wood River, Alaska	Gordon Studer	Gordon Studer	1963	351
24	15 2/16	8 14/16	M	Cantwell, Alaska	Donald R. Johnson	Donald R. Johnson	1964	351

24	14¹¹/₁₆	9⁹/₁₆	M	Little Tok River, Alaska	Herbert F. Fassler	Herbert F. Fassler	1966	351
24	15	9	M	Fernie, B.C.	James Sloan	James Sloan	1967	351
24	14¹⁴/₁₆	9²/₁₆	M	Fairbanks, Alaska	Rudolf von Strasser	Rudolf von Strasser	1968	351
24	14⁹/₁₆	9⁷/₁₆	M	Alaska Range, Alaska	R. A. Schriewer	R. A. Schriewer	1969	351
24	15¹²/₁₆	8⁴/₁₆	M	Bella Coola, B.C.	Alton A. Myhrvold	Alton A. Myhrvold	1969	351
24	14¹⁴/₁₆	9²/₁₆	M	Canyon Lake, B.C.	Luther E. Lilly	Luther E. Lilly	1970	351
24	14⁹/₁₆	9⁷/₁₆	M	Ayiyak River, Alaska	Tom Toscano	Tom Toscano	1971	351
24	14¹²/₁₆	9⁴/₁₆	M	Kuskokwim Mts., Alaska	James V. Travis	James V. Travis	1974	351
24	15¹/₁₆	8¹²/₁₆	M	Ram River, Alta.	Howard Bugg	Howard Bugg	1976	351
24	14¹²/₁₆	9⁹/₁₆	M	Andreafsky River, Alaska	Bruce K. Kent	Bruce K. Kent	1980	351
24	15⁶/₁₆	8¹¹/₁₆	M	Kitsumkalum River, B.C.	Bill Gourlie	Bill Gourlie	1984	351
27¹/₁₆*	17¹/₁₆	10	M	Alexis Creek, B.C.	Doug Edman	Doug Edman	1970	
26⁶/₁₆*	16	10³/₁₆	M	Tok River, Alaska	Garlen Keen	Garlen Keen	1983	
26⁶/₁₆*	16⁵/₁₆	9¹¹/₁₆	M	Wells Creek, Alaska	Wayman H. Hall, Jr.	Wayman H. Hall, Jr.	1978	

*Final Score subject to revision by additional verifying measurements

Photograph by Dick Chace, U. S. Fish & Wildlife Service

ALASKA BROWN BEARS

Alaska Brown Bear

Ursus arctos middendorffi and certain related subspecies

Minimum Score 28

Score	Greatest Length of Skull Without Lower Jaw	Greatest Width of Skull	Sex	Locality Killed	By Whom Killed	Owner	Date Killed	Rank
30 12/16	17 15/16	12 13/16	M	Kodiak Island, Alaska	Roy Lindsley	Los Angeles Co. Museum	1952	1
30 11/16	18 9/16	12 2/16	M	Kodiak Island, Alaska	Erling Hansen	Erling Hansen	1961	2
30 9/16	18 7/16	12 2/16	M	Kodiak Island, Alaska	Fred A. Henton	Los Angeles Co. Museum	1938	3
30 8/16	18 12/16	11 12/16	M	Bear River, Alaska	Cap Wagner	Univ. Calif. Museum	PR1908	4
30 8/16	18	12 8/16	M	Kodiak Island, Alaska	W. S. Brophy, Jr. & W. E. McClure	W. S. Brophy III	1966	4
30 7/16	19 13/16	10 10/16	M	Port Heiden, Alaska	Herschel A. Lamb	Herschel A. Lamb	1961	6
30 5/16	18	12 5/16	M	Deadman Bay, Alaska	Grancel Fitz	Mrs. Grancel Fitz	1955	7
30 4/16	18 7/16	11 8/16	M	Kodiak Island, Alaska	Donald S. Hopkins	National Collection	1940	8
30 4/16	18	12 6/16	M	Kodiak Island, Alaska	Jack Roach	Jack Roach	1947	8
30 4/16	18 7/16	12 6/16	M	Kodiak Island, Alaska	T. H. McGregor	T. H. McGregor	1960	8
30 3/16	18	12 3/16	M	Kodiak Island, Alaska	W. J. Fisher	U. S. Natl. Museum	PR1904	11
30 3/16	18 7/16	11 7/16	M	Kodiak Island, Alaska	Oliver L. Durbin	Oliver L. Durbin	1952	11
30 3/16	18	12 2/16	M	Kodiak Island, Alaska	A. L. Hooker	A. L. Hooker	1958	11
30 2/16	18 6/16	11 11/16	M	Uyak Bay, Alaska	Walter H. White	Walter H. White	1954	14
30 2/16	18	12	M	Kodiak Island, Alaska	Dave Connor	Dave Connor	1957	14
30 1/16	18 6/16	11 14/16	M	Kodiak Island, Alaska	Seymour P. Smith	U. S. Natl. Museum	1927	16
30 1/16	18 3/16	11 15/16	M	Kodiak Island, Alaska	John M. Tait	John M. Tait	1957	16
30 1/16	18 6/16	11 9/16	M	Alinchak Bay, Alaska	Clarence R. Scott	Clarence R. Scott	1961	16
29 15/16	18 6/16	11 6/16	M	Kodiak Island, Alaska	Donald S. Hopkins	National Collection	1939	19
29 15/16	18 6/16	11 11/16	M	Unimak Island, Alaska	Samuel Atkinson	Samuel & Florence Atkinson	1953	19
29 14/16	18 6/16	11 14/16	M	Kodiak Island, Alaska	Fred W. Shield	Fred W. Shield	1950	21
29 14/16	18	11 15/16	M	Kodiak Island, Alaska	Unknown	Kim Clark	1958	21
29 14/16	17 15/16	12 4/16	M	Kodiak Island, Alaska	H. F. Primosch	H. F. Primosch	1959	21
29 3/16	17 9/16	11 8/16	M	Nelson Lagoon, Alaska	Unknown	Harry H. Webb	1946	24
29 3/16	18 5/16	11 6/16	M	Cold Bay, Alaska	Robert C. Reeve	Am. Mus. Nat. History	1948	24
29 3/16	18 6/16	11 8/16	M	Alaska Pen., Alaska	Lud W. Rettig	Denver Mus. Nat. History	1955	24
29 3/16	17 13/16	11 15/16	M	Alaska Pen., Alaska	Don Johnson	Don Johnson	1962	24
29 2/16	18 1/16	11 6/16	M	Kodiak Island, Alaska	William D. Holmes	William D. Holmes	1957	28
29 2/16	17 13/16	11 6/16	M	Alaska Pen., Alaska	Russell J. Uhl	Russell J. Uhl	1963	28
29 1/16	17 13/16	11 4/16	M	Kodiak Island, Alaska	Herman Gibson	Herman Gibson	1951	30

147

ALASKA BROWN BEAR—*Continued*

Ursus arctos middendorffi and certain related subspecies

Score	Greatest Length of Skull Without Lower Jaw	Greatest Width of Skull	Sex	Locality Killed	By Whom Killed	Owner	Date Killed	Rank
29 11/16	17 9/16	12 2/16	M	Kodiak Island, Alaska	James H. Nash	James H. Nash	1954	30
29 11/16	17 12/16	11 15/16	M	Kodiak Island, Alaska	A. J. Taylor & E. A. Chappell	Allen J. Taylor	1976	30
29 10/16	17 13/16	11 13/16	M	Kodiak Island, Alaska	Eddie W. Stinnett	Eddie W. Stinnett	1974	33
29 9/16	19 1/16	10 8/16	M	Unimak Island, Alaska	A. C. Gilbert	A. C. Gilbert	1950	34
29 9/16	17 7/16	12 2/16	M	Kodiak, Alaska	Peter W. Bading	Peter W. Bading	1964	34
29 8/16	17 14/16	11 9/16	M	Kodiak Island, Alaska	Elmer M. & Helen Rusten	Elmer M. Rusten	1941	36
29 8/16	18 14/16	10 9/16	M	Mother Goose Lake, Alaska	Tom Moore	Chicago Nat. Hist. Mus.	1947	36
29 8/16	17 3/16	11 11/16	M	Kodiak Island, Alaska	F. W. Crail	F. W. Crail	1950	36
29 8/16	18 5/16	11 7/16	M	Cold Bay, Alaska	W. P. Waltz	W. P. Waltz	1953	36
29 8/16	17 10/16	11 14/16	M	Kodiak Island, Alaska	W. H. Cothrum	W. H. Cothrum	1953	36
29 8/16	17 12/16	11 12/16	M	Kodiak Island, Alaska	Carlos Alden	Carlos Alden	1956	36
29 8/16	18 5/16	11 7/16	M	Alaska Pen., Alaska	Charles Gates	Charles Gates	1960	36
29 8/16	18	11 8/16	M	Alaska Pen., Alaska	Sam Pancotto	Sam Pancotto	1963	36
29 8/16	18 5/16	11 9/16	M	Port Heiden, Alaska	Robert J. Miller	Robert J. Miller	1971	36
29 8/16	17 2/16	11 9/16	M	Sturgeon River, Alaska	Anthony Gioffre	Anthony Gioffre	1984	36
29 7/16	17 10/16	11 12/16	M	Kodiak Island, Alaska	Robert R. Snodgrass	Robert R. Snodgrass	1949	46
29 7/16	17 9/16	11 13/16	M	Deadman Bay, Alaska	Ira M. Piper	Ira M. Piper	1954	46
29 7/16	17 11/16	11 15/16	M	Kodiak Island, Alaska	Keith Chisholm	Keith Chisholm	1956	46
29 7/16	17 13/16	11 12/16	M	Kodiak Island, Alaska	Richard Van Dyke	Richard Van Dyke	1957	46
29 7/16	17 13/16	11 10/16	M	Kodiak Island, Alaska	H. I. H. Prince Abdorreza Pahlavi	H. I. H. Prince Abdorreza Pahlavi	1967	46
29 6/16	17 13/16	11 6/16	M	Belkofski Bay, Alaska	Laurenti Kuzakin	U. S. Natl. Museum	1897	51
29 6/16	18 2/16	11 4/16	M	Pavlof Bay, Alaska	Willie Pavlof	U. S. Natl. Museum	1897	51
29 6/16	17 15/16	11 7/16	M	Pavlof Bay, Alaska	H. Cutting	U. S. Natl. Museum	1917	51
29 6/16	18	11 6/16	M	Cold Bay, Alaska	Ira A. Minnick	U. S. Natl. Museum	1923	51
29 6/16	18 5/16	11 6/16	M	Alaska Pen., Alaska	E. I. Garrett	Am. Mus. Nat. History	1926	51
29 6/16	17 9/16	11 13/16	M	Kodiak Island, Alaska	John S. Day	John S. Day	1953	51
29 6/16	17 9/16	12	M	Amook Island, Alaska	Albert C. Bledsoe	Albert C. Bledsoe	1959	51
29 6/16	18 5/16	11 3/16	M	Kodiak Island, Alaska	Herb Klein	Herb Klein	1965	51
29 6/16	18 5/16	11	M	Stepovak Bay, Alaska	Roy Fencl	Roy Fencl	1966	51
29 6/16	18 5/16	10 14/16	M	Cold Bay, Alaska	Edwin Mallinkrodt, Jr.	U. S. Natl. Museum	1920	60

				Location	By	Owner	Date	Rank
29 7/16	17 12/16	11 9/16	M	Sand Lake, Alaska	William A. Fisher	William A. Fisher	1953	60
29 5/16	17 13/16	11 8/16	M	Kodiak Island, Alaska	Picked Up	Am. Mus. Nat. History	PR1957	60
29 4/16	17 14/16	11 9/16	M	Kodiak Island, Alaska	A. C. Skinner, Jr.	A. C. Skinner, Jr.	1951	63
29 4/16	17 9/16	11 14/16	M	Kodiak Island, Alaska	H. R. Eavey & H. Wright	Harry R. Eavey	1960	63
29 4/16	17 15/16	11 5/16	M	Alaska Pen., Alaska	Johnnie White	Horns of Hunter Tr. Post	1962	63
29 4/16	18 2/16	11 2/16	M	Alaska Pen., Alaska	H. S. Kamil	H. S. Kamil	1963	63
29 4/16	18 4/16	11	M	Port Heiden, Alaska	Ashley C. Sanders	Ashley C. Sanders	1965	63
29 3/16	18 10/16	10 9/16	M	Alaska Pen., Alaska	J. A. Atkinson	Am. Mus. Nat. History	1948	68
29 3/16	17 15/16	11 4/16	M	Port Moller Bay, Alaska	A. M. Harper	A. M. Harper	1949	68
29 3/16	17 10/16	11 9/16	M	Kodiak Island, Alaska	Fred B. Hawk	Fred B. Hawk	1959	68
29 3/16	17 15/16	11 4/16	M	Port Heiden, Alaska	Ralph E. Smith	Ralph E. Smith	1966	68
29 3/16	17 13/16	11 6/16	M	Kodiak Island, Alaska	William H. Sleith	Lutz Junior Museum	1966	68
29 3/16	18 6/16	10 10/16	M	Mother Goose Lake, Alaska	Robert Denis	Robert Denis	1967	68
29 2/16	17 10/16	11 8/16	M	Alaska Pen., Alaska	Mrs. J. Watson Webb	Mrs. J. Watson Webb	1948	74
29 2/16	17 14/16	11 4/16	M	Alaska Pen., Alaska	Mrs. John J. Louis, Jr.	Mrs. John J. Louis, Jr.	1955	74
29 2/16	17 15/16	11 3/16	M	Kodiak Island, Alaska	Alan O. Hickok	Alan O. Hickok	1957	74
29 2/16	17 11/16	11 7/16	M	Port Moller, Alaska	Milton Knapp	Milton Knapp	1960	74
29 2/16	17 10/16	11 8/16	M	Kodiak Island, Alaska	Edward F. Pedersen, Jr.	Edward F. Pedersen, Jr.	1961	74
29 2/16	18 3/16	10 15/16	M	Alaska Pen., Alaska	Kenneth Richmond	Kenneth Richmond	1962	74
29 2/16	17 9/16	11 8/16	M	Alaska Pen., Alaska	Wesley Pollock	Wesley Pollock	1964	74
29 2/16	18 3/16	11	M	Alaska Pen., Alaska	Richard Hodous	Richard Hodous	1966	74
29 2/16	18 3/16	10 15/16	M	Ugashik, Alaska	Joseph K. Link	Buffalo Mus. of Sci.	1966	74
29 2/16	17 7/16	11 11/16	M	Kodiak Island, Alaska	John F. Ries	John F. Ries	1967	74
29 2/16	17 8/16	11 9/16	M	Kodiak Island, Alaska	John C. Ayres	Signa J. Byers	1934	84
29 2/16	17 9/16	11 7/16	M	Kodiak Island, Alaska	H. H. Kissinger	H. H. Kissinger	1961	84
29 2/16	17 11/16	11 5/16	M	Ugashik Lake, Alaska	George Purdie	George Purdie	1963	84
29 2/16	17 11/16	11 5/16	M	Port Heiden, Alaska	Marshall Carr	Marshall Carr	1963	84
29 2/16	18 2/16	10 15/16	M	Port Moller, Alaska	Russell H. Underdahl	Russell H. Underdahl	1967	84
29 2/16	17 5/16	11 9/16	M	Cold Bay, Alaska	George Caswell	George Caswell	1984	84
29	17 9/16	11 6/16	M	Kodiak Island, Alaska	John Fox	John Fox	1959	90
29	17 14/16	11 2/16	M	Kodiak Island, Alaska	Raymond C. Boystel	Raymond C. Boystel	1963	90
29	18 2/16	10 14/16	M	Cold Bay, Alaska	J. S. Parker	J. S. Parker	1964	90
29	17 12/16	11 4/16	M	Cold Bay, Alaska	Fritz A. Nachant	Fritz A. Nachant	1965	90
29	18 6/16	10 9/16	M	Yakutat, Alaska	Jack DeWald	Jack DeWald	1973	90
29	17 15/16	11 1/16	M	Kodiak Island, Alaska	Creig M. Sharp	Creig M. Sharp	1977	90
29	18 3/16	10 13/16	M	Alaska Pen., Alaska	Johnnie R. Lowe	Johnnie R. Lowe	1979	90
28 15/16	17 11/16	11 2/16	M	Port Moller Bay, Alaska	C. A. Stenger	C. A. Stenger	1951	90
28 15/16	17 13/16	11 2/16	M	Alaska Pen., Alaska	G. W. Folta	G. W. Folta	1954	97
28 15/16	17 6/16	11 9/16	M	Kodiak Island, Alaska	Robert T. Leever	Robert T. Leever	1959	97
28 15/16	17 12/16	11 3/16	M	Kodiak Island, Alaska	H. T. Hilderbrandt	H. T. Hilderbrandt	1961	97
28 15/16	17 15/16	11	M	Sand Lake, Alaska	J. J. Stallone	J. J. Stallone	1962	97
28 15/16	17 14/16	11 1/16	M	Port Moller, Alaska	Andrew S. Allen	Andrew S. Allen	1963	97
28 15/16	17 9/16	11 7/16	M	Kodiak Island, Alaska	Stephen A. Mihal	Stephen A. Mihal	1969	97

ALASKA BROWN BEAR—Continued

Ursus arctos middendorffi and certain related subspecies

Score	Greatest Length of Skull Without Lower Jaw	Greatest Width of Skull	Sex	Locality Killed	By Whom Killed	Owner	Date Killed	Rank
28 15/16	17 11/16	11 4/16	M	Alaska Pen., Alaska	James A. Johnson	James A. Johnson	1970	97
28 15/16	17 7/16	11 11/16	M	Kodiak Island, Alaska	Robert E. Pippen	Robert E. Pippen	1975	97
28 15/16	18 1/16	10 14/16	M	Mother Goose Lake, Alaska	John H. Buckman	John H. Buckman	1976	97
28 14/16	17 13/16	11 5/16	M	Yakataga Beach, Alaska	Melvin Grindel	Stanley P. Young	1933	107
28 14/16	16 13/16	12 2/16	M	Kodiak Island, Alaska	A. J. Casper	A. J. Casper	1936	107
28 14/16	17 7/16	11 7/16	M	Kodiak Island, Alaska	Jack Honhart	Jack Honhart	1952	107
28 14/16	17 7/16	11 6/16	M	Alaska Pen., Alaska	Herb Elliott	Herb Elliott	1960	107
28 14/16	18 5/16	10 9/16	M	Kodiak Island, Alaska	Maurice S. Ireland	Maurice S. Ireland	1961	107
28 14/16	17 6/16	11 8/16	M	Alaska Pen., Alaska	Ethel Prine	Ethel Prine	1964	107
28 14/16	18 5/16	10 9/16	M	Kodiak Island, Alaska	William B. Valen	William B. Valen	1965	107
28 14/16	17 5/16	11 9/16	M	Kodiak Island, Alaska	Richard Kilbane	Richard Kilbane	1965	107
28 14/16	18	10 14/16	M	Alaska Pen., Alaska	Gerald N. Felando	Gerald N. Felando	1971	107
28 14/16	17 14/16	11	M	Skwentna River, Alaska	Richard N. Von	Richard N. Von	1975	107
28 14/16	17 12/16	11 2/16	M	Alaska Pen., Alaska	Robert A. Wainscott	Robert A. Wainscott	1978	107
28 14/16	17 7/16	11 8/16	M	Kodiak Island, Alaska	A. C. Gilbert	A. C. Gilbert	1950	107
28 13/16	18 6/16	10 11/16	M	Hoodoo Lake, Alaska	John Du Puy	John Du Puy	1951	118
28 13/16	17 6/16	11 6/16	M	Port Heiden, Alaska	Rupert Chisholm	Rupert Chisholm	1956	118
28 13/16	17 12/16	11 1/16	M	Frazer Lake, Alaska	Elgin T. Gates	Elgin T. Gates	1960	118
28 13/16	17 15/16	10 14/16	M	Alaska Pen., Alaska	Charles Daniels	Charles Daniels	1962	118
28 13/16	17 13/16	11	M	Kodiak Island, Alaska	Hal Waugh	Hal Waugh	1964	118
28 13/16	17 9/16	11 7/16	M	Kodiak, Alaska	Ernest Rush, Jr.	Ernest Rush, Jr.	1966	118
28 13/16	17 12/16	11 4/16	M	Alaska Pen., Alaska	Michael R. Anderson	Michael R. Anderson	1971	118
28 13/16	17 10/16	11 3/16	M	Deadman Bay, Alaska	Michael F. Short	Michael F. Short	1983	118
28 13/16	17 8/16	11 5/16	M	Herring Bay, Alaska	Jules V. Lane	Jules V. Lane	1939	118
28 12/16	18 2/16	10 10/16	M	Sand Lake, Alaska	A. C. Gilbert	A. C. Gilbert	1939	127
28 12/16	18	10 12/16	M	Sand Lake, Alaska	A. C. Gilbert	Robert R. Stewart	1949	127
28 12/16	18 4/16	10 8/16	M	Pavlof Bay, Alaska	Harry H. Webb	Harry H. Webb	1952	127
28 12/16	18 2/16	10 9/16	M	Alaska Pen., Alaska	Robert D. Boone	Robert D. Boone	1960	127
28 12/16	17 5/16	11 7/16	M	Kodiak Island, Alaska	Hans Otto Meissner	Hans Otto Meissner	1961	127
28 12/16	17 12/16	11	M	Alaska Pen., Alaska	Bert Klineburger	Bert Klineburger	1961	127
28 12/16	17 7/16	11 11/16	M	Alaska Pen., Alaska	Alberto F. Ruiloha	Alberto F. Ruiloha	1962	127
28 12/16	17 11/16	11 6/16	M	Karluk Lake, Alaska	Vernon C. Jensen	Vernon C. Jensen	1963	127
28 12/16	16 14/16	11 14/16	M	Kodiak Island, Alaska				127

150

28 12/16	17 12/16	11 11/16	M	Alaska Pen., Alaska	Bert Klineburger	Bert Klineburger	1964	127
28 12/16	17 9/16	11 3/16	M	Kodiak Island, Alaska	Joe M. Floyd, Jr.	Joe M. Floyd, Jr.	1966	127
28 12/16	17 15/16	10 13/16	M	Kodiak Island, Alaska	Clyde Ormond	Clyde Ormond	1968	127
28 12/16	18 2/16	10 9/16	M	Cold Bay, Alaska	Ted J. Forsi	Ted J. Forsi	1975	127
28 12/16	17 4/16	11 8/16	M	Kodiak Island, Alaska	Roy Herman Tyler	Roy Herman Tyler	1977	127
28 11/16	18 4/16	10 7/16	M	Cinder River, Alaska	George W. Vaughan	George W. Vaughan	1951	141
28 11/16	17 9/16	11 5/16	M	Kodiak Island, Alaska	John Treillet	John Treillet	1953	141
28 11/16	17 9/16	11 5/16	M	Kodiak Island, Alaska	Harold J. Ahrendt	Harold J. Ahrendt	1957	141
28 11/16	18 3/16	10 4/16	M	Alaska Pen., Alaska	Edward R. Crooks	Edward R. Crooks	1958	141
28 11/16	17 3/16	11 8/16	M	Kodiak Island, Alaska	Anthony A. Caldrone	Anthony A. Caldrone	1962	141
28 11/16	18 2/16	10 9/16	M	Alaska Pen., Alaska	Basil C. Bradbury	Basil C. Bradbury	1963	141
28 11/16	17 15/16	10 12/16	M	Afognak Island, Alaska	Clyde Gett	Clyde Gett	1969	141
28 11/16	17 1/16	11 4/16	M	Afognak Island, Alaska	William A. Bardot	William A. Bardot	1972	141
28 11/16	18 5/16	10 5/16	M	Bear Lake, Alaska	Leon A. Naccarato	Leon A. Naccarato	1980	141
28 10/16	17 3/16	11 8/16	M	Deadman Bay, Alaska	James S. Fogel	James S. Fogel	1982	141
28 10/16	18 6/16	10 4/16	M	Pavlof Bay, Alaska	U. S. Natl. Museum	R. H. Rockwell	1921	151
28 10/16	18 2/16	10 8/16	M	Alaska Pen., Alaska	Harry H. Webb	Harry H. Webb	1952	151
28 10/16	17 11/16	10 15/16	M	Alaska Pen., Alaska	Arthur C. Popham, Jr.	Arthur C. Popham, Jr.	1953	151
28 10/16	17 3/16	11 7/16	M	Kodiak Island, Alaska	Kenneth D. Landes	Kenneth D. Landes	1954	151
28 10/16	17 4/16	11 6/16	M	Alaska Pen., Alaska	Selmer Torrison	Selmer Torrison	1959	151
28 10/16	17 9/16	11 1/16	M	Kodiak Island, Alaska	Pat Soderburg	Pat Soderburg	1959	151
28 9/16	18 1/16	10 9/16	M	Alaska Pen., Alaska	Win Condict	Win Condict	1960	151
28 9/16	17 12/16	10 14/16	M	Kodiak Island, Alaska	Alfonso Pasquel	Alfonso Pasquel	1962	151
28 9/16	17 4/16	11 6/16	M	Cordova, Alaska	Wallace Fields	Wallace Fields	1962	151
28 9/16	17 9/16	11 1/16	M	Alaska Pen., Alaska	Frederick O. Kielmam	Frederick O. Kielmam	1963	151
28 9/16	17 3/16	11 7/16	M	Alaska Pen., Alaska	Ed Shapiro	Ed Shapiro	1964	151
28 9/16	18 4/16	10 6/16	M	Kodiak, Alaska	Michael Friedland	Michael Friedland	1964	151
28 9/16	17 5/16	11 5/16	M	Pavlof Bay, Alaska	William M. Kessner	William M. Kessner	1965	151
28 9/16	17 9/16	11	M	Kodiak Island, Alaska	John E. Crook	John E. Crook	1965	151
28 9/16	17 9/16	11 6/16	M	Alaska Pen., Alaska	Alex W. McCoy III	Alex W. McCoy III	1965	151
28 9/16	17 8/16	11 2/16	M	Port Gravina, Alaska	C. J. McElroy	C. J. McElroy	1965	151
28 9/16	17 12/16	10 4/16	M	Kodiak Island, Alaska	Norton T. Montague	Norton T. Montague	1967	151
28 9/16	17 1/16	11 9/16	M	Olga Bay, Alaska	Louis R. Kaminsky	Louis R. Kaminsky	1972	151
28 9/16	17 4/16	11 6/16	M	Long Bay, Alaska	Doug Latimer	Doug Latimer	1980	151
28 9/16	17 14/16	10 12/16	M	Alaska Pen., Alaska	Delbert E. Starr	Delbert E. Starr	1984	151
28 9/16	17 9/16	11 1/16	M	Kodiak Island, Alaska	Camp Fire Club	Charles S. King	1922	171
28 9/16	17 11/16	10 14/16	M	Kodiak Island, Alaska	Peggy M. Noles	Peggy M. Noles	1962	171
28 9/16	17 2/16	11 11/16	M	Cordova, Alaska	Charles Askins	Charles Askins	1963	171
28 9/16	17 6/16	11 7/16	M	Becharof Lake, Alaska	Marvin Kocurek	Marvin Kocurek	1964	171
28 9/16	17 6/16	11 3/16	M	Alaska Pen., Alaska	Robert J. Brocker	Robert J. Brocker	1964	171
28 9/16	17 12/16	10 13/16	M	Alaska Pen., Alaska	Robert L. Helms	Robert L. Helms	1966	171
28 9/16	17 4/16	11 5/16	M	Alaska Pen., Alaska	George H. Landreth	George H. Landreth	1966	171
28 8/16	18	10 9/16	M	Chichagof Island, Alaska	Stewart N. Shaft	Stewart N. Shaft	1973	171

151

ALASKA BROWN BEAR—Continued
Ursus arctos middendorffi and certain related subspecies

Score	Greatest Length of Skull Without Lower Jaw	Greatest Width of Skull	Sex	Locality Killed	By Whom Killed	Owner	Date Killed	Rank
28 6/16	17 9/16	11	M	Alaska Pen., Alaska	James B. Lindahl	James B. Lindahl	1975	171
28 6/16	17 9/16	11	M	Kodiak Island, Alaska	Mrs. Donald S. Hopkins	National Collection	1939	180
28 6/16	18	10 8/16	M	Herendeen Bay, Alaska	Arthur Johnson	Univ. of Alaska	1950	180
28 6/16	16 10/16	11 14/16	M	Kodiak Island, Alaska	Gloria T. Zerega	Gloria T. Zerega	1956	180
28 6/16	17 2/16	11 6/16	M	Caribou Lake, Alaska	W. A. Heldt	W. A. Heldt	1956	180
28 6/16	17 4/16	11 4/16	M	Kodiak Island, Alaska	W. M. Hollinger	W. M. Hollinger	1958	180
28 6/16	17 12/16	10 12/16	M	Port Heiden, Alaska	Chic Kawahara	Chic Kawahara	1963	180
28 6/16	17	11 8/16	M	Kodiak Island, Alaska	Ross Beach	Ross Beach	1963	180
28 6/16	17 14/16	10 9/16	M	Alaska Pen., Alaska	W. H. Picher	W. H. Picher	1964	180
28 6/16	17 4/16	11 4/16	M	Unimak Island, Alaska	Richard A. Guthrie	Richard A. Guthrie	1974	180
28 6/16	17 5/16	11 3/16	M	Deadman Bay, Alaska	Frank Alabiso	Frank Alabiso	1976	180
28 6/16	17 10/16	10 14/16	M	Pavlof Bay, Alaska	Melvin Gillis	Melvin Gillis	1976	180
28 6/16	17 9/16	10 14/16	M	Karluk Lake, Alaska	Paul W. Hansen	Paul W. Hansen	1983	180
28 6/16	17 7/16	11 1/16	M	Alaska Pen., Alaska	William Ronning	Lloyd Ronning	1958	192
28 6/16	16 3/16	11 1/16	M	Kodiak Island, Alaska	Bill Polland	Bill Polland	1959	192
28 6/16	17 15/16	10 8/16	M	Cold Bay, Alaska	Virgil Brill	Virgil Brill	1960	192
28 6/16	17 15/16	11 2/16	M	Kodiak Island, Alaska	Frank Rogers	Frank Rogers	1961	192
28 6/16	17 2/16	11 5/16	M	Kodiak Island, Alaska	Edward F. Pedersen	Edward F. Pedersen	1961	192
28 6/16	17 9/16	10 13/16	M	Alaska Pen., Alaska	Milton L. Knapp	Milton L. Knapp	1961	192
28 6/16	17 9/16	10 14/16	M	Alaska Pen., Alaska	Kenneth Golden	Kenneth Golden	1962	192
28 6/16	17 3/16	10 9/16	M	Alaska Pen., Alaska	Sam Pancotto	Sam Pancotto	1962	192
28 6/16	17	11	M	Afognak Island, Alaska	Robert Munger	Robert Munger	1962	192
28 6/16	17 13/16	10 9/16	M	Alaska Pen., Alaska	Dennis Burke	Dennis Burke	1964	192
28 6/16	17 9/16	10 13/16	M	Ugashik Lake, Alaska	James E. Egger	James E. Egger	1966	192
28 6/16	17 11/16	10 12/16	M	Kodiak Island, Alaska	William A. Ross, Jr.	William A. Ross, Jr.	1968	192
28 6/16	17 2/16	11 5/16	M	Kodiak Island, Alaska	M. H. Brock	M. H. Brock	1971	192
28 6/16	17 11/16	10 12/16	M	Alaska Pen., Alaska	James E. Otto	James E. Otto	1973	192
28 6/16	17 4/16	11 3/16	M	Kodiak Island, Alaska	Virgil J. Sheppard	Virgil J. Sheppard	1978	192
28 6/16	17 5/16	10 7/16	M	Moroski Bay, Alaska	Ivan Katchinof	U. S. Natl. Museum	1897	207
28 6/16	17 14/16	10 8/16	M	Sand Lake, Alaska	Mrs. J. Watson Webb	Mrs. J. Watson Webb	1939	207
28 6/16	17 9/16	10 13/16	M	Kodiak Island, Alaska	Martin J. Coyne	Martin J. Coyne	1960	207
28 6/16	17 11/16	10 11/16	M	Alaska Pen., Alaska	Alberto Pipia	Alberto Pipia	1965	207

152

				Locality	Hunter	Owner	Date	Score
28 9/16	17 9/16	10 14/16	M	Alaska Pen., Alaska	John F. Ault	John F. Ault	1967	207
28 9/16	17 9/16	11 2/16	M	Prince William Sound, Alaska	Ron Kacsmaryk	Ron Kacsmaryk	1970	207
28 9/16	17 4/16	10 6/16	M	Port Heiden, Alaska	Jack Holland, Jr.	Jack Holland, Jr.	1976	207
28 9/16	16 12/16	11 9/16	M	Kodiak Island, Alaska	Darrel Williams	Earl Hahn	1976	207
28 6/16	17 6/16	11 4/16	M	Larsen Bay, Alaska	Sherron G. Perry	Sherron G. Perry	1983	207
28 6/16	17 14/16	10 7/16	M	Pavlof Bay, Alaska	Peter Ruppi	U. S. Natl. Museum	1897	216
28 6/16	17 6/16	11 1/16	M	Cold Bay, Alaska	L. S. Kuter	L. S. Kuter	1952	216
28 6/16	16 9/16	11 7/16	M	Kodiak Island, Alaska	C. D. Fuller & F. C. Miller	C. D. Fuller & F. C. Miller	1959	216
28 6/16	16 14/16	11 7/16	M	Kodiak Island, Alaska	J. D. Roebuck	J. D. Roebuck	1960	216
28 6/16	17 9/16	10 12/16	M	Alaska Pen., Alaska	J. B. Kerley	J. B. Kerley	1964	216
28 6/16	17 14/16	10 1/16	M	Port Heiden, Alaska	John S. Cochran, Jr.	John S. Cochran, Jr.	1964	216
28 6/16	17 9/16	10 13/16	M	Mother Goose Lake, Alaska	H. T. Sliger	H. T. Sliger	1965	216
28 6/16	17 6/16	11 2/16	M	Kodiak Island, Alaska	Jerry Coon	Jerry Coon	1967	216
28 6/16	18	10 5/16	M	Port Heiden, Alaska	Leonard W. Bruns	Leonard W. Bruns	1967	216
28 6/16	17	11 5/16	M	Kodiak Island, Alaska	Chris Klineburger	Chris Klineburger	1967	216
28 5/16	16 15/16	11 9/16	M	Kodiak Island, Alaska	King Mahendra of Nepal	King Mahendra of Nepal	1968	216
28 6/16	17 9/16	10 5/16	M	Kodiak Island, Alaska	Theodore J. Schorsch, Sr.	Theodore J. Schorsch, Sr.	1976	216
28 6/16	18	10 5/16	M	Alaska Pen., Alaska	Keith W. Bates	Keith W. Bates	1981	216
28 6/16	17 6/16	11 2/16	M	Dog Salmon Creek, Alaska	John Della Valle	John Della Valle	1982	216
28 6/16	18	10 5/16	M	Foot Bay, Alaska	Larry A. McComb	Larry A. McComb	1984	216
28 6/16	17 13/16	10 8/16	M	Cold Bay, Alaska	Timothy Orton	Timothy Orton	1984	216
28 6/16	17 9/16	10 12/16	M	Cold Bay, Alaska	Kenneth C. Hayden	Kenneth C. Hayden	1953	216
28 4/16	17 12/16	10 8/16	M	Port Moller, Alaska	Harry H. Webb	Harry H. Webb	1954	233
28 4/16	17	11 4/16	M	Kodiak Island, Alaska	T. E. Shillingburg	T. E. Shillingburg	1957	233
28 4/16	17 8/16	11	M	Afognak Island, Alaska	Edward M. Simko	Edward M. Simko	1959	233
28 6/16	17 9/16	10 7/16	M	Kodiak Island, Alaska	Willie Dene Payton	Willie Dene Payton	1960	233
28 6/16	18 4/16	10 11/16	M	Alaska Pen., Alaska	Jeffrey G. Burmeister	Jeffrey G. Burmeister	1962	233
28 6/16	17	10	M	Alaska Pen., Alaska	Jean Branson	Jean Branson	1963	233
28 6/16	17	11 4/16	M	Uganik Bay, Alaska	J. Coker & J. Meagher	Jerry Coker	1965	233
28 6/16	16 12/16	11 8/16	M	Kodiak Island, Alaska	Keith Honhart	Keith Honhart	1965	233
28 6/16	17 3/16	11 1/16	M	Kodiak Island, Alaska	Roy M. Champayne	Roy M. Champayne	1979	233
28 6/16	16 15/16	11 5/16	M	Kodiak Island, Alaska	James E. Nelson	James E. Nelson	1981	233
28 6/16	17 12/16	10 8/16	M	Cinder River, Alaska	Javier Zubia	Javier Zubia	1981	233
28 6/16	17 9/16	11	M	Olga Bay, Alaska	Allan E. Bergland	Allan E. Bergland	1985	233
28 6/16	17 9/16	10 11/16	M	Unimak Island, Alaska	John D. Frost	John D. Frost	1949	246
28 3/16	17 4/16	10 15/16	M	Aniakchak Bay, Alaska	Francis J. Fabick	Francis J. Fabick	1959	246
28 3/16	17 9/16	10 5/16	M	Alaska Pen., Alaska	Kenneth Holland	Kenneth Holland	1959	246
28 3/16	17 6/16	11 2/16	M	Kodiak Island, Alaska	Raymond A. Du Four	Raymond A. Du Four	1960	246
28 3/16	18	11 1/16	M	Kodiak Island, Alaska	William Offenheim	William Offenheim	1961	246
28 3/16	16 15/16	10 3/16	M	Port Moller, Alaska	John D. Phillips	John D. Phillips	1961	246
28 3/16	17 6/16	11 4/16	M	Kodiak Island, Alaska	Frank Hollendonner	Frank Hollendonner	1961	246
28 3/16	17 12/16	10 12/16	M	Alaska Pen., Alaska	Elmer Graham	Elmer Graham	1964	246
28 3/16	17 4/16	10 15/16	M	Port Heiden, Alaska	Michael Ferrell	Michael Ferrell		246

153

ALASKA BROWN BEAR—Continued
Ursus arctos middendorffi and certain related subspecies

Score	Greatest Length of Skull Without Lower Jaw	Greatest Width of Skull	Sex	Locality Killed	By Whom Killed	Owner	Date Killed	Rank
28 3/16	17 6/16	10 13/16	M	Talkeetna Mts., Alaska	Robert W. Holladay	Robert W. Holladay	1966	246
28 3/16	18 4/16	9 5/16	U	Port Moller, Alaska	Ray Eyler	Ray Eyler	1966	246
28 3/16	16 15/16	11 4/16	M	Kodiak Island, Alaska	T. Kimball Hill	T. Kimball Hill	1967	246
28 3/16	17 6/16	10 14/16	M	Cathedral Valley, Alaska	J. M. Norton	J. M. Norton	1982	246
28 3/16	17 1/16	11 2/16	M	Red Lake, Alaska	Richard H. Neville	Richard H. Neville	1984	246
28 3/16	17 13/16	10 6/16	M	Volcano Bay, Alaska	L. Clark Kiser	L. Clark Kiser	1984	246
28 3/16	16 13/16	11 6/16	M	Kaguyak Bay, Alaska	Jack D. Revelle	Jack D. Revelle	1984	261
28 3/16	16 11/16	11 7/16	M	Kodiak Island, Alaska	J. Watson Webb	J. Watson Webb	1948	261
28 3/16	17 12/16	10 6/16	M	Alaska Pen., Alaska	J. D. Jones	J. D. Jones	1954	261
28 3/16	18 1/16	10 1/16	M	Cold Bay, Alaska	Lewis E. Yearout	Lewis E. Yearout	1956	261
28 3/16	17	11 2/16	M	Kodiak Island, Alaska	Merril R. Reller	Merril R. Reller	1958	261
28 3/16	17 8/16	10 10/16	M	Cinder River, Alaska	Russell Cutter	Russell Cutter	1960	261
28 3/16	17 9/16	10 8/16	M	Port Heiden, Alaska	Herman Kuchanek	Herman Kuchanek	1961	261
28 3/16	17 1/16	11 1/16	U	Kodiak Island, Alaska	Jim Alexander	Jim Alexander	PR1961	261
28 3/16	17 12/16	10 9/16	M	Alaska Pen., Alaska	Mrs. Sam Pancotto	Mrs. Sam Pancotto	1962	261
28 3/16	16 8/16	11 9/16	M	Kodiak Island, Alaska	Gordon G. Maclean	Gordon G. Maclean	1964	261
28 3/16	17 8/16	10 9/16	M	Alaska Pen., Alaska	Charles L. Ball, Jr.	Charles L. Ball, Jr.	1964	261
28 3/16	17 8/16	10 9/16	M	Unimak Island, Alaska	Don Burk	Don Burk	1966	261
28 3/16	17 10/16	10 8/16	M	Cold Bay, Alaska	John D. Jones	John D. Jones	1966	261
28 3/16	16 8/16	10 10/16	M	Eagle Harbor, Alaska	James T. Harrell	James T. Harrell	1966	261
28 3/16	17 12/16	11 9/16	M	Cold Bay, Alaska	Robert Hansen	Robert Hansen	1966	261
28 3/16	17 9/16	10 6/16	M	Alaska Pen., Alaska	Francis S. Levien	Francis S. Levien	1968	261
28 3/16	17 9/16	10 8/16	M	Afognak Island, Alaska	Laszlo Lemhenyi-Hanko	Laszlo Lemhenyi-Hanko	1970	261
28 3/16	17 5/16	10 13/16	M	Kodiak Island, Alaska	Dwight Hildebrandt	Dwight Hildebrandt	1971	261
28 3/16	17 5/16	10 13/16	M	Great Salmon Lake, Alaska	Siegfried Kube	Siegfried Kube	1974	261
28 3/16	17 3/16	10 15/16	M	Kodiak Island, Alaska	Bart D'Averso	Bart D'Averso	1974	261
28 3/16	16 9/16	11 9/16	U	Afognak Island, Alaska	Picked Up	David L. Lazer	PR1976	261
28 3/16	17 5/16	11	M	Kodiak Island, Alaska	Charles A. Goldenberg	Charles A. Goldenberg	1978	261
28 3/16	17 5/16	10 14/16	M	Spiridon Lake, Alaska	Chris T. Hinchey	Bear Arms	1983	261
28 3/16	17	11 2/16	M	Cold Bay, Alaska	Lonnie W. McCurry, Sr.	Lonnie W. McCurry, Sr.	1984	261
28 3/16	16 15/16	11 2/16	M	Port Moller, Alaska	Enos A. Axtell	Enos A. Axtell	1950	284
28 3/16	18	10 6/16	M	Alaska Pen., Alaska	R. H. Blum	R. H. Blum	1954	284

154

$28\frac{1}{16}$	$16\frac{12}{16}$	$11\frac{5}{16}$	M	Kodiak Island, Alaska	Richard O. Daniels	Richard O. Daniels	1958	284
$28\frac{1}{16}$	17	$11\frac{1}{16}$	M	Kodiak Island, Alaska	Joe Maxwell	Joe Maxwell	1959	284
$28\frac{1}{16}$	$17\frac{4}{16}$	$10\frac{13}{16}$	M	Kodiak Island, Alaska	L. W. Zeug	L. W. Zeug	1959	284
$28\frac{1}{16}$	$17\frac{4}{16}$	$10\frac{13}{16}$	M	Alaska Pen., Alaska	Roscoe S. Mosiman	Roscoe S. Mosiman	1960	284
$28\frac{1}{16}$	$17\frac{9}{16}$	$10\frac{7}{16}$	M	Cold Bay, Alaska	Keith C. Brown	Keith C. Brown	1962	284
$28\frac{1}{16}$	$17\frac{11}{16}$	$10\frac{9}{16}$	M	Alaska Pen., Alaska	Bill Boone	Bill Boone	1964	284
$28\frac{1}{16}$	17	$11\frac{1}{16}$	M	Kodiak Island, Alaska	Dan G. Brown	Dan G. Brown	1967	284
$28\frac{1}{16}$	$16\frac{5}{16}$	$11\frac{2}{16}$	M	Kodiak Island, Alaska	Cary E. Weldon	Cary E. Weldon	1968	284
$28\frac{1}{16}$	$17\frac{8}{16}$	$10\frac{9}{16}$	M	Kodiak Island, Alaska	Bill Ulich	Bill Ulich	1976	284
$28\frac{1}{16}$	$17\frac{9}{16}$	$10\frac{9}{16}$	M	Olga Bay, Alaska	Robert N. Wainscott	Robert N. Wainscott	1982	284
$28\frac{1}{16}$	18	$10\frac{1}{16}$	M	Port Heiden, Alaska	William H. F. Wiltshire	William H. F. Wiltshire	1984	284
28	$17\frac{2}{16}$	$10\frac{14}{16}$	M	Alaska Pen., Alaska	Harold Dugdale	Harold Dugdale	1954	297
28	$17\frac{9}{16}$	$10\frac{9}{16}$	M	Alaska Pen., Alaska	Robert D. Jones, Jr.	Robert D. Jones, Jr.	1955	297
28	17	11	M	Kodiak Island, Alaska	Harry F. Weyher	Harry F. Weyher	1958	297
28	$17\frac{12}{16}$	$10\frac{9}{16}$	M	Alaska Pen., Alaska	Wendell S. Fletcher	Wendell S. Fletcher	1960	297
28	$17\frac{15}{16}$	$10\frac{9}{16}$	M	Alaska Pen., Alaska	Fred Bear	Fred Bear	1960	297
28	$17\frac{7}{16}$	$10\frac{9}{16}$	M	Alaska Pen., Alaska	W. T. Yoshimoto	W. T. Yoshimoto	1961	297
28	$17\frac{3}{16}$	$10\frac{13}{16}$	M	Alaska Pen., Alaska	Gilbert Elton	Gilbert Elton	1962	297
28	$17\frac{5}{16}$	$10\frac{9}{16}$	M	Port Moller, Alaska	Harry J. Armitage	Harry J. Armitage	1963	297
28	$17\frac{3}{16}$	$10\frac{13}{16}$	M	Kodiak Island, Alaska	Dean Herring	Dean Herring	1967	297
28	$17\frac{9}{16}$	$10\frac{7}{16}$	M	Alaska Pen., Alaska	James D. Smith	James D. Smith	1968	297
28	$17\frac{14}{16}$	$10\frac{9}{16}$	M	Alaska Pen., Alaska	Rudy Tuten	Rudy Tuten	1968	297
28	18	10	M	Alaska Pen., Alaska	Peter Santin	Peter Santin	1969	297
28	17	11	U	Alaska Pen., Alaska	James J. Fraioli	James J. Fraioli	1970	297
28	$17\frac{1}{16}$	$10\frac{9}{16}$	M	Alaska Pen., Alaska	Larry Lassley	Larry Lassley	1975	297
28	18	10	M	Chilkoot River, Alaska	Philip Nare	Philip Nare	1981	297
28	$16\frac{9}{16}$	$11\frac{9}{16}$	M	Ugak Bay, Alaska	Arnie Gutenkauf	Arnie Gutenkauf	1982	297
28	$17\frac{2}{16}$	$10\frac{9}{16}$	M	Windy Bay, Alaska	Archie H. Stevens, Sr.	Archie H. Stevens, Sr.	1983	297
28	$16\frac{5}{16}$	$11\frac{9}{16}$	M	Skilak Glacier, Alaska	Richard W. Carlock	Richard W. Carlock	1985	297
28	$17\frac{5}{16}$	$10\frac{11}{16}$	M	Copper River, Alaska	Roger R. Card	Roger R. Card	PR1970	297
$30\frac{3}{16}$*	$18\frac{5}{16}$	$12\frac{1}{16}$	M	Afognak Island, Alaska	Almin G. Thompson	Picked Up	1983	
29*	$17\frac{9}{16}$	$11\frac{9}{16}$	M	Kaguyak Bay, Alaska	Ronald L. Winstead	Ronald L. Winstead	1980	
$28\frac{15}{16}$*	$17\frac{1}{16}$	$11\frac{9}{16}$	M	Kiliuda Bay, Alaska	Dean J. Walden	Dean J. Walden	1984	
$28\frac{7}{16}$*	$17\frac{4}{16}$	$11\frac{9}{16}$	M	Kaiugnak Bay, Alaska	Dale E. Machacek	Dale E. Machacek	1980	
$28\frac{6}{16}$*	$17\frac{4}{16}$	$11\frac{2}{16}$	M	Port Heiden, Alaska	Russ McLennan	Russ McLennan		

*Final Score subject to revision by additional verifying measurements

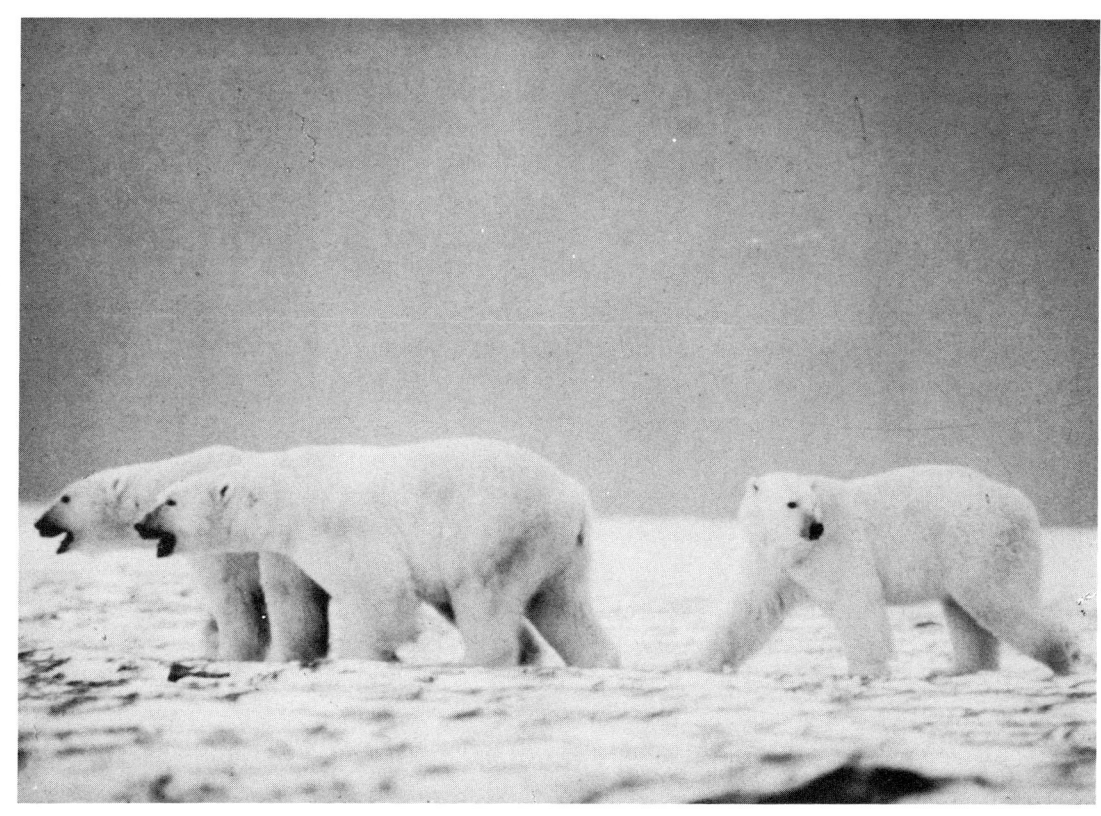

Photograph by Charles Jonkel

POLAR BEAR

Polar Bear
Ursus maritimus

Minimum Score 27

Score	Greatest Length of Skull Without Lower Jaw	Greatest Width of Skull	Sex	Locality Killed	By Whom Killed	Owner	Date Killed	Rank
29 5/16	18 5/16	11 7/16	M	Kotzebue, Alaska	Shelby Longoria	Shelby Longoria	1963	1
29 1/16	18 2/16	10 15/16	M	Kotzebue, Alaska	Louis Mussatoo	Louis Mussatoo	1965	2
28 12/16	17 13/16	10 15/16	M	Point Hope, Alaska	Tom F. Bolack	Tom F. Bolack	1958	3
28 12/16	17 11/16	11 1/16	M	Kotzebue, Alaska	Bill Nottley	Bill Nottley	1967	3
28 9/16	18	10 10/16	M	Little Diomede Is., Alaska	Richard G. Van Vorst	Richard G. Van Vorst	1963	5
28 9/16	17 8/16	11 2/16	M	Chukchi Sea, Alaska	Jack D. Putnam	Jack D. Putnam	1965	5
28 8/16	17 8/16	11 3/16	M	Kotzebue, Alaska	E. A. McCracken	E. A. McCracken	1966	7
28 8/16	17 8/16	11 2/16	M	Kotzebue, Alaska	Curtis S. Williams, Jr.	Curtis S. Williams, Jr.	1967	8
28 8/16	17 10/16	10 14/16	M	Kotzebue, Alaska	Winfred Lee English	Winfred Lee English	1968	8
28 7/16	17 5/16	11 3/16	M	Point Hope, Alaska	Rodney Lincoln	J. A. Columbus	1954	10
28 7/16	17 6/16	11	M	St. Lawrence Is., Alaska	H. B. Collins, Jr.	U. S. Natl. Museum	1929	11
28 6/16	17 8/16	10 14/16	M	Point Hope, Alaska	Clifford Thom	Clifford Thom	1964	11
28 6/16	17 3/16	11 3/16	M	Diomede Is., Alaska	Stephen Pyle III	Stephen Pyle III	1965	11
28 5/16	17 10/16	10 11/16	M	Teller, Alaska	Walter Simas	Walter Simas	1966	14
28 4/16	18 2/16	10 7/16	M	Kotzebue, Alaska	Peter W. Bading	Peter W. Bading	1960	15
28 4/16	17 9/16	10 11/16	M	Big Diomede Is., Alaska	Vance A. Halverson	Vance A. Halverson	1963	15
28 4/16	17 7/16	10 13/16	M	Teller, Alaska	Jack C. Phillips	Jack C. Phillips	1964	15
28 3/16	17 15/16	10 9/16	M	Diomede Islands, Alaska	Louis F. Kincaid	Louis F. Kincaid	1955	18
28 3/16	17 6/16	10 6/16	M	Kotzebue, Alaska	Finis G. Cooper	Los Angeles Co. Museum	1959	18
28 3/16	17 12/16	10 3/16	M	Kotzebue, Alaska	Harold Trulin	Harold Trulin	1962	18
28 3/16	17 6/16	10 7/16	M	Kotzebue, Alaska	S. D. Slaughter	S. D. Slaughter	1962	18
28 3/16	17 6/16	10 3/16	M	Kotzebue, Alaska	C. J. McElroy	C. J. McElroy	1965	18
28 2/16	17 6/16	10 12/16	M	Point Hope, Alaska	Pete Kesselring	Pete Kesselring	1957	23
28 2/16	17 5/16	10 15/16	M	Big Diomede Is., Alaska	Francis Bogon	Francis Bogon	1957	23
28 2/16	17 1/16	11 1/16	M	Chukchi Sea, Alaska	Horace Steele	Horace Steele	1963	23
28 1/16	18 1/16	10	M	St. Paul Is., Alaska	C. H. Townsend	U. S. Natl. Museum	1875	26
28 1/16	17 6/16	10 11/16	M	Kotzebue, Alaska	Don Jahns	Don Jahns	1961	26
28	17 6/16	10 8/16	M	Point Hope, Alaska	Tommy Thompson	Pablo B. Romero	1958	28
28	17 6/16	10 10/16	M	Point Hope, Alaska	William Stevenson	William Stevenson	1959	28
28	17 6/16	10 9/16	M	Kotzebue, Alaska	Rupert Chisholm	Rupert Chisholm	1959	28
28	17 10/16	10 9/16	M	Kotzebue, Alaska	W. H. Hagenmeyer	W. H. Hagenmeyer	1961	28

157

POLAR BEAR—*Continued*
Ursus maritimus

Score	Greatest Length of Skull Without Lower Jaw	Greatest Width of Skull	Sex	Locality Killed	By Whom Killed	Owner	Date Killed	Rank
28	$17\frac{5}{16}$	$10\frac{11}{16}$	M	Kotzebue, Alaska	Alberto Pipia	Alberto Pipia	1964	28
28	$17\frac{8}{16}$	$10\frac{8}{16}$	M	Kotzebue, Alaska	Leonard W. Bruns	Leonard W. Bruns	1966	28
28	$17\frac{8}{16}$	$10\frac{7}{16}$	M	Kotzebue, Alaska	Blair Truitt	Blair Truitt	1960	34
$27\frac{15}{16}$	$17\frac{5}{16}$	$10\frac{9}{16}$	M	Kotzebue, Alaska	Russell C. Cutter	Russell C. Cutter	1960	34
$27\frac{15}{16}$	$17\frac{5}{16}$	$10\frac{9}{16}$	M	Diomede Is., Alaska	William H. Smith, Jr.	William H. Smith, Jr.	1961	34
$27\frac{15}{16}$	$17\frac{4}{16}$	$10\frac{11}{16}$	M	Kotzebue, Alaska	Jess L. Ferguson	Jess L. Ferguson	1961	34
$27\frac{15}{16}$	$17\frac{9}{16}$	$10\frac{6}{16}$	M	Kotzebue, Alaska	James S. Martin	James S. Martin	1962	34
$27\frac{15}{16}$	$17\frac{9}{16}$	$10\frac{6}{16}$	M	Kotzebue, Alaska	R. Lynn Ross	R. Lynn Ross	1966	34
$27\frac{15}{16}$	$17\frac{11}{16}$	$10\frac{4}{16}$	M	Teller, Alaska	James W. Brooks	Univ. of Alaska	1952	40
$27\frac{14}{16}$	$17\frac{4}{16}$	$10\frac{10}{16}$	M	Point Barrow, Alaska	Roy E. Weatherby	Roy E. Weatherby	1959	40
$27\frac{14}{16}$	$17\frac{10}{16}$	$10\frac{4}{16}$	M	Kotzebue, Alaska	Don R. Downey	Don R. Downey	1960	40
$27\frac{14}{16}$	$17\frac{2}{16}$	$10\frac{12}{16}$	M	Kotzebue, Alaska	C. D. Dofflemyer	C. D. Dofflemyer	1961	40
$27\frac{14}{16}$	$17\frac{5}{16}$	$10\frac{8}{16}$	M	Kotzebue, Alaska	Nikolaus Koenig	Nikolaus Koenig	1966	40
$27\frac{14}{16}$	$17\frac{2}{16}$	$10\frac{12}{16}$	M	Chukchi Sea, Alaska	Hugh O'Dower	Hugh O'Dower	1959	45
$27\frac{13}{16}$	$17\frac{13}{16}$	10	M	Kotzebue, Alaska	William P. Boone	William P. Boone	1960	45
$27\frac{13}{16}$	$17\frac{6}{16}$	$10\frac{6}{16}$	M	Point Hope, Alaska	Helen Burnett	Helen Burnett	1962	45
$27\frac{13}{16}$	$17\frac{8}{16}$	$10\frac{5}{16}$	M	Point Hope, Alaska	Dale H. Wolff	Dale H. Wolff	1963	45
$27\frac{13}{16}$	$16\frac{15}{16}$	$10\frac{14}{16}$	M	Cape Lisburne, Alaska	Charles Renaud	Charles Renaud	1963	45
$27\frac{13}{16}$	$17\frac{3}{16}$	$10\frac{10}{16}$	M	Alaska Coast	Lowell M. Cooke	Lowell M. Cooke	1965	45
$27\frac{13}{16}$	$17\frac{4}{16}$	$10\frac{9}{16}$	U	Chukchi Sea, Alaska	Robert M. Mallett	Robert M. Mallett	1967	45
$27\frac{13}{16}$	$17\frac{7}{16}$	$10\frac{6}{16}$	M	Cape Lisburne, Alaska	Edward M. Simko	Edward M. Simko	1956	52
$27\frac{12}{16}$	$17\frac{5}{16}$	$10\frac{7}{16}$	M	Kotzebue, Alaska	J. E. Ottoviano	J. E. Ottoviano	1958	52
$27\frac{12}{16}$	$17\frac{5}{16}$	$10\frac{7}{16}$	M	Kotzebue, Alaska	A. H. Woodward, Jr.	A. H. Woodward, Jr.	1959	52
$27\frac{12}{16}$	17	$10\frac{12}{16}$	M	Point Hope, Alaska	Owen K. Murphy	Owen K. Murphy	1959	52
$27\frac{12}{16}$	$17\frac{8}{16}$	$10\frac{6}{16}$	M	Kotzebue, Alaska	D. V. Merrick	D. V. Merrick	1959	52
$27\frac{12}{16}$	$17\frac{6}{16}$	$10\frac{6}{16}$	M	Little Diomede Is., Alaska	Louis Menegas	Louis Menegas	1963	52
$27\frac{12}{16}$	$17\frac{5}{16}$	$10\frac{7}{16}$	M	Kotzebue, Alaska	Arthur W. Clark	Arthur W. Clark	1963	52
$27\frac{12}{16}$	$17\frac{2}{16}$	$10\frac{10}{16}$	M	Kotzebue, Alaska	Earl W. Nystrom	Earl W. Nystrom	1965	52
$27\frac{12}{16}$	$17\frac{4}{16}$	$10\frac{8}{16}$	M	Teller, Alaska	William M. Kessner	William M. Kessner	1966	52
$27\frac{11}{16}$	$16\frac{4}{16}$	$11\frac{7}{16}$	M	Teller, Alaska	Arthur W. Smith	Arthur W. Smith	1963	61
$27\frac{11}{16}$	$17\frac{7}{16}$	$10\frac{4}{16}$	M	Kotzebue, Alaska	Patricia T. Bergstrom	Patricia T. Bergstrom	1965	61
$27\frac{11}{16}$	$17\frac{7}{16}$	$10\frac{5}{16}$	M	Kotzebue, Alaska	Andrew S. Allen	Andrew S. Allen	1965	61

27¹⁰⁄₁₆	16¹¹⁄₁₆	10¹⁵⁄₁₆	M	Kotzebue, Alaska	Joe Foss	Joe Foss	1960	64
27⁹⁄₁₆	17¹⁄₁₆	10⁶⁄₁₆	M	Kotzebue, Alaska	George P. Whittington	George P. Whittington	1962	64
27⁹⁄₁₆	16¹⁵⁄₁₆	10¹¹⁄₁₆	M	Little Diomede Is., Alaska	Willard R. Skousen	Willard R. Skousen	1962	64
27⁹⁄₁₆	17²⁄₁₆	10⁸⁄₁₆	M	Kotzebue, Alaska	C. T. Kraftmeyer	C. T. Kraftmeyer	1962	64
27⁹⁄₁₆	17	10¹⁰⁄₁₆	M	Point Hope, Alaska	Norma Wahrer	Norma Wahrer	1963	64
27⁹⁄₁₆	17⁴⁄₁₆	10⁶⁄₁₆	M	Kotzebue, Alaska	Kenneth W. Vaughn	Kenneth W. Vaughn	1963	64
27⁹⁄₁₆	17⁶⁄₁₆	10⁴⁄₁₆	M	Kotzebue, Alaska	Robert L. Cohen	Robert L. Cohen	1966	64
27⁹⁄₁₆	17⁹⁄₁₆	10³⁄₁₆	M	Point Hope, Alaska	T. E. Shillingburg	T. E. Shillingburg	1957	71
27⁹⁄₁₆	17⁷⁄₁₆	10⁶⁄₁₆	M	Cape Thompson, Alaska	Daniel H. Cuddy	Daniel H. Cuddy	1959	71
27⁹⁄₁₆	17⁷⁄₁₆	10³⁄₁₆	M	Chukchi Sea, Alaska	Angelo Alessio	Angelo Alessio	1963	71
27⁹⁄₁₆	17⁴⁄₁₆	10⁶⁄₁₆	M	Diomede Is., Alaska	Tony Oney	Tony Oney	1964	71
27⁹⁄₁₆	16¹³⁄₁₆	10¹²⁄₁₆	M	Point Hope, Alaska	Pat Auld	Pat Auld	1964	71
27⁸⁄₁₆	17³⁄₁₆	10⁵⁄₁₆	M	Kotzebue, Alaska	Harry D. Tousley	Harry D. Tousley	1961	76
27⁸⁄₁₆	17⁵⁄₁₆	10³⁄₁₆	M	Point Hope, Alaska	Edward Frecker	Edward Frecker	1963	76
27⁸⁄₁₆	17²⁄₁₆	10⁶⁄₁₆	M	Cape Lisburne, Alaska	Willard E. Flynn	Willard E. Flynn	1963	76
27⁸⁄₁₆	17	10⁸⁄₁₆	M	Kotzebue, Alaska	Russell J. Uhl	Russell J. Uhl	1965	76
27⁸⁄₁₆	17⁵⁄₁₆	10³⁄₁₆	M	Kotzebue, Alaska	Ted Lick	Ted Lick	1965	76
27⁷⁄₁₆	16⁶⁄₁₆	10¹⁴⁄₁₆	M	Kotzebue, Alaska	Mahlon T. Everhart	Mahlon T. Everhart	1959	81
27⁷⁄₁₆	17⁵⁄₁₆	10⁶⁄₁₆	M	Little Diomede Is., Alaska	Herb Klein	Herb Klein	1960	81
27⁷⁄₁₆	17³⁄₁₆	10⁴⁄₁₆	M	Kotzebue, Alaska	Gregory E. Koshell	Gregory E. Koshell	1961	81
27⁷⁄₁₆	17	10	M	Kotzebue, Alaska	Andrew De Matteo	Andrew De Matteo	1965	81
27⁷⁄₁₆	16¹⁵⁄₁₆	10⁵⁄₁₆	M	Polar Circle, Alaska	Aurelio Caccomo	Aurelio Caccomo	1965	81
27⁶⁄₁₆	16¹¹⁄₁₆	10¹¹⁄₁₆	M	Wales, Alaska	Eskimo	Univ. of Alaska	1956	86
27⁶⁄₁₆	16¹⁵⁄₁₆	10⁷⁄₁₆	M	Cape Lisburne, Alaska	J. S. Lichtenfels	J. S. Lichtenfels	1957	86
27⁶⁄₁₆	17	10⁶⁄₁₆	M	Kotzebue, Alaska	W. H. Cato, Jr.	W. H. Cato, Jr.	1960	86
27⁶⁄₁₆	17⁵⁄₁₆	10⁶⁄₁₆	M	Kotzebue, Alaska	Gene Klineburger	Gene Klineburger	1963	86
27⁶⁄₁₆	17	10⁶⁄₁₆	M	Little Diomede Is., Alaska	Bob Payne	Bob Payne	1964	86
27⁶⁄₁₆	17³⁄₁₆	10³⁄₁₆	M	Teller, Alaska	James O. Campbell	James O. Campbell	1964	86
27⁶⁄₁₆	16¹⁰⁄₁₆	10¹²⁄₁₆	M	Kotzebue, Alaska	Glen E. Park	Glen E. Park	1965	86
27⁶⁄₁₆	16¹³⁄₁₆	10⁹⁄₁₆	M	Chukchi Sea, Alaska	Terry Kennedy	Terry Kennedy	1967	86
27⁶⁄₁₆	17	10⁶⁄₁₆	M	Kotzebue, Alaska	Harry Daum	Harry Daum	1971	86
27⁵⁄₁₆	16¹³⁄₁₆	10⁸⁄₁₆	M	Kotzebue, Alaska	W. L. Coleman	W. L. Coleman	1961	95
27⁵⁄₁₆	17¹⁄₁₆	10⁴⁄₁₆	M	Point Hope, Alaska	Sherman R. Whitmore	Sherman R. Whitmore	1963	95
27⁵⁄₁₆	16¹⁵⁄₁₆	10⁶⁄₁₆	M	Point Hope, Alaska	Charles A. McKinsey	Charles A. McKinsey	1963	95
27⁵⁄₁₆	16⁸⁄₁₆	10¹²⁄₁₆	M	Big Diomede Is., Alaska	Bert Klineburger	Bert Klineburger	1963	95
27⁵⁄₁₆	16¹²⁄₁₆	10⁹⁄₁₆	M	Point Barrow, Alaska	Basil C. Bradbury	Basil C. Bradbury	1964	95
27⁵⁄₁₆	17²⁄₁₆	10³⁄₁₆	M	Point Barrow, Alaska	James Senn	James Senn	1965	95
27⁵⁄₁₆	17¹⁄₁₆	10⁴⁄₁₆	M	Point Hope, Alaska	R. K. Siller	R. K. Siller	1965	95
27⁵⁄₁₆	16¹³⁄₁₆	10⁹⁄₁₆	M	Bering Straits, Alaska	William D. Backman, Jr	William D. Backman, Jr.	1965	95
27⁵⁄₁₆	16¹⁵⁄₁₆	10⁵⁄₁₆	M	Kotzebue, Alaska	Lewis Figone	Lewis Figone	1965	95
27⁴⁄₁₆	17⁴⁄₁₆	10¹⁄₁₆	M	Kotzebue, Alaska	Gene Barrow	Gene Barrow	1966	95
27⁴⁄₁₆	16¹³⁄₁₆	10⁷⁄₁₆	M	Point Hope, Alaska	E. F. Simon	E. F. Simon	1968	95
27⁴⁄₁₆			M	Wales, Alaska	Eldon Brant	Univ. of Alaska	1957	106

POLAR BEAR—Continued
Ursus maritimus

Score	Greatest Length of Skull Without Lower Jaw	Greatest Width of Skull	Sex	Locality Killed	By Whom Killed	Owner	Date Killed	Rank
27 4/16	17	10 4/16	M	Point Hope, Alaska	Charles Brauch	Charles Brauch	1960	106
27 4/16	17 1/16	10 3/16	M	Point Hope, Alaska	C. Sam Sparks	C. Sam Sparks	1962	106
27 4/16	16 12/16	10 8/16	M	Cape Lisburne, Alaska	Richard Hanks	Richard Hanks	1962	106
27 4/16	16 15/16	10 5/16	M	Kotzebue, Alaska	Bill Taylor	Bill Taylor	1964	106
27 4/16	16 14/16	10 6/16	M	Kotzebue, Alaska	Ralph Lenheim	Ralph Lenheim	1964	106
27 4/16	17	10 4/16	M	Kotzebue, Alaska	Russell Underdahl	Russell Underdahl	1965	106
27 4/16	16 14/16	10 6/16	M	Teller, Alaska	Joseph O. Porter, Sr.	Joseph O. Porter, Sr.	1965	106
27 3/16	17 5/16	9 14/16	M	Nome, Alaska	J. H. Rogers	J. H. Rogers	1956	114
27 3/16	16 11/16	10 8/16	M	Kotzebue, Alaska	Bud Lotstedt	Bud Lotstedt	1959	114
27 3/16	17 5/16	9 14/16	M	Bering Straits, Alaska	Henry S. Budney	Henry S. Budney	1959	114
27 3/16	16 13/16	10 6/16	M	Point Hope, Alaska	Kenneth Holland	Kenneth Holland	1960	114
27 3/16	17 4/16	9 15/16	M	Point Hope, Alaska	Bert Klineburger	Bert Klineburger	1961	114
27 3/16	16 2/16	10 7/16	M	Point Hope, Alaska	Richard Hanks	Richard Hanks	1962	114
27 3/16	16 3/16	10 6/16	M	Chukchi Sea, Alaska	Chas. P. Adkins	Chas. P. Adkins	1964	114
27 3/16	17 3/16	10	M	Kotzebue, Alaska	Barbara Sjoden	Barbara Sjoden	1966	114
27 3/16	17 1/16	10 3/16	M	Kotzebue, Alaska	Bernard Domries	Bernard Domries	1970	114
27 3/16	16 1/16	10 5/16	M	Point Hope, Alaska	Finis Gilbert	Finis Gilbert	1959	123
27 3/16	16 13/16	10 5/16	M	Kotzebue, Alaska	John F. Meyer	John F. Meyer	1960	123
27 3/16	17 4/16	9 14/16	M	Point Hope, Alaska	C. C. Irving	C. C. Irving	1960	123
27 3/16	16 15/16	10 5/16	M	Kotzebue, Alaska	W. T. Yoshimoto	W. T. Yoshimoto	1962	123
27 3/16	16 12/16	10 6/16	M	Point Barrow, Alaska	Frank Bydalek	Frank Bydalek	1963	123
27 3/16	17	10 3/16	M	Kotzebue, Alaska	E. B. Schur	E. B. Schur	1964	123
27 3/16	16 12/16	10 6/16	M	Shishmaref, Alaska	R. V. Hoyt & W. H. Otis	R. V. Hoyt & W. H. Otis	1965	123
27 3/16	16 14/16	10 4/16	M	Chuckchi Sea, Alaska	R. G. Howlett	R. G. Howlett	1965	123
27 3/16	16 15/16	10 2/16	M	Cape Lisburne, Alaska	Howard W. Pollock	Howard W. Pollock	1957	131
27 3/16	16 13/16	10 4/16	M	Kotzebue, Alaska	Glenn B. Walker	Glenn B. Walker	1959	131
27 3/16	17 7/16	9 10/16	M	Kotzebue, Alaska	True Davis	True Davis	1961	131
27 3/16	16 13/16	10 6/16	M	Point Hope, Alaska	Bill Ellis	Bill Ellis	1962	131
27 3/16	16 13/16	10 7/16	M	Kotzebue, Alaska	Fritz Worster	Fritz Worster	1963	131
27 3/16	16 10/16	10 10/16	M	Little Diomede Is., Alaska	Tony Oney	Tony Oney	1963	131
27 3/16	16 12/16	10 5/16	M	Diomede Is., Alaska	Flavy Davis	Flavy Davis	1963	131
27 3/16	16 14/16	10 3/16	M	Kotzebue, Alaska	George W. Roberts	George W. Roberts	1965	131

27¹/₁₆	16¹¹/₁₆	10⁶/₁₆	M	Kotzebue, Alaska	Marshall Johnson	Marshall Johnson	1965	131
27	16¹⁵/₁₆	10¹/₁₆	M	Point Barrow, Alaska	T. L. Richardson	U. S. Natl. Museum	1917	140
27	16⁷/₁₆	10⁹/₁₆	M	Point Hope, Alaska	T. A. Warren	T. A. Warren	1959	140
27	17³/₁₆	9¹⁴/₁₆	M	Kotzebue, Alaska	Unknown	Dick Drew	1959	140
27	16¹⁴/₁₆	10²/₁₆	M	Point Barrow, Alaska	Clifford H. Dietz	Clifford H. Dietz	1960	140
27	16¹²/₁₆	10⁴/₁₆	M	Kotzebue, Alaska	Henry Blackford	Henry Blackford	1961	140
27	16¹⁴/₁₆	10⁴/₁₆	M	Kotzebue, Alaska	James T. Byrnes	Cin. Mus. Nat. History	1963	140
27	16⁸/₁₆	10²/₁₆	M	Kotzebue, Alaska	Charles E. Shedd	Charles E. Shedd	1964	140
27	16¹²/₁₆	10⁸/₁₆	M	Kotzebue, Alaska	Norman W. Garwood	Norman W. Garwood	1964	140
27		10⁴/₁₆	M	Kotzebue, Alaska	William A. Bond	William A. Bond	1964	140

A LOCALLY FAMED JAGUAR, "OLD ONE FANG"

Collected by John M. Phillips near Tampico, Mexico, in 1910, as displayed in Carnegie Museum's Jaguar Group.

Jaguar

Felis onca hernandesii and related subspecies

Minimum Score 14$\frac{8}{16}$

Score	Greatest Length of Skull Without Lower Jaw	Greatest Width of Skull	Sex	Locality Killed	By Whom Killed	Owner	Date Killed	Rank
$18\frac{15}{16}$	$10\frac{15}{16}$	$7\frac{8}{16}$	M	Sinaola, Mexico	C. J. McElroy	C. J. McElroy	1965	1
$18\frac{5}{16}$	$10\frac{14}{16}$	$7\frac{7}{16}$	M	Cibecue, Arizona	Jack Funk	U. S. Natl. Museum	1924	2
$18\frac{3}{16}$	$10\frac{15}{16}$	$7\frac{4}{16}$	M	Nogales, Arizona	Fred Ott	U. S. Natl. Museum	1926	3
$18\frac{2}{16}$	11	$7\frac{2}{16}$	M	Vera Cruz, Mexico	E. W. Nelson & E. A. Goldman	U. S. Natl. Museum	1894	4
$17\frac{15}{16}$	$10\frac{9}{16}$	$7\frac{6}{16}$	U	Tehuantepec, Mexico	Francis Sumuchrast	U. S. Natl. Museum	PR1869	5
$17\frac{13}{16}$	$10\frac{9}{16}$	$7\frac{4}{16}$	M	Guadalajara, Mexico	Elgin T. Gates	Elgin T. Gates	1954	6
$17\frac{11}{16}$	$10\frac{11}{16}$	7	U	Campeche, Mexico	Jacinta S. Dorantes	Squire Haskins	1960	7
$17\frac{10}{16}$	$10\frac{9}{16}$	$7\frac{1}{16}$	M	Chiapas, Mexico	E. W. Nelson & E. A. Goldman	U. S. Natl. Museum	1900	8
$17\frac{8}{16}$	$10\frac{6}{16}$	$7\frac{2}{16}$	M	Tamaulipas, Mexico	Henderson Coquat	M. Nowotny	1940	9
$17\frac{8}{16}$	$10\frac{8}{16}$	7	M	Campeche, Mexico	Alex Hudson III	Alex Hudson III	1962	9
$17\frac{7}{16}$	$10\frac{7}{16}$	7	M	Tamaulipas, Mexico	Unknown	Bond Carroll	1959	11
$17\frac{6}{16}$	$10\frac{6}{16}$	$6\frac{15}{16}$	M	Nayarit, Mexico	Aldegundo Garza de Leon	Aldegundo Garza de Leon	1969	12
$17\frac{4}{16}$	$10\frac{6}{16}$	$6\frac{12}{16}$	M	Mills Co., Texas	H. D. Attwater	U. S. Natl. Museum	1903	13
$17\frac{2}{16}$	$10\frac{6}{16}$	$6\frac{13}{16}$	M	Nayarit, Mexico	P. Mueller & D. O. Rudin	P. Mueller & D. O. Rudin	1959	13
$17\frac{2}{16}$	$10\frac{6}{16}$	$6\frac{12}{16}$	M	Nayarit, Mexico	Kenneth Campbell	Kenneth Campbell	1971	13
17	$10\frac{4}{16}$	$6\frac{12}{16}$	M	Nayarit, Mexico	Graciano Guichard	Graciano Guichard	1969	16
$16\frac{15}{16}$	$10\frac{4}{16}$	$6\frac{11}{16}$	M	Tamaulipas, Mexico	Squire Haskins	Dallas Mus. Nat. Hist.	1957	17
$16\frac{14}{16}$	$10\frac{4}{16}$	$6\frac{12}{16}$	M	Helvetia, Ariz.	E. J. O'Doherty	U. S. Natl. Museum	1917	18
$16\frac{14}{16}$	$10\frac{5}{16}$	$6\frac{9}{16}$	M	Sonora, Mexico	Frank C. Hibben	Frank C. Hibben	1934	18
$16\frac{14}{16}$	$10\frac{5}{16}$	$6\frac{9}{16}$	M	Sonora, Mexico	Frank C. Hibben	Frank C. Hibben	1934	18
$16\frac{14}{16}$	$10\frac{4}{16}$	$6\frac{9}{16}$	M	Nayarit, Mexico	J. F. Brinkley	J. F. Brinkley	1959	18
$16\frac{14}{16}$	$9\frac{12}{16}$	$7\frac{4}{16}$	M	Tampico, Mexico	Hector Elizondo	Hector Elizondo	1962	18
$16\frac{13}{16}$	$10\frac{4}{16}$	$6\frac{8}{16}$	M	Nayarit, Mexico	G. Hooker & L. Stephens	George Hooker	1957	23
$16\frac{12}{16}$	$10\frac{4}{16}$	$6\frac{11}{16}$	M	Nayarit, Mexico	Herb Klein	Herb Klein	1955	24
$16\frac{12}{16}$	$9\frac{5}{16}$	$6\frac{9}{16}$	M	Nayarit, Mexico	Picked Up	Lawson E. Miller, Jr.	1959	24
$16\frac{11}{16}$	$9\frac{4}{16}$	$6\frac{12}{16}$	M	Oaxaca, Mexico	Charles Oertel	U. S. Natl. Museum	1899	26
$16\frac{11}{16}$	$9\frac{4}{16}$	$6\frac{13}{16}$	U	Sonora, Mexico	Dick Wooddell	Dick Wooddell	1955	26
$16\frac{11}{16}$	$10\frac{4}{16}$	$6\frac{9}{16}$	M	Ft. Apache Res., Ariz.	Russell Culbreath	U. S. Natl. Museum	1964	26
$16\frac{10}{16}$	$9\frac{1}{16}$	$6\frac{5}{16}$	M	Nayarit, Mexico	John Ryan	John Ryan	1962	29
$16\frac{10}{16}$	$9\frac{4}{16}$	$6\frac{12}{16}$	M	Nayarit, Mexico	Morton J. Greene	Morton J. Greene	1965	29
$16\frac{8}{16}$	$9\frac{14}{16}$	$6\frac{11}{16}$	M	Vera Cruz, Mexico	A. Wetmore & J. Canela	U. S. Natl. Museum	1939	31

163

JAGUAR—Continued

Felis onca hernandesii and related subspecies

Score	Greatest Length of Skull Without Lower Jaw	Greatest Width of Skull	Sex	Locality Killed	By Whom Killed	Owner	Date Killed	Rank
16⁵/₁₆	9¹⁵/₁₆	6¹⁰/₁₆	M	Tamaulipas, Mexico	Juan Lebeira	Juan Lebeira	1965	31
16⁵/₁₆	9¹⁴/₁₆	6⁸/₁₆	M	Tamaulipas, Mexico	Alex Hudson	Alex Hudson	1964	33
16⁵/₁₆	9¹⁴/₁₆	6⁸/₁₆	M	Nayarit, Mexico	William J. Campbell	William J. Campbell	1970	33
16⁵/₁₆	9¹⁴/₁₆	6⁷/₁₆	M	Nayarit, Mexico	George H. Hodges, Jr.	George H. Hodges, Jr.	1960	35
16⁵/₁₆	9¹²/₁₆	6⁸/₁₆	M	Nayarit, Mexico	O. J. Fletcher	O. J. Fletcher	1964	35
16⁴/₁₆	9¹¹/₁₆	6⁸/₁₆	M	Nayarit, Mexico	Charles Binney II	443rd Hunting Club	1965	37
16⁴/₁₆	9¹¹/₁₆	6⁸/₁₆	M	Nayarit, Mexico	Ventura G. Cosio	Ventura G. Cosio	1965	38
16³/₁₆	9¹¹/₁₆	6⁸/₁₆	M	Nayarit, Mexico	Arvid F. Benson	Arvid F. Benson	1961	39
16²/₁₆	9⁹/₁₆	6⁸/₁₆	F	Arizona	Juan A. Saenz, Jr.	Juan A. Saenz, Jr.	1970	39
16²/₁₆	9¹¹/₁₆	6⁷/₁₆	M	Tamaulipas, Mexico	A. D. Stenger	A. D. Stenger	1957	41
16¹/₁₆	9⁹/₁₆	6⁸/₁₆	M	Tamaulipas, Mexico	Kenneth Campbell	Kenneth Campbell	1970	41
16¹/₁₆	9¹⁰/₁₆	6⁸/₁₆	M	Nayarit, Mexico	Frank R. Denman	Frank R. Denman	1966	43
16	9⁴/₁₆	6¹⁴/₁₆	M	Tamaulipas, Mexico	Patrick W. Frederick	Patrick W. Frederick	1983	44
15¹⁵/₁₆	9⁶/₁₆	6⁸/₁₆	M	Tamaulipas, Mexico	Winfred Lee English	Winfred Lee English	1966	45
15¹³/₁₆	9¹⁰/₁₆	6³/₁₆	M	Tamaulipas, Mexico	Roy E. Cooper	Roy E. Cooper	1960	46
15⁸/₁₆	9⁵/₁₆	6⁸/₁₆	M	Nayarit, Mexico	Gene Biddle	Gene Biddle	1961	46
15⁸/₁₆	9⁵/₁₆	6³/₁₆	M	Nayarit, Mexico	O. A. Washburn	O. A. Washburn	1964	46
15⁵/₁₆	8¹⁴/₁₆	6¹⁰/₁₆	M	Tamaulipas, Mexico	Laurence L. McGee	Univ. of Ariz.	1965	49
15⁵/₁₆	9⁶/₁₆	6⁵/₁₆	M	Patagonia Mts., Ariz.	Jimmie Underwood	Steve M. Matthes	1963	50
15²/₁₆	9⁶/₁₆	6⁵/₁₆	M	Nayarit, Mexico	James G. Shirley, Jr.	James G. Shirley, Jr.	1959	51
15¹/₁₆	9²/₁₆	6	M	Nayarit, Mexico	Terry D. Penrod	Terry D. Penrod	1963	52
14¹⁵/₁₆	9	6¹/₁₆	M	Big Lake, Ariz.	E. W. Ennis, Jr.	E. W. Ennis, Jr.	1956	53
14⁴/₁₆	9	5¹¹/₁₆	F	Nayarit, Mexico	John F. Nutt	John F. Nutt	1958	54
14⁴/₁₆	8¹¹/₁₆	6³/₁₆	F	Nogales, Ariz.	Glenn W. Slade, Jr.	Glenn W. Slade, Jr.	1960	54
14¹³/₁₆	9	5⁴/₁₆	M	Nayarit, Mexico	Kenneth Campbell	Kenneth Campbell	1970	56
14²/₁₆	8⁴/₁₆	5¹¹/₁₆	F	Nayarit, Mexico	Cecil M. Hopper	Cecil M. Hopper	1971	57
14¹/₁₆	8¹⁵/₁₆	5¹³/₁₆	F	Santa Cruz Co., Ariz.	Ed Scarla	Ed Scarla	1959	58

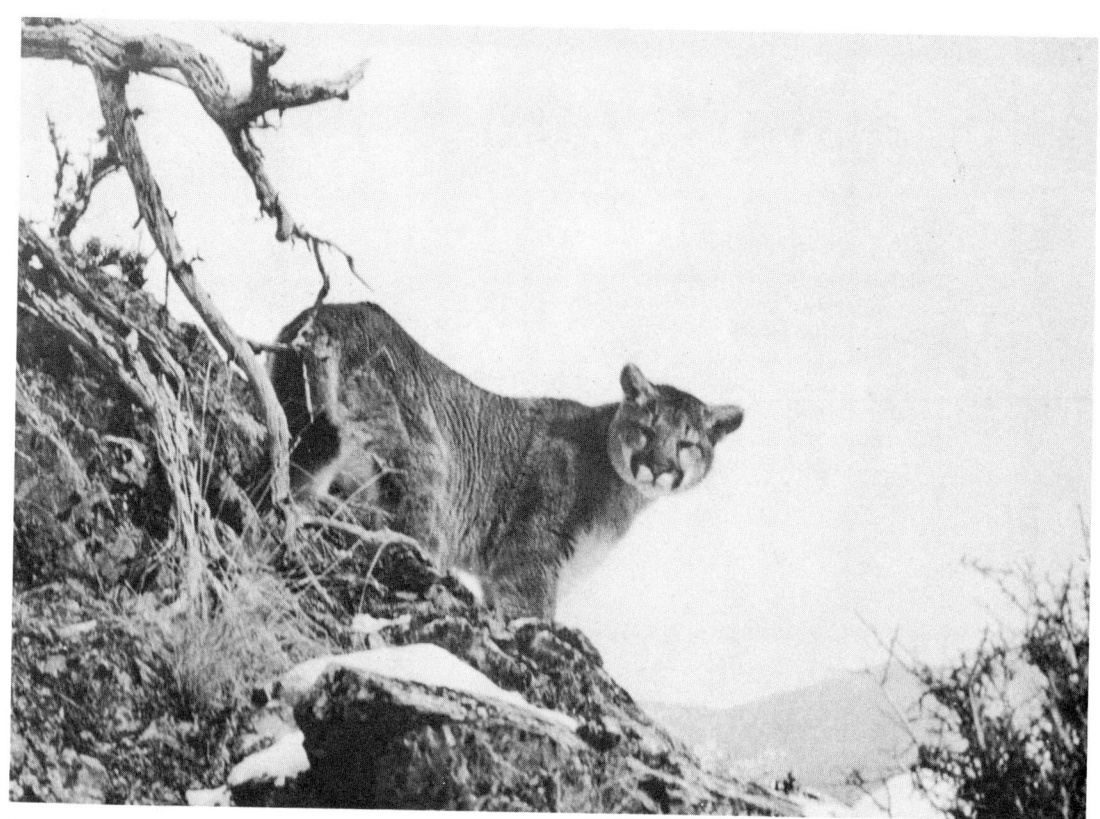

Photograph by Maurice Hornocker

COUGAR (MOUNTAIN LION)

Cougar or Mountain Lion

Felis concolor hippolestes and related subspecies

Minimum Score 15

Score	Greatest Length of Skull Without Lower Jaw	Greatest Width of Skull	Sex	Locality Killed	By Whom Killed	Owner	Date Killed	Rank
16⁵/₁₆	9⁵/₁₆	6¹¹/₁₆	M	Tatlayoko Lake, B.C.	Douglas E. Schuk	Charles M. Travers	1979	1
16	9⁴/₁₆	6¹²/₁₆	M	Garfield Co., Utah	Garth Roberts	R. Scott Jarvie	1964	2
15¹⁵/₁₆	9¹/₁₆	6¹⁴/₁₆	M	Clearwater River, Alta.	Walter R. Weller	Walter R. Weller	1973	3
15¹²/₁₆	9⁵/₁₆	6⁷/₁₆	M	Meeker, Colo.	Theodore Roosevelt	U. S. Natl. Museum	1901	4
15¹²/₁₆	9⁶/₁₆	6¹⁰/₁₆	M	Dutch Creek, Alta.	Edward D. Burton	Edward D. Burton	1954	4
15¹²/₁₆	9⁵/₁₆	6¹¹/₁₆	M	Okanagan Lake, B.C.	Ted Razook	Ted Razook	1973	4
15¹²/₁₆	9⁵/₁₆	6⁷/₁₆	M	Mesa Co., Colo.	Robert R. Meyer	Robert R. Meyer	1978	4
15¹¹/₁₆	9⁴/₁₆	6⁷/₁₆	M	Darb, Mont.	Lowell Hayes	Sherman L. Hayes	1953	8
15¹¹/₁₆	9³/₁₆	6⁸/₁₆	M	Valley Co., Idaho	Louis Rebillet	Louis Rebillet	1961	8
15¹¹/₁₆	9³/₁₆	6⁸/₁₆	M	Selway River, Idaho	Gene R. Alford	Gene R. Alford	1961	8
15¹¹/₁₆	9	6¹¹/₁₆	M	Selway River, Idaho	Gene R. Alford	Gene R. Alford	1961	8
15¹¹/₁₆	9²/₁₆	6⁹/₁₆	M	Okanagan Lake, B.C.	D. Cooper & M. Hubbard	Dusty R. Cooper	1985	8
15¹⁰/₁₆	9³/₁₆	6⁷/₁₆	M	Catherine Creek, Oreg.	Ron Lay	Ron Lay	1966	13
15⁹/₁₆	9²/₁₆	6⁷/₁₆	M	Carbon Co., Utah	H. Alan Foster	H. Alan Foster	1959	14
15⁹/₁₆	9³/₁₆	6⁹/₁₆	M	Okanogan Co., Wash.	Mike Lynch	Mike Lynch	1964	14
15⁹/₁₆	9²/₁₆	6⁷/₁₆	M	Salmon River, Idaho	Doug Kittredge	Doug Kittredge	1971	14
15⁹/₁₆	9	6⁹/₁₆	M	Gallatin Co., Mont.	Tracy J. Peterson	Tracy J. Peterson	1984	14
15⁹/₁₆	9²/₁₆	6⁷/₁₆	M	Carbon Co., Utah	Robert F. McLawhorn	Robert F. McLawhorn	1985	19
15⁸/₁₆	9²/₁₆	6⁹/₁₆	M	Cottonwood, Nev.	Berkley Hunt	Berkley Hunt	1962	19
15⁸/₁₆	9	6⁹/₁₆	M	Porcupine Hills, Alta.	Edward D. Burton	Edward D. Burton	1965	19
15⁸/₁₆	9²/₁₆	6⁹/₁₆	M	Huerfano Co., Colo.	J. D. Dodge	J. D. Dodge	1971	19
15⁸/₁₆	9⁹/₁₆	6	M	Priest Lake, Idaho	Ron Book	Ron Book	1972	19
15⁸/₁₆	9¹/₁₆	6⁷/₁₆	M	Lincoln Co., Mont.	Robert Fleshman	Gary Grenfell	1975	19
15⁸/₁₆	9¹/₁₆	6⁷/₁₆	M	Loblaw Creek, Alta.	John A. Jorgensen	John A. Jorgensen	1977	19
15⁸/₁₆	9	6⁸/₁₆	M	Idaho Co., Idaho	Jerry J. James	Jerry J. James	1982	19
15⁸/₁₆	9³/₁₆	6⁶/₁₆	M	Rio Arriba Co., N.M.	Dick Ray	Dick Ray	1985	19
15⁸/₁₆	9³/₁₆	6⁶/₁₆	M	Rio Blanco Co., Colo.	Robert L. Raley	Robert L. Raley	1985	19
15⁸/₁₆	9	6⁸/₁₆	M	Bannock Co., Idaho	Frank N. Hough	Frank N. Hough	1985	19
15⁷/₁₆	9	6⁸/₁₆	M	Coleman, Alta.	H. Freeman & D. Girardi	H. Freeman & D. Girardi	1963	29
15⁷/₁₆	8¹⁵/₁₆	6⁸/₁₆	M	Kootenay, B.C.	Melvin E. Almas	Melvin E. Almas	1965	29
15⁷/₁₆	9	6⁶/₁₆	M	Lewis & Clark Co., Mont.	Ron Jenkins	R. Jenkins & J. Lee	1967	29

15 7/16	9 3/16	6 5/16	M	Coal Canyon, Colo.	Larry Bamford	Larry Bamford	1967	29
15 5/16	9 1/16	6 5/16	M	Rio Blanco Co., Colo.	Ronald D. Vincent	Ronald D. Vincent	1970	29
15 5/16	9 2/16	6 5/16	M	Columbia Co., Wash.	William R. Randall	William R. Randall	1972	29
15 5/16	8 13/16	6 1/16	M	Gold Creek, B.C.	Donovan W. Ellis	Donovan W. Ellis	1981	29
15 5/16	9 2/16	6 5/16	M	Lemhi Co., Idaho	David W. Thompson	David W. Thompson	1983	29
15 5/16	9 1/16	6 5/16	M	Wind River Mts., Wyo.	M. Abbott Frazier	U. S. Natl. Museum	1892	37
15 5/16	8 14/16	6 8/16	M	Okanogan Co., Wash.	Merle Hooshagen	Merle Hooshagen	1957	37
15 5/16	8 14/16	6 8/16	M	Young, Ariz.	Ed Scarla	Ed Scarla	1958	37
15 5/16	9 4/16	6 2/16	M	Sedalia, Colo.	Walt Paulk	Walt Paulk	1961	37
15 5/16	8 14/16	6 8/16	M	Mineral Co., Mont.	Richard Ramberg	Richard Ramberg	1964	37
15 5/16	8 13/16	6 8/16	M	Natal, B.C.	Dick Ritco	Dick Ritco	1964	37
15 5/16	8 13/16	6 1/16	M	Fernie, B.C.	Oscar Jansen	Oscar Jansen	1964	37
15 5/16	9 2/16	6 8/16	M	West Salt Creek, Colo.	Hartle V. Morris	Hartle V. Morris	1964	37
15 5/16	9	6 8/16	M	Missoula Co., Mont.	Jim Zeiler	William W. Zeiler	1966	37
15 5/16	9	6 8/16	M	Sanders Co., Mont.	Lloyd F. Behling	Lloyd F. Behling	1969	37
15 5/16	9 1/16	6 4/16	M	Bull River, B.C.	Henry Fercho	Henry Fercho	1976	37
15 5/16	9 2/16	6 5/16	M	Colfax Co., N.M.	Marta Sue Burnside	Marta Sue Burnside	1977	37
15 5/16	9 1/16	6 8/16	M	Mesa Co., Colo.	Jack Harrison	Jack Harrison	1980	37
15 5/16	8 14/16	6 8/16	M	Lewis & Clark Co., Mont.	Wayne L. Beach	Wayne L. Beach	1983	37
15 5/16	9	6 8/16	M	Missoula Co., Mont.	Bruce E. Parker	Bruce E. Parker	1984	37
15 5/16	9 2/16	6 1/16	M	Benewah Co., Idaho	Kurt R. Morris	Kurt R. Morris	1984	37
15 5/16	9 3/16	6 7/16	M	Socorro Co., N.M.	Edwin E. Finkbeiner	Edwin E. Finkbeiner	1984	37
15 5/16	8 14/16	6 5/16	M	Hamilton, Mont.	Lloyd Thompson	U. S. Natl. Museum	1922	54
15 5/16	8 12/16	6 8/16	F	Clear Water River, Alta.	William A. Schutte	William A. Schutte	1935	54
15 5/16	8 13/16	6 8/16	M	Missoula Co., Mont.	Ronald Thompson	U. S. Natl. Museum	1936	54
15 5/16	8 15/16	6 8/16	M	East Kootenay, B.C.	Martin Marigeau	C. Garrett	1940	54
15 5/16	8 13/16	6 8/16	M	Clearwater Co., Idaho	Andy Eatmon	H. H. Schnettler	1953	54
15 5/16	8 15/16	6 8/16	M	Spanish Fork Canyon, Utah	R. Jones & G. Pierce	Ronald Jones	1954	54
15 5/16	8 15/16	6 8/16	M	Granite Co., Mont.	Oscar E. Nelson	Oscar E. Nelson	1961	54
15 5/16	8 15/16	6 3/16	M	Idaho Co., Idaho	Wayne & Douglas England	Wayne England	1962	54
15 5/16	9 2/16	6 3/16	M	Eagle Nest, N.M.	Hal Vaught	Hal Vaught	1963	54
15 5/16	9 2/16	6 4/16	M	Lake Quinault, Wash.	C. A. Heppe	C. A. Heppe	1964	54
15 5/16	9 1/16	6 6/16	M	Lac La Hache, B.C.	Andy Hagberg	Andy Hagberg	1964	54
15 5/16	8 15/16	6 4/16	M	Grand Junction, Colo.	John Lamicq, Jr.	John Lamicq, Jr.	1967	54
15 5/16	9 1/16	6 1/16	M	Elk City, Idaho	W. Goodwin & D. Baldwin	David Baldwin	1969	54
15 5/16	9 4/16	6 8/16	M	Elko Co., Nev.	Kenneth A. Johnson	Kenneth A. Johnson	1969	54
15 5/16	8 15/16	6 8/16	M	Lemhi Co., Idaho	Larry L. Schweitzer	Larry L. Schweitzer	1974	54
15 5/16	8 13/16	6 5/16	M	Osoyoos, B.C.	Alvin L. Reiff	Alvin L. Reiff	1975	54
15 5/16	9	6 5/16	M	Okanogan Co., Wash.	Joel N. Hughes	Joel N. Hughes	1975	54
15 5/16	9	6 5/16	M	Hardesty Creek, Alta.	John T. Shillingburg	John T. Shillingburg	1976	54
15 5/16	9	6 5/16	M	Custer Co., Idaho	Florence Buxton	Florence Buxton	1977	54
15 5/16	8 15/16	6 8/16	M	Jumpingpound Creek, Alta.	Max W. Good	Max W. Good	1978	54
15 5/16	8 15/16	6 8/16	M	Mineral Co., Mont.	Dennis E. Moos	Dennis E. Moos	1979	54

Cougar or Mountain Lion—*Continued*

Felis concolor hippolestes and related subspecies

Score	Greatest Length of Skull Without Lower Jaw	Greatest Width of Skull	Sex	Locality Killed	By Whom Killed	Owner	Date Killed	Rank
15 7/16	9	6 7/16	M	Wallowa Co., Oreg.	Duane E. Neuschwander	Duane E. Neuschwander	1980	54
15 7/16	8 15/16	6 7/16	M	Pend Oreille Co., Wash.	Jack Schulte	Jack Schulte	1981	54
15 7/16	9	6 7/16	M	Okanogan Co., Wash.	Merle Hooshagen	Merle Hooshagen	1956	77
15 7/16	8 13/16	6 7/16	M	Wells Gray Park, B.C.	Colin Mann	Colin Mann	1960	77
15 7/16	8 13/16	6 7/16	M	Union Co., Oregon	Don Haefer	W. H. Miller	1961	77
15 7/16	8 15/16	6 7/16	M	Motoqua, Utah	Basil C. Bradbury	Basil C. Bradbury	1963	77
15 7/16	8 14/16	6 7/16	M	Canim Lake, B.C.	H. C. Nickelsen	H. C. Nickelsen	1964	77
15 7/16	9	6 4/16	M	Missoula Co., Mont.	Richard Ramberg	Maurice Hornocker	1964	77
15 7/16	9	6 4/16	M	Missoula Co., Mont.	B. Stanley & C. Johnson	Bob Stanley	1967	77
15 7/16	9	6 4/16	M	Salmon River, Idaho	Aaron U. Jones	Aaron U. Jones	1967	77
15 7/16	9	6 4/16	M	Snake River, Idaho	Dee M. Cannon	Dee M. Cannon	1968	77
15 7/16	8 13/16	6 7/16	M	Sandpoint, Idaho	George C. Taft	George C. Taft	1969	77
15 7/16	8 15/16	6 7/16	M	Okanogan Co., Wash.	Louis J. Ayers	Louis J. Ayers	1969	77
15 7/16	9	6 4/16	M	Vernal, Utah	Harold Schneider	Harold Schneider	1970	77
15 7/16	8 15/16	6 7/16	U	Beaver Creek, Alta.	Oscar Markle	Oscar Markle	1970	77
15 7/16	9 3/16	6 1/16	F	Sanders Co., Mont.	Edna Hill	Edna Hill	1970	77
15 7/16	9 2/16	6 2/16	M	Ravalli Co., Mont.	Larry A. Rose	Larry A. Rose	1973	77
15 7/16	8 15/16	6 5/16	M	Nakusp, B.C.	Glen Olson	Glen Olson	1974	77
15 7/16	8 15/16	6 5/16	M	Mineral Co., Mont.	Irving H. Ratnour	Irving H. Ratnour	1975	77
15 7/16	9	6 4/16	M	Lincoln Co., Mont.	Wayne B. Hunt	Wayne B. Hunt	1975	77
15 7/16	8 14/16	6 6/16	M	Oliver, B.C.	Walter Snoke	Walter Snoke	1977	77
15 7/16	9	6 4/16	M	Meldrum Creek, B.C.	Walter A. Riemer	Walter A. Riemer	1977	77
15 7/16	9	6 4/16	M	Threepoint Creek, Alta.	Robert C. Dickson	R. C. Dickson & R. J. Dickson, Jr.	1978	77
15 7/16	8 14/16	6 6/16	M	Rio Arriba Co., N.M.	Anderson Bakewell	Anderson Bakewell	1978	77
15 7/16	8 15/16	6 5/16	M	Idaho Co., Idaho	Ralph E. Close	Ralph E. Close	1980	77
15 7/16	8 14/16	6 6/16	M	Baker Co., Oreg.	Joe J. Lay	Joe J. Lay	1981	77
15 7/16	9 2/16	6 2/16	M	Colfax Co., N.M.	Ronald G. Troyer	Ronald G. Troyer	1982	77
15 7/16	8 14/16	6 6/16	M	Broadwater Co., Mont.	Ray Toombs	Ray Toombs	1982	77
15 7/16	8 15/16	6 5/16	M	Lewis & Clark Co., Mont.	Robert A. Soukkala	Robert A. Soukkala	1983	77
15 7/16	8 13/16	6 7/16	M	Wallowa Co., Oreg.	Donna Lancaster	Donna Lancaster	1983	77
15 7/16	9 2/16	6 6/16	M	Colfax Co., N.M.	L. Profazi & R. Troyer	Louie Profazi	1984	77

15 6/16	9	6 6/16	M	Coconino Co., Ariz.	Gregg A. Thurston	Gregg A. Thurston	1984	77
15 5/16	9 2/16	6 2/16	M	Mill Creek, Alta.	Warren R. Burton	Warren R. Burton	1984	77
15 5/16	8 14/16	6 6/16	M	Dolores Co., Colo.	Bruce Nay	Bruce Nay	1984	77
15 5/16	9	6 4/16	U	Sevier Co., Utah	John R. Blanton	John R. Blanton	1985	77
15 5/16	8 13/16	6 5/16	M	East Kootenay, B.C.	Martin Marigeau	C. Garrett	1940	110
15 5/16	8 13/16	6 6/16	M	Ventura Co., Calif.	Warren C. Johnston	Warren C. Johnston	1953	110
15 5/16	9 1/16	6 2/16	M	Nelson, B.C.	R. A. Rutherglen	Univ. of B.C.	1956	110
15 5/16	8 14/16	6 5/16	M	Chum Creek, B.C.	J. R. Aitchison	J. R. Aitchison	1956	110
15 5/16	8 14/16	6 5/16	M	Trout Creek, Alta.	Kenny McRae	Kenny McRae	1961	110
15 5/16	8 14/16	6 5/16	M	Pincher Creek, Alta.	Harry R. Freeman	Harry R. Freeman	1961	110
15 5/16	8 14/16	6 4/16	M	Saratoga, Wyo.	Win Condict	Win Condict	1961	110
15 5/16	8 14/16	6 4/16	M	McGregor Lake, Alta.	Gus Daley	A. C. Wilson	1962	110
15 5/16	8 14/16	6 5/16	M	Oliver, B.C.	Allan Nichol	Allan Nichol	1963	110
15 5/16	8 14/16	6 5/16	M	Okanogan Co., Wash.	Mike Lynch	Mike Lynch	1964	110
15 5/16	8 11/16	6 8/16	M	Whitecourt, Alta.	K. J. Stanton	K. J. Stanton	1967	110
15 5/16	8 15/16	6 5/16	M	Oroville, Wash.	L. Fleming & J. Lemaster	Leon Fleming	1967	110
15 5/16	9	6 3/16	M	Tatlayoko Lake, B.C.	C. L. Anderson	C. L. Anderson	1967	110
15 5/16	9 3/16	6	F	Meeker, Colo.	Jack Cadario	Jack Cadario	1968	110
15 5/16	8 15/16	6 4/16	F	Orofino, Idaho	Fairly Bonner	Fairly Bonner	1969	110
15 5/16	8 14/16	6 5/16	M	Falkland, B.C.	Earl Carlson	Wildlife Tax. Studios	1974	110
15 5/16	9 3/16	6	M	Emery Co., Utah	Dan Scartezina	Dan Scartezina	1976	110
15 5/16	8 15/16	6 4/16	M	Prouton Lakes, B.C.	G. C. Ridley & R. Gillespie	G. C. Ridley & R. Gillespie	1976	110
15 5/16	9 2/16	6 1/16	M	Garfield Co., Utah	William A. Coats	William A. Coats	1978	110
15 5/16	8 15/16	6 4/16	M	Mt. Evans, B.C.	Larry N. Dent	Larry N. Dent	1980	110
15 5/16	8 10/16	6 9/16	M	Ferry Co., Wash.	Richard A. Bonander	Richard A. Bonander	1981	110
15 5/16	8 14/16	6 5/16	M	Stevens Co., Wash.	William K. Bean	William K. Bean	1981	110
15 5/16	8 14/16	6 5/16	M	Rio Blanco Co., Colo.	Robert L. Raley	Robert L. Raley	1983	110
15 5/16	8 12/16	6 6/16	U	East Kootenay, B.C.	Martin Marigeau	C. Garrett	1940	133
15 4/16	8 14/16	6 4/16	M	Benewak Co., Idaho	Karl Paulson	Karl Paulson	1945	133
15 4/16	9 1/16	6 4/16	M	Salmon River, Idaho	Bob Hagel	Bob Hagel	1950	133
15 4/16	8 14/16	6 4/16	M	Pine, Ariz.	C. J. Prock	C. J. Prock	1958	133
15 4/16	8 15/16	6 5/16	M	Strawberry, Ariz.	Irene Morden	Irene Morden	1958	133
15 4/16	8 12/16	6 6/16	M	Coleman, Colo.	Ted & Connie Michalsky	Ted & Connie Michalsky	1962	133
15 4/16	9	6 2/16	M	Allison, Colo.	Georgianna Etheridge	Georgianna Etheridge	1962	133
15 4/16	9 1/16	6 1/16	M	New Harmony, Utah	Art Coates	Art Coates	1962	133
15 4/16	8 14/16	6 4/16	M	Parowan, Utah	William Mastrangel	William Mastrangel	1964	133
15 4/16	8 11/16	6 7/16	M	Lendrum Creek, Alta.	Gary G. Giese	Gary G. Giese	1964	133
15 4/16	8 14/16	6 4/16	M	Reserve, N.M.	Wilmer C. Hansen	Wilmer C. Hansen	1966	133
15 4/16	8 15/16	6 3/16	M	Saratoga, Wyo.	Win Condict	Win Condict	1967	133
15 4/16	8 12/16	6 6/16	M	Little Fort, B.C.	Earl E. Hill	Earl E. Hill	1968	133
15 4/16	8 15/16	6 3/16	M	Duchesne Co., Utah	Clyde C. Edwards	Clyde C. Edwards	1969	133
15 4/16	8 14/16	6 4/16	M	Manzano Mts., N.M.	C. J. McElroy	C. J. McElroy	1970	133
15 4/16	8 12/16	6 6/16	M	Okanagan Valley, Wash.	Patrick M. Davis	Patrick M. Davis	1970	133

COUGAR OR MOUNTAIN LION—*Continued*

Felis concolor hippolestes and related subspecies

Score	Greatest Length of Skull Without Lower Jaw	Greatest Width of Skull	Sex	Locality Killed	By Whom Killed	Owner	Date Killed	Rank
15⁹⁄₁₆	8⁶⁄₁₆	6⁹⁄₁₆	M	Duchesne Co., Utah	Richard B. Sydnor, Jr.	Richard B. Sydnor, Jr.	1972	133
15⁹⁄₁₆	8¹²⁄₁₆	6⁹⁄₁₆	M	Ferry Co., Wash.	Paul L. Watts	Paul L. Watts	1972	133
15⁹⁄₁₆	9	6²⁄₁₆	M	Graveyard Creek, B.C.	Rod G. Hardie	Rod G. Hardie	1972	133
15⁹⁄₁₆	8¹⁴⁄₁₆	6⁴⁄₁₆	M	Stevens Co., Wash.	Leroy W. Kindsvogel	Wash. State U. Alumni Assoc.	1972	133
15⁹⁄₁₆	8¹³⁄₁₆	6⁵⁄₁₆	M	Lincoln Co., Mont.	Katherine Kimberlin	Katherine Kimberlin	1973	133
15⁹⁄₁₆	9	6⁷⁄₁₆	M	Pend Oreille Co., Wash.	Robert J. Robertson	Robert J. Robertson	1974	133
15⁹⁄₁₆	9	6²⁄₁₆	M	Carbon Co., Utah	L. A. Grelling	L. A. Grelling	1974	133
15⁹⁄₁₆	8¹²⁄₁₆	6⁶⁄₁₆	M	Idaho Co., Idaho	Lawrence L. Seiler	Lawrence L. Seiler	1977	133
15⁹⁄₁₆	8¹¹⁄₁₆	6⁷⁄₁₆	M	Granby River, B.C.	Everett B. Pannkuk, Jr.	Everett B. Pannkuk, Jr.	1977	133
15⁹⁄₁₆	8¹³⁄₁₆	6⁵⁄₁₆	M	Cascade Range, B.C.	Dennis C. Roach	Dennis C. Roach	1978	133
15⁹⁄₁₆	8¹⁵⁄₁₆	6³⁄₁₆	M	Uintah Co., Utah	Dale Larson	Dale Larson	1978	133
15⁹⁄₁₆	8¹⁴⁄₁₆	6⁴⁄₁₆	M	Mt. Roderick, B.C.	Gail Holderman	Gail Holderman	1979	133
15⁹⁄₁₆	9¹⁄₁₆	6¹⁄₁₆	M	Colfax Co., N.M.	Philip H. Whitley	Philip H. Whitley	1980	133
15⁹⁄₁₆	8¹⁴⁄₁₆	6⁴⁄₁₆	M	Stevens Co., Wash.	Fritz G. Nagel	Fritz G. Nagel	1981	133
15⁹⁄₁₆	8¹⁴⁄₁₆	6⁴⁄₁₆	M	Adams Co., Idaho	Warren J. Mason	Warren J. Mason	1982	133
15⁹⁄₁₆	8¹³⁄₁₆	6⁵⁄₁₆	M	Archuleta Co., Colo.	Judd Cooney	Judd Cooney	1982	133
15⁹⁄₁₆	8¹²⁄₁₆	6⁶⁄₁₆	M	Garfield Co., Colo.	Leslie H. Brewster	Leslie H. Brewster	1983	133
15⁹⁄₁₆	8¹²⁄₁₆	6⁶⁄₁₆	M	Wallowa Co., Oreg.	Samuel E. Briscoe	Samuel E. Briscoe	1984	133
15⁹⁄₁₆	8¹¹⁄₁₆	6⁷⁄₁₆	M	Gallatin Co., Mont.	David M. Tofte	David M. Tofte	1984	133
15⁹⁄₁₆	8¹⁴⁄₁₆	6⁴⁄₁₆	M	Sanders Co., Mont.	Conrad P. Anderson	Conrad P. Anderson	1984	133
15⁹⁄₁₆	8¹³⁄₁₆	6⁶⁄₁₆	U	Princeton, B.C.	Alan Gill	C. F. Gigot	1948	169
15⁹⁄₁₆	8¹³⁄₁₆	6⁶⁄₁₆	M	Okanogan Co., Wash.	Francis Randall	Francis Randall	1948	169
15⁹⁄₁₆	8¹⁵⁄₁₆	6²⁄₁₆	M	Saratoga, Wyo.	Win Condict	Win Condict	1954	169
15⁹⁄₁₆	8⁸⁄₁₆	6⁸⁄₁₆	M	Ferris Mts., Wyo.	W. Condict & E. Levasseur	Win Condict	1959	169
15⁹⁄₁₆	8¹⁴⁄₁₆	6²⁄₁₆	M	Cat Creek, Alta.	Hyrum R. Baker	Hyrum R. Baker	1960	169
15⁹⁄₁₆	9	6¹⁄₁₆	M	Wild Horse Basin, Wyo.	Win Condict	Win Condict	1961	169
15⁹⁄₁₆	8¹³⁄₁₆	6⁴⁄₁₆	M	Custer Co., Idaho	Joe Blackburn	Joe Blackburn	1962	169
15⁹⁄₁₆	8¹⁴⁄₁₆	6³⁄₁₆	M	Oliver, B.C.	Allan Nichol	Allan Nichol	1963	169
15⁹⁄₁₆	9	6¹⁄₁₆	M	Clearwater River, Idaho	Ted Hall	Ted Hall	1964	169
15⁹⁄₁₆	8¹²⁄₁₆	6⁵⁄₁₆	M	Missoula Co., Mont.	William Zeiler	William Zeiler	1966	169
15⁹⁄₁₆	8¹⁴⁄₁₆	6³⁄₁₆	M	Mineral Co., Mont.	Richard Ramberg	Richard & Neal Ramberg	1966	169
15⁹⁄₁₆	8¹³⁄₁₆	6⁴⁄₁₆	M	S. Castle River, Alta.	James F. Simpson	James F. Simpson	1967	169

				Locality	By whom killed	Owner	Date	Rank
15 11/16	8 13/16	6 4/16	M	Lincoln Co., Mont.	H. M. Johnston	H. M. Johnston	1967	169
15 11/16	8 14/16	6 3/16	M	Clearwater Co., Idaho	Robert W. Haskin	Robert W. Haskin	1967	169
15 11/16	9 1/16	6	M	Price, Utah	Robert H. Elder	Robert H. Elder	1968	169
15 11/16	8 15/16	6 2/16	M	Oroville, Wash.	Dan Lynch	Dan Lynch	1968	169
15 11/16	8 13/16	6 4/16	M	Little Fort, B.C.	Earl E. Hill	Earl E. Hill	1968	169
15 11/16	9 1/16	6	M	Sunflower, Ariz.	John C. Shaw	John C. Shaw	1969	169
15 11/16	8 14/16	6 3/16	M	Douglas Co., Colo.	C. R. Anderson & E. H. Brown	Charles R. Anderson	1969	169
15 11/16	9 1/16	6	M	Gunlock, Utah	L. Dean Taylor	L. Dean Taylor	1971	169
15 11/16	8 12/16	6 5/16	M	Mineral Co., Mont.	William E. Bullock	William E. Bullock	1971	169
15 11/16	8 13/16	6 4/16	M	Uintah Co., Utah	Brent L. Winchester	Brent L. Winchester	1972	169
15 11/16	9	6 1/16	M	Superior, Mont.	James L. Schaeffer	James L. Schaeffer	1972	169
15 11/16	8 14/16	6 3/16	M	Pima Co., Ariz.	George W. Parker	George W. Parker	1972	169
15 11/16	8 13/16	6 4/16	M	Granite Co., Mont.	James A. Raikos	James A. Raikos	1973	169
15 11/16	8 14/16	6 3/16	M	Emery Co., Utah	Sharon Ann Burkett	Sharon Ann Burkett	1973	169
15 11/16	8 15/16	6 4/16	M	Idaho Co., Idaho	Chester D. Haight	Chester D. Haight	1975	169
15 11/16	8 13/16	6 2/16	M	Lake Co., Mont.	J. E. McCreedy & R. E. Seabaug	James McCreedy	1977	169
15 11/16	8 14/16	6 2/16	M	Wallowa Co., Oreg.	Rollie Mattson	Rollie Mattson	1978	169
15 11/16	8 15/16	6 4/16	M	Pimainus Hills, B.C.	Norman W. Dougan	Norman W. Dougan	1978	169
15 11/16	8 15/16	6 3/16	M	Pend Oreille Co., Wash.	William M. Day	William M. Day	1978	169
15 11/16	8 13/16	6	M	Piute Co., Utah	Fred J. Markley	Fred J. Markley	1979	169
15 11/16	9 1/16	6 2/16	M	Nez Perce Co., Idaho	Pete M. Baughman, Jr.	Pete M. Baughman, Jr.	1979	169
15 11/16	8 12/16	6 5/16	M	Rio Arriba Co., N.M.	Joseph Strasser, Jr.	Joseph Strasser, Jr.	1980	169
15 11/16	8 15/16	6 4/16	M	Mill Creek, Alta.	Richard C. Davidson	Richard C. Davidson	1980	169
15	8 14/16	6 3/16	M	Erickson Creek, B.C.	R. John Kovak	R. John Kovak	1982	169
15	8 13/16	6 4/16	M	Wallowa Co., Oreg.	William E. Hosford	William E. Hosford	1982	169
15	9	6 3/16	M	Whitney Creek, Alta.	Bryne J. Lengyel	Bryne J. Lengyel	1985	169
15	8 13/16	6	M	Columbia River, Wash.	J. K. Townsend	Acad. Nat. Sci., Phil.	1834	207
15	9	6	M	Dotsero, Colo.	J. T. Meirer	Univ. Kansas Museum	1887	207
15	9	6	M	Lincoln Co., Mont.	Frank Haacke	Univ. of Mont.	1950	207
15	8 12/16	6 5/16	M	Salmon River, Idaho	Bob Hagel	Bob Hagel	1953	207
15	8 13/16	6 1/16	M	Iron Co., Utah	James A. Worthen	James A. Worthen	1958	207
15	8 14/16	6 3/16	M	Salmon River, Idaho	Roy Tumilsen	Roy Tumilsen	1959	207
15	8 15/16	6 2/16	M	Invermere, B.C.	R. A. Merkner	R. A. Merkner	1959	207
15	8 11/16	6 1/16	M	Elko Co., Nev.	Earl Dudley	Earl Dudley	1959	207
15	8 8/16	6 5/16	M	Magdalena Mts., N.M.	F. C. Hibben	F. C. Hibben	1960	207
15	8 13/16	6 3/16	M	Flat Creek, Alta.	Hyrum R. Baker	Hyrum R. Baker	1960	207
15	8 12/16	6 4/16	M	Powell Co., Mont.	Copenhaver Bros.	Norris Pratt	1961	207
15	8 12/16	6 1/16	M	Onyx, Calif.	Ray Mallory	Larry Mansfield	1961	207
15	8 13/16	6 3/16	M	Cranbrook, B.C.	Unknown	Aasland Taxidermy	1961	207
15	8 14/16	6 2/16	M	Lumby, B.C.	Ronald Catt	Ronald Catt	1962	207
15	9	6	M	Jesmond, B.C.	Charlie Coldwell	Charlie Coldwell	1963	207
15	8 10/16	6 6/16	M	Socorro Co., N.M.	Hugh Olney	Hugh Olney	1964	207

COUGAR OR MOUNTAIN LION—*Continued*
Felis concolor hippolestes and related subspecies

Score	Greatest Length of Skull Without Lower Jaw	Greatest Width of Skull	Sex	Locality Killed	By Whom Killed	Owner	Date Killed	Rank
15	8 12/16	6 2/16	U	Mesa Co., Colo.	John Adams	John Adams	1965	207
15	9	6	M	Grass Valley, Oreg.	Danny Henderson	Danny Henderson	1965	207
15	8 12/16	6 4/16	M	West Kootenay, B.C.	M. E. Goddard	M. E. Goddard	1966	207
15	8 13/16	6 3/16	M	Grand Forks, B.C.	Clarence C. Bahr	Clarence C. Bahr	1966	207
15	8 11/16	6 5/16	M	Darfield, B.C.	Ted Scott	Ted Scott	1966	207
15	8 13/16	6 3/16	M	Selway River, Idaho	Ken Wolfinbarger	Ken Wolfinbarger	1966	207
15	8 12/16	6 4/16	M	Idaho Co., Idaho	Jack D. Sheppard	Jack D. Sheppard	1966	207
15	8 12/16	6 4/16	M	Ferndale, Mont.	Loren R. Wittrock	Loren R. Wittrock	1967	207
15	8 14/16	6 2/16	M	Wolf Creek, Mont.	Gus R. Wolfe	G. R. Wolfe & J. Lee	1967	207
15	8 12/16	6 4/16	M	Fisher Creek, Alta.	Perry Jacobson	Perry Jacobson	1967	207
15	8 14/16	6 2/16	M	Hanksville, Utah	Eddie D. Scheinost	Eddie D. Scheinost	1967	207
15	8 13/16	6 3/16	M	Spanish Fork Canyon, Utah	Richard C. Smith	Richard C. Smith	1968	207
15	8 11/16	6 5/16	M	Alpine Co., Calif.	Jeffrey A. Brent	Jeffrey A. Brent	1968	207
15	8 11/16	6 5/16	M	Mizzezula Mts., B.C.	Bengt G. Bjalme	Bengt G. Bjalme	1969	207
15	8 15/16	6 1/16	M	Canon City, Colo.	Dale R. Leonard	Dale R. Leonard	1969	207
15	8 12/16	6 4/16	M	Stevens Co., Wash.	N. Willey & L. Hedrick	N. Willey & L. Hedrick	1969	207
15	8 14/16	6 2/16	M	Lucile, Idaho	Carl P. Bentz	Mrs. W. H. Prescott, Jr.	1969	207
15	8 10/16	6 6/16	M	Ferry Co., Wash.	John D. Mercer	John D. Mercer	1969	207
15	8 13/16	6 3/16	M	Canon City, Colo.	Glen Rosengarten	Glen Rosengarten	1970	207
15	8 12/16	6 5/16	M	Wells, Nev.	Marvin Johnson	Marvin Johnson	1970	207
15	9	6	M	Antelope Pass, Colo.	Phil Nichols	Phil Nichols	1971	207
15	8 13/16	6 3/16	M	Kootenai Co., Idaho	George H. Daly	George H. Daly	1971	207
15	8 14/16	6 2/16	M	Millard Co., Utah	Picked Up	Utah Div. Wildl. Resc.	1974	207
15	8 14/16	6 2/16	U	Las Animas Co., Colo.	Marion M. Snyder	Mike Powell	1974	207
15	8 12/16	6 5/16	M	Stevens Co., Wash.	Roger Lofts	Roger Lofts	1974	207
15	8 12/16	6 5/16	M	Ashcroft, B.C.	Ken Kilback	Ken Kilback	1975	207
15	8 13/16	6 3/16	M	Prouton Lakes, B.C.	G. C. Ridley	G. C. Ridley & R. Gillespie	1977	207
15	8 13/16	6 3/16	M	Union Co., Oreg.	Brian Spencer	Brian Spencer	1977	207
15	8 13/16	6 3/16	M	Huerfano Co., Colo.	Sheila D. Bisgard	Sheila D. Bisgard	1977	207
15	8 14/16	6 2/16	M	Latah Co., Idaho	Earl Landrus	Earl Landrus	1977	207
15	8 15/16	6 1/16	M	Skookumchuck Creek, B.C.	Jack Walkley, Jr.	Jack Walkley, Jr.	1979	207
15	8 11/16	6 5/16	M	Stevens Co., Wash.	Roger A. Rasching	Roger A. Rasching	1979	207

15	8¹⁴⁄₁₆	6⁷⁄₁₆	M	Madison Co., Mont.	George A. Dieruf	George A. Dieruf	1980	207
15	8¹¹⁄₁₆	6⁵⁄₁₆	M	Nine Mile Creek, B.C.	Ray Carry	Ray Carry	1980	207
15	9	6	M	Washington Co., Utah	J. Phil Goodson	J. Phil Goodson	1980	207
15	8¹¹⁄₁₆	6⁵⁄₁₆	M	San Miguel Co., Colo.	James N. McHolme	James N. McHolme	1981	207
15	8¹⁰⁄₁₆	6⁶⁄₁₆	M	Teton Co., Mont.	Richard Klick	John F. Sulik	1982	207
15	8¹²⁄₁₆	6⁴⁄₁₆	M	Rio Arriba Co., N.M.	Michael Ray	Michael Ray	1982	207
15	8¹⁴⁄₁₆	6⁷⁄₁₆	M	Gila Co., Ariz.	William T. Haney	William T. Haney	1983	207
15	8⁸⁄₁₆	6⁸⁄₁₆	M	Sheridan Co., Wyo.	Toby J. Johnson	Toby J. Johnson	1984	207
15	8⁹⁄₁₆	6⁶⁄₁₆	M	Wallowa Co., Oreg.	Edward Cranston	Edward Cranston	1984	207
15¹³⁄₁₆*	8¹³⁄₁₆	6³⁄₁₆	M	Mesa Co., Colo.	Lawrence C. Glass	Lawrence C. Glass	1985	
15¹⁰⁄₁₆*	9⁴⁄₁₆	6⁶⁄₁₆	M	Salmon River, Idaho	Art Ling	Art Ling	1971	
15¹⁰⁄₁₆*	9¹⁄₁₆	6⁹⁄₁₆	M	Lincoln Co., Mont.	Bill Reynolds	Bill Reynolds	1983	
15¹⁰⁄₁₆*	9⁹⁄₁₆	6⁹⁄₁₆	M	Lincoln Co., Mont.	A. Kimberlin & W. Nixon	Anthony Kimberlin	1983	
15⁷⁄₁₆*	9⁴⁄₁₆	6³⁄₁₆	M	Sandoval Co., N.M.	Thomas J. David	Thomas J. David	1980	
15⁶⁄₁₆*	8¹¹⁄₁₆	6¹¹⁄₁₆	M	Taos Co., N.M.	George P. Mann	George P. Mann	1981	

*Final Score subject to revision by additional verifying measurements

Photograph by Grancel Fitz

WORLD'S RECORD ATLANTIC WALRUS TUSKS
SCORE: 118 6/8
Locality: Greenland Date: prior to 1955
Hunter: unknown
Donated by Roy Vail to the National Collection

Atlantic Walrus

Odobenus rosmarus rosmarus

Minimum Score 95

Score	Entire Length of Loose Tusk R.	L.	Circumference of Base R.	L.	Circumference at Third Quarter R.	L.	Sex	Locality Killed	By Whom Killed	Owner	Date Killed	Rank
118⅞	30⅝	30⅜	8⅜	8⅜	5⅜	5⅝	U	Greenland	Gift of Roy Vail	National Collection	PR1955	1
117⅞	27⅛	26⅜	9⅜	9⅞	5⅝	5⅞	M	Greenland	Unknown	Zool. Mus., Copenhagen	PR1951	2
116⅞	29⅜	29⅜	7⅜	7⅞	6	5⅝	M	Greenland	Unknown	Zool. Mus., Copenhagen	PR1951	3
114	28⅛	28	7⅞	7⅞	6	5⅞	M	Greenland	Unknown	Zool. Mus., Copenhagen	PR1951	4
105	25	25	7	7	5⅛	5⅜	M	Greenland	Unknown	Demarest Memorial Mus.	1909	5
103⅜	24⅝	25	7⅛	7⅞	5⅞	5	M	Crockerland, Greenland	D. B. MacMillan	Am. Mus. Nat. History	PR1916	6
100⅞	23⅞	23⅝	7⅛	7⅞	5⅜	5⅜	U	Unknown	Unknown	Zool. Mus., Copenhagen	PR1951	7
98⅞	22⅝	20⅞	8⅜	8⅜	4⅞	4⅜	M	Arctic Ocean	Gift of Peary Arctic Club	Am. Mus. Nat. History	PR1899	8
98⅞	24⅝	24	6⅞	6⅞	5⅛	5⅛	M	Crockerland, Greenland	D. B. MacMillan	Am. Mus. Nat. History	PR1916	8

175

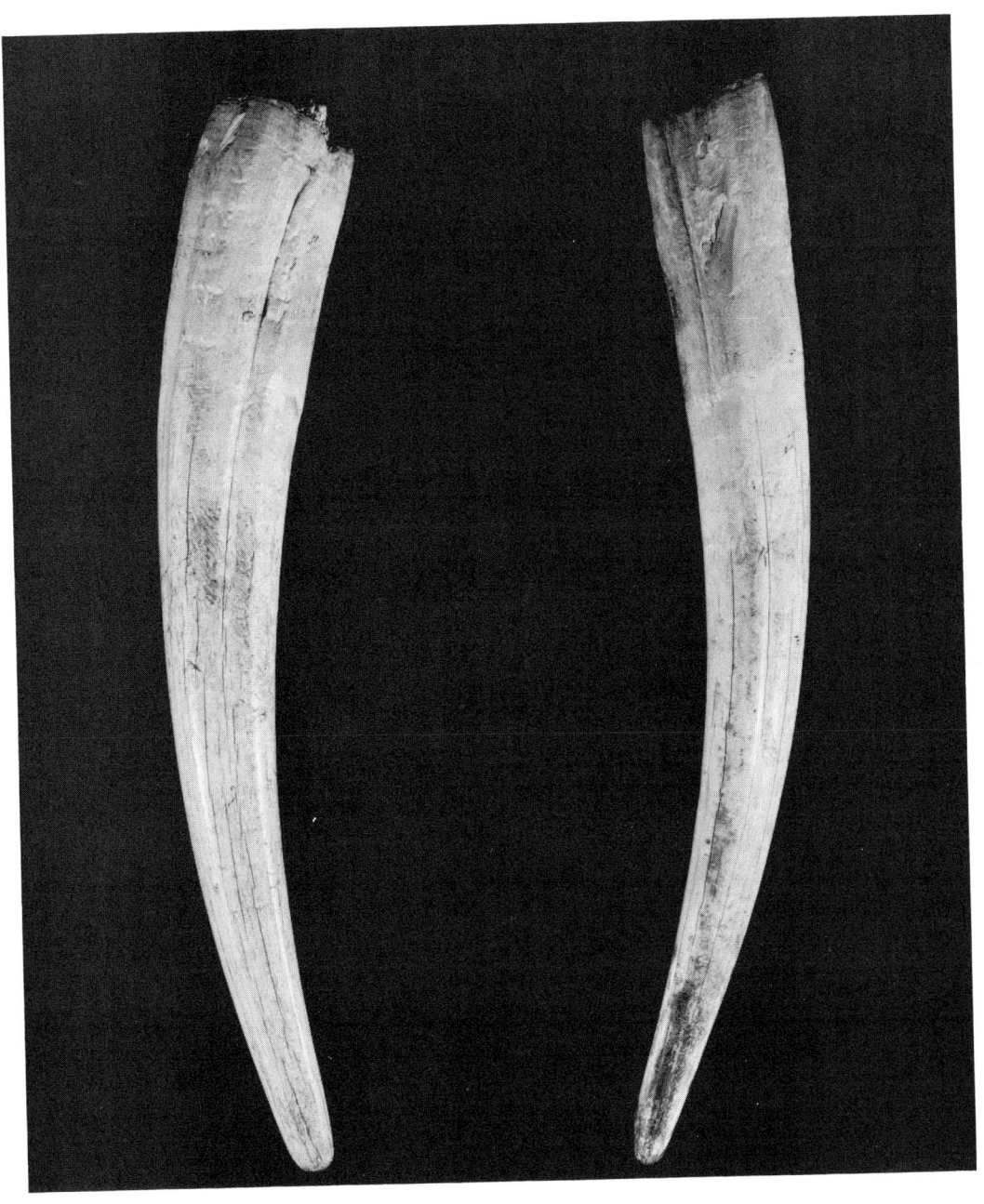

WORLD'S RECORD PACIFIC WALRUS TUSKS
SCORE: 145 6/8
Locality: Point Hope, Alaska Date: 1957
Hunter: an Eskimo   Owner: Jonas Brothers of Seattle

Pacific Walrus

Odobenus rosmarus divergens

Minimum Score 100

Score	Entire Length of Loose Tusk R.	L.	Circumference of Base R.	L.	Circumference at Third Quarter R.	L.	Sex	Locality Killed	By Whom Killed	Owner	Date Killed	Rank
145⅝	32⅞	32⅛	12⅞	13	7⅞	7⅛	M	Point Hope, Alaska	Eskimos	Jonas Bros. of Seattle	1957	1
142⅝	40⅛	39⅜	9⅝	9⅞	5⅝	5⅞	M	Bering Sea, Alaska	Bill Foster	Foster's Bighorn Rest.	1940	2
137⅞	36⅜	36⅜	9⅞	10⅜	6	6⅛	M	Unknown	Gift of N. A. Caesar	National Collection	PR1910	3
136⅝	35⅜	35	9⅜	9⅜	6⅜	6	M	Bristol Bay, Alaska	Eskimo	James W. Brooks	1955	4
135	38	36⅜	9	9⅜	5⅝	5⅝	M	Unknown	Picked Up	Paul Umlauf	1970	5
134⅝	34	34⅞	9⅜	9⅞	6	6	M	Wainwright, Alaska	Helen Burnett	Helen Burnett	1964	6
133⅝	34⅜	36⅜	8⅞	8⅜	6⅞	6⅛	M	Togiak Bay, Alaska	Picked Up	Bill Renfrew	1949	7
133⅜	32⅝	32	9⅛	8⅞	7⅞	7⅛	M	Port Heiden, Alaska	Picked Up	John T. Taylor	1980	7
134⅜	37⅜	37⅜	7⅞	7⅝	6⅛	6⅛	M	Cape Seniavin, Alaska	Picked Up	Patrick C. Martin	1985	7
133	35	35⅜	8⅜	8⅜	6	6	M	St. Lawrence Island, Alaska	Eskimo	Eugene Saxton	1956	9
132⅝	36⅜	37⅜	8⅜	8	6⅜	6	M	Port Moller, Alaska	Picked Up	R. Hammack & J. Hammack	1984	10
132¼	38⅛	37⅜	8⅞	8⅞	5⅝	5⅝	U	Alaska	Unknown	Harvard Univ. Museum	1870	11
132⅛	37⅜	35⅜	8⅞	8⅞	5⅝	5⅝	M	St. Lawrence Island, Alaska	Eskimo	Adventurers Club of N.Y.	1964	12
132⅛	34⅛	34	10⅜	9⅜	6⅛	5⅞	M	Hazen Bay, Alaska	Daniel B. Moore	Daniel B. Moore	1979	12
132⅛	33⅜	32⅝	9⅜	9	6⅜	6⅛	M	St. Lawrence Island, Alaska	Robert F. Hurford	Robert F. Hurford	1959	12
132	34	34	9⅜	8⅞	7⅛	6⅜	M	Savoonga, Alaska	Unknown	Victor Rovier	1967	15
132	35⅜	28⅜	10⅜	10⅜	7⅜	6⅜	M	Savoonga, Alaska	Gordon Iya	C. Vernon Humble	1977	16
131⅛	36⅜	35⅜	8⅜	8⅜	5⅝	5⅝	M	Bering Sea, Alaska	Gift of W. H. White	Am. Mus. Nat. History	1916	16
131⅛	33⅜	33⅜	8⅞	8⅜	6⅜	6⅜	M	Wainwright, Alaska	Eskimo	Ken Armstrong	PR1946	18
131⅛	31⅜	31⅜	9⅜	9⅜	6⅝	6⅜	M	Savoonga, Alaska	Robert M. Vinovich	Robert M. Vinovich	1976	19
131	33⅜	34⅜	8⅝	8⅜	6⅝	6⅜	M	Hagemeister Island, Alaska	Picked Up	Frank M. Thomason	1964	19
130⅞	33⅜	32⅜	9⅛	9⅛	6⅜	6⅜	M	St. Lawrence Island, Alaska	Peter W. Bading	Peter W. Bading	1960	21
130⅞	31⅜	32⅜	9⅜	8	7	7	M	Port Moller, Alaska	Picked Up	John Sarvis	1980	22
130⅜	34⅜	34	8⅜	8	6⅜	6⅛	U	St. Lawrence Island, Alaska	Unknown	Univ. of Alaska	PR1939	22
130⅜	36⅜	35⅜	8⅜	8	6⅜	5⅞	M	St. Lawrence Island, Alaska	George H. Landreth	George H. Landreth	1967	24
130⅜	34⅞	35	9	8⅞	5⅝	5⅜	M	Point Barrow, Alaska	Eskimos	C. R. Gutermuth	1952	24
129⅞	31⅜	32	8⅞	8⅜	7⅜	7⅛	M	St. Lawrence Island, Alaska	Grancel Fitz	Mrs. Grancel Fitz	1957	26
129⅞	34⅜	33⅜	8⅜	8⅜	6⅜	6⅛	M	Bering Sea, Alaska	Joseph J. Cafmeyer	Joseph J. Cafmeyer	1976	26
129⅞	32	32	9	8⅜	6⅜	6⅜	M	Izembek Lagoon, Alaska	Picked Up	John Sarvis	1981	28
129⅞	32⅜	32⅜	8⅝	8⅜	6⅜	6⅜	M	Port Heiden, Alaska	Picked Up	Donald R. Warren	1982	28
128	30⅜	30⅜	9⅜	7⅜	7⅛	7	M	Savoonga, Alaska	W. M. Wheless III	W. M. Wheless III	1977	31

177

PACIFIC WALRUS—Continued
Odobenus rosmarus divergens

Score	Entire Length of Loose Tusk R.	L.	Circumference of Base R.	L.	Circumference at Third Quarter R.	L.	Sex	Locality Killed	By Whom Killed	Owner	Date Killed	Rank
127⅝	35⅝	34⅝	8⅝	8⅞	5⅝	5⅞	M	St. Lawrence Island, Alaska	Chris Klineburger	Chris Klineburger	1961	32
127⅝	32⅝	33	98	8⅞	6	5⅝	M	Nome, Alaska	Charles F. Kleptz	Charles F. Kleptz	1978	32
127⅜	33⅞	34⅜	8⅛	8⅜	5⅝	5⅜	M	Wainwright, Alaska	J. Richard Reuter III	J. Richard Reuter III	1970	34
127	32⅞	32⅞	8⅜	8⅜	6⅛	6	M	Pt. Barrow, Alaska	Karl W. Opryshek	Karl W. Opryshek	1965	35
127	32⅞	32⅝	8⅞	9	6	6⅝	M	St. Lawrence Island, Alaska	Dick Ullery	Dick Ullery	1976	35
127	33	32⅞	8⅝	9	5⅝	6	M	St. Lawrence Island, Alaska	Norman W. Garwood	Norman W. Garwood	1976	35
126⅞	31⅞	31⅞	8⅝	8⅞	6⅛	6⅛	M	Gambell, Alaska	Eskimo	Mike W. Millar	1982	38
126⅝	31⅞	31⅛	9	8⅞	6⅛	6⅝	M	Pt. Barrow, Alaska	Eskimos	Walter O. Sinn	1958	39
126⅝	32⅜	32⅞	8⅝	8⅜	6	5⅝	M	St. Lawrence Island, Alaska	Martin J. Foerster	Martin J. Foerster	1958	39
126⅝	34⅞	34⅜	8	8⅛	5⅜	5⅝	M	Savoonga, Alaska	Unknown	Wayne S. Weiler	1978	39
126⅜	33⅝	33	8	8	6⅛	6⅛	M	Alaska Pen., Alaska	Unknown	Sam Pancotto	1962	42
126⅜	31⅛	31⅜	8⅛	7⅞	6⅝	5⅝	M	Bering Sea, Alaska	Wakon Iron Redbird	Wakon Iron Redbird	1977	42
125⅞	34⅞	34⅝	7⅞	9⅜	6⅛	6	M	St. Lawrence Island, Alaska	Eskimos	Sidney T. Shore	1950	44
125⅞	30⅞	30⅜	9⅝	8⅝	6⅛	4⅞	M	St. Lawrence Island, Alaska	F. J. Bremer	F. J. Bremer	1971	44
125⅝	35	34⅞	8⅞	8⅜	6	5	M	Bering Sea, Alaska	Manfred O. Schroeder	Manfred O. Schroeder	1977	46
125⅝	33⅝	33⅞	8⅝	8⅜	5⅞	5⅜	M	Bering Sea, Alaska	Henry A. Snow	Snow Museum	1923	47
124⅞	30⅞	32	9⅛	9⅞	5⅜	5⅝	M	St. Lawrence Island, Alaska	Bert Klineburger	Bert Klineburger	1962	47
124⅞	33⅞	34⅛	8⅛	8	5⅞	5⅝	M	St. Lawrence Island, Alaska	Kenneth Campbell	Kenneth Campbell	1972	47
124⅞	32⅞	31⅝	8⅞	8⅜	5⅞	5⅜	M	St. Lawrence Island, Alaska	Tim Gollorgeren	George H. Landreth	1966	50
124⅞	32⅝	32⅝	7⅝	8⅞	6⅛	7⅛	M	Pilot Point, Alaska	Picked Up	Dick Gunlogson	PR1969	50
124⅞	36⅞	35⅝	7	7⅛	5⅛	5⅜	M	Nunivak Island, Alaska	Terry Yager	Terry Yager	1977	50
124⅞	32⅝	33⅝	8	8⅞	5⅝	6	M	Bering Sea, Alaska	F. E. Klinesmith	Am. Mus. Nat. History	PR1951	53
124⅞	35	33⅝	7⅝	7⅝	5⅝	6	M	St. Lawrence Island, Alaska	Bert Klineburger	Bert Klineburger	1969	54
124	34⅞	33	7⅝	7⅜	5⅝	5⅝	M	Little Diomede Island, Alaska	Eskimo	James W. Brooks	1953	55
123⅝	33⅞	33⅝	8⅜	8	5⅛	5⅛	M	Bering Sea, Alaska	Dick Salemi	Dick Salemi	1978	55
123⅝	29⅝	29⅛	9	8⅝	6⅛	6⅝	M	St. Lawrence Island, Alaska	C. J. McElroy	C. J. McElroy	1968	57
123⅝	31⅝	32	9	8⅛	5⅞	5⅞	M	Bering Sea, Alaska	Dan H. Brainard	Dan H. Brainard	1977	57
123⅝	30	29⅞	9⅝	9⅝	5⅝	5⅝	M	Bering Sea, Alaska	Arthur H. Bullerdick	Arthur H. Bullerdick	1978	57
123⅝	34	31⅞	8⅜	8⅝	5⅝	5⅜	M	Alaskan Arctic	Eskimo	Robert C. Reeve	PR1955	60
123⅝	32⅜	32⅜	7⅝	7⅞	6⅛	6⅛	M	Nakuck, Alaska	Unknown	Leonard Schwah	1964	60
123⅝	28⅝	28⅞	9⅞	9⅞	6⅝	6⅝	M	Teller, Alaska	W. J. Glunt	W. J. Glunt	1965	60

Score	1	2	3	4	5	6	Sex	Locality	Taken By	Owner	Date	Rank
123	31	31	8⅜	8	6⅞	6	M	St. Lawrence Island, Alaska		Kay Tremblay	1960	63
123	33	32⅝	7⅝	7⅝	6	5⅞	M	Nunivak Island, Alaska	F. Phillips Williamson	F. Phillips Williamson	1961	63
122⅞	32⅜	31⅛	8	7⅝	6	6⅜	M	Alaska	Arvid F. Benson	Arvid F. Benson	1970	63
122⅞	31⅛	31	8⅛	8⅛	5⅝	5⅞	M	Savoonga, Alaska	George Wright	Acad. Nat. Sci., Phil.	1960	66
122⅞	31⅛	31⅛	8⅜	8⅜	5⅞	5⅜	M	St. Lawrence Island, Alaska	Lynn M. Castle	Lynn M. Castle	1971	66
122⅞	32⅛	31⅛	8	8	5⅝	5⅝	M	Savoonga, Alaska	Herb Klein	Herb Klein	1959	68
122⅞	32⅝	32⅜	8⅜	8⅜	6⅜	6⅛	M	Walrus Island, Alaska	William W. Garrison	William W. Garrison	1971	68
122	27⅞	28	10⅛	10⅛	5⅞	6	M	Diomede Island, Alaska	Unknown	Robert C. Reeve	1962	70
122	31⅛	31⅛	9⅛	9⅜	5⅜	5⅜	M	St. Lawrence Island, Alaska	Tony Oney	Tony Oney	1964	71
121⅞	31⅞	32⅜	8⅝	8⅛	5⅜	5⅜	M	Diomede Island, Alaska	Ted Lick	Ted Lick	1970	71
121⅜	31⅛	31	8⅜	8⅜	5⅜	5⅜	M	Savoonga, Alaska	Jim Harrower	Tony Oney	1964	73
121⅞	31⅜	31⅜	8⅜	8⅜	5⅜	5⅜	M	Savoonga, Alaska	Gerald G. Balciar	Gerald G. Balciar	1971	74
121	33⅜	34⅛	7⅝	7⅝	5⅜	5⅜	F	Bering Sea, Alaska	Lowell C. Hansen II	Lowell C. Hansen II	1978	75
121	28	28⅜	11⅜	9⅞	5⅞	5⅞	M	Little Diomede Island, Alaska	Eskimo	Elmer Keith	1956	76
121							M	Little Diomede Island, Alaska	William H. Picher	William H. Picher	1966	76
121	29⅛	29⅞	8⅜	8⅛	6	6	M	Nunivak Island, Alaska	C. Vernon Humble	C. Vernon Humble	1977	76
120⅞	34	33⅝	7	6⅞	5⅝	5⅜	M	Point Hope, Alaska	Don Johnson	Don Johnson	1963	79
120⅝	29	29⅛	8⅜	8⅜	6⅜	5⅞	M	Little Diomede Island, Alaska	Robert Curtis	Robert Curtis	1963	79
120⅝	30	29⅞	8⅜	8⅞	6	6	M	Cape Thompson, Alaska	Eskimo	Nick Petropolis	PR1965	79
120⅞	30⅛	29	9	9	5⅞	5⅝	M	Gambell, Alaska	L. Keith Mortensen	L. Keith Mortensen	1978	79
120⅜	33⅜	33⅜	7	7⅛	5⅝	5⅜	U	Alaska	S. R. Caldwell	Acad. Nat. Sci., Phil.	1902	83
120⅛	28⅞	29⅛	9	9⅛	5⅝	5⅝	M	Savoonga, Alaska	Werner-Rolf Muno	Werner-Rolf Muno	1971	84
120	30⅜	29⅝	8⅜	8⅜	5⅞	5⅝	M	Hazen Bay, Alaska	Richard D. Dimick	Richard D. Dimick	1979	84
120	29	29	9⅜	9⅜	6⅛	6	U	Bristol Bay, Alaska	Eskimo	Foster H. Thompson	PR1959	86
120	33	27⅞	8⅜	8⅜	5⅜	5⅝	M	St. Lawrence Island, Alaska	Sarkis Atamian	Sarkis Atamian	1968	86
119⅞	30⅝	30⅝	8⅞	8⅞	6	5⅝	M	Bering Sea, Alaska	George L. Hall	George L. Hall	1977	86
119⅞	29⅛	29⅛	8⅞	8⅞	6⅝	6⅞	M	Savoonga, Alaska	Ed Cox, Jr.	Ed Cox, Jr.	1977	89
119⅞	28	28⅜	9⅜	9⅜	5⅞	5⅝	U	Bering Sea, Alaska	Unknown	Eugene M. Erwin	PR1975	90
119	31⅝	29⅝	8	8	5⅜	5⅞	M	Savoonga, Alaska	Douglas E. Miller	Douglas E. Miller	1976	90
118⅞	31⅝	31⅛	9⅛	8⅛	5⅝	5⅞	M	Port Moller, Alaska	Picked Up	Bob Stokes	1961	92
118⅞	30⅝	30⅜	8⅜	8⅜	6⅛	6	M	Diomede Island, Alaska	Harry J. Armitage	Harry J. Armitage	1965	93
118⅜	31⅛	31⅛	8⅜	8⅜	6⅞	6⅛	M	St. Lawrence Island, Alaska	Alice J. Landreth	Alice J. Landreth	1967	93
118⅜	28⅜	28⅛	7⅝	7⅝	6⅛	6⅜	M	St. Lawrence Island, Alaska	Wilbur L. Leworthy	Wilbur L. Leworthy	1970	93
118⅜	32	28⅝	8	8	5⅛	5⅞	M	St. Lawrence Island, Alaska	Clifford Patz	Clifford Patz	1979	93
117⅞	29⅛	29	8	8	5⅝	5⅝	M	Savoonga, Alaska	Jack Schwabland	Jack Schwabland	1978	97
117⅞	28⅜	28	7⅞	7⅝	6	6⅜	M	Little Diomede, Alaska	Robert Curtis	Robert Curtis	1963	98
116⅝	30⅛	26⅝	8⅜	8⅜	6⅞	6	M	St. Lawrence Island, Alaska	C. Pitt Sanders	C. Pitt Sanders	1978	98
116⅛	28⅛						M	Little Diomede Island, Alaska	Eskimos	Tony Oney	1962	100
116⅝	27⅞	27⅞	8⅞	8⅜	6	6	M	Savoonga, Alaska	Arnold Carlson	Arnold Carlson	1971	101
116	28	28	8⅜	8⅜	5⅞	5⅝	M	Point Hope, Alaska	Picked Up	William C. Penttila	1965	102
116	30⅜	29⅜	8⅜	8⅜	5⅛	5	M	Bering Sea, Alaska	Hugh L. Nichols, Jr.	Hugh L. Nichols, Jr.	1972	102

PACIFIC WALRUS—Continued
Odobenus rosmarus divergens

Score	Entire Length of Loose Tusk R.	L.	Circumference of Base R.	L.	Circumference at Third Quarter R.	L.	Sex	Locality Killed	By Whom Killed	Owner	Date Killed	Rank
115⅝	28⅞	29	7⅞	8⅞	5⅞	5⅝	M	St. Lawrence Island, Alaska	Hugh H. Logan	U.S. Natl. Museum	1962	104
115⅝	27⅝	31⅛	8⅛	8	6⅜	6	M	Savoonga, Alaska	Peter A. Bossart	Peter A. Bossart	1972	104
115⅝	30⅝	29⅝	8	7⅞	5⅜	5⅜	M	St. Lawrence Island, Alaska	Gerald L. Warnock	Gerald L. Warnock	1977	104
115⅜	30⅝	30⅛	7⅝	7⅝	5⅝	5⅝	M	Diomede Island, Alaska	Unknown	Univ. of Alaska	1953	107
115⅜	27⅝	25⅝	9⅜	9⅜	6⅛	6⅛	M	St. Lawrence Island, Alaska	W. T. Yoshimoto	W. T. Yoshimoto	1962	107
115⅜	28⅝	28⅝	7⅝	7⅝	6⅝	6⅝	M	Little Diomede Island, Alaska	Basil C. Bradbury	Basil C. Bradbury	1964	107
115⅝	30⅝	31	7⅝	7⅝	5⅝	5⅝	M	Little Diomede Island, Alaska	Jack D. Putnam	Jack D. Putnam	1965	110
115⅝	27⅝	31⅛	8⅝	8⅞	5⅝	5⅝	M	Nunivak Island, Alaska	Lloyd Ward	Lloyd Ward	1971	110
115	31⅛	30⅞	6⅝	7	5⅝	5⅝	M	Savoonga, Alaska	John Estes	John Estes	1978	112
115	29⅝	29⅞	7⅝	7⅞	5⅜	5	U	Point Hope, Alaska	Eskimo	Jonas Bros. of Alaska	1958	113
114⅝	29	29⅝	7⅜	7⅝	5⅝	5⅝	M	Kigluaik Mts., Alaska	Russell H. Underdahl	Russell H. Underdahl	1978	113
114⅝	29⅜	29⅝	8⅝	8⅝	5⅛	5⅛	M	Savoonga, Alaska	Richard G. Van Vorst	Richard G. Van Vorst	1976	115
114	26⅝	26⅝	9⅝	9⅞	5⅝	5⅛	M	Kotzebue, Alaska	E. B. Rhodes	E. B. Rhodes	1964	116
113⅝	26	26⅛	8⅝	8⅛	6⅛	6	M	Point Hope, Alaska	Glenn W. Slade	Glenn W. Slade	1961	117
113⅝	28⅝	26⅝	8⅝	9⅛	5⅛	5⅝	M	St. Lawrence Island, Alaska	Maitland Armstrong	Maitland Armstrong	1961	117
113⅝	29	29⅝	9	7⅝	5⅜	5⅝	M	Point Hope, Alaska	Eskimos	John W. Elmore	1966	117
113⅝	29⅝	28⅝	7⅝	7⅜	5⅝	5⅝	M	St. Lawrence Island, Alaska	Denver D. Coleman	Denver D. Coleman	1968	117
113⅝	28⅝	28⅝	7⅝	7⅝	5⅝	5⅝	M	St. Lawrence Island, Alaska	Dick Davis	Dick Davis	1976	117
113⅝	31⅜	30⅝	7⅝	7⅝	5⅛	5⅛	M	Savoonga, Alaska	Warren K. Parker	Warren K. Parker	1979	123
113⅝	28⅝	28⅝	7⅝	7⅝	5⅝	5⅝	M	Savoonga, Alaska	Tom Andersen	Tom Andersen	1978	124
113⅜	28⅝	28⅝	8⅝	8⅜	5⅜	5⅝	M	St. Lawrence Island, Alaska	W. Brandon Macomber	W. Brandon Macomber	1965	124
113⅜	27⅝	27⅝	8⅜	8⅜	5	5⅝	M	Nunivak Island, Alaska	C. R. Feazell	C. R. Feazell	1972	124
113⅜	27⅝	27⅝	7⅝	7⅝	6⅝	5⅝	M	Bering Sea, Alaska	Jack Holland	Jack Holland	1978	127
113	29⅝	29⅝	8⅛	8	5	5	M	St. Lawrence Island, Alaska	Jim Roe	Jim Roe	1969	127
113	30⅝	29⅝	7⅝	7⅜	5⅝	5⅝	M	St. Lawrence Island, Alaska	I. D. Shapiro	I. D. Shapiro	1970	127
113	28	27	8⅝	8	5⅝	5⅝	M	St. Lawrence Island, Alaska	Gail W. Holderman	Gail W. Holderman	1976	127
113	27⅝	26	8⅛	8	6	6⅛	M	Bering Sea, Alaska	Jon Everis Holland	Jon Everis Holland	1978	127
113	31⅛	31	6⅝	6⅝	4⅝	4⅝	M	St. Lawrence Island, Alaska	G. A. Treschow	G. A. Treschow	1979	132
112⅝	27⅝	27⅝	8⅝	8⅛	5⅝	5⅛	M	St. Lawrence Island, Alaska	Alfred F. Corwin	Alfred F. Corwin	1964	133
112⅝	27⅝	27⅝	8⅝	8⅝	5⅝	5⅝	U	Togiak Bay, Alaska	Picked Up	Lloyd Zeman	PR1970	133
112⅝	28⅝	27⅝	7⅝	7⅝	5⅝	6⅝	M	St. Lawrence Island, Alaska	Henry K. Leworthy	Henry K. Leworthy	1970	133

Score							M/U	Locality	Hunter	Owner	Date	Rank
112⅝	28⅝	27⅞	7⅝	7⅞	5⅝	5⅝	M	Savoonga, Alaska	W. K. Leech	W. K. Leech	1972	133
112⅝	29⅝	28⅞	7⅞	7⅞	5⅛	5	M	St. Lawrence Island, Alaska	Harm De Boer	Harm De Boer	1972	133
111⅞	27⅜	32⅜	8⅞	8⅜	4⅜	6	M	Point Hope, Alaska	Eskimo	George H. Landreth	1966	137
111⅛	30⅛	26⅜	8⅛	7⅞	5⅞	5⅝	M	St. Lawrence Island, Alaska	Gary D'Aigle	Gary D'Aigle	1968	138
111	28⅜	28⅛	7	6⅞	5⅝	5⅝	M	Savoonga, Alaska	Don L. Corley	Don L. Corley	1977	138
111	28⅝	30	7⅞	8	4⅝	4⅝	M	St. Lawrence Island, Alaska	Robert E. Speegle	Robert E. Speegle	1972	140
110⅝	29⅛	30⅛	7⅝	7⅞	4⅝	4⅝	M	Savoonga, Alaska	Don Skidmore	Don Skidmore	1977	140
110⅛	29⅞	27⅝	6⅜	7⅜	5⅝	5⅝	M	St. Lawrence Island, Alaska	John M. Blair	John M. Blair	1971	142
110⅛	29⅝	27⅝	7⅜	7⅜	5⅛	5⅛	M	St. Lawrence Island, Alaska	Hugh H. Logan	Los Angeles Co. Museum	1962	143
110⅛	27	26⅝	8⅛	8	5⅛	5⅜	U	Kuskokwim Bay, Alaska	Robert Rood	Robert Rood	1966	144
110⅛	30⅛	30⅜	6⅝	6⅜	4⅞	4⅝	M	Nunivak Island, Alaska	James Lewis	Steve Bayless	1969	144
110⅛	28⅝	28⅝	7⅜	7⅞	5⅛	4⅞	M	St. Lawrence Island, Alaska	Arthur LaCapria	Arthur LaCapria	1971	144
110⅛	28	27⅝	7⅞	7⅞	5	5	M	Point Barrow, Alaska	Wayne S. Weiler	Wayne S. Weiler	1972	144
110⅛	29⅞	29⅛	7⅜	7⅜	4⅜	4⅞	M	St. Lawrence Island, Alaska	Cecil M. Hopper	Cecil M. Hopper	1972	144
109⅛	28⅜	28⅜	7⅜	7⅛	5⅜	5⅜	M	St. Lawrence Island, Alaska	Eskimo	Val Tibbetts	1979	144
109⅛	28⅛	28⅝	7⅜	7⅜	5	5	M	Point Franklin, Alaska	James A. Bush, Jr.	James A. Bush, Jr.	1979	144
109⅛	26⅝	26⅝	8⅜	8⅞	5	5⅝	M	Savoonga, Alaska	Michael R. Bogan	Michael R. Bogan	1978	151
108⅞	27⅞	27⅛	8	8	4⅞	5⅜	M	St. Lawrence Island, Alaska	Richard A. Furniss	Richard A. Furniss	1972	152
108⅜	28⅝	27⅛	7⅞	7⅝	5⅝	5⅜	M	St. Lawrence Island, Alaska	Mahlon T. White	Mahlon T. White	1977	152
108⅛	30⅛	30⅜	7	6⅞	4⅜	5	M	Wainwright, Alaska	T. E. Shillingburg	T. E. Shillingburg	1961	154
107⅞	27	30	7⅜	7⅛	5⅛	5⅛	M	Little Diomede, Alaska	Delano J. Lietzau	Delano J. Lietzau	1978	155
107⅞	28⅛	28⅜	7⅜	7⅝	4⅜	4⅞	M	Bering Sea, Alaska	Barrie White	Barrie White	1963	156
107	27⅞	27⅝	7⅜	7⅜	5⅛	5⅛	M	St. Lawrence Island, Alaska	Gary Boychuk	Gary Boychuk	1977	157
106	26⅝	26	7⅜	7⅜	5⅝	5⅛	M	Savoonga, Alaska	W. A. Bond	W. A. Bond	1964	158
104⅝	23⅝	23⅜	7⅝	7⅛	6⅝	6⅝	M	St. Lawrence Island, Alaska	Jon G. Koshell	Jon G. Koshell	1972	159
104⅝	26⅝	26⅞	7⅜	7⅜	4⅞	4⅝	M	St. Lawrence Island, Alaska	L. M. Cole	L. M. Cole	1964	160
104⅛	26⅜	26⅛	7⅞	7⅞	4⅞	5	M	Bering Sea	Rudolf Sand	Rudolf Sand	1971	160
104	27⅞	26⅜	6⅝	6⅝	5	5⅛	M	Savoonga, Alaska	Andrew A. Samuels, Jr.	Andrew A. Samuels, Jr.	1979	160
103⅞	26	26⅛	6⅝	6⅝	5⅛	4⅞	M	Wainwright, Alaska	Donald R. Theophilus	Donald R. Theophilus	1978	163
103⅞	27⅜	27⅜	6⅜	6⅜	4⅜	4⅜	M	Point Barrow, Alaska	Glenn W. Slade	Glenn W. Slade	1968	164
102⅝	25⅜	25⅜	7⅜	7⅜	5⅛	5⅛	M	St. Lawrence Island, Alaska	Gunther Matschke	Gunther Matschke	1972	164
102	25⅜	25⅜	7⅜	7⅜	4⅝	4⅝	M	Port Moller, Alaska	Picked Up	Dan Lynch	1966	166
102	24⅝	25	7⅝	7⅝	4⅝	4⅝	M	St. Lawrence Island, Alaska	Dalton Foster	Dalton Foster	1961	167
101⅞	26⅝	27⅝	6⅞	7	4⅜	4⅜	M	Savoonga, Alaska	Robert J. Bartlett	Robert J. Bartlett	1979	167
138⅛*	35⅛	35⅜	9⅜	9⅞	6⅝	6⅝	M	St. Lawrence Island, Alaska	Eskimo	Steve Fowler	1967	169
136⅛*	32⅝	32⅜	9⅜	9⅜	6⅝	7⅝	M	St. Lawrence Island, Alaska	Valentin De Madariaga	Valentin De Madariaga	1976	
133⅜*	32⅜	32⅝	9⅜	9⅜	7⅜	7⅝	M	Port Moller, Alaska	Picked Up	Larry R. Rivers	1981	
133⅜*	32⅜	32⅝	9⅞	10	6⅝	6⅝	M	Diomede Island, Alaska	Eskimo	Univ. Iowa Museum	1893	
127⅞*	32⅜	30⅝	9⅜	8⅞	6⅝	6⅜	M	Nunivak Island, Alaska	Ray Cyr	Ray Cyr	1978	
125*	30⅝	30⅛	9⅜	9⅞	6⅝	5⅞	M	Port Heiden, Alaska	Picked Up	Larry R. Rivers	1981	
124⅛*	31⅜	30⅜	8⅜	8⅜	6⅝	6⅞	M	Gambell, Alaska	Charles McLaughlin	Charles McLaughlin	1978	
							M	Hagemeister Island, Alaska	Picked Up	Lloyd D. Friend	1979	

*Final Score subject to revision by additional verifying measurements

181

WORLD'S RECORD AMERICAN ELK (WAPITI)
SCORE: 442 3/8
Locality: Dark Canyon, Colorado Date: 1899
Hunter: John Plute Owner: Ed Rozman

NUMBER TWO AMERICAN ELK (WAPITI)
SCORE: 441 6/8
Locality: Big Horn Mountains, Wyoming Date: 1890
Hunter: unknown
Donated by Homer C. Richards to Jackson Hole Museum and Pioneer Village Foundation, Inc.
Winner of the Sagamore Hill Medal, 1950

American Elk (*Wapiti*)

Cervus elaphus nelsoni and related subspecies

Minimum Score 375

Score	Length of Main Beam		Inside Spread	Circumference at Smallest Place Between First and Second Points		Number of Points		Locality Killed	By Whom Killed	Owner	Date Killed	Rank
	R.	L.		R.	L.	R.	L.					
442⅜	55⅝	59⅝	45⅜	12⅛	11⅛	8	7	Dark Canyon, Colo.	John Plute	Ed Rozman	1899	1
441⅛	61¼	61⅛	47	10⅝	9⅝	8	7	Big Horn Mts., Wyo.	Unknown	Jackson Hole Museum	1890	2
419⅞	62⅜	62⅞	49⅞	10⅜	10⅜	6	8	Panther River, Alta.	Clarence Brown	Clarence Brown	1977	3
419⅞	59⅞	60⅛	53	9⅜	9⅜	7	7	Madison Co., Mont.	Fred C. Mercer	Fred C. Mercer	1958	4
418⅞	58	55	43⅛	10⅝	11⅜	6	7	Wyoming	J. G. Millais	G. Kenneth Whitehead	1886	5
418	54⅛	50⅜	44⅜	8⅜	8⅜	6	6	Muddywater River, Alta.	Bruce W. Hale	Bruce W. Hale	1971	6
412⅛	51⅛	51⅛	42⅜	10	9⅜	9	8	Wieser River, Idaho	Elmer Bacus	Elmer Bacus	1954	7
410	56	53⅜	44⅜	8⅝	8⅛	7	7	Unknown	Picked Up	Neil R. Hinton	1943	8
407	56⅞	56⅝	43⅜	9⅜	8⅝	7	7	Summit Co., Colo.	Robert G. Young	Robert G. Young	1967	9
405⅞	53⅜	55⅜	44⅜	8⅝	8⅝	6	7	Ft. Apache Res., Ariz.	Roy R. Blythe	Roy R. Blythe	1970	10
404⅞	58⅜	57	47⅞	9⅝	9⅛	8	8	Mineral Co., Mont.	Carl B. Snyder	Warren G. Stone	1959	11
402⅝	59⅜	59⅝	44⅛	9⅛	8⅝	7	7	Red Deer River, Alta.	Henry Folkman	Henry Folkman	1946	12
401⅞	58⅜	57⅝	47⅞	8	8	6	7	Teton Co., Wyo.	Douglas Spicer	Douglas Spicer	1972	13
401⅛	53⅛	55⅛	44⅜	7⅞	8⅛	6	6	Park Co., Mont.	Wayne A. Hertzler	Wayne A. Hertzler	1977	14
401⅛	60⅛	64⅝	43⅜	9⅜	9	7	7	Grant Co., Oreg.	James T. Sproul	James T. Sproul	1972	15
400⅞	59⅜	59⅜	47⅜	8⅜	8⅞	7	6	Rock Lake, Alta.	Ray Hindmarsh	Ray Hindmarsh	1963	16
400⅜	59⅛	60⅛	42⅜	9⅜	10	7	7	Owyhee Co., Idaho	Cecil R. Coonts	Cecil R. Coonts	1965	17
400⅛	56	55⅝	46	8⅜	8⅞	7	7	Jackson Hole, Wyo.	C. Atkins & O. Maynard	Thomas Myers	1947	18
400⅛	56⅞	57	49	9⅛	9⅛	7	7	Crook Co., Oreg.	Picked Up	Randall L. Ryerse	1984	19
400	59⅜	57⅞	47⅜	7⅞	7⅝	7	7	Ram River, Alta.	Ralph A. Fry	Ralph A. Fry	1952	20
399⅝	57⅞	53⅜	40⅜	9	9⅝	7	8	Lewis & Clark Co., Mont.	Richard Mosher	J. A. Iverson	1953	21
398⅝	50⅝	50⅞	39⅜	10⅜	11	8	8	Mora Co., N.M.	Bernabe Alcon	Bernabe Alcon	1963	22
398	50⅜	53⅜	46⅜	8⅜	8⅝	6	6	Pincher Creek, Alta.	Monty F. Adams	Pat Adams	1977	23
398	52	55⅛	52⅛	8⅛	7⅞	7	7	Sublette Co., Wyo.	Ray Daugherty	Aldon L. Hale	1950	24
397⅞	53	53	44⅜	8⅞	9	8	7	Cascade Co., Mont.	John W. Campbell	John W. Campbell	1955	25
397⅞	50⅜	50⅞	45⅜	9⅞	9⅜	8	7	Gunnison Co., Colo.	John R. Burritt	John R. Burritt	1970	26
397⅞	54⅛	55	61⅛	9⅞	10⅜	7	7	Montana	Robert Swan	B&C National Collection	1912	27
396⅞	56⅜	56⅜	43⅜	9⅞	10⅞	6	6	Volunteer Canyon, Ariz.	Lamar Haines	Lamar Haines	1960	28
396⅜	48	50⅜	32⅜	10	9⅜	7	7	Duck Mts., Man.	Paul Kirkowich	Paul Kirkowich	1960	29
396⅛	51⅝	50⅜	49⅛	7⅞	7⅜	7	8	Rock Lake, Alta.	Harold R. Vaughn	Harold R. Vaughn	1968	30

Score	Main Beam R	Main Beam L	Inside Spread	Greatest Spread	Circ. R	Circ. L	Pts R	Pts L	Locality	By Whom Killed	Owner	Date	Rank
395⅜	57⅝	57⅝	47	60⅛	8⅜	8⅜	6	6	___ Bow Co., Mont.	Wayne Estep	Wayne Estep	1966	31
395⅛	56⅝	57⅜	46⅜	57⅜	10⅛	9⅜	7	8	Fremont Co., Wyo.	Roger Linnell	Roger Linnell	1955	31
395	56⅝	56⅛	48⅜	56⅝	9	8⅜	7	7	Wallowa Co., Oreg.	Lawton McDaniel	Lawton McDaniel	1935	33
394⅞	54⅞	54⅞	47⅜	60⅛	8⅜	8⅞	7	7	Salmon Natl. For., Idaho	Fred W. Thomson	Fred W. Thomson	1964	34
394⅞	55	55	52⅜	57⅛	10	9⅞	6	6	Jefferson Co., Mont.	John Willard	Mont. Hist. Museum	1953	35
394⅞	53⅜	53⅜	46⅜	53⅜	8⅞	8⅞	7	6	Beaverhead Co., Mont.	Gwyn Brown	Gwyn Brown	1944	36
394⅞	53⅜	57⅜	42⅜	57⅝	9⅞	9⅜	6	6	Idaho Co., Idaho	L. M. White	L. M. White	1977	36
394½	56⅜	53⅜	41⅜	56⅝	9⅞	9⅞	7	6	Panther River, Alta.	Picked Up	George Browne	1938	38
394½	53⅜	53⅜	45⅜	55⅜	9⅞	9⅞	6	6	Hoback Rim, Wyo.	Clyde Robbins	George Franz	1940	38
394¼	53⅛	53⅜	46⅞	58	8⅛	8⅜	6	6	Elkwater, Alta.	Roy Crawford	Roy Crawford	1976	38
394⅛	58	58	43⅜	58	10⅛	10⅛	6	6	Lincoln Co., Wyo.	Roland Smith	Leon C. Smith	1930	41
393⅞	57⅛	57⅛	45⅜	58	8	8	6	6	Apache Co., Ariz.	T. R. Tidwell	T. R. Tidwell	1983	42
393⅝	58⅜	55⅜	51⅛	54⅛	9⅜	9⅜	6	6	Winchester, Idaho	Doyle Shriver	Doyle Shriver	1954	43
393⅜	55⅜	53⅜	46⅜	51⅛	8⅝	8⅛	6	6	Watertown Natl. Park, Alta.	Alan Foster	Alan Foster	1952	43
393⅜	53⅜	53⅜	44⅜	51⅛	10	10⅛	6	6	Big Horn, Wyo.	Edwin Shaffer	Edwin Shaffer	1946	43
393⅜	63⅜	64⅜	47⅛	59⅜	9⅜	9⅜	6	6	Socorro Co., N.M.	Floyd R. Owens	Floyd R. Owens	1977	43
393⅛	56⅜	56⅜	48⅜	58⅜	8⅞	8⅛	7	7	Kittitas Co., Wash.	Paul Anderson	Paul Anderson	1927	43
392⅞	58⅜	58⅜	42⅜	51⅜	8⅞	9	7	7	Panther River, Alta.	Bill Brooks	Bill Brooks	1955	47
392⅞	51⅛	51⅜	42⅜	51⅛	7⅞	7⅞	7	7	Buford, Colo.	Picked Up	Robert T. Fulton	PR1967	48
392	54⅞	54⅜	45⅜	56⅝	10	10	6	6	Jackson Co., Colo.	James A. Baller	North Park State Bank	1969	49
391⅝	54	53	46	53	8⅜	8⅛	6	6	Thoroughfare Creek, Wyo.	Thomas A. Yawkey	Thomas A. Yawkey	1936	50
391½	52⅜	52⅜	35⅜	53⅜	7⅞	7⅞	6	6	Slater, Colo.	W. J. Bracken	W. J. Bracken	1963	51
391½	52⅜	52⅜	51⅜	52⅜	8⅝	9	6	7	Big Horn Mts., Wyo.	Robert K. Hamilton	Robert K. Hamilton	1954	51
391⅛	54⅜	56⅜	43⅜	56⅝	9⅛	9⅛	6	6	Mt. Evans, Colo.	Unknown	Frank Brady	1874	53
391⅛	55⅜	55⅜	39⅜	55⅜	8	8	7	6	Grand Lake, Colo.	John Holzwarth	John Holzwarth	1949	53
390⅞	53⅜	50⅜	39⅜	56⅜	8⅛	8⅛	7	7	Clearwater, Alta.	Bob Dial	Bob Dial	1955	55
390⅞	54⅜	54⅜	49⅜	54⅜	9⅛	9⅝	7	7	Caribou Co., Idaho	Ken Homer	Ken Homer	1963	56
390¾	58	54⅜	42	58	8⅞	9	7	7	Hoback Canyon, Wyo.	Picked Up	Spanky Greenville	1977	56
390½	57⅜	55	49⅜	54⅛	9⅛	9⅛	7	7	Hood River Co., Oreg.	Bill Tensen	Bill Tensen	1980	58
389⅞	50⅛	50⅜	50⅜	53	7⅞	7⅞	6	6	Park Co., Mont.	Thomas B. Adams	Jack Adams	1932	59
389⅞	56⅜	56⅜	52⅜	52⅞	9⅜	9⅜	7	7	Ft. A La Corne, Sask.	Jim Crozier	Jim Crozier	1955	60
389⅜	57⅜	55⅜	42	55⅜	8	8	6	6	Bitterroot Area, Mont.	Unknown	John Le Blanc	1965	60
389⅜	55⅜	56⅜	45	56⅜	10	10	6	6	Helena, Mont.	Picked Up	Robert L. Smith	1964	62
389⅛	53⅜	54⅜	46	54⅜	8⅞	8⅞	6	6	Big Horn Co., Wyo.	Floyd A. Clark	Floyd A. Clark	1976	62
389⅛	56⅜	60⅜	43⅜	60⅝	8⅛	8⅛	6	6	Salmon River, Idaho	Unknown	John M. Anderson	1915	62
389	49⅜	51⅛	42⅛	51⅜	12⅛	12⅛	6	6	Nez Perce Co., Idaho	Picked Up	Michael Throckmorton	1949	65
388⅞	49⅜	48⅛	40	48⅜	10⅛	10⅛	6	6	Saskatchewan	Unknown	B. P. O. Elks Lodge	PR1956	66
388⅝	51	41⅛	41⅛	48⅝	8⅜	8⅜	6	6	Meacham, Oreg.	H. M. Bailey	H. M. Bailey	1963	66
388⅝	56	46⅜	46⅜	55⅝	9⅞	9⅞	7	6	Jackson Hole, Wyo.	Unknown	William Sonnenburg	PR1912	68
388⅝	53⅜	47⅛	47⅛	55	9	9⅜	7	7	Coconino Co., Ariz.	Picked Up	Tim Cotten	PR1982	69
388⅜	62⅝	49⅞	49⅞	51⅜	9⅜	9⅛	7	7	Unknown	Unknown	Carnegie Museum	PR1966	70
388⅜	52⅝	39	39	55	10⅛	10⅛	7	7	Gila Co., Ariz.	Fred B. Dickey	Fred B. Dickey	1984	71
388	57⅛	55⅛	55	55⅜	8⅜	8⅜	6	6	Medicine Lodge Creek, Idaho	D. W. Marshall & E. J. Stacy	D. W. Marshall & E. J. Stacy	1961	73

Score	Length of Main Beam		Inside Spread	Circumference at Smallest Place Between First and Second Points		Number of Points		Locality Killed	By Whom Killed	Owner	Date Killed	Rank
	R.	L.		R.	L.	R.	L.					
388	53⅜	53⅜	48⅞	9	9⅜	6	6	Madison Co., Mont.	Terry Carlson	Christine Mullikin	1961	73
388	55⅜	54⅜	50⅞	8⅝	9	8	9	Converse, Wyo.	Jerry F. Cook	J. F. Cook & Mrs. P. Muchmore	1965	73
387⅞	54⅜	55⅜	44⅜	9⅜	9⅝	7	6	Kelly, Wyo.	Roger Penney	Bernard Bronk	1963	76
387⅞	55⅜	57	37⅜	10	9⅝	7	6	Grant Co., Oreg.	Arnold Troph	Arnold Troph	1966	76
387⅞	52⅜	53	44⅜	7⅞	8	6	6	Lincoln, Wyo.	Dexter R. Gardner	Dexter R. Gardner	1967	76
387⅞	57⅜	56⅜	51	8	7⅞	7	6	Big Horn Mts., Wyo.	Elgin T. Gates	Elgin T. Gates	1954	79
387⅞	50⅜	51⅞	43⅝	9⅝	10⅞	6	6	Fremont, Idaho	Charles A. Preston	Charles A. Preston	1963	79
387⅞	58⅜	56	39⅜	8⅞	9⅛	7	7	Yarrow Creek, Alta.	D. Belyea	D. Belyea	1970	81
387⅜	49⅜	49⅛	41⅞	8⅞	8⅞	7	7	Grant Co., Oreg.	Andy Chambers	Andy Chambers	1959	82
387⅜	56⅜	58⅞	44⅜	9	9	7	6	Sage Creek, Mont.	Joseph A. Vogel	Joseph A. Vogel	1970	82
387⅜	52⅜	52⅜	47⅜	8⅛	8⅛	6	6	Park Co., Mont.	Lawrence P. Deering	Lawrence P. Deering	1978	84
387⅜	54⅜	58⅜	46	9⅜	9⅝	7	8	Meagher Co., Mont.	B. McLees & H. Zehntner	Bud McLees	1971	85
387	55	55⅜	54⅜	8⅞	8⅝	8	7	Chama, N.M.	Herb Klein	Herb Klein	1952	86
386⅞	48⅜	47⅞	41⅜	9⅜	8⅝	8	8	Powell Co., Mont.	Mildred Eder	Mildred Eder	1969	87
386⅞	58⅜	61⅛	41⅞	8⅞	8⅞	6	6	Otero Co., N.M.	Picked Up	William M. Wheless III	1981	87
386⅝	61⅜	61⅞	47⅜	8⅞	9⅝	6	6	Flathead Co., Mont.	Floyd L. Jackson	Floyd L. Jackson	1976	89
386⅝	59⅜	60	52⅜	9⅝	9⅛	6	7	Panther River, Alta.	Leonard L. Hengen	Leonard L. Hengen	1977	90
386⅝	49⅜	50⅜	39⅜	8⅝	9	7	7	Nez Perce Co., Idaho	H. H. Schnettler	H. H. Schnettler	1957	91
386⅜	55⅜	55⅜	42	10	9⅝	7	7	Smoky River, Alta.	Stephen Trulik	Stephen Trulik	1963	91
386⅜	56⅜	54⅞	44	8⅝	8⅛	6	7	Coconino Co., Ariz.	Lee Clemson	Lee Clemson	1974	91
386⅜	52⅜	54⅛	48	8⅞	9⅛	6	6	Delta Co., Colo.	Bert Johnson	Bert Johnson	1974	94
386⅛	57⅞	57⅛	48⅜	7⅞	8⅝	6	6	Forest Gate Store, Sask.	Edwin L. Roberts	Edwin L. Roberts	1962	95
386⅛	59⅛	58	36⅜	10⅜	9⅜	6	6	Mescalero Apache Res., N.M.	Larry W. Bailey, Sr.	Larry W. Bailey, Sr.	1974	95
386	53⅜	55⅜	51	9⅜	9⅝	6	6	Valley Co., Idaho	Denny Young	Kenny Poe	1957	97
386	52⅜	53	48⅜	8⅝	8⅛	6	7	Big Horn Mt., Wyo.	Unknown	Fred Gray	1966	97
385⅞	49⅜	51⅞	44⅜	7⅞	7⅞	6	6	Shoshone Co., Idaho	Jerry Nearing	Jerry Nearing	1976	99
385⅞	56⅜	56⅛	40⅜	7⅞	8	6	6	Big Smoky River, Alta.	Fred T. Huntington, Jr.	Fred T. Huntington, Jr.	1961	100
385⅞	59⅜	56⅜	41⅜	8	9⅜	7	8	Ft. Apache Res., Ariz.	Glen Daly	Glen Daly	1957	101
385⅜	53⅜	53	40⅜	8⅜	8⅛	6	6	Kootenai Co., Idaho	Arth Day	Arth Day	1971	101
385⅜	57⅞	55⅜	42⅝	8⅝	9	7	6	Sanders Co., Mont.	George R. Johnson	George R. Johnson	1977	103

Score	Beam R	Beam L	Spread	Circ R	Circ L	Pts R	Pts L	Locality	By whom killed	Owner	Date	Rank
385⅝	51⅛	54⅞	41¼	10⅞	10⅞	6	6	Otero Co., N.M.	Gregory C. Saunders	Gregory C. Saunders	1985	103
385⅝	55⅝	55⅛	47⅜	10⅛	10⅛	6	6	Teton Co., Wyo.	Gene J. Riordan	Timothy D. Riordan	1960	103
385⅝	48⅞	49⅛	34⅞	8⅜	8⅞	6	6	Trappers Lake, Colo.	Byron W. Kneff	Byron W. Kneff	1954	106
385⅝	51	52⅛	48⅛	11	11⅞	8	8	Grande Cache Lake, Alta.	Kenneth A. Evans	Kenneth A. Evans	1966	106
385⅝	56⅞	56⅜	46⅜	8⅜	10	6	7	Bozeman, Mont.	Robert B. McKnight	Robert B. McKnight	1966	106
385⅛	46	48⅜	44⅜	7⅞	8⅞	6	6	Lincoln Co., Wyo.	Ken Clark	Ken Clark	1979	106
384⅞	55⅛	54⅜	36⅜	9⅜	9	7	6	Clearwater River, Alta.	William Lenz	William Lenz	1966	110
384⅞	54	54	50	10⅛	10	6	6	Hualapai Indian Res., Ariz.	Tod Reichert	Tod Reichert	1975	110
384⅞	56½	58⅝	44	9⅜	9½	7	6	Ft. Apache Res., Ariz.	Jim P. Caires	Jim P. Caires	1978	110
384¾	60	60⅜	44⅜	9⅜	10	7	7	Apache Co., Ariz.	H. C. Meyer & J. T. Caid	Herman C. Meyer	1982	110
384¾	55⅜	54⅛	47⅛	8⅞	8⅞	6	6	Ram River, Alta.	Joe Kramer	Joe Kramer	1966	114
384¾	57	56⅜	43⅝	9⅜	9⅜	7	7	Bonneville Co., Idaho	David W. Anderson	David W. Anderson	1967	115
384¾	53⅜	53⅛	43	8⅜	8⅜	7	6	Bonneville Co., Idaho	Keith W. Hadley	Keith W. Hadley	1972	115
384¾	59⅞	59⅜	49⅜	7⅜	7⅝	7	6	Jackson Hole, Wyo.	Francis X. Bouchard	Francis X. Bouchard	1956	117
384¾	59	58⅜	46⅜	10⅛	9⅜	6	6	Beaverhead Co., Mont.	Phil Matovich	Phil Matovich	1969	117
384¾	54⅝	54½	50⅞	9⅞	9⅜	6	6	Clear Creek Co., Colo.	John Wallace	John Wallace	1973	117
384¾	61⅞	64⅞	40⅞	11	10⅛	6	8	Ft. Apache Res., Ariz.	Ralph C. Winkler, Jr.	Ralph C. Winkler, Jr.	1977	120
384	58⅜	60⅛	49⅜	10	11	7	7	Apache Co., Ariz.	Roy W. Baker	Roy W. Baker	1980	120
384	58⅝	56⅝	44	9⅜	9⅛	6	7	Willow Creek, Mont.	Mike Miles	Mike Miles	1958	122
384	56⅜	54	47	7⅜	8⅜	6	7	Costilla Co., Colo.	William E. Carl	William E. Carl	1967	122
383⅞	53⅜	51⅛	43⅛	8⅝	8⅜	6	6	Meagher Co., Mont.	Frank W. Fuller	Frank W. Fuller	1963	122
383⅞	53⅞	54	43¾	9½	9⅜	6	6	Unknown	Unknown	S. Side Cody Elk Club	1939	125
383⅞	51¾	51⅛	48⅜	9⅝	9⅝	6	6	Unknown	Unknown	N. Side Cody Elk Club	PR1967	126
383¾	53⅞	55	50⅛	9⅜	8	7	6	Maycroft, Alta.	Steve Kubasek	Steve Kubasek	1957	127
383¾	52½	52	41⅜	9¼	9⅜	7	7	Nez Perce Co., Idaho	Thenton L. Todd	Thenton L. Todd	1956	128
383	53⅜	53⅛	47⅜	9⅞	10⅛	6	6	Coconino Co., Ariz.	Jay E. Elmer	Jay E. Elmer	1979	128
383	54⅜	52⅛	43⅞	8⅞	8⅜	6	6	Snowy Range, Wyo.	Kermit Platt	Kermit Platt	1961	130
382⅞	56⅛	54⅜	41⅜	9⅞	10⅛	6	6	Coconino Co., Ariz.	Gene Bird	Gene Bird	1972	131
382⅞	56⅞	55⅛	48	9¾	10⅛	7	8	Panther River, Alta.	Thomas Coupland	Echoglen Taxidermy	1984	131
382⅞	52⅜	52⅝	36⅝	9¾	9	6	8	Blacktail Creek, Mont.	Floyd E. Winn	Floyd E. Winn	1959	133
382⅞	48	48	32⅜	14⅛	13	7	6	Castle River, Alta.	Albert Truant	Albert Truant	1970	133
382⅝	56⅞	56⅞	41⅞	8⅜	9⅜	7	6	Rattlesnake Mt., Wyo.	Bob Edgar	Bob Edgar	1966	135
382⅝	49	48⅛	36⅞	8⅜	8⅝	7	6	Apache Co., Ariz.	William E. Moss	William E. Moss	1985	135
382⅝	54	55⅛	40⅜	8⅜	9⅜	7	7	Kootenai Co., Idaho	Terry Cozad	Terry Cozad	1968	137
382⅝	53⅜	54	50⅝	8⅜	8⅞	7	9	Elbow River, Alta.	Harold F. Mailman	Harold F. Mailman	1964	138
382¼	49⅞	52⅛	35⅜	11	10⅜	6	6	Summit Co., Colo.	Marshall Sherman	Marshall Sherman	1966	138
382¼	56	56⅛	41⅝	8⅜	9⅜	7	7	Teton Co., Wyo.	Randy Johnston	Randy Johnston	1970	138
382¼	49	48⅛	36⅞	8⅜	8⅞	6	6	Cascade Co., Mont.	Robert J. Gliko	Robert J. Gliko	1983	138
382⅛	54	55⅛	40⅜	8⅜	8⅝	7	7	Sublette Co., Wyo.	Frank Dew	Frank Dew	1931	142
382⅛	53⅜	54	50⅝	8⅜	10⅛	6	6	Morman Lake, Ariz.	Wayne A. Barry	John E. Rhea	1965	142
382⅛	49⅞	52⅛	35⅜	11	11	6	6	Gallatin Co., Mont.	Henry Lambert	Charles F. Miller	1923	144
382⅛	55⅛	55	47¼	7⅞	7¾	6	6	Williams, Ariz.	Oscar B. Skaggs	Oscar B. Skaggs	1954	144
382⅛	58⅛	62⅜	48	8	7¾	6	6	Grant Co., Oreg.	Drake J. Davis	Drake J. Davis	1981	144

American Elk (Wapiti)—Continued
Cervus elaphus nelsoni and related subspecies

Score	Length of Main Beam R.	L.	Inside Spread	Circumference at Smallest Place Between First and Second Points R.	L.	Number of Points R.	L.	Locality Killed	By Whom Killed	Owner	Date Killed	Rank
382⅞	54⅞	54⅝	45⅞	8	8⅝	6	6	Gallatin Co., Mont.	A. Francis Bailey	A. Francis Bailey	1966	147
382⅞	57⅜	55⅞	44⅜	8⅛	8⅞	7	7	Bob Marshall Wild., Mont.	Gene E. Trenary	Gene E. Trenary	1958	147
382	52⅞	51⅛	47⅞	9⅝	8⅝	8	7	Missoula Co., Mont.	Fritz Frey	Clifford Frey	1943	149
382	53⅞	51⅛	48	8⅞	9⅛	6	6	Little Cimmaron, Colo.	Newell Beauchamp	Bud Lovato	1957	149
381⅛	59⅝	58	52⅛	7⅞	7⅝	7	8	Gallatin Co., Mont.	H. K. Shields	H. K. Shields	1958	151
381⅞	52⅞	52	49⅞	10⅝	9⅜	6	7	Beaverhead Co., Mont.	C. L. Jensen	C. L. Jensen	1960	152
381⅞	55⅜	57⅛	41	9⅝	9⅝	7	7	Red Deer River, Alta.	Allan E. Brown	Allan E. Brown	1980	152
381⅛	56⅞	56⅜	41⅛	10⅝	10⅛	6	6	Granite Co., Mont.	Jeff Conn	Jeff Conn	1971	154
381⅛	56⅜	57⅛	42⅛	8⅞	9⅝	6	6	Fremont Co., Wyo.	John S. Maxson	John S. Maxson	1954	155
381⅛	57⅞	57⅛	41⅛	9⅝	9⅛	7	6	Park Co., Mont.	Edward F. Skillman	Edward F. Skillman	1968	156
381⅜	55⅞	54⅜	37⅜	9⅝	9⅛	7	7	Larimer Co., Colo.	Earl L. Erbes	Earl L. Erbes	1972	156
381⅜	53⅜	53⅞	43⅞	9⅝	8⅝	6	6	White Pine Co., Nev.	Michael N. Kalafatic	Michael N. Kalafatic	1985	156
381⅛	57	55⅝	44⅜	9	8⅝	6	6	Kittitas Co., Wash.	Clinton W. Morrow	Clinton W. Morrow	1957	159
381⅛	57⅝	56⅜	45⅜	8	7⅜	6	6	Laramie Peak, Wyo.	Lawrence Prager	Lawrence Prager	1958	160
381⅛	49⅞	51⅛	39⅞	8⅝	9	7	7	Flathead Co., Mont.	Earl Weaver, Jr.	Earl Weaver, Jr.	1962	160
381	56⅜	54⅜	48⅛	8⅝	8⅜	6	6	Gallatin Co., Mont.	Jack Bauer	Jack Bauer	1961	162
381	48	54⅜	40⅜	8⅝	8⅞	7	8	Bonneville Co., Idaho	Mrs. E. LaRene Smith	Mrs. E. LaRene Smith	1966	162
381	51⅞	50⅝	43⅝	8	7⅝	7	7	Big Horn Co., Mont.	Jerry Barnes	Jerry Barnes	1962	162
381	54	53⅜	48⅝	8	7⅝	6	7	Gallatin Co., Mont.	Gerald Schroeder	Gerald Schroeder	1977	166
380⅞	51⅛	51	43⅝	10	9⅝	7	7	Park Co., Mont.	John Caputo	John Caputo	1968	167
380⅞	50⅝	54⅞	47⅝	9⅝	9⅝	6	6	Medicine Bow Range, Colo.	Mike Holliday	Mike Holliday	1966	167
380⅜	54⅜	55	51⅜	7⅞	7⅜	6	7	Chaffee Co., Colo.	Anton Purkat	Anton Purkat	1972	167
380⅜	54⅜	53⅜	42⅝	10⅞	9⅝	6	6	Apache Co., Ariz.	Don L. Corley	Don L. Corley	1984	170
380⅛	52⅞	52⅞	41	9	8⅝	6	6	Payson, Ariz.	Harold Foard	Harold Foard	1947	171
380⅜	62⅞	63⅝	47⅛	8⅝	8⅛	7	8	Harney Co., Oreg.	Pat L. Wheeler	Pat L. Wheeler	1967	172
380⅜	56⅛	57⅞	49⅝	8⅛	8⅝	7	7	Madison Co., Mont.	Phil Hensel	Phil Hensel	1959	172
380⅜	57⅛	57⅛	46⅜	8⅜	8⅜	7	7	Lewis Co., Wash.	Charles Rudolph	Charles Rudolph	1973	172
380⅜	58⅜	58⅜	42⅜	9⅜	8⅝	7	6	Granite Co., Mont.	Richard Shoner	Richard Shoner	1977	172
380⅜	58⅞	54⅛	45	8⅝	8⅞	7	6	Coconino Co., Ariz.	Doug Kittredge	Doug Kittredge	1975	176
380	54	53⅞	48⅜	8⅞	8⅛	7	7	Spring Creek, Alta.	A. C. Bair	A. C. Bair	1948	176
380	51⅛	51⅛	41⅛	7⅞	8⅜	6	6	Duck Mt., Man.	G. N. Burton	G. N. Burton	1965	176

Score								Locality	Owner	By Whom Killed	Date Killed	Rank
380	56⅜	53⅜	50⅞	10⅜	9⅞	7	6	Ft. Apache Res., Ariz.	George E. Crosby	George E. Crosby	1957	176
379⅞	51⅜	50⅞	45⅜	9⅞	9⅜	6	6	Rock Lake, Alta.	Jim Soneff	Jim Soneff	1961	179
379⅞	58⅜	58⅜	45⅜	9⅜	9⅜	6	6	Ruby Mts., Mont.	Jack Ballard	Jack Ballard	1960	179
379⅞	54	54	45⅜	7⅞	8⅜	6	6	Daisy Pass, Mont.	Larry R. Price	Larry R. Price	1971	179
379⅞	52	51⅞	36⅜	10	10	9	8	Adams Co., Idaho	William V. Baker	William V. Baker	1976	179
379⅞	57⅞	57⅜	40⅜	7⅞	7⅞	6	6	Big Horn, Mont.	George F. Gamble	George F. Gamble	1968	179
379⅞	58⅜	58⅜	46⅜	8⅜	8⅜	7	7	Grant Co., N.M.	Tony R. Grijalva	Tony R. Grijalva	1983	179
379⅜	57	57	48⅜	9⅜	9⅜	6	6	Big Horn Mts., Wyo.	Unknown	L. M. Brownell	1956	185
379⅜	51⅞	51⅜	39	9⅜	9⅞	6	6	Madison Co., Mont.	LeRoy Schweitzer	LeRoy Schweitzer	1964	186
379⅜	54	52⅜	42⅜	8	7⅜	6	6	Unknown	Gift of Arch. Rogers	National Collection	PR1951	187
379⅜	60⅜	61⅜	45⅜	8⅜	8⅜	6	6	Coconino Co., Ariz.	Tammy J. Otero	Tammy J. Otero	1984	187
379½	55⅞	56⅜	44⅜	9	8⅜	6	6	Bozeman, Mont.	K. L. Berry	K. L. Berry	1959	189
379⅜	58⅜	57⅜	41⅜	9	9⅜	6	6	Sierra Blanca Lake, Ariz.	Joseph A. Rozum	Joseph A. Rozum	1965	189
379⅜	54⅜	54⅜	40⅜	8⅜	8⅜	6	6	Sanders Co., Mont.	Robert L. Coates	Robert L. Coates	1974	189
379⅜	56	57	33⅜	8⅜	9⅜	6	6	Duvernay Bridge, Alta.	Alec Mitchell	Alec Mitchell	1917	192
379	49	50⅜	39	10⅜	10⅜	8	8	Teton Park, Wyo.	S. M. Vilven	S. M. Vilven	1964	193
379	50⅞	51⅜	40⅞	9⅜	8⅜	6	6	Big Creek, Idaho	Picked Up	George Dovel	1963	193
379	51	51	44⅜	9⅜	9⅜	6	6	Petroleum Co., Mont.	Lana J. Sluggett	Lana J. Sluggett	1984	193
378⅞	57⅞	58⅜	47⅜	8⅜	8½	6	6	Carbon Co., Wyo.	Donal F. Mueller	Donal F. Mueller	1964	196
378⅞	56⅜	56⅜	46⅜	8	8	6	6	Wildhay River, Alta.	Richard Clouthier	Richard Clouthier	1973	196
378⅞	54⅜	54⅜	45	7⅞	7⅜	6	6	Gallatin Co., Mont.	Ted Shook	Ted Shook	1966	198
378⅞	51⅞	50½	39⅜	7⅞	8⅜	7	9	Sanders Co., Mont.	John Fitchett	John Fitchett	1980	198
378⅞	52	55⅜	47⅜	8⅜	8⅜	7	6	Dutch Creek, Alta.	Harold King	Harold King	1951	200
378⅞	52⅞	54	42⅜	9⅜	10	7	7	Park Co., Wyo.	Kenneth Smith	Kenneth Smith	1954	201
378⅜	53⅜	48⅜	55	8⅜	8⅜	7	7	Valley Co., Idaho	Joe Gisler	Joe Gisler	1961	201
378⅜	54⅜	55⅜	45⅜	8⅜	8⅜	6	6	Shoshone Co., Idaho	Edward L. Bradford	Edward L. Bradford	1963	201
378⅜	58⅜	56⅜	43⅜	8⅜	8⅜	6	6	Beaverhead Co., Mont.	Milton F. Steele	Milton F. Steele	1963	201
378⅜	51⅛	52⅜	50	9⅜	10	7	7	White River, Colo.	Art Wright	Art Wright	1953	201
378	43⅜	47⅜	40	9⅜	9⅜	9	8	Duck Mt., Man.	John D. Harbarenko	John D. Harbarenko	1973	205
378	49⅜	50⅞	39⅜	7⅞	8⅜	7	7	Richard's Peak, Mont.	Albert Sales	Richard Eastman	1931	205
377⅞	56⅜	56⅞	44⅜	7⅞	7⅜	7	6	Gunnison, Colo.	Ed Lattimore, Jr.	Ed Lattimore, Jr.	1966	207
377⅞	51⅜	52⅜	45	8	8⅜	7	10	Routt Co., Colo.	Tom Nidey	Tom Nidey	1959	207
377⅞	56	55⅜	41⅜	8⅜	8⅜	7	9	Sanders Co., Mont.	Steve Barnes	Steve Barnes	1973	209
377⅞	53⅜	53⅜	41⅜	9	9⅜	6	7	Mistatim, Sask.	Peter Hrbachek	Peter Hrbachek	1984	209
377⅞	54⅜	54⅜	40⅜	8⅜	8⅜	6	6	Apache Co., Ariz.	A. C. Goodell	A. C. Goodell	1963	209
377¾	53⅜	53⅜	51⅜	9	9	7	7	Beaverhead Co., Mont.	Edmund J. Giebel	Edmund J. Giebel	1981	212
377¾	51⅜	51⅜	45⅜	8⅜	8⅜	6	6	Granite Co., Mont.	Tom Villeneue	Tom Villeneue	1966	212
377¾	47⅜	47⅜	45	8⅜	8⅜	6	6	Gunnison Co., Colo.	Leo Welch	Leo Welch	1972	214
377¾	52⅜	53⅜	42⅜	8⅜	8⅜	6	6	Ft. Apache Res., Ariz.	Picked Up	Gary Marsh	1971	214
377¾	52⅜	54	41⅜	8⅜	8⅜	6	7	Park Co., Wyo.	Jon M. Mekeal	Jon M. Mekeal	1984	214
377¾	53⅜	52	46⅜	8⅜	9⅜	6	6	Missoula Co., Mont.	Tom Schenarts	Tom Schenarts	1970	214
377¾	60	58	41⅜	8⅜	8⅜	6	6	Sanders Co., Mont.	Allen White	Allen White	1968	218
377¾	59	55	39⅜	9⅜	9⅜	6	6	Teton Co., Wyo.	Walter V. Solinski	Walter V. Solinski	1962	218

AMERICAN ELK (Wapiti)—Continued
Cervus elaphus nelsoni and related subspecies

Score	Length of Main Beam R.	L.	Inside Spread	Circ. at Smallest Place Between First and Second Points R.	L.	No. of Points R.	L.	Locality Killed	By Whom Killed	Owner	Date Killed	Rank
377⅞	53⅜	51⅛	45⅜	9⅝	8⅝	8	8	Powell Co., Mont.	Rex Sorenson	Univ. Mont. Museum	1952	221
377⅞	53⅜	53⅝	49⅝	8⅝	8⅜	6	7	Gallatin Range, Mont.	E. Dehart, Sr., P. Van Beek, & H. Prestine	Earl Dehart, Sr.	1960	221
377⅞	55⅝	60⅛	50⅝	9⅞	10⅜	6	6	Show Low, Ariz.	Michael Pew	Michael Pew	1964	221
377⅞	56	55⅜	40⅜	11⅛	11	6	6	Park Co., Wyo.	Mary Jane Rickman	M. J. Rickman & E. R. Rickman, Jr.	1965	221
377⅞	54⅝	54⅜	44⅜	8⅞	8⅛	7	7	Apache Co., Ariz.	Donald E. Franklin	Donald E. Franklin	1981	221
377⅞	53	51	45⅛	9	8⅝	6	8	Sublette Co., Wyo.	Ted Dew	Ted Dew	1928	226
377	54⅝	54⅛	47⅞	9⅞	8⅝	7	6	Brazeau River, Alta.	Ted Loblaw	Ted Loblaw	1960	227
377	45⅝	46⅞	42⅛	7⅞	7⅞	7	7	Navajo Co., Ariz.	Melvin Nolte, Jr.	Melvin Nolte, Jr.	1983	227
377	49⅜	48⅛	39	7⅛	7⅞	7	7	Clearwater River, Alta.	Don H. Grimes	Don H. Grimes	1985	227
376⅞	55	55⅝	38⅝	9⅝	10⅛	6	6	Jackson Hole, Wyo.	H. M. Hanna	M. H. Haskell	PR1890	230
376⅞	56⅜	57⅞	52⅞	7⅜	7⅞	6	7	Park Co., Wyo.	Warren C. Cubbage	Warren C. Cubbage	1957	230
376⅞	56⅜	54⅝	44⅜	9⅛	9⅜	7	8	Big Horn Mts., Wyo.	Unknown	A. W. Hendershot	1912	232
376⅞	51⅞	52⅞	48⅝	8⅞	8⅜	8	7	Lewis & Clark Co., Mont.	Cameron G. Mielke	Cameron G. Mielke	1964	232
376⅞	52⅜	52⅛	51	8⅜	7⅞	8	7	Teton Co., Wyo.	Ward Keevert	Ward Keevert	1968	232
376⅞	58⅞	57⅜	45⅜	8⅜	9½	8	7	Crook Co., Oreg.	Picked Up	Larry E. Miller	1983	232
376⅝	59⅜	59⅝	48⅛	10	9½	6	6	Granby, Colo.	Melvin Van Lewen	Colo. Div. of Wildl.	1961	236
376⅝	58⅜	56⅜	39⅜	7⅞	7	7	7	Teton Co., Idaho	Edwin E. Schiess	Tim Schiess	1966	236
376⅜	48	50⅜	39⅜	8⅝	9⅛	7	7	Highwood River, Alta.	L. Edwards	L. Edwards	1956	238
376⅜	56⅝	57	49⅝	9⅜	8⅝	8	7	Albany Co., Wyo.	Jerry F. Cook	Jerry F. Cook	1965	238
376⅜	55⅛	53⅛	40⅜	8⅜	8⅛	7	7	White River, Colo.	Ron Vance	Ronald Crawford	1957	240
376⅜	48⅜	49⅞	41⅛	8	7⅞	6	6	Radium, Colo.	Bill Mercer	Bill Mercer	1964	240
376⅜	49⅜	49⅜	43⅜	7⅞	9⅛	6	6	Rocky Mt. House, Alta.	George P. Ebl	George P. Ebl	1966	240
376	54⅜	55⅝	42⅝	9	8⅜	6	6	Lincoln Co., N.M.	Jim Carter	Jim Carter	1981	243
376	58⅜	56⅜	44⅜	8⅞	8	6	6	Almont, Colo.	John Schwartz	John Schwartz	1961	244
376	60⅛	59	42	7⅝	9⅛	6	6	Dormer River, Alta.	D. C. Thomas	D. C. Thomas	1978	244
375⅞	55	55	43⅜	9⅜	8⅝	8	8	Flathead Co., Mont.	Pat Roth	Pat Roth	1966	246
375⅞	54⅜	54⅜	43	8⅞	8⅜	8	8	Big Horn Mts., Wyo.	Robert F. Retzlaff	Robert F. Retzlaff	1957	247
375⅞	50⅜	50⅞	40⅝	9⅛	10⅛	6	6	Crow Valley, Colo.	Dale R. Leonard	Dale R. Leonard	1961	247
375⅞	57⅞	57⅛	43	7⅜	7⅞	6	6	Buck Creek, Wyo.	Andrew W. Heard, Jr.	Andrew W. Heard, Jr.	1958	247

Score								Locality	By Whom Killed	Owner	Date Killed	Rank
375⅝	55⅝	54⅞	39⅞	8⅞	8⅝	6	6	North Fall Creek, Wyo.	Picked Up	Bob F. Penny	1981	247
375⅝	52⅛	50⅞	37⅞	8⅞	7⅞	7	7	Shoshone Co., Idaho	Ralph H. Brandvold, Jr.	Ralph H. Brandvold, Jr.	1983	247
375⅝	58	59⅞	40⅞	10⅞	10⅞	7	7	Unknown	Unknown	Demarest Mem. Museum	PR1952	252
375⅝	53	51⅞	40⅞	9	9⅞	6	7	Madison River, Mont.	Dale A. Hancock	Dale A. Hancock	1967	252
375⅜	54⅜	54⅛	43⅞	8⅞	8⅞	7	6	Sanders Co., Mont.	Tony B. Cox	Tony B. Cox	1980	255
375⅜	57⅞	55⅞	48⅞	8⅞	8⅛	6	6	Jefferson Co., Mont.	Ralph J. Huckaba	Ralph J. Huckaba	1949	255
375⅜	50	53⅞	48⅞	8⅜	9⅜	6	6	Fremont Co., Wyo.	Edward J. Patik	Edward J. Patik	1962	257
375⅜	52	52	43⅞	9⅞	10⅞	7	6	Jefferson Co., Mont.	Mrs. Lou Sweet	Mrs. Lou Sweet	1924	257
375⅜	58⅞	56⅞	43⅞	8⅞	9⅞	6	7	Snake River, Wyo.	W. H. Robinson	W. H. Robinson	1957	257
375⅜	52⅝	54⅛	44⅞	9	8⅜	7	7	Park Co., Mont.	Bruce Brown	Bruce Brown	1967	257
375⅜	49	50⅞	39⅞	7⅞	7⅞	7	6	Beaverhead Co., Mont.	Harold F. Krieger, Jr.	Harold F. Krieger, Jr.	1970	257
375⅜	51⅛	52	44⅞	7⅞	8⅞	6	7	Teton Co., Wyo.	Unknown	Nathan E. Hindman	PR1950	262
375⅜	55⅞	52⅜	47⅞	8⅞	8⅞	8	8	Craig, Colo.	Kenneth W. Cramer	Kenneth W. Cramer	1960	262
375⅛	51⅛	53⅛	36⅞	7⅞	7⅞	8	7	Ten Sleep, Wyo.	Kenneth Hadland	Kenneth Hadland	1959	262
375⅛	54⅛	55⅛	49	9⅜	9⅞	7	7	Jackson, Wyo.	Bill Blanchard	Bill Blanchard	1954	262
375⅛	53	52	41	10	10⅞	7	8	Natrona Co., Wyo.	Victor R. Jackson	Victor R. Jackson	1976	262
375	56	55	38	8⅞	8⅞	6	6	Albany Co., Wyo.	Don Stewart	Don Stewart	1981	262
375	55⅜	55⅜	41⅞	8⅜	8⅞	6	6	Colfax Co., N.M.	Slim Pickens	Margaret M. Lindley	1981	262
375	52	53⅞	39⅞	9	10	6	6	Prince Albert, Sask.	Unknown	Lucky Lake Sask. Elks	1926	268
375	58⅞	58⅞	37⅞	10⅞	9⅞	7	7	Tonto Lake, Ariz.	Louise F. Campbell	Louise F. Campbell	1967	268
375	52⅝	52⅝	47⅞	8⅞	9	6	6	Fremont Co., Idaho	Eva Calonge	Eva Calonge	1960	270
375	57⅞	54⅞	41⅞	9⅞	9⅞	7	7	Park Co., Mont.	Robert M. Brogan	Robert M. Brogan	1972	270
375	57⅞	54	38	8	8	7	7	Denton Co., Texas	O. Z. Finley	Joe B. Finley, Jr.	1934	270
375	59	58⅞	42⅞	9⅞	9⅞	6	6	Lewis & Clark Co., Mont.	James Bollinger	James Bollinger	1982	270
414⅞*	55⅜	58⅜	53⅞	13⅞	13	9	9	Gunnison Co., Colo.	J. J. Carpenter	Hugh Carpenter	1900	
399⅜*	58⅜	58	49⅞	9⅜	9⅞	6	6	Coconino Co., Ariz.	Terry J. Rice	Terry J. Rice	1979	
391⅛*	57⅞	57⅞	42⅞	10⅞	10⅞	6	7	Ouray Co., Colo.	Eugene D. Guilaroff	Eugene D. Guilaroff	1973	

*Final Score subject to revision by additional verifying measurements

191

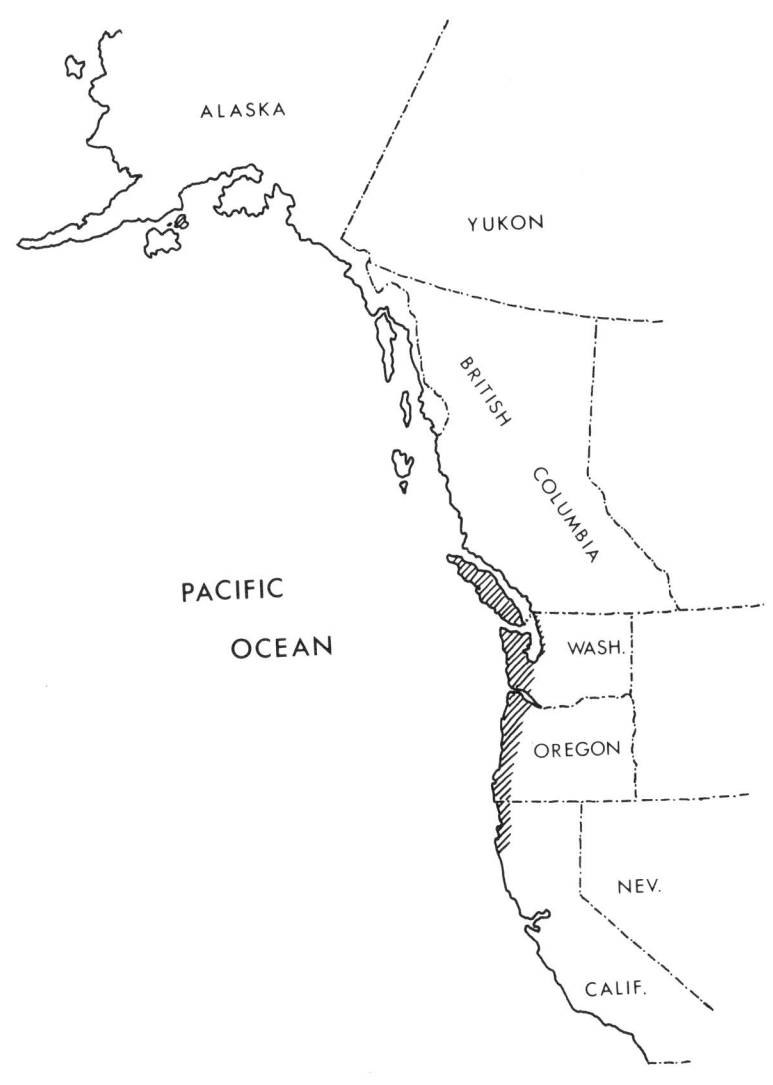

BOUNDARIES FOR AMERICAN AND ROOSEVELT'S ELK

In January 1980, a new category of Roosevelt's elk was established. All other elk varieties, primarily from the Rocky Mountains, are now referred to as American elk. Roosevelt's elk trophies have thicker, shorter antlers, and many of the largest trophies develop crown points, a very distinctive feature.

Roosevelt's elk are acceptable from Del Norte and Humboldt Counties of California; from west of Highway I-5 in Oregon and Washington; from Vancouver Island, B.C.; and from Afognak and Raspberry Islands of Alaska. The Alaskan animals are the result of a successful transplant from the Olympic Peninsula of Washington. To date no trophies from Alaska have been entered which reach the current all-time records book minimum score of 290. Most of the entered trophies to date have come from Coastal Oregon and Washington, with a smaller number from Vancouver Island.

NEW WORLD'S RECORD ROOSEVELT'S ELK
SCORE: 384 3/8
Locality: Clatsop County, Oregon Date: 1949
Hunter: Robert Sharp Owner: Harold E. Stepp

NUMBER TWO ROOSEVELT'S ELK
SCORE: 380 6/8
Locality: Jefferson County, Washington Date: 1983
Hunter and owner: Sam Argo

Roosevelt's Elk

Cervus elaphus roosevelti

Minimum Score 290

Roosevelt's elk includes trophies from: west of Highway 1-5 in Oregon and Washington; Del Norte and Humboldt Counties of California: Afognak and Raspberry Islands of Alaska; and, Vancouver Island, B.C.

Score	Length of Main Beam R.	L.	Inside Spread	Circumference at Smallest Place Between First and Second Points R.	L.	Number of Points R.	L.	Locality Killed	By Whom Killed	Owner	Date Killed	Rank
384⅝	48⅞	49	41⅛	8⅞	9⅞	9	8	Clatsop Co., Oreg.	Robert Sharp	Harold E. Stepp	1949	1
380⅜	52⅝	52⅝	45⅛	8⅜	8⅛	8	8	Jefferson Co., Wash.	Sam Argo	Sam Argo	1983	2
367⅝	50⅜	53	37⅝	9	8⅝	7	7	Clatsop Co., Oreg.	Pravomil Raichl	Pravomil Raichl	1959	3
366⅜	43	45⅝	35⅝	9⅝	9⅝	7	8	Columbia Co., Oreg.	Floyd M. Lindberg	Floyd M. Lindberg	1962	4
358⅝	55⅝	53⅜	42	9⅝	8⅞	8	8	Tillamook Co., Oreg.	Albert Hoffarber	Ray Hoffarber	1940	5
353⅞	52	53⅝	38⅝	8⅝	9⅝	6	6	Washington Co., Oreg.	Kenneth R. Adamson	Kenneth R. Adamson	1985	6
347	47⅜	46⅛	44⅞	9⅛	9⅝	8	7	Columbia Co., Oreg.	Al Glenn	Al Glenn	1955	7
345⅞	51⅝	51⅛	40⅝	11	11⅛	6	7	Columbia Co., Oreg.	Unknown	Harold E. Stepp	1962	8
344⅞	49⅝	47⅝	40	8⅜	8⅝	7	7	Jefferson Co., Wash.	Carroll E. Koenke	Carroll E. Koenke	1966	9
343⅞	41⅜	42⅜	46⅞	8⅜	8	7	7	Tillamook Co., Oreg.	Bud Davis	Herb W. Davis	1957	10
341	45⅜	45⅞	33⅝	10⅜	10	8	8	Columbia Co., Oreg.	Derl Roberts	Derl Roberts	1965	11
340⅞	46⅛	45	36	9⅜	9	6	8	Columbia Co., Oreg.	Bud Holmes	James C. Oroth	1962	12
337⅛	46	44⅜	37⅝	8⅞	8⅞	7	7	Jefferson Co., Wash.	Dave D. Godfrey	Dave D. Godfrey	1966	13
337⅛	49⅝	52	30⅝	9⅛	8⅜	7	6	Wahkiakum Co., Wash.	E. L. McKie & T. Faubian	E. L. McKie	1962	13
336⅞	50⅝	47⅝	39	8	8⅝	6	7	Tillamook Co., Oreg.	Gary L. Cox	Gary L. Cox	1965	15
336⅛	46⅝	46⅞	40⅜	8⅞	9⅛	7	6	Oregon Coast Range	Unknown	Richard Leach	PR1981	16
335⅛	51⅞	51⅛	42⅛	10⅜	10⅛	7	7	Clatsop Co., Oreg.	Picked Up	Andy Mendenhall, Jr.	1978	17
332⅝	51⅛	51⅛	41⅛	8⅝	9⅛	8	6	Humboldt Co., Calif.	Picked Up	Leo Prshora	1955	18
332	49	48⅜	45	8⅛	8⅝	7	6	Tillamook Co., Oreg.	Robert B. Thornton	Robert B. Thornton	1964	19
329⅝	48⅝	50⅛	39⅜	8⅝	8⅜	6	6	Tillamook Co., Oreg.	Gary H. Purdy	Gary H. Purdy	1969	20
328⅞	46⅝	46⅛	38⅝	8⅞	8⅝	7	7	Vancouver Island, B.C.	Wayne H. Zaccarelli	Wayne H. Zaccarelli	1981	21
327⅞	47⅛	46	44⅛	10⅛	11	6	6	Clallam Co., Wash.	Daniel D. Hinchen	Daniel D. Hinchen	1976	22
327⅝	48⅛	50⅝	42⅝	8⅛	8⅛	8	7	Tillamook Co., Oreg.	Picked Up	Dave Griffith	1958	23
327⅛	50⅝	50	40⅝	8⅞	9⅛	7	6	Clatsop Co., Oreg.	Billy L. Jasper	Billy L. Jasper	1946	24
326⅛	49⅝	49⅞	33⅝	8⅛	8⅛	7	7	Wahkiakum Co., Wash.	Otis E. Wright	Otis E. Wright	1966	25
325⅞	50	49	43⅝	9	9⅝	8	7	Columbia Co., Oreg.	Edgar J. Rea	Edgar J. Rea	1973	26
323	45⅞	47	37⅞	7⅝	7⅛	7	7	Clatsop Co., Oreg.	Clarence V. Jurhs	Clarence V. Jurhs	1958	27
322⅝	47⅛	44⅝	38⅛	8⅞	9⅞	8	7	Columbia Co., Oreg.	William E. Curtis	Duane M. Bernard	1952	28
322⅛	43⅝	41	41⅛	10⅜	10⅝	7	7	Clatsop Co., Oreg.	Reed Holding	Reed Holding	1939	29
320⅞	47⅛	51⅛	32⅝	8⅝	8⅝	7	6	Tillamook Co., Oreg.	Stanley E. Kephart	Stanley E. Kephart	1964	30

195

ROOSEVELT'S ELK—Continued
Cervus elaphus roosevelti

Score	Length of Main Beam R.	L.	Inside Spread	Circumference at Smallest Place Between First and Second Points R.	L.	Number of Points R.	L.	Locality Killed	By Whom Killed	Owner	Date Killed	Rank
317⅞	41⅜	41⅝	37⅞	9	8⅝	6	7	Columbia Co., Oreg.	Max Oblack	Max Oblack	1967	31
316⅞	43⅜	43⅝	47⅛	8⅝	8⅝	7	7	Columbia Co., Oreg.	Harry R. Olsen	Harry R. Olsen	1961	32
316⅜	51⅜	49	39	8⅝	9⅝	6	7	Columbia Co., Oreg.	Harry R. Olsen	Harry R. Olsen	1969	32
316⅜	41⅛	41⅛	38⅜	9⅛	8⅛	6	6	Clallam Co., Wash.	Daniel M. Hilt	Daniel M. Hilt	1982	34
316	47⅜	46⅜	43⅛	10⅜	10⅛	6	6	Jefferson Co., Wash.	Hans Norbisrath	Hans Norbisrath	1966	35
315⅜	48⅜	47⅞	42	9⅜	9	6	6	Columbia Co., Oreg.	William E. Curtis	Duane M. Bernard	1965	36
314⅞	46	46⅜	42⅞	8	8⅝	6	8	Columbia Co., Oreg.	Picked Up	Harold E. Stepp	1962	37
314⅜	52⅛	49⅜	36⅜	9⅝	9⅜	6	6	Coos Co., Oreg.	Robert D. Dunson	Robert D. Dunson	1982	38
314⅛	45⅞	46⅛	42⅜	8⅜	8	7	7	Clatsop Co., Oreg.	Robert L. Brown	Robert L. Brown	1966	39
310⅜	43⅜	44⅜	38⅜	7⅜	7⅜	7	7	Clallam Co., Wash.	Daniel M. Hilt	Daniel M. Hilt	1958	40
310⅜	44	44	33⅜	9⅝	9⅝	7	7	Clatsop Co., Oreg.	Elman Peterson, Jr.	Elman Peterson, Jr.	1968	41
310⅛	44⅜	44⅜	34	10⅜	9⅜	7	7	Jefferson Co., Wash.	Howard L. Hill	Michael R. Raffaell	1969	42
309⅞	43⅜	48⅛	31⅜	9⅜	9⅜	7	7	Clatsop Co., Oreg.	Terry E. Andrews	Terry E. Andrews	1984	43
307⅞	46⅛	45⅜	40⅜	7⅜	7⅞	7	7	Tillamook Co., Oreg.	John A. Wehinger	John A. Wehinger	1964	44
306⅞	50⅜	50⅜	38⅜	7⅞	8	6	6	Polk Co., Oreg.	James E. Wallen	James E. Wallen	1980	45
306⅜	47	47⅜	43⅜	7⅜	7⅞	6	6	Humboldt Co., Calif.	Michael L. Johnson	Michael L. Johnson	1976	46
306	40⅜	39⅜	40⅜	9⅜	9⅜	7	7	Washington Co., Oreg.	Michael R. Jamieson	Michael R. Jamieson	1982	47
304⅜	49	41⅛	39⅜	9⅜	9⅜	6	7	Clatsop Co., Oreg.	William D. Mellinger	William D. Mellinger	1958	48
303	47⅞	47⅞	42⅜	9	8⅝	7	5	Jefferson Co., Wash.	C. F. & C. H. Bernhardt	C. F. & C. H. Bernhardt	1972	49
302⅜	50	50	36⅜	7⅜	7⅞	6	6	Jefferson Co., Wash.	Gary Talley	Gary Talley	1981	50
302⅜	45⅜	44⅜	37⅜	8⅜	9	6	6	Grays Harbor Co., Wash.	Donald M. Vestal	Dean Vestal	1981	50
301⅜	43	43⅞	36⅜	8⅜	9⅜	8	8	Clatsop Co., Oreg.	Pravomil Raichl	Pravomil Raichl	1963	52
301⅛	46⅜	44	34⅜	8⅜	8⅝	7	7	Jefferson Co., Wash.	C. F. & C. H. Bernhardt	C. F. & C. H. Bernhardt	1973	53
300⅜	43	40⅜	37⅞	9	8⅜	6	6	Columbia Co., Oreg.	Harry R. Olsen	Harry R. Olsen	1963	54
299⅜	41⅛	42⅜	33⅜	9⅜	9⅜	7	6	Grays Harbor Co., Wash.	Robert Lentz	Robert Lentz	1948	55
296⅞	43⅜	42⅜	34⅜	9⅜	9⅜	6	6	Clallam Co., Wash.	Randy F. Mesenbrink	Randy F. Mesenbrink	1977	56
296⅜	46⅜	48⅜	47⅜	8⅜	8⅜	5	7	Clallam Co., Wash.	Aubrey F. Taylor	Aubrey F. Taylor	1984	56
295⅜	39⅜	41⅛	41	8⅜	8	6	6	Columbia Co., Oreg.	Reed Holding	Reed Holding	1950	58
294⅞	45⅞	45⅜	34⅜	7⅞	8⅜	6	6	Clatsop Co., Oreg.	Picked Up	Robert L. Brown	1965	59

Score								Locality			Date	Rank
293⅞*	43⅜	43⅜	36⅞	7⅝	7⅝	6	6	Tillamook Co., Oreg.	Steven F. Kellow	Steven F. Kellow	1979	60
291⅜	43⅜	43⅜	35⅜	6⅞	7	6	6	Clatsop Co., Oreg.	Picked Up	Robert L. Brown	1979	61
290⅛	45⅜	44⅜	37⅜	9	9⅜	6	6	Coos Co., Oreg.	Gerald W. Hurst	Gerald W. Hurst	1979	62
373⅜*	57⅜	55⅞	44⅛	7⅞	7⅞	7	7	Wahkiakum Co., Wash.	William Williams	William Williams	1968	
370⅞*	50⅞	49	35⅜	8⅜	8⅜	9	9	Ucona River, B.C.	David R. Summers	David R. Summers	1978	
364⅞*	54	54⅜	40⅜	9⅜	8⅝	7	9	Vancouver Island, B.C.	Lawrence A. Ondzik	Alf Spineto	1981	
358⅝*	51⅜	51⅛	42⅜	9⅜	10⅞	7	7	Clatsop Co., Oreg.	Donald A. Schoenborn	Larrys Sports Center	1939	
356⅞*	46	46⅜	39⅜	11⅞	9⅜	8	7	White River, B.C.	George Korhonen	George Korhonen	1982	
344⅜*	52	50⅞	41⅛	10	10	6	6	Kelsey Bay, B.C.	David Webber	David Webber	1981	
342⅞*	47⅞	49⅞	43⅛	8⅞	7⅞	8	7	Clallam Co., Wash.	C. F. & C. H. Bernhardt	C. F. & C. H. Bernhardt	1979	
341²⅞*	46⅞	47⅞	40⅛	9	9⅞	7	7	Moakwa Creek, B.C.	Harry Whitehead	Harry Whitehead	1982	
340⅞*	46⅝	46	38⅜	7⅜	7⅞	8	7	Columbia Co., Oreg.	Harry R. Olsen	Harry R. Olsen	1970	

*Final Score subject to revision by additional verifying measurements

WORLD'S RECORD MULE DEER (TYPICAL ANTLERS)
SCORE: 225 6/8

Locality: Dolores County, Colorado Date: 1972
Hunter and owner: Doug Burris, Jr.
Winner of the Sagamore Hill Medal, 1974

NUMBER TWO MULE DEER (TYPICAL ANTLERS)
SCORE: 217
Locality: Hoback Canyon, Wyoming Date: 1925
Hunter: Unknown
Donated by W. C. Lawrence to Jackson Hole Museum and Pioneer Village Foundation, Inc.

199

Mule Deer (Typical Antlers)

Odocoileus hemionus hemionus and certain related subspecies

Minimum Score 195

Score	Length of Main Beam R.	L.	Inside Spread	Circumference at Smallest Place Between Burr and First Point R.	L.	Number of Points R.	L.	Locality Killed	By Whom Killed	Owner	Date Killed	Rank
225⅝	30⅛	28⅜	30⅛	5⅝	5⅝	6	5	Dolores Co., Colo.	Doug Burris, Jr.	Doug Burris, Jr.	1972	1
217	28⅝	28⅜	26⅝	5⅝	5⅝	6	6	Hoback Canyon, Wyo.	Unknown	Jackson Hole Museum	1925	2
214⅞	27⅞	28⅛	28⅝	5⅜	5⅜	5	6	Franklin Co., Idaho	Ray Talbot	Ray Talbot	1961	3
214⅜	26⅞	28⅛	29⅜	5⅜	5⅜	5	7	Uinta Co., Wyo.	Gary L. Albertson	Spanky Greenville	1960	3
212⅞	26⅛	26⅞	25⅜	5⅜	5⅜	5	5	Gem Co., Idaho	Kirk Payne	Kirk Payne	1967	5
212⅝	26⅜	26⅞	26⅜	6⅛	6⅛	8	6	San Juan Co., Utah	V. R. Rayburn	V. R. Rayburn	1973	6
212⅛	26⅜	27	21⅛	5⅜	5⅝	5	5	Grand Co., Colo.	Wesley B. Brock	Wesley B. Brock	1963	7
212	29	28	27⅝	6⅜	6⅜	5	6	Chama, N.M.	Joseph A. Garcia	Homer Saye	1965	8
211⅞	28⅝	30⅛	25⅜	6⅜	5	5	6	Adams Co., Idaho	Boyd W. Dennis	Boyd W. Dennis	1970	8
211⅞	30⅜	29⅜	30⅛	4⅜	4⅜	7	8	Teton Co., Wyo.	Robert V. Parke	Robert V. Parke	1967	10
211⅜	29⅞	27⅜	31⅜	4⅞	4⅞	5	5	Gypsum Creek, Colo.	Paul A. Muehlbauer	Paul A. Muehlbauer	1967	11
210⅝	27⅝	29⅜	27	5⅝	5⅝	5	5	Southern Ute Res., Colo.	Jack D. Johnston	Jack D. Johnston	1963	12
210⅜	29⅛	26⅜	25⅜	5⅝	5⅛	6	6	Manti-Lasal Mts., Utah	William Norton	William Norton	1970	13
210	26⅜	29⅜	25⅜	5⅝	5⅝	5	7	Montrose Co., Colo.	Mike Thomas	Mike Thomas	1974	14
209⅝	29⅞	27⅜	29⅝	5	5⅝	6	8	Wallowa Co., Oreg.	John Calvin Evans	Budd Gronquist	1920	15
209½	28⅞	27⅞	28	5⅝	5⅝	5	5	Amherst Mt., Colo.	Herbert Graham	Mrs. W. J. Graham	1963	16
209⅜	27⅜	24⅞	27⅜	5⅝	5⅝	5	5	Rich Co., Utah	Dee Hildt	Dee Hildt	1968	16
209⅜	28	24⅜	28⅜	4⅜	4⅝	5	5	Saquache Co., Colo.	William B. Pennington	William B. Pennington	1967	18
209	24⅜	25⅜	24⅜	6⅛	6⅜	5	7	Rio Arriba Co., N.M.	Kirt I. Darner	B & B Outfitter Service	1968	18
209	27	27⅜	27⅜	5	5⅝	6	5	Lincoln Co., Wyo.	Kirt I. Darner	Kirt I. Darner	1979	18
209	26⅝	27	24⅜	5⅝	5⅝	5	5	Boise Co., Idaho	Charles Root	Soron Root	1970	18
208⅞	27⅞	26⅜	26⅞	5⅛	5	6	5	North Kaibab, Ariz.	Horace T. Fowler	Horace T. Fowler	1938	22
208⅜	24⅛	24⅛	17⅜	5⅜	5⅜	6	6	Garfield Co., Colo.	George Shearer	Richard L. Baker	1952	22
208⅜	26	27⅜	26⅜	5⅜	5⅜	4	5	Rio Arriba Co., N.M.	James R. Odiorne, Jr.	James R. Odiorne, Jr.	1978	22
208⅜	27⅜	27⅜	28⅞	5⅜	5⅝	5	7	Rio Arriba Co., N.M.	Kelly Baird	Kelly Baird	1984	25
208⅛	27⅜	26⅜	27⅜	5	5	5	5	Mesa Co., Colo.	Robert L. Zaina	Robert L. Zaina	1960	26
208⅛	26⅜	26⅜	25⅝	5⅜	5⅜	6	6	Jicarilla Apache Res., N.M.	Kenneth Campbell	Kenneth Campbell	1969	27
207⅜	28⅛	29⅞	28⅜	5⅝	5⅝	9	7	Mesa Co., Colo.	Wally Bruegman	Wally Bruegman	1972	27
207⅜	28⅜	27⅜	28⅜	6⅜	6⅛	6	6	Montrose Co., Colo.	Bill Crouch	Bill Crouch	1974	29
207⅛	26⅜	26⅜	24⅜	5⅜	5⅝	6	5	Golden, Colo.	Harold B. Moser	Harold B. Moser	1967	30

Score							Locality			Year	Rank
207	31⅛	27⅞	7	7	6	6	Split Rock, Wyo.	Herb Klein	Herb Klein	1960	31
207	26⅞	28	5⅝	5⅜	5	5	Lincoln Co., Wyo.	Al Firenze, Sr.	Al Firenze, Jr.	1969	31
206⅞	25⅞	25⅞	4⅞	4⅞	5	5	Montrose Co., Colo.	W. L. Boynton	W. L. Boynton	1973	33
206⅜	27⅛	27⅛	5⅛	5	5	5	Delta Co., Colo.	Tom Donaldson	Tom Donaldson	1972	34
206⅜	26⅜	26⅜	5⅜	5⅛	6	5	Rio Arriba Co., N.M.	Jim Roddie	Jim Roddie	1971	35
206⅜	26⅜	26⅜	5⅛	5⅛	5	5	Coconino Co., Ariz.	Robert C. Kaufman	Robert C. Kaufman	1978	35
206²⁄₈	26	27⅛	5⅜	5⅛	6	7	Rio Arriba Co., N.M.	Harley Hinds	Oran M. Roberts	1963	37
206²⁄₈	28	28⅜	6	6	6	5	Montrose, Colo.	Warren S. Bachhofer	Warren S. Bachhofer	1966	37
206¹⁄₈	27⅝	27⅜	5⅛	5⅛	5	5	Eagle Co., Colo.	Harold Taylor	Fred Palmer	1960	39
205⅝	26⅝	25⅜	5⅝	5⅜	5	4	Kanab, Utah	Loyd A. Folkstad	Loyd A. Folkstad	1968	40
205⅝	24⅜	24⅜	5⅝	5⅛	5	7	Eagle Co., Colo.	Mark A. McCormick	Mark A. McCormick	1981	40
205⅝	26⅜	26⅜	6	6	5	5	Peterson, Utah	Picked Up	Paul Crittenden	PR1965	42
205⅝	26	24⅜	4⅞	5	6	8	Gunnison Co., Colo.	Picked Up	Kirt I. Darner	1979	42
205⅝	29⅛	28⅜	5⅛	5⅜	6	5	Carbondale, Colo.	Richard Cobb	Richard Cobb	1962	44
205⅝	25⅜	27⅜	5⅝	5⅛	6	6	Kremmling, Colo.	Larry Bell	Larry Bell	1962	44
205⅝	26⅝	25⅜	5	5	5	5	Lincoln Co., Wyo.	John E. Myers	John E. Myers	1968	44
205⅝	26⅝	26⅜	5⅛	4⅞	6	6	Lincoln Co., Nev.	Erich P. Burkhard	Erich P. Burkhard	1983	44
205⅝	26⅝	26⅜	5⅜	5⅜	5	5	Starkey, Oreg.	H. M. Bailey	H. M. Bailey	1963	48
205	25	22⅛	6	6⅛	5	5	Eagle, Colo.	Harold L. Loesch	Harold L. Loesch	1967	49
204⅞	25⅞	25⅞	5⅛	4⅞	6	6	Pagosa Springs, Colo.	Henry Trujillo, Jr.	Henry Trujillo, Jr.	1963	50
204⅞	27	27	5⅝	5⅝	6	6	Delta Co., Colo.	Frank Peterson	Frank Peterson	1956	50
204⅞	26⅛	26⅛	5⅜	5⅛	5	5	Southern Ute Res., Colo.	Nolan Martins	Nolan Martins	1967	50
204⅝	27	27⅛	6⅛	6⅛	8	8	Pagosa Springs, Colo.	Richard V. Price	Richard V. Price	1962	53
204⅜	25⅜	24⅜	5⅜	5⅜	5	5	Eagle Co., Colo.	Robert V. Doerr	Robert V. Doerr	1982	54
204⅜	26⅜	26⅛	5⅝	5⅛	5	5	Grand Junction, Colo.	Charles M. Bentley	Charles M. Bentley	1962	55
204⅜	26	26⅜	5⅝	5⅛	5	5	Garfield Co., Colo.	James D. Perkins	James D. Perkins	1969	56
204⅛	28⅜	30⅜	4⅝	4⅛	5	5	Jicarilla Apache Res., N.M.	Juan Monarco	Juan Monarco	1960	57
204	27	27⅜	5⅜	5⅜	5	5	Pitkin Co., Colo.	Jens O. Solberg	Jens O. Solberg	1950	58
203⅞	24⅝	26	5⅝	5⅞	6	6	North Park, Colo.	Edison A. Pillmore	Mrs. E. A. Pillmore	1949	59
203⅝	26⅜	27⅝	5⅝	5⅝	6	6	Mesa Creek, Colo.	Ed Craig	Jerome Craig	1951	59
203⅝	29⅜	29⅝	5⅝	5	5	5	Jicarilla Apache Res., N.M.	Dick Wright	Dick Wright	1966	59
203⅝	28⅜	27⅜	5⅞	5⅝	6	6	La Plata Co., Colo.	B.E. Gressett	B. E. Gressett	1950	62
203⅜	28⅛	30⅛	5	5	5	5	Grand Co., Utah	Glen Dumas	S. Kim Bonnett	PR1960	62
203⅜	29⅝	27⅝	5⅝	5⅜	5	5	Kaibab Forest, Ariz.	Herb Graham	Herb Graham	1939	64
203⅜	24	24⅜	5⅝	5⅜	5	5	Elko Co., Nev.	C. H. Wahl	C. H. Wahl	1953	64
203⅜	25⅜	25⅜	4⅞	4⅝	5	5	Mesa Co., Colo.	William P. Burger	William P. Burger	1957	64
203⅜	27	28⅛	5⅜	5⅜	5	5	Rio Arriba Co., N.M.	Arnold Wendt	John Wm. Hughes	1965	64
203⅜	27⅜	27⅛	5⅛	5	6	5	Bayfield, Colo.	Kirt I. Darner	Kirt I. Darner	1969	68
203⅜	25⅝	28	4⅞	4⅞	5	5	White River, Colo.	Ron Vance	Ronald Crawford	1943	69
203⅜	26⅝	26⅝	4⅞	4⅞	6	6	Garfield Co., Utah	James D. Perkins	Mrs. James D. Perkins	1965	69
203⅜	27⅛	26⅝	4⅞	4⅝	5	5	Collbran, Colo.	Joe R. Colingo	Joe R. Colingo	1973	69
203⅜	25⅜	24⅝	4⅛	4⅛	6	6	Crook Co., Wyo.	Ora McGurn	Frances Sheperd	1957	69
203	25	23⅜	5⅞	5⅜	7	5	Mesa Co., Colo.	James K. Scott	James K. Scott	1966	73

MULE DEER (Typical Antlers)—Continued
Odocoileus hemionus hemionus and certain related subspecies

Score	Length of Main Beam R	L	Inside Spread	Circumference at Smallest Place Between Burr and First Point R	L	Number of Points R	L	Locality Killed	By Whom Killed	Owner	Date Killed	Rank
203	26⅞	26⅞	31⅛	5⅜	5⅛	6	5	Franklin Co., Idaho	Herb Voyler, Jr.	Herb Voyler, Jr.	1972	73
202⅞	24⅞	23	22⅛	5⅞	5⅞	5	5	Lincoln Co., Wyo.	Monte J. Brough	Monte J. Brough	1968	75
202⅞	24⅜	26⅜	26⅜	6	5⅞	5	5	Adams Co., Idaho	James S. Denney	James S. Denney	1939	75
202⅞	26⅜	26	23⅛	4⅞	4⅞	6	7	Idaho Co., Idaho	Myron L. Gilbert	Myron L. Gilbert	1975	75
202⅞	27⅝	27⅞	26⅞	6	5⅞	5	7	Jicarilla Apache Res., N.M.	Anthony Julian	Anthony Julian	1961	75
202⅝	26⅜	26⅞	27⅛	5⅞	5⅞	5	5	North Kaibab, Ariz.	Monico Marquez	Monico Marquez	1957	79
202⅝	25⅜	24⅞	19⅞	6⅞	6⅞	5	5	Ouray Co., Colo.	Jewel E. Schottel	Jewel E. Schottel	1966	79
202⅝	28⅜	29⅞	25⅜	5⅜	5⅞	5	5	Rio Arriba Co., N.M.	James F. Leveritt, Jr.	James F. Leveritt, Jr.	1980	79
202⅝	26⅜	25⅝	21⅜	5⅛	5	5	5	Ouray Co., Colo.	Louis V. Schlosser	Louis V. Schlosser	1965	82
202⅝	27⅛	26⅛	25⅜	5	5⅛	5	5	Adams Co., Idaho	David J. Couch	David J. Couch	1970	82
202⅜	30⅜	30	21⅞	6	5⅞	6	4	Collbran, Colo.	Jack Thompson	Jack Thompson	1968	84
202⅜	27⅛	27⅞	27	5⅜	5⅞	6	6	Rio Arriba Co., N.M.	Gerald J. Weber	Gerald J. Weber	1970	84
202¼	26⅞	24⅞	21⅞	5⅛	5	4	6	Garfield Co., Colo.	James S. Harden	James S. Harden	1982	84
202⅛	24⅞	26	27⅛	4⅞	4⅞	6	5	Morgan Co., Utah	Kenneth R. Dickamore	Kenneth R. Dickamore	1967	87
202⅛	26⅜	25⅛	24⅛	5⅝	5⅞	8	7	Baker Co., Oreg.	Brett N. Hayes	Brett N. Hayes	1982	87
202⅛	25⅜	26⅛	23⅜	5⅜	5⅜	7	6	Boulder Co., Colo.	Bob Wallace	Bob Wallace	1963	87
202⅛	26⅜	25⅜	27⅛	5⅝	5⅝	9	8	Montrose Co., Colo.	Earl L. Markley	Earl L. Markley	1968	90
202⅛	30⅜	29⅜	20⅝	4⅞	4⅞	4	5	Archuleta Co., Colo.	Duane Yearwood	Duane Yearwood	1973	90
202	28	28⅜	29⅞	5⅜	5⅜	5	5	Debeque, Colo.	Francis A. Moore	Francis A. Moore	1962	92
202	27⅞	27⅛	24⅜	5⅛	5⅛	5	6	Montrose Co., Colo.	Kenneth Klees	Kenneth Klees	1966	92
202	26⅛	27⅞	25⅝	5⅛	5⅜	5	5	Unknown	Picked Up	Dale Selby	1982	92
202	26⅛	26⅛	21⅛	5	4⅞	5	5	Idaho Co., Idaho	John H. Davis	John H. Davis	1981	92
201⅞	26⅛	27⅞	26⅜	4⅞	4⅞	6	5	Dolores Co., Colo.	Leonard J. Ashcraft	Leonard J. Ashcraft	1958	96
201⅞	27⅞	27⅜	27⅜	6⅛	5⅝	6	6	Dagget Co., Utah	Earl Eldredge	Phil Brotherson	1940	96
201⅞	26	26⅛	21⅛	5	5	5	4	Afton, Wyo.	Bernard Domries	Bernard Domries	1967	98
201½	29⅜	28⅞	30⅜	5⅛	5⅛	5	6	Jicarilla Apache Res., N.M.	Theodore Serafin	Theodore Serafin	1959	99
201⅜	25⅝	26	26⅜	5⅛	5	5	7	Pagosa Springs, Colo.	Allen R. Arnwine	Allen R. Arnwine	1960	99
201⅜	26⅜	26⅛	23⅜	5⅛	5	5	5	Gunnison Co., Colo.	Robert D. Rader	Robert D. Rader	1966	99
201⅜	26⅜	27⅛	27⅜	5⅝	5⅝	5	5	Chelan Co., Wash.	Unknown	Howard W. Hoskins	PR1970	99
201¼	27⅛	25⅜	24⅛	5⅜	5⅜	5	5	Malheur Co., Oreg.	David L. Bauer	David L. Bauer	1971	103
201⅛	28⅜	28⅜	22⅞	5⅝	5⅛	5	7	Ravalli Co., Mont.	Sherman L. Williams	Sherman L. Williams	1973	103

Score	L. R.	L. L.	Cir. R.	Cir. L.	Pts. R.	Pts. L.	Locality	Hunter	Owner	Date	Rank
201 4/8	27	26	5	5	5	5	Garfield Co., Colo.	Unknown	Ronald E. McKinney	1954	103
201 3/8	23	20	5 4/8	5 2/8	6	6	Moffat Co., Colo.	Carl E. Jacobson	Carl E. Jacobson	1967	103
201 3/8	27 6/8	26 5/8	5 4/8	5 4/8	7	7	Blaine Co., Idaho	Brent Jones	Brent Jones	1965	107
201 3/8	25 5/8	25 3/8	5 4/8	5 4/8	5	5	Grand Junction, Colo.	William C. Byrd	William C. Byrd	1967	107
201 3/8	26 3/8	25 3/8	5 5/8	5 5/8	6	6	Rio Arriba Co., N.M.	Donald W. Johnson	Donald W. Johnson	1970	107
201 3/8	25 6/8	23 7/8	5 4/8	5 4/8	5	5	Montrose Co., Colo.	Grant Morlang	Grant Morlang	1972	107
201 3/8	30 1/8	28 7/8	4 6/8	4 6/8	5	5	Wasatch Co., Utah	Paul Probst	Paul Probst	1971	107
201 2/8	28 5/8	28 3/8	5 1/8	5 3/8	5	5	Chama, N.M.	Emitt W. Mundy	Emitt W. Mundy	1961	112
201 2/8	28 3/8	24	6	6	6	6	Jicarilla Apache Res., N.M.	Anthony Julian	Anthony Julian	1961	112
201 2/8	27 6/8	26 5/8	5	4 4/8	5	5	Bayfield, Colo.	D. Rockwell	D. Rockwell	1956	112
201 1/8	29	28	5	4 7/8	5	5	Cameo, Colo.	Thomas C. Krauss	Thomas C. Krauss	1962	115
201 1/8	26 3/8	25 3/8	6 3/8	6 5/8	6	6	Bayfield, Colo.	Les Patrick	Les Patrick	1966	115
201	26 4/8	26 5/8	6 1/8	6 1/8	7	8	Grand Junction, Colo.	Ernest Mancuso	Ernest Mancuso	1954	117
201	26 4/8	22 6/8	5 1/8	5 1/8	5	5	La Plata Co., Colo.	Larry Pennington	Larry Pennington	1978	117
201	25	24 4/8	4 7/8	5	5	5	Dolores Co., Colo.	Mark Loverin	Mark Loverin	1978	117
200 7/8	30 4/8	28 3/8	4 4/8	4 4/8	6	6	Elko Co., Nev.	Harry Irland	Mrs. Harry Irland	1919	120
200 7/8	28	25 7/8	5 2/8	5 2/8	6	6	Collbran, Colo.	Homer O. Hartley	Homer O. Hartley	1962	120
200 6/8	28	28 4/8	5 4/8	5 4/8	5	5	Adams Co., Idaho	Roy Eastlick	Roy Eastlick	1975	120
200 6/8	26 7/8	26 3/8	4 6/8	4 7/8	5	5	Provo Canyon, Utah	Karl D. Zaugg	Karl D. Zaugg	1948	123
200 6/8	27 1/8	25 4/8	5	5 7/8	5	5	Eagle Co., Colo.	John Robertson	John Robertson	1958	123
200 6/8	26	26 6/8	5	5 6/8	6	7	Delta, Colo.	Emil Warber, Jr.	Emil Warber, Jr.	1966	123
200 5/8	27	27 3/8	5 1/8	5 1/8	5	5	Southern Ute Res., Colo.	Jerry E. Morgan	Jerry E. Morgan	1965	123
200 5/8	26 2/8	25 6/8	5 4/8	5 4/8	5	5	Malheur Co., Oreg.	Raymond Duncan	Raymond Duncan	1949	123
200 5/8	25 5/8	26 5/8	5	5 4/8	5	6	Jicarilla Apache Res., N.M.	Arnold Cassador	Arnold Cassador	1967	123
200 4/8	27	27	4 6/8	5	7	9	Ogden, Utah	Carl F. Worden	Carl F. Worden	1948	129
200 4/8	25 5/8	25 2/8	5	5 2/8	6	5	Lincoln Co., Wyo.	John Myers	John Myers	1973	129
200 4/8	27	25 2/8	5	5 1/8	5	5	La Plata Co., Colo.	Unknown	Ronald F. Lax	1979	129
200 4/8	26 1/8	26 2/8	4 7/8	4 7/8	6	6	Bear Lake Co., Idaho	Alan R. Crane	Alan R. Crane	1962	132
200 3/8	27	25 5/8	5 1/8	5	7	6	Bear Lake Co., Idaho	Lee Bridges	Lee Bridges	1966	132
200 3/8	26 5/8	26 6/8	5 3/8	5 3/8	5	5	Caribou Co., Idaho	Herb Voyler, Jr.	Herb Voyler, Jr.	1972	132
200 3/8	25	23	5	5	5	5	Eagle Co., Colo.	Jack Stevens	Jack Stevens	1975	132
200 3/8	26	25	4 7/8	4 7/8	5	5	Sweetwater Co., Wyo.	Arnold A. Bethke	Arnold A. Bethke	1976	132
200 3/8	27 5/8	27 5/8	5 3/8	5 2/8	4	4	Okanogan Co., Wash.	E. R. Crooks	E. R. Crooks	1939	137
200 3/8	27 4/8	26 2/8	5 5/8	5 3/8	7	7	Uncompahgre Natl. For., Colo.	Richard M. Holbrook	Richard M. Holbrook	1972	137
200 3/8	26 7/8	24 4/8	5 1/8	5 1/8	5	7	Gypsum, Colo.	Gene D. Lintz	Gene D. Lintz	1974	137
200 2/8	25	22 2/8	5 5/8	5 5/8	6	6	Battle Mt., Wyo.	Ron Vance	Ronald Crawford	1963	140
200 2/8	29 2/8	23 3/8	4 7/8	4 7/8	5	5	Southern Ute Res., Colo.	Arthur Burch	Steven Burch	1966	140
200 2/8	27 4/8	27	5	5	6	5	Ouray Co., Colo.	Joseph T. Hollingshead	Joseph T. Hollingshead	1967	140
200 2/8	27 5/8	26	4 7/8	4 4/8	4	4	Asotin Co., Wash.	Grant E. Holcomb	Grant E. Holcomb	1975	140
200 2/8	27 3/8	25 7/8	4 4/8	5 5/8	5	5	Mesa Co., Colo.	John M. Domingos	John M. Domingos	1965	144
200 2/8	27 3/8	27 3/8	5 3/8	5 4/8	5	5	Cashmere, Wash.	John F. Schurle	William H. Schott	1913	144
200	26 2/8	27	5 5/8	5 5/8	5	6	Summit Co., Colo.	Picked Up	Bill Knorr	1959	146

MULE DEER (Typical Antlers)—Continued
Odocoileus hemionus hemionus and certain related subspecies

Score	Length of Main Beam R.	L.	Inside Spread	Circumference at Smallest Place Between Burr and First Point R.	L.	Number of Points R.	L.	Locality Killed	By Whom Killed	Owner	Date Killed	Rank
200	24⅞	25⅞	25⅝	4⅞	4⅞	5	5	Piedra River, Colo.	Glenn A. Smith	Glenn A. Smith	1960	146
200	29⅝	29⅞	24⅞	5⅝	5⅝	6	6	Mouqi, Ariz.	Tom Corey	Tom Corey	1964	146
200	27⅛	26	24⅜	4⅞	4⅞	5	5	Eagle Co., Colo.	Dale R. Leonard	David P. Moore	1976	146
200	25⅞	25⅜	21⅞	5⅝	5⅝	5	7	Hot Springs Co., Wyo.	Basil C. Bradbury	Basil C. Bradbury	1977	146
199⅞	22⅞	23⅞	22⅞	5⅛	5⅛	7	6	Jackson Co., Colo.	G. B. Berger, Jr.	Denver Mus. Nat. Hist.	1934	151
199⅞	24⅛		23⅜	5	5⅛	5	5	Uncompahgre Natl. For., Colo.	H. E. Gerhart	H. E. Gerhart	1963	151
199⅞	25⅜	24⅝	25⅛	5⅝	5⅝	5	5	Stillwater Co., Mont.	Basil C. Bradbury	Basil C. Bradbury	1965	151
199⅞	25⅜	27⅞	25⅞	4⅞	5	7	6	Coconino Co., Ariz.	John L. Johnson	John L. Johnson	1972	151
199⅞	26⅝	25⅞	28⅞	5⅝	5	6	6	Eagle Co., Colo.	Richard C. Bergquist	Richard C. Bergquist	1981	156
199⅞	26	26	27	5⅝	5⅝	5	6	Mesa Co., Colo.	Mitchell J. Sacco	Mitchell J. Sacco	1966	156
199⅞	26⅝	24⅞	28⅜	6⅜	6	5	5	Chama, N.M.	James W. Smith II	James W. Smith II	1969	156
199⅞	24⅝	24⅛	25	5⅝	5⅜	5	5	Archuleta Co., Colo.	Kirt I. Darner	Kirt I. Darner	1973	156
199⅞	25⅛	25⅜	25	5⅛	5⅛	5	5	Grant Co., Oreg.	Steve M. Stevenson	Steve M. Stevenson	1982	160
199⅞	27⅜	26	21⅛	5⅝	5⅝	5	5	Princeton, B.C.	Buddy D. Baker	Buddy D. Baker	1979	161
199⅞	28⅞	27⅜	28	6⅛	6⅞	7	8	Pagosa Springs, Colo.	Perry Dixon	Perry Dixon	1957	161
199⅞	27⅜	28⅞	29⅜	6⅜	6⅜	6	5	Garfield Co., Colo.	Picked Up	John F. Frost	1963	161
199⅞	24⅝	24⅞	21⅞	5⅝	5⅝	5	5	Bonneville Co., Idaho	Leonard J. Vella	Leonard J. Vella	1972	161
199⅞	26⅞	27⅜	25⅝	5⅝	5⅝	4	4	Medicine Hat, Alta.	Duncan Baldie	D. Baldie & K. W. McKenzie	1981	161
199⅞	25⅞	26⅞	23⅞	4⅞	5	5	6	Sunpete Co., Utah	Kevin P. Price	Kevin P. Price	1973	161
199⅜	27⅜	26	25⅜	5⅝	6	4	4	Silt, Colo.	V. M. Spiller	V. M. Spiller	1961	166
199⅜	27	27⅞	23⅞	5⅝	5⅝	4	4	Rio Arriba Co., N.M.	John A. Farrell	John A. Farrell	1966	166
199⅜	26⅞	25⅞	24⅞	5⅞	5⅞	5	6	Rio Arriba Co., N.M.	Johnny L. Montgomery	Johnny L. Montgomery	1967	166
199⅜	29⅛	29⅞	31	5⅞	5⅞	7	8	Sanpete Co., Utah	Roger M. Allred	Roger M. Allred	1958	166
199⅜	27⅛	25⅞	26	5	5⅞	5	5	Beechy, Sask.	Marvin Taylor	Marvin Taylor	1961	170
199⅜	27⅞	28	25⅞	5⅜	5⅜	5	5	Strawberry, Utah	Steve Payne	Steve Payne	1962	170
199⅜	27⅞	26⅛	25⅝	5⅛	5⅛	5	5	Eagle Co., Colo.	Howard Stoker	Howard Stoker	1965	170
199⅜	26⅛	25⅞	26⅞	5⅝	5⅝	6	6	Hidden Canyon, Ariz.	Milton Wyman	Milton Wyman	1972	170
199⅜	25⅝	25⅛	25⅛	5⅜	5⅜	7	6	Garfield Co., Colo.	Gary W. Hartley	Gary W. Hartley	1978	170
199⅛	24⅛	25⅜	26⅛	5⅞	5⅞	5	5	Disappointment Creek, Colo.	Clifford Le Neve	Clifford Le Neve	1954	175

Score							Pts R	Pts L	Locality	Hunter	Owner	Date	Score
199½	28⅜	27⅞	27⅞	6	6	5⅞	8	6	Jicarilla Apache Res., N.M.	David L. Chandler	David L. Chandler	1961	175
199½	26⅜	28⅜	28⅜	4⅞	4⅞	4⅞	7	7	Salmon River, Idaho	C. A. Schwope	C. A. Schwope	1959	175
199½	25⅜	25⅜	26⅞	5⅜	5⅜	5⅜	5	7	Boise Co., Idaho	Delbert W. Crawford	Delbert W. Crawford	1969	175
199½	25	24⅜	24⅜	5⅝	5⅝	5⅝	6	5	San Juan Co., Utah	Phyllis O. Crookston	Phyllis O. Crookston	1971	175
199	26⅜	27⅝	26⅜	4⅞	4⅞	5⅛	5	5	Echo, Utah	Wilford Zaugg	Wilford Zaugg	1958	180
199	26⅜	25⅝	29⅞	5⅛	5⅛	5⅜	5	6	Gunnison Natl. Forest, Colo.	James M. Newsom	James M. Newsom	1963	180
199	25⅜	26⅜	23⅞	5⅝	5⅝	5⅛	5	5	Park Co., Wyo.	Lois M. Pelzel	Lois M. Pelzel	1965	180
199	24⅞	24⅜	21	5	5	5⅜	5	6	Mohave Co., Ariz.	William M. Berger, Jr.	William M. Berger, Jr.	1973	180
199	25	25⅜	26	5⅛	5⅛	5	5	5	Dolores Co., Colo.	Kenneth L. Peters	Kenneth L. Peters	1976	180
199	26⅜	28⅛	27⅞	5⅜	5⅜	5⅛	5	6	Bear Lake Co., Idaho	Frank Bidart	Frank Bidart	1965	180
198⅞	27⅞	28⅛	31⅛	5⅝	5⅝	5⅝	10	7	Carbon Co., Utah	Robert R. Henderson	Robert R. Henderson	1961	187
198⅝	27⅛	27⅛	28⅛	6⅛	6⅛	6	5	5	Silt, Colo.	George McCoy	George McCoy	1961	187
198⅝	26⅞	24⅞	19⅜	5⅞	5⅞	5⅞	7	7	Jicarilla Apache Res., N.M.	Anthony Julian	Jicarilla Apache Tribe	1967	187
198⅝	24⅛	26⅜	27⅞	5⅜	5⅜	5⅜	5	5	Burns, Colo.	Charles D. Rush	Charles D. Rush	1981	187
198⅝	27	27⅝	27⅜	5⅜	5⅜	5⅜	5	6	Laramie Co., Wyo.	David L. Shannon	David L. Shannon	1983	187
198⅝	25⅞	25	21⅜	5	5	6	6	5	Yavapai Co., Ariz.	Joseph C. Pecha	Joseph C. Pecha	1960	192
198⅝	23⅜	22⅜	25⅜	5⅛	5⅛	5⅜	5	5	Hines Creek, Alta.	Charles Lundgard	Charles Lundgard	1967	192
198⅝	32⅜	32⅜	25⅜	7	7	7	7	6	Dulce, N.M.	Picked Up	Everett M. Vigil	1966	194
198⅝	24⅛	24⅜	24⅛	5⅜	5⅜	5⅛	7	6	Swan Valley, Idaho	Harry G. Brinkley, Jr.	Harry G. Brinkley, Jr.	1961	194
198⅜	26⅝	24⅜	24⅛	5	5	5	6	7	Carbondale, Colo.	Ralph Clock	Ralph Clock	1968	194
198⅜	25⅛	27⅜	24⅛	5	5	4⅞	6	6	Carbon Co., Wyo.	M. Gary Muske	M. Gary Muske	1984	194
198⅜	25	25⅜	23⅜	4⅞	4⅞	5	5	5	Elmore Co., Idaho	William Hartwig	William Hartwig	1957	198
198⅜	24⅝	25⅞	23⅜	4⅝	4⅝	4⅜	5	5	Tabiona, Utah	Picked Up	H. A. Zumbrock	1966	198
198⅜	25⅜	25⅛	20⅛	5	5	5⅛	5	4	Routt Co., Colo.	Lloyd D. Kindsfater	Lloyd D. Kindsfater	1966	198
198⅜	25	26	21⅛	5⅜	5⅜	5	4	5	Dark Canyon, Colo.	O. P. McGuire	O. P. McGuire	1967	198
198⅜	26	25⅜	22⅜	5⅞	5⅞	5⅝	5	6	Afton, Wyo.	Ray M. Vincent	Ray M. Vincent	1973	202
198⅛	26⅛	28⅜	24⅛	5⅛	5⅛	5⅜	6	5	Bonneville Co., Idaho	Tony Dawson	Tony Dawson	1946	203
198⅛	27⅜	28⅜	19⅜	5	5	5	5	6	Kaibab Forest, Ariz.	W. O. Hart	W. O. Hart	1959	203
198⅛	25⅝	25⅜	28⅜	5	5	4⅜	6	6	Hayden, Colo.	M. W. Giboney	M. W. Giboney	PR1965	203
198⅛	25⅞	26⅛	27⅛	5⅜	5⅜	5	6	6	Summit Co., Colo.	Picked Up	Louis Ceriani	1966	203
198	25	25⅛	26⅜	5⅛	5⅛	6⅜	6	6	Sonora, Mexico	Heinz G. Holdorf	Heinz G. Holdorf	1959	207
198	25⅜	25⅜	22⅜	6	6	6	8	6	Irwin, Idaho	Chet Warwick	Chet Warwick	1967	207
198	24⅛	24⅝	25⅛	5⅝	5⅝	5⅜	6	5	Bayfield, Colo.	C. Ben Boyd	C. Ben Boyd	1975	207
198	25	25⅜	24⅜	5⅞	5⅞	5⅝	5	4	Montrose Co., Colo.	Robert A. Klatt	Robert A. Klatt	1931	210
198	24	24⅜	22⅜	6⅛	6⅛	5⅞	6	6	Unknown	Unknown	Lunds Wildlife Exhibit	1960	210
198	25⅜	26⅛	22⅜	5⅜	5⅜	5⅞	6	6	Mt. Trumbull, Ariz.	E. O. Brown	E. O. Brown	1944	210
198	26⅜	25⅜	26⅜	5⅛	5⅛	5⅛	7	5	Garfield Co., Colo.	Leroy Failor	Leroy Failor	1961	210
197⅞	25⅜	25⅛	25⅜	5⅛	5⅛	5⅛	5	5	Smithfield Canyon, Utah	Stanley Richardson	Stanley Richardson	1973	210
197⅞	28⅛	27⅛	24⅜	4⅞	4⅞	4⅞	6	5	Montpelier, Idaho	Charles R. Mann	Charles R. Mann	1978	210
									Eagle Co., Colo.	Larry Schlasinger	Larry Schlasinger	1983	210
									Natrona Co., Wyo.	Kerry J. Clegg	Kerry J. Clegg	1957	217
									Kaibab Forest, Ariz.	Eoans Pababla	Eoans Pababla	1968	217
									Rossland, B.C.	Robert Simm	Robert Simm		217

MULE DEER (*Typical Antlers*)—Continued
Odocoileus hemionus hemionus and certain related subspecies

Score	Length of Main Beam R	L	Inside Spread	Circ. at Smallest Place Between Burr and First Point R	L	Number of Points R	L	Locality Killed	By Whom Killed	Owner	Date Killed	Rank
197⅞	26⅛	27⅝	24⅛	4⅞	5	5	5	Rio Blanco Co., Colo.	Gary L. Bicknell	Gary L. Bicknell	1967	217
197⅞	24⅜	25	25⅜	5⅛	4⅞	5	5	Coconino Co., Ariz.	Dale C. Morse	Dale C. Morse	1977	217
197⅞	28⅝	28⅝	25⅜	5	5	6	5	Eagle Co., Colo.	Lee Frudden	Lee Frudden	1978	217
197⅞	28⅝	28⅝	25⅜	5⅝	5⅝	7	6	Blaine Co., Idaho	James D. Scarrow	James D. Scarrow	1983	217
197⅞	28⅜	28	25⅜	5⅝	4⅞	5	5	Encampment, Wyo.	Ralph E. Platt, Jr.	Ralph E. Platt, Jr.	1936	223
197⅞	27⅜	28	25⅜	4⅞	4⅞	5	5	Jefferson Co., Mont.	James W. Rowe	James W. Rowe	1964	223
197⅞	27⅛	26⅝	24⅜	4⅞	5⅞	5	5	Elk Ridge, Utah	Bill King	Joseph Fitting	1956	223
197⅞	25⅝	25⅞	23⅝	5⅞	5⅞	6	5	Teton Co., Wyo.	John W. Farlow, Jr.	John W. Farlow, Jr.	1971	223
197⅞	26⅝	27⅝	23⅞	4⅞	5	8	8	Gunnison Co., Colo.	Bobby Joe Watson	Bobby Joe Watson	1975	223
197⅞	26⅝	26	26⅝	5⅞	5⅝	5	5	Major, Sask.	Art Heintz	Art Heintz	1961	228
197⅞	22⅞	22	22⅛	4⅝	4⅞	5	5	Beechy, Sask.	Brett E. Seidle	Brett E. Seidle	1983	228
197⅞	25⅞	26⅛	19⅝	5⅞	5⅞	5	5	Kootenay River, B.C.	Raymond Carry	Raymond Carry	1982	228
197⅞	28⅞	27⅜	23⅛	5⅛	5⅛	5	5	Rio Arriba Co., N.M.	Jerry Longenbaugh	Jerry Longenbaugh	1969	231
197⅞	26	26⅞	23⅞	5⅞	5⅞	6	5	Moffat Co., Colo.	Russ H. Winslow	Russ H. Winslow	1967	231
197⅞	24	26	21⅞	5⅞	5⅞	5	5	Uinta Co., Wyo.	Ken L. Vernon	Ken L. Vernon	1968	231
197⅞	26⅜	25⅞	24⅞	4⅞	4⅞	5	6	Gunnison Co., Colo.	Thomas Gray, Jr.	Thomas Gray, Jr.	1980	231
197⅞	22⅛	24	24	5⅝	5⅝	8	5	Bonneville Co., Idaho	LaDon Harriell	LaDon Harriell	1982	231
197⅞	27⅜	27⅛	23⅞	4⅜	4⅜	4	5	Archuleta Co., Colo.	Joe Moore	Joe Moore	1962	236
197⅞	25⅝	26⅛	30⅛	6⅛	6	5	5	Montrose, Colo.	H. R. Clark	H. R. Clark	1961	236
197⅞	27⅛	27⅞	24⅜	5	5	5	7	Currant Creek, Utah	Morris Kidd	Morris Kidd	1960	236
197⅞	26⅞	25	22⅝	5⅝	5⅜	5	5	Chama, N.M.	Kirt I. Darner	Kirt I. Darner	1962	236
197⅞	25	25⅝	27⅞	5⅞	6	5	6	Fremont Co., Idaho	Stanley A. Gilgen	Stanley A. Gilgen	1964	236
197⅜	26⅜	27⅜	26⅜	4⅞	4⅞	6	6	Pagosa Springs, Colo.	John Damon Guess	John Damon Guess	1966	236
197⅜	26⅞	26	25⅝	5⅝	5⅝	5	5	Apache Mesa, N.M.	Tom Martine	Tom Martine	1970	236
197⅜	25⅝	27⅛	26⅛	5⅝	5⅝	5	6	White River Natl. For., Colo.	Picked Up	Jack Thompson	PR 1957	236
197⅜	26⅜	26⅝	24⅝	5	5	5	5	Gunnison Co., Colo.	Mark L. Hanna	Mark L. Hanna	1980	236
197⅜	26	26⅜	23⅝	5⅝	5⅝	6	6	Garfield Co., Utah	James R. McCourt	James R. McCourt	1985	236
197⅜	28⅞	28⅜	23⅝	5⅝	5⅝	7	6	Beechy, Sask.	Pete Perrin	Pete Perrin	1947	246
197⅜	26⅞	21⅞	21⅞	7	6⅞	7	6	Harney Co., Oreg.	Guy Evan Osborne	Guy Evan Osborne	1963	246
197⅜	29⅞	30⅞	28⅞	5⅝	5⅝	7	5	Afton, Wyo.	Robert Williams	Robert Williams	1960	246
197⅜	27⅜	27⅜	27⅛	5⅝	5⅜	6	5	Weber Co., Utah	Abe B. Murdock	Abe B. Murdock	1972	246
197⅜	26⅝	27⅛	26⅝	4⅜	5⅞	5	8	Chaffee Co., Colo.	Marguerite Hill	Marguerite Hill	1956	246

Record-book listing table (mule deer). Score at left, then measurements, locality, person who killed, owner, date killed, and rank at right.

Score									Locality	Killed By	Owner	Date	Rank
197⅞	26⅜	25⅞	26⅜	26⅜	5⅜	5⅜	5	6	Blaine Co., Idaho	Bart Hofmann	Bart Hofmann	1980	246
197⅞	26⅜	26⅜	28	26⅜	5⅜	5⅜	6	6	Moffat Co., Colo.	Lucille Gooch	George Gooch	1951	252
197⅞	24⅜	24⅜	24⅜	24⅞	4⅜	5	5	5	Ashton, Idaho	Earl Johnson	O. M. Corbett	1959	252
197⅞	26⅜	27⅜	26⅜	26⅜	5⅜	5⅜	5	5	Ashwood, Oreg.	Harvey Rhoads	Harvey Rhoads	1962	252
197⅞	27⅜	27⅜	28⅜	25⅜	5⅛	5⅜	5	5	San Miguel Co., Colo.	Everett Stutler	Everett Stutler	1965	252
197⅞	27⅜	26	30⅝	26	5⅜	5⅜	6	5	Adams Co., Idaho	Roy Eastlick	Roy Eastlick	1974	252
197	25⅜	25⅝	25	25⅜	5⅜	5⅜	6	6	Sonora, Mexico	J. G. Cigarroa, Sr.	J. G. Cigarroa, Sr.	1957	257
197	24⅜	25⅜	25⅞	25⅜	5⅝	5⅝	5	5	Grand Co., Colo.	Woodrow W. Dixon	Woodrow W. Dixon	1962	257
197	24⅜	25⅝	22	25⅜	5⅜	5⅜	5	5	Franklin Co., Idaho	Robert C. Porter	Robert C. Porter	1972	257
197	25⅜	27	22⅜	25	5	4⅜	5	6	Utah Co., Utah	L. Doug Carlton	L. Doug Carlton	1982	257
197	25⅜	24⅛	25	24⅜	4⅜	5⅜	5	5	Camas Co., Idaho	Bret C. Silver	Bret C. Silver	1980	257
197	28⅜	29⅜	34⅜	29⅜	5⅜	5⅜	4	5	Butte Co., Idaho	John A. Little	John A. Little	1981	263
196⅞	26⅝	26⅛	24⅜	26⅜	4⅜	4⅜	5	5	Rio Arriba Co., N.M.	Kirt I. Darner	B & B Outfitter	1965	263
											Service		
196⅞	24⅜	24⅜	22⅜	24⅜	5⅜	5⅜	5	5	Boise Co., Idaho	Andrew T. Rogers	Andrew T. Rogers	1967	263
196⅞	25⅜	24	21⅜	25⅜	5⅜	5⅜	5	5	Lincoln Co., Mont.	Dennis J. Hauke	Dennis J. Hauke	1973	263
196⅞	24⅜	26⅜	27⅜	24⅜	5	5⅜	5	5	Bonneville Co., Idaho	Preston L. Winchell	Preston L. Winchell	1974	263
196⅞	27⅜	27	25⅜	25⅜	5⅛	5⅜	5	5	Scherf Creek, B.C.	Manuela Selby	Manuela Selby	1984	263
196⅞	24⅜	23⅜	24⅜	24⅜	5⅜	5⅜	7	7	Bear Lake Co., Idaho	Nels H. Pehrson	Ralph V. Pehrson	1936	268
196⅞	27	26⅜	28⅜	5	5	5	5	5	N. Kaibab, Ariz.	Simon C. Krevitsky	Simon C. Krevitsky	1963	268
196⅝	25⅛	25⅜	24⅜	25⅜	5⅜	5⅜	5	5	Delta, Colo.	Howard G. Reed	Howard G. Reed	1968	268
196⅝	23⅜	24⅜	22⅜	25⅜	5⅜	5⅜	5	5	Bonneville Co., Idaho	William G. Pine	William G. Pine	1969	268
196⅝	24⅜	23⅜	23⅜	24⅜	6⅛	6⅜	5	6	DeBeque, Colo.	Walter C. Friauf	Walter C. Fraiuf	1970	268
196⅝	26⅛	26	22⅜	26⅜	5	5	5	5	San Juan Natl. For., Colo.	Wilford E. Seymour, Jr.	Wilford E. Seymour, Jr.	1974	268
196⅜	26⅝	25⅜	28	25⅜	4⅜	4⅜	5	5	Wallowa Co., Oreg.	Dan L. Grober	Dan L. Grober	1980	275
196⅜	24⅜	23⅜	28⅜	28⅜	5⅜	5⅜	5	5	Ruby Mt., Nev.	Earl Frantzen	Earl Frantzen	1941	275
196	25⅜	25⅜	22⅜	22⅜	4⅜	4⅜	5	5	Dubois, Wyo.	P. C. Alfred Dorow	P. C. Alfred Dorow	1960	275
196⅜	25⅜	24⅜	25⅜	25⅜	4⅜	4⅜	5	5	Morgan Co., Utah	Gayle Allen	Gayle Allen	1948	275
196	26	26	24⅜	24⅜	4⅜	4⅜	6	5	Slater, Colo.	W. J. Bracken	W. J. Bracken	1959	275
196⅞	27⅜	24⅜	22⅜	22⅜	5⅜	5⅜	6	6	Grand Mesa, Colo.	Marvin L. Shepard	Marvin L. Shepard	1960	275
196⅞	27⅜	26⅜	25⅜	25⅜	6	6	6	6	Chelan Co., Wash.	George Bolton	Welcome Sauer	1930	275
196⅝	25⅜	25⅜	24⅜	24⅜	5	4⅜	7	7	Summit Co., Utah	Jerry L. Henriod	Jerry L. Henriod	1967	275
196	26	25⅜	28	25⅜	5⅜	5⅜	5	5	Rio Arriba Co., N.M.	Stanley Davis	Stanley Davis	1965	275
196⅜	22	22⅜	21⅜	21⅜	5⅜	5⅜	7	6	Lemhi Co., Idaho	Hubert M. Livingston	Hubert M. Livingston	1967	275
196⅜	24⅜	25	23⅜	23⅜	4⅜	4⅜	5	5	Maybell, Colo.	James W. Johnson	James W. Johnson	1968	275
196⅜	23⅜	24	22⅜	22⅜	4⅜	4⅜	5	5	Lincoln Co., Wyo.	Chester P. Michalski	Chester P. Michalski	1974	275
196⅜	24⅜	25⅜	25⅜	25⅜	5⅜	5⅜	7	7	Flathead River, Mont.	Stanley Rauscher	Stanley Rauscher	1959	286
196⅜	23⅜	22⅜	19⅜	5	5	5	5	5	Garfield Co., Colo.	Elmer Nelson	Elmer Nelson	1962	286
196⅜	24⅜	25⅛	21	6⅛	6⅛	6⅜	5	5	Vernal, Utah	Selby G. Tanner	Selby G. Tanner	1966	286
196⅜	25⅜	24⅜	23	5⅜	5⅜	5⅜	5	5	Southern Ute Res., Colo.	William C. Forsyth	William C. Forsyth	1974	286
196⅜	25⅜	25⅜	25⅜	5	5	5	5	5	Johnson Co., Wyo.	Unknown	Toby J. Johnson	1940	286
196⅜	23⅜	23⅜	23	5⅜	5⅜	5⅜	5	5	Powell Co., Mont.	Raymond A. Fitzgerald	Raymond A. Fitzgerald	1983	286

MULE DEER (*Typical Antlers*)—Continued
Odocoileus hemionus hemionus and certain related subspecies

Score	Length of Main Beam R.	L.	Inside Spread	Circumference at Smallest Place Between Burr and First Point R.	L.	Number of Points R.	L.	Locality Killed	By Whom Killed	Owner	Date Killed	Rank
196 3/8	23 5/8	25 5/8	27 1/8	4 7/8	4 7/8	7	7	Gunnison Co., Colo.	E. D. Palmer	E. D. Palmer	1962	292
196 3/8	26 5/8	26	24 5/8	5 2/8	5 3/8	6	5	Durango, Colo.	Ronald Chitwood	Ronald Chitwood	1964	292
196 3/8	28 1/8	28 1/8	26 1/8	4 7/8	5	5	4	Uncompahgre Plateau, Colo.	Earl L. Markley	Earl L. Markley	1969	292
196 3/8	24 5/8	25 1/8	24 5/8	5 3/8	5 3/8	6	5	Powell Co., Mont.	Stanley F. Malcolm	Stanley F. Malcolm	1958	292
196 3/8	26 3/8	27 1/8	25 1/8	5 5/8	5 5/8	6	6	Sublette Co., Wyo.	Kim Bonnett	Kim Bonnett	1978	292
196 3/8	27 1/8	27 1/8	25 3/8	4 5/8	5 1/8	7	5	Lincoln Co., Mont.	Tommy Boothman	Tommy Boothman	1960	297
196 3/8	22 5/8	22 5/8	21 5/8	5 3/8	5 1/8	6	7	Millard Co., Utah	Burnell Washburn	Burnell Washburn	1967	297
196 3/8	27	27 1/8	24 7/8	5 4/8	5 4/8	7	9	Rio Arriba Co., N.M.	B. D. Shipwash	B. D. Shipwash	1969	297
196 3/8	26 1/8	23 7/8	23 4/8	5 4/8	5 7/8	5	6	Chama, N.M.	Laura Wilson	Laura Wilson	1967	297
196 3/8	24	25	20 6/8	4 3/8	4 3/8	5	5	Big Horn Mts., Wyo.	Ruth Davis	Ruth Davis	1968	297
196 3/8	27 3/8	27 3/8	20 6/8	5 5/8	5 2/8	5	8	Meeker, Colo.	Mike Murphy	Mike Murphy	1971	297
196 3/8	25 5/8	25 5/8	22 4/8	5 3/8	5 3/8	6	6	Bingham Co., Idaho	Thomas D. Robison	Thomas D. Robison	1972	297
196 3/8	27	26 3/8	28 3/8	4 3/8	5 3/8	4	5	Hinsdale Co., Colo.	Alan L. VanDenBerg	Alan L. VanDenBerg	1978	297
196 3/8	23	24	25	4 3/8	4 4/8	7	5	Elko Co., Nev.	John C. Burman	John C. Burman	1980	297
196 1/8	27 1/8	27 3/8	25 1/8	5 3/8	5 2/8	5	6	Sweetwater Co., Wyo.	Donald H. Pabst	Donald H. Pabst	1962	307
196 1/8	27 2/8	27 7/8	27	5 1/8	5 1/8	6	9	Chama, N.M.	Jerry Washburn	Jerry Washburn	1960	307
196 1/8	26 3/8	27 3/8	22 3/8	6	6 1/8	6	6	Jicarilla Apache Res., N.M.	Tim Vicenti	Tim Vicenti	1960	307
196 1/8	26	27 1/8	24 4/8	5 7/8	5 5/8	5	7	Boise Co., Idaho	H. L. Rice	H. L. Rice	1966	307
196 1/8	25 5/8	25	23 3/8	5 5/8	5 3/8	4	4	Uncompahgre Natl. For., Colo.	Harry L. Whitlock	Harry L. Whitlock	1968	307
196	25 5/8	25 5/8	25 5/8	5	5 1/8	5	5	Meeker, Colo.	Max R. Zoeller	Max R. Zoeller	1972	307
196	25 5/8	25 3/8	25 5/8	4 4/8	4 7/8	5	5	Eagle Co., Colo.	Jeffery D. Harrison	Jeffery D. Harrison	1981	307
196	25 4/8	24 4/8	26 1/8	5 1/8	4 4/8	5	5	Clackamas Co., Oreg.	Picked Up	Curt M. Funk	1983	314
196	27 4/8	27 4/8	27 3/8	5 5/8	5 5/8	5	5	Huerfano Co., Colo.	F. C. Hibben	F. C. Hibben	1963	314
196	23 3/8	24 1/8	22 2/8	5	5 1/8	5	5	Kaibab Forest, Ariz.	Elgin T. Gates	Elgin T. Gates	1958	314
196	26 3/8	26 3/8	27 7/8	4 7/8	4 7/8	6	6	Mesa Co., Colo.	Bill Styers	Bill Styers	1964	314
196	25	24 4/8	24	5 3/8	5	5	5	Corwin Springs, Mont.	Donald Strazzabosco	Donald Strazzabosco	1966	314
196	29 4/8	29 2/8	25 2/8	5	5	5	5	Jicarilla Apache Res., N.M.	Collins F. Kellogg	Collins F. Kellogg	1973	314
196	25 4/8	28	23	5 5/8	5 5/8	6	5	Franklin Co., Idaho	Larry W. Cross	Larry W. Cross	1974	314
196	27 3/8	26	21 5/8	5 3/8	5 3/8	5	5	N. Kaibab, Ariz.	John D. McNeley	John D. McNeley	1948	314
196	27 5/8	26 5/8	23 3/8	5 3/8	5 2/8	7	6	Kaibab Natl. For., Ariz.	Graves Peeler	John E. Conner Museum	PR1930	314

Score				Circumference			Points		Locality	Hunter	Owner	Date	Rank
195⅞	26⅞	25⅞	26⅞	5⅞	5⅞		7	7	Bannock Co., Idaho	William J. Barry	William J. Barry	1956	322
195⅞	26⅝	25⅜	26⅞	5⅜	5⅜		6	6	Southern Ute Res., Colo.	Richard Schmidt	Southern Ute Tribe	1960	322
195⅞	27⅛	28	27⅛	5⅜	5⅜		5	5	Rio Arriba Co., N.M.	Ross Lopez	Ross Lopez	1964	322
195⅞	28⅜	26⅝	26⅝	5⅛	5⅛		5	7	Cache Co., Utah	Richard E. Reeder	Richard E. Reeder	1968	322
195⅞	27⅛	26⅞	24⅞	5⅛	5⅛		8	5	San Miguel Co., Colo.	Jerry E. Albin	Jerry E. Albin	1972	322
195⅞	27⅛	29	26⅞	5⅜	5⅜		9	7	Keating, Oreg.	Al Delepierre	Francis A. Delepierre	1966	327
195⅝	28⅞	28⅞	28⅞	5⅛	5⅜		5	5	Grant Co., Oreg.	Larry Parlette	Larry Parlette	1967	327
195⅝	24⅞	25⅜	22⅞	5	5		5	7	Montrose Co., Colo.	Larry Della Bitta	Larry Della Bitta	1969	327
195⅝	25⅞	26⅜	24⅜	4⅞	4⅞		5	5	Gunnison, Colo.	Randall R. Kieft	Randall R. Kieft	1967	327
195⅝	22⅞	24⅜	23⅜	5⅜	5⅜		6	6	Gunnison Co., Colo.	George L. Hoffman, Jr.	George L. Hoffman, Jr.	1972	327
195⅝	25⅜	24⅜	24⅜	4⅜	4⅜		5	5	Teton Co., Wyo.	Joel M. Leatham	Joel M. Leatham	1979	327
195⅜	25⅜	25⅜	25⅜	5⅜	5⅜		5	5	Ferry Co., Wash.	Owen R. Burgess	Owen R. Burgess	1982	334
195⅜	26⅜	27⅛	26⅛	4⅜	4⅜		8	5	Ravalli Co., Mont.	William H. Cowan	William H. Cowan	1959	334
195⅜	30⅜	29	26⅜	6⅜	6⅜		7	7	Jicarilla Apache Res., N.M.	Eldrid Vigil	Eldrid Vigil	1962	334
195⅜	24⅜	27⅛	24⅜	6	6		4	7	Slocan Valley, B.C.	John Braun	John Braun	1962	334
195⅜	25⅜	25⅜	21⅜	4⅜	4⅜		5	5	Pitkin Co., Colo.	William F. Kirby	William F. Kirby	1966	334
195⅛	20⅜	25⅜	20⅜	4⅜	4⅜		5	5	Delta Co., Colo.	Royce Jay Carville	Royce Jay Carville	1974	334
195⅛	21⅜	25⅜	21⅜	5	5		6	5	Grand Co., Colo.	C. Jay Stout	C. Jay Stout	1981	341
195⅛	24	26⅛	24	5	5		5	6	Washington Co., Utah	Scott M. Bulloch	Scott M. Bulloch	1985	341
195⅛	24⅜	26⅛	24⅜	5⅜	5⅜		5	5	Princeton, B.C.	Glen Stadler	Glen Stadler	1958	341
195⅛	22⅜	25⅜	22⅜	5⅜	5⅜		5	5	Grover, Utah	Vicki Davis	R. J. Davis	1959	341
195⅛	20⅜	25	20⅜	5⅜	5⅜		5	7	Montrose, Colo.	Tony L. Hill	Tony L. Hill	1969	341
195⅛	24⅜	24⅜	24⅜	5⅜	5⅜		6	5	Garfield Co., Colo.	Billy R. Babb	Billy R. Babb	1969	341
195⅛	26⅜	25⅜	26⅜	5⅜	5⅜		5	5	Raton, N.M.	Unknown	John H. Steinle III	1963	341
195⅜	22⅜	27⅜	22⅜	5⅜	5⅜		6	6	Flathead Co., Mont.	Sharon M. Gaughan	Sharon M. Gaughan	1980	341
195⅜	25⅜	26⅜	25⅜	5⅜	5⅜		5	5	Sanders Co., Mont.	William B. Hart	William B. Hart	1984	341
195⅜	24⅜	24⅜	24⅜	5	5		5	5	Rio Arriba Co., N.M.	Robert W. Highfill	Robert W. Highfill	1964	348
195⅜	25⅜	28⅜	25⅜	5⅜	5⅜		4	7	Mohave Co., Ariz.	Bob B. Coker	Bob B. Coker	1972	348
195⅜	26⅜	27⅜	26⅜	4⅜	4⅜		5	5	Natrona Co., Wyo.	Richard Ullery	Richard Ullery	1977	348
195⅜	26⅜	25⅜	26⅜	5⅜	5⅜		5	5	Moffat Co., Colo.	Frank J. Kubin	Frank J. Kubin	1978	348
195⅜	26⅜	26	26⅜	4⅜	4⅜		6	5	Frontier Co., Neb.	Brent S. Klein	Brent S. Klein	1984	348
195⅜	27	27⅜	27	5⅜	5⅜		7	7	Montrose Co., Colo.	Edward A. Ipser	Edward A. Ipser	1965	353
195⅜	25⅜	27	25⅜	5⅛	5⅛		7	6	Marble, Colo.	David R. Allen	David R. Allen	1968	353
195⅜	28⅜	26	28⅜	5⅜	5⅜		6	5	Archuleta Co., Colo.	Hugh W. Gardner	Hugh W. Gardner	1971	353
195	24⅜	26⅜	24⅜	5⅜	5⅜		5	5	Davis Co., Utah	Mitchell L. Cochran	Mitchell L. Cochran	1972	353
195⅜	26⅜	25⅜	26⅜	4⅜	4⅜		5	5	Antelope Lake, Sask.	Doug Westergaard	Doug Westergaard	1977	353
195⅜	23⅜	24⅜	21⅜	5⅛	5⅛		5	5	Sublette Co., Wyo.	John R. Birchett	John R. Birchett	1981	353
195	29⅜	27⅜	25⅜	5⅜	5⅜		7	6	Gunnison Co., Colo.	Herman F. Tomky	Russell J. Tomky	1937	353
195⅜	25⅜	25⅜	22⅜	5⅜	5⅜		5	5	Elko Co., Nev.	Donald G. Heidtman	Donald G. Heidtman	1954	360
195⅜	24⅜	24⅜	22⅜	5⅜	5⅜		6	6	Utah	Unknown	Jarvie Taxidermy	1959	360
195⅜	25⅜	24⅜	24⅜	5⅜	5⅜		5	5	Rio Arriba Co., N.M.	Eddie W. Brieno, Jr.	Eddie W. Brieno, Jr.	1965	360
195⅜	26⅜	26⅜	24⅜	6	6		6	5	Montrose Co., Colo.	Eldon L. Webb	Eldon L. Webb	1965	360
195⅞	27	29⅜	29⅜	57⅞	57⅞		5	5	Fruitvale, B.C.	Allan Endersby	Allan Endersby	1968	360

MULE DEER (*Typical Antlers*)—Continued
Odocoileus hemionus hemionus and certain related subspecies

Score	Length of Main Beam R.	L.	Inside Spread	Circumference at Smallest Place Between Burr and First Point R.	L.	Number of Points R.	L.	Locality Killed	By Whom Killed	Owner	Date Killed	Rank
195⅛	22⅛	22⅛	23⅜	5⅜	5⅜	5	6	Summit Co., Colo.	Steve Orecchio	Steve Orecchio	1967	360
195⅛	25	25⅛	22⅜	5	4⅞	5	8	Salmon River, Idaho	Gary Bevan	Gary Bevan	1970	360
195⅛	26⅝	26⅛	24⅞	4⅞	5⅛	6	7	Coconino Co., Ariz.	Gary Ray Clark	Gary Ray Clark	1972	360
195⅛	25⅛	25	27⅜	5⅛	5⅜	8	6	Summit Co., Utah	Wendell M. Smith	Nathan H. Smith	1954	360
195⅛	27⅛	26⅜	29⅜	5⅜	5⅝	5	5	Jackson Co., Colo.	Alvin Bush	Jerry Haldeman	1961	360
195	24	24⅜	26⅜	5⅛	5⅜	5	6	N. Kaibab, Ariz.	Alex J. Haas	Alex J. Haas	1961	370
195	24⅜	24⅜	24⅜	4⅝	4⅞	5	6	Moffat Co., Colo.	Orville R. Meineke	Craig Sports	1964	370
195	27⅛	26⅜	22⅜	5⅝	5⅝	5	5	Sun River, Mont.	Dick Lyman	Dick Lyman	1966	370
195	25⅛	25⅛	25	4⅜	4⅞	5	5	Rio Arriba Co., N.M.	Pat Wilson	John Lind, Jr.	1967	370
195	26	25⅝	23⅜	5	5⅛	5	5	Larimer Co., Colo.	Michael D. Blehm	Michael D. Blehm	1972	370
195	24⅝	24⅜	22⅜	5⅛	6⅛	5	5	Rio Blanco Co., Colo.	Gene Lawrence	Gene Lawrence	1977	370
195	24⅜	24⅜	22⅜	6⅛	6⅛	7	5	Sublette Co., Wyo.	Norm Busselle	Norm Busselle	1977	
210⅝*	28⅛	29⅛	24⅜	5	5	5	5	Idaho Co., Idaho	Urban H. Riener	Homer Saye	1979	
204⅝*	26⅝	26⅞	24⅞	4⅞	4⅝	5	5	Elko Co., Nev.	Donnie L. Thompson	Donnie L. Thompson	1982	

*Final Score subject to revision by additional verifying measurements

WORLD'S RECORD MULE DEER (NON-TYPICAL ANTLERS)
SCORE: 355 2/8
Locality: Chip Lake, Alberta Date: 1926
Hunter and owner: Ed Broder

NUMBER TWO MULE DEER (NON-TYPICAL ANTLERS)
SCORE: 330 1/8
Locality: Box Elder County, Utah Date: 1943
Hunter: Alton Hunsaker Owner: Julie Akey

Mule Deer (*Non-Typical Antlers*)

Odocoileus hemionus hemionus and certain related subspecies

Minimum Score 240

Score	Length of Main Beam R.	L.	Inside Spread	Circumference at Smallest Place Between Burr and First Point R.	L.	Number of Points R.	L.	Locality Killed	By Whom Killed	Owner	Date Killed	Rank
355⅝	26⅞	26⅛	22⅛	5	4⅞	22	21	Chip Lake, Alta.	Ed Broder	Ed Broder	1926	1
330½	23⅜	22	9⅜	8⅜	8⅜	21	28	Box Elder Co., Utah	Alton Hunsaker	Julie Akey	1943	2
319⅞	24⅛	24	23⅜	7⅞	7⅛	27	23	Mariposa Co., Calif.	Harold Ray Laird	Homer Saye	1972	3
316⅞	25⅝	25⅛	32⅞	6⅝	6⅝	16	17	N. Kaibab, Ariz.	William L. Murphy	Michael R. Karam	1943	4
311⅞	26⅞	24⅞	24⅛	6⅛	6⅝	22	21	Kaibab, Ariz.	Vernor Wilson	Homer Saye	1941	5
306⅞	29	28⅜	28⅞	5⅝	5⅝	18	18	Chama, N.M.	Joseph A. Garcia	Homer Saye	1963	6
306⅞	28⅛	27⅛	22⅝	5⅝	5⅝	14	23	Norwood Co., Colo.	Steve H. Herndon	Vernon D. & Dan F. Holleman	1954	6
303⅞	26⅞	26⅞	24⅜	5⅛	5	13	11	Eagle Co., Colo.	James Austill	James Austill	1962	8
302⅛	25⅛	26⅞	25⅞	5⅞	6⅜	18	14	Paonia, Colo.	Louis H. Huntington, Jr.	Louis H. Huntington, Jr.	1965	9
300	27	25⅝	23⅛	5⅜	5⅜	14	12	Mesa Co., Colo.	George Blackmon, Jr.	George Blackmon, Jr.	1961	10
299⅛	27⅞	28⅜	24⅜	5⅞	5⅜	13	16	Eureka Co., Nev.	Dan Avery, Jr.	Dan Avery, Jr.	1968	11
298⅝	26⅝	28⅛	29⅛	6⅜	5⅜	19	17	Elk Creek, Colo.	Andrew Daum	National Collection	1886	12
292⅝	26⅞	24⅝	27⅞	5⅝	5⅝	18	16	Wyoming	J. B. Marvin, Jr.	National Collection	PR1924	13
291⅞	29⅜	27⅞	35⅝	5⅜	5⅜	20	18	Malheur Co., Oreg.	Bradley Barclay	Bradley Barclay	1971	14
288⅞	30⅜	31⅞	26⅝	6⅜	6⅜	12	10	Chama, N.M.	Frank B. Maestas	W. H. Mundy, Jr.	1962	15
288⅛	25	25⅞	26	6	6	16	13	Hailey, Idaho	Robby Miller	Homer Saye	1969	16
286⅛	21⅛	22⅞	20⅜	4⅝	4⅜	14	21	Unknown	Walt Mednick	Ike Foster	PR1940	17
284⅝	24⅛	25	26⅛	5	5	12	13	Elko Co., Nev.	Joseph W. Dooley	Joseph W. Dooley	1954	18
284⅝	27⅞	24⅜	26	5⅛	5⅛	15	15	Duchesne Co., Utah	Clyde Lambert	Lucy L. Back	1935	19
284	25⅞	26⅛	24⅛	5⅝	5⅜	15	15	Provo River, Utah	Melvin T. Ashton	Melvin T. Ashton	1961	20
283	28	29⅞	24⅜	8	7⅞	14	13	Rose Creek, Utah	Verl N. Creager	Verl N. Creager	1960	21
282⅞	22⅝	21⅜	22⅛	4⅝	5⅛	18	15	N. Kaibab, Ariz.	Robert C. Rantz	Robert C. Rantz	1969	22
282⅝	25⅜	25⅝	24	7	6⅞	17	13	Sasktchewan	Herman Cox	Herman Cox	1947	23
280⅝	29⅞	29⅜	35⅝	5⅜	5⅛	13	13	Eagle Co., Colo.	Albert L. Mulnix	Homer Saye	1928	24
280⅛	27	26⅞	23⅜	6	6	15	14	Gem Co., Idaho	Ronald S. Holbrook	Ronald S. Holbrook	1982	25
280⅛	25⅞	24⅛	24⅜	6	6	10	15	Otthon, Sask.	Unknown	Spanky Greenville	1940	26
279⅞	26⅞	24⅞	17⅜	6⅜	5⅜	18	10	Kaibab Forest, Ariz.	M. Powell & D. Auld, Jr.	Milroy Powell	1950	27
278⅞	24⅝	26	18	4⅞	5⅛	8	11	Montrose Co., Colo.	Keith Thaute	Keith Thaute	1961	28
278⅞	26⅞	30	24⅜	6⅜	6⅜	12	12	Eagle Co., Colo.	Dale L. Becker	Dale L. Becker	1978	28
278⅜	27⅞	28	26	5⅜	5⅜	11	13	Soda Springs, Idaho	Jack White	Jack White	1957	30

Mule Deer (Non-Typical Antlers)—Continued
Odocoileus hemionus hemionus and certain related subspecies

Score	Length of Main Beam R.	L.	Inside Spread	Circumference at Smallest Place Between Burr and First Point R.	L.	Number of Points R.	L.	Locality Killed	By Whom Killed	Owner	Date Killed	Rank
277⅛	26⅞	24⅜	24⅜	5⅞	5⅞	13	13	Bly, Oreg.	Alice C. O'Brien	David J. O'Brien	1949	31
277	25⅞	24⅞	25⅜	5⅝	5⅝	12	10	Colorado	Indian	Charles McAden	1930	32
276⅝	23⅞	25⅜	25⅜	5⅝	5⅝	11	10	Morgan Co., Utah	Jim Kilfoil	Gilbert Francis	1938	33
276⅜	26⅝	25	23	4⅞	5	11	12	Glenwood Springs, Colo.	Larry Prehm	Spanky Greenville	1967	34
275⅞	25⅝	26⅜	19⅞	5	5⅞	20	16	Dahlton, Sask.	Jim Hewitt	Jim Hewitt	1932	35
275⅝	23⅝	22⅛	20⅝	5⅞	6	14	15	Ruby Mts., Mont.	Peter Zemljak	Peter Zemljak	1960	36
275⅛	26⅞	26⅞	25⅜	5⅝	5⅜	11	10	Kaibab Forest, Ariz.	Unknown	Cliff Cox	PR1950	37
274⅜	27⅝	25	23⅜	6⅝	6⅛	13	13	Sublett, Idaho	Mrs. Jack Keen	Mr. & Mrs. Jack Keen	1957	38
274⅜	22⅝	25⅝	24⅜	5⅝	5⅜	14	13	Fremont Co., Idaho	David L. Maurer	David L. Maurer	1979	38
274⅜	24⅜	28	23	5⅝	5⅞	10	4	Beaver, Utah	Murray Bohn	Parowan Rod & Gun Club	1920	40
274⅛	23⅞	22⅞	22⅜	4⅞	5	11	11	North Fork, Idaho	James D. Edwards	Idaho Fish & Game Dept.	1967	40
273⅞	27⅞	29⅞	26⅜	6⅛	6	8	12	Kane Co., Utah	Waldon Ballard	Alice Ballard	1950	42
273⅜	26	26⅜	26⅛	5	5	15	18	Klamath Co., Ore.	J. J. McDaniels	J. J. McDaniels	1952	43
273⅜	23⅝	24⅜	23⅜	5⅜	5⅞	15	15	Hayden, Colo.	Roy I. Roney	Colo. Div. of Wildl.	1930	43
273⅜	25⅛	25	26⅜	5⅞	5⅞	9	9	San Miguel Co., Colo.	Kirt I. Darner	Kirt I. Darner	1977	43
273⅜	28⅜	28⅜	23⅞	6	6⅛	15	16	Morgan Co., Utah	Harold B. Rollins	Harold B. Rollins	1944	46
272⅝	29	28	21⅝	5⅜	5⅞	16	14	Glenwood Springs, Colo.	William L. Kurtz	William L. Kurtz	1967	47
272⅜	28⅜	27⅞	21⅝	6⅜	5⅞	19	17	Eagle Co., Colo.	Eddie Stephenson, Jr.	Eddie Stephenson, Jr.	1978	48
272⅜	28⅜	28⅜	27⅛	5⅛	5⅞	11	12	Albany Co., Wyo.	S. A. Lawson	Acad. Nat. Sci., Phil.	1905	49
272	24⅜	26⅞	28⅜	5⅞	5⅝	15	16	Caribou Co., Idaho	Picked Up	Newell Gilbert	1948	50
271⅞	21⅞	22⅜	30⅞	6⅞	6⅜	18	17	Cuprum, Idaho	Ed Martin	Ed Martin	1966	51
271⅞	24⅜	24⅜	20	4⅞	5⅛	13	14	East Canyon, Utah	Joseph H. Greenig	Mrs. J. H. Greenig	1947	52
270⅞	28⅜	28⅜	27⅞	5⅞	5⅞	15	15	Crook Co., Oreg.	C. F. Cheney	C. F. Cheney	1962	53
270⅞	29⅜	25⅜	34⅜	5⅜	5⅞	16	13	Highland Mts., Mont.	Peter Zemljak, Sr.	Peter Zemljak, Sr.	1962	53
270⅛	23⅝	24⅜	21⅛	4⅜	4⅜	10	12	Bighorn Co., Mont.	R. Turnsback & J. Van Elsen	John Van Elsen	1961	55
270⅜	29⅜	32⅜	28	4⅜	4⅜	12	13	N. Kaibab, Ariz.	Thomas M. Knoles, Jr.	Thomas M. Knoles, Jr.	1944	56
270⅜	28⅜	28⅜	24⅜	5⅜	5⅝	12	13	Kaibab Forest, Ariz.	Milroy Powell	Milroy Powell	1952	57
268⅝	27	25⅜	25⅜	5	5⅜	14	16	Leader, Sask.	Cocks Brothers	Richard Jensen	1954	58
268⅝	21⅜	23⅜	17⅜	6⅜	6⅝	17	16	Cascade Co., Mont.	Unknown	Tom Williams	PR1980	59
268⅜	25⅝	27⅜	23	6⅛	6	17	11	Delta Co., Colo.	Shirley Smith	Shirley Smith	1962	60

Score								Locality	Owner	By whom killed	Date	Rank
267⅞	24	25	27⅞	5⅝	6	10	10	Kaibab Forest, Ariz.	Dean Naylor	D. B. Sanford	1948	61
267⅝	26	25⅞	26⅜	4⅞	4⅝	13	18	Jicarilla Apache Res., N.M.	Byrd L. Minter, Jr.	Byrd L. Minter, Jr.	1961	62
266⅞	26	25⅛	22⅛	6⅛	6⅛	13	15	Wyoming	J. L. Kemmerer	Am. Mus. Nat. History	1905	63
266⅞	22⅝	22⅞	18⅝	5⅛	5⅛	8	8	Draper, Utah	Glenn W. Furrow	Glenn W. Furrow	1962	63
266⅞	25⅝	25⅜	20⅞	5	5	13	11	Philip, S.D.	Clifford Ramsey	Clifford Ramsey	1959	65
266⅛	24⅛	24⅞	21	5⅜	5⅝	12	18	Park Co., Mont.	Benton R. Venable	Benton R. Venable	1945	66
266⅛	22⅞	22⅞	16⅞	5⅛	5⅛	16	13	Stevens Co., Wash.	Joe C. Mally	Steve Mally	1933	67
265⅞	25⅝	25⅞	24⅛	5⅜	5⅜	11	13	Cache Co., Utah	Jerry S. Wuthrich	Jerry S. Wuthrich	1966	68
265⅜	25⅝	25⅛	21⅜	5⅛	5⅜	13	14	Tyaughton River, B.C.	Terry E. Crawford	Terry E. Crawford	1970	69
265⅜	25⅝	24⅜	18	5⅝	5⅝	22	18	Blue Mts., Wash.	Frank Henriksen	Frank Henriksen	1961	70
265⅜	24⅛	26⅞	27⅞	6⅛	6⅛	16	14	Chama, N.M.	Stephanie D. Tartaglia	Stephanie D. Tartaglia	1966	70
264⅝	25⅞	26⅞	27⅞	5⅛	5	8	12	Sidney, Mont.	Buster Dodson	F. P. Murray	1954	72
264⅝	26	26⅝	22⅛	5⅜	5⅜	18	13	Bannock Co., Idaho	Jarel Neeser	Jarel Neeser	1974	72
264⅜	26	27⅝	21⅜	5⅜	5⅜	13	10	Gunnison Co., Colo.	Gordon E. Blay	Gorden E. Blay	1975	74
264⅜	24⅛	24⅝	21	5⅜	5⅜	7	13	Southern Utah	Unknown	Earl Mecham	1932	75
264	25⅛	26⅛	22⅜	6⅜	5⅞	14	13	Elko Co., Nev.	Jim Stichter	Jim Stichter	1965	76
263⅞	26⅜	26⅞	22⅜	5	5	16	14	Sanpete Co., Utah	Wayne Dwyer	John E. Braithwaite	1974	77
263⅞	26⅞	26⅞	23⅞	5	5	12	12	Montrose, Colo.	Robert L. Price	Robert L. Price	1963	78
263⅞	25⅜	24⅜	27⅞	5⅞	5⅝	16	20	Grant Co., Oreg.	Harold T. Oathes	Harold T. Oathes	1965	78
263⅜	27⅞	26⅛	26⅞	6⅛	6⅛	20	13	Bigwood River, Idaho	Robert C. Young	Robert C. Young	1956	80
263	26⅜	27⅜	25⅜	5	5	12	12	Kaibab Forest, Ariz.	Unknown	Bob Housholder	1940	81
262⅝	26⅜	24	23⅜	4⅜	4⅝	14	13	Dawson Co., Mont.	Johnny Scheitlin	Bob Scheitlin	1949	82
262⅛	28⅜	29	28	5⅜	5⅜	14	12	Kaibab Forest, Ariz.	Jack Verner	Jack Verner	1947	83
262⅜	27⅞	27⅞	28⅜	6⅛	6⅛	10	15	Tierra Amarilla, N.M.	Pat Lovato, Jr.	Pat Lovato, Jr.	1966	84
262⅜	29⅜	29⅜	29⅜	5⅜	5⅜	10	11	Brush Creek, Colo.	Pete Taullie	Pete Taullie	1967	84
262	24⅜	24⅝	16⅞	4⅞	4⅞	14	16	John Day River, Oreg.	Glen E. Park	Glen E. Park	1962	86
262	25⅞	23⅞	21	4⅞	4⅞	14	15	Utah Co., Utah	Michael D. Atwood	Michael D. Atwood	1967	86
261⅞	25	25	23⅜	4⅞	5⅛	10	12	Heber Mountain, Utah	DuWayne C. Bailey	DuWayne C. Bailey	1963	88
261⅞	25⅝	24	27⅞	5⅜	5⅛	10	10	Blaine Co., Idaho	Roger A. Crowder	Roger A. Crowder	1957	89
261⅞	25⅝	26⅝	24⅜	4⅞	4⅝	13	19	Iron Creek, Wash.	Win Coultas	Win Coultas	1924	90
261⅛	23	23⅛	21⅜	5⅛	5⅜	12	13	Rio Blanco Co., Colo.	L. C. Denny, Jr.	L. C. Denny, Jr..	1961	91
261	25⅜	26⅝	25⅝	5	5	12	12	Kaibab Forest, Ariz.	Unknown	Larry Arndt	1930	92
260⅝	29⅞	27⅞	28⅜	5⅜	5⅞	10	14	Rooks Co., Kan.	Lee Odle	Lee Odle	1965	93
260⅝	26⅝	26⅜	22⅜	4⅜	4⅜	10	13	Ada Co., Idaho	Howard R. Cromwell	Howard R. Cromwell	1975	93
260⅝	25⅝	27	26⅞	5⅝	5⅞	13	14	Kaibab Forest, Ariz.	David Bevly	David Bevly	1949	95
260⅝	26⅜	25	21⅜	4⅝	4⅜	12	13	Pinedale, Wyo.	James H. Straley	Monte W. Straley	1965	96
260⅛	26	27⅞	24⅜	5⅛	5⅛	16	20	Newcastle, Utah	Unknown	Utah Div. of Wildl. Resc.	1961	97
260	22⅜	25	20	5	5	12	12	Caribou Co., Idaho	Arthur H. Summers	Arthur H. Summers	1966	98
259⅞	25⅛	25⅝	22⅜	5	5	8	10	Caribou Co., Idaho	Jerry Hunt	Jerry Hunt	1966	99
259⅝	25⅜	24	24⅜	4⅜	4⅞	11	13	Kanab, Utah	Arthur Glover	Arthur Glover	1947	99
259⅜	28⅜	27⅜	29⅜	5⅞	5⅞	12	15	Catron Co., N.M.	Jeff K. Gunnell	Jeff K. Gunnell	1981	99
259⅜	24⅜	25⅝	21⅜	5⅜	5⅜	13	13	Routt Co., Colo.	R. V. Rhoads	Cecil R. Weston	1949	102

MULE DEER (*Non-Typical Antlers*)—Continued
Odocoileus hemionus hemionus and certain related subspecies

Score	Length of Main Beam R	L	Inside Spread	Circ. at Smallest Place Between Burr and First Point R	L	No. of Points R	L	Locality Killed	By Whom Killed	Owner	Date Killed	Rank
259⅝	27⅞	26⅜	24⅛	5⅝	5⅝	12	13	Glendo, Wyo.	Rudolph B. Johnson	Rudolph B. Johnson	1961	103
259⅜	27⅜	29⅜	24⅛	5⅝	5⅝	13	13	Iron Co., Utah	Mont Hunter	Mont Hunter	1939	104
259⅜	26⅜	26⅜	29⅜	5⅜	4⅞	17	12	Mont.	Unknown	Nick M. Messmer	PR1943	104
259⅛	23⅛	24⅜	25⅜	5⅞	6	15	17	Boise, Idaho	George M. Tweedy	George M. Tweedy	1946	106
259⅛	28⅜	27⅜	28⅞	4⅞	4⅞	13	13	N. Kaibab, Ariz.	Marvin Fridenmaker	Marvin Fridenmaker	1968	107
258⅞	27⅞	27⅞	24⅜	5	5	15	10	Valley Co., Idaho	Larry Dwonch	Larry Dwonch	1972	108
258⅝	21	22	16⅛	10	5	18	18	Sweetwater Co., Wyo.	John A. Fabian	John A. Fabian	1974	108
258⅝	25⅜	25⅜	21	5⅜	5⅜	12	10	Elko Co., Nev.	Edward J. Giauque	Edward J. Giauque	1960	110
258⅝	24⅜	24	25⅜	5	5⅝	13	15	Boise Co., Idaho	LeRoy Massey	LeRoy Massey	1959	111
258⅝	24⅜	26⅜	24⅜	5⅜	5⅛	11	9	Grand Co., Utah	Vernon K. Heller	Vernon K. Heller	1971	111
258⅛	28⅜	25⅜	25⅛	5⅛	5⅛	11	10	Monte Vista, Colo.	Geis Nettlebeck	Phil Skinner	1956	113
258⅛	27	29⅝	29⅜	6⅛	6⅞	15	14	Rock Creek, B.C.	George Whiting	B.C. Game Dept.	1909	114
258⅛	29⅝	27⅜	23⅜	5⅛	5⅛	13	14	Atlanta, Idaho	Kenneth E. Potts	Kenneth E. Potts	1968	115
258⅛	27⅜	22⅛	19⅜	4⅜	4⅜	13	13	Cimarron, N.M.	Ralph L. Smith	Ralph L. Smith	1957	116
258	20⅜	26	26⅜	5⅞	5⅝	14	14	Jicarilla Apache Res., N.M.	Henry Callado	Henry Callado	1961	117
257⅞	27⅛	27⅛	26⅜	5⅜	5⅜	14	13	Leclerc Creek, Wash.	Ernest Fait	Ernest Fait	1960	118
257⅞	28⅜	27⅛	24⅜	5⅝	5⅝	9	13	Hell's Hole, Ariz.	D. L. DeMente	D. L. DeMente	1965	119
257⅝	24⅜	26⅜	20⅝	5⅜	5⅝	11	13	Kaibab Natl. For., Ariz.	Graves Peeler	John E. Connor Museum	1947	119
257⅝	29		28⅞	5⅝	5⅝	15	14	Kaibab Natl. For., Ariz.	Graves Peeler	John E. Connor Museum	1946	119
257⅝	24⅛	23	19⅜	5⅝	4⅞	11	11	Encampment, Wyo.	Sam Whitney	Mrs. Sam Whitney	1946	122
257⅜	28⅞	28⅜	27⅛	4⅜	4⅞	18	10	Utah Co., Utah	J. Clyde Burgess	Dave Burgess	1949	122
257⅜	24⅜	26⅜	23⅛	4⅜	4⅞	12	8	New Castle, Colo.	Unknown	A. E. Hudson	1952	124
257⅜	25⅜	24⅜	19	5⅜	5⅜	10	8	Juab Co., Utah	P. L. Jones	Nelson L. Jones	1949	125
257⅛	26	26	24⅜	5	4⅞	12	12	Cache Co., Utah	Harold S. Shandrew	Harold S. Shandrew	1958	126
257	26⅜	27⅜	22⅜	5⅜	5	20	14	Chadron, Neb.	Art Thomsen	Art Thomsen	1960	127
256⅞	26⅜	27⅜	21⅛	4⅛	4⅝	12	13	Elmore Co., Idaho	Paul Vetter	Paul Vetter	1972	127
256⅝	23⅜	22⅜	20⅝	5	5⅛	12	15	Hoback Basin, Wyo.	Buck Heide	Buck Heide	1968	129
256⅝	24⅜	26⅜	25⅜	6⅜	5⅝	15	14	Gooding Co., Idaho	Charles Hollingsworth	Charles Hollingsworth	1970	130
256⅝	25⅜	27⅜	26⅜	5⅝	5⅝	14	13	Jicarilla Apache Res., N.M.	Picked Up	S. L. Canterbury III	1967	130
256⅝	27⅜	28⅜	26⅜	4⅞	5⅛	10	8	Mt. Trumbull, Ariz.	Ervin M. Schmutz	Ervin M. Schmutz	1965	132

Score								Locality	Name	Name	Date	Rank
256⅞	25⅞	26	27⅞	5⅞	5⅞	9	14	Blaine Co., Idaho	Philip T. Homer	Philip T. Homer	1983	132
256⅛	22⅞	22⅜	20⅝	4⅞	5	14	12	Irwin, Idaho	Hale K. Charlton	Hale K. Charlton	1966	134
256	24⅛	26⅜	25⅜	5	4⅞	13	10	Garfield Co., Utah	James D. Perkins	James D. Perkins	1959	135
256	23⅞	24⅞	25	4⅞	5⅛	12	13	East Zion, Utah	Raymond Pocta	Raymond Pocta	1963	135
256	26⅞	26⅜	22⅞	9⅞	6⅝	16	9	Gem Co., Idaho	Jay P. Baker	Jay P. Baker	1981	135
255⅞	23	24⅛	22⅝	5⅞	5	18	12	Unknown	Unknown	Lone Star Brewing Co.	1901	138
255⅞	24	24⅜	25⅜	6	6⅛	12	11	Portreeve, Sask.	Mike Spies	Mike Spies	1947	138
255⅝	26	26⅜	25⅛	4⅞	4⅜	9	9	Rio Arriba Co., N.M.	Gene Garcia	Gene Garcia	1964	140
255	21⅞	22⅜	19⅞	5⅝	5⅝	9	9	Dunkley Flat, Colo.	Richard A. Gorden	Richard A. Gorden	1966	141
255	28	27⅞	28⅜	5⅝	5⅛	14	12	Garfield Co., Colo.	Louis Lindauer	Louis Lindauer	1932	141
254⅞	25⅛	24	18⅝	5⅝	5⅜	13	15	Maloy, Alta.	Otto Schmalzbauer	Otto Schmalzbauer	1930	143
254⅞	25⅝	25⅞	32⅝	5⅝	6⅝	13	11	Mohave Co., Ariz.	John W. Sokatch	John W. Sokatch	1978	143
254⅞	25	25⅞	26⅝	4⅞	5	7	9	Eagle Co., Colo.	Dennis Martinson	Dennis Martinson	1980	145
254⅛	30	28⅜	23⅝	6⅝	6⅛	7	8	Columbine, Colo.	M. A. Story	M. A. Story	1955	146
253⅞	25	26⅛	25⅝	6⅛	6⅛	9	12	Mohave Co., Ariz.	Manuel Machado	Manuel Machado	1973	147
253⅞	24⅜	24⅜	20⅛	5⅜	5⅜	11	11	Rawlins, Wyo.	A. H. Henkel	A. H. Henkel	1952	148
253⅜	27⅞	26⅝	21	5⅞	5⅞	11	13	Georgetown, Colo.	George Lappin	Doug Grubbe	1947	148
253⅜	25⅜	25⅜	20⅛	5⅝	5⅝	15	17	Salmon, Idaho	Ben H. Quick	Ben H. Quick	1960	150
253	25⅜	25⅜	25⅛	6	6	11	11	Paonia, Colo.	F. F. Parham	F. F. Parham	1961	151
252⅞	24⅛	25⅛	25⅝	5⅜	5⅜	11	10	Silt, Colo.	George McCoy	George McCoy	1961	152
252⅝	20⅛	22⅛	22⅝	5⅜	5⅜	15	22	Utah Co., Utah	Paul H. Mitchell	Paul H. Mitchell	1953	153
252⅝	25⅜	23⅝	26⅛	5⅝	5⅝	13	17	Meeker, Colo.	George R. Howey	Robert L. Howey	1917	154
252⅝	24⅜	23⅜	24⅝	5⅝	5⅝	16	12	Sweetwater Co., Wyo.	John C. Erickson	M. Painovich & J. Etcheverry	1932	154
252⅜	26⅞	28⅞	29⅛	5⅞	5⅞	15	13	Kaibab Forest, Ariz.	Graves Peeler	Graves Peeler	PR1951	156
252⅜	25⅝	26⅝	29⅛	5⅞	5⅞	10	11	Hells Canyon, Idaho	Basil C. Bradbury	Basil C. Bradbury	1955	156
252⅜	23⅜	22	14⅜	5⅞	5⅞	16	15	Glacier Co., Mont.	Bob Scriver	Philip Schlegel	1934	158
252⅛	30	30	26⅜	6	6	15	14	Garfield Co., Colo.	B. J. Slack	B. J. Slack	1973	158
252	25⅛	24⅛	21⅛	4⅞	4⅞	11	10	Salina Canyon, Utah	James C. Larsen	James C. Larsen	1969	160
251⅞	24⅜	23	24⅛	5	5	9	13	Eagle Co., Colo.	Richard G. Lundock	Richard G. Lundock	1945	161
251⅝	22	24⅝	17⅜	4⅞	4⅞	13	10	Salem, Utah	John Vincent	John Vincent	1956	162
251⅝	24	25⅜	20	5⅛	5	10	14	Gem Co., Idaho	A. K. England	Roscoe E. Ferris	1969	163
251⅛	24⅛	26⅛	21	5⅛	5⅛	10	14	Roan Creek, Colo.	Anthony Morabito	Anthony Morabito	1965	164
251⅛	27⅞	25⅜	23⅜	5⅜	5⅜	9	14	Gunnison Co., Colo.	John M. Ringler	John M. Ringler	1956	164
251	27⅝	25⅝	25⅝	5⅜	5⅜	10	9	Meeker, Colo.	Henry Zietz, Jr.	Henry Zietz, Jr.	1955	166
250⅞	25⅛	26⅛	26⅛	5⅛	5⅛	13	14	Adams Co., Idaho	Clark Childers	Clark Childers	1955	167
250⅜	26⅜	24	24	5⅝	6	19	13	Chelan Co., Wash.	Ben R. Williamson	Vera T. Williamson	1951	168
250⅜	29⅞	22⅜	22⅜	6⅛	8	7	13	Kunard Valley, Idaho	Ralph D. Hogan	Ralph D. Hogan	1966	169
250⅜	26⅜	25⅜	25⅜	5	5	10	13	Cedaredge, Colo.	E. K. Plante	E. K. Plante	1963	170
250⅜	24⅜	25⅜	27⅞	5⅛	4⅞	10	12	Moffat Co., Colo.	Unknown	Carrol Grounds	1960	170
250⅜	29	27⅞	24	5⅝	5⅝	15	11	Montezuma Co., Colo.	Jack E. Reed	Jack E. Reed	1981	172
250⅜	26	24	24⅛	5⅝	5⅝	18	16	Grease Creek, Alta.	Jack McCallum	J. H. Fry	PR1940	172
250	22⅛	21⅛	27⅛	6⅞	6⅜	14	14	Mohave Co., Ariz.	Douglas C. Mallory	Douglas C. Mallory	1980	174

Mule Deer (*Non-Typical Antlers*)—Continued
Odocoileus hemionus hemionus and certain related subspecies

Score	Length of Main Beam R.	L.	Inside Spread	Circumference at Smallest Place Between Burr and First Point R.	L.	Number of Points R.	L.	Locality Killed	By Whom Killed	Owner	Date Killed	Rank
249⅞	25⅝	26⅝	30⅝	4⅝	4⅝	11	11	East End, Sask.	Henry Leroy	Henry Leroy	1960	175
249⅞	24⅞	25⅞	22	5	4⅞	10	14	Red Willow Co., Neb.	Delman H. Tuller	Delman H. Tuller	1965	176
249⅞	23⅜	21⅜	23⅜	6⅞	5⅞	12	12	Mt. Delenbaugh, Ariz.	Ted Riggs	Ted Riggs	1965	176
249⅞	25	24⅞	19⅝	5⅝	5⅜	12	9	Routt Co., Colo.	Howard Stoker	Howard Stoker	1958	178
249⅞	26⅛	27⅞	28⅛	5⅛	5	12	10	Washington	Unknown	Pat Redding	PR1973	178
249⅜	23⅝	23⅜	20⅞	5	4⅞	12	10	Mesa Co., Colo.	Gene Cavanagh	Gene Cavanagh	1967	180
249⅝	27	27⅞	27⅛	6⅛	6⅞	7	11	Adams Co., Idaho	Howard E. Paradis	Howard E. Paradis	1966	180
249⅜	25⅝	26	25⅛	5⅛	5⅛	8	11	Kaibab, Ariz.	Robert G. McDonald	Robert G. McDonald	1969	182
249	25⅝	23⅜	23⅛	5⅛	5	14	10	Minturn, Colo.	John F. Baldauf	L. F. Nowotny	1941	183
249	27⅞	29⅞	25⅝	5⅜	5⅛	11	8	Jemez Mts., N.M.	Max S. Jenson	Max S. Jenson	1962	183
249	26⅞	26⅞	26⅞	5⅛	5⅛	8	10	Newcastle, Colo.	William Wiedenfeld	William Wiedenfeld	1969	186
248⅞	26⅝	26⅞	28⅛	4⅞	5	10	12	Petroleum Co., Mont.	Lawrence T. Keenan	Lawrence T. Keenan	1979	187
248⅜	26⅜	26⅞	23⅜	5⅝	5⅞	10	16	Kaibab Forest, Ariz.	O. M. Corbett	O. M. Corbett	1953	188
248⅛	25⅝	25	23	5⅜	5	15	18	San Juan Natl. For., Colo.	Leland R. Tate	Leland R. Tate	1973	188
248⅜	25⅝	24⅞	22⅝	5	5⅛	11	10	Rio Blanco Co., Colo.	Claude E. Shults	Claude E. Shults	1956	190
248	23⅜	22⅛	23⅜	5⅝	5⅝	12	14	Val Marie, Sask.	J. Milton Brown	J. Milton Brown	1958	190
248	26	27⅛	22	5	5	12	9	Pinedale, Wyo.	Lyle Rosendahl	Lyle Rosendahl	1960	190
248	25⅝	26⅞	24⅛	5⅜	5	11	10	Colombine, Colo.	Bobby McLaughlin	Bobby McLaughlin	1962	190
248	25⅛	25⅞	26	5⅝	5⅛	13	11	Kaibab Forest, Ariz.	H. W. Meisch	H. W. Meisch	1942	190
247⅞	26	25⅞	25	5⅝	6	16	11	Norwood, Colo.	Walter L. Reisbeck	Walter L. Reisbeck	1951	194
247⅞	23⅝	24	20⅞	5	5	14	13	Asotin Co., Wash.	David G. Bennett	David G. Bennett	1971	194
247⅝	27	25⅝	28	5⅝	5⅝	9	14	Okanogan Co., Wash.	Fred C. Heuer	Fred C. Heuer	1940	196
247⅜	24⅛	23⅝	22⅝	5	5⅛	11	16	Shoshone Co., Idaho	Gary J. Finney	Gary J. Finney	1983	196
247⅜	28⅝	26⅞	24⅛	6	5⅞	10	13	Waterton Park, Alta.	Eric Westergreen	Eric Westergreen	1941	198
247⅜	25⅜	24⅛	24⅜	6⅞	5⅞	12	16	Bend, Oreg.	L. M. Martinson	L. M. Martinson	1949	199
247⅛	28⅜	28⅛	28⅛	5⅛	5	9	10	Archuleta Co., Colo.	Vince Plaskett	Vince Plaskett	1970	199
247⅜	28⅜	28⅛	25⅛	5	5	10	9	Eagle Co., Colo.	Earl M. Johnson	Earl M. Johnson	1966	201
247⅜	22⅝	22⅞	22⅝	4⅜	4⅞	11	9	Fremont Co., Idaho	Donald R. Craig	Donald R. Craig	1982	201
247⅛	30⅜	30⅞	28⅛	6⅛	6⅞	11	11	Drummond, Mont.	Tom Brosovich	Tom Brosovich	1957	203
247⅛	28⅜	27⅞	25	6⅛	6	10	15	San Miguel Co., Colo.	W. F. Grice	W. F. Grice	1978	203
247	29⅜	28⅜	24⅝	6	5⅜	14	16	Elko Co., Nev.	Walter B. Hester	Walter B. Hester	1957	205
247	26	24⅛	26⅝	7⅜	7⅞	16	20	Hinsdale Co., Colo.	Fred Jardine	Fred Jardine	1966	205

Score								Locality	Hunter	Owner	Date	Rank
247	23⅞	24⅞	21⅛	4⅞	4⅞	11	8	Montrose Co., Colo.	Thomas M. Bost	Thomas M. Bost	1967	205
246⅞	25	25⅜	26⅞	7	6⅞	12	12	Kaibab Forest, Ariz.	Graves Peeler	Graves Peeler	PR1951	208
246⅞	24⅞	24⅞	22⅛	4⅞	4⅞	10	14	Lawrence Co., S.D.	Unknown	Old Style Saloon	1945	208
246⅛	24⅞	24⅞	25⅛	5⅝	5⅜	11	14	Kaibab Forest, Ariz.	Elgin T. Gates	Elgin T. Gates	1960	210
246⅛	26⅞	25	27⅛	4⅜	4⅝	12	9	Whitebird, Idaho	Harold Gustin	Wayne Demaray	1965	210
246⅛	28⅛	26⅝	28⅜	5⅛	4⅝	8	9	Eagle Co., Colo.	Charles H. Thornberg	Charles H. Thornberg	1949	210
246⅛	26⅞	25⅝	25⅝	5⅜	5⅝	12	10	Mesa Co., Colo.	Joseph J. Pitcherella	Joseph J. Pitcherella	1972	210
246	23⅜	26⅛	24⅛	6⅜	5⅞	14	13	Mesa Co., Colo.	Harry A. Gay	Harry A. Gay	1962	214
245⅞	24⅛	23⅜	25⅛	5⅜	5⅝	13	11	Eagle Co., Colo.	William M. Nickels	William M. Nickels	1963	215
245⅞	27⅛	28⅜	24⅞	5⅝	5⅞	11	9	Rio Arriba Co., N.M.	Kenneth W. Lee	Kenneth W. Lee	1971	216
245⅞	25⅜	25	26	5⅝	5⅝	9	11	Glenwood Springs, Colo.	Grady P. Lester	Grady P. Lester	1959	217
245⅞	27⅞	28⅜	23⅜	5⅜	5⅛	9	8	Eagle Co., Colo.	James Caraccioli	James Caraccioli	1978	217
245⅞	28	28	23⅜	5⅜	5⅞	13	11	Rio Blanco Co., Colo.	Charlie Grove	Dorothy Shults	1934	217
245⅞	27⅛	27⅞	21⅞	5⅝	5⅝	10	10	Jicarilla Apache Res., N.M.	Arthur Wanoskea	Arthur Wanoskea	1960	220
245⅝	26⅝	24	24⅜	5	5	18	12	Lac Lariche, Alta.	Julius Hagen	Olaf Hagen	1945	220
245	23⅜	23⅜	20⅞	5⅜	5⅜	12	9	Power Co., Idaho	Mark B. Cooper	Mark B. Cooper	1984	220
244⅞	24	22⅝	18⅞	6⅞	7	12	14	Mt. Trumbull, Ariz.	Tony Stromei	Tony Stromei	1960	222
244⅞	24⅞	21⅞	24⅞	5⅝	5⅝	9	10	Cabri, Sask.	Enos Mitchell, Jr.	Enos Mitchell, Jr.	1960	223
244⅞	21⅞	28⅝	25	5⅝	6⅜	9	11	Eagle, Colo.	Robert Rambo	Robert Rambo	1963	224
244⅞	28⅜	21⅜	29⅝	5⅞	5⅜	14	14	Needle Peak, Idaho	Michael G. Cameron	Michael G. Cameron	1966	224
244⅞	27⅞	26⅜	22⅛	4⅞	4⅞	11	9	Lincoln Co., Wyo.	Brian H. Suter	Brian H. Suter	1981	224
244⅝	25⅝	26⅝	35⅞	5⅛	5⅜	11	13	Pagosa Springs, Colo.	Thomas Jarrett	Thomas Jarrett	1962	224
244⅝	29	29⅛	20⅛	5⅜	5⅛	13	10	Delta Co., Colo.	Neil A. Briscoe, Jr.	Neil A. Briscoe, Jr.	1969	228
244⅝	25⅝	25⅝	25⅝	5⅛	5⅛	13	14	Teton Co., Wyo.	Vern Shinkle	Vern Shinkle	1968	229
244⅝	25⅝	24⅝	24⅛	5⅝	5⅝	15	20	Rossland, B.C.	Victor Mattiazzi	Victor Mattiazzi	1970	229
244⅝	26	25	25	5⅝	5⅛	9	10	Park Co., Mont.	Unknown	Larry F. Dvorak	PR1968	229
244½	25⅞	25⅛	25⅜	5⅛	4⅞	11	11	Kaibab Forest, Ariz.	C. M. Randal, Jr.	C. M. Randal, Jr.	1953	229
244½	24⅞	26⅞	26	5	4⅞	9	13	Fremont Co., Wyo.	Warren V. Spriggs	Warren V. Spriggs	1962	233
244⅜	23⅞	21	26⅜	4⅞	4⅞	12	13	San Juan Co., Utah	Phil Acton	Phil Acton	1966	234
244⅜	23⅝	24⅜	26⅜	5⅛	5⅛	12	13	Wasatch Co., Utah	Unknown	Ted Clegg	1938	234
244	26	22⅞	24⅝	5⅛	5	9	10	East Canyon, Utah	Ronald E. Coburn	Ronald E. Coburn	1961	234
244	27⅜	23	26⅛	4⅞	4⅞	11	10	Craig, Colo.	Fred E. Trouth	Fred E. Trouth	1960	237
243⅞	24⅛	21	26⅜	6⅝	6⅛	13	14	Modoc Co., Calif.	Bill Foster	Foster's Bighorn Rest.	1930	237
243⅞	23⅝	24⅜	26⅜	5⅛	5⅛	12	11	Ravalli Co., Mont.	Lloyd G. Hunter	Lloyd G. Hunter	1963	239
243⅞	22⅞	24⅜	22⅛	6⅛	6⅛	10	12	San Miguel Co., Colo.	Ben Crandell	Ben Crandell	1939	239
243⅝	29⅜	29⅝	29⅜	5⅛	5⅛	9	9	Montrose Co., Colo.	Jim Herndon	Mrs. Jim Herndon	1974	241
243⅝	24⅛	27⅞	27⅞	5⅛	5⅛	16	18	Slave Lake, Alta.	R. W. H. Eben-Ebenau	R. W. H. Eben-Ebenau	1930	241
243⅜	22⅞	21	21	5⅝	5⅝	10	13	Clear Creek Co., Colo.	Louis I. Kingsley	Louis I. Kingsley	1981	243
243⅜	28⅞	28⅜	28⅜	4⅞	4⅞	8	9	Harrison Gulch, Colo.	George R. Mattern	George R. Mattern	1958	244
243⅜	25⅛	23⅛	25⅛	5⅝	5⅝	8	11	Fremont Co., Idaho	Larry D. Hawker	Larry D. Hawker	1970	245
243	28⅜	28⅞	30⅛	5⅝	5⅝	9	8	Oak Creek, Colo.	Scott C. Hinkle	Scott C. Hinkle	1961	245
243	25	25⅝	20⅛	7⅛	7⅛	15	11	Winthrop, Wash.	Bruce Miller	Bruce Miller	1941	247
243	25⅝	24⅝	20	5⅛	5	15	12	Crook Co., Oreg.	Wes Mitts	Wes Mitts	1936	247

MULE DEER (Non-Typical Antlers)—Continued
Odocoileus hemionus hemionus and certain related subspecies

Score	Length of Main Beam R.	L.	Inside Spread	Circumference at Smallest Place Between Burr and First Point R.	L.	Number of Points R.	L.	Locality Killed	By Whom Killed	Owner	Date Killed	Rank
242 7/8	24 4/8	24 6/8	22 6/8	4 6/8	5	10	11	Sheridan, Wyo.	J. M. Blakeman	J. M. Blakeman	1952	250
242 5/8	25	26 6/8	18 6/8	6	5 6/8	11	10	Baison, Idaho	Daniel E. Osborne	Daniel E. Osborne	1959	251
242 5/8	27 4/8	26 6/8	25 6/8	5 6/8	5 6/8	12	9	Sanders Co., Mont.	Robert D. Frisk	Robert D. Frisk	1974	251
242 3/8	23 4/8	22 6/8	17 6/8	4 6/8	5	12	12	Arborfield, Sask.	Joseph Fournier	Joseph Fournier	1930	253
242 3/8	23 4/8	23	20 6/8	5 2/8	5 6/8	12	17	Middle Park, Colo.	Picked Up	Karl H. Knorr	PR 1961	254
242 3/8	25 4/8	25 6/8	23 6/8	5	4 6/8	9	12	Rabbit Ears Pass, Colo.	Douglas Valentine	Douglas Valentine	1964	254
242 2/8	20 4/8	23 6/8	17 6/8	6	5 6/8	12	11	Cabri, Sask.	Gordon Millward	Gordon Millward	1960	256
242 2/8	27 5/8	28 4/8	33 6/8	6 6/8	6 4/8	11	12	Missoula Co., Mont.	Harold Wample	Ralph Raymond	1949	256
242 2/8	28	27 6/8	22 6/8	6 6/8	6 4/8	9	11	Bear Lake Co., Idaho	Robert N. Gale	Robert N. Gale	1970	256
242 2/8	26 4/8	26 6/8	28 6/8	5 6/8	5 4/8	9	8	Kaibab Forest, Ariz.	Ray Ramsey	Ray Ramsey	1952	259
242	22 4/8	23 6/8	18 6/8	5 4/8	5 6/8	12	14	Garfield Co., Colo.	Daniel J. Stanek	Daniel J. Stanek	1981	259
242	28 2/8	24	31 6/8	5 6/8	5 2/8	10	7	Saquache Co., Colo.	Walter A. Larsen	Walter A. Larsen	1962	261
241 7/8	21	18	14 6/8	4 3/8	5 4/8	12	15	Sanders Co., Mont.	Buzz Faro	Buzz Faro	1963	261
241 7/8	24 4/8	24 6/8	25	5 6/8	5 6/8	11	19	Jefferson Co., Oreg.	Spencer L. Darrar	Spencer L. Darrar	1953	261
241 7/8	26 4/8	25 6/8	33 6/8	6 2/8	6 4/8	14	10	Franklin Co., Idaho	Joan Butterworth	Quinten Butterworth	1961	264
241 5/8	25 4/8	25 6/8	23 6/8	4 6/8	4 6/8	10	9	Summit Co., Colo.	Robert R. Ross	Robert R. Ross	1974	265
241 5/8	26 4/8	27	27	5	5 6/8	8	7	Socorro Co., N.M.	James T. Everheart	James T. Everheart	1973	265
241 4/8	22 4/8	23 6/8	20 4/8	5 6/8	5 2/8	10	12	Adams Co., Idaho	Peter Renberg	Peter Renberg	1963	267
241 4/8	26 4/8	24 6/8	24 6/8	5	5 4/8	12	13	Salmon River, Idaho	Richard Shilling	Richard Shilling	1965	267
241 4/8	27 4/8	26 6/8	31 6/8	5 6/8	5 6/8	8	8	Mohave Co., Ariz.	Bernard E. Anderson	Bernard E. Anderson	1969	267
241 3/8	19	24 6/8	20	6 2/8	6 2/8	12	15	Nakusp, B.C.	Frank Vicen	Frank Vicen	1967	267
241 3/8	26 4/8	25 6/8	18 6/8	5	5	10	11	Oak Creek, Colo.	Richard J. Peltier	Richard J. Peltier	1967	271
241 2/8	25 4/8	27 6/8	29	5 6/8	5 2/8	11	10	Elko Co., Nev.	Paul Giuliani	Paul Giuliani	1971	271
241 2/8	25	26 6/8	29 2/8	5 6/8	5 6/8	11	12	Split Rock, Wyo.	Herb Klein	Herb Klein	1957	273
241 1/8	25 4/8	25 6/8	29 6/8	5 6/8	5 6/8	17	15	Bonner Co., Idaho	Dick Sherwood	Dick Sherwood	1963	274
241	26 4/8	27 6/8	26 2/8	4 6/8	4 6/8	11	11	Lewis & Clark Co., Mont.	Mike Filcher	Mike Filcher	1972	274
241	27	27	25 6/8	5 6/8	5 2/8	6	6	New Castle, Colo.	Harold F. Auld	Harold F. Auld	1960	276
240 7/8	26 4/8	26 4/8	23 6/8	5 6/8	5 6/8	10	13	Kaibab Forest, Ariz.	Bert Ellis George	Bert Ellis George	1949	277
240 5/8	22	23 6/8	21	4 6/8	4 6/8	10	9	Elko Co., Nev.	George M. Boman	George M. Boman	1956	277
240 5/8	26 4/8	26 6/8	28 6/8	5 6/8	5 6/8	10	8	Klamath Co., Oreg.	Corinne Fields	Corinne Fields	1946	277
240 5/8	27	25 6/8	27 6/8	5 6/8	5 2/8	10	8	Eagle Co., Colo.	Steve B. Humann	Steve B. Humann	1982	277
240 5/8	26 6/8	27	21 6/8	6 2/8	5	10	9	Modoc Co., Calif.	Niilo Niemi	Niilo Niemi	1968	281

240⅞*	23⅞	22	22⅞	5⅛	5⅛	10	11	Eagle Co., Colo.	James Patrick Hale	James Patrick Hale	1979	281
240⅞	23⅞	23⅜	23⅜	5⅛	5⅛	11	14	Morgan Co., Utah	Pietro De Santis	Pietro De Santis	1982	281
240⅞	23	24⅜	21⅝	5⅜	5⅜	15	14	Garfield Co., Colo.	James E. Powell, Jr.	James E. Powell, Jr.	1983	281
240³⁄₈	22⅜	24⅝	21⅞	5⅞	5⅞	13	12	Missoula Co., Mont.	Richard A. Gendrow	Richard A. Gendrow	1973	285
240³⁄₈	24⅛	24⅞	28	4⅞	4⅞	9	10	Big Horn Co., Wyo.	Picked Up	Henry D. Frey	1978	285
240⅞	27⅛	25⅜	29⅜	5	5	10	11	Blaine Co., Idaho	Roger A. Crowder	Roger A. Crowder	1957	287
240⅞	22⅜	23⅞	26⅞	5⅜	5⅜	10	12	Gem Co., Idaho	Roland Bright	Roland Bright	1965	287
240⅞	27⅜	27⅛	21⅞	5⅜	5⅜	9	11	Mt. Dellenbaugh, Ariz.	Edwin R. Riggs	Edwin R. Riggs	1964	287
240⅛	24⅞	24	19⅞	5⅞	5⅞	13	12	Harney Co., Oreg.	R. G. Creager	R. G. Creager	1957	290
240⅛	23⅞	23⅛	23⅜	5⅞	5⅞	12	12	Elmore Co., Idaho	Phillip K. Messer	Phillip K. Messer	1971	290
240	28	28⅞	25	5⅛	5⅛	7	10	Kamloops, B.C.	Ralph McLean	Ralph McLean	1960	292
240	25⅞	24⅛	23⅞	5⅛	5⅛	12	10	Grand Valley, Colo.	Ed Peters, Jr.	Ed Peters, Jr.	1962	292
297⅞*	26⅛	28⅞	27⅛	4⅞	4⅞	9	8	San Juan Wild., Colo.	Tommie Cornelius	Tommie Cornelius	1967	292
268⅞*	26⅛	26⅜	26⅝	6⅞	6⅞	17	15	Larimer Co., Colo.	Jack Autrey	Warren C. Autrey	1941	
266⅞*	25⅞	23	22⅞	5⅞	5⅞	17	14	Deschutes Co., Oreg.	Devon Talley	Devon Talley	1983	
266⅞*	26⅞	25⅞	22⅞	5⅞	5⅞	15	13	Ouray Co., Colo.	Eugene D. Guilaroff	Eugene D. Guilaroff	1971	
262⅞*	27⅞	27⅛	25⅛	5	4⅞	12	15	Teton Co., Wyo.	Thomas R. Ford	Thomas R. Ford	1984	
252⅞*	22⅞	18⅞	19⅛	5⅞	5⅞	11	22	Boise Co., Idaho	Dennis D. Snider	Dennis D. Snider	1983	

*Final Score subject to revision by additional verifying measurements

Boundaries for Mule and Blacktail Deer

The three varieties of mule deer (mule, Columbia blacktail, and Sitka blacktail) belong to the same species and thus are able to interbreed readily where their ranges meet. The intent of the boundary lines is to exclude intergrades from each of the three categories. These boundaries have been redrawn as necessary, as more details have become known about the precise ranges of these animals.

The current boundary for mule and Columbia blacktail deer is as follows:

British Columbia—Starting at the Washington-British Columbia border, blacktail deer range runs west of the height of land between the Skagit and the Chilliwack Ranges, intersecting the Fraser River opposite the mouth of Ruby Creek, then west to and up Harrison Lake to and up Tipella Creek to the height of land in Garibaldi Park and northwesterly along this divide past Alta Lake, Mt. Dalgleish, and Mt. Waddington, thence north to Bella Coola. From Bella Coola, the boundary continues north to the head of Dean Channel, Gardner Canal, and Douglas Channel to the town of Anyox, then due west to the Alaska-British Columbia border, which is then followed south to open water. This boundary excludes the area west of the Klesilkwa River and the west side of the Lillooet River.

Washington—Beginning at the Washington-British Columbia border, the boundary line runs south along the west boundary of North Cascades National Park to the township line between R10E and R11E W.M., which is then followed directly south to its intersection with the north border of Mt. Rainier National Park, then along the north, west, and south park boundaries until it intersects with the township line between R9E and R10E W.M., which is then followed directly south to the Columbia River near Cook.

Oregon—Beginning at Multnomah Falls on the Columbia River, the boundary runs south along the western boundary of the National Forest to Tiller in Douglas County, then south along Highway 227 to Highway 62 at Trail, then south following Highway 62 to Medford, from which the boundary follows the township line between R1W and R2W E.W.M. to the California border.

California—Beginning in Siskiyou County at the Oregon-California border, the boundary lies between townships R8W and R9W M.D.M., extending south to and along the Klamath River to Hamburg, then south along the road to Scott Bar, continuing south and then east on the unimproved road from Scott Bar to its intersection with the paved road to Mugginsville, then south through Mugginsville to State Highway 3, which is then followed to Douglas City in Trinity County, from which the line runs east on State Highway 299 to Interstate 5. The line follows Interstate 5 south to the area of Anderson, where the Sacramento River moves east of Interstate 5, following the Sacramento River until it joins with the San Joaquin River, which is followed to the south border of Stanislaus County. The line then runs west along this border to the east border of Santa Clara County. The east and south borders of Santa Clara County are then followed to the south border of Santa Cruz County, which is then followed to the edge of Monterey Bay.

On the Queen Charlotte Islands of British Columbia and along the coast of Alaska ranges another subspecies of mule deer, the Sitka blacktail. Accordingly, after a compilation of scores of the largest Sitka blacktail deer trophies from southern Alaska (including those from Kodiak Island where they have been transplanted), a new trophy category was established in 1984 for Sitka blacktail deer, with a minimum all-time records book entry score of 108.

Sitka blacktails have been transplanted to the Queen Charlotte Islands and are abundant there. The area of intergradation between the Sitka and the Columbia blacktail lies along the coast north of Bella Coola, but details about the size of trophies from that region are not known. In order to avoid the possibility of these intergrade deer qualifying at the top of this new category, it was decided *not* to accept trophies for the Sitka blacktail category for the present from the coast of British Columbia. Thus, the acceptable area for this category includes only southeastern Alaska and the Queen Charlotte Islands of British Columbia.

NEW WORLD'S RECORD COLUMBIA BLACKTAIL DEER
SCORE: 182 2/8
Locality: Lewis County, Washington Date: 1953
Hunter and owner: Lester H. Miller

NUMBER TWO COLUMBIA BLACKTAIL DEER
SCORE: 170 6/8
Locality: Elk City, Oregon Date: 1962
Hunter and owner: Clark D. Griffith

Columbia Blacktail Deer
Odocoileus hemionus columbianus

Minimum Score 130

Score	Length of Main Beam R.	Length of Main Beam L.	Inside Spread	Circumference at Smallest Place Between Burr and First Point R.	Circumference at Smallest Place Between Burr and First Point L.	Number of Points R.	Number of Points L.	Locality Killed	By Whom Killed	Owner	Date Killed	Rank
182⅞	24⅝	24⅝	20⅜	5⅛	5⅛	5	5	Lewis Co., Wash.	Lester H. Miller	Lester H. Miller	1953	1
170⅝	23⅝	24	21⅛	5⅜	5⅜	5	5	Elk City, Oreg.	Clark D. Griffith	Clark D. Griffith	1962	2
170⅛	23	22⅜	19⅜	5	4⅞	5	5	Linn Co., Oreg.	Woodrow W. Gibbs	Woodrow W. Gibbs	1963	3
167⅞	24⅜	24⅜	19⅜	4⅞	5	5	6	Marion Co., Oreg.	Robert L. Brown	Robert L. Brown	1980	4
165⅝	23⅝	24⅝	21⅜	5⅛	5⅛	4	4	Yamhill Co., Oreg.	Jim McKinley	Jim McKinley	1971	5
164	23⅜	24⅜	26⅜	5⅜	5⅛	6	6	Glenn Co., Calif.	Peter Gerbo	Nordquist Tax. Studio II	1949	6
163⅜	20⅜	20⅜	21⅜	4⅞	4⅝	6	5	Cowlitz Co., Wash.	Harold Melland	Harold Melland	1962	7
163⅜	23⅜	21⅜	20⅛	5	4⅞	7	6	Siskiyou Co., Calif.	Frank Barago	Frank Barago	1945	8
163⅜	21⅜	22⅝	19⅛	5⅛	5	5	5	Eugene, Oreg.	Russell Thomas	Russell Thomas	1964	8
162⅜	22	22⅛	18⅛	4⅜	4⅜	5	5	Trinity Co., Calif.	Sidney A. Nystrom	Sidney A. Nystrom	1961	10
162⅝	24⅜	25⅜	19⅜	4⅜	4⅝	5	5	Glenn Co., Calif.	Roger L. Spencer	Roger L. Spencer	1956	11
160⅞	23⅜	23⅜	19⅜	4⅞	4⅝	6	5	Jackson Co., Oreg.	G. Scott Jennings	G. Scott Jennings	1972	12
160⅝	20⅝	21⅜	16⅜	4⅜	4⅜	4	4	Camas Valley, Oreg.	Bernard L. Den	Bernard L. Den	1958	13
160⅜	23⅜	24⅜	21	4⅞	4⅞	5	6	Siskiyou Co., Calif.	John L. Masters	John L. Masters	1967	14
160⅛	25⅜	24⅞	24⅜	5	5⅝	5	4	Trinity Co., Calif.	Lorio Verzasconi	Lorio Verzasconi	1946	15
159⅞	22⅝	23⅜	21⅜	4⅝	4⅝	5	5	Siskiyou Co., Calif.	Francis M. Sullivan	Francis M. Sullivan	1951	16
159⅞	22⅜	21⅞	16⅜	4	4	5	5	Siskiyou Co., Calif.	John C. Ley	E. R. Cummins	1937	16
159⅝	24⅜	24⅜	22⅜	4⅜	4⅜	6	6	Jackson Co., Oreg.	Frank Chapman	Frank Chapman	1965	18
159⅜	23⅝	23⅜	14⅞	4⅜	4⅜	6	6	Mendocino Co., Calif.	Russ McLennan	Russ McLennan	1984	19
159⅛	21⅝	22⅛	19⅜	4⅜	4⅝	5	5	Trinity Co., Calif.	A. H. Hilbert	A. H. Hilbert	1939	20
158⅝	22	22⅜	17⅜	4⅜	4⅜	5	5	Marion Co., Oreg.	Bradley M. Brenden	Bradley M. Brenden	1973	21
158⅜	24	24⅜	22⅝	4⅜	4⅝	6	6	Trinity Co., Calif.	David Phillips	David Phillips	1974	22
158⅜	22⅜	23⅜	19⅜	4⅜	4⅜	5	5	Josephine Co., Oreg.	James E. Brierley	James E. Brierley	1983	23
158	22⅝	23⅜	18⅜	4⅜	4⅜	5	5	Camas Valley, Oreg.	Frank Kinnan	Frank Kinnan	1968	24
158	21⅜	21⅜	18⅜	4⅜	4⅜	5	5	Trinity Co., Calif.	Charles A. Strickland	Charles A. Strickland	1984	24
157⅞	22⅝	23⅜	21⅜	4⅜	4⅜	5	5	Shasta Co., Calif.	Richard L. Sobrato	Richard L. Sobrato	1969	26
157⅞	21⅜	19⅜	17⅜	4⅞	5	5	5	Yamhill Co., Oreg.	Henry Davenport	Henry Davenport	1932	27
157⅜	23⅜	23⅜	26⅝	5	5	6	5	Trinity Co., Calif	A. H. Hilbert	Jack T. Brusatori	1929	28
157	24⅞	26⅛	24⅝	5	5⅛	5	7	Santa Clara Co., Calif.	Brud Eade	Brud Eade	1961	29
156⅝	21⅜	21⅜	20⅜	4⅜	4⅞	5	5	Pierce Co., Wash.	Horst A. Vierthaler	Horst A. Vierthaler	1963	30

COLUMBIA BLACKTAIL DEER—Continued

Odocoileus hemionus columbianus

Score	Length of Main Beam R.	L.	Inside Spread	Circumference at Smallest Place Between Burr and First Point R.	L.	Number of Points R.	L.	Locality Killed	By Whom Killed	Owner	Date Killed	Rank
156	25	23⅜	21	4⅜	4⅜	6	5	Polk Co., Oreg.	Wayne Bond	Wayne Bond	1965	31
155⅝	23⅛	23⅞	16⅝	4⅞	4⅞	5	6	Pierce Co., Wash.	J. Bennett & F. Duell	J. Bennett & F. Duell	1983	32
155⅜	22⅜	23⅛	20⅝	5⅜	5	4	5	Jackson Co., Oreg.	L. M. Morgan & L. Miller	Lewis M. Morgan	1971	33
155⅜	22⅛	22⅞	19⅞	5⅜	4⅞	5	5	Mendocino Co., Calif.	Gary Land	Gary Land	1972	33
155⅜	21⅞	20⅞	17⅞	4⅞	4⅞	5	5	King Co., Wash.	Horst Vierthaler	Horst Vierthaler	1960	33
155⅜	21	21⅛	18⅛	4⅜	4⅜	4	4	Shasta Co., Calif.	Vance Corrigan	Vance Corrigan	1956	36
155⅛	20⅜	20⅜	20⅛	4⅝	4⅜	4	4	Mendocino Co., Calif.	W. A. McAllister	W. A. McAllister	1968	37
154⅞	22⅜	23⅜	18	4⅝	4⅜	5	6	Cowlitz Co., Wash.	Bud Whittle	Bud Whittle	1957	37
154⅞	24	22⅞	23⅜	4⅜	4⅜	5	5	Humboldt Co., Calif.	Phillip Brown	Phillip Brown	1962	39
154⅝	24⅜	24⅜	21	4⅞	4⅞	6	7	Siskiyou Co., Calif.	Darrell R. Jones	Darrell R. Jones	1984	39
154⅜	21⅛	22⅜	18⅜	4⅜	4⅜	6	7	Glenn Co., Calif.	Mitchell A. Thorson	Mitchell A. Thorson	1969	41
154⅛	20⅛	20⅜	18⅛	4⅜	3⅞	5	5	Lane Co., Oreg.	Eldon Lundy	Eldon Lundy	1943	41
153⅞	21⅜	21⅝	23⅛	3⅜	4⅜	5	5	Trinity Co., Calif.	Fred Heider	Fred Heider	1927	43
153⅞	21⅛	21⅜	18⅜	4⅜	4⅜	5	5	Cultus Lake, B.C.	Steven R. Rupp	Steven R. Rupp	1983	43
153⅜	21⅜	20⅞	17⅞	4⅝	4⅞	5	5	Linn Co., Oreg.	Greg L. Anderson	Greg L. Anderson	1983	45
153⅜	21⅛	21⅜	17⅜	5	5	6	5	Tehama Co., Calif.	James L. Carr	James L. Carr	1979	46
153⅜	21⅛	20⅜	19⅛	5⅜	5⅜	6	7	Columbia Co., Oreg.	J. H. Roberts	Oreg. Dept. Fish & Wildl.	1946	46
153⅛	22	22⅞	19⅞	5⅜	5⅜	6	6	Canton Creek, Oreg.	Marell Abeene	Marell Abeene	1967	48
153	22⅜	23⅜	14⅞	4⅜	4⅝	6	5	Siskiyou Co., Calif.	John Carmichael	J. A. Brose	1969	49
152⅝	22⅜	22	19⅜	4	4⅜	5	5	Mendocino Co., Calif.	Harold D. Schneider	H. D. & M. J. Schneider	1979	50
152⅞	23	23	20	4	4	6	7	Tehama Co., Calif.	Don Strickler	Don Strickler	1979	51
152⅛	20⅞	21⅛	17⅛	5⅜	5⅜	7	6	Pemberton, B.C.	Jim Decker	Jim Decker	1968	52
152⅛	22⅜	21⅛	17⅜	4⅜	4⅜	5	5	Trinity Co., Calif.	Robert V. Strickland	Robert V. Strickland	1966	52
152	23⅜	22⅞	21⅝	4⅜	4⅜	5	5	Yolo Co., Calif.	Herman Darneille	E. L. Gallup	1943	54
152	21⅞	21⅛	15⅝	4⅜	4⅜	6	6	Clackamas Co., Oreg.	Larry W. Peterson	Larry W. Peterson	1980	54
151⅞	20⅞	24⅜	20⅜	4⅜	4⅜	5	5	Jackson Co., Oreg.	David Ellefson	David Ellefson	1972	56
151⅞	25	25⅞	28⅜	4⅜	4⅜	6	6	Trinity Co., Calif.	A. H. Hilbert	A. H. Hilbert	1930	57
151⅝	22⅜	22⅜	17⅜	5⅜	5⅜	6	5	Glide, Oreg.	William Cellers	William Cellers	1947	57
151⅝	20⅜	19⅛	16⅝	4⅜	4⅜	5	5	Marion Co., Oreg.	John Davenport	John Davenport	1958	59
151⅜	23⅛	23⅛	19⅝	5	5	5	6	Josephine Co., Oreg.	E. L. McKie & S. E. McKie	Ernie L. McKie	1977	60

Score	L.R	L.L	Spread	Circ.R	Circ.L	Pts.R	Pts.L	Locality	Owner	Hunter	Year	Rank
151 1/8	22 2/8	21 7/8	22 5/8	4 6/8	4 6/8	5	5	Siskiyou Co., Calif.	Jim A. Turnbow	Jim A. Turnbow	1973	61
151 1/8	21 5/8	21 5/8	16 1/8	4	4	4	4	Josephine Co., Oreg.	Jim Wineteer	Jim Wineteer	1980	61
151	23 5/8	24	17 7/8	5 3/8	5 3/8	7	4	Lewis Co., Wash.	Harold Gossard	George V. Bagley	1967	63
151	20 5/8	21	17 7/8	4 6/8	4 6/8	6	6	Lewis Co., Wash.	Norman Henspeter	Norman Henspeter	1941	63
151	21 7/8	21	19 1/8	4 2/8	4 1/8	5	5	Humboldt Co., Calif.	Elgin T. Gates	Elgin T. Gates	1952	63
150 7/8	22	21 4/8	19 5/8	4 3/8	4 5/8	5	5	Jackson Co., Oreg.	Darrell Leek	Darrell Leek	1974	66
150 6/8	21 5/8	20 7/8	17	5 4/8	5 5/8	5	5	Siskiyou Co., Calif.	Raymond Whittaker	Raymond Whittaker	1978	67
150 5/8	24 1/8	24 5/8	16 5/8	5 1/8	5 1/8	6	5	Yamhill Co., Oreg.	Russell W. Byers	Russell W. Byers	1961	68
150 5/8	21	21	19 3/8	3 7/8	3 7/8	5	6	Trinity Co., Calif.	E. L. Brightenstine	E. L. Brightenstine	1978	69
150 4/8	20 5/8	21	20 1/8	5 2/8	5 5/8	5	5	Trinity Co., Calif.	Thomas L. Hough	Thomas L. Hough	1969	70
150 3/8	22 4/8	22	14 1/8	4 1/8	4 1/8	5	5	Lewis Co., Wash.	Carroll H. Fenn	Carroll H. Fenn	1959	70
150 1/8	22 7/8	23 1/8	16 1/8	4 6/8	4 6/8	5	5	Napa Co., Calif.	Robert G. Wiley	Robert G. Wiley	1965	70
150 1/8	20 5/8	21 5/8	19 3/8	5	5	6	5	Clackamas Co., Oreg.	E. Clint Kuntz	E. Clint Kuntz	1981	70
150	22 5/8	20 5/8	16 5/8	5 3/8	5 3/8	5	6	Douglas Co., Oreg.	Norman Burnett	Norman Burnett	1967	74
150	24	24	20	4 5/8	4 4/8	4	5	Lake Co., Calif.	Bruce Strickler	Bruce Strickler	1970	74
150	25 1/8	25	24	5 5/8	5 5/8	4	4	Napa Co., Calif.	W. C. Lambert	W. C. Lambert	1957	74
149 6/8	22 5/8	22 7/8	19 5/8	5	5 5/8	5	4	King Co., Wash.	Roscoe Rainey	Roscoe Rainey	1963	74
149 5/8	20	22	18 7/8	4 4/8	4 4/8	5	5	Siskiyou Co., Calif.	Emit C. Jones	Emit C. Jones	1961	78
149 5/8	22 7/8	21 3/8	17 7/8	4 3/8	4 5/8	5	5	Humboldt Co., Calif.	Robert C. Stephens	Robert C. Stephens	1961	79
149 4/8	22 5/8	22 7/8	17 1/8	5 1/8	5 3/8	5	5	Clackamas Co., Oreg.	Ray W. Bunnell	Ray W. Bunnell	1970	79
149 3/8	23 2/8	21	20 6/8	5 5/8	5 5/8	5	5	Glenn Co., Calif.	George Stewart, Jr.	George Stewart, Jr.	1957	81
149 3/8	24 3/8	21 2/8	20 3/8	5 5/8	5 5/8	8	5	Trinity Co., Calif.	Lyle L. Johnson	Lyle L. Johnson	1979	82
149 2/8	22 5/8	24 3/8	17 7/8	4 2/8	4 2/8	5	8	Trinity Co., Calif.	Lauren A. Johnson	Lauren A. Johnson	1964	83
149 2/8	20 5/8	22 5/8	19 5/8	4	4	5	5	Lane Co., Oreg.	Richard C. MacKenzie	Richard C. MacKenzie	1983	83
149 1/8	21 3/8	20 7/8	14 5/8	4 7/8	4 7/8	5	5	Clackamas Co., Oreg.	Lance V. Bentz	Lance V. Bentz	1980	83
149 1/8	22 1/8	20 3/8	16 5/8	4 7/8	4 7/8	5	5	Clallam Co., Wash.	Otis Dahman	E. A. Dahman	1943	86
148 7/8	24 4/8	22 7/8	18	5	5 1/8	6	5	Humboldt Co., Calif.	F. Joe Parker	F. Joe Parker	1946	87
148 6/8	23 5/8	21 3/8	20 3/8	5 1/8	5 1/8	5	5	Tillamook Co., Oreg.	Fred Dick	Fred Dick	1948	88
148 4/8	22 7/8	24 2/8	20 6/8	4 5/8	4 5/8	5	5	Mendocino Co., Calif.	N. D. Windbigler	N. D. Windbigler	1969	89
148 4/8	22 5/8	22 5/8	16 5/8	4 4/8	4 4/8	6	5	Skamania Co., Wash.	Alan Dean Borroz	Alan Dean Borroz	1978	89
148 3/8	22 5/8	21 2/8	15 5/8	5 3/8	5 3/8	5	6	Linn Co., Oreg.	Marlin D. Brinkley	Marlin D. Brinkley	1982	89
148 3/8	21	22 5/8	19 5/8	4 3/8	4 2/8	5	5	Douglas Co., Oreg.	Unknown	Bud Jackson	1929	92
148 2/8	21 1/8	21	18 5/8	4 2/8	4 2/8	5	5	Marion Co., Oreg.	Mike Fenimore	Mike Fenimore	1961	92
147 7/8	24	21 1/8	23 4/8	6 2/8	5 5/8	6	5	Shasta Co., Calif.	Jerry W. Sander	Jerry W. Sander	1977	94
147 7/8	22	24 4/8	18 5/8	4 1/8	4 1/8	5	10	Glenn Co., Calif.	Emmet T. Frye	Emmet T. Frye	1937	95
147 7/8	22 1/8	22	18 5/8	4 2/8	4 2/8	6	6	Humboldt Co., Calif.	Melvin H. Kadle	Melvin H. Kadle	1979	95
147 6/8	23	22 2/8	19 5/8	4 4/8	4 3/8	5	5	Santa Clara Co., Calif.	Maitland Armstrong	Maitland Armstrong	1944	97
147 5/8	19 5/8	21 7/8	22 1/8	4 6/8	4 7/8	6	6	Siskiyou Co., Calif.	James C. Elliott	James C. Elliott	1974	98
147 4/8	22 5/8	23 4/8	19 4/8	4 3/8	4 3/8	4	5	Jackson Co., Oreg.	Mike Taylor	Mike Taylor	1969	99
147	21 2/8	21 7/8	16 5/8	4 3/8	4 3/8	5	5	Trinity Co., Calif.	Craig L. Brown	Craig & Joy Brown	1980	100
147	18 2/8	21	17	4 3/8	4 3/8	5	5	Siskiyou Co., Calif.	Ray Whittaker	Ray Whittaker	1966	101
147	20 6/8	18 4/8	21 6/8	5	4 7/8	5	5	Trinity Co., Calif.	Chauncy Willburn	Chauncy Willburn	1955	101
146 5/8	22 4/8	20 2/8	15 1/8	5 5/8	5 5/8	5	5	Clallam Co., Wash.	Charles W. Lockhart	Charles W. Lockhart	1946	103

COLUMBIA BLACKTAIL DEER—Continued
Odocoileus hemionus columbianus

Score	Length of Main Beam R.	L.	Inside Spread	Circ. at Smallest Place Between Burr and First Point R.	L.	No. of Points R.	L.	Locality Killed	By Whom Killed	Owner	Date Killed	Rank
146⅞	21⅝	21⅜	18⅞	4⅞	5	6	5	Camas Valley, Oreg.	Adam J. Hipp	Adam J. Hipp	1961	104
146⅞	20	20⅜	18⅛	4⅜	4⅜	5	5	Siskiyou Co., Calif.	Richard Silva	Richard Silva	1958	104
146⅝	21⅛	21	16⅜	4⅜	4⅜	5	5	Coos Co., Oreg.	Pete Serafin	Pete Serafin	1968	106
146⅝	21⅝	22⅜	22	5⅜	5⅜	5	5	King Co., Wash.	Leo Klinkhammer	Leo Klinkhammer	1961	107
146⅝	22⅝	22⅞	17⅞	4⅝	4⅞	5	5	Glenn Co., Calif.	Lawrence E. Germeshausen	Lawrence E. Germeshausen	1983	107
146⅝	21⅝	21⅜	16⅞	4⅝	4⅝	5	5	Humboldt Co., Calif.	Gerald Wescott	Gerald Wescott	1980	109
146½	21	20⅝	13⅜	4⅝	5⅝	5	5	Shasta Co., Calif.	William H. Taylor	William H. Taylor	1971	110
146½	21⅝	22⅝	14⅞	5⅝	4⅝	5	5	Douglas Co., Oreg.	Bernard H. Schum	Bernard H. Schum	1966	110
146½	20⅞	21⅛	14⅞	4⅜	4⅞	5	5	Trinity Co., Calif.	Kenneth M. Brown	Kenneth M. Brown	1972	112
146½	23⅛	23⅜	19⅛	4⅝	4	4	4	King Co., Wash.	Robert B. Gracey	Robert B. Gracey	1963	113
146	20	20⅜	21⅛	5	5	5	5	Little Fall Creek, Oreg.	Gene B. Johnson	Gene B. Johnson	1963	113
146	20⅝	20⅞	15⅞	5	5	5	5	Shasta Co., Calif.	Gary J. Miller	Gary J. Miller	1968	115
145⅞	22⅝	22⅛	21⅞	4⅜	4⅝	5	5	Lake Co., Calif.	Floyd Goodrich	Mrs. William Olson	1926	115
145⅞	23⅜	23⅜	22	5⅜	5⅝	6	8	Linn Co., Oreg.	Harold Tonkin	C. Vernon Humble	1954	115
145⅞	24⅝	22⅛	19	5⅝	5⅝	6	5	Napa Co., Calif.	C. H. N. Dailey	Tony Stoer	1948	115
145⅝	22	23⅝	16⅜	4⅝	6	5	6	Whatcom Co., Wash.	Dennis Miller	Dennis Miller	1970	119
145⅝	19⅝	20⅞	14⅞	5⅜	4⅛	6	5	Humboldt Co., Calif.	Joe Dickerson	Jay Grunert	1962	120
145⅝	22⅞	23	18⅞	4⅛	4⅛	6	5	Jackson Co., Oreg.	Gary D. Kaiser	Gary D. Kaiser	1967	121
145⅝	20⅝	20⅛	14⅞	4⅝	4⅜	4	4	Mendocino Co., Calif.	Elmer H. Brown	Elmer H. Brown	1960	121
145⅝	22	22⅞	21⅛	4⅛	4⅝	5	5	Douglas Co., Oreg.	Daniel J. Fisher	Daniel J. Fisher	1973	121
145½	21⅝	20	16⅞	4⅞	4⅝	5	5	Trinity Co., Calif.	Carroll E. Dow	Carroll E. Dow	1962	124
145⅜	23⅝	23⅝	24⅞	4⅝	4⅝	5	5	Jackson Co., Oreg.	Bill Hays	Bill Hays	1968	125
145⅜	22⅛	21⅞	16⅞	4⅝	4⅝	5	5	Lake Harrison, B.C.	Lloyd L. Ward, Jr.	Lloyd L. Ward, Jr.	1947	125
145⅜	22⅝	17⅝	17⅞	4	4	4	4	Tehama Co., Calif.	Clint Heiber	Clint Heiber	1979	125
145⅛	22⅝	22⅝	21	5⅜	5⅞	7	9	Lane Co., Oreg.	Boyd Iverson	Boyd Iverson	1982	128
144⅞	19⅝	19⅝	15⅞	4⅜	4⅝	5	5	Lane Co., Oreg.	Clair R. Thomas	Clair R. Thomas	1959	129
144⅞	22⅛	23⅝	22⅞	4⅛	4⅛	5	5	Douglas Co., Oreg.	Larry E. Waller	Larry E. Waller	1980	129
144⅞	19⅝	19⅞	19⅞	4⅝	4⅝	5	5	Clatsop Co., Oreg.	Pravomil Raichl	Pravomil Raichl	1959	129
144⅝	20⅝	20	13⅞	4	4⅛	5	5	Mendocino Co., Calif.	Richard Vannelli	Richard Vannelli	1970	132
144⅝	22⅝	22⅛	22⅞	3⅜	3⅞	5	4	King Co., Wash.	R. Walter Williams	R. Walter Williams	1956	132
144⅝	20	22⅛	17⅞	4⅜	4⅝	6	6	Skamania Co., Wash.	Melvin D. Robertson	Melvin D. Robertson	1983	132

Score	Length Main Beam R.	Length Main Beam L.	Inside Spread	Circ. R.	Circ. L.	Pts. R.	Pts. L.	Locality	Hunter	Owner	Year	Rank
144 6/8	21 6/8	22 6/8	19 6/8	6	6	5	4	Lincoln Co., Oreg.	William D. Harmon	Merle W. Emmert	1976	132
144 4/8	22 4/8	22 4/8	21 5/8	4 4/8	4 4/8	5	5	Josephine Co., Oreg.	Jerry C. Sparlin	Jerry C. Sparlin	1963	136
144 4/8	21 4/8	20 4/8	17 5/8	4 2/8	4 2/8	5	5	Powers, Oreg.	Ray A. Davis	Ray A. Davis	1968	137
144 4/8	21 4/8	21 3/8	19 4/8	4 3/8	4 2/8	5	5	Shasta Co., Calif.	Ernie Young	Chet Young	1953	137
144 4/8	21 6/8	21 5/8	16 6/8	4 2/8	4 3/8	5	5	Clackamas Co., Oreg.	John R. Vollmer, Jr.	John R. Vollmer, Jr.	1960	137
144 4/8	21	21	17	3 6/8	3 6/8	4	4	Snohomish Co., Wash.	Roy Shogren	Roy Shogren	1979	137
144 3/8	22 1/8	23 3/8	21 3/8	5	5 2/8	5	5	Santa Clara Co., Calif.	Maitland Armstrong	Maitland Armstrong	1946	141
144 3/8	20 3/8	21	17 5/8	4 4/8	4 5/8	4	5	Jackson Co., Oreg.	Warren Pestka	Warren Pestka	1974	142
144 2/8	22 3/8	21	23 4/8	4 4/8	4 4/8	5	5	Mendocino Co., Calif.	Paul M. Holleman II	Paul M. Holleman II	1976	142
144 2/8	21	22 4/8	20 6/8	4 4/8	4 4/8	5	5	Mendocino Co., Calif.	Frank Kester	Frank Kester	1981	142
144 2/8	21 6/8	21 3/8	15 5/8	4 4/8	4 4/8	6	6	Marion Co., Oreg.	Arthur L. Schmidt	Arthur L. Schmidt	1978	142
144 1/8	21 7/8	21 3/8	17 7/8	4 5/8	4 5/8	5	5	Siskiyou Natl. For., Oreg.	Dennis E. Bourn	Dennis E. Bourn	1971	146
144	20 7/8	20 4/8	17 7/8	4 4/8	4 5/8	5	5	Skamania Co., Wash.	Wayne Crockford	Wayne Crockford	1960	147
144	21 3/8	21 5/8	17	5 1/8	5 1/8	5	5	Linn Co., Oreg.	Ed A. Taylor	Ed A. Taylor	1981	147
143 7/8	23 4/8	22 7/8	21 3/8	4 5/8	4 5/8	5	5	Clackamas Co., Oreg.	Richard G. Mathis	Richard G. Mathis	1965	149
143 7/8	20 7/8	23	20 6/8	5	5	6	6	Linn Co., Oreg.	Clarence Howe	Clarence Howe	1941	149
143 6/8	20 7/8	20 4/8	16 4/8	5	5	5	5	Lewis Co., Wash.	Bill W. Latimer	Bill W. Latimer	1974	151
143 6/8	19 7/8	20 4/8	16	4 7/8	4 7/8	6	6	Squamish, B.C.	B. Miller	B. Miller	1962	151
143 5/8	20 5/8	20 4/8	19 7/8	5 2/8	5 2/8	6	6	Tehama Co., Calif.	Clint Heiber	Cint Heiber	1978	151
143 5/8	21 4/8	21	17 7/8	5 4/8	5 4/8	5	5	Grays Harbor Co., Wash.	Eddie & Robert Dierick	Eddie & Robert Dierick	1958	154
143 5/8	20 4/8	20 4/8	18 4/8	4 4/8	4 4/8	4	4	Siskiyou Co., Calif.	Emit C. Jones	Emit C. Jones	1960	154
143 4/8	21 4/8	21 4/8	21 3/8	4 4/8	4 4/8	5	5	Snoqualmie, Wash.	Milton L. James	Milton L. James	1964	156
143 4/8	21 4/8	22 4/8	16 2/8	4 1/8	4 1/8	5	5	Clark Co., Wash.	A. W. Gerber	Earl Gerber	1929	156
143 4/8	22	23	16 3/8	3 7/8	4	5	5	Josephine Co., Oreg.	Virgil Welch	Virgil Welch	1983	156
143 4/8	21	20 4/8	17	4 4/8	4 4/8	5	5	Trinity Co., Calif.	Barry Griffin	Barry Griffin	1983	156
143 3/8	20	20 4/8	15 5/8	4 7/8	4 7/8	5	5	Chehalis River, B.C.	Clair A. Howard	Clair A. Howard	1971	160
143 3/8	21 4/8	19	19	4 3/8	4 3/8	5	5	Linn Co., Oreg.	Basil C. Bradbury	Basil C. Bradbury	1960	161
143 3/8	22 3/8	21 4/8	21 4/8	4 4/8	4 4/8	5	5	Lake Co., Calif.	Mario Sereni, Jr.	Mario Sereni, Jr.	1965	161
143 3/8	19 4/8	19	25	6 2/8	6 2/8	7	7	Jones Lake, B.C.	James Haslam	James Haslam	1967	161
143 2/8	26	26	25	4 4/8	4 4/8	5	5	Mendocino Co., Calif.	George W. Rogers	George W. Rogers	1977	161
143 1/8	19 4/8	19 4/8	17 4/8	3 7/8	4	5	5	Humboldt Co., Calif.	Jack Stedman	Jack Stedman	1965	161
142 7/8	22	20 4/8	18 4/8	4 1/8	4 1/8	5	5	Humboldt Co., Calif.	Mitchell A. Thorson	Mitchell A. Thorson	1965	166
142 6/8	21 4/8	20 4/8	17 3/8	4 4/8	4 4/8	6	6	Benton Co., Oreg.	A. C. Nelson	A. C. Nelson	1957	166
142 6/8	20 4/8	22	16 3/8	4	4	4	4	Clackamas Co., Oreg.	Larry Tracy	Larry Tracy	1965	168
142 5/8	21 3/8	21 3/8	19 3/8	4 4/8	5	5	5	Linn Co., Oreg.	R. Reid & D. Liles	R. Reid & D. Liles	1982	169
142 5/8	23 3/8	22	17 3/8	3 7/8	4	4	4	Linn Co., Oreg.	Kenneth W. Wegner	Kenneth W. Wegner	1982	169
142 5/8	22	22 3/8	17 1/8	4 2/8	4 1/8	5	5	Marion Co., Oreg.	Robert E. Bochsler	Robert E. Bochsler	1950	171
142 5/8	20 3/8	20	16 5/8	4 1/8	4	5	5	Santa Clara Co., Calif.	Picked Up	Ray & Neal Haera	PR 1966	171
142 5/8	19 4/8	19 4/8	17 7/8	4 5/8	4 5/8	5	5	Jackson Co., Oreg.	Leonard B. Sequeira	Nancy Sequeira	1959	171
142 5/8	22	22 4/8	19 4/8	4 3/8	4 3/8	5	5	Santa Clara Co., Calif.	Picked Up	Russel Rasmussen	PR 1966	171
142 5/8	21 4/8	20 3/8	19 7/8	4 4/8	4 4/8	4	4	Trinity Co., Calif.	Larry Brown	Larry Brown	1979	171
142 5/8	23 3/8	22 1/8	20 1/8	4 6/8	4 7/8	6	6	Tehama Co., Calif.	Kenneth R. Hall	Kenneth R. Hall	1979	171

COLUMBIA BLACKTAIL DEER—*Continued*

Odocoileus hemionus columbianus

Score	Length of Main Beam R.	Length of Main Beam L.	Inside Spread	Circumference at Smallest Place Between Burr and First Point R.	Circumference at Smallest Place Between Burr and First Point L.	Number of Points R.	Number of Points L.	Locality Killed	By Whom Killed	Owner	Date Killed	Rank
142 4/8	18 3/8	18 3/8	15	4 5/8	4 6/8	5	5	Chilliwack, B.C.	Frank Rosenauer	Frank Rosenauer	1967	177
142 4/8	22 2/8	22 6/8	13 3/8	4 6/8	4 6/8	4	5	Trinity Co., Calif.	Jace Comfort	Jace Comfort	1965	177
142 4/8	21 6/8	22	16 6/8	4 3/8	4 3/8	6	5	Clackamas Co., Oreg.	Henry A. Charriere	Henry A. Charriere	1970	177
142 4/8	22 4/8	22 7/8	21	4 3/8	3 7/8	4	3	Jackson Co., Oreg.	Donald G. Spence	Donald G. Spence	1980	177
142 3/8	23	22	19 3/8	4	4	5	4	Humboldt Co., Calif.	Darol L. Damm	Darol L. Damm	1976	181
142 3/8	20 6/8	20 7/8	17 3/8	4 3/8	4 5/8	5	5	Laytonville, Calif.	Byron J. Rowland, Jr.	Byron J. Rowland, Jr.	1964	181
142 2/8	23 4/8	23 2/8	17	4 2/8	4 1/8	6	5	Mendocino Co., Calif.	James A. Shelton	James A. Shelton	1944	183
142 2/8	20 7/8	20 4/8	16 2/8	4 3/8	4 6/8	5	5	Jackson Co., Oreg.	Eileen F. Damone	Eileen F. Damone	1976	183
142 1/8	21 3/8	22 3/8	19 7/8	5 1/8	5 1/8	5	4	Shasta Co., Calif.	Richard R. Lowell	Richard R. Lowell	1953	185
142	24 6/8	24 6/8	17	5	5	4	5	Skamania Co., Wash.	Ted Howell	Ted Howell	1968	186
142	20 1/8	20 6/8	17	4 3/8	4 2/8	5	5	Cowlitz Co., Wash.	Harold C. Johnson	Harold C. Johnson	1947	186
142	25 3/8	24	18 3/8	7	6 4/8	7	4	Doty, Wash.	Leslie A. Lusk	Leslie A. Lusk	1973	186
142	21 6/8	22 5/8	20 2/8	4 5/8	4 6/8	6	5	Mt. Sheazer, Wash.	Joseph B. Wilcox	Joseph B. Wilcox	1953	186
142	24	23 5/8	16 7/8	5 1/8	5 6/8	8	5	Marion Co., Oreg.	Hugh W. Gardner	Hugh W. Gardner	1966	186
142	23	20 7/8	21 4/8	4 4/8	4 4/8	5	5	Skamania Co., Wash.	Herbert P. Roberts	Herbert P. Roberts	1983	186
141 7/8	20 7/8	21 3/8	18 1/8	5 5/8	5 5/8	4	4	Whatcom Co., Wash.	Kjell A. Thompson	Kjell A. Thompson	1963	192
141 7/8	21 4/8	21 2/8	17 7/8	4 7/8	5	5	5	Trinity Co., Calif.	Pedro H. Henrich	Pedro H. Henrich	1977	192
141 6/8	21 3/8	21 3/8	19 2/8	4 4/8	4 4/8	5	5	Lane Co., Oreg.	Jerry Shepard	Jerry Shepard	1954	194
141 6/8	22 7/8	22 2/8	17 5/8	4 5/8	4 6/8	6	7	Pierce Co., Wash.	Joseph Kominski	Joseph Kominski	1954	194
141 6/8	19 7/8	19 3/8	16 4/8	4 7/8	4 7/8	5	5	Hobart, Wash.	Donald R. Heinle	Donald R. Heinle	1958	194
141 6/8	20 2/8	20 7/8	18 2/8	4 5/8	4 4/8	5	5	Linn Co., Oreg.	Eugene L. Wilson	Eugene L. Wilson	1982	194
141 4/8	20 2/8	20 6/8	17 6/8	4 7/8	5	5	5	Morton, Wash.	Ralph W. Cournyer	Ralph W. Cournyer	1962	198
141 4/8	22	22 5/8	15 4/8	5 2/8	5 1/8	5	5	Pierce Co., Wash.	Ron Dick	Ron Dick	1965	198
141 3/8	19 6/8	19 7/8	17 6/8	4 7/8	4 6/8	7	6	Harrison Lake, B.C.	D. Harrison	D. Harrison	1963	200
141 3/8	22 1/8	21 5/8	18 7/8	4 7/8	4 5/8	5	4	Trinity Co., Calif.	Larry Brown	Larry Brown	1980	200
141 2/8	25 6/8	25 3/8	21 5/8	5 4/8	5 6/8	6	6	Pierce Co., Wash.	John Streepy, Sr.	John Streepy, Sr.	1956	202
141 1/8	19 7/8	19 6/8	20 3/8	4	4 2/8	5	5	Trinity Co., Calif.	A. H. Hilbert	A. H. Hilbert	PR1955	203
141 1/8	22 2/8	22 4/8	17 7/8	4 6/8	4 6/8	5	5	Pierce Co., Wash.	Jerry E. Burke	Jerry E. Burke	1980	203
141	21 3/8	21 1/8	17	3 7/8	4 1/8	5	5	Humboldt Co., Calif.	Allen Pierce, Jr.	Allen Pierce, Jr.	1959	205
141	21	20 2/8	19 4/8	4 4/8	4	5	4	Mendocino Co., Calif.	Richard Vannelli	Richard Vannelli	1970	205
141	23	24 4/8	22	5 4/8	5 4/8	7	6	Mendocino Co., Calif.	Gerald W. Whitmire	Gerald W. Whitmire	1976	205
140 7/8	21 1/8	20 1/8	21 1/8	4 3/8	4 4/8	5	5	Shasta Co., Calif.	Dave Swenson	Dave Swenson	1968	208

Score								Locality	Hunter	Owner	Year	Rank
140⅞	23⅞	22	16⅝	3⅞	4	5	5	Mendocino Co., Calif.	Douglas W. Lim	Douglas W. Lim	1981	208
140⅞	23⅝	23⅝	18⅜	5	5	10	8	Polk Co., Oreg.	Gale A. Draper	Gale A. Draper	1984	208
140⅝	23⅞	23	18⅝	4⅞	5⅛	5	4	Mendocino Co., Calif.	Robert Lynch	Robert Lynch	1971	211
140⅝	17⅞	18⅝	17⅞	4⅞	4⅞	5	6	Lewis Co., Wash.	Nick Nilson	Nick Nilson	1944	211
140⅝	23	22⅜	20	5⅞	5⅞	5	5	Mendocino Co., Calif.	Jerry D. Smith	Jerry D. Smith	1978	214
140⅝	21	21⅞	18⅜	4⅞	4⅝	6	5	Shasta Co., Calif.	Luther Clements	R. H. Bernhardy	1944	214
140⅝	19⅞	20	17⅜	4⅜	4⅜	5	5	Glacier, Wash.	John J. A. Weatherby	John J. A. Weatherby	1965	216
140⅝	21⅝	20⅞	18⅜	4⅜	4	6	5	Trinity Co., Calif.	Loran G. August	Larry Brown	1980	216
140⅜	22	21	17⅞	4	4⅜	5	5	Yamhill Co., Oreg.	Richard Watts	Richard Watts	1981	218
140⅜	20⅛	20⅝	16⅝	3⅞	4⅝	4	5	Siskiyou Co., Calif.	Rodney Irwin	Rodney Irwin	1966	218
140⅜	20⅛	21⅜	16⅞	4⅞	3⅞	5	5	Humboldt Co., Calif.	George S. Johnson	Roy F. Johnson	1934	220
140⅜	21⅛	21⅞	19⅜	3⅞	4⅜	5	5	Lewis Co., Wash.	Randy J. Brossard	Randy J. Brossard	1978	220
140⅜	20⅜	19⅜	16⅜	4⅜	5	4	4	Mendocino Co., Calif.	Earl E. Hamlow, Jr.	Earl E. Hamlow, Jr.	1977	222
140⅜	23⅜	22⅞	18⅛	5	4⅞	6	6	Santa Clara Co., Calif.	Dick Sullivan	Dick Sullivan	1977	222
140⅜	21⅜	21⅛	15⅝	4⅜	4⅜	5	7	Lewis Co., Wash.	George Nichols	George Nichols	1964	222
140⅜	20⅞	22⅛	16⅝	4⅜	4⅜	5	5	Mendocino Co., Calif.	Clarence W. Nelson	Clarence W. Nelson	1948	222
140⅜	19	19⅞	16⅝	4⅞	4⅞	5	5	Lincoln Co., Oreg.	Darrel R. Grishaber	Darrel R. Grishaber	1984	222
140	21	20⅜	17	5	5	6	8	Snohomish Co., Wash.	Kenneth A. Peterson	Kenneth A. Peterson	1985	227
140	20⅜	20⅛	16	4⅞	4⅞	7	5	Polk Co., Oreg.	Harold E. Stepp	Harold E. Stepp	1970	227
140	22	21⅜	17⅞	4⅛	4⅛	5	5	Mendocino Co., Calif.	Roy Bergstrom	Roy Bergstrom	1966	227
140	21⅝	22⅜	19	4⅜	4⅜	4	4	Humboldt Co., Calif.	Carl A. Anderson	Carl A. Anderson	1980	227
139⅞	22⅜	20⅞	21⅜	5⅛	5	4	4	Trinity Co., Calif.	William J. Olson	William J. Olson	1981	227
139⅞	19	18	15⅝	4	4	4	4	Trinity Co., Calif.	Craig L. Brown	Craig & Joy Brown	1981	231
139⅞	20⅜	19⅞	18⅛	4⅜	4⅜	5	6	Siskiyou Co., Calif.	Roy Eastlick	Roy Eastlick	1954	231
139⅞	21⅛	21⅜	18⅝	4⅞	4⅞	5	5	Josephine Co., Oreg.	Richard H. Caswell	Richard H. Caswell	1969	233
139⅞	21⅝	22⅜	16	5	4	5	5	Thurston Co., Wash.	Eric Anderson	Eric Anderson	1937	233
139⅞	21⅜	21⅝	16	4⅛	4⅛	5	5	Shasta Co., Calif.	Warren Hunter	Warren Hunter	1964	233
139⅜	22⅜	21⅜	16	4⅞	4⅞	4	5	Lewis Co., Wash.	Kevin Pointer	Kevin Pointer	1972	236
139⅜	21⅛	21⅛	20⅜	3⅞	4⅜	5	5	Lane Co., Oreg.	Gene Tinker	Gene Tinker	1955	236
139⅜	21⅝	21⅜	17⅜	3⅜	3⅜	7	5	Jackson Co., Oreg.	Arthur A. Ekerson	Arthur A. Ekerson	1966	236
139⅜	21⅛	21⅛	17⅜	4	4⅜	5	5	Monmouth, Oreg.	Roy W. Miller	Roy W. Miller	1967	239
139⅜	20⅜	20⅜	15⅝	4⅜	4⅛	5	5	Whatcom Co., Wash.	Kim S. Scott	Kim S. Scott	1959	239
139⅜	24⅜	23⅜	21⅜	4⅞	4⅞	5	5	Trinity Co., Calif.	Andy Burgess	Andy Burgess	1964	239
139⅜	20⅜	20⅜	19⅜	4	4⅝	5	5	Marion Co., Oreg.	Richard A. Hart	Richard A. Hart	1982	239
139⅜	21⅜	21⅛	20⅜	4⅛	4⅛	5	5	Humboldt Co., Calif.	Jeff Bryant	Jeff Bryant	1964	243
139⅜	22	21⅜	18⅝	3⅜	3⅜	4	6	Trinity Co., Calif.	Gary L. Mayberry	Gary L. Mayberry	1968	243
139⅛	22⅜	21⅜	17⅜	4	5⅝	4	5	Mendocino Co., Calif.	John Winn, Jr.	John Winn, Jr.	1972	245
139⅛	21⅜	22	18⅜	3⅞	4⅜	3	4	Florence, Oreg.	Edwin C. Stevens	Warner Pinkney	1928	245
139	19⅜	19⅜	18⅜	4⅛	4	5	5	Douglas Co., Oreg.	Richard Wigle	Richard Wigle	1968	247
139	21⅛	22⅜	16⅝	4⅛	4⅜	5	5	Jefferson Co., Wash.	Picked Up	Aubrey F. Taylor	1947	247
139	20	20⅜	16⅝	4⅝	4⅜	5	5	Lewis Co., Wash.	Mike Cournyer	Mike Cournyer	1964	247
139	21⅜	21⅜	16⅝	3⅞	3⅞	5	5	Marion Co., Oreg.	Gene Collier	Gene Collier	1983	247
138⅞	21	22⅜	20⅜	4⅝	4⅜	4	4	Siskiyou Co., Calif.	Darrell Nowdesha	Darrell Nowdesha	1961	251

COLUMBIA BLACKTAIL DEER—Continued
Odocoileus hemionus columbianus

Score	Length of Main Beam R.	L.	Inside Spread	Circumference at Smallest Place Between Burr and First Point R.	L.	Number of Points R.	L.	Locality Killed	By Whom Killed	Owner	Date Killed	Rank
138⅞	19⅞	19⅞	15⅞	4⅞	4⅞	5	5	Pacific Co., Wash.	Russell Case	Russell Case	1956	251
138⅞	19⅞	20⅝	15⅜	5	4⅞	6	5	Trinity Co., Calif.	William O. Louderback	William O. Louderback	1963	251
138⅞	23⅞	24⅜	18⅜	4⅞	4⅞	5	5	Tiller, Oreg.	Ronald Elliott	Ronald Elliott	1963	251
138⅜	20⅜	21⅜	15⅜	5⅛	5⅞	6	7	Snohomish Co., Wash.	Walter J. Kau	Walter J. Kau	1950	255
138⅜	23⅜	23	15⅝	4⅞	4⅝	5	6	Pierce Co., Wash.	James Latimer	James Latimer	1962	255
138⅜	21⅜	20⅜	16	4	4⅛	5	5	Humboldt Co., Calif.	Larry Bowermaster	Larry Bowermaster	1964	255
138⅜	22	21⅜	23⅜	4⅜	4⅜	4	5	Trinity Co., Calif.	Charles E. Davy	Charles E. Davy	1983	259
138⅜	21	21	15⅜	5⅜	5	5	5	Clatsop Co., Oreg.	Russell L. Hemphill	Russell L. Hemphill	1972	260
138⅜	19⅜	19⅜	17⅜	4	4	6	6	Siskiyou Co., Calif.	John Carmichael	John Carmichael	1969	260
138¼	22⅜	22⅞	18⅜	4⅜	4	4	5	Mendocino Co., Calif.	Jess Jones	Jess Jones	1950	260
138⅜	21⅜	20	18⅜	4⅞	4	5	5	Siskiyou Co., Calif.	Bob Courts	Bob Courts	1965	263
138⅜	22⅜	22⅜	18	4⅞	4⅛	5	5	Humboldt Co., Calif.	Garry Hughes	Garry Hughes	1968	263
138⅜	22⅜	22	20⅜	4⅞	4⅝	5	5	Clackamas Co., Oreg.	J. B. Mitts	Wes Mitts	1896	263
138⅜	22⅜	22⅜	16⅜	5⅝	5⅝	6	6	Pierce Co., Wash.	George W. Halcott	George W. Halcott	1966	263
138⅜	23⅞	22⅜	22⅝	4⅜	4⅛	5	5	Siskiyou Co., Calif.	Loren L. Lutz	Loren L. Lutz	1964	267
138⅜	21⅜	21⅜	15⅜	4	3⅞	5	5	Tehama Co., Calif.	Robert L. Armanasco	Robert L. Armanasco	1968	267
138⅜	21	21	16⅜	5⅜	4⅞	5	5	Snohomish Co., Wash.	James McCarthy	James McCarthy	1961	267
138⅜	19⅜	19⅜	20⅜	4⅜	4⅜	6	5	Mendocino Co., Calif.	Walter R. Schubert	Walter R. Schubert	1952	267
138⅜	21⅝	22	17⅞	3⅜	3⅞	5	5	Trinity Co., Calif.	Thomas A. Pettigrew, Jr.	Thomas A. Pettigrew, Jr.	1972	267
138⅜	18⅜	18⅜	15⅜	4⅜	4⅜	5	5	Marion Co., Oreg.	Gene Collier	Gene Collier	1974	267
138⅜	18	18	14⅜	4⅛	4⅞	5	5	Mendocino Co., Calif.	Kenzia L. Drake	Kenzia L. Drake	1985	273
138⅛	18⅜	20⅜	17⅜	4⅜	4⅜	5	5	Columbia Co., Oreg.	Virginia L. Brown	Steve Crossley	1981	274
138	19⅜	19⅜	16⅜	4⅞	4⅞	5	6	Douglas Co., Oreg.	Will H. Brown	Will H. Brown	1948	274
138	19⅜	20⅜	15	4⅛	4⅜	5	5	Marion Co., Oreg.	Frank C. Bersin	Frank C. Bersin	1977	276
137⅞	19⅜	19⅜	18⅜	5	5	4	4	Santa Clara Co., Calif.	Farber L. Johnston, Jr.	Farber L. Johnston, Jr.	1967	276
137⅞	18	18⅜	18⅜	4	4	5	5	Trinity Co., Calif.	Picked Up	North Coast Tax.	1965	276
137⅞	18⅜	17⅜	17⅜	4	4⅜	5	5	Shasta Co., Calif.	Paul G. Carter	Paul G. Carter	1964	276
137⅞	20⅜	19⅜	18⅜	4⅜	4⅞	6	6	Yamhill Co., Oreg.	Wallace Hill	Wallace Hill	1963	276
137⅞	20⅜	20⅜	16⅞	4⅜	4⅝	5	6	Vancouver Island, B.C.	Gordie Simpson	Gordie Simpson	1966	276
137⅝	20⅜	20⅜	19⅜	4⅞	4⅞	5	5	Mendocino Co., Calif.	P. R. Borton	John R. Borton	1965	281

Score							Locality			Year	
137⅞	19⅞	19	17	4⅛	4⅛	5 5	Trinity Co., Calif.	Philip Grunert	Philip Grunert	1967	282
137⅞	21⅛	21⅛	19	4⅛	4⅜	5 5	Trinity Co., Calif.	Picked Up	Craig & Joy Brown	1982	282
137⅞	23⅜	23⅜	17⅜	4⅜	4⅜	4 4	Vancouver Island, B. C.	Herb Klein	Herb Klein	1964	284
137⅞	19⅞	20	15	4⅜	4⅛	5 5	Douglas Co., Oreg.	Francis R. Young	Francis R. Young	1972	285
137⅞	20⅜	20⅝	18	4⅛	4	5 5	Douglas Co., Oreg.	Bernard L. Den	Bernard L. Den	1934	285
137⅞	23	22⅜	22⅞	4	5	5 4	Tehama Co., Calif.	Clint Heiber	Clint Heiber	1977	287
137⅞	21⅜	19⅝	15⅝	4⅝	4⅝	5 5	Douglas Co., Oreg.	Peter Serafin	Peter Serafin	1932	287
137⅞	20⅝	20⅛	15⅝	4⅝	4⅝	5 5	Tillamook Co., Oreg.	Iola M. Pfaff	Iola M. Pfaff	1940	287
137	23⅞	21⅜	21⅜	4⅜	4⅜	4 5	King Co., Wash.	Douglas F. Dammarell	Douglas F. Dammarell	1974	290
137	20	19⅝	15⅝	4	4	5 5	Polk Co., Oreg.	Ralph Cooper	Ralph Cooper	1978	290
136⅞	21⅜	20⅞	17⅞	4⅝	4⅝	5 5	Lewis Co., Wash.	Allen J. Roehrick	Allen J. Roehrick	1968	292
136⅞	20⅝	21⅛	16	4⅝	4⅛	4 5	Pierce Co., Wash.	Patrick M. Blackwell	Patrick M. Blackwell	1971	293
136⅞	21⅜	21	14	5⅞	5⅞	5 5	King Co., Wash.	George B. Johnson	Ed Lochus	1930	293
136⅞	21⅛	23	18⅜	4⅞	4⅛	4 4	Shasta Co., Calif.	Vance Corrigan	Vance Corrigan	1957	293
136⅞	21⅜	22⅜	19	5⅞	5⅞	5 5	Arlington, Wash.	Ernest J. Kaesther	Ernest J. Kaesther	1959	293
136⅞	21⅜	22⅛	15⅝	4⅝	4⅝	5 5	Tillamook Co., Oreg.	J. A. Aaron	J. A. Aaron	1943	296
136⅞	20⅜	21⅛	15⅝	4⅛	4	4 4	Marion Co., Oreg.	Ronald A. Bersin	Ronald A. Bersin	1978	296
136⅞	20⅜	18	18	4⅛	4⅝	5 5	Ukiah, Calif.	Charles Tollini	Charles Tollini	1960	296
136⅞	23⅜	22⅜	18⅜	4⅝	4⅞	5 5	Lewis Co., Wash.	Larry F. Smith	Larry F. Smith	1964	299
136⅜	20⅜	20⅜	19⅜	4	4	4 4	Douglas Co., Oreg.	Gerry F. Edwards	Gerry F. Edwards	1971	299
136⅜	19⅜	20⅝	15⅛	4⅜	4⅞	5 5	Tillamook Co., Oreg.	Guy L. Thompson	Guy L. Thompson	1983	301
136⅜	21⅜	20⅝	17	4⅞	5⅞	5 5	Yamhill Co., Oreg.	Monty Dickey	Monty Dickey	1967	301
136⅜	20⅝	20⅝	16	3⅞	3⅝	4 4	Jackson Co., Oreg.	Ellis A. Jones	Martin S. Durbin	1921	303
136⅜	20⅝	20⅝	20⅝	3⅞	4⅛	4 5	Covelo, Calif.	David G. Cox	David G. Cox	1967	303
136⅜	20⅝	21	21⅛	3⅞	3⅞	5 5	Siskiyou Co., Calif.	Shirley Eastlick	Shirley Eastlick	1962	303
136	21⅛	21	19⅞	4	4⅞	5 4	Tehama Co., Calif.	Robert L. Armanasco	Robert L. Armanasco	1968	303
136	23⅜	23	21⅝	4⅞	4⅞	4 4	San Mateo Co., Calif.	Dan Caughey, Sr.	Dan Caughey, Sr.	1973	307
136	20⅝	19⅜	19	4⅛	4⅛	6 6	Trinity Co., Calif.	Richard G. Shelton	Richard G. Shelton	1973	307
136	21⅝	23	19	5⅞	5⅝	6 6	Santa Clara Co., Calif.	Mrs. Maitland Armstrong	Mrs. Maitland Armstrong	1956	307
136	21⅛	21	17	4⅞	4⅜	5 5	Mendocino Natl. For., Calif.	Edward Q. Garayalde	Edward Q. Garayalde	1966	307
135⅞	18⅝	19⅜	15⅜	4⅜	4⅝	4 4	Langley, B. C.	James G. Hill	Charles R. Yeomans	1959	312
135⅞	22⅜	22⅜	17⅜	4⅛	4⅛	5 5	Jackson Co., Oreg.	Mrs. Ila B. Bethany	Mrs. Ila B. Bethany	1972	312
135⅞	20⅝	21⅛	16⅞	5	5	5 5	Snohomish Co., Wash.	Edmund L. Hurst	Edmund L. Hurst	1984	312
135⅞	20⅝	19⅞	15	5⅝	5⅝	6 6	Whatcom Co., Wash.	Jack R. Teeter	Jack R. Teeter	1969	315
135⅞	20⅝	20⅝	19⅝	3⅝	3⅜	4 4	Trinity Co., Calif.	Roy J. Renner	Roy J. Renner	1965	315
135⅞	21⅜	21⅛	18⅜	4⅞	4⅞	5 5	Powell River, B. C.	Duncan Formby	Paddy Price	1939	315
135⅞	20⅝	20⅝	18	4	4	4 4	Linn Co., Oreg.	Gene Collier	Gene Collier	1966	315
135⅞	19⅜	19⅜	17⅝	4⅛	4⅛	4 4	Clallam Co., Wash.	Gary L. Smith	Gary L. Smith	1956	315
135⅞	20⅝	20⅝	16⅝	3⅞	3⅞	5 5	Lewis Co., Wash.	Oren Layton	Oren Layton	1977	319
135⅞	21⅜	21⅜	17⅝	4⅝	4⅝	6 6	Clark Co., Wash.	Francis E. Gillette	Francis E. Gillette	1934	320
135⅞	19⅜	19⅜	19⅜	5⅛	5⅛	7 8	Benton Co., Oreg.	H. G. Slocum	H. G. Slocum	1953	321
135⅞	20	15		3⅝	3⅜	4 4	Trinity Co., Calif.	Andy Burgess	Andy Burgess	1959	322

COLUMBIA BLACKTAIL DEER—*Continued*

Odocoileus hemionus columbianus

Score	Length of Main Beam R.	L.	Inside Spread	Circumference at Smallest Place Between Burr and First Point R.	L.	Number of Points R.	L.	Locality Killed	By Whom Killed	Owner	Date Killed	Rank
135⅝	19⅛	19⅜	13⅞	3⅞	3⅞	4	4	Humboldt Co., Calif.	Christopher A. Umbertus	Christopher A. Umbertus	1981	322
135	19	19⅜	15⅜	4⅛	4⅝	5	5	Humboldt Co., Calif.	Edward F. Burgess	Edward F. Burgess	1965	325
135	19⅛	19⅛	15⅜	4⅜	4⅜	5	5	Clackamas Co., Oreg.	Ray W. Bunnell	Ray W. Bunnell	1978	325
135	20	19⅞	16⅞	4⅛	4⅛	5	5	Whatcom Co., Wash.	Dennis R. Beebe	Dennis R. Beebe	1981	325
134⅞	21⅛	21⅜	14⅞	4⅛	4⅞	5	6	San Bernadino Co., Calif.	James Tacke	James Tacke	1966	328
134⅞	22⅜	22⅞	18⅜	4	4⅞	6	5	Tehama Co., Calif.	Mario Sereni, Jr.	Mario Sereni, Jr.	1964	328
134⅞	21⅛	21⅛	16⅛	3⅜	3⅝	4	4	Butte Falls, Oreg.	Bob Doan, Jr.	Bob Doan, Jr.	1973	328
134⅞	19⅝	20⅜	14⅜	4⅛	4⅛	5	5	Mendocino Co., Calif.	Jesse P. Foster, Jr.	Jesse P. Foster, Jr.	1964	328
134⅞	21⅝	23⅜	19⅝	4⅜	4⅜	5	5	Cowlitz Co., Wash.	Kenneth D. Nicholson	Kenneth D. Nicholson	1970	332
134⅝	19⅜	20	16⅜	4⅛	4⅛	5	5	Trinity Co., Calif.	Donald E. Stevens	Donald E. Stevens	1979	332
134⅜	20⅜	20⅜	15⅜	4⅜	4⅞	5	6	Siskiyou Co., Calif.	Roy Eastlick	Roy Eastlick	1965	334
134⅜	21⅝	22⅝	13	4⅜	4⅜	6	6	Lewis Co., Wash.	Douglas G. McArthur	Douglas G. McArthur	1967	335
134⅜	27⅛	27⅞	20⅜	4⅞	4⅝	5	4	Lewis Co., Wash.	Daniel E. Longmire	Daniel E. Longmire	1974	335
134⅜	26	20⅜	13	4⅜	4⅜	5	5	Shasta Co., Calif.	Jack Floyd	Jack Floyd	1957	335
134⅜	20	20⅜	23⅜	4⅜	4⅜	7	6	Trinity Co., Calif.	William M. Longhurst	William M. Longhurst	1951	335
134⅜	21⅛	21⅜	20⅜	4⅛	4⅜	4	6	Thurston Co., Wash.	Joseph Kominski	Joseph Kominski	1955	335
134⅜	22⅜	23⅜	18⅜	4⅜	4⅜	5	4	Humboldt Co., Calif.	J. A. Phelps	J. A. Phelps	1966	335
134⅜	19⅜	20	17	5⅜	5⅛	5	5	Sonoma Co., Calif.	Richard O'Farrell	Richard O'Farrell	1984	342
134⅜	22	21⅜	18⅜	5⅜	5⅛	5	4	Lewis Co., Wash.	Melvin B. Henle	Melvin B. Henle	1973	342
134⅜	18	15	17⅜	4⅜	4⅜	6	5	Toba Inlet, B.C.	L. Mitchell	Peters Sport Shop	1962	342
134⅜	21⅜	21⅜	19⅜	4⅜	4⅜	5	5	Benton Co., Oreg.	John E. Peterson	John E. Peterson	1965	342
134⅜	21⅜	21⅜	19⅜	4⅜	4⅜	5	5	Humboldt Co., Calif.	G. L. Dorris	G. L. Dorris	1973	345
134½	19⅜	21	16	4	4⅜	4	4	Pierce Co., Wash.	James B. August	James B. August	1971	345
134½	21⅜	22⅜	16	4⅜	4⅜	4	5	Douglas Co., Oreg.	John R. Hughey	John R. Hughey	1965	345
134⅜	20⅜	19⅜	16⅜	4⅜	4⅜	5	5	Colusa Co., Calif.	Gregory R. Bonetti	Gregory R. Bonetti	1983	345
134⅜	24⅛	23⅜	22⅜	4⅜	4⅜	4	4	Coos Co., Oreg.	Dan Woolley	Dan Woolley	1971	349
134⅜	20⅜	21⅜	19⅜	3⅜	3⅜	5	5	Mendocino Co., Calif.	Danny Pardini	Danny Pardini	1976	349
134⅜	19⅜	20	16⅜	4⅜	4⅜	5	5	King Co., Wash.	Greg E. Connell	Greg E. Connell	1979	349
134⅜	20⅜	20⅜	14⅜	4⅜	4	6	5	Trinity Co., Calif.	David Deininger	David Deininger	1980	349
134	18⅜	19⅜	16⅜	3⅜	3⅜	7	5	Siskiyou Co., Calif.	Alicia Whittaker	Alicia Whittaker	1970	353
133⅞	19⅜	21⅜	13⅜	3⅜	3⅜	5	5	Siskiyou Co., Calif.	William E. Turner	William E. Turner	1982	354

Score	Length of Main Beam R	Length of Main Beam L	Inside Spread	Circumference R	Circumference L	Points R	Points L	Locality	Hunter	Owner	Date Killed	Rank
133⅜	20⅞	21⅜	18⅛	4⅞	5⅞	6	6	Pierce Co., Wash.	K. S. Sheets	K. S. Sheets	1966	355
133⅜	21⅞	21⅜	17⅞	4⅜	4⅜	5	4	Mendocino Co., Calif.	Marvin DeAngelis	Marvin DeAngelis	1978	355
133⅜	22⅝	21⅛	18⅛	5⅝	5⅛	6	4	Linn Co., Oreg.	Richard L. Rounds	Richard L. Rounds	1978	357
133⅜	19	19⅜	15⅞	4⅛	4⅜	5	6	Clackamas Co., Oreg.	Richard K. Hughes	Richard K. Hughes	1981	357
133⅜	22	20⅜	20⅛	4⅜	4⅛	5	6	Trinity Co., Calif.	George M. Moxon	George M. Moxon	1977	359
133⅜	20⅜	19⅞	15⅞	5⅝	4⅛	5	5	Clackamas Co., Oreg.	C. A. Pond	C. A. Pond	1940	359
133⅜	19⅜	20⅜	17⅞	4	4	5	5	Coos Co., Oreg.	Toby J. Johnson	Toby J. Johnson	1981	359
133⅜	18⅞	19⅜	18	3⅞	4	6	6	Josephine Co., Oreg.	Randy L. Hansen	Randy L. Hansen	1981	359
133⅜	21	22⅛	17⅛	4⅝	5	6	5	Trinity Co., Calif.	Barry Griffin	Barry Griffin	1976	359
133⅜	19⅜	19⅛	18⅜	4	3⅞	6	5	Lane Co., Oreg.	John D. Woodmark	John D. Woodmark	1969	364
133⅜	18⅝	19⅜	17⅞	4⅜	4	6	6	Coos Co., Oreg.	Frank Neal	Foster H. Thompson	1924	364
133⅜	18⅝	18⅝	20⅜	4⅝	4⅜	9	9	Mendocino Co., Calif.	O. E. Schubert	Walter R. Schubert	1917	364
133⅜	21⅛	20⅜	16⅜	4⅛	4⅛	5	5	Marion Co., Oreg.	Gene Collier	Gene Collier	1984	364
133⅜	19	19⅜	17	4⅛	4	4	4	Clackamas Co., Oreg.	Mary A. Schoenborn	Mary A. Schoenborn	1971	368
133⅜	20⅜	20⅜	14⅛	4⅝	4⅝	5	5	Pierce Co., Wash.	Lowell Apple	Lowell Apple	1968	368
133⅜	21⅛	21⅛	13⅜	4⅝	4⅝	5	5	Skagit Co., Wash.	L. A. Willoughby	L. A. Willoughby	1951	368
133⅜	20	19⅞	14⅜	4⅛	4⅜	5	5	Linn Co., Oreg.	Leon Plueard	Leon Plueard	1965	368
133⅜	20⅜	20⅜	17	4⅛	4⅛	5	5	Trinity Co., Calif.	Ralph L. Perry	Ralph L. Perry	1980	368
133⅛	19⅛	18⅝	16	3⅞	3⅜	5	5	Trinity Co., Calif.	Kirk Finch	Kirk Finch	1975	374
133⅛	22⅝	22	21⅛	4⅝	5	5	5	Trinity Co., Calif.	Hugh A. Dow	Hugh A. Dow	1969	374
133⅛	19⅜	19⅜	15⅞	4⅛	4⅛	5	5	Josephine Co., Oreg.	Michael J. Collins	Michael J. Collins	1983	374
133⅛	18⅝	18⅝	13⅜	4⅛	4⅛	5	5	Langley, B.C.	Frank Jackson	Brooke Whitelaw	1935	374
133	23⅜	23	20⅜	3⅞	4⅜	5	5	Lane Co., Oreg.	Picked Up	Wayne E. Everett	1971	378
133	22⅜	23⅜	20⅛	5⅝	4⅝	5	5	Lewis Co., Wash.	George Sevey	George Sevey	1941	378
132⅞	20⅜	20⅜	19⅜	4⅜	5	4	4	Napa Co., Calif.	Fred C. Framsted	Fred C. Framsted	1966	380
132⅞	21⅜	23⅜	19⅛	4⅜	4⅜	6	5	Tehama Co., Calif.	Joe McBrayer	Joe McBrayer	1981	380
132⅞	18⅜	19⅜	19⅜	4⅛	4⅜	5	5	Clackamas Co., Oreg.	Kerry L. Schoenborn	Kerry L. Schoenborn	1978	382
132⅞	19⅜	19⅜	18⅛	4⅜	4⅜	5	5	Mendocino Co., Calif.	Mason Geisinger	Mason Geisinger	1967	382
132⅞	21	21	16⅜	3⅝	3⅞	5	5	Tehama Co., Calif.	Daniel E. Osborne	Daniel E. Osborne	1956	382
132⅞	19⅜	17⅞	21⅜	4⅜	4⅜	5	4	Mendocino Co., Calif.	Jay M. Gates III	Jay M. Gates III	1984	385
132⅝	22	22⅝	21⅜	5	4⅞	4	4	Lewis Co., Wash.	Robert L. Peck	Robert L. Peck	1964	385
132⅝	19	18⅜	14	4⅜	4⅝	5	5	Linn Co., Oreg.	Gene Collier	Gene Collier	1964	385
132⅝	19⅜	20⅜	16⅝	4⅝	4⅜	5	5	Clackamas Co., Oreg.	Katherine M. Searls	Katherine M. Searls	1982	388
132⅜	20⅜	19⅞	15⅜	3⅞	4	5	5	Cowlitz Co., Wash.	James H. Wilson	James H. Wilson	1959	388
132⅜	19⅞	19	19	5⅝	5⅞	5	5	Grays Harbor Co., Wash.	Jack A. Allen	Jack A. Allen	1963	388
132⅜	21⅜	21⅜	16⅜	4	4	5	5	Trinity Co., Calif.	David L. Matley	David L. Matley	1981	388
132⅜	22⅜	22	19	4⅛	5⅛	4	4	Siskiyou Co., Calif.	Lawrence F. Weckerle	Lawrence F. Weckerle	1982	392
132⅜	18⅞	19⅞	18⅛	5	4	5	5	Island Co., Wash.	Bert Klineburger	Bert Klineburger	1969	392
132⅜	20⅜	20⅜	16⅜	4⅝	5⅛	5	5	Mendocino Co., Calif.	P. R. Borton	William R. Borton	1971	392
132⅜	19⅞	18⅞	18⅜	4⅜	4⅝	4	4	Douglas Co., Oreg.	William McCaleb	William McCaleb	1963	392
132⅜	21⅜	21⅛	12⅜	4⅝	5⅝	5	5	Humboldt Co., Calif.	Guy Hooper	Guy Hooper	1977	396
132⅛	21⅜	19⅜	14⅜	4⅛	4⅝	4	4	Mendocino Co., Calif.	Fred E. Borton II	Matthew E. Borton	1971	396
132⅛	20⅜	20⅜	15⅛	5⅛	5⅛	4	4	Trinity Co., Calif.	R. C. Kauffman	R. C. Kauffman	1936	396

COLUMBIA BLACKTAIL DEER—Continued

Odocoileus hemionus columbianus

Score	Length of Main Beam R.	Length of Main Beam L.	Inside Spread	Circumference at Smallest Place Between Burr and First Point R.	Circumference at Smallest Place Between Burr and First Point L.	Number of Points R.	Number of Points L.	Locality Killed	By Whom Killed	Owner	Date Killed	Rank
132⅛	21⅛	20⅜	13⅛	4⅜	4⅜	5	5	Lewis Co., Wash.	George W. Rodrick III	George W. Rodrick III	1980	396
132⅛	20	19⅝	18⅛	4	4	5	5	Trinity Co., Calif.	Ronald L. Schneider	Ronald L. Schneider	1979	396
131⅞	19⅝	19⅜	14	4	3⅞	5	5	Siskiyou Co., Calif.	Sid E. Ziegler	Sid E. Ziegler	1957	400
131⅞	21	19⅜	18	5	5	5	5	Trinity Co., Calif.	Carter B. Dow	Carter B. Dow	1961	400
131⅞	20⅜	20	18⅜	3⅞	4	5	5	Trinity Co., Calif.	Kenneth L. Cogle, Jr.	Kenneth L. Cogle, Jr.	1981	400
131⅝	18⅜	19⅜	13⅝	5⅛	4⅞	6	5	Trinity Co., Calif.	Melvin M. Clair	Melvin M. Clair	1979	404
131⅝	19⅝	19⅝	14⅞	4⅞	4⅞	5	5	Whatcom Co., Wash.	C. H. Head	C. H. Head	1972	404
131½	19⅝	18⅝	14⅝	4⅛	4⅞	5	5	Humboldt Co., Calif.	Larry Wilson	Larry Wilson	1978	406
131½	19⅝	20⅜	16⅝	4⅜	4⅜	5	5	Tillamook Co., Oreg.	Ted Wolcott	Ted Wolcott	1943	406
131½	18	18⅜	14⅜	4⅜	4⅜	5	5	Lane Co., Oreg.	Helen Sanderlin	Helen Sanderlin	1966	406
131¼	18⅜	18⅝	16⅝	5⅞	5⅛	5	6	Lewis Co., Wash.	Ron N. Nilson	Ron N. Nilson	1963	409
131⅛	19	19	16⅛	4⅜	4⅜	4	4	Lincoln Co., Oreg.	Bert Kessi	Bert Kessi	1942	410
131⅛	19⅛	17⅞	13⅝	4⅜	4⅜	5	5	Estacada, Oreg.	Roy Tracy	Lamont Rumgay	1967	410
131⅛	24⅛	24	19⅞	4⅛	4⅜	5	4	Polk Co., Oreg.	Ray Burtis	Ray Burtis	1960	410
131	21⅛	20⅞	13⅝	4⅞	4⅞	7	6	Skamania Co., Wash.	Thomas E. Krebs	Thomas E. Krebs	1977	413
131	18⅛	17⅞	15⅜	3⅞	4	5	5	Siskiyou Co., Calif.	George Quigley	George Quigley	1971	413
131	21⅛	20⅜	15⅛	4⅜	4⅜	5	5	King Co., Wash.	J. A. Ryezek	George B. Johnson	1935	413
131	17⅞	17⅜	14⅜	4⅜	4⅛	5	5	Jackson Co., Oreg.	Robert R. Maben	Robert R. Maben	1963	413
130⅞	18⅜	18⅜	18⅛	4⅛	4⅜	5	5	Siskiyou Co., Calif.	Raymond Whittaker	Raymond Whittaker	1981	417
130⅞	20⅞	20⅝	16⅝	3⅞	3⅞	5	5	Tehama Co., Calif.	James D. Fiske	James D. Fiske	1956	418
130⅞	20⅝	19	19	4⅜	4	5	4	Mendocino Co., Calif.	Tom Enberg	Tom Enberg	1970	418
130⅞	21⅜	21⅛	19⅛	4	4⅛	8	6	Siskiyou Co., Calif.	Larry E. Richey	Larry E. Richey	1956	418
130⅞	22	22	16	4⅜	4⅜	5	5	Linn Co., Oreg.	Gene Collier	Gene Collier	1967	418
130⅞	19⅜	19⅜	14⅜	4⅛	4⅜	5	5	Yamhill Co., Oreg.	Picked Up	John N. Washburn	1984	418
130⅝	19⅜	20	16⅜	4⅛	4⅜	5	6	Jackson Co., Oreg.	Roy D. Hugie	Univ. of Mont. Mus.	1983	423
130⅝	18	20	17⅛	5	5	6	6	Lake Co., Calif.	Bernard Domries	Bernard Domries	1940	423
130⅜	24⅜	23⅜	23⅜	4⅜	4⅜	4	5	Siskiyou Co., Calif.	Vernon Sutherlin	Vernon Sutherlin	1961	425
130⅜	21⅝	21⅞	18⅝	5⅜	4⅞	5	5	Mendocino Co., Calif.	Mitchell A. Thorson	Mitchell A. Thorson	1969	425
130⅜	20⅝	20⅜	12⅞	4⅜	4⅜	3	5	Cowlitz Co., Wash.	Michael A. Demery	Steven J. Hellem	1978	425
130⅜	20⅝	20⅝	17⅜	4⅜	4⅜	5	5	Pierce Co., Wash.	Don Argo	Don Argo	1950	425
130⅜	21	19⅝	15⅝	4⅞	4⅜	6	4	Santa Cruz Co., Calif.	William J. McGrath	William J. McGrath	1982	425
130⅜	20	20	16⅜	4	4	5	5	Siskiyou Co., Calif.	John Carmichael	John Carmichael	1970	429

130⅜	19⅜	18⅜	15⅜	4⅞	4⅞	5	5	Mt. Jupiter, Wash.	Jack Dustin	Jack Dustin	1946	429
130⅜	20	20	16⅞	4⅞	4⅞	5	5	Clackamas Co., Oreg.	Thomas A. Tremain	Thomas A. Tremain	1976	431
130	17⅞	17⅞	16	4⅜	4⅜	5	5	Cowlitz Co., Wash.	Harold E. Koenig	Harold E. Koenig	1949	432
172⅞*	26⅜	25⅞	20⅞	5⅜	5⅜	7	7	Marion Co., Oreg.	B. G. Shurtleff	B. G. Shurtleff	1969	
170⅞*	25⅞	25⅞	20⅞	4⅝	4⅞	5	5	Jackson Co., Oreg.	Dennis R. King	King Tax. Studios	1970	
162⅝*	24⅛	25⅛	18⅝	5⅞	5⅞	7	8	Clackamas Co., Oreg.	Curtis A. Lee	Steve Crossley	1981	
162⅜*	23⅛	22⅜	21	5⅞	5⅞	5	5	Jackson Co., Oreg.	Mickey Geary	Mickey Geary	1973	
161⅞*	24	23⅜	19⅞	4⅞	4⅞	5	5	Clackamas Co., Oreg.	Darrell Stewart	Darrell Stewart	1977	
152⅝*	23⅞	22⅞	18⅞	5	5⅞	5	4	Trinity Co., Calif.	Larry Brown	Larry Brown	1979	

*Final Score subject to revision by additional verifying measurements

NEW WORLD'S RECORD SITKA BLACKTAIL DEER
SCORE: 123 4/8
Locality: Uganik Bay, Alaska Date: 1983
Hunter and owner: Donna D. Braendel

NUMBER TWO SITKA BLACKTAIL DEER
SCORE: 117 1/8
Locality: Baird Peak, Alaska Date: 1984
Hunter and owner: William C. Dunham

Sitka Blacktail Deer

Odocoileus hemionus sitkensis

Minimum Score 108

Sitka blacktail deer includes trophies from coastal Alaska and Queen Charlotte Islands of British Columbia.

Score	Length of Main Beam R.	L.	Inside Spread	Circumference at Smallest Place Between First and Second Points R.	L.	Number of Points R.	L.	Locality Killed	By Whom Killed	Owner	Date Killed	Rank
123⅜	21⅜	20⅜	17⅜	3⅞	3⅞	4	4	Uganik Bay, Alaska	Donna D. Braendel	Donna D. Braendel	1983	1
117⅛	16⅜	16⅜	13⅜	4⅛	4⅜	5	6	Baird Peak, Alaska	William C. Dunham	William C. Dunham	1984	2
116	17⅜	16⅝	16	4⅛	3⅞	5	5	Kiliuda Bay, Alaska	Timothy Tittle	Timothy Tittle	1984	3
114⅞	15⅞	16⅛	14⅜	3⅞	4	5	6	Control Lake, Alaska	Timothy C. Winsenberg	Timothy C. Winsenberg	1985	4
113⅜	18⅜	18⅛	15⅝	3⅜	3⅜	4	4	Viekoda Bay, Alaska	Edward R. Hajdys	Edward R. Hajdys	1980	5
113⅜	17⅝	18⅞	16⅛	3⅞	3⅞	5	5	Wadding Cove, Alaska	Kurt W. Kuehl	Kurt W. Kuehl	1984	6
109⅞	17⅞	17⅜	14⅛	4⅜	4⅛	5	5	Cleveland Pen., Alaska	Dennis E. Northrup	Dennis E. Northrup	1983	7
109⅜	19	17⅞	17⅞	3⅜	3⅞	4	4	Uganik Bay, Alaska	Harvey D. Harms	Harvey D. Harms	1982	8
109⅛	18⅜	18	16⅞	4	3⅞	5	5	Ugak Bay, Alaska	Donald H. Tetzlaff	Donald H. Tetzlaff	1984	9
109	17⅞	16⅝	16⅞	4	4	5	5	Uganik Bay, Alaska	Karl G. Braendel	Karl G. Braendel	1982	10
108⅝	17⅞	17⅜	15⅞	3⅜	3⅞	5	5	Barling Bay, Alaska	Guy C. Powell	Guy C. Powell	1984	11
108⅜	18⅞	19⅞	15⅞	4⅞	4⅞	7	5	Whale Passage, Alaska	Howard W. Honsey	Howard W. Honsey	1985	12
120⅜*	17⅞	17⅞	15⅞	4⅜	4⅜	5	5	Boulder Bay, Alaska	Ronald D. Swingle	Ronald D. Swingle	1983	
118⅜*	17⅞	19⅞	17⅞	4⅛	4⅛	5	5	Uganik Lake, Alaska	Robert D. Gilliland	Robert D. Gilliland	1983	
118⅛*	16⅞	17⅞	14⅛	4	4⅜	5	5	Long Island, Alaska	Daniel G. Bowden	Daniel G. Bowden	1981	
112⅞*	17	18	15⅞	3⅞	3⅞	5	5	Kodiak Island, Alaska	Gene Coughlin	Gene Coughlin	1984	

* Final Score subject to revision by additional verifying measurements

WORLD'S RECORD WHITETAIL DEER (TYPICAL ANTLERS)
SCORE: 206 1/8
Locality: Burnett County, Wisconsin Date: 1914
Hunter: James Jordon Owner: Charles T. Arnold

NUMBER TWO WHITETAIL DEER (TYPICAL ANTLERS)
SCORE: 205
Locality: Randolph County, Missouri Date: 1971
Hunter and owner: Larry W. Gibson

Whitetail Deer (*Typical Antlers*)

Odocoileus virginianus virginianus and certain related subspecies

Minimum Score 170

Score	Length of Main Beam R.	L.	Inside Spread	Circumference at Smallest Place Between Burr and First Point R.	L.	Number of Points R.	L.	Locality Killed	By Whom Killed	Owner	Date Killed	Rank
206⅛	30	30	20⅝	6⅝	6⅝	5	5	Burnett Co., Wisc.	James Jordan	Charles T. Arnold	1914	1
205	26⅝	25⅛	24⅛	4⅞	4⅞	6	6	Randolph Co., Mo.	Larry W. Gibson	Larry W. Gibson	1971	2
204⅞	27⅛	26⅛	23⅜	6⅛	6⅛	7	6	Peoria Co., Ill.	M. J. Johnson	M. J. Johnson	1965	3
204⅞	26⅛	22⅞	25⅛	5⅛	5⅛	7	10	Beaverdam Creek, Alta.	Stephen Jansen	Stephen Jansen	1967	4
202	31⅛	31	23⅞	5⅞	6	8	8	Beltrami Co., Minn.	John A. Breen	Charles T. Arnold	1918	5
200⅞	26⅛	27⅛	24	5	4⅞	6	7	Whitkow, Sask.	Peter J. Swistun	Peter J. Swistun	1983	6
199⅞	27⅛	26⅞	20	5⅞	5⅞	8	5	Clark Co., Mo.	Jeffrey A. Brunk	Jeffrey A. Brunk	1969	7
199⅜	27⅜	27⅛	22⅞	4⅞	4⅞	6	7	Missoula Co., Mont.	Thomas H. Dellwo	Thomas H. Dellwo	1974	8
198⅜	29⅜	29⅛	18⅛	4⅞	4⅞	6	8	Allegany Co., N.Y.	Roosevelt Luckey	N. Y. Cons. Dept.	1939	9
198⅜	27⅛	26⅞	20⅛	5	5	6	8	Nemaha Co., Kan.	Dennis P. Finger	Dennis P. Finger	1974	10
196⅞	28⅛	27⅜	24⅞	4⅞	4⅞	8	6	Maverick Co., Texas	Tom McCulloch	McLean Bowman	1963	11
195⅞	28⅛	27⅛	22⅞	5⅞	5⅞	6	7	Marshall Co., Minn.	Robert Sands	Robert Sands	1960	12
194⅞	25⅛	25⅛	18⅛	5⅛	5⅜	7	7	Monroe Co., Iowa	Lloyd Goad	Lloyd Goad	1962	13
194⅞	30⅛	30⅜	24⅞	5⅜	5⅜	9	7	Vigo Co., Ind.	D. Bates & S. Winkler	D. Bates & S. Winkler	1983	14
194⅛	30	30⅛	19⅛	4⅞	5	6	7	Dakota Co., Neb.	E. Keith Fahrenholz	E. Keith Fahrenholz	1966	15
193⅞	24⅛	24⅛	18⅛	5	5	7	7	Christopher Lake, Sask.	Jerry Thorson	Jerry Thorson	1959	16
193⅞	28⅛	28⅛	21⅛	4⅛	4⅛	5	7	Itasca Co., Minn.	Picked Up	Paul M. Shaw	1935	17
193	25⅛	26	25	5⅜	5⅝	6	6	South Dakota	Unknown	Eugene J. Lodermeier	1964	18
192⅞	27⅛	27⅛	19⅜	4⅞	4⅞	8	9	York Co., Maine	Alphonse Chase	Earl Taylor	1920	19
192⅞	27⅛	27⅛	22⅞	4⅛	4⅛	8	7	Frio Co., Texas	Basil Dailey	David M. Dailey	1903	20
192	27⅛	28	19⅜	4⅛	4⅛	8	9	Lyman Co., S.D.	Bob Weidner	E. N. Eichler	1957	21
191⅞	27	26	19⅝	4⅛	4⅛	5	6	Hudson Bay, Sask.	George Chalus	George Chalus	1973	22
191⅞	26⅛	26⅛	19	5⅛	5	6	7	Flathead Co., Mont.	Earl T. McMaster	McLean Bowman	1963	23
191⅛	26⅛	27⅛	20	4⅞	5	6	7	Chautauqua Co., Kan.	Michael A. Young	Michael A. Young	1973	24
191⅛	31⅛	31⅛	27⅞	6⅛	6⅛	5	6	Vilas Co., Wisc.	Robert Hunter	May Docken	1910	25
190⅞	22⅛	23⅜	19⅛	4⅞	4⅞	7	6	Buffalo Lake, Alta.	Eugene L. Boll	Eugene L. Boll	1969	26
190	24⅛	25⅞	20⅛	5	5	7	6	Dimmit Co., Texas	C. P. Howard	C. P. Howard	1950	27
189⅞	29⅛	29⅞	21⅛	4⅞	4⅞	5	6	Tabor, S.D.	Duane Graber	Sam Peterson	1954	28
189⅞	28⅛	27⅛	21⅛	4⅞	4⅞	5	5	St. Landry Parish, La.	Leonce Mallet	Johnny M. Hollier	1965	28

WHITETAIL DEER (*Typical Antlers*)—*Continued*

Odocoileus virginianus virginianus and certain related subspecies

Score	Length of Main Beam R.	L.	Inside Spread	Circumference at Smallest Place Between Burr and First Point R.	L.	Number of Points R.	L.	Locality Killed	By Whom Killed	Owner	Date Killed	Rank
189⅞	28⅜	27⅜	20⅛	4⅛	4⅛	5	5	McKenzie Co., N.D.	Gene Veeder	McLean Bowman	1972	30
189⅝	25⅞	24⅛	23⅛	6⅝	6⅝	6	7	Fillmore Co., Minn.	Tom Norby	Tom Norby	1975	30
189⅛	28	28⅛	23⅝	4⅝	4⅝	5	7	Blaine Co., Mont.	Kenneth Morehouse	Kenneth Morehouse	1959	32
189⅛	27⅝	26⅝	25⅞	5⅛	5⅝	6	6	Nuckolls Co., Neb.	Van Shotzman	an Shotzman	1968	32
188⅞	27⅝	26⅞	18⅜	4⅝	4⅝	8	7	Dimmit Co., Texas	William Henry Pease	Jeff Vick Pease	1932	34
188⅞	25	26⅜	22⅝	4⅞	4⅞	5	6	Burstall, Sask.	W. P. Rolick	W. P. Rolick	1957	35
188⅛	27⅜	24⅝	22⅞	5⅝	5⅝	5	5	Metiskow, Alta.	Norman T. Salminen	Norman T. Salminen	1977	35
187⅞	25⅝	26⅜	19	4⅝	5⅛	5	5	Johnson Co., Iowa	Gregg R. Redlin	Gregg R. Redlin	1983	37
187⅞	28⅝	27⅞	19⅞	5	5	6	8	Starr Co., Texas	Picked Up	Jack F. Quist	1945	38
187⅞	25	25⅞	20⅛	5⅝	5⅝	6	6	Emmons Co., N.D.	Joseph F. Bosch	Joseph F. Bosch	1959	38
187⅞	29⅝	31⅛	23⅛	5⅝	5⅛	6	6	Cherokee Co., Iowa	Dennis R. Vaudt	Dennis R. Vaudt	1975	38
187⅝	25⅝	25⅝	19⅝	5⅝	5⅜	8	8	Winona Co., Minn.	Ken W. Koenig	Ken W. Koenig	1976	38
187⅝	26⅝	26⅜	15⅝	5⅝	5⅝	6	6	Montana	Unknown	Johnny M. Hollier	PR1984	38
187⅜	28⅜	27	24⅝	5⅜	5⅜	8	5	Winona Co., Minn.	Dan Groebner	Dan Groebner	1974	43
187⅜	31⅛	30⅝	30⅜	4⅝	4⅝	7	8	Warren Co., Iowa	Dwight E. Green	Dwight E. Green	1964	44
187⅜	29	28⅝	26⅝	5⅝	5⅜	5	5	Lyon Co., Minn.	Lynn Jackson	J. D. Andrews	1967	44
187⅛	26	26⅝	19⅝	4⅝	4⅝	6	8	Scotland Co., Mo.	Robin Berhorst	Robin Berhorst	1971	44
187⅛	26⅝	26⅝	19⅝	4⅝	4⅝	6	7	Cooper Co., Mo.	Joe Ditto	Joe Ditto	1974	47
186⅞	26⅝	26⅝	18⅞	4⅝	4⅞	6	6	Pulaski Co., Ky.	Scott Abbott	Scott Abbott	1982	47
186⅞	25⅝	25⅜	20⅛	4⅞	5	5	5	Arkansas Co., Ark.	Walter Spears	Walter Spears	1952	49
186⅞	27⅜	27⅞	19⅝	5	5⅝	7	8	Atchison Co., Mo.	Mike Moody	Mike Moody	1968	49
186⅜	27⅝	27⅛	20⅛	5⅞	5⅞	7	6	Morris Co., Kan.	Garold D. Miller	Garold D. Miller	1969	51
186⅜	30⅛	29	22⅝	4⅝	4⅝	5	5	Flathead Co., Mont.	Unknown	Wayne D. Williamson	1973	51
186⅜	26⅝	27⅞	20⅝	5⅝	5⅝	8	7	Ontonagon Co., Mich.	Unknown	Mac's Taxidermy	1980	51
186⅜	25⅝	25⅜	21	4⅝	4⅝	6	6	La Salle Co., Texas	Herman C. Schliesing	Herman C. Schliesing	1967	54
186⅜	25	25⅜	22⅜	5	5⅜	6	7	Laclede Co., Mo.	Larry Ogle	Larry Ogle	1972	54
186⅜	27⅜	27⅛	18	4⅞	4⅞	8	10	Kenedy Co., Texas	Jack Van Cleve III	McGill Estate	1972	54
186⅜	28⅝	29⅝	19	5⅛	5⅛	8	5	Hancock Co., Maine	Gerald C. Murray	Gerald C. Murray	1984	54
186⅛	25⅛	26⅜	20⅛	4⅞	4⅞	6	5	Roane Co., Tenn.	W. A. Foster	W. A. Foster	1959	58
186⅛	28	26⅝	21⅛	6	6⅛	8	5	Waupaca Co., Wisc.	Fred Penny	Dale Trinrud	1963	58

Score								Locality	Hunter	Owner	Date	Rank
186⅝	29⅞	29⅞	21	4⅜	4⅜	8	9	Zavala Co., Texas	Picked Up	Paul W. Sanders, Jr.	1965	58
186	30⅜	31⅜	26⅜	5⅛	5	5	9	Itasca Co., Minn.	Knud W. Jensen	Wayne Williamson	1955	61
186	25⅜	25	19	4⅜	4⅜	6	6	Flathead Co., Mont.	Douglas G. Mefford	Douglas G. Mefford	1966	61
185⅝	24⅜	25	19⅜	4⅜	4⅜	6	8	Nenzel, Neb.	Richard Kehr	Richard Kehr	1965	63
185⅝	26⅜	27⅛	22	4⅝	4⅜	6	6	Otter Tail Co., Minn.	Orris T. Neirby	Orris T. Neirby	1942	64
185⅝	26⅛	27	19⅛	5⅛	5⅛	7	10	Marshall Co., Minn.	Donald W. Wilkens	Donald W. Wilkens	1973	65
185⅝	27⅜	28	20⅛	4⅞	4⅞	5	5	Canwood, Sask.	Clark Heimbechner	Clark Heimbechner	1984	65
185⅝	27⅜	27⅛	19⅛	5⅜	5	6	7	Harrison Co., Iowa	Marvin E. Tippery	Marvin E. Tippery	1971	67
185⅝	26⅞	27⅛	23⅛	4⅝	5⅛	6	7	Franklin Co., Ind.	Gayle Fritsch	Gayle Fritsch	1972	67
185	30	29⅜	30⅜	5⅜	5⅝	8	8	Todd Co., Ky.	C. W. Shelton	McLean Bowman	1964	69
185	28⅜	28⅜	18⅜	4⅜	4⅜	5	5	Vernon Co., Wisc.	Harold Christianson	Harold Christianson	1968	69
184⅞	26⅞	27	24⅜	5⅜	5⅜	6	9	Desha Co., Ark.	Lee Perry	Walter Brock	1961	71
184⅞	24⅝	26⅜	21⅜	5⅜	5⅜	6	6	Dore Lake, Sask.	Garvis C. Coker	Garvis C. Coker	1971	71
184⅞	26⅜	26⅜	20⅜	4⅜	4⅜	6	6	Greene Co., Pa.	Ivan Parry	Ivan Parry	1974	71
184⅞	26⅜	26⅜	27	5⅜	5⅜	5	7	Delaware Co., Iowa	R. E. Stewart	R. E. Stewart	1953	74
184⅞	28⅜	28⅜	22⅞	5⅜	5⅜	7	7	Bossier Co., La.	Earnest O. McCoy	Lucille McCoy	1961	75
184⅞	23⅜	23⅜	17	5	4⅜	6	5	Fayette Co., Tenn.	Benny M. Johnson	Benny M. Johnson	1979	75
184⅞	30⅛	30⅜	20⅛	5⅜	5⅛	7	6	Chase Co., Kan.	Thomas D. Mosher	Thomas D. Mosher	1984	75
184⅝	28⅜	29	25⅝	5⅝	5⅞	5	6	Kingsbury Co., S.D.	Rudy F. Weigel	Rudy F. Weigel	1960	78
184⅝	26	26⅝	20⅜	5⅛	5⅛	5	6	Paulding Co., Ga.	Floyd Benson	Floyd Benson	1962	78
184⅝	28⅜	27⅜	24	5	5	6	5	Franklin Parish, La.	H. B. Womble	Carey B. McCoy	1914	80
184⅝	27	26	27⅜	6	6¼	8	6	Muskingum Co., Ohio	Dale Hartberger	Dale Hartberger	1981	80
184⅛	26⅞	27⅜	21	5	5	5	7	Marshall Co., Minn.	Alvin C. Westerlund	Alvin C. Westerlund	1953	82
184	29	31	31	4⅜	5	8	5	Vinton Co., Ohio	Dan F. Allison	Dan F. Allison	1965	82
184	27⅞	28⅜	18⅜	5	4⅜	6	6	Newton Co., Ga.	Gene Almand	Gene Almand	1966	84
183⅞	24⅝	25⅜	18⅜	5	4⅜	5	6	Menominee Co., Wisc.	Keith Miller	Charles Loberg	1969	84
183⅞	27⅞	27⅜	20⅛	5⅜	5⅜	6	7	Taylor Co., Iowa	Wayne Swartz	Spanky Greenville	1947	86
183⅞	25⅝	25	27	5	6⅛	7	6	Webb Co., Texas	Henderson Coquat	Henderson Coquat	1949	86
183⅜	28	28	19⅜	5⅜	4⅜	7	5	Forest Co., Wisc.	James M. Thayer	James M. Thayer	1980	86
183⅜	26⅞	26⅞	18	5	5⅜	5	7	Pepin Co., Wisc.	LaVerne Anibas	LaVerne Anibas	1965	89
183⅜	26⅞	27⅛	19⅜	5⅜	5⅜	7	7	Clinton Co., Ind.	Stuart C. Snodgrass	Stuart C. Snodgrass	1977	89
183⅜	26	26	23⅜	4⅜	4⅜	6	6	Buffalo Co., Wisc.	Lee F. Spittler	Mrs. Lee F. Spittler	1953	91
183⅜	26⅝	26⅞	18⅜	5⅜	5⅜	7	6	Sumner, Mo.	Marvin F. Lentz	Marvin F. Lentz	1968	92
183⅜	23⅜	23⅜	19⅜	5⅜	5⅜	5	5	Flathead Co., Mont.	Unknown	Edwin M. Sager	1957	93
183⅜	27⅛	26⅜	18⅜	4⅜	4⅜	7	9	Dorchester Co., Md.	John R. Seifert, Jr.	John R. Seifert, Jr.	1973	93
183⅛	26⅝	26⅜	16	5	5	8	9	Ashland Co., Wisc.	Unknown	Martin Bonack	1900	95
183	25	25	20⅜	5	5	7	7	Duval Co., Texas	Charles Drennan	Bill Carter	1973	96
183	26	26⅛	18⅞	4⅜	4⅜	6	6	Desha Co., Ark.	R. J. Diekhoff	Franzen Bros.	1954	97
183	28⅜	25	19⅜	5	4⅝	5	5	Piedmont Lake, Ohio	J. Rumbaugh & J. Ruyan	J. Rumbaugh & J. Ruyan	1958	97
182⅞	28⅜	26	21	4⅜	4½	8	9	Red Deer River, Alta.	Picked Up	Ovar Uggen	1966	97
182⅞	27⅜	28⅜	19⅜	5⅜	5⅜	6	6	Hale Co., Ala.	James Cecil Bailey	James Cecil Bailey	1974	100
182⅞	28⅜	28⅜	19	5⅜	6	6	6	Wayne Co., Ohio	Gary E. Landry	Gary E. Landry	1975	100

WHITETAIL DEER (Typical Antlers)—Continued
Odocoileus virginianus virginianus and certain related subspecies

Score	Length of Main Beam R.	L.	Inside Spread	Circumference at Smallest Place Between Burr and First Point R.	L.	Number of Points R.	L.	Locality Killed	By Whom Killed	Owner	Date Killed	Rank
182⅞	27⅛	26⅞	24	5⅛	5⅛	6	7	Montana	Unknown	Johnny M. Hollier	PR1983	100
182⅝	28⅜	28	22⅜	4⅜	4⅝	6	5	Vilas Co., Wisc.	George Sparks	Mac's Taxidermy	1942	103
182⅝	27⅞	28⅜	21⅝	5⅜	5⅜	7	8	Virden, Man.	Darryl Gray	Darryl Gray	1957	104
182⅝	23	24⅜	19⅜	5⅝	5⅝	6	8	Yuma Co., Colo.	Ivan W. Rhodes	Ivan W. Rhodes	1978	104
182⅝	28⅝	29	23⅝	5⅜	5⅛	7	5	Carrot River, Sask.	Lori Lonson	J. D. Andrews	1960	106
182⅝	27	26⅝	18⅜	5⅜	5⅜	7	5	Warren Co., Mo.	Donald L. Tanner	Donald L. Tanner	1968	106
182⅝	28⅜	27⅛	23⅝	5⅜	5⅝	7	7	Kanabec Co., Minn.	Steven R. Berg	Steven R. Berg	1973	106
182⅝	24⅜	23⅜	18	5⅝	5⅜	6	6	Menominee Co., Wisc.	Unknown	John L. Stein	PR1985	106
182⅜	27	26⅝	23⅜	5⅜	5⅞	6	5	Waubausee Co., Kan.	Norman Anderson	Norman Anderson	1966	110
182⅜	25⅝	25⅛	18⅜	4⅜	4⅝	6	6	Marshall Co., Iowa	Barbara Daniel	Terry Daniel	1967	110
182⅜	25⅝	25⅝	21⅜	6	5⅝	6	6	Freeborn Co., Minn.	Robert H. Dowd	Robert H. Dowd	1969	110
182⅜	28⅜	27⅛	21⅝	4⅜	4⅝	6	6	Braxton Co., W.Va.	William D. Given	William D. Given	1976	110
182⅜	28⅜	27⅜	19⅝	4⅜	4⅜	5	6	Buffalo Co., Wisc.	Anthony F. Wolfe	Anthony F. Wolfe	1984	115
182⅜	27	27	20⅜	4⅞	5	7	5	Sullivan Co., Pa.	Floyd Reibson	Maynard Reibson	1930	115
182⅜	27⅛	26⅝	19⅝	5⅛	5⅝	5	5	Claiborne Co., Miss.	R. L. Bobo	R. L. Bobo	1955	115
182⅜	27⅛	26⅝	19⅜	4⅞	5⅛	6	6	Nicollet Co., Minn.	T. J. Merkley	T. J. Merkley	1966	115
182⅜	26	26⅜	18⅜	5⅜	5⅛	5	5	Park Co., Mont.	Jim Whitt	Jim Whitt	1983	115
182⅛	25⅝	25⅝	22⅝	5⅝	5⅝	5	5	Round Lake, Sask.	Jesse Bates	Jesse Bates	1984	119
182	24⅜	25	23	4⅜	4	7	7	Zap, N.D.	Wally Duckwitz	Sioux Sporting Goods	1962	120
181⅞	26⅜	27⅛	23⅜	5⅜	5⅝	8	7	Cottonwood Co., Minn.	Picked Up	Minn. Game & Fish Dept.	1963	121
181⅞	24⅜	24⅝	15⅝	4⅜	4⅜	6	6	McMullen Co., Texas	Oscar Hasette	Bill Carter	1971	121
181⅞	26⅜	26⅝	21⅜	4⅜	4⅜	5	5	Hotchkiss, Alta.	Andy G. Petkus	Andy G. Petkus	1984	121
181⅞	27⅜	27⅜	20⅜	4⅜	4⅜	5	6	Whitman Co., Wash.	George A. Cook III	George A. Cook III	1985	121
181⅞	23⅜	23⅜	20⅝	5⅜	5⅜	5	5	Lyon Co., Kan.	Kenneth C. Haynes	Kenneth C. Haynes	1969	125
181⅞	26⅜	26⅜	17⅝	6	6⅛	5	5	Wabasha Co., Minn.	Lee G. Partington	Lee G. Partington	1971	125
181⅞	27⅜	26⅜	21⅝	5⅜	5⅜	6	6	Ionia Co., Mich.	Lester Bowen	Richard Bowen	1947	127
181⅝	25⅝	27⅜	19⅞	5⅜	5⅜	6	7	Wilkinson Co., Miss.	Ronnie P. Whitaker	Ronnie P. Whitaker	1981	127
181⅝	29	28⅜	23⅝	4⅜	4⅝	7	5	Oxford Co., Maine	Dean W. Peaco	Dean W. Peaco	1953	129
181⅛	28⅜	27⅜	22	5⅛	5⅜	5	5	Wadena Co., Minn.	Lester Zentner, Jr.	E. E. Patson	1962	129
181⅛	25⅝	25⅝	22⅜	5⅝	5⅞	7	7	Licking Co., Ohio	Arlee McCullough	Arlee McCullough	1962	129

Score	L.R	L.L	Spread	C.R	C.L	Pts.R	Pts.L	Locality	Owner	By Whom Killed	Date	Rank
181 4/8	26	28 5/8	18 1/8	5 2/8	5 2/8	9	7	Canton, Ill.	Arnold C. Hegele	Arnold C. Hegele	1968	129
181 4/8	25 5/8	27	22 3/8	5 5/8	5 5/8	6	7	Pine Lake, Alta.	Robert Crosby	Robert Crosby	1977	129
181 3/8	27 3/8	27 5/8	20 7/8	4 5/8	4 4/8	7	6	Portage Co., Ohio	Robert M. Smith	Robert M. Smith	1953	134
181 3/8	25 7/8	24 3/8	21 3/8	5	5	7	6	Southey, Sask.	A. K. Flaman	Sam Peterson	1955	134
181 3/8	24 7/8	27 3/8	18 7/8	5 2/8	5 2/8	6	7	Orange Co., N.Y.	Roy Vail	Roy Vail	1960	134
181 3/8	24 7/8	24 5/8	18 5/8	6 4/8	6 4/8	6	7	Pope Co., Ill.	Jack A. Higgs	Jack A. Higgs	1963	134
181 3/8	26	25	17 5/8	4 4/8	4 4/8	6	6	Winona Co., Minn.	Kenneth W. Schreiber	Kenneth W. Schreiber	1980	134
181 2/8	25 5/8	25 7/8	25 7/8	5 1/8	5 1/8	5	6	Hardin Co., Ky.	Thomas L. House	Thomas L. House	1963	139
181 2/8	25	25 3/8	21	4 3/8	4 3/8	6	6	Lafayette Co., Wisc.	Michael Morrissey	Michael Morrissey	1982	139
181 1/8	27 5/8	26 2/8	17 3/8	5 4/8	5 4/8	6	5	Waldo Co., Maine	Clarendon Pomeroy	Larry C. Pomeroy	1946	141
181 1/8	27 3/8	27	20 7/8	6 5/8	5 5/8	10	7	Empress, Sask.	Don Leach	Don Leach	1960	141
181	25 7/8	24 7/8	22 3/8	4 7/8	4 7/8	6	8	Beltrami Co., Minn.	Robert C. Shaw	Robert C. Shaw	1910	143
181	25 5/8	26 3/8	19	5 5/8	5 5/8	5	5	Langlade Co., Wisc.	Elroy W. Timm	Elroy W. Timm	1959	143
181	27	26 5/8	20	5 5/8	5 7/8	5	6	Stettler, Alta.	Archie Smith	Archie Smith	1962	143
181	28 5/8	28	20	4 4/8	4 4/8	5	5	Wood Co., Wisc.	James D. Wyman	James D. Wyman	1977	143
181	26 5/8	26 2/8	21 2/8	6 3/8	6 3/8	7	8	Lac qui Parle Co., Minn.	Mary A. Barvels	Mary A. Barvels	1978	143
181	27 7/8	20 3/8	20 3/8	5 2/8	5 1/8	8	7	Gallatin Co., Ky.	Kenneth D. Hoffman	Kenneth D. Hoffman	1979	143
180 7/8	29	29 3/8	20 4/8	5 3/8	5 2/8	7	6	Jones Co., Ga.	James H. C. Kitchens	James H. C. Kitchens	1957	149
180 7/8	29 5/8	29 4/8	24 1/8	5 3/8	5 3/8	6	5	Keya Paha Co., Neb.	Steve R. Pecsenye	Steve R. Pecsenye	1966	149
180 7/8	25 7/8	25 3/8	17 5/8	5 1/8	5	6	7	Castor, Alta.	Norman D. Stienwand	Norman D. Stienwand	1981	149
180 7/8	27 7/8	28 3/8	23 1/8	5 3/8	5	5	7	Unknown	Unknown	Johnny M. Hollier	PR1984	149
180 6/8	30	29 3/8	23 3/8	5 5/8	5 5/8	5	6	Hancock Co., Maine	Cyrus H. Whitaker	Orrin W. Whitaker	1912	153
180 6/8	26 5/8	26	25	4 4/8	4 4/8	6	9	Dimmit Co., Texas	Edward Gardner	Edward Gardner	1937	153
180 6/8	31 1/8	31 3/8	25	5 5/8	5	7	8	New Brunswick	Unknown	Acad. Nat. Sci., Phil.	1937	153
180 5/8	25	23 3/8	19 4/8	4 4/8	4 4/8	6	7	Maverick Co., Texas	Jim Webb	Richard H. Bennett	1912	156
180 5/8	24 7/8	25 1/8	18 3/8	4 7/8	4 7/8	6	6	Treasure Co., Mont.	Jack Welch	Jack Welch	1958	156
180 5/8	25	23	23	5 3/8	5 3/8	7	7	Cheat Mt., W. Va.	Joseph V. Volitis	Joseph V. Volitis	1969	156
180 5/8	28 3/8	28	18 7/8	5	4 7/8	8	6	St. Landry Parish, La.	Shawn P. Ortego	Shawn P. Ortego	1975	156
180 4/8	29 4/8	20	20	4 4/8	4 4/8	6	6	Iron Co., Mich.	John Schmidt	Bob Schmidt	1927	160
180 4/8	28	26	26	4 7/8	5	7	7	Jim Hogg Co., Texas	Roy Lee Henry	Roy Lee Henry	1958	160
180 4/8	23 5/8	24	17 7/8	5	5	6	6	Andrew Co., Mo.	Virgil M. Ashley	Virgil M. Ashley	1967	160
180 4/8	28	27	22 7/8	5 3/8	5 3/8	7	6	Leflore Co., Miss.	W. F. Smith	W. F. Smith	1968	160
180 4/8	26 7/8	25 1/8	19	5 1/8	5 1/8	6	6	Clay Co., S.D.	James E. Olson	James E. Olson	1975	160
180 4/8	30	30 2/8	24 3/8	4 7/8	4 7/8	8	8	Okanogan Co., Wash.	Joe Peone	Joe Peone	1983	160
180 3/8	30 2/8	30	23 3/8	5 1/8	5 1/8	8	8	Livingston Co., N.Y.	Edward Beare	Edward Beare	1943	166
180 3/8	26 4/8	27	20 3/8	4 3/8	4 3/8	7	6	Sheboygan Co., Wisc.	Unknown	James K. Lawton	1955	166
180 3/8	24 4/8	24 1/8	19 3/8	5 5/8	5 5/8	8	6	Orvando, Mont.	Clinton Berry	Clinton Berry	1957	166
180 3/8	25 5/8	26 3/8	21	5 1/8	5 1/8	6	6	Stoughton, Sask.	Joe Zbeetnoff	Joe Zbeetnoff	1961	166
180 3/8	25 5/8	25 2/8	23 3/8	4 6/8	4 6/8	6	6	Union Parish, La.	Picked Up	Johnny M. Hollier	1963	166
180 3/8	27 5/8	26	21 1/8	4 5/8	4 5/8	8	8	Antler Lake, Alta.	German Wagenseil	German Wagenseil	1964	166
180 3/8	30	29 5/8	22 5/8	4 4/8	4 4/8	7	6	Meeker Co., Minn.	Stanley M. Messner	Stanley M. Messner	1981	166
180 2/8	26 5/8	25	22 2/8	5 2/8	5 2/8	8	7	Lumsden, Sask.	Mike Lukas	E. M. Gazda	1959	173

WHITETAIL DEER (Typical Antlers)—Continued
Odocoileus virginianus virginianus and certain related subspecies

Score	Length of Main Beam R.	L.	Inside Spread	Circumference at Smallest Place Between Burr and First Point R.	L.	Number of Points R.	L.	Locality Killed	By Whom Killed	Owner	Date Killed	Rank
180⅞	28⅞	28⅞	18⅞	4⅞	4⅞	5	5	Newton Co., Ga.	David Moon	David Moon	1972	173
180⅞	26⅞	26⅞	18⅞	4⅝	4⅝	6	6	Eau Claire Co., Wisc.	Dennis B. Bryan	Dennis B. Bryan	1979	173
180⅞	27⅛	27⅛	19⅜	4⅜	4⅜	5	5	Iowa	Unknown	Tom Williams	PR1984	173
180⅞	23⅝	23⅝	17⅜	5⅞	5⅞	5	5	Maryfield, Sask.	Donald Cook	Richard Christoforo	1956	177
180⅞	26⅝	26⅝	17⅜	4⅞	4⅝	5	6	Ashland Co., Wisc.	Audrey Kundinger	Audrey Kundinger	1961	177
180⅞	26⅝	26⅝	20⅛	4⅜	4⅝	6	6	Phelps Co., Mo.	William A. Hagenhoff	William A. Hagenhoff	1973	177
180⅛	24	24	19⅛	4⅜	5	7	6	Vermillion, Alta.	Ralph M. McDonald	Ralph M. McDonald	1975	177
180⅛	25⅛	25⅛	19⅜	5⅜	5⅜	6	6	Cottonwood Co., Minn.	Charles C. Burnham	Charles C. Burnham	1983	177
180⅛	24⅝	24⅝	19⅜	5⅛	5	7	5	Hubbard Co., Minn.	Larry D. Dierks	Larry D. Dierks	1984	183
180⅛	24	24	20	4⅜	5	5	6	Oneida Co., Wisc.	Milo K. Fields	Milo K. Fields	1938	183
180	27⅝	27⅝	19⅝	4⅜	4⅜	5	5	Desha Co., Ark.	Turner Neal	Turner Neal	1962	183
180	26⅞	26⅜	19⅜	4⅝	4⅝	7	7	Zavala Co., Texas	Mrs. Richard King III	Mrs. Richard King III	1966	183
180	26	25⅞	19	4⅜	4⅞	10	7	Big Horn Co., Mont.	Clair W. Jensen	Clair W. Jensen	1967	183
180	25⅜	25⅜	19⅜	6⅛	6⅛	6	8	Castor, Alta.	Kenneth Larson	Kenneth Larson	1969	183
180	26⅜	26⅜	20⅜	5⅞	5⅞	5	7	Hancock Co., Maine	Butler B. Dunn	Butler B. Dunn	1930	188
179⅞	25⅜	27⅛	19	5⅛	5	9	6	Steele Co., Minn.	Elmer Janning	Elmer Janning	1972	189
179⅞	27⅛	29⅜	21⅛	5	4⅜	7	7	Aitkin Co., Minn.	Harland A. Kern	Harland A. Kern	1973	189
179⅞	28⅛	26⅜	22⅜	4⅜	4⅝	6	5	Longview, Alta.	Eldred Umbach	Eldred Umbach	1977	189
179⅞	29⅛	28	21	5⅝	5⅜	7	6	Jim Hogg Co., Texas	William B. Van Fleet	William B. Van Fleet	1979	189
179⅞	26⅜	26⅜	19⅜	4⅝	4⅝	6	5	Penobscot Co., Maine	Dale Rustin	Dale Rustin	1984	189
179⅞	25⅝	26⅝	21⅝	5⅜	5⅝	6	6	Rumsey, Alta.	Arley Harder	Arley Harder	1969	194
179⅞	25⅞	25⅞	19⅜	6	6	5	5	Coronation, Alta.	Harold McKnight	Harold McKnight	1969	195
179⅞	23⅜	23⅝	19⅜	4⅜	4⅝	6	6	Spokane Co., Wash.	Bert E. Smith	Bert E. Smith	1972	195
179⅞	24⅜	24⅞	19⅜	5⅜	5⅛	7	6	Elk Co., Kan.	Lowell E. Howell	Lowell E. Howell	1973	195
179⅞	27⅜	27⅜	19⅜	5	5	6	6	Pawnee Co., Neb.	Kenneth C. Mort	Kenneth C. Mort	1975	195
179⅞	27⅜	28⅜	20⅛	5⅜	5⅜	6	5	Chouteau Co., Mont.	Richard L. Charlson	Richard L. Charlson	1977	195
179⅞	24⅜	25⅜	19⅜	5	4⅜	7	8	Essex Co., N.Y.	Herbert Jaquish	Herbert Jaquish	1953	200
179⅞	29	29⅜	19⅜	4⅜	4⅝	10	8	Parkman, Sask.	Harold Larsen	Sam Peterson	1958	200
179⅞	28⅜	28	20⅜	5⅝	5⅝	5	5	Vernon Co., Wisc.	Alois V. Schendel	Alois V. Schendel	1966	200
179⅞	26⅜	26⅜	17⅜	4⅜	6	6	6	Oberon, Man.	Arnold W. Poole	Arnold W. Poole	1968	200

Score	Length of Main Beam R.	L.	Inside Spread	Circumference R.	L.	No. Points R.	L.	Locality	By Whom Killed	Owner	Date Killed	Rank
179⅞	27⅞	27⅞	23⅜	5	5⅞	9	11	Prairie Co., Ark.	Charles Newsom	Charles Newsom	1962	204
179⅞	27⅞	27	20	5⅝	5⅝	9	9	Cypress Hills, Sask.	Raymond McCrea	Raymond McCrea	1964	204
179⅞	25⅞	24⅞	21⅜	4⅝	4⅞	7	9	Lamar Co., Ga.	Gary Littlejohn	Gary Littlejohn	1968	204
179⅞	26⅝	25⅞	17⅞	5	4⅞	7	7	Worth Co., Iowa	John Janssen	John Janssen	1976	204
179⅞	26⅞	28	16	4⅞	4⅜	6	5	Ashland Co., Wisc.	Jack D. Hultman	Jack D. Hultman	1981	204
179⅞	24⅜	24⅞	19⅜	4⅞	4⅜	6	6	Dimmit Co., Texas	William M. Knolle	William M. Knolle	1982	204
179⅞	23⅞	25⅛	19⅝	5⅝	5⅛	7	6	Buffalo Co., Wisc.	Jerome Kulig	Jerome Kulig	1984	204
179⅞	28⅞	27⅛	18⅝	4⅜	4⅜	6	6	Twiggs Co., Ga.	Cy Smith	Duncan A. Dobie	1970	211
179	25	23⅞	18⅝	5⅜	5⅜	5	6	Chippewa Co., Wisc.	John F. Kukuska	John F. Kukuska	1931	212
179	27⅛	25⅛	19⅝	5⅝	5⅝	6	7	Sherburne Co., Minn.	Victor Nagel	Victor Nagel	1956	212
179	26⅞	26⅝	21⅜	4⅞	4⅜	5	6	Jasper Co., Ga.	Hubert R. Moody	Hubert R. Moody	1957	212
179	25⅞	25⅞	19⅜	5⅛	5⅛	5	6	Waldersee, Man.	Wm. Wutke	Wm. Wutke	1959	212
179	28⅜	28⅜	20⅜	4⅜	4⅜	5	5	Dooley Co., Ga.	Shannon Akin	Shannon Akin	1981	212
179	27⅜	29⅜	20⅜	4⅜	4⅜	6	7	Logan Co., Ohio	Gregory K. Snyder	Greta J. Snyder	1982	212
178⅞	24⅜	28	21⅜	5⅜	5⅜	6	6	Monroe Co., Ohio	Roger E. Schumacher	Roger E. Schumacher	1958	218
178⅞	28⅜	26⅝	19⅝	4⅜	4⅞	6	6	Van Buren Co., Iowa	Noel E. Harlan	Noel E. Harlan	1984	218
178⅞	26	25	22⅝	5⅜	5⅛	6	6	Elkhorn, Man.	Jerry May	Jerry May	1959	220
178⅞	27⅞	27⅞	25⅞	5⅜	5⅜	6	5	Windthorst, Sask.	Clarence E. Genest	Clarence E. Genest	1965	220
178⅞	26	26⅝	21⅜	5⅛	5⅝	6	8	McPherson Co., Kan.	Larry D. Daniel	Larry D. Daniel	1967	220
178⅞	27	24⅜	22⅜	5⅞	5⅞	7	7	Breton, Alta.	George Clark	George Clark	1981	220
178⅞	26⅜	27⅞	20⅝	5	5	6	6	Aroostook Co., Maine	John R. Hardy	John R. Hardy	1983	220
178⅞	25⅞	27⅞	20⅜	5⅝	5⅛	6	5	Bolivar Co., Miss.	Grady Robertson	Merigold Hunting Club	1951	225
178⅞	28⅜	27	24	5⅛	5⅛	7	7	Beechy, Sask.	Archie D. McRae	Archie D. McRae	1957	225
178⅞	27	26⅜	20⅜	4⅜	4⅜	6	6	Harlan Co., Neb.	Don Tripe	Don Tripe	1961	225
178⅝	27⅞	29⅜	26⅜	5⅜	5⅜	6	6	Debden, Sask.	Henry Rydde	Henry Rydde	1966	225
178⅝	24⅜	24⅜	20⅜	4⅞	5⅛	6	7	Pincher Creek, Alta.	Unknown	H. Bruce Freeman	1973	225
178⅝	27	26⅜	21⅜	5⅜	5⅜	5	5	Scott Co., Tenn.	Charles H. Smith	Charles H. Smith	1978	225
178⅝	25⅜	25⅝	22⅜	4⅜	4⅜	5	5	Itasca Co., Minn.	Gino P. Maccario	Gino P. Maccario	1980	225
178⅝	23⅜	24	21⅜	4⅜	4⅜	7	7	Addy, Wash.	Irving Naff	Irving Naff	1957	232
178⅝	25⅞	25	23⅝	5⅜	5⅞	5	5	McMullen Co., Texas	D. H. Waldron	D. H. Waldron	1964	232
178⅝	27⅜	27⅜	18⅝	4⅞	4⅜	6	6	Cumberland Co., Maine	Patrick D. Wescott	Patrick D. Wescott	1980	232
178⅝	24⅜	25⅜	18⅛	5⅝	5⅜	5	6	St. Clair Co., Ill.	Emil W. Kromat	Emil W. Kromat	1981	232
178⅝	26⅜	25⅜	21	5⅜	5⅜	6	5	Scotland Co., Mo.	Picked Up	Roland E. Meyer	1984	232
178⅜	26⅞	26⅜	24⅜	5⅜	5⅜	6	5	Aitkin Co., Minn.	George E. Jenks	George E. Jenks	1969	237
178⅜	27	27⅛	17⅝	4⅜	4⅜	5	5	Queens Co., N.B.	Bert Bourque	Bert Bourque	1970	237
178⅜	28⅜	28⅜	23⅞	5⅛	5⅞	7	8	Lincoln Co., Minn.	Larry Lustfield	Larry Lustfield	1976	237
178⅜	25⅛	24⅜	26⅞	5⅞	5⅜	6	7	Hardisty, Alta.	George R. Walker	George R. Walker	1977	237
178⅜	27⅜	26⅝	18⅜	4⅜	4⅜	6	6	Goochland Co., Va.	Edward W. Fielder	Edward W. Fielder	1981	237
178⅜	26⅜	26⅛	20⅜	4⅜	4⅞	5	5	Pawnee Co., Neb.	Picked Up	Gale Sup	1960	242
178⅜	27⅞	27⅜	24⅜	4⅜	4⅜	6	6	Wallowa Co., Oreg.	Sterling K. Shaver	Sterling K. Shaver	1982	242
178⅜	27⅜	27	19⅜	4⅜	4⅜	5	5	Tuscarawas Co., Ohio	Raymond D. Gerber, Jr.	Raymond D. Gerber, Jr.	1983	242
178⅜	24⅜	23⅜	19⅜	4⅞	4⅜	8	8	Dismal River, Neb.	Gift of G. B. Grinnell	National Collection	PR1909	245

Whitetail Deer (*Typical Antlers*)—Continued

Odocoileus virginianus virginianus and certain related subspecies

Score	Length of Main Beam R.	L.	Inside Spread	Circumference at Smallest Place Between Burr and First Point R.	L.	Number of Points R.	L.	Locality Killed	By Whom Killed	Owner	Date Killed	Rank
178⅛	28⅜	26⅞	18⅜	4⅞	5	5	7	Concrete, N.D.	Lawrence E. Vandal	Lawrence E. Vandal	1947	245
178⅛	27⅝	27⅜	17⅜	4⅞	4⅞	8	7	Iron Co., Wisc.	DuWayne A. Weichel	Robert G. Steidtmann	1957	245
178⅛	35⅛	35	15⅛	5⅜	5⅜	6	6	Jasper Co., Ga.	M. C. Lennon, Jr.	M. C. Lennon, Jr.	1964	245
178⅛	29⅜	28⅜	18⅜	4⅞	4⅞	7	7	Harlan Co., Neb.	Duane E. Johnson	Duane E. Johnson	1967	245
178⅛	27⅞	27⅞	21⅛	5⅝	5⅜	5	5	Price Co., Wisc.	Terry Staroba	Terry Staroba	1983	245
178	27	27⅞	17⅛	4⅞	5	7	6	Price Co., Wisc.	Emery Swan	Emery Swan	1949	251
178	26⅞	27⅞	21⅛	4⅜	4⅜	6	6	Clark Co., Mo.	Allen L. Courtney	Allen L. Courtney	1966	251
178	25	24⅜	17⅜	4⅞	4⅞	6	7	Washington Co., Iowa	Brad Gardner	Vaughn Wilkins	1978	251
178	27⅞	27⅞	20	5⅛	5⅜	7	7	Price Co., Wisc.	John E. Martinson	John E. Martinson	1981	251
178	25⅛	26⅞	22⅛	6	6	5	5	Union Co., Ky.	Gary L. Gibson	Gary L. Gibson	1983	251
177⅞	27	28⅞	20	4⅞	5	6	6	Chicot Co., Ark.	George Matthews	W. T. Haynes	1923	256
177⅞	28	27⅞	20⅜	5⅝	5⅝	5	5	Iron Co., Mich.	Felix Brzoznowski	Joseph Brzoznowski	1939	256
177⅞	24⅜	23⅞	19⅜	4⅞	4⅞	7	7	Ymir, B.C.	Frank Gowing	Frank Gowing	1961	256
177⅞	25⅞	25⅛	24⅜	5	5⅛	5	6	Wibaux Co., Mont.	Dan Amunrud	David Welliever	1967	256
177⅞	26⅜	26⅞	22⅛	5⅜	5⅜	6	6	Christian Co., Ill.	Rodney J. Gorden	Rodney J. Gorden	1974	256
177⅞	26⅛	27⅜	23	5⅜	5	7	9	Jefferson Co., Mont.	Tracy Forcella	Tracy Forcella	1983	256
177¾	25⅝	26⅜	19	4⅜	4⅜	6	6	Paxton, Neb.	Ole Herstedt	Ole Herstedt	1956	262
177¾	26⅜	26	22	4⅜	4⅜	6	6	Kleberg Co., Texas	Elaine A. O'Brien	Patrick O'Brien	1972	262
177¾	24	24	22⅝	5	5	5	5	Atoka Co., Okla.	Skip Rowell	Skip Rowell	1972	262
177¾	26⅝	25⅜	24	4⅜	4⅜	6	6	Duval Co., Texas	Harry Heimer	Harry Heimer	1974	262
177¾	23⅞	24	23⅜	4⅝	4⅜	6	5	Stearns Co., Minn.	Robert G. Schwarz	Robert G. Schwarz	1975	262
177¾	26⅝	27⅜	18⅜	5	5⅛	9	7	Shaunavon, Sask.	Stan J. Crawford	Stan J. Crawford	1979	262
177⅝	26¼	26⅜	19⅛	5⅝	5⅜	5	5	Endeavour, Sask.	Terry L. Halgrimson	Terry L. Halgrimson	1971	268
177⅝	25⅝	26⅜	22⅛	4⅞	4⅜	7	6	Wabasha Co., Minn.	Bruce J. Hall	Bruce J. Hall	1972	268
177⅝	26⅝	26	22⅛	4⅛	4⅛	6	8	Macon Co., Ga.	James W. Athon	Mike's Gun Shop	1976	268
177⅝	25	24⅜	17⅜	5⅜	5⅜	5	5	Washburn Co., Wisc.	Patrick Henk	Patrick Henk	1984	268
177⅝	25⅝	25⅝	19⅜	4⅜	4⅜	7	8	Harrison Co., Ohio	Mark Dulkoski	Mark Dulkoski	1984	268
177½	29	28⅜	22	5	5	6	5	Dimmit Co., Texas	Tom Brady	McLean Bowman	1926	273
177½	27⅞	27¼	23¾	4⅝	4⅛	8	6	Oneida Co., Wisc.	Elmer Ahlborn	Gene Ahlborn	1926	273
177½	26	26⅜	21⅛	4⅝	5⅝	8	6	Dundurn, Sask.	L. B. Galbraith	L. B. Galbraith	1956	273

Final Score	L.R	L.L	Spread	Circ. R	Circ. L	Pts. R	Pts. L	Locality	By	Owner	Date	Rank
177 7/8	26 3/8	26	21	4	4 1/8	5	5	Bedford Co., Pa.	Raymond Miller	Raymond Miller	1957	273
177 7/8	24 6/8	23 3/8	24 2/8	5 1/8	5 3/8	7	7	Dimmit Co., Texas	Carter Younts	Carter Younts	1963	273
177 7/8	28 3/8	28 2/8	22 2/8	5 5/8	5 5/8	6	5	Beltrami Co., Minn.	Sheldon M. Stockdale	Sheldon M. Stockdale	1968	273
177 7/8	26	26 2/8	24	5	5	6	6	McMullen Co., Texas	Unknown	Ken Mamatz	1983	273
177 7/8	25 4/8	25 4/8	18	6	6 2/8	6	6	Hall Co., Neb.	Charles R. Babel	Spanky Greenville	1969	280
177 7/8	26	26	20 2/8	5 3/8	5 5/8	6	6	Rusk Co., Wisc.	David A. Reichel	David A. Reichel	1981	280
177 7/8	27	26 2/8	23 2/8	5	5 1/8	5	5	Menominee Co., Wisc.	William Matchapatow, Sr.	William Matchapatow, Sr.	1981	280
177 3/8	25 3/8	25 1/8	16 7/8	6 2/8	6 2/8	10	10	Unknown	Unknown	Johnny M. Hollier	PR1983	284
177 3/8	26 6/8	26 6/8	26 2/8	5 1/8	5 1/8	7	7	Webb Co., Texas	Unknown	Eugene Roberts	1924	284
177 3/8	28 5/8	28	20 6/8	4 6/8	4 6/8	5	5	Augusta Co., Va.	Donald W. Houser	Donald W. Houser	1963	284
177 3/8	25 3/8	24 3/8	21 2/8	4 1/8	4 1/8	8	9	Golden Valley Co., N.D.	Allen Goltz	Allen Goltz	1964	284
177 3/8	25 5/8	25 7/8	18 2/8	4 6/8	4 6/8	6	6	Richland Co., Wisc.	Dewitt S. Pulham	Dewitt S. Pulham	1982	284
177 2/8	29 4/8	30 2/8	18 2/8	6 5/8	6 3/8	6	6	Geary Co., Kan.	Kelly D. Gulker	Kelly D. Gulker	1982	284
177 1/8	27 5/8	29	21 2/8	6	6	5	6	Litchfield Co., Conn.	Picked Up	Rickey A. Vincent	1984	290
177 1/8	25 5/8	26 1/8	19	5 1/8	5 2/8	7	10	Newcastle, Wyo.	H. W. Julien	H. W. Julien	1954	290
177 1/8	27 6/8	27	21 1/8	4 4/8	4 4/8	5	5	Walworth Co., Wisc.	Daniel J. Brede	Daniel J. Brede	1984	292
177 1/8	28 3/8	28	17 2/8	4 6/8	4 6/8	6	7	Bayfield Co., Wisc.	Elof E. Sjostrom	Mrs. Elof E. Sjostrom	1932	292
177	25	26	19 1/8	6	5 2/8	6	6	Gage Co., Neb.	Art Wallman	Art Wallman	1968	292
177	26 6/8	27 3/8	18 4/8	4 4/8	4 4/8	5	5	Cass Co., Ind.	Herbert R. Frushour	Herbert R. Frushour	1974	296
177	28 5/8	26 1/8	20 2/8	5 5/8	5 5/8	7	5	Innisfree, Alta.	Donald M. Baranec	Donald M. Baranec	1984	296
176 7/8	28	26	16 2/8	3 7/8	3 5/8	5	6	Day Co., S.D.	William B. Davis	William B. Davis	1959	296
176 7/8	25 5/8	25	19 2/8	5 5/8	5 4/8	5	5	Pierson, Man.	Bud Smith	Bud Smith	1960	296
176 7/8	29 6/8	28 3/8	23	5 7/8	5 4/8	5	5	Logan Co., Ohio	David Sutherly	David Sutherly	1975	301
176 7/8	25 5/8	25 5/8	22 1/8	4 6/8	5	5	5	Butler Co., Kan.	Craig D. Waltman	Craig D. Waltman	1982	301
176 6/8	27 3/8	27 3/8	20 2/8	4 4/8	4 5/8	5	5	Pierce Co., Wisc.	John M. Oelke	John M. Oelke	1984	301
176 6/8	27 1/8	26	20 2/8	5 2/8	5 3/8	6	5	Vilas Co., Wisc.	Porter Dean	Safari North Tax.	1938	301
176 5/8	26 3/8	25	19	5 3/8	5 3/8	6	6	Langlade Co., Wisc.	Jack Ryan	LaVern Emerich	1950	301
176 5/8	25 5/8	27 3/8	20 2/8	5 2/8	5 1/8	11	12	Clinton Co., Mich.	Ray Sadler	Ray Sadler	1963	307
176 5/8	25 5/8	25	23 4/8	4 6/8	4 4/8	6	6	Frankfort, Kan.	Ray A. Mosher	Ray A. Mosher	1966	307
176 5/8	24 1/8	23 4/8	18 2/8	5	5	5	5	Knox Co., Neb.	Alvin Zimmerman	Spanky Greenville	1966	307
176 5/8	25 5/8	27	21 2/8	5 4/8	5 3/8	5	5	Pine Co., Minn.	Kim Shira	Kim Shira	1977	307
176 5/8	25	25	21 1/8	5	5 3/8	7	6	Mifflin Co., Pa.	John Zerba	Kenneth Zerba	1936	307
176 5/8	26 6/8	26 4/8	21 2/8	5 2/8	4 4/8	5	5	Bolivar Co., Miss.	Sidney D. Sessions	Sidney D. Sessions	1952	307
176 5/8	26 1/8	25 7/8	19 4/8	4 6/8	6 1/8	8	8	Washington	Unknown	Jonas Bros. of Seattle	PR1953	314
176 5/8	26 5/8	23 4/8	17 4/8	4 5/8	5 5/8	5	5	Montgomery Co., Iowa	Unknown	Chris Hein	1961	314
176 5/8	23 3/8	23 4/8	17 2/8	4 5/8	4 5/8	6	5	Roberts Co., S.D.	Fred Kuehl	J. D. Andrews	1964	314
176 5/8	24 4/8	24	23 2/8	5 4/8	5 3/8	6	6	Tensas Parish, La.	Sam Barber	Johnny M. Hollier	1974	314
176 5/8	24 3/8	24 4/8	20 2/8	5	5 3/8	6	6	Buffalo, Alta.	Bob Fraleigh	Bob Fraleigh	1978	314
176 5/8	23 3/8	23 4/8	21 1/8	4 4/8	4 1/8	6	5	Esterhazy, Sask.	Albert Kristoff	Albert Kristoff	1960	314
176 5/8	25 3/8	24 4/8	22	6 1/8	5 5/8	5	5	Charlotte Co., N.B.	Albert E. Dewar	Albert E. Dewar	1960	314
176 5/8	23 5/8	23 5/8	17 4/8	5 4/8	5 3/8	5	5	St. Louis Co., Minn.	Michael J. Nielsen	Michael J. Nielsen	1962	314
176 5/8	25 5/8	24 4/8	19	3 7/8	4 1/8	6	6	Shackelford Co., Texas	H. V. Stroud	H. V. Stroud	1964	314

WHITETAIL DEER (Typical Antlers)—Continued
Odocoileus virginianus virginianus and certain related subspecies

Score	Length of Main Beam		Inside Spread	Circumference at Smallest Place Between Burr and First Point		Number of Points		Locality Killed	By Whom Killed	Owner	Date Killed	Rank
	R.	L.		R.	L.	R.	L.					
176⅞	23	23	16⅜	4⅞	4⅞	9	7	Carrizo Springs, Texas	Lin F. Nowotny	Lin F. Nowotny	1966	314
176⅞	25	25	19⅜	4⅜	4⅜	7	6	Crawford Co., Wisc.	Louis Franks	Louis Franks	1969	314
176⅞	26⅞	27	26⅝	4⅜	4⅜	6	6	Houston Co., Minn.	James L. Reinhart	James L. Reinhart	1971	314
176⅞	27⅞	28	21⅞	4⅜	4⅜	5	5	Sanders Co., Mont.	Dallas J. C. Nelson	Dallas J. C. Nelson	1983	314
176⅞	26	26⅝	20⅝	5⅛	5⅝	7	5	Baraga Co., Mich.	Paul Korhonen	Paul Korhonen	1945	322
176⅞	26⅛	25⅛	22⅜	5⅞	5⅝	5	6	Koochiching Co., Minn.	Picked Up	James R. Smith	1957	322
176⅞	25	25⅛	17⅝	4⅝	5⅛	6	5	Stockton, Man.	Robert R. Blain	Robert R. Blain	1977	322
176⅞	25⅝	28⅝	25⅛	4⅞	5	5	5	Erie Co., N.Y.	Wesley H. Iulg	Wesley H. Iulg	1944	325
176⅞	23	25⅜	18⅜	5	4⅞	5	5	Swanson, Sask.	L. S. Wood	L. S. Wood	1959	325
176⅞	25⅝	25⅞	20⅜	5⅛	5⅝	7	6	Rappahannock Co., Va.	George W. Beahm	George W. Beahm	1959	325
176⅞	24⅞	26⅜	17⅛	5⅛	5⅝	8	7	Warren Co., N.Y.	Frank Dagles	Frank Dagles	1961	325
176⅞	28⅞	27⅞	25	5⅛	5⅝	5	4	Washington Co., Neb.	Albert Ohrt	Spanky Greenville	1962	325
176⅞	28⅞	29⅞	20⅝	5⅛	5⅝	5	5	Richland Parish, La.	Willard Roberson	Willard Roberson	1968	325
176⅞	30	28⅜	23	6⅛	6⅛	7	6	Coshocton Co., Ohio	James R. Gardner	James R. Gardner	1976	325
176⅞	28	26⅜	21	5⅝	5⅝	8	7	Macon Co., Ga.	Charles M. Wilson	Charles M. Wilson	1981	325
176⅞	24⅞	25⅛	20⅝	4⅝	4⅞	6	6	Troup Co., Ga.	Claude A. McKibben, Jr.	James E. Lasater	1984	325
176⅞	28	27⅞	21⅛	5⅝	5⅝	6	5	Florence Co., Wisc.	Theron A. Meyer, Sr.	Theron A. Meyer, Sr.	1943	334
176⅞	25⅜	24⅝	19⅞	6⅝	6⅞	7	7	Goodhue Co., Minn.	David Anderson	David Anderson	1960	334
176⅞	25⅛	23⅞	24⅛	5⅝	5⅝	5	6	Assiniboine River, Man.	G. G. Graham	G. G. Graham	1984	334
176	28⅞	29⅞	17⅝	5⅜	5⅜	8	7	Florence Co., Wisc.	John G. Kozicki	Vernon J. Kozicki	1936	337
176	24⅞	24⅞	17⅛	3⅞	4	8	6	Bradford Co., Pa.	Clyde H. Rinehuls	Clyde H. Rinehuls	1944	337
176	25⅜	25⅜	20⅜	5⅝	5⅝	5	5	Dawson Co., Neb.	Unknown	Spanky Greenville	1957	337
176	23⅞	25⅜	19⅜	5⅝	5⅝	8	7	Lyon Co., Iowa	Duane K. Rohde	Duane K. Rohde	1964	337
176	26	26⅜	20	5⅝	5⅝	5	5	Veblen, S.D.	John W. Cimburek	John W. Cimburek	1966	337
176	24⅝	25⅞	21⅝	4⅞	4⅞	5	5	Russell Co., Kan.	Don Mai	Don Mai	1981	337
175⅞	23	23⅛	16⅝	5⅛	5⅛	5	5	Hanley, Sask.	G. Koyl & W. King	Gavin Koyl	1964	343
175⅞	24⅞	25⅛	17⅛	4⅝	4⅜	4	4	Logan Co., Colo.	Picked Up	Marvin Gardner	1971	343
175⅞	26⅝	27	21⅛	4⅜	4⅜	5	6	Swift Co., Minn.	Kim Manska	Kim Manska	1982	343
175⅞	27	26⅝	22⅝	4⅜	4⅜	5	5	Sundre, Alta.	Russell D. Holmes	Russell D. Holmes	1984	343
175⅞	25⅝	26	20⅞	4	4	6	6	Webb Co., Texas	William Bretthauer, Sr.	George H. Glass	1915	347

								Location			Year	Score
175 5/8	21 3/8	23 3/8	18	4 4/8	4 4/8	6	6	St. Onge, S.D.	Don Ridley	Don Ridley	1957	347
175 5/8	25 3/8	26 3/8	19 6/8	5 3/8	5 3/8	5	5	Southey, Sask.	J. A. Maier	J. A. Maier	1958	347
175 5/8	22 3/8	24 3/8	20	5	5	6	6	Burleigh Co., N.D.	Earl Haakenson	Earl Haakenson	1963	347
175 5/8	26 3/8	25 3/8	16 7/8	5 4/8	5 4/8	8	6	Cuming Co., Neb.	Herman Blankenau	Herman Blankenau	1963	347
175 5/8	24 3/8	24 3/8	17 7/8	6 2/8	6 2/8	8	10	Marshall Co., Minn.	Ell-Kay B. Foss	Ell-Kay B. Foss	1974	347
175 5/8	27 2/8	26 7/8	22 2/8	5 4/8	5 4/8	7	6	Webb Co., Texas	Norman Frede	Norman Frede	1978	347
175 5/8	25 4/8	26 3/8	20	5	5	6	6	Dimmit Co., Texas	George E. Light III	George E. Light III	1979	347
175 5/8	26 3/8	26 3/8	22 3/8	5 3/8	5 3/8	5	6	Pope Co., Ill.	Picked Up	Picked Up	PR1982	347
175 5/8	24 3/8	26 3/8	22 2/8	5 1/8	5 1/8	4	5	Hayes Co., Texas	Bill Kuykendall	James W. Seets	1925	356
175 5/8	24 7/8	26 3/8	27 3/8	4 7/8	4 7/8	7	4	Lake Co., Mont.	Kenneth D. Johnson	Bill Kuykendall	1974	356
175 5/8	26	25 2/8	25 3/8	4 6/8	4 6/8	5	7	Allegany Co., N.Y.	William L. Damon	Kenneth D. Johnson	1981	356
175 5/8	25 3/8	25 2/8	18 7/8	4 6/8	4 6/8	6	6	Benewah Co., Idaho	Carl Groth	William L. Damon	1982	356
175 4/8	24 7/8	26 7/8	17 7/8	4 5/8	4 5/8	5	7	Unknown	Unknown	Carl Groth	PR1985	356
175 4/8	25 3/8	25	17 1/8	5 2/8	5 2/8	6	5	McKean Co., Pa.	Arthur Young	Brad Lewis	1830	361
175 4/8	25 3/8	25	17 1/8	5	5	6	5	Pepin Co., Wisc.	Carl E. Frick	C. R. Studholme	1954	361
175 4/8	27	27	21 2/8	5 1/8	5 1/8	5	5	Corning, Mo.	Orrie L. Schaeffer	Carl E. Frick	1962	361
175 4/8	25 3/8	25 5/8	20 3/8	5 1/8	5 1/8	8	7	Dodge Co., Neb.	Leroy W. Ahrndt	Orrie L. Schaeffer	1963	361
175 4/8	29	29	22 5/8	5 5/8	5 5/8	5	5	Hanover, Ill.	J. O. Engebretson	Leroy W. Ahrndt	1963	361
175 4/8	26 7/8	27 7/8	21	5 1/8	5 1/8	5	5	Renville Co., Minn.	Larry D. Youngs	J. O. Engebretson	1973	361
175 4/8	26 1/8	25 4/8	23 3/8	5 3/8	5 3/8	5	5	Bridgeford, Sask.	Elgin T. Gates	Larry D. Youngs	1958	367
175 3/8	25 3/8	25 4/8	20 1/8	5 2/8	5 2/8	6	5	Gallia Co., Ohio	Jack Auxier	Elgin T. Gates	1969	367
175 3/8	24 5/8	25 2/8	20 4/8	5 5/8	5 5/8	6	6	Williamson Co., Ill.	Lewis F. Simon	Jack Auxier	1973	367
175 3/8	24	22 2/8	19 6/8	4 7/8	4 7/8	8	8	Monroe Co., Ohio	David Mancano	Lewis F. Simon	1976	367
175 3/8	25	25	18 1/8	4 2/8	4 2/8	6	6	Dimmit Co., Texas	Betsy Campbell	David Mancano	1978	367
175 2/8	29 5/8	28	22 3/8	4 4/8	4 4/8	5	5	Todd Co., Ky.	Gary W. Crafton	Betsy Campbell	1981	367
175 2/8	22 7/8	22 2/8	19	4 5/8	4 5/8	6	6	Encinal, Texas	W. S. Benson, Sr.	Gary W. Crafton	1928	373
175 2/8	24	23 5/8	19 6/8	5 5/8	5 5/8	6	5	Qu'Appelle, Sask.	Douglas Garden	W. S. Benson III	1965	373
175 2/8	28 5/8	28 7/8	17 1/8	5 5/8	5 5/8	8	6	Val Marie, Sask.	Leon Perrault	Douglas Garden	1977	373
175 2/8	26 1/8	25 4/8	21 1/8	5 3/8	5 3/8	7	8	Wilkinson Co., Miss.	Johnnie J. Leake, Jr.	Leon Perrault	1978	373
175 2/8	28 3/8	28 3/8	19 6/8	5 5/8	5 5/8	5	7	Fulton Co., Ind.	Larry A. Croxton	Johnnie J. Leake, Jr.	1984	373
175 2/8	27 1/8	27	19	6 1/8	6 1/8	5	5	Union Co., Ill.	Randy Edmonds	Larry A. Croxton	1984	373
175 1/8	26 3/8	26 3/8	20 3/8	4 3/8	4 3/8	5	6	Claiborne Parish, La.	Picked Up	Randy Edmonds	PR1985	373
175 1/8	28	27 7/8	25	4 7/8	4 7/8	8	7	Waldo Co., Maine	Unknown	Johnny M. Hollier	1924	380
175 1/8	26 7/8	27 7/8	19 5/8	4 4/8	4 4/8	5	5	Alger Co., Mich.	Warren Beebe	Kenneth T. Winters	1936	380
175 1/8	23 5/8	22 7/8	22 5/8	5	5	5	5	Chedderville, Alta.	Larry Trimble	Donald J. Docking	1963	380
175 1/8	25 5/8	26 5/8	22 2/8	4 5/8	4 5/8	5	5	Gerald, Sask.	Ken Cherewka	Larry Trimble	1964	380
175 1/8	27	27	20 2/8	5	5	8	7	Menominee Co., Wisc.	Gerald Ponfil	Ken Cherewka	1968	380
175 1/8	25 1/8	25 1/8	19	5 5/8	5 5/8	7	6	Knox Co., Neb.	Paul Klawitter	Gerald Ponfil	1970	380
175 1/8	27 1/8	25 5/8	18 5/8	5	5	5	5	Houston Co., Minn.	Craig F. Swenson	Paul Klawitter	1973	380
175 1/8	24 7/8	26 5/8	20 7/8	4 4/8	4 4/8	6	7	Lac qui Parle Co., Minn.	Harold Kittelson	Craig F. Swenson	1976	380
175 1/8	25 5/8	24 6/8	19 7/8	5 1/8	5 1/8	6	6	Shaunavon, Sask.	Richard Klink	Harold Kittelson	1981	380
175 1/8	22 5/8	22 2/8	20 5/8	5 5/8	5 5/8	6	6	Marinette Co., Wisc.	John Nielson	Richard Klink	1983	380

WHITETAIL DEER (Typical Antlers)—Continued
Odocoileus virginianus virginianus and certain related subspecies

Score	Length of Main Beam R.	L.	Inside Spread	Circumference at Smallest Place Between Burr and First Point R.	L.	Number of Points R.	L.	Locality Killed	By Whom Killed	Owner	Date Killed	Rank
175⅛	27⅜	27⅛	21⅞	5⅞	6	6	5	Wetzel Co., W.Va.	Matthew Scheibelhood	Matthew Scheibelhood	1984	380
175	25⅝	25⅛	21	4⅜	3⅞	5	5	New Salem, N.D.	John T. Cartwright	John T. Cartwright	1957	391
175	24⅜	22⅜	18⅝	4⅞	4⅞	7	7	La Salle Co., Texas	Leonard Wolf Bouldin	Leonard Wolf Bouldin	1972	391
175	23⅜	24	19⅞	5⅛	5⅞	5	5	Harrison Co., Mo.	Carl J. Graham	Carl J. Graham	1973	391
175	25⅜	25⅛	19⅞	5⅜	5⅛	5	5	Itasca Co., Minn.	David A. Frandsen	David A. Frandsen	1982	391
175	26	27⅛	21	5⅛	5⅛	6	6	Jim Hogg Co., Texas	Carl D. Ellis	Lee H. Lytton, Jr.	1984	391
174⅞	26⅜	25	22⅝	5⅜	5⅜	6	9	Rivers, Man.	N. Manchur	N. Manchur	1954	396
174⅞	28⅜	28⅜	21⅜	5	5	4	4	Burnett Co., Wisc.	Myles Keller	Myles Keller	1977	396
174⅞	25⅜	25⅛	21⅜	4⅞	4⅝	5	6	Jo Daviess Co., Ill.	W. V. Patrick	Jerry Patrick	1983	396
174⅞	26⅜	27⅛	21	5⅛	5⅝	8	6	Hayward, Wisc.	Bill Metcalf	John Metcalf	1924	399
174⅞	23⅜	24⅛	17⅝	6	5⅛	6	6	Lancaster Co., Neb.	Vaughn Wright	Phillip Wright	1960	399
174⅞	27⅜	29⅛	21⅛	5⅛	5	5	7	Coahoma Co., Miss.	O. P. Gilbert	O. P. Gilbert	1960	399
174⅞	28⅜	27⅛	21	4⅛	4⅜	5	5	Maine	Unknown	Warren H. Delaware	PR1977	399
174⅞	24⅜	24⅜	19⅜	5⅛	5⅛	9	9	Unknown	Unknown	Gerald Hillman	PR1978	399
174⅞	25	25⅜	24⅜	4⅜	4⅛	7	7	Kleberg Co., Texas	C. T. Burris	Darrell Pitts	1959	404
174⅜	24⅜	24⅜	19⅜	5⅜	5⅜	7	6	Manitoba	C. S. Browning	C. S. Browning	1960	404
174⅜	25⅜	26⅜	18⅜	5⅛	4⅞	5	6	Butler Co., Iowa	Vernon Simon	Vernon Simon	1972	404
174⅜	22⅜	21⅜	17⅜	5	5	6	6	Jefferson Co., Kan.	Keith D. Hendrix	Keith D. Hendrix	1973	404
174⅜	24	22⅜	18⅜	4⅜	4⅜	5	5	Meeker Co., Minn.	James L. Mattson	James L. Mattson	1973	404
174⅜	26	26⅜	21⅛	5⅜	5⅜	5	6	Baldonnel, B.C.	D. Ian Williams	D. Ian Williams	1978	404
174⅜	22⅜	24⅛	16⅜	4⅜	4⅛	5	5	Fort Steele, B.C.	John Lum	John Lum	1958	410
174⅜	22⅜	23⅜	19⅜	4⅜	4⅛	7	7	Powell Co., Mont.	Dave Rittenhouse	Dave Rittenhouse	1973	410
174⅜	22⅜	23⅜	18	5	5⅛	6	6	McKenzie Co., N.D.	Ben Dekker	Ben Dekker	1976	410
174⅜	26⅜	25⅜	19⅛	5⅜	5⅝	5	7	Charlotte Co., Va.	Jerry C. Claybrook	Jerry C. Claybrook	1977	410
174⅜	27⅜	27⅜	21	4⅜	4	6	6	Knox Co., Maine	Robert E. Young	Robert E. Young	1979	410
174⅜	28⅜	27⅜	17	5⅜	5⅜	5	7	Boone Co., Iowa	Curtis A. Lind	Curtis A. Lind	1982	410
174⅜	26⅜	27⅜	23⅜	5⅜	5⅛	6	5	Knox Co., Mo.	Jon Simmons	Jon Simmons	1972	416
174⅜	28⅜	26⅜	20⅛	5⅜	4⅜	6	5	Goshen Co., Wyo.	Casey L. Hunter	Casey L. Hunter	1984	416
174⅜	25⅜	25⅜	25⅜	4⅜	5⅜	4	4	Cerralvo, Mexico	Unknown	Antonio G. Gonzalez	1900	418
174⅜	28⅜	26	20	5⅜	4⅜	6	8	Zavala Co., Texas	Ernest Holdsworth	E. M. Holdsworth	1908	418

Score	R. Beam	L. Beam	Spread	Circ. 1	Circ. 2	Pts. R	Pts. L	Locality	By Whom Killed	Owner	Date	Rank
174 2/8	25 6/8	26 6/8	22	4 4/8	4 4/8	5	5	Livingston Co., N.Y.	Kenneth Bowen	Kenneth Bowen	1941	418
174 2/8	24 4/8	24 4/8	22	4 4/8	4 4/8	6	5	Dimmit Co., Texas	Red Tollet	McLean Bowman	1958	418
174 2/8	21 4/8	22	17	4 4/8	4 4/8	6	6	Cass Co., Texas	R. J. Perkins	John D. Small	1963	418
174 2/8	23 5/8	23 5/8	15 6/8	4 4/8	4 5/8	10	9	La Salle Co., Texas	Walter L. Taylor	Walter L. Taylor	1979	418
174 1/8	27	26 1/8	21 1/8	5 2/8	5 2/8	7	6	Aroostook Co., Maine	Unknown	Vern Black	1930	424
174 1/8	26 3/8	27 3/8	16 7/8	4 3/8	4 2/8	6	7	Essex Co., N.Y.	Denny Mitchell	Lewis P. Evans	1933	424
174 1/8	25	25	16 3/8	4 4/8	4 4/8	8	7	Calloway Co., Mo.	Jac LaFon	Jac LaFon	1968	424
174 1/8	26 3/8	26 3/8	20	5	5	6	6	Anarchist Mt., B.C.	George Urban	George Urban	1980	424
174 1/8	23 3/8	24 5/8	20 5/8	5 1/8	5 2/8	5	5	Johnson Co., Kan.	Ralph E. Schlagel	Ralph E. Schlagel	1984	424
174	26 1/8	26 2/8	20 5/8	4 4/8	4 4/8	7	7	Bulyea, Sask.	W. H. Dodsworth	E. B. Shaw	1961	429
174	26 2/8	26	17 5/8	4 5/8	4 5/8	5	7	Jefferson Co., Wisc.	Gary A. Coates	Gary A. Coates	1970	429
173 7/8	24 4/8	23 7/8	23 3/8	5 1/8	5 1/8	7	8	Dundurn, Sask.	Herb Wilson	Herb Wilson	1960	431
173 7/8	25 4/8	26	19 3/8	5	5	6	6	Starr Co., Texas	Leonard A. Schwarz	Leonard A. Schwarz	1965	431
173 7/8	26 6/8	27 1/8	19 5/8	5 5/8	5 3/8	7	5	Mercer Co., Ill	Floyd A. Clark	Floyd A. Clark	1961	433
173 6/8	26	26	18 5/8	5 7/8	6 1/8	6	5	Colfax Co., Neb.	Leonard Bowman	Leonard Bowman	1962	433
173 6/8	25	25 3/8	22 3/8	5 1/8	5	5	5	McAuley, Man.	Alex D. Vallance	Alex D. Vallance	1967	433
173 6/8	26 4/8	27	18 3/8	5 7/8	5 7/8	9	9	Bonner Co., Idaho	Robert L. Campbell	Robert L. Campbell	1967	433
173 6/8	25 4/8	25 1/8	18 5/8	5 3/8	5 5/8	7	6	Knox Co., Neb.	Paul H. Klawitter	Paul H. Klawitter	1970	433
173 6/8	23 3/8	24	19 5/8	4 6/8	4 4/8	6	6	Dimmit Co., Texas	Booth W. Petry	Booth W. Petry	1970	433
173 6/8	25 4/8	25 5/8	18 1/8	4 3/8	4 3/8	6	5	Pulaski Co., Ill.	Rose M. Blanchard	Rose M. Blanchard	1973	433
173 6/8	25 4/8	25 5/8	19 1/8	4 7/8	4 7/8	6	6	Livingston Co., Mich.	Terry J. Kemp	Terry J. Kemp	1979	433
173 6/8	26 6/8	26 1/8	17 1/8	4 4/8	4 4/8	5	6	Minburn, Alta.	Joseph R. McGillis	Joseph R. McGillis	1981	433
173 6/8	24 1/8	24 1/8	18 3/8	4 3/8	4 3/8	6	6	Regina, Sask.	Don Wolk	Don Wolk	1982	433
173 6/8	25 7/8	25 3/8	23 3/8	5 4/8	5 5/8	7	7	Carroll Co., Ga.	Ken Yearta	Ken Yearta	1983	433
173 6/8	24 4/8	24 4/8	17 5/8	4 4/8	4 4/8	5	5	Hart Creek, B.C.	Greg Lamontange	Greg Lamontange	1984	433
173 5/8	26 4/8	26 4/8	22 3/8	5 7/8	5 7/8	5	5	Sawyer Co., Wisc.	Maurice Peterson	Mac's Taxidermy	1940	445
173 5/8	26 4/8	25 3/8	18 3/8	5	5	7	6	Alberta	Frank Lind	Frank Lind	1952	445
173 5/8	25 4/8	21 1/8	20 1/8	4 7/8	4 7/8	8	5	Gentry Co., Mo.	William F. Oberbeck	William F. Oberbeck	1969	445
173 5/8	22 6/8	25	22 5/8	4 4/8	4 4/8	6	6	Valley Co., Mont.	Scott Fossum	Scott Fossum	1978	445
173 5/8	25	27 5/8	22 2/8	5 3/8	5 3/8	6	6	Lowndes Co., Miss.	Geraline Holliman	Geraline Holliman	1982	445
173 5/8	27 3/8	28 3/8	20 5/8	5 4/8	5 4/8	6	4	Woods Co., Okla.	Jack Clover	Jack Clover	1983	445
173 4/8	28 3/8	28 5/8	20 7/8	4 4/8	4 4/8	7	6	Flathead Co., Mont.	Mike J. Beaty	Mike J. Beaty	1984	445
173 4/8	26 4/8	27	20 1/8	5 5/8	5 5/8	8	9	Augusta Co., Va.	David H. Wolfe	David H. Wolfe	1957	452
173 4/8	27	28	26 1/8	5 3/8	5 3/8	6	6	Marengo Co., Ala.	Picked Up	L. M. Cabiniss	1960	452
173 4/8	23 3/8	23 5/8	18 3/8	4 6/8	4 6/8	7	7	Shelby Co., Tenn.	John J. Heirigs	John J. Heirigs	1962	452
173 4/8	24 7/8	23 6/8	17	5 5/8	5 5/8	6	6	Clover Leaf, Man.	Walter Lucko	Walter Lucko	1962	452
173 3/8	24 4/8	25	20 5/8	5 3/8	5 3/8	5	7	Tuffnell, Sask.	Ed Mattson	Ed Mattson	1964	452
173 3/8	25	29 6/8	20 7/8	5 3/8	5 1/8	7	6	Todd Co., Ky.	Troy L. Harris	Troy L. Harris	1965	452
173 3/8	29 4/8	27 4/8	21 2/8	5 1/8	5 1/8	5	7	Union Co., Iowa	Danny E. Abbott	Danny E. Abbott	1966	452
173 3/8	27 4/8	26	21	5 3/8	5 3/8	5	5	Vilas Co., Wisc.	Unknown	Donald Krueger	1967	452
173 3/8	26	29 3/8	23 3/8	6 3/8	6 3/8	7	8	Ontario Co., N.Y.	Martin Solway	N. Y. Cons. Dept.	1946	460
173 3/8	28 3/8	28 1/8	20 1/8	4 5/8	4 5/8	5	6	Clarion Co., Pa.	Mead Kiefer	Mead Kiefer	1947	460

WHITETAIL DEER (Typical Antlers)—Continued
Odocoileus virginianus virginianus and certain related subspecies

Score	Length of Main Beam R	L	Inside Spread	Circumference at Smallest Place Between Burr and First Point R	L	Number of Points R	L	Locality Killed	By Whom Killed	Owner	Date Killed	Rank
173⅜	26⅜	26⅜	19⅛	5⅜	5⅜	7	7	Arkansas Co., Ark.	Jimmy Hanson	Jimmy Hanson	1948	460
173⅜	25⅝	26⅞	17⅞	4⅜	4⅜	5	5	Clarion Co., Pa.	Picked Up	Fred Gallagher	1954	460
173⅜	27	27⅞	21⅛	5⅜	5⅜	5	5	Lewis Co., Ky.	Darrell Tully	Darrell Tully	1968	460
173⅜	23⅜	23⅜	23⅜	5⅛	5⅛	5	5	Rosebud Co., Mont.	Ted Millhollin	Ted Millhollin	1975	460
173⅜	24⅜	25	16⅞	5⅛	5⅛	5	5	Valley Co., Mont.	Steve K. Sukut	Steve K. Sukut	1978	460
173⅜	26⅛	25⅝	18⅝	5	5	5	5	Keya Paha Co., Neb.	Gene F. Pool	Gene F. Pool	1980	460
173⅜	27⅛	27⅛	17⅛	4⅞	4⅞	7	7	Clay Co., Kan.	Charles A. Hammons	Charles A. Hammons	1984	460
173⅜	30⅜	29⅝	21⅛	5	5⅞	5	8	Chicot Co., Ark.	Yan Sturdivant	Bruce Sturdivant	1951	469
173⅜	24⅜	25⅜	20⅜	4⅝	4⅞	6	5	Bemersyde, Sask.	R. L. McCullough	R. L. McCullough	1959	469
173⅜	25⅜	24⅜	25⅜	5⅛	5⅛	5	5	Price Co., Wisc.	Clarence Parmelee	J. D. Andrews	1959	469
173⅜	25⅛	24⅜	25⅜	5⅜	5⅜	7	6	Whitewood, Sask.	L. Reichel	L. Reichel	1964	469
173⅜	25⅜	25⅞	21	6	5⅝	8	5	Antler, Sask.	Elmer Lowry	Elmer Lowry	1966	469
173⅜	26⅞	24⅜	20⅜	5⅜	5	5	5	Furnas Co., Neb.	Marvin F. Wieland	Marvin F. Wieland	1969	469
173⅜	29	29⅜	20	5⅛	5⅜	6	5	Lyman Co., S.D.	William G. Psychos	William G. Psychos	1972	469
173⅜	25⅜	25⅜	21⅝	4⅜	4⅛	5	5	Decatur Co., Tenn.	Glen D. Odle	Glen D. Odle	1972	469
173⅜	27⅜	25⅜	18⅜	4	4⅛	6	6	Allen Co., Ky.	Terry Wayne Sims	Terry Wayne Sims	1979	469
173⅜	28	28⅜	20⅜	5⅜	5⅜	9	8	Warren Co., Mo.	Jerome E. Ley	Jerome E. Ley	1980	469
173⅜	26⅞	28⅜	23⅜	4⅜	4⅜	6	6	Chisago Co., Minn.	Roger A. Peterson	Roger A. Peterson	1984	469
173⅜	26⅜	26⅜	19	4⅛	4	6	5	Marie, Sask.	King Trew	King Trew	1957	480
173⅜	23⅜	24⅜	20⅜	5	5	6	5	Estuary, Sask.	Melvin J. Anderson	Melvin J. Anderson	1962	480
173⅜	25⅜	24⅜	19⅜	5	5	7	7	Slope Co., N.D.	Robert L. Stroup	Robert L. Stroup	1967	480
173⅜	23⅜	23⅜	18⅜	4	4	6	6	Wabaunsee Co., Kan.	James D. Downey	James D. Downey	1970	480
173⅜	28⅜	28⅜	22⅜	5⅜	5⅜	6	6	Lake Co., Mont.	Darrell Brist	Darrell Brist	1971	480
173⅜	26⅛	24⅜	21⅜	4⅞	4⅞	5	5	Fillmore Co., Minn.	Gerry D. Arnold	Gerry D. Arnold	1973	480
173⅜	29⅜	28⅜	25⅜	5⅜	5⅛	4	4	White Co., Tenn.	Sam H. Langford	Sam H. Langford	1980	480
173⅜	26	26⅜	18⅜	4⅛	3⅞	6	6	Shelby Co., Mo.	William A. Light, Jr.	William A. Light, Jr.	1981	480
173⅜	26⅜	27⅜	19⅜	4⅜	4⅜	7	6	Big Muddy Valley, Sask.	Lyndon T. Ross	Lyndon T. Ross	1984	480
173⅜	24⅜	25⅜	16⅜	4⅜	4⅜	5	5	Pawnee Co., Neb.	Gary G. Habegger	Gary G. Habegger	1967	489
173	25⅜	27⅜	25⅜	5⅞	5⅞	6	5	Sandusky Co., Ohio	Harold M. Chalfin	Harold M. Chalfin	1975	489
173	28	28⅜	21⅞	5⅜	5⅜	7	6	Howard Co., Mo.	Thomas R. Banning	Thomas R. Banning	1978	489

Score	Length of Main Beam R.	Length of Main Beam L.	Inside Spread	Circ. R.	Circ. L.	Pts. R.	Pts. L.	Locality	By Whom Killed	Owner	Date	No.
173	25⁵⁄₈	24⁴⁄₈	21⁷⁄₈	4⁴⁄₈	4⁵⁄₈	9	6	Hidalgo Co., Texas	William L. Turk	William L. Turk	1979	489
173	27⁷⁄₈	27⁴⁄₈	21⁵⁄₈	4⁴⁄₈	4⁵⁄₈	5	6	Cook Co., Minn.	Wesley A. Nelson	Wesley A. Nelson	1980	489
173	26	26	21	4⁴⁄₈	4⁵⁄₈	6	6	Somerset Co., Maine	Charles A. Moulton	Charles A. Moulton	1981	489
173	23⁷⁄₈	25⁵⁄₈	19⁵⁄₈	4⁴⁄₈	4⁵⁄₈	7	8	Bunder Lake, Alta.	Steve Swinhoe	Steve Swinhoe	1983	489
173	24⁴⁄₈	24⁴⁄₈	16⁵⁄₈	5³⁄₈	5³⁄₈	5	5	Bonnyville, Alta.	Lionel P. Tercier	Lionel P. Tercier	1983	489
173	24⁴⁄₈	25⁴⁄₈	16⁷⁄₈	3⁷⁄₈	3⁷⁄₈	6	7	Trinity Co., Texas	Don Knight	Don Knight	1983	489
173	27	27⁵⁄₈	23⁷⁄₈	5⁷⁄₈	5⁵⁄₈	6	7	Doniphan Co., Kan.	Charles A. Staudenmier	Charles A. Staudenmier	1983	489
173	25⁵⁄₈	25⁴⁄₈	19⁴⁄₈	4⁴⁄₈	4⁵⁄₈	4	4	Sullivan Co., Tenn.	C. Alan Altizer	C. Alan Altizer	1984	489
172⁷⁄₈	25⁵⁄₈	25⁵⁄₈	22⁵⁄₈	4⁷⁄₈	4⁷⁄₈	6	6	Windthorst, Sask.	Jack Glover	Jack Glover	1951	500
172⁷⁄₈	25⁵⁄₈	25	20⁵⁄₈	4³⁄₈	4³⁄₈	7	7	McHenry Co., N.D.	David Medalen	David Medalen	1959	500
172⁷⁄₈	25	24³⁄₈	16⁷⁄₈	5⁴⁄₈	5	5	5	Ashland Co., Wisc.	Einar Sein	Rick Iacono	1965	500
172⁷⁄₈	26⁷⁄₈	26¹⁄₈	18	4²⁄₈	4⁷⁄₈	6	6	Olmsted Co., Minn.	Wesley W. Holtz	Wesley W. Holtz	1966	500
172⁷⁄₈	26⁵⁄₈	27	21⁷⁄₈	5³⁄₈	5⁵⁄₈	6	7	Newton Co., Ga.	L. W. Shirley, Jr.	L. W. Shirley, Jr.	1967	500
172⁷⁄₈	27⁷⁄₈	26⁵⁄₈	21¹⁄₈	4⁷⁄₈	4⁵⁄₈	6	5	Seneca Co., N.Y.	Martin J. Way	Martin J. Way	1968	500
172⁷⁄₈	24⁴⁄₈	25¹⁄₈	22²⁄₈	4⁵⁄₈	4⁵⁄₈	7	8	Cascade Co., Mont.	Skip Halmes	Skip Halmes	1976	500
172⁶⁄₈	26	27³⁄₈	18⁴⁄₈	4⁴⁄₈	4⁴⁄₈	5	10	Heard Co., Ga.	Keith McCullough	Keith McCullough	1982	508
172⁶⁄₈	25⁵⁄₈	25¹⁄₈	24	4⁵⁄₈	4⁵⁄₈	5	6	Woodruff, Wisc.	Unknown	Mac's Taxidermy	1918	508
172⁶⁄₈	27⁷⁄₈	27³⁄₈	22⁴⁄₈	5	5	5	5	Waldo Co., Maine	Wallace Humphrey	Arthur Humphrey	1963	508
172⁶⁄₈	28⁵⁄₈	29	22⁴⁄₈	4⁴⁄₈	4⁵⁄₈	5	6	Webb Co., Texas	B. A. Vineyard	B. A. Vineyard	1964	508
172⁶⁄₈	25⁵⁄₈	25⁵⁄₈	20³⁄₈	4⁵⁄₈	4⁷⁄₈	6	6	Spokane Co., Wash.	Maurice Robinette	Maurice Robinette	1968	508
172⁶⁄₈	24⁴⁄₈	24³⁄₈	22²⁄₈	6	6	6	5	Boone Co., Iowa	Lonne L. Tracy	Lonne L. Tracy	1975	508
172⁶⁄₈	25⁴⁄₈	25¹⁄₈	16³⁄₈	4⁷⁄₈	4⁵⁄₈	5	6	Allamakee Co., Iowa	Picked up	Tom Kernat, Sr.	1976	508
172⁶⁄₈	24²⁄₈	23⁴⁄₈	21¹⁄₈	5	5	7	6	Edgerton, Alta.	Richard T. Abbott	Richard T. Abbott	1980	508
172⁵⁄₈	24⁴⁄₈	24⁴⁄₈	22³⁄₈	5	5	6	5	Frio Co., Texas	Unknown	Roy Hindes	PR1940	515
172⁵⁄₈	26	26	19¹⁄₈	4⁴⁄₈	4⁴⁄₈	6	5	Esterhazy, Sask.	J. Weise	J. Weise	1960	515
172⁵⁄₈	24⁵⁄₈	24⁴⁄₈	18¹⁄₈	5⁷⁄₈	5⁷⁄₈	7	5	Shoal Lake, Man.	Gary Phillips	Gary Phillips	1967	515
172⁵⁄₈	26⁷⁄₈	25⁵⁄₈	18¹⁄₈	5³⁄₈	5⁵⁄₈	6	5	Cass Co., Mich.	Ben R. Williams	Ben R. Williams	1971	515
172⁵⁄₈	24¹⁄₈	23	17⁴⁄₈	4³⁄₈	4³⁄₈	5	6	Tuscarawas Co., Ohio	Charles Kerns	Charles Kerns	1972	515
172⁵⁄₈	26⁶⁄₈	25	21³⁄₈	4⁵⁄₈	4⁷⁄₈	9	6	Knox Co., Maine	Willis A. Moody, Jr.	Willis A. Moody, Jr.	1974	515
172⁵⁄₈	26³⁄₈	26⁴⁄₈	22	4⁷⁄₈	4⁷⁄₈	5	7	Highland Co., Ohio	Wilbur D. Rhoads	Wilbur D. Rhoads	1979	515
172⁵⁄₈	28	28	25⁴⁄₈	6²⁄₈	6³⁄₈	8	8	Adams Co., Miss.	Adrian L. Stallone	Adrian L. Stallone	1983	515
172⁴⁄₈	25⁵⁄₈	25⁵⁄₈	20⁵⁄₈	4⁷⁄₈	4⁷⁄₈	5	5	Barren Co., Ky.	Billy N. Short	Billy N. Short	1984	524
172⁴⁄₈	27	27	18⁴⁄₈	5	5	6	6	Cotulla, Texas	George E. Light III	George E. Light III	1959	524
172⁴⁄₈	24⁵⁄₈	24⁴⁄₈	22⁵⁄₈	4⁴⁄₈	4⁴⁄₈	7	6	Webb Co., Texas	A. M. Russell	A. M. Russell	1961	524
172⁴⁄₈	24⁷⁄₈	26⁷⁄₈	24	5¹⁄₈	5¹⁄₈	5	4	Laird, Sask.	A. E. Nikkel	A. E. Nikkel	1963	524
172⁴⁄₈	26⁴⁄₈	24	20	5³⁄₈	5⁵⁄₈	5	5	Fort Knox, Ky.	E. G. Christian	E. G. Christian	1966	524
172⁴⁄₈	27⁷⁄₈	24³⁄₈	19	5	5	6	6	Chauvin, Alta.	Ron D. Jakimchuk	Ron D. Jakimchuk	1971	524
172⁴⁄₈	24³⁄₈	25³⁄₈	21⁴⁄₈	4⁵⁄₈	4⁵⁄₈	5	5	Randolph Co., Ga.	Robert D. Bell	Robert D. Bell	1979	524
172⁴⁄₈	26⁷⁄₈	26³⁄₈	23⁵⁄₈	5²⁄₈	5²⁄₈	6	6	Muskingum Co., Ohio	Michael Wilson	Michael Wilson	1982	524
172⁴⁄₈	26	25⁵⁄₈	20	5⁵⁄₈	5⁵⁄₈	8	7	Muhlenberg Co., Ky.	Dennis Nolen	Dennis Nolen	1982	524
172⁴⁄₈	24⁴⁄₈	25⁵⁄₈	19⁵⁄₈	5⁷⁄₈	5⁷⁄₈	6	5	Franklin Co., Ill.	Joseph S. Smothers	Joseph S. Smothers	1984	524
172³⁄₈	26	26⁶⁄₈	19⁵⁄₈	4⁵⁄₈	4⁵⁄₈	6	5	Monroe Co., Mo.	Clark Ernest Bray	Clark Ernest Bray	1967	533

WHITETAIL DEER (Typical Antlers)—Continued
Odocoileus virginianus virginianus and certain related subspecies

Score	Length of Main Beam R.	Length of Main Beam L.	Inside Spread	Circumference at Smallest Place Between Burr and First Point R.	Circumference at Smallest Place Between Burr and First Point L.	Number of Points R.	Number of Points L.	Locality Killed	By Whom Killed	Owner	Date Killed	Rank
172⅞	27⅞	27⅞	20⅜	6	6⅛	5	6	Brookings, S.D.	Paul W. Back	Paul W. Back	1967	533
172⅞	27⅞	28⅜	17⅞	4⅝	4⅝	6	5	Decatur Co., Tenn.	Danny Pope	Danny Pope	1982	533
172⅞	24⅜	24⅜	18	4⅞	4⅞	8	7	Rusk Co., Wisc.	Randy A. Jochem	Randy A. Jochem	1984	533
172⅞	30⅛	30⅜	22⅜	5⅝	5⅝	9	9	Porcupine Plain, Sask.	Kim Mikkonen	Kim Mikkonen	1985	533
172⅞	27⅞	28	20	4⅝	4⅝	5	6	Lincoln Co., Wisc.	Alfred Theilig	Philip Schlegel	1928	538
172⅞	24⅜	24⅜	18	4⅝	4⅝	6	6	Vilas Co., Wisc.	Ray Hermanson	J. James Froelich	1936	538
172⅞	28⅜	26⅜	21⅜	4⅝	4⅜	6	6	Bedford Co., Pa.	John F. Sharpe	John F. Sharpe	1942	538
172⅞	26⅝	25⅜	20	6	5⅝	7	7	Weyburn, Sask.	Wilfred LaValley	Wilfred LaValley	1958	538
172⅞	26⅜	26⅜	19⅝	4⅝	4⅝	6	7	Manor, Sask.	Albert McConnell	Albert McConnell	1962	538
172⅞	27⅜	25⅜	23⅜	5⅛	5⅛	5	8	Flathead Co., Mont.	Lonny Hanson	Lonny Hanson	1963	538
172⅞	25⅜	25⅝	19	5	5	6	7	Adams Co., Wisc.	W. R. Ingraham	W. R. Ingraham	1965	538
172⅞	23	30⅞	23	4⅞	5⅛	6	7	Perry Co., Ill.	Raymond E. Haertling	Raymond E. Haertling	1968	538
172⅞	31⅛	22⅜	23⅜	4⅞	5	7	6	Perry Co., Ill.	Ralph J. Przygoda, Jr.	Ralph J. Przygoda, Jr.	1978	538
172⅞	25⅝	24⅜	20	4⅝	4⅞	6	8	Perkins Co., S.D.	Randy G. Swenson	Randy G. Swenson	1979	538
172⅞	25⅝	24⅜	23⅜	4⅝	4⅜	5	5	Cattaraugus Co., N.Y.	Thomas J. Hinchey	Thomas J. Hinchey	1982	538
172⅞	25⅞	25⅜	20⅜	4⅜	4⅝	7	5	Pendleton Co., Ky.	Kevin L. Galloway	Kevin L. Galloway	1983	538
172⅞	26⅜	25½	22	5	5	6	6	Stewart Co., Tenn.	Joe K. Sanders	Joe K. Sanders	1984	538
172⅛	26⅜	25	18⅞	5	5	5	5	Juneau Co., Wisc.	Unknown	Clark G. Gallup	1949	551
172⅛	25⅝	25⅝	19⅝	5⅜	5⅜	5	5	Pickens Co., Ala.	Walter Jaynes	Walter Jaynes	1968	551
172⅛	26⅜	26⅝	21⅝	5⅜	5⅜	5	5	Hughes Co., S.D.	Mark Lilevjen	Mark Lilevjen	1971	551
172⅛	26⅜	25⅝	23⅜	4⅜	4⅜	8	7	Coshocton Co., Ohio	Virgil E. Carpenter	Virgil E. Carpenter	1972	551
172⅛	27	27⅞	19⅜	4⅜	5	6	7	Queen Annes Co., Md.	James R. Spies, Jr.	James R. Spies, Jr.	1976	551
172⅛	28⅜	28⅜	18⅝	5	4⅝	6	5	Fillmore Co., Minn.	Murrel Mathison	Murrel Mathison	1977	551
172⅛	27⅜	26⅜	18⅜	4⅜	5⅜	8	7	Winona Co., Minn.	Robert J. Cordie	Robert J. Cordie	1979	551
172	24	24⅛	20⅜	5⅛	4⅞	6	6	Oconto Co., Wisc.	Henry J. Bredael	Henry J. Bredael	1939	558
172	25⅛	25⅝	16⅝	5⅛	5⅛	5	5	Neepawa, Man.	Jim Sinclair	Jim Sinclair	1947	558
172	26⅝	25⅝	19⅝	5⅜	5⅜	5	5	Wadena, Sask.	Edgar Smale	Edgar Smale	1959	558
172	24⅝	23	17	4⅜	4⅞	9	8	Buffalo Co., Wisc.	Ralph Duellman	Ralph Duellman	1960	558
172	24⅜	24⅜	18⅜	5⅜	5⅜	5	6	N. Battleford, Sask.	Dick Napastuk	Dick Napastuk	1962	558
172	26½	25	21⅜	4⅜	4⅜	5	5	Bearden, Ark.	Buddy Wise	Buddy Wise	1962	558

Score						R	L	Locality	By whom killed	Owner	Date	Rank
172	25	26⅞	21¼	5⅛	5⅝	5	5	Parkman, Sask.	A. T. Mair	A. T. Mair	1963	558
172	24⅞	24⅞	20⅛	6⅜	6⅜	8	7	Butts Co., Ga.	Jack Hammond	Jack Hammond	1963	558
172	24⅞	24⅞	17⅞	4⅜	4⅜	6	5	Joseph Plains, Idaho	Jim Felton	Jim Felton	1965	558
172	25	25⅜	18⅜	5⅜	5⅜	6	5	Adams Co., Miss.	Nan Foster New	Nan Foster New	1977	558
172	26	25⅜	22⅜	4⅜	4⅜	6	7	Muskingkum Co., Ohio	David R. Hatfield	David R. Hatfield	1980	558
172	25⅛	26	19⅜	4⅞	5⅞	7	5	Furnas Co., Neb.	Marvin A. Briegel	Marvin A. Briegel	1980	558
172	24	25⅞	18	4⅜	4⅜	6	5	Tift Co., Ga.	Mayo Tucker	Mayo Tucker	1982	558
172	24⅞	25⅞	22⅝	5⅜	5⅜	5	5	Miami Co., Kan.	Dan R. Moore	Dan R. Moore	1982	558
172	27⅜	28⅜	18⅜	5	5	5	5	Westmoreland Co., N.B.	Edgar Cormier	Edgar Cormier	1983	558
172	25⅞	25⅜	19	4⅜	4⅜	5	5	Waukesha Co., Wisc.	Donald R. Friedlein	Donald R. Friedlein	1983	558
171⅞	27⅞	27⅞	20⅛	5	5	5	5	Madison Parish, La.	M. L. Arnold	David D. Arnold	1941	574
171⅞	25⅜	27	16⅜	5⅞	5⅞	8	8	Scotch Bay, Man.	W. J. Harker	W. J. Harker	1951	574
171⅞	27	27	20⅜	4⅜	4⅜	5	5	Houston Co., Minn.	Donald R. Sobolik	Donald R. Sobolik	1958	574
171⅞	26⅜	25⅝	20⅛	5⅛	5⅝	7	6	Aroostook Co., Maine	Julian B. Perry	Julian B. Perry	1962	574
171⅞	25⅜	25⅜	18⅜	5	5	6	7	Union Co., Iowa	Darrell M. Gutz	Darrell M. Gutz	1973	574
171⅞	25⅜	24⅜	25⅝	5⅛	5⅛	5	6	Perry Co., Ohio	Bill Pargeon	Bill Pargeon	1976	574
171⅞	25⅜	26⅛	21⅛	4⅜	4⅜	5	5	Oxford Co., Maine	Picked Up	Francis Ontengco	1980	574
171⅞	25	24⅜	20	5	5	6	5	Washington Co., Ohio	Thomas E. Burnette	Thomas E. Burnette	1982	574
171⅞	26⅜	26⅜	24⅛	4⅛	4⅛	5	8	Scotland Co., Mo.	David R. Smith	David R. Smith	1984	574
171⅞	26⅜	26⅜	18	4⅜	4⅜	5	4	Niagara, Wisc.	Francis H. Van Ginkel	David Watson	1945	574
171⅞	26	27	18⅜	6⅜	6⅜	5	5	St. Louis Co., Minn.	Paul S. Paulson	Paul S. Paulson	1946	583
171⅞	25	24⅜	22	4⅜	4⅜	5	6	Maverick Co., Texas	Harry Garner	Harry Garner	1962	583
171⅞	24⅜	24⅜	19	5⅜	5⅜	7	5	Turtle Mt., Man.	Roy Hainsworth	Roy Hainsworth	1963	583
171⅞	26⅝	26⅝	21⅜	4⅜	4⅜	6	9	Asquith, Sask.	M. S. Vanin	M. S. Vanin	1963	583
171⅞	25⅝	25⅝	18⅛	4⅜	4⅜	5	5	Maple Creek, Sask.	G. J. Burch	G. J. Burch	1967	583
171⅞	24⅜	24⅜	17⅛	4⅛	4⅛	5	8	Muscatine Co., Iowa	Larry Dipple	Larry Dipple	1967	583
171⅞	28⅜	27⅜	19⅜	5⅜	5⅜	8	4	Buffalo Co., Wisc.	Richard Schultz	Richard Schultz	1973	583
171⅞	25⅛	24⅜	18⅜	4⅜	4⅜	4	5	Dawes Co., Neb.	Tim Morava	Tim Morava	1974	583
171⅞	27⅜	26⅜	21	4⅜	4⅜	6	5	Adams Co., Ill	R. C. Stephens	R. C. Stephens	1975	583
171⅞	25⅜	25⅜	24⅜	5⅜	5⅜	6	6	Clinton Co., N.Y.	William J. Branch	William J. Branch	1982	583
171⅞	24⅜	23⅜	19⅜	4⅜	4⅜	8	10	Gray Creek, B.C.	Ross Oliver	Ross Oliver	1982	583
171⅞	26⅜	26⅜	19⅜	5⅜	5⅜	7	7	Perry Co., Ill.	Daniel P. Hollenkamp	Daniel P. Hollenkamp	1982	583
171⅞	26⅜	26⅜	20⅜	4⅜	4⅜	4	4	Van Buren Co., Mich.	Ronald E. Eldred	Ronald E. Eldred	1983	583
171⅞	24⅜	24⅜	19⅜	5	5	9	10	Morton Co., N.D.	Dick Eastman	Sioux Sporting Goods	1955	597
171⅞	22⅜	23	19	5⅜	5⅜	5	6	Tensas Parish, La.	Jim Keahey	Gerald P. Begnaud, Jr.	1960	597
171⅞	25⅜	26⅜	20⅜	5⅜	5⅛	6	5	Hanley, Sask.	L. R. Libke	L. R. Libke	1961	597
171⅞	26	25⅜	24⅜	4⅜	4⅜	7	6	Langbank, Sask.	Thomas K. Grimm	Thomas K. Grimm	1968	597
171⅞	25⅛	26⅛	16⅜	4	4	8	7	Baldwin Co., Ga.	Picked Up	E. Donald Graham	1977	597
171⅞	27	25⅜	18⅜	5⅜	5⅜	6	6	Otter Tail Co., Minn.	Carl D. Hill	Carl D. Hill	1977	597
171⅞	25⅜	24⅜	18⅜	4⅜	4⅜	5	5	Grant Co., Minn.	Gary P. Kollman	Gary P. Kollman	1980	597
171⅞	27⅜	27⅜	18⅜	5	5	6	6	Riley Co., Kan.	Mick McCallister	Mick McCallister	1980	597
171⅞	25⅜	26⅜	19⅜	5⅜	5⅜	7	7	Bonnell Brook, N.B.	Steve R. McCutcheon	Steve R. McCutcheon	1984	597

WHITETAIL DEER (Typical Antlers)—Continued

Odocoileus virginianus virginianus and certain related subspecies

Score	Length of Main Beam R	L	Inside Spread	Circumference at Smallest Place Between Burr and First Point R	L	Number of Points R	L	Locality Killed	By Whom Killed	Owner	Date Killed	Rank
171⅝	24⅞	26⅜	19⅞	5⅝	5⅝	5	5	Hayter, Alta.	H. D. L. Loucks	H. D. L. Loucks	1953	606
171⅝	26	26⅜	21⅛	5	4⅞	11	6	Woodlands Dist., Man.	Bill Rutherford	Bill Rutherford	1961	606
171⅝	26⅜	27⅞	23⅜	5⅝	5⅞	7	9	Clay Co., Minn.	Clint Foslien	Clint Foslien	1965	606
171⅝	26	26	23⅜	4⅞	4⅜	5	7	Schroon Lake, N.Y.	Richard E. Johndrow	Richard E. Johndrow	1968	606
171⅝	25⅞	24⅝	19⅝	4⅜	4⅜	5	5	Clearwater Co., Minn.	Peter Tranby	Peter Tranby	1978	606
171⅝	25	24⅜	20⅝	4⅜	4⅜	6	6	Rusk Co., Wisc.	Luke Dernovsek III	Luke Dernovsek III	1983	606
171⅝	27⅛	26⅜	18⅝	4⅜	4⅝	5	6	Becker Co., Minn.	Kraig J. Ketter	Kraig J. Ketter	1983	606
171⅝	24⅝	21⅞	21⅜	5	4⅞	8	6	Crooked Lake, Alta.	Bruce J. Ferguson	Bruce J. Ferguson	1984	606
171½	26⅝	26⅝	21⅜	4⅞	4⅜	9	7	Juneau Co., Wisc.	Fay Hammersley	Fay Hammersley	1938	614
171½	26	26⅜	17⅞	4⅜	4⅜	6	7	Herkimer Co., N.Y.	John Christie	John Christie	1957	614
171½	31⅛	29	16	5	5	7	9	Frio Co., Texas	Leonard Van Horn	Leonard Van Horn	1962	614
171½	26	24⅜	15⅜	4⅜	4	5	6	La Salle Co., Texas	Charles D. Johnson	Charles D. Johnson	1964	614
171½	22⅝	22⅝	18	5⅜	5⅜	7	6	Grenfell, Sask.	George DeMontigny	George DeMontigny	1965	614
171½	25⅝	25⅝	19⅜	4⅜	4⅜	6	7	Oceana Co., Mich.	Delos Highland	Delos Highland	1967	614
171½	25⅜	26⅝	18⅝	5⅜	5⅜	5	5	Forest Co., Wisc.	Chester Cox, Jr.	Chester Cox, Jr.	1969	614
171½	22⅞	23⅜	14⅜	5	5	7	6	Metaline Falls Co., Wash	Scott Hicks	Scott Hicks	1970	614
171½	23⅜	24⅜	23⅜	4⅞	4⅞	5	5	Kandiyohi Co., Minn.	Werner B. Reining	Werner B. Reining	1974	614
171½	25⅞	24⅜	22⅝	5	5	7	6	Pope Co., Minn.	Corbin G. Corson	Corbin G. Corson	1975	614
171½	24⅞	23⅜	21⅝	4⅜	4⅜	5	5	Athabasca River, Alta.	Ron J. Holm	Ron J. Holm	1977	614
171½	27⅜	27⅜	21⅝	5	4⅞	7	6	Boyd Co., Neb.	Scott A. Sperling	Scott A. Sperling	1982	614
171½	28	27⅛	18⅝	4⅜	4⅜	5	6	Kalamazoo Co., Mich.	Harvey B. Braden	Harvey B. Braden	1984	614
171½	25⅝	26⅜	21⅜	5⅜	5⅜	8	10	Douglas Co., Minn.	Gregory A. Dropik	Gregory A. Dropik	1984	614
171½	27⅜	28⅝	18⅛	4⅜	4⅜	5	5	Sumner Co., Kan.	Jeff D. Ehlers	Jeff D. Ehlers	1984	614
171⅜	29⅞	28⅞	19⅞	4⅜	4⅜	6	5	Arkansas Co., Ark.	Wilbur Stephens	Wilbur Stephens	1953	629
171⅜	25⅝	25⅞	19⅛	5	5	5	5	Bayfield Co., Wisc.	Lawrence Stumo	Lawrence Stumo	1956	629
171⅜	27	26⅛	21⅛	5⅜	5⅜	6	6	Waldo Co., Maine	Paul K. Nickerson	Paul K. Nickerson	1957	629
171⅜	26⅝	25	22⅜	5⅝	5⅝	5	6	Macintosh, Ont.	Richard Kouhi	Richard Kouhi	1967	629
171⅜	25⅝	25⅜	19⅜	4⅝	4⅝	5	6	Webb Co., Texas	Ernie Pavlas	Ernie Pavlas	1970	629
171⅛	27⅞	27⅞	21⅜	4⅜	4⅜	5	5	Charlevoix Co., Mich.	Noel Thomson	Ivan Thomson	1957	634
171⅛	22⅝	21	18⅝	5⅛	5⅝	6	6	Medicine Hat, Alta.	Frank Chevalier	Marcel Houle	1958	634

Score	R	L	Spread	Circ. R	Circ. L	Pts R	Pts L	Locality	Name	Name	Date	Rank
171⅛	24⅞	25	20⅝	6	6	5	5	Penobscot Co., Maine	Kenneth Scott	Kenneth W. Bennett	1960	634
171⅛	26	26⅞	16⅝	5⅝	5⅝	5	5	Douglas Co., Minn.	James M. Bircher	James M. Bircher	1962	634
171⅛	27⅞	27⅛	18	4⅜	4⅜	8	7	Alger Co., Mich.	Shirley L. Robare	Shirley L. Robare	1963	634
171⅛	23⅜	23⅜	20⅛	5⅝	5	5	6	Whitewood, Sask.	Wm. Cook	Wm. Cook	1966	634
171⅛	23⅜	23⅜	19⅛	6⅜	7⅞	5	5	Bayfield Co., Wisc.	James A. Peters	James A. Peters	1979	634
171	26⅜	26⅜	19⅛	5	4⅞	7	6	Sherwood, N.D.	Roy Foss	Roy Foss	1947	641
171	27⅛	26	19⅞	4⅜	4⅜	5	5	Hampshire Co., W.Va.	Conda L. Shanholtz	Conda L. Shanholtz	1958	641
171	23⅜	27⅝	19⅞	5⅛	5⅛	5	6	Windthorst, Sask.	Thomas Dovell	Thomas Dovell	1961	641
171	28⅝	20⅝	20⅜	5⅜	5⅜	7	7	Perkins, S.D.	Ethel Schrader	Ethel Schrader	1963	641
171	22⅝	25⅞	19⅞	5	5⅝	7	7	Antelope Co., Neb.	Leo M. Beelart	Leo M. Beelart	1964	641
171	26⅞	25⅜	20⅛	4⅛	4⅛	7	8	Buffalo Co., Wisc.	Clarence H. Castleberg, Jr.	Clarence H. Castleberg, Jr.	1964	641
171	24⅞	23⅝	17⅝	4⅛	4⅜	6	6	Ray Co., Mo.	Darle R. Siegel	Darle R. Siegel	1966	641
171	24⅜	26⅛	21	5	5	5	5	Seven Persons, Alta.	Haven Lane	Haven Lane	1968	641
171	28⅛	26⅝	21	4⅞	4⅞	5	5	Speers, Sask.	Charles E. Strautman	Charles E. Strautman	1969	641
171	27	26⅞	26⅝	5⅝	5⅜	7	7	Otter Tail Co., Minn.	Lawrence J. Anderson	Lawrence J. Anderson	1974	641
171	26	26	20	4⅜	4⅜	5	5	Aroostook Co., Maine	Roland L. Demers	Roland L. Demers	1983	641
171	25⅜	25⅜	15⅝	5⅜	5⅜	5	5	Christian Co., Mo.	Melba J. Herndon	Melba J. Herndon	1983	641
171	28⅛	27⅛	19⅝	4⅜	4⅜	5	5	Okanagan Range, B.C.	Picked Up	Dennis A. Dorholt	1984	641
170⅞	26⅞	25⅜	17⅞	5	5	5	5	Issaquena Co., Miss.	Warren A. Miller	Alford M. Cooley	1920	654
170⅞	26⅞	25⅞	19⅝	5	5	7	7	Frio Co., Texas	Lex Stewart	Lex Stewart	1930	654
170⅞	30	30	20⅞	4⅞	4⅞	5	5	Bath Co., Va.	Maurice Smith	Maurice Smith	1953	654
170⅞	26⅞	27⅛	21⅛	5	5	5	5	Des Moines Co., Iowa	Craig A. Field	Craig A. Field	1967	654
170⅞	26⅞	27⅛	21⅛	5⅝	5⅝	5	5	Kingman, Alta.	Robert D. Kozack	Robert D. Kozack	1971	654
170⅞	25⅜	24⅜	18⅝	5⅜	5⅜	7	7	Holmes Co., Ohio	Ken Taylor	Ken Taylor	1975	654
170⅞	27	26⅝	23⅛	5	5	6	6	Tippecanoe Co., Ind.	Harold A. Anthrop	Harold A. Anthrop	1976	654
170⅞	25⅜	25⅝	19⅛	5⅝	5⅝	8	8	Steuben Co., N.Y.	Duane L. Horton	Duane L. Horton	1976	654
170⅞	27⅛	26⅝	17⅛	5⅝	5⅝	5	5	Washington Co., Maine	Merle G. Michaud	Merle G. Michaud	1979	654
170⅞	25⅝	24⅝	22⅝	5⅝	5⅝	8	8	Warren Co., Iowa	Gary L. Johnson	Gary L. Johnson	1981	654
170⅞	28⅝	28⅛	22⅝	4⅛	4⅛	6	6	Burleigh Co., N.D.	Ronald C. Wagner	Ronald C. Wagner	1982	654
170⅞	25⅝	26	24⅝	5⅝	5⅝	6	7	Zapata Co., Texas	G. O. Elliff	Michael Elliff	1926	665
170⅞	26	25⅛	21	5⅜	5⅜	8	8	Dimmit Co., Texas	J. H. Hixon	J. H. Hixon	1958	665
170⅞	25⅝	24⅞	19⅝	4⅝	4⅝	5	5	Gerald, Sask.	Jerry Norek	Jerry Norek	1959	665
170⅞	24⅝	26⅜	24⅜	5⅝	5⅝	6	6	Elbow, Sask.	W. H. Crossman	W. H. Crossman	1959	665
170⅞	27⅛	24	18	5⅛	5	7	7	Chicot Co., Ark.	Mrs. L. M. Hamilton	Mrs. L. M. Hamilton	1960	665
170⅞	24	25⅞	21⅛	4⅞	5	6	6	Ames, Man.	T. Litwin	T. Litwin	1963	665
170⅞	25⅞	26⅝	20	4⅜	4⅜	5	5	Carroll Co., Md.	Wes McKenzie	Wes McKenzie	1971	665
170⅞	27⅞	26⅝	20	4⅝	4⅝	6	6	Howell Co., Mo.	Roy W. Woodson	Roy W. Woodson	1974	665
170⅞	23⅜	23⅜	19⅞	4	4	6	5	Winn Parish, La.	William C. Erwin	William C. Erwin	1980	665
170⅞	24⅛	24⅛	16⅝	4⅝	4	4	5	Harris Co., Ga.	Gorman S. Riley	Gorman S. Riley	1983	665
170⅞	23⅜	23⅜	19⅝	4⅝	4⅝	5	7	Great Sand Hills, Sask.	Ralph Cervo	Ralph Cervo	1984	665
170⅝	21⅛	21⅝	15⅝	4⅝	4⅝	6	6	Allegan Co., Mich.	William Caywood	William Caywood	1948	676
170⅝	25⅝	25⅞	18⅝	4⅜	4⅜	6	6	Lake Co., Minn.	Unknown	George W. Flaim	1960	676

Score	Length of Main Beam R	L	Inside Spread	Circumference at Smallest Place Between Burr and First Point R	L	Number of Points R	L	Locality Killed	By Whom Killed	Owner	Date Killed	Rank
170⅝	27⅛	26⅛	19⅜	4⅞	4⅝	6	5	Jasper Co., Ga.	Gordon W. Cown	Gordon W. Cown	1961	676
170⅝	22⅝	23⅜	17⅞	4⅞	5	5	5	St. Charles Co., Mo.	Oscar Mallinckrodt	Oscar Mallinckrodt	1962	676
170⅝	27⅛	26⅝	19⅜	4⅞	4⅝	7	7	Douglas Co., Wisc.	George Pettingill	George Pettingill	1963	676
170⅝	26⅜	27⅜	21⅝	5⅜	5⅜	5	7	Sherburne Co., Minn.	Sylvester Zormeier	Sylvester Zormeier	1967	676
170⅝	26⅞	27⅜	18⅜	5⅜	5⅝	6	8	Price Co., Wisc.	Nyle H. Rodman	Nyle H. Rodman	1970	676
170⅝	26⅛	25⅜	19⅜	4⅜	4⅝	5	6	Boyd Co., Neb.	Leonard Reiser	Leonard Reiser	1973	676
170⅝	24⅝	26⅜	17⅜	5⅛	4⅞	5	5	St. Marys Co., Md.	Brian M. Boteler	Brian M. Boteler	1980	676
170⅝	26⅞	25⅜	18⅜	5⅜	5⅝	5	7	Atchison Co., Mo.	Roy E. Munsey	Roy E. Munsey	1980	676
170⅝	25⅝	26	20⅜	4⅜	4⅝	5	6	Berrien Co., Mich.	G. Steven Abdoe	G. Steven Abdoe	1982	676
170⅝	26⅜	27⅜	21	6	5⅝	6	7	Lyon Co., Kan.	Bill D. Hollond	Bill D. Hollond	1984	676
170⅝	26⅛	25⅜	20⅜	4⅜	4⅝	6	6	Beltrami Co., Minn.	Hank Sandland	Hank Sandland	1931	688
170⅝	25⅝	24⅜	18	4⅜	4⅝	6	6	Douglas Co., Minn.	August P. J. Nelson	Roger M. Holmes	1946	688
170⅝	27	27⅜	20⅝	5⅜	5⅝	8	7	Desha Co., Ark.	Bob Norris	Bob Norris	1948	688
170⅝	25⅜	24⅜	19⅜	4⅞	4⅝	5	5	Craven, Sask.	Ted Paterson	Ted Paterson	1960	688
170⅝	24⅝	24	20⅝	5⅝	5⅝	6	6	Preeceville, Sask.	Vernon Hoffman	Vernon Hoffman	1965	688
170⅝	24⅜	25⅜	19	4⅜	4⅝	5	6	La Salle Co., Texas	Jerome Knebel	Jerome Knebel	1974	688
170⅝	27	27⅜	23⅜	4⅜	4⅜	7	7	Webb Co., Texas	R. W. Mann	R. W. Mann	1979	688
170⅝	25⅜	24⅜	16⅜	5	5	7	7	Oneida Co., Wisc.	Leonard E. Westberg	Leonard E. Westberg	1981	688
170⅝	29⅜	29⅜	21⅜	4⅜	4⅝	7	8	Sherburne Co., Minn.	Curtis G. Nelson	Curtis G. Nelson	1981	688
170⅝	26⅛	26⅝	18	4⅜	4⅝	5	5	Marshall Co., Ind.	Alan R. Collins	Alan R. Collins	1982	688
170⅝	24	24⅜	19⅜	4⅜	4⅝	5	8	Day Co., S.D.	Credan Ewalt	Credan Ewalt	1982	688
170⅝	28⅝	28	20	5	5	8	5	Todd Co., Minn.	Freddie H. Peterson	Freddie H. Peterson	1982	688
170⅝	24⅞	24⅜	21	4⅞	5	5	9	Chippewa Co., Mich.	Paul Slawski	Paul Slawski	1984	688
170⅜	25⅝	25⅜	16⅜	3⅞	3⅞	9	9	Price Co., Wisc.	N. J. Groelle	Melvin Guenther	1905	701
170⅜	25⅝	25⅜	22⅜	5⅜	5⅝	6	6	Travis Co., Texas	W. A. Brown	W. A. Brown	1922	701
170⅜	25⅜	25⅜	26⅜	5⅛	5⅝	5	6	Whatshan Lake, B.C.	Ernest Roberts	Ernest Roberts	1957	701
170⅜	26	26	19⅛	5⅝	5⅝	6	5	Woodruff Co., Ark.	R. L. Taylor	R. L. Taylor	1960	701
170⅜	26⅝	26⅜	25⅝	5⅝	5⅝	5	5	Fort Qu'Appelle, Sask.	L. A. Magnuson	L. A. Magnuson	1962	701
170⅜	28⅜	28⅜	21⅜	4⅜	4⅝	6	4	Hall Co., Neb.	Gust Bergman	Gust Bergman	1965	701
170⅜	25⅝	25⅜	23⅜	5⅜	5⅝	6	5	Grant Co., S.D.	James Boerger	James Boerger	1965	701

WHITETAIL DEER (Typical Antlers)—Continued

Odocoileus virginianus virginianus and certain related subspecies

Score	Length of Main Beam R.	L.	Inside Spread	Circumference at Smallest Place Between Burr and First Point R.	L.	Number of Points R.	L.	Locality Killed	By Whom Killed	Owner	Date Killed	Rank
170	26⅝	27	23	6⅛	6⅛	5	5	Virden, Man.	Jessie Byer	Jessie Byer	1951	748
170	27	28	22⅝	4⅞	4⅞	6	5	Webb Co., Texas	Herbert Zieschang	Herbert Zieschang	1957	748
170	27⅜	27⅝	23⅜	6⅝	6⅞	6	6	Fullerton, Neb.	Truman Lauterback	Truman Lauterback	1959	748
170	26⅞	25⅜	21	5⅞	5⅞	5	5	Cat Island, La.	Jerry Loper	Jerry Loper	1960	748
170	23⅜	26	19⅞	5⅛	5⅞	7	6	Henderson Co., Ill.	Donald R. Vaughn	Donald R. Vaughn	1960	748
170	27⅝	26⅞	24⅛	4	4	6	8	Atascosa Co., Texas	Ben H. Moore, Jr.	Ben H. Moore, Jr.	1961	748
170	22⅝	22⅞	18⅝	4⅞	4⅞	5	6	Stevens Co., Wash.	Clair Kelso	Clair Kelso	1966	748
170	26⅛	24⅛	17⅞	4⅛	4⅛	6	6	Flathead Co., Mont.	Dave Delap	Dave Delap	1966	748
170	26⅛	26⅝	17⅞	4⅛	4⅞	7	5	Bates Co., Mo.	Gary Rosier	Gary Rosier	1969	748
170	28⅜	25⅝	21⅛	5⅞	5⅝	6	7	Hancock Co., Ill.	Henry F. Collins	Henry F. Collins	1973	748
170	26⅛	25⅜	19⅝	4⅞	4⅛	6	6	York Co., Maine	Aubin Huertas	Aubin Huertas	1973	748
170	26⅝	24⅜	19⅞	5⅞	5⅛	5	5	Shelby Co., Mo.	Rusty D. Gander	Rusty D. Gander	1973	748
170	24⅜	23⅞	20⅞	4⅞	4⅞	5	5	Scotland Co., Mo.	Chester James Young	Chester James Young	1974	748
170	25⅜	25⅜	18	4⅛	4⅛	7	6	Ballard Co., Ky.	Rudolf Koranchan, Jr.	Rudolf Koranchan, Jr.	1977	748
170	28⅜	27⅞	21	5	5	4	6	Androscoggin Co., Maine	Ricky D. Cavers	Ricky D. Cavers	1981	748
170	26⅝	26⅝	20⅞	4⅞	4⅞	5	7	Wapello Co., Iowa	George C. Ellis	George C. Ellis	1984	748
199⅞*	31⅞	31⅞	24⅝	5⅞	5⅞	5	5	Saunders Co., Neb.	Vernon A. Virka	Vernon A. Virka	1983	
196⅝*	25	25⅜	21⅞	4⅞	4⅞	6	6	Antelope Co., Neb.	John R. Harvey	Walter Schreiner	1963	
194⅞*	24⅞	25	24	4⅞	4⅞	6	6	Kenedy Co., Texas	Alexander M. D. Guest	Alexander M. D. Guest	1973	
191⅞*	27⅛	26⅞	19⅞	4⅞	4⅞	6	6	Waukesha Co., Wisc.	Kenneth Lange	Kenneth Lange	1979	
190⅞*	27⅜	27⅞	22⅞	5⅞	5⅞	5	5	Pelly, Sask.	James R. Strelioff	James R. Strelioff	1980	
190⅜*	27⅞	27⅜	18⅝	6	6	6	8	Clinton Co., Ind.	Alan W. Brannan	Alan W. Brannan	1982	
188⅞*	28⅝	28⅞	20⅛	5	4⅛	8	8	Riley Co., Kan.	Robert E. Luke	Robert E. Luke	1984	
187⅞*	29⅞	28⅜	21⅛	5⅝	5⅞	8	5	Somerset Co., Maine	M. Dana Goodwin	M. Dana Goodwin	1981	

* Final Score subject to revision by additional verifying measurements

NEW WORLD'S RECORD WHITETAIL DEER (NON-TYPICAL ANTLERS)
SCORE: 333 7/8
Locality: St. Louis County, Missouri Date: 1981
Picked Up Owner: Missouri Department of Conservation

NUMBER TWO WHITETAIL DEER (NON-TYPICAL ANTLERS)
SCORE: 328 2/8
Locality: Portage County, Ohio Date: 1940
Picked Up Owner: Dick Idol

Whitetail Deer (*Non-Typical Antlers*)

Odocoileus virginianus virginianus and certain related subspecies

Minimum Score 195

Score	Length of Main Beam R.	L.	Inside Spread	Circ. at Smallest Place Between Burr and First Point R.	L.	No. of Points R.	L.	Locality Killed	By Whom Killed	Owner	Date Killed	Rank
333⅞	24⅛	23⅜	23⅜	5⅛	5⅛	19	25	St. Louis Co., Mo.	Picked Up	Mo. Dept. of Cons.	1981	1
328⅜	25⅛	24⅛	24⅜	6⅛	5⅛	23	22	Portage Co., Ohio	Picked Up	Dick Idol	1940	2
286	23⅜	18⅜	15⅜	4⅞	4⅞	23	26	Brady, Texas	Jeff Benson	Lone Star Brewing Co.	1892	3
282	26⅛	27	24⅜	6⅝	6⅝	15	14	Clay Co., Iowa	Larry Raveling	Larry Raveling	1973	4
277⅝	27⅝	28⅜	24⅝	6	6⅛	17	16	Hardisty, Alta.	Doug Klinger	Doug Klinger	1976	5
277⅜	28⅜	28⅜	21⅛	6⅝	6⅝	19	18	Hall Co., Neb.	Del Austin	Del Austin	1962	6
272	23⅜	25	17⅜	6⅝	5⅝	23	16	Junction, Texas	Picked Up	Fred Mudge	1925	7
268⅝	20⅝	24⅛	14⅜	6⅛	5⅜	20	21	Norman Co., Minn.	Mitchell A. Vakoch	Mitchell A. Vakoch	1974	8
267⅞	25	24⅛	22⅜	6⅛	6⅜	20	18	Shoal Lake, Alta.	Jerry Froma	Jerry Froma	1984	9
267⅞	25⅛	28⅜	20	6⅛	6⅛	18	7	Peoria Co., Ill.	Richard A. Pauli	Richard A. Pauli	1983	10
265⅝	25⅞	26	18⅜	6⅝	6⅝	16	17	White Fox, Sask.	Elburn Kohler	Charles T. Arnold	1957	11
258⅝	22⅜	26⅛	23⅜	6⅜	6	17	15	Republic Co., Kan.	John O. Band	John O. Band	1965	12
258⅜	27	26⅜	19⅜	4⅞	4⅞	17	17	Becker Co., Minn.	J. J. Matter	J. J. Matter	1973	13
257⅞	25⅜	23⅜	16⅜	4⅞	4⅞	21	17	Elkhorn, Man.	Harvey Olsen	Harvey Olsen	1973	14
256⅝	29⅛	27⅜	24⅜	6⅜	6⅛	14	17	Holmes Co., Ohio	Picked Up	Ohio Dept. Nat. Res.	1975	15
256⅜	28⅜	28⅛	20⅜	6⅝	6⅜	11	16	Monona Co., Iowa	Carroll E. Johnson	Carroll E. Johnson	1968	16
255⅝	23⅜	22⅜	18⅛	5⅝	5⅜	18	15	Pigeon Lake, Alta.	Leo Eklund	Leo Eklund	1973	17
254⅞	28⅜	27	20⅜	5⅝	5	14	17	Stanley, N.D.	Roger Ritchie	Roger Ritchie	1968	18
253	28	28	21⅛	5⅝	5⅝	14	26	Goldenville, N.S.	Neil MacDonald	Dick Idol	1945	19
252⅝	25⅝	28⅜	19⅝	5⅜	5⅝	9	9	Hill Co., Mont.	Frank A. Pleskac	Frank A. Pleskac	1968	20
251⅛	28⅜	28	19	5⅝	5⅝	12	13	Mitchell Co., Kan.	Theron E. Wilson	Theron E. Wilson	1974	21
249⅜	26⅛	26⅜	19⅜	6⅜	6⅜	12	20	Greenwood Co., Kan.	Jerry Roitsch	J. D. Andrews	1965	22
248⅞	27⅞	27⅜	20⅜	5⅜	5⅝	8	10	Lily, S.D.	Clifford G. Pickell	Clifford G. Pickell	1968	23
248⅞	25	24	20⅜	5⅛	5⅝	16	12	Snowy Mts., Mont.	Unknown	McLean Bowman	PR1980	24
248⅛	22⅜	24⅜	22	5⅞	5⅛	13	11	Moose Mtn. Park, Sask.	Walter Bartko	George Hooey	1964	25
248⅛	31⅛	32⅛	22⅜	5⅜	5⅝	15	15	Penobscot Co., Maine	Unknown	James L. Mason, Sr.	1945	26
247⅛	26⅛	26	19⅜	5⅜	5⅛	13	17	Frio Co., Texas	Raul Rodriquez II	Raul Rodriquez II	1966	27
247⅜	25⅜	25⅜	24⅜	5⅛	6⅛	16	14	Johnston Co., Okla.	Bill M. Foster	Bill M. Foster	1970	28
245⅜	31⅜	27⅜	25⅜	5⅝	5⅝	11	14	Elk River, B.C.	James I. Brewster	J. I. Brewster Est.	1905	29
245⅜	22⅜	22⅜	24⅜	6⅝	6⅝	9	17	Nez Perce Co., Idaho	John D. Powers, Jr.	Zeke West	1983	30

267

WHITETAIL DEER (Non-Typical Antlers)—Continued
Odocoileus virginianus virginianus and certain related subspecies

Score	Length of Main Beam R.	L.	Inside Spread	Circumference at Smallest Place Between Burr and First Point R.	L.	Number of Points R.	L.	Locality Killed	By Whom Killed	Owner	Date Killed	Rank
245⅝	24⅝	21⅝	16⅝	5⅜	5	18	12	Carrot River, Sask.	Picked Up	Ken Halloway	1962	31
245	27⅞	27	20⅛	5⅜	5⅜	15	15	Buffalo Co., Wisc.	Elmer F. Gotz	Elmer F. Gotz	1973	32
244⅞	27	27⅞	16⅝	5⅝	5⅝	13	13	Allegany Co., N.Y.	Homer Boylan	Harry Boylan	1939	33
244⅜	26⅞	26⅜	16⅞	8⅜	8⅜	18	15	Wirral, N.B.	H. Glenn Johnston	Arnold Alward	1962	34
243⅞	26⅞	24⅛	22⅛	5⅛	5	11	15	Govan, Sask.	A. W. Davis	Sam Peterson	1951	35
243⅜	24⅛	24⅛	17⅞	6	5⅜	13	16	Nance Co., Neb.	Robert E. Snyder	Robert E. Snyder	1961	36
242⅝	27⅞	26⅛	17⅞	6⅛	6⅝	18	14	Auburnville, N.B.	John L. MacKenzie	Arnold Alward	1958	37
242⅜	24⅜	21⅜	20⅜	6⅛	5	14	19	Flathead Co., Mont.	George Woldstad	George Woldstad	1960	38
241⅞	26⅜	25⅜	20⅛	4⅝	5	9	11	Wisconsin	Unknown	Robert Kietzman	1940	39
241⅜	29⅞	25⅞	19⅜	5⅜	6	19	18	Bighill Creek, Alta.	Donald D. Dwernychuk	Donald D. Dwernychuk	1984	40
241⅛	26⅜	26⅛	18⅛	6⅛	5⅜	17	20	St. Louis Co., Minn.	John Cesarek	John Cesarek	1964	41
240⅞	25⅜	26⅜	17⅞	5⅜	7⅞	18	20	Monroe Co., Ga.	John L. Hatton, Jr.	John L. Hatton, Jr.	1973	42
240⅜	24⅜	24⅛	18⅝	7⅝	5⅜	15	11	Kerr Co., Texas	Walter R. Schreiner	Charles Schreiner III	1905	43
240	26⅜	26	21⅛	5⅜	5⅜	17	15	Crook Co., Wyo.	Picked Up	J. D. Andrews	1962	44
238⅞	22⅝	21⅛	18⅛	5	5⅜	12	17	Bay Co., Mich.	Paul M. Mickey	Paul M. Mickey	1976	45
238⅜	27⅛	26⅞	21⅛	5⅝	5⅞	13	15	Whitewood, Sask.	Jack Davidge	Jack Davidge	1967	46
238⅛	24⅜	21⅞	22	5⅝	5⅜	15	8	Keya Paha Co., Neb.	Donald B. Phipps	Donald B. Phipps	1969	47
238	26⅜	27⅞	23⅜	5⅝	5⅜	12	16	Whiteshell, Man.	Angus McVicar	Angus McVicar	1925	48
237⅞	23⅞	23⅜	23⅛	5⅛	5⅜	12	12	Reserve, Sask.	Harry Nightingale	McLean Bowman	1959	49
236⅜	25	23⅜	20⅜	5	5⅜	17	12	Union Co., Ky.	Wilbur E. Buchanan	Wilbur E. Buchanan	1970	50
236	23⅜	24⅜	20	5⅝	5⅛	14	16	Winona Co., Minn.	Francis A. Pries	Francis A. Pries	1964	51
235⅞	22⅜	22⅜	19⅛	5⅛	5⅝	11	12	Ashtabula Co., Ohio	James L. Clark	James L. Clark	1957	52
235⅞	29⅜	27⅜	22⅜	5⅝	5⅝	11	13	Pipestone Valley, Sask.	E. J. Marshall	E. J. Marshall	1958	52
235⅜	25⅜	24⅜	19⅝	5⅝	5⅝	9	20	Frio Co., Texas	C. J. Stolle	John F. Stolle	1919	54
235⅛	24	23⅜	21⅜	5	4⅜	14	15	Stevens Co., Wash.	Larry G. Gardner	Larry G. Gardner	1953	55
234⅞	29	28⅜	20⅞	5⅜	5⅝	14	12	Alfalfa Co., Okla.	Loren Tarrant	Loren Tarrant	1984	56
234⅜	27⅜	27⅜	20⅛	7	7⅛	6	10	Glacier Co., Mont.	Unknown	Larry W. Lander	PR1968	57
234⅜	25⅞	27⅛	17⅞	4⅝	4⅜	16	15	Loraine, Wisc.	Homer Pearson	McLean Bowman	1937	58
233⅞	27	26⅜	21⅛	5⅝	5⅝	9	14	Tompkins, Sask.	Don Stueck	McLean Bowman	1961	58
233⅜	23⅜	23⅜	16⅞	6	5⅞	14	13	Thompson Creek, Wash.	George Sly, Jr.	George Sly, Jr.	1964	60
233⅜	26⅜	26⅝	24⅛	4⅜	4⅜	9	9	Acadia Valley, Alta.	James J. Niwa	James J. Niwa	1973	61

Score								Locality	Hunter	Owner	Date	Rank
233	26	27⅞	20⅜	5⅞	6	14	11	Burnett Co., Wisc.	Victor Rammer	Jerry C. Ganske	1949	62
233	20⅞	23⅞	19⅞	6⅞	5⅝	12	7	Punnichy, Sask.	Steve Kapay	John L. Stein	1968	62
232⅞	24⅜	24⅜	16⅜	4⅞	4⅝	11	11	McLean Co., N.D.	Olaf P. Anderson	Burton L. Anderson	1886	64
232	25⅜	25	17	6	6	18	11	Waukesha Co., Wisc.	John Herr, Sr.	Mac's Taxidermy	1955	65
231⅞	24	22⅜	18	5⅝	5⅝	10	20	Harris, Sask.	Herman Cox	R. M. Burnett	1954	66
231⅝	26⅛	25⅜	23⅜	6	6⅛	11	13	Peace River, Alta.	Terry Doll	Terry Doll	1978	67
231⅝	28⅛	26⅜	19⅜	5⅛	5⅛	11	11	Dane Co., Wisc.	Dennis D. Shanks	Dennis D. Shanks	1979	68
231⅜	29⅜	27⅜	23⅜	4⅜	4⅜	9	10	Licking Co., Ohio	Norman L. Myers	Norman L. Myers	1964	69
231⅜	28	28⅜	26⅜	6⅞	6⅜	9	9	Holland, Man.	Wm. Ireland	J. D. Andrews	1968	69
231⅛	25⅜	26⅜	18⅜	5	4⅞	17	13	Forest Co., Wisc.	Robert Bussano	Robert Jacobson	1958	71
231	26	25⅞	18	5	5	12	12	Stevens Co., Wash.	Joe Bussano	Joe Bussano	1946	72
230⅞	24⅜	24⅞	15⅜	6⅝	5⅝	24	13	Sumter Co., Ala.	James L. Spidle, Sr.	James L. Spidle, Sr.	PR1942	73
230⅞	27⅞	27⅜	19⅜	5⅞	5⅝	14	16	Red Deer, Atla.	Delmer E. Johnson	Delmer E. Johnson	1973	74
229⅞	27	28⅜	21⅜	6⅞	6	8	15	Linn Co., Kan.	Merle C. Beckman	Merle C. Beckman	1984	75
228⅞	28⅜	27⅜	18⅜	5⅞	6	11	10	Cherryfield, Maine	Flora Campbell	Fred Goodwin	1953	76
228⅞	26⅜	29⅜	21	5⅝	5⅝	13	10	Cable, Wisc.	Charles Berg	Eva Mae Fisher	1910	77
228⅛	28⅜	29	20⅜	5⅝	6	13	14	Maine	Henry A. Caesar	National Collection	PR1911	78
227⅞	25⅜	25⅜	18⅜	6⅝	6	16	17	Bayfield Co., Wisc.	Earl Holt	Mrs. Earl Holt	1934	79
227⅞	27⅛	26⅜	20⅝	5⅝	5⅝	12	9	Pullman, Wash.	Glenn C. Paulson	Glenn C. Paulson	1965	79
227	25⅜	26⅜	24⅜	7⅝	7⅝	12	10	Miami Co., Kan.	Gary A. Smith	Gary A. Smith	1970	81
226⅞	25⅜	27⅞	15⅜	4⅞	5⅝	22	25	Rusk Co., Wisc.	Joe Michalets	John R. Michalets	1911	82
226⅞	28⅜	28⅜	22⅛	5⅝	5⅝	10	12	Manor, Sask.	Stan Balkwill	McLean Bowman	1960	82
226⅜	26⅜	26	18⅜	6	5⅝	7	9	Pulaski Co., Ky.	H. C. Sumpter	H. C. Sumpter	1984	84
226⅜	21⅜	22⅜	19⅜	4⅝	4⅝	13	11	Muskingum Co., Ohio	Rex Allen Thompson	Rex Allen Thompson	1981	85
226⅜	25⅜	27⅜	18⅞	5⅝	5⅝	10	8	Nez Perce Co., Idaho	Mrs. Ralph Bond	Mrs. Ralph Bond	1964	86
226⅛	25⅝	26⅜	20⅜	4⅞	4⅞	10	10	Trumbull Co., Ohio	Paul E. Lehman	Paul E. Lehman	1948	87
225⅞	29⅜	29⅜	23⅜	6⅛	6⅛	9	8	St. Louis Co., Minn.	Elmer H. Sellin	Elmer H. Sellin	1938	88
225	25⅜	25⅝	21⅜	5⅝	6	15	12	Nipawin, Sask.	Picked Up	John L. Stein	1981	89
224⅝	24⅞	24⅜	25⅝	5⅝	5⅝	15	7	Perry Co., Ala.	Robert E. Royster	Robert E. Royster	1976	90
224⅜	26⅞	27	21⅛	5⅛	5⅝	8	7	Lac qui Parle Co., Minn.	Mike Unzen	Mike Unzen	1969	91
224⅜	26⅝	27⅝	20⅝	5	5⅛	11	11	Salmon River, N.B.	Ford Fulton	McLean Bowman	1966	92
224⅜	23⅝	23⅜	22	5⅝	5⅝	18	15	Pine Co., Minn.	Greg S. Blom	Greg S. Blom	1980	92
224⅛	25	24⅜	19⅞	4⅝	4⅜	12	13	Crook Co., Wyo.	John S. Mahoney	John S. Mahoney	1947	94
224	29⅝	29⅝	20	6⅝	5⅝	15	13	Minnesota	Unknown	Harvard Univ. Mus.	1890	95
224	23⅛	24	17⅞	4⅝	5	16	12	Lincoln Co., Mont.	Ray Baenen	Ed Boyes	1935	95
224	29⅜	29⅜	27	5⅜	5⅜	7	14	Hancock Co., Maine	Picked Up	Wesley B. Starn	PR1975	95
223⅞	23⅜	23⅜	22⅜	4⅝	4⅝	13	14	New York	Unknown	Johnny M. Hollier	PR1983	95
223⅝	28	28	25⅝	7⅛	6⅛	10	11	Greene Co., Ill.	Terry L. Walters	Terry L. Walters	1982	99
223⅜	25⅛	24⅜	16⅜	4⅜	4⅜	10	13	Nuevo Leon, Mexico	Ron Kolpin	Ron Kolpin	1983	99
223⅜	23⅞	24⅜	17	5⅛	5⅛	18	13	Richland Co., Mont.	Verner King	Verner King	1960	101
223⅜	20⅜	24⅜	19	5⅝	5⅝	19	12	Cochin, Sask.	Vic Pearsall	Vic Pearsall	1960	102
223	21⅜	23	23⅜	4⅜	4⅜	19	11	Hawkins Co., Tenn.	Luther E. Fuller	Luther E. Fuller	1984	103
222⅞	21⅜	22⅞	16⅜	5⅝	5⅝	11	10	Itasca Co., Minn.	Picked Up	James R. Smith	1936	104

269

WHITETAIL DEER (*Non-Typical Antlers*)—*Continued*

Odocoileus virginianus virginianus and certain related subspecies

Score	Length of Main Beam R.	L.	Inside Spread	Circumference at Smallest Place Between Burr and First Point R.	L.	Number of Points R.	L.	Locality Killed	By Whom Killed	Owner	Date Killed	Rank
222⅞	24⅞	23⅜	17⅞	5⅝	5⅝	8	8	Rusk Co., Wisc.	Raymond Charlevois	Philip Schlegel	1936	104
222⅞	27	25⅞	19⅞	5⅞	5⅞	9	12	Mair, Sask.	R. A. McGill	Mr. & Mrs. Murray Melom	1952	106
222⅝	24⅞	23⅞	18⅛	5⅛	5⅛	9	9	Edgerton, Alta.	Nick Leskow	Russell Thornberry	1964	106
222⅜	24⅜	25⅞	20⅞	5⅞	5⅜	16	10	Ostrea Lake, N.S.	Verden M. Baker	C. L. Gage	1949	108
222⅜	25⅜	23⅞	21⅛	5⅜	5⅜	14	11	Richland Co., Wisc.	Janice K. Beranek	Janice K. Beranek	1983	108
222⅜	25⅜	25⅞	19⅞	5⅞	5⅞	14	12	Itasca Co., Minn.	Lumie Jackson	Rick Ferguson	1942	110
221⅞	25⅜	26⅜	16⅞	5⅞	5⅜	12	14	Trigg Co., Ky.	Bill McWhirter	Bill McWhirter	1982	111
221⅛	23⅜	25⅞	21⅜	5⅜	5⅝	13	10	Snipe Lake, Alta.	Robert Dickson, Sr.	Robert Dickson, Sr.	1984	112
221⅛	30	25⅞	23⅞	6⅝	6⅞	12	12	Humboldt Co., Iowa	Donald Crossley	Donald Crossley	1971	113
221⅜	22⅝	29⅞	17⅞	4⅝	4⅞	16	11	Itasca Co., Minn.	Richard I. Goble	Richard I. Goble	1955	114
221⅜	22⅝	23⅞	19⅞	6⅛	6⅜	12	15	Anoka Co., Minn.	Donald Torgerson	J. D. Andrews	1946	115
220⅞	26⅜	25⅞	20⅞	4⅞	4⅞	12	9	Mercer Co., Ill.	Roger D. Hultgren	Roger D. Hultgren	1970	116
220⅜	30	30⅞	20⅞	5	5	14	13	Olmstead Co., Minn.	E. E. Comartin III	E. E. Comartin, Jr.	1963	117
220⅜	25⅛	25⅞	18⅞	5	5	9	8	Zavala Co., Texas	J. D. Jarratt	J. D. Jarratt	1930	118
220⅜	28⅜	28⅞	21	5⅝	5⅝	11	12	Union Co., Iowa	George Foster	George Foster	1968	118
220⅜	25	26⅜	19⅜	6	6	10	10	Genesee Co., N.Y.	Robert Wood	Robert Wood	1944	120
219⅞	27⅜	27⅞	19⅞	5⅜	6	13	12	Warren Co., Mo.	James E. Williams	James E. Williams	1959	121
219⅜	24⅜	25⅛	21⅛	5⅞	6⅝	11	10	Webb Co., Texas	Richard O. Rivera	Richard O. Rivera	1972	122
219⅜	27⅜	27⅞	20	5⅜	5⅜	13	11	Buffalo Co., Wisc.	Glenn Lehman	Glenn Lehman	1958	123
219⅜	26	30⅝	19⅞	6⅝	6⅞	9	11	Aroostook Co., Maine	Harold C. Kitchin	Harold C. Kitchin	1973	123
219⅜	24⅜	24⅞	21⅛	5⅜	5⅞	9	15	Flathead Co., Mont.	R. C. Garrett	R. C. Garrett	1962	125
219⅛	27	27	18⅞	5⅞	5⅞	12	11	Florence Co., Wisc.	W. C. Gotstein	J. D. Andrews	1914	126
218⅞	28⅛	27⅞	20	5⅜	4⅞	6	8	Waldo Co., Maine	Roy C. Guse	J. Bruce Probert	1957	126
218⅞	29⅜	28⅞	18⅜	5⅝	4⅞	9	11	Chariton Co., Mo.	Stanley McSparren	Stanley McSparren	1979	128
218⅜	26⅜	25⅞	18⅜	4⅜	4⅜	12	12	Sawyer Co., Wisc.	Walter Kittleson	Walter Kittleson	1920	129
218⅜	27	26⅜	18⅜	5⅜	5⅜	8	8	St. Martin Parish, La.	Drew Ware	Gary S. Crnko	1941	129
218⅜	26⅜	26⅜	17⅞	5⅝	5⅝	9	11	La Crosse Co., Wisc.	Daniel P. Cavadini	J. D. Andrews	1951	131
218⅜	27	24⅜	17	5⅜	5⅜	11	17	Sumter Co., Ala.	Josh Jones	Harrison H. Perry	PR1952	131
218⅜	23⅜	22⅜	15⅜	5⅜	5⅛	13	15	South Goodeve, Sask.	Fred Bohay	Fred Bohay	1958	131
218⅜	20⅜	24⅜	19⅜	4⅜	5	10	11	Keweenaw Co., Mich.	Bernard J. Murn	Bernard J. Murn	1980	131
218⅜	24⅜	25⅜	19⅜	5⅜	5⅜	11	12	West Kootenay, B.C.	Karl H. Kast	Karl H. Kast	1940	135

Score	Length R	Length L	Inside Spread	Circ. R	Circ. L	Pts. R	Pts. L	Locality	By Whom Killed	Owner	Date Killed	Rank
218	25⅞	25⅞	19	5⅜	5⅜	11	15	Otter Tail Co., Minn.	Dennis A. Pearson	Dennis A. Pearson	1977	135
217⅞	27⅞	28⅞	21⅜	5⅜	5⅞	10	16	Maries Co., Mo.	Gerald R. Dake	Gerald R. Dake	1974	137
217⅞	26⅜	28⅞	18⅝	5⅛	5	12	12	Macoupin Co., Ill.	Albert Grichnik	Albert Grichnik	1966	138
217⅝	27⅜	24⅝	23	4⅞	5⅜	14	14	Carroll Co., Miss.	Mark T. Hathcock	Mark T. Hathcock	1978	139
217⅞	25⅝	25	19⅞	6⅞	6⅜	11	12	Aitkin Co., Minn.	Fred C. Melichar	Fred C. Melichar	1973	140
217⅞	27	28⅞	18⅞	5⅝	5⅜	12	15	Meeker Co., Minn.	Steven R. Turek	Steven R. Turek	1982	141
217⅞	23⅜	23⅞	19	5⅜	5⅜	11	11	Spruchome, Sask.	Tom Pillar	Tom Pillar	1957	142
217⅛	22	20	20	4⅞	4⅞	13	12	Talbot Co., Md.	Vincent L. Jordan, Sr.	Vincent L. Jordan, Sr.	1974	142
216⅞	19⅛	21⅛	13⅞	7	6⅜	11	15	Brown Co., S.D.	Francis Shattuck	Sand Lake N.W.R.	1960	144
216⅞	26	24⅞	22⅞	5⅜	5⅛	11	13	Kathryn, N.D.	Gerald R. Elsner	Gerald R. Elsner	1963	145
216⅞	25⅛	25⅜	18⅞	6⅜	6⅜	10	13	Barber Co., Kan.	Robert L. Rose	Robert L. Rose	1972	145
216⅝	23	25⅜	25⅜	5⅜	5⅜	11	11	Isle of Wight Co., Va.	Peter F. Crocker, Jr.	Peter F. Crocker, Jr.	1963	147
216⅜	26	24⅞	18⅞	5⅜	5⅞	14	17	Comanche Co., Okla.	Dwight O. Allen	Dwight O. Allen	1962	148
216⅜	26⅜	26⅜	20⅜	4⅞	5	9	10	Powhatan Co., Va.	William E. Schaefer	William E. Schaefer	1970	148
216⅜	26	25⅜	17⅜	5⅜	5⅜	10	9	Clay Co., Iowa	Blaine Salzkorn	Blaine Salzkorn	1970	148
216⅜	23⅜	24	18⅜	4⅜	4⅜	10	8	Buchanan, Sask.	Mike Spezrivka	Linda Christoforo	1961	151
216⅛	26⅜	27⅜	20⅜	5⅜	5⅞	10	14	Richland Co., Mont.	Joseph P. Culbertson	Joseph P. Culbertson	1972	151
216⅛	23⅜	19⅜	15⅞	5⅜	6⅜	15	16	Itasca Co., Minn.	Thomas Thurstin	Thomas Thurstin	1977	153
216⅛	25	24⅜	24⅜	6⅜	6	11	12	Long Pine, Neb.	Picked Up	Duane Lotspeich	1964	154
215⅞	29⅜	27⅜	16⅞	6⅛	6⅜	13	13	Putnam Co., Ga.	Thomas H. Cooper	Thomas H. Cooper	1974	154
215⅞	24⅜	24⅜	23⅜	6⅜	7⅜	16	12	Chippewa Co., Minn.	Micheal Allickson	Micheal Allickson	1974	156
215⅝	26	25⅜	20	5⅜	5⅜	16	12	Iron Co., Mich.	C. & R. Lester	C. & R. Lester	1970	157
215⅝	28	28	20⅜	5⅜	5⅛	10	9	Worth Co., Mo.	B. M. & R. Nonneman	B. M. & R. Nonneman	1974	157
215⅜	29⅜	28⅞	23⅞	5⅜	5⅝	8	8	Lafayette Co., Wisc.	Roger Vickers	Roger Vickers	1969	159
215⅜	27⅜	26⅝	15⅜	6	5⅜	9	6	Schuyler Co., Ill.	Donald E. Ziegenbein	Donald E. Ziegenbein	1981	160
215	23⅝	23⅜	14⅞	5⅜	6	17	13	Fergus Co., Mont.	Robert D. Fleherty	Robert D. Fleherty	1958	161
215	28⅝	27⅜	24⅜	6⅜	6	12	15	Hardin Co., Ky.	Michael F. Meredith	Michael F. Meredith	1980	161
214⅞	25⅝	25⅜	16⅜	4⅞	4⅜	9	12	Aweme, Man.	Criddle Bros.	Criddle Bros.	1954	163
214⅞	25⅜	26⅜	20⅜	5	4⅞	15	14	Koochiching Co., Minn.	Unknown	Wilbur Tilander	1956	164
214⅞	24	25⅝	23⅜	5⅜	5	11	9	Swift Co., Minn.	Leonard N. Kanuit	Leonard N. Kanuit	1972	165
214⅞	23⅜	25⅜	15⅜	5⅝	5⅜	11	10	Price Co., Wisc.	Henry J. Copt	James A. Copt	1926	166
214	26	24	14⅜	5⅛	5⅜	14	10	Missoula Co., Mont	Lyle Pettit	Lyle Pettit	1962	166
213⅞	24⅜	27⅜	24⅜	6	5⅜	11	11	Bayfield Co., Wisc.	Clarence Lauer	Mrs. Clarence Lauer	1963	166
213⅞	28⅞	28⅜	16⅜	6⅜	6⅜	8	8	Crook Co., Wyo.	Clinton Berry	Clinton Berry	1953	169
213⅝	25	25⅜	20⅜	4⅜	4⅜	10	9	Clay Co., Minn.	Dean Klemetson	Dean Klemetson	1984	170
213⅝	25⅜	18	18	5	5⅜	17	12	Sawyer Co., Wisc.	Charles Ross	Charles Ross	1949	171
213⅜	27⅜	16⅝	16⅝	5⅜	5⅜	12	8	Bresaylor, Sask.	Barry Braun	Barry Braun	1966	171
213⅜	24⅜	17⅜	17⅜	5⅝	5⅝	12	6	Beltrami Co., Minn.	Unknown	Jim Smith	1924	173
213⅜	27⅛	23⅜	23⅜	5⅜	7	9	9	Bonner Co., Idaho	Rodney Thurlow	Rodney Thurlow	1968	173
213	23	18⅜	16⅜	6⅜	6⅜	10	12	Buffalo Co., Wisc.	Norman C. Ratz	Ed Klink	1968	173
213	26⅜	18⅜	18⅜	6⅜	5⅛	12	11	Rochester, Alta.	Lamar A. Windberg	Lamar A. Windberg	1973	176
213	22	17	17	5⅛	5⅜	12	10	Havre, Mont.	Unknown	Frank English	1950	177
213	24	17⅞	17⅞	4⅜	4⅜	10	10	Kinney Co., Texas	Rankin F. O'Neill	John L. Stein	1960	178

WHITETAIL DEER (Non-Typical Antlers)—Continued
Odocoileus virginianus virginianus and certain related subspecies

Score	Length of Main Beam R.	L.	Inside Spread	Circumference at Smallest Place Between Burr and First Point R.	L.	Number of Points R.	L.	Locality Killed	By Whom Killed	Owner	Date Killed	Rank
213	25⅞	24⅛	20⅛	5⅜	5⅜	5	15	Rush Lake, Sask.	Jim Runzer	Murray Bromley	1966	178
212⅞	30	23⅜	21⅛	5⅜	5	7	12	Waukesha Co., Wisc.	Max Mollgaard	Max Mollgaard	1976	180
212⅞	27⅛	26⅞	18⅛	5⅜	5⅜	14	16	Lewis & Clark Co., Mont.	LeFleur	L. S. Kuter	1952	181
212½	25⅜	25¾	23⅜	4⅜	4⅜	11	11	Lincoln Co., Mont.	Charles F. Woods, Jr.	Charles F. Woods, Jr.	1973	182
212½	28⅜	29⅛	23⅞	5⅜	5⅞	10	9	Lake Co., Mont.	Dennis Courville	Dennis Courville	1975	182
212½	25⅞	24⅞	17⅞	5	5	11	13	Glentworth, Sask.	Garnet Fortnum	Garnet Fortnum	1984	182
212½	29	28⅜	24⅜	5⅜	5⅞	11	10	Hershey, Neb.	Ray Liles	Spanky Greenville	1959	185
212⅜	23⅜	29	18⅛	5	4⅞	11	10	Rosebud Co., Mont.	Picked Up	Art F. Hayes III	1979	185
212⅜	25	23⅜	19⅜	5⅜	5⅞	11	13	Webb Co., Texas	Claude W. King	Claude W. King	1949	187
212⅜	26⅛	25	23⅜	5⅜	5⅜	9	7	Houston Co., Minn.	Alfred C. Pieper	Alfred C. Pieper	1977	187
212⅜	21	26⅞	24	4	4	9	16	Parker Co., Texas	Pleasant Mitchell	Pleasant Mitchell	1982	187
212¼	28⅛	21	21⅜	5⅜	6	8	10	Woodbury Co., Iowa	Harold M. Leonard	Harold M. Leonard	1965	190
212⅛	27	28⅛	19⅜	5⅜	5⅜	14	16	St. Louis Co., Minn.	Robert J. LaPine	Robert J. LaPine	1968	190
212⅛	26⅞	27	16⅜	4⅞	5⅛	14	13	Becker Co., Minn.	Unknown	George W. Flaim	1922	192
212	29	25	23⅜	6⅜	6⅜	8	9	Iron Co., Mich.	Ben Komblevicz	Duane K. Wenzel	1942	192
212	25⅝	27⅜	24⅜	6	5⅞	14	11	Raymore, Sask.	Adolf Wulff	Adolf Wulff	1951	194
211⅞	25	26⅜	20⅜	4⅜	4⅜	10	12	Rockingham Co., Va.	Dorsey O. Breeden	Dorsey O. Breeden	1966	194
211⅞	22	25⅜	21⅜	4⅜	4⅜	15	15	Crook Co., Wyo.	Curtis U. Nelson	Curtis U. Nelson	1971	194
211⅞	22⅜	25⅝	21	5	5	10	11	Cottonwood Co., Minn.	James A. Sykora	James A. Sykora	1981	197
211⅝	23⅛	22⅝	13⅜	7	5⅜	18	11	Alda, Neb.	Donald Knuth	Donald Knuth	1964	198
211⅝	28⅜	23	23	5⅞	6	11	11	Glaslyn, Sask.	Carl R. Frohaug	Carl R. Frohaug	1981	198
211¼	25⅜	25	18⅜	5⅛	4⅞	14	17	St. Louis Co., Minn.	John E. Peterson, Jr.	John E. Peterson, Jr.	1963	200
211¼	23⅜	23⅜	13⅜	6⅜	5⅞	12	10	Dodge Co., Wisc.	Michael A. Koehler	Michael A. Koehler	1984	200
211⅛	24⅜	25⅜	16⅜	5⅜	5⅞	12	10	Borden, Sask.	Leonard Verishine	Leonard Verishine	1972	202
211⅛	27	24⅜	19⅜	6⅛	6⅛	8	9	Marshall Co., Minn.	Picked Up	Robert Sands	1959	203
211⅛	23⅜	27	16⅜	6⅜	5⅞	10	9	Hughenden, Alta.	Morris Sather	Morris Sather	1966	203
211	23⅜	24⅜	16⅜	6	6	12	13	Zavala Co., Texas	Unknown	McLean Bowman	PR1973	205
210⅞	24⅜	24¼	18⅛	5⅜	5⅜	11	9	Stevens Co., Wash.	Charles Tucker	Charles Tucker	1966	206
210⅞	23⅜	23⅜	16⅜	5	5	11	8	Coahuila, Mexico	Picked Up	Jim Jacob	1981	207
210⅝	26¼	28⅜	22	5	5	8	9	Lincoln Co., Mont.	Glen Savage	Patrick W. Savage	1934	208
210⅝	24⅜	25⅜	18	5⅝	5⅝	14	10	Renville Co., N.D.	Glen Southam	Glen Southam	1978	208

Score	Length of Main Beam R	L	Inside Spread	Circumference R	L	Points R	L	Locality	By Whom Killed	Owner	Date	Rank
210⅞	26⅞	25⅞	20	5⅛	5⅛	12	11	Dane Co., Wisc.	LaVerne W. Marten	LaVerne W. Marten	1970	210
210⅞	28⅛	27⅜	21⅞	5	5⅛	9	10	Marinette Co., Wisc.	George E. Bierstaker	Mrs. George E. Bierstaker	1947	211
210⅜	24⅜	25	19⅜	5	5	13	12	Lyon Co., Ky.	Roy D. Lee	Roy D. Lee	1975	211
210⅛	26⅛	25⅜	21⅛	5⅜	5⅜	8	9	Columbiana Co., Ohio	Harold L. Hawkins	Harold L. Hawkins	1981	213
210	26	26⅛	18	5⅞	5⅝	10	9	Glenewen, Sask.	H. Frew	H. Frew	1955	214
210	23⅜	23⅝	20⅜	5⅞	5⅞	9	8	Gregory Co., S.D.	Richard C. Berte	Richard C. Berte	1982	214
209⅞	25⅛	24⅜	22⅜	4⅞	4⅞	9	9	Maryfield, Sask.	W. W. Nichol	W. W. Nichol	1967	216
209⅞	25⅝	25⅜	18⅝	4⅞	4⅞	10	9	Pine Co., Minn.	Scott A. Miller	Scott A. Miller	1980	216
209⅞	20⅜	19⅞	19⅝	5⅞	5⅞	13	15	Hawkins Co., Tenn.	Johnny W. Byington	Johnny W. Byington	1982	216
209⅞	24⅜	27⅞	17⅜	5⅝	5⅛	11	11	Koochiching Co., Minn.	Harry Van Keuren	Louis E. Muench	1929	219
209⅞	23⅜	24⅜	20⅜	5⅝	5⅝	10	10	Franklin Co., Miss.	Ronnie Strickland	Ronnie Strickland	1981	219
209⅞	24⅛	24	22⅛	4⅞	4⅞	8	11	Edwards Co., Kan.	Tim C. Schaller	Tim C. Schaller	1984	219
209⅞	26⅛	25⅜	22⅛	5	5	10	10	Butler Co., Ky.	Dean A. Hannold	Dean A. Hannold	1979	219
209⅜	23⅜	26⅛	21	5⅛	5⅜	11	11	La Salle Co., Texas	Unknown	E. T. Reilly	1931	222
209⅜	26	21⅛	16⅞	4⅜	4⅜	13	9	Grant Co., Wisc.	Tim Yanna	Tim Yanna	1982	223
209	26⅞	26⅛	19⅜	5	5	11	10	Clinton Co., Iowa	Gregory Stewart	Gregory Stewart	1963	223
208⅞	25⅜	28⅜	23⅜	5⅜	5⅜	8	8	Lee Co., Iowa	Glenn L. Carter II	Glenn L. Carter II	1984	225
208⅞	25⅜	26	21⅛	5	5	8	9	Atchison Co., Mo.	Kenneth W. Lee	Kenneth W. Lee	1964	226
208⅞	27	26⅞	18¾	4⅞	4⅞	8	11	Charles Co., Md.	Robert A. Boarman	Robert A. Boarman	1984	227
208⅞	27	26⅞	20⅛	5⅜	5⅜	10	8	Daniel Boone Natl. For., Ky.	Richard G. Lohre	Richard G. Lohre	1968	227
208⅞	26⅞	24⅞	19¾	5⅛	5	13	12	Unknown	Unknown	David A. Boys	PR1982	229
208⅝	24⅞	24⅜	21⅛	5⅝	5⅝	9	8	Taylor Co., Wisc.	Unknown	Mac's Taxidermy	PR1945	229
208⅝	27	27⅛	22	6	5⅞	10	8	Beaufort Co., S.C.	John M. Wood	John M. Wood	1971	231
208⅜	19½	19⅜	18⅛	5	5	11	10	Dixon Co., Neb.	Dan Greeny	Dan Greeny	1969	231
208⅜	28	27⅛	23⅜	6⅛	6⅛	11	10	Frio Co., Texas	Unknown	Roy Hindes	PR1950	233
208⅜	27	26⅝	18¾	5⅝	5⅝	10	7	St. Louis Co., Minn.	Walter H. Enzenauer	Walter H. Enzenauer	1961	234
208⅜	21⅜	20⅛	20⅛	4⅞	4⅞	11	11	Chauvin, Alta.	Picked Up	Shane Hansen	1981	234
208⅛	27⅛	24⅛	19⅝	4⅝	4½	10	11	Monona Co., Iowa	Rob L. Cadwallader	Rob L. Cadwallader	1984	234
208	25	25	19⅞	4⅝	4½	9	10	Griswold, Man.	J. V. Parker	J. V. Parker	1946	234
207⅞	23⅞	23⅞	21⅛	5	5	13	8	Mexico	Unknown	William M. Day	1959	238
207⅞	24⅛	24⅜	20⅜	4⅞	5	13	8	Antelope Co., Neb.	Leon McCoy	Leon McCoy	1965	238
207⅞	28⅛	30½	24⅜	6⅛	5	10	8	Atkinson Highway, Neb.	Russell Angus	Russell Angus	1966	238
207⅞	21⅜	23⅞	24⅜	5	4⅞	8	8	Prairie Co., Mont.	Charles Danielson	Charles Danielson	1969	238
207⅞	25	25	19⅞	4⅝	4⅝	9	10	Chesaw, Wash.	Charles Eder	Charles Eder	1967	243
207⅝	23⅞	21⅜	19⅞	4⅝	4⅜	13	19	Suffolk Co., N.Y.	George Hackal	Gary C. Boyer	1950	244
207⅝	23⅝	31½	24½	4⅜	4½	11	7	Port Royal, Pa.	C. Ralph Landis	C. Ralph Landis	1951	244
207⅝	24⅞	25⅜	19	5⅝	5⅞	11	14	Perkins Co., S.D.	W. E. Brown	J. D. Andrews	1957	244
207⅝	26⅞	26	24⅜	5⅜	5⅜	7	9	Monitor, Alta.	Raymond Worobo	Raymond Worobo	1979	244
207⅝	27	27⅜	25⅜	6⅜	6¼	9	9	Aroostook Co., Maine	Alfred Wardwell	Alfred Wardwell	1945	248
207⅝	27⅛	26⅜	22⅜	6⅝	7	9	9	Lincoln Co., Minn.	Joe Ness	Joe Ness	1961	249
207⅝	24⅛	23⅜	17⅞	5⅝	5⅝	11	8	Moosomin, Sask.	Leslie Hanson	Sam Peterson	1961	249
207⅝	25	20⅜	19⅝	6	6	10	17	Seward Co., Neb.	Ladislav Dolezal	Ladislav Dolezal	1964	249

WHITETAIL DEER (Non-Typical Antlers)—Continued
Odocoileus virginianus virginianus and certain related subspecies

Score	Length of Main Beam R.	L.	Inside Spread	Circumference at Smallest Place Between Burr and First Point R.	L.	Number of Points R.	L.	Locality Killed	By Whom Killed	Owner	Date Killed	Rank
207⅞	25⅜	25⅛	21⅞	6	6	11	7	Keephills, Alta.	Unknown	William J. Greenhough	PR1970	249
207⅞	24	23⅜	23⅜	6⅜	6⅜	10	8	Buffalo Co., Wisc.	Dennis M. Eberhart	Dennis M. Eberhart	1984	249
207⅞	25⅜	24⅛	16⅜	5⅜	5⅞	12	11	Burnett Co., Wisc.	Harold Miller	Mac's Taxidermy	1938	254
207⅜	28⅜	29⅛	18⅝	6⅜	6⅜	10	10	Lincoln Co., Mo.	Melvin Zumwalt	Melvin Zumwalt	1955	255
207⅜	28⅜	27⅜	21⅛	5⅞	5⅞	10	11	Roberts Co., S.D.	Delbert Lackey	Delbert Lackey	1975	255
207⅞	24⅛	19⅜	11⅞	5⅝	5⅝	11	17	Oroville, Wash.	Victor E. Moss	Victor E. Moss	1967	257
207⅞	27⅛	26⅜	18⅜	5⅝	5⅝	7	10	Drayton Valley, Alta.	Hassib Halabi	Hassib Halabi	1977	257
207⅞	25⅜	24⅜	20⅝	5⅜	5⅜	9	10	Provost, Alta.	Michael D. Kerley	Michael D. Kerley	1977	259
207⅛	22	23⅜	19⅜	8	8⅜	14	13	Buffalo Co., Neb.	Unknown	John L. Stein	1978	259
207	26	25⅜	26	5⅝	5⅝	11	13	Lycoming Co., Pa.	Al Prouty	Al Prouty	1949	261
207	23⅜	23⅜	18⅜	5⅝	6⅜	16	13	Bayfield Co., Wisc.	Francis F. Zifko	Francis F. Zifko	1954	261
206⅞	24⅜	25	16⅜	5⅝	5⅜	14	9	Oneida Co., Wisc.	Clarence Staudenmayer	Clarence Staudenmayer	1942	263
206⅞	25	24⅜	18	5⅜	5⅜	10	12	Loup Co., Neb.	T. A. Brandenburg	J. D. Andrews	1963	263
206⅞	23⅜	25⅜	18⅜	5⅛	4⅞	14	12	Horicon Marsh, Wisc.	Picked Up	Ronald A. Lillge	1966	263
206⅞	28⅜	30⅜	23⅜	6⅛	5⅝	11	10	Claiborne Parish, La.	J. H. Thurmon	J. H. Thurmon	1970	263
206⅞	26⅜	29⅜	27⅜	5⅝	5⅝	11	10	Wright Co., Minn.	Richard A. Erickson	Richard A. Erickson	1983	263
206⅞	25⅜	25⅜	24	5⅜	5⅝	7	11	Beechy, Sask.	Harold Penner	Spanky Greenville	1959	268
206⅞	25⅜	26⅜	17⅜	5⅝	5⅝	8	10	Grant Parish, La.	Richard D. Ellison, Jr.	Richard D. Ellison, Jr.	1969	268
206⅞	25⅜	23⅜	23⅜	5⅝	5⅝	12	9	Somerset Co., Maine	Mark T. Lary	Mark T. Lary	1979	268
206⅜	26	24⅜	19⅜	5⅜	5⅜	7	12	Chase Co., Kan.	Jay A. Talkington	Jay A. Talkington	1983	271
206⅛	22⅛	22⅞	19⅜	5	5	10	13	Brooks Co., Texas	John E. Wilson	James Martin Hancock, Jr.	1947	272
206⅛	23⅜	23⅜	16⅜	5⅝	5⅝	14	8	Norman Co., Minn.	Unknown	Tom Williams	1950	272
206⅛	25⅜	24⅜	17⅜	6⅜	6⅜	12	9	Yankton Co., S.D.	William Sees	William Sees	1973	272
206⅛	26	26⅜	19⅜	6⅜	6⅜	11	6	Lac qui Parle Co., Minn.	Steven J. Karels	Steven J. Karels	1974	272
206⅛	28⅜	26⅜	20⅜	5⅜	5⅜	10	9	Lawrence Co., Ill.	Shirley Lewis	Shirley Lewis	1976	272
206⅜	22⅜	23⅜	19	4⅜	4⅜	11	11	Webb Co., Texas	Willard V. Brenizer	Gerry Elliff	1942	277
206⅛	28⅜	28⅜	25	5⅜	5⅝	9	11	Cortland Co., N.Y.	Hank Hayes	Interlaken Sportsmans Club	1947	278
206⅜	25⅜	25	16⅜	5	5	7	9	Cotulla, Texas	George E. Light III	George E. Light III	1950	278
206⅜	31⅛	31	22⅞	6	5⅜	9	7	Piscataquis Co., Maine	Ralph E. Dow	Ralph E. Dow	1964	278
206⅛	22	20⅜	20⅜	4⅜	4⅜	10	10	Loon Lake, Wash.	Bill Quirt	Bill Quirt	1955	281

206 2/8	22 2/8	22 2/8	18 3/8	5 4/8	5 4/8	15	10	Kisbey, Sask.	J. Harrison	J. Harrison	1956	281
206 1/8	24 2/8	22 2/8	18	4 3/8	4 3/8	14	13	Boydel, Ark.	Picked Up	Clem Billgisher	1959	281
206 1/8	23 3/8	22 2/8	22	5 5/8	5 5/8	10	9	Lincoln Co., Wisc.	Picked Up	Louis Pond	PR1974	281
206 1/8	25 3/8	25 3/8	18 1/8	5 5/8	5 1/8	8	9	Dunn Co., N.D.	Kenneth E. DeLap	Kenneth E. DeLap	1982	281
205 7/8	28 3/8	27 3/8	17 1/8	5	5 5/8	8	17	Steuben Co., N.Y.	Fred J. Kelley	Fred J. Kelley	1938	286
205 7/8	25 3/8	25 3/8	20 5/8	4 3/8	4 3/8	10	10	Houston Co., Texas	Gary Rogers	Gary Rogers	1969	286
205 7/8	25	23 3/8	20 5/8	6	6	13	12	Missoula Co., Mont.	Unknown	John L. Stein	1973	286
205 7/8	23 5/8	28 3/8	19 5/8	5 1/8	5 1/8	10	8	Switzerland Co., Ind.	Paul Graf	Paul Graf	1981	286
205 7/8	27 4/8	23 3/8	17 5/8	5 5/8	5 5/8	9	13	Clark Co., Mo.	Allen L. Courtney	Allen L. Courtney	1983	291
205 6/8	23 5/8	26 3/8	18 1/8	4 5/8	4 5/8	11	9	Minnesota	Unknown	Greg Jensen	1965	291
205 5/8	23 1/8	21 3/8	21	4 4/8	4 4/8	12	12	Lowndes Co., Miss.	Joe W. Shurden	Joe W. Shurden	1976	291
205 5/8	24 2/8	24	21	5	5	12	9	Ritchie Co., W.Va.	Ed Bailey	Ed Bailey	1979	291
205 5/8	23 3/8	23	20 3/8	5 5/8	5 5/8	8	10	Cloud Co., Kan.	Gary G. Pingel	Gary G. Pingel	1982	295
205 5/8	26	25 3/8	21 3/8	5 3/8	5 3/8	14	9	Cottonwood Co., Minn.	Larry G. Gravley	Larry G. Gravley	1975	295
205 4/8	25 1/8	26 3/8	22 3/8	5 7/8	5 7/8	10	12	Midway, B.C.	Gordon Kamigochi	Gordon Kamigochi	1980	297
205 4/8	25 5/8	25 3/8	22 3/8	5	5	10	9	Roseau Co., Minn.	Erwin Klaassen	Erwin Klaassen	1955	297
205 4/8	25	25 3/8	19 3/8	5 5/8	5 5/8	9	9	Adams Co., Ill.	Eldon K. Dagley	Eldon K. Dagley	1981	299
205 3/8	23 3/8	21 3/8	18 3/8	6 1/8	5 5/8	11	7	Kelvington, Sask.	D. Minor	D. Minor	1954	299
205 3/8	25 5/8	27 1/8	22 3/8	4 7/8	5	6	12	Trempealeau Co., Wisc.	Dennis L. Ulberg	Dennis L. Ulberg	1968	299
205 3/8	25 5/8	23 3/8	17	4 1/8	4 4/8	10	9	Todd Co., Minn.	Mark A. Miksche	Mark A. Miksche	1979	302
205 3/8	22 5/8	24 3/8	20 3/8	6	6	10	12	Leross, Sask.	R. Weger	R. Weger	1961	303
205	26 3/8	26 3/8	16 7/8	5	5	10	9	St. Louis Co., Minn.	Ed Nelson	George W. Flaim	1964	304
204 7/8	26 3/8	26 3/8	29 7/8	6 1/8	6	12	10	Portageville, N.Y.	Howard W. Smith	Howard W. Smith	1959	304
204 7/8	26 3/8	26 3/8	21 3/8	4 3/8	4 4/8	7	8	Trempealeau Co., Wisc.	Ralph Klimek	Ralph Klimek	1960	306
204 6/8	23 3/8	23 3/8	15 5/8	5 5/8	6 5/8	9	9	Moose Jaw, Sask.	Earl Sears	Earl Sears	1958	306
204 6/8	28 3/8	26 3/8	21 3/8	5 7/8	5 7/8	10	10	Gilmer Co., W.Va.	Brooks Reed	Brooks Reed	1960	306
204 6/8	26 5/8	26 3/8	18 3/8	5 1/8	5	9	12	Nemaha Co., Kan.	Unknown	John L. Stein	PR1974	306
204 5/8	26 7/8	25 7/8	21 1/8	5	5	9	7	Innisfree, Alta.	Donald Baranec	Donald Baranec	1977	310
204 5/8	25 5/8	25 3/8	19 3/8	5	5 4/8	6	8	Unknown	Unknown	John A. Jarosz	PR1930	311
204 4/8	30	28 3/8	21 1/8	5 4/8	5 4/8	11	8	Jackson Co., Ohio	Bernard Tennant	Bernard Tennant	1960	311
204 4/8	22 3/8	21 3/8	16 5/8	5	5	10	12	Love Co., Okla.	William B. Heller	William B. Heller	1970	313
204 3/8	26	24 3/8	18 3/8	5 5/8	5 5/8	10	11	Newport, Wash.	David R. Buchite	David R. Buchite	1960	313
204 3/8	23 5/8	24	20 5/8	4 7/8	4 7/8	11	12	Waukesha Co., Wisc.	Unknown	Mac's Taxidermy	PR1975	313
204 2/8	23	20 3/8	17 3/8	5 5/8	5 5/8	10	12	Crook Co., Wyo.	David Sipe	David Sipe	1956	315
204 2/8	25 3/8	23 3/8	17 1/8	4 4/8	4 4/8	11	15	Silver Lake, Alta.	Edwin Nelson	Gary Padleski	1980	315
204 1/8	28 5/8	28 3/8	17 1/8	5 5/8	5 5/8	7	15	Charlotte Co., N.B.	Gary L. Lister	Gary L. Lister	1984	317
204	26 1/8	25 7/8	22 5/8	6 1/8	6 1/8	12	9	Carlton Co., Minn.	Erick Zack	Glen Van Guilder	1964	318
204	26 1/8	25 3/8	16 2/8	5 3/8	5 3/8	10	11	Sheep River, Alta.	Walter L. Brown	Walter L. Brown	1966	318
204	27 3/8	25 3/8	21 3/8	5 3/8	5 3/8	7	12	Grant Co., Minn.	Douglas S. Olson	Douglas S. Olson	1977	318
204	26 3/8	25 3/8	18 3/8	5 2/8	5 2/8	13	10	Holbein, Sask.	Jesse Bates	Jesse Bates	1981	318
204	23 3/8	23 3/8	18 3/8	5 7/8	5 7/8	13	14	Webster Co., Ky.	Jeff Robinson	Jeff Robinson	1982	318
203 7/8	26 3/8	27 1/8	21 3/8	5 5/8	5 4/8	9	11	Eastland Co., Texas	Picked Up	William B. Wright, Jr.	1920	323
203 5/8	27 3/8	27 3/8	17 7/8	4 6/8	4 6/8	11	8	George Lake, N.B.	Henry Kirk	Ron Kirk	1903	324

Odocoileus virginianus virginianus and certain related subspecies

Score	Length of Main Beam R	L	Inside Spread	Circumference at Smallest Place Between Burr and First Point R	L	Number of Points R	L	Locality Killed	By Whom Killed	Owner	Date Killed	Rank
203⅜	24⅞	25⅛	16⅞	4	3⅞	8	8	Maverick Co., Texas	Picked Up	Richard H. Bennett	1941	324
203⅜	25	26⅞	17⅞	4⅜	4⅞	9	8	McCurtain Co., Okla.	Gary L. Birge	Gary L. Birge	1981	324
203⅜	26⅝	28	15⅜	6⅛	6	18	13	Chariton Co., Mo.	Vernon Sower	Vernon Sower	1953	327
203⅜	23	30⅜	15	6⅝	6⅝	8	14	Meigs Co., Ohio	Wesley Gilkey	Wesley Gilkey	1970	327
203⅜	23⅞	25⅞	17⅜	6	5⅝	10	9	Grand Forks Co., N.D.	Thomas G. Bernotas	Thomas G. Bernotas	1975	327
203⅜	24⅜	26⅜	21⅛	5⅝	5⅞	12	11	St. Louis Co., Minn.	Picked Up	Phillip A. Roalstad	1981	331
203⅜	25	25⅛	22	4⅝	4⅜	13	12	Live Oak Co., Texas	Alec Coker	Henderson Coquat	1916	331
203⅜	23⅜	22⅛	18⅝	5⅜	5⅝	9	10	Lawrence Co., S.D.	Ernest C. Larive	Ernest C. Larive	1957	333
203⅜	25⅛	24⅛	21	5⅜	5⅜	8	10	Olmsted Co., Minn.	Logan Behrens	Logan Behrens	1961	333
203⅜	25⅞	25⅞	21⅛	5	5	10	8	Okanogan Co., Wash.	Michael A. Anderson	Michael A. Anderson	1961	333
203⅜	22⅜	23⅜	19⅞	6	6⅛	8	8	S. Piapot, Sask.	Frank Kelly	Frank Kelly	1966	333
203⅜	26⅜	26⅛	17⅞	5⅝	5⅞	8	10	Olmsted Co., Minn.	Daniel J. Bernard	Daniel J. Bernard	1967	337
203¾	23⅜	23⅜	17⅞	5⅛	5⅜	13	13	Esterhazy, Sask.	Walter Tucker	Walter Tucker	1966	338
203⅛	23⅜	25⅝	16	4⅞	4⅞	11	10	Koochiching Co., Minn.	Unknown	George W. Flaim	1934	338
203⅛	28⅛	27⅜	21	4⅞	4⅜	9	7	Pawnee Co., Neb.	Virgil J. Fisher	Virgil J. Fisher	1970	338
203⅜	23⅞	24⅛	19⅜	5⅜	5⅜	10	12	Wetzel Co., W.Va.	Tom Kirkhart	Tom Kirkhart	1981	341
203	26⅜	24⅛	15	5⅛	5⅛	9	11	Hancock Co., Ill.	S. E. Brockschmidt	S. E. Brockschmidt	1958	341
203	26⅛	27⅞	17⅜	4⅝	4⅜	9	8	Jefferson Co., Kan.	Dale Heston	Dale Heston	1982	343
202⅞	25⅛	24⅜	23⅜	5	5	7	10	Marinette Co., Wisc.	Theodore Maes	Theodore Maes	1932	344
202⅞	22⅜	22	18	5⅝	5⅛	7	8	Garrison, N.D.	Clarence Hummel	Clarence Hummel	1961	345
202⅝	29	29⅜	20⅜	4⅝	4⅜	10	9	Dane Co., Wisc.	Ray S. Outhouse	Ray S. Outhouse	1964	345
202⅝	23	24	14⅞	5⅝	5⅛	9	9	McMullen Co., Texas	Picked Up	Patrick L. Seals	1984	347
202⅝	24⅜	24⅜	16⅞	5	4⅞	13	12	Missoula Co., Mont.	Unknown	Robert A. Bracken	1962	348
202⅝	26	24⅜	21⅛	5⅝	5⅜	11	12	Koochiching Co., Minn.	George A. Balaski	George A. Balaski	1955	348
202⅜	26⅛	27	20⅜	5	5⅛	10	10	Aitkin Co., Minn.	Joe Clarke	Joe Clarke	1960	348
202⅜	23⅝	25⅜	16⅝	4⅝	4⅜	11	6	Crook Co., Wyo.	Marshall Miller	Marshall Miller	1968	351
202⅜	21⅝	22⅜	22	5⅛	5⅛	12	9	Fergus Co., Mont.	Harold K. Stewart	Harold K. Stewart	1948	351
202⅜	24	23⅜	27	5⅝	5⅜	11	8	Hungry Hollow, Sask.	K. W. Henderson	K. W. Henderson	1954	351
202⅛	25⅛	24⅜	19⅞	4⅝	4⅞	9	9	East Kooteney, B.C.	Andrew W. Rosicky	Andrew W. Rosicky	1956	351
202⅛	25⅛	25⅜	22⅜	4⅞	5	9	9	Zehner, Sask.	Lee Danison	Lee Danison	1958	354
202⅛	26⅛	26⅝	19⅜	6⅞	6⅛	8	9	Gary, S.D.	Dennis Cole	Dennis Cole	1960	354
202⅛	26⅛	26⅜	19½	4⅞	4⅞	10	7	Pennington Co., Minn.	R. Scott Sorvig	R. Scott Sorvig	1980	354

276

Score								Locality	Hunter	Owner	Date	Rank
202⅛	28⅜	28⅜	16⅞	5⅝	5⅝	15	11	Oktibbeha Co., Miss.	Oliver H. Lindig	Oliver H. Lindig	1983	354
202	26⅜	27	22⅝	6⅛	6⅛	6	9	Bayfield Co., Wisc.	Indian	Richard Wanasek	1960	358
202	28⅜	27⅞	15⅝	5⅝	6	12	11	Nodaway Co., Mo.	Richard L. Stewart	Richard L. Stewart	1972	358
202	26⅞	27	23⅜	5⅞	5⅞	13	10	Powell Co., Ky.	Hershel Ingram	Hershel Ingram	1980	358
202	26⅞	28⅜	26⅞	5	5	8	7	Knox Co., Maine	Skip Black	Skip Black	1981	358
201⅞	24⅜	23⅜	23⅜	5⅝	5⅝	9	7	Burmis, Alta.	Joe Tapay	Joe Tapay	1964	362
201⅞	28⅜	27	17⅜	6	6	11	11	Itasca Co., Minn.	Picked Up	J. Gorden & G. Dopp	1981	362
201⅝	26⅜	23⅛	26⅜	5⅝	5⅞	8	9	Waldo Co., Maine	James A. Tripp, Sr.	James A. Tripp, Sr.	1959	364
201⅝	27⅞	22⅞	20⅜	5⅝	5⅝	8	12	Sisseton, S.D.	Truman M. Nelson	Truman M. Nelson	1967	364
201⅝	27	26⅞	18	5⅞	5⅞	15	16	Charlevoix Co., Mich.	Robert V. Doerr	Robert V. Doerr	1973	364
201	25	24⅞	17⅛	5⅜	5⅛	10	8	Ohaton, Alta.	Curtis Siegfried	Curtis Siegfried	1976	364
201	27	26	18⅜	5⅝	5⅝	7	10	Johnson Co., Iowa	Duane E. Papke	Duane E. Papke	1981	364
201⅜	25⅛	24⅞	19⅞	6⅜	6⅛	7	7	Baraga Co., Mich.	Dennis D. Bess	Dennis D. Bess	1981	364
201⅜	22⅞	23⅜	16⅜	4⅛	4⅛	9	8	Campbell Co., S.D.	Edward J. Torigian	J. D. Andrews	1957	370
201¼	25⅞	23⅛	16⅛	4⅝	5⅛	14	13	Stevens Co., Wash.	Robert W. Newell	Robert W. Newell	1963	370
201¼	28⅝	28⅛	22⅛	5⅜	5⅜	8	9	Brown Co., Neb.	R. L. Tinkham	R. L. Tinkham	1965	370
201¼	29⅜	28⅝	19⅞	5⅞	5⅝	10	10	Hubbard Co., Minn.	Duane G. Lorsung	Duane G. Lorsung	1973	370
201⅛	22	29⅞	23⅞	6⅞	6⅛	9	8	Barber Co., Kan.	Joe Ash	Joe Ash	1975	370
201⅛	28⅜	25⅜	18⅜	6⅞	6⅞	7	7	Flathead Co., Mont.	Barry L. Wensel	Barry L. Wensel	1976	370
201⅛	26⅜	25⅜	18⅜	5⅝	5⅜	10	8	St. Louis Co., Minn.	Andrew G. Groen	Andrew G. Groen	1958	376
201⅛	21⅛	21⅝	21⅜	5⅝	4⅛	16	11	Bonner Co., Idaho	Leroy Coleman	Leroy Coleman	1960	376
201⅛	26⅛	18⅜	18⅜	4⅞	4⅛	9	10	Concordia Parish, La.	G. O. McGuffee	G. O. McGuffee	1963	376
201⅛	24⅜	25⅛	19	5⅝	5⅝	12	10	Queen Annes Co., Md.	Franklin E. Jewell	Franklin E. Jewell	1978	376
201⅛	26⅜	16	16⅜	5⅝	5⅝	17	14	Pennington Co., Minn.	Glenn Tasa	Glenn Tasa	1940	380
201⅛	26⅜	16⅝	16⅜	5⅝	5⅝	10	7	Itasca Co., Minn.	Cecil L. Johnson	Cecil L. Johnson	1976	380
201⅛	27⅜	27⅜	23⅛	4⅛	4⅜	11	11	Coshocton Co., Ohio	Lou L. Rogers	Lou L. Rogers	1979	380
201⅛	28⅜	28⅜	23⅜	5⅛	4⅞	8	10	Arkansas Co., Ark.	Daniel Boone Bullock	Daniel Boone Bullock	1953	383
201⅛	28⅜	27⅜	16⅝	5⅝	5⅝	8	9	Slope Co., N.D.	Arthur Hegge	J. D. Andrews	1961	383
201⅛	21⅜	22⅜	16⅜	5⅝	5⅝	9	11	Westmoreland Co., Pa.	Richard K. Mellon	Richard K. Mellon	1966	383
201⅛	23	22⅝	14⅝	4⅞	4⅛	13	16	Freeborn Co., Minn.	Jim Palmer	Jim Palmer	1972	383
201⅛	25	25⅜	20⅜	6⅛	6⅛	10	8	Butler Co., Neb.	James L. Sklenar	James L. Sklenar	1973	383
201	25⅜	25⅜	18⅜	5	4⅞	8	7	Delta Co., Mich.	Ernest B. Fosterling	Ernest B. Fosterling	1953	388
201	22⅜	22⅜	15⅜	5⅜	5⅜	14	12	Cessford, Alta.	Russell C. Chapman	Russell C. Chapman	1966	388
201	25⅜	26⅜	20⅜	4⅛	4⅝	9	13	Mercer Co., Ill.	Gerald L. Olson	Gerald L. Olson	1972	388
201	27⅞	27⅞	21⅛	5⅝	5⅝	11	8	Anoka Co., Minn.	Unknown	John L. Stein	1977	388
200⅞	23⅜	21⅛	19⅝	6⅞	7⅛	8	11	Mandan, N.D.	Virgil Chadwick	Peter Voigt	1957	392
200⅞	23⅜	24⅜	20⅜	5⅜	5⅜	9	8	Rusk Co., Wisc.	Gerald Cleven	Gerald Cleven	1963	392
200⅞	23	19	19	4⅞	4⅛	11	9	Kleberg Co., Texas	Picked Up	John A. Larkin	1982	392
200⅞	23⅜	23⅜	19	4⅛	4⅝	11	10	Juneau Co., Wisc.	Anchor Nelson	J. D. Andrews	1946	395
200⅞	24⅜	24⅜	17⅞	5	5	11	9	Wapello Co., Iowa	Rod A. McKelvey	Rod A. McKelvey	1983	395
200⅝	25⅜	25⅜	25⅜	6⅛	6⅛	9	11	Jackson Co., Ohio	Glenn McCall	Glenn McCall	1970	397
200⅝	27⅞	22⅜	22⅜	5⅜	5⅝	8	7	Brentford, S.D.	S. C. Mitchell	S. C. Mitchell	1948	398
200⅝	25⅞	23	19⅝	6⅛	6	9	6	Wainwright, Alta.	Paul Pryor	Paul Pryor	1968	398

WHITETAIL DEER (Non-Typical Antlers)—Continued
Odocoileus virginianus virginianus and certain related subspecies

Score	Length of Main Beam R.	L.	Inside Spread	Circumference at Smallest Place Between Burr and First Point R.	L.	Number of Points R.	L.	Locality Killed	By Whom Killed	Owner	Date Killed	Rank
200⅜	24⅝	24⅞	19⅞	5⅝	5⅝	12	10	Geauga Co., Ohio	Rudy C. Grecar	Rudy C. Grecar	1969	398
200⅜	24⅝	22⅝	18	4⅜	4⅝	8	10	Crook Co., Wyo.	Paul L. Wolz	Paul L. Wolz	1967	401
200⅜	23⅝	24	18⅝	4⅜	4⅝	8	8	Lake of the Woods Co., Minn.	Mark H. Hagen	Mark H. Hagen	1974	401
200⅜	25⅝	27	19⅛	6⅛	5⅝	10	10	Tuscarawas Co., Ohio	Michael D. Korns, Sr.	Michael D. Korns, Sr.	1978	401
200⅜	27	23⅛	24⅜	5⅛	5		7	Knox Co., Ohio	Albert Hall	Albert Hall	1983	401
200⅛	26	24⅜	23	6	6	11	12	Parrsboro, N.S.	Allison Smith	Edward B. Shaw	1960	405
200⅛	27⅜	26⅝	21⅜	4⅞	5⅛	12	12	Kandiyohi Co., Minn.	Robert J. Custer	Robert J. Custer	1966	405
200⅛	24⅜	24⅝	20⅝	5	5	9	8	Blaine Co., Neb.	Pauline C. Sander	Pauline C. Sander	1983	405
200⅛	25⅛	25⅜	18⅝	4⅞	4⅝	11	10	Outlook, Sask.	Earl B. Schmitt	Earl B. Schmitt	1966	408
200	20⅝	25⅝	14	5⅛	5	7	14	Hickory Co., Mo.	Darwin L. Stogsdill	Darwin L. Stogsdill	1971	409
199⅞	28⅞	20⅞	19⅞	6⅛	6	7	8	Meigs Co., Ohio	Cody R. Boothe	Cody R. Boothe	1970	410
199⅞	23⅜	29⅞	17⅞	5⅛	5⅝	8	9	Rochester, Alta.	James Weismantel	James Weismantel	1979	410
199⅞	29	27⅞	19⅛	6⅛	6⅛	8	6	Jefferson Co., Wisc.	Jerome Stockheimer	Jerome Stockheimer	1968	412
199⅝	25⅜	25⅜	20⅛	5⅛	5⅝	8	8	Aitkin Co., Minn.	Sanford Patrick	Sanford Patrick	1963	413
199⅝	25⅛	25⅜	21⅛	5⅝	5⅝	9	9	Wilcox Co., Ala.	Billy W. Morton	Billy W. Morton	1975	413
199⅜	23⅜	23⅜	17⅜	5⅛	5⅝	10	9	Flathead Co., Mont.	Unknown	Tom Williams	PR1980	413
199⅛	28	26⅝	21⅛	5⅛	5⅝	10	10	Clark Co., Mo.	Bob Arnold	Bob Arnold	1973	416
199⅛	21⅛	21⅛	20⅜	5⅛	5⅝	8	8	Jasmin, Sask.	Richard Gill	Richard Gill	1958	417
199	28⅞	27⅛	23⅜	5⅛	5⅝	7	9	Winston Co., Ala.	James W. Huckbay	James W. Huckbay	1973	417
199	25⅝	25⅜	17⅛	5⅛	5⅝	10	13	St. Louis Co., Minn.	Orville Schultz	Orville Schultz	1978	419
199	22⅞	21	17⅛	5⅛	5	13	7	Clark Co., Wisc.	George Mashin	Douglas Wampole	1946	420
199	25	25	19⅛	5	5	10	8	Yellow Medicine Co., Minn.	William A. Botten	William A. Botten	1976	420
198⅞	24⅜	27⅜	19⅛	6⅛	7⅜	8	7	Westaskiwin, Alta.	John Miller	John Miller	1984	420
198⅞	24⅜	28⅜	24⅜	5⅛	5⅛	7	9	Unknown	Unknown	Max E. Chittick	1900	423
198⅞	25	23⅜	16⅜	5⅜	5⅝	11	11	Weston Co., Wyo.	G. Huls & B. L. Arfmann	Chester S. Jones	1973	423
198⅞	26⅞	25⅝	21⅛	5⅜	4⅞	10	7	Chippewa Co., Minn.	Ray N. Strand	Ray N. Strand	1976	423
198⅞	29⅜	28⅜	24⅜	4⅞	5⅜	8	7	Ripley Co., Ind.	William L. Wagner	William L. Wagner	1982	423
198⅞	29⅝	27⅛	15⅜	5⅜	6⅛	11	7	Fillmore Co., Minn.	Phillip S. Hansen	Phillip S. Hansen	1973	427
198⅛	24⅜	24⅜	17⅛	5⅝	5⅝	9	15	Hayward, Wisc.	Unknown	Harold Burrows	PR1920	428
198⅛	26⅝	26⅝	18⅜	5⅝	5⅝	11	13	Iron Co., Mich.	Eino Macki	J. D. Andrews	1930	428
198⅛	26⅝	27⅝	22⅛	6⅛	6⅛	6	11	Concordia Parish, La.	Raymond Cowan	Raymond Cowan	1961	428
198⅛	26⅜	26⅝	17⅜	5⅛	5⅛	9	6	Jackson Co., Ohio	Stanley Elam	Stanley Elam	1962	428

Score	Main Beam R.	Main Beam L.	Inside Spread	Circum. R.	Circum. L.	Points R.	Points L.	Locality	Hunter	Owner	Date	Rank
198⅝	26⅜	25⅜	22⅜	5	4⅞	8	7	Webb Co., Texas	Larry Bickham	Larry Bickham	1962	428
198⅝	23⅞	22⅞	17⅞	4⅞	5	14	12	Will Co., Ill.	William H. Rutledge	William H. Rutledge	1977	428
198⅝	25⅜	25⅜	23⅜	5	5	10	10	Oconto Co., Wisc.	Paul M. Krueger	Paul M. Krueger	1977	428
198⅛	26¼	22⅜	18⅜	5⅞	5⅝	9	10	Clay Co., Minn.	F. W. Kolle	Kolle Farms, Inc.	1946	435
198⅛	24⅜	23⅛	18	5⅜	5⅜	13	12	Cow Creek, Wyo.	Thelma Martens	Thelma Martens	1951	435
198⅛	23⅞	23⅜	17⅞	4⅞	4⅞	8	9	Iroquois Co., Ill.	Charles E. Crow	Charles E. Crow	1974	435
198⅛	26⅜	24⅜	21⅜	4⅞	4¾	7	8	Lincoln Co., Minn.	Dennis G. Geiken	Dennis G. Geiken	1980	435
198⅛	25	26⅜	23⅜	4⅞	4⅞	7	8	Webb Co., Texas	Alvin C. Santleben, Jr.	Alvin C. Santleben, Jr.	1983	435
198⅛	22⅞	26	21⅞	5⅜	5	12	8	Wheeler Co., Ga.	David Frost	David Frost	1978	441
198⅜	26⅛	26⅛	17⅞	4⅞	4½	8	8	Montgomery Co., Tenn.	Clarence McElhaney	Clarence McElhaney	1941	442
198⅛	23⅞	22⅜	21⅜	5	5	8	10	Crow Wing Co., Minn.	Harold B. Stotts	Harold B. Stotts	1966	442
198⅛	23⅜	23⅜	19⅜	5⅞	5⅞	8	12	Rock Co., Neb.	Gerald M. Lewis	Gerald M. Lewis	1935	444
198⅛	21⅛	21⅜	17	5	5	13	8	Nelway, B.C.	Edward John	Edward John	1959	444
198⅛	27	28⅜	22⅜	4⅞	4⅞	7	9	Harrison Co., Ohio	Roy Hines	Roy Hines	1964	444
198⅛	27	26⅜	20⅜	5	5	10	7	Hocking Co., Ohio	Hugh Cox	Hugh Cox	1967	444
198	24⅜	24⅜	19⅜	5⅝	5⅝	10	9	Kootenai Co., Idaho	Frank J. Cheney	Idaho Dept. Fish & Game	1961	448
198	26⅛	24⅜	23	7⅛	6⅜	9	7	Valley, Neb.	Ivan Masher	Ivan Masher	1977	448
197⅞	25⅜	25⅜	17⅞	6⅜	6⅜	9	10	Osage Co., Kan.	Joe A. Rose, Jr.	Joe A. Rose, Jr.	1984	450
197⅞	27⅜	28⅜	25	5⅜	5½	9	8	Cheyenne Co., Neb.	Reid Block	Reid Block	1961	451
197⅞	23⅜	26⅜	20½	5⅜	5⅜	10	8	Hunters, Wash.	Rachel Mally	Rachel Mally	1965	451
197⅞	25⅝	26⅜	17	5	5	10	8	Riceville, Mont.	James R. Eastman	James R. Eastman	1967	451
197⅞	24	24⅜	18½	5⅜	5⅜	9	11	Langham, Sask.	Leonard Waldner	Leonard Waldner	PR1984	451
197⅞	20⅜	22⅜	22⅞	5	5	10	7	Unknown	Unknown	John L. Stein	1917	455
197⅞	20	24	18	8⅜	8⅛	8	11	Luce Co., Mich.	Sid Jones	Jim Deavereaux	1945	455
197⅞	24⅜	24⅛	20⅜	6⅜	5⅜	7	8	Sawyer Co., Wisc.	James Borman	James Borman	1956	455
197⅞	31⅛	32⅜	25⅜	5⅜	5⅜	5	11	Geauga Co., Ohio	Edward Dooner	Edward Dooner	1962	455
197⅞	28	28⅜	21	5⅞	5⅜	10	6	Jo Daviess Co., Ill.	David H. Carpenter	David H. Carpenter	1981	455
197⅞	25⅛	24⅞	22⅜	5⅞	5⅛	10	7	Blue Earth Co., Minn.	Daniel R. Nelson	Daniel R. Nelson	1961	460
197⅞	25⅞	25⅞	25	5⅜	5⅜	10	8	Pope Co., Ill.	Joe C. Schwegman	Joe C. Schwegman	1967	460
197⅞	25⅝	26⅜	25⅞	5	5	11	9	Wainwright, Alta.	George Bauman	George Bauman	1971	460
197⅞	25	23⅜	22⅜	5⅜	5⅜	7	7	Johnson Co., Iowa	Dennis R. Ballard	Dennis R. Ballard	1973	460
197¾	24⅜	24⅜	21⅜	6⅜	6⅞	8	7	Chippewa Co., Minn.	Dean D. Anspach	Dean D. Anspach	1980	460
197¾	25⅞	25⅜	20⅜	6⅜	6⅜	11	10	Garfield Co., Okla.	Derald D. Crissup	Derald D. Crissup	1984	460
197¾	26¾	27¾	18	4⅞	4⅞	10	12	Dooly Co., Ga.	Wayne Griffin	Wayne Griffin	1984	467
197¾	25⅞	26⅜	16⅜	5⅜	5⅞	6	8	Lyon Co., Kan.	John R. Clifton	John R. Clifton		467
197¾	26	26⅜	17⅞	5⅜	5⅜	9	10	Stevens Co., Wash.	Coulston W. Drummond	Coulston W. Drummond	1948	467
197¾	24	26⅜	16⅞	5⅞	5⅞	9	9	Newton Co., Ga.	R. H. Bumbalough	R. H. Bumbalough	1969	467
197¾	27⅜	26⅜	20⅜	5⅜	5⅜	9	9	Faribault Co., Minn.	Randy L. Sandt	Randy L. Sandt	1982	471
197¾	22⅜	23⅜	21⅜	5⅞	5⅛	14	10	Marshall Co., Kan.	Lloyd Wenzl	Lloyd Wenzl	1983	471
197¾	27⅞	26⅝	21	5	5	8	9	Hancock Co., Maine	Hollis Patterson	Reginald R. Clark	PR1950	471
197¾	23⅞	26⅜	17⅞	5⅝	5⅜	10	9	Stanton, Neb.	Peter Bartman III	Peter Bartman III	1963	471

279

WHITETAIL DEER (Non-Typical Antlers)—Continued
Odocoileus virginianus virginianus and certain related subspecies

Score	Length of Main Beam R.	L.	Inside Spread	Circumference at Smallest Place Between Burr and First Point R.	L.	Number of Points R.	L.	Locality Killed	By Whom Killed	Owner	Date Killed	Rank
197⅞	24⅞	24⅜	18⅜	4⅜	4⅜	9	14	Redvers, Sask.	Eugene M. Gazda	Eugene M. Gazda	1984	471
197⅞	28⅞	26⅜	18⅞	5	5⅛	9	11	Worth Co., Mo.	Gary G. Kinder	Gary G. Kinder	1982	474
197⅞	23	22⅞	17⅞	5⅛	4⅜	10	9	Noble Co., Okla.	Kenneth R. Bright	Kenneth R. Bright	1982	474
197⅞	25⅜	25⅜	21	5⅛	5⅛	10	10	Jefferson Co., Ill.	Unknown	Jeff Sartaine	1983	474
197⅞	26⅛	26⅜	17⅜	5⅜	4⅜	8	7	Jackson Co., Mo.	Jim Martin	Jim Martin	1984	474
197	23⅜	24⅜	19⅜	5	5	11	9	Oak River, Man.	Sam Henry	J. J. Henry	1946	478
197	28⅞	26⅜	22⅜	5⅜	6	6	9	Fayette Co., Iowa	Stanley E. Harrison	Stanley E. Harrison	1973	478
197	24⅜	26⅜	25⅜	5	5⅛	8	9	Kootenai Co., Idaho	D. L. Whatcott & R. C. Carlson	D. L. Whatcott & R. C. Carlson	1980	478
197	21⅛	22⅛	15⅜	5⅜	5	11	11	Rosebud Co., Mont.	Mark D. Holmes	Mark D. Holmes	1983	478
196⅞	24⅜	24⅜	19	5	5	10	8	Edmunds Co., S.D.	Melvin Borkirchert	Melvin Borkirchert	1983	482
196⅞	22⅜	22⅜	17⅜	5	5	8	8	Vilas Co., Wisc.	Joe Wilfer	Rick Iacono	1934	483
196⅞	26⅜	25⅜	18⅜	5⅜	5⅜	9	8	Perry Co., Pa.	Kenneth Reisinger	Kenneth Reisinger	1949	483
196⅝	25	25	19⅛	4⅜	5	9	10	Unicoi Co., Tenn.	Elmer Payne	Elmer Payne	1972	483
196⅝	21⅞	20⅜	19⅜	4⅞	4⅜	10	12	Wilkinson Co., Miss.	Robert D. Sullivan	Robert D. Sullivan	1982	486
196⅝	25⅜	25⅛	20⅜	5⅜	5⅜	9	8	Van Buren Co., Iowa	Kenneth R. Barker	Kenneth R. Barker	1984	486
196⅝	26⅜	28⅜	19	5	4⅜	8	8	Desha Co., Ark.	Turner Neal	Turner Neal	1955	488
196⅝	25⅜	25⅜	17⅜	4⅜	5⅛	9	12	Charlotte Co., N.B.	Clayton Tatton	J. D. Andrews	1959	488
196⅜	25⅜	24⅜	22⅜	5	5⅜	9	9	Prairie River, Sask.	Herb Kopperud	Herb Kopperud	1959	490
196⅜	24⅜	25⅜	24	5⅜	5⅜	9	10	Clark Co., Ill.	Mary K. LeCrone	Mary K. LeCrone	1982	490
196⅜	18⅜	18⅜	27	6	6	7	14	Dorchester Co., Md.	Kevin R. Coulbourne	Kevin R. Coulbourne	1979	492
196⅛	25⅜	27	19⅜	5⅜	5⅜	8	11	Nemaha Co., Neb.	Picked Up	Gale Sup	1975	493
196	24⅜	24⅜	16⅜	5⅜	5⅜	7	12	Westmoreland Co., Pa.	Edward G. Ligus	Edward G. Ligus	1956	494
196	25⅜	25⅜	18⅜	5⅜	5	6	7	Buffalo Co., Wisc.	William A. Gatzlaff	William A. Gatzlaff	1970	494
196	26⅜	25⅜	25⅜	5	5⅜	12	10	Annapolis Valley, N.S.	David Cabral	David Cabral	1984	494
195⅞	28⅜	30⅜	25⅜	5⅜	5⅜	8	6	Webb Co., Texas	Charles J. Schelper, Sr.	Vernon L. Watson	1930	497
195⅞	24⅜	25	23⅜	3⅜	3⅜	10	7	Beltrami Co., Minn.	Ollie Jamtaas	James Gorden	1938	497
195⅞	26⅜	26⅜	19⅜	6	6	11	10	Grant Co., Wisc.	Roger Derrickson	Roger Derrickson	1973	497
195⅞	27⅛	25⅜	20⅜	5⅜	5⅜	8	8	Perry Co., Ohio	Pearl R. Wiseman	Pearl R. Wiseman	1976	497
195⅞	29⅛	21⅜	21⅜	4⅜	5	11	10	Moosomin, Sask.	Tom Ryan	Tom Ryan	1961	501
195⅝	26⅜	27⅜	19⅜	5⅜	5⅜	11	11	St. Louis Co., Minn.	Mike Desanto	Mike Desanto	1963	501
195⅝	25⅜	25	20⅜	5⅜	5⅜	10	7	Wetaskiwin, Alta.	Lewis D. Callies	Lewis D. Callies	1972	501

195⅝*	25¼	26⅝	19⅝	6⅝	7	11	12	Roseau Co., Minn.	George H. Tepley	George H. Tepley	1984	501
195⅝	25¼	25⅝	19	6	6⅛	10	10	Parkman, Sask.	H. E. Kennett	H. E. Kennett	1949	505
195⅝	25⅛	25⅝	19⅝	5	5⅝	8	8	Duffield, Alta.	Robert A. Schaefer	Robert A. Schaefer	1980	505
195⅝	23⅞	24⅛	13	5	5⅝	14	10	Adams Co., Miss.	Kathleen McGehee	Kathleen McGehee	1981	505
195⅝	26⅛	26⅛	21⅛	5⅝	5⅝	8	7	Story Co., Iowa	Jordan L. Larson	Jordan L. Larson	1983	505
195⅝	24⅛	24⅛	17⅞	4⅞	4⅞	9	9	Maverick Co., Texas	Ronald K. Hudson	Ronald K. Hudson	1971	509
195⅝	25⅛	16⅞	20⅛	6	6	7	7	Bureau Co., Ill.	Picked Up	John Cotter	1976	509
195⅜	26	25⅜	16⅞	4⅞	4⅞	10	7	Winona Co., Minn.	Patrick Bartholomew	Patrick Bartholomew	1976	509
195⅜	21⅛	22⅛	17⅞	5	5	10	8	Carlisle Co., Ky.	William H. Deane IV	William H. Deane IV	1979	509
195⅜	26⅛	26	19⅜	5⅝	5⅝	7	10	Valley City, N.D.	William F. Cruff	William F. Cruff	1955	513
195⅜	27⅛	29⅞	20⅛	6	5⅝	6	7	Colquitt Co., Ga.	Olen P. Ross	Olen P. Ross	1976	513
195⅜	20⅛	22⅛	16⅞	7⅜	7⅞	10	12	Beltrami Co., Minn.	John G. Binsfeld	John G. Binsfeld	1980	513
195⅜	25⅛	26⅜	20⅛	5⅜	5⅝	11	8	Grassland, Alta.	Frederick Neuhmann	Frederick Neuhmann	1980	513
195⅜	25⅛	25⅜	22⅛	5	4⅞	9	12	Webb Co., Texas	Sidney A. Lindsay, Jr.	Sidney A. Lindsay, Jr.	1983	518
195⅜	26	24⅛	19½	6⅞	6⅜	9	9	Rusk Co., Wisc.	Alexander King	Roger King	1890	518
195⅜	28⅛	27⅞	20⅜	4⅞	4⅞	11	8	Du Charme Coulee, Wisc.	Eugene E. Morovitz	Eugene E. Morovitz	1959	518
195⅜	25	23⅞	18⅜	5⅝	5⅜	11	11	Pottawattmie Co., Iowa	Ted Houser	Ted Houser	1968	518
195⅜	24⅛	22	17⅞	4⅜	4⅝	12	10	Kenedy Co., Texas	Don E. Harrison	Don E. Harrison	1975	518
195⅜	25⅜	25⅛	22⅜	5⅝	5⅝	12	13	Stevens Co., Wash.	Floyd E. Newell	Floyd E. Newell	1981	518
195⅜	23⅝	28⅞	15	5	5⅛	15	14	Washington Co., Maine	M. Chandler Stith	M. Chandler Stith	1963	523
195⅝	26	25⅞	21	4⅞	4⅞	9	9	Zapata Co., Texas	Corando Mirelez	Corando Mirelez	1966	523
195⅝	24⅜	23	23⅜	5⅝	5⅝	10	9	Whitman Co., Wash.	Robert & Rodney Boyer	Robert & Rodney Boyer	1975	523
195	22⅜	23	20⅜	5⅝	5⅝	8	9	Calhoun Co., Ill.	Roger F. Becker	Roger F. Becker	1983	526
261⅛*	25	25⅜	25⅜	6	6	12	14	Pike Co., Ohio	Chester T. Veach	Chester T. Veach	1971	
259*	25⅛	26⅜	19⅜	6⅛	5⅞	15	16	Washington Co., Maine	Hill Gould	Charles T. Arnold	1910	
242⅜*	27⅛	30⅞	18⅛	5⅛	5	12	9	Mahoning Co., Ohio	David L. Klemm	Dick Idol	1980	
237⅞*	25⅛	25⅛	18⅜	5⅛	5	15	12	Sawyer Co., Wisc.	David D. Sprangers	David D. Sprangers	1980	

*Final Score subject to revision by additional verifying measurements

WORLD'S RECORD COUES' WHITETAIL DEER (TYPICAL ANTLERS)
SCORE: 143

Locality: Pima County, Arizona Date: 1953
Hunter and owner: Ed Stockwell

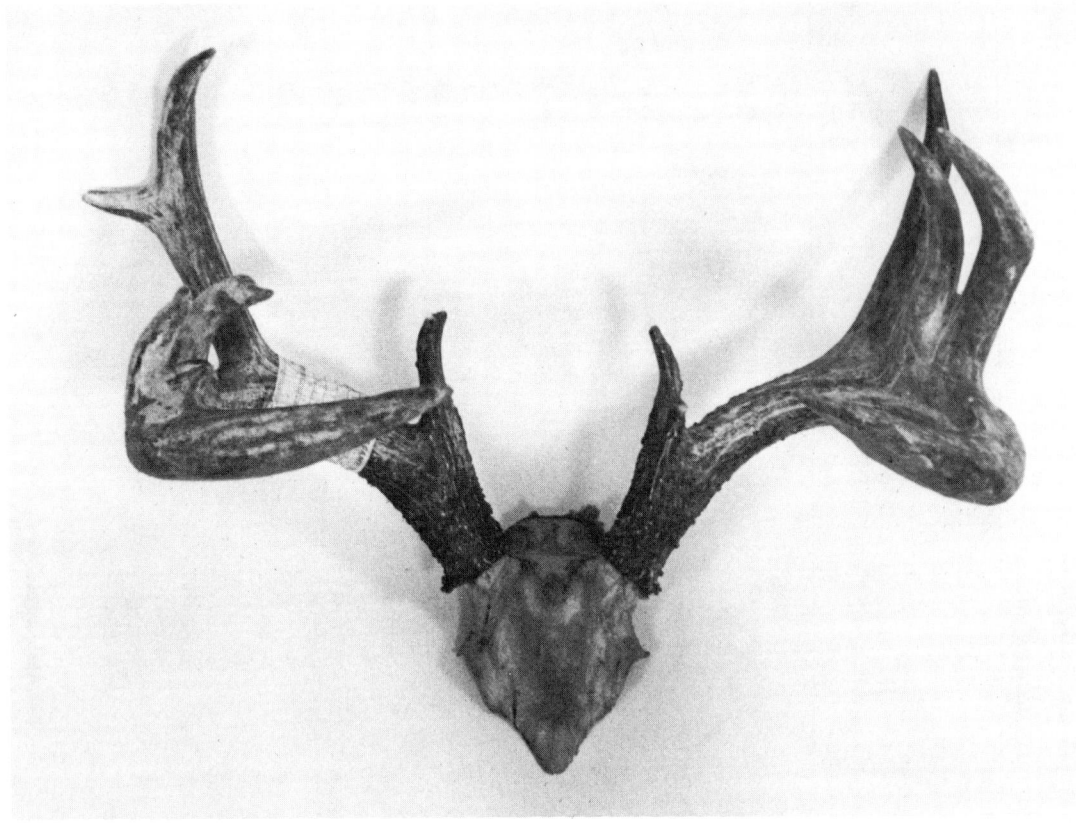

NUMBER FOUR COUES' WHITETAIL DEER (TYPICAL ANTLERS)
SCORE: 130 4/8

Locality: Pima County, Arizona Date: 1981
Hunter and owner: Kim J. Poulin

Coues' Whitetail Deer (Typical Antlers)

Odocoileus virginianus couesi

Minimum Score 110

Score	Length of Main Beam R.	L.	Inside Spread	Circumference at Smallest Place Between Burr and First Point R.	L.	Number of Points R.	L.	Locality Killed	By Whom Killed	Owner	Date Killed	Rank
143	20⅞	20⅜	15⅜	5⅞	5⅞	5	6	Pima Co., Ariz.	Ed Stockwell	Ed Stockwell	1953	1
131⅞	19⅜	19⅜	16⅛	4⅞	4⅞	5	5	Cochise Co., Ariz.	George W. Kouts	George W. Kouts	1935	2
130⅞	20⅜	19⅜	14⅝	3⅞	3⅜	5	5	Chihuahua, Mexico	Wayne Kleinman	Wayne Kleinman	1958	3
130⅜	20⅜	20⅜	15⅝	4⅞	4⅝	8	6	Pima Co., Ariz.	Kim J. Poulin	Kim J. Poulin	1981	4
126⅝	19⅜	18⅜	11⅛	4⅜	4⅜	5	5	Pima Co., Ariz.	DeWayne M. Hanna	DeWayne M. Hanna	1977	5
125⅜	18⅜	19	16⅞	3⅞	3⅞	6	5	Arivaca, Ariz.	Gerald Harris	Gerald Harris	1953	6
125	19⅜	19⅞	15⅜	4⅛	4⅛	5	5	Ft. Apache Res., Ariz.	Picked Up	Jerry S. Pippen	PR1969	7
124⅜	19⅜	19	14⅜	4	4⅛	6	6	Rincon Mts., Ariz.	James Pfersdorf	Mrs. J. E. Pfersdorf, Sr.	1936	8
124⅜	18⅜	18⅜	13⅜	3⅜	3⅜	5	5	Sonora, Mexico	Enrique Lares	Enrique Lares	1959	8
123⅞	17⅜	17⅜	13⅞	4⅜	4⅜	6	6	Gila Co., Ariz.	Stephen P. Hayes	Stephen P. Hayes	1965	10
122⅞	18⅞	18⅜	14⅜	4⅛	4	5	6	Chiracahua Mts., Ariz.	Roger Becksted	Roger Becksted	1960	11
122⅜	22	20⅜	15⅜	3⅛	3⅜	5	5	Sonora, Mexico	Lloyd L. Ward, Jr.	Lloyd L. Ward, Jr.	1945	12
121⅞	20⅜	19⅜	15⅜	4⅜	4	4	4	Pima Co., Ariz.	Joe Fanning	Joe Fanning	1964	13
121⅛	19	17⅞	14⅜	4	3⅞	6	6	Santa Rita Mts., Ariz.	Max E. Wilson	Max E. Wilson	1965	14
121⅜	16⅜	17	10⅞	3⅜	3⅜	6	6	Santa Rita Mts., Ariz.	George Shaar	George Shaar	1964	15
121⅛	19⅜	19⅜	15⅜	3⅜	3⅜	5	5	Pima Co., Ariz.	T. Reed Scott	T. Reed Scott	1975	16
121	20⅜	19⅜	13	3⅜	3⅜	5	5	Sierra Madre Mts., Mexico	Herb Klein	Herb Klein	1965	17
120⅞	20⅞	19⅜	16⅜	4⅜	4⅛	5	6	Santa Rita Mts., Ariz.	Harold Lyons	Harold Lyons	1956	18
120⅝	19⅜	18⅜	14⅜	4	4	5	5	Sonora, Mexico	Manuel A. Caravantez	Manuel A. Caravantez	1960	19
120⅝	19	19⅜	12⅜	4⅜	4⅜	5	5	Sonora, Mexico	George W. Parker	George W. Parker	1969	20
120⅝	20⅝	19⅜	16⅜	3⅝	3⅞	4	4	Cochise Co., Ariz.	Becki D. Goffrier	Becki D. Goffrier	1984	20
120⅜	17⅞	18⅜	13	4⅜	4	4	4	Sonora, Mexico	Diego G. Sada	Diego G. Sada	1969	22
120⅛	18	18⅜	13⅜	4	4	5	6	Baboquivari Mts., Ariz.	Homer R. Edds	Homer R. Edds	1961	23
119⅞	20⅜	21⅜	17⅜	4⅛	3⅞	4	4	Gila Co., Ariz.	Tom Connolly	Tom Connolly	1960	24
119⅜	20⅜	20⅜	15⅜	4⅜	4⅜	4	5	Sonora, Mexico	Picked Up	George W. Parker	1960	24
119⅝	20⅜	19	12⅜	4	4⅛	5	4	Canelo Hills, Ariz.	George W. Parker	George W. Parker	1960	26
119⅜	19⅜	20⅜	12	3⅞	3⅜	6	6	Canelo Hills, Ariz.	A. R. Anglen	A. R. Anglen	1967	27
119⅞	16⅜	18⅜	15	4	3⅞	7	6	Gila Co., Ariz.	Bert M. Pringle	Mrs. Bert M. Pringle	1952	28
119⅛	18	19⅜	10⅜	5	5⅜	6	4	Santa Rita Mts., Ariz.	Monte L. Colvin	Monte L. Colvin	1965	29
119	17⅞	17⅜	13⅜	3⅜	3⅜	7	6	Hidalgo Co., N.M.	Jesse Williams	Jesse Williams	1971	30

Score								Locality	By Whom Killed	Owner	Date	Rank
118⅝	19⅝	19⅛	14⅞	4⅞	4⅜	4	4	Chiricahua Mts., Ariz.	Ward Becksted	Ward Becksted	1958	31
118⅛	17⅞	17⅜	15⅜	3⅞	3⅞	5	5	Santa Cruz Co., Ariz.	David W. Ahnell	David W. Ahnell	1977	32
118	16⅞	16⅛	14⅛	4⅛	4⅜	8	7	Washington Mts., Ariz.	Ralph Vaga	Ralph Vaga	1962	33
118	18⅞	19⅝	12⅝	3⅝	3⅞	4	4	Santa Cruz Co., Ariz.	Michael L. Valenzuela	Michael L. Valenzuela	1982	33
117⅞	19	18⅛	16⅛	4	4	4	4	Rincon Mts., Ariz.	Picked Up	H. L. Russell	1963	35
117⅞	19⅝	19⅛	12⅝	4⅛	3⅞	6	5	Santa Rita Mts., Ariz.	George Shaar	George Shaar	1965	35
117⅞	18⅞	17⅞	14	3⅞	3⅝	4	5	Canelo Hills, Ariz.	Raymond J. Kassler	Raymond J. Kassler	1958	37
117⅞	20⅜	20	18⅛	4⅜	4	4	4	Libertad, Mexico	Abe R. Hughes	Abe R. Hughes	1967	38
117⅞	17⅞	17⅛	14⅜	4⅜	4⅜	4	4	Atasco Mts., Ariz.	F. O. Haskell	F. O. Haskell	1939	39
117⅞	17⅜	17⅜	12⅝	3⅝	3⅝	5	6	Sicritta Mts., Ariz.	George S. Tsaguris	George S. Tsaguris	1958	39
117⅜	19⅞	19⅜	16⅜	3⅞	3⅝	4	4	Sonora, Mexico	Charles B. Leonard	Charles B. Leonard	1974	39
117⅜	19	19⅛	11⅝	4⅞	4⅞	8	6	Santa Rita Mts., Ariz.	George L. Garlits	George L. Garlits	1957	42
117⅜	17⅝	18⅜	17⅝	4⅜	4⅜	4	5	Chiricahua Mts., Ariz.	Picked Up	Warren A. Cartier	1963	42
117⅞	18	18	12	3⅜	3⅜	5	5	Tumacacori Mts., Ariz.	Charles H. Pennington	Charles H. Pennington	1968	42
117	18⅜	18⅜	14⅜	4⅛	4	4	5	Cochise Co., Ariz.	W. R. Tanner	Fred Tanner	1941	45
117	18⅛	19⅛	16	3⅞	4	7	6	Pima Co., Ariz.	Arthur L. Butler	Arthur L. Butler	1974	45
116⅞	17⅜	17⅜	13⅞	3⅝	3⅞	5	5	Santa Cruz Co., Ariz.	Seymour H. Levy	Seymour H. Levy	1967	47
116⅞	19⅝	19	16⅝	4⅛	4⅞	5	5	Pima Co., Ariz.	Arcenio G. Valdez	Arcenio G. Valdez	1971	47
116⅝	17⅜	16⅜	14⅜	4⅜	4⅜	5	4	Santa Rita Mts., Ariz.	Mike Holloran	Mike Holloran	1962	49
116⅝	19⅜	17⅜	14⅛	3⅞	4⅜	4	6	Gila Co., Ariz.	Richard A. Thom	Richard A. Thom	1978	49
116⅝	19⅞	19⅞	14⅜	4⅛	4⅝	5	5	Gila Co., Ariz.	Nathan Ellison	Nathan Ellison	1950	51
116⅝	15⅝	16⅝	14⅝	4⅛	4⅜	6	6	Blue River, Ariz.	Earl H. Harris	Earl H. Harris	1965	52
116	17⅞	17⅝	13⅜	4⅜	4⅝	6	6	Chiricahua Mts., Ariz.	Freeman Neal	R. M. Woods	1947	53
115⅞	18⅝	16⅞	13⅞	4⅝	4⅜	4	4	Santa Cruz Co., Ariz.	Ben Richardson	Ben Richardson	1978	54
115⅞	18⅜	18⅝	14⅞	4⅞	4⅜	5	7	Sonora, Mexico	Berry B. Brooks	Berry B. Brooks	1954	55
115⅝	15⅝	18⅜	14⅜	3⅝	3⅞	4	5	Breadpan Mt., Ariz.	Mitchell R. Holder	Mitchell R. Holder	1966	56
115⅝	17⅞	16⅝	13	4	4⅝	5	5	Santa Rita Mts., Ariz.	Picked Up	James Bramhall	PR1963	57
115⅝	18	17	13⅜	5	4⅞	5	4	Santa Rita Mts., Ariz.	Denis Wolstenholme	Denis Wolstenholme	1958	58
115⅝	20⅛	19⅝	15	4	4	4	5	Cerro Colo. Mts., Ariz.	Manuel V. Guillen	Manuel V. Guillen	1962	58
115⅝	20⅜	20⅛	12⅝	4⅜	4⅜	5	5	Santa Rita Mts., Ariz.	Bill J. Ford	Bill J. Ford	1965	58
115	19⅞	19	16⅝	4⅝	4⅜	5	5	Catalina Mts., Ariz.	Jim Stough	Jim Stough	1972	58
115	19⅞	19⅜	17⅝	4⅜	4⅜	4	5	Baboquivari Mts., Ariz.	Karl G. Ronstadt	Karl G. Ronstadt	1967	62
115	20⅛	19⅜	18⅛	4⅛	4⅛	4	4	Coconino Co., Ariz.	Picked Up	Jerry C. Walters	PR1970	62
115	18⅛	18⅛	16⅝	4⅞	4	5	5	Pima Co., Ariz.	Glen Alan Elmer	Glen Alan Elmer	1980	62
114⅞	18	18	12⅝	3⅞	4	4	4	Ruby, Ariz.	Richard McDaniel	Richard McDaniel	1963	65
114⅞	20	19⅝	16⅛	4⅛	4⅞	5	5	Santa Rita Mts., Ariz.	John H. Lake	John H. Lake	1965	65
114⅝	16⅞	16⅝	13⅛	4⅛	3⅞	5	5	Chihuahua, Mexico	Tom Jones	George B. Johnson	1932	67
114⅝	19⅜	19⅝	14⅛	4⅜	4⅛	6	8	Chiricahua Mts., Ariz.	John Miller	John Miller	1949	67
114⅝	16	16	15⅝	4⅝	4⅝	4	5	Santa Rita Mts., Ariz.	Art Pollard	Art Pollard	1951	67
114⅝	18	15⅝	15⅛	4	4⅜	6	5	Canelo Hills, Ariz.	Guy Perry	Guy Perry	1960	67
114⅝	16⅝	16⅝	11	4⅜	4⅜	5	7	Santa Rita Mts., Ariz.	John Bessett	John Bessett	1965	67
114⅝	17⅝	17⅛	14⅞	4⅛	4⅛	5	5	Nogales, Ariz.	Arthur N. Lindsey	Arthur N. Lindsey	1967	67
114⅜	19⅜	20⅛	15	4⅜	4⅜	4	4	Graham Mts., Ariz.	Robert Stonoff	Robert Stonoff	1962	73

Coues' Whitetail Deer (Typical Antlers)—Continued

Odocoileus virginianus couesi

Score	Length of Main Beam R.	L.	Inside Spread	Circumference at Smallest Place Between Burr and First Point R.	L.	Number of Points R.	L.	Locality Killed	By Whom Killed	Owner	Date Killed	Rank
114⁴⁄₈	15⅞	16⅞	12⅝	3⅞	4⅛	6	4	Patagonia Mts., Ariz.	Verna Conlisk	Verna Conlisk	1964	73
114⁴⁄₈	15⅞	15⅞	14⅛	3⅝	3⅝	5	5	Chiricahua Mts., Mexico	Elgin T. Gates	Elgin T. Gates	1968	73
114⁴⁄₈	17⅝	17⅞	13⅞	3⅝	3⅝	6	5	Cherry Creek, Ariz.	Alan G. Adams	Alan G. Adams	1968	73
114³⁄₈	18	18⅞	12⅝	4	3⅞	4	5	Atasco Mts., Ariz.	Antonio Lopez	Antonio Lopez	1961	77
114²⁄₈	18⅛	15⅞	15⅞	4⅛	4⅛	5	6	Catalina Mts., Ariz.	Wayne L. Heckler	Wayne L. Heckler	1958	78
114²⁄₈	16⅝	17⅛	11⅝	4	4⅛	5	6	Canelo, Ariz.	Earl Stillson	Earl Stillson	1967	78
114²⁄₈	18⅞	16⅞	14⅛	4⅛	4⅛	4	4	Sonora, Mexico	Unknown	Bill Quimby	PR1965	80
114¹⁄₈	17⅞	17⅞	16⅞	3⅞	3⅞	5	5	Yavapai Co., Ariz.	Jim D. Snodgrass	Jim D. Snodgrass	1983	80
114¹⁄₈	17⅞	17⅞	10⅞	3⅝	3⅞	4	4	Animas Mts., N.M.	F. C. Hibben	F. C. Hibben	1955	82
114	18⅛	17⅞	14⅛	3⅝	3⅝	4	5	Galiuro Mts., Ariz.	Clifford Kouts	Clifford Kouts	1964	83
113⁷⁄₈	20⅛	19	12	4⅝	4½	5	5	Santa Rita Mts., Ariz.	Joe Moore	Joe Moore	1968	83
113⁷⁄₈	18⅜	16	13⅛	3⅞	3⅞	8	8	Chihuahua, Mexico	Herb Klein	Herb Klein	1957	85
113⁶⁄₈	15⅝	16	13⅛	4	4	5	5	Mt. Graham, Ariz.	Bill Sizer	Bill Sizer	1963	85
113⁶⁄₈	16	17	13⅛	4⅜	4⅝	7	6	Galiuro Mts., Ariz.	Doran V. Porter	Doran V. Porter	1966	85
113⁶⁄₈	17⅜	17⅞	16⅛	4⅛	4	4	5	Graham Mts., Ariz.	J. H. Hunt	J. H. Hunt	1962	88
113⁵⁄₈	19⅞	19	15	3⅞	3⅞	4	4	Sonora, Mexico	George W. Parker	George W. Parker	1947	89
113⁴⁄₈	19⅞	19	14⅛	4⅜	4½	4	6	Santa Rita Mts., Ariz.	George W. Parker	George W. Parker	1962	89
113⁴⁄₈	16⅞	16⅜	12⅝	3⅞	3⅞	6	6	Santa Rita Mts., Ariz.	Jack Englet	Jack Englet	1962	89
113⁴⁄₈	16⅜	16⅞	13⅜	4⅝	4½	6	5	Santa Teresa Mts., Ariz.	D. B. Sanford	D. B. Sanford	1950	92
113³⁄₈	16	17	14⅛	4	4⅜	5	4	Tumacacori Mts., Ariz.	Tom W. Caid	Tom W. Caid	1958	92
113³⁄₈	18	16⅝	17	4	4	4	4	Four Peaks Mt., Ariz.	Carl J. Slagel	Carl J. Slagel	1963	92
113³⁄₈	16⅝	17	12⅝	4⅜	4⅛	4	4	Pima Co., Ariz.	Sam E. Harrison, Jr.	Sam E. Harrison, Jr.	1969	92
113³⁄₈	16⅞	18	15⅝	3⅝	3⅝	5	6	Santa Rita Mts., Ariz.	Donna Greene	Donna Greene	1958	96
113³⁄₈	18⅛	19	14⅛	4	4	5	5	Tumacacori Mts., Ariz.	Carlos G. Touche	Carlos G. Touche	1961	96
113³⁄₈	19⅜	19⅞	16	4⅜	4⅛	5	5	Gila Co., Ariz.	David W. Miller, Jr.	David W. Miller, Jr.	1984	96
113³⁄₈	20⅞	18	19	4	4⅛	4	4	Chiricahua Mts., Ariz.	Ralph Hopkins	Fred Tanner	1928	99
113	18⅛	18⅞	15⅝	4⅜	4⅜	4	4	Canelo Hills, Ariz.	Carlos Ochoa	Carlos Ochoa	1955	100
113	19	18⅛	12⅞	3⅞	3⅞	4	5	Tumacacori Mts., Ariz.	Basil C. Bradbury	Basil C. Bradbury	1968	100
112⁷⁄₈	17	17⅝	14⅝	4⅜	4⅜	4	4	Ruby, Ariz.	Roger Scott	Roger Scott	1962	102
112⁶⁄₈	17⅝	18	14⅛	5⅛	4⅝	5	6	Baboquivari Mts., Ariz.	Charles R. Whitfield	Charles R. Whitfield	1969	103
112⁶⁄₈	17⅞	18⅝	15⅞	4⅞	4⅝	6	6	Cochise Co., Ariz.	Mike York	Mike York	1973	103

Score	L	R	Spread	C1	C2	P1	P2	Locality	Taken By	Owner	Year	Rank
112 5/8	18 1/8	17 1/8	14 1/8	4	3 7/8	4	4	Sonora, Mexico	Henry Lares	Henry Lares	1959	105
112 5/8	18	19 7/8	13 1/8	3 7/8	3 5/8	5	5	Sonora, Mexico	William W. Sharp	William W. Sharp	1968	105
112 4/8	17 3/8	17 3/8	15	4 7/8	4 3/8	5	4	Gila Co., Ariz.	R. T. Beach & L. A. Mossinger	Ronald T. Beach	1974	107
112 3/8	17 3/8	17	15 5/8	4 1/8	4 2/8	4	5	White Mts., Ariz.	Dennis E. Nolen	Dennis E. Nolen	1961	108
112 3/8	19	19 5/8	13 5/8	4 2/8	4 4/8	5	4	Santa Cruz Co., Ariz.	W. C. Grant	W. C. Grant	1973	108
112 2/8	19 5/8	19 1/8	11 5/8	3 3/8	3 5/8	5	4	Sonora, Mexico	George W. Parker	George W. Parker	1960	110
112 2/8	18	17 5/8	17	4	3 7/8	5	5	Maricopa Co., Ariz.	Gary D. Nichols	Gary D. Nichols	1980	110
112 2/8	16 5/8	16	13 3/8	4 4/8	4 6/8	4	4	Pima Co., Ariz.	William W. Sharp	William W. Sharp	1981	110
112	18 3/8	18 7/8	14 7/8	3 6/8	3 6/8	5	5	Bartlett Mts., Ariz.	Keith Robbins	Keith Robbins	1957	113
112	17 5/8	18	13 5/8	4	4	5	5	Baboquivari Mts., Ariz.	Jesse Genin	Jesse Genin	1961	113
112	15	15 5/8	12 7/8	3 6/8	3 7/8	5	5	Greenlee Co., Ariz.	Jerald S. Wager	Jerald S. Wager	1982	113
111 7/8	18 5/8	17 5/8	12 5/8	4 1/8	4	5	5	Canelo Hills, Ariz.	Walter G. Sheets	Walter G. Sheets	1959	116
111 5/8	17 5/8	16 4/8	13 5/8	4	3 7/8	4	4	Gila Co., Ariz.	Karl J. Payne	Karl J. Payne	1955	117
111 5/8	17	17 1/8	11 5/8	3 4/8	3 2/8	5	5	Catron Co., N.M.	Charles Tapia	Charles Tapia	1959	117
111 5/8	18	18 5/8	14 1/8	4 5/8	3 5/8	5	5	Patagonia Mts., Ariz.	Norval L. Wesson	Norval L. Wesson	1967	117
111 5/8	18 2/8	18 5/8	14 2/8	3 5/8	3 4/8	4	4	Baboquivari Mts., Ariz.	Stanley W. Gaines	Stanley W. Gaines	1971	117
111 4/8	17 1/8	16 6/8	14	3 7/8	3 7/8	5	5	Pima Co., Ariz.	George V. Borquez	George V. Borquez	1979	117
111 4/8	18 7/8	19	14 3/8	4 3/8	4 5/8	6	6	Santa Rita Mts., Ariz.	Rick Detwiler	Rick Detwiler	1968	122
111 3/8	20 1/8	19 5/8	14 2/8	4	3 7/8	5	5	Sonora, Mexico	George W. Parker	George W. Parker	1926	123
111 3/8	17 4/8	18	15	3 5/8	4	4	4	Santa Rita Mts., Ariz.	Tom L. Swanson	Tom L. Swanson	1965	123
111 3/8	20 5/8	21 3/8	12 5/8	3 5/8	3 4/8	4	4	Sierra Madre Mts., Mexico	Herb Klein	Herb Klein	1965	125
111 3/8	17 5/8	18 5/8	16 5/8	4 1/8	3 4/8	4	4	Santa Cruz Co., Ariz.	Frank Yubeta III	Frank Yubeta III	1983	125
111 2/8	17	17	15 5/8	4	4	4	4	Graham Co., Ariz.	C. R. Hale	C. R. Hale	1958	127
111 2/8	18 5/8	19 5/8	11 5/8	3 5/8	3 5/8	4	5	Sonora, Mexico	George W. Parker	George W. Parker	1960	127
111 1/8	19 5/8	19 4/8	16 4/8	4	4	5	6	Graham Mts., Ariz.	Bill Barney	Bill Barney	1962	127
111 1/8	19 1/8	19	15 5/8	4 2/8	4 3/8	4	4	Atascosa Mt., Ariz.	Henry B. Carrillo	Henry B. Carrillo	1964	127
111 1/8	17 5/8	17 5/8	11 5/8	4	3 6/8	6	6	Santa Rita Mts., Ariz.	Lon E. Bothwell	Lon E. Bothwell	1969	127
111 1/8	16 4/8	16 5/8	15 5/8	3 4/8	3 5/8	5	5	Santa Cruz Co., Ariz.	Robert L. Rabb	Robert L. Rabb	1977	127
110 7/8	17 5/8	17 7/8	16	4	4	5	6	Sonora, Mexico	Joe Daneker, Jr.	Joe Daneker, Jr.	1973	133
110 7/8	19 5/8	19 5/8	13 5/8	3 6/8	3 6/8	4	4	Chiricahua Mts., Ariz.	Wayne A. Dirst	Wayne A. Dirst	1954	134
110 7/8	17 2/8	18 5/8	11 2/8	4 1/8	4 1/8	5	5	Canelo Hills, Ariz.	Bill Fidelo	Bill Fidelo	1958	134
110 6/8	19	19	15 7/8	3 5/8	3 5/8	5	5	Rincon Mts., Ariz.	Ollie O. Barney, Jr.	Ollie O. Barney, Jr.	1961	134
110 6/8	16	16 5/8	13 5/8	3	3	6	6	Pima Co., Ariz.	William W. Sharp	William W. Sharp	1974	134
110 6/8	18 5/8	18 2/8	13 5/8	3 6/8	3 7/8	4	4	Catalina Mts., Ariz.	H. C. Ruff	H. C. Ruff	1959	138
110 4/8	18 2/8	18 2/8	15 5/8	4	4	5	5	Santa Rita Mts., Ariz.	John S. McFarling	John S. McFarling	1965	138
110 4/8	16 7/8	17 5/8	14 5/8	4 4/8	4 4/8	4	4	Canelo Mts., Ariz.	Otto L. Fritz	Otto L. Fritz	1947	140
110 4/8	16 5/8	16 5/8	14 2/8	4 1/8	4 1/8	5	5	Tumacacoci Mts., Ariz.	John Doyle	John Doyle	1966	140
110 3/8	17 7/8	17 7/8	13 7/8	4	4	4	4	Santa Rita Mts., Ariz.	Edward L. Blixt	Edward L. Blixt	1946	142
110 3/8	18 5/8	18 4/8	12 7/8	3 4/8	3 4/8	4	4	Santa Rita Mts., Ariz.	Lyle K. Sowls	Lyle K. Sowls	1956	142
110 3/8	17 7/8	18 5/8	15 7/8	3 5/8	3 5/8	4	4	Hidalgo Co., N.M.	Ronald M. Gerdes	Ronald M. Gerdes	1979	142
110 2/8	17	16 5/8	14	4 5/8	4 5/8	5	5	Gila Co., Ariz.	William P. Hampton, Jr.	William P. Hampton, Jr.	1976	145
110 2/8	16	15 5/8	15 5/8	3 6/8	4	5	4	Hidalgo Co., N.M.	Jay M. Gates III	Jay M. Gates III	1981	145

COUES' WHITETAIL DEER (Typical Antlers)—Continued
Odocoileus virginianus couesi

Score	Length of Main Beam		Inside Spread	Circumference at Smallest Place Between Burr and First Point		Number of Points		Locality Killed	By Whom Killed	Owner	Date Killed	Rank
	R.	L.		R.	L.	R.	L.					
110⅞	18⅞	18	16	4⅛	4	4	5	Pima Co., Ariz.	David G. Mattausch	David G. Mattausch	1984	145
110⅛	16⅞	16⅜	15⅞	4⅛	4⅜	4	4	Payson, Ariz.	Picked Up	Richard Noonan	PR1963	148
110⅛	16⅜	17	12⅜	4⅞	4⅜	4	4	Pima Co., Ariz.	Andy C. Strebe	Andy C. Strebe	1981	148
110	19⅜	18⅜	14⅞	4⅜	4⅜	5	5	Sonora, Mexico	Enrique C. Cicero	Enrique C. Cicero	1966	150
115⅝*	18⅞	18⅞	15	4	4	5	5	Cochise Co., Ariz.	Bill Byrd	Bill Byrd	1983	
113⅝*	18	17⅞	14⅞	4	4	4	4	Pima Co., Ariz.	Richard N. Huber	Richard N. Huber	1979	
113⅜*	18⅜	18	13⅜	3⅞	4	5	5	Pima Co., Ariz.	Andy A. Ramirez	Andy A. Ramirez	1979	

*Final Score subject to revision by additional verifying measurements

Photograph by Leo T. Sarnaki

WORLD'S RECORD COUES' WHITETAIL DEER (NON-TYPICAL ANTLERS)
SCORE: 151 4/8

Locality: Cochise County, Arizona Date: 1929
Hunter: Charles C. Mabry Owner: Tom Mabry

289

Photograph by Wm. H. Nesbitt

NUMBER FOUR COUES' WHITETAIL DEER (NON-TYPICAL ANTLERS)
SCORE: 143 6/8
Locality: Pima County, Arizona Date: 1983
Hunter and owner: Oscar C. Truex

Coues' Whitetail Deer (Non-Typical Antlers)

Odocoileus virginianus couesi

Minimum Score 120

Score	Length of Main Beam R.	L.	Inside Spread	Circ. at Smallest Place Between Burr and First Point R.	L.	Number of Points R.	L.	Locality Killed	By Whom Killed	Owner	Date Killed	Rank
151⅛	18¾	18⅜	15⅝	5⅝	5⅝	9	8	Cochise Co., Ariz.	Charles C. Mabry	Tom Mabry	1929	1
150⅝	18⅜	19	12⅝	4⅜	4⅜	8	8	Sasabe, Ariz.	Robert Rabb	Robert Rabb	1954	2
149⅞	17⅝	18⅜	13⅜	4⅜	4⅝	10	8	Chiricahua Range, Ariz.	Marvin R. Hardin	Marvin R. Hardin	1950	3
143⅞	17⅜	16⅝	14⅜	5	5	6	9	Pima Co., Ariz.	Oscar C. Truex	Oscar C. Truex	1983	4
142⅞	20⅛	18⅞	13⅜	4⅜	4⅜	9	7	Apache Indian Res., Ariz.	Indian	Arizona Game & Fish Dept.	1950	5
12⅞	17⅝	17¼	14⅞	4⅜	4⅝	8	8	Pinal Mts., Ariz.	Phil Rothengatter	Phil Rothengatter	1967	6
139⅞	18⅜	18⅜	15	4⅞	4⅞	8	6	Patagonia Mts., Ariz.	Howard W. Drake	Howard W. Drake	1968	7
137⅞	19⅜	19⅞	14⅜	4⅜	4⅜	6	7	Patagonia Mts., Ariz.	Ivan J. Buttram	Ivan J. Buttram	1969	8
130⅜	17⅜	17⅝	13⅞	4⅛	4¼	7	9	Santa Cruz Co., Ariz.	Jack Everhart	Fred Baker	1946	9
130⅜	14⅜	15⅞	10⅛	5	3⅞	10	8	Rincon Mts., Ariz.	Velton Clark	Velton Clark	1962	10
130	17⅜	16⅝	13⅞	4⅜	5⅜	6	11	Whetstone Range, Ariz.	Unknown	Roger Clyne	PR1967	11
128	18⅜	19⅛	16⅝	5⅜	4⅜	5	8	Santa Cruz Co., Ariz.	Carlos G. Touche	Carlos G. Touche	1968	12
125⅞	16⅝	16⅝	13⅜	4⅜	4¼	6	8	Pima Co., Ariz.	Fred W. Havens	Fred W. Havens	1966	13
125⅜	15⅝	16⅝	13⅜	4¼	4⅜	9	6	Sonora, Mexico	Enrique C. Cicero	Enrique C. Cicero	1967	14
124⅞	15⅜	17⅛	11⅜	4⅜	4⅞	8	5	Las Guijas Mts., Ariz.	Aubrey F. Powell	Aubrey F. Powell	1966	15
124⅜	20	18⅜	17⅜	4	3⅞	6	6	Pinal Co., Ariz.	C. J. Adair	C. J. Adair	1966	16
124⅛	17⅜	19	15	4⅜	4⅜	6	6	Yavapai Co., Ariz.	James W. P. Roe	James W. P. Roe	1971	17
122⅝	16⅜	16⅝	12⅜	4¼	4¼	6	6	Hidalgo Co., N.M.	Jack Samson	Jack Samson	1984	18
121	16⅝	16⅝	14	3⅜	3⅜	8	6	Gila Co., Ariz.	James E. Stinson	James E. Stinson	1983	19
120⅞	16⅝	17	13⅜	4⅜	4⅜	6	6	Pima Co., Ariz.	Carl E. Fasel	Carl E. Fasel	1981	20
120⅞	17⅜	17⅞	15⅝	5⅝	4⅜	6	6	Gila Co., Ariz.	David M. Conrad	David M. Conrad	1982	20
120⅜	20⅛	20	13⅜	3⅞	4	6	4	Santa Cruz Co., Ariz.	Jerry M. Myers	Jerry M. Myers	1970	22
144⅜*	14⅜	17⅜	11⅜	4⅜	4⅜	8	8	Pima Co., Ariz.	Unknown	Mike Yeager	PR1966	23
135⅛*	20⅜	21	16	5⅝	5⅜	7	5	Sonora, Mexico	Arturo Rodriguez Campoy	Rebeca Rodriguez	1979	
127⅞*	18⅜	18⅜	14⅜	4⅜	4⅜	7	7	Cochise Co., Ariz.	Todd A. Doser	Todd A. Doser	1979	
126⅛*	17⅜	17⅜	13⅜	4⅛	4⅜	6	6	Hidalgo Co., N.M.	Michael C. Finley	Michael C. Finley	1983	
120⅛*	14⅜	15⅝	11⅝	4⅜	4⅜	8	6	Pima Co., Ariz.	William F. Crull	William F. Crull	1979	
120⅛*	18⅜	19	13⅝	4	4	8	6	Santa Cruz Co., Ariz.	Gerald M. Kluzik	Gerald M. Kluzik	1981	

*Final Score subject to revision by additional verifying measurements

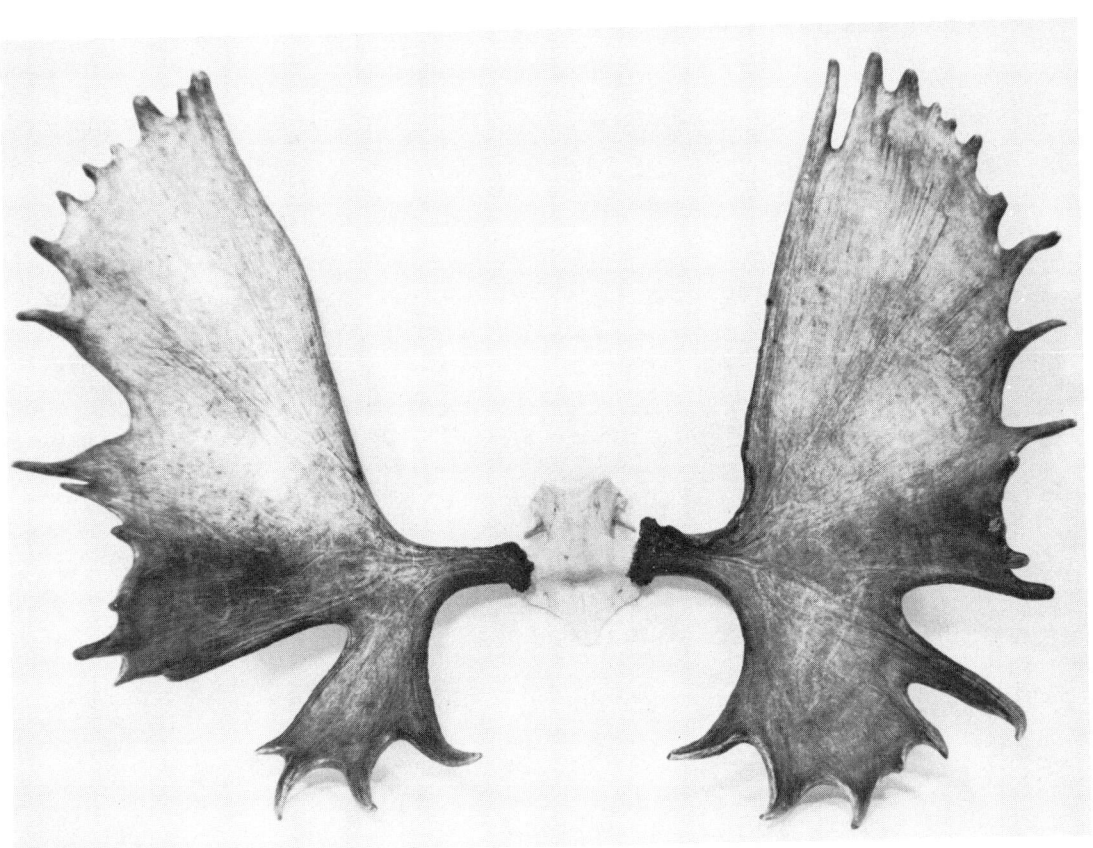

NEW WORLD'S RECORD CANADA MOOSE
SCORE: 242
Locality: Grayling River, British Columbia Date: 1980
Hunter and owner: Michael E. Laub

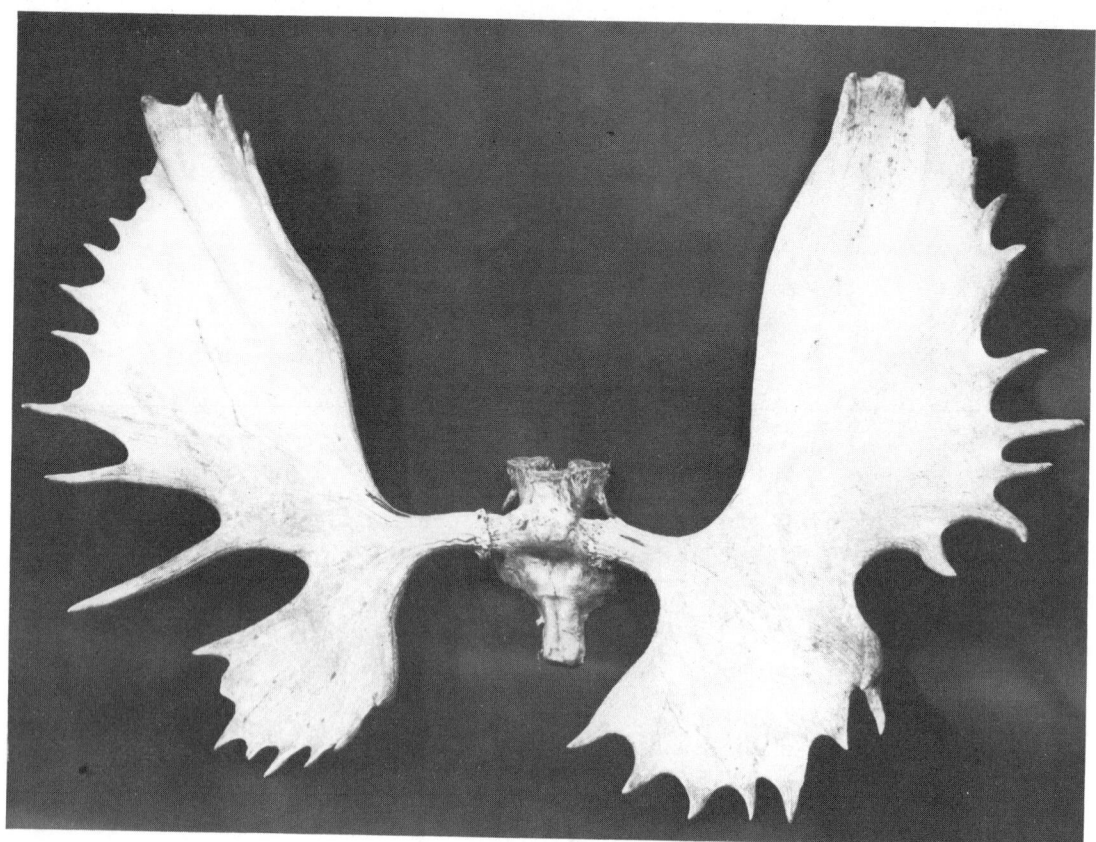

NUMBER TWO CANADA MOOSE
SCORE: 240 2/8
Locality: Teslin River, British Columbia Date: 1982
Hunter and owner: Albertoni Ferruccio

Canada Moose

Alces alces americana and Alces alces andersoni

Minimum Score 195

Three categories of moose are recognized for records keeping, with boundaries based on geographic lines. Canada moose includes trophies from Newfoundland and Canada (except for the Yukon and Northwest Territories), Minnesota, and Maine.

Score	Greatest Spread	Length of Palm R	Length of Palm L	Width of Palm R	Width of Palm L	Circumference of Beam at Smallest Place R	Circumference of Beam at Smallest Place L	Number of Normal Points R	Number of Normal Points L	Locality Killed	By Whom Killed	Owner	Date Killed	Rank
242	63	44⅝	45	21⅝	23	8⅛	9⅞	15	16	Grayling River, B.C.	Michael E. Laub	Michael E. Laub	1980	1
240⅞	66⅜	46⅜	45⅜	19	18⅝	7⅞	7⅞	15	15	Teslin River, B.C.	Albertoni Ferruccio	Albertoni Ferruccio	1982	2
238⅝	65⅜	44⅝	43⅜	21	18⅝	7⅝	7⅞	18	19	Bear Lake, Que.	Silas H. Witherbee	B&C National Collection	1914	3
226⅞	63⅛	48⅝	47	16⅝	16⅝	8⅜	8⅜	11	10	Whitecourt, Alta.	Tim Harbridge	Tim Harbridge	1978	4
225	60	45⅞	46⅜	14⅞	14⅜	7⅞	7⅞	17	15	Driftwood River, Alta.	Carl J. Buchanan	Carl J. Buchanan	1960	5
224⅛	58⅜	43⅜	43	18⅝	17⅜	8⅜	8⅞	14	14	Nipawin, Sask.	Roy M. Hornseth	Roy M. Hornseth	1959	6
223⅞	60⅝	47⅜	46	16⅞	14⅝	7⅜	7	17	14	Buffalo Lake, Man.	Pierre A. Lachance	Pierre A. Lachance	1985	7
223⅜	64⅜	46⅜	47⅛	17⅞	14	7	7⅝	12	12	Island Lake, Man.	Indian	Jack E. Dunn	1980	8
222	59	46	47⅛	14⅜	14	7⅞	7⅞	15	14	Clearwater River, Alta.	Manuel Dominguez	Manuel Dominguez	1947	9
221⅝	64⅜	48⅜	47⅞	15⅞	11	8⅝	8⅞	14	11	Arborfield, Sask.	Ed Lutz	Ed Lutz	1959	10
220⅜	67⅜	41⅝	46⅜	17⅞	15⅝	8⅜	7⅞	11	13	Cassiar, B.C.	Unknown	Luxton Museum	PR1954	11
219⅝	62⅜	40⅜	39⅜	18⅝	15⅝	7⅝	7⅜	17	19	Canada	Gift Of W. B. O. Field	National Collection	1924	12
219⅛	64⅛	45	43⅜	15⅝	13⅜	7⅞	7⅞	14	13	Cold Fish Lake, B.C.	George & Phil Halvorson	George & Phil Halvorson	1974	13
218⅝	58⅝	42⅝	40⅜	15	15⅜	8⅝	8⅝	16	16	Kennicott Lake, B.C.	Mike Popoff	Mike Popoff	1984	14
218⅛	61⅜	44⅜	42⅝	15	15	7⅜	7⅝	13	13	Chuchinra River, B.C.	Friedbert Prill	Friedbert Prill	1973	15
217⅞	64⅜	44⅛	47⅜	15	15	7⅝	7⅜	10	12	Cassiar Mts., B.C.	J. Barry Dyar	J. Barry Dyar	1977	16
217⅜	63⅜	42⅛	44	19⅜	15⅜	7⅝	6⅝	17	12	Hart Mt., B.C.	Donna Loewenstein	Donna Loewenstein	1966	17
217⅜	63⅜	42⅜	39⅜	17⅜	15⅜	7	8⅛	15	15	Firebag River, Alta.	Frank Baldwin	Carlysle Baldwin	1977	18
217⅛	63⅛	40⅛	43⅜	14⅜	15	8⅜	8⅛	14	15	Liard River, B.C.	Wayne E. Dalgleish	Wayne E. Dalgleish	1984	19
216⅞	59⅜	41⅜	44⅜	17⅜	15⅜	7⅜	7⅜	17	14	Prophet River, B.C.	John G. Oltmanns	John G. Oltmanns	1971	20
216⅜	58⅜	43⅜	46⅜	14⅝	15⅜	8⅜	8⅜	16	12	Cassiar Mts., B.C.	Ross Ferguson	Ross Ferguson	1978	21
216⅜	62⅜	46⅜	43⅜	14⅜	13⅜	7⅝	7⅝	15	12	Cassiar Mts., B.C.	Don L. Corley	Don L. Corley	1984	22
216⅜	71⅜	38⅜	37	14⅛	14⅜	8	7⅝	14	14	Maine	H. M. Boice	Everhart Museum	1900	23
216⅛	58⅜	41⅜	42⅜	18⅜	19⅜	7	7⅜	17	12	Dease Lake, B.C.	George A. Sinclair	George A. Sinclair	1981	23
215⅜	64	41⅜	42	13⅜	13⅜	6⅞	7⅛	14	15	Maine	Albert Bierstadt	National Collection	1880	25
215⅜	54⅜	39⅜	38⅜	17⅜	17⅜	7⅛	7⅜	17	20	Latornell River, Alta.	Artie G. Brown	Artie G. Brown	1971	26
215⅜	60⅛	44⅜	45⅜	12⅞	13⅛	7⅞	7⅝	13	13	Cassiar Mts., B.C.	Milton J. Duffin	Milton J. Duffin	1976	27
215⅜	62⅝	42⅜	44⅛	14⅜	13⅜	7⅜	7⅞	13	14	Dease Lake, B.C.	Bert Klineburger	Bert Klineburger	1960	28

Score										Locality	Hunter	Owner	Year	Rank
215	57⅝	43	45⅜	15⅜	14	7⅜	7⅜	15	14	Ice Mt., B.C.	David H. Hilsberg	David H. Hilsberg	1985	29
214⅞	53⅜	44⅜	44⅜	16	13⅜	7⅜	7⅜	16	15	Narraway River, Alta.	Karl Weber	Karl Weber	1956	30
214⅞	68	39⅜	39⅜	16⅜	15	8⅜	8⅜	13	13	Dease River, B.C.	Herb Klein	Herb Klein	1960	30
214⅛	62	42⅜	38⅜	15⅞	17	7⅜	7⅜	14	16	Piscataquis Co., Maine	Desmond Harvey	Desmond Harvey	1984	32
214⅛	60⅜	44⅜	42⅜	17⅞	14⅜	7⅜	7⅜	12	12	Teslin River, B.C.	John P. Costello II	John P. Costello II	1976	33
214	62⅜	43	43⅜	13⅜	13⅜	7⅜	7	13	14	Mile 100, Alaska Hwy., B.C.	Karl Fritzsche	Karl Fritzsche	1968	34
213⅛	60⅜	44⅜	45⅜	15⅜	13⅜	7⅜	7⅜	13	11	Prophet River, B.C.	Daniel T. Applebaker	Daniel T. Applebaker	1972	35
213⅞	51⅜	44	44	19	17⅜	7⅜	7⅜	12	12	Atlin, B.C.	Ewald Krentz	Ewald Krentz	1971	36
213	62⅜	45⅜	42⅜	14⅜	11⅜	8⅜	8⅜	14	13	Stikine River, B.C.	Sam Sanders, Jr.	Sam Sanders, Jr.	1975	37
213	63⅜	41⅜	39⅜	15⅜	15⅞	7⅜	7⅜	12	12	Hines Creek, Alta.	Elwood Baird	Elwood Baird	1975	37
213	52	45	46⅜	15	15⅞	7⅜	7⅜	14	13	Liard River, B.C.	Hayden O. Woods, Sr.	Hayden O. Woods, Sr.	1976	37
212⅞	61	42⅜	42⅜	13⅜	14⅜	7⅜	7⅜	14	13	Love, Sask.	Robert J. Rogers	Robert J. Rogers	1966	40
212⅞	60⅜	38⅜	38	18	20	8	8⅜	13	14	Sikanni Chief River, B.C.	David B. Willis	David B. Willis	1977	40
212⅝	60⅜	40⅜	43⅜	13⅜	13⅜	8	8	14	16	Slave Lake, Alta.	R. W. H. Eben-Ebenau	R. W. H. Eben-Ebenau	1937	42
212⅝	55⅞	39⅜	41⅜	16⅜	18⅜	7	7⅜	15	16	Marion Lake, B.C.	J. Clifton Jensen	J. Clifton Jensen	1974	42
212⅜	56⅜	47⅜	40⅜	18⅜	15⅜	8⅜	8	17	15	Cassiar Mts., B.C.	Dean A. Bloomfield	Dean A. Bloomfield	1979	44
212	54	39⅜	39	16⅜	16⅜	7⅜	7⅜	16	18	Grayling River, B.C.	Arnold E. Dado	Arnold E. Dado	1984	45
211⅞	65⅜	38⅜	44⅜	13⅜	12⅜	7⅜	7⅜	15	15	Pasquia Hills, Sask.	William H. Schweitzer	William H. Schweitzer	1978	46
211⅝	56⅜	40	39⅜	18	17⅜	7⅜	7	15	17	Ft. St. John, B.C.	Jack Fries	Jack Fries	1977	47
211⅛	61⅞	46	42	14⅜	18⅜	8⅜	8⅜	14	10	Powell Lake, Ont.	Jerry R. Brocksmith	Jerry R. Brocksmith	1969	48
211⅛	65	40⅜	40⅜	12⅜	12⅜	7⅜	7⅜	12	13	Pine Lake, Que.	Walter Geismar	Walter Geismar	1949	49
211⅛	64⅜	41⅜	43	11⅜	12⅜	7⅜	7⅜	14	17	Atlin, B.C.	William L. Frederick	William L. Frederick	1969	49
211¾	54⅜	40⅜	40	18⅜	15⅜	8⅜	7⅜	12	16	Tochieka Range, B.C.	C. Thomas Manier	C. Thomas Manier	1978	51
211	49	43⅜	43⅜	16⅜	14⅜	8	8	15	15	Grande Prairie, Alta.	Lester C. Hearn	Lester C. Hearn	1972	52
210⅞	70⅜	40	40⅜	14⅜	11⅜	8⅜	8⅜	11	12	Round Lake, Ont.	M. A. Kennedy	Royal Ontario Museum	1912	53
210⅝	63⅜	45⅜	44⅜	13⅜	13⅜	7⅜	7⅜	11	9	Sikanni Chief River, B.C.	Gerald Stecklein	Gerald Stecklein	1965	54
210⅛	62⅜	42⅜	42⅜	12⅜	11⅜	7⅜	7⅜	13	13	Sheep Creek, Alta.	R. V. D. Goltz	R. V. D. Goltz	1964	55
210	59⅞	41⅜	40⅜	15⅜	14⅜	6⅜	6⅜	14	16	Sheep River, Alta.	Elton Boggs	Elton Boggs	1956	56
210	54⅜	44⅜	47⅜	14⅜	13⅜	7⅜	7⅜	12	14	Cassiar Mts., B.C.	Richard J. Wristen	Richard J. Wristen	1978	56
209⅞	53⅜	43⅜	43⅜	12⅜	12⅜	7⅜	7⅜	15	15	Kakwa River, Alta.	Rolf Koelblinger	Rolf Koelblinger	1969	58
209⅜	54⅜	45⅜	42⅜	15⅜	15⅜	7⅜	7⅜	13	13	Turnagain River, B.C.	Gordon R. Cole	Gordon R. Cole	1974	58
209⅞	58⅜	42	40⅜	14	14⅜	7⅜	7⅜	14	14	Cassiar Mts., B.C.	William M. Silva	William M. Silva	1976	58
209⅞	60	43⅜	43⅜	14	14⅜	7	7⅜	10	10	Jennings Lake, B.C.	Collins F. Kellogg	Collins F. Kellogg	1969	61
209⅜	59⅜	41⅜	41⅜	13⅜	15⅜	8⅜	8⅜	12	15	Malone Lake, Que.	Harvey A. Kipp	Harvey A. Kipp	1953	62
209⅜	59⅜	42⅜	42⅜	15⅜	16⅜	7⅜	7⅜	10	10	Cassiar Mts., B.C.	Hurnie H. Whitehead	Hurnie H. Whitehead	1978	63
209⅜	59	44	50⅜	12⅜	12⅜	7⅜	7⅜	12	11	Smoky River, Alta.	William R. Farmer	William R. Farmer	1970	64
209	55⅜	40⅜	41⅜	13	13	7	7⅜	16	16	Kenora, Ont.	David O. Moreton	David O. Moreton	1970	65
208⅞	63	39⅜	39	15	17⅜	8	8	11	11	Manawaki, Que.	George A. Krikory	George A. Krikory	1953	66
208⅞	56⅜	39⅜	43⅜	15⅜	15	6⅜	7⅜	15	15	Hudson Bay, Sask.	Don Hendricks	Don Hendricks	1961	67
208⅞	60⅜	39⅜	41⅜	15	13⅜	7⅜	7⅜	13	14	Telegraph Creek, B.C.	T. T. Stroup	T. T. Stroup	1968	67
208⅞	63⅜	39⅜	44⅜	15⅜	16⅜	6⅜	7⅜	11	15	The Pas, Man.	Denver M. Wright	Denver M. Wright	1950	69
208⅞	61	41⅜	40⅜	16⅜	14	6⅜	6⅜	14	13	Ft. St. John, B.C.	Richard O. Vycital	Richard O. Vycital	1967	69

Score	Greatest Spread	Length of Palm		Width of Palm		Circumference of Beam at Smallest Place		Number of Normal Points		Locality Killed	By Whom Killed	Owner	Date Killed	Rank
		R.	L.	R.	L.	R.	L.	R.	L.					
208⅝	61⅛	41	41⅛	17⅞	15⅞	7⅞	8	9	12	Hudson Bay, Sask.	Frank B. Miller	Frank B. Miller	1967	69
208⅝	57⅞	42⅜	41⅛	13⅞	13⅜	7⅛	7⅞	14	14	Catagua River, B.C.	Dominic Arone	Dominic Arone	1969	69
208⅝	56	43⅜	47⅞	12⅝	14⅛	7⅞	7⅞	13	16	Pepaw Lake, Sask.	Maurice R. LaRose	Maurice R. LaRose	1976	69
208⅝	61	41⅜	41⅛	14⅞	14⅛	7⅛	7⅞	11	13	Ketchum Lake, B.C.	Gailand K. Hamn	Gailand K. Hamn	1985	69
208⅜	58⅝	43⅝	44⅛	15⅛	13⅛	7⅛	7⅜	12	11	Muskwa River, B.C.	Gary D. Linsinbigler	Gary D. Linsinbigler	1969	75
208⅛	52⅝	46⅛	45⅜	16⅜	12⅜	8	8	14	12	Prophet River, B.C.	Vollrad J. von Berg	Vollrad J. von Berg	1967	76
208⅜	61⅜	40⅛	40⅜	11⅜	12	7⅝	7⅞	14	14	Chetwynd, B.C.	Louis Carriere	Louis Carriere	1976	77
208⅛	59⅝	39⅛	40⅜	15⅛	17⅜	6⅜	6⅞	13	13	Halfway River, B.C.	Eugene F. Konopaski	Eugene F. Konopaski	1967	78
208⅛	61⅜	42⅜	40	16⅜	17⅛	7	7⅜	12	10	Cadomin, Alta.	Picked Up	E. F. Madole	1977	78
208	58⅜	41⅞	40⅜	14⅛	12⅜	7⅞	7⅝	14	16	Muskwa River, B.C.	William D. Phifer	William D. Phifer	1969	80
207⅞	56⅛	43⅜	43	13⅜	13⅜	7⅝	7⅝	14	12	Hudson Bay, Sask.	Harold Read	Philip Schlegel	1956	81
207⅞	52⅜	47⅜	46⅜	14⅛	16	7⅜	7⅛	11	10	Neaves Creek, B.C.	Mrs. George A. Strom, Jr.	Mrs. Geo. A. Strom, Jr.	1960	81
207⅞	71⅜	41⅛	38⅜	13⅜	12⅜	7⅜	7⅝	11	10	Moccasin Lake, Ont.	Charles W. Reiley	Charles W. Reiley	1961	83
207⅝	52⅜	44⅜	44	15⅞	13⅜	7⅝	7⅝	16	12	Ash Mt., B.C.	Robert E. Rabon	Robert E. Rabon	1984	84
207⅞	56⅜	42⅜	48	12⅜	14	7⅜	7⅝	14	13	Long Lake, Alta.	Garry A. Debienne	Garry A. Debienne	1975	85
207⅞	60⅜	38⅜	40⅜	16⅜	15⅝	7⅜	7⅞	12	16	Sulphur Creek, Alta.	Willard L. Gamin	Willard L. Gamin	1980	85
207⅞	51⅜	43⅜	43	14⅛	14⅜	7	7	14	15	Prophet River, B.C.	Arvion Harrell	Arvion Harrell	1981	85
207⅜	70⅜	31	31	15	16	7⅞	7⅛	16	15	Alberta	Unknown	Acad. Nat. Sci., Phil.	1905	88
207⅜	59⅜	39⅜	40⅜	14⅛	14	7⅞	7⅞	13	13	Smoky River, Alta.	Robert L. Carmichael, Jr.	Robert L. Carmichael, Jr.	1974	88
207⅜	59⅜	43	40⅜	13⅜	13⅜	7⅞	7⅞	13	12	Hudson Bay, Sask.	A. L. Moore	A. L. Moore	1961	90
207⅛	60⅜	40⅜	39⅜	13⅜	15	7⅜	7⅜	13	13	Manning, Alta.	Gary Cumming	Gary Cumming	1971	91
207	61⅞	43⅜	45⅞	12⅜	15	7⅞	7⅝	9	12	Goose River, Alta	O. D. Evans	O. D. Evans	1960	92
207	58⅝	42⅞	44⅜	13⅝	14⅜	8	7⅝	14	12	Nipisi Lake, Alta.	J. M. Kirkpatrick	J. M. Kirkpatrick	1966	92
206⅞	62⅝	41	40⅜	13⅜	13⅜	7⅛	7⅞	11	13	Somerset Co., Maine	Stephen D. Cole	Stephen D. Cole	1984	94
206⅞	60⅜	39⅜	39⅜	14	14⅜	7⅝	7⅞	13	13	Smithers, B.C.	W. G. Reed	Louis Calder	1951	95
206⅝	60⅜	37⅜	38⅜	16⅛	13⅜	7⅜	7⅞	17	15	Black Sturgeon Lake, Ont.	Joseph J. Casey	Joseph J. Casey	1967	95
206⅝	57⅜	43⅜	44⅜	13	12⅜	7⅜	7⅜	11	11	Assiniboine River, Sask.	Francis Peecock	Francis Peecock	1976	97
206⅛	60	40⅜	35⅜	16	17⅜	8⅜	9⅜	14	14	White River, Ont.	Ronald L. Porter	Ronald L. Porter	1975	98
206⅜	56⅜	41⅜	41⅜	13⅜	14⅜	7⅜	7⅛	15	13	Horseranch Mts., B.C.	Bill McCoy	Bill McCoy	1976	98
206⅜	56⅜	46⅛	49	15	12⅜	7⅜	7⅞	9	9	Windfall Creek, Alta.	Brian Richardson	Brian Richardson	1978	100

Score										Locality	By whom killed	Owner	Date	Rank
206⅞	55⅞	41⅞	42⅞	13⅜	13	8⅛	8⅞	13	13	Trutch, B.C.	Richard M. Wilkey	Richard M. Wilkey	1976	101
206⅞	59⅛	40⅞	39⅞	18⅜	16⅜	6⅜	6⅞	11	12	Brule, Alta.	Steven Rose	Steven Rose	1969	102
206⅛	59⅛	42⅜	42⅜	14⅜	15⅜	7⅛	7⅛	12	11	Klappan River, B.C.	Bert Varkonyi	Joe & Nini Varkonyi	1979	102
206	52⅞	41⅛	41⅛	16⅞	21⅜	7⅜	7⅜	12	13	Trimble Lake, B.C.	Clifford E. Palmer	Clifford E. Palmer	1962	104
206	59⅛	38⅞	42⅜	15⅛	13⅜	7⅞	7⅞	13	13	Moose Call Lake, B.C.	W. W. Harvie	W. W. Harvie	1965	104
206	54⅛	40⅜	40⅜	16⅜	15⅜	7⅜	7⅛	13	14	Muskwa River, B.C.	C. Dale Hippensteel	C. Dale Hippensteel	1968	104
205⅝	56	41⅜	40⅜	12⅜	14⅜	6⅜	7⅛	15	17	Sheep Creek, Alta.	Rudiger Schwarz	Rudiger Schwarz	1959	107
205⅝	55	42	41⅜	14⅜	16⅜	8⅜	8⅛	12	11	Kechika River, B.C.	Len Eklund	Len Eklund	1968	107
205⅜	54⅜	42	41⅛	14⅛	16⅜	7⅞	7⅜	14	13	Turnagain River, B.C.	Audrey E. Crabtree	Audrey E. Crabtree	1984	107
205⅜	65⅜	45	40	14⅜	14⅜	7⅜	7⅜	13	8	Vice Lake, Ont.	A. W. Winchester	A. W. Winchester	1959	110
205⅜	55⅜	43⅜	43⅜	13⅜	12⅜	7⅛	7⅜	12	13	Simonette River, Alta.	John G. Stelfox	John G. Stelfox	1965	110
205⅜	54⅛	41⅛	41	12	17⅜	8⅛	7⅞	15	17	Cassiar Mts., B.C.	Richard Trapp	Richard Trapp	1972	110
205⅜	66⅞	40⅜	43⅜	13⅜	11⅛	7⅜	7⅜	12	11	Bay Tree, Alta.	A. Iverson	Wally's Sporting Goods	1926	113
205⅜	61⅛	39⅜	40⅜	16⅜	17	7⅝	7⅜	9	8	Kedahda Lake, B.C.	Jack Perisits, Jr.	Jack Perisits, Jr.	1970	113
205⅜	62⅜	44⅜	37⅜	14⅜	13⅜	8⅜	8⅜	13	12	Kleena Kleene, B.C.	Roger Dane	Roger Dane	1965	115
205⅜	59⅜	38⅜	44⅜	15⅜	16⅜	7⅜	7⅜	11	15	Liard Plateau, B.C.	Charles W. Melton	Charles W. Melton	1971	115
205⅜	57⅜	39⅜	39⅜	13⅜	14⅜	7⅜	7⅜	17	14	Stikine Plateau, B.C.	Mike Papac	Mike Papac	1977	117
205⅜	53⅜	43⅜	42	13⅜	14⅜	8⅜	8⅜	13	12	Cold Fish Lake, B.C.	A. Baltensweiler	A. Baltensweiler	1965	118
205	57⅜	36⅜	35⅜	17⅜	19⅜	7⅜	7⅜	16	14	Prophet River, B.C.	John E. Hammett, Jr.	John E. Hammett, Jr.	1944	119
205	56	42⅞	41⅜	11⅜	14	7⅛	7	14	16	Moose Lake, Man.	Leif R. Langsjoen	Leif R. Langsjoen	1960	119
205	57⅜	43⅜	42⅜	11⅜	12	7⅜	7⅜	12	13	Cassiar, B.C.	James H. Bryant	James H. Bryant	1965	119
205	60⅛	41	43	12	12	8⅜	8⅜	11	13	Cassiar Mts., B.C.	Earl I. Jones	Earl I. Jones	1978	119
204⅞	62⅜	38⅜	40⅜	14⅜	14⅜	7⅜	7	15	11	Prophet River, B.C.	Lewis Morgan	Lewis Morgan	1970	123
204⅞	56⅜	46⅜	43⅜	15⅜	15⅜	7⅜	7⅜	8	8	Hudson Bay, Sask.	Fred Smorodin	Fred Smorodin	1957	124
204⅜	54⅜	40⅜	40⅜	13⅜	12⅜	6⅜	6⅜	16	16	Cassiar, B.C.	Unknown	B.C. Game Dept.	PR1918	125
204⅜	51⅞	45⅜	44⅜	15	14⅜	7⅜	7⅜	13	11	Germansen Mts., B.C.	Edward A. McLarney	Edward A. McLarney	1978	125
204⅜	57⅞	40⅜	39⅜	14	13⅜	8	8	12	13	Prophet River, B.C.	W. T. Yoshimoto	W. T. Yoshimoto	1966	127
204⅜	55⅜	42⅜	41⅜	16⅜	14⅜	7⅜	7⅜	12	10	Summit Lake, B.C.	R. A. Schweitzer	R. A. Schweitzer	1970	127
204⅜	52⅜	36⅜	38⅜	16⅜	16⅜	7⅜	7⅜	16	16	Buckinghorse, B.C.	John C. Belcher	John C. Belcher	1955	129
204⅜	60	37⅜	38⅜	16⅜	14⅜	7⅜	7⅜	14	13	The Pas, Man.	Eddy Burkhartsmeir	Eddy Burkhartsmeir	1960	129
204⅜	62⅜	41⅜	41⅜	16⅜	14⅜	7⅜	7⅜	8	9	Ice Mt., B.C.	J. E. Mason	J. E. Mason	1964	129
204⅜	62	37⅜	38⅜	15⅜	16⅜	8⅜	8⅜	10	10	Duty Lake, B.C.	John M. Haugen	John M. Haugen	1966	129
204⅜	55⅜	44⅜	39⅜	15⅜	14⅜	7⅜	7⅜	13	14	Muskwa River, B.C.	James C. Kolbe	James C. Kolbe	1966	129
204⅜	58⅜	36⅜	41⅜	19⅜	18⅜	7	7	11	16	Wawa, Ont.	Edward A. Hall	Edward A. Hall	1969	129
204⅜	56⅛	45	44⅜	11⅜	12⅜	7⅜	7⅜	12	11	Tetsa River, B.C.	Alex Nesterenko	Alex Nesterenko	1970	129
204⅜	65	41⅜	39⅜	15⅜	13	7⅛	7	11	10	Peace River, Alta.	Wilbur C. Savage	Wilbur C. Savage	1973	129
204⅜	55⅜	41⅜	46⅜	15	13⅜	7⅜	7⅜	13	16	Ft. St. James, B.C.	Ed Cornish	Ed Cornish	1984	129
204	68⅞	35	33⅜	15⅜	13	8	8	13	13	Elderslay, Sask.	R. E. McKenzie	R. E. McKenzie	1964	137
204	55	40⅜	41⅜	13⅜	13⅜	7⅛	7⅜	15	13	Lake Nipigon, Ont.	Gary C. Jacobson	Gary C. Jacobson	1930	138
203⅜	63⅜	41⅜	39⅜	10⅜	11⅜	7⅜	7⅜	12	13	Lodge, Sask.	F. Foarie	F. Foarie	1965	138
203⅜	55	38⅜	39	15⅜	15⅜	7	7	14	15	Jackfish Lake, Alta.	A. Stopson	A. Stopson	1962	140
203⅜	59⅜	42⅜	41⅜	10⅜	12⅜	8⅜	8⅜	13	12	Hudson Bay, Sask.	Abraham Hassen	Abraham Hassen	1959	141

CANADA MOOSE—Continued
Alces alces americana and Alces alces andersoni

Score	Greatest Spread	Length of Palm R.	L.	Width of Palm R.	L.	Circumference of Beam at Smallest Place R.	L.	Number of Normal Points R.	L.	Locality Killed	By Whom Killed	Owner	Date Killed	Rank
203⅜	60	38⅛	41⅛	13	14	7⅞	8	13	15	Rabbit River, B.C.	Bob V. Kelley	Bob V. Kelley	1969	141
203⅜	58⅜	39⅛	39	12⅞	12⅝	8⅜	8⅜	13	14	Pink Mt. B.C.	Garth C. Hardy	Garth C. Hardy	1973	141
203⅜	53⅜	43⅜	43⅜	11⅜	12⅞	7⅜	7⅜	14	13	Overflowing River, Man.	Lester Ochsner	Lester Ochsner	1957	145
203⅜	59⅜	39⅝	41⅞	13⅝	13⅛	7⅜	7⅞	12	12	Gladys Lake, B.C.	Harry Hoeft	Harry Hoeft	1984	145
203⅜	56⅜	43⅜	45	13⅛	13⅜	7⅜	7⅜	16	10	Surmont Lake, Alta.	Daryl Goodine	Daryl Goodine	1984	145
203⅜	61	39⅝	39⅞	13⅜	14⅜	7⅜	7⅜	13	11	Graham River, B.C.	R. M. Frye	R. M. Frye	1970	148
203⅜	64⅜	41	36⅜	15⅜	14	7⅞	8⅜	11	11	Leaf Lake, Sask.	Tom Skoretz	Tom Skoretz	1959	149
203⅜	55⅜	42	48⅜	12⅜	14⅜	7⅜	7⅜	12	13	Hudson Bay Junct., Sask.	Murray Griffin	Murray Griffin	1965	149
203⅜	53⅜	40⅝	42	17⅜	16⅜	7⅜	7⅜	11	17	Big Smoky River, Alta.	Ross D. Carrick	Ross D. Carrick	1971	149
203⅜	58⅜	39⅜	40	17⅜	16⅜	7⅛	7⅜	10	10	Muskwa River, B.C.	John A. Kolman	John A. Kolman	1975	149
203⅜	69⅜	32⅞	32⅜	17	16⅛	7⅛	7⅜	11	11	Kvass Creek, Alta.	F. C. Hibben	F. C. Hibben	1958	153
203⅜	59⅜	39⅜	38⅜	13⅜	15⅜	8	7⅞	12	12	Wapiti River, Alta.	David L. Savage	David L. Savage	1984	153
203⅜	56⅜	37⅜	37⅜	14⅜	15	7⅝	7⅜	15	14	Scoop Lake, B.C.	Dwight E. Farr, Jr.	Dwight E. Farr, Jr.	1980	155
203	55	39	40	15⅜	14	7	9⅜	14	15	Fawcett, Alta.	A. Juckli	Mrs. A. Juckli	PR1933	156
203	58⅜	42	41⅜	11	12⅝	6⅜	6⅝	14	13	Cassiar, B.C.	Tom Lindahl	Tom Lindahl	1961	156
203	57⅜	38⅜	39⅛	15⅜	14	7⅜	7⅛	13	14	Cassiar, B.C.	Arvid F. Benson	Arvid F. Benson	1965	156
203	58⅜	41⅜	38⅜	12⅜	13⅛	7⅛	7⅜	16	14	Pink Mt., B.C.	T. C. Britt, Jr.	T. C. Britt, Jr.	1966	156
203	55	43⅜	44⅜	13⅜	12⅛	7⅜	7⅞	13	11	Robb Lake, B.C.	Jerome Metcalfe	Jerome Metcalfe	1967	156
203	61⅜	39⅛	42	14⅜	15⅜	7⅜	7⅜	13	10	Manning, Alta.	James Harbick	James Harbick	1967	156
203	62	39⅜	44⅜	11⅜	12⅜	7⅜	7⅜	12	12	Graham River, B.C.	Harold L. Sperfslage	Harold L. Sperfslage	1975	156
202⅞	60⅜	42	47⅜	13⅜	14⅜	7⅛	7⅜	9	9	Prophet River, B.C.	Elbert Stiles	Elbert Stiles	1960	163
202⅞	55⅜	39⅜	39⅜	13⅜	16	7⅜	7⅜	11	11	Atlin, B.C.	Robert H. Morgan	Robert H. Morgan	1973	163
202⅞	57⅜	43⅜	46⅜	15	11⅜	8⅛	7⅜	10	11	Lower Manitou Lake, Ont.	Donald R. Anderson	Donald R. Anderson	1979	163
202⅞	56⅜	41⅜	46⅜	18⅜	13⅜	8⅛	7⅜	13	10	Frog River, B.C.	Malcom Dan Anderson	Malcom Dan Dinges, Jr.	1980	163
202⅝	58	43⅜	40⅜	11⅜	11⅞	7⅜	7⅞	14	13	Bee Peak, B.C.	Dennis J. Eakin	Dennis J. Eakin	1984	167
202⅝	59⅜	43⅜	43⅜	12	14	7⅜	7⅜	9	13	Alder Flats, Alta.	Fred J. Simpson	Carnegie Museum	1966	168
202⅝	56⅜	39⅜	40⅜	13⅜	13⅜	7⅜	7⅜	13	14	Harmon Lake, Ont.	Dale C. Curtis	Dale C. Curtis	1969	168
202⅝	55⅜	40	40⅜	14⅜	13⅝	7⅜	7⅛	13	13	High Prairie, Alta.	Dean L. Walker	Dean L. Walker	1973	168
202⅝	57	39⅝	38⅜	14⅜	15⅞	8	8⅛	11	13	Chelan, Sask.	Picked Up	Harold Bergman	1955	171
202⅝	61⅜	41	40⅞	14⅜	15⅜	7⅜	7⅜	8	10	Prophet River, B.C.	Lyle Nosler	Lyle Nosler	1964	171

202⅝	58⅜	41⅞	41⅝	13⅝	13⅜	8	7⅞	10	10	Watson Lake, B.C.	Lloyd Nosler	Lloyd Nosler	1964	171
202⅛	62⅜	43⅜	40⅝	13⅜	14	7⅞	7⅞	10	9	Stewart Lake, B.C.	Keith Wilson	Keith Wilson	1980	171
201⅞	59⅜	39⅞	39⅝	15⅝	15⅝	7⅞	7⅞	12	14	Cassiar, B.C.	Unknown	B. C. Game Dept.	PR1918	175
201⅝	53⅜	39	39⅜	19	16⅝	8⅜	7⅝	13	12	Swan Hills, Alta.	Harold R. Wiese	Harold R. Wiese	1967	175
201⅝	62⅜	40⅞	40⅜	12⅞	11⅝	7⅞	7⅞	11	12	Grovedale, Alta.	Douglas R. Morris	Douglas R. Morris	1974	175
201⅜	55⅜	43⅜	43⅝	15	14	7⅜	7⅞	10	11	Cormorant, Man.	Howard J. Lang	Howard J. Lang	1950	178
201⅜	60⅜	41⅞	41⅜	12⅞	16⅝	7⅞	7⅞	12	9	Goose Mt., Alta.	Fred Bartel	Fred Bartel	1956	178
201⅜	56⅜	40⅞	44⅝	12⅞	13⅜	7⅝	7⅞	13	13	Hines Creek, Alta.	Ralph Jumago	Ralph Jumago	1960	178
201⅜	59⅜	36⅜	38⅜	16	17	6⅞	6⅞	12	13	Telegraph Creek, B.C.	George D. Young	George D. Young	1962	178
201⅜	61⅜	41	41	10⅜	12⅞	7⅞	7⅝	13	13	Turcotte Lake, Que.	S. B. Fredenburgh, Jr.	S. B. Fredenburgh, Jr.	1962	178
201⅜	59	40⅞	44⅞	13⅝	14⅜	7⅜	7⅜	11	11	Atlin, B.C.	J. D. Kethley	J. D. Kethley	1966	178
201⅜	51⅜	44⅜	42⅝	13⅝	14	7	6⅞	14	12	Graham River, B.C.	Thomas H. Morrison	Thomas H. Morrison	1981	184
202	66⅜	43⅜	39⅜	13⅝	13⅜	7⅝	7⅝	9	8	Kawdy Mt., B.C.	Herman Kirn	Herman Kirn	1981	184
202	58	37	37⅞	14	16⅝	7	7⅞	14	15	St. Jovite, Que.	Ed Schmeller	Ed Schmeller	1942	186
201⅞	61	39⅞	42	14	15	7⅞	7⅝	15	10	Muskwa River, B.C.	Gordon C. Arndt	Gordon C. Arndt	1976	186
201⅞	51⅜	39⅞	40⅝	13⅜	14⅜	7⅝	7⅞	10	17	Saskatchewan	Gordon Lund	Gordon Lund	PR1954	188
201⅝	56⅜	40⅞	43⅝	15	12⅝	7⅝	7⅝	15	16	Cassiar Mts., B.C.	Clark A. Goetzmann	Clark A. Goetzmann	1968	188
201⅝	56⅜	40⅞	41⅝	15⅝	16	7⅞	7⅝	13	14	Ft. St. John, B.C.	William J. Heiman	William J. Heiman	1969	188
201⅜	60⅜	40⅞	41⅞	15⅝	14	7⅞	7⅝	15	12	Kechika Mts., B.C.	Norman Lougheed	Norman Lougheed	1964	191
201⅜	57⅜	39	40⅞	14⅞	16⅝	7⅝	7⅝	10	15	Colt Lake, B.C.	James C. Wood	James C. Wood	1965	191
201⅜	59⅜	39	39⅜	15	13⅝	7⅝	8	15	15	Pink Mt., B.C.	John P. Blanchard	John P. Blanchard	1970	191
201⅛	55⅜	38⅞	42	13⅝	13⅜	8	7⅝	12	12	Cabin Lake, B.C.	Donald F. Gould	Donald F. Gould	1974	191
201⅛	54⅜	41⅞	40⅝	13⅝	12	7⅝	7⅜	11	14	Toad River, B.C.	Dennis R. Gustafson	Dennis R. Gustafson	1982	191
201⅛	53⅜	41⅞	39	18	20	7	7	14	15	Omineca Mt., B.C.	C. L. Burnette	C. L. Burnette	1973	196
201⅛	49⅜	37	42⅝	15⅝	13⅝	7⅝	7⅝	12	12	Cold Fish Lake, B.C.	Charles E. Wilson, Jr.	Charles E. Wilson, Jr.	1957	197
201⅛	56	42⅝	34⅝	18	19⅝	7⅜	7⅝	15	13	Island Lake, Que.	Silvene Bracalente	Silvene Bracalente	1962	197
201⅛	54⅜	43⅜	42⅝	16⅝	15⅝	7⅝	7⅝	17	13	Ospika River, B.C.	Bill Goosman	Bill Goosman	1964	197
201⅛	55⅜	46⅝	42⅝	12⅝	11⅝	7⅞	7⅝	10	10	Mt. Lady Laurier, B.C.	Peter L. Halbig	Peter L. Halbig	1968	197
201⅜	57⅜	40	40⅝	13⅝	13⅜	7	7	12	12	Swan Hills, Alta.	Earl C. Wood	Vale E. Wood	1967	201
201⅜	56⅜	41	40⅝	13⅜	14	7	7	11	13	Rocky Mt. House, Alta.	John B. Gibson	John B. Gibson	1955	202
201⅜	62	40	43	15	13⅜	7⅝	7⅝	14	12	Racing River, B.C.	Anthony Battaglia	Anthony Battaglia	1966	202
201⅜	58	36⅝	37⅞	15	14⅝	6⅞	6⅞	13	14	Upsala, Ont.	Daniel F. Volkmann	Daniel F. Volkmann	1969	202
201⅜	63⅜	34⅞	34⅝	15⅝	15⅝	7⅞	7⅝	13	13	Quebec	Diana Baglino	Diana Baglino	1971	202
201⅜	53	40⅝	38⅝	13⅝	13⅝	7⅝	8	15	15	Lesser Slave Lake, Alta.	B. Strain & B. Baergen	Bert Strain	1976	202
201⅛	54	39⅞	39⅝	15	14⅝	6⅝	7	13	14	Fox River, B.C.	Toby J. Johnson	Toby J. Johnson	1980	208
201⅛	53⅝	39⅞	39⅜	15⅝	15⅝	7⅝	8	11	11	Reserve, Sask.	O. A. Kjelshus	O. A. Kjelshus	1953	208
201⅛	55⅝	41⅞	40	15	15	7⅜	7⅜	13	13	Big Sandy Lake, Sask.	John Longley	John Longley	1961	208
201⅛	56⅝	40⅞	43	15	12⅝	7	7	15	12	Slave Lake, Alta.	A. F. Harry	A. F. Harry	1967	208
201⅛	61⅜	41	45	16⅝	13⅝	7⅝	7⅜	11	13	Skeena Mts., B.C.	Wayne A. Tri	Wayne A. Tri	1978	208
201⅛	57⅝	38⅝	40⅝	11	14⅝	8⅝	8⅜	13	13	Piscataquis Co., Maine	Walter V. Scott	Walter V. Scott	1980	208
201	55⅝	38⅝	42	14⅝	15⅝	8	8⅛	13	12	Muskwa River, B.C.	J. H. Blu	J. H. Blu	1972	213
201	54⅜	43⅝	42	13⅝	13⅝	8⅝	8⅛	10	12	Toad River, B.C.	Steven Ronshausen	Steven Ronshausen	1981	213

Score	Greatest Spread	Length of Palm R.	L.	Width of Palm R.	L.	Circumference of Beam at Smallest Place R.	L.	Number of Normal Points R.	L.	Locality Killed	By Whom Killed	Owner	Date Killed	Rank
200⅞	61⅜	39⅞	41⅞	10⅞	13⅜	7⅜	7⅝	12	14	Grande Prairie, Alta.	John W. Benson	John W. Benson	1969	215
200⅞	60⅞	38⅞	34⅜	14⅜	14⅞	7½	7	14	14	Spatsizi River, B.C.	G. C. Taylor	G. C. Taylor	1974	215
200⅝	50⅞	41⅛	42	13⅝	13⅜	7	7	14	13	Goodwin Lake, B.C.	Bill R. Moomey	Bill R. Moomey	1974	217
200⅝	63⅝	38⅝	39	11⅜	12	7⅞	7½	11	13	Alberta	Ray Pierson	Ray Pierson	1967	218
200⅝	61⅝	39⅜	39	11⅜	11⅝	6⅝	6⅜	13	15	Prophet River, B.C.	Chauncey Everard	Chauncey Everard	1967	218
200⅝	58⅝	37⅝	39⅜	13	12	7⅜	7⅞	14	14	Fort Nelson, B.C.	Everett L. Ashley	Everett L. Ashley	1975	218
200⅝	59⅝	39⅜	41⅛	16⅝	13	7⅝	7⅝	15	11	Cassiar Mts., B.C.	G. L. Garrett	G. L. Garrett	1977	218
200⅝	59⅝	40⅜	41⅞	14	13⅜	8⅜	8	9	14	Robb Lake, B.C.	Richard L. Bostrom	Richard L. Bostrom	1985	218
200½	61	39⅜	41⅜	15⅜	13⅝	6⅝	6⅝	10	12	Deadmans Lake, B.C.	John Caputo	John Caputo	1950	223
200½	61⅝	38⅜	39⅜	14⅞	16⅛	7	7	10	12	Watson Lake, B.C.	Dan E. O'Neal, Jr.	Dan E. O'Neal, Jr.	1968	223
200½	52	40	41⅞	15	15⅛	7⅝	7⅜	14	12	Muskwa River, B.C.	William W. Veigel	William W. Veigel	1971	223
200½	59⅝	42⅝	40⅝	15⅛	15⅛	6⅝	7⅛	9	10	Cassiar Mts., B.C.	Calvin D. Boatwright	Calvin D. Boatwright	1976	223
200⅜	58⅛	36⅝	39	15	15	6⅝	6⅝	13	13	English River, Ont.	Jack Radke	Jack Radke	1966	227
200⅜	59⅝	43⅝	41⅛	11⅜	11⅝	8⅜	8	10	11	Peace River, B.C.	Walter W. Kassner	Walter W. Kassner	1968	227
200⅜	51⅞	41⅞	43	13⅜	14	6⅝	6⅝	12	12	Cassiar Mts., B.C.	Don Stallings	Don Stallings	1971	227
200⅜	53⅛	40⅞	38⅝	13⅞	14⅜	7	7⅛	16	14	Cypress Creek, B.C.	Raymond A. Racette	Raymond A. Racette	1984	227
200⅛	62	42	40½	13⅜	11⅜	7⅝	7⅝	10	10	Atlin, B.C.	John Vigna	John Vigna	1965	231
200⅛	56⅝	36⅝	37⅜	14	15⅜	7⅝	7⅝	14	13	Pink Mt., B.C.	Danny Taylor	Danny Taylor	1970	231
200⅛	56⅞	39⅝	41⅜	12⅝	12⅜	8	8	12	13	Turcott Lake, Que.	George Clark, Jr.	George Clark, Jr.	1960	233
200⅛	52⅝	46⅝	46	11⅞	10⅝	7⅛	7⅝	12	10	Red Fern Lake, B.C.	M. Steven Weaver	M. Steven Weaver	1966	233
200⅛	55⅜	41⅜	39⅝	14⅞	13⅞	7⅝	7⅝	14	12	Whitebeech, Sask.	John J. Kuzma	John J. Kuzma	1966	233
200	59	43	42½	14½	12½	7	7	9	11	Cold Fish Lake, B.C.	G. Kenneth Whitehead	G. Kenneth Whitehead	1964	236
200	56⅜	37⅝	41⅝	15⅜	13⅛	6⅝	6⅝	14	16	Lac Seul, Ont.	Robert B. Peregrine	Robert B. Peregrine	1966	236
200	59½	40⅜	41⅛	14⅛	12	7⅝	7⅝	11	12	Nass Lake, B.C.	Dan A. Pick	Dan A. Pick	1969	236
200	53	36⅜	35⅜	16	16⅝	7⅝	7⅝	15	14	Muskwa River, B.C.	Roy V. Haskell	Roy V. Haskell	1978	236
199⅞	62⅜	32⅝	33⅜	16⅝	13⅜	7⅝	7⅜	15	15	Patapedia Lakes, Que.	Frederick K. Barbour	William Darrow	1911	240
199⅞	46⅝	41⅛	40⅜	17⅝	15⅞	7⅜	7⅜	13	13	Vanderhoof, B.C.	William Ilnisky	William Ilnisky	1978	240
199⅞	61⅛	36⅜	36⅛	12⅝	13⅞	8⅛	8⅜	12	12	Cutbank River, Alta.	Steve Kalischuk	Steve Kalischuk	1960	242
199⅞	51⅛	40⅜	40⅞	14⅛	14⅝	7⅜	7⅝	12	13	Halfway River, B.C.	Jack Taylor	Jack Taylor	1973	242
199⅞	57	39⅝	39⅞	14	13⅞	7⅝	7⅝	11	13	Kledo Creek, B.C.	Rick L. McGowan	Rick L. McGowan	1975	242

199 6/8	60 5/8	37 7/8	41	13	12 7/8	8 3/8	8 5/8	11	11	Lake Co., Minn.	L. D. Holtegaard	L. D. Holtegaard, R. Smith, B. Nessler, & P. Nietz	1981	242
199 5/8	61 5/8	38 7/8	39 7/8	15 5/8	14	8	8	10	8	Prairie River, Sask.	Clarence Slater	Clarence Slater	1955	246
199 5/8	53 5/8	38 7/8	39 7/8	13 5/8	15 5/8	7 5/8	7 3/8	14	15	Greenbush, Sask.	Tom Flanagan	Tom Flanagan	1955	246
199 4/8	59	41	42	9 4/8	11 7/8	7 4/8	7 5/8	12	14	Drayton Valley, Alta.	Ollie Fedorus	Ollie Fedorus	1962	248
199 4/8	60	37 7/8	39 7/8	12 4/8	13	6 7/8	6 6/8	13	13	Dease Lake, B.C.	Peter Hohorst	Peter Hohorst	1968	248
199 4/8	58 5/8	40 7/8	40 7/8	12 2/8	14 4/8	7	7	11	11	Aroostook Co., Maine	Richard Neal	Richard Neal	1983	248
199 3/8	49 7/8	43	45 4/8	13	12	7 5/8	7 5/8	12	14	Buckinghorse River, B.C.	Fain J. Little	Fain J. Little	1967	251
199 2/8	52 4/8	37 7/8	37 7/8	15 5/8	15 5/8	7 5/8	7 5/8	14	18	Glaslyn, Sask.	Allan Johnson	Allan Johnson	1956	252
199 2/8	63	38 7/8	37 7/8	14 1/8	15 4/8	7 5/8	7 5/8	10	14	English River, Ont.	Melvin Vetse	Melvin Vetse	1969	252
199 2/8	57 4/8	41 7/8	43 7/8	11 3/8	15 5/8	6 7/8	6 7/8	11	11	Pasco Hills, Sask.	Mac B. Ford	Mac B. Ford	1969	252
199 2/8	53 4/8	38 4/8	40	13 4/8	12 2/8	7 3/8	7 3/8	14	14	Kluayaz Lake, B.C.	William F. Jury	William F. Jury	1970	252
199 1/8	55 5/8	39 5/8	37	12 2/8	12 6/8	7 6/8	7 5/8	15	15	Mayerthorpe, Alta.	Unknown	Bennie Ziemmer	PR 1965	256
199 1/8	57 3/8	37 7/8	36 7/8	12 7/8	12 7/8	7 6/8	7 4/8	14	14	Dixonville, Alta.	Edward W. Filpula	Edward W. Filpula	1977	256
199 1/8	52 3/8	43 5/8	43 5/8	12 4/8	11	7 5/8	8	11	12	Iskut, B.C.	Larry Zilinski	Larry Zilinski	1979	256
199 1/8	51 5/8	43 4/8	43 4/8	11 1/8	13 3/8	7 5/8	7 4/8	12	11	Coutts River, Alta.	George J. Thimer	George J. Thimer	1983	256
199	58 5/8	38	35 4/8	16	14	8	8	14	13	Hornepayne, Ont.	Harry T. Young	Harry T. Young	1967	260
199	61 5/8	36 7/8	35 4/8	12	13 2/8	7 4/8	7 4/8	12	12	Timmons, Ont.	Domenic Ripepiv	Domenic Ripepiv	1968	260
199	57 4/8	38 4/8	37 4/8	14 1/8	14	7 6/8	7 5/8	14	11	Stikine River, B.C.	Francis O. N. Morris	Francis O. N. Morris	1968	260
199	51 4/8	44 7/8	44 4/8	17 5/8	15 5/8	7 5/8	7 5/8	17	16	Fox Creek, Alta.	Ken McDonald	Merv Zaddery	1969	260
199	53 4/8	41 3/8	41 4/8	14 1/8	13 3/8	7 6/8	7 6/8	14	9	Trout Lake, B.C.	William R. Lee	William R. Lee	1982	260
198 7/8	56 5/8	41 7/8	43	13 7/8	17	7 5/8	7 3/8	15	11	Hotchkiss, Alta.	R. A. Anderson	R. A. Anderson	1960	260
198 7/8	54 4/8	43	39 3/8	14	13 2/8	8 3/8	8 3/8	12	10	Monkman Pass, B.C.	A. E. Haddrell	A. E. Haddrell	1971	265
198 7/8	54 4/8	42 7/8	37 3/8	13	13 6/8	6 7/8	6 7/8	15	15	Manning, Alta.	Eugene G. McGee	Eugene G. McGee	1975	265
198 7/8	53 3/8	37 7/8	41	15	12	8 3/8	8 3/8	13	13	Coconino Creek, B.C.	Allan C. Endersby	Allan C. Endersby	1980	265
198 6/8	52	41 5/8	40	14	13 1/8	6 6/8	7	14	15	Prophet River, B.C.	T. D. Braden	T. D. Braden	1973	265
198 6/8	53 4/8	40 7/8	39 4/8	13 1/8	17	7 3/8	7 3/8	11	11	Mt. Laurier, B.C.	Don Miller	Don Miller	1985	269
198 5/8	61 3/8	39 7/8	36	12 4/8	13 4/8	7 6/8	7 7/8	12	12	Stoney Lake, B.C.	George Kalischuk	George Kalischuk	1962	269
198 4/8	62 5/8	36 7/8	36 7/8	13 4/8	13	6 5/8	6 6/8	12	15	Serpentine Lake, B.C.	Randolph P. Wilson	Randolph P. Wilson	1976	271
198 3/8	53 4/8	43 3/8	39 4/8	17	18 3/8	7 2/8	7 4/8	8	11	Robb, B.C.	Bernholdt R. Nystrom	Bernholdt R. Nystrom	1973	272
198 3/8	60 5/8	40 3/8	43	10 5/8	12 7/8	7 4/8	7	11	12	Besa River, B.C.	Tommy D. Prance	Tommy D. Prance	1977	273
198 2/8	57 4/8	38	38	12 4/8	12	7 3/8	7 3/8	14	17	Whitecourt, Alta.	Glen Cox	Richard Jensen	1960	273
198 2/8	54 4/8	39 7/8	41 5/8	13 4/8	14	7	7	12	12	Beale Lake, B.C.	John O. Forster	John O. Forster	1963	275
198 2/8	53 4/8	43 5/8	42 4/8	12 4/8	12 5/8	7 1/8	6 7/8	11	11	Prairie River, B.C.	C. J. McElroy	C. J. McElroy	1967	275
198 1/8	59 4/8	36 5/8	41 5/8	17	15 5/8	7 1/8	7 1/8	11	14	Lake Co., Minn.	D. P. & H. Bradley	D. P. & H. Bradley	1973	275
198 1/8	56 5/8	42	42	12 1/8	13 3/8	7 5/8	7 5/8	13	9	Saskatchewan	Neil Oliver	Neil Oliver	1954	275
198 1/8	56 5/8	40	40	12 7/8	11 5/8	7 5/8	7 4/8	10	12	Dore Lake, Sask.	O. Dore	O. Dore	1966	279
198 1/8	63 5/8	40 3/8	34	12 4/8	17	8 5/8	7 6/8	13	15	Chapleau, Ont.	Chester Anderegg	Chester Anderegg	1968	279
198 1/8	58 5/8	34	39	12 4/8	16 5/8	7 2/8	7	13	9	McCloud River, Alta.	Kenneth Campbell	Kenneth Campbell	1971	279
198 1/8	50 5/8	39 5/8	41	15	13 5/8	8 1/8	7 3/8	11	13	Fraser River, B.C.	J. Henry Scown	J. Henry Scown	1973	279
198 1/8	55 5/8	42 4/8	42 5/8	12	13 3/8	7 5/8	7 5/8	14	9	Hluey Lakes, B.C.	Dale Campbell	Dale Campbell	1982	279
198	62 5/8	37 7/8	38 5/8	12 1/8	11 5/8	7	7	9	12	Cold Fish Lake, B.C.	Dan Edwards	Dan Edwards	1961	285

CANADA MOOSE—Continued
Alces alces americana and Alces alces andersoni

Score	Greatest Spread	Length of Palm		Width of Palm		Circumference of Beam at Smallest Place		Number of Normal Points		Locality Killed	By Whom Killed	Owner	Date Killed	Rank
		R	L	R	L	R	L	R	L					
198	57	37	37⅞	13	14⅜	6⅜	6⅜	14	15	Hardwood Lake, Ont.	Weston Cook	Weston Cook	1963	285
198	63⅜	37	36⅝	14¼	15	7	6⅝	10	11	Upper Besa River, B.C.	Lloyd Schoenauer	Lloyd Schoenauer	1977	285
198	56⅜	38⅜	36⅜	15⅞	14⅞	7⅝	7⅝	12	14	Crooked Lake, B.C.	J. W. Cornwall	J. W. Cornwall	1982	285
197⅞	54⅜	39⅞	42⅞	16⅞	17	7⅛	7⅞	11	9	Pink Mt., B.C.	Wallace E. Anderson	Wallace E. Anderson	1963	290
197⅞	55⅞	44⅛	40⅞	11⅞	13⅜	7⅞	7⅝	11	11	Prophet River, B.C.	Paul W. Sharp	Paul W. Sharp	1964	290
197⅞	59⅞	39⅝	40⅛	11⅛	12	7⅞	7⅞	10	11	Pink Mt., B.C.	Robert H. Ruth	Robert H. Ruth	1971	290
197⅞	62⅝	39	39	11⅛	10⅝	8	8⅛	12	10	Swan Plain, Sask.	Gene Petryshyn	Gene Petryshyn	1974	290
197¾	56⅜	40⅞	40⅞	14	15	7⅝	7⅞	9	9	Sikanni Chief River, B.C.	Nicholas M. Esposito	Nicholas M. Esposito	1960	294
197¾	63⅜	38⅞	41⅞	10⅜	10⅜	6⅞	6⅞	12	11	Willow Creek, Alta.	Helmut Vollmer	Helmut Vollmer	1964	294
197¾	52	37⅞	39⅜	14⅜	13⅜	7⅛	7⅛	15	15	Marion Lake, B.C.	Virgil W. Binkley	Virgil W. Binkley	1973	294
197⅝	59⅞	34⅝	36⅞	14⅛	12⅞	7	6⅞	15	16	Pipestone River, Ont.	Howard E. Bennett	Howard E. Bennett	1960	297
197½	56⅞	42⅛	38⅛	13⅛	13⅜	7	7	12	12	Glaslyn, Sask.	Ernest Noble	Ernest Noble	1968	298
197½	51⅛	36⅜	37⅛	16⅜	17⅞	8	8	12	15	Cassiar Mts., B.C.	Russell H. Underdahl	Russell H. Underdahl	1968	298
197½	57⅞	42⅝	41⅛	10⅜	14⅛	7	7	11	15	Telegraph Creek, B.C.	Gordon Best	Gordon Best	1973	298
197½	56⅞	39⅜	39⅜	13⅜	13	7⅜	7⅜	14	11	Atlin, B.C.	John Konrad	John Konrad	1975	298
197½	54⅜	41	42⅞	12⅜	12	7⅛	7⅞	11	13	Dease River, B.C.	Terry Jackson	Terry Jackson	1980	298
197⅜	50⅞	43⅝	41⅛	13⅜	13⅜	7⅛	7⅜	11	11	Kelly Creek, B.C.	Leonard O. Farlow	Leonard O. Farlow	1962	303
197⅜	58⅜	40⅜	41⅛	13⅞	13⅜	8	8	11	8	Sikanni Chief River, B.C.	Leslie Bowling	Leslie Bowling	1964	303
197⅜	48⅜	43⅜	47⅜	13	11⅛	7⅞	7⅞	12	12	Cabin Lake, B.C.	W. Harrison	W. Harrison	1973	303
197⅜	57⅞	41⅜	38⅜	13⅜	16⅛	7⅜	7⅞	11	15	Firth Lake, B.C.	Gordon J. Pengelly	Gordon J. Pengelly	1976	303
197¼	50⅜	39⅜	39⅜	13	13⅜	7⅛	7	14	14	Fleming Lake, Alta.	Peter Holland	Peter Holland	1955	307
197¼	56⅜	37⅜	38⅜	10⅜	12⅜	7⅞	8⅞	14	15	Jackfish Lake, Alta.	Unknown	Ovar Uggen	1962	307
197¼	50⅜	40⅜	43⅜	13	16⅜	7⅞	7⅞	12	15	Terminus Mt., B.C.	Basil C. Bradbury	Basil C. Bradbury	1970	307
197⅛	50	44	43⅞	14⅜	17⅞	7⅞	7⅛	8	8	Liard Plateau, B.C.	George Roberts	George Roberts	1960	310
197⅛	56⅜	40⅜	38⅛	13⅜	13⅜	7⅞	7⅛	11	13	Tisdale, Sask.	Bill Hrechka	Bill Hrechka	1963	310
197	54⅜	38⅛	43⅜	12⅞	15⅜	6⅝	6⅜	13	14	Pink Mt., B.C.	Allison R. Smith	Allison R. Smith	1967	312
197	57⅞	38	38⅛	11⅛	11⅜	7⅜	7⅛	13	13	Cold Fish Lake, B.C.	George W. Hale	George W. Hale	1971	312
197	54⅜	39⅛	39⅜	17⅛	15⅜	7⅛	6⅛	11	10	Brothers Lake, B.C.	William D. Phifer	William D. Phifer	1975	312
196⅞	60⅛	39⅜	37⅞	12⅜	12⅛	7¼	7⅞	11	13	Swan Lake, B.C.	Carl E. Larson	Wild Kingdom Tax.		315
196⅞	58⅞	36⅜	38⅜	13⅜	12⅜	7	7	13	14	Weeks, Sask.	Ken Holloway	Ken Holloway	1961	315

Score	Spread	Width	Len R	Len L	Circ R	Circ L	Pts	Pts	Locality	Owner	By whom killed	Date	Rank
196⅛	54⅛	39⅞	14⅞	13⅞	7⅞	7⅞	11	13	Slave Lake, Alta.	Kathleen Wickersham	Ernest Wickersham	1967	315
196⅛	50⅞	39⅛	20⅛	13⅞	7	7	13	13	Cassiar Mts., B.C.	Larry Herwick	Larry Herwick	1979	315
196⅛	62⅛	43	13⅞	12	7⅞	7⅞	14	10	Pink Mountain, B.C.	Tony J. Farace	Tony J. Farace	1984	315
196⅛	49⅛	44	14⅞	12⅞	6⅞	6⅞	15	11	Hines Creek, Alta.	Harry Kashuba	Harry Kashuba	1959	319
196⅛	57	39⅞	13⅞	14	7⅞	7⅞	9	11	Atlin, B.C.	Dennis Downton	Dennis Downton	1969	319
196⅛	57⅞	38⅞	16⅞	16⅞	7⅞	7⅛	10	12	Wapiti River, Alta.	John J. Seeliger	Jchn J. Seeliger	1985	319
196⅛	58⅛	40⅞	11⅞	15⅞	7⅛	7⅝	13	10	Stoney Lake, B.C.	George Kalischuk	George Kalischuk	1963	322
196⅛	53⅛	43⅞	12	12⅞	7	7⅛	10	11	Atlin, B.C.	Ernest Wilfong	Ernest Wilfong	1965	322
196⅛	53⅛	42⅞	14	13⅞	7⅛	6⅝	11	13	Medicine Lake, Alta.	Stan Reiser	Stan Reiser	1967	322
196⅛	50⅛	40⅞	15⅞	13⅞	8⅛	8⅛	13	11	Cassiar, B.C.	Richard Pain	Richard Pain	1967	322
196⅛	57⅛	39⅞	11⅛	11⅞	7⅛	7⅛	12	11	Telegraph Creek, B.C.	Paul Inzanti, Jr.	Paul Inzanti, Jr.	1969	322
196⅛	62⅛	39⅞	11⅞	11⅞	7	7	11	9	Adsit Creek, B.C.	Loren D. Bliss	Loren D. Bliss	1980	322
196⅛	53⅛	36⅞	16⅞	16⅞	7	7	14	12	Lake Co., Minn.	Brian S. Agnoli	Brian S. Agnoli	1981	329
196⅛	46⅛	37	18⅛	18⅞	8	8	12	13	Belcourt Lake, B.C.	Robert Agnello	Robert Agnello	1965	329
196⅛	50⅛	39⅞	14	14	7⅞	7⅞	13	12	Perrault Falls, Ont.	A. H. Nettleship	A. H. Nettleship	1967	329
196⅛	56⅛	38⅞	12	12⅞	7⅞	7⅞	12	13	Sikanni Chief River, B.C.	W. C. Spencer	W. C. Spencer	1970	329
196⅛	56⅛	39⅞	11⅞	12⅞	7⅛	7⅛	14	12	Kula Tan Tan River, B.C.	Arnold J. Kaslon	Arnold J. Kaslon	1972	329
196⅛	45⅛	42⅞	13⅞	16⅞	7⅛	7⅛	13	13	Pink Mt., B.C.	Gary Bloxham	Gary Bloxham	1973	329
196⅛	53⅛	43⅞	14⅞	14⅞	7⅞	7⅛	11	13	Turnagain River, B.C.	George H. Biddle	George H. Biddle	1973	329
196⅛	60	36⅞	16⅞	17⅞	7⅞	7⅞	9	8	Lake Co., Minn.	Roy H. Anderson	Roy H. Anderson	1977	329
196⅛	59⅛	38⅞	10⅞	11⅞	7⅞	7⅛	12	12	Abitibi Co., Ont.	Pelham Glasier	Pelham Glasier	1951	336
196⅛	52⅛	41⅞	12⅞	12⅞	8⅛	8⅛	11	11	Green Lake, Sask.	Mike Spies	Mike Spies	1959	336
196⅛	58⅛	37⅞	15⅞	14⅞	7⅞	7⅛	10	11	Cassiar Mts., B.C.	E. David Slye	E. David Slye	1967	336
196⅛	55⅛	43	13⅞	12⅞	7	7	10	8	Anguille Mts., Nfld.	Robert D. Smith	Robert D. Smith	1963	339
196⅛	59	39⅞	12⅞	16⅞	6⅞	6⅝	10	10	Jack Pine, Ont.	William Picht	William Picht	1963	339
196⅛	55⅛	39⅞	16⅞	15⅞	7	7⅛	10	10	Cassiar Mts., B.C.	Bryan Upchurch	Bryan Upchurch	1975	339
196⅛	56⅛	35⅞	14	13⅞	7⅛	7⅛	14	13	Aroostook Co., Maine	R. E. Gatchell & C. Dole	Robert E. Gatchell & C. Dole	1982	339
196⅛	55⅛	36⅞	15⅞	16⅞	7⅛	7⅛	11	13	Endeavor, Sask.	G. N. Galbraith	G. N. Galbraith	1955	343
196⅛	55⅛	42⅞	13⅞	13⅞	7⅛	7⅛	10	16	Jack Pine River, Ont.	M. H. Brown	M. H. Brown	1962	343
196⅛	56⅛	38	13⅞	12⅞	6⅞	6⅞	13	14	Atlin, B.C.	Cliff Schmidt	Cliff Schmidt	1966	343
196⅛	49⅛	42⅞	11⅞	11⅞	7⅛	7	13	13	Atlin, B.C.	H. J. Schwegler	H. J. Schwegler	1967	343
196⅛	52⅛	41⅞	15⅞	14⅞	7⅞	7⅛	12	12	Frog River, B.C.	Robert McMurray	Robert McMurray	1968	343
196⅛	51⅛	38⅞	14⅞	12⅞	7⅞	7⅛	15	16	Ft. St. John, B.C.	Kanton R. Flemming	Kanton R. Flemming	1975	343
196⅛	51⅛	41⅞	12⅞	12⅞	8⅛	8⅛	13	11	Penobscot Co., Maine	Richard A. Record	Richard A. Record	1982	343
196	56⅛	38⅞	13⅞	14⅞	8	7⅝	11	13	Pelican River, Alta.	Douglas A. Stoller	Douglas A. Stoller	1982	350
196	54⅛	43⅞	10⅞	12⅞	7	7	13	14	Tatuk Lake, B.C.	Erling E. Gull	Erling E. Gull	1971	350
196	53⅛	39⅞	13⅞	15⅞	6⅞	6⅝	12	12	Wollaston Lake, Sask.	Daryl V. Johannesen	Daryl V. Johannesen	1980	350
195⅞	56⅞	40⅞	12⅞	13⅞	7⅛	7⅛	13	12	Cassiar, B.C.	Donald F. Conway	Donald F. Conway	1982	353
195⅞	54⅛	37	14	13⅞	7⅛	7⅛	12	13	Sheep Creek, Alta.	S. J. Blaupot Ten Cate	S. J. Blaupot Ten Cate	1965	353
195⅞	56	38	11⅞	11⅞	8⅛	8⅛	15	13	Prophet River, B.C.	Earl Mumaw	Earl Mumaw	1966	355
195⅞	53⅛	38⅞	12⅞	13⅞	7⅞	7⅛	12	14	Hudson Bay, Sask.	Charles Hamilton	Charles Hamilton	1957	355
195⅞	59	44	13⅞	13⅞	7	7⅛	10	14	Smoky River, Alta.	Ken G. Johnson	Ken G. Johnson	1964	355
195⅞	59	44	13⅞	13⅞	7	7⅛	10	14				1966	355

CANADA MOOSE—Continued

Alces alces americana and Alces alces andersoni

Score	Greatest Spread	Length of Palm R	L	Width of Palm R	L	Circumference of Beam at Smallest Place R	L	Number of Normal Points R	L	Locality Killed	By Whom Killed	Owner	Date Killed	Rank
195⅞	56⅝	42⅞	39⅞	12⅞	12	7⅞	7⅞	11	12	Ft. St. John, B.C.	Louis M. Soetebeer	Louis M. Soetebeer	1969	355
195⅞	58	37⅞	37⅞	15⅛	15	7¼	7¼	9	13	Pasqua Hills, Sask.	Henry Dyck	Henry Dyck	1955	359
195⅞	65⅜	39	40⅜	11⅜	10	7⅛	7⅞	9	9	Sheep Creek, Alta.	H. C. Early	H. C. Early	1957	359
195⅞	57⅜	38⅜	39⅜	12⅜	13⅜	8	7⅞	11	10	Blanchard River, B.C.	William E. Lauffer	William E. Lauffer	1969	359
195⅞	61	37⅝	36⅜	13⅞	13⅜	7⅞	7⅞	10	13	Whitecourt, Alta.	John E. Esslinger	John E. Esslinger	1971	359
195⅞	54⅜	38⅜	39⅜	13⅜	13⅝	8⅛	8	13	10	Stikine River, B.C.	Manfred Beier	Manfred Beier	1976	359
195⅞	57⅜	37⅜	40⅜	11⅜	16	7⅜	7⅜	13	13	Somerset Co., Maine	Frank White	Frank White	1983	359
195⅜	55⅜	41¼	41⅞	14⅛	12⅝	6⅝	6⅞	9	9	Turnagain Lake, B.C.	Fenton C. Carter	Fenton C. Carter	1985	366
195⅜	57⅜	38⅞	39⅜	12⅜	12⅞	7⅜	7⅜	10	10	Atlin, B.C.	Jerome A. Ree	Jerome A. Ree	1965	366
195⅜	63⅜	36⅞	37⅛	14⅜	13⅝	7¼	7⅜	9	9	Trembleur Lake, B.C.	Harry McCarter	Harry McCarter	1965	366
195⅜	52⅝	39⅝	38⅜	13	12⅝	6⅞	7	13	14	Prophet River, B.C.	Ronald B. Sorensen	Ronald B. Sorensen	1967	366
195⅜	54⅜	38⅝	40⅛	12⅝	12⅞	7⅞	7⅞	12	12	Kechika Mts., B.C.	Frank S. Kohar	Frank S. Kohar	1968	366
195⅜	55⅜	39⅜	43⅜	15	13⅜	6⅞	7	10	13	Chip Lake, Alta.	Elon Johnson	Elon Johnson	1984	371
195⅜	60	39⅜	39⅜	12⅞	11⅛	7⅜	7⅜	10	13	Atlin, B.C.	Wilbert Hoffman	Wildlife Tax. Studios	1966	371
195⅜	57⅜	39⅞	42⅞	12⅞	13⅝	7⅛	7⅝	9	11	British Columbia	Len Anderson	Len Anderson	1967	371
195⅜	60	33⅝	39⅜	14⅜	19⅝	7⅜	7⅜	12	15	Ignace, Ont.	Ervey W. Smith	Ervey W. Smith	1969	371
195⅜	56⅜	41⅞	40	10⅜	13	7⅛	7⅜	12	14	Blanchard River, B.C.	Pat Archibald	Pat Archibald	1969	371
195⅜	59⅝	38⅜	40	14⅜	14⅜	8⅜	8⅛	7	13	Lake Nipigon, B.C.	Danny E. Breivogel	Danny E. Breivogel	1974	371
195⅜	52	39⅜	41⅜	13⅜	13⅜	7⅜	7⅜	11	15	Ospika River, B.C.	John L. Fullmer	John L. Fullmer	1977	371
195⅜	54	37⅜	39	13	14⅜	7⅛	7⅜	13	13	Turnagain River, B.C.	Donald E. Franklin	Donald E. Franklin	1977	371
195⅜	54⅜	35	42	15⅜	15⅜	7⅛	7⅜	13	17	Piscataquis Co., Maine	W. H. Gagnon, Jr.	W. H. Gagnon, Jr. & R. R. Gagnon	1980	371
195⅜	57⅜	41⅞	42	12	12⅜	7⅜	7⅞	8	8	Nuthinaw Mt., B.C.	Robert S. Curtis	Robert S. Curtis	1984	371
195⅜	55⅜	40	42⅜	13	12⅜	7⅛	7⅜	10	14	Berland River, Alta.	W. C. Kadatz	W. C. Kadatz	1962	380
195⅜	55⅜	39⅜	39⅛	11⅜	11⅜	8⅛	7⅝	12	11	Hudson Bay, Sask.	Walter Sukkau	Walter Sukkau	1964	380
195⅜	56⅜	38⅜	39⅛	13⅜	14⅜	7	6⅞	10	11	British Columbia	Charles Waugaman	Charles Waugaman	1969	380
195⅜	56⅜	36	36⅜	15⅜	16	7⅛	7⅛	11	14	Muskwa River, B.C.	Buck Heide	Buck Heide	1979	380
195⅜	61⅜	39	34⅜	14⅛	15⅛	6⅝	5⅞	13	14	Terminus Mt., B.C.	Modesta S. Williams	Modesta S. Williams	1982	380
195⅜	58⅞	38⅜	38⅜	11⅜	12⅜	7⅜	7⅜	11	11	Ash Mt., B.C.	H. Frank Grainger	H. Frank Grainger	1984	380
195	57⅜	34⅜	38⅜	14⅜	14	7⅜	7⅞	15	13	Little Codroy Pond, Nfld.	J. Russell Allison	J. Russell Allison	1957	386

Score										Locality	Hunter	Owner	Date	
195	57⅝	37⅛	38⅜	11⅞	12⅞	6⅜	6⅝	14	13	Turner Valley, Alta.	Bart Rockwell	Bart Rockwell	1958	386
195	52	41⅛	40	14	15⅞	7⅛	8	13	10	Houston, B.C.	R. Starnes	R. Starnes	1966	386
195	58	37⅝	42⅛	13⅛	12⅞	7⅞	7⅞	13	11	Pontiac Co., Que.	Roger Cashdollar	Roger Cashdollar	1966	386
195	54⅜	38	37⅞	15	14⅞	7⅜	7⅛	11	11	Piscataquis Co., Maine	Keith B. Gould	Keith B. Gould	1980	386
195	54⅛	39	38⅜	14	14⅞	7⅛	7⅜	11	11	Lake Co., Minn.	Lewis N. Hostrawser	Lewis N. Hostrawser	1981	386
195	61⅜	37⅛	36⅜	16⅞	14⅞	8	7⅞	10	8	Aroostook Co., Maine	Sterling W. Waterman	Sterling W. Waterman	1982	386
195	53⅜	40⅛	40	12⅞	13⅞	7⅞	7⅞	11	11	Piscatiquis Co., Maine	Lester Whitten	Cecile D. Therrien	1982	386
229⅝*	66⅜	45⅜	45⅜	14⅛	16	8½	8⅜	13	15	Muncho Lake, B.C.	Roger J. Ahern	Roger J. Ahern	1977	
225⅝*	62⅝	44⅞	42⅛	18⅞	17⅝	7⅞	7⅞	15	16	Halfway River, B.C.	Richard Petersen	Richard Petersen	1977	
224⅝*	65⅜	45⅛	48	13⅝	13⅜	7⅜	7⅞	15	14	Birch River, Sask.	Olaus R. Coffron	Olaus R. Coffron	1970	
222*	62	51⅛	47⅞	15⅜	12⅞	8	7⅞	15	12	Duck Mtn. Prov. Park, Man.	Ray Wiebe	Ray Wiebe	1976	
221⅛*	63⅜	47⅛	45⅞	13⅜	13⅞	8½	8⅜	13	12	Goat Creek, B.C.	Roland Wilz	Roland Wilz	1971	
219⅜*	59⅜	43⅞	46⅜	17⅜	21	7⅜	7⅜	11	13	Muskwa River, B.C.	Sandra D. Vince	Sandra D. Vince	1978	
219⅛*	65⅜	41	40⅛	13	13⅜	7⅜	7⅜	18	16	Carrot River, Sask.	Stewart Hilliar	James Hilliar	1984	
209⅜*	64⅜	39⅛	44	12	13⅜	7	7⅞	14	14	Oba Lake, Ont.	Bruce McPherson	Bruce McPherson	1963	

*Final Score subject to revision by additional verifying measurements

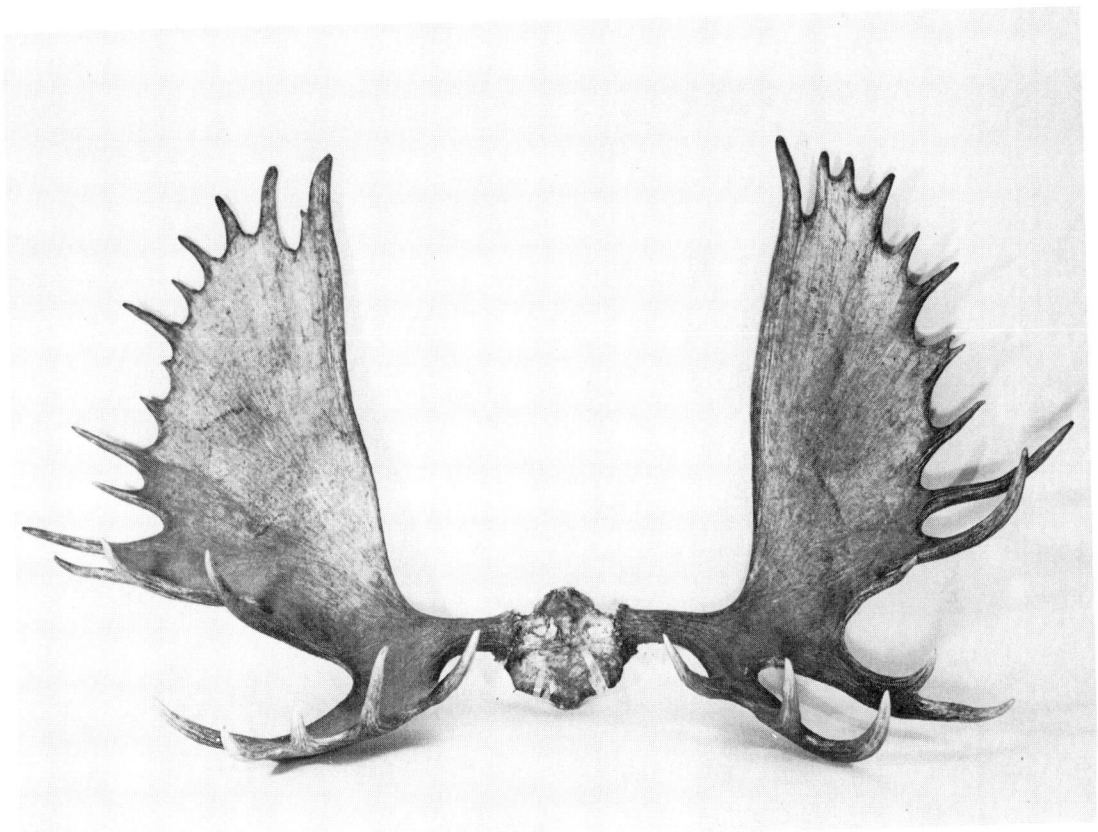

WORLD'S RECORD ALASKA-YUKON MOOSE
SCORE: 255

Locality: McGrath, Alaska Date: 1978
Hunter and owner: Kenneth Best

Photograph by Alex Rota

NUMBER TWO ALASKA-YUKON MOOSE
SCORE: 251
Locality: Mount Susitna, Alaska Date: 1961
Hunter and owner: Bert Klineburger

Alaska-Yukon Moose

Alces alces gigas

Minimum Score 224

Alaska-Yukon moose includes trophies from Alaska, the Yukon Territory, and the Northwest Territories.

Score	Greatest Spread	Length of Palm R.	L.	Width of Palm R.	L.	Circumference of Beam at Smallest Place R.	L.	Number of Normal Points R.	L.	Locality Killed	By Whom Killed	Owner	Date Killed	Rank
255	77	49⅝	49⅝	20⅝	15⅝	7⅞	7⅞	18	16	McGrath, Alaska	Kenneth Best	Kenneth Best	1978	1
251	77⅝	46½	51	17	19⅞	7⅞	8⅛	18	17	Mt. Susitna, Alaska	Bert Klineburger	Bert Klineburger	1961	2
250⅜	65⅜	55⅞	49⅞	21⅛	20	8⅜	8⅜	18	16	Kenai Pen., Alaska	Dyton A. Gilliland	National Collection	1947	3
249⅞	67	47⅞	48⅞	22⅛	21⅛	7⅜	7⅜	15	15	Mother Goose Lake, Alaska	Josef Welle	Josef Welle	1967	4
249⅞	72	48½	49⅝	19⅞	17	8⅛	8⅛	15	16	Alaska Range, Alaska	Henry S. Budney	Henry S. Budney	1967	5
249⅛	69⅝	46	43⅜	21⅞	22	8⅜	8⅜	22	17	Granite Mt., Alaska	David B. Parent	Earl D. Hahn	1982	6
248⅞	73⅛	47⅜	47⅛	20	19⅞	7⅞	7⅞	14	19	Farewell Lake, Alaska	Loren G. Hammer	Loren G. Hammer	1967	7
248⅞	68⅞	54⅜	46⅝	19⅞	19⅞	7⅞	8	17	16	Kenai Pen., Alaska	Bill Foster	Foster's Bighorn Rest.	1912	8
248⅛	77⅝	47⅜	48⅜	18⅜	18⅞	8⅜	8⅜	13	16	Mulchatna River, Alaska	Bruce B. Hodson	Bruce B. Hodson	1970	9
248⅛	79⅝	45⅞	46⅛	22⅛	22⅞	9	8⅞	10	7	Iliamna Lake, Alaska	Gale L. Galloway	Gale L. Galloway	1970	10
247⅞	66⅜	48	48	18⅜	19	7⅞	7⅞	17	16	Mackenzie Mts., N.W.T.	Harry Rogers	Harry Rogers	1978	11
247⅞	75	50	46⅝	17⅞	21⅛	7⅜	8⅛	15	18	Kenai Pen., Alaska	A. S. Reed	B&C National Collection	1900	12
247	77⅝	48⅞	48⅛	16	17⅞	7⅜	7⅞	13	15	Melozitna River, Alaska	Elmer Raphael	Elmer Raphael	1978	13
246⅞	67⅜	44⅝	49⅝	22⅞	20⅜	10⅜	9⅜	19	16	Kenai Pen., Alaska	Henry Hope	Henry Hope	1957	14
246⅜	75⅜	48	46⅝	18⅝	19⅝	8⅜	8⅝	12	16	Alaska Range, Alaska	Ralph Davies	Ralph Davies	1970	15
246⅛	72⅝	46⅜	46⅜	17	17⅞	7⅜	7⅜	16	17	Wrangell Mts., Alaska	Philip S. Davidson	Philip S. Davidson	1970	16
245⅞	67⅞	51⅞	49⅛	20	18⅜	8⅝	8⅝	13	14	Talkeetna Mts., Alaska	W. H. Moore	W. H. Moore	1953	17
244⅞	72⅝	48⅝	47⅞	19⅞	19⅞	8⅛	8⅜	12	12	Long Lake, Alaska	William F. Rae, Jr.	William F. Rae, Jr.	1973	18
244⅜	72⅜	48⅜	48⅜	14⅝	17⅞	7⅜	7⅜	16	17	Mayo, Yukon	Carl Straub	Carl Straub	1971	19
243⅞	71⅞	49⅝	50⅝	15⅝	21⅛	8⅛	7⅜	17	14	Wrangell Mts., Alaska	John Ringstad	Loren St. Amand	1977	19
243⅜	69⅝	47⅞	50⅝	19⅝	20⅜	7⅞	7⅜	15	12	Kenai Pen., Alaska	D. Thompson & F. Walunga	Denny Thompson	1958	21
242⅞	63⅞	51½	50⅝	16⅞	16⅞	8	7⅞	16	15	Alaska	Unknown	Jonas Bros. Of Seattle	1954	22
242⅜	69⅞	46½	49⅞	15⅞	15⅞	8⅞	8⅞	16	17	Upper Susitna, Alaska	Helen S. Rusten	Carnegie Museum	1948	23
242⅛	78⅜	44⅞	44	19⅞	21⅞	8⅛	8⅜	11	11	Alaska Pen., Alaska	H. S. Kamil	H. S. Kamil	1963	24
242	73⅞	48⅞	45⅞	19⅞	19⅞	8	7⅞	15	11	Homer, Alaska	Dan Jones	Dan Jones	1957	25
242	68	48⅝	49⅝	19⅞	19⅞	7⅝	7⅜	14	16	Grass Lakes, Yukon	Melvin R. Spohn	Melvin R. Spohn	1981	25
241⅞	72⅞	48⅜	48⅜	16⅞	16	8⅝	9	12	16	Neresna, Alaska	Lorene Ellis	Lorene Ellis	1962	27
241⅛	67⅝	46⅝	46⅞	19⅛	16⅝	8⅜	8	16	16	Dawson City, Yukon	Ray C. Dillman	Ray C. Dillman	1971	27
241⅛	76⅜	47	47⅞	16⅜	15⅜	8	8⅜	14	12	King Salmon, Alaska	O. O. Parker & B. Bradley	O. O. Parker & B. Bradley	1960	29

308

Score	Spread	Palm Len. R	Palm Len. L	Palm Wid. R	Palm Wid. L	Circ. R	Circ. L	Pts. R	Pts. L	Locality	Hunter	Owner	Date	Rank
240⅞	71⅛	43⅞	51⅜	21⅞	20⅞	9	8⅞	15	11	___ Bay, Alaska	Glenn B. Walker	Glenn B. Walker	1958	30
240⅞	64⅞	48⅞	42⅜	17⅞	20⅛	8⅛	8⅛	21	21	Ugashik Lake, Alaska	Gene Buckles	Gene Buckles	1973	31
240⅛	66⅞	49⅞	47⅜	15⅞	18⅛	7⅞	7⅞	16	21	Noatak River, Alaska	Jake & Mae Jacobson	Jake & Mae Jacobson	1974	32
240	62⅞	48⅞	49⅜	16⅜	21	7⅞	8⅜	16	17	Wrangell Mts., Alaska	Forest Bigelow	Forest Bigelow	1973	33
239⅞	66⅞	47⅞	46⅜	17⅞	21⅛	8⅜	8⅛	14	18	Beluga Mt., Alaska	Walter Renz	Walter Renz	1976	34
239⅞	75⅞	44⅞	43⅜	21⅞	19⅛	7⅞	7⅞	12	16	Rainy Pass, Alaska	Mrs. J. Watson Webb	Mrs. J. Watson Webb	1935	35
239⅞	70	52⅞	47⅞	14⅞	21⅝	8⅞	8⅝	15	18	Mayo, Yukon	Dave Moses	Yukon Hist. Society	1950	35
239⅞	75⅞	42	45⅝	20⅛	19	8	8⅝	13	14	Alaska Range, Alaska	James E. Egger	James E. Egger	1965	35
239⅞	62⅞	53⅞	56	16⅛	20⅛	8⅜	7⅞	11	16	Gold King, Alaska	Billy Joe Morris	Billy Joe Morris	1971	38
239⅞	74	44⅞	45⅜	17⅜	15⅛	9⅜	8⅞	14	10	Alaska Pen., Alaska	Lars Degefors	Lars Degefors	1967	39
239⅞	74	44⅞	45⅜	17⅜	15⅛	9⅜	9⅜	14	14	Bonnet Plume Range, Yukon	Tafford E. Oltz	Tafford E. Oltz	1978	39
239⅛	65⅝	47⅞	47⅜	20⅞	14⅞	7⅞	7⅞	18	17	Alaska Pen., Alaska	J. Paul Dittrich	J. Paul Dittrich	1962	41
239⅛	67	45⅛	45⅜	15	14⅞	12⅛	12⅛	14	14	Baluga Lake, Alaska	Peter W. Bading	Peter W. Bading	1961	42
239⅛	74	51⅜	50⅜	13⅞	15	8⅜	8⅜	10	13	Alaska Pen., Alaska	George J. Markham	George J. Markham	1967	42
239⅛	73⅜	49⅜	52⅜	14	16⅞	8⅜	8⅜	12	15	Ugashik, Alaska	Alois A. Mauracher	Alois A. Mauracher	1973	42
239	67	46⅛	48⅜	18⅜	16⅜	8⅜	8⅜	15	15	Mackenzie Mts., N.W.T.	Burl A. Jones	Burl A. Jones	1973	45
238⅞	71⅛	44	48	19⅜	17⅞	9⅜	9⅜	14	14	Lake Clark, Alaska	Frits Kielman	Frits Kielman	1973	46
238⅞	72⅞	46⅜	45⅜	18	22⅛	8⅛	8⅛	11	13	Alaska Range, Alaska	Jeff Sievers	Jeff Sievers	1963	47
238⅞	63⅞	44	45⅜	19⅞	20⅛	8⅜	8⅜	16	17	Anvil Range, Yukon	James F. Byers	James F. Byers	1977	47
238⅞	74⅛	43⅜	47	21⅞	25	8⅜	8⅜	9	16	Iliamna, Alaska	Joseph C. Anzalone	Joseph C. Anzalone	1972	49
238	69	48⅜	44⅜	16	17⅞	9	9	11	15	Copper River, Alaska	Howard E. Thilenius II	Howard E. Thilenius II	1973	50
238	70⅝	45⅜	42⅜	19⅜	16⅛	7⅞	7⅞	15	15	Mulchatna River, Alaska	Gary A. Smith	Gary A. Smith	1974	50
237⅞	71⅛	46	48⅜	18⅜	18⅜	8⅝	8⅜	11	13	Dog Salmon River, Alaska	Peter Von Kap-Herr	Peter Von Kap-Herr	1971	52
237⅞	67⅛	49⅛	47⅞	18⅜	18⅛	8	8	17	12	Kenai Pen., Alaska	Leslie Maff	Temple Bros.	PR 1958	53
237	69⅝	46⅜	47⅝	15⅜	15⅝	8⅜	8⅜	13	15	Talkeetna Mts., Alaska	Merle C. LaFortune	Merle C. LaFortune	1970	54
236⅞	67⅞	48⅜	46⅜	15⅞	15⅞	9	9	14	14	Talkeetna Mts., Alaska	Mario Pasquel	Mario Pasquel	1961	55
236⅞	68⅛	42⅜	48⅜	18⅞	18⅞	8⅜	8⅜	15	13	Baluga Mt., Alaska	Albert W. Erickson	Albert W. Erickson	1961	55
236⅞	67⅝	45⅜	43	14⅜	14⅜	8	8⅜	13	15	Koyukuk River, Alaska	Harry B. Markoskie	Harry B. Markoskie	1969	55
236⅞	62⅞	46⅜	46⅝	22	21⅛	7⅞	7⅞	14	13	Kiana Lake, Alaska	Lane H. Drury	Lane H. Drury	1977	55
236⅞	68⅛	44⅜	49⅜	22⅜	21⅛	8⅜	8⅜	14	13	Wood River, Alaska	Ronald Long	Ronald Long	1963	59
236⅞	70⅝	46⅛	45⅜	16⅜	17⅞	7⅞	7⅞	14	18	Lake Clark, Alaska	Gordon F. Wentzel	Gordon F. Wentzel	1973	59
236⅞	68⅛	46⅜	52⅜	16⅜	17⅛	8⅛	8⅝	14	16	Brusha Kama River, Alaska	Robert Harnish	Robert Harnish	1953	61
236⅛	72	47	41⅛	16⅜	18⅛	8⅛	8⅛	16	17	Upper Kiana Lake, Alaska	Marvin Henriksen	Marvin Henriksen	1964	61
236⅛	66⅞	44⅜	43⅜	16⅜	18⅛	7⅜	8⅛	17	20	Birch Creek, Alaska	D. T. Sharp	D. T. Sharp	1962	63
236⅛	70⅞	47⅞	48	14⅜	15⅜	7⅞	7⅞	14	13	Black Lake, Alaska	Robert B. Ryan	Robert B. Ryan	1969	63
236⅛	68⅞	50	49⅜	16⅞	17⅜	8⅜	8⅞	13	9	Alaska Range, Alaska	Dennis R. Johnson	Dennis R. Johnson	1980	63
235⅞	73⅝	50⅝	46⅜	16⅞	17⅜	8⅛	8⅛	10	10	Dog Salmon River, Alaska	Gary R. Swanson	Gary R. Swanson	1966	66
235⅞	69⅜	50	50⅜	17⅜	15⅝	7⅞	8⅛	11	10	Farewell Lake, Alaska	Wilhelm H. Koehler	Wilhelm H. Koehler	1974	66
235⅞	74	44⅜	46⅜	15⅞	16⅛	8⅛	8⅜	13	13	Alaska	Frank Alexander	Univ. of Alaska	1952	68
235⅞	65⅝	46⅜	51⅜	20⅜	21⅞	9⅜	9⅜	13	10	Kenai Pen., Alaska	J. D. Rasmusson	J. D. Rasmusson	1959	68
235⅞	71⅛	50⅝	50⅜	14⅛	14⅜	8⅜	8⅜	9	10	Rainy Pass, Alaska	Ralph Vogel	Ralph Vogel	1956	70
235⅞	66⅝	51⅜	49	17⅞	16⅜	7⅞	7⅞	12	12	Post Lake, Alaska	Charles Bradley	Charles Bradley	1978	70

ALASKA-YUKON MOOSE—Continued

Alces alces gigas

Score	Greatest Spread	Length of Palm R.	L.	Width of Palm R.	L.	Circumference of Beam at Smallest Place R.	L.	Number of Normal Points R.	L.	Locality Killed	By Whom Killed	Owner	Date Killed	Rank
235	71	47	45	14	15⅝	8	8⅜	15	16	Alaska Pen., Alaska	Otis Chandler	Otis Chandler	1964	72
235	74	45⅞	45½	15⅜	14⅜	8	8	15	13	Yellow River, Alaska	Peter Apokedak	Peter Apokedak	1966	72
235	71	47	46	16	17	8	8	12	14	Kateel River, Alaska	Ronald S. Peterson	Ronald S. Peterson	1976	72
234⅞	74⅜	50⅜	49⅜	16⅞	16⅜	8⅛	7⅞	12	8	Hewitt Lake, Alaska	W. L. Braun	W. L. Braun	1951	75
234⅞	62⅜	48⅜	45⅜	16⅜	17⅛	8⅜	8⅜	18	16	Mayo Landing, Yukon	Edwin Edger	J. H. McEvoy	1962	76
234⅞	70⅜	43	42⅜	18⅜	17⅜	7⅜	7⅞	14	16	Alaska Pen., Alaska	Herb Klein	Herb Klein	1967	76
234⅞	66⅜	47⅛	44⅜	17⅜	16⅜	7⅜	7⅞	16	15	Alaska	L. M. Hanson	L. M. Hanson	1969	76
234⅞	69	47⅛	48	18⅛	17⅜	8	8⅛	11	12	Alaska Pen., Alaska	Robert P. Bliss	Robert P. Bliss	1969	76
234⅞	71⅜	47⅜	49⅜	14⅜	15⅜	8⅜	8⅜	11	11	Council, Alaska	Arden L. Peterson	Arden L. Peterson	1979	76
234⅜	58	47⅜	51⅜	16⅜	16⅜	8⅜	8⅜	15	11	Alaska Range, Alaska	Wakon Iron Redbird	Wakon Iron Redbird	1969	81
234⅜	71⅜	45⅜	44⅜	16⅜	15⅜	7⅜	7⅜	14	15	Forty Mile River, Alaska	Orval R. Evans	Orval R. Evans	1973	81
234⅜	70⅜	45⅜	46⅛	17⅜	17⅜	8⅛	8	12	11	Koyukuk River, Alaska	Oren Johnson	Oren Johnson	1975	81
234⅜	71⅜	41⅜	43⅜	19⅜	18⅜	7⅜	7⅜	16	14	Galena, Alaska	Michael J. Stowell	Michael J. Stowell	1977	84
234⅜	68⅜	46⅜	43⅜	18	17⅜	8	8⅛	14	14	Ugashik Lake, Alaska	Richard C. Rubin	Richard C. Rubin	1968	85
234	75⅜	49⅜	48⅜	12⅜	14⅜	7⅜	8	10	11	King Salmon, Alaska	Larry R. Price	Larry R. Price	1971	85
234	71⅜	43⅜	41	17⅜	16⅜	7⅜	7⅜	17	16	Kenai Pen., Alaska	A. S. Reed	National Collection	1900	87
233⅞	76	42⅜	50⅜	20⅜	19⅜	7⅜	8	10	12	Kenai Pen., Alaska	Otto Rohm	Otto Rohm	1964	87
233⅞	63	50⅜	49⅜	20⅜	15⅜	8	7⅜	13	14	Wrangell Mts., Alaska	Dan L. Quen	Dan L. Quen	1965	87
233⅞	77⅜	41	44⅜	14⅜	18⅜	8	7⅜	15	18	Kenai Pen., Alaska	Picked Up	Am. Mus. Nat. History	1938	90
233⅞	65⅜	46⅜	45⅜	18	20⅜	7⅜	7⅜	15	13	Alaska Pen., Alaska	J. S. Parker	J. S. Parker	1968	90
233⅞	71⅜	45⅜	50	15⅜	18⅜	8⅜	8⅜	14	17	Iliamna Lake, Alaska	Wayne Rattray	Wayne Rattray	1972	90
233⅞	71⅜	46⅜	48⅜	18⅜	16⅜	8	8	11	13	McGrath, Alaska	Art Beattie	Linda Beattie	1978	90
233⅞	74⅜	43⅜	42⅜	16⅜	16⅜	7⅜	7⅜	13	17	Kenai Pen., Alaska	Gift of C. H. Mackay	National Collection	PR1939	94
233	69	48⅜	47⅜	16⅜	13⅜	8⅛	8	14	14	Merrill Pass, Alaska	Andrew F. Bjorge	Andrew F. Bjorge	1963	95
233	73⅜	49⅜	46⅜	15⅜	14⅜	7⅜	7⅜	11	12	Dillinger River, Alaska	James N. McHolme	James N. McHolme	1976	95
232⅞	65⅜	46⅜	42⅜	15⅜	18⅜	7⅜	7⅜	17	17	Port Heiden, Alaska	Don C. Killom	Don C. Killom	1965	97
232⅞	75	45⅜	44⅜	19⅜	17⅜	8⅜	8⅜	10	9	Port Heiden, Alaska	Gerald L. Lavenstein	Gerald L. Lavenstein	1967	97
232⅞	65⅜	43⅜	45⅜	18⅜	18⅜	8⅜	8⅜	15	14	Swede Lake, Alaska	Paul Bierdeman	Paul Bierdeman	1956	99
232⅞	70⅜	46⅜	47⅜	18⅜	15⅜	7⅜	7⅜	12	12	Ugashik Lake, Alaska	Jack A. Shane, Sr.	Jack A. Shane, Sr.	1967	99
232⅞	69⅜	45	45	18⅜	17⅜	6⅜	6⅜	13	12	Talkeetna, Alaska	Ole Dahl	Boston Mus. Of Science	1950	101
232⅞	67⅜	47⅜	48⅜	15⅜	17⅜	7⅜	8	12	15	Stewart River, Yukon	Patrick Seaman	Patrick Seaman	1968	101
232⅞	68	45⅜	46⅜	17⅜	17⅜	7⅜	8⅜	12	12	Teklanika River, Alaska	Richard O. Cook	Richard O. Cook	1976	101

[illegible]	71	45	[illegible]	[illegible]	17	[illegible]	[illegible]	14	12	Alaska Pen., Alaska	Stewart G. Richards	Stewart G. Richards	1968	104
232	66 6/8	47 3/8	50 7/8	17 4/8	18 3/8	7 6/8	7 7/8	10	11	Alaska Pen., Alaska	A. R. Buckles	A. R. Buckles	1967	105
232	63	55	55 3/8	14	14 5/8	7 4/8	7 4/8	8	9	Alaska Pen., Alaska	L. W. Bailey, Jr.	L. W. Bailey, Jr.	1969	105
231 7/8	63 1/8	50 6/8	49 7/8	12	12 2/8	8 4/8	8 4/8	15	14	Talkeetna Mts., Alaska	T. A. Miller	T. A. Miller	1959	107
231 6/8	76	44 6/8	44 5/8	12 6/8	15 4/8	8 4/8	8 4/8	12	14	Kenai Pen., Alaska	Gift of C. H. Mackay	National Collection	PR1939	108
231 6/8	64 2/8	45 2/8	51 4/8	16 2/8	18	8 2/8	9	14	15	Lake Louise, Alaska	Paul Kunning	Paul Kunning	1966	108
231 5/8	73 1/8	48 6/8	44 4/8	17	15 4/8	7 6/8	7 7/8	12	16	Alaska Range, Alaska	Cecil M. Hopper	Cecil M. Hopper	1969	110
231 4/8	67 4/8	42 4/8	45 5/8	20 6/8	26 4/8	9 4/8	8 6/8	10	12	Alaska Pen., Alaska	George H. Landreth	George H. Landreth	1967	111
231 4/8	69 2/8	43 1/8	46 2/8	17	16 5/8	6 7/8	7 1/8	18	15	Steese Hwy., Alaska	Denver Perry	Denver Perry	1968	111
231 4/8	62 6/8	44	44 7/8	17 2/8	16 7/8	7 5/8	7 4/8	16	17	Alaska Range, Alaska	Peter J. Cassinelli	Peter J. Cassinelli	1977	111
231 2/8	67	47 1/8	47 3/8	16 2/8	16	8	8	13	11	Brooks Range, Alaska	Lezlie D. Fickes	Lezlie D. Fickes	1972	114
231 1/8	66 5/8	49 3/8	49 6/8	15 4/8	14 1/8	7 6/8	7 6/8	12	11	Alaska Pen., Alaska	Frank N. Rome	Frank N. Rome	1976	115
231	67 6/8	42 7/8	45 5/8	18 1/8	17 4/8	7 2/8	7 3/8	14	17	Tazlina Glacier, Alaska	Stanley B. Hoagland	Stanley B. Hoagland	1963	116
231	67 2/8	45 6/8	46 3/8	17 3/8	19	7 6/8	8 1/8	11	12	Amber Bay, Alaska	Charles E. Guess	Charles E. Guess	1974	116
230 6/8	67 6/8	48 6/8	46 6/8	16 2/8	17 6/8	7 4/8	7 4/8	11	13	Petersville, Alaska	Johnny Lamb	Johnny Lamb	1969	118
230 6/8	67 4/8	53 5/8	52 6/8	13 1/8	14 2/8	7 7/8	7 6/8	9	8	Innoko River, Alaska	Leslie R. Hunter	Leslie R. Hunter	1983	118
230 5/8	68 7/8	54 4/8	53 2/8	15	14 5/8	9	8 4/8	6	6	Cordova, Alaska	John B. Pecel	John B. Pecel	1969	120
230 5/8	65 5/8	47 4/8	47	16 2/8	16 2/8	7 2/8	7 2/8	12	12	Port Heiden, Alaska	Brent Greenburg	Brent Greenburg	1972	120
230 5/8	71 5/8	43 4/8	44 2/8	17	14 6/8	7 3/8	7 2/8	22	14	Bonnet Plume Lake, Yukon	Walter P. Griffin	Walter P. Griffin	1978	120
230 5/8	64 1/8	46 7/8	48 2/8	15 3/8	16 4/8	8	8 2/8	13	14	Alaska Pen., Alaska	Lucky Christoph	Carl V. Christoph	1981	120
230 3/8	69 1/8	49	47 1/8	15 1/8	18 3/8	8 3/8	8 5/8	10	15	Alaska Pen., Alaska	James H. Lieffers	James H. Lieffers	1963	124
230 2/8	66 4/8	45 1/8	47	15 6/8	16	8	8 2/8	14	15	Chelatna Lake, Alaska	G. O. Wiegner	G. O. Wiegner	1969	125
230 2/8	81 4/8	40 1/8	39 5/8	18 7/8	17	7 6/8	8	13	11	Iliamna Lake, Alaska	Peter Zipperle	Peter Zipperle	1972	125
230 2/8	70 2/8	46 5/8	46 2/8	17 1/8	17 2/8	8 1/8	8 3/8	9	11	Alaska Range, Alaska	Earl R. Hossman	C. Coldren	1975	125
230 1/8	65 3/8	45 7/8	47 4/8	18 5/8	25	8	7 7/8	10	12	Alaska Pen., Alaska	Walter Pfisterer	Walter Pfisterer	1960	128
230	70 4/8	43 5/8	45	18 7/8	19 7/8	7 3/8	7 2/8	14	10	Port Heiden, Alaska	Norman Garwood	Norman Garwood	1964	129
230	73	44 2/8	44 3/8	14 4/8	14 6/8	7 6/8	7 6/8	12	12	Miner River, Yukon	Gary L. Knepp	Gary L. Knepp	1979	129
229 7/8	66 7/8	42 4/8	41 5/8	17 6/8	17 1/8	7 7/8	7 6/8	17	15	Wood River, Alaska	Bert Klineburger	Bert Klineburger	1964	131
229 7/8	66 1/8	46	46 2/8	19 2/8	20 7/8	8 6/8	8 5/8	8	13	King Salmon River, Alaska	Wilfred von Brand	Wilfred von Brand	1966	131
229 6/8	60 4/8	48 4/8	51	17	18	8 1/8	8 3/8	11	11	Alaska Pen., Alaska	Robert H. Stewart	Robert H. Stewart	1963	133
229 6/8	67 2/8	47	45	17	19 6/8	8 2/8	8 2/8	12	11	Kenai Pen., Alaska	Barjona Meek	Barjona Meek	1973	133
229 6/8	64 6/8	45 6/8	45 6/8	17 2/8	17 2/8	7 4/8	7 4/8	12	12	Anvil Range, Yukon	Fritz Kemper	Fritz Kemper	1978	133
229 5/8	64 7/8	45	45 4/8	16 2/8	16 6/8	7 1/8	7 2/8	14	15	McGrath, Alaska	Fred M. Poorman	Fred M. Poorman	1958	136
229 5/8	68 7/8	47 4/8	48 1/8	15	18	7 7/8	8	12	10	Kuichack River, Alaska	C. J. McElroy	C. J. McElroy	1966	136
229 4/8	63 4/8	42	43	21	21	8 4/8	8 4/8	12	13	Alaska Pen., Alaska	W. M. Ellis	W. M. Ellis	1963	138
229 4/8	72 2/8	45 6/8	46 2/8	15 1/8	18 6/8	8	7 6/8	10	12	Alaska Pen., Alaska	Arnold H. Craine	Arnold H. Craine	1968	138
229	72 2/8	44 7/8	43 4/8	13 1/8	13 6/8	7 6/8	8	15	14	Wood River, Alaska	A. Knutson	A. Knutson	1957	140
229	62 4/8	47	45	19 3/8	20 1/8	7 4/8	6 7/8	12	13	Shaw Creek Flats, Alaska	William Bugh	William Bugh	1962	140
229	69	44	42 6/8	22 5/8	24	7 5/8	8	8	13	Mother Goose Lake, Alaska	Paul R. Sharick	Paul R. Sharick	1966	140
229	65 2/8	44 2/8	44 4/8	14	13 6/8	8	7 7/8	16	16	Wind River, Yukon	William G. Latimer	William G. Latimer	1973	140
228 7/8	65 7/8	47 3/8	44 4/8	17 4/8	16 5/8	8 6/8	8 3/8	15	13	Wood River, Alaska	Berry B. Brooks	Berry B. Brooks	1958	144
228 7/8	63 7/8	48 6/8	48 4/8	13 5/8	13 6/8	8 3/8	8 4/8	12	12	Talkeetna Mts., Alaska	David F. Bremner, Jr.	David F. Bremner, Jr.	1959	144
228 7/8	70 7/8	42 1/8	45 2/8	22 1/8	15 5/8	8 2/8	8 2/8	13	13	Cantwell, Alaska	Ray L. Aldridge	Ray L. Aldridge	1964	144

Score	Greatest Spread	Length of Palm		Width of Palm		Circumference of Beam at Smallest Place		Number of Normal Points		Locality Killed	By Whom Killed	Owner	Date Killed	Rank
		R.	L.	R.	L.	R.	L.	R.	L.					
228⅜	70⅛	46⅜	42⅜	20⅜	18⅜	8⅜	9⅜	12	10	Ugashik Lake, Alaska	Russell Matthes	Russell Matthes	1969	144
228⅜	65⅝	47⅜	44	17⅜	18⅛	8⅜	8	12	13	Mulchatna River, Alaska	R. D. Eichenour	R. D. Eichenour	1968	148
228⅜	72⅝	43⅜	48⅝	14	16	8⅜	8⅜	13	12	Mulchatna River, Alaska	E. L. Dosdall	E. L. Dosdall	1975	148
228⅜	63¼	47⅜	44⅞	15⅜	15⅜	7	6⅞	19	16	Holitna River, Alaska	Scott R. Sexson	Scott R. Sexson	1978	148
228⅜	78⅝	42⅜	40⅞	22⅜	20⅛	8⅜	8⅜	11	15	Kenai Pen., Alaska	Dale R. Wood	Dale R. Wood	1960	151
228⅜	54⅜	48⅜	48⅜	16⅜	18⅜	8⅛	9	15	14	Ugashik Bay, Alaska	Max Fugler	Max Fugler	1966	151
228⅜	69⅛	47⅜	47⅞	14	16	7⅜	7⅜	11	14	Kijik River, Alaska	Edward A. Kneeland	Edward A. Kneeland	1970	151
228⅜	72⅛	42	46⅜	15⅜	15⅜	8	7⅜	14	13	Wood River, Alaska	Larry B. Jamison	Larry B. Jamison	1979	151
228⅜	68⅜	45	47⅜	15⅜	16	7⅜	8⅜	12	16	Brooks Range, Alaska	Robert L. Nelson	Robert L. Nelson	1981	156
228⅜	58	47	45⅜	16⅜	21⅛	8⅜	8⅜	19	15	Wrangell Mts., Alaska	G. W. Berry	G. W. Berry	1960	156
228⅜	65⅜	43⅜	45⅜	15⅜	15⅜	8⅛	8⅛	14	15	Bonnet Plume Lake, Yukon	Ted T. Dabrowski	Ted T. Dabrowski	1965	156
228¼	70	45⅜	44⅜	17⅜	16⅜	8	8⅜	10	13	Alaska Pen., Alaska	Tom W. Degefors	Tom W. Degefors	1967	156
228¼	65⅜	45⅛	45⅜	14⅛	13⅜	7⅜	8⅜	17	15	Wernecke Mts., Yukon	Hugh Beasley	Hugh Beasley	1968	156
228¼	71	47⅜	47⅜	15⅜	15⅜	7⅜	7⅜	12	10	Tagagawik River, Alaska	Jesse C. Sprague	Jesse C. Sprague	1983	161
228⅜	70⅜	47⅜	46⅜	15⅜	15⅜	7	7	13	10	Paxson Lake, Alaska	Vern Mahoney	Vern Mahoney	1953	162
228⅜	66⅜	44⅜	44	16⅜	15⅜	8⅜	8⅜	15	14	Blair Lakes, Alaska	Jerry D. Redick	Jerry D. Redick	1979	163
228⅛	71⅜	40⅜	41⅛	18⅛	19⅜	8⅜	8⅜	12	11	Mother Goose Lake, Alaska	Bert Klineburger	Bert Klineburger	1967	163
228⅛	65⅜	46	45⅜	15⅜	15	8⅛	8	13	15	Rainy Pass, Alaska	W. J. Brule	W. J. Brule	1968	163
228	69⅜	45	44	17	18	7⅜	7⅛	17	15	Rainy Pass, Alaska	J. W. Dixon	J. W. Dixon	1949	165
228	69⅜	42⅜	44⅜	14⅜	15⅜	8⅜	8⅜	16	14	Talkeetna Mts., Alaska	Wayne C. Eubank	Wayne C. Eubank	1957	165
228	62⅜	46⅜	45⅞	15⅜	15⅜	7⅜	7⅜	14	14	Alaska Pen., Alaska	M. E. Davis, Jr.	M. E. Davis, Jr.	1958	165
228	69	41½	43⅜	16⅜	16⅛	8⅜	8⅛	17	14	Mt. Susitna, Alaska	Peter W. Bading	Peter W. Bading	1963	165
228	67	47	45⅜	15⅜	20	7⅜	8	12	12	Tonzona River, Alaska	Glen Miller	Glen Miller	1971	165
227⅜	65⅜	42⅜	42⅜	14⅜	15	7⅜	7⅜	17	17	McKinley Park, Alaska	Thomas V. Scrivner	Thomas V. Scrivner	1966	170
227⅜	65⅜	46⅜	49⅛	17⅜	18⅜	7⅜	8⅜	17	10	Dog Salmon River, Alaska	John C. Davis	John C. Davis	1984	170
227⅜	62⅜	44⅜	44⅜	14	13⅜	7	7⅜	18	10	Soslota Creek, Alaska	Alex Cox	Alex Cox	1957	172
227⅜	72⅝	42	43	17	16⅜	8⅜	8⅜	11	12	Nikabuna Lake, Alaska	James E. Curley	James E. Curley	1968	172
227⅝	73⅜	50⅜	42⅜	16⅜	17⅜	7⅜	8⅜	12	16	Martin River, Alaska	Jim Goodfellow, Jr.	Jim Goodfellow, Jr.	1977	172
227⅝	72⅛	41⅛	43⅜	18⅜	18⅜	8⅛	8	11	10	Livengood, Alaska	James W. Keasling	James W. Keasling	1973	175
227⅝	67⅜	47⅜	47⅜	15⅜	19⅜	7⅜	7⅜	10	12	Alaska Pen., Alaska	Floyd F. Marrs	Floyd F. Marrs	1977	175

Score										Owner	By whom killed	Locality	Date Killed	Rank
227⅛	67⅞	45	46⅞	14⅞	17⅞	7⅞	8	13	13	Darryl G. Sanford	Darryl G. Sanford	Susitna River, Alaska	1981	175
227⅛	75⅞	39⅞	45⅜	17⅜	20⅞	7⅞	7⅞	13	12	John Humphreys	John Humphreys	Cinder River, Alaska	1963	178
227⅛	56⅝	48⅛	46⅜	21⅛	19⅞	8⅜	8⅜	13	11	R. H. Platt	R. H. Platt	Alaska Pen., Alaska	1965	178
227⅛	71⅛	51⅛	46⅜	14⅛	14⅛	8⅜	8⅜	10	9	Robert L. Hammond	Robert L. Hammond	Iliamna Lake, Alaska	1968	178
227⅛	63	46	46⅝	17	16⅛	9⅜	8⅜	11	12	Richard C. Wolff	Richard C. Wolff	Kluane Lake, Yukon	1971	178
227⅛	66	44⅛	42⅞	16⅜	16⅛	7⅝	7⅝	15	15	Paul E. Wollenman	Paul E. Wollenman	Elliott Lake, Yukon	1984	178
227⅛	69⅛	44⅞	44⅞	15	15⅝	8	7⅞	12	14	Walter W. Kellogg	Walter W. Kellogg	Tok River, Alaska	1967	183
227⅛	69⅝	44⅝	44⅛	16	15⅛	8⅝	8⅜	11	12	Jules R. Ashlock	Jules R. Ashlock	Salana River, Alaska	1961	184
227⅛	68⅝	44⅜	44⅛	20	17⅝	7⅞	7⅜	10	12	Pressley R. Rankin, Jr.	Pressley R. Rankin, Jr.	Port Heiden, Alaska	1966	184
227⅛	70⅛	41⅞	41⅛	14⅞	15⅛	8⅜	7⅝	14	15	Donn W. Ulrich	Donn W. Ulrich	Aniak River, Alaska	1980	184
227⅛	67⅞	48	49⅝	17	13⅜	8⅜	8⅜	13	10	A. H. Clise	A. H. Clise	Bonnet Plume Lake, Yukon	1982	184
227⅛	74⅜	46⅛	44⅜	14	15⅜	8⅜	7⅞	10	11	Michael L. Caverly	Michael L. Caverly	Aniak Lake, Alaska	1982	188
227	69	47⅜	45⅜	15⅜	14⅛	8⅜	8⅝	11	12	John A. Mueller	John A. Mueller	Rainy Pass, Alaska	1966	189
227	68⅝	48⅛	46⅜	15⅝	18	7⅞	8⅛	9	12	Emil Underberg	Emil Underberg	Ugashik Lake, Alaska	1967	189
227	67⅝	45⅜	44⅜	16⅜	16⅛	8⅜	8⅜	11	11	Robert Loch	Robert Loch	Ugashik Lake, Alaska	1967	189
227	64⅝	52	46	15⅜	14⅜	7⅜	7⅜	13	13	C. O. Tweedy	C. O. Tweedy, J. Albright & W. Burnette, Sr.	Ketchumstuk, Alaska	1968	189
227	66⅝	44⅜	44⅜	20⅜	17	8	7⅞	14	11	Duke of Penaranda	Duke of Penaranda	Farewell Lake, Alaska	1969	189
227	62⅝	47⅝	47⅜	14⅜	14⅜	7⅜	7⅜	13	13	Louis T. Hill	Louis T. Hill	South Macmillan River, Yukon	1973	189
227	69⅝	48⅜	43⅜	14⅜	14⅜	8⅛	8⅛	13	15	L. E. Wold	L. E. Wold & W. A. Vollendorf	Susitna River, Alaska	1978	189
226⅞	63⅝	47⅞	46⅜	13⅜	12	7⅜	7⅜	16	16	M. D. Gilchrist	M. D. Gilchrist	Wood River, Alaska	1958	196
226⅞	63⅞	41	43	17⅞	17⅞	8⅞	8⅞	16	15	Ray E. Buckwalter	Ray E. Buckwalter	Yakutat, Alaska	1963	196
226⅞	61⅛	47⅜	44⅜	16⅞	16	7⅜	7⅜	14	14	Eric Pilkington	Eric Pilkington	Nessling Range, Yukon	1965	196
226⅞	63⅝	43⅜	47	16⅝	16⅞	8	8	14	14	David G. Martini	David G. Martini	Eagle, Alaska	1969	196
226⅞	67⅞	48⅜	43⅜	16⅞	16⅛	7⅜	7⅜	17	18	William A. Galster	William A. Galster	Ray River, Alaska	1972	196
226⅞	58⅝	52⅝	50⅞	12⅞	15⅜	7½	7⅜	14	14	Michael E. Carter	Michael E. Carter	Camp Creek, Alaska	1982	196
226⅞	67	41⅞	49	13½	13⅜	9	9½	12	12	George A. Waldriff	George A. Waldriff	Alaska Pen., Alaska	1962	202
226⅞	68	45⅞	46⅝	20⅞	19⅞	9⅞	9⅜	11	10	Ross L. Phillippi, Jr.	Ross L. Phillippi, Jr.	Nabesna River, Alaska	1968	202
226⅞	70⅞	45⅜	41⅜	14	15⅜	7⅜	7½	10	12	Mac's Taxidermy	Gerald F. McNamara	Alaska Pen., Alaska	1979	202
226⅞	61⅜	44	48	18	17⅞	7⅝	7⅝	12	14	Lino Fred Vannelli	Lino Fred Vannelli	Talkeetna Mts., Alaska	1979	205
226⅞	68⅝	44⅜	44⅜	16⅜	17	8⅜	8	15	13	Wolfgang Porsche	Wolfgang Porsche	Talkeetna Mts., Alaska	1981	205
226⅞	70⅞	44⅜	44⅜	16⅜	13⅜	8	7⅞	14	12	Dan Auld, Jr.	Dan Auld, Jr.	Wood River, Alaska	1949	207
226⅞	68	43⅜	54⅜	11⅜	13⅜	7⅝	7⅜	12	17	Alaska Natl. Bank	G. P. Nehrbas	Charley River, Alaska	1951	207
226⅞	63	45⅜	47	15	14⅜	8	8	16	15	W. B. Macomber	W. B. Macomber	Rainy Pass, Alaska	1953	207
226⅞	62⅞	46	43⅜	18⅜	14⅜	7⅝	7⅜	14	13	L. M. Cole	L. M. Cole	Paxson Lake, Alaska	1958	207
226⅞	65⅜	46	44⅜	16⅜	15⅜	8	8	12	14	R. E. Kelley	R. E. Kelley	Chugach Mts., Alaska	1961	207
226⅞	64⅞	48⅜	49	15⅜	15	8	7⅜	13	14	Harold Froehle	Harold Froehle	Talkeetna Mts., Alaska	1965	207
226⅞	60⅞	48	50⅜	15⅜	16	7⅝	7⅜	12	10	H. H. Ahlemann	H. H. Ahlemann	Dog Salmon River, Alaska	1968	207
226⅜	69⅝	46	41⅜	21	19⅞	7½	7⅜	12	12	H. C. Ragsdale II	H. C. Ragsdale II	Lake Louise, Alaska	1958	214
226⅜	65⅛	45⅜	45⅜	20⅜	17⅜	8⅜	7⅜	10	14	Lit Ng	Lit Ng	Alaska Pen., Alaska	1967	214
226⅜	65⅛	42⅞	47	16⅛	18	8⅜	8⅜	11	10	Noel Thompson	Noel Thompson	Naknek, Alaska	1971	214

313

ALASKA-YUKON MOOSE—Continued

Alces alces gigas

Score	Greatest Spread	Length of Palm R.	Length of Palm L.	Width of Palm R.	Width of Palm L.	Circumference of Beam at Smallest Place R.	Circumference of Beam at Smallest Place L.	Number of Normal Points R.	Number of Normal Points L.	Locality Killed	By Whom Killed	Owner	Date Killed	Rank
226⅜	69	48⅜	44⅝	13⅜	12⅞	7⅞	7⅞	16	14	Talkeetna Mts., Alaska	T. L. Wynne, Jr.	T. L. Wynne, Jr.	1958	217
226⅜	68	47⅛	44⅝	16⅜	13	7⅜	7⅜	14	14	Kenai Pena., Alaska	Ottokar J. Skal	Ottokar J. Skal	1963	217
226⅜	65⅝	44	43	14⅜	14⅜	8	8	15	15	Bonnet Plume Lake, Yukon	Ted Dabrowski	Ted Dabrowski	1965	217
226⅛	70⅛	44⅜	46⅜	14⅜	14⅜	7⅞	8	11	12	King Salmon Creek, Alaska	Tiney Mitchell	Tiney Mitchell	1971	220
226	65⅜	40⅞	41⅛	15⅜	17⅞	8	8⅛	16	20	Nelchina, Alaska	Jack D. Putnam	Denver Mus. Nat. Hist.	1961	221
226	66	46	48⅝	17⅜	16	8	8	10	11	Alaska Pen., Alaska	Robert L. Wesner	Robert L. Wesner	1963	221
226	67⅞	46⅜	44⅜	17⅜	20⅞	7⅜	7⅜	11	14	Ft. Greely, Alaska	Jerry L. Bailey	Jerry L. Bailey	1970	221
226	58⅝	46⅜	46⅜	18⅜	18⅜	8	8	11	11	Black Lake, Alaska	John Mike Behan	John Mike Behan	1972	221
226	64⅛	47	45⅜	14⅜	16⅜	7⅜	7⅞	13	14	Dillinger River, Alaska	Jerry E. Romanowski	Jerry E. Romanowski	1976	221
226	68⅜	44⅜	43⅜	14⅜	13⅜	8⅜	8⅛	14	14	Wrangell Mts., Alaska	Lee Chambers	Lee Chambers	1969	226
225⅞	76⅜	46⅜	44⅜	14⅜	14⅜	8	8⅛	10	9	Alaska Pen., Alaska	Herman Kulhanek	Herman Kulhanek	1961	227
225⅝	66⅜	46⅜	43⅜	13⅜	14⅜	8⅛	8⅛	15	14	Alaska Pen., Alaska	Don Johnson	Don Johnson	1963	227
225⅝	63⅜	46⅜	45⅜	15	13⅜	9⅜	8⅜	12	10	Alaska Range, Alaska	J. B. Copeland, Jr.	J. B. Copeland, Jr.	1968	227
225⅝	57⅞	47⅜	47⅜	18⅜	16⅜	7⅜	8⅜	12	18	St. George Creek, Alaska	Joseph G. Gaillard	Joseph G. Gaillard	1973	227
225⅝	75⅜	43⅜	38⅜	14⅜	15⅜	8⅜	8⅜	14	14	Kenai Pen., Alaska	Willi Hilpert	Willi Hilpert	1973	227
225⅝	70⅜	46⅜	45	15⅜	15⅜	8⅛	8⅜	12	10	Farewell Station, Alaska	Daniel M. DiBenedetto, Sr.	Daniel M. DiBenedetto, Sr.	1973	227
225⅝	66	46⅜	46	13⅜	16	8⅜	8⅜	12	12	Upper Mulchatna River, Alaska	O. B. Beard III	O. B. Beard III	1974	227
225⅝	65⅜	40⅞	41	21⅜	18⅜	7⅜	7⅜	15	17	Spring Creek, Alaska	William D. Phifer	William D. Phifer	1975	227
225⅝	71⅜	42⅞	42⅜	14⅜	15⅜	9	9	12	14	Alaska Range, Alaska	Toby J. Johnson	Toby J. Johnson	1978	227
225⅝	67⅜	43⅜	42	15⅜	16	8⅜	8⅜	13	13	Glennallen, Alaska	Eugene E. Wheeler	Eugene E. Wheeler	1981	227
225⅝	66⅜	45	42⅜	15⅜	18⅜	8⅜	8⅜	14	14	Unknown	Gift of C. H. Mackay	National Collection	PR1951	237
225⅝	72⅜	44	43⅜	16	21⅜	7⅜	7⅜	11	10	Port Heiden, Alaska	Harold Sill	Harold Sill	1964	237
225⅝	65⅝	45⅜	46⅝	16⅜	14⅜	7⅜	7⅜	13	12	High Lake, Alaska	Glen E. Park	Glen E. Park	1965	237
225⅝	70⅛	41⅜	43	19⅜	17⅜	8	8	13	13	Alaska Range, Alaska	R. Pinamont & J. Albright	Robert Pinamont	1972	237
225⅝	69⅜	44⅜	41⅜	17⅜	20⅜	8	8⅜	11	11	Farewell, Alaska	G. Jack Tankersley	G. Jack Tankersley	1975	237
225⅝	66⅜	44	49⅜	15⅜	13⅜	8⅜	8⅜	14	14	Chandalar River, Alaska	William O. Dudley	William O. Dudley	1980	237
225⅜	68⅜	41⅜	41	15⅜	18⅜	8	8	14	15	Alaska Pen., Alaska	Dolores F. Jones	Dolores F. Jones	1958	243
225⅜	66⅜	47⅜	48⅜	14⅜	16⅜	8⅜	8	10	14	Blackstone River, Yukon	Marc Korting	Marc Korting	1970	243

Final Score										Locality	Owner	Hunter	Date
225⅛	70⅜	43⅜	45	16⅜	16⅛	7⅞	8	10	10	Clark Lake, Alaska	Geo. W. Robinson	Geo. W. Robinson	1965
225⅛	66⅝	43⅝	43	17	16⅝	8⅜	8⅜	12	12	Wernecke Mt., Yukon	David V. Collis	David V. Collis	1984
225⅛	64⅞	48⅜	46⅜	16⅛	17½	7⅝	7⅝	10	10	Alaska Pen., Alaska	James Ford	James Ford	1970
225⅛	69⅜	40⅞	44	14⅛	13⅜	8⅜	8⅜	15	16	Alaska Range, Alaska	Richard C. Beall	Richard C. Beall	1978
225	66⅝	45⅝	43⅜	15⅝	13	8⅝	8⅝	14	15	Kenai Pen., Alaska	Walter R. Peterson	Walter R. Peterson	1935
225	74	41	41⅛	17	18⅜	7⅝	7⅜	17	11	Livengood, Alaska	Univ. of Alaska	Bill Thomas	1952
225	65⅜	50	49	15	14⅞	7⅝	7⅞	8	9	Alaska Range, Alaska	Basil C. Bradbury	Basil C. Bradbury	1963
225	72	45	47⅞	14	16⅛	7⅛	7⅞	10	15	Farewell Lake, Alaska	Lyman Strong	Lyman Strong	1965
225	58	47⅞	45⅞	15⅝	16⅛	7½	7⅞	14	17	Tok, Alaska	Bruce Dodson	Bruce Dodson	1974
224⅞	70	44	44⅛	13⅞	15⅞	8⅜	10¾	12	14	Talkeetna, Mts., Alaska	Eberhart Herzog	Eberhart Herzog	1981
224⅞	71⅜	48⅛	42⅞	16	17¾	7⅜	7⅜	12	13	Mt. Katmai, Alaska	Morris Roberts	Morris Roberts	1951
224⅞	61⅝	48⅛	47⅞	14⅛	14⅛	7⅜	7⅜	12	12	Ugashik Narrows, Alaska	Wayne Ewing	Wayne Ewing	1966
224⅞	67⅜	45⅛	45⅜	17⅛	16⅜	7⅝	7⅛	9	12	King Salmon, Alaska	Albert B. Fay	Albert B. Fay	1969
224⅞	67⅛	45⅛	46⅞	14⅜	14⅞	8⅛	8⅛	11	13	Koyukuk River, Alaska	Dennis E. Reiner	Dennis E. Reiner	1973
224⅞	70⅛	41⅛	40⅞	19⅛	18⅞	7⅞	7½	14	11	Farewell Lake, Alaska	Gust Pabst	Gust Pabst	1963
224⅞	74⅜	41⅛	42⅛	14⅛	17⅜	7⅝	7⅜	12	13	Alaska Pen., Alaska	Charles Bonnici	Charles Bonnici	1969
224⅞	58⅝	46	47	15	15	8⅝	8⅝	14	14	Cantwell, Alaska	Gene Sivell	Gene Sivell	1970
224¾	61⅝	46⅝	44⅞	20⅛	21¼	9⅛	9⅝	9	9	Lower Ugashik Lake, Alaska	Hugo Klinger	Hugo Klinger	1972
224⅝	69⅛	44⅛	44⅛	16	14	8⅝	8⅝	12	11	Little Tok River, Alaska	Edward J. Janus	Edward J. Janus	1974
224⅝	68⅛	45⅛	47⅞	16⅛	18⅞	9⅝	9⅝	8	13	Port Heiden, Alaska	Jon G. Koshell	Jon G. Koshell	1964
224⅝	62	44⅜	43⅜	15	15⅝	7⅞	7⅜	14	16	Fog Lakes, Alaska	C. A. Schwope	C. A. Schwope	1960
224⅝	68⅜	45⅛	46⅛	18	14⅞	8	8⅛	14	12	Alaska Pen., Alaska	James E. McFarland	James E. McFarland	1967
224⅝	71⅛	41⅛	48⅞	19⅝	18⅛	7⅝	7⅜	9	9	Koyukuk River, Alaska	William M. Harrington	William M. Harrington	1970
224⅝	66⅝	46⅛	45	16⅛	18⅛	7⅝	7⅜	9	14	Hess River, Yukon	Philip C. Wahlbom	Philip C. Wahlbom	1976
224⅝	63⅝	45⅛	48⅞	16	16⅝	7⅛	7⅞	12	13	Kenai Pen., Alaska	Richard B. Limbach	Richard B. Limbach	1985
224½	58⅛	44⅛	43⅜	19⅛	16⅝	8⅛	8⅜	14	19	Alaska Pen., Alaska	Carole Colclasure	Carole Colclasure	1962
224½	71⅛	47⅛	43⅛	18⅛	14⅞	8⅛	8⅜	12	11	Kenai Pen., Alaska	Alice J. Landreth	Alice J. Landreth	1967
224½	61⅝	47⅛	46⅜	13⅝	13⅜	7⅜	7⅜	14	15	Alligator Lake, Yukon	Gloria Reiter	Gloria Reiter	1969
224½	70⅛	45	46	14⅛	15⅜	7⅛	7⅜	11	10	Susitna River, Alaska	Arthur C. Popham, Jr.	Arthur C. Popham, Jr.	1950
224½	63⅝	43⅞	43⅜	17⅛	14⅜	8⅞	8⅞	14	16	Post Lake, Alaska	J. R. Gray	J. R. Gray	1951
224½	61⅛	48⅜	46⅞	13⅜	13⅝	8	8⅛	12	12	Lake Telaquana, Alaska	Donald E. Wicks	Donald E. Wicks	1963
224½	60⅛	42⅝	46⅜	16⅛	13⅞	7⅝	7⅝	16	15		Wulf Nosofsky	Wulf Nosofsky	1965
224¼	67⅛	44⅜	44	18⅛	15⅝	8⅜	8⅛	10	10		Paul G. Curren	Paul G. Curren	1960
224¼	68⅜	47⅛	47⅜	14⅛	15⅞	7⅝	7⅝	11	11	Port Salmon, Alaska	Graf Scheel-Plessen	Graf Scheel-Plessen	1965
224	65⅝	43⅞	43⅞	18⅛	15⅝	7⅝	7⅝	11	13	Alaska Range, Alaska	L. J. Pfeifer	L. J. Pfeifer	1977
254⅛*	71⅛	51⅛	53⅜	17⅞	21¼	9⅜	9⅜	13	13	Alagnak River, Alaska	Robert L. Marvin	Robert L. Marvin	1981
243⅛*	67⅛	52	53⅜	16⅜	16⅞	8	8⅜	12	12	Talkeetna Mts., Alaska	Duane E. Stroupe	Duane E. Stroupe	1982
240⅞*	70⅛	43⅜	43⅜	19⅞	17⅜	7⅞	7⅜	17	17	Yukon River, Alaska	G. Kenneth Whitehead	Unknown	PR1899
239⅛*	62⅝	47⅛	50⅞	16⅜	17¾	8⅛	8⅛	16	18	Clear Creek, Alaska	Douglas A. Hulme	Douglas A. Hulme	1980
233⅜*	66⅛	48	48	15⅝	16⅜	8⅛	8⅛	12	11	Worm Lake, Yukon	James E. Nelson	James E. Nelson	1985
231⅞*	69⅛	43⅝	44	22⅛	18	8⅛	8⅛	13	15	Red Paint Creek, Alaska	Larry D. Kropf	Larry D. Kropf	1983

*Final Score subject to revision by additional verifying measurements

WORLD'S RECORD WYOMING MOOSE
SCORE: 205 4/8
Locality: Green River Lake, Wyoming Date: 1952
Hunter: John M. Oakley
Donated by W. C. Lawrence to Jackson Hole Museum and Pioneer Village Foundation, Inc.

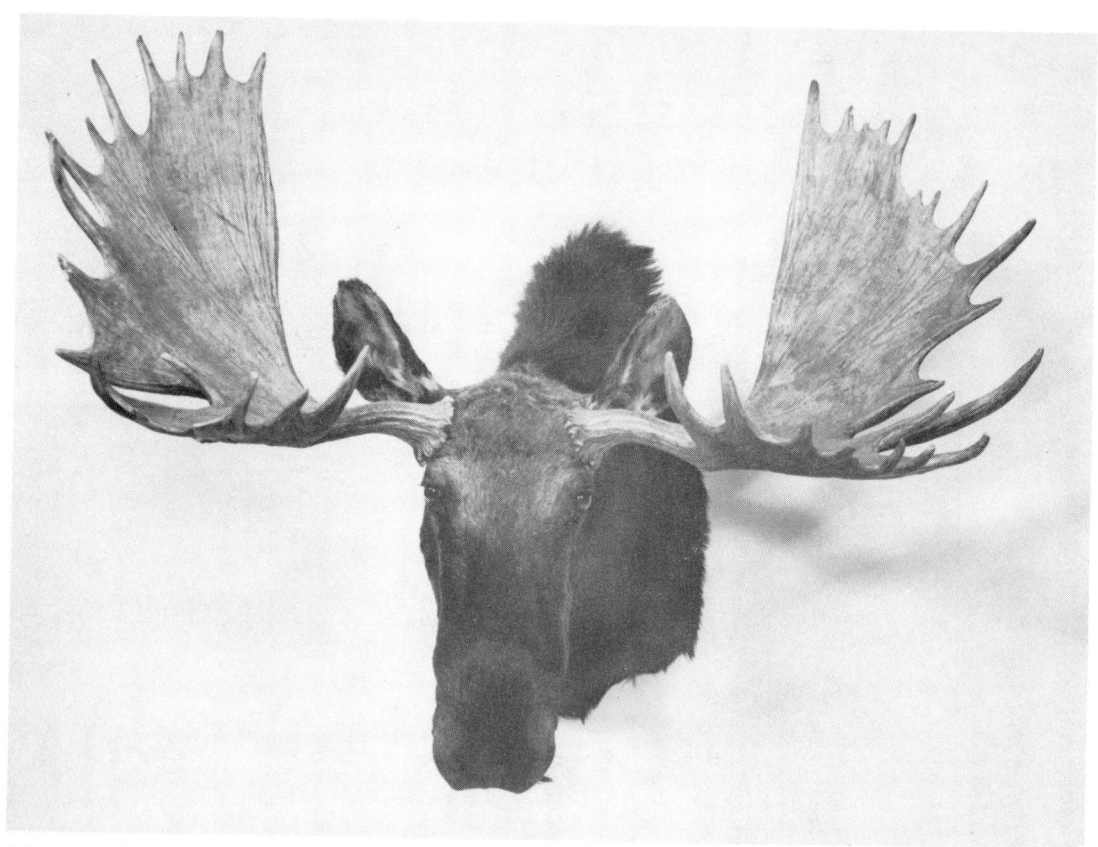

NUMBER THREE WYOMING MOOSE
SCORE: 200 3/8
Locality: Lincoln County, Wyoming Date: 1981
Hunter and owner: Aldon L. Hale

Wyoming or Shiras Moose

Alces alces shirasi

Minimum Score 155

Wyoming (Shiras) moose includes trophies taken in Utah, Idaho, Montana, Wyoming, and Washington.

Score	Greatest Spread	Length of Palm R	L	Width of Palm R	L	Circumference of Beam at Smallest Place R	L	Number of Normal Points R	L	Locality Killed	By Whom Killed	Owner	Date Killed	Rank
205⅝	53	38⅝	38⅝	16⅜	15⅜	6⅞	6⅞	15	15	Green River Lake, Wyo.	John M. Oakley	Jackson Hole Museum	1952	1
205⅜	56⅝	40	40	13⅜	14⅜	7⅞	7⅞	13	13	Fremont Co., Wyo.	Arthur E. Chandler	Arthur E. Chandler	1944	2
200⅜	55⅞	38⅛	36⅝	13⅛	13⅜	7	6⅜	16	17	Lincoln Co., Wyo.	Aldon L. Hale	Aldon L. Hale	1981	3
193⅞	62⅜	38⅛	36⅝	12⅜	16⅜	7⅞	8⅝	12	15	Elk City, Idaho	Reid T. Fisher	Reid T. Fisher	1957	4
195⅝	52⅛	41⅛	40	13	11	7	6⅜	14	15	Atlantic Creek, Wyo.	Alfred C. Berol	Alfred C. Berol	1933	5
195⅛	57⅝	43⅛	35⅝	15⅛	14⅜	7⅞	7⅞	14	14	Red Rock Lakes, Mont.	C. M. Schmauch	C. M. Schmauch	1952	6
188⅞	50⅜	34⅜	36⅜	15	15⅜	6⅞	6⅞	13	13	Madison Co., Idaho	Vicki Grover	Vicki Grover	1976	7
186⅞	56⅞	37⅛	38⅜	11⅜	11⅜	6⅞	6⅞	18	10	Sublette Co., Wyo.	Curt Mann	Curt Mann	1972	8
186⅛	58⅛	41⅛	37⅜	12⅜	12⅜	7⅞	7	8	7	Hamilton, Mont.	Picked Up	G. Beechwood	1957	9
185⅞	56⅞	41⅛	40	10⅜	12⅜	6⅞	7	7	9	Sublette Co., Wyo.	Robert C. Neely	Robert C. Neely	1959	10
185	52⅞	37⅛	36⅛	12⅜	11	6⅞	6⅞	13	15	Teton Co., Wyo.	Isabelle Perry	Isabelle Perry	1961	11
184⅞	56⅜	33⅞	33⅜	13⅛	14⅛	7⅜	7⅜	11	10	Green River Lake, Wyo.	Vern A. Bapst	Vern A. Bapst	1961	12
184⅛	49	42⅛	40⅜	10⅜	11	7	7	10	10	Fremont Co., Wyo.	Jack C. Dow	Jack C. Dow	1948	13
183⅞	45⅝	37⅛	38	13	13⅜	6⅛	6⅛	12	15	Bear Lake Co., Idaho	Claudia R. Howell	Claudia R. Howell	1977	14
182⅞	50	35⅜	38	11⅞	13	6⅜	6⅜	12	13	Spencer, Idaho	Charles A. Oswald	Charles A. Oswald	1957	15
182⅜	48⅜	34⅜	38⅜	12⅜	13	6	6	14	15	Caribou Co., Idaho	Patricia A. Wood	Patricia A. Wood	1983	15
182⅜	55⅝	35⅝	36⅜	11⅜	12⅜	6⅞	6⅞	10	9	Teton Co., Wyo.	Dick Gaudern	Dick Gaudern	1946	17
182	45⅜	37⅜	38⅛	11⅛	11⅜	6⅞	6⅞	15	13	Sublette Co., Wyo.	James R. Brougham	James R. Brougham	1969	18
181⅞	51⅞	38⅜	38⅞	8⅜	9⅞	6⅜	6⅜	11	12	Bear River, Utah	John W. Way	Utah Div. of Wildl. Resc.	1958	19
180⅞	48⅜	37⅞	37⅞	12⅜	10⅜	6⅞	6⅞	15	12	Sublette Co., Wyo.	Glen W. Beane	Glen W. Beane	1957	20
180⅞	53⅜	39⅜	41	10⅜	10⅜	6⅞	6⅞	8	7	Sublette Co., Wyo.	Donald Irwin	Donald Irwin	1976	20
180⅞	51⅜	35⅛	34⅜	13⅜	14⅜	6⅜	6⅜	11	10	Weber Co., Utah	Robert S. Mastronardi	Robert S. Mastronardi	1981	22
180	45⅜	40⅛	38⅜	10⅜	9⅜	7⅜	7⅜	13	12	Green River, Wyo.	L. W. Isaacs	L. W. Isaacs	1948	23
180	47	33⅜	34⅜	11⅜	12⅜	6⅞	6⅞	15	16	Pinedale, Wyo.	Stuart W. Shepherd	Stuart W. Shepherd	1966	23
179⅞	51⅜	32⅜	35	12⅜	12⅜	6⅞	6⅞	13	14	Gallatin Co., Mont.	John Williams	Powderhorn Sportsman Supply	1930	25
179⅞	49⅜	36⅜	34⅜	12⅜	12⅜	6⅜	6⅜	12	14	Greys River, Wyo.	Serena Malech	Serena Malech	1972	26
179⅛	47⅜	38⅜	38⅛	11⅜	12⅜	6⅜	6⅜	10	11	Teton Co., Wyo.	John D. Seifert	John D. Seifert	1976	27
179⅛	45⅛	35⅜	34⅜	14⅜	11⅜	6⅞	6⅞	14	14	Nalley, Wyo.	Stephen S. Fisher	Stephen S. Fisher	1964	28
178⅞	52⅝	38⅜	37⅛	9⅜	10⅜	6⅛	6⅜	14	10	Eagle Creek, Wyo.	Loren L. Lutz	Loren L. Lutz	1956	29

Score										Locality	By whom killed	Owner	Date killed	Rank
178 6/8	55 7/8	33 3/8	31 1/8	10 1/8	13 3/8	6	5 7/8	14	16	Upper Hoback River, Wyo.	Daniel T. Burch	Daniel T. Burch	1967	30
178 6/8	48 3/8	36 3/8	37 3/8	10 3/8	11 3/8	6 7/8	6 3/8	12	14	Sublette Co., Wyo.	Charles Thornton	Charles Thornton	1973	30
178 3/8	58 1/8	35 4/8	36 5/8	9 3/8	8 7/8	6 5/8	6 7/8	11	9	Sublette Co., Wyo.	Robert Dennis	Robert Dennis	1969	32
178 3/8	49 1/8	32 2/8	32 4/8	13 5/8	15 3/8	6 6/8	6 6/8	15	12	Sublette Co., Wyo.	Ross J. Berlin	Ross J. Berlin	1972	33
178 1/8	50 3/8	37	36 3/8	10 6/8	11 4/8	6 5/8	6 6/8	12	9	Buffalo Park, Wyo.	Walter Russell	Walter Russell	1956	34
178 1/8	49 1/8	36 7/8	38 3/8	13 3/8	12 3/8	7	7	10	12	Teton Co., Wyo.	Harold L. Roby	Garvice E. Roby	1961	34
177 6/8	50 1/8	37	33 5/8	14 7/8	12 3/8	6 1/8	6 2/8	11	13	Thorofare River, Wyo.	Earl Brahler	H. E. Wolfe	1959	36
177 6/8	49	35	34 3/8	13 7/8	14 7/8	6 5/8	6 5/8	9	14	Big Piney, Wyo.	George F. Stewart, Jr.	George F. Stewart, Jr.	1965	36
177 5/8	52 1/8	30 4/8	31 2/8	14 7/8	14	6 6/8	6 7/8	12	12	Green River, Wyo.	Walter C. Motta, Sr.	Walter C. Motta, Sr.	1956	38
177 5/8	51 7/8	38 3/8	35 3/8	13 7/8	11 2/8	6 4/8	6 1/8	10	11	Teton Co., Wyo.	John R. Blanton	John R. Blanton	1985	38
177 3/8	51 1/8	33 3/8	33 3/8	11 3/8	11 3/8	6 1/8	5 7/8	12	12	Park Co., Mont.	Lawrence A. Allestad	Lawrence A. Allestad	1961	40
177 1/8	50 3/8	34	34	11 3/8	11 3/8	7 3/8	7 2/8	13	12	Big Piney, Wyo.	Mrs. Robert R. Jamieson	Mrs. Robert R. Jamieson	1966	41
177	53	32 7/8	32	12 5/8	11 5/8	7	7 3/8	14	11	Teton Co., Wyo.	Elgin T. Gates	Elgin T. Gates	1947	42
176 7/8	50 1/8	36 7/8	37 5/8	11	11	6 7/8	6 1/8	10	10	Teton Co., Wyo.	Jack G. Binkley	Jack G. Binkley	1977	43
176 6/8	48 1/8	35	35 3/8	11 5/8	10 6/8	6 3/8	6 7/8	12	12	Caribou Co., Idaho	Charles L. Walters	Charles L. Walters	1966	44
176 2/8	50 1/8	35 5/8	33 5/8	11 5/8	10 7/8	6 2/8	6 3/8	12	11	Bonneville Co., Idaho	Diggs Lewis	Diggs Lewis	1972	45
175 6/8	50 1/8	34 4/8	35	12 1/8	12 3/8	7 1/8	7 1/8	14	13	Weber Co., Utah	Steven A. Barnard	Steven A. Barnard	1985	46
175 2/8	41 1/8	31 6/8	35 7/8	14 3/8	13 3/8	6 5/8	6 3/8	12	13	Lincoln Co., Wyo.	Robert A. Cox	Robert A. Cox	1973	47
175 1/8	50	36 3/8	34 6/8	12 2/8	11 6/8	6 5/8	6 5/8	10	14	Hoback River, Wyo.	Leon Gordon	Leon Gordon	1967	48
175 1/8	48 3/8	33 7/8	35 5/8	12 6/8	11 4/8	6 6/8	6 6/8	12	15	Squaw Creek, Wyo.	George Tolan	George Tolan	1964	49
175	46 3/8	34	37 7/8	12 6/8	11 4/8	6 5/8	6 5/8	10	11	Park Co., Mont.	Denton C. Barker	Triangle C Ranch	1969	49
174 6/8	54 1/8	33 5/8	34	11 2/8	10	6 4/8	6 6/8	11	14	Livingston, Mont.	Thomas J. Radoumis	Thomas J. Radoumis	1974	51
174 6/8	50 3/8	33 5/8	34 3/8	11 5/8	13	6	6 6/8	12	12	Gallatin Co., Mont.	Bill Cutler	Bill Cutler	1964	52
174 4/8	48	37 7/8	36 1/8	10 1/8	14 3/8	7	7 1/8	10	13	Gallatin Co., Mont.	L. C. Hulslander	L. C. Hulslander & K. Bennet	1981	52
174 4/8	45 1/8	35 1/8	36 3/8	11	11 5/8	7	7	11	13	Teton Co., Wyo.	John Fuller Cross	John Fuller Cross	1965	54
174 3/8	46	32 2/8	33 3/8	12 5/8	11 4/8	6 4/8	6 1/8	13	10	Park Co., Wyo.	Walter L. Gale	Walter L. Gale	1983	54
174 2/8	58 1/8	30 6/8	29 3/8	14 3/8	12 5/8	7 4/8	6 6/8	13	14	Idaho Co., Idaho	Paul L. White	Paul L. White	1981	56
173 6/8	46	32 2/8	32 1/8	13 7/8	13 3/8	7 7/8	7 6/8	14	10	Teton Co., Wyo.	John R. Harju	John R. Harju	1980	57
173 3/8	50 3/8	34 3/8	34 3/8	10 6/8	13 3/8	7 1/8	7 7/8	10	10	Atlantic Creek, Wyo.	Clyde Ormond	Clyde Ormond	1955	58
173 3/8	54 1/8	32 2/8	31 1/8	8 6/8	10 3/8	7 1/8	7 1/8	10	12	Flathead Co., Mont.	Tom Scheer	Tom Scheer	1976	59
173 1/8	48 3/8	33 1/8	38	11 6/8	10	6	6	12	10	Madison Co., Mont.	Thomas L. Carter	Thomas L. Carter	1955	60
173	52 1/8	35	34 3/8	11 2/8	11 5/8	6 4/8	6 2/8	10	12	Sublette Co., Wyo.	John C. Eklund	John C. Eklund	1970	60
172 6/8	49 3/8	35 1/8	35 3/8	11 3/8	12	6 6/8	6 6/8	11	13	Buffalo River, Wyo.	Robert L. Hitch	Robert L. Hitch	1951	62
172 2/8	41	35 5/8	35	12 5/8	11 3/8	6 5/8	6 6/8	13	13	Bridger Natl. For., Wyo.	J. D. Bradley	J. D. Bradley	1970	63
172 2/8	42	32 2/8	33 1/8	14 3/8	14 4/8	6 6/8	6 6/8	13	17	Lincoln Co., Mont.	Tom DeShazer	Tom DeShazer	1956	64
172 3/8	50	37 1/8	36 1/8	10 6/8	10 5/8	6 1/8	6 2/8	12	12	Kilgore Creek, Wyo.	Bill Jhun	Bill Jhun	1967	64
172	44 1/8	36 3/8	38 3/8	10 7/8	10 7/8	6 7/8	6 7/8	10	10	Pinedale, Wyo.	Basil C. Bradbury	Basil C. Bradbury	1969	66
172	51	38 1/8	38 3/8	9 6/8	9 7/8	6 5/8	6 7/8	8	10	Sublette Co., Wyo.	William D. Stewart	William D. Stewart	1954	67
172	46 3/8	35 7/8	38 3/8	10	10	6 5/8	6 6/8	11	12	Sublette Co., Wyo.	Holland C. McHenry	Holland C. McHenry	1980	67
171 1/8	58 3/8	30	33 3/8	9 6/8	9 5/8	6 1/8	6 1/8	11	13	Weber Co., Utah	Kent G. Yearsley	Kent G. Yearsley	1981	69

319

WYOMING OR SHIRAS MOOSE—Continued

Alces alces shirasi

Score	Greatest Spread	Length of Palm R.	Length of Palm L.	Width of Palm R.	Width of Palm L.	Circumference of Beam at Smallest Place R.	Circumference of Beam at Smallest Place L.	Number of Normal Points R.	Number of Normal Points L.	Locality Killed	By Whom Killed	Owner	Date Killed	Rank
171⅛	49⅛	32⅛	31⅛	12⅝	12⅜	7⅞	8	10	11	Fremont Co., Idaho	Rodney Chandler	Rodney Chandler	1967	70
171⅛	50	34⅜	37⅜	10⅜	10⅜	6⅝	6⅝	9	9	Silver Bow Co., Mont.	Martin E. Carlson	Martin E. Carlson	1980	71
171	49⅞	34⅝	32	10⅞	11⅛	7⅛	7⅛	11	11	Teton Co., Wyo.	Keith H. Hanson	Keith H. Hanson	1972	72
170⅞	45⅞	37⅞	38⅝	10⅞	10⅜	7	7⅛	8	10	Lincoln Co., Mont.	Bruce C. Todd	Bruce C. Todd	1982	73
170⅞	47⅞	35⅝	34⅝	10⅛	8⅜	7⅛	7⅛	13	11	Sublette Co., Wyo.	Don L. Corley	Don L. Corley	1983	73
170⅝	50⅜	35⅝	34⅝	8⅞	11⅞	6⅛	6⅛	12	11	Bridger Natl. For., Wyo.	Unknown	Neil Blair	1965	75
170⅝	47⅝	38⅝	35⅜	9⅞	11⅝	7⅝	7⅛	9	12	Sublette Co., Wyo.	Kenneth E. Myers	Kenneth E. Myers	1968	75
170⅜	46⅝	34⅝	34⅜	9⅜	9⅞	7⅝	7⅝	12	10	Warm Spring Creek, Wyo.	Herbert L. Palmer	Herbert L. Palmer	1951	77
170⅜	39⅝	34⅝	35⅛	10⅜	12⅜	6⅝	6⅝	13	13	Lincoln Co., Mont.	Picked Up	Wayne Lundberg	1974	78
169⅞	47⅛	34⅞	33⅜	10⅞	10⅜	7	6⅝	11	12	Lincoln Co., Mont.	William A. Stevens	William A. Stevens	1967	79
169⅞	50⅛	33⅞	32⅞	10⅞	11⅛	7⅞	6⅝	10	10	Weber Co., Utah	Riley A. Bushman	Riley A. Bushman	1969	79
169⅝	54⅝	32⅞	27⅝	10⅜	10⅝	6⅝	6⅞	15	13	Wilson, Wyo.	Howard Bennage	Howard Bennage	1958	81
169⅜	52⅝	30⅜	32⅛	12⅜	11⅛	7	6⅞	10	11	Merna, Wyo.	C. Von De Graaff	C. Von De Graaff	1959	82
169⅛	40⅝	35	35⅜	12⅛	11⅜	7	7	11	11	Dubois, Wyo.	Albert Wagner, Jr.	Albert Wagner, Jr.	1962	83
169¼	42⅜	30⅞	34	12	11⅛	6⅛	6⅛	15	15	Lincoln Co., Wyo.	Vannetta Marshinsky	Vannetta Marshinsky	1968	84
169⅛	54⅝	31⅛	31⅛	9⅜	9⅞	6⅛	6⅛	10	12	Clark Co., Idaho	Carolyn Karvinen	Carolyn Karvinen	1966	85
169	52	33⅛	33⅜	8⅜	8⅞	7⅜	7⅜	9	9	Jackson Hole, Wyo.	Shirley Straley	Shirley Straley	1963	86
168⅝	58	30⅜	30	11⅜	11⅞	6⅝	6⅝	7	8	Park Co., Wyo.	John A. Mahoney, Jr.	John A. Mahoney, Jr.	1957	87
168⅝	48⅜	36⅜	34⅜	10⅜	10⅜	6⅝	6⅝	12	9	Sublette Co., Wyo.	Larry Petersen	Larry Petersen	1964	87
168⅜	43⅜	36⅜	39⅝	13⅜	12⅜	6⅜	6⅜	13	7	Park Co., Mont.	Victoria L. Miller	Victoria L. Miller	1977	89
167⅞	43⅝	39⅝	33⅜	10⅜	11	6⅜	6⅜	13	12	Gros Ventre, Wyo.	Bonita Young	Bonita Young	1960	90
167⅞	51	34⅜	33⅜	8⅜	9⅜	6⅜	6⅜	10	11	Teton Co., Wyo.	Roger Wilmot	Roger Wilmot	1972	91
167⅞	44	33⅞	37	12⅞	11⅜	6⅜	6⅜	10	12	Park Co., Wyo.	Peter A. Parini	Peter A. Parini	1981	91
167⅞	47⅞	34⅝	32⅜	11	11	6⅜	6⅜	10	10	Beaverhead Co., Mont.	Leo C. Chapel	Leo C. Chapel	1967	93
167⅜	43⅝	37⅜	33⅜	12	10⅜	6⅜	6⅜	12	11	Park Co., Wyo.	Timothy G. Coulson	Timothy G. Coulson	1974	94
167⅜	49⅝	36⅜	30⅜	12	12	6⅝	6⅝	12	10	Lincoln Co., Wyo.	John K. Ryan	John K. Ryan	1984	94
167⅜	45⅜	32⅝	34	11⅞	10⅞	6⅝	6⅝	11	11	Bonneville Co., Idaho	L. Stanley	L. Stanley	1964	96
167⅛	48⅛	32⅜	30⅞	10⅞	11	6⅝	6⅝	11	11	Teton Co., Wyo.	Bob Housholder	Bob Housholder	1968	96
167⅛	48⅜	32⅜	36⅛	10	9⅝	7⅝	6⅝	11	10	Sublette Co., Wyo.	Ernest Saxton	Ernest Saxton	1969	96
167	46⅝	35⅜	35⅝	8⅞	12⅛	6⅝	6⅝	9	12	Caribou Co., Idaho	Picked Up	Robert Dory	1976	99
167	46⅝	38⅝	34⅞	9⅝	10⅜	6⅝	6⅝	13	10	Fremont Co., Wyo.	LeRoy Castagno	LeRoy Castagno	1977	99
167	44⅝	33⅝	32⅝	11⅛	11⅛	6⅜	6⅜	11	12	Lincoln Co., Mont.	Jeff Wisehart	Jeff Wisehart	1983	99

Score									Locality	Owner	By whom taken	Year	No.
166⅞	51⅛	33⅜	33⅜	9⅞	6⅜	6⅜	10	8	Gallatin Co., Mont.	Rodney R. Richardson	Rodney R. Richardson	1979	102
166⅝	48⅞	34⅜	36	7⅞	7⅞	7⅞	10	11	Teton Co., Wyo.	R. G. De Graff	R. G. De Graff	1963	103
166⅜	50	28⅜	28⅜	13⅜	6⅜	6⅜	10	11	Bonneville Co., Idaho	Daniel J. Duggan	Daniel J. Duggan	1982	104
166⅜	50⅛	34⅜	32⅞	8⅞	6	6	10	10	Teton Co., Wyo.	Terry Nilsen	Terry Nilsen	1970	105
166⅜	48⅞	37	35⅜	11⅞	5⅞	6⅜	8	11	Bonner Co., Idaho	Brian T. Farley	Brian T. Farley	1977	105
166	48⅞	35⅜	32⅞	9⅞	7	6⅜	10	10	Tosi Creek, Wyo.	Roscoe O. McKeehan	Roscoe O. McKeehan	1960	107
166	47	30	31	11⅞	7	7	11	13	Glade Creek, Wyo.	E. E. Hosafros	E. E. Hosafros	1961	107
166	48⅞	34⅜	33⅜	9⅞	6⅜	6⅜	10	9	Bonneville Co., Idaho	E. Ray Robinson	E. Ray Robinson	1977	107
165⅞	52⅞	29⅞	29⅞	11	7⅞	7⅜	11	9	Clark Co., Idaho	Elden L. Perry	Elden L. Perry	1975	110
165⅝	48⅞	33	33⅜	11	6⅜	6⅜	8	9	Sublette Co., Wyo.	Ray Snow	Don Boyer	1959	111
165⅝	48⅞	32	30⅞	13⅜	7⅞	7⅜	8	9	Bridger Lake, Wyo.	Hugh W. Mildren	Larry Arndt	1959	111
165⅝	46⅞	32⅞	36⅜	9⅞	6	6	11	13	Sublette Co., Wyo.	Paul A. Graham	Paul A. Graham	1970	113
165⅝	43⅞	32⅞	32⅞	10⅞	6	6	12	13	Buffalo River, Wyo.	Jock H. White	Jock H. White	1953	114
165⅝	47⅞	32⅞	32⅞	12	6⅜	6⅜	8	10	Fremont Co., Idaho	Harvey W. Lewis	Harvey W. Lewis	1964	114
165⅜	43⅞	33⅞	32⅜	11⅞	6⅜	6⅜	14	12	Dubois, Wyo.	Vernon Limbach	Vernon Limbach	1969	114
165⅜	45⅞	27⅞	28⅜	14⅞	5⅞	5⅝	12	12	Lincoln Co., Wyo.	Ryley Z. Dawson	Ryley Z. Dawson	1969	114
165⅛	47⅛	34	35⅜	9	7	7⅞	9	12	Lincoln Moose, Wyo.	Bern Whittaker	Bern Whittaker	1964	114
165	51⅛	35	32	9⅞	7⅞	7⅞	9	8	Fremont Co., Wyo.	Charles A. Boyle	Charles A. Boyle	1965	118
164⅞	52⅞	30⅞	34⅜	9⅞	6⅜	6⅜	10	10	Sublette Co., Wyo.	Edmund J. Giebel	Edmund J. Giebel	1971	119
164⅞	50⅞	34	32⅞	10⅞	6⅜	6⅜	9	9	Pinedale, Wyo.	Clifford G. McConnell	Clifford G. McConnell	1959	120
164⅞	47⅞	29⅞	32⅛	11	6⅛	6⅜	16	12	Teton Co., Wyo.	Ernest L. Cummings	Ernest L. Cummings	1960	121
164⅝	50⅞	33	33⅜	8⅞	6⅜	6⅜	10	9	Lincoln Co., Wyo.	Vernal J. Larsen	Vernal J. Larsen	1973	121
164⅝	51⅞	30⅞	30⅜	7⅞	5⅞	5⅞	11	11	Flathead Co., Mont.	Picked Up	John Castles	PR1954	121
164⅝	51⅞	32	30	10⅞	6⅜	6⅜	11	10	Cache Co., Utah	Bruce N. Moss	Bruce N. Moss	1977	124
164⅝	48⅞	34	34⅜	11⅞	6⅜	6⅜	10	11	Spread Creek, Wyo.	George Malouf	George Malouf	1966	124
164	51⅞	34	34⅞	8⅞	6⅝	6⅝	10	10	Park Co., Wyo.	Burton H. Ward	Burton H. Ward	1984	126
164	50	34	34⅜	11	6⅝	6⅝	10	10	Teton Co., Wyo.	Don L. Corley	Don L. Corley	1985	126
163⅞	43⅞	35⅞	33⅜	13⅜	6⅜	6	9	12	Skull Crack, Utah	Blaine E. Worthen	Blaine E. Worthen	1975	126
163⅞	45⅞	31⅞	36⅜	12	6	6⅜	12	11	Wilson, Wyo.	V. Tullis & A. Van Noye	Victor Tullis	1955	129
163⅞	49⅞	26⅜	35⅝	9⅞	6⅝	6⅜	9	11	Teton Co., Wyo.	Clifford H. Rockhold	Clifford H. Rockhold	1984	130
163⅞	51⅞	30⅞	31⅜	10⅞	6⅜	6	10	9	Teton Co., Wyo.	Robert D. Rice	Robert D. Rice	1982	130
163⅞	47⅞	32⅞	29⅜	11⅞	6⅜	6⅜	12	8	Bear Canyon, Mont.	John Olsen	John Olsen	1962	132
163⅞	51⅞	34	30⅞	11⅞	6⅜	6⅜	9	12	Teton Co., Wyo.	Gordon Hay	Gordon Hay	1970	133
163⅞	50	34	32	10⅞	6⅜	6⅜	11	10	Teton Co., Wyo.	Michael S. Greenwald	Michael S. Greenwald	1978	133
163⅞	43⅞	35⅞	35⅜	11	6⅜	6⅜	12	8	Lincoln Co., Mont.	Alfred E. Journey	Alfred E. Journey	1983	133
163⅞	44⅞	37⅛	35⅛	9⅛	6⅜	6⅜	10	9	West Yellowstone, Mont.	Pete Hansen	Forest B. Fenn	1948	137
163⅞	48⅞	31⅞	32⅞	11⅜	6⅜	6⅜	8	10	Teton Co., Wyo.	Bruce C. Liddle	Bruce C. Liddle	1974	137
163⅞	44⅞	31⅜	32⅞	14⅜	6⅜	6⅜	9	9	Bonneville Co., Idaho	Gerald E. Hill	Gerald E. Hill	1981	137
163⅞	43⅞	31⅜	29⅞	10⅜	6⅜	6⅜	8	11	Lincoln Co., Wyo.	Russell J. Smuin	Russell J. Smuin	1976	140
163⅞	49⅞	31⅜	31⅜	11⅜	6⅜	6⅜	11	11	Jackson, Wyo.	Richard Butts	Richard Butts	1968	141
163⅞	31⅛	29⅞	13⅜	6⅜	6⅜	9	9		Sublette Co., Wyo.	Gerald A. Hoefner	Gerald A. Hoefner	1974	141
162⅞	46⅞	30⅞	31⅜	11⅜	6⅜	6⅜	9	11	Sublette Co., Wyo.	Donald K. Irvine	Donald K. Irvine	1969	143

Score	Greatest Spread	Length of Palm R.	L.	Width of Palm R.	L.	Circumference of Beam at Smallest Place R.	L.	Number of Normal Points R.	L.	Locality Killed	By Whom Killed	Owner	Date Killed	Rank
162⅜	44⅜	31⅞	31⅞	10⅜	9⅝	6⅞	6⅛	12	11	Teton Co., Wyo.	Patrick L. Shanahan	Patrick L. Shanahan	1966	144
162	44⅞	33⅝	32⅜	11⅜	12⅜	6⅛	6⅛	9	11	Upper Hoback, Wyo.	Walter L. Flint	Walter L. Flint	1951	145
162	48⅞	29⅝	34	10⅜	10⅞	6⅛	6⅛	10	11	Lincoln Co., Wyo.	Joan Burnett	Dee J. Burnett	1963	145
162	42	33	34⅜	9⅝	11⅜	6⅜	6⅜	13	11	Madison Co., Mont.	Joseph A. Aanes	Joseph A. Aanes	1984	145
161⅞	51	30⅜	32	9⅝	10⅜	5⅞	6⅛	10	9	Fremont Co., Wyo.	Robert E. Novotny	Ernest Novotny	1944	148
161⅝	46⅜	28⅝	29⅞	11⅜	12⅜	6⅛	6⅜	11	11	Flathead Co., Mont.	Sharon L. Chase	Sharon L. Chase	1979	149
161⅝	51⅜	30⅝	32⅜	10⅜	9⅜	6	6⅛	9	10	Cache Co., Utah	Kenneth Hamilton	Kenneth Hamilton	1980	149
161⅝	51	32⅜	28⅜	10⅜	10⅜	6⅝	6⅝	10	10	Teton Co., Wyo.	Don M. Sheaffer	Don M. Sheaffer	1958	151
161⅝	52⅝	29	35⅜	11⅞	9⅜	6⅜	6⅛	10	11	Jackson, Wyo.	Robert D. Lynn	Robert D. Lynn	1969	151
161⅞	40⅛	34⅜	34⅜	12⅜	12⅜	6⅜	6⅜	10	8	Teton Co., Wyo.	Lynn C. Hill	Oliver Hill	1979	151
161⅝	40⅞	36⅜	30⅜	12⅜	11⅜	6⅜	6⅛	12	12	Bonneville Co., Idaho	Joe M. Coelho III	Joe M. Coelho III	1982	151
161⅝	50	34⅜	27⅜	11⅜	11⅛	6⅝	6⅝	11	10	Lincoln Co., Mont.	Stanley J. Evans	Stanley J. Evans	1982	155
161⅞	43⅜	32⅜	32⅜	10⅜	10⅜	6⅞	7⅜	9	10	Park Co., Mont.	Wes Symness	Wes Symness	1970	156
160⅞	46⅛	30	30⅜	10⅜	10⅜	6	6	12	11	Lincoln Co., Wyo.	Hugh E. Taylor	Hugh E. Taylor	1976	156
160⅞	49	32⅜	34⅜	8⅜	9⅜	6⅞	6⅜	9	12	Pend Oreille Co., Wash.	Archie D. Wyles	Archie D. Wyles	1977	158
160⅛	48	29⅜	30⅜	11⅛	11⅛	6⅞	7	10	9	Lincoln Co., Wyo.	Vic Dana	Fred's Taxidermy	1971	159
160⅞	43⅜	31⅞	31⅜	11⅛	11	7⅜	7⅜	10	9	Beaverhead Co., Mont.	Morton L. Arkava	Morton L. Arkava	1980	159
160⅞	45⅜	30⅜	31⅜	11⅛	12⅞	7⅜	7⅜	11	8	Madison Co., Mont.	Tom Bugni	Tom Bugni	1959	161
160⅛	45⅛	31⅜	34⅜	9⅞	12⅞	6⅜	6⅜	10	14	Jackson Hole, Wyo.	Jack Griset	Jack Griset	1967	161
160⅛	49⅜	29⅜	31⅞	9⅜	11⅜	6⅝	6⅝	10	12	Lincoln Co., Wyo.	Eugene Heap	Eugene Heap	1970	161
160⅛	50⅜	29⅜	29⅜	10⅜	10⅜	5⅝	5⅞	10	10	Teton Co., Wyo.	Joy Lee Gage	Joy Lee Gage	1981	161
159⅞	59⅜	29	38	8⅞	8⅞	6⅜	6⅜	6	7	Lower Hoback, Wyo.	Obby Agins	Obby Agins	1966	165
159⅞	49⅜	31⅞	31⅜	9⅜	8⅜	7	6⅝	8	10	Teton Co., Wyo.	Willis McAmis	Willis McAmis	1972	166
159⅜	46	32	32⅜	10⅜	9⅞	6⅛	6	9	10	Fremont Co., Idaho	Lennard C. Bradley	Lennard C. Bradley	1983	166
159⅜	45⅜	30⅜	29⅜	10⅜	10⅜	6⅝	6⅝	9	10	Pinedale, Wyo.	C. J. McElroy	C. J. McElroy	1969	168
159⅜	55⅜	26⅜	28	10	10⅜	6⅝	6⅝	9	10	Idaho Co., Idaho	Rick E. Kramer	Rick E. Kramer	1980	168
159⅜	46⅞	31⅜	31⅞	11⅜	9⅞	6⅜	6⅛	10	9	Teton Co., Wyo.	Tony D. Poulos	Tony D. Poulos	1983	168
159⅜	41⅜	30⅜	30⅜	10⅜	11⅜	6⅝	6⅜	11	13	Weber Co., Utah	Carl O. Berube	Carl O. Berube	1983	168
159⅞	53⅜	34⅛	30⅜	11⅛	10	7	6⅝	6	9	Pine Creek, Wyo.	Bud Toliver	Bud Toliver	1971	172
159⅞	52⅝	32	31	7⅞	9⅞	6⅝	6⅝	8	8	Lincoln Co., Wyo.	Orlando J. Bernardi	Orlando J. Bernardi	1979	172
159⅜	51⅛	33⅜	29	8⅞	8⅞	7⅜	7⅜	9	9	Sublette Co., Wyo.	Robert W. Sievers	Mrs. R. B. McCullough	1967	174
159	48⅜	33⅜	27⅜	13⅜	11⅜	6	6	10	12	Jackson, Wyo.	Earl F. Hayes	Earl F. Hayes	1953	175

Score										Locality	Owner	By whom killed	Date	Rank
159	41½	36⅝	35⅝	10⅝	9¼	6⅞	6⅞	8	7	Green River, Wyo.	W. M. Hightower	W. M. Hightower	1962	175
158⅞	45⅞	36⅛	33⅝	9⅝	9¼	6	6	8	11	N. Hoback, Wyo.	Geo. W. Hundley	Geo. W. Hundley	1970	177
158⅞	44⅞	33	33	9⅝	9⅛	6⅞	6⅞	8	8	Trail Creek, Wyo.	John J. Huseas	John J. Huseas	1953	178
158⅞	47⅞	35⅝	28⅝	11⅞	12⅛	7⅞	7⅛	10	8	Teton Co., Wyo.	Albert Pantelis	Albert Pantelis	1967	178
158⅞	40⅞	30⅞	30⅞	10⅛	10⅝	6	6	12	13	Lincoln Co., Wyo.	Caroline Nare	Caroline Nare	1979	178
158⅞	47	32	34	11⅞	9⅝	6⅛	6⅛	8	8	Teton Co., Wyo.	Roy G. Hoover	Roy G. Hoover	1966	181
158⅞	43⅞	28⅞	28⅞	11⅞	14⅛	6⅛	6⅛	11	11	New Fork River, Wyo.	Oscar Boyd	Oscar Boyd	1966	181
158⅞	50⅞	26	26⅞	10⅛	10⅝	6⅝	6⅝	11	12	Pinedale, Wyo.	Donald C. Rehwaldt	Donald C. Rehwaldt	1966	183
158⅝	51	30⅝	26⅜	11⅛	11⅛	7⅛	7⅛	10	9	Clark Co., Idaho	Harold Vietz	Harold Vietz	1968	183
158⅛	42⅝	33⅜	35⅝	11⅛	11⅛	6⅝	6⅛	9	6	Gravel Mt., Wyo.	W. A. Kalkofen	W. A. Kalkofen	1966	185
158⅛	46⅞	30⅞	31⅞	8⅞	10⅜	6⅝	6⅛	10	10	Teton Co., Wyo.	Fred L. Eales	Fred L. Eales	1984	185
157⅞	43⅝	34⅜	33⅜	9⅝	13⅜	6	6	8	13	Flathead Co., Mont.	Jim M. Milligan	Jim M. Milligan	1982	187
157⅞	43⅞	31⅞	31⅞	9⅛	8⅛	6⅝	6⅛	10	10	Teton Co., Wyo.	Willard H. Leedy	Willard H. Leedy	1982	187
157⅞	47⅛	27	29	13⅜	12⅛	6⅛	6	10	12	Cache Co., Utah	David W. Jensen	David W. Jensen	1977	189
157⅞	47⅛	35⅝	33	8⅜	9⅜	6⅝	6⅝	7	8	Sublette Co., Wyo.	Mrs. Kenneth Fortuna	Mrs. Kenneth Fortuna	1984	189
157⅜	50⅞	28⅛	26⅝	10⅛	11⅛	6⅝	6⅝	11	10	Grey's River, Wyo.	Mary B. Mikalis	Mary B. Mikalis	1969	191
157⅜	51⅛	28	28	10	9⅝	6⅝	6⅝	11	11	Sublette Co., Wyo.	Teressa Ennis	Teressa Ennis	1983	192
157⅜	41⅜	28⅛	28⅛	12⅛	12	6⅝	6⅛	12	11	Idaho Co., Idaho	Norman R. Fuchs	Norman R. Fuchs	1984	192
157	45⅛	33	37⅛	10⅜	9⅞	6	6	7	8	Lincoln Co., Wyo.	Bob Stafford	Bob Stafford	1963	194
156⅞	47⅛	29⅛	31⅛	9⅝	12⅞	6⅝	6⅛	10	9	Fremont Co., Wyo.	Fred S. Finley	Fred S. Finley	1962	195
156⅞	46⅛	29⅞	28	14⅞	14⅛	6⅝	7⅛	6	9	Ruby Mts., Mont.	Milton Burdick	Milton Burdick	1960	196
156⅞	38⅞	30⅞	31	11⅜	12⅜	6⅜	6⅛	11	13	Deer Lodge Co., Mont.	Mike Munson	Mike Munson	1971	196
156⅞	45⅛	33⅛	31⅛	10⅛	9	7⅜	7	9	8	Teton Co., Wyo.	Palmer Hegge	Palmer Hegge	1952	198
156⅞	37	34	36	11⅛	13⅜	6⅝	6⅝	8	9	Devil's Basin, Wyo.	Charlotte Bruce	Charlotte Bruce	1967	198
156⅝	46⅞	33⅜	31⅜	11	11⅛	6⅛	5⅞	9	7	Sublette Co., Wyo.	Richard A. Bonander	Richard A. Bonander	1979	198
156⅝	43⅝	31	29⅝	10⅛	11	6⅞	6⅝	10	10	Fremont Co., Wyo.	Jan Liggett	J. Liggett & L. Liggett	1985	198
156⅝	42⅝	29⅝	29⅝	11⅜	11⅛	7⅞	7⅛	9	10	Teton Co., Wyo.	George A. Nevills	George A. Nevills	1977	202
156¼	42⅝	32⅝	34⅝	12⅛	12⅜	6⅝	6⅛	6	6	Gallatin River, Mont.	Paul Mako	Paul Mako	1960	203
156¼	51⅞	29	32	8⅝	9	6⅛	5⅞	11	9	Buffalo Horn Lake, Mont.	Vincent De Stefano	Vincent De Stefano	1966	203
156¼	49⅞	28	30	9	9	5⅞	5⅞	9	12	Thorofare River, Wyo.	Dean Johnson	Dean Johnson	1973	203
156⅛	43	40⅞	31⅞	10⅛	10⅛	7	7	9	8	Teton Co., Wyo.	Gerda Prince	Gerda Prince	1970	206
156⅛	46⅞	31⅞	30⅞	9⅝	9⅝	6⅛	6⅛	10	10	Summit Co., Utah	John G. Allred	John G. Allred	1980	206
156⅛	47⅞	31⅝	34⅝	9⅞	7⅞	6	6	10	9	Lewis Creek, Wyo.	Donald J. Krist	Donald J. Krist	1967	208
156⅛	45⅞	30⅝	31⅛	11	10⅛	6⅝	6⅝	9	8	Glade Creek, Wyo.	Joseph A. Merrill, Jr.	Joseph A. Merrill, Jr.	1973	208
156	45⅛	32⅝	31⅛	8⅜	8	7	6⅝	11	9	Missoula Co., Mont.	W. L. Rohrer	W. L. Rohrer	1957	210
155⅞	52⅛	29⅝	30⅞	7⅝	9⅜	6	6	9	9	Ashton, Idaho	Robert H. Thomas	Robert H. Thomas	1972	211
155⅞	46	31⅛	31⅞	8⅛	7⅞	7⅛	7⅛	10	9	Jackson Hole, Wyo.	Don Phillips	Don Phillips	1956	212
155⅞	48⅞	27⅞	27⅞	10⅛	11⅛	6⅝	6⅛	9	9	Jackson Hole, Wyo.	Ralph Brumbaugh	Ralph Brumbaugh	1960	212
155⅞	39⅝	28	28⅝	13	16⅝	7	6⅛	11	10	Upper Hoback, Wyo.	Stephen N. Bean	Stephen N. Bean	1969	212
155⅞	52⅝	36⅝	33⅝	7⅞	6⅞	6⅛	5⅞	8	12	Summit Co., Utah	Monika M. Anderson	Monika M. Anderson	1982	212
155⅞	41⅛	30	31⅛	11⅜	11⅜	6	6	10	6	Lincoln Co., Mont.	Robert D. Nolin	Robert D. Nolin	1979	216
155⅞	51⅛	30⅞	31⅛	8⅞	8⅛	6⅜	6⅛	9	11	Green River, Wyo.	H. S. Jackman	H. S. Jackman	1964	217
155⅞	46	27⅞	31	11⅞	11⅞	6⅛	6⅛	11	10	Jackson, Wyo.	Bud Weaver	Bud Weaver	1968	217

WYOMING OR SHIRAS MOOSE—*Continued*

Alces alces shirasi

Score	Greatest Spread	Length of Palm R.	L.	Width of Palm R.	L.	Circumference of Beam at Smallest Place R.	L.	Number of Normal Points R.	L.	Locality Killed	By Whom Killed	Owner	Date Killed	Rank
155⅝	42⅞	29	29	10⅞	10⅞	6	6	11	11	Lincoln Co., Wyo.	Ralph Wood	Ralph Wood	1977	217
155⅝	52⅜	28	27⅞	9⅞	9⅞	6⅜	6⅜	8	8	Upper Yellowstone, Wyo.	Harold E. Anthony	Amer. Mus. Nat. History	1934	220
155⅜	49⅝	30⅝	30½	8⅝	9⅝	6	6⅛	8	9	Spread Creek, Wyo.	Marty Fiorello	Marty Fiorello	1963	220
155⅜	43⅜	31⅜	30	10⅝	10⅝	6⅝	7	9	10	Sublette Co., Wyo.	Tom J. Schwindt	Tom J. Schwindt	1973	220
155⅜	49⅝	23⅜	29	13⅜	14⅞	6⅝	6⅝	10	11	Pend Oreille Co., Wash.	Thomas F. Kneeshaw	Thomas F. Kneeshaw	1983	220
155⅜	47	28⅜	29⅜	10	9⅜	6⅝	6⅝	11	10	Teton Co., Wyo.	Clarence Harris	David M. Clark	1947	224
155⅜	51⅞	28⅜	25⅝	10⅛	10⅜	6⅝	6⅝	11	10	Dubois, Wyo.	Clyde Thompson	Clyde Thompson	1954	224
155⅞	46	29⅜	30⅜	9⅜	8⅝	6⅝	6⅝	10	11	Lolo Creek, Mont.	Edward Churchwell	Virgil Fite	1955	224
155⅞	41⅛	32⅞	30⅞	11⅛	11⅜	6⅝	6⅝	9	10	Teton Co., Wyo.	Thomas F. Smith	Thomas F. Smith	1973	224
155⅞	40⅜	33⅜	30⅜	11	11	5⅝	5⅝	10	14	Yellowstone River, Wyo.	T. Robert Johnson	T. Robert Johnson	1974	228
155	46⅝	29⅝	30	9	9⅜	6⅝	6⅜	9	9	Jackson Hole, Wyo.	Vernon Williams, Jr.	Vernon Williams, Jr.	1969	229
189⅞*	43⅞	42⅞	43⅜	12⅞	11⅞	6⅝	6⅝	12	12	Jackson, Wyo.	Kenneth Booth	Kenneth Booth	1969	
179*	50⅛	34	38	13⅞	14⅛	6⅝	6⅝	12	10	Bonneville Co., Idaho	Michael B. Whitfield	Michael B. Whitfield	1982	
176⅜*	42⅛	37⅜	37⅝	12⅞	12⅝	6⅝	6⅝	13	11	Bonneville Co., Idaho	Karen Kopinski	Karen Kopinski	1984	
175⅞*	47⅝	34⅜	33	13⅞	13⅜	7	7⅛	12	11	Teton Co., Wyo.	J. Bryan Midgley	J. Bryan Midgley	1979	
175⅞*	46⅝	35	34⅜	13⅞	12	6⅝	6⅞	11	12	Teton Co., Wyo.	Richard D. Oster	Richard D. Oster	1985	

* Final Score subject to revision by additional verifying measurements

Boundaries for Caribou

The various varieties of caribou, which vary widely in size and antler configuration, have been divided into five different categories for records keeping purposes. These five categories are: mountain, woodland, barren ground, Central Canada barren ground, and Quebec- Labrador caribou.

The so-called mountain caribou, now regarded as a variety of woodland caribou by taxonomists, is found in British Columbia and Alberta. Beginning in 1980, the mountain caribou boundary was expanded to include the southern Yukon and the Mackenzie Mountains of Northwest Territories. In the Yukon, the boundary begins at the intersection of the Yukon River with the boundary between the Yukon Territory and the state of Alaska. The boundary runs southeasterly following the Yukon River upstream to Dawson; then easterly and southerly along the Klondike Highway to Stewart Crossing; then easterly following the road to Mayo; then northeasterly following the road to McQuesten Lake; then easterly following the south shore of McQuesten Lake and then upstream following the main drainage to the divide leading to Scougale Creek to its confluence with the Beaver River; then south following the Beaver River downstream to its confluence with the Rackla River; then southeasterly following the Rackla River downstream to its confluence with the Stewart River; then northeasterly following the Stewart River upstream to its confluence with the North Stewart River to the boundary between the Yukon Territory and the Northwest Territories. North of this line caribou are classed as barren ground, while those specimens taken south of the line are considered mountain caribou.

Woodland caribou are eligible for entry from Nova Scotia, Newfoundland, and New Brunswick. Woodland caribou occur sparingly all the way across Canada to southern British Columbia. Although there may be some open seasons in provinces other than the three noted, they are not taken in large numbers anywhere. Woodland caribou can only be entered from the three provinces noted above.

The largest antlered caribou from North America are the Grant's variety, more commonly known as barren ground caribou. Thus, caribou trophies from Alaska, the northern Yukon, Saskatchewan, Manitoba, and Ontario are acceptable in the barren ground caribou category.

In 1984 a new category was established for the barren ground caribou of Baffin Island and the mainland of the Northwest Territories, east of the Mackenzie River and west of Hudson's Bay, to be called the central Canada barren ground caribou. This area is inhabited primarily by the Bathurst, Beverly, and Kaminuriak herds, all of which are highly migratory. Although producing fine trophies, none were known with a high enough score to qualify for listing with the barren ground animals from Alaska and the Northern Yukon. This separate category allows these caribou to receive proper recognition in the records book(s).

Boundaries for the Quebec-Labrador caribou are just as the name implies. Only caribou taken in the Canadian provinces of Quebec and Labrador are included in this category.

WORLD'S RECORD MOUNTAIN CARIBOU
SCORE: 452
Locality: Turnagain River, British Columbia Date: 1976
Hunter and Owner: Gary Beaubien
Winner of the Sagamore Hill Medal, 1977

NUMBER TWO MOUNTAIN CARIBOU
SCORE: 446 2/8
Locality: Atlin, British Columbia Date: 1955
Hunter: Irvin Hardcastle Owner: Mrs. Irvin Hardcastle

Mountain Caribou
Rangifer tarandus caribou

Minimum Score 390

Mountain caribou includes trophies from British Columbia, Alberta, southern Yukon, and the Mackenzie Mountains of the Northwest Territories.

Score	Length of Main Beam R.	L.	Inside Spread	Circumference at Smallest Place Between Brow and Bez Points R.	L.	Length of Brow Points R.	L.	Width of Brow Points R.	L.	Number of Points R.	L.	Locality Killed	By Whom Killed	Owner	Date Killed	Rank
452	43⅛	42⅜	30⅜	7⅜	7⅜	16⅝	16⅛	11⅞	5	22	19	Turnagain River, B.C.	Garry Beaubien	Garry Beaubien	1976	1
446⅝	55	53⅝	40⅜	7⅝	7⅞	14⅝	13⅜	9⅜	5	20	14	Atlin, B.C.	Irvin Hardcastle	Mrs. Irvin Hardcastle	1955	2
445⅜	48⅝	46⅝	27⅜	6⅜	5⅞	17⅝	20⅜	4⅝	17⅞	19	20	Cold Fish Lake, B.C.	John I. Moore	John I. Moore	1958	3
444	52	52⅛	38⅝	6	6⅛	8⅝	20⅜	⅛	15⅞	16	25	Mountain River, N.W.T.	John A. Kolar	John A. Kolar	1984	4
442⅞	44⅜	46⅜	37⅞	7	6⅞	15⅝	17⅛	11⅛	4⅞	24	23	Spatsizi Plateau, B.C.	Jay L. Brasher	Jay L. Brasher	1984	5
441⅞	49⅜	46⅝	33⅜	7	6⅞	19⅝	21	15⅜	4⅞	24	19	Cold Fish Lake, B.C.	Drew W. Gergen	Carnegie Museum	1961	6
441⅛	42⅝	47⅞	35⅜	7⅝	7⅛	17⅝	16⅛	12⅜	10⅛	21	22	Atlin, B.C.	Rafael Garcia Cano	Cascade Lodge	1968	7
428⅝	56⅝	55	37	7⅜	7⅜	15⅝	15	17	15⅜	19	19	Dease Lake, B.C.	Fred G. Kelly	Fred G. Kelly	1964	8
428⅜	56⅝	59	44⅜	7⅜	7⅜	6	19⅜	⅛	14⅜	10	15	Atlin, B.C.	Anna Chabara	Anna Chabara	1960	9
427⅜	55⅜	52⅝	34	7⅜	7⅞	10	20⅜	⅛	17⅞	12	25	Dease Lake, B.C.	Gift of Mrs. Hyland	B&C National Collection	1917	10
425	55⅝	52⅝	43⅝	7	6⅜	16⅝	16⅝	10⅜	8⅝	22	22	Cold Fish Lake, B.C.	A. H. Clise	A. H. Clise	1968	11
424⅜	47⅞	49⅝	37⅜	6⅜	6⅛	15⅝	15⅝	9⅝	7⅝	20	19	Cold Fish Lake, B.C.	Howard Keeler	Howard Keeler	1954	12
424¼	47	46⅝	34⅜	7	6⅜	14⅝	14	10⅜	4⅜	19	16	Cold Fish Lake, B.C.	Edward E. Wilson	Edward E. Wilson	1963	13
423⅞	46⅝	45⅝	33⅜	6⅜	6⅜	17⅝	16⅜	13⅜	6	21	23	Stikine Plateau, B.C.	Dwight Lewis	Dwight Lewis	1970	14
423⅜	42	40⅝	36⅜	6⅜	6⅛	15⅝	19⅜	⅛	13⅜	17	20	Watson Lake, Yukon	Gary Lundstrom	Gary Lundstrom	1980	15
422⅞	45⅝	44⅜	36⅜	7⅛	7	18⅝	19⅜	⅛	16⅜	14	22	Keele Park, Yukon	Donald P. Smith, Jr.	Donald P. Smith, Jr.	1954	16
422⅜	53⅝	54⅝	46	5⅞	6⅛	21⅜	20⅜	6⅛	13⅜	16	15	Little Dall Lake, N.W.T.	Dale L. Martin	Dale L. Martin	1976	17
422¼	50⅝	52	50	5⅝	6	15⅝	16	8⅜		22	14	Cassiar, B.C.	D. W. Bell	Acad. Nat. Sci., Phil.	1923	18
422	65⅝	62⅝	50½	7	7	14⅝	18	1⅛	12⅜	19	25	Cassiar, B.C.	Arvid F. Benson	Arvid F. Benson	1967	19
421⅞	47⅛	47⅛	48⅝	6⅝	6⅜	18⅝	18⅜	12⅜	15⅞	27	19	Aishihik Lake, Yukon	A. W. Fees, Jr.	A. W. Fees, Jr.	1971	20
421⅛	54	52⅝	35⅝	6⅝	7⅝	18⅝	3⅜	16⅛	⅞	27	20	Taku Lake, Yukon	Lloyd Walker	Lloyd Walker	1961	21
420⅝	49⅜	43⅝	41⅜	6⅝	6	19⅝		13⅜		27	17	Cold Fish Lake, B.C.	Maurice C. Perkins	Maurice C. Perkins	1961	22
420	49⅜	44⅝	40⅜	5⅝	6	22⅝	14⅜	20⅜	8⅛	21	15	Mackenzie Mts., N.W.T.	Martin C. Ernest	Martin C. Ernest	1978	23
419⅞	45⅜	44⅜	44⅜	7⅜	7⅛	19⅝	16⅛	13⅜	11	21	18	Atlin Lake Area, B.C.	John Haefeli, Jr.	John Haefeli, Jr.	1964	24
419⅜	52⅜	50⅝	42⅜	8⅜	6⅜	18⅝	17⅞	15⅜	⅛	21	16	Livingstone, Yukon	Charlie L. Bertani	Charlie L. Bertani	1977	25
419⅜	50	50⅜	37⅛	6⅞	7⅜	18⅜	20⅜	2⅜	13	15	13	Mount Mye, Yukon	Clark A. Johnson	Clark A. Johnson	1981	25
417⅞	51⅜	49⅜	40⅛	7⅜	7⅛	6⅝	17⅝	⅛	12⅜	13	21	Gladstone River, Yukon	Herman Peterson	Herman Peterson	1960	27

Score												Locality	Hunter	Owner	Year	Rank
417⅞	43⅝	43⅜	30⅜	6⅛	6	18⅞	18⅜	12⅞	6	24	21	Cassiar, B.C.	Elgin T. Gates	Elgin T. Gates	1953	28
417⅞	51⅛	49⅜	42⅜	6⅛	6⅝	21⅛	10⅛	⅛	14	15	16	Cold Fish Lake, B.C.	John E. Rhea	John E. Rhea	1959	28
417⅞	49⅝	49⅝	40⅝	7⅛	7⅞	11⅛	17⅜	1⅛	14⅜	15	19	Connally Lake, Yukon	Marlin P. Alt	Marlin P. Alt	1973	30
416⅞	53⅛	52⅛	38⅝	7⅜	7⅝	15⅜	19⅛	⅛	14⅜	14	20	Little Dal Lake, N.W.T.	Patricia M. Dreeszen	Patricia M. Dreeszen	1980	31
416⅝	50⅛	47⅛	46	6⅜	6⅞	14⅞	12⅜	10⅜	⅛	14	18	Redstone River, N.W.T.	David D. Hill	David D. Hill	1970	32
416⅜	42⅛	40⅞	31⅛	8⅜	8⅞	11⅛	15	3⅞	11	24	26	Cold Fish Lake, B.C.	Charles E. Wilson, Jr.	Charles E. Wilson, Jr.	1985	33
416⅜	52⅛	51⅞	47⅛	7⅞	7⅝	17⅛	18⅛	2⅜	11⅜	12	13	Mountain Lake, N.W.T.	Stewart N. Shaft	Stewart N. Shaft	1966	33
416⅛	50⅛	50	42	6⅛	6⅛	18⅜	20⅛	2⅜	8⅜	13	13	Cold Fish Lake, B.C.	Clyde Williams	Clyde Williams	1956	35
416	57⅛	53⅜	45⅜	7⅛	7⅞	16	16	8⅛	6	13	16	Atlin, B.C.	R. W. Johnson	R. W. Johnson	1971	36
415⅝	46⅛	49	40⅜	7⅜	7⅞	14⅛	14⅛	1⅛	14⅜	20	21	Cassiar, B.C.	James Keegan	James Keegan	1974	37
415⅜	48⅛	44⅞	33⅜	6⅝	7⅞	15	17⅛	1⅛	9⅜	13	23	Mackenzie Mts., N.W.T.	Gerald Schroeder	Gerald Schroeder	1973	37
415⅝	48⅛	47⅜	34	7⅞	7⅞	16⅛	18⅛	13	14	18	17	Arrowhead Lake, Yukon	Robert L. Pagel	Robert L. Pagel	1971	39
414⅞	50⅞	51⅛	41⅛	5⅝	5⅞	19⅜	17⅞	13⅜	14	19	12	Watson Lake, B.C.	John H. Myaard	John H. Myaard	1984	40
414⅛	48⅛	48⅜	40⅞	7⅛	7⅞	3⅛	16⅛	11	10⅞	17	21	Hoole River, Yukon	Kris M. Gustafson	Kris M. Gustafson	1966	40
414⅛	54	53⅜	28⅜	7⅜	7⅞	15	15	1⅜	10⅛	16	19	Tweedsmuir Park, B.C.	Gary J. Deleenheer	Gary J. Deleenheer	1956	42
414⅛	49⅛	51⅛	26	6⅜	6⅞	15⅝	17⅛	11⅛	5⅜	15	18	Cold Fish Lake, B.C.	D. W. Thiem	D. W. Thiem	1960	43
413⅞	47⅞	49	35⅞	6⅜	7⅞	17⅛	6⅜	10	14⅜	15	14	Dease Lake, B.C.	Bert Klineburger	Bert Klineburger	1963	44
413⅞	49	49	36⅝	6⅝	6⅞	20⅜	19⅛	8⅛	1⅛	20	15	Cassiar Mts., B.C.	Ira Jones	Ira Jones	1956	44
413⅞	53⅛	51⅜	45⅝	6⅜	6⅞	1	14⅜	11⅛	2	17	27	Atlin, B.C.	Mrs. R. S. Marvin, Jr.	Mrs. R. S. Marvin, Jr.	1984	46
413⅞	42⅜	39⅜	35⅛	6⅝	7	18⅜	18⅛	1⅛	15⅜	17	27	Livingstone Creek, Yukon	Lawrence W. Dossman	Lawrence W. Dossman		47
413⅜	51⅛	55	39⅜	6⅝	6⅞	16	10	11⅛	⅛	15	10	Atlin, B.C.	Mrs. Ramon Somavia	Mrs. Ramon Somavia	1955	48
413⅜	41	44⅛	40⅜	8⅞	7⅞	15⅜	13⅜	6⅞	9⅞	19	20	Nisutlin Lake, Yukon	James V. Bosco, Jr.	James V. Bosco, Sr.	1935	49
413⅜	44⅛	49	31⅛	7⅞	7⅛	18⅜	7⅛	13⅜	1	16	14	Livingstone, Yukon	Lawrence W. Dossman	Lawrence W. Dossman	1975	49
413⅜	43	46⅞	25⅞	7⅞	6⅛	17⅛	19⅜	4⅛	14⅞	22	26	Livingstone, Yukon	Mike J. Chirpich	Mike J. Chirpich	1977	49
413	51⅛	53⅞	43	6⅝	6⅞	15⅜	16⅞	8⅜	7⅞	14	18	Drury Lake, Yukon	James H. Russell	James H. Russell	1971	52
412⅞	50⅜	53⅞	47⅜	6⅞	6⅞	18⅛	2⅜	12⅜	⅛	18	15	Cassiar Mts., B.C.	John R. Rinkevich	John R. Rinkevich	1968	53
412⅞	49⅛	50⅛	38⅛	6	6⅞	15⅛	17⅛	10⅜	9⅞	21	23	Cassiar Mts., B.C.	Nolan Martins	Nolan Martins	1967	54
412⅞	55⅞	57⅛	26	6⅜	6⅞	12⅜	12⅛	6	11	20	22	Telegraph Creek, B.C.	James F. Clarke	James F. Clarke	1929	55
412⅞	48⅛	51⅜	33⅜	7⅜	6⅞	19⅛	14⅛	14⅜	8⅜	18	15	Cassiar Mts., B.C.	Leon Mazzeo	Leon Mazzeo	1971	55
412⅞	51⅛	50	37⅜	7⅜	7⅞	14⅜	21⅜	4⅛	15⅜	16	17	Ross River, Yukon	Barry E. Enders	Barry E. Enders	1984	55
412	49⅜	48	36⅜	6⅝	6⅞	18⅛	12⅜	14⅜	3⅞	16	16	Fort Nelson, B.C.	Elmer T. Newman	Elmer T. Newman	1970	58
412	47⅞	47⅛	33⅝	6⅛	6⅞	14	14	11⅜	7⅞	26	25	Dease River, B.C.	Herb Klein	Herb Klein	1960	59
411⅛	43	47	37⅛	7⅜	7⅞	11⅛	16⅜	11⅛	21	21	19	Livingstone, Yukon	Arvo Walter Kannisto	Arvo Walter Kannisto	1974	59
411	48⅛	49⅛	43	6⅛	6⅞	10	18⅜	13⅛	⅛	22	13	Norman Wells, N.W.T.	Elmer R. Kochans	Elmer R. Kochans	1981	61
410⅞	39⅛	40⅜	31⅛	7⅜	7⅞	17⅜	14	10	17	17	14	Nisling Range, Yukon	Jack Odor	Jack Odor	1977	62
410⅛	53	53⅜	41⅛	6⅞	7⅞	16⅜	18⅞	9	5⅞	14	18	Atlin, B.C.	Dale L. McCord	Dale L. McCord	1966	63
410⅛	55⅜	54⅜	30⅞	6⅜	7⅞	17⅜	17⅜	9⅜	5⅛	15	12	Cassiar Mts., B.C.	Charles J. Woodruff	Charles J. Woodruff	1970	63
410⅛	52⅛	53⅜	39	7⅜	7⅞	19⅝	18⅛	16	10⅛	22	21	Ram River, N.W.T.	Michael N. Anderson	Michael N. Anderson	1979	63
410	44⅛	45⅜	22⅜	7⅜	7⅞	20⅜	14⅛	15⅜	2⅜	26	23	Level Mt., B.C.	James W. Reilly	James W. Reilly	1968	66
409⅞	46	45	44	7⅜	7⅞	20	18⅜	9⅜	15⅛	17	20	Atlin, B.C.	Cliff Schmidt	Cliff Schmidt	1966	67
409⅜	41⅛	42	36⅜	7⅜	7⅞	20⅛	7⅜	3⅛	17	13		Dease Lake, B.C.	Wilf W. Klingsat	Wilf W. Klingsat	1974	68
409⅛	51⅛	52⅜	42⅜	6⅜	6⅞	20	7⅞	13⅜	22	12		Ice Mt., B.C.	David M. George	David M. George	1966	69

MOUNTAIN CARIBOU—Continued
Rangifer tarandus caribou

Score	Length of Main Beam R	Length of Main Beam L	Inside Spread	Circumference at Smallest Place Between Brow and Bez Points R	L	Length of Brow Points R	L	Width of Brow Points R	L	Number of Points R	L	Locality Killed	By Whom Killed	Owner	Date Killed	Rank
409⅜	45⅝	46	30⅞	7⅞	7⅞	14⅛	14⅜	10⅜	12⅜	22	24	Johanson Lake, B.C.	George L. Seifert	George L. Seifert	1968	69
409	48⅞	44	48⅞	8⅜	7⅝	18⅜	11⅜	14⅛	⅛	18	14	Level Mts., B.C.	Larry A. Zullo	Larry A. Zullo	1978	71
408⅞	43	43⅞	34⅛	6⅛	6	14	15⅞	6	8⅜	18	16	Skeena River, B.C.	Gordon Baird	Gordon Baird	1966	72
408⅞	48	47⅞	35⅞	6⅝	6⅜	14⅞	16⅛	⅛	6⅞	16	16	Atlin, B.C.	Bradford O'Connor	Bradford O'Connor	1951	73
408⅛	57⅝	57	44⅜	5⅞	6	16⅞	17⅜	4⅛	12⅛	17	20	Canada	Unknown	Snow Museum	1890	74
407⅞	49	48⅞	33⅞	6⅞	6⅜	17⅛	19⅛	15	16	18	20	Cassiar Mts., Yukon	H. R. Safford III	H. R. Safford III	1968	75
407⅞	54⅞	56⅞	37⅞	6⅜	6⅜	2⅞	17⅛	⅛	13⅜	14	15	Keele River, N.W.T.	Roland Schwengler	Roland Schwengler	1984	76
407⅛	47⅞	46⅞	30	5⅝	5⅞	20⅛	21	12⅛	6⅞	18	18	Lower Post, B.C.	Jack Jordon	Jack Jordon	1960	77
407⅛	51⅛	54⅛	43⅞	6⅜	6⅜	20⅜	21⅛	1⅛	16⅜	16	13	Watson Lake, B.C.	Len Anderson	Len Anderson	1967	78
407	51⅛	54	42⅛	7⅛	6⅝	6	19⅞	⅞	10⅞	14	18	Norman Wells, N.W.T.	Thomas P. Warner	Thomas P. Warner	1980	78
406⅞	45⅞	48⅛	39⅜	6⅜	6⅜	18⅜	18⅛	10⅛	10⅜	17	14	Lake Tatlatui, B.C.	Winston P. Woodman	Winston P. Woodman	1966	80
406⅝	50⅜	51⅛	39⅜	8⅜	8⅜	17⅞	17⅜	12⅛	1⅜	18	19	Mountain River, N.W.T.	Grover F. Glasner	Grover F. Glasner	1985	81
406⅜	54	52⅞	37⅝	6⅜	6⅜	17⅜		11⅛	27		20	Ketchika Mts., B.C.	Basil C. Bradbury	Basil C. Bradbury	1962	82
406⅜	43⅜	41⅛	35⅞	6⅛	6⅛	19	19⅞	12⅛	4⅞	21	18	Cassiar Mts., B.C.	Arvid F. Benson	Arvid F. Benson	1965	83
406⅛	48⅛	43⅜	37⅞	6⅞	6⅜	16	16	10⅛	12⅛	19	18	Tweedsmuir Park, B.C.	Bob Stewart	Bob Stewart	1964	84
406	54	53	42⅛	7	6⅜	16⅛	17⅞	5⅞	11	17	18	Dawson Range, Yukon	John M. Domingos	John M. Domingos	1980	84
406	57⅞	55⅞	30	6⅜	6⅜	15	14⅛	7⅞	4⅛	17	17	Watson Lake, B.C.	Marvin Walker	Marvin Walker	1968	86
405⅞	52⅞	51	38⅜	6⅜	6⅜	17⅞	19	13⅜	7⅞	14	14	Mackenzie Mts., N.W.T.	Robert J. Begeny	Robert J. Begeny	1976	87
405⅝	44	40⅝	36⅜	6⅜	6⅜	16⅛	16⅛	5⅞	9	14	15	Cold Fish Lake, B.C.	O. A. Campbell	O. A. Campbell	1959	88
404⅞	44	44	36	6⅜	6⅜	16⅛	15	12	6⅛	22	23	June Lake, N.W.T.	Myron A. Peterson	Myron A. Peterson	1980	89
404⅞	48⅛	48	40⅛	5⅝	5⅞	16⅞	18	8⅞	7⅛	15	17	Cassiar Mts., B.C.	Francis B. Wadelton	Francis B. Wadelton	1969	90
404⅜	47⅞	48	35	7	7	2⅞	14⅛	1	11⅞	24	29	White River, Yukon	Perry Shankle	Perry Shankle	1955	91
404⅛	46⅞	49	41⅛	6	6⅜	19⅝	23⅛	5⅞	15⅝	16	21	Keele River, N.W.T.	T. C. Britt, Jr.	T. C. Britt, Jr.	1968	92
404⅛	49⅜	50⅞	36	6	5⅞	23	7⅞	⅛	19⅞	16	23	Gem Lake, B.C.	Johann Gerdenits	Johann Gerdenits	1976	92
403⅞	44	46⅞	32	6⅜	6⅛	17⅛	10⅜	12⅛	1	26	14	Cassiar Mts., B.C.	Mrs. G. L. Gibbons	Mrs. G. L. Gibbons	1964	94
403⅝	48⅛	49⅞	38⅜	7⅞	7	14	17	5⅞	5⅜	13	14	Gataga River, B.C.	Laurel E. Brown	Laurel E. Brown	1970	94
403⅝	47⅞	51⅛	40⅛	7	7	17⅞	17⅞	9⅞	10⅜	16	15	Pelly Mts., Yukon	B. F. Briggs	B. F. Briggs	1963	96
403⅜	45⅜	43⅝	34⅛	7⅞	8⅜	19⅜	21⅛	10⅛	14	13	16	Drury Lake, Yukon	Henry Macagni	Henry Macagni	1963	96
403⅜	52⅝	50⅜	31	9	8⅜	13⅜	16⅜	7⅞	8⅜	18	24	Ketchum Lake, B.C.	Andy Proksch	Andy Proksch	1978	96

Score												Locality	Owner	By whom killed	Killed	Rank
402 6/8	48 6/8	50 3/8	41 1/8	6 6/8	6 6/8	11 3/8	19 3/8	1/8	14 3/8	17	27	Level Mts., B.C.	Phillip Neuweiler	Phillip Neuweiler	1956	99
402 2/8	45 4/8	47	40 1/8	6 4/8	6 6/8	16 5/8	20 3/8	12	12 6/8	15	13	Dease Lake, B.C.	G. C. F. Dalziel	G. C. F. Dalziel	1958	100
402 2/8	41 6/8	47	39 6/8	7 1/8	7	13	7 6/8	8 3/8	1/8	19	15	Cottonwood Lake, B.C.	Collins F. Kellogg	Collins F. Kellogg	1969	101
401 7/8	50 4/8	51 1/8	39 6/8	5 4/8	5 6/8	20	16 3/8	17 1/8	1 3/8	19	13	Mackenzie Mts., N.W.T.	Thomas E. South	Thomas E. South	1976	102
401 4/8	43 7/8	46	32 1/8	6 2/8	5 6/8	8 1/8	10 4/8	8 5/8	10 2/8	19	19	Dease Lake, B.C.	Hugh Bennett	Hugh Bennett	1961	103
401 3/8	46 7/8	46 1/8	41 5/8	7	7 2/8	15 6/8	15 6/8	1/8	11 5/8	14	15	Cassiar Mts., B.C.	Bernard W. McNamara	Bernard W. McNamara	1958	104
401 1/8	41 4/8	40	36 4/8	6 6/8	8 2/8	17	4 6/8	13 5/8	1 2/8	23	15	Cold Fish Lake, B.C.	P. Walsh	P. Walsh	1970	105
401	42	41 1/8	36 4/8	8 4/8	8 1/8	16 1/8	11 1/8	11 2/8	1/8	15	15	Ketchika Mts., B.C.	H. I. H. Prince	H. I. H. Prince	1960	106
400 5/8	44 4/8	44	34 6/8	6	6 3/8	17 3/8	19 3/8	11 3/8	13 3/8	14	18	Cassiar Mts., B.C.	Abdorreza Pahlavi	Abdorreza Pahlavi	1965	107
400 5/8	54 4/8	54 5/8	36 5/8	7 1/8	7 3/8	16 5/8	2 3/8	10	7 7/8	19	22	Nascha Creek, B.C.	Jack Fleishman, Jr.	Jack Fleishman, Jr.	1968	107
400 3/8	47 3/8	47	39 3/8	8 3/8	8 3/8	19	3 1/8	14 3/8	4 4/8	21	17	Cold Fish Lake, B.C.	W. A. K. Seale	W. A. K. Seale	1961	109
400 3/8	41 3/8	42 5/8	28 5/8	6 3/8	6 7/8	18 3/8	18 3/8	6 3/8	9 2/8	16	17	Caribou Mt., Yukon	Juan Brittingham	Juan Brittingham	1984	109
400 3/8	58 5/8	57 5/8	39 3/8	8	8 1/8	20 3/8	2 3/8	13 3/8	2/8	14	11	Dease Lake, B.C.	Charles B. Heuring	Charles B. Heuring	1973	111
400	37 1/8	39	31 1/8	6 5/8	6 3/8	13 7/8	13 3/8	9 5/8	7	19	22	Cold Fish Lake, B.C.	Stanley A. Chase	Stanley A. Chase	1965	112
400	54	53 5/8	37 7/8	6 6/8	6 5/8	17	14 4/8	6 3/8	5 4/8	18	14	Nahanni River, N.W.T.	Charles P. Yarn, Jr.	Charles P. Yarn, Jr.	1977	112
399 7/8	49 5/8	50 2/8	32 5/8	6 1/8	6 5/8	3 5/8	17 4/8	5/8	8 7/8	16	22	Eagle Nest Mts., B.C.	Kevin Davidson	Kevin Davidson	1967	114
399 6/8	47 3/8	49 2/8	33 5/8	8 5/8	8 2/8	14 4/8	17 7/8	3	14 3/8	17	27	Divide Lake, N.W.T.	Robert J. Stevens	Robert J. Stevens	1984	115
399 4/8	46 5/8	48	34 1/8	6 5/8	6 7/8	17 1/8	17 3/8	4	12 3/8	21	17	Cassiar Mts., B.C.	Brooks Carmichael	Brooks Carmichael	1969	116
399 4/8	45 1/8	45 5/8	38 5/8	5 5/8	5 7/8	15 5/8	3 1/8	8 5/8	1/8	16	16	Turnagain River, B.C.	William R. Franklin	William R. Franklin	1984	116
398 7/8	51 5/8	49	34 5/8	5 7/8	5 7/8	14 5/8	20	1 3/8	13 5/8	16	18	Cold Fish Lake, B.C.	Gerald L. Simpson	Gerald L. Simpson	1956	118
398 2/8	54 5/8	56	38 5/8	7 1/8	6 6/8	19	11 1/8	14 3/8	1	18	14	Spatsizi Plateau, B.C.	George W. Hooker	George W. Hooker	1970	119
398	47 1/8	44 4/8	36 5/8	6 3/8	6 5/8	19 5/8	18 3/8	10 2/8	12 6/8	22	18	Pelly Mts., Yukon	Warren Page	Warren Page	1982	120
397 7/8	46 4/8	47	29 4/8	5 7/8	5 5/8	4 7/8	16 7/8	5/8	14 5/8	17	23	Muncho Lake, Yukon	Michael F. Short	Michael F. Short	1960	121
397 6/8	47	49	39 5/8	8 3/8	7 7/8	17 7/8	18 5/8	10 5/8	12	11	13	Glacier Lake, B.C.	Bob Landis	Tom Mould	1967	122
397 6/8	52 5/8	51 3/8	42 5/8	7 3/8	7 5/8	16 5/8	15 1/8	4	10 4/8	11	14	Mackenzie Mts., N.W.T.	Helmuth Katz	Helmuth Katz	1978	122
396 6/8	46 5/8	44 4/8	29 4/8	7 1/8	7 1/8	19 5/8	20 3/8	2 5/8	14 3/8	14	15	Cold Fish Lake, B.C.	William J. Chronister	William J. Chronister	1960	124
396 6/8	54 4/8	58 5/8	44 4/8	7	6 5/8	18 5/8	15 4/8	13 5/8	1 4/8	19	12	Cassiar Mts., B.C.	L. W. Zimmerman	L. W. Zimmerman	1964	125
395 7/8	46	42 4/8	40 5/8	6 7/8	6 4/8	4	19	1/8	15 7/8	18	21	Ice Lake, Yukon	Peter C. Jurs	Peter C. Jurs	1982	126
395 4/8	51 3/8	51 5/8	42 5/8	6 1/8	6 1/8	18 4/8	17 4/8	9	10 7/8	16	13	Atlin, B.C.	Tadeus S. Konieczka	Tadeus S. Konieczka	1960	127
395 4/8	43 6/8	42 1/8	34 5/8	6 6/8	6 6/8	14 7/8	13 5/8	9	2 5/8	17	15	Dease Lake, B.C.	Ray Foerster	Ray Foerster	1963	128
395 2/8	47 3/8	47 5/8	36 5/8	6 5/8	6 5/8	20 5/8	20 7/8	17 5/8	3 5/8	20	14	Cold Fish Lake, B.C.	George H. Glass	George H. Glass	1963	128
395	48	48 5/8	29 5/8	7 1/8	7 1/8	2 2/8	14	1/8	10 5/8	15	21	Prophet River, B.C.	D. A. Boyd	D. A. Boyd	1961	130
395	56 5/8	54 4/8	46 5/8	5 7/8	5 5/8	19 5/8	15 5/8	18 5/8	1 5/8	17	9	Mountain River, N. W. T.	V. B. Seigel	V. B. Seigel	1983	130
395	56 5/8	54 4/8	46 5/8	5 7/8	5 5/8	19 5/8	15 5/8	18 5/8	1 5/8	17	9		Robert L. Williamson	Robert L. Williamson		130
394 6/8	42 5/8	43	39 5/8	6 7/8	7 5/8	18 5/8	17 5/8	9	11 5/8	15	15	Cassiar, B.C.	Arcadio Guerra	Arcadio Guerra	1957	132
394 4/8	37 5/8	39 5/8	24 5/8	7 5/8	7 5/8	14 5/8	14 5/8	10 5/8	2 5/8	28	22	Muncho Lake, B.C.	H. W. Julien	H. W. Julien	1965	133
394 4/8	44	46 5/8	30 5/8	7 5/8	7 3/8	9 5/8	16 5/8	1 5/8	8 5/8	17	19	Cassiar Mts., B.C.	Raymond A. Schneider	Raymond A. Schneider	1968	133
394	56 5/8	56 5/8	51 5/8	6 4/8	7	14 5/8	19 3/8	13 7/8	13 7/8	11	18	Turnagain River, B.C.	Robert E. Miller	Robert E. Miller	1968	135
393 7/8	38	37 5/8	30 5/8	8 5/8	8 5/8	14 5/8	13 5/8	12 3/8	2/8	18	21	Tweedsmuir Park, B.C.	Harold Daye	Harold Daye	1960	136
393 4/8	49 5/8	51 5/8	39 5/8	6 5/8	6 5/8	2 5/8	2 5/8	1/8	2 5/8	14	17	Cassiar Dist., B.C.	Robert E. Miller	Robert E. Miller	1966	136
393 2/8	54 5/8	54 4/8	33 5/8	6 5/8	6 5/8	11 5/8	17 5/8	1	14 5/8	13	18	Grass Lakes, Yukon	Melvin R. Spohn	Melvin R. Spohn	1981	138
393	52 5/8	50 5/8	39 5/8	5 5/8	5 5/8	18 5/8	16 5/8	4	12 5/8	13	17	Mt. Thule, B.C.	William L. Searle	William L. Searle	1963	139

Rangifer tarandus caribou

Score	Length of Main Beam R.	L.	Inside Spread	Circumference at Smallest Place Between Brow and Bez Points R.	L.	Length of Brow Points R.	L.	Width of Brow Points R.	L.	Number of Points R.	L.	Locality Killed	By Whom Killed	Owner	Date Killed	Rank
392⅞	47⅜	49⅞	37⅞	6⅞	6⅞	⅞	15	⅞	11⅛	16	16	Cassiar Mts., B.C.	Charles Haas	Charles Haas	1959	140
392⅞	41⅞	42⅞	36	6⅝	6⅝	18	16⅝	9⅝	1⅜	21	21	Atlin, B.C.	Earl H. Carlson	Wildlife Tax. Studios	1966	140
392⅞	45⅜	45⅜	40⅜	7⅜	7⅜	14⅜	3⅛	13⅛	⅛	17	17	W. Toad River, B.C.	Daniel R. Bond	Daniel R. Bond	1966	142
392⅝	46⅜	44⅜	36	6⅞	6⅞	16⅞	17⅜	9⅞	5	18	20	Little Dal Lake, N.W.T.	Douglas M. Dreeszen	Douglas M. Dreeszen	1984	142
392⅝	39⅜	39⅜	33⅜	5⅜	5⅜	7⅜	15⅜	⅛	10⅝	22	34	Cold Fish Lake, B.C.	Richard G. Van Vorst	Richard G. Van Vorst	1974	144
392⅜	46⅜	48⅞	32	6⅞	6⅝	16⅜	21	6	12	12	14	Ketchika Mts., B.C.	H. I. H. Prince Abdorreza Pahlavi	Game Council of Iran	1960	145
392⅜	48⅜	52⅞	43⅜	6⅛	6⅛	19⅜	15⅜	⅛	15⅞	10	17	Ice Mt., B.C.	J. E. Mason	J. E. Mason	1966	145
392⅜	47⅜	45⅜	32⅜	6⅜	6⅝	16	17⅞	9⅜	6	15	12	Logan Mts., Yukon	Gordon Graham	Gordon Graham	1978	145
392⅜	44⅜	44	34⅜	6⅜	6⅜	16⅜	17⅞	10⅜	6⅝	18	16	Dease Lake, B.C.	Ross H. Mann	Ross H. Mann	1984	145
392⅜	45⅜	43⅜	30⅜	5⅜	5⅜	16⅜	17	8⅜	11⅜	18	22	Keele River, N.W.T.	Dale R. Hill	Dale R. Hill	1980	149
392⅜	39⅜	46⅜	38	7⅜	7⅜	17⅜	17	7⅜	7⅛	17	13	Rabbit River, B.C.	Bob C. Jones	Bob C. Jones	1969	150
392⅜	42⅜	47⅜	32⅜	5⅜	6⅜	19⅜	5⅜	13⅜	1	19	15	Twopete Mt., Yukon	David H. Crum	David H. Crum	1984	151
392	43⅜	45⅜	42⅜	6⅜	6⅝	15⅜	16⅜	12	11	24	19	Cassiar, B.C.	Dorothy N. Benson	Dorothy N. Benson	1967	152
391⅞	53⅜	53	40⅜	6⅜	6⅛	17⅜	15⅞	5⅝	5⅜	11	11	Glacier Lake, B.C.	Lowell C. Hansen II	Lowell C. Hansen II	1970	152
391⅞	44⅜	44	30⅜	6⅜	6⅜	15⅜	15⅝	9	7⅜	19	18	Mt. Rognaas, B.C.	Michael D. Miklosi	Michael D. Miklosi	1983	152
391⅞	46⅜	43⅜	34	5⅜	6	18⅜	21⅜	19⅜	17⅞	18	21	Cassiar, B.C.	E. F. Ardourel	E. F. Ardourel	1960	155
391⅞	49	52⅞	40⅜	5⅜	5⅜	22	21⅜	5⅜	11⅜	14	13	Ruby Range, Yukon	William K. Hilton	William K. Hilton	1985	156
391⅞	46⅜	43⅜	38⅜	6⅜	6⅜	3	18⅜	⅛	15⅜	13	16	Atlin, B.C.	Bob Reinhold	Bob Reinhold	1963	157
391	38⅜	39⅜	37⅜	7	7	7⅜	17⅜	⅛	11⅜	19	20	Tuya Range, B.C.	Robert L. Gilkey	Robert L. Gilkey	1978	158
390⅜	40⅜	39	34⅜	6⅜	6	15⅜	2⅜	10	⅛	23	17	Tuya Lake, B.C.	John H. Epstein	John H. Epstein	1953	159
390⅜	46	46⅜	34	5⅜	5⅜	2⅜	16⅜	⅛	11⅜	18	23	Snake River, B.C.	J. W. L. Monaghan	J. W. L. Monaghan	1963	159
390⅜	51⅜	48⅜	45⅜	7⅜	7⅛	6⅜	18⅜	3⅜	13⅜	12	12	Atlin, B.C.	Vern Cox	Vern Cox	1962	161
390⅜	39⅜	39⅜	36	5⅜	6⅜	16	18⅜	11⅜	7⅜	20	18	Muncho Lake, B.C.	Dennis Dean	Dennis Dean	1963	162
390⅛	37⅜	38⅜	37⅜	7⅜	7⅜	18⅜	17⅜	11⅜	13⅜	17	19	Cassiar Mts., B.C.	Milo L. Blickenstaff	Milo L. Blickenstaff	1965	162
390⅛	36⅜	37⅜	29⅜	7⅜	7⅜	17⅜	15⅜	12⅝	11⅜	20	17	Halfway River, B.C.	Steven L. Rose	R. Lynn Ross	1965	162
390⅜	36⅜	37⅜	37⅜	7	6⅜	17	1	11⅜	⅜	15	14	Level Mts., B.C.	Donald S. Hopkins	National Collection	1928	165
390⅜	54⅜	54⅜	47⅜	7⅜	8⅜	18⅜	16⅜	8⅜	⅜	12	12	Cassiar, B.C.	Orlando Bodeau	Orlando Bodeau	1953	165
390⅛	55	50	40⅜	6⅜	6⅜	18⅜	6	14⅜	⅛	21	16	Dease Lake, B.C.	W. A. Tharp	W. A. Tharp	1962	167

390 1/8	55 3/8	51 1/8	34 1/8	6 3/8	6 3/8	17 6/8	18 6/8	12 6/8	2 3/8	15	11	Firesteel Lake, B.C.	Melvin K. Wolf	Melvin K. Wolf	1970
448 6/8*	51 3/8	51 1/8	40 2/8	6 6/8	6 6/8	18	4	10 6/8	1	24	20	Great Salmon Lake, Yukon	John Tomko	John Tomko	1965
448 2/8*	47 6/8	50 4/8	39 6/8	6 3/8	6 3/8	19 3/8	18 4/8	15 3/8	1 6/8	18	18	Teena Lake, Yukon	Julian Gutierrez	Julian Gutierrez	1976
447 5/8*	47 6/8	45 5/8	45 3/8	7 4/8	7 4/8	14 4/8	15 5/8	9 6/8	10 5/8	18	15	Pelly Mts., Yukon	Emil Eichenberger	Emil Eichenberger	1960
436 3/8*	57	54 4/8	46 4/8	6 2/8	6 5/8	20 4/8	16 6/8	10 6/8	8	17	14	St. Cyr Range, Yukon	Randall W. Lawton	Randall W. Lawton	1985
432 4/8*	47 3/8	46 1/8	41 5/8	6 4/8	6 4/8	17 3/8	17 1/8	12 4/8	14 1/8	21	22	Tay River, Yukon	Edmund D. Patterson, Jr.	Edmund D. Patterson, Jr.	1964
430 5/8*	46 6/8	47 3/8	43 5/8	7	7	15 5/8	20 6/8	3 3/8	15	15	19	Pelly Mts., Yukon	J. M. Conway	J. M. Conway	1960
421 5/8*	51	52	31 1/8	6 5/8	6 5/8	15 5/8	6	11	1 6/8	22	14	Cry Lake, B.C.	Gordon W. Heenan	Gordon W. Heenan	1985

167

*Final Score subject to revision by additional verifying measurements

WORLD'S RECORD WOODLAND CARIBOU
SCORE: 419 5/8
Locality: Newfoundland Date: prior to 1910
Donated by H. Casmir de Rham to the B&C National Collection

NUMBER TWO WOODLAND CARIBOU
SCORE: 405 4/8
Locality: Gander River, Newfoundland Date: 1951
Hunter and owner: George H. Lesser
Winner of the Sagamore Hill Medal, 1951

Woodland Caribou
Rangifer tarandus caribou

Minimum Score 295

Woodland caribou includes trophies from Nova Scotia, New Brunswick, and Newfoundland

Score	Length of Main Beam		Inside Spread	Circumference at Smallest Place Between Brow and Bez Points		Length of Brow Points		Width of Brow Points		Number of Points		Locality Killed	By Whom Killed	Owner	Date Killed	Rank
	R.	L.		R.	L.	R.	L.	R.	L.	R.	L.					
419⅜	50⅛	47⅜	43⅜	6⅛	6	20	17⅜	17⅝	12⅞	19	18	Newfoundland	Gift of H. Casmir de Rham	B&C National Collection	PR1910	1
405⅞	45	44	30⅜	5⅞	5⅞	20⅛	20⅛	19⅜	19⅝	22	21	Gander River, N.B.	George H. Lesser	George H. Lesser	1951	2
405⅛	38	39⅝	34	5⅝	6⅛	21⅜	20⅜	18⅝	18⅝	22	25	Millertown, Nfld.	Robert V. Knutson	Robert V. Knutson	1966	3
373⅝	39⅛	43⅛	22⅛	5⅛	5⅛	24⅜	22⅜	20	21	21	22	Newfoundland	Gift of J. B. Marvin, Jr.	National Collection	PR1924	4
359⅞	42⅝	43⅛	32	5⅜	5⅛	19⅜	22⅜	17⅛	16⅝	16	18	Serpentine Lake, N.B.	F. W. Ayer	Carnegie Museum	1899	5
357⅛	43	43⅜	31⅛	5⅜	5⅛	19⅛	19⅜	17⅜	16⅝	15	18	Serpentine Lake, N.B.	Frederick K. Barbour	Carnegie Museum	1929	6
350⅛	39⅜	44	30⅜	5⅝	6⅜	21⅜	19⅝	22	17⅞	21	18	Gander, Nfld.	Robert M. Lee	Robert M. Lee	1951	7
349⅝	44⅛	41⅞	45⅜	5⅝	5⅝	17⅛	17⅛	14⅜	7⅞	14	16	Louse Lake, Nfld.	William J. Chasko	William J. Chasko	1963	8
347⅝	41⅜	39⅜	39⅜	6⅞	5⅞	15⅜	14⅝	14	5⅝	20	20	Gander River, Nfld.	E. B. Warner	E. B. Warner	1951	9
347	45⅜	43⅛	33⅜	5⅝	5⅜	14	19	13⅜	3	15	12	Rocky Pond, Nfld.	Gordon J. Birgbauer, Jr.	Gordon J. Birgbauer, Jr.	1984	10
345⅜	42⅜	43	35⅜	7⅛	6⅞	14	14⅜	15⅜	1⅜	23	14	Lake Kaegudeck, Nfld.	J. J. Veteto	J. J. Veteto	1968	11
345⅜	39⅜	39⅜	28⅜	6⅜	6⅝	17⅜	16⅜	15⅞	16⅜	18	19	Newfoundland	Wilson Potter	National Collection	1909	12
340⅞	38⅝	40⅜	31	5⅞	5⅛	15⅝	16⅜	12⅜	10⅜	19	17	Shenadithit River, Nfld.	Gene Manion	Gene Manion	1964	13
340⅞	46	44⅜	27⅞	6⅛	5⅝	17⅜	17⅝	15⅛	10⅜	15	16	Victorian River, Nfld.	Dempsey Cape	Dempsey Cape	1966	14
340⅞	40⅞	41⅛	35⅜	5⅛	4⅞	16⅛	17	13⅜	10⅜	17	17	Wall's Pond, Nfld.	Jeff Lawton	Jeff Lawton	1971	14
340⅞	40⅜	41⅜	30⅜	8⅜	8⅜	1⅜	16⅜	⅛	13⅜	10	20	New Gander, Nfld.	Elgin T. Gates	Elgin T. Gates	1962	16
339⅞	50⅜	50	42⅜	6⅛	6⅛	17	18	8⅜	12⅜	11	10	Gander, Nfld.	Michael Savino	Michael Savino	1969	17
335⅜	40⅜	41	31	5⅜	5⅛	17⅜	16⅜	17⅜	16	15	18	King George Lake, Nfld.	John R. Blanton	John R. Blanton	1984	18
334⅛	39⅜	39⅜	29⅜	5⅝	5⅝	14⅜	14⅜	10⅜	12⅜	25	16	Red Indian Lake, Nfld.	Grancel Fitz	Mrs. Grancel Fitz	1960	19
334	34⅞	37⅜	28⅜	5	5⅛	15⅜	15⅜	14⅜	11⅜	20	19	La Poile, Nfld.	Donald A. Piombo	Donald A. Piombo	1979	20
332⅞	46	43⅝	27⅜	6⅜	6⅝	17⅜	16⅜	16⅜	13⅜	23	18	Newfoundland	Gift of J. B. Marvin, Jr.	National Collection	PR1924	21
332⅝	35	36⅜	28	6	6⅜	15	16⅜	13⅜	13⅜	25	21	Newfoundland	Gift of Grover Asmus	National Collection	1932	21
331⅞	46⅜	48	40⅜	5⅝	5⅜	17⅜	18⅜	11	14	11	11	Newfoundland	Frederick Brooks	Harvard Univ. Mus.	1881	23
330⅜	31⅛	34⅜	26⅜	5⅜	5⅜	15⅜	15⅜	13⅜	11	22	23	New Brunswick	R. W. Gelbach	M. C. McQueen	1900	24
330⅜	41⅜	42⅜	33⅜	5⅝	5⅜	14⅜	16⅜	13⅜	14⅜	18	19	Meelpaeg, Nfld.	Alex Kariotakis	Alex Kariotakis	1969	24
330⅜	37⅜	38⅜	26⅜	6⅜	5	15⅜	16	11⅜	7⅞	17	16	Robinsons River, Nfld.	Timothy E. Fiedler	Timothy E. Fiedler	1980	26
329⅜	37⅜	38⅜	26⅜										Michael E. Lombardo	Michael E. Lombardo	1968	27

336

Score												Locality	Hunter	Owner	Date	Rank
327⅞	44⅞	44⅜	32⅞	5⅞	5⅝	14⅝	12⅞	13⅝	11⅜	18	17	Princess Lake, Nfld.	Dermod O. Sullivan	Dermod O. Sullivan	1967	28
327⅜	39⅜	39⅜	27	4⅝	4⅝	16⅝	17⅜	6⅝	14⅜	18	18	Caribou Lakes, Nfld.	Conrad R. Bragg	Conrad R. Bragg	1962	29
326⅜	41⅜	40⅜	31⅛	6	5⅞	14⅝	15⅝	11⅜	9⅞	21	23	Avalon Pen., Nfld.	Harrold Clarke	Harrold Clarke	1971	30
326⅜	39⅛	41⅛	31⅛	5⅞	5⅝	15⅝	12⅝	9	8⅞	13	17	Rocky Pond, Nfld.	Thomas E. Phillippe, Jr.	Thomas E. Phillippe, Jr.	1975	31
325⅜	43⅛	45⅞	34⅜	6⅛	6⅛	13⅜	13⅜	12⅜	7⅞	18	15	Dashwoods Pond, Nfld.	Daniel P. Amatuzzo	Daniel P. Amatuzzo	1983	32
325	45⅜	44⅜	42⅝	6⅞	6⅝	12⅝	2	16⅝	⅛	17	14	Bear Pond, Nfld.	Stanley T. Beers	Stanley T. Beers	1970	33
322⅝	37⅜	36⅞	37⅛	5⅞	6⅛	14⅞	15⅜	14⅜	10⅞	17	14	Avalon Pen., Nfld.	Richard F. Lewis	Richard F. Lewis	1977	34
322⅜	40⅜	38⅛	35⅛	4⅞	5	13⅞	15⅜	8⅜	9⅞	12	20	Avalon Pen., Nfld.	Angus J. Chafe	Angus J. Chafe	1969	35
322⅜	40	40⅜	25	5⅞	5⅞	15	14⅞	13⅜	9⅞	15	16	Lloyds River, Nfld.	Richard P. Navas	Richard P. Navas	1980	36
321⅝	42⅜	43⅜	35⅞	6⅛	6⅞	13⅜	17⅝	6⅝	15⅛	13	16	Princess Lake, Nfld.	Henry Bondesen	Henry Bondesen	1966	37
320⅞	37⅜	40⅝	34⅜	5⅝	6⅛	15⅜	16⅜	8⅜	11⅞	15	17	La Poile, Nfld.	David J. Coleman	David J. Coleman	1974	38
320⅛	39⅜	39⅜	34	4⅞	5⅝	15⅝	17⅜	12	6⅝	12	17	Top Pond, Nfld.	Donald F. Senter	Donald F. Senter	1984	39
319⅝	40⅜	39	38⅜	5⅞	5⅝	15	15⅝	11⅝	3⅜	17	15	Conne River, Nfld.	Lloyd W. McClelland	Lloyd W. McClelland	1970	40
319⅜	40⅜	37⅛	30⅜	6	5⅞	11⅜	11⅝	8⅜	1⅛	21	16	Long Range Mts., Nfld.	William H. Taylor	William H. Taylor	1983	41
319⅛	37⅜	38⅜	29⅜	4⅞	5⅜	15⅜	11⅝	12⅜	9⅞	20	20	Deer Lake, Nfld.	Alexander Thane	Alexander Thane	1951	42
318⅞	38⅜	39⅜	27	5	4⅞	13⅝	14⅜	11⅜	13⅜	16	17	Lake Margaret, Nfld.	Edward J. Bugden	Edward J. Bugden	1973	42
318⅞	38⅜	38⅜	34⅜	5⅞	5⅛	18⅜	17	15⅜	4⅜	12	9	Great Rattling Brook, Nfld.	Henry D. Frey	Henry D. Frey	1970	44
318⅜	40	41⅜	26⅜	5⅜	5⅞	13⅜	12⅜	11	6⅜	22	16	La Poile, Nfld.	Van R. Johnson	Van R. Johnson	1977	45
318⅛	40⅞	37	38⅜	5⅝	5	16	16	10⅜	12⅜	20	18	Gander River, Nfld.	W. H. Wilson	W. H. Wilson	1955	46
317⅞	32	34⅜	31⅜	5⅞	5⅛	13⅜	13⅜	11	10	18	18	Walls Pond, Nfld.	Laurence Brown	Laurence Brown	1967	47
317⅞	45⅜	45⅜	30⅜	5⅞	5⅜	17	18⅞	⅛	15⅞	9	15	Doyles, Nfld.	Franklin H. Burns	Franklin H. Burns	1956	48
317⅛	43⅜	42⅜	50⅛	5⅝	5⅜	16⅝	16⅜	11⅞	10⅜	13	10	Hynes Lake, Nfld.	Martin W. Nasadowski	Martin W. Nasadowski	1969	49
316⅜	40⅜	42	33⅜	5⅞	5⅝	16⅝	18	1⅜	16⅝	16	21	Sandy Pond Barrens, Nfld.	George L. Harrison	Acad. Nat. Sci., Phil.	1897	50
315⅞	43⅜	46⅜	33⅜	5⅜	5⅜	14⅝	16⅜	11⅛	9	16	16	Newton Lake, Nfld.	W. H. Wilson	W. H. Wilson	1957	51
315⅝	43⅜	42⅜	33⅜	5⅞	5⅞	12⅜	12	7⅜	6⅛	14	14	Sitdown Pond, Nfld.	H. R. Wambold	H. R. Wambold	1966	52
314⅞	42⅜	42⅜	34⅜	5⅝	5⅜	14⅝	14⅜	9⅜	3⅜	12	12	Long Range Mts., Nfld.	James J. McBride	James J. McBride	1982	53
314	35	35	34⅜	6	6	14	14	9⅞	16	12	16	Rainy Lake, Nfld.	Arnold H. Craine	Arnold H. Craine	1967	54
313⅜	33⅜	32⅜	29⅜	5⅞	5⅞	12⅜	10⅝	11⅞	12⅜	14	17	Buchans Plateau, Nfld.	Robert R. Kampstra	Robert R. Kampstra	1980	55
312⅞	39⅜	40⅞	40⅜	5⅞	5⅞	16⅜	16⅞	11⅜	9	16	20	Crooked Lake, Nfld.	Vernon L. Hanlin	Vernon L. Hanlin	1967	56
312⅜	36⅜	36⅜	29⅞	6⅜	6⅞	12⅜	14⅝	9⅜	6⅜	17	14	Stag Pond, Nfld.	Max Meister	Max Meister	1976	57
311⅞	40⅜	43⅜	40⅜	5⅛	5⅝	13⅜	14⅝	4⅛	6⅜	15	14	Buchans Plateau, Nfld.	Basil C. Bradbury	Basil C. Bradbury	1971	58
309⅞	38	36	34⅜	5⅜	5⅞	16⅜	15	14	17	15	12	Neola Paul Brook, Nfld.	Ted Dreimans	Ted Dreimans	1962	59
309⅜	43	43⅜	33	5⅜	5⅜	16	15⅜	5⅜	13⅜	13⅜	15	Rainy Lake, Nfld.	A. L. Levenseler	A. L. Levenseler	1967	60
309	42⅜	44	33	5⅛	5⅞	15⅜	2⅛	17⅛	⅛	17⅝	15	Corner Brook, Nfld.	Gilbert J. Heuer	Gilbert J. Heuer	1970	61
309	46⅜	43⅜	38⅜	5⅞	5⅛	3⅛	13	⅛	9⅛	13	13	Alex Lake, Nfld.	James E. Conklin	James E. Conklin	1981	61
308	38⅜	41⅛	35⅜	5⅜	5⅜	13⅜	11⅜	10⅜	5⅜	15	13	Shenadithit River, Nfld.	L. Ben Hull	L. Ben Hull	1969	63
308	39⅜	40	34⅜	6⅜	5⅜	15⅜	13⅜	2⅜	11⅜	16	15	Meelpaeg, Nfld.	Richard M. Moorehead	Richard M. Moorehead	1969	63
307⅞	38⅜	39⅜	34⅜	5⅜	5⅜	16⅜	16	11⅜	2⅜	19	13	White Bear Bay, Nfld.	John K. Howard	John K. Howard	1938	65
306⅜	37⅜	42⅜	29	5⅛	5⅜	14⅝	14⅜	10⅜	15	11	11	Grand Lake, Nfld.	Theodore R. Greenwood	Theodore R. Greenwood	1983	66

337

WOODLAND CARIBOU—Continued
Rangifer tarandus caribou

Score	Length of Main Beam R.	L.	Inside Spread	Circumference at Smallest Place Between Brow and Bez Points R.	L.	Length of Brow Points R.	L.	Width of Brow Points R.	L.	Number of Points R.	L.	Locality Killed	By Whom Killed	Owner	Date Killed	Rank
306⅝	39	39⅜	29⅜	4⅞	4⅞	16⅜	13⅝	12⅝	⅛	13	13	Millertown, Nfld.	Gerhart H. Huber	Gerhart H. Huber	1966	67
306⅜	41⅜	39⅜	37⅜	5	4⅞	13⅛	12⅝	10⅞	9⅝	17	20	Portage Lake, Nfld.	Arnold Tonn	Arnold Tonn	1967	68
305⅛	37⅞	36⅝	28⅞	5⅜	5	11⅝	13⅝	10⅞	11⅛	17	19	Buchans Plateau, Nfld.	Raymond M. Cappelli	Raymond M. Cappelli	1981	69
304⅝	44⅝	48⅞	26⅝	5⅝	5⅜	18⅝	20⅛	1⅞	18⅛	9	15	Middle Ridge, Nfld.	Nat Levenson	Nat Levenson	1950	70
302⅞	51⅛	50⅛	29⅜	5⅞	6	18⅛	11⅜	16⅛	⅛	14	10	Newfoundland	Gift of H. Casmir de Rham	National Collection	PR1910	71
301⅛	38	39⅜	27⅞	5⅝	5	15⅝	13⅝	12⅝	9⅜	15	13	Eastern Pond, Nfld.	H. W. Doyle	H. W. Doyle	1953	72
300⅛	38⅞	36⅞	34⅝	5	5⅝	16	16⅝	2⅝	13⅝	12	13	Buchans Plateau, Nfld.	Ernest J. Morgan	Ernest J. Morgan	1979	73
299⅞	37⅝	35⅝	28⅝	5⅜	5⅜	13⅝	13⅜	6⅝	9⅝	14	17	La Poile, Nfld.	W. T. Yoshimoto	W. T. Yoshimoto	1973	74
298⅝	40⅞	41⅝	31⅛	5⅝	6	15	16⅝	16⅝	12⅜	14	11	Pasadena, Nfld.	C. J. McElroy	C. J. McElroy	1968	75
298	42⅝	39⅝	35	5⅝	5⅝	17	15⅞	7⅝	11⅜	9	10	Buchans Plateau, Nfld.	Stewart N. Shaft	Stewart N. Shaft	1982	76
297⅝	32⅝	33⅝	29⅝	5⅝	5⅝	13⅝	12⅝	9⅛	6⅛	17	14	Buchans Plateau, Nfld.	Morton J. Greene	Morton J. Greene	1983	77
295⅞	40⅝	38⅝	26⅝	5	5	14⅝	15⅝	9⅝	14	16	17	Top Pond, Nfld.	Robert L. Rex	Robert L. Rex	1966	78
295⅝	41⅝	41⅛	28	5⅝	5	16⅝	14⅝	12⅝	9⅝	18	14	South Branch, Nfld.	Victor Pelletier	Victor Pelletier	1967	78
373⅛*	42⅝	43⅝	36⅝	7⅝	7⅝	19	18⅜	13⅝	15⅝	16	16	Grey Islands, Nfld.	Percy G. Gilbert	Percy G. Gilbert	1975	
370⅛*	47⅝	48⅝	34⅝	6	6	17⅝	16⅝	13	14⅝	20	16	Avalon Pen., Nfld.	John T. MacIsaac	John T. MacIsaac	1970	
368⅛*	49⅝	46⅝	35⅞	6	6	15⅝	15	17⅝	16⅝	22	18	Bonavista Bay, Nfld.	Unknown	Crow's Nest Officers Club	1935	
358⅝*	46⅝	50⅝	30⅝	6⅝	6	13⅝	14	8⅛	8	17	16	Avalon Pen., Nfld.	Gerald R. Bourgoin	Gerald R. Bourgoin	1976	
357⅛*	49⅝	48⅝	39⅝	5⅝	6⅛	15⅝	18⅝	8	7⅝	12	14	Avalon Pen., Nfld.	Barrett Greening	Barrett Greening	1972	
334⅝*	48⅝	44⅝	37⅞	5⅝	6	16⅝	13⅝	8⅝	3⅝	18	16	Burnt Pond, Nfld.	E. B. Pannkuk, Jr.	E. B. Pannkuk, Jr.	1983	
325⅛*	42⅝	41	36⅛	5⅝	5⅝	17	17⅝	10⅝	10⅝	11	12	Caribou Lake, Nfld.	Lyle M. Paro	Lyle M. Paro	1981	
322⅛*	42⅝	41⅝	34⅝	5⅝	5⅝	14⅝	14⅝	4⅝	11	13	15	Cappahayden, Nfld.	T. E. Best, Jr. & H. A. Chafe	Thomas E. Best, Jr.	1982	

* Final Score subject to revision by additional verifying measurements

WORLD'S RECORD BARREN GROUND CARIBOU
SCORE: 463 6/8
Locality: Ugashik Lake, Alaska Date: 1967
Hunter and owner: Ray Loesche

NUMBER TWO BARREN GROUND CARIBOU
SCORE: 461 6/8
Locality: Post River, Alaska Date: 1976
Hunter and owner: John V. Potter, Jr.

Barren Ground Caribou

Rangifer tarandus granti

Minimum Score 400

Barren ground caribou includes trophies from Alaska, northern Yukon Territory, Saskatchewan, Manitoba, and Ontario.

Score	Length of Main Beam R.	L.	Inside Spread	Circumference at Smallest Place Between Brow and Bez Points R.	L.	Length of Brow Points R.	L.	Width of Brow Points R.	L.	Number of Points R.	L.	Locality Killed	By Whom Killed	Owner	Date Killed	Rank
463⅜	51⅞	51½	46⅞	5⅞	6⅛	18⅞	24⅛	12⅞	21⅛	22	23	Ugashik Lake, Alaska	Ray Loesche	Ray Loesche	1967	1
461⅞	53⅜	55⅜	35	8⅜	8⅛	20	18⅜	16⅛	12⅜	29	21	Post River, Alaska	John V. Potter, Jr.	John V. Potter, Jr.	1976	2
459⅜	58	59⅜	40⅜	7⅛	7	19⅜	18⅜	16⅞	4	30	17	Slana, Alaska	Floyd A. Blick	Floyd A. Blick	1954	3
458⅜	68⅝	68⅛	41⅛	6⅛	5⅞	18⅛	15⅞	9	2⅜	21	17	Alaska Pen., Alaska	Joseph Shoaf	Joseph Shoaf	1968	4
458⅜	55⅞	54⅛	45⅜	5⅞	5⅜	20⅛	21⅜	10⅛	15⅛	15	21	Cinder Creek, Alaska	Josef Meran	Josef Meran	1967	5
458⅛	49⅜	50	31⅜	7⅜	7⅛	17⅜	15⅜	13⅜	8⅞	18	17	Alaska Range, Alaska	Bobbie E. Robinson	Bobbie E. Robinson	1963	6
456⅜	54⅛	56	38⅜	6⅞	7⅛	15⅜	20⅜	⅛	20⅛	21	29	Gulkana River, Alaska	W. J. Krause	W. J. Krause	1953	6
456⅛	53⅜	55	43⅞	7	7	9⅞	19⅜	⅛	16⅛	27	31	Mulchatna River, Alaska	Dan Bottrell	Dan Bottrell	1965	8
456⅛	63⅜	59⅜	48	6⅞	6⅜	23⅛	25⅜	8⅜	13⅛	22	21	Alaska Pen., Alaska	Kenneth R. Best	Bavarian Builders, Inc.	1978	9
455⅞	49⅜	48⅜	41⅛	7⅜	7⅜	21⅛	19	10⅜	15⅜	22	26	Alaska Pen., Alaska	Fred H. Blatt, Jr.	Fred H. Blatt, Jr.	1979	10
454⅜	57⅜	58⅛	44⅜	9⅜	7⅜	22⅜	21⅛	19⅜	2⅜	19	17	Wrangell Mts., Alaska	Mary Brisbin	Mary Brisbin	1959	11
453⅜	46⅜	46⅜	38⅜	6⅜	6⅛	17	18⅜	10⅜	5⅜	23	21	Tangle Lakes, Alaska	Mrs. Robert Dosdall	Mrs. Robert Dosdall	1955	12
453	50⅜	51⅜	35⅜	11⅜	6⅛	20	15⅜	20⅛	5⅜	36	18	Alaska Pen., Alaska	Ken Higginbotham	Ken Higginbotham	1984	13
451⅞	54⅜	54⅛	31⅜	7⅜	7⅛	19⅜	18⅜	13⅜	9⅜	23	22	Alaska Range, Alaska	Mrs. Leah Clemmons	Mrs. Leah Clemmons	1956	14
451⅜	51⅜	52⅜	47⅞	6⅜	6⅛	20	8⅜	14⅜	⅛	22	13	Wood River, Alaska	Q. Odell Robinson	Q. Odell Robinson	1980	15
450⅜	64⅜	61	44⅜	6⅜	6⅛	22⅜	20⅜	7⅜	10⅜	16	18	Alaska Pen., Alaska	Phillip D. Wagner	Phillip D. Wagner	1977	16
449⅜	49⅜	48⅜	40⅜	9⅜	8⅜	19⅜	20	17	8⅜	25	23	Lake Clark, Alaska	Dennis Burdick	Dennis Burdick	1984	17
449⅜	50	47⅜	46	6⅜	6⅛	17⅜	19⅜	11⅜	12⅜	19	23	Lake Ugashik, Alaska	Frank Knies	Frank Knies	1965	18
449⅜	45⅜	43⅜	42⅜	5⅜	5⅜	20⅜	23⅜	⅛	16⅜	18	24	Alaska Pen., Alaska	Eddie L. House	Eddie L. House	1979	19
449	47⅜	48⅜	36⅜	7⅜	6⅜	17	16⅜	13⅜	4⅜	20	24	Talkeetna Mts., Alaska	George L. Clark	George L. Clark	1960	20
448⅜	50⅜	51⅛	40⅜	8⅜	7⅜	20	13⅜	15⅜	7⅜	22	24	Little Mulchatna Lake, Alaska	Morton P. Donohue	Morton P. Donohue	1968	21
448⅜	54⅜	56⅜	42	6⅜	6⅜	16⅜	24⅜	4⅜	21⅜	18	20	Dog Salmon River, Alaska	Picked Up	Butch Hautanen	1982	22
447⅜	59⅜	58⅜	49	7⅜	6⅜	20	23⅜	4⅜	14⅜	18	19	Alaska Pen., Alaska	A. D. Heetderks	A. D. Heetderks	1966	23
447⅜	52⅜	52⅜	48⅜	7⅜	6⅜	17⅜	17⅜	14⅜	13⅜	26	22	Alaska Range, Alaska	Richard K. Tollison	Sandra L. Tollison	1978	24
447⅜	54⅜	57⅜	48⅜	6	6	17⅜	20	13	14⅜	24	22	Denali Hwy., Alaska	K. K. Anton	K. K. Anton	1957	24
447⅜	52⅜	50⅜	42⅜	6⅜	7	19	18⅜	15⅜	16⅜	26	21	Ugashik Lake, Alaska	Neil C. McLaughlin	Neil C. McLaughlin	1971	24
447⅜	58⅜	59⅜	52⅜	5	5	17⅜	19⅜	11⅜	12⅜	20	24	Nelchina, Alaska	Bert Klineburger	Bert Klineburger	1964	27
446⅜	58⅜	55⅜	48⅜	5⅞	6	20⅜	23⅜	⅛	17⅜	15	19	Cinder River, Alaska	Cliff Thom	Cliff Thom	1966	28

Score	Length of Main Beam R.	L.	Inside Spread	Circ. at Smallest Place Between Brow and Bez Points R.	L.	Length of Brow Points R.	L.	Width of Brow Points R.	L.	Number of Points R.	L.	Locality Killed	By Whom Killed	Owner	Date Killed	Rank
446 1/8	60	54 6/8	43 3/8	7 3/8	8 1/8	21	18 4/8	15 6/8	12 2/8	19	21	Alaska Range, Alaska	Toby J. Johnson	Toby J. Johnson	1978	29
444 4/8	60 6/8	57 6/8	59	6	6 3/8	24 2/8	21 5/8	17 6/8	1/8 18	18	13	Mother Goose Lake, Alaska	S. W. Terry	S. W. Terry	1967	30
444 1/8	47 6/8	51	41 4/8	6 5/8	6	21 3/8	20 5/8	19 2/8	16 5/8	22	22	King Salmon River, Alaska	John C. Belcher	John C. Belcher	1967	31
443 7/8	51 5/8	50 3/8	45 1/8	5 7/8	6	22	19 5/8	3 5/8	15 7/8	19	21	Wrangell Mts., Alaska	A. E. Bruggeman	A. E. Bruggeman	1962	32
443 1/8	46 5/8	49 5/8	39 5/8	6	5 7/8	15 5/8	19 5/8	9 5/8	15 5/8	16	22	Denali Hwy., Alaska	Stephen Vacula	Stephen Vacula	1967	33
443	57 5/8	57 5/8	51 5/8	6 5/8	6 3/8	10	21	1	16 4/8	18	18	Denali Hwy., Alaska	C. W. Hilbish	C. W. Hilbish	1958	34
443	50 4/8	50 5/8	37	8	6 5/8	17 4/8	19 5/8	12	14 4/8	23	23	Lime Village, Alaska	Billy Ellis III	Billy Ellis III	1978	34
442 2/8	62 5/8	62 7/8	41 4/8	7	7 1/8	24 2/8	7 7/8	20 5/8	1/8	14	14	Wood River, Alaska	Charles M. Bentley	Charles M. Bentley	1960	36
442 1/8	45	50	38 2/8	7 4/8	7 1/8	1 3/8	21 5/8	1/8	17 5/8	26	26	Talkeetna Mts., Alaska	Jack C. Robb	Jack C. Robb	1958	37
441 5/8	51 5/8	53 7/8	47	7 4/8	6	22 5/8	5 5/8	16 7/8	1 1/8	20	13	Alaska Pen., Alaska	George Waldriff	George Waldriff	1962	38
441 1/8	55 5/8	53 5/8	37 5/8	5 7/8	6 2/8	20	15 1/8	14 4/8	1/8	17	15	Healy, Alaska	G. H. Gunn	G. H. Gunn	1968	39
440 7/8	59 5/8	56 5/8	44 2/8	6 5/8	6 3/8	13 5/8	22 4/8	1/8	17 2/8	11	15	Snow Shoe Lake, Alaska	Ray Al Winchester	Demarest Mem. Museum	1953	40
440 5/8	54 4/8	58 5/8	44 2/8	6 5/8	7	9 5/8	20 5/8	1/8	16 5/8	19	28	Blue Berry Creek, Alaska	Ed Shapiro	Ed Shapiro	1964	41
440 2/8	55 5/8	55 1/8	40 5/8	5 5/8	6 1/8	20 5/8	18 4/8	10 5/8	11	18	17	Kenai, Alaska	Picked Up	Marcia L. King	1972	41
439 7/8	44	46 5/8	51 2/8	6 5/8	7	18 5/8	3 3/8	14 5/8	5/8	25	17	Port Heiden, Alaska	Marshall Carr	Marshall Carr	1963	43
439 5/8	60 5/8	61 3/8	40 5/8	6 5/8	6 6/8	7 5/8	7 3/8	11 5/8	1/8	16	12	Talkeetna Mts., Alaska	Chris Klineburger	Chris Klineburger	1961	44
439 2/8	45 7/8	36 5/8	38 5/8	5 5/8	6 5/8	23 5/8	19 1/8	16	13 5/8	33	25	Egegik River, Alaska	Norman Tibbetts	Norman Tibbetts	1959	45
439 1/8	53 4/8	53 4/8	45 5/8	5 5/8	5 5/8	22 5/8	21 4/8	16 5/8	3 5/8	23	15	Iliamna Lake, Alaska	Edward L. Fuchs	Edward L. Fuchs	1955	46
439 1/8	59 5/8	59	46	7	5 5/8	2 4/8	18 4/8	1 5/8	10 5/8	12	15	Twin Lakes, Alaska	Thomas H. Lutsey	Thomas H. Lutsey	1955	46
439	62 5/8	60 2/8	53 5/8	5 5/8	5 5/8	21 5/8	15 3/8	16 5/8	9 5/8	22	22	Alaska Pen., Alaska	Joseph H. Johnson	Joseph H. Johnson	1976	48
438 5/8	52 4/8	51 5/8	41 5/8	6 5/8	6 3/8	17 5/8	15 5/8	8 5/8	7 5/8	21	19	Maclaren River, Alaska	Donald W. Bunselmeier	Donald W. Bunselmeier	1981	49
438	53 4/8	49	47	5 5/8	5 4/8	19 4/8	14	14 4/8	7 4/8	18	18	Lower Ugashik Lake, Alaska	Bert A. McLay	Bert A. McLay	1981	50
438	60 4/8	55 4/8	40 4/8	8 5/8	7 5/8	21 4/8	6 5/8	15	1/8	12	12	Ugashik Lake, Alaska	Norman W. Gilmore	Norman W. Gilmore	1967	50
437 7/8	46 2/8	51	38 5/8	6 5/8	6 3/8	21 5/8	16 7/8	15 5/8	9 4/8	14	14	Alaska Pen., Alaska	Herb Klein	Herb Klein	1967	52
437 5/8	61 1/8	61 3/8	37 2/8	6 5/8	6 1/8	5 1/8	23 5/8	1/8	9 5/8	25	25	Nelchina River, Alaska	Don Flynn	Don Flynn	1959	53
437 5/8	48 1/8	48 5/8	38 5/8	7 5/8	6	21 5/8	20 5/8	14 5/8	18 5/8	22	22	Tangle Lake, Alaska	Dennis Weston	Dennis Weston	1964	54
437 5/8	60	61 5/8	50 5/8	6 7/8	7 5/8	13 5/8	19 5/8	1 5/8	12 5/8	19	19	Naknek, Alaska	C. J. McElroy	C. J. McElroy	1966	55

Score											Locality	Hunter	Owner	Date	Rank
437⅞	59⅜	57⅞	6⅜	5⅞	20⅛	19⅞	5	12⅞	19	23	Mulchatna River, Alaska	Lyle W. Bentzen	Lyle W. Bentzen	1974	56
436⅞	52⅞	53	6	6	16	19⅞	12⅞	10⅞	15	16	Chisana River, Alaska	Terry Overly	Terry Overly	1976	57
436⅞	55⅝	58⅞	7⅜	6	20	24⅜	1⅞	19⅞	19	23	Alaska Pen., Alaska	A. R. Buckles	A. R. Buckles	1967	58
436⅛	54⅞	53⅛	6	5⅞	19⅛	20⅛	15⅞	15⅞	22	18	Nabesna, Alaska	Bill Ellis	Bill Ellis	1964	58
436⅛	54⅞	55	5⅞	5⅞	9⅞	24⅞	1⅞	21⅞	15	27	Port Moller, Alaska	Marvin L. Fergastad	Marvin L. Fergastad	1962	60
435⅞	56⅞	54	6⅜	7	18⅛	3	16	⅞	23	16	McClaren Ridge, Alaska	Peter W. Bading	Peter W. Bading	1959	61
435⅞	55⅜	51⅞	6⅜	8⅜	10⅜	17⅞	10	5⅞	23	33	Wrangell Mts., Alaska	Fred Williams	Fred Williams	1964	61
435⅝	48⅞	52⅞	8⅛	8⅛	14⅛	13⅞	11⅜	10	22	19	Farewell, Alaska	Henry Budny	Henry Budny	1960	63
435⅝	53⅛	53	6⅜	5⅞	4⅛	17⅞	⅞	11⅜	17	24	Talkeetna Mts., Alaska	John M. Killian	John M. Killian	1960	63
435⅝	53⅛	54⅜	6⅜	6⅜	18⅛	20⅛	11⅛	14⅜	22	19	Talkeetna Mts., Alaska	Mrs. Arnt Antonsen	Mrs. Arnt Antonsen	1960	65
435⅜	51⅛	50⅛	7⅞	7	23⅞	12⅛	18⅛	2⅞	19	13	Ugashik Lake, Alaska	Robert E. Sass	Robert E. Sass	1963	66
435⅜	52⅛	49⅛	9⅜	9⅞	19⅞	22⅞	9⅜	6⅜	19	19	Naknek River, Alaska	Chris M. Kendrick	Chris M. Kendrick	1977	67
435⅜	53⅛	55⅛	5⅜	5⅞	22⅞	18⅛	11⅜	12⅜	25	19	Alaska Range, Alaska	Kermit G. Johnson	Kermit G. Johnson	1970	68
434⅜	58⅛	57⅞	6⅜	6	17⅞	17⅞	11⅛	9	22	22	Tangle Lakes, Alaska	Bryant Flynn	Bryant Flynn	1953	69
434⅜	42⅞	45⅞	6⅜	6⅜	16	17⅞	7⅞	12⅞	21	22	Tazlina, Alaska	Chuck Sutter	Chuck Sutter	1958	70
434	51⅛	48⅞	6⅜	6⅜	20⅛	19⅞	15⅞	14⅞	21	16	King Salmon, Alaska	Roger W. Seiler	Roger W. Seiler	1959	71
434	61⅛	60	6⅜	5⅞	19⅜	19⅞	11⅞	6⅞	14	18	Little Nelchina River, Alaska	Joseph Brisco, Jr.	Joseph Brisco, Jr.	1955	71
433⅞	59⅛	56⅞	6⅜	6⅜	15⅝	20⅛	10⅛	15	25	21	Port Moller, Alaska	Paul M. Sweezey	Paul M. Sweezey	1968	73
433⅜	59⅛	59⅞	6⅜	6⅜	23	8⅛	18⅛	1	22	13	Alaska Pen., Alaska	Herb Klein	Herb Klein	1964	74
433⅜	59⅛	56	5⅝	6	3⅜	19⅞	⅞	14⅞	16	22	Port Heiden, Alaska	D. R. Klein	D. R. Klein	1966	75
432⅞	52⅛	52⅞	5⅝	6⅛	5⅞	23⅞	4	16⅞	15	19	Black Lake, Alaska	John Tyler Swiss	John Tyler Swiss	1967	76
432⅝	50⅛	48⅞	9	12⅞	14⅞	15⅛	⅞	8⅞	16	21	Healy River, Alaska	Frank Talerico	Anitra Talerico	1982	76
432⅜	55⅞	55⅞	5⅝	5⅞	7	21⅞	17⅞	⅞	23	15	Hick Creek, Alaska	Justin D. Hall	Justin D. Hall	1984	78
432	58⅞	50⅞	7	7	5⅞	22	1	16⅜	15	19	King Salmon, Alaska	Dan E. McCarty	Dan E. McCarty	1967	79
432	52⅛	51⅛	7⅞	10⅛	4⅜	15	12⅛	21	22	—	Lake Louise, Alaska	Mike Walganski	Mike Walganski	1961	80
432	49⅛	49⅛	6	5⅞	18⅜	15	11⅞	⅞	18	19	Upper Susitna River, Alaska	Theodore A. Warren	Theodore A. Warren	1955	80
431⅞	48	53⅜	5⅝	6	37⅜	17⅜	11⅜	11	18	21	Nondalton, Alaska	Gordon S. Swift	Gordon S. Swift	1981	82
431⅝	49⅜	45⅜	7⅞	7	33⅜	19⅞	16⅝	20	29	—	Clarence Lake, Alaska	Jack Hill	Jack Hill	1964	83
431⅜	51⅛	51⅜	6⅝	6⅝	55⅛	20⅜	12⅝	15	23	—	King Salmon, Alaska	Warren F. Phillips	Warren F. Phillips	1983	84
431⅜	49	52⅜	6⅝	6⅝	36⅜	13⅜	5⅞	28	24	—	Cold Bay, Alaska	Gary D'Aigle	Gary D'Aigle	1973	85
431⅜	54⅛	51⅜	7⅜	7⅜	35⅜	18⅜	10⅜	20	20	—	Lake Clark, Alaska	William R. Lykken	William R. Lykken	1976	85
431	54⅜	54⅜	6⅜	6⅝	41⅜	18⅜	10⅜	15	17	—	Talkeetna Mts., Alaska	Joseph R. Good	Joseph R. Good	1956	85
430⅞	39	54⅜	7⅜	7⅜	39	21	13⅜	20	21	—	Port Heiden, Alaska	Ray B. Nienhaus	Ray B. Nienhaus	1966	88
430⅞	49	48⅜	6⅝	7⅜	40⅜	14	7⅞	14	19	—	Susitna River, Alaska	James I. Roland	James I. Roland	1983	89
430⅞	50⅛	48⅜	6⅝	6	32⅜	16⅝	10⅜	20	26	—	Talkeetna Mts., Alaska	Nelson Spencer	Nelson Spencer	1962	90
430⅜	57	54⅜	8	8⅜	46⅜	6⅜	⅞	22	17	—	Alaska Pen., Alaska	Michaux Nash, Jr.	Michaux Nash, Jr.	1968	91
430⅜	47	49⅜	6⅝	7	35⅜	13⅜	14⅜	24	24	—	Gulkana River, Alaska	Troy Bogard	Troy Bogard	1954	91
430⅜	53⅛	54⅜	6⅛	5⅝	44⅜	22⅜	17⅜	15	20	—	Alaska Pen., Alaska	Ernest Milani	Ernest Milani	1961	93
430⅜	57⅞	53⅜	6⅝	6⅝	44⅜	16⅜	10⅜	23	16	—	Mother Goose Lake, Alaska	R. C. Parker	R. C. Parker	1959	93
429⅞	50⅞	51⅜	5⅞	5⅞	18	19⅞	15⅞	12⅞	21	24	Bonnet Plume, Yukon	R. G. Studemann	R. G. Studemann	1963	95

343

Barren Ground Caribou—Continued
Rangifer tarandus granti

Score	Length of Main Beam R.	L.	Inside Spread	Circumference at Smallest Place Between Brow and Bez Points R.	L.	Length of Brow Points R.	L.	Width of Brow Points R.	L.	Number of Points R.	L.	Locality Killed	By Whom Killed	Owner	Date Killed	Rank
429⅜	53⅛	59	42⅝	7⅞	7	15⅜	15	11⅜		24	17	Mulchatna River, Alaska	Lem Crofton	Lem Crofton	1978	96
429⅛	58	58	35	6⅞	6	26	15	19	½	22	15	Alaska Range, Alaska	J. C. Phillips	Harvard Univ. Mus.	1928	97
429⅛	49	48⅜	43⅜	9⅜	7	16⅜	17⅞	8⅞	8⅞	21	20	Tyone Lake, Alaska	Ralph Marshall	Ralph Marshall	1960	97
428⅝	57	54⅛	41	6⅜	6⅜	21⅛	7	16⅜	⅛	20	12	Iliamna Lake, Alaska	Linda J. Corley	Linda J. Corley	1983	99
427⅞	56⅜	59⅞	44⅛	5⅞	5⅛	19⅞	18⅞	13⅞	⅛	19	11	Talkeetna Mts., Alaska	Donald Parker	Donald Parker	1969	100
426⅞	49	46	40⅝	6⅛	5⅞	16	21⅞	9⅝	11⅜	22	25	Cinder River, Alaska	John G. Merry, Jr.	John G. Merry, Jr.	1968	101
426⅜	52⅛	52⅛	49⅛	7⅞	5⅝	11⅛	20	⅛	15⅞	17	20	Alaska Range, Alaska	Dan Parker	Dan Parker	1971	102
426⅜	52⅛	53⅛	45⅛	6⅛	7⅞	15⅞	6⅛	17⅞	⅛	25	17	Anchorage, Alaska	Peter W. Bading	Peter W. Bading	1963	102
426⅜	53⅛	54⅛	44⅜	8⅜	8	24		13⅜		19	18	Black Lake, Alaska	Lester W. Miller, Jr.	Lester W. Miller, Jr.	1963	104
426⅜	52⅜	54⅝	37⅝	6⅜	6⅜	18⅝	18⅞	3⅞	15⅜	15	22	Eureka, Alaska	C. C. Grey	C. C. Grey	1953	104
426⅜	52⅜	48⅜	40⅞	8⅜	8	33⅛	17	⅛	11⅜	17	22	Wrangell Mts., Alaska	Richard Conroy	Richard Conroy	1961	104
426⅜	56⅜	60⅞	41⅛	6⅛	6⅛	19⅛	13	15⅜	⅛	17	15	White River, Yukon	F. C. Havemeyer	National Collection	1912	104
426	53	52⅜	42⅜	6⅛	6⅞	19⅛	19⅜	8⅛	11⅜	22	20	Fog Lakes, Alaska	Larry F. Grout	Larry F. Grout	1981	107
425⅝	45⅜	49⅜	32⅜	6	6	17⅞	19⅜	11⅜	18⅝	18	18	Denali Hwy., Alaska	Sam Pancotto	Sam Pancotto	1960	108
425⅝	53⅜	55⅞	39⅛	7⅜	7⅞	33⅛	14	⅛	10⅜	15	19	Nabesna, Alaska	Frank Martin, Jr.	Frank Martin, Jr.	1965	109
425⅝	48⅛	47⅞	46⅞	5⅝	5⅝	20⅜	19	4⅛	14⅞	17	21	Becharof Lake, Alaska	Lavon L. Chittick	Lavon L. Chittick	1981	109
425⅝	52⅜	48	31	7⅜	7⅞	13	19	⅛	13⅜	14	19	Iliamna Lake, Alaska	Donald R. Barnes	Donald R. Barnes	1973	111
425⅝	56⅜	59	43⅜	7⅛	7	20⅜	19⅞	8	10⅜	20	14	Iliamna Lake, Alaska	A. A. Bishop	A. A. Bishop	1982	111
425⅜	55⅜	56⅞	41	6⅞	7⅞	17⅞	18⅞	5⅝	9⅝	17	17	Moody Creek, Alaska	Ervin Hostetler	Ervin Hostetler	1983	113
425⅝	46⅜	48⅞	35⅜	6⅞	6⅜	16	2⅜	7⅞	12⅜	20	21	McClaren Ridge, Alaska	Peter W. Bading	Peter W. Bading	1959	113
425	47⅛	52⅞	36	7	6⅜	8	23	1⅜	18⅝	18	32	Lake Louise, Alaska	H. E. O'Neal	H. E. O'Neal	1964	115
425	52⅞	52⅞	40⅝	6⅛	6⅜	17⅞	9⅜	12⅜	⅛	23	17	Susitna Area, Alaska	Elmer M. Rusten	Elmer M. Rusten	1952	116
425	45⅛	45⅞	36⅞	5⅝	5⅜	20⅜	21⅛	15⅜	7⅞	22	22	Talkeetna Mts., Alaska	Thorne Donnelley	Thorne Donnelley	1959	116
424⅞	53⅜	53⅝	36⅜	6⅜	6⅛	21⅛	2⅜	16⅛	⅛	18	20	Alaska Range, Alaska	Dennis R. Johnson	Dennis R. Johnson	1980	119
424⅞	52⅜	58⅛	43⅜	7⅞	8⅛	15⅜	14	5⅜	9	19	16	Denali Hwy., Alaska	Moyer Johnstone	Moyer Johnstone	1958	119
424⅞	57⅛	54	49⅛	6⅜	6⅛	20⅜	14⅛	14⅜	1⅛	18	16	La Pas, Man.	Unknown	Luxton Museum	PR 1954	119
424⅞	58⅛	54⅝	45⅜	6⅜	6⅜	37⅛	25⅜	⅛	18⅞	14	17	Ugashik Lakes, Alaska	Robert C. Jones	Robert C. Jones	1981	119
424⅜	58⅜	54⅝	45⅝	7⅛	6⅜	19⅞	19⅜	14⅞	1⅛	18	13	Talkeetna Mts., Alaska	Karl Weber	Karl Weber	1959	123
424⅜	55	52⅜	47⅜	7⅛	6⅜	17	17	14⅜	1⅛	18	18	Talkeetna Mts., Alaska	Wayne C. Eubank	Wayne C. Eubank	1959	123
424⅜	51⅛	47⅜	43⅜	6⅜	6⅜	16⅜	1⅞	11⅜	8⅛	18	20	Lake Louise, Alaska	Dick Luckow	Dick Luckow	1959	125
424⅜	61	59	46	7⅜	5⅜	19⅞	14⅞	13	⅜	23	13	Post River, Alaska	Guntram Rhomberg	Guntram Rhomberg	1966	125
424⅜	51⅛	58⅜	40⅜	5⅜	5⅜	15⅜	19⅛	10⅜	15⅜	17	19	King Salmon, Alaska	Samuel C. Johnson	Samuel C. Johnson	1978	127

[illegible]	[illegible]	[illegible]	[illegible]	[illegible]	[illegible]	[illegible]	[illegible]	[illegible]	16	18	26	Summit, Alaska	Myron Bethel	Myron Bethel	1976	127
424 2/8	51 1/8	49	43 3/8	6 2/8	6 1/8	12 2/8	22 4/8	1	17 7/8	16	23	Talkeetna Mts., Alaska	Morris Spencer	Morris Spencer	1962	127
424 1/8	52 5/8	52 4/8	46 6/8	6 2/8	6 2/8	17 6/8	19 4/8	9 1/8	4 6/8	16	17	Talkeetna Mts., Alaska	Lyle E. Reynolds	Lyle E. Reynolds	1960	130
424 1/8	43 5/8	43 4/8	32 7/8	6 7/8	6 2/8	16	1 7/8	13 4/8	5/8	37	24	Wrangell Mts., Alaska	Dan G. Best	Dan G. Best	1961	130
423 6/8	56 5/8	55 1/8	40 7/8	6 4/8	6 6/8	18 4/8	14 2/8	12 5/8	1 4/8	16	12	Alaska Pen., Alaska	Rex Hancock	Rex Hancock	1961	132
423 6/8	55	54 7/8	47	5 6/8	5 6/8	17 2/8	10 7/8	11 3/8	3 2/8	25	17	Cinder River, Alaska	Gary F. Romaniw	Gary F. Romaniw	1981	132
423 6/8	52 7/8	50 6/8	40 3/8	5 2/8	5 3/8	1 7/8	15 1/8	1/8	10 4/8	19	23	King Salmon River, Alaska	Henry N. Warren	Henry N. Warren	1978	132
423 3/8	59 3/8	59 4/8	41 1/8	5 6/8	5 5/8	19	19 2/8	8	16 2/8	17	21	Ferry, Alaska	Roy Maxwell	Roy Maxwell	1965	135
423 1/8	44 6/8	44	32 4/8	6 7/8	7 1/8	19 3/8	20 3/8	9 1/8	17	18	24	Tyone River, Alaska	Alva H. Rich	Alva H. Rich	1961	136
423	53 1/8	55 2/8	44 1/8	6 7/8	6 7/8	16	15 3/8	6 2/8	9 4/8	13	15	Gulkana River, Alaska	Lewis E. Yearout	Lewis E. Yearout	1956	137
423	47 6/8	50	48	6 4/8	6 3/8	18 2/8	16 3/8	9 2/8	8 7/8	15	16	Panorama Mt., Alaska	Ronald R. Minard	Ronald R. Minard	1985	137
423	43 5/8	43 7/8	40	5 6/8	7 2/8	6 7/8	16 7/8	3	11	14	15	Port Heiden, Alaska	Robert D. Jones	Robert D. Jones	1981	137
422 7/8	50 6/8	51 5/8	37	6 2/8	6 2/8	21 1/8	20 2/8	9 1/8	15 1/8	20	21	Rainy Pass, Alaska	L. Arthur Cushman, Jr.	L. Arthur Cushman, Jr.	1961	140
422 6/8	46 6/8	51 7/8	40	5 7/8	6 1/8	19 6/8	17	12 4/8	3 6/8	18	17	Matanuska River, Alaska	Stephen E. Skaggs	Stephen E. Skaggs	1978	141
422 6/8	49 2/8	48 6/8	47 3/8	6 3/8	6 3/8	16 4/8	14 5/8	11 2/8	6 6/8	19	13	Slana River, Alaska	Kirby Kiltz	Kirby Kiltz	1959	141
422 5/8	50 4/8	45 4/8	34 4/8	9 4/8	6 6/8	20 2/8	17	15	5 5/8	16	19	Mt. Sanford, Alaska	John J. Heidel	John J. Heidel	1982	143
422 5/8	44 2/8	44 6/8	35 4/8	5 6/8	5 7/8	22	4 3/8	13 6/8	1 2/8	23	16	Snipe Lake, Alaska	Steven S. Lambe	Steven S. Lambe	1983	143
422 4/8	52 1/8	47 4/8	45 4/8	5 4/8	5 4/8	20 7/8	18	4 2/8	11 7/8	22	20	Iliamna Lake, Alaska	Bill Sims	Bill Sims	1973	145
422 3/8	49 2/8	49 3/8	37 4/8	6 3/8	6 2/8	21 4/8	19 3/8	13 4/8	11 4/8	22	20	Tangle Lakes, Alaska	Leroy G. Bohuslor	Leroy G. Bohuslor	1952	146
422 1/8	57 3/8	59 3/8	54 4/8	6 1/8	5 7/8	22 2/8	1 4/8	17 4/8	1/8	21	14	King Salmon, Alaska	Jerry R. Jones	Jerry R. Jones	1981	147
422 1/8	42 3/8	45 7/8	37	7 6/8	6 5/8	16 5/8	13	15 2/8	11	27	21	Susitna River, Alaska	Warren Jones	Warren Jones	1961	147
421 7/8	55 6/8	48	33 6/8	7 2/8	7 3/8	17 5/8	20	16 5/8	10 7/8	22	21	Farewell Lake, Alaska	Richard K. Siller	Richard K. Siller	1958	149
421 6/8	64 5/8	59 3/8	57	7 3/8	7 1/8	22 1/8	2 6/8	16 5/8	1	18	12	King Salmon, Alaska	Edwin W. Seiler	Edwin W. Seiler	1958	150
421 5/8	51 4/8	50	36 3/8	7 4/8	8 7/8	18 4/8	17 4/8	9	14	17	23	Port Moller, Alaska	John S. Clark	John S. Clark	1966	151
421 5/8	56 7/8	55 5/8	56	5 5/8	5 6/8	18 6/8		12 5/8		14	9	Upper Ugashik Lake, Alaska	Barry Barbour	Barry Barbour	1969	151
421 4/8	55	53 4/8	43	5 4/8	5 4/8	16 3/8	15 5/8	10	9 2/8	18	18	Denali Hwy., Alaska	John Schmidel	John Schmidel	1961	153
421 4/8	55 3/8	54 6/8	42 6/8	7 2/8	6 7/8	20 3/8	19 6/8	12 2/8	15 5/8	17	16	Denali Hwy., Alaska	D. G. Skagerberg	D. G. Skagerberg	1956	153
421 4/8	58 1/8	58 1/8	44 6/8	7 1/8	8 4/8	19	2 4/8	12 3/8	1/8	17	12	Kuskokwim River, Alaska	Dennis Harms	Dennis Harms	1967	153
421 4/8	55 1/8	54 2/8	45 5/8	5 4/8	5 4/8	15 5/8	20 1/8	4 5/8	17	17	26	Twin Lakes, Alaska	Paul O'Hollaren	Paul O'Hollaren	1964	153
421 2/8	48 7/8	49 7/8	37 1/8	6 2/8	6 2/8	21 2/8	19 2/8	12 7/8	11 6/8	22	19	Alaska	Unknown	Jonas Bros. of Seattle	1953	157
421 2/8	57 2/8	57	43 4/8	6	7	11 6/8	12 7/8	8 3/8	11 4/8	19	22	Cantwell, Alaska	Richard L. Miller	Richard L. Miller	1979	157
421 1/8	47 2/8	48 6/8	43 6/8	6	6		19 6/8		14 1/8	17	21	Alaska Pen., Alaska	Alice J. Landreth	Alice J. Landreth	1968	159
421 1/8	47	51 4/8	37 3/8	7 4/8	7 3/8	18 2/8	19	10 5/8	10 5/8	24	21	Lake Louise, Alaska	Orel O. Parker	Orel O. Parker	1959	159
421 1/8	58 7/8	57 3/8	45 6/8	5 7/8	5 6/8	19 2/8		10 5/8		19	12	Ugashik Lake, Alaska	Jack A. Shane, Sr.	Jack A. Shane, Sr.	1967	159
421	56 4/8	58 4/8	49 1/8	5 4/8	6 1/8	20 3/8	20 4/8	15 5/8	14 1/8	13	19	Alaska Pen., Alaska	Lloyd W. Birdwell	Lloyd W. Birdwell	1970	162
420 7/8	54 1/8	54 7/8	38 4/8	8	7 7/8	20 1/8	9 1/8	14 6/8	1/8	22	15	Farewell, Alaska	Vern G. Smith	Vern G. Smith	1967	163
420 7/8	56 2/8	55 2/8	45 3/8	5 6/8	5 5/8	23 6/8	2 4/8	21 4/8	4/8	16	14	Port Heiden, Alaska	Otis Chandler	Otis Chandler	1964	163
420 6/8	56 4/8	57 4/8	46 1/8	5 4/8	6	20 1/8	23	5 2/8	5	18	14	Becharof Lake, Alaska	Steven H. Schaust	Steven H. Schaust	1983	165
420 6/8	45 6/8	47 6/8	36 4/8	6	6 3/8	16		10 2/8		27	21	Becharof Lake, Alaska	Glenn E. Anderson	Glenn E. Anderson	1982	165
420 4/8	46 4/8	48	39 5/8	6 1/8	6 2/8	18 1/8	18 3/8	3 3/8	13 2/8	19	24	Dog Salmon River, Alaska	Gary R. Swanson	Gary R. Swanson	1966	167

Score	Length of Main Beam R.	L.	Inside Spread	Circumference at Smallest Place Between Brow and Bez Points R.	L.	Length of Brow Points R.	L.	Width of Brow Points R.	L.	Number of Points R.	L.	Locality Killed	By Whom Killed	Owner	Date Killed	Rank
420⅜	59⅛	57⅛	42⅜	8⅜	8⅝	12	18⅜	1	17⅞	11	16	Tangle Lake, Alaska	J. W. Latham	J. W. Latham	1961	167
420⅜	55	52⅜	40⅛	5⅝	5⅝	23	15⅜	17⅞	3	19	12	Alaska Pen., Alaska	Wm. M. Ellis	Wm. M. Ellis	1963	169
420⅛	59⅜	57⅜	40⅛	6⅜	6⅜	22⅞	22⅞	5⅝	17⅞	15	19	Iliamna Lake, Alaska	A. E. Wilson	A. E. Wilson	1955	170
420⅛	50⅜	55⅜	41⅛	6⅝	6⅜	22⅞	21	16⅛		14	20	King Salmon River, Alaska	Frank N. Rome	Frank N. Rome	1983	170
420⅛	56⅛	54⅜	37⅜	7⅜	7⅜	20	17⅜	13⅜	⅛	18	15	Yanert Fork, Alaska	Michael H. Werner	Michael H. Werner	1984	170
420	50⅜	50⅜	42	7⅛	7⅜	17⅜	13	13⅜	⅛	20	17	Chisana, Alaska	John S. Newkam, Jr.	John S. Newkam, Jr.	1960	173
419⅞	44	46⅛	46⅜	6⅜	7⅜	14⅜	15⅜	⅛	12⅜	15	22	Aleutian Range, Alaska	Fred Dykema	Fred Dykema	1973	174
419⅞	54	50⅜	47⅜	7⅜	6⅝	17⅜	16⅜	9⅜	10⅜	15	16	Dog Salmon River, Alaska	Ralph H. Eisaman	Ralph H. Eisaman	1971	174
419⅝	43⅜	45⅜	29⅜	7⅝	7⅝	14	15⅜	8⅜	10⅜	22	22	Chisana, Alaska	Thomas F. Esper	Thomas F. Esper	1965	176
419⅝	51⅛	50⅛	35⅜	6⅛	6⅜	16⅝	15⅞	9⅜	12⅜	22	23	Mt. Drum, Alaska	Jerald T. Waite	Jerald T. Waite	1966	176
419⅝	53⅜	53⅜	39⅜	6⅝	6⅜	16⅜	20⅛	14⅜	10⅜	16	16	Nabesna, Alaska	Bernard Kendall	Bernard Kendall	1969	176
419⅜	50	51⅜	45⅜	7⅜	7⅜	6⅝	19⅜	⅛	12⅜	13	21	Rainy Pass, Alaska	Warren Page	Warren Page	1956	179
419⅜	46⅜	47⅜	32	7	7⅜	16⅝	15⅜	8⅝	8⅜	20	20	Talkeetna, Alaska	Dale Westenbarger	Dale Westenbarger	1965	179
419⅜	54⅜	52⅜	37	7	6⅜	20⅜	19⅜	7⅜	11⅜	14	17	Alaska Pen., Alaska	C. Driskell	C. Driskell	1965	181
419⅜	45	45⅜	35⅜	8⅛	8⅜	15⅜	18	13⅜	1⅜	26	21	Fairbanks, Alaska	Unknown	Ladd Air Force Base	PR1953	181
419	45⅜	44⅜	35⅜	7⅜	7⅜	15⅜	14⅜	8⅜	9⅜	18	19	Becharof Lake, Alaska	Ron L. Lerch	Ron L. Lerch	1966	183
418⅞	49⅜	49⅜	44	5⅜	5⅜	17⅜	18⅜	12⅜	11⅜	20	19	Cold Bay, Alaska	James E. Carson	James E. Carson	1974	184
418⅞	54⅛	50⅜	40⅜	7	6⅜	15⅜	17	10⅜	11⅜	18	17	Hoholitna River, Alaska	O. B. Beard III	O. B. Beard III	1974	184
418⅞	52⅜	53⅜	40⅜	5⅜	5⅜	19⅜	22⅜	9	8⅜	10	15	Mother Goose Lake, Alaska	Robert A. Epperson	Robert A. Epperson	1963	184
418⅞	49⅝	50	43		5⅜	18	1⅜	12	⅛	28	20	Nabesna River Valley, Alaska	Wayne Platt	Wayne Platt	1958	184
418⅜	59	55⅜	34⅜	6⅛	6⅜	14	22⅜	1⅜	6⅜	21	17	Alaska Pen., Alaska	Otis Chandler	Otis Chandler	1964	188
418⅜	59⅜	60	53⅜	6⅝	6⅜	19⅞	17⅜	12⅜	3⅜	15	15	Eureka, Alaska	William Curtis	F. A. Harrington	1949	188
418⅜	50⅜	49⅜	32⅜	5⅜	5⅜	19⅜		12⅜		27	17	Hicks Creek, Alaska	Charles Brumbelow	Charles Brumbelow	1956	190
418⅜	54⅜	55	38⅜	7⅜	7⅜	2⅜	18	⅛	13⅜	17	19	Ivishak River, Alaska	William O. Dudley	William O. Dudley	1979	191
418⅛	53	56	38⅜	6⅝	6⅜	8	18⅜	1	14⅜	19	23	Aleutian Range, Alaska	Wayne Patton	Wayne Patton	1968	192
418⅛	52⅝	51⅜	50⅜	6⅜	5⅜	18⅜	19	5⅜	8⅜	12	13	Chistochina, Alaska	James H. Lahey	James H. Lahey	1961	192
418⅛	52⅜	46⅜	39⅜	7	7⅜	19⅜		11⅜		21	12	High Lake, Alaska	Glen E. Park	Glen E. Park	1965	192
418⅛	47⅜	46⅝	45⅜	5⅜		12⅜	19⅜	1⅜	15⅜	15	17	Rainy Pass, Alaska	Aaron Saenz, Jr.	Aaron Saenz, Jr.	1964	192
418⅜	52⅜	52⅜	45⅜	6		20⅜	21⅜	4	15⅜	14	20	Big Susitna, Alaska	Forrest Boyce	Jack Dustin	1957	196

Score													Locality	Owner	By whom killed	Date	Rank
418 4/8	57 6/8	55 3/8	5 6/8	6	41 3/8	19	22	5 5/8	9 7/8	5 1/8	17	11	Becharof Lake, Alaska	William M. Beyl	William M. Beyl	1981	197
418 1/8	53 7/8	50 7/8	6 1/8	7	39 7/8	10 5/8	20	6 1/8	18 5/8	1/8	23	13	Caribou Creek, Alaska	Gary Joll	Gary Joll	1963	197
418 1/8	50 1/8	53 1/8	6 3/8	6 7/8	45 3/8	17	13 5/8	6 3/8	2 5/8	14 5/8	22	23	Chistochina, Alaska	Delbert H. Bullock	Delbert H. Bullock	1964	197
418 1/8	50 1/8	48 1/8	6	6	34 5/8	16 5/8	18 3/8	6 3/8	16 3/8	8	24	19	Denali Hwy., Alaska	Jerry Shepard	Jerry Shepard	1961	197
418	54 3/8	54	6 1/8	6 3/8	42 7/8	14 5/8	19 7/8	6 1/8	15 7/8	1/8	18	15	Alaska Range, Alaska	Richard L. McClellan	Richard L. McClellan	1978	201
418	54 5/8	53 5/8	7 5/8	7 7/8	47 3/8	20 5/8	17	1/8	1/8	14 5/8	12	17	Kenai, Alaska	Gary L. Zerbe	Gary L. Zerbe	1981	201
417 7/8	50 5/8	54 3/8	5 5/8	7 3/8	38 5/8	1 5/8	19 1/8	5 5/8	17	1/8	20	14	Tonzona River, Alaska	Fred T. Hecox	Fred T. Hecox	1983	203
417 7/8	55 5/8	60 3/8	5 5/8	5 5/8	46 5/8	21 7/8	15 7/8	6 1/8	9	13 5/8	15	19	Alaska Pen., Alaska	William J. Miller	William J. Miller	1967	204
417 7/8	51 5/8	50 1/8	6 5/8	6 1/8	42 1/8	16 3/8	12 5/8	9	13 5/8	15	25	16	Talkeetna Mts., Alaska	Mrs. R. S. Mosiman	Mrs. R. S. Mosiman	1958	204
417 5/8	50	49	6	6	27 5/8	13 5/8	4 7/8	17 5/8	17	1 5/8	11	14	Alaska Range, Alaska	Richard K. Mellon	Richard K. Mellon	1959	206
417 5/8	56 5/8	56 3/8	6 1/8	5 7/8	43 5/8	19 5/8	12 5/8	11	1 5/8	25	26		Tangle Lakes, Alaska	Kurt C. Dunn	Kurt C. Dunn	1981	206
417 5/8	52 5/8	51 3/8	6 7/8	6 3/8	38 5/8	15 5/8	12 5/8	3 5/8	26	15	21		Wrangell Mts., Alaska	Fred Packer	Fred Packer	1955	206
417 4/8	52 3/8	55 7/8	7 1/8	6 3/8	38 1/8	17 5/8	18 5/8	13 5/8	19	17			Mulchatna River, Alaska	R. D. Eichenour	R. D. Eichenour	1968	209
417 3/8	48 7/8	49 3/8	5 3/8	6	41 5/8	17	18	3 5/8	26	17			Alaska Pen., Alaska	Tyson Nichols	Tyson Nichols	1979	210
417 3/8	48 7/8	49 3/8	5 3/8	6	45 3/8	24 5/8	6	11 5/8	14	16			Alaska Pen., Alaska	Herb Klein	Herb Klein	1964	210
417 3/8	47 3/8	50 3/8	5	5	38 7/8	19 3/8	16 5/8	5 5/8	23	21			Fracture Creek, Alaska	L. Irvin Barnhart	L. Irvin Barnhart	1983	210
417 3/8	50 5/8	50 3/8	6 3/8	6 5/8	36 1/8	17 5/8	17 1/8	6	12 5/8	19	22		Mt. Sanford, Alaska	Dennis Brieske	Dennis Brieske	1984	210
417 1/8	51 3/8	53	7 5/8	7 1/8	25 3/8	14 5/8	19	5	11	15	17	19	Twin Lakes, Alaska	Samuel B. Webb, Jr.	Samuel B. Webb, Jr.	1960	215
417	50 5/8	52	6 1/8	6 3/8	33 3/8	10 5/8	17 5/8	9 3/8	13	16			Rainy Pass, Alaska	Sigurd Jensen	Sigurd Jensen	1956	216
416 7/8	61 3/8	61 5/8	8 3/8	9 1/8	40 3/8	1	15 1/8	9 5/8	13	22			Little Delta River, Alaska	Fred Bear	Fred Bear	1959	217
416 5/8	59 5/8	57 5/8	6 3/8	6 1/8	45 5/8	14 3/8	20 3/8	1/8	17	11	17		Clarence Lake, Alaska	James K. Harrower	James K. Harrower	1961	218
416 5/8	54 3/8	51 3/8	5 3/8	8	43	17	21 3/8	1/8	15 3/8	17	20		King Salmon, Alaska	F. Robert Bell	F. Robert Bell	1983	218
416 3/8	51 3/8	51 1/8	6 3/8	6 1/8	36 3/8	17 5/8	18 5/8	12 3/8	1 3/8	31	21		Wood River, Alaska	A. Knutson	A. Knutson	1957	220
416 3/8	56 5/8	58 5/8	7	7	41	12 3/8	19 3/8	1	14 5/8	15	16		Alaska Pen., Alaska	Jim Ford	Jim Ford	1970	220
416 3/8	49 3/8	52	6 5/8	6 5/8	44 3/8	12	17 5/8	10	18	20			Mulchatna River, Alaska	R. D. Eichenour	R. D. Eichenour	1968	220
416 1/8	56 3/8	54 3/8	5 5/8	6 3/8	48 5/8	16 7/8	19 5/8	3 5/8	10 3/8	13	18		American Pass, Alaska	Brett G. Alexander	Brett G. Alexander	1984	222
416 1/8	56	54	7 3/8	5 5/8	37 5/8	13 5/8	16 3/8	13 3/8	15	21			Mulchatna River, Alaska	Willard L. Hubbard	Willard L. Hubbard	1983	222
416 1/8	45 1/8	45 3/8	8 3/8	7	41 1/8	20 5/8	18	5	13 3/8	17	20		Rainy Pass, Alaska	J. Watson Webb, Jr.	J. Watson Webb, Jr.	1934	222
416 1/8	45 5/8	45 7/8	8 7/8	7 7/8	41 1/8	5	18 5/8	14 5/8	20 5/8	17			Upper Ugashik Lake, Alaska	Russell Matthes	Russell Matthes	1969	222
416 1/8	56	56 5/8	5 5/8	5 5/8	35 5/8	6 3/8	19	14 5/8	20 5/8	13	18		Blackstone River, Yukon	Ken Vickerman	Ken Vickerman	1983	226
416 1/8	58 5/8	59 3/8	7 5/8	8 3/8	46	13 3/8	10 1/8	1/8	20 5/8	13	11		Iliamna Lake, Alaska	Michael J. Ryan, Sr.	Michael J. Ryan, Sr.	1973	226
416 1/8	49 3/8	49 1/8	6 3/8	6 5/8	43 3/8	1 7/8	16 5/8	9 3/8	13 3/8	9 1/8	17	19	Port Heiden, Alaska	Charlie Martin	Charlie Martin	1981	226
416 1/8	53 5/8	52 7/8	6 3/8	6 7/8	38 5/8	16 5/8	19	18 7/8	14 5/8	24	18		Post Lake, Alaska	Gerald Scheuerman	Gerald Scheuerman	1961	226
416 1/8	52 5/8	51 3/8	7 5/8	7 1/8	44 7/8	9	17 7/8	15 3/8	8 3/8	13	17		Talkeetna Mts., Alaska	Karris Keim	Karris Keim	1958	226
416 1/8	49 1/8	49 5/8	6 3/8	6 3/8	38 5/8	17 5/8	17 7/8	4 7/8	16	231			Crooked Creek, Alaska	Bill E. Slone	Bill E. Slone	1964	231
416 1/8	54 5/8	56 5/8	7	7	46 5/8	20 5/8	16	11	20				Farewell Lake, Alaska	K. T. Miller	K. T. Miller	1962	231
416 1/8	51 5/8	50 5/8	5 7/8	5 5/8	35	15	18 5/8	12 5/8	20	22			Little Mulchatna River, Alaska	M. E. Kulik	M. E. Kulik	1967	231
416 1/8	52 5/8	52 3/8	6 1/8	6 3/8	37 5/8	1 5/8	19 5/8	15 5/8	11	20			Wrangell Mts., Alaska	William H. Warrick	William H. Warrick	1961	231
416	50 5/8	51 3/8	5 5/8	5 5/8	48	13 3/8	17 5/8	10	19	22			Alaska Pen., Alaska	Bill E. Hodson	Bill E. Hodson	1978	235
416	50 5/8	50 3/8	9 7/8	7 3/8	40 5/8	15 5/8	6 3/8	1/8	19	16			Stony River, Alaska	Charles F. Nadler	Charles F. Nadler	1985	235
416	57 5/8	56 5/8	6 1/8	6 5/8	39 5/8	17 3/8	3 3/8	21 5/8	5/8	17	14		Ugashik, Alaska	Richard S. Farr	Richard S. Farr	1966	235

Score	Length of Main Beam R.	L.	Inside Spread	Circ. Between Brow and Bez R.	L.	Length of Brow Points R.	L.	Width of Brow Points R.	L.	Number of Points R.	L.	Locality Killed	By Whom Killed	Owner	Date Killed	Rank
415⅞	51⅝	52⅝	40⅜	6⅜	6⅜	18⅜	12⅜	12⅞	10⅛	14	14	Alaska Pen., Alaska	Richard A. Bengraff	Richard A. Bengraff	1981	238
415⅞	55⅝	53⅝	45⅜	6	6⅜	16	16⅞	10⅛	10⅜	25	25	Steese Hwy., Alaska	Howard Hill	Howard Hill	1958	238
415⅝	56⅝	56⅞	40⅜	5⅜	6⅜	19⅜	7⅞	13⅜	12⅜	19	19	Monsoon Lake, Alaska	Paul A. Szopa	Paul A. Szopa	1983	240
415⅝	49⅞	52⅞	39⅜	5⅞	6⅜	17⅜	17⅞	6⅜	11⅜	20	19	King Salmon River, Alaska	Robert G. Barta	Robert G. Barta	1978	241
415⅝	50⅝	50⅜	43⅜	6⅜	6⅞	6⅜	17⅜	4⅝	13⅜	20	20	Whitefish Lake, Alaska	Jeffrey S. Sorg	Jeffrey S. Sorg	1982	241
415⅝	54⅛	53	39⅜	5⅝	6⅜	20⅜	22⅜	15⅝	9⅝	18	22	Egegik River, Alaska	George J. Markham	George J. Markham	1967	243
415⅝	56⅝	56⅞	35⅞	6⅜	6⅜	19⅜	7⅝	12⅜	5⅝	16	20	Tyone Creek, Alaska	E. H. Miller	E. H. Miller	1956	243
415⅝	49⅞	48	33	6	6	21⅛	17⅛	8⅜	13⅜	20	16	Watana Lake, Alaska	Kurt K. Knutson	Kurt K. Knutson	1981	243
415⅜	58⅝	60⅞	40⅞	5⅝	5⅞	3⅜	17⅜	10⅜	⅛	23	15	Becharof Lake, Alaska	Max E. Chittick	Max E. Chittick	1980	246
415⅜	49⅝	50⅛	41⅞	5⅝	5⅞	17⅝	13⅜	14⅜	⅛	15	17	Nenana River, Alaska	James H. Hunt	James H. Hunt	1983	246
415⅜	59	57⅞	51⅞	6⅜	6⅜	17⅜	17⅞	11⅛	11⅜	15	18	Becharof Lake, Alaska	L. Keith Mortensen	L. Keith Mortensen	1980	248
415	56⅞	57	44⅜	6⅜	5⅝	16⅜	19⅜	8⅝	9⅝	22	15	Alaska Pen., Alaska	Picked Up	William P. Bredesen, Jr.	1974	249
414⅞	54⅜	53⅞	46⅜	5⅝	5⅞	20⅜	23⅜	9⅝	8⅜	15	14	Alaska Pen., Alaska	Herb Klein	Herb Klein	1967	250
414⅞	56	55⅞	46⅛	6	6⅛	21⅜	16⅞	16⅜	1⅜	17	16	Denali Hwy., Alaska	Paul Patz	Paul Patz	1965	251
414⅝	50⅞	53	37	7⅜	7⅞	14⅜	16⅞	10⅝	13⅜	10	15	Miner River, Yukon	Gary L. Selig	Gary L. Selig	1979	252
414⅝	57⅜	54⅜	42⅜	7	7	19⅜	16⅞	15⅝	⅜	27	29	Rainy Pass, Alaska	Mahlon T. White	Mahlon T. White	1969	252
414⅝	53⅝	52⅞	50⅝	5⅝	5⅞	2⅜	19⅜	⅞	15⅝	16	20	Naknek, Alaska	C. J. McElroy	C. J. McElroy	1966	254
414⅝	57	49⅞	47⅞	6⅜	6⅜	20⅜	17⅜	12⅝	9⅞	22	15	Alaska Pen., Alaska	Robert Wessner	Robert Wessner	1969	255
414⅝	46⅞	54⅜	40⅛	6	6	5⅜	21⅛	⅞	17⅝	17	17	Alaska Pen., Alaska	George H. Landreth	George H. Landreth	1967	255
414⅝	54	55⅞	39⅝	7⅛	7	16	16	10⅝	9⅝	24	16	Denali Hwy., Alaska	C. W. Hilbish	C. W. Hilbish	1958	255
414⅜	54⅞	54⅞	49	6⅜	6⅜	14⅜	16⅞	⅛	14⅞	17	15	Talkeetna Mts., Alaska	G. W. Berry	G. W. Berry	1960	255
414⅜	45⅞	46⅞	35⅞	11⅛	11⅜	14⅜	17⅞	3⅝	11⅜	15	14	Clarence Lake, Alaska	Jack Hill	Jack Hill	1964	259
414⅜	38⅞	40⅞	36⅜	5⅞	6	17⅜	15⅞	7⅝	10⅜	20	15	Little Nelchina River, Alaska	Picked Up	Temple Bros. Tax.	1954	260
414	53⅞	54⅞	38⅜	8	8	4⅜	20⅜	⅛	15⅝	24	23	Upper Susitna, Alaska	Harold Gould	Harold Gould	1953	260
413⅞	57⅞	59⅞	44⅝	7	6⅜	19⅞	17⅜	12⅝	15⅝	22	17	Alaska Pen., Alaska	Ira Swartz	Ira Swartz	1967	262
413⅞	48⅞	52	42⅛	5	5⅛	17⅜	20⅜	11⅝	14⅜	14	19	Alaska Pen., Alaska	Robert C. Kaufman	Robert C. Kaufman	1978	262
413⅝	51⅞	51⅛	39⅜	6⅜	6⅝	12	18⅜	⅛	13⅜	15	12	Wrangell Mts., Alaska	Robert Reed	Robert Reed	1968	262
413⅝	47⅞	47⅞	44⅜	7⅝	6⅜	22⅜	27⅜	13⅜	17⅞	20	20	King Salmon River, Alaska	Basil C. Bradbury	Basil C. Bradbury	1967	265
413⅜	48⅞	52	33⅜	5⅞	5⅞	16⅝	17⅞	13⅜	15⅝	18	22	Kuskokwim River, Alaska	Walther Schmitz	Walther Schmitz	1969	265

Score											Locality			Date	Rank
413⅝	50⅝	50⅜	38	7	7	8	18	1	16⅛	19	Talkeetna Mts., Alaska	Louis Mussatto	Louis Mussatto	1964	267
413⅜	52⅜	53	44	6	5⅝	20⅝	19⅝	13	½	15	Denali Hwy., Alaska	Albert E. Greer	Albert E. Greer	1963	268
413⅜	55⅝	57⅜	44⅜	6⅜	6⅝	18	5⅝	13⅜	19	14	Whitefish Lake, Alaska	Larry D. Domson	Larry D. Domson	1984	269
413⅛	59⅜	57⅜	40⅜	5⅝	5⅝	20⅝	16⅝	8⅜	7⅞	14	Tyone River, Alaska	Walter Elam	Walter Elam	1959	270
413	61⅛	60	45⅜	6⅝	6	17⅝	20⅝	7⅜	11⅜	17	Aniakchak Crater, Alaska	M. G. Johnson	M. G. Johnson	1964	271
413	38	41⅞	40⅞	7	6⅝	16⅛	17⅝	12⅝	8⅝	17	Tangle Lakes, Alaska	David J. Morlock	David J. Morlock	1956	271
412⅞	56⅜	56⅜	41	5⅝	6⅜	16⅝	14⅝	18	7⅜	18	Lake Clark, Alaska	William F. Rae, Jr.	William F. Rae, Jr.	1968	273
412⅞	51⅜	48⅜	31⅜	8⅝	7⅝	11⅝	14⅝	2⅝	9⅝	20	Rainy Pass, Alaska	Ernst Von Hake	Ernst Von Hake	1963	273
412⅝	56⅜	58	47	6	6	17	21⅜	4⅝	14⅝	12	Alaska Pen., Alaska	John P. Nelson, Jr.	John P. Nelson, Jr.	1961	275
412⅝	50⅜	46⅜	38⅜	5⅝	5⅝	17⅝	20	4⅝	14⅝	19	Port Moller, Alaska	Billy W. Green	Billy W. Green	1983	275
412⅜	61⅜	62⅜	50⅜	5⅝	5⅝	22⅝	8⅝	14	17⅜	19	King Salmon, Alaska	Larry Spiva	Larry Spiva	1983	277
412⅜	50⅜	55⅜	41⅜	6⅝	6	20⅝	14⅝	15	⅛	18	Twin Lakes, Alaska	Inge Hill, Jr.	Inge Hill, Jr.	1965	277
412⅜	59⅜	58⅜	24⅝	8⅝	8⅝	19	18⅝	13⅝	8⅝	18	Slana, Alaska	William Kiltz	William Kiltz	1959	279
412½	46	46⅞	25⅜	7⅝	6⅝	17⅝	17⅝	7	15	15	Tay Lake, Yukon	Dan Newlon	Dan Newlon	1963	280
412	43⅜	47⅜	40	8	8⅜	19⅝	20	13	13⅜	27	Alaska Pen., Alaska	Paul T. Hartman	Paul T. Hartman	1966	281
411⅞	45⅜	44⅜	40	5⅝	5⅝	17	17⅝	11⅝	14⅝	23	Dog Salmon River, Alaska	Benny B. Kerns	Benny B. Kerns	1983	282
411⅞	59⅜	60⅜	49⅜	5⅝	5⅝	20⅝	4⅝	18⅛	1⅛	16	Jimmy Lake, Alaska	Jack M. Matthews	Jack M. Matthews	1966	282
411⅞	57	53⅜	46⅜	7⅝	7	3⅝	23⅝	½	20	20	Talkeetna Range, Alaska	Walter J. Wojciuk	Walter J. Wojciuk	1960	282
411½	61⅜	59⅜	47	6	6	20⅝	20⅜	15⅝	12	16	Alaska Pen., Alaska	Berne Mus. Nat. Hist.	H. Sagesser	1962	285
411¼	49	45⅜	34⅜	6⅝	6⅝	17⅝	18⅝	7⅝	13⅝	16	Twin Lakes, Alaska	Richard R. Oberle	Richard R. Oberle	1973	286
411¼	56⅜	57	42⅜	6⅝	6⅝	16⅝	10	10⅝	⅛	12	Wood River, Alaska	Carol L. Schwabland	Carol L. Schwabland	1981	286
411¼	45⅜	45⅜	45⅜	6⅝	9⅝	20⅝	18⅝	8⅝	7⅝	14	Lake Louise, Alaska	John Trautner	John Trautner	1960	288
411	53⅜	55⅜	46⅜	9⅝	8	16⅝	16	18⅝	7⅜	13	Wood River, Alaska	Luther W. Palmer	Luther W. Palmer	1984	289
411	43	43⅜	32⅜	8	8⅝	18⅝	17	15	9⅝	22	Healy, Alaska	Michael A. Couch	Michael A. Couch	1969	290
411	55⅜	56⅜	35⅜	5⅝	5⅝	21⅝	16	11	9⅝	17	Wood River, Alaska	James C. Midcap	James C. Midcap	1970	290
410⅞	64⅜	65⅜	53⅜	6	6⅝	16⅝	20⅝	8⅝	12⅝	12	Becharof Lake, Alaska	Gordon G. Chittick	Gordon G. Chittick	1981	292
410⅞	49⅜	50⅜	47⅜	6⅝	7	19	16⅝	10⅝	12⅝	16	Talkeetna Mts., Alaska	Clifford F. Hood	Clifford F. Hood	1958	292
410⅞	53⅜	52⅜	32⅜	6⅝	6⅝	21	16⅝	15⅝	6⅝	24	Wrangell Mts., Alaska	John Belcher	John Belcher	1956	292
410⅞	57⅜	56⅜	41⅜	6⅝	6⅝	3⅝	17⅝	1	14⅝	20	Alaska Pen., Alaska	Jim Keeler	Jim Keeler	1966	295
410¾	53⅜	54⅜	40⅜	6⅝	6⅝	18⅝	12⅝	14⅝	1⅛	16	Denali Hwy., Alaska	Ray W. Holler	Ray W. Holler	1965	295
410¾	47⅜	58⅜	47⅜	5⅝	5⅝	16⅝	17⅝	11⅝	12⅝	14	Lake Chandalar, Alaska	L. A. Miller	L. A. Miller	1953	295
410¾	53	64⅜	53	5⅝	5⅝	19⅝	1⅝	16⅞	7⅞	31	Talkeetna Mts., Alaska	Elgin T. Gates	Elgin T. Gates	1960	295
410¾	45⅜	54⅜	45⅜	7⅝	7	16⅝	17⅝	8	9⅝	18	Denali Hwy., Alaska	J. W. Jett	J. W. Jett	1960	299
410⅝	35	49⅜	47⅜	6⅝	6	15⅝	15⅝	14⅝	9⅝	18	Hunt River, Alaska	James W. Styler	James W. Styler	1981	299
410⅝	31⅜	51⅜	31⅜	7⅝	8⅝	21⅜	4⅝	8⅝	4⅝	19	McKinley Nat. Park, Alaska	Joseph M. Messana	Joseph M. Messana	1968	299
410⅜	51⅜	52⅜	33⅜	6⅝	6⅝	15	18⅝	14⅝	15⅝	22	Tanana Valley, Alaska	Bob Hagel	Bob Hagel	1961	299
410⅜	58⅜	56⅜	33⅜	6⅝	6⅝	16⅝	21⅜	1	16⅝	12	Wrangell Mts., Alaska	Lee Chambers	Lee Chambers	1969	299
410⅜	58⅜	53⅜	46⅜	6⅝	5⅝	13	21	⅛	12⅝	13	Becharof Lake, Alaska	Lavon L. Chittick	Lavon L. Chittick	1981	304
410⅜	48⅜	49⅜	36⅜	5⅝	5⅝	17⅝	17⅝	15⅝	10⅝	19	Lake Clark, Alaska	Donald J. Hotter III	Donald J. Hotter III	1979	304
410⅜	55⅜	57⅜	55⅜	5⅝	5⅝	20⅝	14⅛	13⅝	6	26	King Salmon, Alaska	Richard J. Gutherie	Richard J. Gutherie	1979	306

BARREN GROUND CARIBOU—Continued
Rangifer tarandus granti

Score	Length of Main Beam R.	L.	Inside Spread	Circumference at Smallest Place Between Brow and Bez Points R.	L.	Length of Brow Points R.	L.	Width of Brow Points R.	L.	Number of Points R.	L.	Locality Killed	By Whom Killed	Owner	Date Killed	Rank
410⅜	57⅜	56	41⅛	6	6⅛	18⅜	17⅞	7⅞	12⅜	14	18	Rainy Pass, Alaska	Mrs. J. Watson Webb	Mrs. J. Watson Webb	1934	306
410	47⅝	51⅞	43⅝	9⅛	9	28⅛		13⅜		20	18	Alaska Pen., Alaska	C. G. Suits	C. G. Suits	1965	308
410	50⅞	51	43⅝	6⅝	6⅛	15⅜	19⅛	10⅛	10⅝	16	15	Fog Lakes, Alaska	Squee Shore	Squee Shore	1958	308
410	53⅝	54⅞	40	6⅛	6⅛	16⅞	21	⅛	17⅞	12	13	Nenana River, Alaska	Tom Grady	Tom Grady	1961	308
410	54⅜	59	44⅜	5⅝	6⅜	16⅛	18⅞	7⅛	14⅜	14	17	White River, Alaska	Dirk E. Brinkman	Dirk E. Brinkman	1974	308
410	54⅞	59⅞	42⅜	7⅛	6⅛	20⅛	4⅜	13	1	15	16	Post Lake, Alaska	Werner Frey	Werner Frey	1963	312
409⅞	59⅝	59⅞	27⅜	6⅜	6⅛	15	15⅜	5⅞	10⅞	19	21	Wood River, Alaska	Stuart L. G. Rees	Stuart L. G. Rees	1983	313
409⅝	54⅝	52⅞	47⅛	6⅛	5⅞	21	11	15⅜	4⅜	19	13	Point Moller, Alaska	John S. Clark	John S. Clark	1966	314
409⅝	46⅝	48⅛	33⅜	6⅞	7⅛	22⅜	16	16⅜	⅛	17	14	Tyone Lake, Alaska	Ralph Marshall	Ralph Marshall	1960	314
409⅝	54⅞	55	42⅜	6⅜	6⅛	18⅜	18⅜	10⅜	⅜	17	14	Paxton Lake, Alaska	Gary J. Lundgren	James Lundgren	1950	316
409¾	54⅝	53⅞	41⅛	6	5⅞	16⅞	15⅜	10⅜	7⅞	17	17	Port Heiden, Alaska	Frank W. Ussery, Jr.	Frank W. Ussery, Jr.	1963	316
409¾	57⅜	58⅞	35⅜	6⅜	6⅛	20⅜	21⅛	15⅜	⅛	19	13	Alaska Range, Alaska	James W. Rehm	James W. Rehm	1978	318
409¾	55⅝	53	38⅜	6⅜	6⅛	24⅜	12⅜	18⅞	1	20	13	King Salmon River, Alaska	Lit Ng	Lit Ng	1967	318
409½	47⅝	46⅝	46	6⅝	6⅛	16	17⅞	12⅜	12⅞	20	24	Alaska Pen., Alaska	L. W. Bailey	L. W. Bailey	1969	320
409¼	53⅜	53	40⅝	5⅝	6	21⅛	19⅛	7	12	15	20	Alaska Pen., Alaska	Herb Klein	Herb Klein	1967	320
409¼	45⅝	47⅞	28⅜	9	8	22	13⅜	15⅜	5⅜	28	20	Chisana, Alaska	James B. Higgins	James B. Higgins	1967	320
409⅛	46⅝	51⅜	36¼	8	7⅛	16⅛	18	9⅜	13⅜	21	19	Alaska Pen., Alaska	Herb Klein	Herb Klein	1968	323
409	48⅛	46⅜	35⅜	11	6⅛	17⅞	16⅛	8⅜	12⅜	19	21	Chisana Valley, Alaska	William Burns	William Burns	1963	324
409	55⅜	54⅜	41⅛	6⅜	6	23	9⅜	18⅛	⅛	23	11	Port Heiden, Alaska	D. J. Lehman	D. J. Lehman	1967	324
409	55	53⅞	45	6⅝	6	15⅝	16⅛	6⅜	9⅜	19	19	Deadman Lake, Alaska	R. J. Brocker	R. J. Brocker	1950	326
408⅞	41⅛	42⅞	37⅝	8⅜	8⅛	16⅝	12⅜	11	1⅛	18	16	Talkeetna Mts., Alaska	H. I. H. Prince Abdorreza Pahlavi	H. I. H. Prince Abdorreza Pahlavi	1960	326
408⅞	52⅛	53⅞	34	8⅜	7⅜	17⅞	17⅞	12⅜	4⅜	18	17	David River, Alaska	W. K. Leech	W. K. Leech	1979	328
408⅞	54⅞	54⅞	39⅝	6⅜	7⅛	18⅛	10⅜	9⅜	3⅜	14	13	Ingersol Lake, Alaska	John A. Du Puis	John A. Du Puis	1973	328
408⅞	52⅝	51	39⅜	10⅜	9⅜	4	18⅞	1	12⅜	14	17	Red Paint Creek, Alaska	Larry D. Kropf	Larry D. Kropf	1983	328
408⅞	55	56⅜	37⅞	6⅜	6⅛	18⅛	12⅜	13⅜	1⅜	18	17	Lake Clark, Alaska	J. G. Blow	J. G. Blow	1968	331
408⅞	46⅝	46⅝	40⅛	7	7⅜	5⅝	19⅜	⅞	19⅜	20	23	Talkeetna Mts., Alaska	Bill Lachenmaier	Bill Lachenmaier	1961	331
408⅞	46⅝	49⅜	40⅜	6⅛	5⅞	17⅜	17⅜	6⅞	9	13	15	Alaska Pen., Alaska	Robert E. L. Wright	Robert E. L. Wright	1978	333
408⅞	56	56⅜	38⅜	7	6⅛	17⅛	19⅜	8⅜	10⅜	18	22	Sandy River, Alaska	Mrs. Ken McConnell	Mrs. Ken McConnell	1966	333
408⅞	54⅜	51	40⅜	6⅛	6⅛	12⅜	18⅜	1	15⅜	16	25	Susitna River, Alaska	Richard G. Drew	Richard G. Drew	1961	333
408⅞	52⅜	53⅞	44⅜	5⅝	5⅛	3	22⅜	⅛	16⅞	15	22	Becharof Lake, Alaska	Pete M. Baughman, Jr.	Pete M. Baughman, Jr.	1984	336

350

Score												Locality	Owner	By	Date	Page
408⅜	52⅝	52⅝	50	5⅝	6	13	14⅜	11⅜	4	17	18	Alaska Pen., Alaska	Robert J. Nellett	Robert J. Nellett	1966	337
408⅜	52½	51½	37⅝	7⅝	6⅞	15⅜	18	7⅝	9⅝	14	18	Bruskasna Creek, Alaska	Rod Boertje	Rod Boertje	1984	337
408⅜	58¼	59⅝	48⅝	6⅞	6⅞	18	20⅝	8⅝	8⅝	19	18	Dog Salmon River, Alaska	Arlington F. Svoboda	Arlington F. Svoboda	1983	337
408⅜	50⅝	51⅝	35⅝	6⅜	6⅛	20⅝	20⅜	7⅝	13⅞	13	13	Rainy Pass, Alaska	John S. Howell	John S. Howell	1966	337
408⅛	52⅝	54	36⅛	7	7⅝	21⅝	16	15	½	17	13	Wood River, Alaska	Max Lukin	Max Lukin	1964	341
407⅞	54¼	51	36⅛	7⅛	6⅝	20⅝	17⅝	4⅝	10⅛	15	15	Alaska Pen., Alaska	Frank R. Fowler	Frank R. Fowler	1976	342
407⅞	46¼	48	41⅜	7⅛	9	15⅝	15⅜	2⅝	9⅜	16	19	Caribou Creek, Alaska	Donald Kettlekamp	Donald Kettlekamp	1957	342
407⅞	58⅝	56	37⅛	7⅜	6⅝	19⅝	19⅝	10⅝	12⅝	16	18	Kuskokwim River, Alaska	Robert Jacobsen	Robert Jacobsen	1982	342
407⅝	50⅝	49⅝	44⅝	5⅝	6	6	20⅝	⅛	14⅜	13	18	Becharof Lake, Alaska	Max E. Chittick	Max E. Chittick	1981	345
407⅝	45	49	46⅛	6⅝	7	19⅝	19	1⅝	13⅜	15	18	Butte Creek, Alaska	J. H. Doolittle	J. H. Doolittle	1956	345
407⅝	58⅛	56⅝	45⅜	6⅝	7⅛	19	5	12⅝	⅜	13	11	Alaska Pen., Alaska	Pete Serafin	Pete Serafin	1966	347
407⅝	50	47⅜	37⅝	6⅝	6⅝	14	14⅝	3⅝	10⅜	20	18	Chisana, Alaska	Lewis S. Kunkel, Jr.	Lewis S. Kunkel, Jr.	1964	348
407⅝	57	55⅝	44⅝	5⅝	6	16⅝	2⅝	12⅝	⅛	20	14	Tetelin River, Alaska	O. F. Goeke	O. F. Goeke	1954	348
407⅝	56⅜	56⅝	43⅝	6	6⅝	19⅝	12⅝	⅛	13⅜	30	13	Ugashik Lakes, Alaska	Gary J. Gray	Gary J. Gray	1981	348
407⅝	47⅝	50	31⅛	7	7	8⅝	17	7⅝	1	22	24	Chandler Lake, Alaska	Steve Scheidness	Steve Scheidness	1974	351
407⅝	62⅝	58⅝	45⅝	6⅝	6	6	15⅝	13⅝	13⅜	12	16	Kanuti River, Alaska	Leslie A. Olson	Leslie A. Olson	1981	351
407⅝	49⅛	44⅝	34⅜	5⅝	7	16⅝	8⅝	12⅝	12⅜	22	15	Lake Clark, Alaska	Arthur L. Patterson	Arthur L. Patterson	1978	351
407⅜	47	49	35⅝	8⅝	6	19	19	11	½	22	18	Snowshoe Lake, Alaska	John P. Hale	John P. Hale	1962	351
407⅛	53⅛	51⅛	38⅛	6⅝	6⅝	20⅝	16⅝	⅛	5⅜	18	16	Mt. Watana, Alaska	James A. Jana	James A. Jana	1966	355
407	52	54⅛	35⅝	6⅝	6⅛	21⅝	19⅝	5⅝	1	22	14	Farewell Lake, Alaska	Ken Golden	Ken Golden	1962	356
406⅞	52	52	44⅜	8⅝	8	16⅝	18⅝	10⅝	10⅜	18	20	Cantwell, Alaska	W. F. Shoemaker	W. F. Shoemaker	1958	357
406⅝	46⅝	47⅛	41⅜	7	7	16⅛	14⅝	4	8⅜	15	18	Denali Hwy., Alaska	D. L. Lucas	D. L. Lucas	1957	358
406⅜	48⅛	52⅝	32⅜	5⅝	5⅝	15⅝	23⅝	⅛	18⅜	17	22	King Salmon, Alaska	Joe B. Reynolds	Joe B. Reynolds	1981	358
406⅜	65⅜	59⅝	57⅝	6⅝	6	1⅝	1	⅛	12	16	17	Becharof Lake, Alaska	Gordon G. Chittick	Gordon G. Chittick	1980	360
406⅜	53⅜	55⅝	41⅝	6	6	18	1	⅛	12⅝	17	16	Kuskokwim River, Alaska	Cheryl & Dennis Harms	Cheryl Harms	1967	360
406	48	50	35⅝	7⅝	8	20⅝	19⅝	5⅝	13	13	16	Lake Louise, Alaska	Eugene Fetzer	Eugene Fetzer	1961	362
406	51⅛	53	28⅝	6	6⅝	24⅝	18⅝	10⅝	8⅝	14	13	Talkeetna Mts., Alaska	Herb Klein	Herb Klein	1960	362
406	52⅝	50	44⅝	7⅝	6⅝	16⅝	4⅝	13⅝	⅛	20	18	Moller Bay, Alaska	Harry H. Webb	Harry H. Webb	1953	364
406	50⅞	52	45⅝	5⅝	5	21⅝	17⅝	17⅝	13⅜	16	16	Ugashik Lake, Alaska	John A. Moody	John A. Moody	1983	364
406	51⅛	51½	47⅛	6⅝	6⅛	14	15⅝	10⅝	8	16	16	Fairbanks, Alaska	H. A. Cox, Jr.	H. A. Cox, Jr.	1968	366
406	58	53½	46⅝	6⅝	6⅝	16⅝	15⅝	8	½	13	10	Kenai, Alaska	Ernest A. Stirman	Ernest A. Stirman	1981	366
406	50⅛	47⅜	36⅛	7⅝	7⅝	23	11	18⅝	18⅜	17	12	Lake Louise, Alaska	C. J. Sullivan	C. J. Sullivan	1960	366
406	50	49⅝	30⅛	7⅜	7⅝	6⅝	19⅝	1	15⅜	14	19	Squaw Creek, Alaska	Elmo Strickland	Elmo Strickland	1960	366
405⅞	57⅞	58⅝	57	6	6	19	11⅝	⅛	⅛	15	16	Becharof Lake, Alaska	Max E. Chittick	Max E. Chittick	1983	370
405⅝	60⅝	62⅝	42⅝	5⅝	5⅝	19⅝	16⅝	14⅛	1⅝	20	12	Joseph Creek, Alaska	Madeline M. Kelleyhouse	Madeline M. Kelleyhouse	1984	371
405⅝	47⅝	51⅝	45⅝	6⅝	6⅝	6⅝	17⅝	11⅝	⅜	20	16	Paxton, Alaska	Maurice A. Stafford	Maurice A. Stafford	1956	371
405⅝	47⅛	48⅛	36⅛	5⅝	5⅝	17⅝	19⅝	2	16⅝	17	24	Port Heiden, Alaska	James V. Pepa	James V. Pepa	1968	371
405⅝	54⅛	52⅝	44⅝	5⅝	5⅝	20⅝	3	13	1	17	14	Denali Hwy., Alaska	Edna Conegys	Edna Conegys	1958	374
405⅝	45⅜	44⅝	32⅝	6⅝	6⅝	15⅝	16⅝	11⅝	9⅝	16	16	Little Nelchina, Alaska	Simon Jensen	Simon Jensen	1960	374

Score	Length of Main Beam R	L	Inside Spread	Circumference at Smallest Place Between Brow and Bez Points R	L	Length of Brow Points R	L	Width of Brow Points R	L	Number of Points R	L	Locality Killed	By Whom Killed	Owner	Date Killed	Rank
405⅞	58⅝	57⅞	52⅛	6⅜	5⅞	18	17⅜	9⅞	⅛	12	9	Alaska Pen., Alaska	Jose Garcia	Jose Garcia	1971	376
405⅞	47⅞	48⅜	36⅝	7⅜	6⅜	15⅝	14⅞	8⅜	5⅞	22	15	Mulchatna River, Alaska	Thomas J. Gallo	Thomas J. Gallo	1983	376
405⅞	46⅝	46⅜	43⅜	6⅜	6⅜	6⅝	17⅜	1⅛	13⅝	17	22	Ochetna River, Alaska	Elbert E. Husted	Elbert E. Husted	1962	376
405⅜	51⅜	56⅜	39⅝	6⅛	6⅛	13⅜	18⅜	⅛	10⅜	10	13	Bear Lake, Alaska	Ruth S. Kennedy	Ruth S. Kennedy	1983	379
405⅜	49⅜	50⅝	35⅝	6⅜	6	16⅝	15	8⅝	6⅜	22	17	Denali Hwy., Alaska	W. Auckland	W. Auckland	1958	379
405⅜	54⅜	53⅜	42	6⅜	6⅜	14	15⅝	7⅝	10⅜	14	13	Rainy Pass, Alaska	W. D. Vogel	W. D. Vogel	1958	379
405⅜	50⅝	52⅜	42⅜	6⅜	6⅜	18	9⅜	11⅜	⅞	20	18	Talkeetna Mts., Alaska	Digvijay Sinh	Digvijay Sinh	1963	379
405⅜	45⅝	46⅜	35	9	7⅜	12⅜	17	⅛	9⅝	20	23	Wood River, Alaska	Herb Klein	Herb Klein	1955	379
405	56⅜	60⅜	55⅜	5⅜	5⅜	7⅜	15⅝	6⅜	9⅝	16	20	Port Heiden, Alaska	Lee W. Richie	Lee W. Richie	1963	384
405	55⅜	60⅜	33⅜	6⅜	6⅞	9⅜	19⅜	⅛	17⅜	15	27	Susitna Valley, Alaska	E. Michael Rusten	E. Michael Rusten	1948	384
405	45⅜	43⅜	31⅝	7⅜	8	8	16	⅛	9⅜	15	20	Wrangell Mts., Alaska	Roger H. Belke	Roger H. Belke	1974	384
404⅞	49⅞	49⅜	35	6⅜	6⅜	7⅜	17	1	11⅝	16	15	Wrangell Mts., Alaska	J. D. Waring	J. D. Waring	1959	387
404⅞	48⅜	47⅜	42⅜	6⅜	6⅛	19	7⅜	14⅛	1	19	14	Alaska Pen., Alaska	M. C. Worster	M. C. Worster	1963	388
404⅞	53⅜	52⅜	49⅜	7	7	19⅞	19⅜	13⅜	9⅜	12	12	Alaska Pen., Alaska	W. T. Yoshimoto	W. T. Yoshimoto	1961	388
404⅞	46⅜	47⅛	39⅜	8⅜	6⅜	17⅞	2⅛	11⅜	⅛	17	16	Becharof Lake, Alaska	Dan M. Rudanovich	Dan M. Rudanovich	1983	388
404⅞	54⅜	54⅜	38⅝	5⅜	5⅜	23	15⅜	9⅝	11	22	15	Cathedral Valley, Alaska	Victor Koenig	Victor Koenig	1981	388
404⅞	56⅝	54⅜	36⅝	6⅜	5⅜	7	23⅜	1⅛	19	14	21	King Salmon, Alaska	Henry A. Elias	Henry A. Elias	1965	388
404⅞	49⅝	50	43⅜	6	5⅜	16⅜	15⅞	7⅜	19	20	17	King Salmon, Alaska	Paul Hopkins	Paul Hopkins	1973	388
404⅞	42⅜	46⅜	33⅝	7⅛	6⅜	16⅝	15⅜	10⅜	10⅜	21	20	Lake Clark, Alaska	Doug Butler	Doug Butler	1980	388
404⅞	50⅜	48⅜	44⅜	7⅜	7⅛	16⅜	16⅜	9⅜	10⅜	15	15	Eureka, Alaska	Charles C. Parsons	Charles C. Parsons	1950	395
404⅞	54⅜	55	33⅜	6⅜	6	16⅝	17⅜	11	11⅜	17	17	Talkeetna Mts., Alaska	J. W. Lawson	J. W. Lawson	1965	395
404⅞	54⅜	55	32⅜	6⅜	6⅛	16⅜	17⅜	15⅜	20	18	24	Taylor Hwy., Alaska	John C. Howard	John C. Howard	1960	395
404⅜	53⅜	51⅛	39⅜	6⅜	5⅜	2⅜	18⅜	⅛	15⅜	13	18	Wood River, Alaska	Robert D. Hancock, Jr.	Robert D. Hancock, Jr.	1983	395
404⅜	53	54⅜	40	5⅞	5⅜	16⅜	18⅞	10⅜	7⅝	16	14	Alaska Pen., Alaska	Peter Roemer	Camp Fire Club	1970	399
404⅜	49⅜	51⅛	37⅜	5⅜	5⅜	14⅜	18⅜	⅛	12⅜	19	22	Black River, Alaska	Alfred Eugene Wochner	Alfred Eugene Wochner	1981	399
404⅜	53⅜	53⅜	35⅜	6⅜	6⅜	17⅜	7⅜	11⅜	⅛	16	13	Wrangell Mts., Alaska	William B. Henley, Jr.	William B. Henley, Jr.	1962	399
404⅜	52⅜	52⅜	46⅜	6⅜	6⅜	19	⅝	13⅜	5⅜	20	15	Wood River, Alaska	C. A. Stenger	C. A. Stenger	1968	402
404⅜	52⅛	52⅝	38⅜	7⅜	7⅜	22⅜	16⅜	7⅜	10	15	16	Oshetna River, Alaska	Marven A. Henriksen	Marven A. Henriksen	1962	403
404⅜	58⅜	58⅜	59⅜	5⅜	5⅜	18⅜	4⅜	16⅜	⅛	20	12	Port Heiden, Alaska	Jon B. Chaney	Jon B. Chaney	1962	403
404⅜	38⅜	37	36⅜	6	6⅜	16⅜	16⅜	14⅜	14⅞	21	22	Talkeetna Mts., Alaska	Ken Oldhem	Ken Oldhem	1959	403
404⅜	48	48	34⅜	5⅜	5⅜	15⅜	19⅜	3⅜	12⅜	17	24	Upper Susitna, Alaska	Elmer M. Rusten	Elmer M. Rusten	1950	403

Score	Measurements (left)	By whom killed	Owner	Locality	Measurements (right)	Date	Score
404⅛	45⅜ 48 41 6⅞ 6⅞ 18 17⅞	B. C. Varner	B. C. Varner	Nabesna, Alaska	1⅞ 13⅝ 11⅞ 19 22	1955	407
404	52 55½ 41 7 6⅛ 18⅜ 18¾	Berry B. Brooks	Berry B. Brooks	Wood River, Alaska	6⅜ 14⅜ 14⅜ 18 16	1958	407
403⅞	55½ 52½ 36½ 8 8⅜ 19½ 17	Earl Faas	Earl Faas	Salmon Mts., Yukon	9⅜ 13⅜ 13⅜ 17 15	1960	409
403⅞	52½ 52½ 32 6⅞ 6⅛ 3½ 21¼	John R. Copenhaver	John R. Copenhaver	Butte Creek, Alaska	1⅛ 11⅞ 11⅞ 17 22	1956	410
403⅞	52½ 52½ 30 11¼ 6⅞ 21¼ 21	Ben Bearse	Ben Bearse	Cantwell, Alaska	12 8 13 14	1968	410
403⅞	44½ 44½ 44 6 5⅜ 2⅜ 14⅜	Richard S. Hembroff	Richard S. Hembroff	Halfway Mt., Alaska	⅞ 11¼ 8 16 18	1974	410
403⅞	41½ 37⅛ 37⅛ 6⅞ 7⅜ 15 13⅞	Tony Weiss	Tony Weiss	Holitna River, Alaska	7 5⅛ 22 20	1979	410
403⅞	50½ 43⅝ 43⅝ 5⅜ 6⅞ 22½ 21⅜	Melvin Hetland	Melvin Hetland	Port Moller, Alaska	18 1 15	1962	410
403⅞	48 44⅝ 44⅝ 6⅛ 6⅛ 24 18	Jim Carpenter	Jim Carpenter	Denali Hwy., Alaska	1 13⅝ 19	1960	415
403⅞	52½ 51⅛ 29⅜ 6⅝ 6⅛ 19⅜ 15⅛	Robert R. Opland	Robert R. Opland	Denali Hwy., Alaska	14⅜ 1 20 14	1959	415
403⅞	47⅞ 47⅛ 44¼ 6 6⅛ 18⅜ 2⅜	Gene Gall	Gene Gall	Port Heiden, Alaska	13⅜ ⅜ 23 16	1967	415
403⅞	41⅜ 43⅜ 27⅝ 6⅝ 6⅛ 16⅜ 17⅜	Joe Nevins	Joe Nevins	Talkeetna Mts., Alaska	9⅜ 14⅜ 21 25	1958	415
403¾	52½ 52⅛ 34 7 20⅜ 17⅜	Frederick W. Fernelius	Frederick W. Fernelius	Tyone Creek, Alaska	10⅜ 9⅜ 16 13	1981	415
403⅝	51⅜ 50⅛ 34⅜ 6⅛ 15 14	Marvin Kocurek	Marvin Kocurek	Lake Louise, Alaska	8⅜ 6⅜ 21 21	1961	420
403⅝	49⅛ 46⅜ 33⅜ 7⅜ 16⅜ 15⅜	Ralph E. Marshall	Ralph E. Marshall	Tyone Lake, Alaska	8⅜ 6 19 18	1957	420
403¾	53⅜ 55⅜ 49⅜ 6 15⅜ 17⅜	Gerald R. Gold	Gerald R. Gold	Alaska Pen., Alaska	11⅜ 11⅜ 14 17	1977	422
403¾	60⅜ 60⅜ 59⅜ 5⅜ 27⅜ 21⅜	Max E. Chittick	Max E. Chittick	Becharof Lake, Alaska	15⅜ ⅜ 13 9	1979	422
403¾	50⅜ 50⅜ 39⅜ 6⅜ 13 21	Mrs. Jon B. Chaney	Mrs. Jon B. Chaney	Port Heiden, Alaska	⅜ 17⅜ 14 19	1962	422
403⅜	43⅜ 29⅜ 29⅜ 7⅜ 21 20⅜	Harry L. Swank, Jr.	Harry L. Swank, Jr.	Tazlina, Alaska	15⅜ 5⅜ 18 14	1959	422
403⅛	56⅜ 50 42⅜ 6 16⅜ 18⅜	Charles R. Green	Charles R. Green	Deadman Lake, Alaska	8 12⅜ 19 21	1959	426
403⅛	49⅜ 48⅜ 38⅜ 6⅜ 16⅜ 19⅜	James S. Evans	James S. Evans	Eureka, Alaska	5⅜ 14⅜ 17 19	1960	426
403	49⅜ 49⅜ 37⅜ 5⅜ 20⅜ 8⅜	William M. Sowers	William M. Sowers	Pear Lake, Alaska	16 ⅜ 27 19	1981	428
403	53⅜ 50⅜ 43⅜ 6⅛ 16⅜ 14⅜	E. C. Lentz	E. C. Lentz	Deadman Lake, Alaska	1⅜ 8⅜ 13 16	1955	429
402⅞	56⅜ 54⅜ 39⅛ 7 18⅜ 4⅜	Norman L. Akau, Jr.	Norman L. Akau, Jr.	Wood River, Alaska	14 ⅜ 20 10	1980	429
402⅞	54⅜ 56 41⅜ 5⅜ 19⅜ 19⅜	Chris Klineburger	Chris Klineburger	Nelchina, Alaska	14⅜ 11⅜ 18 17	1957	431
402⅞	48 46⅜ 28⅜ 8 11⅜ 19⅜	E. J. Miller	E. J. Miller	Ogilvie Range, Yukon	⅜ 17⅜ 17 25	1956	431
402⅞	49 54 33 7⅜ 14⅜ 15⅜	William Sleith	William Sleith	Rainy Pass, Alaska	8 9 15 18	1961	433
402⅜	52 50 43⅜ 5 16 16	Vincent T. Ciaburri	Vincent T. Ciaburri	Ugashik Lakes, Alaska	8⅜ 7⅜ 22 18	1977	433
402⅜	46⅜ 47⅜ 34⅜ 5⅜ 16⅜ 15⅜	J. M. Mouchet	J. M. Mouchet	Old Crow, Yukon	1⅜ 13⅜ 19 26	1958	435
402⅜	46⅜ 47⅜ 39⅜ 7⅜ 16⅜ 15⅜	John C. Heck	John C. Heck	Clarence Lake, Alaska	6⅜ 7⅜ 14 15	1951	436
402⅜	53⅜ 53⅜ 36⅜ 7 22⅜ 21⅜	Walter Pfisterer	Walter Pfisterer	Glen Hwy., Alaska	18⅜ 2⅜ 14 11	1959	436
402⅜	52⅜ 51⅜ 41⅜ 7⅜ 8⅜ 16⅜	Joseph Caputo	Joseph Caputo	Nelchina, Alaska	13⅜ 13⅜ 13 24	1964	436
402⅜	59⅜ 59 37⅜ 6⅛ 19⅜ 23⅜	Walter Schubert	Walter Schubert	Port Heiden, Alaska	17⅜ 17⅜ 13 12	1965	436
402⅜	58 54 34⅜ 6⅜ 16⅜ 16⅜	Mahlon White	Mahlon White	Rainy Pass, Alaska	6⅜ 10⅜ 13 16	1954	436
402⅜	49⅜ 49⅜ 30⅜ 7⅜ 16⅜ 18⅜	Arvid F. Benson	Arvid F. Benson	Talkeetna Mts., Alaska	13⅜ ⅜ 23 17	1956	436
402⅜	45 48 34⅜ 8⅜ 18⅜ 17	A. Sweat	A. Sweat	Talkeetna Mts., Alaska	10 12⅜ 20 21	1959	436
402⅜	56⅜ 56 43⅜ 6⅜ 7⅜ 19⅜	W. L. Miers	W. L. Miers	Talkeetna Mts., Alaska	10⅜ 7 11 10	1961	444
402⅜	51⅜ 55⅜ 44 6⅜ 7⅜ 15⅜	Jerry Shepard	Jerry Shepard	Denali Hwy., Alaska	3⅜ 14⅜ 15 20	1959	444
402⅜	43⅜ 44⅜ 33⅜ 7⅜ 15⅜ 14⅜	Leon J. Brochu	Leon J. Brochu	Tyone Lake, Alaska	7 13⅜ 18 20	1981	444
402⅜	53⅜ 53⅜ 44⅜ 5⅜ 17⅜ 18	Carol Ann Rollings	Carol Ann Rollings	White Fish Lake, Alaska	9⅜ 2⅜ 16 14	1977	447
402⅜	46 46 39 5⅜ 17 16	William K. Leech	William K. Leech	Alaska Pen., Alaska	12⅜ 12⅜ 17 16	1983	447
402⅜	57⅜ 54⅜ 38⅜ 7⅜ 19⅜ 2⅜	John T. Holzschuh	John T. Holzschuh	Post Lake, Alaska	⅜ 16⅜ 13 23	1964	447
402⅜	54⅜ 53⅜ 49⅜ 6⅜ 19⅜ 2⅜	John Elmore	John Elmore	Ugashik Lake, Alaska	15⅜ ⅜ 20 18	1967	447
402⅛	52⅜ 47 32⅜ 7 1⅜ 17⅜	George V. Lenher	George V. Lenher	Rainy Pass, Alaska	⅜ 14⅜ 16 24	1967	450

353

BARREN GROUND CARIBOU—Continued

Rangifer tarandus granti

Score	Length of Main Beam		Inside Spread	Circumference at Smallest Place Between Brow and Bez Points		Length of Brow Points		Width of Brow Points		Number of Points		Locality Killed	By Whom Killed	Owner	Date Killed	Rank
	R	L		R	L	R	L	R	L	R	L					
402⅛	48	49⅛	43⅜	8⅜	6⅜	23⅜	4⅛	13⅜		19	16	Susitna River, Alaska	Fredrick W. Thornton	Fredrick W. Thornton	1969	450
402⅛	55⅞	54	42⅜	6⅜	7	21⅜		17⅜	⅛	19	11	Twin Lakes, Alaska	Cecil Glessner	Cecil Glessner	1966	450
402	48⅜	55⅜	41⅜	7⅜	7⅜	19⅜	23⅜	11⅜	11⅜	12	12	Mulchatna River, Alaska	Phillip Miller	Phillip Miller	1972	453
402	51⅜	52⅜	43⅜	4⅜	5⅜	22⅜	23⅜	12⅜	9⅜	14	17	Talkeetna Mts., Alaska	Clyde A. McLeod	Clyde A. McLeod	1983	453
401⅞	54⅜	54⅜	44⅜	5⅛	4⅜	17⅜	20⅛	14	4⅜	15	13	Alaska Range, Alaska	Glenn E. Allen	Glenn E. Allen	1979	455
401⅞	54⅜	54⅜	35⅜	6⅜	7⅜	19	18⅜	5⅜	16⅜	18	24	Nabesna, Alaska	Bill Copeland	Bill Copeland	1969	455
401⅞	59⅜	56⅜	35⅜	7⅜	9⅜	19	18⅜	11⅜	15⅜	16	15	Tyone Lake, Alaska	Eileen Marshall	Eileen Marshall	1961	455
401⅞	55⅜	55⅜	35⅜	9⅜	6⅜	15⅜	6⅜	12⅜	15⅜	15	14	Mt. Sanford, Alaska	Harold R. Clark	Harold R. Clark	1981	458
401⅞	47⅜	48⅜	44⅜	5⅜	6⅜	15⅜	15⅜	5⅜	7⅜	18	14	Talkeetna Mts., Alaska	David Maroney	David Maroney	1961	458
401⅞	45⅜	49⅜	39⅜	6⅜	6⅜	13⅜	15⅜	11⅜	9⅜	29	27	Tazlina, Alaska	Lloyd Ronning	Lloyd Ronning	1958	458
401⅞	41⅜	40⅜	40⅜	6⅜	5⅜	19	17⅜	10⅜	11⅜	18	10	Totatlanika River, Alaska	Heinrich K. Springer	Heinrich K. Springer	1969	458
401⅝	50⅜	50⅜	37⅜	6⅜	6⅜	16⅜	18⅜	13	9⅜	19	21	Lake Louise, Alaska	Dale A. Hillmer	Dale A. Hillmer	1961	462
401⅝	45⅜	44⅜	36⅜	6⅜	7⅜	13⅜	18⅜	7⅜	9⅜	17	24	Rainy Pass, Alaska	Reed Sandvig	Reed Sandvig	1964	462
401½	50⅜	51⅜	30⅜	7	7	19⅜	20⅜	16⅜	15⅜	23	17	Becharof Lake, Alaska	Bill D. Reed	Bill D. Reed	1983	464
401½	49⅜	49	38⅜	5⅜	5⅜	17⅜	18⅜	2⅜	6⅜	13	13	Little Delta River, Alaska	Danny R. Hart	Danny R. Hart	1982	464
401½	61⅜	59⅜	39⅜	7⅜	7	9⅜	6	9⅜	9⅜	13	14	Stuyahok River, Alaska	Fred A. Wright	Fred A. Wright	1961	464
401½	61⅜	63⅜	48⅜	7⅜	7⅜	17⅜	18⅜	10⅜	⅛	17	14	Talkeetna River, Alaska	J. Donald Neill	J. Donald Neill	1968	464
401½	50	54⅜	35⅜	7⅜	7⅜	17⅜	18⅜	7	11⅜	13	18	Wrangell Mts., Alaska	Gerald F. McNamara	Gerald F. McNamara	1959	464
401⅜	52	53	32⅜	5⅜	5⅜	14⅜	14⅜	9⅜	8	20	18	Denali Hwy., Alaska	Norman Smith	Norman Smith	1965	469
401⅜	51⅜	51⅜	35⅜	6⅜	6⅜	16⅜	15⅜	9⅜	9⅜	18	21	Wrangell Mts., Alaska	Ronald Bergstrom	Ronald Bergstrom	1959	469
401¼	57⅜	56⅜	42⅜	6⅜	6	9⅜	16⅜	⅛	13	14	18	Alaska Range, Alaska	Robert B. Boone	Robert B. Boone	1983	471
401¼	48⅜	43⅜	34⅜	6⅜	8	16⅜	13	13⅜	9⅜	18	17	Wood River, Alaska	William P. Ghiorso	William P. Ghiorso	1983	471
401⅛	50⅜	54⅜	42⅜	6⅜	6⅜	17⅜		16⅜		16	14	King Salmon, Alaska	Edward W. Ratcliff	Edward W. Ratcliff	1984	473
401⅛	61⅝	57⅜	47⅜	5⅜	6⅜	22⅜	18⅜	9⅜	⅛	13	10	Little Nelchina River, Alaska	Elton Aarestad	Elton Aarestad	1964	473
401⅛	52	52⅜	45⅜	7⅜	7⅜	15⅜	18	8⅜	13⅜	15	16	Nicholson Lake, Alaska	John P. Scribner	John P. Scribner	1956	473
401⅛	54⅜	51	44	6⅜	7⅜	17	19⅜	7⅜	14⅜	14	17	Nondalton, Alaska	Anton L. Cerro	Anton L. Cerro	1973	473
401⅛	53⅜	54⅜	40⅜	6⅜	7⅜	6⅜	19⅜	⅛	17⅜	11	21	Rainy Pass, Alaska	John Weirdsma	John Weirdsma	1961	473
401⅛	49⅜	48⅜	52⅜	6⅜	6⅜	19	2⅛	13		22	20	Talkeetna Mts., Alaska	Joe Van Daalwyk	Joe Van Daalwyk	1957	473
401	55⅜	56⅜	37	8⅜	7⅜	18⅜	19⅜	11⅜	4	18	14	Red Devil, Alaska	Joseph L. LaNou	Joseph L. LaNou	1984	479
401	61⅜	58	46	7	8	20	14⅜	8	8	16	19	Talkeetna Mts., Alaska	Louis Mussatto	Louis Mussatto	1964	479
400⅞	51⅜	50⅜	38	6⅜	7⅜	11⅜	13⅜	6⅜	9⅜	14	19	Chisana, Alaska	Harry L. Thompson	Harry L. Thompson	1966	481

Score												Locality	By whom killed	Owner	Date killed	Rank
400⅞	57⅜	57⅞	38⅛	7⅜	7⅞	8⅞	21⅛	1	18	12	22	Alaska Pen., Alaska	E. J. Hansen	E. J. Hansen	1964	482
400⅞	48⅛	49⅞	29⅛	7	6⅞	22⅞	21⅛	16⅞	4⅞	16	14	Fortymile River, Alaska	Arnold O. Burton	Arnold O. Burton	1985	483
400⅜	49⅜	47⅞	39¾	6⅞	6⅞	17⅞	19	9⅞	15⅜	19	26	Alaska Pen., Alaska	James Swartout	James Swartout	1978	484
400⅜	49½	49	42	5⅞	5⅞	8⅞	19⅞	1	9⅞	19	14	Cinder River, Alaska	Mervin Bergstrom	Mervin Bergstrom	1975	484
400⅜	52	35	45⅜	7⅞	7⅞	3⅞	23⅜	⅛	16	13	15	Ingersoll Lake, Alaska	Peter H. Merlin	Peter H. Merlin	1970	484
400⅜	42½	41⅛	33⅜	5⅞	5⅞	17⅞	18⅛	13⅞	13⅞	15	19	Talkeetna, Alaska	S. H. Sampson	S. H. Sampson	1959	484
400⅜	57¾	58⅜	40	7⅞	7⅞		4	12		20	13	Wood River, Alaska	Berry B. Brooks	Berry B. Brooks	1958	484
400⅛	60	60⅛	50	7⅞	9⅞	24⅞	24⅜		17	14	22	King Salmon, Alaska	Richard O. Burns III	Richard O. Burns III	1982	489
400⅛	48⅞	48⅛	31⅛	5⅞	5⅞	16	16⅞	6⅞	7	13	18	Alaska Pen., Alaska	Lillie E. Kriss	Lillie E. Kriss	1972	490
400⅛	51⅛	50⅜	42	6⅞	6⅞	5⅞	14⅛	⅞	10⅛	15	19	Denali Hwy., Alaska	Wilbur T. Gamble	Wilbur T. Gamble	1963	490
400	59⅜	59⅜	43	5⅞	5⅞	18	15⅜	10⅛	1	17	16	Monahan Flats, Alaska	C. H. Dana, Jr.	C. H. Dana, Jr.	1965	490
400	57⅞	56⅜	37⅞	7⅞	6	18⅞	19	12⅜	11⅛	14	16	Alaska Pen., Alaska	Bert Klineburger	Bert Klineburger	1961	493
400	47⅞	50⅛	30⅜	8⅛	5⅞	3	17	⅛	10⅛	13	19	Anchorage, Alaska	C. C. Irving	C. C. Irving	1959	493
400	48	50	39⅞	6⅞	6	15⅜	17⅞	12	1⅛	19	15	Caribou Lake, Alaska	Donald J. Giottonini, Jr.	Donald J. Giottonini, Jr.	1983	493
400	54⅜	56⅞	35⅛	7⅛	7⅛	19⅞	16⅞	17⅛	⅛	17	8	King Salmon, Alaska	G. O. Wiegner	G. O. Wiegner	1970	493
400	53⅛	53⅛	37	5⅞	5⅞	20⅞	21⅛	1	14⅛	9	19	Lake Louise, Alaska	George Moerlein	George Moerlein	1962	493
400	45	46⅝	44⅛	5	5	16⅜	5⅞	12⅛	⅞	24	16	Nelchina, Alaska	Webb Hilgar	Webb Hilgar	1962	493
400	54⅜	53⅛	31⅛	6⅜	7	6	17	⅛	9	18	20	White Fish Lake, Alaska	Thomas K. Willard	Thomas K. Willard	1984	493
459⅛*	60⅛	57⅞	57⅜	6⅞	6⅜	5⅞	21	⅛	14⅜	17	22	Becharof Lake, Alaska	Gordon G. Chittick	Gordon G. Chittick	1983	
452⅝*	49⅛	49⅜	50⅞	6⅛	6⅞	20⅜	23	22⅛	13⅜	13	16	Meshik River, Alaska	Robert D. Jones	Robert D. Jones	1980	
441⅛*	53⅛	51⅛	42⅞	6⅞	6⅜	19⅞		14⅛		19	14	Stephans Lake, Alaska	Timothy J. Schrage	Timothy J. Schrage	1983	
439⅛*	55⅛	56⅜	41⅛	5⅞	6⅜	20⅜	18⅜	10⅛	8⅛	17	17	Alaska Pen., Alaska	Rodney D. Fulcher	Rodney D. Fulcher	1984	

*Final Score subject to revision by additional verifying measurements

NEW WORLD'S RECORD CENTRAL CANADA BARREN GROUND CARIBOU
SCORE: 408 6/8

Locality: Rendez-vous Lake, Northwest Territories Date: 1982
Picked Up Owner: Tom W. Barry

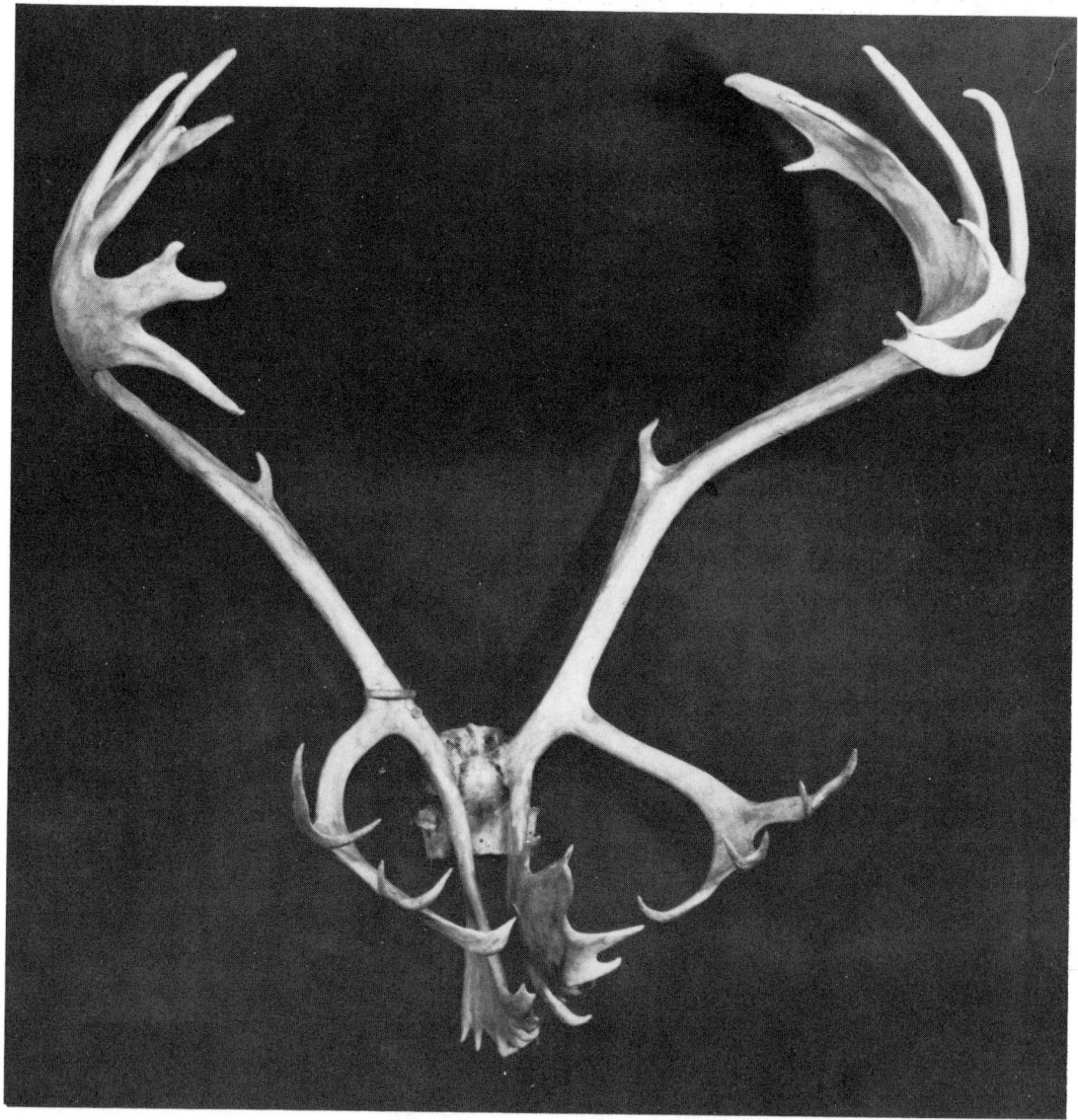

NUMBER TWO CENTRAL CANADA BARREN GROUND CARIBOU
SCORE: 408 2/8

Locality: Courageous Lake, Northwest Territories Date: 1985
Hunter and owner: Raymond H. Bonar

Central Canada Barren Ground Caribou

Rangifer tarandus groenlandicus

Minimum Score 345

Central Canada barren ground caribou occur on Baffin Island and the mainland of N.W.T., with geographic boundaries of the Mackenzie River to the west; the north edge of the continent to the north (excluding any islands except Baffin Island); Hudson's Bay to the east; and the southern boundary of Northwest Territories to the south.

Score	Length of Main Beam R.	L.	Inside Spread	Circumference at Smallest Place Between Brow and Bez Points R.	L.	Length of Brow Points R.	L.	Width of Brow Points R.	L.	Number of Points R.	L.	Locality Killed	By Whom Killed	Owner	Date Killed	Rank
408⅛	52⅞	51⅛	38⅝	4⅞	4⅞	21⅞	18⅝	8⅝	15⅛	17	23	Rendez-vous Lake, N.W.T.	Picked Up	Tom W. Barry	1982	1
408⅜	46⅛	47	39⅛	4⅞	4⅞	16⅜	19	10⅞	18⅜	20	25	Courageous Lake, N.W.T.	Raymond H. Bonar	Raymond H. Bonar	1985	2
395⅜	49⅜	49⅝	31⅛	4⅜	4⅞	15⅞	16⅞	11⅛	7⅞	18	20	Courageous Lake, N.W.T.	George O. Poston	George O. Poston	1985	3
382⅞	56	56⅛	37⅛	6⅛	6	16⅛	16⅜	8⅝	9⅞	17	15	Courageous Lake, N.W.T.	Earle H. Harder	Earle H. Harder	1985	4
371⅛	56⅜	58	37⅛	5⅞	6	16	12⅞	12⅝	5	16	16	Courageous Lake, N.W.T.	Jon R. Stephens	Jon R. Stephens	1984	5
369⅛	50⅜	51⅛	43	5	5⅝	14⅞	14⅜	9	7⅞	15	14	Seahorse Lake, N.W.T.	Barry D. Taylor	Barry D. Taylor	1985	6
361⅛	49⅜	49⅝	29⅞	5⅝	5⅝	6⅞	18⅞	2⅞	14⅛	17	23	Winter Lake, N.W.T.	Warren D. St. Germaine	Warren D. St. Germaine	1984	7
357⅞	48	47	27⅝	5⅜	5⅛	13⅝	19	7⅞	11⅜	17	18	Undine Lake, N.W.T.	Barry D. Taylor	Barry D. Taylor	1985	8
357⅛	49⅜	48⅞	33	4⅜	4⅞	16⅛	18⅜	13⅞	7⅞	16	18	Courageous Lake, N.W.T.	Kaye Poston	Kaye Poston	1983	9
351⅛	48⅜	48⅞	31	5⅜	5⅛	16⅛	16⅛	11⅝	11	11	14	Robin Lake, N.W.T.	Gary D. Cooney	Gary D. Cooney	1981	10
350⅛	46⅜	43⅜	31⅛	5⅜	5⅛	8⅛		10	⅛	20	15	Perry Pen., N.W.T.	Donald F. Senter	Donald F. Senter	1985	11
391⅜*	49	54⅞	41⅛	5⅝	5⅛	13	15⅜	⅛	10⅜	14	16	Winter Lake, N.W.T.	William M. Leschasin	William M. Leschasin	1985	
390⅞*	59	57	41⅛	5⅛	5⅛	5⅝	17⅞	10⅝	10⅛	16	13	Grizzle Bear Lake, N.W.T.	Douglas C. Heard	Douglas C. Heard	1978	
388⅜*	52⅜	50⅛	30⅜	5⅞	5⅛	20⅜	19⅞	3⅜	17	12	23	Courageous Lake, N.W.T.	James E. Nelson	James E. Nelson	1984	
377⅞*	47⅞	48⅛	31⅛	5⅝	5⅞	17⅞	18⅝	12	16⅞	17	18	Winter Lake, N.W.T.	Warren D. St. Germaine	Warren D. St. Germaine	1985	

*Final Score subject to revision by additional verifying measurements

358

WORLD'S RECORD QUEBEC-LABRADOR CARIBOU
SCORE: 474 6/8

Locality: Nain, Labrador Date: 1931
Hunter: Zack Elbow
Donated by Charles R. Peck to the B&C National Collection

NUMBER THREE QUEBEC-LABRADOR CARIBOU
SCORE: 460 6/8
Locality: Ungava Bay, Quebec Date: 1978
Hunter and owner: Lynn D. McLaud

Quebec-Labrador Caribou

Rangifer tarandus from Quebec and Labrador

Minimum Score 375

Score	Length of Main Beam R.	L.	Inside Spread	Circumference at Smallest Place Between Brow and Bez Points R.	L.	Length of Brow Points R.	L.	Width of Brow Points R.	L.	Number of Points R.	L.	Locality Killed	By Whom Killed	Owner	Date Killed	Rank
474⅞	60⅜	61⅝	58⅞	6⅜	6⅜	14⅞	21⅞	9	14⅞	22	30	Nain, Lab.	Zack Elbow	B&C National Collection	1931	1
464⅝	55⅞	54⅞	54⅛	5⅞	5⅞	19⅞	19⅝	2⅛	14⅛	18	23	Tunulic River, Que.	James A. DeLuca	James A. DeLuca	1983	2
460⅝	59⅞	56⅝	49⅛	5⅛	5⅛	16⅝	21⅛	13⅛	18⅝	22	24	Ungava Bay, Que.	Lynn D. McLaud	Lynn D. McLaud	1978	3
439⅛	56⅝	59⅛	42	6⅞	5⅛	17⅞	20⅛	12⅜	13⅞	11	22	Ungava Bay, Que.	Don Tomberlin	Don Tomberlin	1985	4
438⅞	59⅜	55⅛	52⅞	5⅝	5⅞	8	21⅛	19⅞	19⅜	17	25	Beach Camp, Que.	Ron Ragan	Ron Ragan	1975	5
434⅞	51⅛	52	44⅝	4⅞	5⅛	16⅜	20⅛	14⅞	8⅝	25	22	Mistinibi Lake, Que.	Don L. Corley	Don L. Corley	1983	6
433⅞	50⅝	53⅞	54	5⅛	5⅛	16⅝	20⅛	9⅝	16⅛	22	28	George River, Que.	Dewey Mark	Dewey Mark	1973	7
429⅞	55⅛	59⅛	50⅛	5⅛	5⅛	21⅛	2⅛	19⅛	⅛	15	12	Ford Lake, Que.	George Shultz	George Shultz	1972	8
429⅜	51⅛	50⅛	48⅜	5⅛	5⅛	18⅛	18⅝	13⅛	14⅛	21	21	Mistinibi Lake, Que.	Charles E. Wilson, Jr.	Charles E. Wilson, Jr.	1980	9
428⅞	51⅛	52⅛	38⅜	6	6	14⅞	15⅜	9⅝	12	26	30	George River, Que.	Cayetano G. Arriola, Jr.	Cayetano G. Arriola, Jr.	1975	10
421⅜	52⅜	54⅛	53⅜	5⅞	5⅜	17⅛	5⅞	12⅞	⅛	20	16	George River, Que.	Maurice Southmayd	Maurice Southmayd	1979	11
416⅝	45⅜	47⅞	47⅞	4⅞	4⅞	13⅝	16	6⅞	11	28	27	George River, Que.	Collins F. Kellogg	Collins F. Kellogg	1978	12
415⅝	54⅝	52⅛	46	5	5⅞	17⅜	18⅝	8⅞	16⅝	15	21	George River, Que.	George E. Poleshock	George E. Poleshock	1980	13
414⅞	62⅞	66	43⅝	5⅛	5⅞	2⅜	21⅛	⅛	16⅝	16	22	Schefferville, Que.	Peggy A. Vallery	Peggy A. Vallery	1980	14
414	42⅞	43⅝	41	5⅝	6	15⅛	13⅞	8⅝	8⅛	22	23	George River Lodge, Que.	James E. McCarthy	James E. McCarthy	1974	15
412⅞	53⅝	52⅞	45⅛	6	6¼	17⅞	16	13⅛	11⅛	16	22	Whale River, Que.	Daniel E. Merrell	Daniel E. Merrell	1972	16
411⅛	51	51⅞	52⅞	7	8⅞	13⅜	14	5⅝	4⅛	9	14	Mistinibi Lake, Que.	Rudolf Sand	Rudolf Sand	1973	17
411⅛	61⅝	63⅞	48	5⅞	6	16⅞	3⅞	17⅞	⅛	18	18	Mistinibi Lake, Que.	David H. Crum	David H. Crum	1980	17
410⅞	57⅝	55⅞	49	5⅝	5⅞	20⅝	16⅜	17	10⅞	21	21	Mistinibi Lake, Que.	Picked Up	Toby J. Johnson	1984	19
410⅝	59⅝	60⅞	40⅞	5⅞	5⅝	17⅞	17⅞	14	8⅞	26	22	George River, Que.	Kenneth E. Goslant	Kenneth E. Goslant	1974	20
409⅞	51⅞	50⅞	51⅛	5⅛	5⅞	14	16⅞	8⅞	11	18	20	Mistinibi Lake, Que.	George H. Fearons	George H. Fearons	1982	21
408⅞	44⅝	42⅞	46⅝	6⅛	5⅞	13⅛	13⅜	14⅝	13⅞	25	24	George River, Que.	Gail W. Holderman	Gail W. Holderman	1979	22
408⅛	57⅞	47⅞	45	5⅜	5⅞	21⅛	20⅞	15⅛	1⅞	19	14	Mistinibi Lake, Que.	Lee Frudden	Lee Frudden	1980	23
408⅛	53⅝	53⅛	46⅛	6⅞	6⅜	18	13⅛	12⅞	⅞	19	19	Ungava Bay, Que.	Richard H. Propp	Richard H. Propp	1985	23
407⅞	54⅝	56⅜	42⅛	6	6⅜	17⅞	15⅛	11⅛	10	19	17	Tunulik Lake, Que.	Robert L. Sprinkle, Jr.	Robert L. Sprinkle, Jr.	1979	25
405⅞	55	56⅛	51⅛	5⅛	5⅞	18⅛	17⅝	12⅛	11⅜	19	19	Tunulik River, Que.	Jerry Ippolito	Jerry Ippolito	1980	26
405⅞	52	53	44⅝	6	5⅞	16⅝	22	12⅜	17⅝	19	23	De Pas River, Que.	Herbert J. Englemann	Herbert J. Englemann	1979	27
405	53⅛	54⅛	51⅛	5⅛	5	20	20⅛	17⅞	9⅝	15	15	Knob Lake, Que.	Chester Gluck	Chester Gluck	1964	28

Score	Length of Main Beam R.	L.	Inside Spread	Circumference at Smallest Place Between Brow and Bez Points R.	L.	Length of Brow Points R.	L.	Width of Brow Points R.	L.	Number of Points R.	L.	Locality Killed	By Whom Killed	Owner	Date Killed	Rank
404⅝	46⅜	46	40⅞	6⅛	6⅛	20⅝	20⅝	15⅜	19⅞	19	14	Ungava Bay, Que.	Daniel W. Inserra	Daniel W. Inserra	1979	29
404½	53⅜	57⅞	42⅝	5⅝	5⅝	17⅝	18⅝	10⅞	9⅞	13	15	Camp Tuktu, Que.	Robert E. Pritinen	Robert E. Pritinen	1980	30
403⅛	58⅝	61	44⅞	5⅜	5⅜	19⅝	18⅝	10⅛	12⅛	18	21	Ungava Bay, Que.	John A. Gulius	John A. Gulius	1975	31
403⅛	51⅛	51⅛	48⅝	5⅛	5⅝	18⅝	19⅛	11	13⅜	15	16	Thibault Lake, Que.	Ralph Cervo	Ralph Cervo	1983	32
402⅝	49⅜	50⅛	51⅛	5⅜	5⅜	16⅝	17⅝	14⅜	8⅝	20	17	Sagler Fiord, Lab.	Ernest W. Foster, Jr.	Ernest W. Foster, Jr.	1985	33
402⅝	60⅜	57⅜	48⅝	4⅝	5	16⅝	15⅜	11⅝	8⅝	19	16	George River, Que.	Paul B. Brunner	Paul B. Brunner	1980	34
402	54⅞	53⅝	48⅝	5⅞	6⅛	15⅛	16	6⅝	10⅞	18	18	Mistinibi Lake, Que.	Theodore L. Greenwood	Theodore L. Greenwood	1981	35
401⅞	57	58⅝	48⅝	5⅛	5	18⅝	16⅛	9⅞	8⅞	17	15	Indian River, Que.	Bruce Hartel	Bruce Hartel	1981	36
401	51⅛	52⅞	44⅞	5⅝	5⅝	15⅝	19⅜	10⅛	16	20	24	George River, Que.	Robert A. Krizek	Robert A. Krizek	1979	37
401	46⅝	48⅞	50⅞	5⅛	5	17⅛	16⅞	9⅞	13⅞	20	18	Schefferville, Que.	L. C. Harold	L. C. Harold	1982	37
400⅞	52⅝	52⅝	37⅞	5⅝	5⅝	17⅝	13	15⅜	8⅝	24	22	Tunulik River, Que.	M. Farrel Gosman	M. Farrel Gosman	1978	39
400⅞	46	46⅛	46⅛	6	6	15⅛	14⅛	11⅜	13⅜	21	18	Mistinibi Lake, Que.	Dennis E. Moos	Dennis E. Moos	1980	39
400⅜	54⅝	56⅝	52⅝	5⅜	5⅝	23	23⅜	17⅛	13⅜	15	11	George River, Que.	Dale D. Wieand	Dale D. Wieand	1977	41
400	56⅝	58⅝	51⅝	5⅛	5⅝	⅞	16⅜	⅛	9⅞	15	19	George River, Que.	John C. Sullivan, Jr.	John C. Sullivan, Jr.	1978	42
399⅞	57⅝	59⅝	45⅝	6	6⅝	17⅝	17⅛	14⅝	⅛	15	14	Dihourse Lake, Que.	George E. Rommler	George E. Rommler	1980	43
398⅞	52⅝	51⅛	48⅝	5⅜	5⅜	13⅝	15⅜	3⅝	9⅝	16	14	George River, Que.	Bob Bates	Bob Bates	1980	44
398⅛	52⅝	51⅛	45	5⅜	6	16⅝	16⅛	12⅝	11⅜	14	14	Tunulik River, Que.	Jack Schwabland	Jack Schwabland	1980	45
398⅛	54⅜	55⅞	52⅜	4⅞	6	10⅞	20⅝	⅛	15⅝	15	21	Ford Lake, Que.	George H. Fearons	George H. Fearons	1977	46
397⅞	55	56	58	5	4⅞	7⅝	18⅝	2⅝	12⅝	13	14	George River, Que.	David L. George	David L. George	1968	47
397⅞	43⅝	47⅞	46⅝	6	4⅞	2⅛	17⅛	⅛	12⅝	21	18	Twin River Lodge, Que.	Fred W. Sheaman, Jr.	Fred W. Sheaman, Jr.	1969	48
397	54⅝	54⅜	40	5⅛	5⅝	14	15⅝	14⅝	15⅛	19	22	Ungava Bay, Que.	Charles T. Sheley	Charles T. Sheley	1979	49
396⅝	46⅝	47⅞	39⅝	5⅞	5⅝	15⅝	19⅝	⅛	15⅝	21	23	Tunulik River, Que.	Charles W. Dixon	Charles W. Dixon	1979	50
396⅝	59⅛	59⅞	46⅝	6	5⅝	20⅝	20⅝	17⅛	8⅝	16	17	George River Lodge, Que.	Robert S. Carroll	Robert S. Carroll	1974	51
396⅜	54⅛	55⅝	48⅝	6⅝	7⅝	17⅝	11	13⅝	6⅝	19	14	George River, Que.	John E. Clark	John E. Clark	1980	52
395⅞	55⅝	58⅝	51	5⅝	5⅝	1	18⅝	⅛	14⅝	15	22	Ungava Bay, Que.	Bruce S. Markham	Bruce S. Markham	1979	53
394⅞	51⅛	48⅞	42⅝	5⅛	4⅝	19⅝	17⅝	2⅝	11⅛	17	15	De Pas River, Que.	William A. O'Connor	William A. O'Connor	1980	54
394⅜	54⅜	53	57⅛	5⅝	5⅝	9⅝	16⅝	⅛	11⅝	12	20	George River, Que.	Stanley M. Boots	Stanley M. Boots	1983	55
394⅜	49⅛	50⅝	41	5⅝	5⅝	18⅝	1⅛	12	1	13	16	Mistinibi Lake, Que.	Paul E. Robey	Paul E. Robey	1981	56
394⅛	52⅝	52⅝	46⅝	4⅝	4⅝	19⅜	19⅛	4⅝	13	16	19	Ungava Region, Que.	James F. Tappan	James F. Tappan	1967	57
393⅝	50⅞	54⅛	40⅝	4⅝	5	16⅝	9⅝	12⅝	⅛	22	16	George River, Que.	Rick Ullery	Rick Ullery	1975	58

Score												Locality	Owner	By whom killed	Date killed	Rank
393⅜	55⅞	50⅜	5⅜	5⅛	5⅜	17⅞	15⅜	4⅞	9⅞	12	14	Ungava Bay, Que.	Arthur Bashore	Arthur Bashore	1971	59
393⅜	59⅜	57⅛	6⅜	6⅛	6⅜	17⅝	17⅜	8⅜	11⅜	17	13	George River, Que.	Michael J. Merritt	Michael J. Merritt	1978	59
392⅞	56⅜	56⅜	5⅜	5⅜	5⅜	18⅜	2	8⅜	19	19	17	George River, Que.	Morris Weinstein	Morris Weinstein	1972	61
392½	55	53⅜	5⅜	5⅜	5⅜	18⅜	7⅜	15⅜	⅛	20	20	Schefferville, Que.	Robert Henn	Robert Henn	1979	62
392⅜	48	47	4⅜	4⅜	4⅜	17⅜	17⅜	14	13⅜	24	25	George River, Que.	Kerry W. Blanton	Kerry W. Blanton	1983	63
392⅜	57⅜	57⅛	5⅜	5⅛	5⅜	16⅜	18⅜	2⅜	13	13	20	Ungava Area, Que.	Frank J. Blaha, Jr.	Frank J. Blaha, Jr.	1978	64
392⅛	56⅜	55⅜	4⅜	4⅜	4⅜	3⅜	20⅜	⅛	15⅜	15	23	Tunulik River, Que.	Salvatore A. Gusmano	Salvatore A. Gusmano	1981	65
392⅛	55	53⅜	5⅜	5⅜	5⅜	12⅜	16⅜	3⅜	14	15	18	George River, Que.	Donald F. Senter	Donald F. Senter	1983	65
391⅞	56⅜	56	6⅜	6⅛	6⅜	16⅜	19⅜	⅛	13⅜	15	18	George River, Que.	Alex Kariotakis	Alex Kariotakis	1974	67
391¼	60⅜	57	5⅜	5⅜	5⅜	15	8	2⅜	13⅜	13	15	Tunulik River, Que.	Kenneth J. Gerstung	Kenneth J. Gerstung	1979	68
390⅝	54	54⅜	6⅜	6⅜	6⅜	14⅜	20	⅛	13⅜	15	17	Mistinibi Lake, Que.	Thomas J. Merkley	Thomas J. Merkley	1979	69
390⅜	54	55⅜	5⅜	5⅜	5⅜	18⅜	8	12	6⅜	14	14	George River, Que.	James E. Prevost	James E. Prevost	1979	70
390⅜	54	52⅜	6⅜	6⅛	6⅜	14⅜	14⅜	⅛	12⅜	14	17	George River, Que.	John Daniels	John Daniels	1972	71
390	53	55	5⅜	5⅜	5⅜	18⅜	18⅜	1⅜	14	12	17	Schefferville, Que.	Samuel March, Jr.	Samuel March, Jr.	1972	72
389⅞	54⅜	56⅜	5⅜	5⅜	5⅜	15⅜	12⅜	9⅜	1⅜	14	17	Ford Lake, Que.	Carl F. Gernold	Carl F. Gernold	1982	73
389⅜	48⅜	51⅜	6	5⅜	5⅜	20⅜	19⅜	2	17⅜	18	16	Ungava Region, Que.	Eugene M. Decker	Eugene M. Decker	1973	74
389⅛	48⅜	49⅜	5⅜	5⅜	5	18⅜	13⅜	6⅜	14	21	21	Mistinibi Lake, Que.	Don L. Corley	Don L. Corley	1983	74
388⅝	51⅜	49⅜	5⅜	5⅜	5⅜	17⅜	15⅜	11⅜	13⅜	16	19	Mistinibi Lake, Que.	William A. S. Heuer	William A. S. Heuer	1981	76
387⅞	53⅜	47	5⅜	5⅜	5⅜	17	1	⅛	11⅜	14	18	Tunulik River, Que.	Larry Hoff	Larry Hoff	1984	77
386⅞	54⅜	47⅜	6⅜	6⅜	6⅜	18⅜	7	14⅜	⅛	17	18	George River, Que.	Arthur C. Sadowski	Arthur C. Sadowski	1979	78
386⅜	49⅜	44⅜	5⅜	5	5⅜	12⅜	18⅜	2⅜	12⅜	17	14	Mistinibi Lake, Que.	Watson T. Yoshimoto	Watson T. Yoshimoto	1980	79
385⅞	51	47⅛	6	6	5⅜	15⅜	13⅜	10	14	17	20	George River, Que.	James J. McBride	James J. McBride	1982	80
385	57⅜	56	5⅛	5⅜	5	20⅜	20⅜	6	5	13	15	George River, Que.	Daniel B. Kahle	Daniel B. Kahle	1983	81
384⅞	53⅜	52⅛	6	5⅜	5⅜	17⅜	17⅜	12⅜	18	18	15	Mistinibi Lake, Que.	Stewart N. Shaft	Stewart N. Shaft	1979	82
383⅞	52⅜	51⅛	5⅜	5	5⅜	18⅜	18⅜	4⅜	14	15	14	George River Lodge, Que.	Clayton C. Dovey, Jr.	Clayton C. Dovey, Jr.	1969	83
382⅞	51⅜	53⅜	6⅜	6⅜	6⅜	17⅜	6⅜	14⅜	1⅜	15	14	George River, Que.	Ralph Zampella	Ralph Zampella	1972	84
382⅜	53⅜	53⅜	5⅜	5⅜	5⅜	4⅜	15⅜	⅛	12	17	23	Mistinibi Lake, Que.	Watson T. Yoshimoto	Watson T. Yoshimoto	1979	85
381⅞	59⅜	54⅜	5⅜	5⅜	6⅜	18⅜	16	10⅜	5⅜	19	14	Ungava Region, Que.	John R. Oakes	John R. Oakes	1971	86
381⅞	53⅜	46	7	7	7	1⅜	16	⅛	57⅜	19	16	Kogaluk, Lab.	Basil C. Bradbury	Basil C. Bradbury	1949	87
380⅞	47⅜	44⅜	6	6	6	14⅜	12	8⅜	14⅜	15	18	Mistinibi Lake, Que.	Paul F. Barnhart	Paul F. Barnhart	1980	88
380⅜	52⅜	53⅜	6⅜	6⅜	6	17⅜	16⅜	8⅜	1⅜	16	16	Fiddle Lake, Que.	Herb Dittmar	Herb Dittmar	1966	89
380⅜	58	60⅜	5⅜	5⅜	5⅜	16	22⅜	10⅜	5⅜	16	17	Whale River, Que.	John A. Yeager	John A. Yeager	1979	90
380⅜	51⅜	52⅜	5⅜	5⅜	5⅜	16	20⅜	12⅜	8⅜	15	18	Mistinibi Lake, Que.	Toby J. Johnson	Toby J. Johnson	1984	90
380⅜	53⅜	51	7⅜	7	5⅜	8⅜	15⅜	1	14⅜	16	15	Fort Chimo, Que.	B. N. McCrum	B. N. McCrum	1967	92
380⅜	53⅜	48⅜	6⅜	6⅜	5⅜	16⅜	14⅜	1⅜	16⅜	11	20	George River, Que.	Roger R. Card	Roger R. Card	1980	92
380⅜	62⅜	39⅜	5⅜	5⅜	5⅜	8	15⅜	11⅜	⅛	10	11	George River, Que.	Randal L. Diehl	Randal L. Diehl	1980	92
380	51⅜	55	5⅜	5⅜	5⅜	19⅜	17⅜	10⅜	2	12	12	Tunulic River, Que.	Peter Smith	Peter Smith	1982	95
379⅜	52⅜	52⅜	5⅜	5⅜	5⅜	15⅜	19	6⅜	10	12	13	George River, Que.	Frank R. Heller	Frank R. Heller	1978	96
378⅜	54	40⅜	4⅜	4⅜	4⅜	17⅜	15⅜	7	9⅜	15	14	Tunuliq Lake, Que.	Scott M. Schowalter	Scott M. Schowalter	1982	97
378⅜	56	56⅜	5⅜	5⅜	4⅜	15⅜	⅜	10⅜	11⅜	18	15	Ford River, Que.	Vivian Sleight	Vivian Sleight	1973	98
378	53	51⅛	5⅜	5⅜	5⅜	2⅜	18⅜	⅛	13⅜	15	17	George River, Que.	Dick Ullery	Dick Ullery	1975	99
377⅛	45⅜	45⅜	4⅜	4⅜	4⅜	16⅜	16⅜	10⅜	12⅜	20	17	Lake Brisson, Que.	David Read	David Read	1983	100

QUEBEC-LABRADOR CARIBOU—*Continued*
Rangifer tarandus from Quebec and Labrador

Score	Length of Main Beam R.	L.	Inside Spread	Circumference at Smallest Place Between Brow and Bez Points R.	L.	Length of Brow Points R.	L.	Width of Brow Points R.	L.	Number of Points R.	L.	Locality Killed	By Whom Killed	Owner	Date Killed	Rank
377⅞	45⅛	45⅛	41⅝	5⅞	6⅛	6⅞	19	⅛	14⅛	16	20	George River, Que.	Normand Poulin	Normand Poulin	1976	101
377⅛	56⅞	58⅞	49⅞	5⅜	5⅛	20⅛		13⅜		24	18	Mistinibi Lake, Que.	James H. Meckes, Jr.	James H. Meckes, Jr.	1980	102
377	53⅝	55⅛	49⅜	5⅝	5⅝	18⅜	18	4	16⅝	12	11	George River, Que.	Stanley R. Smith	Stanley R. Smith	1975	103
376⅞	51⅜	53⅜	52⅝	5⅝	5⅞	14⅞	18⅝	1⅞	17⅞	21	24	George River, Que.	C. J. McElroy	C. J. McElroy	1969	104
376⅝	50⅛	50⅝	45⅝	5⅛	5⅛	16⅞	15	13⅝	10⅞	15	13	Ungava Bay, Que.	John D. Powers	John D. Powers	1981	105
376⅜	45⅛	48⅞	48	5⅛	5⅝	16⅜	19⅝	⅛	14⅞	15	19	Schefferville, Que.	Carl J. Los	Carl J. Los	1970	106
376⅜	40⅛	42⅛	28	4⅜	4⅞	11⅜	20⅛	1⅞	18	21	27	George River, Que.	Norman Clausen	Norman Clausen	1973	107
376⅜	53	53⅜	46⅝	6	6⅛	2⅞	17⅞	⅛	13⅜	18	20	Ungava Region, Que.	Don Peters	Don Peters	1969	108
376⅛	49⅝	50⅜	47⅞	6⅜	6⅜	13⅜	12⅛	8⅜	9⅞	17	15	Schefferville, Que.	Charles Lanzarone	Charles Lanzarone	1980	109
376⅛	55⅜	54⅛	55⅜	5⅛	5⅛	19⅝	10⅜	12⅜	2⅞	15	12	North Tudor Lake, Que.	Collins F. Kellogg	Collins F. Kellogg	1970	110
375⅞	50⅜	52⅞	37⅞	7⅞	7	19⅛	14⅞	14⅞	⅛	16	13	George River, Que.	Norma J. Laros	Norma J. Laros	1975	111
375⅞	52⅜	53⅞	46⅛	5⅝	5⅞	9⅜	19	⅛	14⅞	17	19	Fritz Lake, Que.	Donald A. Boyer	Donald A. Boyer	1978	112
375	46⅛	44	49⅞	6⅛	6⅝	14	13⅞	9⅜	1⅝	16	16	Ungava Pen., Que.	Theodore M. Schall	Theodore M. Schall	1985	112
446⅛*	61⅛	60⅞	67⅞	5⅝	5⅛	23⅜	22⅛	16⅜	4⅞	20	15	Ungava Bay, Que.	Leonard M. Clarke	Leonard M. Clarke	1983	
427⅝*	51	54⅜	47	6⅜	6⅝	11	20⅜	1⅞	17⅞	22	33	George River, Que.	Larry Barnett	Larry Barnett	1978	
425*	50⅜	51⅜	52⅞	5⅝	5⅝	15⅝	15⅛	10⅜	7⅞	14	19	Tunulic River, Que.	Kenneth J. Gerstung	Kenneth J. Gerstung	1978	
423⅜*	53⅜	54	53⅝	6⅛	6⅛	12	20⅛	2⅛	17⅞	19	28	George River, Que.	Claude E. Genet	Claude E. Genet	1967	
419⅜*	59⅜	59⅞	52⅛	6⅛	6	17⅞	3⅜	15	5⅞	19	16	De Paw River, Que.	William R. Branson	William R. Branson	1979	
417⅜*	52⅞	49⅞	46⅜	6⅜	6	18⅛	17⅜	14⅜	13⅝	21	20	George River, Que.	Edgar Brochu	Edgar Brochu	1976	
417*	60⅛	56⅞	50⅝	6⅜	6⅝	24⅜	19⅝	18⅛	1⅜	16	15	Mistinibi Lake, Que.	Howard M. Barnett	Howard M. Barnett	1980	
416⅛*	59⅜	59⅜	52⅝	5⅝	5	18⅛	18⅞	13⅜	8⅛	20	14	Ungava Region, Que.	Richard S. Neely	Richard S. Neely	1977	
416⅛*	49⅛	50⅜	42⅜	5⅝	5⅝	15⅛	15⅜	12⅞	13	16	20	Tunulik Lake, Que.	Robert F. Cook	Robert F. Cook	1979	
415⅝*	55⅜	55⅝	55⅝	5⅝	5⅜	23	19⅜	13⅛	14⅛	20	20	Ungava Pen., Que.	Gerald R. Warnock	Gerald R. Warnock	1978	
413⅝*	51⅜	51⅜	50⅛	6⅛	6⅛	16⅞	17⅜	2⅜	11⅞	14	21	George River, Que.	Picked Up	Claude E. Genet	PR1967	
413*	51⅞	49⅜	54⅜	4⅞	5⅜	27⅞	26⅜	23⅜	23⅜	25	19	Slippery Creek, Que.	Picked Up	Claude E. Genet	PR1967	
405⅛*	50⅜	48⅜	45⅜	5⅜	5⅜	20	15⅜	17⅜	⅛	23	19	George River, Que.	Howard Shelley	Howard Shelley	1971	
401⅛*	49⅜	51	49⅜	5⅞	6⅛	16⅛	18⅜	1⅜	13⅞	15	16	George River, Que.	Claude E. Genet	Claude E. Genet	1966	
394⅞*	58⅜	55⅜	54⅜	6	5⅝	20⅜	7⅞	⅛	13⅞	14	13	Fiddle Lake, Que.	Robert Hammond	Robert Hammond	1967	

*Final Score subject to revision by additional verifying measurements

NEW WORLD'S RECORD PRONGHORN
SCORE: 93 4/8
Locality: Coconino County, Arizona Date: 1985
Hunter and owner: Michael J. O'Haco, Jr.
Winner of the Sagamore Hill Medal, 1986

NUMBER TWO PRONGHORN
SCORE: 93
Locality: Yavapai County, Arizona Date: 1975
Hunter and owner: Edwin L. Wetzler

Pronghorn

Antilocapra americana americana and related subspecies

Minimum Score 82

Score	Length of Horn R.	L.	Circumference of Base R.	L.	Circumference at Third Quarter R.	L.	Inside Spread	Tip to Tip Spread	Length of Prong R.	L.	Locality Killed	By Whom Killed	Owner	Date Killed	Rank
93⅞	17⅞	17⅞	7	7	3⅛	3⅜	12⅜	8⅛	8	8⅜	Coconino Co., Ariz.	Michael J. O'Haco, Jr.	Michael J. O'Haco, Jr.	1985	1
93	18⅛	18⅛	7⅜	7	2⅝	2⅝	10⅛	6⅜	7⅞	7⅞	Yavapai Co., Ariz.	Edwin L. Wetzler	Edwin L. Wetzler	1975	2
91⅞	20½	20	7¼	7	2⅝	2⅝	12	11⅜	4½	5⅜	Arizona	Wilson Potter	National Collection	1899	3
91⅞	15½	15⅛	7⅞	7⅞	3⅜	3⅜	10⅛	9⅛	7	7	Weld Co., Colo.	Bob Schneidmiller	Bob Schneidmiller	1965	3
91⅞	17⅛	17	7⅜	7⅞	3⅜	3⅜	13⅜	10⅛	4⅜	7⅜	Garfield Co., Mont.	Donald W. Yates	Donald W. Yates	1977	3
91	16⅝	16⅛	7⅞	7⅞	2⅝	2⅝	10⅜	3	7⅜	7⅜	Carbon Co., Wyo.	J. Ivan Kitch	J. Ivan Kitch	1964	6
91	16⅛	15⅛	7⅛	7⅛	3	3⅛	14⅛	11⅜	5⅝	5⅝	Rawlins, Wyo.	Fred Starling	Fred Starling	1967	6
90⅞	18⅛	18⅛	6⅝	6⅝	2⅝	2⅝	10⅜	2⅞	7	6⅜	Yavapai Co., Ariz.	Joe P. Fornara	Joe P. Fornara	1984	8
90	19¼	19⅛	7	6⅞	2⅞	2⅛	10⅛	8	4⅝	4⅜	Guano Creek, Oreg.	E. C. Starr	E. C. Starr	1942	9
90	16⅛	16⅛	7⅜	7¼	2⅝	2⅝	17⅛	15⅜	7⅜	7⅜	Weston Co., Wyo.	Allen Douglas	Richard J. Macy	1943	9
89⅞	18	18	6⅝	6⅛	2⅞	2⅝	9⅜	4	7⅛	7⅜	Seligman, Ariz.	J. W. Johnson	J. W. Johnson	1959	11
89⅞	17⅛	17⅞	7⅜	7⅜	2⅝	2⅝	11⅛	6⅝	6⅛	6⅜	Rawlins, Wyo.	Mary C. Kircher	Mary C. Kircher	1961	11
89⅞	17⅜	17⅛	7	7⅞	2	2	12⅜	11⅜	7⅜	7⅜	Rosebud Co., Mont.	Jim Ollom	Jim Ollom	1973	11
89⅞	17⅛	17⅛	7⅛	7¼	3⅜	3⅜	10	3⅜	6	6	Ferris, Wyo.	John T. Peddy	John T. Peddy	1957	14
89⅞	17⅛	17⅛	7	7⅜	2⅜	2⅝	13⅜	9⅞	6⅛	6⅛	Laramie Co., Wyo.	Roy Vail	Roy Vail	1958	14
89⅞	16	15⅛	7¼	7¼	3	3	12	8⅝	6⅜	5⅝	Sierra Co., N.M.	P. K. Colquitt, Jr.	Thomas V. Schrivner	1961	14
89⅞	17⅛	17⅛	6⅝	7	2⅝	3	9⅜	3⅜	6⅜	6⅜	Humboldt Co., Nev.	Richard Steinmetz	Richard Steinmetz	1977	14
89⅞	18⅛	18⅛	7⅜	7⅜	2⅝	2⅝	11⅛	3	5⅜	5⅜	Grant Co., N.M.	Jerry Saint	N.M. Dept. Game & Fish	1975	18
89	17⅛	17⅛	7	7	3⅛	2⅝	7⅝	1⅝	6	6	Moffat Co., Colo.	Gerald Scott	Gerald Scott	1982	18
89	18	18⅛	6⅞	7⅛	2⅝	3⅜	10⅛	3⅜	6⅜	6⅜	Lincoln Co., N.M.	Arthur E. Long	Arthur E. Long	1985	20
88⅞	17	16⅛	7¼	7¼	3⅛	3⅛	11	5⅜	6⅜	5⅜	Lassen Co., Calif.	Picked Up	George W. Conant	1985	20
88⅞	18⅛	18⅛	7¼	7	3	3	11⅜	10⅛	6⅜	6⅜	Socorro Co., N.M.	J. Lyn Perry	J. Lyn Perry	1976	22
88⅞	16⅛	17⅛	7	7	2⅝	2⅝	10	5⅜	5⅞	5⅝	Fremont Co., Wyo.	Terry N. TenBoer	Terry N. TenBoer	1974	23
88⅞	19¼	18⅛	6⅝	6⅝	2⅝	2⅝	15⅛	11⅛	5	5⅝	Humboldt Co., Nev.	Clifford J. Heaverne	Clifford J. Heaverne	1983	23
88⅞	18⅛	18⅛	6⅝	6⅛	3⅛	3⅛	13⅜	10⅛	5⅝	5⅜	Coconino Co., Ariz.	Harold R. Edgemon	Harold R. Edgemon	1984	23
88⅞	16⅛	16⅛	7	6⅝	2⅜	2⅝	10⅛	8⅛	5⅜	5⅜	Navajo Co., Ariz.	John M. Griffith, Jr.	John M. Griffith, Jr.	1983	26
88	17¾	17	7⅜	6⅝	2⅝	2⅝	12⅜	7⅜	6	6	Yavapai Co., Ariz.	Larry D. Saylor	Larry D. Saylor	1984	26
88	16⅛	17⅛	7	7⅞	2⅜	2⅝	9⅛	5⅛	5⅝	5⅝	Sweet Grass Co., Mont.	William S. Amos	William S. Amos	1971	28
88	17	16⅛	7	7	2⅝	2⅝	9⅛	5⅛	5⅝	5⅝	Coconino Co., Ariz.	Richard J. Hallock	Richard J. Hallock	1973	28
87⅞	17	16⅛	7¼	7¼	2⅝	2⅝	15⅜	12⅜	5⅜	5⅜	Fremont Co., Wyo.	William I. Crump	William I. Crump	1963	30
87⅞	15	15⅛	7⅛	7⅛	3⅛	3⅛	10⅛	6⅜	7⅛	7⅛	Fremont Co., Wyo.	Frank Schuele	Frank Schuele	1975	30

PRONGHORN—Continued
Antilocapra americana americana and related subspecies

Score	Length of Horn R.	L.	Circumference of Base R.	L.	Circumference at Third Quarter R.	L.	Inside Spread	Tip to Tip Spread	Length of Prong R.	L.	Locality Killed	By Whom Killed	Owner	Date Killed	Rank
87⅜	17⅝	17⅜	6⅛	6⅜	2⅝	2⅜	11⅝	6⅜	6⅛	6⅜	Gillette, Wyo.	Stanley Scott	Stanley Scott	1961	32
87⅜	16	17⅞	7⅛	7	4⅞	3⅜	11⅞	12	6	6⅜	Modoc Co., Calif.	Lynn M. Greene	Lynn M. Greene	1971	32
87⅜	17⅜	17⅜	6⅜	6⅜	2⅝	2⅞	9⅜	2⅞	6⅜	6⅝	Modoc Co., Calif.	Ron L. Reasor	Ron L. Reasor	1979	32
87⅜	16⅝	17	7	7⅜	2⅞	2⅛	13⅜	11⅜	7⅜	7⅞	Lake Co., Oreg.	Ronald E. Hills	Ronald E. Hills	1966	35
87⅜	16⅜	17	6⅜	6⅜	2⅝	2⅝	13⅜	11	7⅛	7⅞	Fremont Co., Wyo.	Scott A. Trabing	Scott A. Trabing	1973	35
87⅜	16⅜	16⅝	6⅜	6⅜	2⅝	2⅜	12⅜	10⅞	7	6⅞	Humboldt Co., Nev.	Steve Young	Steve Young	1975	35
87⅜	16⅞	16⅝	6⅜	6	2⅝	2⅜	10⅞	4⅞	6⅞	6⅜	Sweetwater Co., Wyo.	Jay R. Anderson	Jay R. Anderson	1975	35
87⅜	17⅝	17⅜	6	6	2⅝	4⅛	14⅜	10⅜	6	5⅞	Carbon Co., Wyo.	Lee Miller	Lee Miller	1976	35
87⅜	16⅝	16⅛	7⅜	7⅜	4⅛	4⅞	12⅛	9	6⅜	6⅜	Niobrara Co., Wyo.	Stephen M. Cameron	Stephen M. Cameron	1976	35
87⅜	16	16⅛	7⅜	7⅛	2⅝	2⅜	16	12⅜	6⅜	7	Hudspeth Co., Texas	E. R. Rinehart	E. R. Rinehart	1959	41
87	16⅜	16⅛	7⅜	7⅜	2⅝	2⅛	10⅝	4⅞	6⅜	6⅜	Washoe Co., Nev.	William E. Walker	William E. Walker	1970	41
87	16⅜	16⅛	6⅜	6⅜	3⅛	3⅛	15⅜	10⅜	5⅜	5⅜	Magdalena, N.M.	Picked Up	Jim Riggs	1970	41
87	17⅞	17⅜	6⅜	6	2⅝	2⅜	10⅜	6⅜	6⅜	5⅜	Lake Co., Oreg.	JoAnn Hathaway	JoAnn Hathaway	1976	41
87	15⅞	15⅜	6⅜	7	2⅜	2⅜	10⅜	5	6⅛	6⅜	Sweetwater Co., Wyo.	Dell J. Barnes	Dell J. Barnes	1976	41
87	16⅜	16⅛	6⅝	6⅜	2⅜	2⅜	11⅜	7⅜	7⅜	6⅝	Sweetwater Co., Wyo.	William S. Salisbury	William S. Salisbury	1983	41
87	17	17	6⅜	6⅜	2⅜	2⅜	10⅜	8⅜	6⅜	6⅜	Millard Co., Utah	Duane Stanworth	Duane Stanworth	1984	41
87	18⅞	18	6⅜	6⅜	2⅝	2⅛	12⅜	7⅜	4⅜	5	Anderson Mesa, Ariz.	Gene Tolle	Gene Tolle	1941	48
86⅞	17⅜	17⅜	6⅜	6⅝	2⅝	2⅛	15⅜	13⅜	7⅜	6	Rock Springs, Wyo.	Stanley Sinclair	Stanley Sinclair	1952	48
86⅞	16⅜	16⅜	7⅜	7⅜	2⅜	2⅛	9⅜	6⅜	6⅜	6⅜	Rawlins, Wyo.	C. M. Chandler	C. M. Chandler	1953	48
86⅞	16⅜	17	7	7	2⅜	2⅜	8⅛	3⅜	6⅜	6⅛	Jefferson Co., Idaho	Dale Nealis	Dale Nealis	1961	48
86⅞	17⅜	15⅜	6⅜	6⅜	2⅜	2⅜	9⅝	6⅛	5⅜	6⅛	Yavapai Co., Ariz.	Louis R. Dees	Louis R. Dees	1963	48
86⅞	16⅜	16⅜	7	7	3	3	11⅜	9⅜	6	6⅜	Carbon Co., Wyo.	Chuck Sanger	Chuck Sanger	1968	48
86⅞	16⅜	16⅜	7	7	2⅜	2⅜	8⅜	2⅜	6⅜	7	Fremont Co., Wyo.	Richard A. Fruchey	Richard A. Fruchey	1973	48
86⅞	15⅜	16⅜	6⅜	6	2⅜	2⅜	9⅜	6	7⅞	8⅜	Sublette Co., Wyo.	Mrs. Arvid J. Siegel	Mrs. Arvid J. Siegel	1974	48
86⅞	17⅜	17⅜	7	6⅜	2⅜	2⅜	10⅜	6⅜	5⅜	5⅜	Coconino Co., Ariz.	Ralph C. Stayner	Ralph C. Stayner	1980	48
86⅞	17	17⅜	6⅜	6⅜	3⅛	3⅛	14	9⅜	5⅜	5⅜	Humboldt Co., Nev.	Rebecca J. Hall	Rebecca J. Hall	1981	48
86⅞	15⅜	15⅜	7⅜	7⅜	2⅜	2⅜	11⅜	10⅜	6⅜	7	Albany Co., Wyo.	Lloyd D. Kindsfater	Lloyd D. Kindsfater	1983	48
86⅞	18⅜	18⅛	6⅜	6⅜	3	3	8⅜	5⅜	4⅜	5⅜	Sublette Co., Wyo.	Glenn A. Eiden	Glenn A. Eiden	1983	48
86⅜	16⅜	16⅜	6⅜	6⅜	2⅜	2⅜	10⅜	10⅜	6	5⅜	Moffat Co., Colo.	Joseph R. Maynard	Joseph R. Maynard	1972	60
86⅜	15⅜	15⅜	6⅜	6⅜	2⅞	2⅜	10⅜	5⅜	6⅜	7	Lake Co., Oreg.	James W. Greer	James W. Greer	1976	60
86⅜	18	17⅜	6⅜	6⅜	2⅜	3	10⅜	6⅜	5⅜	6	Navajo Co., Ariz.	John D. Higginbotham	John D. Higginbotham	1979	60
86⅜	17	16⅜	7⅜	7⅞	2⅜	2⅜	11	6⅜	6	5⅜	Sweetwater Co., Wyo.	Rex A. Behrends	Rex A. Behrends	1980	60

369

PRONGHORN—Continued
Antilocapra americana americana and related subspecies

Score	Length of Horn R.	L.	Circumference of Base R.	L.	Circumference at Third Quarter R.	L.	Inside Spread	Tip to Tip Spread	Length of Prong R.	L.	Locality Killed	By Whom Killed	Owner	Date Killed	Rank
85⅞	16⅝	16⅝	6⅝	6⅝	2⅝	2⅝	9⅝	4⅛	6⅛	6⅛	Yavapai Co., Ariz.	Randy Modisett	Randy Modisett	1974	94
85⅞	18⅜	18⅜	6⅝	6⅜	2⅝	2⅝	7⅞	4⅞	4⅜	5⅞	Carbon Co., Wyo.	Robert F. Johnston	Robert F. Johnston	1977	94
85⅞	16⅛	16	7	7⅛	2⅝	2⅝	11⅜	8⅞	6⅛	6⅛	Natrona Co., Wyo.	Terrie L. Morrison	Terrie L. Morrison	1980	94
85⅞	15⅞	16	6⅞	6⅞	2⅞	2⅞	9⅜	4⅜	5⅞	5⅝	Sweetwater Co., Wyo.	Mark E. Nedrow	Mark E. Nedrow	1981	94
85⅞	15⅞	16	7⅜	7⅞	2⅝	2⅞	7⅞	3	5⅞	5⅞	Carbon Co., Wyo.	James M. Jagusch	James M. Jagusch	1981	94
85⅞	16⅞	16⅜	7⅝	7⅜	2⅜	2⅜	11⅛	8⅛	6⅝	7⅜	Rawlins, Wyo.	Paul C. Himelright	Paul C. Himelright	1960	112
85⅞	16	16⅜	6⅝	6⅝	2⅜	2⅝	10⅞	6⅞	6⅜	6⅞	Campbell Co., Wyo.	Eugene D. Springen	Eugene D. Springen	1962	112
85⅞	17	16⅝	7⅜	7⅞	2⅝	2⅞	10⅞	4⅛	6⅜	6⅜	Saratoga, Wyo.	Carlyn J. Ourada	Carlyn J. Ourada	1969	112
85⅞	15⅜	15⅜	6⅞	7⅞	2⅝	2⅞	7⅜	4⅜	6⅜	6⅛	Rosebud Co., Mont.	Calvin F. Mayes	Calvin F. Mayes	1973	112
85⅞	16	16⅞	6⅞	6⅜	3	2⅞	11⅜	10⅞	6⅛	5⅞	Washoe Co., Nev.	Mario E. Gildone	Mario E. Gildone	1977	112
85⅞	16⅞	17⅞	7⅞	6⅜	2⅝	2⅝	15⅛	11⅛	6⅛	6	Washoe Co., Nev.	Maryanne Robinson	Melbourne & Maryanne Robinson	1981	112
85⅞	17⅜	17⅜	6⅜	6⅛	2⅝	2⅝	9⅜	4⅜	5⅞	5⅞	Lemhi Co., Idaho	Michael Wolf	Michael Wolf	1982	112
85⅞	15⅜	15⅞	6⅜	6⅜	2⅝	2⅝	8⅞	2⅜	6⅜	6⅜	Fremont Co., Wyo.	Roger E. Udovich	Roger E. Udovich	1982	112
85⅞	16⅛	17⅛	7	7⅛	3	2⅝	13	9⅜	5⅞	5⅞	Fremont Co., Wyo.	Jerry A. Martin	Jerry A. Martin	1982	112
85⅞	16	16	6⅞	7	2⅝	2⅝	7⅜	3⅜	6⅜	6⅜	Stillwater Co., Wyo.	Lee Frudden	Lee Frudden	1982	112
85⅞	17⅛	17⅜	6⅞	6⅜	2⅝	2⅝	11⅛	9⅛	6⅞	6⅝	Mora Co., N.M.	Roger B. Heemeier	Roger B. Heemeier	1982	112
85⅞	16⅛	15⅞	7	7⅛	2⅜	2⅜	10	5	6⅝	7⅛	Sioux Co., Neb.	John W. Hlavacek	John W. Hlavacek	1983	112
85⅞	17	16	6⅞	6⅞	2⅝	2⅝	9⅜	6	5⅜	5⅜	Sweetwater Co., Wyo.	E. Jay Dawson	E. Jay Dawson	1983	112
85⅞	18⅛	18⅛	6⅜	6⅜	2⅝	2⅝	17⅛	13⅛	5⅞	5⅝	Apache Co., Ariz.	Don L. Corley	Don L. Corley	1985	112
85⅞	17⅞	17⅜	7	7	2⅝	2⅜	14⅛	12⅜	5⅜	5⅜	Lake Co., Oreg.	Edna J. Kettenburg	Edna J. Kettenburg	1985	112
85⅝	16⅜	16⅛	7	7	2⅜	2⅜	12⅜	8⅜	6	6	Saratoga, Wyo.	Russell Cutter	Russell Cutter	1957	127
85⅝	15⅞	15⅛	7⅛	7⅛	2⅝	2⅝	12⅜	11⅛	6	6	Lower Sweetwater, Wyo.	John Kereszturi	John Kereszturi	1963	127
85⅝	17⅛	17	7⅛	7⅜	2⅝	2⅝	7⅜	2	5⅜	5⅜	Yavapai Co., Ariz.	Robert C. Bogart	Robert C. Bogart	1963	127
85⅝	17	17	6⅜	6⅜	2⅝	2⅝	10⅞	8	5⅝	5⅜	Bow City, Alta.	Howard M. Stephens	Eric Wilson	1964	127
85⅝	16⅜	16⅛	6⅜	6⅜	2⅝	2⅝	12½	8	6⅛	6⅛	Maple Creek, Sask.	Glen A. Lewis	George Hooey	1964	127
85⅝	14⅜	14⅜	6⅝	6⅝	2⅜	2⅜	14	11⅛	6⅜	6⅜	Sublette Co., Wyo.	Mike Wilson	Mike Wilson	1966	127
85⅝	14	14⅜	6⅝	6⅝	2⅜	2⅝	11⅛	5⅜	6⅜	6⅜	Sweetwater Co., Wyo.	Mario Shassetz	Mario Shassetz	1968	127
85⅝	17⅛	16⅞	6⅜	6⅜	2⅝	2⅝	10⅜	7⅜	7⅛	7⅜	Johnson Co., Wyo.	Robert P. Murphy	Robert P. Murphy	1968	127
85⅝	15⅝	16	7⅞	7⅛	2⅝	2⅝	11⅜	9⅞	4⅛	4⅞	S. Wamsutter, Wyo.	William G. Hepworth	William G. Hepworth	1970	127
85⅝	15⅞	15⅝	7⅜	7⅛	2⅝	2⅝	8⅜	3⅜	6⅛	6⅛	Carbon Co., Wyo.	Daryl L. Frank	Daryl L. Frank	1973	127
85⅝	15⅝	15⅞	6⅜	6⅝	2⅝	2⅝	12⅜	8⅜	7⅛	6⅞	Lincoln Co., Wyo.	James R. Gunter	James R. Gunter	1976	127

											Locality	By	Owner	Date	Rank
85⅞	17⅞	18⅞	6⅞	6⅞	3	3⅛	11⅛	4⅞	5	4⅞	Colfax Co., N.M.	John D. Pearson	John D. Pearson	1977	127
85⅞	15⅞	15⅛	7⅞	7	2⅜	2⅜	10⅛	6⅜	4	6⅜	Baker Co., Oreg.	Robert Spears	Robert Spears	1977	127
85⅞	17⅞	17⅝	7	7	2⅞	2⅞	9⅞	6⅛	4⅞	5⅞	Colfax Co., N.M.	Rick H. Jackson	Rick H. Jackson	1977	127
85⅞	16⅞	16⅜	7⅛	7	3	3	8⅞	4⅜	5⅛	4⅜	Carbon Co., Wyo.	Paul M. Ostrander	Paul M. Ostrander	1977	127
85⅞	14⅞	14⅛	5⅞	5⅞	2⅞	2⅞	13⅜	6⅞	6	6⅞	Carbon Co., Wyo.	Roland W. Anthony	Roland W. Anthony	1978	127
85⅞	16⅛	16⅛	6⅞	7⅛	2⅝	2⅝	11⅛	6⅜	6⅞	6⅜	Lake Co., Oreg.	James H. Hastings	James H. Hastings	1979	127
85⅞	15⅞	15⅜	6⅝	6⅝	2⅜	2⅜	8	4⅛	5⅞	7⅜	Baker Co., Oreg.	Eldon L. Buckner	Eldon L. Buckner	1981	127
85⅞	16	15⅛	6⅛	6⅛	2⅝	2⅝	12	8⅜	5	6⅝	Fremont Co., Wyo.	Richard A. Fruchey	Richard A. Fruchey	1981	127
85⅞	17⅞	17⅜	6⅛	6⅛	2⅞	2⅞	9⅜	6⅝	5⅛	6⅛	Natrona Co., Wyo.	Margery H. T. Torrey	Margery H. T. Torrey	1981	127
85⅞	16⅜	16⅜	7	6⅞	2⅝	2⅝	14⅜	10	6⅝	6⅞	Carbon Co., Wyo.	Patrick R. Adams	Patrick R. Adams	1982	127
85⅞	16⅞	16⅜	6⅞	6⅝	3	2⅞	11	6⅝	5⅛	6⅝	Coconino Co., Ariz.	Philip S. Leiendecker	Philip S. Leiendecker	1982	127
85⅞	16⅛	16⅛	6⅜	6⅜	2⅝	2⅝	10⅛	7⅛	5⅝	7	Sweetwater Co., Wyo.	L. Bill Miller	L. Bill Miller	1982	127
85⅜	17	17⅛	6⅜	7	2⅝	2⅝	14⅜	13⅛	5⅛	6⅛	Colfax Co., N.M.	S. X. Callahan III	S. X. Callahan III	1983	127
85⅛	17⅜	17⅜	7⅜	7⅜	2⅝	2⅝	12	7⅜	5⅜	7	Rosebud Co., Mont.	Dale R. Brauer	Dale R. Brauer	1983	127
85	17⅞	16	6⅝	6⅝	3	3	20	20	7⅜	6⅜	Sweetwater Co., Wyo.	Annette D. Lynch	Annette D. Lynch	1983	152
85	15⅜	14⅞	6⅝	6⅝	3⅛	3⅛	11⅛	6⅛	6⅛	7⅛	Douglas, Wyo.	Floyd Bishop	Floyd Bishop	1937	153
85	15⅞	15⅛	6⅝	6⅝	3⅜	3⅜	9⅞	10	7⅛	5⅝	Henderson, N.M.	Ron Vance	Ron Vance	1943	153
85	17⅞	17⅜	6⅞	6⅞	3	3	14⅛	7	5⅝	6⅛	Washoe Co., Nev.	Walter Craig Bell	Walter Craig Bell	1949	153
85	15	15	6⅝	6⅝	2⅞	2⅞	14⅛	12⅜	5⅜	6⅜	Brothers, Oreg.	Orlo Flock	Orlo Flock	1955	153
85	19⅜	18⅛	6	6	3⅛	3⅛	14⅛	10⅞	5⅝	6⅝	Raleigh, N.D.	Archie Malm	Archie Malm	1958	153
85	15⅜	15⅛	6⅝	6⅝	3⅜	3⅜	9⅞	8⅞	5⅞	4⅞	Williams, Ariz.	Donovan E. Smith	Donovan E. Smith	1959	153
85	17⅜	17⅝	6	6	3	3	17⅜	14⅜	5	5⅜	Sage Creek Basin, Wyo.	Robert A. Hill	Robert A. Hill	1959	153
85	15⅞	15⅝	6⅞	6⅞	2⅝	2⅝	10	5⅜	5	5⅛	Forsyth, Mont.	John M. Broadwell	Unknown	1961	153
85	15⅞	15⅝	6⅞	6⅞	3⅜	3⅜	10⅜	7	5	4⅝	Brusett, Mont.	Frank McKeever	Frank McKeever	PR 1962	153
85	16⅛	16⅛	6⅛	6⅛	2⅝	2⅝	10⅜	7	6⅝	6⅛	Garfield Co., Mont.	W. A. Delaney	W. A. Delaney	1965	153
85	16	15⅜	6⅜	6⅜	2⅝	2⅝	8⅜	4	5⅝	5⅞	Rawlins, Wyo.	Clarence J. Becker	Clarence J. Becker	1965	153
85	14⅞	14⅜	7	7	2⅝	2⅝	11⅛	10⅜	5⅞	5⅞	Saratoga, Wyo.	Benny E. Bechtol	Benny E. Bechtol	1968	153
85	16⅝	16⅛	7⅜	8⅜	2⅝	2⅝	14⅛	9⅜	5⅞	6	Rawlins, Wyo.	H. H. Eighmy	H. H. Eighmy	1969	153
85	15⅞	16⅝	8⅜	8⅜	3	3	13⅜	8⅞	6⅝	6⅛	Uinta Co., Wyo.	Joan Beachler	Joan Beachler	1974	153
85	16⅛	15⅞	6⅜	6⅝	2⅝	2⅝	9⅜	3⅜	5⅝	6⅜	Torrance Co., N.M.	Stephen A. Nisbet	Stephen A. Nisbet	1975	153
85	17⅜	16⅝	6⅜	6⅞	3⅜	3⅜	13⅜	8⅜	4⅞	6⅜	Yavapai Co., Ariz.	David M. Sanders	David M. Sanders	1976	153
85	18⅝	18⅝	7⅞	7⅞	2⅝	2⅝	13⅛	9	5	5⅝	Sierra Co., N.M.	Charles R. Bowen	Charles R. Bowen	1977	153
85	16⅞	16⅝	6⅜	6⅜	2⅝	2⅝	10⅛	7⅝	6	5⅞	Lake Co., Oreg.	Frank R. Biggs	Frank R. Biggs	1978	153
85	16⅞	16⅝	6⅜	6⅜	2⅝	2⅝	10⅜	5⅝	5	5⅝	Lincoln Co., Wyo.	Ross M. Wilde	Ross M. Wilde	1980	153
85	16⅛	16⅞	6⅝	6⅝	2⅝	2⅝	12⅜	9⅜	6⅜	6⅛	Carbon Co., Wyo.	Kelly W. Hepworth	Kelly W. Hepworth	1982	153
85	16	16	6⅜	6⅜	2⅝	2⅝	10⅜	3⅝	6⅛	6⅜	Hudspeth Co., Texas	Vernon Dodd	Vernon Dodd	1984	153
85	17	17⅞	6⅜	6⅜	2⅝	2⅝	11⅜	8⅜	6⅜	6⅜	Millard Co., Utah	Scott C. Rowley	Scott C. Rowley	1984	153
84⅞	18	18⅛	6⅜	6⅜	2⅝	2⅝	18⅜	14⅛	5⅛	6⅛	Plush, Oreg.	Ernest E. Puddy	Ernest E. Puddy	1949	175
84⅝	15⅞	16⅛	6⅞	7⅜	2⅜	2⅜	7	1	6⅛	7⅜	Modoc Co., Calif.	William A. Shaw	William A. Shaw	1942	176
84⅝	16⅝	16⅞	6⅛	6⅛	2⅝	3	14⅛	11⅛	6⅛	6⅝	Anderson Mesa, Ariz.	Elgin T. Gates	Elgin T. Gates	1955	176
84⅝	17⅛	17⅜	6⅛	6⅛	2⅝	2⅜	12⅛	10⅜	6⅜	6⅛	Slate Creek, Wyo.	Jim Calkins	Jim Calkins	1956	176
84⅝	16⅞	16⅞	6⅛	6⅛	2⅝	2⅝	8⅜	3⅜	6⅛	6⅜	Laramie, Wyo.	Roger D. Ramsay	Roger D. Ramsay	1958	176
84⅝	16⅜	16⅝	6	6	2⅞	2⅞	11⅜	7⅜	4⅝	4⅞	Laramie Peak, Wyo.	Elmer Rupert	Elmer Rupert	1961	176

371

PRONGHORN—Continued

Antilocapra americana americana and related subspecies

Score	Length of Horn R.	L.	Circumference of Base R.	L.	Circumference at Third Quarter R.	L.	Inside Spread	Tip to Tip Spread	Length of Prong R.	L.	Locality Killed	By Whom Killed	Owner	Date Killed	Rank
84⅝	16	16⅛	7⅛	7⅛	3	3	12⅛	6⅞	5	4⅞	Alliance, Neb.	Joseph Nelson	Joseph Nelson	1962	176
84⅝	15⅞	15⅞	6⅞	6⅞	3⅞	3⅞	7⅞	17⅛	5⅝	5⅝	Harney Co., Oreg.	D. R. Knoll	D. R. Knoll	1963	176
84⅝	16⅜	16⅛	6⅝	6⅝	3	3	11⅛	7	5	5	Sinclair, Wyo.	John Kastner	John Kastner	1963	176
84⅝	17⅜	16⅞	7⅛	7⅛	3	2⅞	14⅛	12⅛	5⅛	4⅜	Fremont Co., Wyo.	Dick Cone	Dick Cone	1963	176
84⅝	17	17⅜	6⅞	6⅞	2⅞	2⅝	14⅛	11⅛	6⅛	5⅜	Jenner, Alta.	J. E. Edwards	J. E. Edwards	1964	176
84⅝	16⅞	17⅛	6⅞	7	3	2⅞	12	11	6⅞	5⅜	Johnson Co., Wyo.	John G. Carroll	John G. Carroll	1965	176
84⅝	16⅞	16⅛	6	6⅛	2⅞	2⅞	8⅝	3⅝	7	6⅞	Navajo Co., Ariz.	George M. Owen	George M. Owen	1966	176
84⅝	16⅞	16⅜	7⅞	7⅞	2⅝	2⅞	10⅛	5⅞	5⅝	5⅝	Poison Spider Creek, Wyo.	Robert Ziker	Robert Ziker	1966	176
84⅝	15⅞	15⅞	6⅞	6⅝	2⅝	2⅝	11⅛	5⅜	6⅛	6⅛	Casper, Wyo.	John E. Mohritz	John E. Mohritz	1966	176
84⅝	16	16	6⅝	6⅝	2⅝	2⅝	10⅛	6⅝	6⅛	6⅛	Rock Springs, Wyo.	W. Daniel English	W. Daniel English	1966	176
84⅝	15⅞	15⅞	6⅝	6⅝	2⅝	2⅝	17	16	7	7	Custer Co., Idaho	Claus Karlson	Claus Karlson	1966	176
84⅝	17	16⅜	6⅝	6⅝	2⅜	2⅜	10⅛	5⅛	5⅝	6⅝	Modoc Co., Calif.	Leland C. Lehman	Leland C. Lehman	1969	176
84⅝	16⅞	17	6⅝	5⅞	2⅜	2⅜	18	13⅞	6⅝	6⅝	Boquillas Ranch, Ariz.	Bob Dixon	Bob Dixon	1970	176
84⅝	19⅞	19⅛	6⅛	6⅛	2⅝	2⅝	13⅝	8⅞	5⅜	4⅞	Ft. Apache Res., Ariz.	Donald Smith	Donald Smith	1972	176
84⅝	15⅞	15⅞	6⅝	6⅝	3⅝	3⅝	11	5⅛	5⅜	5⅜	Moffat Co., Colo.	James C. MacLachlan	James C. MacLachlan	1975	176
84⅝	16⅜	16⅜	7	7⅛	2⅝	2⅝	10⅜	7⅛	5⅜	5⅜	Garden Co., Neb.	Richard Mosley	Richard Mosley	1978	176
84⅝	15⅝	15⅝	7⅛	7⅛	2⅝	2⅝	10	5	6⅛	6⅛	Washoe Co., Nev.	Lloyd B. Miller	Lloyd B. Miller	1980	176
84⅝	17⅛	17⅛	6⅞	6⅝	2⅝	2⅝	13⅛	11⅛	4⅞	4⅜	Lincoln Co., N.M.	Pat McCarty	Pat McCarty	1980	176
84⅝	16⅛	16⅛	6⅝	6⅛	3	3	9⅛	5	6⅛	6⅛	Modoc Co., Calif.	Earnest Anacleto	Earnest Anacleto	1980	176
84⅝	16⅞	16⅜	6⅝	6⅛	2⅝	2⅝	11⅛	8⅜	6⅛	6⅛	Baker Co., Oreg.	Martin Vavra	Martin Vavra	1980	176
84⅝	16⅞	16⅜	6⅜	6⅜	2⅝	2⅝	8⅝	3⅞	6⅛	6⅜	Natrona Co., Wyo.	W. Bruce Mouw	W. Bruce Mouw	1980	176
84⅝	15⅞	15⅞	6⅜	6⅜	2⅝	2⅝	9⅜	7⅜	6⅛	6⅜	Fremont Co., Wyo.	James E. Egger	James E. Egger	1981	176
84⅝	14⅛	14⅞	7⅛	7⅛	3⅜	3⅜	11⅛	8⅜	5	5	Carbon Co., Wyo.	Robb D. Hitchcock	Robb D. Hitchcock	1981	176
84⅝	16⅞	16⅜	6⅝	6⅝	2⅜	2⅜	11⅛	7⅞	7⅛	7⅛	Sweetwater Co., Wyo.	David L. Thompson	David L. Thompson	1982	176
84⅝	15⅞	15⅞	7⅜	7⅜	2⅜	2⅜	8	1⅝	6⅞	6⅝	Lemhi Co., Idaho	Sherl L. Chapman	Sherl L. Chapman	1983	176
84⅝	17	16⅝	6⅝	6⅜	2⅞	2⅞	9⅞	6	6	5⅜	Carbon Co., Wyo.	A. A. Carrey	A. A. Carrey	1944	206
84⅝	16⅞	16⅜	7⅛	7⅛	2⅝	2⅝	12⅞	9⅞	5⅜	5⅜	Chihuahua, Mexico	Julio Estrada	Julio Estrada	1945	206
84⅝	16⅞	16⅜	6⅞	6⅝	2⅝	2⅝	10⅛	5⅝	7⅞	7⅞	North Dakota	Dale Linderman	Dale Linderman	PR1952	206
84⅝	15⅞	15⅞	6⅝	6⅝	3	3	14⅛	13⅞	5⅞	5⅜	Fremont Co., Wyo.	Ernest R. Novotny	Ernest R. Novotny	1954	206
84⅝	16	16	5⅝	5⅝	2⅜	2⅜	14⅜	10⅜	5⅛	5⅛	Rawlins, Wyo.	Eloise Kees	Eloise Kees	1962	206
84⅝	15⅞	15⅞	7⅜	7⅝	2⅝	2⅝	10⅜	4⅞	5⅝	5⅝	Tripp Co., S.D.	Roy Hazuka	Roy Hazuka	1962	206
84⅝	18⅛	18	7	7	3	3	13	8⅜	5	5	Seligman, Ariz.	Garth A. Brown	Garth A. Brown	1964	206

Pronghorn records — score chart (continued)

Score									Locality	By Whom Killed	Owner	Date Killed	Min.
84 6/8	14 6/8	14 6/8	7 1/8	6 6/8	2 2/8	2 2/8	9 1/8	5 7/8 5 7/8 6 2/8	Baggs, Wyo.	Tom Elberson	Tom Elberson	1966	206
84 6/8	17	17 1/8	6 5/8	6 6/8	2 4/8	2 4/8	11 1/8	5 5/8 5 5/8 5 5/8	Sweetwater Co., Wyo.	Harvey B. Bartley	Harvey B. Bartley	1970	206
84 6/8	16 6/8	16 6/8	6	6	2 3/8	2 3/8	13	7 1/8 7 7	Carbon Co., Wyo.	William G. Mackey	William G. Mackey	1972	206
84 6/8	16	16	6 5/8	6 7/8	2 4/8	2 4/8	12 3/8	6 3/8 6 6 1/8	Lincoln Co., Wyo.	George Kirkman	George Kirkman	1973	206
84 6/8	14 5/8	14 7/8	7 1/8	7 1/8	2 4/8	2 4/8	12 5/8	6 1/8 6 1/8 6 5/8	Lake Co., Oreg.	Gene Cormie	Gene Cormie	1973	206
84 6/8	17	16 3/8	7 2/8	7 2/8	2 3/8	2 3/8	9 5/8	6 6 6 1/8	Fields, Oreg.	John H. Johnson	John H. Johnson	1974	206
84 6/8	16 3/8	16 3/8	7 2/8	7 2/8	2 4/8	2 4/8	13 3/8	5 5/8 5 5/8 5 5/8	Washoe Co., Nev.	Frances M. Hansell	Frances M. Hansell	1974	206
84 6/8	15 5/8	16	7 4/8	7 4/8	3 1/8	3	10 6/8	5 1/8 5 1/8 5 3/8	Carbon Co., Wyo.	John C. Sjogren	John C. Sjogren	1976	206
84 6/8	15	15 3/8	7 7/8	7 7/8	2 6/8	2 6/8	6 6/8	6 6 6	Carbon Co., Wyo.	Stephen C. LeBlanc	Stephen C. LeBlanc	1976	206
84 6/8	17 1/8	16 6/8	6 6/8	6 3/8	2 3/8	2 3/8	15 5/8	6 6 7	Modoc Co., Calif.	J. Bob Johnson	J. Bob Johnson	1978	206
84 6/8	16 3/8	16 3/8	7	7	3	3	14 4/8	7 7 7	Sweetwater Co., Wyo.	Frankie Miller	Frankie Miller	1979	206
84 6/8	17 2/8	17	6 5/8	6 3/8	2 3/8	2 3/8	13 7/8	5 1/8 5 1/8 4	Lake Co., Oreg.	Rodger D. Bates	Rodger D. Bates	1980	206
84 6/8	16 1/8	16	6 5/8	6 3/8	3	2 7/8	8 3/8	5 5/8 5 5/8 5 5/8	Sweetwater Co., Wyo.	Lee Frudden	Lee Frudden	1981	206
84 6/8	15	15	6 5/8	6 5/8	2 6/8	3	15	5 7 5 5/8	Carbon Co., Wyo.	Jack A. Berger	Jack A. Berger	1982	206
84 6/8	15 5/8	15 3/8	6 5/8	6 6/8	2 6/8	2 6/8	9 5/8	5 5/8 5 7/8 6 1/8	Carbon Co., Wyo.	William J. Stokes	William J. Stokes	1982	206
84 6/8	16 6/8	16 1/8	7 1/8	7	3	3	13 5/8	5 4/8 4 5/8 5 5/8	Fremont Co., Wyo.	Michael P. Hauffe	Michael P. Hauffe	1983	206
84 6/8	16 4/8	16 7/8	7 3/8	7 7/8	2 5/8	2 5/8	14 7/8	7 1/8 4 5/8 4 5/8	Fremont Co., Wyo.	William R. Suranyi	William R. Suranyi	1983	206
84 6/8	17	16 4/8	6 3/8	6	2 5/8	2 5/8	9	5 1/8 7 1/8 7	Phillips Co., Mont.	Donald W. Hellhake	Donald W. Hellhake	1984	206
84 6/8	16 5/8	17	7	6 7/8	2 5/8	2 3/8	15	5 2/8 5 2/8 5 2/8	Deschutes Co., Oreg.	Rick Ward	Rick Ward	1985	206
84 6/8	15 5/8	16	6 6/8	6 6/8	2 6/8	2 6/8	10 6/8	5 7/8 5 5/8 5 5/8	Sweetwater River, Wyo.	Kermit Platt	Kermit Platt	1952	232
84 6/8	17 7/8	15	6 3/8	6 3/8	3 1/8	3 1/8	11 4/8	4 3/8 4 3/8 4 4/8	Pumpkin Buttes, Wyo.	John B. Miller	John B. Miller	1957	232
84 6/8	16 4/8	16 4/8	6 3/8	6 3/8	2 5/8	2 5/8	10 6/8	4 4/8 4 4/8 4 4/8	Sage Creek Basin, Wyo.	Aydeen Auld	Aydeen Auld	1959	232
84 6/8	17 1/8	16 4/8	6 4/8	6 4/8	2 5/8	2 5/8	13	5 5/8 5 5/8 5 1/8	Anderson Mesa, Ariz.	Bill Gray	Bill Gray	1960	232
84 6/8	16 6/8	16 5/8	7	7	2 5/8	2 5/8	7 5/8	6 6 6 2/8	Natrona, Wyo.	William Fisher	William Fisher	1960	232
84 6/8	16	16 3/8	7	7	2 5/8	2 5/8	11 5/8	6 1/8 6 1/8 6 1/8	Uinta Co., Wyo.	Ross Lukenbill	Ross Lukenbill	1965	232
84 6/8	15 5/8	16	7 1/8	7	2 5/8	2 5/8	10 5/8	6 1/8 6 1/8 6 1/8	Rawlins, Wyo.	Armin O. Baltensweiler	Armin O. Baltensweiler	1966	232
84 6/8	17 7/8	17 7/8	6 1/8	6	3	3 1/8	12 1/8	7 6/8 4 4/8 7 6/8	Ft. Apache Res., Ariz.	Frank E. White	Frank E. White	1967	232
84 6/8	14 4/8	14 7/8	6 5/8	6 6/8	3	3	7 7/8	7 1/8 6 6/8 7 1/8	Big Piney, Wyo.	Lawrence M. Kick	Lawrence M. Kick	1967	232
84 6/8	16 2/8	16 1/8	7 3/8	7 1/8	2 5/8	2 5/8	12 3/8	8 5 5/8 5	Fremont Co., Wyo.	Edward S. Friend	Edward S. Friend	1967	232
84 6/8	15	15	7	7 7/8	2 3/8	2 3/8	13 3/8	11 7/8 8 8	Fremont Co., Wyo.	Lee Arce	Lee Arce	1968	232
84 6/8	17 7/8	17 7/8	7 2/8	7 2/8	2 4/8	2 4/8	8 7/8	5 1/8 4 1/8 6	Humboldt Co., Nev.	Gerald A. Lent	Gerald A. Lent	1970	232
84 6/8	15 5/8	15 3/8	6	6	2 6/8	2 7/8	11 7/8	8 2/8 4 7/8 4 7/8	Natrona Co., Wyo.	Donald F. Mahnke	Donald F. Mahnke	1971	232
84 6/8	16 6/8	16 6/8	7	7	2 6/8	2 6/8	15 5/8	11 7/8 5 2/8 5 2/8	Albany Co., Wyo.	George Panagos, Jr.	George Panagos, Jr.	1972	232
84 6/8	16 6/8	16 7/8	6 5/8	6 5/8	2 6/8	2 6/8	8 4/8	3 7/8 5 4/8 5 3/8	Apache Co., Ariz.	Alaine D. Neal	Alaine D. Neal	1973	232
84 6/8	17 1/8	17 1/8	5 7/8	5 5/8	2 4/8	2 4/8	8 7/8	1 1/8 7 5 4/8	Abbott, N.M.	George H. Ray III	George H. Ray III	1974	232
84 6/8	16	16 4/8	6 7/8	6 7/8	2 7/8	2 7/8	9 4/8	7 4/8 4 4/8	Carbon Co., Wyo.	William O. Queen	William O. Queen	1975	232
84 6/8	16 4/8	17 2/8	6 6/8	6 6/8	2 6/8	3	16	11 4/8 5 5/8 6	Meade Co., S.D.	John Hostetter	John Hostetter	1975	232
84 6/8	16 4/8	16 3/8	6 4/8	6 3/8	2 6/8	2 6/8	8 3/8	5 5/8 5 5/8 5 5/8	Humboldt Co., Nev.	David Perondi	David Perondi	1976	232
84 6/8	15 2/8	15 5/8	7 1/8	7	2 5/8	2 5/8	13	12 1/8 5 5/8 5	Carbon Co., Wyo.	Kenneth Mellin	Kenneth Mellin	1976	232
84 6/8	17 4/8	17 4/8	6 6/8	6 7/8	2 4/8	2 4/8	11 4/8	8 1/8 4 4/8 4 3/8	Sweetwater Co., Wyo.	Bill Jordan	Bill Jordan	1976	232
84 6/8	15 4/8	15 7/8	7 4/8	7 4/8	2 4/8	2 4/8	14 4/8	13 5/8 5 7/8 5 7/8	Carbon Co., Wyo.	Glenn F. Galbraith	Glenn F. Galbraith	1977	232
84 6/8	17	17 3/8	6 6/8	6 6/8	2 6/8	2 7/8	12 5/8	10 5/8 5 5/8 5 5/8	Sweetwater Co., Wyo.	John V. Wilgus	John V. Wilgus	1980	232
84 6/8	15 5/8	15 5/8	7	6 7/8	2 4/8	2 4/8	6 4/8	2 6 6/8	Humboldt Co., Nev.	James R. Puryear	James R. Puryear	1980	232

PRONGHORN—Continued

Antilocapra americana americana and related subspecies

Score	Length of Horn R.	L.	Circumference of Base R.	L.	Circumference at Third Quarter R.	L.	Inside Spread	Tip to Tip Spread	Length of Prong R.	L.	Locality Killed	By Whom Killed	Owner	Date Killed	Rank
84⅔	15⅝	15⅝	7⅜	7⅛	2⅝	2⅝	12⅞	8	6⅜	6⅜	Fremont Co., Wyo.	William D. Baldwin	William D. Baldwin	1980	232
84⅔	15⅝	16⅛	6⅞	6⅞	2⅜	3⅛	9⅛	5⅞	6⅜	6⅛	Modoc Co., Calif.	Larry A. Owens, Sr.	Larry A. Owens, Sr.	1981	232
84⅔	17	16⅝	6⅜	6⅜	2⅝	2⅜	12⅞	8⅛	6	6⅛	Coconino Co., Ariz.	Michael A. Cromer	Michael A. Cromer	1982	232
84⅔	16⅝	16⅜	6⅞	6⅞	2⅜	2⅜	13⅞	10⅜	6	6	Malheur Co., Oreg.	Matt J. Brundridge	Matt J. Brundridge	1982	232
84⅔	17⅞	17⅞	6⅜	6⅜	2⅜	2⅜	14⅞	10⅜	6⅛	6	Powder River Co., Mont.	Sam C. Borla	Sam C. Borla	1982	232
84⅔	16	15⅞	6⅝	6⅝	2⅜	2⅜	10	5⅞	5⅝	5⅝	Carbon Co., Wyo.	Ernest L. Tollini	Ernest L. Tollini	1983	232
84⅔	17⅞	17⅜	6⅜	6⅜	2⅜	2⅝	8⅝	2⅜	5⅝	5⅝	Washoe Co., Nev.	Judy Taylor	Judy Taylor	1983	232
84⅔	16⅞	16⅞	6⅜	6⅜	2⅝	2⅝	9⅛	6⅞	5⅝	5⅝	Coconino Co., Ariz.	William R. Vaughn	William R. Vaughn	1983	232
84⅔	16⅝	16⅛	7⅜	7⅜	3	3	9⅜	5⅛	4⅞	4	Natrona Co., Wyo.	Allen J. Hogan	Allen J. Hogan	1983	232
84⅔	15⅞	15⅝	6⅞	6⅞	2⅝	2⅞	9⅜	4⅝	6⅝	6⅛	Carbon Co., Wyo.	Mike Clegg	Mike Clegg	1983	232
84⅔	15	15	6⅞	6⅞	3	3	12⅞	10⅞	6⅛	6	White Pine Co., Nev.	Paul E. Podborny	Paul E. Podborny	1985	232
84⅔	16	16⅞	6⅝	6⅝	3	3	13⅞	11	5⅞	5⅝	Fremont Co., Wyo.	John Monje	John Monje	1985	232
84	15⅞	16	7⅜	7⅞	3⅞	3⅞	14⅛	10⅞	3⅜	3⅜	Lost Cabin, Wyo.	Jack Henrey	Jack Henrey	1955	268
84	17⅛	17⅛	6⅜	6⅜	2⅜	2⅜	14⅜	11⅛	5	5⅞	Meadowdale, Wyo.	Mrs. Lodisa Pipher	Mrs. Lodisa Pipher	1956	268
84	16⅜	17⅜	6⅜	6	2⅜	2⅜	10⅞	5⅞	5	5⅝	Yavapai Co., Ariz.	Walter Tibbs	Walter Tibbs	1959	268
84	16⅛	16⅛	6⅝	6⅜	2⅞	2⅜	11⅛	9	5⅝	5⅜	Sage Creek, Wyo.	Pat Swarts	Pat Swarts	1960	268
84	14⅞	14⅛	6⅝	7⅞	3⅛	3⅛	14⅛	13⅞	5⅞	5⅞	Pinedale, Wyo.	Edward Sturla	Edward Sturla	1960	268
84	15⅞	16	6⅞	6⅞	2⅞	2⅞	11⅜	8	6⅛	6	Campbell Co., Wyo.	Fred J. Brogle	Fred J. Brogle	1960	268
84	16	16⅛	6⅜	6⅜	2⅝	2⅞	8⅜	5⅝	6⅜	6⅝	Rawlins, Wyo.	John M. Sell	John M. Sell	1964	268
84	16⅜	16⅜	6⅜	6⅜	3	3	11⅜	6	6⅞	6⅛	Fremont Co., Wyo.	Robert E. Novotny	Robert E. Novotny	1964	268
84	17⅛	17⅞	6⅜	6⅜	3⅛	3	13⅜	12⅞	5⅜	5⅝	Carbon Co., Wyo.	Mrs. Thom. H. Green	Mrs. Thom. H. Green	1964	268
84	17	17⅞	7⅛	7⅛	2⅞	2⅞	12⅞	6⅞	4⅞	4⅞	Milk River, Alta.	George Vandervalk	George Vandervalk	1966	268
84	15⅞	15⅛	6⅞	6⅞	2⅝	2⅜	14⅞	12⅞	6⅝	6⅜	Leola, S.D.	Leonard Lahr	Leonard Lahr	1967	268
84	16⅜	16⅛	6⅜	6⅜	3	3	8	3	5⅜	5⅞	Washington Co., Colo.	Christian Heyden	Christian Heyden	1968	268
84	15⅜	15⅞	6⅝	6⅝	2⅝	2⅝	11⅞	8⅞	7⅛	6⅞	Choteau Co., Mont.	W. E. Cherry	W. E. Cherry	1969	268
84	14⅜	14⅞	7	6⅞	2⅞	2⅞	11⅝	11⅜	6⅝	6⅝	Red Desert, Wyo.	Fred Morgan	Fred Morgan	1969	268
84	15⅞	16⅜	6⅝	6⅜	2⅜	2⅜	14⅜	9	6	6⅝	Washoe Co., Nev.	Robert L. Mallory	Robert L. Mallory	1970	268
84	16⅜	16⅛	6⅞	6⅞	2⅜	2⅜	8⅜	2⅜	6⅛	6⅜	Humboldt Co., Nev.	Gary D. Bader	Gary D. Bader	1970	268
84	16⅜	16⅛	6⅞	6⅞	2⅜	2⅜	7⅜	3⅜	4⅜	4	Carbon Co., Wyo.	Russ Allen	Russ Allen	1972	268
84	15	15⅞	7	7	2⅝	2⅝	14⅛	11⅜	6	6	Albany Co., Wyo.	Andy Pfaff	Andy Pfaff	1974	268
84	18⅜	18⅜	6⅜	6⅜	2⅜	2⅜	17⅜	15⅝	5	4⅜	Sublette Co., Wyo.	Dick Reilly	Dick Reilly	1977	268
84	15⅜	14⅞	6⅜	6⅝	3⅜	3⅛	11⅝	9⅞	6⅞	5⅞	Sioux Co., Neb.	Harvey Y. Suetsugu	Harvey Y. Suetsugu	1977	268

Score												Name	Locality	Name	Date	Rank
84	16⅜	16⅝	6⅝	6⅝	2⅝	2⅝	11⅜	8⅜	5⅝	5⅝	5⅝	W. Wayne Roye	Presidio Co., Texas	W. Wayne Roye	1977	268
84	16⅝	16⅞	6⅝	6⅝	3	2⅞	10⅝	4⅞	5⅝	5⅝	5⅜	Robert F. Veazey	Coconino Co., Ariz.	Robert F. Veazey	1979	268
84	17⅞	17⅞	6⅛	6⅛	2⅞	2⅞	13⅜	8⅞	5	5	4⅞	James O. Pierce	Yavapai Co., Ariz.	James O. Pierce	1980	268
84	17⅛	17⅛	6⅞	6⅞	2⅜	2⅜	6	5⅜	6	6	5⅜	Jamie L. Kent	Washoe Co., Nev.	Jamie L. Kent	1980	268
84	14⅞	14⅞	7⅜	7⅜	3	3	11⅛	10	6⅜	6⅜	6	Bill E. Boatman	Natrona Co., Wyo.	Bill E. Boatman	1980	268
84	16⅛	16⅛	6⅞	6⅞	2⅝	2⅝	11⅛	5⅝	6⅝	6⅝	5⅝	Joel E. Hensley	Fremont Co., Wyo.	Joel E. Hensley	1981	268
84	15⅝	15⅞	7⅛	7⅛	2⅜	2⅜	15⅜	13⅝	6⅞	7⅛	6⅝	Victor M. McCullough	Fremont Co., Wyo.	Victor M. McCullough	1981	268
84	16	15⅞	6⅜	6⅜	2⅜	2⅜	14⅝	12⅜	6⅜	6⅜	5	Charles R. Hisaw	Blaine Co., Idaho	Charles R. Hisaw	1981	268
84	16⅝	16⅝	6⅝	6⅝	2⅜	2⅜	10⅝	6	6⅝	6⅝	6	Lorio Verzasconi	Sweetwater Co., Wyo.	Lorio Verzasconi	1982	268
84	16	15⅝	7	7	2⅜	2⅜	12⅝	9⅛	7	7	6⅜	Dudley R. Elmgren	Carbon Co., Wyo.	Dudley R. Elmgren	1982	268
84	15⅝	15⅝	6⅞	6⅞	3⅛	3⅛	15⅛	11⅝	6⅝	6⅝	5⅝	Fred J. Nobbe, Jr.	Coconino Co., Ariz.	Fred J. Nobbe, Jr.	1982	268
84	16⅞	16⅞	7	7	2⅝	2⅝	10⅜	6⅝	6⅜	6⅜	5⅝	Richard H. Maddock	Sweetwater Co., Wyo.	Richard H. Maddock	1982	268
84	16⅝	16⅜	6⅜	6⅜	2⅝	2⅝	11⅝	7⅝	6⅜	6⅜	5⅝	Dennis W. Gallegos	Sweetwater Co., Wyo.	Dennis W. Gallegos	1983	268
84	16⅜	16⅜	6⅝	6⅝	3⅜	3⅜	12	9⅝	5⅜	5⅜	5⅜	Roger B. Coit	Mora Co., N.M.	Roger B. Coit	1983	268
84	17⅜	17⅜	6⅝	6⅝	2⅝	2⅝	9⅛	5⅝	4	4	4	Paul R. Nelson	Bennett Co., S.D.	Paul R. Nelson	1983	268
84	14⅝	14⅝	7⅛	7⅛	3	3	11⅛	7⅞	6⅞	6⅞	5⅝	Wayne M. Kelly	Sheridan Co., Neb.	Wayne M. Kelly	1983	268
84	16	16	6⅝	6⅝	2⅞	2⅞	10	7⅝	5⅝	5⅝	5⅝	Bert F. Carder	Washoe Co., Nev.	Bert F. Carder	1983	268
84	16⅝	16⅝	6⅝	6⅝	2⅝	2⅝	10⅜	6⅝	5⅝	5⅝	6⅜	Dale A. Ableidinger	Natrona Co., Wyo.	Dale A. Ableidinger	1984	268
84	17⅞	17⅝	6⅝	6⅝	3	3	10⅜	4⅛	5⅜	5⅜	5⅝	Fredrick T. Lau	Yavapai Co., Ariz.	Fredrick T. Lau	1984	268
84	16⅜	16⅝	6⅝	6⅝	2⅝	2⅝	12⅜	6	5⅝	5⅝	5⅝	Marvin Redburn	Coconino Co., Ariz.	Marvin Redburn	1985	268
83⅞	16⅜	16⅜	6⅞	6⅞	3	3	12⅞	11	5⅝	5⅝	5⅝	John T. Yarrington	Sheridan Co., Wyo.	John T. Yarrington	1950	307
83⅞	16	16	6⅜	6⅜	2⅝	2⅝	10⅜	6⅜	5⅝	5⅝	5⅝	Bob Herbison	Saratoga, Wyo.	Bob Herbison	1951	307
83⅞	16⅜	16⅜	7	7	3	3	12⅝	6⅜	5⅝	5⅝	5⅝	Robert Ziker	Poison Spider, Wyo.	Robert Ziker	1955	307
83⅞	15⅜	16⅛	6⅞	6⅞	2⅝	2⅝	16⅛	15⅜	6⅝	6⅝	5⅜	Bernie Wanhanen	Plainview, S.D.	Bernie Wanhanen	1960	307
83⅞	16⅜	16⅜	7	7	2⅝	2⅝	15⅝	10⅜	6⅝	6⅝	6	Max Durfee	Chino Valley, Ariz.	Max Durfee	1960	307
83⅞	15	15	6⅞	6⅞	3	3	12⅝	8⅞	5⅝	5⅝	5⅞	Dave Blair	Williams, Ariz.	Dave Blair	1960	307
83⅞	15⅝	15⅝	7⅜	7⅜	2⅝	2⅝	15⅝	10⅜	6⅝	6⅝	6⅜	C. J. Adair	Yavapai Co., Ariz.	C. J. Adair	1961	307
83⅞	14⅜	14⅜	7⅞	7⅞	3	3	15⅛	10⅜	6⅝	6⅝	5⅜	Jim Perry	Hudspeth Co., Texas	Jim Perry	1961	307
83⅞	16	16	6⅝	6⅝	2⅝	2⅝	13⅜	8	5⅝	5⅝	5⅝	Donald G. Gebers	Alcova, Wyo.	Donald G. Gebers	1963	307
83⅞	16⅜	16⅜	7	7	2⅝	2⅝	9⅜	5⅜	6⅛	6⅛	6⅜	Basil C. Bradbury	Hudspeth Co., Texas	Basil C. Bradbury	1964	307
83⅞	16	16	7⅜	7⅜	2⅝	2⅝	10⅞	6⅝	6⅜	6⅜	5⅞	Ron Vandiver	Motley Co., Texas	Ron Vandiver	1966	307
83⅞	15⅜	15⅜	6⅞	6⅞	2⅝	2⅝	7⅞	4⅛	6⅜	6⅜	6⅞	Dale E. Beattie	Meridian, Oreg.	Dale E. Beattie	1967	307
83⅞	16⅛	16⅛	6⅝	6⅝	3⅛	3⅛	10	5	6⅜	6⅜	4⅞	George Malin Lewis	Black Tank, Ariz.	George Malin Lewis	1967	307
83⅞	15	15	6⅝	6⅝	3	3	13⅜	10⅜	5⅝	5⅝	5	R. L. Brown, Jr.	Sweetwater Co., Wyo.	R. L. Brown, Jr.	1968	307
83⅞	15⅝	15⅝	7⅞	7⅞	2⅝	2⅝	9	4⅛	5⅜	5⅜	4⅛	Dennis E. Carter	Lake Co., Oreg.	Dennis E. Carter	1970	307
83⅞	15	15⅛	7⅞	7⅞	2⅝	2⅝	14⅞	11⅛	5⅝	5⅝	5⅜	Betty J. Oliver	Sweetwater Co., Wyo.	Betty J. Oliver	1972	307
83⅞	15⅝	16⅜	6⅝	6⅝	2⅛	2⅛	10	10	6⅜	6⅜	6	D. F. & T. Holt	Park Co., Wyo.	Don F. Holt	1974	307
83⅞	15⅝	16⅝	6⅝	6⅝	2⅝	2⅝	10⅜	7⅜	6⅝	6⅝	6	Leslie Banford	Divide, Sask.	Leslie Banford	1975	307
83⅞	14⅞	14⅜	6⅝	6⅝	2⅝	2⅝	10⅜	2	6⅛	6⅛	6	William B. Steig	Modoc Co., Calif.	William B. Steig	1975	307
83⅞	16	16	6⅝	6⅝	2⅝	2⅝	7⅜	2	6⅜	6⅜	6	James A. White	Wamsutter, Wyo.	James A. White	1977	307
83⅞	16	17⅜	6⅝	6⅝	2⅝	2⅝	11⅜	7⅞	6⅜	6⅜	6⅜	Harold J. Ward	Humboldt Co., Nev.	Harold J. Ward	1980	307
83⅞	16	16	6⅝	6⅝	2⅛	2⅛	9⅜	5	6⅜	6⅜	6	Jack F. Schakel	Carbon Co., Wyo.	Jack F. Schakel	1981	307
83⅞	15⅜	14⅞	7⅜	7⅜	2⅝	2⅝	9⅜	6	5⅝	5⅝	5	—	—	—	1981	307
83⅞	16⅝	16⅝	6⅝	6⅝	2⅝	2⅝	8⅜	2	6⅜	6⅜	6⅝	James R. Doverspike	Lincoln Co., N.M.	James R. Doverspike	1982	307

375

PRONGHORN—Continued
Antilocapra americana americana and related subspecies

Score	Length of Horn R.	L.	Circumference of Base R.	L.	Circumference at Third Quarter R.	L.	Inside Spread	Tip to Tip Spread	Length of Prong R.	L.	Locality Killed	By Whom Killed	Owner	Date Killed	Rank
83⅜	15	15⅛	6⅞	6⅞	2⅞	2⅞	10⅞	6⅞	6⅞	6⅞	Big Horn Co., Mont.	Michael Ferri	Michael Ferri	1982	307
83⅜	14⅞	15⅞	6⅝	6⅜	2⅝	3	6⅝	3⅛	5	4⅝	Washoe Co., Nev.	Robert A. Colon	Robert A. Colon	1982	307
83⅜	17⅞	16⅜	6⅝	6	2⅝	2⅜	7⅛	2⅝	6⅜	6⅛	Natrona Co., Wyo.	Ronald K. Morrison	Ronald K. Morrison	1982	307
83⅜	16⅛	16⅝	7	6⅞	2⅝	2⅞	12⅝	8⅜	5⅞	5⅝	Carbon Co., Wyo.	Douglas L. Hancock	Douglas L. Hancock	1983	307
83⅜	15⅝	15⅞	6⅞	6⅞	2⅞	2⅞	11	7⅞	6	6⅛	Jackson Co., Colo.	Cylestine A. Manguso	Cylestine A. Manguso	1983	307
83⅜	15⅝	15⅞	6⅞	6⅞	2⅜	2⅜	12⅛	11	6⅝	6⅝	Sweetwater Co., Wyo.	Robert Gilbert	Robert Gilbert	1983	307
83⅜	15⅞	16	7⅜	7⅞	2⅜	2⅜	15⅝	11⅝	5⅞	6⅞	Lake Co., Oreg.	Barbara J. Smallwood	Barbara J. Smallwood	1983	307
83⅜	16⅛	16⅛	6⅜	6⅜	2⅜	2⅜	12⅞	9⅝	6	6⅜	Washoe Co., Nev.	Arthur L. Biggs	Arthur L. Biggs	1984	307
83⅜	15⅞	16⅛	6⅛	6⅜	2⅝	2⅝	12	7⅝	5⅜	5⅜	Millard Co., Utah	Mitchell S. Bastian	Mitchell S. Bastian	1985	307
83⅜	15⅞	16⅛	6⅝	6⅞	2⅝	2⅜	14⅛	11⅛	6⅛	6⅛	Farson, Wyo.	Geo. E. MacGillivray	Geo. E. MacGillivray	1951	340
83⅜	17	16⅞	7	7	2⅝	2⅜	10⅛	6⅞	5⅜	5⅜	Miles City, Mont.	J. Louis Mann	J. Louis Mann	1954	340
83⅜	16⅞	17	6⅜	6⅜	2⅝	2⅝	16	14⅛	5⅞	5⅞	Arizona	O. Patton	William N. Henry	1956	340
83⅜	18⅛	17⅞	6⅜	6⅜	2⅜	2⅜	10⅜	5⅞	5	4⅞	Navajo Co., Ariz.	Mrs. Don Lambert	Mrs. Don Lambert	1961	340
83⅜	17	17	6⅝	6⅜	2⅝	2⅝	12⅝	10⅛	6⅝	6⅞	Watford City, N.D.	Dean Etl	Dean Etl	1964	340
83⅜	14	14⅜	6⅞	6⅞	3⅜	3⅜	11⅜	6⅜	4⅞	4⅞	Shoshoni, Wyo.	Collins F. Kellogg	Collins F. Kellogg	1965	340
83⅜	15⅛	15⅞	6⅛	6⅛	3⅛	3⅛	11⅜	5⅞	6⅝	7	Boone, Colo.	Mahlon T. White	Mahlon T. White	1966	340
83⅜	16	15⅞	6⅜	6⅜	2⅜	2⅜	10⅝	5⅞	5⅜	5⅜	Wamsutter, Wyo.	Kenneth L. Swanson	Kenneth L. Swanson	1967	340
83⅜	15⅞	15⅝	7	7⅛	2⅝	2⅝	9⅝	6⅞	5⅜	5⅜	Craig, Colo.	Albert Johnson	Albert Johnson	1969	340
83⅜	15⅝	15⅞	7⅛	7⅛	2⅜	2⅜	11⅛	7⅛	5⅜	5⅛	Carbon Co., Wyo.	Billy C. Randall	Billy C. Randall	1970	340
83⅜	16⅝	16⅜	6⅝	6⅜	2⅜	2⅝	12	10⅜	5	5⅛	Red Desert, Wyo.	David W. Knowles	David W. Knowles	1970	340
83⅜	16⅜	16⅛	6⅜	6⅜	2⅝	2⅝	15⅜	12⅞	5⅝	5⅞	Hoback Rim, Wyo.	F. Larry Storey	F. Larry Storey	1973	340
83⅜	17⅛	17	6⅝	6⅝	2⅝	2⅝	15⅝	10⅞	5	5	Coconino Co., Ariz.	Thomas A. Dunlap	Thomas A. Dunlap	1974	340
83⅜	17⅞	17⅛	6⅞	6⅜	2⅝	2⅝	9⅝	9⅝	5	5⅜	Fremont Co., Wyo.	Ruth Muller	Ruth Muller	1974	340
83⅜	16	16	7⅛	7⅛	2⅝	2⅝	9	3⅜	5⅜	5⅜	Coconino Co., Ariz.	Cheryl Alderman	Cheryl Alderman	1974	340
83⅜	17	17⅞	6⅝	6⅝	2⅝	2⅝	6⅝	1⅜	4⅜	4⅜	Fremont Co., Wyo.	James G. Allard	James G. Allard	1974	340
83⅜	15⅜	15⅞	7⅜	7	2⅜	2⅜	8⅛	2⅜	5⅜	5⅛	Fremont Co., Wyo.	Robert B. Cragoe, Sr.	Robert B. Cragoe, Sr.	1975	340
83⅜	17⅜	17⅞	6⅜	6⅜	2⅜	2⅜	9⅝	5⅜	5⅝	5⅞	Box Butte Co., Neb.	Derald E. Morgan	Derald E. Morgan	1977	340
83⅜	16⅛	16⅛	6⅜	6⅝	3	2⅝	10⅜	5⅜	5⅛	5⅛	Harney Co., Oreg.	Craig Foster	Craig Foster	1977	340
83⅜	16⅜	16⅜	7⅜	7⅜	2⅝	2⅝	9⅜	3⅝	4⅜	4⅜	De Baca Co., N.M.	Glenn C. Conner	Glenn C. Conner	1977	340
83⅜	17	17	6⅜	6⅜	2⅝	2⅝	10⅜	6⅜	5⅛	5⅛	Sweetwater Co., Wyo.	Otis T. Page	Otis T. Page	1978	340
83⅜	16⅝	16⅛	6⅜	6⅝	2⅝	2⅝	8⅜	2⅜	5⅜	5⅜	Uinta Co., Wyo.	Velma B. O'Neil	Velma B. O'Neil	1978	340
83⅜	15⅜	16⅛	6⅜	6⅜	2⅝	3	10⅜	6	6⅝	6⅛	Washoe Co., Nev.	James R. Cobb	James R. Cobb	1978	340

376

									Locality	By Whom Killed	Owner	Score	Date Killed
83⅜	14⅞	6⅜	2⅜	2⅛	9	3⅜	2⅜	7⅜	Lake Co., Oreg.	Thomas A. Jones	Thomas A. Jones	340	1980
83⅜	16⅞	6⅜	2⅜	2⅞	11⅞	5⅝	2⅞	5⅛	Custer Co., Idaho	Wayne L. Coleman	Wayne L. Coleman	340	1981
83⅜	16⅞	6⅞	2⅞	2⅞	10⅜	4⅝	2⅞	5	Harding Co., S.D.	John R. Simpson	John R. Simpson	340	1981
83⅜	15⅞	6⅝	3⅛	3⅛	13	10⅜	3⅛	5⅛	Rosebud Co., Mont.	James D. Cameron	James D. Cameron	340	1981
83⅜	17⅞	6⅛	2⅜	2⅝	0	0	2⅝	5⅛	Natrona Co., Wyo.	Gerald J. Ahles	Gerald J. Ahles	340	1982
83⅜	14⅛	6⅜	3⅜	3⅜	4	2⅞	3⅜	6⅝	Jackson Co., Colo.	Cynthia L. Welle	Cynthia L. Welle	340	1982
83⅜	16⅞	6⅜	2⅜	2⅜	10⅛	4⅝	2⅜	6⅝	Prairie Co., Mont.	L. H. Lindquist	L. H. Lindquist	340	1982
83⅜	17	6⅝	2⅜	2⅜	9⅜	4⅝	2⅜	5	Colfax Co., N.M.	James H. Hoffman	James H. Hoffman	340	1982
83⅜	18	7	3⅞	3⅜	9⅜	6⅝	3⅜	4⅝	Carbon Co., Wyo.	Ronald K. Pettit	Ronald K. Pettit	340	1983
83⅜	16⅞	6⅜	2⅞	2⅞	13⅜	8⅜	2⅞	5⅝	Yavapai Co., Ariz.	Glenn E. Leslie, Jr.	Glenn E. Leslie, Jr.	340	1984
83⅜	17⅞	6⅝	3	3	18	14	3	4⅝	Colfax Co., N.M.	David S. Dickenson	David S. Dickenson	340	1984
83⅜	17⅞	6	2⅜	2⅞	8	8	2⅞	5	Coconino Co., Ariz.	Arthur A. Smith	Arthur A. Smith	340	1984
83⅜	16⅞	6⅛	2⅜	2⅝	10⅜	8	2⅝	5⅝	Lake Co., Oreg.	Donald R. Davidson	Donald R. Davidson	340	1984
83⅜	17	6⅝	2⅜	3	14⅛	11⅛	3	4⅝	Coconino Co., Ariz.	Duane D. Backhaus	Duane D. Backhaus	340	1984
83⅜	17⅜	7⅞	2⅜	2⅝	13⅜	13⅜	2⅝	6	Sweetwater Co., Wyo.	Richard D. Ulery	Richard D. Ulery	377	1980
83⅜	17⅞	6⅝	2⅜	2⅞	16⅝	15⅝	2⅞	6	Arminto, Wyo.	Edward H. Bohlin	Edward H. Bohlin	378	1951
83⅜	15⅜	6⅝	2⅜	3	16⅝	15⅝	3	6	Newcastle, Wyo.	Rupert Chisholm	Rupert Chisholm	378	1953
83⅜	16⅞	8⅜	2⅜	2⅝	12⅜	10⅜	2⅝	4⅜	Campbell Co., Wyo.	Phillip M. Hodge	Phillip M. Hodge	378	1955
83⅜	16	7	2⅜	2⅝	8⅜	6⅜	2⅝	6⅜	Atlantic City, Wyo.	James S. Kleinhammer	James S. Kleinhammer	378	1958
83⅜	15⅜	6⅝	2⅜	2⅝	5	5	2⅝	6⅝	Kaycee, Wyo.	R. B. Nienhaus	R. B. Nienhaus	378	1961
83⅜	15⅜	6⅝	2⅜	2⅝	9⅜	7⅜	2⅝	5⅝	Jeffrey City, Wyo.	Harry G. M. Jopson	Harry G. M. Jopson	378	1961
83⅜	16⅜	6⅝	2⅜	2⅝	8⅛	6⅝	2⅝	6	Ferris Mt., Wyo.	Ron Vance	Ron Vance	378	1962
83⅜	15⅝	6⅜	3	3⅜	9⅜	4⅜	3⅜	4⅝	Fergus Co., Mont.	Steven G. Ard	Steven G. Ard	378	1962
83⅜	16⅜	6⅜	2⅜	2⅝	6	6	2⅝	6	Capitan, N.M.	Lee H. Ingalls	Lee H. Ingalls	378	1969
83⅜	16	6⅜	2⅜	2⅝	7⅜	7⅜	2⅝	5⅛	Sweetwater Co., Wyo.	Allen Tanner	Allen Tanner	378	1970
83⅜	17⅛	6⅜	2⅜	3	11⅞	11⅜	3	5½	Culberson Co., Texas	Jim Smith	Jim Smith	378	1972
83⅜	16⅝	6⅝	2⅜	2⅝	14⅞	12⅜	2⅝	5⅜	Washoe Co., Nev.	David Pohl	David Pohl	378	1972
83⅜	17	6⅝	2⅜	2⅝	13⅜	9⅞	2⅝	5⅛	Coconino Co., Ariz.	Vernon E. North	Vernon E. North	378	1972
83⅜	17⅛	6⅝	2⅜	2⅝	8	2⅜	2⅝	6	Carbon Co., Wyo.	Ray Freitas	Ray Freitas	378	1973
83⅜	16⅞	6⅝	2⅜	2½	12	7⅜	2½	7⅛	Coconino Co., Ariz.	Russell Fischer	Russell Fischer	378	1973
83⅜	16	6⅝	2⅜	3⅜	11	8⅜	3⅜	5	Park Co., Wyo.	Dwight Brunsvold	Dwight Brunsvold	378	1974
83⅜	15⅜	7	3⅜	2⅝	15	6⅝	2⅝	5⅜	Jackson Co., Colo.	James R. Mosman	James R. Mosman	378	1975
83⅜	17	6⅝	2⅜	2⅝	11	5⅝	2⅝	5⅜	Coconino Co., Ariz.	Edmond C. Morton	Edmond C. Morton	378	1975
83⅜	15⅞	6⅜	2⅜	2⅝	11⅛	7⅝	2⅝	7⅜	Medicine Hat, Alta.	Roger H. Stone	Roger H. Stone	378	1975
83⅜	16	6⅞	3⅛	3⅜	7⅜	7⅜	3⅜	6	Harding Co., S.D.	Kathleen Prestjohn	Kathleen Prestjohn	378	1975
83⅜	17⅞	6⅜	2⅜	2⅝	12⅜	6⅜	2⅝	4⅜	Yavapai Co., Ariz.	J. Mike Foley	J. Mike Foley	378	1975
83⅜	16⅞	6⅛	2⅜	2⅝	10⅜	4⅛	2⅝	6⅝	Rolling Hills, Alta.	Dennis A. Andrews	Dennis A. Andrews	378	1975
83⅜	16⅜	7	2⅜	2⅝	15⅛	12⅜	2⅝	5⅛	Yavapai Co., Ariz.	Ralph Koepke	Ralph Koepke	378	1975
83⅜	14⅞	6⅜	2⅜	2⅝	12⅜	10	2⅝	7⅞	Carter Co., Mont.	Joseph Henderson	Joseph Henderson	378	1975
83⅜	14⅞	7⅛	3⅜	3	10⅛	10⅛	3	4⅝	Goshen Co., Wyo.	William E. Patterson	William E. Patterson	378	1976
83⅜	15⅞	6⅜	2⅞	2⅞	9	2⅞	2⅞	5⅛	Cochise Co., Ariz.	Keith Lee Miller	Keith Lee Miller	378	1976
83⅜	16	6⅝	2⅝	2⅝	9⅝	4⅜	2⅝	6⅜	Sweet Grass Co., Mont.	Dennis E. Moos	Dennis E. Moos	378	1977
83⅜	15⅜	7⅛	2⅞	2⅞	14	10⅜	2⅞	6⅛	Natrona Co., Wyo.	Dean L. Johnson	Dean L. Johnson	378	1977

Pronghorn—Continued
Antilocapra americana americana and related subspecies

Score	Length of Horn R.	L.	Circumference of Base R.	L.	Circumference at Third Quarter R.	L.	Inside Spread	Tip to Tip Spread	Length of Prong R.	L.	Locality Killed	By Whom Killed	Owner	Date Killed	Rank
83⅜	17⅜	17⅜	6⅝	6⅝	2⅝	2⅝	15	9⅝	4⅝	4⅝	Humboldt Co., Nev.	Robert E. Stopper	Robert E. Stopper	1979	378
83⅜	17⅛	17⅛	6⅝	6⅝	2⅝	2⅝	16⅛	13	4⅝	4⅝	Roosevelt Co., N.M.	Danny L. Tivis	Danny L. Tivis	1979	378
83⅜	16⅜	16⅛	7⅝	6⅝	2⅝	2⅝	10⅛	4⅝	4⅝	4	Socorro Co., N.M.	Charles M. McLaughlin	Charles M. McLaughlin	1979	378
83⅜	16⅞	16⅞	6⅝	6⅝	3	2⅞	8⅝	5⅞	5⅞	5⅞	Musselshell Co., Mont.	Caroll M. Lumpkin, Jr.	Caroll M. Lumpkin, Jr.	1980	378
83⅜	16⅜	16⅞	6⅝	6⅝	2⅝	2⅝	12⅛	7⅝	6	6⅛	Beaverhead Co., Mont.	Scott Withers	Scott Withers	1980	378
83⅜	16⅜	16⅞	7⅝	7⅞	2⅞	2⅝	12⅞	7⅝	5⅞	5⅝	Harney Co., Oreg.	Gary L. Wilfert	Gary L. Wilfert	1981	378
83⅜	16	16	7	7	2⅞	3	10⅛	5⅝	5	6⅞	Natrona Co., Wyo.	Bill E. Boatman	Bill E. Boatman	1981	378
83⅜	15⅛	15⅞	6⅝	6⅝	2⅞	2⅝	9⅝	6⅞	6	5⅞	Natrona Co., Wyo.	Andy Van Patten	Andy Van Patten	1981	378
83⅜	17⅜	16⅞	6⅝	6⅝	3⅛	2⅝	7⅝	2⅝	5⅜	6	Fremont Co., Wyo.	Benjamin T. Tonn	Benjamin T. Tonn	1981	378
83⅜	17⅜	17⅞	6⅝	6⅝	3	2⅝	8	2⅝	5⅛	4⅝	Campbell Co., Wyo.	Dwayne A. Anderson	Dwayne A. Anderson	1982	378
83⅜	16⅜	16⅛	6⅝	6⅝	3⅜	3⅜	8⅞	3⅝	4⅝	4⅞	Brewster Co., Texas	Richard T. Delgado	Richard T. Delgado	1982	378
83⅜	16⅜	16⅞	6	6	3⅜	3⅜	11⅝	8⅛	4⅞	4⅞	Coconino Co., Ariz.	Gilbert S. Garside	Gilbert S. Garside	1982	378
83⅜	15⅞	15⅞	7⅛	7⅞	3⅛	3⅛	12	11⅛	4⅝	5⅝	Natrona Co., Wyo.	Gary A. Campbell	Gary A. Campbell	1983	378
83⅜	16⅛	16⅞	6⅝	6⅝	3	3⅛	14⅜	10⅛	5	5⅝	Mora Co., N.M.	James E. Davenport, Jr.	James E. Davenport, Jr.	1983	378
83⅜	16⅛	16⅞	6	6	2⅞	2⅝	9⅛	3⅝	6⅝	6⅝	Carter Co., Mont.	Martin Crane	Martin Crane	1983	378
83⅜	16⅛	16⅞	6⅝	6⅝	2⅝	2⅝	8⅝	3⅝	6⅝	6⅞	Uinta Co., Wyo.	Earl H. Heninger	Earl H. Heninger	1983	378
83⅜	16⅞	17	6⅝	6⅝	2⅝	2⅝	9⅝	3⅝	5⅝	5⅝	Sweetwater Co., Wyo.	Donald W. Kramer	Donald W. Kramer	1983	378
83⅜	17⅜	17⅞	7	6⅞	2⅝	2⅝	12⅜	7	5⅛	3⅝	Apache Co., Ariz.	Robert A. Stacy	Robert A. Stacy	1983	378
83⅜	15⅜	15⅞	7⅛	6⅞	2⅝	2⅝	11⅝	6⅝	5⅝	5⅝	Lake Co., Oreg.	Richard L. Smith	Richard L. Smith	1983	378
83⅜	17⅛	17⅞	6⅝	6⅝	3	3⅛	12⅛	6⅝	4⅝	4⅝	Coconino Co., Ariz.	Delroy Western	Delroy Western	1983	378
83⅜	14⅞	14⅞	7⅝	7⅞	2⅝	2⅝	13⅛	11⅝	5⅝	5⅝	Lake Co., Oreg.	Clyde L. Dehlinger	Clyde L. Dehlinger	1984	378
83⅜	16⅛	15	6⅝	6⅝	3⅜	3⅛	11⅛	7⅝	6⅛	6	Cochise Co., Ariz.	Jim Tomlin	Jim Tomlin	1984	378
83⅜	15⅝	15⅞	6⅝	6⅝	3⅜	3⅜	8⅛	4⅝	4⅝	4⅞	Coconino Co., Ariz.	Matthew Dominy	Matthew Dominy	1984	378
83⅜	15⅜	15⅞	7⅛	7	3⅜	3⅛	15⅛	14	4⅝	4⅝	Thomas Co., Kan.	Charles M. Barnett	Charles M. Barnett	1985	378
83	16⅞	16⅞	6⅝	6⅝	3⅜	3	16⅛	16⅛	5⅛	5⅞	Shirley Basin, Wyo.	Duncan G. Weibel	Duncan G. Weibel	1946	430
83	15⅜	15⅞	7⅛	6⅞	3⅜	2⅝	9⅛	3⅝	5⅝	5⅞	Rawlins, Wyo.	Richard Eisner	Richard Eisner	1951	430
83	15⅜	15⅞	6⅝	6⅝	3⅜	3⅜	11⅛	7⅝	5	5⅞	Hartley Co., Texas	William G. Kendrick	William G. Kendrick	1953	430
83	14⅝	15⅞	7⅞	7⅞	2⅝	2⅝	10⅛	8⅝	6⅝	6⅞	Casper, Wyo.	Tom R. Frye	Tom R. Frye	1954	430
83	15⅝	14⅞	6⅝	6⅝	3⅛	3⅜	12⅛	9⅝	6	5⅝	Heber, Ariz.	Grady L. Beard	Grady L. Beard	1954	430
83	15⅝	15⅞	6⅝	6⅝	2⅝	2⅝	14⅞	13⅝	6⅝	6⅝	Saratoga, Wyo.	Dave Erickson	Dave Erickson	1957	430
83	16⅜	15⅞	6⅝	6⅝	3	3	13⅞	11⅛	5⅝	5⅝	Rawlins, Wyo.	Melvin Birks	Melvin Birks	1960	430
83	16	16⅞	6⅝	6⅝	2⅝	2⅝	11	5⅝	5⅞	5⅞	Lame Deer, Mont.	G. E. Badgley	G. E. Badgley	1961	430

Score											Locality	Hunter	Owner	Date	Rank
83	16⅜	16⅜	6⅝	6⅝	2⅝	2⅜	11	5⅝	5⅝	6⅛	Lake Co., Oreg.	Ken Smith	Ken Smith	1962	430
83	15⅝	15⅝	7⅛	7⅛	2⅝	3	13⅝	5⅝	5⅝	6⅛	Plevna, Mont.	Joseph P. Burger	Joseph P. Burger	1963	430
83	16⅜	16⅜	6⅝	6⅝	2⅝	2⅝	8⅝	5⅝	5⅝	6⅛	Boyero, Colo.	Henry H. Zietz	Henry H. Zietz	1965	430
83	16⅜	17⅛	6⅝	6⅝	3	3	14⅛	5⅝	5⅝	6⅛	Thatcher, Colo.	M. A. May	M. A. May	1965	430
83	16⅜	16⅜	7	6⅝	3⅛	3	8⅝	4⅝	4⅝	6⅜	Wamsutter, Wyo.	Marlene Simons	Marlene Simons	1970	430
83	18⅜	18⅜	6⅝	6⅝	2⅝	2⅝	12⅝	4⅝	4⅝	6⅜	Navajo Co., Ariz.	Joseph R. Rencher	Joseph R. Rencher	1970	430
83	16⅜	16⅜	6⅝	6⅝	2⅜	2⅜	8⅝	6⅜	6⅜	6⅝	Moffat Co., Colo.	Michael Coleman	Michael Coleman	1971	430
83	16	16	6⅝	6⅝	2⅝	2⅝	13⅝	6⅝	6⅝	6⅝	Springer, N.M.	Ronald E. McKinney	Ronald E. McKinney	1973	430
83	16	15⅝	7	7	2⅜	2⅜	9	5	5	6⅜	Fremont Co., Wyo.	Robert Cragoe, Jr.	Robert Cragoe, Jr.	1974	430
83	16⅜	17	6⅜	6⅜	2⅝	2⅝	6⅝	5⅞	5⅞	7	Yavapai Co., Ariz.	Artie L. Thrower	Artie L. Thrower	1975	430
83	16⅜	16⅜	6⅜	6⅜	3	3	4⅛	5⅝	5⅝	6⅜	Colfax Co., N.M.	Jim Hoots	Jim Hoots	1975	430
83	16⅜	17	6⅜	6⅜	3⅜	3⅜	12⅝	5⅝	4⅝	6⅝	Valley Co., Mont.	Timothy R. Logan	Timothy R. Logan	1976	430
83	16⅜	16⅞	6⅛	6⅜	2⅞	2⅜	9⅝	4⅝	4⅝	6⅛	Wagon Mound, N.M.	Dale R. Leonard	Dale R. Leonard	1976	430
83	16⅜	16⅛	6⅝	6⅜	2⅝	2⅝	10⅜	5⅞	5⅞	6⅜	Harding Co., N.M.	Stephen C. LeBlanc	Stephen C. LeBlanc	1977	430
83	16	16⅛	6⅜	6⅜	2⅜	2⅜	4⅝	6⅜	6⅝	6⅜	Sweetwater Co., Wyo.	Douglas Grantham	Douglas Grantham	1978	430
83	16⅜	16⅜	6⅜	6⅜	2⅜	2⅜	7⅛	6⅜	6⅜	6⅝	Lake Co., Oreg.	Francis G. Dalrymple	Francis G. Dalrymple	1978	430
83	17⅛	17⅛	6⅜	6⅜	2⅝	2⅝	2⅜	6⅜	6⅜	6⅜	Sublette Co., Wyo.	Thomas A. Scott	Thomas A. Scott	1978	430
83	16⅝	16⅜	7⅛	7⅛	2⅝	2⅝	9⅝	7	7	6⅜	Sublette Co., Wyo.	Kenneth D. Knight	Kenneth D. Knight	1978	430
83	16	16⅜	7⅝	7⅝	2⅝	2⅝	5	7⅛	7⅛	6⅝	Sweetwater Co., Wyo.	Glen W. Coates	Glen W. Coates	1979	430
83	16⅜	16⅜	6⅜	6⅜	2⅝	2⅝	10⅝	7	7	6⅝	Custer Co., S.D.	Edward J. Schauer	Edward J. Schauer	1979	430
83	16⅜	16⅜	6⅜	6⅜	3	3	7⅝	7⅛	7	6⅝	Washington Co., Colo.	Gina R. Cass	Gina R. Cass	1979	430
83	15⅝	15⅝	7⅜	7⅜	2⅝	2⅝	14⅝	6⅜	6⅜	6⅝	Sweetwater Co., Wyo.	Keith Penner	Keith Penner	1980	430
83	15⅜	15⅜	6⅜	6⅜	2⅜	2⅜	1⅝	6⅝	6⅝	6⅝	Lake Co., Oreg.	Jerry J. Peacore	Jerry J. Peacore	1980	430
83	16	16	5⅝	5⅝	3⅜	3⅜	1⅝	5	5	6⅝	Hudspeth Co., Texas	Charles E. Davis	Charles E. Davis	1980	430
83	15⅝	15⅝	6⅜	6⅜	3⅜	3⅛	4⅝	6⅜	6⅜	6⅝	Campbell Co., Wyo.	Richard S. Alford	Richard S. Alford	1982	430
83	15⅜	15⅜	6⅛	7	2⅝	2⅜	6⅛	6⅝	6⅝	7	Washoe Co., Nev.	Richard J. Depaoli	Richard J. Depaoli	1982	430
83	15⅜	15⅜	6⅜	6⅝	2⅝	2⅝	9	6⅝	6	6⅝	Albany Co., Wyo.	Mark T. Gleason	Mark T. Gleason	1982	430
83	16⅜	16⅜	6⅝	6⅝	2⅜	2⅜	11⅝	6⅝	6⅝	6⅜	Meade Co., S.D.	Randy A. Cammack	Randy A. Cammack	1982	430
83	15⅜	15⅜	7	7	2⅝	2⅝	10⅝	5⅝	5⅝	7	Humboldt Co., Nev.	Thomas S. Kelley	Thomas S. Kelley	1983	430
83	15⅜	15⅜	7⅛	7⅛	2⅜	2⅝	13⅝	5⅜	5⅜	7⅛	Colfax Co., N.M.	John W. Ladd	John W. Ladd	1983	430
83	16	15⅜	7⅛	7⅛	2⅜	2⅜	10⅝	9⅝	8⅝	7⅛	Carbon Co., Wyo.	Frederick L. Proffit	Frederick L. Proffit	1983	430
83	15⅜	15⅜	7	7	3⅛	3	9	8⅝	7	7	Box Butte Co., Neb.	Lynda G. Sydow	Lynda G. Sydow	1984	430
82⅝	17⅜	17	6⅜	6⅜	2⅝	2⅝	12⅝	5⅝	5	7	Natrona Co., Wyo.	G. S. Peterson	Unknown	1948	470
82⅝	16⅝	17	6⅝	6⅜	2⅝	2⅝	14⅜	5	5	6⅜	Prairie Co., Mont.	Gordon Spears	Gordon Spears	1954	470
82⅝	16	16⅜	6⅝	6⅜	3⅜	3⅜	12⅜	5	5	6⅜	Angora, Neb.	Neb. Game & Parks Comm.	Harold C. Rusk	1954	470
82⅝	15⅜	15⅜	6⅜	6⅜	2⅜	2⅜	14⅜	6	6	6⅜	Jelm Mt., Wyo.	Guy Murdock	Guy Murdock	1955	470
82⅝	17⅜	17⅜	6	5⅝	3⅛	3	10⅝	5⅝	5⅝	6⅜	Butte Co., S.D.	P. T. Theodore	P. T. Theodore	1958	470
82⅝	15⅜	15⅜	7⅜	7⅜	2⅝	2⅝	11⅝	5	5	7⅜	Glad Valley, S.D.	D. M. Davis	D. M. Davis	1958	470
82⅝	17⅜	17⅜	6⅜	6⅜	2⅝	2⅝	13⅜	4⅝	4⅝	6⅜	Yavapai Co., Ariz.	Vaughan Rock	Vaughan Rock	1959	470
82⅝	14⅜	14⅜	7	7	2⅜	2⅜	2⅝	5⅜	5⅜	7	Gillette, Wyo.	R. R. Kirchner	R. R. Kirchner	1961	470
82⅝	15⅜	15⅜	6⅜	6⅜	2⅜	2⅜	5⅜	6⅝	6⅝	6⅜	Sweetwater Co., Wyo.	A. L. Bruner	A. L. Bruner	1962	470
82⅝	16⅝	16⅝	6⅜	6⅜	2⅜	2⅜	5⅜	6⅝	6⅝	6⅜	Lake Co., Oreg.	Kenneth Smith	Kenneth Smith	1963	470
82⅝	15⅜	15⅜	7	7	2⅞	2⅜	8⅝	6⅜	6⅜	7	Natrona Co., Wyo.	William S. Martin	William S. Martin	1964	470

Antilocapra americana americana and related subspecies

Score	Length of Horn R.	L.	Circumference of Base R.	L.	Circumference at Third Quarter R.	L.	Inside Spread	Tip to Tip Spread	Length of Prong R.	L.	Locality Killed	By Whom Killed	Owner	Date Killed	Rank
82 6/8	15 6/8	15 5/8	7 3/8	7 5/8	2 5/8	3	8 5/8	8 3/8	5	6	Converse Co., Wyo.	Paul W. Tomlin	Paul W. Tomlin	1965	470
82 6/8	17 3/8	17 3/8	6 6/8	6 6/8	2 7/8	2 6/8	14 4/8	10 4/8	4 4/8	4 4/8	Mora Co., N.M.	R. L. Wakefield	R. L. Wakefield	1965	470
82 6/8	14 2/8	14 1/8	7 6/8	7 7/8	2 6/8	2 6/8	12 4/8	10 4/8	5 5/8	5 7/8	Alcova, Wyo.	June & Vaughn Johnson	New Park Hotel	1965	470
82 6/8	15 2/8	15 3/8	6 7/8	6 6/8	2 4/8	2 4/8	15 3/8	11 7/8	6 6/8	6 6/8	Sweetwater Co., Wyo.	James C. Klum	James C. Klum	1965	470
82 6/8	17 7/8	17 4/8	6	6	2 7/8	2 5/8	14 4/8	9 1/8	4 4/8	4 7/8	Ft. Apache Res., Ariz.	Robert L. Martin	Robert L. Martin	1965	470
82 6/8	15 2/8	15 4/8	7	6 7/8	2 6/8	2 6/8	10 4/8	8 1/8	6 1/8	5 5/8	Fremont Co., Wyo.	Terry N. TenBoer	Terry N. TenBoer	1967	470
82 6/8	16 3/8	16 4/8	6 4/8	6 5/8	2 4/8	2 7/8	10	4 7/8	5 5/8	5 5/8	Farson, Wyo.	Ronald O. West	Ronald O. West	1967	470
82 6/8	17 3/8	17 3/8	6 5/8	6 6/8	3	2 7/8	8 5/8	1 5/8	4	4 2/8	Round Mt., Ariz.	Dennis L. Fife	Dennis L. Fife	1967	470
82 6/8	15 1/8	15 2/8	6 5/8	6 7/8	2 6/8	2 6/8	10 5/8	8 5/8	6 1/8	5 5/8	Rocky Ford, Colo.	Henry A. Helmke	Henry A. Helmke	1967	470
82 6/8	15 3/8	15 4/8	6 6/8	6 6/8	2 4/8	2 5/8	8 6/8	5 2/8	6 3/8	6 3/8	Carbon Co., Wyo.	John M. Sell	John M. Sell	1969	470
82 6/8	16	15 7/8	6 7/8	6 7/8	3	3 1/8	10 3/8	5 1/8	5 5/8	5 5/8	Uinta Area, Wyo.	Barry Hyken	Barry Hyken	1969	470
82 6/8	16 5/8	16 4/8	6 3/8	6 4/8	2 3/8	2 3/8	15 4/8	13 3/8	5 4/8	5 1/8	Socorro Co., N.M.	Lawrence D. Vigil	Lawrence D. Vigil	1970	470
82 6/8	15 3/8	15 3/8	6 6/8	6 3/8	3 1/8	3 1/8	8 3/8	5 1/8	6	6	Custer Co., Mont.	George E. Sanquist	George E. Sanquist	1970	470
82 6/8	14 3/8	14	7 3/8	7 5/8	2 4/8	2 5/8	9	7 5/8	5 5/8	5 5/8	Sweetwater Co., Wyo.	Keith F. Dunbar	Keith F. Dunbar	1970	470
82 6/8	16 3/8	16 3/8	6 3/8	6 5/8	2 5/8	2 5/8	8 4/8	2 7/8	6 2/8	5 5/8	Natrona Co., Wyo.	Kenneth Niedan	Kenneth Niedan	1971	470
82 6/8	16 1/8	15 5/8	6 2/8	6 4/8	2 7/8	2 7/8	10 7/8	8 4/8	6 6/8	6 7/8	Medicine Bow, Wyo.	Raymond Freitas	Raymond Freitas	1973	470
82 6/8	15 4/8	15 4/8	6 3/8	6 1/8	3 5/8	3 3/8	9 2/8	4 4/8	5	4 3/8	Carbon Co., Wyo.	Roger D. George	Roger D. George	1975	470
82 6/8	16 1/8	16	6 2/8	6 1/8	2 5/8	2 6/8	13	7 4/8	6	5 2/8	Modoc Co., Calif.	Dennis McClelland	Dennis McClelland	1977	470
82 6/8	15 3/8	16 3/8	6 3/8	6 3/8	2 5/8	2 5/8	10 5/8	5 5/8	6 4/8	6 5/8	Weld Co., Colo.	Chester N. Erwin	Ronald G. Erwin	1978	470
82 6/8	16 2/8	16 3/8	6 6/8	6 6/8	2 3/8	2 2/8	10 5/8	6	5 1/8	5 2/8	Catron Co., N.M.	David Chavez	David Chavez	1978	470
82 6/8	16 5/8	17 2/8	6 6/8	6 6/8	2 2/8	2 1/8	11 2/8	7 5/8	7 2/8	7 7/8	Grant Co., Oreg.	A. Paul Malstrom	A. Paul Malstrom	1980	470
82 6/8	14 2/8	14 4/8	6 5/8	6 5/8	2 2/8	2 2/8	10 5/8	8 2/8	6 1/8	6 1/8	Carbon Co., Wyo.	Robert J. Smith	Robert J. Smith	1980	470
82 6/8	15 2/8	15 3/8	6 4/8	6 5/8	2 2/8	2 6/8	8	5 3/8	5 5/8	5 5/8	Hudspeth Co., Texas	L. A. Grelling	L. A. Grelling	1982	470
82 6/8	15 7/8	15 7/8	6 4/8	6 5/8	2 7/8	2 4/8	8 7/8	2 1/8	5 2/8	5 2/8	Natrona Co., Wyo.	Bill E. Boatman	Bill E. Boatman	1982	470
82 6/8	16 1/8	16 1/8	7 4/8	7 3/8	2 4/8	2 4/8	12	9	5 5/8	6 1/8	Carter Co., Mont.	Lloyd R. Norvell	Lloyd R. Norvell	1982	470
82 6/8	15 3/8	15 4/8	6 6/8	6 6/8	2 2/8	2 2/8	11 3/8	8 3/8	4 7/8	5	Mora Co., N.M.	Donald R. Warren	Donald R. Warren	1982	470
82 6/8	16 7/8	16 6/8	6 2/8	6 2/8	2 5/8	2 5/8	9 2/8	6 3/8	6 3/8	5 5/8	Natrona Co., Wyo.	Eugene Turner, Jr.	Eugene Turner, Jr.	1982	470
82 6/8	15 5/8	16	6 5/8	6 4/8	2 5/8	2 5/8	10	6	5 3/8	5 5/8	Carbon Co., Wyo.	Dailen R. Jones	Dailen R. Jones	1982	470
82 6/8	15	15	7 2/8	6 5/8	2 2/8	2 2/8	11 1/8	4 4/8	5 2/8	5 3/8	Washoe Co., Nev.	Michael J. Lange	Michael J. Lange	1983	470
82 6/8	17 1/8	17 4/8	6 6/8	6 5/8	2 2/8	2 2/8	11 4/8	12 3/8	6 3/8	5 5/8	Carbon Co., Wyo.	Kenneth E. Grail	Kenneth E. Grail	1983	470
82 6/8	16 3/8	15	7 5/8	7 3/8	2 2/8	2 2/8	14 4/8	10 1/8	5 2/8	5 5/8	Yellowstone Co., Mont.	Robert M. Labert	Robert M. Labert	1984	470
82 6/8	17 3/8	17	6	6	2 5/8	2 5/8	9 5/8	5 1/8	5 4/8	5 3/8	Custer Co., Idaho	William P. Benscoter	William P. Benscoter	1985	470

											Locality	Owner	By	Date	Score
82⅝	16⅞	16⅞	6⅞	6⅞	2⅞	2⅞	8⅞	2⅝	6⅞	6⅞	Sweetwater Co., Wyo.	Craig B. Argyle	Craig B. Argyle	1985	470
82⅝	15⅞	15⅞	6⅞	6⅜	2⅞	2⅞	15⅞	13	6⅞	6⅜	Yavapai Co., Ariz.	Joseph C. Cancilliere	Joseph C. Cancilliere	1984	514
82⅜	17½	17	6	6	2⅝	2⅞	8	3⅞	6	6	California	Foster's Bighorn Rest.	Bill Foster	1930	515
82⅝	16⅞	16⅞	6⅞	6⅞	2⅞	2⅝	9⅜	4⅞	5⅞	5⅜	Saratoga Co., Wyo.	Helen R. Peterson	Helen R. Peterson	1945	515
82⅜	16⅛	15⅞	6⅞	6⅞	2⅞	2⅞	10⅛	6⅞	6⅛	6⅛	Park Co., Mont.	William E. Randall	William E. Randall	1947	515
82⅝	16⅞	16⅞	6⅞	6⅛	2⅝	2⅜	11⅞	5⅞	5⅞	5⅜	Catron Co., N.M.	Chas. J. Boyd	Chas. J. Boyd	1952	515
82⅝	16⅛	16⅞	6⅛	6⅛	2⅝	2⅞	10	6⅞	5⅞	5⅝	Seligman, Ariz.	Cleo E. Wallace	Cleo E. Wallace	1959	515
82⅝	14¼	14¼	7⅞	7⅞	2⅝	2⅝	12⅞	11½	6	6	Ferris Mt., Wyo.	Donald Anderson	Donald Anderson	1959	515
82⅝	16⅞	16	6⅞	6⅞	2⅝	2⅝	10⅞	7¼	4⅞	5⅛	Shirley Basin, Wyo.	Walter B. Hester	Walter B. Hester	1960	515
82⅝	16⅛	15⅞	6⅞	6⅛	3	2⅞	11⅛	8	5⅞	5⅛	Campbell Co., Wyo.	Fred J. Brogle	Fred J. Brogle	1960	515
82⅝	16⅞	16⅛	6⅞	6⅞	2⅞	2⅞	13⅛	8⅜	6⅜	3⅞	Poison Spider, Wyo.	Clarence Meddock	Clarence Meddock	1961	515
82⅜	17	17	6	6⅞	2⅝	2⅜	14⅜	10	5⅞	5	Springerville, Ariz.	Malcolm Silvia	Malcolm Silvia	1962	515
82⅜	16⅛	16⅛	6⅞	6⅛	2⅝	2⅝	11⅛	7⅞	5⅞	5⅞	Green Mt., Wyo.	Forrest H. Burnett	Forrest H. Burnett	1962	515
82⅜	15⅞	15⅞	6⅞	6⅞	2⅝	2½	10⅛	4⅛	6⅜	5⅞	Medicine Hat, Alta.	Nick Mandryk	Nick Mandryk	1963	515
82⅜	16⅜	16⅞	7⅞	7½	2⅜	2⅜	10⅛	11½	4⅛	5	Park Co., Colo.	Mrs. Cotton Gordon	Mrs. Cotton Gordon	1964	515
82⅝	16⅞	16⅞	6⅞	6⅞	2⅞	2⅞	16⅛	11½	5	5⅜	Ingomar, Mont.	L. P. Treaster	L. P. Treaster	1965	515
82⅝	16⅝	16⅞	6⅞	6⅛	2⅞	2⅞	10⅛	7⅞	5⅞	5⅞	Seligman, Ariz.	Glenn Olson	Glenn Olson	1965	515
82⅝	15⅞	16	6⅜	6⅛	3	2⅜	6⅞	4⅞	6⅞	6⅜	Butte, N.D.	E. J. Weigel	E. J. Weigel	1966	515
82⅝	15⅞	16⅛	6⅞	7⅛	2⅝	2⅝	7⅞	7⅞	5⅞	5⅞	Laramie, Wyo.	Noel Weidner	Noel Weidner	1966	515
82⅝	13⅜	13⅜	9⅞	9⅜	2⅝	3	11	6⅞	5⅛	5⅞	Pecos Co., Texas	Ben H. Moore, Jr.	Ben H. Moore, Jr.	1967	515
82⅝	16⅛	16⅛	6⅞	6⅛	2⅜	3	9⅜	6⅛	5⅛	5⅝	Lake Co., Oreg.	Charles R. Waite	Charles R. Waite	1969	515
82⅝	15⅞	15⅛	6⅛	6⅛	2⅝	2⅜	12⅛	6⅛	5⅜	5⅞	Washoe Co., Nev.	James R. Stoner, Jr.	James R. Stoner, Jr.	1969	515
82⅝	15⅞	15⅞	6⅞	6⅛	2⅝	2⅜	14	10⅞	5⅜	5⅜	Humboldt Co., Nev.	Robert C. Lawson	Robert C. Lawson	1970	515
82⅝	15⅛	15⅛	6⅛	6⅛	2⅜	2⅝	8⅞	6⅞	5⅞	5⅞	Brewster Co., Texas	Joseph W. Burkett III	Joseph W. Burkett III	1971	515
82⅝	15⅛	16	6⅞	6⅞	3⅛	3	8⅛	4	3⅜	3⅜	Platte Co., Wyo.	William B. Brewer	Dwight E. Farr	1972	515
82⅝	16⅛	16	6⅝	6	2⅞	2⅜	9⅞	10⅛	5⅞	5⅝	Converse Co., Wyo.	J. A. Merrill, Jr.	J. A Merrill, Jr. & C. Davis	1973	515
82⅝	17⅛	16⅝	6⅜	6⅝	2⅞	2⅜	10⅛	5	5	4⅞	Coconino Co., Ariz.	Robert J. Hallock	Robert J. Hallock	1973	515
82⅝	16	16⅜	6⅝	6⅜	2⅜	2⅜	11⅛	6⅞	5⅞	5⅞	Custer Co., Mont.	Harry Zirwas	Harry Zirwas	1974	515
82⅝	14⅞	14⅞	7⅜	7⅛	3⅛	3	11	9⅜	6	6	Cimarron, N.M.	Ronald E. McKinney	Ronald E. McKinney	1974	515
82⅝	14⅞	14⅜	7	7	3⅛	3½	9⅝	5⅝	5⅞	5⅞	Rosebud Co., Mont.	Norman G. Kern	Norman G. Kern	1974	515
82⅝	17	17⅛	6⅛	6⅛	2⅞	3⅛	10⅛	5⅛	5⅛	5	Slope Co., N.D.	Marlin J. Kapp	Marlin J. Kapp	1975	515
82⅝	16⅛	16⅝	6⅞	6⅜	2⅝	2⅞	11⅞	7⅞	5⅜	5⅜	Coconino Co., Ariz.	David S. Hibbert	David S. Hibbert	1976	515
82⅝	16⅜	17⅞	6⅞	7	2⅜	2⅞	11⅛	5⅞	5⅝	5⅛	Fremont Co., Wyo.	Wayne D. Kleinman	Wayne D. Kleinman	1977	515
82⅝	16	15⅛	6⅝	6⅜	2⅜	2⅜	14⅜	14⅜	5⅝	5⅝	Washakie Co., Wyo.	Greg Warner	Greg Warner	1977	515
82⅝	16	16⅛	6⅝	6⅝	2⅜	2⅜	12⅜	8⅛	5⅜	5⅝	Carter Co., Mont.	James A. White	James A. White	1977	515
82⅝	15⅞	15⅞	6⅜	6⅜	2⅜	2⅜	13⅜	10⅛	6⅜	6⅜	Lassen Co., Calif.	Brad L. Ayotte	Brad L. Ayotte	1977	515
82⅝	15	15	6⅜	6⅜	2⅜	2⅛	9⅜	4	6⅜	7	Sublette Co., Wyo.	Larry W. Cross	Larry W. Cross	1977	515
82⅝	14⅞	14⅜	7	7	3	3	11⅞	8⅞	5⅞	6⅜	Richland Co., Mont.	Lloyd Holland	Lloyd Holland	1977	515
82⅝	16⅜	16⅜	6⅜	6⅜	2⅝	2⅝	9⅜	5⅜	5⅝	5⅛	Sweetwater Co. Wyo.	Fred B. Keyes	Fred B. Keyes	1978	515
82⅝	15⅝	15⅜	6⅝	6⅝	2⅝	2⅜	12⅛	7⅜	5⅝	5⅝	Modoc Co., Calif.	Mark Hansen	Mark Hansen	1978	515
82⅝	16⅝	16⅜	7	7	2⅜	2⅜	8⅛	6⅜	5⅝	5⅝	Siskiyou Co., Calif.	Rodney F. Royer	Rodney F. Royer	1979	515
82⅝	14⅞	14⅜	6⅝	6⅝	2⅞	2⅜	13⅜	11⅛	6⅛	6⅝	Carbon Co., Wyo.	Michael Boender	Michael Boender	1979	515

PRONGHORN—Continued

Antilocapra americana americana and related subspecies

Score	Length of Horn R.	L.	Circumference of Base R.	L.	Circumference at Third Quarter R.	L.	Inside Spread	Tip to Tip Spread	Length of Prong R.	L.	Locality Killed	By Whom Killed	Owner	Date Killed	Rank
82⅜	15⅞	15⅝	6⅜	6⅜	2⅝	2⅝	9⅜	4⅝	5⅝	5⅝	Millard Co., Utah	William R. Houston	William R. Houston	1979	515
82⅜	15⅞	16⅛	6⅛	6⅜	2⅝	2⅝	14⅛	9⅞	6⅛	6⅞	White Pine Co., Nev.	Tom I. Papagna, Jr.	Tom I. Papagna, Jr.	1980	515
82⅜	15⅝	15⅞	6⅝	6⅝	2⅜	2⅜	12⅛	10⅜	6⅜	6⅜	Carbon Co., Wyo.	Barry L. Alger	Barry L. Alger	1980	515
82⅜	17⅞	17⅜	6	6	2⅝	2⅝	11⅞	6	5⅜	5⅜	Hudspeth Co., Texas	Ray A. Acker, Sr.	Ray A. Acker, Sr.	1980	515
82⅜	17	16⅞	6⅜	6	2⅝	2⅝	9⅞	3⅜	5⅝	5⅝	Sweetwater Co., Wyo.	Donald R. Williamson	Donald R. Williamson	1981	515
82⅜	15⅝	15⅛	6⅜	6⅜	3	3	10⅜	8⅜	6	6⅛	Socorro Co., N.M.	Clyde C. Brumley	Clyde C. Brumley	1981	515
82⅜	15⅜	15⅜	6⅜	6⅜	3	3	8⅞	4⅛	6⅛	6⅜	Moffat Co., Colo.	Charles W. Klaassens	Charles W. Klaassens	1981	515
82⅜	14⅞	14⅜	6⅞	7⅜	2⅝	2⅝	9⅛	6⅜	6⅜	6⅜	Campbell Co., Wyo.	Larry L. Helgerson	Larry L. Helgerson	1982	515
82⅜	16⅝	16⅝	6⅜	6⅜	3	3	10⅜	5⅝	5	5	Union Co., N.M.	John W. Saunders	John W. Saunders	1982	515
82⅜	15⅛	15⅛	6⅝	6⅝	2⅝	2⅝	10⅛	9⅜	5⅞	5⅞	Carbon Co., Wyo.	John T. Butters	John T. Butters	1982	515
82⅜	16⅛	16⅛	6⅜	6⅜	2⅞	3	9⅜	4⅜	5⅜	5⅜	Natrona Co., Wyo.	Edgar M. Artecona	Edgar M. Artecona	1983	515
82⅜	16⅛	16⅛	7	7	2⅜	2⅜	5⅜	2	5⅜	5⅜	Natrona Co., Wyo.	Bill E. Boatman	Bill E. Boatman	1983	515
82⅜	15⅜	16	6⅜	6⅜	3	3	12	10⅜	5⅝	5⅜	Carbon Co., Wyo.	Merlyn J. Kiel	Merlyn J. Kiel	1983	515
82⅜	16⅝	16⅛	6⅝	6⅝	2⅜	2⅜	8⅛	2⅝	5⅜	5⅜	Washoe Co., Nev.	Vernon E. Benney	Vernon E. Benney	1983	515
82⅜	15⅞	16⅜	6⅝	6⅝	2⅜	2⅜	9⅜	5⅜	6	6	Sweetwater Co., Wyo.	Richard E. Knox, Jr.	Richard E. Knox, Jr.	1984	515
82⅜	15⅜	15⅜	6⅜	6⅜	3	2⅞	8	3⅜	5⅝	5	Navajo Co., Ariz.	Perry H. Finger	Perry H. Finger	1985	515
82⅜	15⅝	16⅛	6⅜	6⅜	2⅞	2⅝	8⅜	5⅜	5⅜	5⅜	Sweetwater Co., Wyo.	W. A. Chambers	W. A. Chambers	1985	515
82⅜	15⅜	15⅛	6⅝	6⅝	2⅝	2⅝	14⅛	9⅜	5⅜	6⅜	Hudspeth Co., Texas	Ernest Elbert, Jr.	Ernest Elbert, Jr.	1985	515
82⅜	16⅜	15⅞	6⅜	6⅜	2⅝	2⅝	8⅜	3⅜	5⅜	5⅜	Natrona Co., Wyo.	Toby J. Johnson	Toby J. Johnson	1985	515
82⅜	16⅜	16⅜	7	6⅞	2⅝	2⅝	14⅛	13⅜	6⅜	6⅜	Chaves Co., N.M.	Glenn Marshall	Harvey Pirtle	1939	574
82⅜	14⅜	14⅜	5⅞	7⅛	3⅛	2⅝	8⅜	4⅜	5⅜	5⅜	Henderson, N.M.	Ron Vance	Ron Vance	1947	574
82⅜	16⅝	16⅝	7⅛	7⅛	2⅝	2⅝	15⅜	11⅛	5⅜	5⅜	Split Rock, Wyo.	Herb Klein	Herb Klein	1952	574
82⅜	16⅝	16⅝	6⅝	6⅜	2⅝	2⅝	14⅛	10	4⅜	4⅜	Anderson Mesa, Ariz.	Roy Stevens	Roy Stevens	1953	574
82⅜	17⅜	17⅜	6⅜	6⅜	3⅛	2⅝	8⅜	4⅜	5	5	Saratoga, Wyo.	J. E. Prothroe	J. E. Prothroe	1955	574
82⅜	15⅜	15⅜	6⅜	6⅜	2⅝	2⅝	8⅜	5⅜	6⅜	5⅜	Rawlins, Wyo.	Thomas B. McNeill	Thomas B. McNeill	1955	574
82⅜	16	16⅜	6⅜	6⅜	3	3	10⅛	4⅜	4⅜	4⅜	Hettinger, N.D.	Art Score	Art Score	1957	574
82⅜	16⅜	16⅜	6⅜	6⅜	2⅝	2⅝	13⅜	10⅜	5⅜	5⅜	Williams, Ariz.	Fred Udine	Fred Udine	1959	574
82⅜	16⅜	16⅜	6⅜	6⅜	2⅝	2⅝	13⅜	8⅜	6	6⅛	Sage Creek, Wyo.	Glenn P. Anderson	Glenn P. Anderson	1959	574
82⅜	15⅜	15⅜	7	7⅛	2⅝	2⅝	11⅛	5	5⅜	5⅜	Arpan, S.D.	Dell Shanks	Dell Shanks	1960	574
82⅜	16⅜	16⅜	6⅜	6	2⅝	2⅜	10⅜	6	6⅜	6	Crook Co., Wyo.	John P. Wood	John P. Wood	1960	574
82⅜	16⅜	16⅜	6⅜	6⅜	2⅜	2⅜	6⅜	4⅜	5⅜	5⅜	Park Co., Wyo.	Don A. Johnson	Don A. Johnson	1960	574
82⅜	16⅜	16⅜	6⅜	6⅜	2⅜	2⅜	13⅜	10⅜	4⅜	4⅜	Sierra Blanca, Texas	Charles Nichols	Charles Nichols	1960	574

										Owner	By	Locality	Killed	
82⅞	16⅞	16⅞	6	6	2⅞	11⅞	7⅞	5⅞	5⅞	Robert F. Ziker	Unknown	Poison Spider, Wyo.	1961	574
82⅞	17⅜	16	6	6	2⅞	12⅞	12⅞	6⅜	6⅜	Joan V. Gordon	Joan V. Gordon	New Mexico	1961	574
82⅞	16⅛	16	6⅞	6⅜	3⅛	14	9	5	5	T. C. Gonya	T. C. Gonya	Shirley Basin, Wyo.	1961	574
82⅞	15⅞	16⅜	6⅜	6⅜	2⅞	13⅛	13⅛	6⅜	5⅞	W. J. Morrelle	W. J. Morrelle	Lavina, Mont.	1963	574
82⅞	15⅞	15⅜	7⅞	7⅜	2⅞	11⅜	6⅜	5⅜	5⅜	Frank Gardner	Frank Gardner	Casper, Wyo.	1963	574
82⅞	15⅞	15⅛	6⅜	6⅜	2⅜	10⅛	5	5⅜	6	Leo M. Bergthold	Leo M. Bergthold	Lewis & Clark Co., Mont.	1963	574
82⅞	16⅜	16⅜	6⅜	6⅜	2⅜	12	9⅜	5	5	Susan W. Tupper	Susan W. Tupper	Laramie, Wyo.	1964	574
82⅞	15⅞	16	7	7	3	11⅜	7⅜	5⅜	5⅛	C. W. Edwards	Rita Shumka	Hanna, Alta.	1964	574
82⅞	16⅜	16⅜	6⅜	6⅜	2⅜	13⅜	9⅛	5⅜	5⅜	Ken Bosch	Ken Bosch	Knappen, N.D.	1965	574
82⅞	16⅜	16⅜	6⅜	6⅜	2⅜	11	11⅛	5	5	Sioux Sport Goods	Lee Atkinson	Bowen, N.D.	1966	574
82⅞	16⅛	16⅜	6⅜	6⅜	2⅜	10⅛	4⅛	5⅜	5⅜	Les Gordon	Les Gordon	Foremost, Alta.	1966	574
82⅞	14⅞	15	6⅜	6⅜	2⅜	9⅛	5⅜	6⅜	6⅜	Mrs. Paul Goodwin	Mrs. Paul Goodwin	Weld Co., Colo.	1967	574
82⅞	15	15⅛	6⅞	6⅜	2⅜	11⅜	7⅜	6⅜	6⅛	Larry K. Lantz	Larry K. Lantz	Vivian, S.D.	1969	574
82⅞	15⅞	15⅜	6⅜	6⅜	2⅜	9⅛	4⅜	6	6⅛	Morrel W. Ivie	Morrel W. Ivie	Powderville, Mont.	1969	574
82⅞	17⅜	17⅜	7⅜	7⅜	1⅜	7⅜	3⅜	4⅜	4⅜	Adam Schmick	Adam Schmick	Wild Horse, Alta.	1970	574
82⅞	16⅜	16⅜	6⅜	6⅜	2⅜	10⅜	8⅜	5⅜	5⅜	R. O. Marshall, Jr.	R. O. Marshall, Jr.	Natrona Co., Wyo.	1970	574
82⅞	15⅜	15⅜	6⅜	6⅜	2⅜	10⅜	4⅜	5⅜	5⅞	Carl Aus	Carl Aus	Fergus Co., Mont.	1971	574
82⅞	16⅜	16⅜	6⅜	6⅜	2⅜	13	8⅜	5⅜	5⅜	William Lee Butler	William Lee Butler	Coconino Co., Ariz.	1973	574
82⅞	15	15⅜	6	6	2⅜	10⅜	9⅜	5⅜	5⅜	Collins F. Kellogg	Collins F. Kellogg	Fremont Co., Wyo.	1974	574
82⅞	15⅜	15⅜	6⅜	6⅜	2⅞	9⅜	5⅜	5⅜	5⅜	Joseph A. Balmelli	Joseph A. Balmelli	Treasure Co., Mont.	1974	574
82⅞	15⅜	15⅜	6⅜	6⅜	2⅜	7⅜	3⅜	5⅜	5⅞	Gary Simonson	Gary Simonson	Gillette, Wyo.	1975	574
82⅞	15⅜	15⅜	7⅜	7⅛	2⅜	8⅜	5⅜	6⅛	6⅜	David L. Peterson	David L. Peterson	Duchesne Co., Utah	1976	574
82⅞	15⅜	14⅞	6⅜	6⅜	2⅜	13⅜	9⅞	6⅜	6⅜	Dean Dunson	Dean Dunson	Harney Co., Oreg.	1977	574
82⅞	16	15⅜	6⅜	6⅜	3	13⅜	10	6	6	Kenneth L. Kelly	Kenneth L. Kelly	Morgan Co., Colo.	1977	574
82⅞	16⅜	16⅜	6⅜	6	2⅜	12⅜	8	5⅜	5⅜	Richard L. Simmons, Sr.	Richard L. Simmons, Sr.	Apache Co., Ariz.	1978	574
82⅞	16⅜	16⅜	6⅜	6⅜	2⅜	15	11	6⅜	6⅜	Heber Simmons, Jr.	Heber Simmons, Jr.	Otero Co., N.M.	1978	574
82⅞	15⅞	16	6⅜	6⅜	2⅜	12⅜	9	6⅜	7	Del S. Oliver	Del S. Oliver	Lassen Co., Calif.	1978	574
82⅞	15⅜	15⅜	6⅜	6⅜	2⅜	10⅜	4⅜	5⅜	5⅜	Jon L. Wadkins	Jon L. Wadkins	Butte Co., Idaho	1981	574
82⅞	15⅜	15	6⅜	6⅞	2⅜	9⅜	7	6⅜	6⅜	Richard R. Delfs	Richard R. Delfs	Lake Co., Oreg.	1981	574
82⅞	17⅜	17⅜	6⅜	6⅜	2⅜	14⅜	11⅞	5⅜	5⅜	W. L. McMillan	W. L. McMillan	Niobrara Co., Wyo.	1981	574
82⅞	16	16⅜	6⅜	6⅜	2⅜	8⅜	5⅜	4⅜	4⅜	David D. Rittenhouse	David D. Rittenhouse	Valley Co., Mont.	1982	574
82⅞	14⅜	14⅜	6⅜	6⅜	2⅜	9⅜	6⅜	6⅜	6⅜	Gregg R. Landrum	Gregg R. Landrum	Stillwater Co., Wyo.	1982	574
82⅞	15⅜	15⅜	6⅜	6⅜	2⅜	14⅜	13⅜	5⅜	5⅜	Larry J. Thoney	Larry J. Thoney	Carbon Co., Wyo.	1982	574
82⅞	16⅜	16⅜	6⅜	6⅜	2⅜	11⅜	8⅜	4⅞	4⅞	Thomas O. Malone	Thomas O. Malone	Washoe Co., Nev.	1982	574
82⅞	16⅜	18	6⅛	6	2⅜	11⅜	5⅜	5⅜	5⅛	McLean Bowman	McLean Bowman	Brewster Co., Texas	1982	574
82⅞	16⅜	16⅜	6⅜	6⅜	2⅞	13⅜	11	5⅜	4⅞	Mike Meeker	Michael C. Meeker	Fremont Co., Wyo.	1982	574
82⅞	16⅜	16⅜	6⅜	6⅜	2⅜	13⅜	8⅜	5⅜	5⅜	Evelyn A. Maxon	Evelyn A. Maxon	Fremont Co., Wyo.	1983	574
82⅞	14	14⅞	7⅜	7⅞	2⅜	10⅜	8⅜	6⅜	6⅜	Peter B. Shaw	Peter B. Shaw	Sweetwater Co., Wyo.	1983	574
82⅞	16⅜	16⅜	6⅜	6⅜	2⅜	9⅜	3⅜	5⅜	5⅜	William E. Butler	William E. Butler	Garfield Co., Mont.	1983	574
82⅞	16⅜	16⅜	6⅜	6⅜	2⅞	15	11	5	5⅜	A. T. Boultinghouse	A. T. Boultinghouse	Navajo Co., Ariz.	1983	574
82⅞	15⅜	15⅜	6⅜	6⅜	2⅜	10⅜	6⅜	5⅜	5⅜	Carol Greet	Carol Greet	Washakie Co., Wyo.	1983	574
82⅞	15⅜	15⅜	6⅜	6⅜	2⅜	10⅜	6⅜	5⅞	5⅞	Chris Tiller	Chris Tiller	Butte Co., Idaho	1983	574
82⅞	16⅜	16⅜	6⅜	6⅜	2⅜	13⅜	9⅜	5⅜	5⅜	Richard L. Bostrom	Richard L. Bostrom	Fremont Co., Wyo.	1983	574

Antilocapra americana americana and related subspecies

Score	Length of Horn R.	L.	Circumference of Base R.	L.	Circumference at Third Quarter R.	L.	Inside Spread	Tip to Tip Spread	Length of Prong R.	L.	Locality Killed	By Whom Killed	Owner	Date Killed	Rank
82²⁄₈	16	15⅞	6⅞	6⅜	2⅝	2⅝	12⅛	8⅝	6⅛	6⅛	Natrona Co., Wyo.	Michael D. Samuelson	Michael D. Samuelson	1984	574
82²⁄₈	15⅞	15⅞	6⅜	6⅜	2⅞	3	10	4⅞	6⅛	6	Fremont Co., Wyo.	Charles D. Day	Charles D. Day	1984	574
82²⁄₈	15⅞	15⅞	6⅛	6⅛	2⅝	2⅝	12⅝	8⅞	6⅜	6⅜	Hartley Co., Texas	Ernie Davis	Ernie Davis	1984	574
82²⁄₈	17⅜	16⅞	6⅞	6	2⅜	2⅜	11⅞	9⅜	6⅜	5⅜	Siskiyou Co., Calif.	Laird E. Marshall	Laird E. Marshall	1984	574
82	17⅞	17⅞	6⅞	6⅞	3⅜	3⅜	14⅛	11⅛	3⅜	4	Pahsimeroi Valley, Idaho	Elmer Keith	Elmer Keith	1936	634
82	15⅜	15⅞	6⅞	6⅞	2⅝	2⅝	12⅜	6⅜	5⅝	5⅜	Catron Co., N.M.	Floyd Todd	Floyd Todd	1947	634
82	16⅜	15⅞	6⅜	6⅞	3	3	11	7⅞	5	5⅛	Mormon Lake, Ariz.	Bob Housholder	Bob Housholder	1949	634
82	15⅝	15⅞	6⅜	6⅞	2⅝	3⅜	16⅜	14⅝	6⅜	5⅝	Navajo Co., Ariz.	Joe D. Sutton	Joe D. Sutton	1951	634
82	17⅜	17⅞	6⅝	6⅝	3	3	16	11⅛	3⅜	3⅜	Williams, Ariz.	Paul D. Hosman	Paul D. Hosman	1951	634
82	16⅜	16⅞	6⅜	6⅜	2⅜	2⅝	13⅛	10⅛	5⅝	6	Shirley Basin, Wyo.	Earl Fisher	Earl Fisher	1951	634
82	16⅛	15⅞	6⅞	6⅞	2⅝	2⅝	11⅜	5	5⅜	4⅞	Anderson Mesa, Ariz.	Mrs. C. C. Cooper	Mrs. C. C. Cooper	1953	634
82	17⅞	17⅜	6⅛	6	2⅝	2⅞	12⅜	5⅝	4⅜	4⅞	Santa Rosa, N.M.	F. C. Hibben	F. C. Hibben	1955	634
82	15	14⅞	6⅞	6⅞	2⅝	2⅞	10⅜	7⅞	5⅝	5⅝	Bow Island, Alta.	R. F. Dunmire	R. F. Dunmire	1957	634
82	15⅜	15⅜	7	7	3	3	14	12⅜	5⅜	5⅜	Limon, Colo.	Walt Paulk	Walt Paulk	1958	634
82	16	16⅜	6⅝	6⅝	2⅜	2⅝	12⅜	8⅜	6	5⅞	Encampment, Wyo.	G. A. Surface	G. A. Surface	1960	634
82	14⅞	14⅞	6⅝	6⅝	2⅝	2⅝	9⅜	8⅜	6⅜	5⅞	Sage Creek, Wyo.	Mrs. Ramon Somavia	Mrs. Ramon Somavia	1960	634
82	15⅜	15⅜	6⅛	6⅛	2⅜	2⅜	11⅛	6⅜	6⅜	6⅞	Shirley Basin, Wyo.	Norman Miller	Norman Miller	1961	634
82	15⅜	15⅜	6⅞	6⅞	2⅞	2⅞	10⅜	6⅛	5⅞	5	Natrona Co., Wyo.	Fred Deiss	Fred Deiss	1961	634
82	16⅛	16	6⅝	6⅜	2⅞	2⅞	9⅝	7⅞	5⅜	5	Shirley Basin, Wyo.	Henry Macagni	Henry Macagni	1962	634
82	16	16⅜	6⅝	6⅝	2⅜	2⅜	16⅝	14⅝	5⅝	5⅝	Shirley Basin, Wyo.	G. C. Cunningham	G. C. Cunningham	1962	634
82	14⅜	14⅞	6⅝	6⅝	2⅝	2⅝	11	6⅝	6⅝	6⅜	Hartley Co., Texas	Walter O. Ford, Jr.	Walter O. Ford, Jr.	1964	634
82	16⅛	16	6⅜	6⅜	2⅝	2⅝	12⅛	11⅛	5⅜	5⅜	Navajo Co., Ariz.	John Welch III	John Welch III	1965	634
82	17	17	6⅜	6⅛	2⅝	2⅝	12⅛	6⅜	4⅜	3⅜	McKinley Co., N.M.	W. R. Phillips	W. R. Phillips	1965	634
82	15⅜	15⅜	5⅝	5⅝	2⅜	2⅜	11	9	6	5⅜	Arco, Idaho	Ernest L. Ellis, Jr.	Ernest L. Ellis, Jr.	1965	634
82	16⅜	16⅜	6⅛	6⅛	2⅝	2⅝	9⅜	8⅜	5⅞	5⅝	Lake Co., Oreg.	Dennis Crowe	Eldon Hayes	1966	634
82	15⅜	15	6	6	2⅝	2⅝	8⅜	7	6⅞	7	Eston, Sask.	Dennis Crowe	Dennis Crowe	1966	634
82	15⅜	15	6⅝	6⅝	3	3	10⅛	8⅜	5⅝	5⅝	Carbon Co., Wyo.	C. W. Hermanson	C. W. Hermanson	1968	634
82	14⅜	14⅞	6⅜	6⅜	3	3	8⅞	3⅜	7	6	Garfield Co., Mont.	Dean V. Ashton	Dean V. Ashton	1968	634
82	15⅜	15⅜	7⅜	6⅞	2⅝	2⅝	15	13	5⅝	5⅝	Wamsutter, Wyo.	Frank Simons	Frank Simons	1969	634
82	16	16	6⅝	6⅝	2⅝	2⅞	12⅜	8⅝	5⅝	5⅜	Carbon Co., Wyo.	Martin J. Stuart	Martin J. Stuart	1969	634
82	15⅜	15⅜	7⅛	7⅛	2⅝	2⅝	8	7	5⅜	5	Farson, Wyo.	Larry Nolan Garner	Larry Nolan Garner	1969	634

											Locality	Owner	By whom killed	Date killed	Rank
82	15⅜	15⅜	6⅝	6⅝	2¼	2¼	14⅜	13½	6	6	Albany Co., Wyo.	Edwin J. Keppner	Edwin J. Keppner	1969	634
82	15⅜	15	7	7	2¼	2⅜	10⅜	5	6⅝	6⅝	Washoe Co., Nev.	Oliver V. Iveson	Oliver V. Iveson	1970	634
82	15⅜	15⅜	5⅞	5⅞	3⅜	3⅜	11⅜	7⅜	5⅞	4⅜	Brewster Co., Texas	Joseph W. Burkett III	Joseph W. Burkett III	1972	634
82	17	17⅞	6⅝	6⅝	2⅜	2⅜	11⅜	5⅜	6⅝	5⅞	Coconino Co., Ariz.	Jerry Ray Killman	Jerry Ray Killman	1973	634
82	14⅜	14	7⅜	7⅜	2⅜	2⅜	13	9⅜	6⅝	7	Garfield Co., Mont.	Don E. Traughber	Don E. Traughber	1973	634
82	14⅜	14⅜	7⅜	7⅜	3⅜	3⅜	9⅜	7⅜	5⅞	5⅞	Sweet Rock, Wyo.	Alphonse Cuomo, Jr.	Alphonse Cuomo, Jr.	1973	634
82	15⅜	15⅜	7	7	2⅜	2⅜	10⅜	8	6⅝	6	Sublette Co., Wyo.	Gary D. Jorgensen	Gary D. Jorgensen	1973	634
82	16⅜	16⅜	6⅝	6⅝	3⅜	3⅜	11	7⅜	2⅜	3⅜	Wolf Point, Mont.	Raymond A. Gould	Raymond A. Gould	1974	634
82	16⅜	16⅜	6⅝	6⅝	2⅜	2⅜	12	7⅜	5⅞	5⅞	Carbon Co., Wyo.	Reg. R. Smith	Reg. R. Smith	1974	634
82	14⅝	14⅝	6⅝	6⅝	3	3	10⅜	5⅜	5⅞	5⅞	Campbell Co., Wyo.	Gilbert Steinen, Jr.	Gilbert Steinen, Jr.	1975	634
82	15⅜	15⅜	6⅝	6⅝	3⅜	3	9	2⅜	5⅞	5⅞	Wallace Co., Kansas	Curtis R. Penner	Curtis R. Penner	1976	634
82	14⅜	13⅜	7	7	3	3⅜	11⅜	9⅜	4⅜	4⅜	Sweetwater Co., Wyo.	Starla L. Cairns	Starla L. Cairns	1976	634
82	15	15	7⅜	7⅜	2⅜	2⅜	10⅜	5	5	5	Carbon Co., Wyo.	Peck Rollison	Peck Rollison	1977	634
82	16⅜	16⅜	6⅝	6⅝	2⅜	2⅜	8⅜	5⅜	5⅜	5⅜	Fremont Co., Wyo.	Daniel R. Hahn	Daniel R. Hahn	1977	634
82	16	16	6	6	3⅜	3⅜	9	6⅝	5⅜	5⅜	Hartley Co., Texas	John A. Wright	John A. Wright	1977	634
82	16⅜	16⅜	6⅝	6⅝	2⅜	2⅜	8⅜	4	5⅜	5⅜	Hudspeth Co., Texas	Luther V. Oliver	Luther V. Oliver	1978	634
82	16⅜	16⅜	7	7	2⅜	2⅜	12⅜	10⅜	5⅜	5	Fremont Co., Wyo.	John J. Eichhorn	John J. Eichhorn	1978	634
82	17⅛	17⅜	5⅜	5⅜	2⅜	2⅜	12⅜	6⅝	5⅜	5⅜	Otero Co., N.M.	Robert E. Anton	Robert E. Anton	1978	634
82	17⅛	17⅜	6⅜	6⅜	3⅜	3⅜	0	0	4⅜	4⅜	Culberson Co., Texas	Charles Seidensticker	Charles Seidensticker	1978	634
82	14⅝	15⅜	6⅝	6⅝	2⅜	2⅜	10⅜	6⅝	6⅜	6⅜	Sweetwater Co., Wyo.	Dan B. Artery	Dan B. Artery	1979	634
82	17	17	6⅝	6⅝	2⅜	2⅜	8⅜	6⅝	4	4⅜	Brewster Co., Texas	Peggy F. Brady	Peggy F. Brady	1979	634
82	16⅛	16⅛	6⅝	6⅝	2⅜	2⅜	12⅜	7⅜	5⅜	5⅜	Lassen Co., Calif.	Robert D. Luna, Jr.	Robert D. Luna, Jr.	1979	634
82	16⅝	16⅜	6⅝	6⅜	2⅜	2⅜	15	11⅜	5⅜	5⅜	Natrona Co., Wyo.	Theresa Fulfaro	Theresa Fulfaro	1980	634
82	15⅜	15⅜	6⅝	6⅝	2⅜	2⅜	15⅜	14⅜	5⅜	5⅜	Carbon Co., Wyo.	Jerry G. Hagen	Jerry G. Hagen	1980	634
82	16⅛	16	6⅜	7	2⅜	2⅜	9	2⅜	5⅜	5⅜	Fremont Co., Wyo.	Steven E. Clingman	Steven E. Clingman	1980	634
82	16	16⅜	6⅜	6⅜	2⅜	2⅜	9⅜	3⅜	5⅜	5⅜	Coconino Co., Ariz.	Fred W. Fernow, Jr.	Fred W. Fernow, Jr.	1981	634
82	16⅜	15⅜	7⅜	7⅜	2⅜	2⅜	16⅜	14⅜	6	5⅜	Natrona Co., Wyo.	Wade Dumont	Wade Dumont	1981	634
82	15⅞	16	6⅜	6⅜	2⅜	2⅜	14	10⅜	6	6	Washoe Co., Nev.	Jerry L. Nelms	Jerry L. Nelms	1981	634
82	15	17	6⅜	6⅝	2⅜	2⅜	6⅝	1⅜	5⅜	5⅜	Lincoln Co., Wyo.	Tom Crank	Tom Crank	1982	634
82	16⅜	15⅜	6⅝	6⅜	3⅜	3⅜	10	6⅜	5⅜	5⅜	Carbon Co., Wyo.	Eric J. Swanson	Eric J. Swanson	1982	634
82	14⅜	14	7⅜	7⅜	2⅜	2⅜	10⅜	7⅜	6⅜	6⅜	Sweetwater Co., Wyo.	Brett A. Ward	Brett A. Ward	1982	634
82	15⅜	15⅜	6⅜	6⅝	2⅜	2⅜	10⅜	6⅜	6⅜	6⅜	Fremont Co., Wyo.	Thomas O. Martens	Thomas O. Martens	1982	634
82	16⅜	16⅜	6⅝	6⅝	2⅜	2⅜	12	8⅜	5⅜	5⅜	Natrona Co., Wyo.	Joseph P. Prinzi	Joseph P. Prinzi	1982	634
82	15⅜	15⅜	7	7	2⅜	2⅜	8⅜	2⅜	5⅜	5⅜	Crook Co., Wyo.	Jay D. Hacklin	Jay D. Hacklin	1982	634
82	15	14⅜	7	7⅜	2⅜	2⅜	12	10⅜	5⅜	5⅜	Carbon Co., Wyo.	Albert Gregg	Albert Gregg	1983	634
82	16⅜	16⅜	6⅜	6⅜	2⅜	2⅜	14⅜	10⅜	5⅜	5⅜	Quay Co., N.M.	Donald E. Fritz	Donald E. Fritz	1984	634
82	16	15⅜	6⅜	6⅜	2⅜	2⅜	9⅜	5	5	5⅜	Coconino Co., Ariz.	Charles L. Holland	Charles L. Holland	1984	634
82	16⅜	15⅜	6⅜	6⅜	2⅜	2⅜	7⅜	1	5⅜	5⅜	Washoe Co., Nev.	Jack D. Bothwell	Jack D. Bothwell	1984	634
89¼*	17	16⅜	7⅜	7	2⅜	2⅜	11	6⅜	6⅜	6⅜	Sweetwater Co., Wyo.	Richard D. Ullery	Richard D. Ullery	1983	634
87⅞**	16⅝	16	7⅜	7⅜	2⅜	2⅜	12⅜	9	5⅜	6⅜	Sweetwater Co., Wyo.	Stanley L. Ackerman	Stanley L. Ackerman	1980	634
87*	16⅜	16⅜	7⅜	7⅜	2⅜	2⅜	14⅜	10⅜	6	6	Fremont Co., Wyo.	Ronald K. Morrison	Ronald K. Morrison	1980	634

*Final Score subject to revision by additional verifying measurements

385

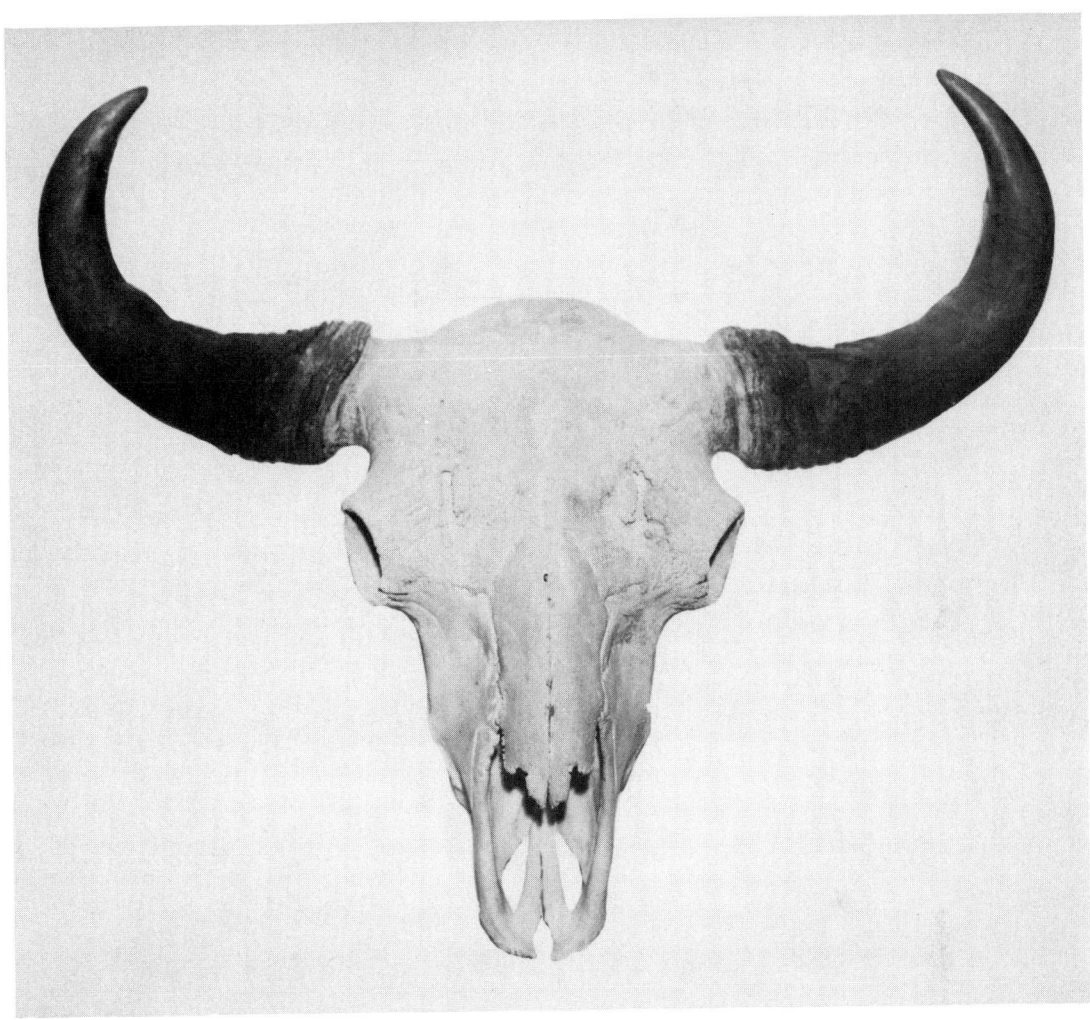

Photograph by Grancel Fitz

WORLD'S RECORD BISON
SCORE: 136 4/8

Locality: Yellowstone National Park, Wyoming Date: 1925
Hunter: S. Woodring Owner: Fishing Bridge Museum, Yellowstone Nat. Park

Photograph by Alex Rota

NUMBER TWO BISON
SCORE: 136 2/8
Locality: Northwest Territories Date: 1961
Hunter and owner: Samuel Israel

Bison

Bison bison bison and Bison bison athabascae

Minimum Score 115

Trophies from the lower 48 states are acceptable only for records, not awards, and only from states that recognize bison as wild and free-ranging and for which a hunting license and/or big game tag is required for hunting.

Score	Length of Horn R.	L.	Circumference of Base R.	L.	Circumference at Third Quarter R.	L.	Greatest Spread	Tip to Tip Spread	Sex	Locality Killed	By Whom Killed	Owner	Date Killed	Rank
136⅞	21⅞	23⅜	16	15	8⅜	8	35⅜	27	M	Yellowstone N.P., Wyo.	S. Woodring	Fishing Bridge Museum	1925	1
136⅜	19	18⅞	18⅛	18⅛	6⅞	6⅞	30⅛	22⅞	M	Northwest Territories	Samuel Israel	Samuel Israel	1961	2
134½	21⅜	20⅝	14⅜	14⅞	8⅜	7⅝	33⅞	26⅝	M	Park Co., Wyo.	Picked Up	H. A. Moore	1977	3
133¾	19⅝	18⅝	17	17	7	7	29⅝	21⅛	M	Great Slave Lake, Alta.	Mike Dempsey	Natl. Mus. Of Canada	1935	4
132⅜	21⅝	22⅝	16⅛	16⅝	6	7⅝	35⅜	26⅝	M	Unknown	James H. Lockhart	Carnegie Museum	PR1939	5
132⅜	22⅝	21⅝	14⅛	14⅛	6⅝	6⅝	32⅝	24⅝	M	Sweet Grass, Alta.	Ken Cooper	Univ. Of Sask.	1961	5
131⅝	20⅝	20⅝	15	15	7	7	30	20⅝	M	Hell Roaring Creek, Mont.	Picked Up	Univ. Of Mont.	1945	7
129	21⅜	20⅜	14⅜	14⅛	7⅝	7⅝	29⅜	18⅝	M	Big Horn Mts., Wyo.	Picked Up	George S. Burnap, Jr.	1953	8
128⅜	18⅛	18⅜	14⅛	14⅛	8⅜	8⅛	28⅛	20⅛	M	Yellowstone N.P., Wyo.	Unknown	U.S. Natl. Museum	1913	9
127⅞	19⅜	19⅜	15	15⅜	6⅜	6⅜	32⅝	25⅜	M	Northwest Territories	Wilbur Hilgar	Wilbur Hilgar	1961	10
127⅞	19⅝	20⅜	15⅝	15⅜	5⅝	6	31⅜	22⅝	M	Northwest Territories	Leslie Bowling	Leslie Bowling	1961	12
127	21⅝	22⅜	13⅝	13⅞	7⅝	7⅞	29	18⅛	M	Canada	Unknown	Raymond Brown	1899	12
127	18⅝	19	15	15⅛	6⅞	7⅛	26⅜	23⅝	M	Custer Co., S. D.	Henry E. McLemore	Henry E. McLemore	1980	14
126⅝	19⅝	19⅝	15⅝	15⅛	7⅝	7⅜	27⅝	18⅝	M	Gillette, Wyo.	D. C. Basolo, Jr.	D. C. Basolo, Jr.	1963	15
126⅝	17⅝	18⅜	15⅝	15⅛	7⅞	7	30⅜	24⅜	M	Yellowstone River, Mont.	Picked Up	Edward J. Melby	1935	15
126⅝	18⅛	18⅛	16⅛	16	6⅞	6⅝	29⅝	21⅞	M	Fort Smith, N.W.T.	V. N. Holderman	V. N. Holderman	1961	17
126	20⅛	20⅜	15	15⅜	5⅞	5⅝	27⅝	13⅝	M	Slave River, N.W.T.	Edward A. Feser	Edward A. Feser	1975	17
126	18⅛	21	15	15⅜	6⅞	7⅝	31⅞	24⅝	M	Wrangell Mts., Alaska	Walter H. Hammer	Walter H. Hammer	1977	19
125⅝	19⅝	19⅝	15	15⅜	6	6⅝	30⅜	24	M	Yellowstone N.P., Wyo.	Lee L. Coleman	Jackson Hole Museum	1958	19
125⅝	17⅝	17⅞	14	14	8	8	26⅝	21⅛	M	Park Co., Wyo.	Unknown	James Patterson	PR1970	21
125⅝	19⅞	20	14⅜	13⅝	6⅞	7⅛	28⅜	19⅜	M	Montana	Unknown	O. P. Chisholm	PR1891	22
125	19⅞	20	14⅛	14⅛	6	6	28	20⅛	M	Manitoba	Unknown	James Fredrick	1928	22
125	18⅝	18⅝	14⅛	14⅛	6⅞	6⅛	28⅜	18⅝	M	Fort Smith, N.W.T.	Leonard J. Ostrom	Leonard J. Ostrom	1959	24
124⅜	20⅜	20⅜	15⅛	15⅛	6⅛	5⅞	30⅛	21⅛	M	Wyoming	Lord Rendlesham	B&C National Collection	1892	25
124⅜	20⅛	20⅛	14⅜	15⅛	6⅛	6⅛	31⅛	24	M	Copper River, Alaska	Earl E. Knutson	Earl E. Knutson	1965	25
124⅜	19⅝	20	15⅛	15⅛	5⅞	5⅝	29⅜	20⅛	M	Delta Junction, Alaska	Mike Stagno	Mike Stagno	1975	27
124⅜	17⅝	17⅝	16⅜	16⅝	6⅝	5⅝	32⅜	28⅛	M	Fort Smith, N.W.T.	Margaret Buckner	Margaret Buckner	1960	27
124⅜	17⅝	17⅝	14⅞	14⅜	7⅛	7⅝	31⅜	27⅜	M	Custer Co., S.D.	Stuart Godin	Stuart Godin	1975	27
124⅜	17⅝	19⅝	15⅜	15⅝	6⅜	5⅝	31	25⅝	M	Chitina River, Alaska	Robert E. Day	Robert E. Day	1976	27
124	21⅞	20⅜	14	13⅜	6⅝	5⅞	29⅞	20⅛	U	Jardine, Mont.	Unknown	Kerry Constan	1962	30
124	19⅝	20⅝	15⅜	15⅝	7⅝	7⅝	25⅝	18⅝	M	Slave River, N.W.T.	Rudolf Sand	Rudolf Sand	1972	30

Score									Sex	Locality	Owner	By whom taken	Date	Rank
124	19⅜	19⅜	14	14⅞	6⅞	5⅞	30⅛	22⅞	M	Hook Lake, N.W.T.	Manfred Kurtz	Manfred Kurtz	1973	30
124	18⅞	18⅞	14	14	6⅞	7⅞	33⅜	27⅞	M	Coconino Co., Ariz.	Philip A. Sturgill	Philip A. Sturgill	1984	30
123⅞	20⅞	20⅞	16	16	5⅞	5⅞	31	20⅞	M	Northwest Territories	J. S. Sanders	J. S. Sanders	1961	34
123⅝	17⅞	18	15	15	7⅞	7⅞	25	15⅜	M	Gillette, Wyo.	D. C. Basolo, Jr.	D. C. Basolo, Jr.	1963	34
123⅜	19⅞	19⅞	14⅞	14⅞	5⅞	6⅞	28⅞	21⅛	M	Yellowstone N.P., Wyo.	James B. Minter	Harry Trishman	1924	36
123⅜	18	18	16	16	6⅞	6⅞	29⅜	21⅛	U	Yellowstone N.P., Wyo.	C. Watters & D. Moore	Picked Up	1956	36
123⅜	20⅜	20⅜	15⅝	15⅝	5⅞	6	32⅞	22⅝	M	Delta Junction, Alaska	Donald A. Prescott	Donald A. Prescott	1963	36
123⅜	20⅜	20⅜	15⅝	15⅝	5⅞	5⅞	29⅞	19	M	Gillette, Wyo.	H. I. H. Prince Abdorreza Pahlavi	H. I. H. Prince Abdorreza Pahlavi	1967	36
123⅜	19⅞	18⅞	15	14⅞	7⅞	7⅞	26	21⅛	M	Fort Smith, N.W.T.	Earl H. Harris	Earl H. Harris	1969	36
123⅜	17⅞	18	16⅞	16⅝	6	6	29⅞	22⅛	M	Custer Co., S.D.	Tim P. Matzinger	Tim P. Matzinger	1983	41
122⅞	20⅜	19⅜	15⅝	15⅝	5⅞	5⅞	31⅛	24⅛	M	Big Delta, Alaska	Chuck Sutter	Unknown	1950	42
122⅝	20⅜	20⅜	14⅝	14⅝	5	5	26⅞	16⅝	M	Henry Mts., Utah	Greg Harper	Greg Harper	1978	43
122⅝	20⅜	20⅜	13⅞	13⅜	6⅞	6⅞	32⅞	26⅞	M	Absarokee Wild., Mont.	H. E. Lillis	H. E. Lillis	1953	44
122⅝	19⅞	19⅞	15	15	9⅞	9⅞	28⅞	19⅜	M	Northwest Territories	A. Sanford	A. Sanford	1961	44
122⅜	18	18	14⅞	14⅝	7⅞	7⅞	29⅞	23⅜	M	Fort Greely, Alaska	McClaren Johnson, Jr.	Picked Up	PR1961	44
122⅜	18⅝	18⅝	14⅝	14⅜	7⅞	7⅞	28⅞	20⅜	M	Gillette, Wyo.	Tom R. Bowles	Tom R. Bowles	1963	44
122⅜	18⅝	18⅝	16	16	5⅝	5	29⅛	22⅝	M	Hook Lake, N.W.T.	Robert C. Jones	Picked Up	1974	44
122	19⅛	20⅜	14⅝	14⅝	5⅞	5⅞	29⅜	21⅜	M	Wayne Co., Utah	Ardell K. Woolsey	Ardell K. Woolsey	1974	48
121⅞	18⅝	18⅝	14⅜	14⅜	7⅞	7⅞	29⅜	23⅜	M	Custer Co., S.D.	Jon R. Stephens	Jon R. Stephens	1982	49
121⅞	21⅛	22⅛	13⅜	14	5⅜	5⅜	29⅞	18⅜	M	Custer, Mont.	Martin Sorensen, Jr.	Picked Up	1962	49
121⅛	16	14⅞	16	16⅜	8⅞	8	29⅜	25⅝	M	Ogalala Sioux G. R., S.D.	Robert B. Peregrine	Robert B. Peregrine	1972	51
121⅛	18⅛	18⅝	14⅜	14⅜	6⅜	7	28⅜	17⅞	M	Fort Smith, N.W.T.	W. C. Whitt	W. C. Whitt	1972	52
121⅛	18⅛	18⅝	15	15⅜	5⅝	6	28⅜	21⅛	M	Custer Co., S.D.	Robert L. Trupe	Robert L. Trupe	1979	52
121	16⅝	17⅜	14⅜	14⅜	7⅛	7⅛	29⅝	21⅝	M	Slave River, N.W.T.	Franz M. Wilhelmsen	Franz M. Wilhelmsen	1959	52
121	17⅞	18⅜	14⅜	15⅜	6⅞	7⅞	28	21⅜	M	House Rock, Ariz.	Larry R. French	Larry R. French	1965	55
121	20⅜	18	14⅜	14⅜	6⅞	6⅞	28⅜	21⅞	M	Shoshone Natl. For., Wyo.	G. A. Cadwalader	Picked Up	PR1965	55
121	18⅝	18	14⅞	14⅞	6⅞	6⅞	27	19⅞	M	Big Horn Co., Mont.	Larry Edgar	Picked Up	1972	55
121	19⅜	18⅜	14⅝	14⅝	5⅞	5⅞	30⅜	24⅞	M	Custer Co., S.D.	Dave Ramey	Dave Ramey	1978	55
121	17⅞	17⅞	15⅜	15⅜	6⅛	6⅜	25	19⅞	M	Custer Co., S.D.	Wilson W. Crook III	Wilson W. Crook III	1982	55
120⅞	17	17⅜	15⅜	15⅜	5⅞	7⅞	31⅜	29⅞	M	Delta Junction, Alaska	George R. Horner	George R. Horner	1950	55
120⅞	17⅜	18⅜	15⅜	15⅜	5⅞	5⅞	29⅞	24⅜	M	Hook Lake, N.W.T.	George W. Parker	George W. Parker	1961	61
120⅞	17	16⅞	14⅛	14⅛	7⅞	7	29⅜	24⅛	M	Custer Co., S.D.	Louis Vaughn	Louis Vaughn	1968	61
120⅞	17⅞	17⅝	15⅝	15⅝	5⅜	5⅜	29	25⅞	M	Afton, Wyo.	Bernard Domries	Bernard Domries	1968	61
120⅞	20⅝	19⅞	15⅝	15⅝	5⅜	5	31⅜	24	M	Gillette, Wyo.	C. J. McElroy	C. J. McElroy	1970	61
120⅞	16⅝	16⅜	13⅞	14⅞	7⅞	7⅞	28⅜	24	M	Park Co., Wyo.	James Patterson	Picked Up	PR1970	61
120⅝	17⅞	18	15⅜	15⅞	6⅞	6⅞	29⅜	26⅜	M	Coconino Co., Ariz.	Greg V. Parker	Greg V. Parker	1975	61
120⅜	18	18⅜	15⅞	15⅜	5⅜	5⅜	29⅜	17⅜	M	Custer Co., S.D.	Lucky Simpson	Lucky Simpson	1985	69
120⅜	14	14	14⅝	14⅛	7	7	29⅜	23⅜	M	Northwest Territories	Charles H. Stoll	Charles H. Stoll	1961	69
120⅜	17⅛	17⅞	14⅜	14⅛	6⅛	6⅛	28⅜	21⅛	M	Custer State Park, S.D.	Philip L. Nare	Philip L. Nare	1974	71
120⅜	17⅞	17⅞	14⅛	14⅞	5⅝	5	27⅜	21⅞	M	Slave River, N.W.T.	Mrs. Malcom McKenzie	Unknown	1960	71
120⅜	19⅞	20	15⅜	15⅜	5	5	31⅜	27⅞	M	Delta Junction, Alaska	James M. Hill	James M. Hill	1978	73
120	21	20⅜	16	15⅞	4⅜	4⅜	28⅞	18⅛	M	Lamar River, Wyo.	National Park Service	Frank Oberhansley	1939	73

Score	Length of Horn R.	L.	Circumference of Base R.	L.	Circumference at Third Quarter R.	L.	Greatest Spread	Tip to Tip Spread	Sex	Locality Killed	By Whom Killed	Owner	Date Killed	Rank
120	15⅞	17	14⅞	14⅞	7⅛	7⅛	28⅜	24⅜	U	Big Delta, Alaska	Unknown	Robert C. Reeve	1950	73
120	18⅛	20½	16	16⅝	4⅝	5⅛	29⅝	23	M	Big Delta, Alaska	Thomas B. Hite	Thomas B. Hite	1983	73
119⅞	18⅛	18	15⅛	15⅝	6⅝	6⅝	28⅝	20⅜	M	Northwest Territories	Pitt Sanders	Pitt Sanders	1961	76
119⅞	19⅝	20	15⅛	14⅝	5	5	30⅜	23⅜	M	Big Delta, Alaska	Ann Denardo	Ann Denardo	1961	76
119⅞	17⅝	18⅛	15	14⅞	6⅝	6⅜	25⅝	16	M	Northwest Territories	Patrick Britell	Patrick Britell	1961	76
119⅞	17⅝	18⅛	14⅝	14⅝	5⅜	5⅝	28⅝	21⅜	M	Fort Smith, N.W.T.	Sheldon H. Weinstein	Sheldon H. Weinstein	1975	76
119⅞	20	19	14⅞	14⅞	5⅝	5⅜	32	25⅝	M	Gillette, Wyo.	Glenn Ellingson	Glenn Ellingson	1961	80
119⅞	17	17⅞	15⅝	15⅛	6	6	29	24⅝	M	Gillette, Wyo.	Walt Paulk	Walt Paulk	1962	80
119⅞	19⅞	19⅛	13⅜	13⅛	6⅝	7	25⅛	15⅛	M	Yellowstone N.P., Wyo.	Picked Up	Jim Ford	1970	80
119⅞	18	17⅜	16⅛	15⅝	5⅜	5⅝	30⅝	24⅝	M	Coconino Co., Ariz.	Dorothy B. Gilliam	Dorothy B. Gilliam	1980	84
119⅞	18⅛	18⅛	15⅝	15⅛	6⅝	5⅝	27⅝	18⅛	M	Ravalli Co., Mont.	Unknown	Harold G. Arnold	1975	85
119	17⅝	17⅛	13⅝	13⅛	6⅝	6⅜	25⅝	16⅝	M	Fort Smith, N.W.T.	John H. Epp	John H. Epp	1960	85
119	18⅛	18⅛	15⅛	15⅝	4⅞	5	25⅝	18	M	Hook Lake, N.W.T.	John G. Zelenka	John G. Zelenka	1971	85
119	16⅝	16⅞	14⅝	14	6⅝	6⅝	27⅝	18⅛	M	Coconino Co., Ariz.	Melvin C. Kincaid	Melvin C. Kincaid	1983	88
118⅞	15⅝	17⅛	15⅝	15⅝	6⅝	5⅝	27⅜	20⅛	M	Fort Smith, N.W.T.	D. N. Rowe	D. N. Rowe	1960	88
118⅞	17⅝	16⅝	15⅜	15⅛	6	5⅝	29	22⅜	M	Fort Smith, N.W.T.	W. J. Nixon	W. J. Nixon	1960	88
118⅞	18	18⅛	14⅛	14	7⅛	7⅛	28⅝	19⅛	M	Northwest Territories	Herb Klein	Herb Klein	1960	88
118⅞	19⅛	18	14⅛	15⅛	5⅜	4⅛	28⅝	22⅝	M	Fort Smith, N.W.T.	Charles Sides	Charles Sides	1961	88
118⅞	16⅝	16⅝	14⅝	14⅛	7	7⅛	29⅝	26⅝	M	Big Delta, Alaska	Richard P. Platz	Richard P. Platz	1968	88
118⅞	15⅜	14	15⅛	15⅝	7⅛	7⅛	28⅝	25	M	Big Horn Co., Mont.	Basil C. Bradbury	Basil C. Bradbury	1968	88
118⅞	19⅝	19⅞	15⅝	15⅝	4⅛	4⅝	31⅛	23⅝	M	Arlee, Mont.	Jack A. Shane, Sr.	Jack A. Shane, Sr.	1972	88
118⅞	17⅝	15⅝	16⅛	16⅝	6⅝	6⅝	31⅛	26	M	Hook Lake, N.W.T.	G. A. Treschow	G. A. Treschow	1975	88
118⅞	20¼	20⅜	14⅝	14⅛	5	5	29	23⅛	M	Garfield Co., Utah	David G. Hansen	David G. Hansen	1981	88
118⅞	17⅝	17⅛	15⅝	16	5⅝	5⅝	30⅝	24⅛	M	Custer Co., S.D.	Joel J. Torgerson	Joel J. Torgerson	1964	98
118⅞	18⅛	18⅛	14⅝	14⅛	5⅞	6	28⅝	23⅝	M	Copper River, Alaska	Jim Harrower	Jim Harrower	1972	98
118⅞	20⅜	20⅜	14⅞	15⅛	4⅛	4⅛	28⅝	21⅛	M	Pine Ridge Indian Res., S.D.	Mary L. Pipp	Mary L. Pipp		98
118⅜	19⅞	18⅞	14⅞	15⅛	4⅛	5⅜	31	28	M	Wyoming	Sidney Snow	Snow Museum	PR1900	100
118⅜	18⅝	19⅛	14⅝	14⅛	5⅝	5⅝	28⅝	22⅛	M	Pierre, S.D.	Earl Mumaw	Earl Mumaw	1962	100
118⅜	19⅛	19⅝	14⅝	14⅛	5⅝	5⅛	29	18⅛	M	Houserock Valley, Ariz.	Fred Shook	Fred Shook	1967	100
118	17⅝	18⅝	15	15⅛	6⅝	6⅝	29⅝	21	M	Yellowstone N.P., Wyo.	Unknown	Alfred C. Berol	1927	103
118	17⅝	17⅜	13⅞	14⅞	6⅞	7	30	26⅝	M	Crow Indian Res., Mont.	Pete Laird	Curt Laird	1956	103
118	16	16	16	16	5⅞	5⅞	27⅝	20⅞	M	Gillette, Wyo.	D. C. Basolo, Jr.	D. C. Basolo, Jr.	1962	103

Score									M	Locality	By Whom Killed	Owner	Date Killed	Rank
118	17⅞	16⅞	14⅞	16	6	6	25⅜	19	M	Henry Mts., Utah	John Goldenstein	John Goldenstein	1962	103
118	18⅞	19⅝	15⅞	15⅛	5⅛	5⅛	31⅛	29⅛	M	Custer State Park, S.D.	Harry T. Scharfenberg	Harry T. Scharfenberg	1984	103
117⅞	18⅜	17⅞	14⅝	14⅛	6⅛	6⅛	30⅛	25⅝	M	Farewell, Alaska	Thomas R. Keele	Thomas R. Keele	1975	108
117⅞	17⅜	17⅜	13⅜	13⅜	5⅝	5⅝	26	20⅜	M	Garfield Co., Utah	Sheldon D. Worthen	Sheldon D. Worthen	1977	108
117¾	16⅜	16⅝	15⅝	15⅝	6	6⅝	29	23	M	Custer Co., S.D.	Thomas J. Radoumis	Thomas J. Radoumis	1973	110
117½	17⅞	17⅜	14	14	6⅝	6⅜	30	25	M	Henry Mts., Utah	Don Genessy	Don Genessy	1960	111
117⅜	18⅞	18⅜	14⅞	14⅞	4⅞	4⅝	27	16	M	Gillette, Wyo.	D. C. Basolo, Jr.	D. C. Basolo, Jr.	1963	111
117⅜	19	19⅝	14⅞	14⅞	5	5	31	27	M	Campbell Co., Wyo.	Leroy Van Buggenum	Leroy Van Buggenum	1968	111
117⅜	18⅝	18	14⅞	14⅜	5	5	30⅛	25	M	Fort Smith, N.W.T.	Fred Burke	Fred Burke	1960	114
117	17⅞	17⅞	15⅛	15⅛	6⅜	5⅜	28⅛	22⅛	M	Gillette, Wyo.	D. C. Basolo, Jr.	D. C. Basolo, Jr.	1963	114
117	18⅝	18⅝	15	15⅜	5⅜	5	29⅜	26	M	Dadina River, Alaska	Joe Van Conia	Joe Van Conia	1965	114
117	19	19⅜	14⅜	14⅜	5	5	29⅜	29⅜	M	Delta Junction, Alaska	William T. Warren	William T. Warren	1978	114
117	19⅝	20⅜	14⅜	14⅜	4⅜	4⅜	30⅜	24⅜	M	Donnelly Dome, Alaska	Debra S. Darland	Debra S. Darland	1981	114
117	17⅞	17⅞	14⅜	14⅛	6⅜	6	29	23⅜	M	Delta Junction, Alaska	Elizabeth B. McConkey	Elizabeth B. McConkey	1981	114
117	19⅝	19⅞	14	14	5	5	29⅜	26⅜	M	Farewell, Alaska	Kevin G. Meyer	Kevin G. Meyer	1982	114
116⅞	16⅝	15⅜	14⅞	14⅛	6⅝	6⅝	32⅜	38⅜	M	Raymond Ranch, Ariz.	Unknown	Jack Brooks	1954	121
116⅞	16⅜	15⅝	13⅜	13⅛	7	7⅛	28	24	M	Custer Co., S.D.	Merle G. Smith	Merle G. Smith	1974	121
116⅝	21	20⅜	12⅞	13⅛	5⅛	5⅜	29⅜	17⅛	M	Donnelly Dome, Alaska	F. Glaser & R. Tremblay	Univ. of Alaska	1954	123
116⅝	16⅜	16⅜	15	14⅞	7	7⅝	28	22	M	Gillette, Wyo.	D. C. Basolo, Jr.	D. C. Basolo, Jr.	1963	123
116⅝	18	18⅜	15	14⅞	4⅞	4⅞	30⅜	26⅜	M	Alberta	Casper Whitney	B&C National Collection	1907	125
116⅜	20⅜	20⅜	13⅜	14	4⅛	4⅜	30⅜	23⅜	M	Osage Co., Okla.	Harold A. Yocum	Harold A. Yocum	1943	125
116⅜	17⅛	17⅞	16	17	5	5	25⅜	18⅛	M	Slave River, N.W.T.	Jim Wellman	Jim Wellman	1960	125
116⅜	18⅞	20	14⅜	14⅜	5⅝	5⅝	23⅜	23⅜	M	Delta Junction, Alaska	Alma Eades	Alma Eades	1963	125
116⅜	17⅜	17⅜	14⅜	14⅜	6⅝	6⅝	33	28⅜	M	Hook Lake, N.W.T.	Jerry Bick	Jerry Bick	1970	125
116⅜	16⅝	16⅜	14⅜	14⅜	6⅝	6⅝	25⅜	17	M	Hook Lake, N.W.T.	Jens K. Touborg	Jens K. Touborg	1972	125
116	19⅜	18⅜	14⅜	14⅜	4⅜	4⅜	25⅜	20⅜	M	Custer Co., S.D.	James B. Wade	James B. Wade	1976	125
116	15	15	14⅜	15	6⅜	6⅜	27⅜	22⅜	M	Gillette, Wyo.	D. C. Basolo, Jr.	D. C. Basolo, Jr.	1962	132
116	17⅞	18	14⅜	14⅞	5⅝	5⅜	30⅜	24⅜	M	Copper River, Alaska	Tony Oney	Tony Oney	1964	132
115⅞	17⅝	17⅜	14⅞	14⅞	5⅜	5⅜	30⅜	23⅜	M	Coconino Co., Ariz.	John Renkema, Jr.	John Renkema, Jr.	1977	132
115⅞	18⅝	18⅞	14	14⅜	6	6	33	25	M	Big Delta, Alaska	Barbara A. Nagengast	Barbara A. Nagengast	1963	135
115⅞	17⅞	18	14⅜	14	5⅛	4⅜	28⅜	20⅜	M	Sanders Co., Mont.	Glenn W. Slade, Jr.	Glenn W. Slade, Jr.	1961	136
115⅞	19⅜	19⅜	14⅛	14	4⅛	5⅜	0	0	M	Delta Junction, Alaska	W. S. Jarusiewicz	W. S. Jarusiewicz	1963	136
115⅝	19⅛	19	13⅜	14⅛	5	5	27⅜	15⅛	M	Hook Lake, N.W.T.	Robert C. Jones	Robert C. Jones	1974	136
115⅝	19	20	13⅜	13⅜	5⅝	5⅜	29⅜	22⅜	M	Chitna River, Alaska	Ronald A. Sturgeon	Ronald A. Sturgeon	1979	136
115⅝	17⅜	17⅜	14⅛	14⅞	5⅝	5⅜	29⅜	24⅜	M	Garfield Co., Utah	Roger Stewart	Roger Stewart	1984	136
115⅝	16⅝	17⅜	13⅜	13⅛	6⅜	7⅜	28⅜	23⅜	M	Black Hills, S.D.	Unknown	John H. Brandt	1969	141
115⅝	18⅜	19⅛	14⅞	15⅜	5⅝	5⅜	28⅜	21	M	Custer Co., S.D.	J. P. Moon, Jr.	J. P. Moon, Jr.	1983	141
115	16	14	13⅜	14⅜	5⅜	4⅜	28⅜	18⅛	M	Fort Smith, N.W.T.	Jules R Ashlock	Jules R Ashlock	1973	143
115	18⅜	15	15	15	6⅝	5⅜	29⅜	27⅛	M	Custer Co., S.D.	Rodger E. Warwick	Rodger E. Warwick	1982	143
115	19⅛	14⅜	14⅜	15	5⅜	5⅜	30⅜	25⅜	M	Custer Co., S.D.	August Benz, Jr.	August Benz, Jr.	1983	143
129⅞*	18⅛	15	16	7	6⅝	7	30⅜	21⅛	M	Fort Smith, N.W.T.	Lloyd L. Ward, Jr.	Lloyd L. Ward, Jr.	1971	
128⅞*	21⅛	16⅜	16⅜	5⅜	5⅜	20⅜	32⅛	24	M	Fort Smith, N.W.T.	Billy Day	Billy Day	1960	
128⅞*	18⅜	17⅜	16⅞	6⅝	6⅝	33⅜	25		M	Nothwest Territories	Bert Klineburger	Bert Klineburger	1960	

*Final Score subject to revision by additional verifying measurements

391

WORLD'S RECORD ROCKY MOUNTAIN GOAT
SCORE: 56 6/8

Locality: Babine Mountains, British Columbia Date: 1949
Hunter: E. C. Haase Owner: The B&C National Collection
Winner of the Sagamore Hill Medal, 1949

NUMBER TWO ROCKY MOUNTAIN GOAT (TIE)
SCORE: 56 2/8
Locality: Hedley, British Columbia Date: 1969
Picked Up Owner: Robert Kitto

Rocky Mountain Goat

Oreamnos americanus americanus and related subspecies

Minimum Score 50

Score	Length of Horn R.	L.	Circumference of Base R.	L.	Circumference at Third Quarter R.	L.	Greatest Spread	Tip to Tip Spread	Sex	Locality Killed	By Whom Killed	Owner	Date Killed	Rank
56⅜	12	12	6⅜	6⅜	2	2	9⅜	9	M	Babine Mts., B.C.	E. C. Haase	B&C National Collection	1949	1
56⅜	11⅜	11⅜	5⅝	5⅝	2⅛	2⅛	7⅞	6⅞	M	Helm Bay, Alaska	W. H. Jackson	W. H. Jackson	1933	2
56⅜	11⅜	11⅜	6⅜	6⅜	2⅛	2⅛	8⅝	8⅜	M	Hedley, B.C.	Picked Up	Robert Kitto	1969	2
56	10⅞	10⅞	6⅛	6	2⅝	2⅝	6⅞	6⅝	M	Kenai Pen., Alaska	Peter W. Bading	Peter W. Bading	1963	4
55	11⅞	11⅞	5⅜	5⅝	2	2	8⅝	6⅝	M	Cleveland Pen., Alaska	Elmer W. Copstead	Jonas Bros. of Seattle	1939	5
55	12⅛	12⅛	5⅝	5⅛	2	2⅛	7⅞	5⅞	M	Alex. Archipelago, Alaska	James Wilson	James Wilson	1969	5
54⅝	10⅝	11⅜	6⅝	6⅝	2	1⅞	8⅜	7⅞	M	Coquihalla Mts., B.C.	Fred D. Fouty	Fred D. Fouty	1959	7
54⅝	10⅞	11⅞	6	6	2⅜	2⅜	7⅞	6⅜	M	Telkwa Mts., B.C.	Mrs. V. Goudie	Mrs. V. Goudie	1964	7
54⅝	11⅜	11⅜	5⅝	5⅝	2	2	7⅞	5⅝	M	Reflection Lake, Alaska	Lue Wilson, Jr.	Lue Wilson, Jr.	1979	7
54⅜	11	11	6⅜	6⅜	1⅞	1⅞	10⅛	10	M	Fairmont Range, B.C.	Ira McLemore	Ira McLemore	1947	10
54⅜	11⅞	11⅞	6	5⅞	1⅞	1⅞	10	9⅜	M	Hastings Arm, B.C.	Rupert Maier	Rupert Maier	1963	10
54⅜	10⅜	10⅞	6	5⅞	2⅛	2⅛	8⅜	7⅞	M	Cassiar Mts., B.C.	Richard J. Wristen	Richard J. Wristen	1978	10
54⅜	11	10⅞	6⅜	6⅜	2	2	9⅜	9⅞	M	Cassiar Mts., B.C.	Raymond M. Stenger	Raymond M. Stenger	1979	10
54	11⅞	11⅞	6⅜	6⅜	2	2	9⅜	9⅜	M	Bow Summit, Alta.	Indian	N. K. Luxton	1907	14
54	11	11	6⅛	6⅛	2	2	8⅛	8⅜	M	Terminus Mt., B.C.	Herb Klein	Herb Klein	1965	14
53⅞	11⅛	11⅛	5⅝	5⅝	2	1⅞	9⅜	8⅜	M	Telegraph Creek, B.C.	V. D. E. Smith	V. D. E. Smith	1954	16
53⅞	10⅞	10⅞	6	6	1⅞	1⅞	7⅞	6⅝	M	Tumeka Lake, B.C.	Robert H. Edwards	Robert H. Edwards	1972	16
53⅞	10⅞	10⅞	5⅞	6	2⅛	2⅛	7⅞	7⅝	M	Elko Co., Nev.	Robert D. Kennedy	Robert D. Kennedy	1978	16
53⅞	11⅜	11⅞	5⅞	5⅞	2	2	7⅜	6⅝	M	Stikine River, B.C.	John Creyke	John Creyke	1926	19
53⅞	10⅞	11	6	6	1⅞	1⅞	9⅜	8⅜	M	Coldstream Creek, B.C.	R. J. Pop	Herb Klein	1952	19
53⅞	10⅜	9⅜	6⅜	6⅜	2	2⅜	7	6	M	Bella Coola, B.C.	Darryl Hodson	Darryl Hodson	1966	19
53⅜	11⅜	11⅜	5⅞	5⅞	1⅞	1⅞	8⅜	7⅞	M	Kitimat, B.C.	Fred Hahn	Fred Hahn	1966	19
53⅜	11⅜	11⅜	5⅝	5⅝	2	2	9⅜	8⅜	M	Cassiar Mts., B.C.	William Rohlfs	William Rohlfs	1971	19
53⅜	10⅞	10⅜	6⅜	6⅜	2	2	7	5⅜	M	Mt. Horetzky, B.C.	Jackie O. Arnold	Jackie O. Arnold	1980	19
53⅜	11⅜	11⅞	5⅞	5⅞	2	2	8⅞	7⅞	M	Cassiar Mts., B.C.	W. Reuen Fisher	W. Reuen Fisher	1945	25
53⅜	10⅞	11	5⅞	5⅞	2	2	6⅝	5⅝	M	Ketchikan, Alaska	Charles E. Slajer	Charles E. Slajer	1966	25
53⅜	11	11	5⅞	5⅞	1⅜	1⅜	7⅞	7⅞	M	Mt. Findlay, B.C.	Glenn Welsh	Glenn Welsh	1971	25
53⅜	10⅜	11⅜	6⅜	6⅜	1⅝	1⅞	7	6⅜	M	Halfmoon Lake, Alaska	Robert A. Hewitt	Robert A. Hewitt	1980	25
53	11⅜	11⅜	5⅝	5⅝	1⅞	1⅞	8⅜	8	M	Skagway, Alaska	Charles R. Heath	Charles R. Heath	1965	29
53	10⅜	10	5⅝	5⅝	2	2	8⅝	6⅝	M	Skeena-Copper Rivers, B.C.	John A. Paetkau	John W. Kroeker	1967	29

Score									M	Locality	By whom killed	Owner	Date	Rank
53	9⅞	10	6⅞	6⅞	2	2	8⅞	8⅞	M	Cassiar Mts., B.C.	Jack Thorndike	Jack Thorndike	1970	29
53	11⅛	10⅛	6	6	2	2	6⅝	4⅞	M	Aaron Mt., Alaska	John Sturgeon	John Sturgeon	1973	29
53	10⅛	10⅛	6	6	2	2	8⅜	8⅜	M	Homer, Alaska	Robert W. Hertz, Jr.	Robert W. Hertz, Jr.	1974	29
52⅞	11⅛	11⅛	5⅝	5⅝	1⅞	1⅞	7⅜	7⅜	M	Idaho Co., Idaho	Farrell M. Trenary	Farrel M. Trenary	1933	34
52⅞	11	11	5⅞	5⅞	1⅞	1⅞	8⅝	8⅛	M	Kootenay, B.C.	Jules V. Lane	A. C. Gilbert	1935	34
52⅞	11⅛	11⅛	5⅝	5⅝	1⅝	1⅝	7⅞	7⅞	M	Whatcom Co., Wash.	Arie Vander Hoek, Jr.	Arie Vander Hoek, Jr.	1966	34
52⅞	10⅛	10⅛	5⅞	5⅞	2⅛	2⅛	6⅝	5⅝	M	Cold Fish Lake, B.C.	Stanley W. Glasscock	Stanley W. Glasscock	1967	34
52⅞	11⅛	11⅛	5⅝	5⅝	2	2	5⅝	5⅝	M	Vernon, B.C.	Robert B. Procter	Robert B. Procter	1968	34
52⅞	10⅛	10⅛	5⅞	5⅞	2⅛	2⅛	8⅛	8⅜	M	Ashnola Valley, B.C.	Brian Chipperfield	Brian Chipperfield	1968	34
52⅞	10⅛	10⅛	6	6	2	2	7	7	M	Terrace, B.C.	R. P. Kolterman	R. P. Kolterman	1971	34
52⅞	10⅜	10⅜	5⅝	5⅝	2	2	8⅜	8⅜	M	Cassiar Mts., B.C.	H. Scott Whyel	H. Scott Whyel	1981	34
52⅞	10⅛	10⅛	5⅝	5⅝	2⅛	2⅛	7⅛	6⅝	M	Reflection Lake, Alaska	Timothy F. McGinn	Timothy F. McGinn	1985	34
52⅜	10⅛	10⅜	5⅝	5⅞	2	2	7⅞	7⅞	M	Okanogan Co., Wash.	Richard Shatto	Richard Shatto	1962	43
52⅜	11	11	5⅞	5⅞	1⅞	1⅞	8⅞	8⅞	M	Terminus Mt., B.C.	Herb Klein	Herb Klein	1965	43
52⅜	10⅛	10⅛	5⅞	5⅞	2	2	6⅞	6⅞	M	Colt Lake, B.C.	George P. Jackson, Jr.	George P. Jackson, Jr.	1965	43
52⅜	11⅜	11⅜	5⅝	5⅝	1⅞	1⅞	6	6	M	Whatcom Co., Wash.	John W. Bullene	John W. Bullene	1965	43
52⅜	10⅛	10⅛	5⅜	5⅜	2	1⅞	7	7	M	Sheep Creek, Wash.	R. C. Dukart	R. C. Dukart	1967	43
52⅜	10⅛	10	5⅝	5⅞	2	2	10¼	10	M	Cassiar, B.C.	Otto Machek	Otto Machek	1968	43
52⅜	10⅛	10⅜	5⅞	5⅞	2⅛	2⅛	7⅞	7⅞	M	Spectrum Range, B.C.	Kelly Good	Kelly Good	1973	43
52⅜	10	10⅝	6	6	2	2	8⅜	7⅜	M	Rock Island Lake, B.C.	Joe E. Coleman	Joe E. Coleman	1976	43
52⅜	9⅞	10⅜	5⅞	5⅝	2⅛	2⅛	7⅝	7⅝	M	Skeena Mts., B.C.	Hardy Murr	Hardy Murr	1977	43
52⅜	11	11⅛	6	6	2	2	8⅜	8	M	Taku River, B.C.	Fritz Stork	Fritz Stork	1985	43
52¼	10⅛	11⅛	5⅝	5⅝	1⅞	1⅞	8	8	M	Swan Lake, B.C.	A. C. Gilbert	A. C. Gilbert	1938	53
52¼	10⅛	10⅜	5⅝	5⅝	1⅞	1⅞	6	6	M	Cassiar, B.C.	Frank H. Schramm	Frank H. Schramm	1947	53
52¼	10⅛	10⅜	5⅝	5⅝	1⅞	1⅞	6⅝	7⅛	M	Hastings Arm, B.C.	Ernest Dietschi	Ernest Dietschi	1963	53
52¼	10⅝	10⅜	5⅞	5⅝	2	2	7⅞	8⅛	M	Copper River, Alaska	Fritz Maier	Fritz Maier	1964	53
52¼	10⅜	10⅜	5⅝	5⅝	1⅞	1⅞	6	5⅜	M	Bella Bella, B.C.	William B. Chivers	William B. Chivers	1965	53
52¼	11	11⅛	5⅝	5⅝	1⅞	1⅞	7⅛	7⅛	M	Boca De Quadra, Alaska	Doug Vann	Doug Vann	1968	53
52¼	10⅜	10⅜	5⅜	5⅜	2	2	8	8	M	Boca De Quadra, Alaska	Dan Hook	Dan Hook	1968	53
52¼	10⅜	10⅜	5⅝	5⅝	2	2	8⅜	7⅜	M	Seward, Alaska	Donald R. Platt, Sr.	Donald R. Platt, Sr.	1969	53
52¼	10⅝	10⅜	5⅝	5⅝	1⅞	1⅞	7⅜	7⅜	M	Whatcom Co., Wash.	Al Hershey	Al Hershey	1969	53
52¼	10⅛	10⅛	6⅛	6	1⅞	1⅞	8	8	M	Cassiar Mts., B.C.	Peter Fenchak	Peter Fenchak	1970	53
52¼	11	11⅛	5⅝	5⅝	1⅞	1⅞	5⅜	5⅛	M	Mt. Cronin, B.C.	Vinko Strgar	Vinko Strgar	1972	53
52¼	10⅝	10⅜	5⅝	5⅝	1⅞	1⅞	6⅛	6⅛	M	Chelan Co., Wash.	John W. Lane	John W. Lane	1973	53
52¼	10⅜	10⅜	5⅝	5⅜	1⅝	1⅞	8⅜	8⅜	M	Kutcho Creek, B.C.	J. C. Page	J. C. Page	1975	53
52¼	10⅛	10⅛	5¾	5½	1⅝	1⅝	8⅜	8⅜	M	Cold Fish Lake, B.C.	Larry Bonetti	Larry Bonetti	1975	53
52¼	10⅛	10⅜	5⅞	6	1⅞	2	9⅞	9⅞	M	Chelan Co., Wash.	Thomas A. Lovas	Thomas A. Lovas	1976	53
52¼	10	10	6	5⅞	2	1⅞	6⅞	6⅞	M	Chelan Co., Wash.	Nat Steele	Nat Steele	1980	53
52¼	10⅜	10⅜	5⅝	5⅝	2	2	7	7	M	Lewis & Clark Co., Mont.	Charles N. Johns	Charles N. Johns	1981	53
52¼	10⅛	10⅛	6⅛	6⅛	2	2	7⅜	7⅜	M	Sheslay River, B.C.	Frank L. Stukel	Frank L. Stukel	1984	53
52	10⅝	10⅝	6⅛	6⅛	2	2	8⅜	8⅜	M	Cassiar, B.C.	Walter R. Peterson	Walter R. Peterson	1937	71
52	10⅛	10⅝	5⅝	5⅞	2	2	9	9	M	Tweedsmuir Park, B.C.	Chester G. Moore	Chester G. Moore	1946	71

Rocky Mountain Goat—Continued

Oreamnos americanus americanus and related subspecies

Score	Length of Horn		Circumference of Base		Circumference at Third Quarter		Greatest Spread	Tip to Tip Spread	Sex	Locality Killed	By Whom Killed	Owner	Date Killed	Rank
	R.	L.	R.	L.	R.	L.								
52	10⅜	10⅜	5⅜	5⅝	2	2⅛	6⅝	4⅝	M	Jumbo Mt., Wash.	Clyde Lewis	Clyde Lewis	1948	71
52	10⅞	11	5⅜	5⅜	1⅞	1⅞	7⅛	6⅝	M	Watson Peak, Alaska	Harold M. Wright	Harold M. Wright	1957	71
52	10⅝	10⅜	5⅝	5⅜	2	2	6⅛	6⅜	M	Idaho Co., Idaho	Charlie T. Knox	Charlie T. Knox	1959	71
52	10⅜	11	5⅝	6	2⅛	2⅛	8⅝	8⅜	M	Bulkley Range, B.C.	Ingvar Wickstrom	Ingvar Wickstrom	1960	71
52	10⅜	10⅜	5⅝	6	2	1⅞	7⅞	7⅜	M	Mission Ridge, B.C.	B. Naimark	B. Naimark	1960	71
52	10⅜	10⅜	5⅝	5⅞	1⅞	1⅞	7⅞	6⅛	M	Kootenay River, B.C.	Howard Paish	Howard Paish	1961	71
52	11⅜	11⅜	5⅜	5⅝	2	2	7	4⅝	M	Boca De Quadra, Alaska	James Todahl	James Todahl	1962	71
52	10	10	6	6	2	2	7⅜	7	M	Sundial Lake, Alaska	Arnold W. Johnson	Arnold W. Johnson	1962	71
52	10⅜	10⅜	5⅞	5⅞	2⅛	2	7⅜	7⅛	M	Coquihalla, B.C.	Fred D. Fouty	Fred D. Fouty	1962	71
52	10⅜	10⅜	5⅝	5⅝	2	2	9⅛	7⅞	M	Skeena River, B.C.	R. H. Simonds	R. H. Simonds	1963	71
52	9⅞	10	5⅝	5⅝	2⅛	2⅛	8	7⅝	M	Hart Mt., B.C.	Donna Loewenstein	Donna Loewenstein	1965	71
52	10⅜	10⅜	6	6⅛	1⅞	1⅞	7⅜	6	M	Kitsumgallum Lake, B.C.	Manfred Beier	Manfred Beier	1965	71
52	10⅜	10⅜	5⅝	5⅜	2	2	6⅜	5⅝	M	Southgate River, B.C.	R. T. Ostby	R. T. Ostby	1966	71
52	10⅜	10⅜	6⅛	6⅛	2	2	6⅛	5⅜	M	Okanogan Co., Wash.	E. W. Butler	E. W. Butler	1967	71
52	10⅜	10⅜	5⅜	5⅜	1⅞	1⅞	9⅝	9⅜	M	Auke Bay, Alaska	Kenneth L. Klawunder	Kenneth L. Klawunder	1968	71
52	9⅞	9⅜	5⅝	5⅝	2	2	7⅜	7	M	Skagit Co., Wash.	John C. Casebeer	John C. Casebeer	1970	71
52	9⅝	9⅜	5⅞	5⅝	2⅛	2⅛	7	5⅞	M	Skeena Mts., B.C.	William F. Jury	William F. Jury	1971	71
52	10⅜	10⅜	5⅝	5⅝	2⅛	2⅛	8⅝	8	M	Camp Island Lake, B.C.	C. N. Hoffman	C. N. Hoffman	1971	71
52	10⅜	10⅜	6	6⅛	1⅞	2	7	6⅜	M	Chelan Co., Wash.	Robert A. Beckton	Robert A. Beckton	1971	71
52	11	10⅜	6⅛	6	1⅝	2	8⅜	7⅞	M	Kispiox Range, B.C.	John W. Allen	John W. Allen	1974	71
52	10⅜	10⅜	6	6	2⅛	2	7	5⅝	M	Whatcom Co., Wash.	George W. Bowen	George W. Bowen	1978	71
52	10⅜	10⅜	5⅝	5⅝	2	2	7	6⅜	M	Elko Co., Nev.	Les Boni	Les Boni	1978	71
52	10⅜	10⅜	6⅝	6⅝	1⅝	1⅞	6⅜	5⅝	M	Mt. Saint Elias, Alaska	Terry L. Friske	Terry L. Friske	1980	71
52	12⅛	11⅜	5⅜	5⅜	1⅞	1⅞	8⅛	7⅝	M	Horn Cliffs, Alaska	Jack W. McKernan	Jack W. McKernan	1981	71
52	10⅜	10⅜	5⅝	5⅝	2	2	8⅛	7⅜	M	Burnie Lake, B.C.	Paul R. Levan	Paul R. Levan	1983	71
51⅞	10⅜	10⅜	5⅝	5⅝	2	2	8⅜	8⅜	M	Telegraph Creek, B.C.	John S. McCormick, Jr.	John S. McCormick, Jr.	1936	98
51⅞	10⅜	10⅜	5⅝	5⅝	1⅞	2	7⅝	7⅜	M	Mile 402, Alaska Hwy., Alaska	E. J. Blumenshine	E. J. Blumenshine	1948	98
51⅞	10⅜	10⅜	6⅛	6⅛	1⅞	1⅞	6⅜	6⅝	M	Lake Co., Mont.	Glenn Conklin	Glenn Conklin	1958	98
51⅞	10⅜	10⅜	5⅜	5⅝	2	2	8⅜	8⅜	M	Wolf Creek, Mont.	Jim B. Beard	Jim B. Beard	1963	98
51⅞	10⅜	10⅜	5⅝	5⅜	1⅞	1⅞	9⅜	9⅛	U	Atlin, B.C.	Bill Slikker	Bill Slikker	1965	98
51⅞	10⅜	10	5⅝	5⅝	2	2	7⅞	7	M	Telegraph Creek, B.C.	John Caputo, Sr.	John Caputo, Sr.	1965	98

									Locality	Owner	Hunter	Year	
51⅝	11⅜	11	5⅞	5⅝	1⅞	1⅞	7⅞	M	Flathead Co., Mont.	John J. Allmaras	John J. Allmaras	1965	98
51⅝	11⅜	12	5⅛	5⅛	1⅞	1⅞	13	F	Cassiar Mts., B.C.	Bruce N. Spencer	Bruce N. Spencer	1966	98
51⅝	10⅞	10⅞	5⅝	5⅝	2	1⅞	7⅝	M	Kildala River, B.C.	Lorne Hallman	Lorne Hallman	1966	98
51⅝	10⅛	10	5⅞	5⅞	2	2	6⅞	M	Ecstall River, B.C.	W. A. Kristmanson	W. A. Kristmanson	1967	98
51⅝	10⅛	10⅜	5⅝	5⅝	1⅞	1⅞	7⅞	M	Copper-Skeena Rivers, B.C.	Henry Dyck	Henry Dyck	1967	98
51⅝	11⅜	11⅜	5⅝	5⅝	1⅞	1⅞	10	M	Clearwater Creek, B.C.	Stephen W. Cook	Stephen W. Cook	1968	98
51⅝	10⅜	10⅜	5⅜	5⅜	1⅞	1⅞	7⅞	M	Skeena-Exstew Rivers, B.C.	Frans Fait	Frans Fait	1968	98
51⅝	10⅜	10⅜	6⅛	6⅛	1⅞	1⅞	9⅜	M	Hobo Creek, B.C.	Roy K. Pysher	Roy K. Pysher	1968	98
51⅝	10⅞	10⅞	5⅝	5⅝	2	2	6⅞	M	The Pinnacles Mt., B.C.	Michael Bigford	Michael Bigford	1968	98
51⅝	10⅞	10⅛	5⅝	5⅝	1⅞	1⅞	8⅜	M	Wrangell Mts., Alaska	Basil C. Bradbury	Basil C. Bradbury	1968	98
51⅝	10⅜	10⅜	6	6	2	2	7	M	Turnagain River, B.C.	John R. Braun	John R. Braun	1968	98
51⅝	10⅜	10⅜	5⅞	5⅞	2	2	7⅝	M	Burns Lake, B.C.	Ellis Dee Skidmore	Ellis Dee Skidmore	1969	98
51⅝	10	10	5⅝	5⅝	1⅞	1⅞	6⅜	M	Bradfield River, Alaska	James M. Remza	James M. Remza	1970	98
51⅝	10⅞	10⅞	5⅝	5⅝	1⅞	1⅞	8⅞	M	Tongass Natl. For., Alaska	Roderick Martin	Roderick Martin	1970	98
51⅝	10⅜	10⅜	6⅛	6⅜	1⅞	1⅞	7⅞	M	Cassiar Mts., B.C.	Kenneth Campbell	Kenneth Campbell	1971	98
51⅝	10⅞	10⅞	5⅝	5⅝	2	2	7⅝	M	Cleveland Pen., Alaska	H. D. Costello	H. D. Costello	1973	98
51⅝	10⅞	10⅞	5⅜	5⅞	1⅞	1⅞	7⅞	M	Snohomish Co., Wash.	Des F. Hinds	Des F. Hinds	1974	98
51⅝	10⅜	10⅜	6	6	1⅞	1⅞	6	M	Mt. Allard, B.C.	David Brousseau	David Brousseau	1975	98
51⅝	11	11	5⅝	5⅝	2	2	7⅞	M	Ketchikan, Alaska	Donald K. Oldenburg	Donald K. Oldenburg	1977	98
51⅝	10⅝	10⅜	5⅝	5⅝	1⅞	1⅞	8⅜	M	Zymoetz River, B.C.	William E. Bond	William E. Bond	1978	98
51⅝	10⅜	10⅜	5⅝	5⅝	1⅞	1⅞	6⅝	M	Kaza Lake, B.C.	J. C. Priebe & W. A. Bolles	J. C. Priebe & W. A. Bolles	1980	98
51⅝	10⅜	10⅜	5⅝	5⅝	2	2	6⅜	M	Mt. Carthew, B.C.	Harry McCowan	Harry McCowan	1980	98
51⅝	10⅜	10⅜	5⅞	6	2	2	7⅞	M	Behm Canal, Alaska	Michael L. Ward	Michael L. Ward	1980	98
51⅝	9⅞	9⅞	5⅝	5⅝	2⅛	2⅛	6⅜	M	Snohomish Co., Wash.	John M. Mitchell	Michael J. Simon	1981	98
51⅝	10⅜	10⅜	5⅝	5⅝	2⅛	2⅛	6⅜	M	Tyee Lake, Alaska	Daniel G. Bowden	Daniel G. Bowden	1982	98
51⅝	10⅜	10⅜	5⅜	5⅜	2	2	7⅛	M	Leduc River, Alaska	Steve Lepschat	Steve Lepschat	1982	98
51⅝	10⅛	10⅜	5⅝	5⅝	2⅛	2⅛	6⅜	M	Lake Rowena, Alaska	George T. Law	George T. Law	1983	98
51⅝	9⅞	9⅞	6	6	1⅞	1⅞	7⅞	M	Bonneville Co., Idaho	K. Rands Wiley	K. Rands Wiley	1983	98
51⅝	10⅜	10⅜	5⅝	5⅝	2	2	6	M	Cleveland Pen., Alaska	Michael L. Ward	Michael L. Ward	1983	98
51⅝	10⅝	11⅜	5⅝	5⅝	1⅞	1⅞	7⅛	M	Snohomish Co., Wash.	Edward M. Beitner	Edward M. Beitner	1984	98
51⅝	11	11⅜	5⅝	5⅝	1⅞	1⅞	8⅜	M	Kootenay, B.C.	Herb Klein	Herb Klein	1946	134
51⅝	11⅜	11⅜	5⅜	5⅜	2	2	7⅜	M	Ella River, B.C.	Lee G. Smith	Lee G. Smith	1950	134
51⅝	10⅞	10	5⅝	5⅝	2	2	6	M	Cold Fish Lake, B.C.	Geo. W. Hooker	Geo W. Hooker	1956	134
51⅝	10	10	5⅝	5⅝	1⅞	1⅞	0	M	Jarvis Lake, B.C.	G. F. Juhl	G. F. Juhl	1960	134
51⅝	10⅜	10⅜	5⅝	5⅝	2	2	6⅜	M	Cleveland Pen., Alaska	Allen E. Linn	Allen E. Linn	1961	134
51⅝	10⅜	10⅞	5⅝	5⅜	1⅞	1⅞	6⅞	M	Boca De Quadra, Alaska	Charles E. Simmons	Charles E. Simmons	1961	134
51⅝	10	10	5⅝	5⅞	2	2	7	M	Cassiar, B.C.	Adolf Doerre	Adolf Doerre	1961	134
51⅝	10⅜	10⅜	5⅝	5⅝	1⅞	1⅞	9⅜	M	Cold Fish Lake, B.C.	Dan Edwards	Dan Edwards	1961	134
51⅝	10⅝	10⅞	5⅝	5⅝	1⅞	1⅞	7⅛	M	Kenai Pen., Alaska	Alan Olson	Alan Olson	1962	134
51⅝	9⅝	9⅝	5⅝	5⅝	1⅞	1⅞	7⅞	M	Chugach Mts., Alaska	Donald A. Turcke	Donald A. Turcke	1964	134

ROCKY MOUNTAIN GOAT—*Continued*

Oreamnos americanus americanus and related subspecies

Score	Length of Horn R.	L.	Circumference of Base R.	L.	Circumference at Third Quarter R.	L.	Greatest Spread	Tip to Tip Spread	Sex	Locality Killed	By Whom Killed	Owner	Date Killed	Rank
51⅞	11⅛	11⅜	5⅜	5⅜	1⅞	1⅞	6⅜	4⅛	M	Boca De Quadra, Alaska	Arthur N. Wilson, Jr.	Arthur N. Wilson, Jr.	1965	134
51⅞	10⅞	10⅞	5⅝	5⅝	1⅝	1⅞	8⅛	7⅞	M	Kechika Range, B.C.	W. C. Dabney, Jr.	W. C. Dabney, Jr.	1965	134
51⅞	10⅝	10⅝	5⅞	5⅞	1⅞	1⅞	6⅞	5⅝	M	Clearwater Creek, B.C.	Richard H. Leedy	Richard H. Leedy	1967	134
51⅞	10⅛	10⅞	6	6	2	1⅞	7⅞	6⅝	M	Coast Range, B.C.	S. Lantenhammer	S. Lantenhammer	1967	134
51⅞	10⅛	9⅞	5⅞	6⅛	1⅞	1⅞	7⅞	7⅝	M	Sheep Creek, Alta.	Russell A. Fischer	Russell A. Fischer	1967	134
51⅞	9⅝	9⅞	6	6	2	2	7⅞	6⅝	M	Toad River, B.C.	Bill Goosman	Bill Goosman	1970	134
51⅞	10⅜	10⅜	5⅝	6	2	2	8	7⅞	M	Bowen Lake, Alaska	Ted A. Dedmon	Ted A. Dedmon	1971	134
51⅞	10⅞	10⅞	5⅞	5⅝	1⅞	1⅞	8⅝	8	M	Terrace, B.C.	George A. Shaw	George A. Shaw	1972	134
51⅞	10⅜	10⅜	5⅝	5⅝	1⅞	1⅞	6⅝	5⅝	M	Stikine River, Alaska	Donald E. Fossen	Donald E. Fossen	1973	134
51⅞	11	10⅜	5⅞	5⅞	1⅞	1⅞	7⅞	6⅜	M	Ketchikan, Alaska	Kevin Downey	Kevin Downey	1973	134
51⅞	10⅜	10⅜	5⅞	5⅞	1⅞	1⅞	6⅞	7⅞	M	Chelan Co., Wash.	Virgil N. Carpenter	Virgil N. Carpenter	1973	134
51⅞	10⅜	10⅜	5⅝	5⅝	1⅞	1⅞	8⅝	5⅝	M	Mt. Edziza, B.C.	A. Coe Frankhauser	A. Coe Frankhauser	1974	134
51⅞	10⅞	10⅜	5⅞	6	2	2	7⅞	8⅝	M	Stikine Range, B.C.	L. A. Candelaria	L. A. Candelaria	1974	134
51⅞	9⅞	9⅞	5⅝	5⅞	1⅞	2⅛	9⅜	7⅝	M	Pine Lake, B.C.	Charles H. Duke, Jr.	Charles H. Duke, Jr.	1975	134
51⅞	10⅜	10⅜	5⅝	5⅝	1⅞	1⅞	8⅛	8⅛	M	Bulkley Mts., B.C.	Gordon Hannas	Gordon Hannas	1976	134
51⅞	10⅜	10⅜	5⅝	5⅝	2⅛	2⅛	8⅞	8⅝	M	Kodiak Island, Alaska	Ron Eller	Ron Eller	1978	134
51⅞	9⅞	9⅞	5⅝	5⅝	1⅞	1⅞	8⅝	8⅛	M	Telegraph Creek, B.C.	Casey G. Terry	Casey G. Terry	1979	134
51⅞	10⅜	10⅛	6	6	2	2	8⅛	7⅝	M	Montana	Unknown	James Fredrick	PR1981	134
51⅞	10⅛	10⅛	6⅛	6⅛	1⅞	1⅞	7⅞	6⅝	M	Halfmoon Lake, Alaska	Kurt W. Kuehl	Kurt W. Kuehl	1982	134
51⅞	10⅜	10⅜	5⅞	5⅝	1⅞	1⅞	6⅞	6⅝	M	Chouteau Co., Mont.	Larry W. Lander	Larry W. Lander	1983	134
51⅞	10⅜	10⅜	5⅝	5⅝	1⅞	1⅞	7⅞	7⅛	M	Snohomish Co., Wash.	Theadore H. Kiser	Theadore H. Kiser	1985	134
51⅞	10⅞	10⅞	5⅜	5⅝	1⅞	1⅝	8⅛	7⅝	M	Kootenay, B.C.	Teddy MacLachlan	W. K. Porter	1925	165
51⅞	10⅜	10⅞	6	6	1⅝	1⅞	7⅞	7⅝	M	Hard Scrabble Pass, Alta.	Justus von Lengerke	Justus von Lengerke	1937	165
51⅞	10⅜	10⅛	5⅝	5⅝	2	2	8⅞	8⅛	M	Katalla, Alaska	John Goeres	John Goeres	1943	165
51⅞	10	10	6⅛	6⅛	2	2	6⅞	6	M	Mt. Robson, B.C.	E. T. Reilly	E. T. Reilly	1948	165
51⅞	10⅞	10⅞	5⅝	5⅝	1⅝	1⅝	8⅞	8⅜	M	Cassiar, B.C.	Elmer E. Rasmuson	Elmer E. Rasmuson	1952	165
51⅞	10⅞	10⅞	5⅝	5⅝	1⅞	1⅞	7⅞	6⅞	M	Bulkley Range, B.C.	Mrs. Billie Gardiner	Mrs. Billie Gardiner	1959	165
51⅞	9⅞	9⅞	5⅞	5⅞	2	2	7⅝	7	M	Gataga River, B.C.	Robert C. McAtee	Robert C. McAtee	1965	165
51⅞	10	10	6	6	1⅞	1⅞	7⅞	7⅝	M	Kechika Range, B.C.	Paul A. Bagalio	Paul A. Bagalio	1965	165
51⅞	9⅜	9⅜	6⅛	6⅛	2⅜	2⅛	7⅞	7⅝	U	Anchorage, Alaska	Wade Charles	Wade Charles	1966	165
51⅞	10⅜	10⅜	5⅝	5⅝	2	2	8⅜	8⅛	M	Atlin, B.C.	Nolan Martins	Nolan Martins	1967	165
51⅞	9⅞	10	5⅝	5⅝	2	2	7⅞	6⅞	M	Atlin Lake, B.C.	Walter O. Johnston	Walter O. Johnston	1968	165

Score	Length of Horn R	Length of Horn L	Circ. of Base R	Circ. of Base L	Circ. at Quarter R	Circ. at Quarter L	Greatest Spread	Tip to Tip	Hunter	Sex	Locality	Owner	Date Killed	Rank
51⅞	10⅛	10⅛	5⅞	5⅞	1⅞	1⅞	7⅞	6⅞	Tracy Skead	M	Vetter Peak, B.C.	Tracy Skead	1969	165
51⅞	10¼	10¼	5⅞	5⅞	2	2	6⅞	5⅞	W. A. McKay	M	Kechika Range, B.C.	W. A. McKay	1970	165
51⅞	10¼	10⅛	5⅜	5⅜	2¼	2⅛	8⅜	8⅜	John E. Meyers	M	Wrangell Mts., Alaska	John E. Meyers	1971	165
51⅞	10¼	10⅛	5⅞	5⅞	1⅞	1⅞	8⅜	8⅜	Michael A. Wright	M	Skeena Mts., B.C.	Michael A. Wright	1972	165
51⅞	10⅜	10⅜	5⅞	5⅞	1⅞	1⅞	7⅜	6⅞	Douglas V. Turner	M	Tsetia Creek, B.C.	Douglas V. Turner	1973	165
51⅞	10¼	10½	6	6	2	2	6⅞	5⅞	William R. Stevens	M	Pend Oreille Co., Wash.	William R. Stevens	1975	165
51⅞	10¼	10¼	5⅞	5⅞	1⅞	1⅞	7⅜	6⅞	Lorraine Ravary	M	Idaho Co., Idaho	Lorraine Ravary	1978	165
51⅞	10⅜	10⅜	5⅝	5⅝	1⅞	1⅞	10⅛	10	James K. Montgomery	M	Marker Lake, Yukon	James K. Montgomery	1978	165
51⅞	10⅛	10	5⅞	5⅞	2	2	7⅛	6⅞	George Fitchett	M	Morice Lake, B.C.	G. Fitchett & L. Austin	1978	165
51⅞	10⅜	10⅜	5⅞	5⅞	2	2	8⅜	8⅜	Michael W. Duby	M	Kittitas Co., Wash.	Michael W. Duby	1980	165
51⅞	10⅜	10⅜	5⅞	5⅞	1⅞	1⅞	7⅜	7⅜	Terry L. Friske	M	Chilkat Mt., Alaska	Terry L. Friske	1980	165
51⅞	9⅞	9⅞	6⅛	6⅛	1⅞	1⅞	8¼	8¼	John Dobish	M	Swan Lake, B.C.	John Dobish	1981	165
51⅞	10⅛	10⅛	5⅞	5⅞	2	2	7	7	T. J. Tucker	M	Duti Lake, B.C.	T. J. Tucker	1981	165
51⅞	10⅛	10⅛	5⅞	5⅞	1⅞	1⅞	6⅞	6⅞	Richard D. Grant	M	Okanogan Co., Wash.	Richard D. Grant	1982	165
51⅞	10⅛	10	5⅞	5⅞	2	2	8⅜	8⅜	Kirk Z. Smith	F	Glenallen, Alaska	Kirk Z. Smith	1982	165
51⅞	10½	10⅛	6	6	1⅞	1⅞	7¼	7¼	Duane Pankratz	M	Kaustua Creek, B.C.	Duane Pankratz	1982	165
51⅞	10	10	5⅞	5⅞	2⅛	2⅛	5⅞	5⅞	David L. Bowden	M	Tyee Lake, Alaska	David L. Bowden	1982	165
51⅞	9⅞	9⅞	5⅞	5⅞	2¼	2	7⅜	7⅜	Charles W. Schmidt	M	Taku River, B.C.	Charles W. Schmidt	1985	165
51	9⅞	10	5⅞	5⅞	2	2	8⅜	8⅜	Warren Bodeker	M	Morice River, B.C.	Warren Bodeker	1958	194
51	9⅞	9⅞	5⅝	5⅝	2⅛	2⅛	6⅞	6⅞	Peter W. Bading	M	Resurrection Bay, Alaska	Peter W. Bading	1961	194
51	11	10⅛	5⅞	5⅞	1⅞	1⅞	7⅜	7⅜	John Strban	M	Smithers, B.C.	John Strban	1962	194
51	9⅞	9⅞	5⅜	5⅜	2⅛	2⅛	5⅞	5⅞	Gerald Prosser	M	Terrace, B.C.	Gerald Prosser	1962	194
51	10⅛	10⅛	5⅞	5⅞	1⅞	1⅞	7⅛	7⅛	Norbert M. Welch	M	Kootenay Range, B.C.	Norbert M. Welch	1963	194
51	10⅜	10⅜	5⅜	5⅜	2	2	7⅛	7⅝	Reuben C. Carlson	M	Butte Inlet, B.C.	Reuben C. Carlson	1963	194
51	10	10	5⅞	5⅞	2	2	7⅛	7⅛	W. M. Rudd	M	Dease Lake, B.C.	W. M. Rudd	1964	194
51	10⅛	10⅛	5⅞	5⅞	1⅞	1⅞	6⅜	6⅜	Johnny Powell	M	Flathead Co., Mont.	Johnny Powell	1965	194
51	10⅛	10⅛	5⅜	5⅜	1⅞	1⅞	7⅛	7⅛	John Caputo, Jr.	M	Telegraph Creek, B.C.	John Caputo, Jr.	1965	194
51	10⅛	10⅛	5⅞	5⅞	1⅞	1⅞	7⅛	7⅛	Donald W. Moody	M	Alaska Panhandle, Alaska	Donald W. Moody	1966	194
51	10⅛	10⅛	5⅞	5⅞	2	2	8	8	George McCullough	M	Telegraph Creek, B.C.	George McCullough	1967	194
51	9⅞	9⅞	5⅞	5⅞	2	2	9⅜	9⅜	Gary Townsend	M	Terrace, B.C.	Gary Townsend	1967	194
51	10⅛	10⅛	5⅞	6	1⅞	1⅞	7⅜	7⅜	Marvin F. Lawrence	M	Hart Mt., B.C.	Marvin F. Lawrence	1967	194
51	10⅛	10⅛	5⅞	5⅞	1⅞	1⅞	8⅜	8⅜	Earl Dawson	M	Okanagan, B.C.	Earl Dawson	1967	194
51	10⅛	10⅛	5⅞	5⅞	1⅞	1⅞	7⅜	7⅜	George Hanschen	M	Tete Jaune, B.C.	George Hanschen	1968	194
51	9⅞	9⅞	6	6	1⅞	1⅞	5⅜	5⅜	Ervin Voelk	M	McBride, B.C.	Ervin Voelk	1968	194
51	10⅛	10⅛	5⅞	5⅞	1⅞	1⅞	7⅜	7⅜	Curt Henning	M	Nuka Bay, Alaska	Curt Henning	1969	194
51	10⅜	10⅜	5⅞	5⅞	1⅞	1⅞	8⅜	8⅜	Helmut Krieger	M	Lillooet, B.C.	Helmut Krieger	1971	194
51	10	9⅞	5⅞	5⅞	2⅛	2⅛	6⅝	6⅝	Robert Sinko	M	Yakutat, Alaska	Robert Sinko	1972	194
51	10⅛	10⅛	5⅝	5⅝	2	2	6⅝	6⅝	David T. Lewis	M	Snohomish Co., Wash.	David T. Lewis	1978	194
51	10⅜	10⅜	6	6	1⅞	1⅞	8	8	Sharon Robey	M	Findlay Creek, B.C.	Sharon Robey	1979	194
51	10⅛	10⅛	5⅞	5⅞	1⅞	1⅞	0	0	John K. Frederikson	M	Ravalli Co., Mont.	John K. Frederikson	1981	194
51	10⅛	10⅜	5⅞	5⅞	1⅞	1⅞	7⅝	7⅝	Vernon J. Boose	M	Tahtsa Lake, B.C.	Vernon J. Boose	1982	194
51	10⅛	10⅛	5⅞	5⅞	1⅞	1⅞	7⅜	7⅜	John W. Lane	M	Snohomish Co., Wash.	John W. Lane	1982	194
51	9⅞	9⅞	5⅞	5⅞	1⅞	1⅞	6	6	Gerry D. Downey	M	Granite Basin, Alaska	Gerry D. Downey	1983	194

Rocky Mountain Goat—*Continued*

Oreamnos americanus americanus and related subspecies

Score	Length of Horn R.	L.	Circumference of Base R.	L.	Circumference at Third Quarter R.	L.	Greatest Spread	Tip to Tip Spread	Sex	Locality Killed	By Whom Killed	Owner	Date Killed	Rank
51	10⅛	10⅜	5⅜	5⅜	1⅞	1⅞	6⅛	5⅞	M	Gallatin Co., Mont.	Ronald K. Lewis	Ronald K. Lewis	1984	194
51	10⅛	10⅜	5⅜	5⅜	1⅞	1⅞	7⅜	6⅞	M	Sheslay River, B.C.	Steven M. Sullivan	Steven M. Sullivan	1985	194
50⅞	10⅛	10⅜	5⅝	5⅞	1⅞	2	7⅛	6⅞	M	Cassiar, B.C.	Wm. N. Beach	Wm. N. Beach	1918	221
50⅞	10⅞	11⅛	5⅞	5⅞	1⅝	1⅞	9	8⅝	M	Cassiar, B.C.	Clement B. Newbold	Clement B. Newbold	1926	221
50⅞	11	11⅛	5⅞	5⅞	1⅞	1⅞	5⅞	4⅜	U	Flathead Co., Mont.	Picked Up	Charlie Shaw	1936	221
50⅞	9⅞	9⅞	5⅞	5⅞	2⅛	2⅛	7⅞	7⅞	M	Similkameen, B.C.	Peter Braun	John D. Rempel	1939	221
50⅞	10⅛	10⅞	5⅞	5⅞	2	2	8⅜	7⅞	M	Cassiar, B.C.	Peter Schramm	Peter Schramm	1950	221
50⅞	10⅜	10⅜	5⅜	5⅞	1⅞	1⅞	6⅞	6⅞	M	Cordova, Alaska	Ralph E. Renner	Ralph E. Renner	1950	221
50⅞	10⅜	11⅛	5⅞	5⅞	1⅝	1⅞	9⅛	8	M	Telegraph Creek, B.C.	Wayne C. Eubank	Wayne C. Eubank	1953	221
50⅞	9⅞	9⅞	5⅞	5⅞	1⅞	1⅞	7⅞	7⅜	M	Telegraph Creek, B.C.	A. J. Duany	A. J. Duany	1954	221
50⅞	9⅞	10⅛	5⅞	5⅞	2⅛	1⅞	8	7⅜	M	Knik River, Alaska	C. M. Van Meter	C. M. Van Meter	1956	221
50⅞	10⅛	10⅜	5⅞	5⅞	2	2	7⅞	5⅞	M	Boca De Quadra Inlet, Alaska	Lyman Reynoldson	Lyman Reynoldson	1957	221
50⅞	9⅞	9⅞	6	6	2	2	7⅞	5⅞	M	Maxan Lake, B.C.	K. J. Nysven	K. J. Nysven	1961	221
50⅞	10⅛	10⅜	5⅞	5⅞	2	2	8⅜	7⅞	M	Kenai Pen., Alaska	Elgin T. Gates	Elgin T. Gates	1961	221
50⅞	10⅞	10	6	6	2	1⅞	7⅞	6⅞	M	Cold Fish Lake, B.C.	Howard Boazman	Howard Boazman	1962	221
50⅞	9⅞	9⅞	5⅞	6	1⅞	2	6⅛	5⅞	M	Keremeos, B.C.	Bill Postill	Bill Postill	1963	221
50⅞	10⅛	10⅜	5⅞	5⅞	1⅞	1⅞	9⅜	8⅜	M	Gataga River, B.C.	Herb Klein	Herb Klein	1963	221
50⅞	10	9⅞	6	6	2⅛	2⅛	9⅜	8⅞	M	Atlin, B.C.	G. Vernon Boggs	G. Vernon Boggs	1964	221
50⅞	9⅞	9⅞	5⅞	5⅞	1⅞	1⅞	8⅞	8⅛	M	Klappan Range, B.C.	Larry P. Miller	Larry P. Miller	1965	221
50⅞	9⅞	9⅞	6⅛	6⅛	1⅞	2	6⅞	6⅜	M	Hedley, B.C.	Donald J. Robb	Donald J. Robb	1965	221
50⅞	10⅞	10⅞	6⅛	6⅛	1⅜	1⅞	6	5⅞	M	Mt. Antero, Colo.	Leroy C. Wood	Leroy C. Wood	1965	221
50⅞	10⅜	10⅜	5⅜	5⅞	2⅛	2⅛	8	7⅞	M	Cold Fish Lake, B.C.	Armin Baltensweiler	Armin Baltensweiler	1965	221
50⅞	9⅞	9⅞	5⅞	5⅞	1⅞	1⅞	6⅝	6	M	Kechika Range, B.C.	Basil C. Bradbury	Basil C. Bradbury	1965	221
50⅞	10⅞	10⅛	5⅞	5⅞	1⅞	2	7⅞	7⅞	M	Cassiar Mts., B.C.	Ernest Granum	Ernest Granum	1965	221
50⅞	9⅞	9⅞	5⅞	5⅞	2⅛	2⅛	8⅜	8⅜	M	Toad River, B.C.	Walt Paulk	Walt Paulk	1966	221
50⅞	10⅞	10⅞	5⅞	5⅞	1⅞	1⅞	8⅜	6⅞	U	Horsethief Creek, B.C.	Bill Pitt	Bill Pitt	1966	221
50⅞	10⅛	10⅛	5⅜	5⅜	1⅞	2	7⅝	7⅜	M	Ashnola River, B.C.	Robert C. Bateson	Robert C. Bateson	1966	221
50⅞	10⅜	10⅛	5⅜	5⅜	1⅞	1⅞	6⅞	5⅞	M	Skeena River, B.C.	G. Best	G. Best	1966	221
50⅞	10⅜	10⅜	5⅞	5⅞	1⅞	1⅞	6⅞	5⅜	M	Black Hills, S.D.	Lloyd Weaver	Lloyd Weaver	1967	221
50⅞	10⅜	10⅜	5⅞	5⅞	1⅞	2	7⅞	7⅞	M	Kenai Mts., Alaska	Stephen D. LaBelle	Stephen D. LaBelle	1971	221
50⅞	9⅞	9⅞	5⅞	5⅞	2	2⅜	7⅜	7⅛	M	Dease Lake, B.C.	John H. Epp	John H. Epp	1972	221

400

50⅝	10⅛	9⅞	5⅝	2	2	8⅝	8⅝	M	Kechika River, B.C.	Dennis Laabs	Dennis Laabs	1973	221
50⅝	10⅞	10⅞	5⅝	1⅞	1⅞	8⅝	8⅝	M	Chelan Co., Wash.	Raymond J. Hammer	Raymond J. Hammer	1973	221
50⅝	10⅛	10	5⅞	1⅞	1⅞	7⅞	7⅞	M	Kenai Pen., Alaska	Jack Allen	Jack Allen	1974	221
50⅛	10	8⅞	6⅛	2⅛	2⅛	7⅞	6⅞	M	Cassiar Mts., B.C.	Kenneth E. Bishop	Kenneth E. Bishop	1979	221
50⅝	10⅜	10½	5⅝	1⅞	1⅞	7⅞	7⅞	M	Johnston Lake, B.C.	Brian A. Halina	Brian A. Halina	1979	221
50⅝	10⅜	10½	5⅞	1⅞	1⅞	7⅛	6⅞	M	Dutch Creek, B.C.	Tom Housh	Tom Housh	1982	221
50⅝	10⅜	10⅜	5⅝	2	2	7⅞	7	M	Stewart, B.C.	Harry J. McCowan	Harry J. McCowan	1983	221
50⅝	10⅜	10⅜	5⅝	1⅞	1⅞	9⅝	9⅝	M	Day Harbor, Alaska	Steen Henriksen	Steen Henriksen	1984	221
50⅝	10	10	5⅞	1⅞	1⅞	7⅝	7⅝	M	Okanogan Co., Wash.	Jerrel R. Harmon	Jerrel R. Harmon	1984	221
50⅝	11⅜	11⅞	5⅝	1⅝	1⅝	7⅞	7	M	Beaverfoot Range, B.C.	Kelley Knight	Kelley Knight	1984	221
50⅝	10	10	5⅞	1⅞	1⅞	6⅝	6⅝	M	Okanogan Co., Wash.	Susan M. Fletcher	Susan M. Fletcher	1985	221
50⅛	11	10⅞	6	2	1⅞	7⅜	7⅛	M	Little Oliver Creek, B.C.	David J. Flemming	David J. Flemming	1985	221
50⅝	12⅛	12⅞	4⅞	1⅞	1⅞	7⅜	7	F	Cassiar, B.C.	A. Bryan Williams	Mrs. N. S. Gooch	PR1916	262
50⅝	10⅛	10⅜	5⅝	2	1⅞	7⅞	7⅝	M	Cassiar, B.C.	George E. Burghard	George E. Burghard	1925	262
50⅝	10⅛	10⅜	5⅝	1⅞	1⅞	7⅝	7	M	Telegraph Creek, B.C.	John S. McCormick, Jr.	John S. McCormick, Jr.	1936	262
50⅝	11⅛	11⅛	5	2	2	7⅛	7⅝	M	Brazeau River, Alta.	Walter B. McClurkan	Walter B. McClurkan	1942	262
50⅛	10⅛	10⅛	5⅝	2	2	7	7	M	Stikine River, Alaska	W. F. Littleton	W. F. Littleton	1953	262
50⅝	10⅛	9⅞	5⅝	1⅞	1⅞	7⅛	7⅝	M	Bull River, B.C.	Albert Markstein	Albert Markstein	1954	262
50⅝	10	10	5⅝	2⅛	2⅛	8⅛	7	M	Cold Fish Lake, B.C.	Joseph Smith	Joseph Smith	1955	262
50⅜	10⅛	10	5⅛	1⅞	1⅞	6⅝	5⅜	M	Okanogan Mts., Wash.	Neil Castner	Neil Castner	1956	262
50⅝	10⅛	10	5⅝	1⅞	1⅞	0	0	U	Seward, Alaska	Picked Up	A. D. Stenger	PR1957	262
50⅝	10⅛	10⅛	5⅜	1⅞	1⅞	8	7⅞	M	Cold Fish Lake, B.C.	Patrick Britell	Patrick Britell	1957	262
50⅛	10⅛	10⅞	5⅝	2	2	7⅛	6⅞	M	Cold Fish Lake, B.C.	L. A. Wunsch	L. A. Wunsch	1958	262
50⅛	9⅛	9⅜	5⅝	1⅞	1⅞	8⅛	7⅝	M	Chugach Mts., Alaska	Elmer A. Patson	Elmer A. Patson	1958	262
50⅝	10⅛	10⅛	5⅛	2⅛	1⅞	7⅛	6⅜	F	Lake Bennet, Yukon	H. Kennedy	H. Kennedy	1958	262
50⅝	10⅛	10⅛	5⅝	1⅞	1⅞	7	7	M	Chilco Lake, B.C.	C. Marc Miller	C. Marc Miller	1960	262
50⅝	10⅛	10⅜	5⅝	2	2	7⅞	6⅝	M	Smithers, B.C.	A. S. Langan	A. S. Langan	1960	262
50⅝	10⅛	10⅜	5⅝	2⅛	2	6⅛	5⅜	M	Okanogan, Wash.	Bob Hazelbrook	Bob Hazelbrook	1960	262
50⅝	9⅜	9⅜	5⅜	1⅞	1⅞	6⅝	5⅜	M	Mt. Stoyoma, B.C.	Frank S. T. Bradley	Frank S. T. Bradley	1962	262
50⅝	10⅛	9⅞	5⅞	1⅞	2	7	6⅜	M	White Sales Mt., B.C.	Robert McDonald	Robert McDonald	1962	262
50	10	10⅜	5⅝	2	1⅞	8	7	M	Kenai Pen., Alaska	G. Best & R. Reed	Gordon Best	1962	262
50	10	10⅝	5⅝	2	1⅞	7⅝	7⅝	M	Atlin Lake, B.C.	Wendell Bever	Wendell Bever	1962	262
50⅛	9⅞	10	5⅜	1⅞	1⅞	7⅛	6⅝	M	Kechika Range, B.C.	G. W. Hawkins	G. W. Hawkins	1963	262
50⅝	10⅝	10⅛	5⅝	1⅞	1⅞	7⅞	6⅝	M	Cape Yakataga, Alaska	Lynn M. Castle	Lynn M. Castle	1964	262
50	9¾	9¼	5⅞	2⅛	1⅞	8	8	M	Smoky River, Alta.	Terry Thrift, Jr.	Terry Thrift, Jr.	1965	262
50⅝	10	10	5⅝	1⅞	1⅞	7⅛	5⅜	M	Wrangell Mts., Alaska	Charles S. Moses	Charles S. Moses	1965	262
50⅝	10⅜	10⅜	5⅝	1⅞	1⅞	7⅛	6	M	Lake Kinniskan, B.C.	Michel Boel	Michel Boel	1965	262
50⅝	10⅜	10⅜	5⅛	1⅞	1⅞	6	5⅜	U	Revelstoke, B.C.	Picked Up	George Lines	1966	262
50⅝	10⅝	10⅛	5⅝	1⅞	1⅞	7⅝	5⅜	M	Seward, Alaska	Frank W. Pinkerton	Frank W. Pinkerton	1966	262
50⅝	10⅜	9⅞	5⅜	1⅞	1⅞	7⅜	5⅜	M	Winstanley Lakes, Alaska	James R. Simms	James R. Simms	1966	262
50⅛	9⅞	9⅞	5⅝	2	2	8⅛	7	M	Atlin, B.C.	Raymond Bartram	Raymond Bartram	1966	262
50⅝	10⅜	10⅜	5⅝	1⅞	1⅞	7⅜	6⅛	U	McDonald Lake, B.C.	Henry P. Foradora	Henry P. Foradora	1966	262

ROCKY MOUNTAIN GOAT—Continued

Oreamnos americanus americanus and related subspecies

Score	Length of Horn R.	L.	Circumference of Base R.	L.	Circumference at Third Quarter R.	L.	Greatest Spread	Tip to Tip Spread	Sex	Locality Killed	By Whom Killed	Owner	Date Killed	Rank
50 4/8	9 6/8	9 7/8	5 5/8	5 5/8	2	2	8	7 5/8	M	Sloko Lake, B.C.	John Haefeli	John Haefeli	1966	262
50 4/8	10 1/8	10 3/8	5 5/8	5 5/8	1 7/8	1 7/8	9 4/8	9 4/8	M	Cassiar Mts., B.C.	Donovan N. Branch	Donovan N. Branch	1967	262
50 4/8	10 5/8	10 5/8	5 3/8	5 3/8	1 6/8	1 6/8	7 5/8	6 7/8	M	Black Hills, S.D.	T. T. Stroup	T. T. Stroup	1967	262
50 4/8	10 2/8	10 3/8	5 4/8	5 4/8	1 7/8	1 7/8	8 4/8	7 7/8	M	Telegraph Creek, B.C.	Howard S. Duffield	Howard S. Duffield	1968	262
50 4/8	10 4/8	9 7/8	5 7/8	6	2	1 7/8	6 5/8	5 7/8	M	Turnagain River, B.C.	Donald E. Fossen	Donald E. Fossen	1969	262
50 4/8	11	11	5 4/8	5 5/8	1 7/8	1 7/8	7 5/8	7 1/8	M	Stikine River, Alaska	Robert F. Thelen	Donald C. Thelen	1973	262
50 4/8	10 3/8	10 4/8	5 5/8	6	1 6/8	1 6/8	7 7/8	7 7/8	M	Lewis & Clark Co., Mont.	James T. Knutson	James T. Knutson	1974	262
50 4/8	10	10 4/8	5 5/8	5 5/8	1 7/8	2	7 5/8	7 7/8	M	Dease Lake, B.C.	Leonard O. Farlow	Leonard O. Farlow	1975	262
50 4/8	9 7/8	9 6/8	5 5/8	5 5/8	1 7/8	1 7/8	7	6 4/8	M	Wrangell Mts., Alaska	Floyd J. Campbell	Floyd J. Campbell	1978	262
50 4/8	10	10	5 7/8	5 7/8	1 7/8	1 7/8	7 1/8	6 6/8	M	Pennington Co., S.D.	C. P. Podrasky	C. P. Podrasky	1978	262
50 4/8	10 3/8	10 4/8	5 5/8	5 5/8	1 7/8	1 7/8	6 7/8	5 7/8	M	Bingay Creek, B.C.	Reuben F. Gerecke	Reuben F. Gerecke	1981	262
50 4/8	10	9 7/8	5 5/8	5 5/8	1 7/8	1 7/8	9 1/8	9	M	Stikine Canyon, B.C.	Rod Aune	Rod Aune	1982	262
50 4/8	10 5/8	10 3/8	5 7/8	5 7/8	2	2	7 7/8	7 3/8	M	Mt. Cummins, B.C.	James M. Judd	James M. Judd	1984	262
50 4/8	10 6/8	10 7/8	5 3/8	5 3/8	1 6/8	1 7/8	7 4/8	6 4/8	M	Leduc Lake, Alaska	A. C. Gilbert	A. C. Gilbert	1985	262
50 4/8	10 5/8	10 6/8	5 5/8	5 5/8	1 7/8	1 6/8	8 3/8	8 4/8	M	Swan Lake, B.C.	T. A. Walker	Univ. of B.C.	1938	306
50 4/8	10	10	5 5/8	5 5/8	2	2	7 4/8	7 4/8	M	Cold Fish Lake, B.C.	L. W. Howell	L. W. Howell	1952	306
50 4/8	9 6/8	9 7/8	5 5/8	5 5/8	2	2	7	6 7/8	M	Taseko Lake, B.C.	Picked Up	Chas. F. Martinsen	1952	306
50 4/8	10	10	5 5/8	5 5/8	1 7/8	1 7/8	8	6 4/8	M	Blue Goat Mt., Wash.	Victor E. Moss	Victor E. Moss	1956	306
50 4/8	10	10 1/8	5 5/8	5 4/8	2	1 7/8	7 2/8	7 7/8	M	Okanogan Co., Wash.	John La Rocca	John La Rocca	1957	306
50 4/8	10 3/8	10 3/8	5 4/8	5 4/8	1 7/8	1 7/8	6 6/8	7 7/8	M	Turnagain River, B.C.	Guy Brash	Guy Brash	1957	306
50 4/8	10 4/8	10 3/8	5 4/8	5 5/8	1 7/8	1 6/8	8	7 4/8	M	Pentagon Mt., Mont.	Nolan Rad	Nolan Rad	1957	306
50 4/8	10 1/8	10 3/8	5 5/8	5 5/8	1 7/8	1 7/8	7 2/8	6 4/8	M	Shuswap Creek, B.C.	Leslie B. Maxwell	Leslie B. Maxwell	1958	306
50 4/8	10 4/8	10 4/8	5 5/8	5 5/8	1 7/8	1 6/8	6 3/8	6	M	Sheridan Glacier, Alaska	William Stallone	William Stallone	1959	306
50 4/8	10 3/8	10 4/8	5 5/8	5 5/8	1 7/8	1 7/8	8 4/8	5 4/8	M	Smithers, B.C.	Robert C. Sutton	Robert C. Sutton	1960	306
50 4/8	10 2/8	10 1/8	5 5/8	5 5/8	1 7/8	1 7/8	7 4/8	8 4/8	M	Sukunka River, B.C.	Billy Ross	Billy Ross	1962	306
50 4/8	9 4/8	9 1/8	6	6	2 1/8	2	7 3/8	7 3/8	M	Ft. St. John, B.C.	James E. Kelley	James E. Kelley	1962	306
50 4/8	10 5/8	9 5/8	5 5/8	5 4/8	2	1 7/8	8 4/8	7 4/8	M	Cassiar, B.C.	Emile Gele	Emile Gele	1963	306
50 4/8	11 2/8	10 6/8	5 4/8	5 4/8	1 6/8	1 6/8	6 4/8	5 4/8	M	Elk Valley, B.C.	Laszlo Molnar	Laszlo Molnar	1964	306
50 4/8	10 5/8	10 3/8	5 4/8	5 4/8	1 7/8	1 7/8	8 4/8	8 4/8	M	Invermere, B.C.	Walter F. Ramage	Walter F. Ramage	1965	306
50 4/8	10 7/8	11	5 4/8	5 3/8	1 7/8	1 7/8	8 3/8	8 1/8	M	Atlin, B.C.	Mark J. Jakobson	Mark J. Jakobson	1965	306
50 4/8	10 7/8	10 3/8	5 5/8	5 5/8	1 6/8	1 6/8	8	7 4/8	M	Ravalli Co., Mont.			1965	306

402

Score									M	Locality	Hunter	Owner	Date	Rank
50 4/8	10 4/8	10 4/8	5 5/8	5 5/8	1 6/8	1 6/8	7 6/8	7 7/8	M	Koch Creek, B.C.	Pat Archibald	Pat Archibald	1965	306
50 4/8	10 4/8	10 4/8	5 4/8	5 4/8	1 7/8	1 7/8	6 6/8	6 5/8	M	Chehalis Lake, B.C.	Fred E. Harper	Fred E. Harper	1965	306
50 3/8	10	10	5 7/8	5 5/8	1 6/8	1 6/8	7 4/8	6 6/8	M	Chelan Co., Wash.	Ned Shiflett	Ned Shiflett	1966	306
50 3/8	10 6/8	10 7/8	5 5/8	5 5/8	1 6/8	1 6/8	6 3/8	5 5/8	M	Skeena River, B.C.	Jack E. Monet	Jack E. Monet	1966	306
50 3/8	10 3/8	10 3/8	5 5/8	5 5/8	1 5/8	1 5/8	6 3/8	5 5/8	M	Telkwa, B.C.	A. W. Phillips	A. W. Phillips	1967	306
50 3/8	10 4/8	10 4/8	5 5/8	5 4/8	2	2	7 7/8	7 7/8	M	Lynn Canal, Alaska	Jacques M. Norvell, Sr.	Jacques M. Norvell, Sr.	1968	306
50 2/8	9 4/8	9 4/8	5 5/8	5 5/8	2	2	7	6 4/8	M	Cassiar, B.C.	John A. Mueller	John A. Mueller	1968	306
50 2/8	10	9 6/8	6	5 7/8	1 7/8	1 7/8	6 6/8	5 7/8	M	Lake Chelan, Wash.	Gary L. Aichlmayr	Gary L. Aichlmayr	1969	306
50 2/8	10 5/8	10 5/8	5 3/8	5 3/8	1 7/8	1 7/8	6 5/8	5	M	Ecstall River, B.C.	Thomas J. Perry	Thomas J. Perry	1970	306
50 2/8	9 7/8	9 5/8	5 5/8	5 5/8	2	2	6 7/8	6	M	Juneau, Alaska	Jerry Kressin	Jerry Kressin	1971	306
50 2/8	10 4/8	10 4/8	5 5/8	5 5/8	1 7/8	1 7/8	7 1/8	6 2/8	M	Tumeka Lake, B.C.	Dan M. Edwards, Jr.	Dan M. Edwards, Jr.	1972	306
50 2/8	10 4/8	10 4/8	5 3/8	5 3/8	1 7/8	1 7/8	7 7/8	7 7/8	M	Dease Lake, B.C.	Carl K. Beaudry	Carl K. Beaudry	1975	306
50 2/8	10 6/8	10 6/8	5 5/8	5 5/8	1 6/8	1 6/8	8 2/8	8	M	Stikine River, B.C.	R. H. Weaver	R. H. Weaver	1976	306
50 1/8	9 7/8	9 7/8	5 7/8	5 7/8	2	2	7 5/8	7 5/8	M	Ice Mt., B.C.	J. S. Van Alsburg	J. S. Van Alsburg	1978	306
50 1/8	9 7/8	9 7/8	5 5/8	5 5/8	1 7/8	1 7/8	7 3/8	7 3/8	M	Cassiar Mts., B.C.	Ron Ragan	Ron Ragan	1978	306
50 1/8	9 3/8	9 1/8	5 7/8	5 7/8	1 7/8	1 6/8	6 7/8	6 3/8	M	Okanogan Co., Wash.	Richard J. Wristen	Richard J. Wristen	1982	306
50 1/8	10	10	5 5/8	5 5/8	1 6/8	1 5/8	6 6/8	5 5/8	M	Pemberton, B.C.	Weldon Talbot	Weldon Talbot	1982	306
50	10 3/8	10 3/8	5 5/8	5 5/8	1 6/8	1 6/8	7 4/8	7	M	Mt. Stockdale, B.C.	James C. King	James C. King	1983	306
50	10 1/8	10 1/8	5 5/8	5 5/8	2	2	8 1/8	8 1/8	M	Kildala River, B.C.	Philip Perrone	Philip Perrone	1983	306
50	10 2/8	10 2/8	5 4/8	5 4/8	1 6/8	1 6/8	7 4/8	6 7/8	M	Chouteau Co., Mont.	Robert E. Young	Robert E. Young	1983	306
50	10 5/8	10 6/8	5 4/8	5 4/8	1 6/8	1 6/8	8	8	M	Skeena, B.C.	Clarence J. Fields	Clarence J. Fields	1983	306
50	10	10	5 5/8	5 5/8	2	2	6 7/8	6 7/8	M	Bleasdell Creek, B.C.	Daniel Fediuk	Daniel Fediuk	1984	306
50	10 5/8	10 5/8	5 4/8	5 4/8	1 6/8	1 6/8	6 3/8	6 3/8	M	Klinaklini River, B.C.	Powhatan Robinson	Camp Fire Club	1916	345
50	10	10	5 5/8	5 7/8	1 6/8	1 6/8	7 3/8	7	M	Rudyerd Bay, Alaska	Joseph H. Keeney	Joseph H. Keeney	1946	345
50	9 6/8	9 6/8	5 5/8	5 5/8	2	2	7 7/8	7	M	Cassiar Mts., B.C.	James King	James King	1947	345
50	10	10	5 4/8	5 4/8	2	2	6	6	M	Okanogan Co., Wash.	John Hutchinson	Ralph Hutchinson	1950	345
50	9 7/8	10	5 4/8	5 4/8	2 1/8	2	7	7	M	Keremeos Mt., B.C.	Robert Quaedvlieg	Robert Quaedvlieg	1956	345
50	10 5/8	10 6/8	5 5/8	5 5/8	1 7/8	1 7/8	7 3/8	7 3/8	M	Prophet River, B.C.	F. C. Hibben	F. C. Hibben	1956	345
50	10 5/8	10 5/8	5 5/8	5 5/8	1 7/8	1 6/8	7	6 6/8	M	Kenai Pen., Alaska	Coke Elms	Coke Elms	1957	345
50	9 4/8	9 4/8	6	6	2	2	7 3/8	7 3/8	M	Flathead River, Mont.	Gene Biddle	Gene Biddle	1959	345
50	10 2/8	10 2/8	5 4/8	5 4/8	2	2	7 7/8	6 6/8	M	Squaw Creek, Idaho	William A. Callaway	William H. Lockhart	1960	345
50	10 6/8	10 6/8	5 7/8	5 7/8	1 6/8	1 5/8	6 6/8	5 5/8	M	Cape Yakataga, Alaska	Edward I. Worst	Edward I. Worst	1961	345
50	9 4/8	9 4/8	5 7/8	5 7/8	1 7/8	1 7/8	5 7/8	5 7/8	M	K-Mountain, B.C.	Fred D. Fouty	Fred D. Fouty	1961	345
50	9 4/8	9 4/8	5 5/8	5 5/8	1 7/8	1 7/8	6 6/8	6	M	Girdwood, Alaska	Franklin Maus	Franklin Maus	1961	345
50	10	10	5 5/8	5 5/8	1 6/8	1 6/8	6 5/8	5 5/8	M	Bear Point, Idaho	Aaron U. Jones	Aaron U. Jones	1962	345
50	9 7/8	9 7/8	6	6	2	2	6 7/8	6 7/8	M	Lake Chelan, Wash.	Ed Pariseu	Ed Pariseu	1962	345
50	9 6/8	9 6/8	6	6	1 6/8	1 6/8	7	6 6/8	M	Grand Forks, B.C.	Norman Dawson, Jr.	Norman Dawson, Jr.	1963	345
50	10 3/8	10 4/8	5 4/8	5 5/8	1 7/8	1 7/8	6 7/8	6 6/8	M	Spatsizi, B.C.	William L. Searle	William L. Searle	1963	345
50	10	10	5 7/8	5 7/8	1 6/8	1 6/8	7	7	M	Oroville, Wash.	G. Pickering	G. Pickering	1963	345
50	10 3/8	10 3/8	5 3/8	5 3/8	1 7/8	1 7/8	9 2/8	6 6/8	M	Gataga River, B.C.	Herb Klein	Herb Klein	1963	345
50	9 4/8	9 4/8	5 5/8	5 5/8	2 2/8	2 2/8	6 7/8	6 7/8	M	Telegraph Creek, B.C.	Anthony Bechik	Anthony Bechik	1963	345
50	10 1/8	10 1/8	5 4/8	5 4/8	2	2	6 7/8	6 7/8	M	Lincoln, Mont.	James A. Gunn III	James A. Gunn III	1963	345

Rocky Mountain Goat—*Continued*

Oreamnos americanus americanus and related subspecies

Score	Length of Horn R.	L.	Circumference of Base R.	L.	Circumference at Third Quarter R.	L.	Greatest Spread	Tip to Tip Spread	Sex	Locality Killed	By Whom Killed	Owner	Date Killed	Rank
50	9⅞	9⅞	5⅛	5⅛	2⅛	2⅛	7⅞	7⅜	M	Halfway River, B.C.	Victor Tullis	Victor Tullis	1963	345
50	10⅜	10⅜	5⅝	5⅝	1⅞	1⅞	7⅞	6⅞	M	Smithers, B.C.	John Rienhart	John Rienhart	1964	345
50	9⅝	9⅝	5⅝	5⅞	1⅞	1⅞	6	5⅛	M	Blue Sheep Lake, B.C.	O. A. McClintock	O. A. McClintock	1964	345
50	9⅞	10⅛	5⅝	5⅝	2	2⅛	7⅞	6⅞	M	Heart Peaks, B.C.	Bob Loewenstein	Bob Loewenstein	1965	345
50	10⅜	10⅜	5⅜	5⅜	1⅞	1⅞	6⅞	5⅞	M	Hope, B.C.	Peter Konrad	Peter Konrad	1965	345
50	10	10⅜	5⅝	5⅝	2	2	7⅞	7⅞	M	Morice River, B.C.	Dennis A. Sperling	Dennis A. Sperling	1965	345
50	10⅜	10	5⅝	5⅝	1⅞	1⅞	8⅜	8	M	Chilkat Range, Alaska	Jacques M. Norvell	Jacques M. Norvell	1965	345
50	10⅜	10⅞	5⅝	5⅜	1⅝	1⅝	7	6	M	Missoula Co., Mont.	Charles Barry	Charles Barry	1965	345
50	9⅞	9⅞	5⅝	5⅛	2	2	6	6⅞	M	Keremeos, B.C.	Picked Up	Bob Kitto	1965	345
50	9⅜	9⅞	6	5⅞	1⅞	1⅞	6⅞	5⅞	M	Lake Chelan, Wash.	Don Francis	Don Francis	1966	345
50	9⅞	9⅞	5⅝	5⅝	1⅞	1⅞	6⅜	5⅞	M	Nass River, B.C.	Vernon Rydde	Vernon Rydde	1966	345
50	10⅛	10⅛	5⅝	5⅞	1⅞	1⅞	8⅜	8⅜	M	Seward, Alaska	John Lee	John Lee	1966	345
50	11⅜	11⅜	5	5	1⅞	1⅞	8⅜	7⅞	M	Petersburg, Alaska	James Briggs	James Briggs	1966	345
50	9⅞	9⅞	5⅜	5⅜	2	2	7⅜	7⅜	M	Nass River, B.C.	D. E. O'Shea	D. E. O'Shea	1967	345
50	10⅞	10⅜	5⅝	5⅝	1⅞	1⅞	7⅜	6⅞	M	Cassiar Mts., B.C.	Arthur M. Scully, Jr.	Arthur M. Scully, Jr.	1967	345
50	10	10	5⅜	5⅝	2	2	8⅜	8⅜	M	Cassiar Mts., B.C.	E. David Slye	E. David Slye	1967	345
50	10⅜	10⅜	5⅜	5⅝	1⅞	1⅞	7⅞	7⅜	M	Kenai Pen., Alaska	A. P. Funk	A. P. Funk	1967	345
50	9⅞	9⅞	5⅝	5⅝	1⅞	1⅞	6⅞	5⅞	C	Tatla Lake, B.C.	Jack Close	Jack Close	1968	345
50	9⅞	10⅜	5⅝	5⅜	2	2	7⅜	6⅞	M	Hastings Arm, B.C.	Walter J. Eisele	Walter J. Eisele	1968	345
50	10⅞	10⅞	5⅝	5⅝	1⅞	1⅞	6	4⅞	M	Chelan Co., Wash.	Carl Lewis	Carl Lewis	1968	345
50	9⅞	9⅞	5⅝	5⅝	1⅞	1⅞	7⅞	7⅞	M	Whittier, Alaska	Myron Dean Cowell	Myron Dean Cowell	1968	345
50	10⅜	10⅜	5⅜	5⅝	1⅞	1⅞	7⅛	6⅞	M	Skagway, Alaska	Don Sather	Don Sather	1969	345
50	10⅜	10⅜	5⅝	5⅜	1⅝	1⅝	6⅞	6	M	St. Mary's River, B.C.	Frederick Brahniuk	Frederick Brahniuk	1969	345
50	9⅞	9⅞	5⅝	5⅞	1⅝	1⅞	5	4⅜	M	Chelan Co., Wash.	John F. Hooper	William R. Hooper	1970	345
50	9⅞	9⅞	5⅝	5⅝	2	2	6⅞	5⅞	M	Lake Kitchener, B.C.	Aubrey W. Minshall	Aubrey W. Minshall	1971	345
50	10⅜	10⅜	5⅜	5⅝	2	2	8⅜	8⅜	M	Port Dick, Alaska	Neil Smith	Neil Smith	1972	345
50	9⅞	9⅞	5⅜	5⅝	2	2	6⅜	6	M	Hendon River, B.C.	R. A. Wiseman	R. A. Wiseman	1973	345
50	10⅜	10⅜	5⅝	5⅝	1⅞	1⅞	8⅜	8	M	Goodwin Lake, B.C.	Bill Moomey	Bill Moomey	1974	345
50	9⅞	10⅜	5⅝	5⅝	1⅞	1⅞	6⅜	6	M	Rudyerd Bay, Alaska	Gerry D. Downey	Gerry D. Downey	1975	345
50	10⅞	10⅞	5⅜	5⅜	2	2	7⅜	6⅜	M	Gataga River, B.C.	Jerald T. Waite	Jerald T. Waite	1975	345
50	10⅜	10⅜	5⅝	5⅝	1⅞	1⅞	7⅜	7⅜	M	Terrace, B.C.	Joe Zucchiatti	Joe Zucchiatti	1976	345

50	9⅞	9⅞	5⅞	5⅞	1⅞	1⅞	8²⁄₈	7⅞	M	Cassiar Mts., B.C.	Gordon A. Read	Gordon A. Read	1976	345
50	10⅜	10⅝	5⅞	5⅞	1⅞	1⅞	8²⁄₈	7⅝	M	Cassiar Mts., B.C.	Murray B. Wilson	Murray B. Wilson	1977	345
50	10⅛	10⅛	5⅜	5⅜	1⅞	1⅞	8²⁄₈	7⅜	M	Prince William Sound, Alaska	Ernest H. Youngs	Ernest H. Youngs	1978	345
50	10⅛	10⅜	5⅞	5⅞	1⅞	1⅞	7⅜	6⅞	M	Skeena Mts., B.C.	Dee J. Burnett	Dee J. Burnett	1982	345
50	10⅜	10⅜	5⅞	5⅞	2	2	8²⁄₈	7	M	Yeth Creek, B.C.	Michael Follett	Michael Follett	1983	345
50	9⅞	9⅞	5⅞	5⅞	1⅞	1⅞	7⅜	7⅛	M	Bonneville Co., Idaho	Charles E. Wood	Charles E. Wood	1983	345
50	10⅛	10⅛	5⅞	5⅞	1⅞	1⅞	7⅜	8	M	Inklin River, B.C.	John V. Macaluso	John V. Macaluso	1984	345
55⅝*	10⅝	10	6⅛	6⅛	2⅜	2⅜	7⅞	6⅜	M	Blunt Mt., B.C.	Picked Up	Jack Adams	1970	
54⅝*	10⅛	10⅞	6⅛	6⅛	2⅜	2⅜	6⅞	5⅛	M	Cleveland Pen., Alaska	Lana L. DeLong	Roger DeLong	1979	
54⅞*	10⅜	10⅜	5⅞	5⅞	2⅜	2⅜	8	8⅛	M	McCarthy Creek, Alaska	George A. Morelock	George A. Morelock	1981	
52⅞*	10⅛	10⅝	6	6⅛	2	2	9	8⅞	M	Similkameen River, B.C.	Doug & Judy Crossley	Doug & Judy Crossley	1983	
52⅞*	9⅞	9⅞	6	6	2⅛	2⅛	7⅞	7⅛	M	Nimbus Mt., B.C.	J. D. Souza	J. D. Souza	1985	

*Final Score subject to revision by additional verifying measurements

WORLD'S RECORD MUSKOX
SCORE: 122
Locality: Perry River, Northwest Territories Date: 1979
Picked Up Owner: Robert J. Decker

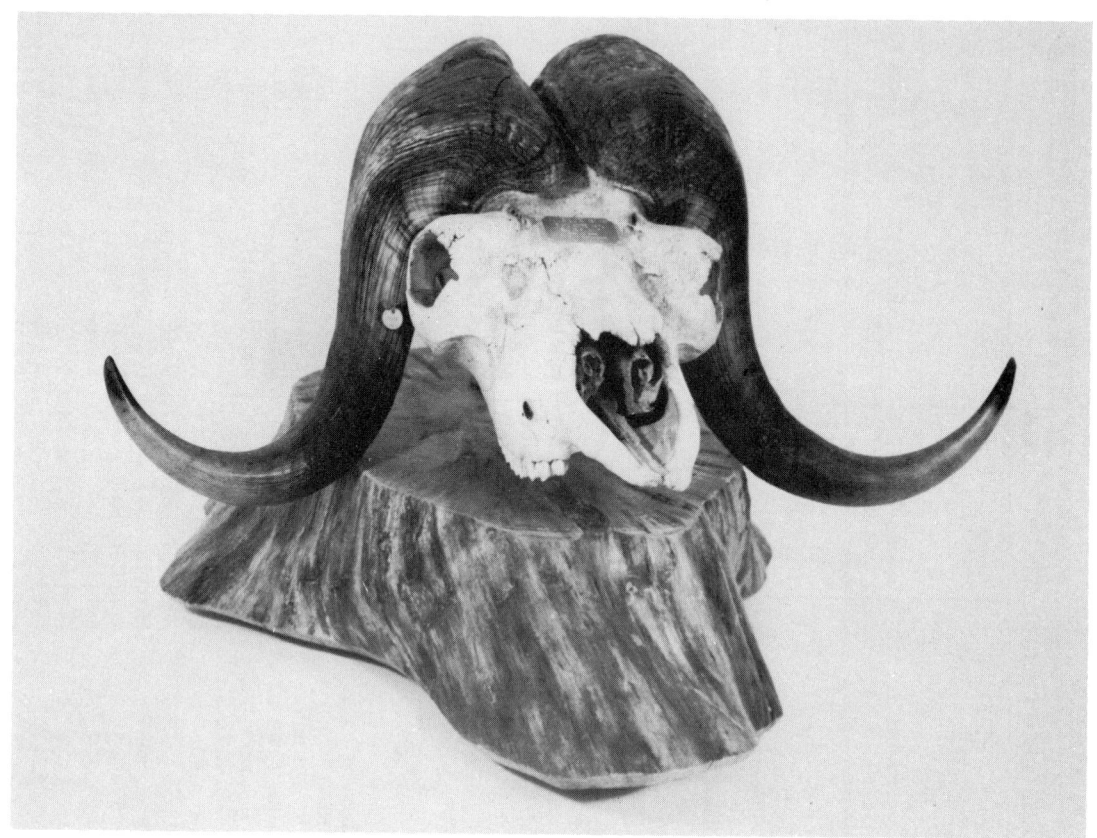

Photograph by Wm. H. Nesbitt

NUMBER TWO MUSKOX
SCORE: 121
Locality: Ellice River, Northwest Territories Date: 1983
Picked Up Owner: John G. Stelfox

Muskox

Ovibos moschatus moschatus and certain related subspecies

Minimum Score 90

Score	Length of Horn R.	L.	Width of Boss R.	L.	Circumference at Third Quarter R.	L.	Greatest Spread	Tip to Tip Spread	Sex	Locality Killed	By Whom Killed	Owner	Date Killed	Rank
122	29	28⅛	10	9⅞	6⅛	5⅞	30⅛	30⅛	M	Perry River, N.W.T.	Picked Up	Robert J. Decker	1979	1
121	28⅜	29⅝	9⅞	9⅞	5⅝	6⅛	31⅛	31	M	Ellice River, N.W.T.	Picked Up	John G. Stelfox	1983	2
115	26	27	10⅜	10⅜	5⅜	5⅜	27	27	M	Ellesmere Is., N.W.T.	I. S. Wombath	Harvard Univ. Mus.	1900	3
114⅞	29⅝	29⅛	9⅝	9⅞	5⅜	5	26	25⅝	U	Hudson Bay, N.W.T.	Monjo	Carnegie Mus.	1910	4
113⅞	28	29	8⅝	8⅛	4⅞	4⅞	29⅝	28⅝	M	Barren Grounds, N.W.T.	Gift of H. Casmir de Rham	B&C National Collection	PR1910	5
112⅞	27⅝	27⅛	8⅜	8⅛	5	5	31⅛	30⅝	M	Thirty Mile Lake, N.W.T.	Joe Scotti	Neale Wortley	1983	6
111⅞	24⅜	24⅛	10⅛	10⅜	5⅝	5⅛	26⅜	25⅜	U	Pr. Wales Is.., N.W.T.	Picked Up	J. William Kerr	1970	7
110⅞	27⅞	26⅝	9⅜	9⅜	5	4⅝	28⅛	27	M	Holman Island, N.W.T.	Adam Ovilek	Roger Britton	1981	8
110⅞	25	25⅛	10	10	5	5⅝	28⅜	27⅝	M	Holman Island, N.W.T.	William M. Phillippe, Jr.	William M. Phillippe, Jr.	1982	8
110⅞	26	26	9⅝	9⅛	4⅝	5	25⅝	21⅝	M	Banks Island, N.W.T.	David V. Collis	David V. Collis	1985	8
110	26⅛	26⅛	8⅝	9⅛	4⅞	5⅜	28	26⅛	M	Banks Island, N.W.T.	Billy Ellis III	Billy Ellis III	1982	11
110	26⅝	26⅛	8⅝	8⅛	5⅜	5⅛	27	26⅛	M	Sadlerochit River, Alaska	Ronald L. Deis	Ronald L. Deis	1985	11
109⅞	25	26⅜	9⅛	9⅛	4⅞	5⅜	27	25⅝	M	Banks Island, N.W.T.	James M. Domokos	James M. Domokos	1981	13
109⅞	25⅞	26	9⅞	9⅛	5⅞	5⅜	28⅛	27⅝	M	Nunivak Island, Alaska	Carolyn Elledge	Carolyn Elledge	1983	13
109⅞	27	26⅝	9⅛	8⅞	4⅞	4⅛	26⅛	23⅝	M	Parry Pen., N.W.T.	Douglas J. Dollhopf	Douglas J. Dollhopf	1983	15
109⅞	28	26⅝	9⅛	9⅞	5⅜	4⅛	25⅝	23	M	Banks Island, N.W.T.	Audrey E. Crabtree	Audrey E. Crabtree	1985	15
108⅞	25⅛	25⅛	10⅛	10	5	5	28⅛	27⅜	M	Banks Island, N.W.T.	William M. Wheless III	William M. Wheless III	1980	17
108⅞	26⅜	27⅛	9⅞	8⅞	4⅝	4⅛	24⅝	21⅞	M	Banks Island, N.W.T.	Toby J. Johnson	Toby J. Johnson	1981	17
108⅞	25⅜	25⅝	8⅞	8⅜	5⅞	5⅛	27⅞	27⅝	M	Nunivak Island, Alaska	James P. Moon, Jr.	James P. Moon, Jr.	1985	17
108⅞	27	26⅜	9⅜	9⅛	4⅝	4⅛	25⅝	23⅝	M	Banks Island, N.W.T.	James W. Owens	James W. Owens	1981	20
108⅞	25⅝	26⅜	9⅞	10⅛	4⅝	5⅜	27⅝	26⅝	M	Hudson Bay, N.W.T.	Herman A. Bennett	Herman A. Bennett	1982	20
108	24⅝	25⅝	9⅞	10⅛	4⅞	4⅞	26⅝	24	M	Hudson Bay, N.W.T.	Indian	N. K. Luxton	1890	22
108	24⅝	25⅝	9⅝	9⅛	5⅝	5⅛	26⅝	26	M	Barren Grounds, N.W.T.	Gift of J. B. Marvin	B&C National Collection	PR1951	22
108	30⅛	30⅛	7⅛	7⅞	4⅛	5⅞	25⅝	23⅝	M	Cape Mendenhall, Alaska	Donald E. Franklin	Donald E. Franklin	1978	22
108	26⅝	25⅝	9⅛	9⅛	5⅛	5	25⅝	25⅜	M	Paulatuk, N.W.T.	Don McVittie	Don McVittie	1983	22
108	26⅜	25⅜	9⅜	9⅜	5	4⅛	28	26⅝	M	Sachs Harbour, N.W.T.	John G. Munsinger	John G. Munsinger	1985	22
107⅞	25	25⅛	9⅜	9⅞	5⅝	5⅛	25⅝	24⅝	M	Melville Is.., N.W.T.	Picked Up	D. C. Thomas	1974	27
107⅞	26⅜	26⅜	8⅜	8⅜	5	4⅛	27⅜	27⅛	M	Nunivak Island, Alaska	John H. Taucher II	John H. Taucher II	1976	27
107⅞	27⅛	26⅝	9⅞	9⅛	4⅛	4⅛	26⅝	24⅝	M	Victoria Island, N.W.T.	Picked Up	John Behrns	1982	27
107⅞	26⅜	27⅛	8	8⅜	5⅜	5⅛	25⅝	25⅝	M	Canada	George Vaux	Acad. Nat. Sci., Phil.	PR1951	30
107⅞	25⅜	25⅝	9⅛	9⅛	4⅞	5	27⅜	25⅝	M	Banks Island, N.W.T.	Jack Fiske	Jack Fiske	1981	30

Score										Locality	Hunter	Owner	Date	Rank
107⅞	26⅞	24⅞	8⅞	9⅞	5⅛	5	29⅞	29⅛	M	Greenland	Bill Foster	Foster's Bighorn Rest.	PR1945	32
107⅞	27⅞	26⅞	9	8⅞	5⅝	5	27⅞	26⅞	M	Nunivak Island, Alaska	William A. Keller	William A. Keller	1977	32
107⅞	26⅞	26⅞	8⅛	8⅛	5⅜	4⅞	28	27⅜	M	Nunivak Island, Alaska	Normand Poulin	Normand Poulin	1977	32
107⅞	26⅜	26⅜	8⅛	8⅜	5⅜	5⅜	27⅞	27⅛	M	Nunivak Island, Alaska	Jacob Metzger	Jacob Metzger	1978	32
107⅞	25	25⅝	9⅛	9	5⅜	5⅛	24⅞	23	M	Cambridge Bay, N.W.T.	Picked Up	Manfred Huellbusch	1979	32
107⅞	28⅞	27⅞	8⅞	8⅞	4⅞	4⅞	24⅞	23⅜	M	Banks Island, N.W.T.	Picked Up	Toby J. Johnson	1981	32
107	26⅞	26⅞	8⅝	8⅛	5	5	27⅞	26⅞	M	Nunivak Island, Alaska	Russell Reed	Russell Reed	1978	38
107	24⅞	25	9	9⅞	5⅝	5⅞	24⅞	23⅝	M	Delesse Lake, N.W.T.	Franco Mazzucchelli	Franco Mazzucchelli	1981	38
107	26⅞	24⅞	9⅞	10½	4⅞	4⅝	24⅞	22⅞	U	Holman Island, N.W.T.	I. D. Shapiro	I. D. Shapiro	1982	38
106⅞	27⅞	28⅞	8⅜	8⅜	5⅜	5⅜	26⅞	26⅛	M	Greenland	Unknown	Rudolf Sand	1930	41
106⅝	25	27⅞	8⅜	8⅜	5⅜	6	26⅜	25⅛	M	Greenland	Alvin Pedersen	Zool. Mus., Copenhagen	1935	41
106⅝	25⅞	26⅞	8⅝	8⅝	5⅜	5	28	27⅞	M	Nunivak Island, Alaska	Bert Klineburger	Bert Klineburger	1959	41
106⅝	26⅞	26⅝	9⅝	9	4⅞	5	27⅞	27	M	Sachs Harbour, N.W.T.	Ethel D. Leedy	Ethel D. Leedy	1975	41
106⅜	26	25⅞	8⅛	8⅞	4⅝	4⅜	29⅞	29⅛	M	Nunivak Island, Alaska	John R. Blanton	John R. Blanton	1984	41
106	26⅜	25⅛	10⅛	10½	4⅜	4⅝	27	27	M	Nunivak Island, Alaska	L. G. Sullivan	L. G. Sullivan	1977	46
106	26⅝	26⅝	8⅛	9	5⅛	4⅝	26⅞	25⅛	M	Banks Island, N.W.T.	Gail W. Holderman	Gail W. Holderman	1976	47
106	26⅛	25⅝	8⅛	8⅝	5⅜	5	27⅝	27⅜	M	Canning River, Alaska	Norman F. Taylor	Norman F. Taylor	1981	47
105⅞	25⅝	27⅞	9⅞	9⅞	4⅛	5⅝	27	27	M	Barren Grounds, N.W.T.	Darrel W. Sauder	Darrel W. Sauder	1983	47
105⅞	25⅝	25⅝	8⅛	8⅞	5	4⅛	27⅞	27⅝	M	Nunivak Island, Alaska	Unknown	Snow Museum	1890	50
105⅞	25⅝	25⅛	8⅝	8⅞	5⅝	5	25⅝	25⅜	M	Nunivak Island, Alaska	William K. Leech	William K. Leech	1977	50
105⅞	26	25⅞	9⅜	9⅛	4⅝	4⅜	25⅞	25⅞	M	Nunivak Island, Alaska	Lynn M. Castle	Lynn M. Castle	1977	50
105⅞	25⅞	25⅞	8⅜	8⅜	5	4⅜	27	27	M	Nunivak Island, Alaska	Gary E. Brown	Gary E. Brown	1978	50
105⅞	25⅞	26	8⅝	8⅝	4⅞	4⅝	27	26	M	Nunivak Island, Alaska	Robert E. Speegle	Robert E. Speegle	1976	54
105⅞	26	25⅝	8⅛	8⅛	5⅝	5⅛	25⅝	25⅞	M	Nunivak Island, Alaska	Sam C. Arnett III	Sam C. Arnett III	1976	54
105⅞	25⅝	25⅞	8⅛	8⅛	5½	5	26⅜	25⅜	M	Nunivak Island, Alaska	Curtis S. Williams	Curtis S. Williams	1978	54
105⅝	25⅝	25⅝	9⅛	9⅛	4⅝	4⅜	28	27	M	Nunivak Island, Alaska	Jean Louis L'Ecuyer	Jean Louis L'Ecuyer	1978	54
105⅝	25⅝	25⅝	8⅝	8⅝	5⅛	4⅜	29⅞	29	M	Nunivak Island, Alaska	Roland Stickney	Roland Stickney	1979	54
105½	26⅝	26⅝	8⅝	8⅛	5⅜	5⅝	25⅝	24	M	Nunivak Island, Alaska	Joseph A. Carr	Joseph A. Carr	1984	54
105	25⅝	25⅝	7⅝	7⅞	6	5⅝	27⅝	26⅞	M	Nunivak Island, Alaska	F. Phillips Williamson	F. Phillips Williamson	1978	60
105	26	26⅜	8⅜	8⅜	5⅜	5⅛	27⅝	23⅜	M	Nunivak Island, Alaska	G. A. Treschow	G. A. Treschow	1978	60
105	26⅞	25⅜	8⅜	9⅜	4⅜	4⅞	26⅜	26⅛	M	Hudson Bay, N.W.T.	Indian	N. K. Luxton	1905	62
105	26	26⅝	8⅞	8⅞	4⅜	4⅜	26⅛	26⅜	M	Nunivak Island, Alaska	Carlo Bonomi	Carlo Bonomi	1976	62
104⅞	26⅝	27⅝	8⅝	8⅜	4⅜	4⅜	27⅞	26	M	Bering Sea, Alaska	Jack M. Holland, Jr.	Jack M. Holland, Jr.	1977	62
104⅞	25⅞	25⅜	8⅜	9	4⅛	4⅞	27⅞	27	M	Nunivak Island, Alaska	Dan H. Brainard	Dan H. Brainard	1977	62
104⅞	24⅞	25	8⅜	9⅛	5⅛	5⅝	24⅞	24	M	Cambridge Bay, N.W.T.	Picked Up	Manfred Huellbusch	1979	62
104⅞	24⅞	24⅞	9	9	5⅝	5⅝	26	26	M	Ellesmere Is., N.W.T.	Hugh H. Logan	Los Angeles Co. Mus.	1960	67
104⅝	31⅛	29⅞	8⅜	8⅜	4⅜	3⅞	25⅝	24⅞	M	Nunivak Island, Alaska	Jerry D. Mercer	Jerry D. Mercer	1975	67
104⅝	28⅜	26⅝	8⅜	8⅜	5⅛	4⅝	25⅝	25⅝	M	Nunivak Island, Alaska	Wilson W. Crook, Jr.	Wilson W. Crook, Jr.	1976	67
104⅝	24⅛	24⅝	8⅜	8⅜	6⅛	5⅝	25⅝	25⅝	M	Nunivak Island, Alaska	Milton N. Stevens	Milton N. Stevens	1977	67
104⅝	23⅞	24⅛	8	7⅞	6⅛	6⅛	26⅝	25⅜	M	Sachs Harbour, N.W.T.	Joseph J. Cafmeyer	Joseph J. Cafmeyer	1982	67
104⅝	24⅛	24⅝	9⅜	9⅜	4⅜	6⅛	25	22⅞	M	Banks Island, N.W.T.	Michel Laurent	Michel Laurent	1983	67
104⅝	28⅛	26⅛	8⅝	9⅜	4⅝	4⅜	30⅛	30	M	Nunivak Island, Alaska	Lawrence T. Epping	Lawrence T. Epping	1984	74

MUSKOX—Continued

Ovibos moschatus moschatus and certain related subspecies

Score	Length of Horn R.	L.	Width of Boss R.	L.	Circumference at Third Quarter R.	L.	Greatest Spread	Tip to Tip Spread	Sex	Locality Killed	By Whom Killed	Owner	Date Killed	Rank
104⅝	24⅞	25⅞	9	9⅛	4⅞	5⅛	28⅛	27⅞	M	Banks Island, N.W.T.	Donald F. Senter	Donald F. Senter	1985	74
104⅜	26	26⅜	8⅝	8⅜	4⅜	4⅞	27⅞	26⅜	M	Nunivak Island, Alaska	Donald A. Stone	Donald A. Stone	1976	76
104⅜	25⅞	25⅛	9⅜	9⅜	4⅞	4⅞	26⅛	21⅞	M	Banks Island, N.W.T.	Lawrence T. Keenan	Lawrence T. Keenan	1981	76
104	23⅞	23⅞	10⅜	10⅜	4⅜	5⅛	28⅜	25⅛	M	Sachs Harbour, N.W.T.	Paul Giesel	Paul Giesel	1980	78
103⅞	25⅞	25⅞	8⅜	8⅜	4⅞	4⅞	27⅞	26⅞	M	Nunivak Island, Alaska	Donald K. Kremer	Donald K. Kremer	1976	79
103⅞	25⅞	25⅛	8⅝	8⅜	5⅛	5⅛	26⅛	25⅛	M	Nunivak Island, Alaska	Richard F. Davis	Richard F. Davis	1976	79
103⅞	25⅛	26⅛	9⅜	9⅜	4⅜	5⅛	26⅛	24⅛	M	Pr. Wales Is., N.W.T.	Picked Up	Alan Kennedy	1977	79
103⅞	25	25⅛	8⅜	8⅜	4⅞	5⅛	25⅛	24⅞	M	Nunivak Island, Alaska	Maurice Ireland	Maurice Ireland	1979	79
103⅞	24⅞	24⅞	9	9	5	5	23⅞	23	M	Holman Island, N.W.T.	Thomas E. Phillippe, Sr.	Thomas E. Phillippe, Sr.	1982	79
103⅞	25⅜	24⅜	8⅞	9	5⅜	5	27⅛	26⅜	M	Nunivak Island, Alaska	Reginald W. Elkins	Reginald W. Elkins	1984	79
103⅞	24⅞	24	9	8⅜	5⅜	5⅜	27	27	M	Nunivak Island, Alaska	Dick Ullery	Dick Ullery	1976	85
103⅞	25	24⅜	8⅜	8⅜	5⅜	4⅜	24⅜	23⅜	M	Nunivak Island, Alaska	Beverly Stevens	Beverly Stevens	1977	85
103⅞	24⅜	24	8⅜	8⅜	5	5⅛	27⅛	27	M	Nunivak Island, Alaska	Ricardo Medem	Ricardo Medem	1977	85
103⅞	24⅛	23⅞	9⅜	9⅞	5⅛	5⅛	25⅜	24⅞	M	Unknown	Unknown	Samuel B. Webb	PR1950	88
103⅞	25	24⅞	8⅜	8⅜	4⅜	4⅜	26⅛	25⅛	M	Nunivak Island, Alaska	Bobby L. Graham	Bobby L. Graham	1985	88
103	26⅜	26⅜	8⅜	8⅜	5	4⅜	23⅜	22⅜	M	Greenland	R. E. Peary	Am. Mus. Nat. History	1909	90
103	25⅝	25⅝	7⅜	7⅝	4⅜	5	26⅜	24⅜	M	Nunivak Island, Alaska	G. L. Gibbons	G. L. Gibbons	1977	90
103	25	26⅜	9⅜	9⅜	4	5⅜	24⅜	21⅛	M	Prince of Wales Is., N.W.T.	Jay R. Wolfenden	Jay R. Wolfenden	1984	90
102⅞	25⅜	25⅜	7⅞	8⅜	5⅜	5	26⅜	26⅜	M	Grant Land, Greenland	R. E. Peary	Am. Mus. Nat. History	1909	93
102⅞	25⅜	25⅞	9⅛	10	5⅜	5⅜	31⅛	29⅜	M	Bathurst Inlet, N.W.T.	David E. Wheeler	Everett P. Wheeler	1913	93
102⅞	23	25	9⅜	8⅜	6⅜	5⅜	26⅜	25⅜	M	Nunivak Island, Alaska	Rudolf Sand	Rudolf Sand	1976	93
102⅞	26⅜	25⅜	8	8⅛	6	5	27⅜	27⅜	M	Nunivak Island, Alaska	Mitch Wagner	Mitch Wagner	1976	93
102⅞	25⅞	25⅜	8	8⅜	5	4⅜	29⅜	28⅜	M	Nunivak Island, Alaska	C. J. McElroy	C. J. McElroy	1977	93
102⅞	24⅜	25⅛	8⅜	8⅜	5	5⅜	28	27⅜	M	Nunivak Island, Alaska	David A. Widby	David A. Widby	1983	93
102⅜	25⅜	25	8⅜	8⅜	4⅜	4⅜	26⅛	25⅜	M	Nunivak Island, Alaska	Edward L. Russell	Edward L. Russell	1984	99
102⅜	24⅜	24⅜	9⅜	9⅜	4⅜	5	26⅜	28⅜	M	Hudson Bay, N.W.T.	George Comer	Am. Mus. Nat. History	1902	100
102⅜	23⅜	24	9⅜	7⅜	5⅛	5	28⅜	28⅛	M	Nunivak Island, Alaska	Russell H. Underdahl	Russell H. Underdahl	1979	100
102⅜	24⅜	25⅛	9⅜	9	4⅛	5	27⅜	25⅜	M	Victoria Island, N.W.T.	Robert J. Matyas	Robert J. Matyas	1981	100
102⅜	22⅜	24⅛	9⅜	9⅛	5⅝	5⅜	24⅜	23⅜	M	Victoria Island, N.W.T.	Dennis D. Schlafmann	Dennis D. Schlafmann	1983	100
102	25⅜	27⅜	9⅝	8⅜	3⅞	5⅜	26⅜	26⅛	M	Ellesmere Is., N.W.T.	Elijah Nutara	Archie Knill	1971	104
102	24⅜	25⅜	8⅜	8⅜	5⅜	5⅜	27⅜	26⅜	U	Unknown	Unknown	Larry W. Lander	PR1972	104

102	28⅜	27⅜	8	7⅞	4²⁄₈	4	25⅞	24²⁄₈	M	Nunivak Island, Alaska	Gerald L. Warnock	Gerald L. Warnock	1976	104
102	23⅝	25²⁄₈	8⁶⁄₈	8⅜	5⅜	5⅛	25	24⅜	M	Nunivak Island, Alaska	Manfred O. Schroeder	Manfred O. Schroeder	1977	104
102	28⅝	28⅛	7⅝	7²⁄₈	4⅜	4⅝	26	24²⁄₈	M	Nunivak Island, Alaska	A. A. Samuels, Jr.	A. A. Samuels, Jr.	1979	104
102	24⁴⁄₈	25	8	8⁴⁄₈	4⅞	5⅛	25⁴⁄₈	23⅛	M	Nunivak Island, Alaska	Curtis W. Lynn	Curtis W. Lynn	1984	104
101⁶⁄₈	24⅝	25⅝	8⅛	8⅛	4⅜	4⅞	27⅞	27⁴⁄₈	M	Nunivak Island, Alaska	Patrick P. Wright	Patrick P. Wright	1981	110
101⁶⁄₈	24⅝	24⅞	8⅛	8⅜	4⁶⁄₈	4⅞	29⅞	29⅝	M	Nunivak Island, Alaska	John R. Jameson	John R. Jameson	1984	110
101⁴⁄₈	25⁶⁄₈	24⅝	8⅝	8⁶⁄₈	5⅝	4⅜	27⁴⁄₈	26⁴⁄₈	M	Nunivak Island, Alaska	Robert Chisholm	Robert Chisholm	1977	112
101⁴⁄₈	24⅞	24⅝	8²⁄₈	8⅝	4⁶⁄₈	4⁴⁄₈	26⅞	25	M	Nunivak Island, Alaska	Daniel B. Moore	Daniel B. Moore	1977	112
101⁴⁄₈	24⅝	25⅝	8⁴⁄₈	8⅛	4⅝	4⅞	26⁶⁄₈	25⅛	M	Nunivak Island, Alaska	Denny Pilling	Denny Pilling	1978	112
101⁴⁄₈	25⅛	26²⁄₈	8⁴⁄₈	8⁴⁄₈	4⅛	4⅜	27⅜	26⅝	M	Nunivak Island, Alaska	Vernie T. Epperson	Vernie T. Epperson	1982	112
101²⁄₈	26⁶⁄₈	27⅛	6⅜	6⅞	5⅝	4⅞	27⁴⁄₈	25⁴⁄₈	M	Barren Grounds, N.W.T.	Warburton Pike	National Collection	1889	116
101²⁄₈	24⁴⁄₈	24⅞	9⅛	9⅛	4⅝	4⅞	27⅞	27⁴⁄₈	M	Hudson Bay, N.W.T.	George Comer	Am. Mus. Nat. History	1902	116
101²⁄₈	24²⁄₈	24⅛	9²⁄₈	8⅞	4⁶⁄₈	4²⁄₈	28⁴⁄₈	28	M	Nunivak Island, Alaska	Unknown	Univ. Calif. Mus.	1952	116
101²⁄₈	25⅛	23⅛	8	8	5⁴⁄₈	5²⁄₈	26⅝	26²⁄₈	M	Nunivak Island, Alaska	William Koller	William Koller	1977	116
101²⁄₈	25⅛	25⅝	8²⁄₈	7⁶⁄₈	4⁴⁄₈	4⁶⁄₈	27⅛	25⁶⁄₈	M	Nunivak Island, Alaska	Cecil M. Hopper	Cecil M. Hopper	1977	116
101²⁄₈	25	25⁶⁄₈	8²⁄₈	7⅞	4⅜	4⅝	29	28⅝	M	Nunivak Island, Alaska	James A. Bush, Jr.	James A. Bush, Jr.	1978	116
101²⁄₈	25⅛	25⅝	7²⁄₈	7⅜	5	5²⁄₈	26⅜	25⅛	M	Delesse Lake, N.W.T.	Massimo Bertoni	Massimo Bertoni	1981	116
101²⁄₈	25⁴⁄₈	25⅜	7⁴⁄₈	7⁶⁄₈	4⁶⁄₈	4⁴⁄₈	26⁴⁄₈	26⅜	M	Seemalik Butte, Alaska	Edward C. Luther	Edward C. Luther	1982	116
101²⁄₈	26⁴⁄₈	25⁴⁄₈	8⁶⁄₈	8⅝	4²⁄₈	4⅞	28⅜	27⁴⁄₈	M	Nunivak Island, Alaska	Don B. Skidmore	Don B. Skidmore	1983	116
101	22⅛	23⅛	8²⁄₈	8²⁄₈	5⅞	5⅞	25⁶⁄₈	25²⁄₈	M	Nunivak Island, Alaska	Gene D. Klineburger	Gene D. Klineburger	1975	125
100⁶⁄₈	25⅛	25⁶⁄₈	8⅜	8	4²⁄₈	4⅝	27⅛	26	M	Nunivak Island, Alaska	Kenneth Campbell	Kenneth Campbell	1975	126
100⁶⁄₈	23²⁄₈	25⁴⁄₈	9⅛	9⅛	5	5⅛	26⁶⁄₈	26⁶⁄₈	M	Nunivak Island, Alaska	Henry Brockhouse	Henry Brockhouse	1976	126
100⁶⁄₈	23⅝	23⅝	8⅛	8⅛	5⅛	5²⁄₈	25⁶⁄₈	25	M	Nunivak Island, Alaska	Arthur LaCapria	Arthur LaCapria	1976	126
100⁶⁄₈	23⁴⁄₈	25⅛	9⅛	8⅞	4⅝	5⁴⁄₈	27	26⁶⁄₈	M	Sabine Bay, N.W.T.	Picked Up	Ken Ryalls	1976	126
100⁶⁄₈	26⁶⁄₈	25⅛	8⅛	8	5	3⅞	27²⁄₈	26⁴⁄₈	M	Nunivak Island, Alaska	Carolyn Elledge	C. Elledge & G. Elledge	1985	126
100⁶⁄₈	24²⁄₈	25⅛	8⅜	8²⁄₈	4⅝	5²⁄₈	25⁶⁄₈	24²⁄₈	M	Barter Island, Alaska	John W. Sargent	John W. Sargent	1985	126
100⁴⁄₈	22⁶⁄₈	24⅛	8²⁄₈	8⅜	5⅛	5⁶⁄₈	27⁴⁄₈	26⅝	M	Nunivak Island, Alaska	Unknown	Iran Game & Fish Dept.	1967	132
100⁴⁄₈	23⅞	24	7⅞	8	5	5⅛	26²⁄₈	24⅜	M	Nunivak Island, Alaska	W. T. Yoshimoto	W. T. Yoshimoto	1976	132
100⁴⁄₈	24⅛	24⅝	8⅜	8²⁄₈	4⁴⁄₈	4⁴⁄₈	25⅞	22⁶⁄₈	M	Nunivak Island, Alaska	William A. Bond	William A. Bond	1976	132
100²⁄₈	22⁶⁄₈	23⁶⁄₈	8⅝	8⁴⁄₈	5⅛	5	25⅛	23⅞	U	Pr. Patrick Is., N.W.T.	Picked Up	William P. Hampton	1964	135
100	23²⁄₈	25⅜	10⅝	9⁴⁄₈	4	4⅞	26²⁄₈	26	M	Nunivak Island, Alaska	Marion L. Connerly	Marion L. Connerly	1976	136
99⁶⁄₈	26⁴⁄₈	27⅛	8⅛	7⅞	4⅝	5	25	24⅛	U	Greenland	Eskimo	Charles T. Arnold	1959	137
99⁶⁄₈	24⅝	26²⁄₈	7⅞	8	4²⁄₈	5⅛	26⁴⁄₈	25⁶⁄₈	M	Nunivak Island, Alaska	J. W. Lawson	J. W. Lawson	1977	137
99⁶⁄₈	24⁴⁄₈	25⅛	8²⁄₈	8	4⁴⁄₈	4⅝	27⅛	25⅜	M	Nunivak Island, Alaska	Ronald H. Stover	Ronald H. Stover	1977	137
99⁶⁄₈	26⅛	26⅞	7⁴⁄₈	7⁴⁄₈	4⅛	4⅝	27⁶⁄₈	26⅞	M	Nunivak Island, Alaska	Harvey D. Harms	Harvey D. Harms	1983	137
99⁴⁄₈	24⁴⁄₈	23⁴⁄₈	8⅛	8⅛	6	4⁶⁄₈	27	27	M	Nunivak Island, Alaska	Ray Tremblay	Univ. Alaska Mus.	1959	141
99²⁄₈	24⅜	24	8⅝	8⅝	4⁴⁄₈	4⁴⁄₈	28⅝	27⅞	M	Nunivak Island, Alaska	Robert C. Jones	Robert C. Jones	1980	142
99	27²⁄₈	26	7	7	4⁶⁄₈	5	25	23²⁄₈	U	Greenland	Unknown	Harvard Univ. Mus.	PR1952	143
99	24⅞	25⅝	7⁴⁄₈	7⁴⁄₈	4⁴⁄₈	4⅝	28⅜	28	M	Nunivak Island, Alaska	Richard H. Leedy	Richard H. Leedy	1976	143
99	25⅛	24	8⁴⁄₈	8⅝	4⅞	4⅛	25⁶⁄₈	24⅞	M	Nunivak Island, Alaska	Lowell Hansen II	Lowell Hansen II	1978	143
99	24⅝	25²⁄₈	8	8	4²⁄₈	4⅜	26⁶⁄₈	25⅛	M	Nunivak Island, Alaska	R. W. Howe	R. W. Howe	1979	143
98⁶⁄₈	24²⁄₈	24⅜	7⁶⁄₈	7⁶⁄₈	4⁶⁄₈	4⁶⁄₈	24⁴⁄₈	22⁶⁄₈	M	Hudson Land, Greenland	Arthur D. Norcross	Arthur D. Norcross	1931	147
98⁶⁄₈	24⅜	24	7⅝	7⁴⁄₈	4⅞	5⅛	26⅜	25⅝	M	Greenland	U. M. Hansen	Zool. Mus., Copenhagen	1947	147

MUSKOX—Continued
Ovibos moschatus moschatus and certain related subspecies

Score	Length of Horn R.	L.	Width of Boss R.	L.	Circumference at Third Quarter R.	L.	Greatest Spread	Tip to Tip Spread	Sex	Locality Killed	By Whom Killed	Owner	Date Killed	Rank
98⅞	23⅛	22⅜	8⅛	8⅛	5⅛	5	26⅜	26	M	Nunivak Island, Alaska	Warren K. Parker	Warren K. Parker	1978	147
98⅞	24⅛	23⅜	8	8⅛	5⅛	4⅞	27⅛	26⅞	M	Nunivak Island, Alaska	Ronald Cunningham	Ronald Cunningham	1978	147
98⅞	22⅞	23⅜	9⅜	9⅜	4⅜	4⅝	24⅜	20⅞	M	Banks Island, N.W.T.	Gary Boychuk	Gary Boychuk	1981	147
98⅞	24⅜	24⅜	7⅛	7⅜	4⅞	5	27⅛	26⅛	M	Ellesmere Is., N.W.T.	Harry Whitney	B&C National Collection	1909	152
98⅞	23⅝	25⅜	8⅛	8⅛	4⅞	4⅞	26⅝	26⅝	M	Nunivak Island, Alaska	Lawrence B. Harbison	Lawrence B. Harbison	1976	152
98⅞	21⅝	24⅛	8⅞	8⅝	5⅛	6	27⅛	27⅜	M	Nunivak Island, Alaska	John L. Estes	John L. Estes	1976	152
98⅞	25⅜	24⅛	8⅝	8⅝	4⅞	4	27⅛	26⅛	M	Nunivak Island, Alaska	H. I. H. Prince Abdorreza Pahlavi	H. I. H. Prince Abdorreza Pahlavi	1976	152
98⅞	22⅝	23⅜	7⅛	7⅛	5⅜	5⅜	25⅛	24⅛	M	Nunivak Island, Alaska	Valentin Madariaga	Valentin Madariaga	1976	152
98⅞	24⅝	24⅛	7⅞	8	4⅜	4⅜	24⅛	20⅛	M	Banks Island, N.W.T.	L. Irvin Barnhart	L. Irvin Barnhart	1981	152
98⅞	24	26	8	7⅞	4⅞	5⅞	26⅛	26	M	Greenland	Unknown	Zool. Mus., Copenhagen	1926	158
98⅞	24⅜	23⅞	7⅞	8	5⅛	4⅜	24⅜	22⅝	M	Hudson Land, Greenland	Arthur D. Norcross	Arthur D. Norcross	1931	158
98	24⅝	24⅛	7⅞	7⅝	4⅝	4⅜	24⅜	22⅝	M	Greenland	Harry Whitney	Acad. Nat. Sci., Phil.	1930	160
98	25	27⅛	7⅛	7⅛	5	4⅛	25⅜	24⅛	U	Greenland	Finn Kristoffersen	Finn Kristoffersen	1940	160
98	24⅛	26⅛	8⅛	8	4⅜	5⅛	25⅛	24⅛	M	Axel Heiberg Is., N.W.T.	Picked Up	Bryan Robertson	1961	160
98	22⅞	23⅜	8⅜	8⅛	4⅞	5⅛	25⅛	25⅛	M	Nunivak Island, Alaska	Picked Up	Steve C. Leirer	1977	160
97⅞	23⅝	25⅝	8⅜	7⅞	4⅜	4⅜	26⅛	26⅛	U	Black Fox Creek, Yukon	Picked Up	David M. Twamley	1973	164
97⅞	23	24⅛	8⅜	8⅜	4⅝	5⅜	25⅛	25⅛	M	Nunivak Island, Alaska	Steve C. Leirer	Steve C. Leirer	1977	164
97⅞	25⅞	25⅛	7⅛	7⅛	4⅛	4⅝	26⅛	25⅛	M	Grant Land, Greenland	R. E. Peary	Am. Mus. Nat. History	1906	166
97⅞	23⅝	25⅛	8⅛	7⅛	4⅜	5	24⅜	23⅛	M	Unknown	Unknown	Camp Fire Club		166
97⅞	23⅞	23⅛	7⅛	7⅛	5⅜	5⅛	27⅜	25⅛	M	Back Bay, N.W.T.	James W. Perkins	James W. Perkins	1983	166
97⅞	25⅛	24⅜	7⅛	7⅛	5⅛	4⅜	28⅛	28⅛	M	Greenland	Unknown	Zool. Mus., Copenhagen	PR1939	169
97⅞	24⅜	24⅛	8	7⅞	4	4⅜	28⅛	27⅞	M	Nash Harbor, Alaska	L. Irvin Barnhart	L. Irvin Barnhart	1980	169
97	22⅞	24⅛	9⅜	9⅜	4⅜	4⅜	24⅛	23⅞	U	Nunivak Island, Alaska	Picked Up	Darrell D. McCullaugh	1962	171
97	26⅛	24⅛	8⅜	8⅛	4⅞	4⅞	28⅛	27⅞	M	Nunivak Island, Alaska	Norman W. Garwood	Norman W. Garwood	1977	171
97	25⅞	24⅛	7⅞	8⅜	4⅜	3⅞	26⅛	25⅛	M	Sor Fiord, N.W.T.	Earl A. Shelsby, Jr.	Earl A. Shelsby, Jr.	1981	171
97	23⅞	24⅜	7⅞	7⅛	4⅞	4⅞	27	26⅛	M	Axel Heiberg Is., N.W.T.	Brian F. Glenister	Brian F. Glenister	1955	174
96⅞	25	23⅜	8⅛	8	4⅜	5	24⅜	23⅜	M	Clavering Is., Greenland	Harry Whitney	Acad. Nat. Sci., Phil.	1930	175
96⅞	24⅜	25⅜	8⅛	8	4	4⅜	25⅛	23⅝	M	Shannon Is., Greenland	Arthur D. Norcross	Arthur D. Norcross	1931	175
96⅞	23⅞	22⅜	8⅝	8⅞	5⅜	4⅜	25⅛	25⅜	M	Barren Grounds, N.W.T.	Picked Up	James P. Borman	PR1963	175
96⅞	22⅞	24	7⅞	7⅛	5⅜	5⅛	25⅜	23⅜	M	Sor Fiord, N.W.T.	Vincent T. Ciaburri	Vincent T. Ciaburri	1982	175
96⅞	23⅞	25⅞	8⅝	8⅛	4⅝	4⅜	28⅜	27⅛	M	Nunivak Island, Alaska	Stewart N. Shaft	Stewart N. Shaft	1982	175

Final Score									Sex	Locality	By Whom Killed	Owner	Date	Rank
96⅞	21⅞	23⅞	8⅞	8⅞	5	5⅛	24⅞	25⅞	M	Nunivak Island, Alaska	Michael W. Elkins	Michael W. Elkins	1984	175
96⅜	24⅞	24⅜	7	6⅝	4⅝	5⅛	26⅜	27	M	Greenland	Ryder	Zool. Mus., Copenhagen	1892	181
96⅜	24⅜	22⅞	9⅝	9⅝	4⅝	3⅝	25⅜	22⅞	M	Melville Island, N.W.T.	Picked Up	M. G. Sullivan	1977	181
96⅜	23⅞	24⅞	7⅞	7⅝	4⅝	5⅛	23	23⅞	M	Ellesmere Island, N.W.T.	Robert I. Michel	Robert I. Michel	1984	181
96	25	25⅝	7⅛	7⅜	4	4⅝	24⅝	23⅝	M	Nunivak Island, Alaska	Larry G. Dunn	Larry G. Dunn	1977	184
96	24⅞	24⅞	7⅝	7	4⅝	4⅝	24⅜	25⅛	M	Killinupak Mt., Alaska	Ray E. Stock	Ray E. Stock	1984	184
95⅝	23⅞	25⅝	8⅝	9⅛	4	4⅝	27⅞	27⅞	M	Hudson Bay, N.W.T.	George Comer	National Collection	1909	186
95⅜	23⅜	23⅜	7⅝	7⅞	4⅝	4⅝	26⅜	26⅜	M	Nunivak Island, Alaska	Herman A. Lawrence	Herman A. Lawrence	1976	186
95⅛	23⅞	26	8⅜	8	3⅝	4⅝	25	26⅛	M	Nunivak Island, Alaska	James E. Conklin	James E. Conklin	1979	188
95	23⅜	24⅜	8⅞	8⅛	4⅝	5⅞	24⅝	24⅞	U	Unknown	Unknown	Loren Lutz	PR1962	189
95	24⅞	25⅞	7⅞	7⅛	4	4⅝	26⅜	25⅝	M	Nunivak Island, Alaska	M. L. Warne	M. L. Warne	1979	189
94⅞	23⅞	24	7⅝	7⅞	4⅝	5	26⅝	25⅝	M	Hudson Land, Greenland	Arthur D. Norcross	Arthur D. Norcross	1931	191
94⅝	23	23⅞	8	7⅝	4⅝	5⅝	24⅝	23⅝	M	Greenland	W. S. Webb, Jr.	J. Watson Webb	1932	191
94⅝	23⅝	24⅜	6⅝	6⅝	4⅝	4⅝	26⅝	25⅝	M	Nunivak Island, Alaska	C. Vernon Humble	C. Vernon Humble	1976	191
94⅜	23⅝	21⅝	7⅞	8⅛	5⅝	4⅝	26⅝	26⅜	M	Nunivak Island, Alaska	Picked Up	Robert C. Jones	1980	194
93⅝	22⅝	24⅝	8⅞	9	3⅝	5	22⅝	22⅝	M	Banks Island, N.W.T.	James K. Montgomery	James K. Montgomery	1980	195
93⅜	23⅝	24⅝	7⅝	7⅝	3⅞	4	24⅝	24⅝	M	Greenland	Unknown	Jules V. Lane	PR1951	196
93⅛	23⅝	23⅝	6⅝	7⅛	4⅝	4⅝	22⅝	22⅝	U	Greenland	Joem Ladegaard	Joem Ladegaard	1975	196
92⅝	24⅝	25	7⅝	7⅞	4	4⅝	22⅝	24⅝	M	Greenland	Harry Whitney	Acad. Nat. Sci., Phil.	1930	198
92⅛	23⅝	22⅝	7⅝	7⅝	4⅝	5	23⅝	22⅝	M	Unknown	A. Brock	Acad. Nat. Sci., Phil.	PR1951	199
92	23⅝	24⅝	7⅝	7⅝	4⅛	4⅝	26	25⅝	M	Nunivak Island, Alaska	Terry Yager	Terry Yager	1976	200
92	22⅝	25⅝	8⅝	8⅝	3⅝	4⅝	24⅝	23⅝	M	Unknown	Picked Up	Doreen Vair	PR1981	200
91⅝	23⅝	24⅝	7⅝	7⅝	4⅝	4⅝	22⅝	21⅝	M	Greenland	W. T. Hornaday	E. H. Herrick	PR1959	202
90⅝	22⅝	21⅝	7	7	4⅝	4⅝	23⅝	22⅝	M	Cambridge Bay, N.W.T.	Unknown	Jules Verquin	1975	203
90	21⅝	21⅝	6⅝	7⅛	4⅝	4⅝	24⅝	24	M	Greenland	Herb Klein	Herb Klein	1947	204
123⅞*	28⅝	28⅝	10⅛	10⅛	6⅝	6⅝	31⅝	31	M	Northwest Territories	Unknown	Sam Pancotto	PR1976	
114⅞*	27⅝	27⅝	10⅛	11	5⅝	5⅝	29⅝	29⅝	M	Victoria Island, N.W.T.	Jimmy Memogana	Terry Pellow	1977	
113⅞*	25⅝	25⅝	9⅝	10	6⅝	6⅝	30	29⅝	M	Cambridge Bay, N.W.T.	Picked Up	Edmonton Tannery & Taxidermy	1979	
113⅞*	26⅝	26⅝	9⅝	10⅛	5⅝	4⅝	28	26⅝	M	Swan Lake, N.W.T.	Basil C. Bradbury	Basil C. Bradbury	1982	
117⅞*	26⅝	28	10⅝	10⅛	4⅝	5⅝	25⅝	25⅝	M	Parry Pen., N.W.T.	Roy L. Mondike	Roy L. Mondike	1985	
111*	24⅝	24⅝	9⅝	9⅝	5⅝	5	26⅝	26	M	Victoria Island, N.W.T.	William H. Taylor	William H. Taylor	1985	
109*	26⅝	26⅝	8⅝	8⅝	5⅝	5⅝	26⅝	26⅝	M	Nunivak Island, Alaska	Douglas E. Miller	Douglas E. Miller	1976	
108⅛*	25	23	9⅝	9⅝	6⅝	6⅞	23⅝	25⅝	U	Hornaday River, N.W.T.	Picked Up	Dan Murphy	PR1976	
108*	24⅝	26⅝	9	8⅝	5⅝	6⅝	26	27	M	Nunivak Island, Alaska	Helga Schroeder	Helga Schroeder	1977	

*Final Score subject to revision by additional verifying measurements

413

Photograph by Leo T. Sarnaki

WORLD'S RECORD BIGHORN SHEEP
SCORE: 208 1/8
Locality: Blind Canyon, Alberta Date: 1911
Hunter: Fred Weiller Owner: Clarence Baird

NUMBER TWO BIGHORN SHEEP
SCORE: 207 2/8
Locality: Oyster Creek, Alberta Date: 1924
Hunter and owner: Martin Bovey

Bighorn Sheep

Ovis canadensis canadensis and certain related subspecies

Minimum Score 180

Score	Length of Horn R.	Length of Horn L.	Circumference of Base R.	Circumference of Base L.	Circumference at Third Quarter R.	Circumference at Third Quarter L.	Greatest Spread	Tip to Tip Spread	Locality Killed	By Whom Killed	Owner	Date Killed	Rank
208⅛	44⅞	45	16⅛	16⅜	11⅞	11⅞	22⅝	19⅝	Blind Canyon, Alta.	Fred Weiller	Clarence Baird	1911	1
207⅞	45	45⅝	15⅞	16	11⅝	11⅝	23⅜	19⅛	Oyster Creek, Alta.	Martin Bovey	Martin Bovey	1924	2
206⅜	44⅜	44⅜	15⅞	15⅞	12⅛	12⅛	21⅛	21⅛	Burnt Timber Creek, Alta.	Picked Up	Roy C. Stahl	1955	3
204	49⅜	48⅞	15⅜	15⅜	10⅛	10⅜	23⅜	23⅜	Sheep Creek, B.C.	James Simpson	Am. Mus. Nat. History National Collection	1920	4
202⅝	46⅜	44⅝	15⅜	15⅜	11	10⅜	23⅜	23⅜	Panther River, Alta.	Tom Kerquits	A. H. Hilbert	1918	5
201⅞	44	43⅞	15⅜	15⅜	11⅜	11⅜	25	25	Jasper, Alta.	Picked Up	Royal Ontario Mus.	1932	6
200⅞	43⅜	43⅜	16⅜	16⅞	9	9⅜	22⅝	20⅜	Fernie, B.C.	H. J. Johnson	Norman Lougheed	1902	7
200⅛	44⅜	44	15⅛	15⅞	11⅜	11⅜	23	23	Brazeau River, Alta.	Unknown	Otis Chandler	1937	8
200⅛	40⅞	41⅜	16⅜	16⅜	11⅜	11⅜	22⅝	18⅜	Alberta	Picked Up	Duncan Weibel	1955	8
200	40⅞	41⅜	16⅜	16⅜	11⅜	11⅜	22	19⅝	Wind River Range, Wyo.	Crawford	Parliament Bldg., B.C.	1883	10
199	45	45⅝	15⅛	15⅛	10⅜	10⅜	22⅝	22⅝	Spence's Bridge, B.C.	Picked Up	Foster's Bighorn Rest.	1969	11
198⅞	43⅜	43⅜	15⅜	15⅜	10⅜	11⅜	24⅜	24⅜	Alberta	Bill Foster	Foster's Bighorn Rest.	PR1947	12
198⅛	42⅜	41⅜	15⅜	15⅞	12	11⅜	23⅜	23⅜	Sask. Lake, Alta.	Herb Klein	Herb Klein	1965	13
197⅞	44⅞	43⅜	14⅜	14⅜	10⅝	11⅛	23⅜	18⅜	Alberta	Bill Foster	Foster's Bighorn Rest.	PR1947	14
197⅞	39⅜	42⅜	17	17	9⅜	9⅜	23⅜	20	E. Kootenay, B.C.	Picked Up	Victoria Fish & Game Assn.	PR1930	15
197⅞	44⅜	45⅜	15⅜	15⅜	8⅝	8⅜	28⅜	28⅜	Sanders Co., Mont.	Armand H. Johnson	Armand H. Johnson	1979	16
196⅞	41⅛	40⅜	17⅜	17⅜	10	9⅜	23⅜	18⅛	Yarrow Creek, Alta.	George W. Biron	George W. Biron	1968	17
196⅞	41⅛	40⅜	16⅛	16⅜	9⅜	10⅜	22⅞	19⅞	Badlands, N.D.	Howard Eaton	Richard K. Mellon	1880	18
196⅞	45⅜	44⅜	16⅛	15⅞	9⅜	8⅞	23	23	Wardner, B.C.	Jim Buss	Jim Buss	1961	18
196⅜	41⅛	42	16⅜	16⅛	10⅜	10⅜	22⅜	20	Brazeau River, Alta.	Donald S. Hopkins	Donald S. Hopkins	1924	20
196⅜	39⅝	41⅛	16	16	10⅛	11⅜	21⅜	19⅛	Alberta	Bill Foster	Foster's Bighorn Rest.	1938	20
196⅜	45⅝	44⅜	14⅜	14⅜	10⅜	10⅜	24⅜	24⅜	Sun River, Mont.	Don Anderson	Don Anderson	1961	20
196⅜	40⅜	40⅜	15⅜	15⅜	12	12	24	19⅜	Badlands Natl. Park, S.D.	Picked Up	S.D. Dept. Game, Fish & Parks	1984	23
196⅜	42⅜	42⅜	16⅜	16⅜	10	9⅜	21⅜	16⅜	Highwood, Alta.	Joseph F. Kubasek	Joseph F. Kubasek	1953	24
196	44⅜	43⅜	15	15	10⅜	10⅜	24⅜	24⅜	Cadomin, Alta.	Al Leary	Al Leary	1962	25
195⅞	45⅜	44⅜	15⅜	15⅜	9⅞	8⅜	24	24	Montana	Unknown	Dole & Bailey, Inc.	1890	26
195⅝	41⅜	40⅜	16⅜	16⅜	11⅜	10⅜	22⅜	18⅜	Castle River, Alta.	R. E. Woodward	R. E. Woodard	1965	27
195⅜	43	43⅜	14⅜	14⅜	11⅛	11	23	19⅜	Bow River, Alta.	Indian	N. K. Luxton	1890	28
195⅜	42⅜	42⅜	15⅜	15⅜	10⅜	10⅜	22⅜	20⅜	West Sundre, Alta.	Jim Neeser	Jim Neeser	1961	29
195	44⅜	38⅜	15⅜	16⅜	11	11⅜	26⅜	26⅜	Sun River, Mont.	Gold White	Lee M. Ford	1911	30

Score								Locality	Killed By	Owner	Date	Rank
194 7/8	42 7/8	15 5/8	11 1/8	15	11 1/8	23 1/8	19 3/8	Ram River, Alta.	G. M. De Witt	G. M. De Witt	1944	31
194 6/8	42	15 1/8	10 7/8	15 3/8	10 7/8	20 1/8	20	Storm Mt., Alta.	Bryan M. Watts	Bryan M. Watts	1957	32
194 3/8	40 7/8	15 7/8	10 6/8	15 7/8	10 6/8	22 1/8	17 7/8	Sheep River, Alta.	Picked Up	Harry McElroy	1966	33
194 2/8	44	15	9 7/8	14 7/8	9 7/8	21 3/8	21 3/8	Panther River, Alta.	Picked Up	N. K. Luxton	1930	34
194	42 7/8	14 4/8	10 1/8	14 4/8	10 1/8	22 3/8	21 3/8	Alberta	Bill Foster	Foster's Bighorn Rest.	PR1947	35
193 6/8	42 7/8	16 7/8	9 5/8	16 3/8	9 5/8	22 1/8	16 5/8	Yarrow Creek, Alta.	F. H. Riggall	F. H. Riggall	1906	36
193 6/8	42	16	10 1/8	16	10 1/8	24	18 1/8	Cameron Pass, Colo.	F. Cotter	Herbert J. Havemann	1954	36
193 5/8	40 5/8	15 4/8	10 5/8	15 4/8	10 5/8	22 1/8	17 1/8	Tornado Pass, B.C.	John Stuber	John Stuber	1956	36
193 2/8	40 7/8	15 1/8	10 3/8	15 7/8	10 3/8	22 3/8	17 3/8	Coleman, Alta.	George Hagglund	George Hagglund	1952	39
193 2/8	42 4/8	15 7/8	10	15 7/8	10	21 7/8	22 1/8	Spence's Bridge, B.C.	M. Da Rosa	M. Da Rosa	1961	40
193	43 3/8	14 6/8	9 7/8	15 3/8	9 7/8	23 3/8	21 3/8	Missoula Co., Mont.	Bonnie A. Ford	Bonnie A. Ford	1982	40
192 6/8	43 3/8	14 6/8	10 1/8	14 6/8	10 1/8	22 1/8	23 3/8	Spence's Bridge, B.C.	Norman Holland	Norman Holland	1971	42
192 6/8	43 2/8	14 2/8	11 1/8	14 2/8	11 1/8	22 1/8	21	Clearwater, Alta.	Edward L. Fuchs	Edward L. Fuchs	1943	43
192 6/8	44 2/8	14 3/8	10 3/8	14 3/8	10 3/8	24	17 5/8	Sun River, Mont.	Unknown	Robert Gabbert	1963	44
192 5/8	40 7/8	15 4/8	11 1/8	15 4/8	11 1/8	21 7/8	20 3/8	Clearwater River, Alta.	James Allan	James Allan	1977	44
192 2/8	40 7/8	15	10 5/8	15 4/8	10 5/8	22 7/8	21 3/8	Alberta	Henry Graves, Jr.	National Collection	PR1931	46
192	43	16	8 5/8	15	8 5/8	21	22 1/4	Sanders Co., Mont.	Richard W. Browne	Richard W. Browne	1968	47
191 7/8	40 5/8	16 7/8	9 2/8	16 7/8	9 2/8	22	22	Sanders Co., Mont.	Michael A. Jorgenson	Michael A. Jorgenson	1978	47
191 7/8	42 2/8	15	10 3/8	15	10 3/8	21 5/8	24	Narrow Creek, Alta.	Henry Mitchell	Henry Mitchell	1910	49
191 6/8	40 7/8	15 3/8	9 7/8	15 3/8	9 7/8	23 3/8	22 3/8	Colorado	Emory Whilton	Kern Co. (Calif.) Mus.	1901	50
191 5/8	42 2/8	15 3/8	9 5/8	15 3/8	9 5/8	24	24	Wildhorse Is., Mont.	Picked Up	Univ. Mont. Mus.	1961	50
191 4/8	40 3/8	16	10 5/8	15 5/8	10 5/8	22 3/8	22 1/4	Alberta	Clarence Hardy	Russel Vanslett	PR1961	50
191 3/8	41 1/8	15 5/8	9 5/8	15 5/8	9 5/8	24	23 3/8	Granite Co., Mont.	Steven L. Gingras	Steven L. Gingras	1984	50
191 3/8	42 1/8	15 3/8	10	15 3/8	10	23 3/8	22 1/4	Smoky River, Alta.	Picked Up	Carl M. Borgh	1944	54
191	40 7/8	15	10 3/8	14 7/8	10 3/8	22 1/8	20 7/8	Dinwoody Creek, Wyo.	Oris Miller	Oris Miller	1954	55
191	42 1/8	15 3/8	10 5/8	15 3/8	10 5/8	22 1/4	15 3/8	Lincoln Co., Mont.	Picked Up	Ed Boyes	PR1961	56
190 7/8	40	16 7/8	10 7/8	16	10 7/8	22 1/4	18 3/8	Canada	Unknown	A. H. Hilbert	PR1930	57
190 7/8	38 5/8	16 3/8	10 3/8	16 1/8	10 3/8	21 7/8	20 5/8	Natal, B.C.	John A. Morais	John A. Morais	1960	57
190 6/8	41 5/8	15 3/8	10 5/8	15 3/8	10 5/8	20	24 3/8	Cadomin, Alta.	Tony Oney	Tony Oney	1966	57
190 6/8	44 2/8	15 2/8	7 7/8	15 2/8	7 7/8	22	19 1/8	Brazeau River, Alta.	Donald S. Hopkins	Donald S. Hopkins	1937	60
190 6/8	41	14 5/8	10 1/8	14 5/8	10 1/8	24 3/8	19 5/8	Grassmere, B.C.	Donald F. Letcher	Donald F. Letcher	1965	60
190 5/8	42	15 3/8	9 6/8	15 3/8	9 6/8	22 1/8	18 3/8	Leyland Mt., Alta.	Rick J. Tymchuk	Rick J. Tymchuk	1982	60
190 5/8	39 5/8	15 3/8	11 1/8	15 3/8	11 1/8	19 7/8	18	Cadomin, Alta.	Frank Nuspel	Frank Nuspel	1962	63
190 5/8	39	15 3/8	11	15 3/8	11	22	22 5/8	Castle River, Alta.	Picked Up	E. B. Cunningham	PR1967	63
190 3/8	42 1/8	14 7/8	10 5/8	14 7/8	10 5/8	22 5/8	22 5/8	Kvass Creek, Alta.	Joseph W. Dent	Joseph W. Dent	1962	65
190 3/8	42 2/8	14 7/8	9 2/8	14 7/8	9 2/8	22 5/8	22 5/8	Prospect Creek, Alta.	Kenneth Campbell	Kenneth Campbell	1971	65
190 3/8	37 5/8	16 7/8	11	16 7/8	11	23 3/8	23 3/8	Fernie, B.C.	J. J. Osman	J. J. Osman	1950	67
190 3/8	39 5/8	17	8 6/8	17	8 6/8	22	15 3/8	Elko, B.C.	Charles Weikert	Charles Weikert	1970	67
190 2/8	41 1/8	15 5/8	8 6/8	15 5/8	8 6/8	23 3/8	16 5/8	Brazeau River, Alta.	Julio Estrada	Julio Estrada	1936	69
190 2/8	43 3/8	15 5/8	8 4/8	15 5/8	8 4/8	24 3/8	24 3/8	Missoula Co., Mont.	John J. Ottman	John J. Ottman	1985	69
190 1/8	46 3/8	15	8 3/8	15	8 3/8	22	22 1/8	Highwood, Alta.	Nick Sekella	Nick Sekella	1953	71
190 1/8	39 5/8	16	10 3/8	16	10 3/8	21 3/8	21 3/8	Sun River, Mont.	F. P. Murray	F. P. Murray	1957	71
190	40	15 5/8	10 5/8	15 5/8	10 5/8	22 1/8	14	Alberta	Stony Indian	Acad. Nat. Sci., Phil.	1901	73

Ovis canadensis canadensis and certain related subspecies

Score	Length of Horn R.	L.	Circumference of Base R.	L.	Circumference at Third Quarter R.	L.	Greatest Spread	Tip to Tip Spread	Locality Killed	By Whom Killed	Owner	Date Killed	Rank
190	40⅞	39⅞	15⅛	15⅞	10⅞	10⅜	19⅞	19⅞	Brazeau River, Alta.	Donald S. Hopkins	Acad. Nat. Sci., Phil.	1927	73
189⅞	40⅜	39⅜	16	16⅞	9⅞	10⅜	21⅜	21⅜	Clearwater Forest, Alta.	George Bugbee	Sally Bugbee	1928	75
189⅞	40⅜	41⅜	15⅜	15	9	9⅛	21⅜	17⅞	Ribbon Lake, Alta.	Ovar Uggen	Ovar Uggen	1957	75
189⅝	41	40⅜	15⅞	15⅜	9⅝	9⅛	23⅜	20⅜	Highwood Range, Alta.	Unknown	Earl Johnson	1928	77
189⅝	40⅝	40⅝	15⅝	15⅝	9⅛	9⅜	21⅛	14⅝	Swan Lake, B.C.	Billy Stork	A. C. Gilbert	1936	77
189⅝	38⅝	40⅛	16	16	9⅜	9⅜	23	20⅜	Yarrow Creek, Alta.	Allan Foster	Allan Foster	1963	79
189⅜	41	40⅜	14⅝	14⅞	11⅛	11⅞	23⅜	21	Park Co., Wyo.	Picked Up	Dale McWilliams	1975	80
189⅜	41⅞	39⅞	15⅞	16	9⅞	9⅜	19⅜	19⅜	Nikanassin Range, Alta.	Colleen Bodenchuk	Colleen Bodenchuk	1976	80
189⅜	40⅜	41⅞	14⅝	14⅛	11⅜	11⅛	18⅜	17⅞	Panther River, Alta.	Picked Up	George Browne	1928	82
189⅜	43⅜	43	14⅜	14⅜	10⅛	9⅞	22⅜	22⅜	Spence's Bridge, B.C.	Bert Walkem	Bert Walkem	1964	82
189⅜	40⅜	40⅜	16⅛	16⅜	8⅝	8⅞	23	19⅛	Teton Co., Mont.	R. L. Kennedy	R. L. Kennedy	1983	82
189⅛	41	39	15⅜	15⅛	9⅞	9⅞	24	20⅞	Canal Flat, B.C.	Robert Lemaster	Robert Lemaster	1962	85
189⅛	40⅞	42	14⅞	14⅛	10⅛	10⅜	21⅜	17⅞	Alberta	Bill Foster	Foster's Bighorn Rest.	PR1947	86
189	39	41	15⅜	15⅞	9⅜	9⅞	19⅜	17	Highwood River, Alta.	Hanson Bearspaw	W. S. Armstrong	1917	87
188⅞	41	40⅜	14⅞	14⅜	10⅜	11⅛	21⅜	18	Ram Creek, Alta.	William N. Beach	William N. Beach	1928	88
188⅞	43⅜	41⅜	14⅜	15⅜	9⅝	9⅜	25⅜	25⅝	Bow Valley, Alta.	Picked Up	Joseph Kovach	PR1952	88
188⅞	40⅜	41	14⅜	14⅞	10⅝	10	24	17	Gannet Peak, Wyo.	James Huffman	James Huffman	1962	88
188⅞	41⅞	44⅜	15⅛	15	9	8⅞	24⅜	23⅞	Gallatin Range, Mont.	Alden B. Walrath	Alden B. Walrath	1965	88
188⅝	40⅞	38⅜	17⅛	17⅞	8⅜	8⅜	24⅞	20⅝	Highwood, Alta.	Steve Kubasek	Steve Kubasek	1953	92
188⅝	40⅞	41⅛	15⅝	15⅞	9⅜	9⅜	23⅜	21⅜	Alberta	Bill Foster	Foster's Bighorn Rest.	PR1947	93
188⅝	38⅞	39⅜	15⅝	15⅞	9⅞	10⅛	21⅞	19⅞	Sun River, Mont.	Bruce McCracken	Bruce McCracken	1955	93
188⅜	41	38⅞	15⅜	15⅜	10⅜	10⅛	20⅜	19	Simpson River, B.C.	Patrick Deuling	Patrick Deuling	1985	93
188⅜	41	45⅜	14⅜	14⅜	11	9⅜	27	27	Clearwater, Alta.	Unknown	Norman Lougheed	1936	96
188⅜	40⅜	40	16⅜	16	8⅝	8⅞	21⅛	19⅜	Opal Range, Alta.	Robert Zebedee	Robert Zebedee	1977	96
188⅜	39	40⅜	15⅞	15⅞	9⅞	10	22⅜	22⅞	Rivalli Creek, Mont.	Sandy Rose	Sandy Rose	1978	96
188⅜	40⅞	39⅞	16⅜	16⅜	9	9	25⅝	21	White Swan Lake, B.C.	A. C. Gilbert	James V. Bosco	1940	99
188⅜	40⅞	40⅜	15⅜	15⅜	9	9	21⅜	17⅞	Surprise Lake, B.C.	Herb Klein	Herb Klein	1950	99
188⅛	42⅜	38	16	16	9⅜	9⅜	20⅜	20⅜	Alberta	Arthur Smith	Arthur Smith	1959	99
188⅛	39⅜	39⅞	15⅞	15⅜	9⅝	9⅞	21⅜	15⅜	Burnt Timber Creek, Alta.	Walter O. Ford, Jr.	Walter O. Ford, Jr.	1966	99
188⅛	39⅜	39⅜	15⅜	15⅜	11	10⅜	22⅜	14	Gibraltar Mt., Alta.	Leslie Kish	Leslie Kish	1981	99
188⅛	40	40⅜	15⅜	15⅜	10⅜	10⅜	21⅜	19	Sun River, Mont.	Bruce Neal	Bruce Neal	1912	104
188⅛	45⅞	44⅞	13⅜	13⅜	9⅜	9⅞	23⅜	22⅞	Panther River, Alta.	Unknown	Harvey A. Trimble	1932	104

188⅝	40⅞	40⅞	15⅛	15	10	10⅞	22⅞	21⅞	Sun River, Mont.	J. R. Pfeifer	J. R. Pfeifer	1958	104
188⅝	38⅞	37⅞	15⅜	15⅛	10⅞	10⅞	21⅞	21⅞	Kananaskis, Alta.	Terry Webber	Terry Webber	1961	104
188⅜	42⅞	42⅞	15⅜	15⅛	8⅜	8⅞	25⅞	25⅞	Spences Bridge, B.C.	Romeo Leduc	Romeo Leduc	1982	104
188⅜	44⅜	43⅜	14⅜	14⅞	9⅜	9⅞	25⅞	25⅜	Lincoln Co., Mont.	Alfred E. Journey	Alfred E. Journey	1980	109
188⅛	38⅜	39⅞	16	16⅜	9	9⅜	26⅞	26⅜	Sanders Co., Mont.	Patti L. Lewis	Patti L. Lewis	1984	109
188	41	40⅞	14⅞	14⅞	10	10⅞	21⅞	21⅞	Kananaskis River, Alta.	C. Allenhof	C. Allenhof	1958	111
188	39⅞	39⅞	15	15⅜	10⅞	10	23⅞	23⅜	Kananaskis Summit, Alta.	Ted Howell	Ted Howell	1963	111
187⅞	43⅜	44⅜	14⅞	14⅞	8⅜	8⅜	24⅞	24⅜	Salmon River, Idaho	Picked Up	Dwight Smith	1951	113
187⅞	42⅜	42⅜	14⅜	14⅜	9⅞	9⅜	24⅜	21⅞	Chase, B.C.	L. McNary & J. Langer	Lloyd McNary	1956	113
187⅞	44	43⅜	15	15	8⅞	8⅜	24⅜	24⅞	Ram River, Alta.	George W. Parker	George W. Parker	1961	113
187⅞	39⅜	38⅜	15⅛	15⅜	11⅜	11⅜	23⅜	23⅜	Wild Hay River, Alta.	Jim Papst	Jim Papst	1967	113
187⅞	39⅜	42	15⅜	15	8⅜	8⅞	23⅜	23⅜	Deer Lodge Co., Mont.	William H. Shurte	William H. Shurte	1984	113
187⅞	39⅜	40⅜	15⅜	15⅜	9⅞	9⅜	21⅜	21⅜	Glacier Natl. Park, Mont.	Olmstead, Dow, & Hawley	Mont. Dept. Fish & Game	1956	118
187⅞	40⅜	40⅜	14⅜	14	10⅜	10⅜	22⅜	22	Butcher Creek, Alta.	Vince Bruder	Vince Bruder	1958	118
187⅞	42⅜	42	16⅛	16	8⅞	8⅜	26⅜	25⅜	Teton Co., Wyo.	William R. Flagg	William R. Flagg	1967	118
187⅞	45⅞	43⅜	14⅞	14⅞	8⅜	8⅞	23	22⅞	Spence's Bridge, B.C.	J. David Smith	J. David Smith	1969	118
187¾	39⅜	40⅜	15⅜	15⅜	9	8⅜	26⅜	26⅜	Crystal Creek, Wyo.	Picked Up	Melvin R. Fowlkes	1970	122
187¾	40⅜	39⅜	15⅜	15⅜	9⅜	9⅜	20⅜	19⅞	Ram Range, Alta.	John F. Snyder	John F. Snyder	1978	122
187¾	39⅜	39⅜	15⅜	15⅜	9⅜	9⅞	21⅜	20	Sundre, Alta.	Stan Burrell	Stan Burrell	1953	124
187¾	40⅜	40⅜	16⅛	16⅜	8⅜	8⅜	22⅜	22⅜	Elbow River, Alta.	Sam Ross Sloan	Sam Ross Sloan	1962	124
187¾	42	41⅜	15⅜	15⅜	8⅜	8⅜	21⅜	21⅜	Lytton, B.C.	R. G. Jones & P. B. Wilmot	R. George Jones	1973	124
187¼	40⅜	41⅜	14⅜	15⅜	9⅜	9⅜	22⅜	22⅜	McDonald Creek, Alta.	Ernest F. Greenwood	Ernest F. Greenwood	1965	127
187¼	38⅜	43⅜	15⅜	15⅜	10⅜	10⅜	22⅞	22⅜	Plateau Mt., Alta.	Randy Jackson	Randy Jackson	1984	127
187¼	41⅜	39⅜	15⅜	15⅜	9⅜	9⅜	21	21	White Swan Lake, B.C.	Lucius A. Chase	Lucius A. Chase	1961	129
187⅛	43⅜	40⅜	15	15	8⅜	9⅜	23⅜	23⅜	Fallen Timber Creek, Alta.	Picked Up	Joe Blakemore	1968	129
187⅛	41	38⅜	15⅜	15⅞	9	9⅜	22⅞	22⅜	Red Deer River, Alta.	Richard B. Smith	Richard B. Smith	1984	129
187⅛	40⅜	40⅜	14⅜	14	10⅜	10⅜	23⅜	23⅜	Deer Lodge Co., Mont.	David J. Etzwiler	David J. Etzwiler	1985	129
187	39	39	15	15	10⅜	10⅜	23⅜	22⅜	Wind River Mts., Wyo.	Ralph E. Platt	Ralph E. Platt	1963	133
187	36⅞	38	15⅜	15⅜	10⅜	10⅜	17⅜	17⅜	Colorado	Picked Up	E. H. Brown	PR1964	133
187	37⅞	38⅜	16	16⅛	10⅜	10⅜	22⅜	22⅜	Unknown	Unknown	Dale Selby	PR1968	133
187	40⅜	40⅜	15⅜	15⅜	8⅜	8⅜	22⅜	22⅜	Sanders Co., Mont.	Bruce L. Hartford	Bruce L. Hartford	1978	133
187	37⅜	38⅜	16⅜	16⅜	9⅞	9⅜	25	25	Sanders Co., Mont.	Richard F. Lukes	Richard F. Lukes	1980	133
187	40⅜	38⅞	16	15⅜	8⅜	8⅜	15	15	Elbow River, Alta.	Ralph Cervo	Ralph Cervo	1981	133
187	41⅜	41⅜	16	16	8⅜	8⅜	24⅜	24⅜	Sanders Co., Mont.	Mark S. Eaton	Mark S. Eaton	1985	133
186⅞	34⅜	34⅜	15⅜	15⅜	10⅜	10⅜	22⅜	24⅜	Burnt Timber, Alta.	C. J. McElroy	C. J. McElroy	1965	140
186⅞	39⅜	38⅜	16⅜	16⅜	10	9⅜	23⅜	22⅜	E. Kootenay, B.C.	Jerry Mortimer	Jerry Mortimer	1959	141
186⅞	39⅜	39⅜	15⅜	15⅜	10⅜	10⅜	22	23	Whitehorse Creek, Alta.	Philip H. R. Stepney	Prov. Mus. Alta.	1978	141
186⅞	41⅜	42⅜	15⅜	15⅜	7⅜	7⅜	22⅜	21⅜	Whitman Co., Wash.	Picked Up	Inland Empire Big Game Council	1983	141
186⅞	38⅜	38⅜	16⅜	16⅜	8⅞	8⅜	23⅜	23⅜	Highwood River, Alta.	Ross Nikonchuk	Ross Nikonchuk	1984	141
186⅞	42⅜	41⅜	14⅜	14⅜	9⅞	9⅜	24⅜	24⅞	Panther River, Alta.	Picked Up	Belmore Browne	1936	145

BIGHORN SHEEP—*Continued*

Ovis canadensis canadensis and certain related subspecies

Score	Length of Horn R.	L.	Circumference of Base R.	L.	Circumference at Third Quarter R.	L.	Greatest Spread	Tip to Tip Spread	Locality Killed	By Whom Killed	Owner	Date Killed	Rank
186⅞	42⅛	42⅛	15	15	8⅜	8⅞	25⅝	25⅝	Shell Rock, Idaho	Lea J. Bacos	Lea J. Bacos	1953	145
186⅞	38⅜	38⅜	15⅜	15⅜	10⅛	10	22	17⅜	Blind Canyon, Alta.	Picked Up	Alberta Fish & Wildlife	1983	145
186⅜	40⅜	39⅜	15⅝	15⅝	9⅜	8⅞	19	22⅝	Fording River, B.C.	M. C. Baher	M. C. Baher	1942	148
186⅜	38	38⅜	17⅜	17⅜	8⅛	8⅜	20⅞	17⅞	Rocky Mt. House, Alta.	Robert B. Johnson	Robert B. Johnson	1960	148
186⅜	41⅞	40⅞	14⅜	14⅜	10⅜	10⅜	20	18	Tyrrell Creek, Alta.	Picked Up	John H. Batten	1949	150
186⅜	41	41⅞	14⅜	14	10⅝	11⅛	22⅛	17⅞	Ventre-Flat, Wyo.	John Evasco	John Evasco	1953	150
186⅜	38⅜	36	16	16⅛	10	10	22⅛	18⅜	Castle River, Alta.	Ed Burton	Ed Burton	1954	150
186⅜	42	41⅛	15⅜	15⅜	8⅜	8⅜	21⅝	16⅝	Fernie, B.C.	Thomas Krall	Thomas Krall	1963	150
186⅜	41	42⅜	15⅛	15⅛	8⅜	8⅞	20⅛	20⅛	Simpson River, B.C.	James A. Walls	James A. Walls	1981	150
186⅜	41⅞	42⅛	14	14	9⅝	9⅞	22⅛	21⅛	Cadomin, Alta.	R. A. Craig	R. A. Craig	1936	155
186⅜	42⅜	41⅜	14⅜	14⅞	9⅞	9⅞	24⅞	20⅞	Clearwater River, Alta.	Picked Up	John H. Batten	1954	155
186⅜	40⅞	40⅜	15⅛	15⅜	9⅞	9⅝	21⅛	19⅝	Sheep Creek, Alta.	G. A. Reiche	G. A. Reiche	1960	155
186⅜	37	38⅜	15⅞	16	10	9⅞	20⅛	17	Junction Mt., Alta.	Robert R. Willis	Robert R. Willis	1978	155
186⅜	40	41⅛	16	16	8	8⅜	22⅝	22⅝	Rabbit Creek, B.C.	Lanny E. Kniert	Lanny E. Kniert	1982	155
186⅜	39⅜	39⅜	16⅛	16⅛	8⅜	8⅜	23⅜	17⅜	Little Elbow River, Alta.	John Liefso	John Liefso	1982	155
186⅜	40	41	16⅛	16⅛	8⅜	8⅛	20⅞	13	Riverside Mt., B.C.	Paul A. Templin	Paul A. Templin	1983	155
186⅛	43⅜	44⅜	16⅛	16	6⅜	6⅞	24⅞	24⅞	Yellowstone Park, Mont.	William H. Dirrett	James K. Weatherford	1913	162
186⅛	39⅜	38⅜	15⅜	15⅜	10⅛	10	22⅜	15⅜	Highwood, Alta.	Terry J. Webber	Terry J. Webber	1959	162
186⅛	41⅜	41⅞	15⅜	15⅝	8⅜	8⅜	20⅞	19⅜	Sun River Canyon, Mont.	Glen Roberts	Glen Roberts	1961	162
186⅛	39⅜	40⅜	15⅝	15⅝	8⅜	8⅜	22	17⅜	Waterton Natl. Park, Alta.	Picked Up	Robert Thompson	PR1966	162
186	40⅜	40⅜	15⅛	15	9⅜	9⅜	22	18⅜	Sparwood, B.C.	Unknown	H. Bruce Freeman	PR1910	166
186	40⅜	39	16	16	8⅜	8⅞	19⅝	19⅝	Clear Water, Alta.	Herb Hamilton	Herb Hamilton	1964	166
186	39⅜	39	14⅜	14⅜	10⅛	10⅜	21	21	Granite Co., Mont.	Dale W. Hoth	Dale W. Hoth	1981	166
185⅞	40⅜	40⅜	15	15	9⅝	9⅜	21	17⅜	Panther River, Alta.	J. F. Blakemore	J. F. Blakemore	1961	169
185⅞	35	37⅜	14⅜	14⅜	13	13	20⅜	17⅜	Ural, Mont.	Curtis Gatson	Curtis Gatson	1962	169
185⅞	41⅜	41⅜	14	14⅜	10⅜	10⅜	22⅜	17⅜	Mystery Lake, Alta.	Jim Baballa	Jim Baballa	1962	169
185⅞	38⅜	38⅜	15⅜	15⅜	10	10	21⅜	17⅜	Burnt Timber Creek, Alta.	John T. Blackwell	John T. Blackwell	1967	169
185⅞	40⅜	40⅜	15	14⅜	9⅜	10⅜	21	21	Ghost River, Alta.	William D. Cox	William D. Cox	1959	173
185⅝	39⅜	39⅜	14⅜	14⅜	10⅛	10⅜	22⅜	18	Black Diamond, Alta.	Picked Up	Gordon Lait	1962	174
185⅝	40⅜	40	15⅜	15⅜	8⅞	9	23⅜	23⅜	Lemhi Co., Idaho	W. R. Franklin	W. R. Franklin	1963	174
185⅝	42⅜	41	13⅞	14	10	9⅞	21⅜	21⅜	Wind River Mts., Wyo.	Elgin T. Gates	Elgin T. Gates	1954	176
185⅝	40⅝	40	14⅜	14⅜	10⅜	10	22⅜	20	Sask. River, Alta.	Herb Klein	Herb Klein	1963	176

185⅞	38⅞	40⅝	15⅜	15⅜	8⅝	10	24	19⅝	Highwood River, Alta.	W. Erdman	M. R. Wagner	1964	176
185⅞	40⅜	40⅝	14⅜	14⅜	10⅛	10⅛	22	20⅛	Canyon Creek, Alta.	Edith J. Nagy	Edith J. Nagy	1981	176
185⅞	39⅞	39⅝	16⅜	16⅜	8	8⅛	21⅛	13⅜	Natal, B.C.	H. Beard	Myles Travis	1921	180
185⅞	39⅜	38⅜	14⅞	15⅜	10⅜	10⅜	22	17⅜	Lewis & Clark Co., Mont.	Richard Tyler	Richard Tyler	1954	180
185⅞	39⅜	39	16	16	9⅜	9⅜	21	20⅛	Fremont Co., Colo.	Leonard L. Kiser	Leonard L. Kiser	1955	180
185⅞	39⅜	39⅜	14⅜	14⅞	10⅛	9⅝	23⅛	19⅜	Lillooet, B.C.	Glen E. Park	Glen E. Park	1964	180
185⅞	39⅜	40⅜	15⅝	15⅜	10⅝	9⅝	21⅛	15⅜	Banff, Alta.	Unknown	E. Kent. Univ.	PR1974	180
185⅞	42⅜	38	16	15⅜	8⅝	10⅛	21	17⅜	Unknown	Unknown	Art Esslinger	1930	185
185⅞	38⅛	37⅛	16	15⅜	8⅝	8⅛	20⅛	20⅛	Big Creek, Idaho	Edson Piers	Edson Piers	1962	185
185⅞	40⅜	41	15⅜	15⅜	8⅜	9⅜	23⅜	20⅛	Spence's Bridge, B.C.	J. C. Atkinson	J. C. Atkinson	1965	185
185⅜	38⅛	37⅜	16⅝	16⅜	9⅛	8⅝	22⅛	21	Fremont Co., Colo.	Robert W. Wallace	Robert W. Wallace	1978	185
185⅜	38⅜	41⅜	15⅜	15⅜	8⅝	9⅜	21⅛	20⅛	Teton Co., Mont.	Picked Up	Tim French	1980	185
185⅜	41⅜	40⅝	14⅜	14⅜	9⅜	9⅜	22⅞	19⅜	Dubois, Wyo.	B. N. Lively	B. N. Lively	1953	190
185⅞	40⅛	38⅜	15⅜	15⅜	9⅜	8⅞	23	15⅜	Tornado Mt., B.C.	Vincent Kehm	Vincent Kehm	1958	190
185⅞	40⅜	37⅜	15⅞	15⅞	9⅜	9	23⅜	18⅜	Big Horn River, Alta.	Chris Klineburger	Chris Klineburger	1962	190
185	40⅜	39⅛	16⅞	16⅞	8⅜	8⅜	22	19⅜	Alberta	Gift of Lynford Biddle	Acad. Nat. Sci., Phil.	1901	193
185	39⅜	39⅛	14⅜	14⅜	10⅛	10⅛	23	17⅜	Green River, Wyo.	Floyd J. Stalnaker	Elsie Stalnaker	1913	193
185	38⅜	41⅛	15⅜	15⅜	9⅜	9⅜	18⅜	17⅜	Mitchell River, B.C.	Mr. & Mrs. N. A. Meckstroth	Mr. & Mrs. N. A. Meckstroth	1963	193
185	40⅜	39⅜	15⅜	15⅜	9⅜	8⅝	20⅜	17⅜	Cadomin, Alta.	Rita Oney	Rita Oney	1966	193
184⅞	40⅜	39⅜	14⅜	14⅜	9⅜	9⅜	23⅜	23⅜	Westhorse Mts., Idaho	Cecil Dodge	Cecil Dodge	1953	197
184⅞	37⅜	37⅜	15⅜	15	10⅜	10⅜	22⅜	20	Glenwood Springs, Colo.	Picked Up	Mark E. Cook	1960	197
184⅞	38⅜	39⅜	15⅝	15⅝	10⅜	10⅜	21⅜	21⅜	Unknown	Unknown	George Ostashek	PR1920	199
184⅞	40⅜	40⅜	15⅝	15⅜	9⅞	9⅜	21⅜	19⅜	Brazeau River, Alta.	Grancel Fitz	Mrs. Grancel Fitz	1931	199
184⅞	41⅜	41⅜	14⅜	14⅜	9⅜	9⅜	21	20⅜	Castle Mt., Mont.	E. L. Anderson	E. L. Anderson	1954	199
184⅞	40	40⅜	14⅜	14⅜	10⅜	10⅜	23⅜	21⅜	Jackson Hole, Wyo.	Johnny Kretschman	Johnny Kretschman	1962	199
184⅜	39⅜	39⅜	16⅜	16⅜	7⅜	8⅜	21⅜	17⅜	Little Elbow River, Alta.	Alex Cornett	Alex Cornett	1976	199
184⅜	38⅜	37⅜	15⅜	15⅜	9⅜	9⅜	22⅜	20⅜	Salmon River, Idaho	Ted Biladeau	Ted Biladeau	1939	204
184⅜	39⅜	41⅜	14⅜	14⅜	9⅜	9⅜	20⅜	17⅜	Clearwater, Alta.	G. C. Matthews	G. C. Matthews	1942	204
184⅜	39⅜	39⅜	14⅜	14⅜	10⅜	10⅜	22⅜	18⅜	Rock Lake, Alta.	Bill Bodenchuk	Clifford Wolfe	1960	204
184⅜	41⅜	42⅜	14⅜	14⅜	9⅜	9⅜	22⅜	22⅜	Burnt Timber Creek, Alta.	Berry B. Brooks	Berry B. Brooks	1960	204
184⅜	38⅜	40⅜	15⅜	15⅜	9⅜	9⅜	22⅜	21⅜	Ruby Lake, Alta.	Picked Up	John G. Stelfox	1965	204
184⅜	39	40⅜	15	15	10	10	22	18⅜	Luscar Creek, Alta.	Doug W. Whiteside	Doug W. Whiteside	1976	204
184⅜	39⅜	39⅜	16	16	8⅜	8⅜	22⅜	17⅜	Smoky River, Alta.	Wm. C. Barthman	Wm. C. Barthman	1946	210
184⅜	39⅜	38⅜	14⅜	14⅜	10⅜	10⅜	21⅜	17⅜	Sun River, Mont.	Picked Up	W. H. Stecker	1948	210
184⅜	38⅜	39⅜	15⅜	15⅜	8⅜	8⅜	22⅜	18⅜	Custer Co., Idaho	Stanley V. Potts	Stanley V. Potts	1981	210
184⅜	37⅜	37⅜	15⅜	15⅜	10⅜	11	21⅜	13⅜	Gunnison Co., Colo.	Billy Prior	Daniel C. Harrington	1915	213
184⅜	37⅜	41⅜	15⅜	15⅜	8⅜	9	22⅜	17⅜	Cadomin, Alta.	John H. Marcum	John H. Marcum	1969	213
184⅜	39⅜	39⅜	14	14⅜	11⅜	9	22	21	Carbon Co., Mont.	Picked Up	Monte Berzel	1977	213
184⅜	37⅜	37⅜	15⅜	15⅜	10⅜	10⅜	24	24	Middle Mts., Wyo.	William Underwood	William Underwood	1959	216
184⅜	38⅜	40⅜	15	15	9⅜	10⅜	20⅜	18⅜	Drinnan Creek, Alta.	John H. Epstein	John H. Epstein	1963	216
184⅛	40⅜	38⅜	15⅜	15⅜	8⅜	8⅜	23	22	Vaseux Lake, B.C.	Bob McDowell	Bob McDowell	1960	218
184⅛	39⅜	42	15⅜	15⅜	8⅜	8⅜	22⅜	22⅜	Alberta	Bob Wood	N. Am. Wildl. Mus.	1964	218

Ovis canadensis canadensis and certain related subspecies

Score	Length of Horn R.	L.	Circumference of Base R.	L.	Circumference at Third Quarter R.	L.	Greatest Spread	Tip to Tip Spread	Locality Killed	By Whom Killed	Owner	Date Killed	Rank
184⅛	38⅞	39	17	17	7⅞	7⅞	23⅛	23⅛	Castle River, Alta.	E. B. Cunningham	E. B. Cunningham	1965	218
184⅛	39⅞	39⅝	15⅝	15⅝	9⅜	9⅜	24	21⅞	Panther River, Alta.	Picked Up	Paul Ujfalusi	1966	218
184	40⅝	37⅝	14⅝	14⅝	9⅜	9⅛	22⅝	22⅜	Valley Co., Idaho	Picked Up	LaVarr Jacklin	1949	222
184	41⅜	41⅛	14⅜	14⅛	10	10	20⅝	19	Ghost River, Alta.	W. D. Norwood	W. D. Norwood	1955	222
184	39⅜	39⅜	14⅝	14⅝	10⅛	10⅜	21	21⅛	Sun River, Mont.	Carl Mehmke	Carl Mehmke	1957	222
184	35	36⅜	16⅝	16⅛	10⅜	11	21	20	Cardston, Alta.	August Glander	August Glander	1969	222
184	37⅝	39⅜	16⅛	16⅜	8⅜	8⅞	21	20	Sanders Co., Mont.	Don Robinson	Don Robinson	1980	222
183⅞	41⅛	40	14⅛	14⅛	9⅝	9⅜	23	20⅝	Sask. River, Alta.	Basil C. Bradbury	Basil C. Bradbury	1968	227
183⅞	43⅝	35⅝	17	17	7⅝	6⅝	24⅝	23	Beaverhead Co., Mont.	James C. Garrett	James C. Garrett	1983	227
183⅞	37⅝	37⅝	15⅝	15⅝	9⅝	9⅝	20⅝	17⅝	Fernie, B.C.	Unknown	Fred Braatz	1930	229
183⅞	39⅝	39⅝	14⅝	14⅝	9⅞	10	21⅛	15⅝	Natal, B.C.	Mrs. A. L. Musser	A. L. Musser	1947	229
183⅝	40⅛	39⅝	14⅜	14⅜	10⅜	10⅛	19⅝	18⅝	Castle River, Alta.	George Hagglund	George Hagglund	1959	229
183⅝	37⅝	38	15⅝	15⅝	10	10	21⅛	18⅝	Highwood Range, Alta.	K. Fred Coleman	K. Fred Coleman	1977	229
183⅝	37⅞	37⅝	16⅝	16⅜	9⅝	9⅜	21⅛	17⅝	Mystery Lake, Alta.	Paul Inzanti	Paul Inzanti	1960	233
183⅝	38⅜	39⅜	15	15⅝	9⅜	9⅝	19⅝	18⅝	Marble Creek, Idaho	Joseph T. Pelton	Joseph T. Pelton	1961	233
183⅝	37⅝	39	15⅜	15⅜	9⅝	10⅛	22	16⅝	Burnt Timber Area, Alta.	Jay H. Giese	Jay H. Giese	1966	233
183⅝	36⅝	37	16⅛	16⅝	9⅝	9⅝	24⅝	24⅝	Granite Co., Mont.	Sandy C. Antonich	Sandy C. Antonich	1982	233
183⅝	33⅝	39	16	16	10⅛	10⅛	22⅝	18⅝	Sweetgrass Co., Mont.	Basil C. Bradbury	Basil C. Bradbury	1965	237
183⅝	42	36⅝	14⅝	14⅝	9⅝	9⅛	21⅜	21⅛	Mystery Lake, Alta.	Armando Tomasso	Armando Tomasso	1967	237
183⅝	38⅝	37⅝	15⅝	15	9⅝	9⅝	20⅝	20	C. M. R. Game Range, Mont.	Mrs. Gordon Pagenkopf	Mrs. Gordon Pagenkopf	1970	237
183⅝	41	38⅝	16	15⅝	8	8⅝	24⅝	23⅝	Lewis & Clark Co., Mont.	John Coston	John Coston	1961	240
183⅝	37⅝	38⅜	15⅝	15⅝	10⅜	10⅛	22	16⅝	Clearwater River, Alta.	C. J. McElroy	C. J. McElroy	1969	240
183⅝	38⅝	39⅝	16⅝	16⅝	7⅝	8⅜	21	15⅝	Sanders Co., Mont.	John P. Dilley	John P. Dilley	1981	240
183⅝	39⅝	39⅜	14⅝	14⅜	11⅝	11⅛	20	17⅝	Snake-Indian River, Alta.	O. Fowler & J. Brewster	Fred Brewster	1919	243
183⅝	39⅝	38⅝	14⅝	14⅝	9⅝	9⅝	23⅝	23⅝	Sun River, Mont.	Earl Hofland	Earl Hofland	1957	243
183⅝	39⅜	38	15⅝	15⅝	9⅜	9⅝	19⅝	19	Smoky River, Alta.	F. C. Hibben	F. C. Hibben	1957	243
183⅝	39⅝	40⅝	14⅝	15⅝	9⅜	8⅝	23⅝	18⅝	Clearwater River, Alta.	Joseph C. Sellitti	Joseph C. Sellitti	1981	243
183⅝	38⅜	40⅝	15⅝	15⅝	8⅜	8⅜	22⅝	18⅝	Granite Co., Mont.	John L. Wozniak	John L. Wozniak	1984	243
183⅝	41	42⅝	15⅝	15⅝	7⅜	7⅝	23⅝	23⅝	Deer Lodge Co., Mont.	Phillip Demers	Phillip Demers	1985	243
183⅝	40	37⅝	16	16	9	8⅝	22⅝	20	Unknown	Unknown	Jonas Bros. of Seattle	PR1939	249
183⅝	34⅝	36	16⅝	16⅝	9⅝	10⅛	24⅝	20	S. Platte Canyon, Colo.	Harold C. Eastwood	Harold C. Eastwood	1957	249

183⅛	38⅝	38⅝	15⅝	15⅝	9	9⅛	22⅞	16⅞	Kootenay River, B.C.	W. Vernon Walsh	W. Vernon Walsh	1962	249
183⅛	36⅞	37⅞	15⅜	15⅜	10⅜	10	22	18	Fraser River, B.C.	Karl P. Willms	Karl P. Willms	1977	249
183⅛	36⅞	36⅜	16⅜	15⅝	9⅝	9⅝	21⅛	16⅜	Mt. Sparrowhawk, Alta.	Randy Ward	Randy Ward	1984	249
183	39⅜	38	16⅜	16⅜	8⅜	8⅛	21⅛	17	Teton Basin, Wyo.	William A. Baillie-Grohman	John H. Batten	1876	254
183	37⅝	39⅝	15⅝	15⅝	10⅜	10⅜	19⅝	15⅛	Clearwater River, Alta.	John H. Batten	John H. Batten	1931	254
183	39½	40	15⅝	15⅝	8⅜	8⅜	21⅛	21⅛	Cadomin, Alta.	Otis Chandler	Otis Chandler	1969	254
183	38	38⅝	15⅝	15⅝	9	9⅝	21⅛	21⅛	Solomon Creek, Alta.	Picked Up	William Gosney	1977	254
182⅞	40⅝	40⅞	13⅞	14⅛	10⅛	9⅝	20⅞	19⅛	Ram River, Alta.	Robert G. Morgan	Robert G. Morgan	1980	254
182⅞	40⅝	38⅞	15	15	9⅜	9⅝	22	17⅜	Alberta	G. L. Gibbons	G. L. Gibbons	1963	259
182⅞	37⅝	37⅝	15⅜	15½	10	9⅞	23⅝	20⅛	Lake Louise, Alta.	Picked Up	Howard Bronsdon	1952	260
182⅞	39⅝	38	14⅜	14½	10⅜	10	22⅛	18	Salmon River, Idaho	Picked Up	Wayne Demaray	1963	260
182⅞	38⅜	37⅞	14⅞	15	10⅝	10⅜	21⅛	15⅜	Burnt Timber, Alta.	Mrs. W. E. Anderson	Mrs. W. E. Anderson	1964	260
182⅞	39⅜	39	15	15	9⅞	9⅝	22	18	Wild Hay River Valley, Alta.	Jim Papst	Jim Papst	1968	260
182⅞	40⅛	40⅛	14⅝	14	9	9⅛	22⅞	22⅞	Lower Salmon River, Idaho	Glenn H. Schubert	Deloras A. Schubert	1970	260
182⅞	40⅛	39⅞	16⅛	16	7⅞	7⅝	22⅞	19⅛	Sanders Co., Mont.	Terrence Pond	Terrence Pond	1978	260
182⅞	44⅛	42⅝	13⅞	14	9⅜	8⅛	23⅜	23⅛	Alberta	John D. Hazen	National Collection	1918	266
182⅞	37⅞	38⅝	16⅝	16⅛	8⅜	7⅝	19⅜	16	Brazeau Forest, Alta.	H. A. Yocum	H. A. Yocum	1941	266
182⅞	40⅜	39⅜	15	15⅝	8⅜	8⅜	22⅝	15⅜	Bull River, B.C.	Ralph W. Stearns	Ralph W. Stearns	1950	266
182⅞	42⅛	40⅝	15⅝	15⅝	7⅝	7⅝	20⅛	20	Sun River, Mont.	Martin Alzheimer	Martin Alzheimer	1955	266
182⅞	39⅛	36⅝	15⅝	15⅝	9⅜	9⅛	21⅝	20⅛	Narraway River, Alta.	John C. Seidensticker	John C. Seidensticker	1959	266
182⅞	38⅛	38⅜	15	14⅞	10⅛	9⅝	21⅝	15⅛	Storm Mt., Alta.	W. Glaser	W. Glaser	1961	266
182⅞	38⅛	37⅜	16	16	9⅛	9⅜	19⅝	13⅛	Junction Creek, Alta.	Robert F. Brooks	Robert F. Brooks	1978	266
182⅞	37	35⅝	15⅝	15⅜	10⅝	8⅞	23	21	Wind River, Wyo.	Hubert Weibel	Hubert Weibel	1956	273
182⅞	35⅞	35⅝	16⅛	16⅜	10	9⅛	24	22⅜	Waterton, Colo.	William D. Jenkins	William D. Jenkins	1956	273
182⅞	36⅞	35⅝	16⅛	16⅝	8⅜	8⅝	23⅝	17⅛	S. Castle River, Alta.	Leon Atwood	Leon Atwood	1962	273
182⅞	39⅛	39⅜	15⅝	15½	8⅜	8⅜	22⅝	19⅛	Kananaskis Summit, Alta.	Ted Howell	Ted Howell	1964	273
182⅞	38⅜	37⅝	15	14½	10	10⅜	22⅝	18⅛	Turtle Creek, Wyo.	Russell C. Cutter	Russell C. Cutter	1968	273
182⅞	41⅛	40⅝	15	15	8⅛	8⅜	22	18⅛	Edgewater, B.C.	William N. Ward	William N. Ward	1969	273
182⅞	40⅝	40	15⅝	15⅜	8⅜	8⅛	23⅝	20	Spence's Bridge, B.C.	Don Ticehurst	Don Ticehurst	1973	273
182⅞	38⅝	35⅝	15⅝	15⅝	11⅛	10⅛	23⅝	23⅛	Wallowa Co., Oreg.	Randy Craddock	Randy Craddock	1981	273
182⅞	35⅞	36⅜	16⅝	16⅛	9⅜	9⅝	22⅜	19	Blind Canyon, Alta.	Alan W. Foster	Alan W. Foster	1981	273
182⅞	38⅝	41⅛	15⅜	15⅜	8⅜	8⅝	22⅝	17⅜	Mary Ann Creek, B.C.	Jack Bridgewater	Jack Bridgewater	1981	273
182⅞	38⅜	37⅜	14⅝	14⅜	10⅝	10⅜	22	16⅞	Banff, Alta.	Gift of Madison Grant	National Collection	PR1951	283
182⅞	37⅜	37⅜	15⅜	15⅜	10⅛	10⅝	21⅝	17	Teton River, Mont.	Geoffrey A. Morrison	Geoffrey A. Morrison	1969	283
182⅞	38⅝	37⅜	16	15⅝	8⅜	8⅛	23⅝	18⅝	West Sulphur River, Alta.	Robert Highberg	Robert Highberg	1980	283
182⅞	40⅝	40⅜	14⅞	14⅝	9⅞	9⅝	21⅝	21	Shoshone N. Fork, Wyo.	Herb Klein	Herb Klein	1934	286
182⅞	40⅛	40⅝	15	15	8⅝	8⅜	23⅝	20⅛	Dubois, Wyo.	George Pate	Larry Pate	1960	286
182⅞	39⅝	39⅞	15⅝	15⅝	9⅛	9⅜	21⅝	17⅝	Ram River, Alta.	Louise McConnell	Louise McConnell	1961	286
182⅞	36	36⅜	15⅝	15⅝	10	10	21⅝	16	Sulphur River, Alta.	Unknown	Roy Everest	1963	286
182⅞	40⅛	39⅜	15	14⅝	9⅜	9⅛	21⅛	21⅛	Wild Hay River, Alta.	James H. Duke, Jr.	James H. Duke, Jr.	1967	286

423

BIGHORN SHEEP—Continued

Ovis canadensis canadensis and certain related subspecies

Score	Length of Horn R.	L.	Circumference of Base R.	L.	Circumference at Third Quarter R.	L.	Greatest Spread	Tip to Tip Spread	Locality Killed	By Whom Killed	Owner	Date Killed	Rank
182⅞	36⅜	35⅝	16⅛	16⅝	9⅛	9⅛	23⅝	18⅞	Rocky Creek, Alta.	Randy A. Desabrais	Randy A. Desabrais	1982	286
182⅞	37⅝	39⅛	14⅜	14⅞	10⅛	10⅛	22⅛	21⅜	Park Co., Mont.	Rodney W. Cole	Rodney W. Cole	1985	286
182⅛	41⅛	39	12⅞	13⅛	11⅛	11⅛	22⅛	22⅝	Salmon River, Idaho	Picked Up	Anson Eddy	PR1959	293
182⅛	35⅝	39⅛	15⅜	15⅜	11⅛	9⅛	24⅛	24⅛	Lemhi Co., Idaho	Leonard C. Miller, Sr.	Leonard C. Miller, Sr.	1963	293
182⅛	38⅜	37⅛	15⅜	15⅛	9⅜	9⅜	22⅛	17⅜	Panther River, Alta.	W. H. Slikker	W. H. Slikker	1966	293
182⅛	37⅞	37⅞	16	16⅞	8⅝	8⅜	20⅛	18⅞	Crowsnest Lake, Alta.	John Truant	John Truant	1970	293
182	40	41	14⅜	14⅜	8⅝	8⅞	24	24	Salmon River, Idaho	Picked Up	Elmer Keith	1957	297
182	37⅜	36⅞	15⅜	15⅞	9⅜	10	21	16⅜	Pincher Creek, Alta.	Delton Smith	Delton Smith	1958	297
182	41	37⅞	15	14⅞	9⅜	9⅜	21⅛	17⅛	Canal Flat, B.C.	Allen Cudworth	Allen Cudworth	1958	297
182	39⅜	41⅛	15	15	8⅜	7⅛	23⅜	23⅜	Lewis & Clark Co., Mont.	Allan L. Davies	Allan L. Davies	1981	297
182	38⅛	38⅜	14⅜	14⅜	10⅜	10⅜	19	17⅜	Mt. Kidd, Alta.	Picked Up	Dirk Kieft	1982	297
182	37⅜	39⅜	15⅜	15⅜	8⅜	8⅛	20⅜	17⅛	Mt. Kidd, Alta.	Dwayne W. Oneski	Dwayne W. Oneski	1982	297
181⅞	39⅜	39⅛	14⅜	14⅜	10⅜	10⅛	20⅜	20⅛	Coal Branch, Alta.	John Caputo	John Caputo	1962	303
181⅞	36⅜	36⅜	16⅜	16⅛	8⅜	8⅛	20⅜	20	Elko, B.C.	Percy McGregor	Percy McGregor	1974	303
181⅞	39⅜	40⅜	15⅜	14⅞	8⅜	8⅜	21⅛	21⅜	Sundre, Alta.	Dennis George Overguard	Dennis George Overguard	1980	303
181⅞	38⅜	39	15⅜	15⅜	9⅜	9⅜	21⅛	19	Hinton, Alta.	Darla J. Smith	Ben Morris	1980	303
181⅞	39⅜	38⅜	15⅜	15⅜	9	9⅛	20	19	Kakwa River, Alta.	Donald C. Fobert	Donald C. Fobert	1983	303
181⅛	38	38⅜	15⅜	15⅛	8⅜	8⅛	23⅜	22⅛	Cataract Creek, Alta.	Michael J. Hogan	Michael J. Hogan	1984	303
181⅝	37	37⅞	15⅜	15⅜	9⅜	9⅛	18	14⅛	Ghost River, Alta.	L. C. Nowlin	L. C. Nowlin	PR1940	309
181⅝	38⅜	38⅜	15	15⅜	9⅜	10	20⅜	16⅛	Prospect Creek, Alta.	Wayne Tarnasky	Wayne Tarnasky	1983	309
181⅝	42	40⅛	15⅜	15⅜	8	7⅜	21	20⅜	Ghost River, Alta.	J. S. Parker	J. S. Parker	1954	311
181⅝	39⅜	37	15	15⅜	8⅜	9⅜	23⅜	21⅜	Custer Co., Mont.	Picked Up	W. S. Maloit	1959	311
181⅝	36⅜	39⅜	15	15⅜	9	8⅜	23⅜	23⅜	Elbow River, Alta.	Ernest F. Dill	Ernest F. Dill	1961	311
181⅝	39	40⅜	15⅜	15⅜	8⅜	7⅜	22⅞	22⅛	Sun River, Mont.	Walter L. Bodie	Walter L. Bodie	1965	311
181⅝	41⅜	37⅞	14⅜	14⅜	10	10⅜	21⅛	20⅜	Burnt Timber Creek, Alta.	George H. Glass	George H. Glass	1967	311
181⅝	38⅜	39⅜	14⅜	14⅜	9⅜	9⅜	23⅝	19	Park Co., Wyo.	Keith Frick	Keith Frick	1972	311
181⅝	39⅜	37	16⅜	16⅜	7⅜	7⅜	20	15⅜	Fisher Range, Alta.	Reginald Zebedee	Reginald Zebedee	1982	311
181⅝	39⅜	39⅜	15⅜	15⅜	8⅜	8⅜	21⅛	17⅜	Goat Range, Alta.	Christian D. Pagenkopf	Christian D. Pagenkopf	1984	311
181⅝	38⅛	34⅜	16⅜	16⅜	9⅜	9⅜	23	18	Pigeon Mt., Alta.	Paul S. Inzanti, Jr.	Paul S. Inzanti, Jr.	1984	311
181⅛	40	40⅜	15⅛	15⅞	8⅜	8⅜	22	21⅛	Sulphur River, Alta.	John E. Hammett	John E. Hammett	1938	320
181⅛	38⅜	41⅛	14⅜	14⅜	8⅜	8⅜	22⅜	21⅜	Castle River, Alta.	Cliff Johnson	Cliff Johnson	1957	320
181⅛	36	36⅜	15⅜	15⅜	11⅛	11⅜	23	21	Dubois, Wyo.	Jack Adams	Jack Adams	1959	320

Score									Locality	Owner	By whom killed	Date	Rank
181⅛	38⅜	39⅜	15⅛	15⅛	8⅞	9	23⅛	19⅞	Cadomin, Alta.	John Caputo	John Caputo	1961	320
181⅛	43	43⅜	16	16	6⅞	6⅞	29⅞	29⅞	Gallatin Co., Mont.	Richard D. Gilman	Richard D. Gilman	1967	320
181⅛	41⅜	39⅜	15⅜	15⅜	8	7⅜	22⅜	22⅜	Lewis & Clark Co., Mont.	Picked Up	William L. Wesland	1973	320
181	39	37	15⅛	15⅛	9	9⅜	22	18	Spray Lake, Alta.	George R. Willows	George R. Willows	1974	320
181⅛	41	41⅜	16⅛	16	6⅜	6⅜	21⅜	21	Deer Lodge Co., Mont.	Gerald P. Wendt	Gerald P. Wendt	1978	320
181⅛	37	39	16⅜	16⅜	8⅜	8⅜	24⅜	24⅜	Lewis & Clark Co., Mont.	Donel G. Hayes	Donel G. Hayes	1980	320
181⅜	39⅜	39⅜	14⅜	15⅜	9⅜	9⅜	25	21	Clearwater River, Alta.	Phil Temple	Phil Temple	1951	329
181⅜	38⅜	39⅜	15⅜	15⅜	9⅜	9⅜	20⅜	14	Big Horn Creek, Alta.	Earl Foss	Earl Foss	1960	329
181⅜	37⅜	36⅜	17	17	8	8⅜	20⅜	15⅜	Park Co., Colo.	Richard L. Rudeen	Richard L. Rudeen	1963	329
181⅜	38⅜	37⅜	14⅜	14⅜	9⅜	9⅜	20⅜	19⅜	Clearwater River, Alta.	Joseph T. Pelton	Joseph T. Pelton	1966	329
181⅜	38⅜	38⅜	15	14⅜	9⅜	9⅜	21⅜	15	Beartooth Plateau, Mont.	Olav E. Nelson	Olav E. Nelson	1970	329
181⅛	39	39⅜	15⅜	15⅜	8⅜	8⅜	22⅜	19⅜	Lincoln Co., Mont.	Lowell Olin	Lowell Olin	1977	329
181⅜	37⅜	37⅜	15	15	10⅜	10⅜	19	15⅜	Cardinal River, Alta.	Randy Babala	Randy Babala	1980	329
181⅜	39⅜	41⅜	15⅜	15⅜	8⅜	7⅜	21⅜	20⅜	Granite Co., Mont.	David D. Rittenhouse	David D. Rittenhouse	1980	329
181⅞	42	41⅜	14	14	8⅜	8⅜	24⅜	24⅜	Teton Basin, Wyo.	Michael Huppuch	Philip Schlegel	1901	337
181⅞	41⅛	40⅜	13⅞	14	10⅜	9⅜	21⅜	19⅜	Highwood River, Alta.	Ralph Rink	George Beach	1946	337
181⅞	40⅜	40⅞	15⅜	15⅜	7⅜	7⅜	22⅜	22⅜	McBride, B.C.	Alfred Saulnier	Alfred Saulnier	1966	337
181⅛	38⅜	38⅜	14	14⅜	11	10⅜	20⅜	15⅜	Cooke City, Mont.	Larry L. Altimus	Larry L. Altimus	1969	340
181⅛	38⅜	35	15⅜	15⅜	9⅜	9	20⅜	15	Spray Lakes Reservoir, Alta.	G. Robert Willows	G. Robert Willows	1977	340
181⅛	39⅜	39⅜	14⅜	14⅜	9⅜	9⅜	22⅜	22⅜	Deer Lodge Co., Mont.	Thomas R. Puccinelli	Thomas R. Puccinelli	1984	340
181	40⅜	45⅜	14⅜	13⅜	7⅜	7⅜	26⅜	26⅜	Kootenay, B.C.	A. E. Matthew	A. E. Matthew	1950	343
181	39⅜	39⅜	14⅜	14⅜	8⅜	8⅜	23⅜	17⅜	Lincoln Co., Mont.	Hal Kanzler	Hal Kanzler	1960	343
181	39⅜	39⅜	15⅜	15⅜	8⅜	8⅜	21	17	Brule, Alta.	Picked Up	G. W. Warner	1963	343
181	37	37	15⅜	15⅜	9	9	23	15	Mystery Lake, Alta.	Peter Lazio	Peter Lazio	1967	343
181	38⅜	37⅜	14⅜	14⅜	11⅜	11	19⅜	19⅜	Simpson Creek, B.C.	Walt Failor	Walt Failor	1968	348
180⅞	38⅜	39⅜	14	14	10⅜	10⅜	19⅜	18	Park Co., Wyo.	Picked Up	Jay Thomas	1979	348
180⅞	38⅜	42	15	15	8⅜	8⅜	22⅜	22⅜	Seebe, Alta.	Ted Trueblood	Ted Trueblood	1956	349
180⅞	37	38⅜	15⅞	15⅜	8⅜	8⅜	22⅜	15	Bull River, B.C.	Walter J. Ruehle	Walter J. Ruehle	1962	349
180⅝	35	34⅜	15⅜	15⅜	11⅜	10⅜	22⅜	17	Texas Creek, Colo.	Picked Up	Jack Putnam	PR1963	349
180⅞	37⅜	35⅜	16⅜	16	8⅜	8⅜	21	15⅜	Flat Creek, Alta.	G. I. Franklin	G. I. Franklin	1964	349
180⅞	37⅜	38⅜	15	15	9⅜	9⅜	21⅜	16⅜	Panther Creek, Alta.	C. D. Sharp	C. D. Sharp	1966	349
180⅞	37⅜	36⅜	16	16	9⅞	8⅞	21	17⅜	Junction Creek, Alta.	Spencer T. Nichols	Spencer T. Nichols	1981	349
180⅞	37	37⅜	14⅜	14⅜	10	10	22⅜	18	Park Co., Wyo.	Dwight Lyman	Dwight Lyman	1982	349
180⅝	39⅜	39⅜	15	15	8⅜	8⅜	22	19⅜	Mineral Co., Mont.	Roberta A. Hartford	Roberta A. Hartford	1982	349
180⅝	37⅜	37⅜	15⅜	15⅜	8⅜	8⅜	21⅜	17⅜	Forbidden Creek, Alta.	Dennis H. Russell	Dennis H. Russell	1984	349
180⅝	39⅜	39⅜	13⅜	13⅜	10⅜	11	22	17⅜	Wind River Mts., Wyo.	Alfred Hume	Alfred Hume	1960	358
180⅝	38⅜	38⅜	14⅜	14⅜	10⅜	10	21⅜	21⅜	Sun River, Mont.	Robert W. Boucher	Robert W. Boucher	1966	358
180⅝	38	39⅜	14⅜	14⅜	9⅜	10⅜	19⅜	19⅜	Salmon River, Idaho	Emerson Hall	Emerson Hall	1968	358
180⅝	37⅜	35	15⅜	15⅜	9⅜	9⅜	22⅜	15⅜	Waterton Lake, B.C.	Victor T. Zarnock, Jr.	Victor T. Zarnock, Jr.	1972	358
180⅝	40⅜	39⅜	15⅜	15⅜	8⅜	7⅜	20	18⅜	Lewis & Clark Co., Mont.	William J. McRae	William J. McRae	1980	358
180⅝	37⅜	36	15⅜	15⅜	9⅞	9⅜	22⅜	16⅜	Ghost River, Alta.	Robert W. Hodge	Robert W. Hodge	1985	358
180⅜	39	41⅜	14⅜	14⅜	8⅜	8⅜	22⅜	22	Smoky River, Alta.	H. P. Brandenburg	H. P. Brandenburg	1924	364

BIGHORN SHEEP—Continued

Ovis canadensis canadensis and certain related subspecies

Score	Length of Horn R.	L.	Circumference of Base R.	L.	Circumference at Third Quarter R.	L.	Greatest Spread	Tip to Tip Spread	Locality Killed	By Whom Killed	Owner	Date Killed	Rank
180 6/8	40 2/8	38 2/8	15 6/8	15 4/8	8 3/8	8	21 2/8	20	White Swan Lake, B.C.	John Barton	John Barton	1936	364
180 6/8	35 6/8	38 2/8	15 2/8	15	10 2/8	9 3/8	22	17	Lake Louise, B.C.	Unknown	Martin Bonack	PR1951	364
180 6/8	38	39	14 2/8	14 4/8	10 2/8	10 2/8	22 2/8	18 2/8	Coal Branch, Alta.	R. G. F. Brown	R. G. F. Brown	1962	364
180 6/8	38	38 4/8	15	15	8 2/8	9	19 2/8	18 2/8	Moosehorn Lake, Alta.	Maynard Mathews	Maynard Mathews	1964	364
180 6/8	38 2/8	39 2/8	13 2/8	13	10 2/8	10 2/8	20	20	Park Co., Wyo.	Picked Up	Sam L. Beasom	1974	364
180 6/8	34 7/8	35 2/8	15 4/8	15 5/8	10 1/8	10 2/8	21 2/8	13 1/8	Thistle Creek, Alta.	Paul H. Chance	Paul H. Chance	1975	364
180 6/8	40 1/8	40 1/8	15 4/8	15 4/8	7 6/8	7 6/8	22 2/8	20	Luscar Mt., Alta.	Jerry L. Christian	Jerry L. Christian	1979	364
180 6/8	40	38 2/8	14 2/8	14 4/8	9 2/8	9 3/8	23 2/8	22 2/8	Deer Lodge Co., Mont.	Jan J. Henry	Jan J. Henry	1983	364
180 2/8	39 2/8	39 7/8	16	16 2/8	7 1/8	7 2/8	22 2/8	22 1/8	Sulphur River, Alta.	W. D. Parker	W. D. Parker	1955	373
180 2/8	41	36 7/8	15 4/8	15	8	8 1/8	19 2/8	19 2/8	Ghost River, Alta.	Art Brewster	Art Brewster	1960	373
180 2/8	37 4/8	38	14 2/8	14 4/8	9 4/8	10 1/8	22 2/8	19	Sheep Creek, Wyo.	Picked Up	Loren L. Lutz	1962	373
180 2/8	36 1/8	37 2/8	15 2/8	15 2/8	9 5/8	10	22	19 4/8	Jakey's Fork, Wyo.	Eugene Schilling	Eugene Schilling	1962	373
180 2/8	38 2/8	39 4/8	15	14 2/8	9 4/8	9	21 2/8	17	Ghost River, Alta.	J. E. Edwards	J. E. Edwards	1964	373
180 2/8	39 2/8	39 4/8	14 4/8	15	8 7/8	9	23 2/8	23 2/8	Wallowa Co., Oreg.	Kirk W. Jones	Kirk W. Jones	1979	373
180 2/8	40 7/8	40 2/8	14 4/8	14 6/8	8 5/8	8 3/8	22 7/8	22 2/8	Lemhi Co., Mont.	Picked Up	R. Munn & F. Porter	1982	373
180 2/8	35 5/8	38 2/8	16 3/8	16 4/8	8 3/8	8 3/8	24 4/8	21 5/8	Silver Bow Co., Mont.	Robert C. Carlson	Robert C. Carlson	1983	373
180 2/8	39 2/8	39 1/8	15 3/8	15 3/8	8 5/8	8 1/8	22 2/8	19 6/8	Mineral Co., Mont.	J. Ray Lake	J. Ray Lake	1984	373
180 2/8	37	37 7/8	15 1/8	15 3/8	9 5/8	9 5/8	23	19	Park Co., Wyo.	Robert G. Curtis	Robert G. Curtis	1984	373
180 2/8	36 7/8	38 6/8	15	15 4/8	9	9	20 4/8	20 4/8	Cecelia Lake, B.C.	Dan Auld	Dan Auld	1950	383
180 2/8	39 2/8	38 1/8	14 1/8	14 6/8	10 6/8	10	20 2/8	20 2/8	Salmon River, Idaho	Ralph Puckett	Ralph Puckett	1958	383
180 2/8	38 4/8	37 2/8	14 6/8	14 6/8	10 3/8	9 6/8	21 1/8	15	Burnt Timber Creek, Alta.	Ruth Mahoney	Ruth Mahoney	1963	383
180 1/8	36 4/8	34 5/8	15 2/8	15 2/8	10 3/8	10 7/8	22 1/8	18 4/8	Sugarloaf Mt., Colo.	Picked Up	Henry Zietz	1947	386
180 1/8	36 5/8	37 2/8	15	15 3/8	9 1/8	9	23 3/8	20 5/8	Green River, Wyo.	John N. Leonard	John N. Leonard	1953	386
180 1/8	36 1/8	40	15 4/8	15 2/8	8 3/8	8 3/8	20 4/8	18	Sun River, Mont.	Dennis Reichelt	Dennis Reichelt	1958	386
180 1/8	39 5/8	40 2/8	14 7/8	15	8 3/8	8 5/8	23	23	Salmon River, Idaho	C. A. Schwope	C. A. Schwope	1959	386
180 1/8	37 4/8	34 5/8	15 3/8	15 3/8	10 4/8	9 6/8	22 1/8	16 5/8	Gannet Peak, Wyo.	Wilbur Rickett	Wilbur Rickett	1964	386
180 1/8	37 3/8	37 6/8	14 5/8	14 6/8	10	10	22 4/8	19 2/8	Ghost River, Alta.	Lloyd E. Zeman	Lloyd E. Zeman	1968	386
180 1/8	36 6/8	34 3/8	15 6/8	15 4/8	9 6/8	9 5/8	22 5/8	18 2/8	Castle River, Alta.	Don W. Caldwell	Don W. Caldwell	1969	386
180 1/8	37 6/8	38 1/8	15 7/8	15 7/8	8 1/8	8	18 5/8	18 5/8	Nye, Mont.	Ira H. Kent	Ira H. Kent	1974	386
180 1/8	37 5/8	37 7/8	16 6/8	16 5/8	8 5/8	8	20	20	Sanders Co., Mont.	Gene N. Meyer	Gene N. Meyer	1976	386
180 1/8	41 3/8	41 1/8	15	15	7	7 5/8	28 5/8	28 5/8	Deer Lodge Co., Mont.	Arden Holden	Arden Holden	1979	386
180 1/8	37 3/8	35 5/8	15 3/8	15 3/8	9 7/8	9 5/8	19 4/8	16	Coral Creek, Alta.	Leonard W. King	Leonard W. King	1983	386

Score									Locality	Owner	By	Date	Rank
180⅛	37⅝	37⅝	16	16	7⅞	8	21⅛	14%	Cougar Mt., Alta.	Norman Howg	Norman Howg	1984	386
180	37⅛	38⅛	15	15	9⅛	10	22	18%	Seebe, Alta.	Anson Brooks	Anson Brooks	1956	398
180	39⅛	37⅛	15	15⅞	9⅛	9⅞	21	19%	Forbidden Creek, Alta.	James Haugland	James Haugland	1958	398
180	38⅜	38⅜	15⅞	15⅞	9	9	21⅛	18%	Kootenay, B.C.	Walter L. Bjorkman	Walter L. Bjorkman	1963	398
180	37⅞	37⅞	14⅞	14⅞	10⅛	10⅛	22⅛	22%	Panther Creek, Alta.	Walter R. Schubert	Walter R. Schubert	1966	398
180	39⅜	39⅞	15⅜	15⅜	8	8	22⅛	20%	Wallowa Co., Oreg.	F. Carter Kerns	F. Carter Kerns	1978	398
180	38⅜	41⅛	14⅜	14⅜	8⅜	8⅜	24	23%	Lewis & Clark Co., Mont.	James G. Braddee, Jr.	James G. Braddee, Jr.	1978	398
180	38⅜	37⅜	15⅜	15⅜	9	8⅜	20⅛	16%	Whitehorse Creek, Alta.	Philip H. R. Stepney	Prov. Mus. Alta.	1978	398
180	40⅛	37⅜	15⅜	15⅜	8⅜	8⅜	22⅛	22%	Granite Co., Mont.	Jerry E. Gallagher	Jerry E. Gallagher	1980	398
180	40⅛	40⅛	14⅜	14⅜	8⅜	8⅜	25	25	Wallowa Co., Oreg.	Jerome V. Epping	Jerome V. Epping	1984	398
199*	43⅜	43⅜	15⅛	16⅛	10⅛	10⅛	23⅛	23%	Granite Co., Mont.	Larry D. Smith	Larry D. Smith	1984	398
196*	44⅛	41⅛	15⅞	16	10⅛	9⅞	22⅞	20	Missoula Co., Mont.	Claude I. Burlingame	Claude I. Burlingame	1984	
191⅝*	41⅛	42⅛	16⅝	16	8⅞	8⅜	23	22%	Sanders Co., Mont.	Bryan G. Nelson	Bryan G. Nelson	1982	
191⅜*	42⅜	42⅜	15⅜	15⅜	9⅛	9⅜	24	20%	El Paso Co., Colo.	Raymond E. Moore	Raymond E. Moore	1983	

*Final Score subject to revision by additional verifying measurements

427

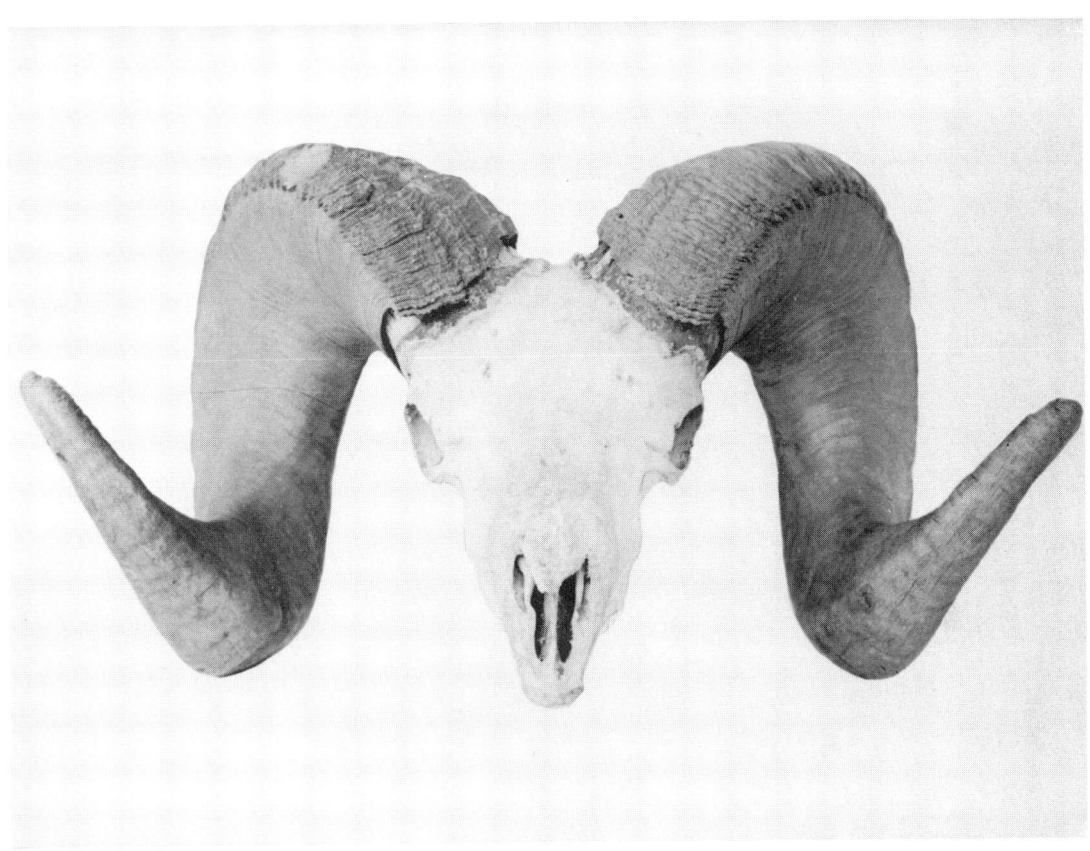

WORLD'S RECORD DESERT SHEEP
SCORE: 205 1/8
Locality: Lower California, Mexico Date: 1940
Hunter: an Indian Owner: Carl M. Scrivens

NUMBER TWO DESERT SHEEP
SCORE: 201 3/8
Locality: Pima County, Arizona Date: 1982
Picked Up Owner: Greg Koons

Desert Sheep

Minimum Score 168

Ovis canadensis nelsoni and certain related subspecies

Score	Length of Horn R.	L.	Circumference of Base R.	L.	Circumference at Third Quarter R.	L.	Greatest Spread	Tip to Tip Spread	Locality Killed	By Whom Killed	Owner	Date Killed	Rank
205⅝	43⅜	43⅛	16⅜	17	10⅜	10⅜	25⅜	25⅜	Lower Calif., Mexico	Indian	Carl M. Scrivens	1940	1
201⅜	45¼	46½	15⅝	15⅝	11⅛	11⅛	20⅜	20	Pima Co., Ariz.	Picked Up	Greg Koons	1982	2
197⅞	43½	43⅜	15⅜	15⅜	10	10	23⅞	23⅞	Lower Calif., Mexico	Gift of H. M. Beck	Acad. Nat. Sci., Phil.	1892	3
192⅝	41½	42⅜	15	15⅛	10⅛	10⅛	25⅜	25	Baja Calif., Mexico	Javier Lopez del Bosque	Javier Lopez del Bosque	1979	4
191⅝	42	43⅜	15⅜	15⅜	9⅝	9⅜	23⅜	23⅜	Baja Calif., Mexico	Lit Ng	Lit Ng	1968	5
191⅜	40	41⅞	16⅛	16⅛	9⅜	9⅜	24⅛	24⅛	Mexico	Picked Up	Snow Museum	PR1952	6
191⅛	38⅜	40⅛	16⅜	16⅜	10⅜	10⅜	21⅛	17⅛	Baja Calif., Mexico	Claude Bourguignon	Claude Bourguignon	1982	7
189⅜	39⅜	39⅜	15⅜	15⅜	10⅜	11	21⅜	21⅜	Lower Calif., Mexico	M. B. Silva	M. B. Silva	1939	8
189⅜	43	43	14⅝	14⅜	9⅜	9⅜	27⅜	27⅜	Baja Calif., Mexico	A. Cal Rossi, Jr.	A. Cal Rossi, Jr.	1974	9
188⅞	39⅝	39⅝	15⅜	15⅞	9⅜	9⅜	21⅜	16⅜	Pima Co., Ariz.	Carl A. Mattias, Sr.	Carl A. Mattias, Sr.	1982	10
187⅞	42	40	15⅜	15⅞	10⅛	10⅛	23⅜	23⅜	Baja Calif., Mexico	Ed Stedman, Jr.	Ed Stedman, Jr.	1976	11
187⅞	38⅜	40⅜	16⅜	16⅜	9	9	21⅜	20⅜	Baja Calif., Mexico	Romulo Sanchez Mireles	Romulo Sanchez Mireles	1969	12
187⅜	39⅜	39⅜	15⅜	15⅜	10⅜	10⅜	21	21	Sonora, Mexico	Herb Klein	Herb Klein	1952	13
187⅜	39⅛	39⅜	15⅜	16	10⅜	10⅜	17⅜	17⅜	Sonora, Mexico	Oscar J. Brooks	Oscar J. Brooks	1955	13
187	39⅛	39⅜	16	16	9⅜	9⅜	24⅜	24⅜	Lower Calif., Mexico	Unknown	Snow Museum	PR1952	15
187	40⅜	40⅜	15⅜	15⅜	9⅜	10	26	26	Kofa Mts., Ariz.	Louis R. Dees	Louis R. Dees	1965	15
186⅞	38⅜	38⅜	14⅜	14⅜	11⅜	11⅜	22	20⅜	Sonora, Mexico	F. B. Heider	O. M. Corbett	1927	17
186⅞	40⅜	38⅜	16	16	9	9⅜	21⅜	20⅜	Maricopa Co., Ariz.	Ralph Grossman	Ralph Grossman	1961	18
186⅞	40⅜	40⅜	14⅜	14⅜	10	10	20⅜	23	Baja Calif., Mexico	Robert P. Miller	Robert P. Miller	1981	18
186	38⅜	38⅞	15⅜	15⅜	10⅛	10⅜	22⅜	19⅜	Yuma Co., Ariz.	Gerry W. Nikolaus	Gerry W. Nikolaus	1979	20
185⅞	39⅜	40	16	16	10⅜	9⅜	22⅜	19⅜	Baja Calif., Mexico	Graciano Guichard	Graciano Guichard	1970	21
185⅜	38⅜	37⅜	15⅜	15⅜	9	9⅜	19⅜	16⅜	Baja Calif., Mexico	Wilmer C. Hansen	Wilmer C. Hansen	1972	22
185⅜	39⅜	39⅜	15⅜	15⅜	10⅜	9⅞	25⅜	25⅜	Baja Calif., Mexico	Albert Pellizzari	Albert Pellizzari	1978	22
185⅜	41	40⅜	15⅜	15⅜	8⅜	9	21⅜	20⅜	Graham Co., Ariz.	John W. Harris	John W. Harris	1982	22
185	39⅜	39⅜	15⅜	15⅜	8⅜	9	20⅜	18⅜	San Borja Mts., Mexico	Alice J. Landreth	Alice J. Landreth	1969	25
185	38⅜	37⅜	16⅜	16⅜	9	8⅜	24⅜	21	Baja Calif., Mexico	Miguel Zaldivar De Valasco	Miguel Zaldivar De Valasco	1979	25
184⅞	42	40⅜	14⅜	15	9⅜	9⅜	29⅜	29⅜	Kofa Mts., Ariz.	W. A. Rudd	W. A. Rudd	1965	27
184⅞	39⅜	38⅜	16⅜	16⅜	8⅜	8⅜	22⅜	21⅜	Baja Calif., Mexico	Burton L. Smith, Sr.	Burton L. Smith, Sr.	1973	27
184⅞	40⅜	37⅞	15⅜	15⅜	10	10⅜	22⅜	21⅜	Baja Calif., Mexico	Steven L. Rose	Steven L. Rose	1967	29
184⅞	38⅜	39	15⅜	16	9⅜	9⅜	20⅜	21	Baja, Mexico	H. Clayton Poole	H. Clayton Poole	1966	30
184⅞	43⅜	45⅜	13⅜	13⅜	8⅜	8⅜	26⅜	26⅜	Santa Teresa Mts., Ariz.	Picked Up	Ariz. Game & Fish Dept.	1967	30

Score									Locality	By	Owner/Collection	Year	Rank
184⅞	40⅞	40	15⅞	15⅞	9	9	22	22	Baja Calif., Mexico	Clint Heiber	Clint Heiber	1978	30
184⅛	38⅞	40	15⅜	15⅜	9⅜	9⅞	22	20⅛	Papago Indian Res., Ariz.	Ralph J. Murrietta	Ollie O. Barney, Jr.	1965	33
184	40⅜	38⅞	14	14	10⅜	9⅞	25⅝	25⅛	Santa Rosa Mts., Calif.	Picked Up	Fred L. Jones	1955	34
184	41	40⅜	15⅜	15⅜	8⅞	8⅞	25⅛	25⅝	Baja Calif., Mexico	Thomas J. Brimhall	Thomas J. Brimhall	1981	34
183⅞	39⅜	38⅞	16	16	9⅜	9⅜	23⅝	23⅝	Gonzaga, Mexico	Glenn Napierskie	Glenn Napierskie	1970	36
183⅜	40	40⅜	14	13⅞	10⅜	9⅜	24⅞	24⅞	Pinkley, Ariz.	Picked Up	Organ Pipe Cactus Natl. Mon.	1957	37
183⅜	39⅞	41⅜	15⅞	15⅞	9	9	25⅞	25⅞	Lower Calif., Mexico	George H. Gould	National Collection	1894	38
183⅜	39⅞	38⅜	15⅞	15⅞	10⅜	9⅞	23	23	Clark Co., Nev.	Gerald A. Lent	Gerald A. Lent	1976	38
182⅞	39⅜	37⅜	14⅞	14⅞	8⅜	10⅞	22	20⅛	Colo. River, Ariz.	Picked Up	John E. Luster	1956	40
182⅞	41⅛	38⅜	15⅜	15⅜	8⅜	8⅞	23⅜	23⅜	Baja Calif., Mexico	Rita Oney	Rita Oney	1976	40
182⅝	39	39⅜	15⅜	15⅜	9⅜	9⅜	22⅞	22⅞	Baja Calif., Mexico	Duane H. Loomis	Duane H. Loomis	1972	42
182⅝	36	35⅜	16⅜	16⅜	9⅜	9⅜	22⅜	19⅜	Pima Co., Ariz.	Charles W. Fisher	Charles W. Fisher	1972	42
182¼	39⅞	39⅞	14⅞	14⅞	9⅞	9⅜	21⅜	21⅜	Lower Calif., Mexico	Picked Up	C. G. Clare	1958	44
182¼	37	37⅞	14⅞	14⅞	10	10⅜	22⅜	22⅜	Riverside Co., Calif.	Picked Up	Orson Morgan	1963	44
182⅜	38⅜	37⅜	14⅝	15	10⅜	10⅜	22	22	Lower Calif., Mexico	Elgin T. Gates	Elgin T. Gates	1940	46
182⅛	39⅜	40	15	15	9⅜	9⅜	22⅜	22⅜	Baja Calif., Mexico	Robert Zachrich	Robert Zachrich	1978	46
182⅛	40	39⅝	14⅞	14⅞	8⅜	9⅜	23⅜	23⅝	Graham Co., Ariz.	James W. Ferguson	James W. Ferguson	1984	48
182⅛	39⅞	37	15	15	10⅛	9⅞	22¼	19⅜	Baja Calif., Mexico	Jesus H. Garza-Villarreal	Jesus H. Garza-Villarreal	1984	48
182	37⅜	37	15	15	10⅜	9⅞	24	19⅜	Baja Calif., Mexico	John M. Griffith, Jr.	John M. Griffith, Jr.	1974	50
181⅞	38	36⅜	15	15	8⅞	8⅞	24⅛	24	Sonora, Mexico	George W. Parker	George W. Parker	1939	51
181⅞	42⅜	41⅜	15⅜	15⅜	8⅜	8⅞	24⅛	24⅜	Sheep Mt. Range, Nev.	David Ingram	David Ingram	1962	52
181⅜	39⅜	36⅜	16⅜	16⅜	10⅜	10⅜	22	20⅛	Baja Calif., Mexico	Elvin Hawkins	Elvin Hawkins	1978	52
181½	36⅜	38⅝	15⅜	15⅜	9⅜	9⅜	25⅝	25⅝	Maricopa Co., Ariz.	Kirt I. Darner	Kirt I. Darner	1971	54
180⅞	38⅜	37	15	15	10⅜	10⅜	21⅜	21⅜	Sonora, Mexico	Ira C. Green	Ira C. Green	1939	55
180⅞	37	38⅜	15⅜	15⅜	8⅞	9⅞	22⅜	22⅜	Baja Calif., Mexico	Geo. H. Landreth	Geo. H. Landreth	1969	56
180⅜	40	34⅜	15⅝	15⅝	9⅞	9⅝	20⅜	20⅛	Baja Calif., Mexico	Jack Atcheson, Jr.	Jack Atcheson, Jr.	1978	56
180⅜	37⅞	37⅜	15⅜	15⅜	9	8⅞	19⅜	17⅜	Dragon Teeth Mt., Ariz.	Raymond White	Raymond White	1966	58
180⅜	35⅝	40⅜	14⅜	14⅜	9⅜	9⅜	20⅜	20⅛	Baja, Mexico	Arthur R. Dubs	Arthur R. Dubs	1966	59
180⅛	38⅜	39⅞	15⅜	15⅜	9⅜	9⅞	22⅜	0	Baja Calif., Mexico	Fritz A. Nachant	Fritz A. Nachant	1970	59
180	38	37½	16⅛	16⅛	10⅜	9⅛	21⅜	23⅜	Yuma Co., Ariz.	James K. McCasland	James K. McCasland	1978	59
180	37⅞	39⅜	14⅜	14⅜	9⅜	7⅞	22	24⅜	Tank Mts., Ariz.	Picked Up	Calvin C. Wallerich	1960	62
179⅞	39⅜	36⅞	15⅜	15⅜	9⅞	9⅞	19⅜	24	Pima Co., Ariz.	Clifford W. Saylor	Clifford W. Saylor	1976	63
179⅞	36⅜	36½	15⅜	15⅜	9	9⅜	25⅜	19⅝	Clark Co., Nev.	John Virgil Zenz	John Virgil Zenz	1980	63
179⅞	38⅜	38⅝	15⅜	15⅜	8⅞	9⅞	24⅜	19⅜	Baja Calif., Mexico	George W. Vogt	George W. Vogt	1978	65
179⅞	37⅝	35⅜	16	16	10⅜	9⅜	24	21⅜	Clark Co., Nev.	Sal Quilici	Nevada State Museum	1978	65
179⅝	37	37	16	16	8⅜	7⅜	21	20⅜	Baja Calif., Mexico	Paul E. Robey	Paul E. Robey	1979	65
179⅝	36⅞	36⅜	15⅜	15⅜	7⅞	9⅞	21⅜	20⅜	Baja Calif., Mexico	Don L. Corley	Don L. Corley	1978	68
179⅜	38⅜	39⅜	16⅛	16⅜	9⅜	9⅜	20⅜	21⅜	Baja Calif., Mexico	Mrs. Carroll Pistell	Mrs. Carroll Pistell	1969	69
179½	36½	36½	15⅜	15⅜	9⅜	9⅜	20⅜	18⅜	Baja, Mexico	Jim Buss	Jim Buss	1966	70
179½	38⅜	37	15⅜	15⅜	9⅜	9⅜	21⅜	18⅜	Baja Calif., Mexico	Francisco Salido	Francisco Salido	1968	70
179⅜	36⅜	36⅜	14⅜	14⅜	9⅞	8⅜	20⅜	18⅜	Clark Co., Nev.	Andy S. Burnett	Andy S. Burnett	1979	70
179⅜	36⅛	38⅜	15⅜	15⅜	8⅜	8⅝	21⅜	18⅜	Baja Calif., Mexico	W. J. Boynton, Jr.	W. J. Boynton, Jr.	1974	73
179	37⅜	36⅛	16⅜	16⅜	8⅜	8⅜	19⅜	19⅜	Baja Calif., Mexico	Graciano G. Michel	Graciano G. Michel	1970	74

Desert Sheep—Continued

Ovis canadensis nelsoni and certain related subspecies

Score	Length of Horn R.	L.	Circumference of Base R.	L.	Circumference at Third Quarter R.	L.	Greatest Spread	Tip to Tip Spread	Locality Killed	By Whom Killed	Owner	Date Killed	Rank
178⅜	39⅛	36	16⅛	16⅜	8	7⅞	20⅜	20	Hidalgo Co., N.M.	L. P. McKinney	Frank McKinney	1921	75
178⅜	36⅞	37	15⅜	15⅝	9⅞	10⅛	23	22⅜	Sauceda Mts., Ariz.	Picked Up	Edward Hunt	1962	75
178⅜	35⅞	36⅜	15⅜	15⅜	9⅞	10⅜	29⅜	29⅜	Mohave Co., Ariz.	Earle H. Smith	Earle H. Smith	1981	75
178⅜	39⅜	39⅛	14⅜	14⅜	9⅛	9	27	27	Colo. River, Nev.	E. A. Goldman	U. S. Natl. Mus.	1913	78
178⅜	37⅜	37	14⅜	14⅜	10⅜	10⅛	22⅜	18⅜	Sonora, Mexico	Oscar J. Brooks	Oscar J. Brooks	1950	78
178⅜	37⅜	36⅝	15⅜	15⅝	8⅜	8⅜	21⅜	21⅜	Baja Calif., Mexico	Hobson L. Sanderson, Jr.	Hobson L. Sanderson, Jr.	1981	78
178⅜	35⅝	36⅜	15⅜	15⅜	9⅜	9⅜	23⅜	22	Lincoln Co., Nev.	William A. Bertelson	William A. Bertelson	1984	81
178⅜	38⅜	35⅜	15⅜	15⅝	9⅜	9⅜	22⅜	20	Pima Co., Ariz.	Ken Broyles	Ken Broyles	1971	82
178⅜	38⅜	36⅝	15⅜	15⅝	9	9⅜	20⅜	19⅜	Baja Calif., Mexico	Henry Culp	Henry Culp	1978	82
178⅜	34	40⅜	15	14⅜	9⅜	10⅜	19⅜	18	Maricopa Co., Ariz.	Michael Holt	Michael Holt	1970	84
178	36	37	16	16	8⅜	9	22	22	Sonora, Mexico	Aaron Saenz, Jr.	Aaron Saenz, Jr.	1969	85
178	38⅜	37⅜	15	14⅜	9⅜	9⅜	21⅜	19⅜	Baja Calif., Mexico	Basil C. Bradbury	Basil C. Bradbury	1969	85
178	35⅜	38⅜	16	16	8⅜	8⅜	24	24	Baja Calif., Mexico	James G. Lagiss	James G. Lagiss	1980	85
177⅜	39⅜	38⅜	15⅛	15⅜	8⅜	8	26⅜	26⅜	San Boros Mts., Mexico	Jerald T. Waite	Jerald T. Waite	1972	88
177⅜	38⅜	37⅜	15	15⅜	9⅜	9⅜	20⅜	19⅜	Baja Calif., Mexico	Richard C. Hansen	Richard C. Hansen	1973	88
177⅜	37	37⅜	14⅜	15	9⅜	9⅜	21	19⅜	Mohave Co., Ariz.	William C. Duffy, Jr.	William C. Duffy, Jr.	1981	88
177⅜	36⅜	36	15⅜	15⅝	9⅜	9⅜	22⅜	20⅜	Yuma Co., Ariz.	J. Dorsey Smith	J. Dorsey Smith	1983	88
177⅜	38	42	14⅜	14⅜	8⅜	8⅜	27⅜	27⅜	Lower Calif., Mexico	Earl A. Garrettson	William Foster	1912	92
177⅜	38	37	14⅜	14⅜	9⅜	9⅜	25⅜	24	Baja, Mexico	Herb Klein	Herb Klein	1966	92
177⅜	36⅜	35⅜	14⅜	15⅜	9⅜	9⅜	15⅜	18⅜	Baja Calif., Mexico	Joe Osterbauer	Joe Osterbauer	1978	92
177⅜	38⅜	38⅜	14⅜	14⅜	10⅜	9⅜	21	21	Lower Calif., Mexico	F. Stephens	U. S. Natl. Mus.	1902	95
177⅜	36⅜	37⅜	14⅜	14⅜	9⅜	9⅜	22⅜	22	Yuma Co., Ariz.	George I. Parker	George I. Parker	1968	95
177⅜	37⅜	38	15⅜	15⅜	8⅜	8⅜	21⅜	21⅜	Baja Calif., Mexico	Arthur W. Carlsberg	Arthur W. Carlsberg	1970	95
177⅜	37	37⅜	16	16⅜	8⅜	8	19⅜	16	Baja Calif., Mexico	Don McBride	Don McBride	1980	95
177⅜	34⅜	36⅜	15⅛	15	10⅜	11	19	19	Clark Co., Nev.	Ralph W. McClintock	Ralph W. McClintock	1980	95
177⅜	39⅜	34⅜	15⅜	15⅜	8⅜	8⅜	28⅜	28⅜	Clark Co., Nev.	Robert M. Bransford	Robert M. Bransford	1966	100
177⅜	37⅛	37⅜	15⅜	15⅜	9	9⅜	20⅜	20⅜	San Borjas Mts., Mexico	Lloyd Zeman	Lloyd Zeman	1970	100
177⅜	37	36	15⅜	15⅜	9⅜	9⅜	23	20⅜	Yuma Co., Ariz.	Robert Fritzinger	Robert Fritzinger	1976	100
177⅛	36⅜	36⅜	15⅝	15⅜	8⅜	8⅜	21⅜	20⅜	Pima Co., Ariz.	Michael A. Jensen	Michael A. Jensen	1978	103
177⅛	37⅜	38⅜	15⅜	15⅜	8⅜	8⅜	22⅜	22⅜	Baja Calif., Mexico	G. Dale Monson	G. Dale Monson	1982	103
177	36⅜	36⅜	15⅜	15⅜	9	9⅜	19	18	Baja, Mexico	Alain Ferraris	Alain Ferraris	1966	105
177	35⅜	36⅜	15⅜	15⅜	9⅜	9⅜	19⅜	17⅜	Baja Calif., Mexico	Roy A. Woodward	Roy A. Woodward	1969	105

432

Score									Locality	Hunter	Owner	Date	Rank
177	36⅞	37	15⅛	14⅞	9⅜	9⅜	21⅛	20	Sonora Desert, Mexico	Herb Klein	Herb Klein	1969	105
176⅞	38⅜	36⅞	14⅞	14⅞	9	8⅞	23⅞	23⅞	Muddy Mts., Nev.	Arthur Alles	Lauren A. Johnson	1956	108
176⅞	38⅜	42	14⅜	14⅜	8⅜	8⅜	27⅞	27⅜	Mexico	Bill Foster	Foster's Bighorn Rest.	PR1967	108
176⅞	38	39⅜	14⅞	14⅞	8⅜	7⅜	21⅜	20	Kofa Range, Ariz.	Picked Up	Duard B. Sanford	1957	110
176⅞	36⅜	36⅜	14⅛	13⅜	10⅜	10⅜	23⅜	23⅜	Santa Rosa Mts., Calif.	Picked Up	John C. Belcher	PR1958	110
176⅞	37⅜	38⅜	15⅜	15⅜	8⅜	8⅜	23⅞	21⅜	Pinal Co., Ariz.	Travis R. Holder	Travis R. Holder	1984	110
176⅜	36⅜	38	15⅜	15⅜	8⅜	8⅜	20	20	Baja Calif., Mexico	Fernando Garcia	Fernando Garcia	1968	113
176⅞	39	38	14⅜	15⅜	8⅜	8⅜	28⅜	28⅜	Clark Co., Nev.	Allan R. Sundell	Kent A. Sundell	1979	113
176⅞	35⅝	36⅜	15⅜	14⅜	9⅛	9⅜	19⅜	14⅜	Baja Calif., Mexico	Douglas J. Dollhopf	Douglas J. Dollhopf	1983	113
176⅞	38⅞	37⅜	15⅜	15⅜	8⅜	8⅜	23⅜	23⅜	Lower Calif., Mexico	E. W. Funcke	U. S. Natl. Mus.	1905	116
176⅜	38	38⅜	13⅜	13⅜	10⅜	9⅜	21⅜	21⅜	Baja Calif., Mexico	Picked Up	Leland Brand	1973	116
176⅜	34⅜	34⅜	16⅜	16⅜	9	9	19⅜	18⅜	Baja Calif., Mexico	William L. Baker, Jr.	William L. Baker, Jr.	1974	118
176⅜	35⅜	37⅜	15⅜	16	9⅜	9⅜	21⅜	15⅜	Baja Calif., Mexico	Joe E. Coleman	Joe E. Coleman	1976	118
176⅜	36⅜	36⅜	15⅜	15⅜	8⅜	8⅜	19⅜	14⅞	Baja Calif., Mexico	Richard Wehling	Richard Wehling	1978	118
176⅜	37⅜	36	15⅜	15⅜	8⅜	8⅜	29⅜	29⅜	Clark Co., Nev.	C. J. McElroy	C. J. McElroy	1978	118
176⅜	35⅜	36⅜	14⅜	13⅜	9⅜	10	23⅜	22⅜	Yuma Co., Ariz.	F. Lorin Ronnow	F. Lorin Ronnow	1957	122
176⅜	38⅜	37⅜	15	15	8⅜	8⅜	21⅜	21⅜	Clark Co., Nev.	Vicki L. Clark	Vicki L. Clark	1980	122
176⅜	38⅜	36	15⅜	15⅜	8⅜	8⅜	21⅜	21⅜	Pinal Co., Ariz.	Christine J. Burrows	Christine J. Burrows	1981	122
176⅜	38⅜	37⅜	14⅜	14	9	9	21	21	Clark Co., Nev.	D. Mark Exline	D. Mark Exline	1982	122
176⅜	34	37	15⅜	15⅜	9⅜	9⅜	23	21⅜	Baja Calif., Mexico	Jack Oberly	Jack Oberly	1983	127
176	37⅜	36⅜	15⅜	15⅜	9⅜	9⅜	25⅜	25⅜	Sonora, Mexico	N. J. Segal, Jr.	N. J. Segal, Jr.	1972	128
176	38⅜	39⅜	15⅜	15⅜	8⅜	8⅜	22⅜	20⅜	Black Mts., Ariz.	Fritz Katz	Fritz Katz	1941	128
176	37⅜	38⅜	14⅜	15	9⅜	9⅜	25	25	Kofa Mts., Ariz.	Picked Up	R. A. Wagner	1954	128
176	37⅜	34⅜	15⅜	15⅜	9⅜	9⅜	21⅜	18⅜	Sonora, Mexico	Robin Underdown	Robin Underdown	1966	128
176	34⅜	34⅜	17⅜	17⅜	8⅜	8⅜	19⅜	17	Baja Calif., Mexico	Ollie O. Barney	Ollie O. Barney	1968	128
176	36	36	15⅜	15⅜	9	9⅜	18⅜	18⅜	Baja Calif., Mexico	Paul S. Inzanti, Jr.	Paul S. Inzanti, Jr.	1982	133
175⅞	35⅜	35⅜	15	15	9⅜	9⅜	22⅜	22⅜	Yuma Co., Ariz.	J. Don McGaffee	J. Don McGaffee	1978	133
175⅞	39⅜	38⅜	14	14	8⅜	9⅜	22⅜	22⅜	Yuma Co., Ariz.	Fred W. Jerome	Fred W. Jerome	1979	133
175⅞	36⅜	37	15⅜	15⅜	9⅜	9⅜	22⅜	22⅜	Pinal Co., Ariz.	Tracy L. Contreras	Tracy L. Contreras	1980	136
175⅞	35⅜	36⅜	14	14	10⅜	10⅜	21⅜	17⅜	San Diego Co., Calif.	Picked Up	Anza-Borrego Desert State Park	1951	136
175⅞	35⅜	35⅜	16⅜	16⅜	8⅜	8⅜	18⅜	18⅜	Baja Calif., Mexico	Jack Leeds	Jack Leeds	1976	136
175⅞	33⅜	35⅜	16	16	9⅜	9⅜	22	20⅜	Pima Co., Ariz.	Robert F. Lebo	Robert F. Lebo	1977	136
175⅞	36⅜	36⅜	14⅜	14⅜	9⅜	9⅜	21	21	Lincoln Co., Nev.	Denny L. Frook	Denny L. Frook	1977	136
175⅞	35⅜	35⅜	16	16	8⅜	9⅜	20	17⅜	Baja Calif., Mexico	William C. Cloyd	William C. Cloyd	1984	136
175⅞	36	36⅜	15⅜	15⅜	8⅜	8⅜	20⅜	19⅜	Yuma, Ariz.	Picked Up	Tom D. Moore	1956	141
175⅞	37⅜	36	15	14⅜	9⅜	10	21⅜	21⅜	Maricopa Co., Ariz.	Picked Up	Robert B. Thompson	1963	141
175⅞	36⅜	36⅜	14⅜	14⅜	9⅜	9⅜	21⅜	19	Baja Calif., Mexico	Tony Oney	Tony Oney	1968	141
175⅞	37⅜	37⅜	14⅜	14⅜	8⅜	9⅜	22⅜	21⅜	Plomosa Mts., Ariz.	J. James Froelich	J. James Froelich	1969	141
175⅞	36⅜	36⅜	14⅜	14⅜	10⅜	10⅜	21⅜	18⅜	Yuma Co., Ariz.	Anton E. Rimsza	Anton E. Rimsza	1982	141
175⅞	35⅜	35⅜	15⅜	15⅜	9⅜	9⅜	21⅜	18⅜	Plomosa Mts., Ariz.	M. S. MacCollum	M. S. MacCollum	1968	146
175⅞	37	37⅜	14⅜	14⅜	8⅜	8⅜	21⅜	21⅜	Lincoln Co., Nev.	Robert Fagan	Robert Fagan	1968	146
175⅞	38⅜	38⅜	14⅜	14⅜	8⅜	8⅜	22	19⅜	Yuma Co., Ariz.	Patrick E. Hurley	Patrick E. Hurley	1981	146

DESERT SHEEP—Continued

Ovis canadensis nelsoni and certain related subspecies

Score	Length of Horn R.	L.	Circumference of Base R.	L.	Circumference at Third Quarter R.	L.	Greatest Spread	Tip to Tip Spread	Locality Killed	By Whom Killed	Owner	Date Killed	Rank
175⅞	37⅞	39⅛	13⅞	14	9⅞	9⅜	19⅜	17⅞	Baja Calif., Mexico	Isidro Lopez-Del Bosque	Isidro Lopez-Del Bosque	1984	146
175⅞	37⅛	37⅛	14⅛	14⅜	9⅛	9⅛	21⅛	21⅜	Baja Calif., Mexico	K. C. Brown	K. C. Brown	1966	150
175⅞	36⅜	37⅛	15⅛	15⅛	8⅜	8⅞	19⅜	19⅜	Mexico	Bill Foster	Foster's Bighorn Rest.	1950	151
175⅞	36⅞	37⅛	14⅞	15	9⅜	8⅞	19⅜	17⅞	Sonora, Mexico	Unknown	Paul W. Hughes	1952	151
175⅞	37⅞	38⅛	14⅞	14⅞	9⅞	8⅞	20⅛	20⅛	Lamb Springs, Nev.	D. B. Walkington	D. B. Walkington	1965	151
175⅞	37⅛	37	14⅞	14⅞	9⅜	9⅜	25⅞	25⅞	Clark Co., Nev.	Wayne C. Matley	Wayne C. Matley	1966	151
175⅞	37⅛	40	13⅞	13⅞	8⅞	9⅜	31⅞	22⅞	Riverside Co., Calif.	Picked Up	George F. Stewart, Jr.	PR1967	151
175⅞	36⅛	35⅜	15⅛	15⅜	8⅞	8⅜	23⅜	18⅜	Baja Calif., Mexico	C. J. Wimer	C. J. Wimer	1977	151
175⅞	36⅛	37⅜	15⅛	15⅜	8⅜	8⅜	23⅜	23⅜	Clark Co., Nev.	Lenda Z. Azcarate	Lenda Z. Azcarate	1979	151
175⅞	36⅜	36⅛	15⅛	15	9	9⅜	23⅜	23⅜	Clark Co., Nev.	Lloyd G. Bare	Lloyd G. Bare	1980	151
175	35	36	15	15⅞	10	9⅞	22⅜	22⅜	Sonora, Mexico	Juan A. Saenz, Jr.	Juan A. Saenz, Jr.	1969	159
175	37⅞	33⅜	15⅜	15⅜	8⅜	8⅞	20⅛	18⅜	Yuma Co., Ariz.	Harry B. Cook	Harry B. Cook	1982	159
175	37⅞	37⅛	15	15	9⅜	9⅜	26⅞	26⅞	Clark Co., Nev.	Timothy P. Ryan	Timothy P. Ryan	1983	159
174⅞	37	35⅛	13⅜	13⅜	9⅜	8⅞	20⅜	19⅜	Pima, Ariz.	Picked Up	Robert J. Kirkpatrick	PR1968	162
174⅞	37⅛	38⅜	13⅜	13⅜	9⅜	9⅜	23⅜	21	Arizona	Picked Up	Nathan Frisby	1974	162
174⅞	35⅜	35	15⅜	15⅜	8⅞	8⅜	23⅜	23⅛	Clark Co., Nev.	Herman H. Storey, Jr.	Herman S. Storey, Jr.	1980	162
174⅞	39	38⅛	14⅞	15⅜	9⅜	8⅞	22⅜	0	Barstow, Calif.	Picked Up	Thomas Hodges	1941	165
174⅞	33⅞	34	15	14⅞	10⅛	10⅛	25⅞	25⅞	Clark Co., Nev.	Ron W. Biggs	Ron W. Biggs	1980	165
174⅞	34⅜	34⅛	15⅞	15⅛	9⅜	9⅜	18⅞	16⅜	Baja Calif., Mexico	Stanley S. Gray	Stanley S. Gray	1972	167
174⅞	36⅜	37⅛	14⅞	14⅜	8⅞	9⅜	25⅛	25⅜	Clark Co., Nev.	Roseanne K. Wilkinson	Roseanne K. Wilkinson	1980	167
174⅞	36⅜	36	14	14⅜	9⅜	9⅜	19⅜	19⅜	Maricopa Co., Ariz.	Picked Up	Robert B. Thompson	1963	169
174⅞	37	36	15⅛	15⅜	8⅜	8⅜	20⅜	20⅜	Baja, Mexico	Jack Walters	Jack Walters	1966	169
174⅞	36⅞	37⅛	14⅞	14⅜	9	9⅛	21⅜	18⅜	Clark Co., Nev.	Larry G. Marshall	Larry G. Marshall	1983	169
174⅞	37⅞	37⅛	15⅜	15⅜	7⅞	7⅞	25⅞	26⅜	Clark Co., Nev.	Stanley R. Galvin, Jr.	Stanley R. Galvin, Jr.	1983	169
174⅞	38⅛	38⅞	14⅞	14⅜	8	7⅞	24⅜	23⅜	Clark Co., Nev.	Kathy E. Seaberg	K. E. & G. Seaberg	1981	173
174⅞	37	36	15⅞	15⅞	7⅞	7⅞	20⅜	18⅜	Baja Calif., Mexico	Basil C. Bradbury	Basil C. Bradbury	1968	174
174⅞	37	38⅞	14	14⅛	10⅛	10⅛	21⅜	21⅛	Las Vegas, Nev.	Thos. R. McElhenney	Thos. R. McElhenney	1969	174
174⅞	35⅜	36⅛	14⅞	14⅞	9⅞	10	25⅜	25⅛	Mohave Co., Ariz.	Susan C. Nelson	Susan C. Nelson	1979	174
174⅞	34⅞	35⅜	15⅜	15⅜	9	9⅞	26	26	Lincoln Co., Nev.	Larry M. Evans	Larry M. Evans	1982	174
174⅞	35⅜	40⅛	14⅜	14⅜	8⅜	8⅜	30⅜	30⅜	Mohave Co., Ariz.	Howard Grounds	Howard Grounds	1984	174
174	40	38⅜	15⅜	15⅜	7⅜	7⅞	25⅜	25⅜	Lower Calif., Mexico	E. W. Funcke	Harvard Univ. Mus.	1911	179
174	36⅜	37⅞	15⅜	15⅜	7⅞	8	21⅜	21	Yuma, Ariz.	Wynn Robestal	U. S. Fish & Wild. Serv.	1913	179

Score	L.R	L.L	Base R	Base L	Circ. R	Circ. L	Gr. Spr.	T.T.	Locality	Hunter	Owner	Date	Rank
174	37⅞	36⅞	14⅞	14⅞	9⅞	9	19⅞	18	Sonora, Mexico	F. C. Hibben	F. C. Hibben	1940	179
174	36⅞	37	13⅝	13⅝	10	10	24⅞	23	McCullough Mts., Nev.	Picked Up	William H. Pogue	PR1958	179
174	36⅜	35⅜	15⅜	15	8⅞	9⅛	23	23	Baja Calif., Mexico	James W. Owens	James W. Owens	1983	179
173⅞	37⅛	37⅛	14⅜	14⅜	8⅞	8⅜	24⅞	24⅞	Kofa Mts., Ariz.	William L. Snider	William L. Snider	1965	184
173⅞	37	37	13⅜	13⅜	10⅜	10⅜	22⅜	19⅞	Anza-Borrego Desert, Calif.	Picked Up	Anza-Borrego Desert State Park	1971	184
173⅞	34⅞	34⅞	15⅝	15⅝	9⅛	9⅛	22⅜	22⅜	Baja Calif., Mexico	Erwin Dykstra	Erwin Dykstra	1978	184
173⅞	37	37	15	15	8⅜	8⅜	20	21⅜	Yuma Co., Ariz.	John C. Marsalla	John C. Marsalla	1982	184
173¾	34⅞	34¾	14⅜	14⅜	9⅞	10⅜	22⅜	21⅜	Yuma Co., Ariz.	Picked Up	Bob Housholder	1953	188
173¾	35⅞	36⅞	16⅞	16⅞	8	8	20⅜	20⅜	Baja Calif., Mexico	Fritz A. Nachant	Fritz A. Nachant	1969	188
173⅝	37	37	15⅛	15⅛	8⅞	9	20⅜	20⅜	Baja Calif., Mexico	James H. Duke, Jr.	James H. Duke, Jr.	1969	190
173⅝	34⅞	34	15⅛	15	9	8⅞	22⅜	22⅜	Clark Co., Nev.	John H. Batten	John H. Batten	1975	190
173⅝	36⅞	36	15⅛	15	8⅝	8⅜	23⅝	23⅝	Yuma Co., Ariz.	Buddy H. Fujii	Buddy H. Fujii	1980	190
173⅝	34⅝	34⅜	15⅛	15⅜	9⅜	9⅜	24⅞	24⅞	Sonora, Mexico	David C. Root	David C. Root	1983	190
173½	34⅜	34⅜	15	15	9	9	19⅞	19⅞	Muleje Baja, Mexico	Douglas G. Williams	Douglas G. Williams	1983	190
173½	35⅞	35⅞	15⅝	15⅝	8⅜	8⅜	21⅜	21⅜	Sonora, Mexico	Victor M. Ruiza	Victor M. Ruiza	1966	195
173½	34⅜	34⅜	16⅝	16⅝	8⅜	8⅜	19⅞	19⅞	Clark Co., Nev.	Walter Snoke	Walter Snoke	1978	195
173½	35	36	15⅜	15⅜	8⅜	8⅜	23⅜	23⅜	Baja Calif., Mexico	Ira H. Kent	Ira H. Kent	1978	198
173½	36⅜	36⅜	14⅜	14⅜	8⅜	8⅜	21⅜	21⅜	Sonora, Mexico	M. Alessio Robles	M. Alessio Robles	1956	198
173½	36⅜	36⅜	15⅜	15⅜	8⅛	8⅛	21⅜	21⅜	Baja Calif., Mexico	Gaston Cano	Gaston Cano	1968	198
173½	37	37	14⅜	14⅜	8⅜	8⅜	22⅜	22⅜	Baja Calif., Mexico	Roy A. Schultz	Roy A. Schultz	1971	198
173½	37	37	15⅛	15	8⅜	8⅜	22	22	Mohave Co., Ariz.	Dale R. Leonard	Dale R. Leonard	1972	198
173½	40⅛	38	13⅞	13⅞	8⅛	8⅛	0	0	Little Horn Mts., Ariz.	Tim C. Boyd	Tim C. Boyd	1981	198
173½	36	36⅜	15⅜	15⅜	8⅜	8⅜	21⅜	19⅛	Baja Calif., Mexico	Donald E. Franklin	Donald E. Franklin	1982	204
173½	34⅞	34⅜	15⅝	15⅜	8⅝	8⅝	25⅜	25⅜	Baja Calif., Mexico	Joseph J. Sobotka	Joseph J. Sobotka	1969	204
173½	36⅜	36⅛	15⅝	15½	8⅜	8⅜	21⅜	21⅜	Little Horn Mts., Ariz.	Ernest Righetti	Ernest Righetti	1974	204
173½	36⅛	35¾	15⅜	15⅜	8⅜	8⅜	21⅜	21⅜	Tulelake, Calif.	Marion H. Scott	Marion H. Scott	1978	207
173½	35⅞	34⅞	14⅛	14⅛	9⅛	9	21	21	Sonora Desert, Mexico	Picked Up	Duane J. Hall	1960	207
173½	32⅞	30⅞	15⅛	15⅛	11⅛	11	24⅞	23	Clark Co., Nev.	Picked Up	Natl. Park Service	1968	207
173½	37⅞	37⅞	13⅛	13⅛	9⅞	7⅞	21⅜	21⅜	Lower Calif., Mexico	Picked Up	Herb Klein	1969	211
173⅛	37⅛	37	14⅜	14	8⅜	9⅛	27⅜	27⅜	Sheep Mt. Range, Nev.	Chris Hurtado	Chris Hurtado	1975	211
173	36	38	15	15	8⅜	8⅜	24⅜	24⅜	Aguila Mts., Ariz.	Henry H. Blagden	Henry H. Blagden	1914	211
173	38⅜	38⅜	14⅜	14⅜	9⅛	8⅜	19⅛	19⅛	Baja Calif., Mexico	Gilbert A. Helsel	Gilbert A. Helsel	1960	211
173	36	36	14⅜	14⅜	9	9	21⅜	21⅜	Maricopa Co., Ariz.	Picked Up	C. G. Clare	1961	211
173	35⅝	35⅝	15⅛	15	8⅜	8⅜	20⅜	20⅜	Baja Calif., Mexico	James H. Russell	James H. Russell	1970	211
173	37⅛	37⅛	13⅝	13⅝	10⅜	10⅜	20	20	Baja Calif., Mexico	Stephen K. Weisser	Stephen K. Weisser	1973	211
173	39	35	15	15	8⅜	8⅜	24	24	Baja Calif., Mexico	Charles Oyer	Charles Oyer	1975	211
173	34⅞	35	15⅝	15⅝	8⅝	8⅝	20⅜	20⅜	Baja Calif., Mexico	P. Franklin Bays, Jr.	P. Franklin Bays, Jr.	1976	211
172⅞	34	34⅜	15⅜	15⅜	9⅜	9⅜	20⅜	20⅜	Baja Calif., Mexico	Mahlon T. White	Mahlon T. White	1969	218
172⅞	37⅛	38⅜	13⅜	13⅜	9	9	23⅜	23⅜	Baja Calif., Mexico	Otis Chandler	Otis Chandler	1966	219
172⅝	35⅝	35⅝	15⅝	15⅝	8⅝	8⅝	21⅜	21⅜	Baja Calif., Mexico	Graciano Guichard	Graciano Guichard	1969	219
172⅝	36⅜	36⅜	14⅜	14⅜	8⅝	8⅝	20⅜	20⅜	Yuma Co., Ariz.	Norman F. Mathews	Norman F. Mathews	1977	219
172⅝	36⅝	36½	14	13⅞	9⅜	10⅜	19⅞	19⅞	Yuma Co., Ariz.	Larry J. Landes	Larry J. Landes	1981	219

DESERT SHEEP—Continued

Ovis canadensis nelsoni and certain related subspecies

Score	Length of Horn R.	Length of Horn L.	Circumference of Base R.	Circumference of Base L.	Circumference at Third Quarter R.	Circumference at Third Quarter L.	Greatest Spread	Tip to Tip Spread	Locality Killed	By Whom Killed	Owner	Date Killed	Rank
172⅝	36	36⅜	15⅛	15⅜	8⅜	8⅜	19⅝	18⅝	Pima Co., Ariz.	Paul H. Harrison	Paul H. Harrison	1981	219
172⅝	34⅛	36⅜	15⅜	15⅜	8⅛	9⅜	20⅝	18⅝	Sonora, Mexico	Lloyd O. Barrow	Lloyd O. Barrow	1969	224
172⅝	35⅜	35⅜	14⅛	14⅛	9⅝	10	19⅝	19⅝	Baja Calif., Mexico	G. David Edwards	G. David Edwards	1973	224
172⅝	37⅜	36	15⅜	15⅜	8	8	21⅜	21⅜	Baja Calif., Mexico	Daniel Smith	Daniel Smith	1975	224
172⅝	32⅜	35⅜	15⅞	15⅞	8⅜	9	19⅝	18⅝	Clark Co., Nev.	Charles W. Knittle	Charles W. Knittle	1976	224
172⅝	40⅝	38⅜	13⅜	12⅞	8⅝	8⅝	26⅝	26⅝	White Mts., Calif.	Picked Up	Danny Lowe	1978	224
172⅝	36⅞	34⅝	15⅜	15⅜	8⅜	8⅜	22⅝	19⅝	Yuma Co., Ariz.	Margaret Wood	Margaret Wood	1958	229
172⅝	36	34⅜	15	15	8⅛	8⅛	23	23	Yuma Co., Ariz.	Picked Up	Donald Ogan	1964	229
172⅝	40	36	14⅜	14⅜	8	7⅝	25	25	Clark Co., Nev.	Scott D. Oxborrow	Scott D. Oxborrow	1983	229
172⅝	33⅜	33⅜	15⅛	15⅜	9⅜	9⅜	21⅜	21	Baja Calif., Mexico	Hector Aguilar Parada	Hector Aguilar Parada	1985	229
172⅝	34⅝	32⅜	15	15⅛	9⅝	9⅝	21⅝	21	Sauceda Mts., Ariz.	Wayne Grippin	Wayne Grippin	1962	233
172⅝	36⅜	35⅜	14⅜	14⅜	9⅝	9⅝	20⅜	19⅝	Baja Calif., Mexico	H. Varley Grantham	H. Varley Grantham	1980	233
172⅝	35⅛	34⅝	15⅞	15⅛	9	9	23⅜	23⅜	Clark Co., Nev.	Ronald L. Giovanetti	Ronald L. Giovanetti	1980	233
172⅝	35⅜	36	14⅞	14⅞	8⅜	9⅝	21⅝	21⅝	Clark Co., Nev.	John F. Lohse	John F. Lohse	1982	233
172⅝	38	37⅜	15	15⅜	7⅜	7⅛	27⅜	27⅛	Baja Calif., Mexico	Wm. E. Humphrey	Wash. State Mus.	1909	233
172⅝	36⅝	35⅜	15⅛	15⅛	8⅜	8⅜	20⅝	20⅝	Baja Calif., Mexico	Herb Klein	Herb Klein	1966	237
172⅝	35⅜	35⅜	15⅛	15⅜	9	8⅝	19⅝	16⅝	Baja Calif., Mexico	Armando de la Parra	Armando de la Parra	1966	237
172⅝	36	36⅜	15	15⅜	8⅜	8⅜	23	14	Kofa Range, Ariz.	Picked Up	Ariz. Game & Fish Dept.	1953	237
172	33	36	15	15⅛	9	8⅜	30⅜	30⅜	Tulelake, Calif.	Picked Up	Natl. Park Service	1963	240
172	34⅝	34⅝	16⅛	16⅛	8⅜	8⅝	21⅜	20⅝	Baja Calif., Mexico	Bill Silveira	Bill Silveira	1974	241
172	34⅝	35	15	15	8⅜	8⅜	20⅝	20⅝	Baja Calif., Mexico	Robert O. Cromwell	Robert O. Cromwell	1974	241
171⅞	33⅜	32⅝	16⅛	15⅞	8⅝	8⅜	19⅜	17⅝	Baja Calif., Mexico	Joan Leeds	Joan Leeds	1976	241
171⅞	33⅜	35⅞	16⅛	15⅜	9⅝	9⅝	22⅝	21⅝	Baja Calif., Mexico	Don L. Corley	Don L. Corley	1978	244
171⅞	33⅜	35⅞	15⅝	15⅜	9⅝	9⅝	20⅝	20⅝	Kofa Range, Ariz.	Harvey Davison	Harvey Davison	1953	244
171⅞	37⅝	36⅜	14	13⅜	7⅝	8⅜	21	18⅝	Baja Calif., Mexico	Earl H. Harris	Earl H. Harris	1968	246
171⅞	36⅝	36	15⅝	15⅝	10	10⅜	23	20⅝	Lincoln Co., Nev.	William A. Molini	William A. Molini	1977	246
171⅞	35⅝	35⅜	14	14	7	7	23	23	Sonora, Mexico	Julio Estrada	Julio Estrada	1931	246
171¾	38⅛	35	15⅜	15⅜	8⅜	8⅞	20	18⅝	Baja Calif., Mexico	Dan L. Quen	Dan L. Quen	1968	249
171¾	33⅜	35⅜	15⅜	15	9⅜	8⅜	19⅝	19⅝	Baja Calif., Mexico	C. J. McElroy	C. J. McElroy	1969	249
171¾	35⅝	35⅜	14⅜	15⅜	8⅜	8⅜	21⅝	20	Baja Calif., Mexico	Roberto M. del Campo	Roberto M. del Campo	1969	249
171¾	35⅝	36⅜	14⅜	14⅜	8⅝	8⅝	21⅝	21⅝	Sonora, Mexico	Picked Up	Bob C. Jones	1970	249
171¾	35⅜	35⅜	14⅜	14⅜	9⅜	9	20⅝	20⅝	Clark Co., Nev.	George Hueftle	George Hueftle	1977	249

436

Score	Length of Horn R	Length of Horn L	Circumference of Base R	Circumference of Base L	Third Quarter R	Third Quarter L	Tip to Tip Spread	Greatest Spread	Locality	Owner	Hunter	Date	Rank
171⅝	34¾	32⅞	15⅝	15⅜	9⅜	9⅜	21⅜	20⅝	Clark Co., Nev.	Edward M. Evans	Edward M. Evans	1977	249
171⅜	35⅜	34⅜	14	14	10⅛	10	19⅞	19⅜	Bullion Mts., Calif.	Fred L. Jones	Picked Up	1950	256
171⅜	37⅜	37⅜	13⅜	13⅜	8⅜	8⅜	23	22⅜	Clark Co., Nev.	Jerry P. Devin	Jerry P. Devin	1976	256
171⅜	33⅜	35	15	15	9⅜	9⅜	21⅜	20⅜	Maricopa Co., Ariz.	Clarence House	Unknown	PR1979	256
171¾	36⅞	36⅝	14⅜	14⅜	8⅝	8⅜	22⅞	22⅜	Anvil Mt., Ariz.	George Stewart, Jr.	George Stewart, Jr.	1961	259
171¾	34⅜	34⅜	15⅝	15⅝	8⅜	8⅝	19⅞	16⅜	Crater Mts., Ariz.	Raymond I. Skipper, Jr.	Raymond I. Skipper, Jr.	1971	259
171¾	38⅛	37	14⅛	14⅜	8⅜	8⅜	24	23⅜	Clark Co., Nev.	Daniel T. Magee	Daniel T. Magee	1980	259
171¾	37⅜	38⅛	14⅛	14⅛	9⅜	9¼	21⅜	25	Lincoln Co., Nev.	Roy D. Lerg	Roy F. Lerg	1984	259
171¾	35⅜	35⅝	14⅜	14⅜	8⅝	8⅜	21⅜	18⅜	Growler Mts., Ariz.	David E. Brown	David E. Brown	1967	263
171¾	35⅜	36⅝	14⅜	14⅜	8⅝	8⅝	20⅜	20⅜	Clark Co., Nev.	Bill R. Balsi, Jr.	Bill R. Balsi, Jr.	1979	263
171¼	34¾	35	15⅜	15⅜	8⅜	8⅜	24	24	Baja Calif., Mexico	David L. Harshbarger	David L. Harshbarger	1983	263
171⅛	38	38⅜	14⅞	14⅞	9⅜	9⅜	21⅜	21⅛	Yuma Co., Ariz.	Lauren W. Hogan	Lauren W. Hogan	1984	263
171⅛	35⅜	35⅜	16⅛	16⅜	7⅜	7⅜	19⅞	19⅛	Yuma Co., Ariz.	Elizabeth Barganski	Elizabeth Barganski	1959	267
171⅛	36⅜	36⅞	14⅜	14⅜	8⅜	8⅜	22⅜	17⅛	Palomas Mts., Ariz.	James F. Pierce	James F. Pierce	1967	267
171⅛	35⅜	35⅜	15	15	9⅜	9⅜	25⅜	25⅛	Clark Co., Nev.	Ray W. Diehl	Ray W. Diehl	1979	267
171	36	36⅝	14⅜	14⅜	8⅜	8⅞	20⅞	19⅛	Sauceda Mts., Ariz.	Kelly S. Neal, Jr.	Kelly S. Neal, Jr.	1969	270
171	36⅜	35⅜	15⅝	15⅝	8⅞	8⅝	22⅜	22⅛	Baja Calif., Mexico	George S. Gayle III	George S. Gayle III	1975	270
170⅞	35⅞	35⅜	16⅜	16⅜	8	8⅜	21⅜	21⅜	Sonora Desert, Mexico	Herb Klein	Herb Klein	1962	272
170⅞	38⅛	37⅞	14	14⅞	9⅜	9⅜	19⅝	17⅜	Baja Calif., Mexico	Michaux Nash, Jr.	Michaux Nash, Jr.	1964	272
170⅞	36⅜	36⅜	14⅜	14⅜	9⅜	9⅜	21⅜	21	Baja Calif., Mexico	John T. Blackwell	John T. Blackwell	1966	272
170⅞	36⅜	37	15	15	8⅜	8⅜	23⅜	23⅛	Baja Calif., Mexico	Daniel B. Moore	Daniel B. Moore	1979	272
170⅞	33⅜	35⅛	14	14	9½	10⅛	21⅜	20⅜	San Bernadino Co., Calif.	John M. Parrish	Picked Up	1960	276
170⅞	36⅞	36⅜	15⅝	15⅜	7⅜	7⅝	20⅞	20⅜	Little Horn Mts., Ariz.	Dale Wagner	Dale Wagner	1963	276
170⅞	35⅜	34⅜	15⅝	15⅝	7⅜	7⅜	21⅜	21⅛	Baja Calif., Mexico	Enrique Cervera Cicero	Enrique Cervera Cicero	1968	276
170⅞	36⅛	36⅛	16⅜	16⅜	7⅜	7⅜	22⅜	22⅛	Baja Calif., Mexico	Gino Perfetto	Gino Perfetto	1968	276
170⅞	39⅞	39⅜	13⅜	13⅜	9⅜	9⅜	24⅞	24⅜	Clark Co., Nev.	Roy Gamblin	Roy Gamblin	1977	276
170⅝	34	34	16	16	9⅝	9⅜	19⅜	17⅜	Death Valley, Calif.	Fred L. Jones	Picked Up	1955	281
170⅝	34⅜	35⅜	15	15	8⅞	8⅝	23⅜	23⅛	Baja Calif., Mexico	Bill Lewis	Bill Lewis	1969	281
170⅝	32⅞	34⅞	14⅜	14⅜	8⅞	9⅜	22⅞	22⅜	Pima Co., Ariz.	David Chavez	David Chavez	1972	281
170⅝	34⅜	34⅜	14⅛	14⅛	9	9	19⅜	19⅜	Clark Co., Nev.	George W. Wilkinson, Jr.	George W. Wilkinson, Jr.	1976	281
170⅝	34⅞	34⅜	16	16	9⅜	9	20⅜	15⅜	Mohave Co., Ariz.	John H. Houzenga, Jr.	John H. Houzenga, Jr.	1961	285
170⅝	36	35	14⅞	14⅞	10¼	9⅜	23⅜	19⅜	Clark Co., Nev.	Robert E. Coons	Robert E. Coons	1971	285
170⅜	36	35⅜	14⅜	14⅜	7⅝	7⅝	18⅞	18⅜	Baja Calif., Mexico	Don Turner	Don Turner	1980	285
170⅜	32	34⅜	15⅜	15⅝	7⅜	7⅜	19⅞	19⅜	Sonora, Mexico	F. C. Hibben	F. C. Hibben	1935	288
170⅜	35⅜	36⅝	16⅝	16⅞	7⅜	7⅜	19⅜	18	Chemehuevi Mts., Ariz.	James B. Lingo	James B. Lingo	1970	288
170⅜	35⅜	35⅜	15	15	8⅜	9⅜	23⅜	23	Yuma Co., Ariz.	Gary V. Harmon	Gary V. Harmon	1979	288
170⅜	32⅝	32⅜	14⅛	14⅛	9⅜	9⅝	20⅜	15⅜	Hermosillo, Mexico	Michael Follett	Michael Follett	1979	288
170⅜	35⅜	35⅛	14⅜	14⅜	9⅜	9⅜	23⅜	19⅜	Clark Co., Nev.	Tracy L. Wilkinson	Tracy L. Wilkinson	1982	288
170¼	35	35⅞	14⅜	14⅜	9⅜	9⅜	23⅜	23⅜	Lincoln Co., Nev.	Robert S. Mastronardi	Robert S. Mastronardi	1982	288
170¼	35⅝	36⅝	15	15	8	8⅜	20⅜	20⅜	Baja Calif., Mexico	Richard Buffington	Richard Buffington	1966	294
170¼	37⅞	34⅞	14⅞	14⅞	8⅜	8⅜	24⅜	24⅜	Clark Co., Nev.	Landon D. Mack	Landon D. Mack	1977	294
170¼	37⅜	37⅜	15⅞	15⅝	7⅝	7⅝	21⅜	20⅜	Baja Calif., Mexico	James W. Owens	James W. Owens	1978	294
170⅛	34⅜	34⅜	15	15	9⅝	9⅝	18	18	Baja Calif., Mexico	A. Verne Crowell	A. Verne Crowell	1979	294

DESERT SHEEP—*Continued*
Ovis canadensis nelsoni and certain related subspecies

Score	Length of Horn R.	L.	Circumference of Base R.	L.	Circumference at Third Quarter R.	L.	Greatest Spread	Tip to Tip Spread	Locality Killed	By Whom Killed	Owner	Date Killed	Rank
170⅝	34⅞	33⅞	14⅞	14⅞	9⅞	9⅛	21⅝	16	Sonora, Mexico	Leonard E. Brewster	Leonard E. Brewster	1982	294
170⅝	36	35⅝	15⅛	15⅛	8⅛	8⅜	21⅞	21⅞	Baja Calif., Mexico	David C. Southard, Jr.	David C. Southard, Jr.	1982	294
170⅜	40⅜	34⅞	13⅜	13⅞	8⅜	8⅜	25⅞	25⅞	Mineral Co., Nev.	Picked Up	Nev. Dept. of Wildl.	1969	300
170⅜	34⅞	34⅞	14⅞	15	8⅞	9	19⅞	18⅞	Baja Calif., Mexico	Fred T. LaBean	Fred T. LaBean	1969	300
170⅜	37⅛	37	15⅜	15⅝	7⅛	7⅛	22⅞	22⅛	Baja Calif., Mexico	Arthur E. Davis	Arthur E. Davis	1972	300
170⅜	36	36⅜	15⅜	15⅜	7⅞	7⅞	19⅞	16⅝	Baja Calif., Mexico	Edward V. Wilson	Edward V. Wilson	1974	300
170⅜	34⅞	35⅜	15⅜	15⅜	8⅞	8⅞	20⅞	18⅞	Clark Co., Nev.	William F. Zenz, Jr.	William F. Zenz, Jr.	1980	300
170⅜	35⅜	35⅜	14⅞	14⅞	8⅞	9⅛	20⅛	19⅝	Baja Calif., Mexico	Alfred Barone	Alfred Barone	1984	300
170⅜	33	33	15⅝	15⅜	9⅛	9⅛	21⅛	19⅝	Little Horn Mts., Ariz.	Ivan L. Shiflet	Ivan L. Shiflet	1966	306
170	37⅞	33⅞	15⅝	15⅜	7⅞	7⅝	22⅞	21⅞	Baja Calif., Mexico	Warren K. Parker	Warren K. Parker	1970	306
170	33	34⅞	15⅝	14⅜	9⅞	10⅞	20⅞	18⅝	Clark Co., Nev.	Lee R. Williamson	Lee R. Williamson	1972	306
170	35⅜	35⅜	14⅜	14⅞	8⅝	8⅛	19⅞	19⅝	Baja Calif., Mexico	Rudolf Sand	Rudolf Sand	1973	306
170	34⅞	34⅛	14⅜	14⅜	10⅛	9⅜	21⅛	21⅛	Clark Co., Nev.	Jim Lathrop, Jr.	Jim Lathrop, Jr.	1976	306
170	35⅜	35⅜	14⅜	14⅜	8⅜	8⅛	20⅛	19⅝	Baja Calif., Mexico	Harold Hallick	Harold Hallick	1971	311
169⅞	35⅜	35⅝	14⅞	14	9⅜	9⅝	21⅛	21⅛	Baja Calif., Mexico	W. M. Wheless III	W. M. Wheless III	1974	312
169⅞	34⅝	36⅜	14⅜	14⅞	9⅛	9⅛	23	19	Muddy Mts., Nev.	Peter Dietrick	Peter Dietrick	1962	313
169⅞	35⅛	36⅞	15	15	8	8⅜	20	18⅞	Baja Calif., Mexico	Leonard W. Gilman	Leonard W. Gilman	1969	313
169⅞	35⅜	34	15⅝	15⅝	8⅜	8⅞	20⅞	20⅞	San Borjas Mts., Mexico	John T. Blackwell	John T. Blackwell	1970	313
169⅞	35⅝	34	15	15	9	8⅞	18⅞	16⅝	Baja Calif., Mexico	Gunter M. Paefgen	Gunter M. Paefgen	1975	313
169⅞	33⅝	34⅝	15⅝	15⅝	7⅞	8⅜	21⅛	21⅛	Baja Calif., Mexico	Emerson Hall	Emerson Hall	1978	313
169⅞	34	33⅞	15⅛	15⅛	8⅞	8⅛	20⅞	18⅞	Yuma Co., Ariz.	Brad J. Ullery	Brad J. Ullery	1981	319
169⅞	33	36	15⅝	15⅝	8⅞	8⅜	25⅞	25⅞	Lower Calif., Mexico	Henry H. Blagden	Henry H. Blagden	1914	319
169¾	34⅞	34⅞	14⅛	14⅜	9⅞	10⅞	21	18⅝	Hart Tank, Ariz.	Picked Up	Greg Diley	PR1970	319
169¾	35⅝	35⅝	14⅜	14⅜	8⅜	8⅝	18	18	Baja Calif., Mexico	Lowell C. Hansen II	Lowell C. Hansen II	1974	319
169¾	33⅝	36	14⅞	14⅞	9⅞	8⅜	22⅞	22⅝	Quartzite, Ariz.	Maurice D. Mathews	Maurice D. Mathews	1975	319
169⅝	39	37⅞	15⅜	15	6⅝	6⅞	19⅞	19	Baja Calif., Mexico	James A. Bush, Jr.	James A. Bush, Jr.	1981	319
169⅝	35⅜	35	15⅞	16	7⅞	7⅞	20⅛	20	Sonora, Mexico	Unknown	National Collection	PR1939	324
169⅝	34⅜	34⅜	14⅜	14⅜	9⅜	9	20⅛	20⅛	Baja Calif., Mexico	Kenneth Campbell	Kenneth Campbell	1973	324
169⅝	33⅜	38⅝	15	15	8	8	23	22	Pima Co., Ariz.	Don L. Mattausch	Don L. Mattausch	1979	324
169⅝	34⅞	34⅞	14	13⅞	9⅞	9⅞	21⅞	21⅝	White Mts., Calif.	Picked Up	Fred L. Jones	1951	327
169⅝	34⅞	34⅞	15⅝	15⅝	8⅞	9⅛	18⅝	18⅜	Baja Calif., Mexico	Joe Osterbauer	Joe Osterbauer	1977	327
169⅝	35⅝	36⅜	15⅝	15⅝	7⅞	7⅞	20⅛	18⅞	Baja Calif., Mexico	Steve F. Reiter	Steve F. Reiter	1984	327

Score									Locality	By Whom Killed	Owner	Date	Rank
169 1/8	33 3/8	33 3/8	14 3/8	14 3/8	10	10	20 6/8	15 6/8	Lower Calif., Mexico	Picked Up	William W. Renfrew	1953	330
169 1/8	35	34 7/8	14 7/8	14 7/8	9 4/8	9	22 6/8	22 6/8	Chocolate Mts., Ariz.	Dan Oliver	Dan Oliver	1966	330
169 1/8	35 5/8	38 7/8	15	15	7 1/8	7 1/8	25 4/8	25 2/8	Baja Calif., Mexico	James W. Owens	James W. Owens	1977	330
169 1/8	34 7/8	35 5/8	14	14	10	10 4/8	21 6/8	21 6/8	Clark Co., Nev.	Lee M. Smith, Jr.	Lee M. Smith, Jr.	1979	330
169	36 7/8	36 3/8	15 5/8	15 1/8	6 7/8	6 5/8	22 3/8	22 7/8	Baja Calif., Mexico	W. E. Humphrey	Wash. State Mus.	1909	334
169	37	36	13 7/8	14	8	8 4/8	27	27	Yuma Co., Ariz.	Picked Up	Dean Bowdoin	1964	334
169	35 2/8	35 2/8	13 6/8	13 7/8	10	10	20 6/8	18 7/8	Baja Calif., Mexico	Arthur L. Wehner	Arthur L. Wehner	1980	334
169	34 3/8	35 3/8	13 5/8	13 5/8	7 7/8	8	14 7/8	21	Baja Calif., Mexico	Gordon L. Shuster	Gordon L. Shuster	1980	334
168 7/8	34 7/8	35	14 6/8	14 6/8	8 6/8	8 6/8	22 6/8	16 3/8	Aquila Mts., Ariz.	John Carr	John Carr	1969	338
168 7/8	35	33 7/8	16	16	7 7/8	8 1/8	21 4/8	21 4/8	Baja Calif., Mexico	Larry R. Price	Larry R. Price	1973	338
168 7/8	36 2/8	36 7/8	14 6/8	14 6/8	7 6/8	7 6/8	20 6/8	18 6/8	Baja Calif., Mexico	Gary Davis	Gary Davis	1975	338
168 7/8	36 5/8	33 2/8	14 6/8	14 6/8	8 7/8	8 7/8	22	22	Clark Co., Nev.	Robert Darakjy	Robert Darakjy	1978	338
168 7/8	33 7/8	33 7/8	14 7/8	14 7/8	9 2/8	9 3/8	20 6/8	20 6/8	Lincoln Co., Nev.	Melvin J. Lowe	Melvin J. Lowe	1981	338
168 6/8	35 2/8	33 4/8	14	14	10 1/8	10 1/8	19 7/8	16 7/8	Sonora, Mexico	Jack O'Connor	Jack O'Connor	1946	343
168 6/8	36 3/8	36 2/8	14 7/8	14 7/8	7 6/8	7 6/8	22 6/8	21 7/8	Little Horn Mts., Ariz.	Dean Bowdoin	Dean Bowdoin	1966	343
168 6/8	35 5/8	36 6/8	13 7/8	13 7/8	9	9	22 6/8	22 6/8	Lincoln Co., Nev.	Von A. Mitton	Von A. Mitton	1966	343
168 6/8	34 6/8	35 4/8	15 2/8	15 2/8	7 6/8	8 6/8	19	16 3/8	Sierra De Jaraguay, Mexico	Jack A. Shane, Sr.	Jack A. Shane, Sr.	1972	343
168 6/8	37 7/8	34 7/8	13 7/8	13 7/8	9 7/8	8 7/8	21 7/8	22 7/8	Yuma Co., Ariz.	Frances B. Boggess	Frances B. Boggess	1980	343
168 6/8	34 7/8	34 3/8	13 7/8	13 7/8	9 6/8	9 4/8	23 7/8	23	Arizona	Picked Up	D. B. Sanford	PR 1961	348
168 6/8	33 6/8	34	14	14	9 6/8	10	20 7/8	18	Castle Dome Peak, Ariz.	Tommy G. Moore	Tommy G. Moore	1966	348
168 6/8	34 7/8	34 4/8	14 5/8	14 5/8	8 7/8	8 7/8	21 7/8	17 7/8	Aquila Mts., Ariz.	David C. Thornburg	David C. Thornburg	1969	348
168 6/8	34 7/8	34 3/8	14 3/8	14 3/8	8 7/8	9	18 7/8	18 7/8	Sonora, Mexico	Lionel Heinrich	Lionel Heinrich	1982	348
168 5/8	33 6/8	33 7/8	15 6/8	15 6/8	8 7/8	8 7/8	18 6/8	17 7/8	Baja Calif., Mexico	Russell C. Cutter	Russell C. Cutter	1964	352
168 5/8	35 3/8	35	15	15	8 4/8	8 4/8	25 4/8	25	Kofa Game Range, Ariz.	Judy Franks	Judy Franks	1965	352
168 5/8	36 2/8	36 2/8	13 5/8	13 5/8	9 3/8	9 3/8	23 7/8	21 2/8	Clark Co., Nev.	Kenneth K. Reuter	Kenneth K. Reuter	1969	352
168 5/8	35	35 4/8	14	14	7	7 4/8	21 2/8	20 3/8	Pima Co., Ariz.	Jerald S. Wagner	Jerald S. Wagner	1977	352
168 5/8	35 5/8	35 4/8	16 3/8	16 3/8	9 4/8	9	18	18	Baja Calif., Mexico	W. T. Yoshimoto	W. T. Yoshimoto	1978	352
168 5/8	36 3/8	36 3/8	13 5/8	13 5/8	7 1/8	7 1/8	23 4/8	23 4/8	Baja Calif., Mexico	Dan L. Duncan	Dan L. Duncan	1979	352
168 5/8	37	37	15 5/8	15 7/8	7 7/8	7 7/8	18 4/8	17 3/8	Baja Calif., Mexico	John Whitcombe	John Whitcombe	1983	352
168 5/8	36	35 4/8	14 5/8	14 5/8	8 2/8	8	17 7/8	17 7/8	Sand Tank Mts., Ariz.	Homer Coppinger	Homer Coppinger	1960	352
168 5/8	34 7/8	34	14 5/8	14 5/8	9 6/8	9 6/8	19 1/8	17	Yuma Co., Ariz.	Leanna G. Mendenhall	Leanna G. Mendenhall	1975	359
168 5/8	35 2/8	34 7/8	14 7/8	14 7/8	8	8	21 2/8	21 2/8	Baja Calif., Mexico	George H. Glass	George H. Glass	1964	359
168 5/8	34 1/8	34 7/8	15 5/8	15 5/8	7 4/8	7 4/8	20 4/8	20 2/8	Sonora, Mexico	Sergio Rios Aguilera	Sergio Rios Aguilera	1968	361
168 5/8	34 7/8	34 5/8	14 4/8	14 4/8	7 5/8	7 5/8	21 3/8	14 3/8	Clark Co., Nev.	Marie F. Reuter	Marie F. Reuter	1969	361
168 5/8	33 6/8	33 5/8	15 3/8	15 3/8	8 5/8	8 5/8	22 3/8	19 3/8	Clark Co., Nev.	Charles J. Lindberg	Charles J. Lindberg	1971	361
168 1/8	33 5/8	35 5/8	14	14	8 3/8	8 3/8	22	22	Yuma Co., Ariz.	Ervin Black	Ervin Black	1972	361
168 1/8	33 5/8	34 4/8	14 4/8	14 4/8	9 5/8	9 5/8	23 3/8	23 3/8	Lincoln Co., Nev.	Dale Deming	Dale Deming	1977	361
168 1/8	35 7/8	37 1/8	15 5/8	15 1/8	7 7/8	7 7/8	25 5/8	25 5/8	Clark Co., Nev.	Ronald E. Brown	Ronald E. Brown	1983	361
168 1/8	35 1/8	33 1/8	15 1/8	15 1/8	8 4/8	8 4/8	19 6/8	19 6/8	Baja Calif., Mexico	Roger R. Card	Roger R. Card	1985	361
168 1/8	34 3/8	37	15	15	8	8	19	19	Lower Calif., Mexico	G. L. Harrison	Acad. Nat. Sci., Phil.	1903	369
168 1/8	34 4/8	34 1/8	14 1/8	14 1/8	8 6/8	8 6/8	20 7/8	18 3/8	Baja Calif., Mexico	James C. Nystrom	James C. Nystrom	1969	369
168 1/8	32 3/8	31 1/8	16 1/8	16 1/8	8 4/8	8 4/8	19	18	Pima Co., Ariz.	Jeff R. Snodgrass	Jeff R. Snodgrass	1970	369

DESERT SHEEP—*Continued*

Ovis canadensis nelsoni and certain related subspecies

Score	Length of Horn R.	L.	Circumference of Base R.	L.	Circumference at Third Quarter R.	L.	Greatest Spread	Tip to Tip Spread	Locality Killed	By Whom Killed	Owner	Date Killed	Rank
168⅛	34⅞	35⅜	14⅞	14⅞	8⅞	8⅞	22⅞	22⅞	Baja Calif., Mexico	C. R. Palmer	C. R. Palmer	1979	369
168⅛	32⅞	34⅜	15⅞	15⅞	8⅞	9	20	15⅞	Sonora, Mexico	David V. Collis	David V. Collis	1985	369
168	35	35	14	14	10	9	25	25	Lamb Springs, Nev.	Leslie H. Farr	Leslie H. Farr	1966	374
168	34⅞	34⅞	15	14⅞	8⅜	8⅞	21⅛	21	Clark Co., Nev.	Edward Friel	Edward Friel	1969	374
168	34⅞	35⅞	15⅛	15⅛	8	8⅜	21⅛	21⅛	Baja Calif., Mexico	Lee Frudden	Lee Frudden	1972	374
168	35	35⅜	14⅞	14⅜	9⅛	9	23	23	Clark Co., Nev.	Leonard M. Faike	Leonard M. Faike	1973	374
168	33⅛	34⅜	14⅞	14⅞	8⅜	9⅜	18⅛	17⅞	Mohave Co., Ariz.	Robert L. Fletcher	Robert L. Fletcher	1974	374
168	37⅞	35⅞	14⅞	14⅞	6⅜	6⅝	26⅜	26⅜	Mohave Co., Ariz.	Tom H. Martin	Tom H. Martin	1980	374
168	36⅜	35⅝	14⅞	14⅞	8⅜	8⅛	23⅜	22⅜	Clark Co., Nev.	Dennis K. Evans	Dennis K. Evans	1981	374
168	34	35	14⅜	14⅜	9⅞	7⅞	21	20	Mohave Co., Ariz.	Perry H. Finger	Perry H. Finger	1985	374
168	35⅞	35	15⅞	15⅞	7⅞	7⅞	19⅜	19⅞	Baja Calif., Mexico	Carl E. Jacobson	Carl E. Jacobson	1985	374
191⅛*	39⅜	39⅞	16⅜	16⅞	10	10	19⅜	19⅜	Baja Calif., Mexico	Bruno Scherrer	Bruno Scherrer	1981	
186⅞*	42⅜	38⅞	16⅞	16⅛	8⅜	8⅜	24⅞	23⅞	Baja Calif., Mexico	James N. McHolme	James N. McHolme	1981	

*Final Score subject to revision by additional verifying measurements

WORLD'S RECORD DALL'S SHEEP
SCORE: 189 6/8

Locality: Wrangell Mountains, Alaska Date: 1961
Hunter: Harry L. Swank, Jr. Owner: Mrs. Harry L. Swank, Jr.
Winner of the Sagamore Hill Medal, 1961

NUMBER TWO DALL'S SHEEP
SCORE: 185 6/8
Locality: Chugach Mountains, Alaska Date: 1956
Hunter and owner: Frank Cook
Winner of the Sagamore Hill Medal, 1957

Dall's Sheep

Ovis dalli dalli and Ovis dalli kenaiensis

Minimum Score 170

Score	Length of Horn R.	L.	Circumference of Base R.	L.	Circumference at Third Quarter R.	L.	Greatest Spread	Tip to Tip Spread	Locality Killed	By Whom Killed	Owner	Date Killed	Rank
189⅜	48⅛	47⅜	14⅜	14⅛	6⅝	6⅝	34⅜	34⅜	Wrangell Mts., Alaska	Harry L. Swank, Jr.	Mrs. Harry L. Swank, Jr.	1961	1
185⅝	49⅛	44⅞	14	13⅞	6⅝	7⅜	24⅞	24⅞	Chugach Mts., Alaska	Frank Cook	Frank Cook	1956	2
185⅜	43⅝	40⅞	14⅞	14⅞	9⅜	9⅜	20⅞	20⅞	Chugach Mts., Alaska	Jack W. Lentfer	Jack W. Lentfer	1964	3
184⅜	43⅞	46	14⅛	14⅜	9	7⅜	21⅞	21⅞	Wrangell Mts., Alaska	B. L. Burkholder	B. L. Burkholder	1958	4
184	44⅛	44⅞	14⅜	14⅛	7⅛	7⅜	24⅞	24⅞	Chugach Mts., Alaska	Thomas C. Sheets	Thomas C. Sheets	1962	5
183⅞	46⅛	47⅛	13⅞	13⅞	6⅝	6⅝	31	31	Wrangell Mts., Alaska	Tony Oney	Tony Oney	1963	6
183⅜	48	47⅛	14	13⅞	6⅝	6⅝	33⅞	33⅞	Alaska Range, Alaska	Jonathan T. Summar, Jr.	Jonathan T. Summar, Jr.	1965	7
183⅜	45⅛	45⅛	13⅞	14	7⅛	7⅞	27⅞	27⅞	Whitehorse, Yukon	W. Newhall	Robert E. Barnes	1924	8
183	42⅜	39⅞	14⅞	14⅞	9⅞	9⅞	22⅞	19⅞	Wrangell Mts., Alaska	Gene M. Effler	Gene M. Effler	1959	9
182⅞	44⅛	43⅞	14⅛	14⅛	7⅛	7⅛	23⅞	23⅞	Champagne, Yukon	Earl J. Thee	Earl J. Thee	1948	10
182	38⅝	39	15⅛	15⅜	10⅛	10⅛	0	0	Kenai Pen., Alaska	Picked Up	C. E. Lyons	PR1969	11
181⅞	44⅞	44⅛	14⅞	14⅞	6⅝	6⅛	27⅞	27⅞	Knik River, Alaska	Matthew Lahti	National Collection	1930	12
181⅞	47⅛	47⅜	14⅞	14⅞	5⅞	6⅛	28⅞	28⅞	Atlin, B.C.	Robert Landis	Ralph & Pearl Landis	1969	12
181⅜	46⅜	46⅞	14	14⅛	6	6⅛	32⅞	32⅞	McCarthy, Alaska	Bud Nelson	Bud Nelson	1953	14
181⅜	42⅞	42⅛	15⅛	15⅛	7⅛	7⅞	24⅞	24⅞	Wrangell Mts., Alaska	James K. Harrower	James K. Harrower	1961	15
181	46⅜	46⅞	13⅞	13⅞	6⅛	6⅛	28⅞	28⅞	Mt. Selous, Yukon	George C. Morris, Sr.	George C. Morris, Sr.	1962	16
180⅞	44⅛	44⅛	14⅞	14⅞	6⅝	6⅛	30⅞	30⅞	Wrangell Mts., Alaska	Robert W. Engstrom	Robert W. Engstrom	1973	17
180⅞	43⅜	43⅞	14⅛	14⅛	7⅞	7⅞	27	27	Kluane Lake, Yukon	Indian	Joe Jacquot	1953	18
180⅞	42⅜	44⅛	15	15	6⅞	7	26⅞	26⅞	Yukon	Billy Jack	Yukon Govt.	1966	18
180⅜	45⅜	46⅜	13⅞	13⅞	6⅝	6⅛	29⅞	29⅞	Johnson River, Alaska	P. A. Johnson & J. N. Brennan	P. A. Johnson & J. N. Brennan	1950	20
180⅛	39⅜	46⅛	15⅛	14⅞	7⅞	7	27	27	Wrangell Mts., Alaska	Harry H. Wilson	Harry H. Wilson	1961	21
180	39⅜	40⅞	14⅞	14⅞	8⅞	8⅛	23	21	Grand View, Alaska	Nellie Neal	Nellie Neal	1917	22
179⅞	45⅛	45⅜	13	13	6⅞	7⅞	27⅞	27⅞	Kenai Pen., Alaska	A. B. Learned	A. B. Learned	1936	23
179⅞	41⅜	41⅛	14⅞	14⅞	7	7	28⅞	28⅞	Chugach Mts., Alaska	J. H. Esslinger	J. H. Esslinger	1959	24
179⅞	40⅝	41⅛	14⅞	14⅛	8	8	26⅞	26⅞	Kluane Lake, Yukon	George E. Thompson	George E. Thompson	1956	25
179⅞	44⅛	44⅜	14⅛	14⅛	6⅝	6⅛	27	27	Chugach Mts., Alaska	Boyd Howard	Boyd Howard	1957	26
178⅞	40⅝	40⅞	14⅛	14⅞	7⅛	7⅞	24	23⅞	Chugach Mts., Alaska	Daniel A. Story	Daniel A. Story	1954	27
178⅞	42⅜	42⅛	13⅞	13⅜	8⅛	8⅞	25⅞	25⅞	Knik River, Alaska	V. A. Morgan	V. A. Morgan	1934	28
178⅞	40⅝	40⅛	15⅝	15⅞	7	7	30⅞	30⅞	Champagne, Yukon	B. V. Seigel	B. V. Seigel	1964	28
178⅜	45⅜	43⅝	13⅜	13⅞	7	6⅞	23⅞	23⅞	Alaska Hwy., Yukon	William H. Miller	William H. Miller	1947	30

DALL's SHEEP—Continued

Ovis dalli dalli and Ovis dalli kenaiensis

Score	Length of Horn R.	L.	Circumference of Base R.	L.	Circumference at Third Quarter R.	L.	Greatest Spread	Tip to Tip Spread	Locality Killed	By Whom Killed	Owner	Date Killed	Rank
178⅜	43⅝	42⅝	13⅞	14	6⅞	6⅝	27⅛	27⅛	Chugach Mts., Alaska	Sam Jaksick, Jr.	Sam Jaksick, Jr.	1966	30
178⅜	45⅝	42⅞	14⅛	14⅞	6⅜	6	31⅝	31⅝	Wrangell Mts., Alaska	Wilbur Ternyik	Wilbur Ternyik	1958	32
178⅜	45⅞	46⅜	13	13	6⅝	6⅜	26⅜	26⅜	Pelly Mts., Yukon	Eric W. French	Eric W. French	1958	32
178⅜	45⅞	43⅝	13⅝	13⅝	7⅛	6⅞	23⅝	23⅝	Wrangell Mts., Alaska	Unknown	Jeff Sievers	PR1950	34
178⅛	45⅞	44	14	13⅞	7⅜	7⅜	28	28	Chugach Mts., Alaska	J. S. Lichtenfels	J. S. Lichtenfels	1956	34
178	43⅜	43	15	15	6⅜	6⅜	30⅜	30⅜	Chitina River, Alaska	F. C. Hibben	F. C. Hibben	1963	36
177⅞	44⅛	45	14⅜	14	6⅝	6⅝	28⅜	28⅜	Chugach Mts., Alaska	William R. Champlain	William R. Champlain	1965	37
177⅞	43⅜	44⅜	14⅛	14⅜	6⅞	6⅛	27⅜	27⅜	Chugach Mts., Alaska	Chris Klineburger	Chris Klineburger	1957	38
177⅞	41⅞	43⅜	13⅜	13⅜	8⅞	9⅛	22	22	Rainy Pass, Alaska	F. Edmond Blanc	F. Edmond Blanc	1937	39
177⅝	44	43⅝	14⅛	14⅛	6	6	27⅛	27⅛	Kenai Pen., Alaska	John Swiss	John Swiss	1959	39
177⅝	44⅛	43⅜	14	14	6⅜	6⅜	26⅜	26⅜	Wrangell Mts., Alaska	Elgin T. Gates	Elgin T. Gates	1961	39
177⅜	44	43⅜	14⅜	14⅜	6⅞	6⅞	28⅜	28⅜	Wrangell Mts., Alaska	Rita Oney	Rita Oney	1963	42
177⅜	43⅜	44	14⅜	14⅛	6⅜	6⅛	25⅜	25⅜	Aishihik Lake, Yukon	Eleanor O'Connor	Eleanor O'Connor	1963	42
177⅜	40⅞	42⅞	13⅞	13⅞	7⅛	7⅜	23	23	Ruby Mt. Range, Yukon	Kenneth Campbell	Kenneth Campbell	1971	42
177⅜	45⅞	44⅜	13⅜	14	6⅛	6	28⅜	28⅜	Chugach Mts., Alaska	Robert Kraai	Robert Kraai	1977	42
177⅜	42⅜	43⅜	13⅜	13⅝	7	7	23⅜	23⅜	Kenai Pen., Alaska	Luke Elwell	Luke Elwell	1936	46
177⅛	38	40⅝	15⅜	15⅝	7⅜	7⅜	20⅛	20⅛	Chugach Mts., Alaska	Harry H. Wilson	Harry H. Wilson	1960	46
177⅛	43⅜	43⅜	14	13⅝	6⅝	6⅛	27⅜	27⅜	Kenai Pen., Alaska	C. R. Cross, Jr.	Harvard Club of Boston	1907	48
177⅛	43⅞	44	13	13⅛	7	7⅛	22⅛	22⅛	Ship Creek, Alaska	Oliver Tovsen	Oliver Tovsen	1940	48
177⅛	45⅞	44⅜	14	14	6	5⅞	30⅜	30⅜	Chugach Mts., Alaska	Jim Milito	Jim Milito	1971	48
177⅛	44⅜	45⅜	13⅜	13⅜	6⅞	6⅛	25⅜	25⅜	Mackenzie River, N.W.T.	Joseph Scott	Joseph Scott	1973	48
177	44⅞	44⅛	13⅜	13⅝	6	6	27⅛	27⅛	Chugach Mts., Alaska	Paul E. Huling	Paul E. Huling	1959	52
176⅞	43⅜	42⅜	14⅜	14⅜	6⅛	6⅜	23⅜	23⅜	Sifton Range, Yukon	Jack O'Connor	Jack O'Connor	1950	53
176⅞	41⅜	42	14⅜	14⅜	6⅜	6⅜	28	28	Wrangell Mts., Alaska	Vic S. Sears	Vic S. Sears	1960	53
176⅝	43	43	15	15	6⅜	5⅜	23⅜	23⅜	Wrangell Mts., Alaska	Ed Bilderback	Ed Bilderback	1959	55
176⅝	43⅛	43⅜	14⅜	14⅜	6⅜	6⅝	27	27	Chugach Mts., Alaska	Charles H. Rohrer	Charles H. Rohrer	1982	55
176⅝	44⅜	44⅜	13⅜	13⅛	6⅜	6⅜	26⅛	26⅛	Mayo, Yukon	C. L. Bestoule	C. L. Bestoule	1960	57
176⅜	45	45⅞	13	13⅜	7⅜	7	32	32	Donjek, Yukon	Olof Erickson	Mrs. Jacquot	1933	58
176⅜	46⅞	40⅞	13⅞	13⅜	6⅜	6⅜	22⅜	22⅜	Knik River, Alaska	Philip English	Philip English	1954	58
176⅜	43⅜	43⅜	14	14	6⅞	6⅞	25⅜	25⅜	Mt. River, N.W.T.	Daniel E. Yaeger	Daniel E. Yaeger	1973	58
176⅜	41⅜	41⅛	14	14	8	7⅝	24⅜	24⅜	Chugach Mts., Alaska	Lloyd Ronning	Lloyd Ronning	1953	61
176⅜	40⅜	42⅜	14⅜	14⅜	6⅝	7	24	24	Champagne, Yukon	H. W. Meisch	H. W. Meisch	1957	62

Score	(1)	(2)	(3)	(4)	(5)	(6)	(7)	(8)	Locality	Hunter	Owner	Date	Rank
176 6/8	40 7/8	41 3/8	13 3/8	13 3/8	8 2/8	8 2/8	21 1/8	18 1/8	Ruby Range, Yukon	J. Martin Benchoff	J. Martin Benchoff	1963	62
176 6/8	41 6/8	42	14 3/8	14 1/8	7	7 1/8	27 6/8	27 6/8	Chugach Mts., Alaska	Donald P. Chase	Donald P. Chase	1978	62
176	40 6/8	42	14 2/8	14 2/8	7	7	23	22	Knik River, Alaska	John S. Lahti	John S. Lahti	1930	65
176	42	43	14 3/8	14 3/8	6 4/8	6 4/8	22 6/8	22 6/8	Alaska	Picked Up	T. H. Rowe	PR 1960	65
176	39	38 4/8	15	14 5/8	9 4/8	9 6/8	26	26	Tonsina Lake, Alaska	Horace E. Groff	Horace E. Groff	1960	65
176	42	41 6/8	14 7/8	14 7/8	6 5/8	6 4/8	28 6/8	28 6/8	Chugach Mts., Alaska	William D. Backman, Jr.	William D. Backman, Jr.	1960	65
176	46 6/8	45 4/8	13 5/8	13 3/8	6	6	31 6/8	31 4/8	Wrangell Mts., Alaska	Harold Meeker	Harold Meeker	1965	65
176	41 2/8	41 4/8	15	15	6	6	25	25	Wrangell Mts., Alaska	Paul D. Weingart	Paul D. Weingart	1974	65
175 6/8	40 6/8	46 6/8	13 3/8	13 4/8	6 6/8	6 7/8	23 6/8	23 6/8	Ruby Range, Yukon	John K. Hansen	John K. Hansen	1960	71
175 6/8	42 3/8	42 7/8	13 5/8	13 5/8	6 6/8	6 2/8	23 6/8	22 6/8	Yukon	William E. Portman	William E. Portman	1966	71
175 6/8	43 7/8	43 7/8	14 7/8	15	6 4/8	6 4/8	30 6/8	30 6/8	Wrangell Mts., Alaska	Ben C. Boynton	Ben C. Boynton	1971	71
175 5/8	41 4/8	42 3/8	13 5/8	13 5/8	7 4/8	7 6/8	24	24	Chugach Mts., Alaska	Harry Anderson	Harry Anderson	1955	74
175 4/8	42	42	14	14	7	6 6/8	28 6/8	28 6/8	Wrangell Mts., Alaska	Swen Honkola	Swen Honkola	1958	75
175 3/8	37 6/8	40 3/8	14 4/8	14 4/8	8 2/8	8 2/8	23 6/8	23 3/8	Wrangell Mts., Alaska	Burt Ahlstrom	Burt Ahlstrom	1959	76
175 2/8	40 4/8	46 4/8	14 6/8	14 6/8	6 6/8	6 3/8	26 6/8	26 6/8	Chitina River, Alaska	Henry Boyden	Am. Mus. Nat. History	1936	77
175 2/8	41 4/8	42	14 3/8	14 3/8	6 6/8	6 6/8	26 6/8	26 2/8	Wrangell Mts., Alaska	Grant Smith	Grant Smith	1963	77
175 2/8	42 7/8	43 4/8	14 5/8	14 2/8	6 7/8	6 7/8	30 6/8	30 6/8	Chugach Mts., Alaska	Miles Hajny	Miles Hajny	1969	77
175 1/8	42 3/8	44 4/8	14	13 7/8	6 4/8	6 6/8	29	29	Talkeetna Mts., Alaska	Dale Caldwell	Dale Caldwell	1957	80
175 1/8	42 4/8	42 4/8	14 3/8	13 3/8	8 2/8	8 2/8	20 6/8	19 4/8	Wrangell Mts., Alaska	Herman F. Wyman	Herman F. Wyman	1964	80
175 1/8	41	40 7/8	13 3/8	13 3/8	6 6/8	6 6/8	23	23	Chugach Mts., Alaska	Edward A. Champlain	Edward A. Champlain	1965	80
175 1/8	41 3/8	39	15	15	7 6/8	7 6/8	26	26	Wrangell Mts., Alaska	John M. Griffith, Jr.	John M. Griffith, Jr.	1976	80
175	42 4/8	42 4/8	14 2/8	14 2/8	7	6 5/8	23 6/8	23 6/8	Kenai Pen., Alaska	Russel Gainer	Russel Gainer	1959	84
175	42 7/8	42 7/8	13 7/8	13 7/8	5 6/8	5 6/8	23 6/8	23 4/8	Chugach Mts., Alaska	Arthur R. Dubs	Arthur R. Dubs	1961	84
174 7/8	44 5/8	44	13 3/8	13 3/8	7 2/8	7 1/8	26 6/8	26 4/8	Lake Arkell, Yukon	J. J. Elliott	J. J. Elliott	1924	86
174 7/8	41 3/8	40 4/8	13 7/8	13 7/8	8 2/8	8	19 6/8	19 4/8	Chugach Mts., Alaska	Leroy Holen	Leroy Holen	1957	86
174 7/8	43 4/8	43	13 5/8	13 5/8	6 6/8	6 6/8	29	29	Wrangell Mts., Alaska	R. W. Ulman	R. W. Ulman	1962	86
174 7/8	42 4/8	40 3/8	13 7/8	13 5/8	6 4/8	6 6/8	28 6/8	28 4/8	Aishihik Lake, Yukon	Abe Goldberg	Abe Goldberg	1962	86
174 7/8	44 4/8	42 1/8	14	14	7 4/8	7 7/8	29	29	Chitina River, Alaska	Ray B. Nienhaus	Ray B. Nienhaus	1966	86
174 6/8	47 4/8	47	13 6/8	13 6/8	5 6/8	6 4/8	26	26	Carcross, Yukon	Billy Smith	Acad. Nat. Sci., Phil.	1927	91
174 6/8	46 6/8	43	13	13	7 1/8	6 6/8	25 6/8	25 4/8	Sifton Mt. Range, Yukon	Herb Klein	Herb Klein	1950	91
174 6/8	45 4/8	45	13 1/8	13 1/8	9 2/8	9 2/8	28 6/8	28 6/8	Wrangell Mts., Alaska	Warren W. Wilbur	Warren W. Wilbur	1952	91
174 6/8	41 3/8	43 4/8	14 5/8	14 4/8	6 4/8	6 1/8	28 6/8	28 4/8	Wheaton, Yukon	Herbert Carlson	Herbert Carlson	1963	91
174 6/8	40 6/8	40 3/8	14	14	6 2/8	6 7/8	26 6/8	26 4/8	Wrangell Mts., Alaska	Peter W. Bading	Peter W. Bading	1963	91
174 6/8	42	42 4/8	14 4/8	13 6/8	6 7/8	7	23 6/8	24	Chugach Mts., Alaska	Bill Silveira	Bill Silveira	1969	91
174 6/8	40 1/8	40 7/8	14	13 7/8	6 6/8	6 6/8	20 6/8	20 1/8	Mt. Wrangell, Alaska	Tod Reichert	Tod Reichert	1976	91
174 6/8	41 2/8	41 2/8	14 2/8	14	6 7/8	7 2/8	27 6/8	27 2/8	Wrangell Mts., Alaska	Don L. Corley	Don L. Corley	1978	91
174 5/8	40 4/8	43 5/8	14 5/8	14 2/8	6 4/8	6 4/8	22 6/8	22 3/8	Kenai Mts., Alaska	C. A. Brauch	C. A. Brauch	1959	99
174 5/8	40 5/8	40 4/8	14 5/8	14 5/8	7 2/8	7 2/8	27 6/8	27 1/8	Raft Creek, Yukon	Marvin Wood	Marvin Wood	1961	99
174 5/8	43 4/8	42 3/8	13 7/8	13 7/8	6 6/8	6 6/8	26 6/8	26 2/8	Kusawa Lake, Yukon	Lawrence J. Kolar	Lawrence J. Kolar	1973	99
174 4/8	41	41	13 5/8	13 5/8	8 2/8	8 2/8	22	21 3/8	Wrangell Mts., Alaska	Lloyd Walker	Lloyd Walker	1959	102
174 4/8	42 4/8	41 6/8	13 7/8	13 7/8	8	7 6/8	20 6/8	20 5/8	Wrangell Mts., Alaska	Robert L. Jenkins	Robert L. Jenkins	1963	102
174 4/8	40 3/8	40 6/8	15 1/8	14 7/8	6 6/8	6 6/8	23 6/8	23 4/8	Chugach Mts., Alaska	Lawrence T. Keenan	Lawrence T. Keenan	1976	102

Ovis dalli dalli and Ovis dalli kenaiensis

Score	Length of Horn R.	Length of Horn L.	Circumference of Base R.	Circumference of Base L.	Circumference at Third Quarter R.	Circumference at Third Quarter L.	Greatest Spread	Tip to Tip Spread	Locality Killed	By Whom Killed	Owner	Date Killed	Rank
174⅞	43⅛	43⅛	14⅜	14⅜	6⅛	6⅜	24	24	Wrangell Mts., Alaska	John J. Liska	John J. Liska	1963	105
174⅞	42⅛	42⅛	14⅛	14⅛	6⅜	6⅜	25⅝	25⅝	Nahannie Range, N.W.T.	Nick Trenke	Nick Trenke	1979	105
174⅞	41⅝	41⅝	14⅜	14⅜	6⅜	6⅜	26⅝	26⅝	Talkeetna Mts., Alaska	William J. Konesky	William J. Konesky	1958	107
174⅞	40⅞	41⅝	14⅜	14⅜	7⅜	7	22	22	Wrangell Mts., Alaska	Jerry L. Beason	Jerry L. Beason	1961	107
174⅞	41⅛	43⅝	13⅞	14	6⅜	6⅜	31⅛	31⅛	Coast Mts., Yukon	Clarence Hinkle	Clarence Hinkle	1963	107
174¾	40	42⅞	14⅝	14⅝	6⅜	6⅜	25	25	Ruby Range, Yukon	Lawrence S. Kellogg	Lawrence S. Kellogg	1958	110
174¾	43⅞	43⅛	14⅛	14⅛	5⅞	6	30⅞	30⅞	Wrangell Mts., Alaska	Sven Johanson	Sven Johanson	1960	110
174	40⅞	42⅞	13⅝	13⅞	7⅞	7⅞	21⅞	21⅞	Kenai Pen., Alaska	Basil C. Bradbury	Basil C. Bradbury	1960	112
174	42⅜	45	14	14	6⅜	6⅜	27	27	Wrangell Mts., Alaska	Howard Gilmore, Jr.	Howard Gilmore, Jr.	1969	112
174	43⅜	44⅜	14	14	5⅞	5⅞	32⅜	31⅜	Wrangell Mts., Alaska	Dan Parker	Dan Parker	1972	112
174	43⅜	42⅛	14⅜	14⅜	5⅞	5⅞	29	29⅞	Alaska Range, Alaska	Harry Robert Hannon	Harry Robert Hannon	1976	112
173⅞	44⅛	42⅜	13⅞	13⅞	6⅜	6⅜	26	26	Twitya River, N.W.T.	Lewis W. Lindemer	Lewis W. Lindemer	1970	116
173⅞	42⅜	43⅜	14⅜	14⅜	6⅛	6⅜	29⅜	29⅜	Talkeetna Mts., Alaska	Frank Cook	Frank Cook	1961	117
173⅞	36⅞	41⅛	15⅛	15	7⅜	7⅜	24⅜	24⅜	Wrangell Mts., Alaska	Gene Effler	Gene Effler	1964	117
173⅞	40⅜	40⅛	14⅞	14⅛	5⅜	5⅞	30⅜	30⅜	Keele River, N.W.T.	John M. Azevedo	John M. Azevedo	1975	117
173⅝	41⅛	45⅜	12⅞	13	7	6⅜	24⅜	24⅜	Ruby Range, Yukon	John E. Hammett	John E. Hammett	1949	120
173⅝	45⅜	45⅛	13⅛	13⅜	5⅞	5⅝	30⅜	30⅜	Chitina, Alaska	Dene Leonard, Jr.	Dene Leonard, Jr.	1959	120
173⅝	38⅜	42⅜	13⅞	13⅞	9⅜	9⅜	21⅞	19⅞	Wrangell Mts., Alaska	B. L. Burkholder	B. L. Burkholder	1960	120
173⅝	42⅜	42⅞	14⅜	14⅝	5⅝	5⅜	28	28	Chugach Mts., Alaska	Richard T. Kopsack	Richard T. Kopsack	1961	120
173⅝	43⅜	41⅜	13⅜	13⅜	7⅜	7⅜	23⅜	22⅜	Champagne, Yukon	Edmund D. Patterson, Jr.	Edmund D. Patterson, Jr.	1963	120
173⅝	41⅜	41⅞	14⅜	14⅜	6⅜	6⅜	24⅜	24⅜	Lake Clark, Alaska	Melvin C. Paxton	Melvin C. Paxton	1968	120
173⅝	43⅜	43⅜	13⅞	14	5⅜	5⅜	29⅜	29⅜	Primrose River, Yukon	W. R. Collier	W. R. Collier	1962	126
173⅝	42	44⅜	13⅞	13⅞	6⅜	6⅜	29⅜	29⅜	Wrangell Mts., Alaska	James Harrower	James Harrower	1963	126
173⅝	41⅛	40⅞	14⅞	14⅜	6⅜	6⅜	31⅜	30⅜	Chitina Glacier, Alaska	Robert W. Kubick	Robert W. Kubick	1967	126
173⅝	43⅜	43	13⅜	13⅜	6⅜	6⅜	28⅜	28⅜	Tonseno Lake, Alaska	James St. Amour	James St. Amour	1957	129
173⅝	44⅜	44⅞	13⅜	13⅜	5⅞	5⅜	28⅜	28⅜	Chugach Mts., Alaska	Howard Haney	Howard Haney	1961	129
173⅝	40⅜	40⅛	15	15	6⅛	6⅜	27⅜	27⅜	Whitehorse, Yukon	Francis Bouchard	Francis Bouchard	1961	129
173⅝	43⅜	42⅜	13⅜	13⅜	6⅜	6⅜	19⅞	19⅞	Kenai Pen., Alaska	Spud Dillon	Spud Dillon	1966	129
173⅝	39⅜	44⅜	13⅞	13⅜	6⅜	6⅜	25⅜	24⅜	Wrangell Mts., Alaska	Basil C. Bradbury	Basil C. Bradbury	1968	129
173⅝	42	42⅞	13⅜	13⅜	7	7⅜	22⅜	22⅜	Alaska Range, Alaska	Arthur L. Spicer	Arthur L. Spicer	1970	129
173⅝	35⅝	45	14⅜	14⅜	6⅜	6⅜	25⅜	23⅜	Wrangell Mts., Alaska	J. H. Shelton	J. H. Shelton	1958	135
173⅝	46⅛	41⅜	13⅜	13⅜	6	6	20⅜	26⅜	Kenai Pen., Alaska	W. R. Shellhorn	D. Shellhorn	1936	136

Score	Length R	Length L	Circ. Base R	Circ. Base L	Circ. 3rd Qtr R	Circ. 3rd Qtr L	Greatest Spread	Tip to Tip	Locality	Owner	Hunter	Killed	Rank
173½	41¼	39⅜	14¾	14¾	7⅜	7½	21⅞	18⅞	Dawson Mts., Yukon	Bill Goosman	Bill Goosman	1972	136
173	42	42⅜	13⅞	13⅞	6⅞	6⅜	28	28	Wrangell Mts., Alaska	Ken Knudson	Ken Knudson	1961	138
173	40⅞	40⅜	15	15	6⅞	6⅜	28⅜	28⅜	Whitehorse, Yukon	Earl DuBois	Earl DuBois	1961	138
173	45⅛	45⅛	13¾	13¾	5⅜	5⅜	33	33	Wrangell Mts., Alaska	Bob Merz	Bob Merz	1966	138
173	40⅝	41⅛	13½	13¾	7⅜	7⅛	20⅜	20⅜	Chugach Mts., Alaska	J. C. Hemming	J. C. Hemming	1970	138
173	40⅛	43	13½	13½	5⅞	5⅞	28⅜	27⅞	Wrangell Mts., Alaska	Charles A. Pohland	Charles A. Pohland	1971	138
173	43⅛	44	13½	14¾	6	6	28	28	Chugach Mts., Alaska	Thomas Clark	Thomas Clark	1975	138
172⅞	40⅜	40⅛	14¾	14⅜	6⅜	6⅜	25⅜	25⅜	Chugach Mts., Alaska	Peter W. Bading	Peter W. Bading	1961	144
172⅞	39⅛	39	14⅞	14¾	7⅞	7⅜	25⅜	25⅜	Wrangell Mts., Alaska	Ralph Cox	Ralph Cox	1971	144
172⅞	43⅝	42⅝	14¾	14⅜	6⅝	6⅛	24⅞	24	Alaska Range, Alaska	George Faerber	George Faerber	1976	144
172⅞	40⅜	40⅝	13⅞	13⅝	7⅞	7⅜	22	20⅜	Kusawa Lake, Yukon	John I. Moore	John I. Moore	1955	147
172⅞	38⅞	43⅛	14⅞	14½	8	6⅝	27⅞	27⅞	Nabesna River, Alaska	J. C. Phillips	J. C. Phillips	1956	147
172⅞	41⅛	41⅛	13½	13½	6⅞	6⅜	25⅜	25⅜	Chugach Mts., Alaska	Ruby Wyatt	Ruby Wyatt	1960	147
172⅞	43⅝	43⅛	13½	13½	6⅞	6⅜	33	33	Chugach Mts., Alaska	Richard Kopsack	Richard Kopsack	1963	147
172⅞	40	40⅞	14⅛	15	7	6⅛	30⅜	30⅜	Gerstle River, Alaska	John A. Shilling	John A. Shilling	1968	147
172⅞	41⅛	42⅛	14⅛	14⅛	6⅜	6⅜	28⅜	28⅜	Wrangell Mts., Alaska	Alvin W. Huba, Jr.	Alvin W. Huba, Jr.	1968	147
172⅞	41⅞	41⅞	14⅛	14⅛	6⅜	6⅜	29	29	Radelet Creek, B.C.	Norman W. Dougan	Norman W. Dougan	1972	147
172⅞	43⅛	43	13⅞	13⅝	5⅞	5⅞	28⅜	28⅜	Chandalar River, Alaska	Robert M. Welch	Robert M. Welch	1974	147
172⅞	43⅝	43⅝	14	14	5⅝	5⅝	30⅜	30⅜	Wrangell Mts., Alaska	Robert J. Wykel	Robert J. Wykel	1976	147
172⅝	40⅜	41⅛	15	15	6⅝	6⅜	29	28⅜	Mountain River, N.W.T.	Edmond D. Henley	Edmond D. Henley	1983	147
172⅝	43⅝	42⅛	12⅞	13½	7	7	29⅞	29⅞	Knik Glacier, Alaska	Howard G. Romig	Picked Up	1932	157
172⅝	42⅛	42⅛	13⅞	13⅛	6⅞	6⅜	26⅜	26⅜	Mt. Arkell, Yukon	Stuart Hall	Stuart Hall	1957	157
172⅝	42	41⅜	14⅝	14⅜	5⅝	5⅜	32	32	Wrangell Mts., Alaska	William T. Ellis	William T. Ellis	1960	157
172⅝	38⅞	39⅝	14⅞	15¾	6⅞	6⅝	33⅞	33⅜	Caribou Creek, Yukon	Harold J. Lund	Harold J. Lund	1963	157
172⅝	41⅛	42	14⅛	14⅛	6⅜	6⅜	27⅞	27⅜	Yukon	S. P. Viezner	S. P. Viezner	1964	157
172⅝	41⅛	41⅜	13	13	7⅜	7½	29⅞	29⅜	Knik River, Alaska	Miles G. France	Miles G. France	1969	157
172⅝	42	41⅛	14⅞	14⅜	6⅜	6⅜	21⅞	21⅝	Talbot Creek, Yukon	Lloyd E. Zeman	Lloyd E. Zeman	1969	157
172⅝	42⅛	42⅛	13⅞	13⅛	6⅜	6⅜	26⅞	26⅛	Wrangell Mts., Alaska	W. A. Bailey, Jr.	W. A. Bailey, Jr.	1959	164
172⅝	43⅛	43⅛	13⅛	14⅝	7⅜	6	24⅜	24⅜	Wrangell Mts., Alaska	H. E. Eldred	H. E. Eldred	1960	164
172¼	39⅝	45⅝	14	14	6	5⅛	27⅜	27⅜	Chugach Mts., Alaska	Raymond Capossela	Raymond Capossela	1963	164
172¼	41⅛	42⅛	14⅞	14⅜	6⅜	6⅜	31⅜	31⅜	Primrose Lake, Yukon	Walter Sutton	Walter Sutton	1968	164
172¼	40⅜	42	14⅛	15	6⅝	6⅜	26⅜	26⅜	Mackenzie Mts., N.W.T.	Leslie C. Finger	Leslie C. Finger	1985	164
172¼	41⅛	41⅛	13⅞	13⅝	6⅜	6⅜	25⅜	25⅛	Chugach Mts., Alaska	Chuck Moe	Chuck Moe	1979	169
172⅜	42⅜	41⅝	14⅜	14½	5⅝	5⅛	21⅞	21⅛	Granite Lake, Yukon	William E. Medley II	William E. Medley II	1980	169
172⅜	45⅞	44⅛	13⅜	13⅜	6	6	32	32	Copper River, Alaska	C. J. McElroy	C. J. McElroy	1977	171
172¼	40	39⅞	14⅛	14¼	7	7	24¾	24¾	Wrangell Mts., Alaska	Kirk Gay	Kirk Gay	1958	172
172⅛	39⅞	39	15⅜	15⅜	7	7	26	26	Wrangell Mts., Alaska	Horace Groff	Horace Groff	1961	172
172⅛	38⅞	42	14⅛	14⅛	6	6⅜	21⅜	21⅜	Chugach Mts., Alaska	E. F. Craig	E. F. Craig	1963	172
172⅛	42	41⅞	14⅞	14⅝	5⅝	5⅜	25⅜	25⅜	Wrangell Mts., Alaska	Walter E. Cox	Walter E. Cox	1966	172
172	43	38⅞	14	14	6	6	29¾	29¾	Kuskokwim River, Alaska	Ken M. Wilson	Ken M. Wilson	1973	172
172	43⅝	44⅝	13⅝	13¾	5⅝	5⅜	26⅜	26⅜	Chugach Mts., Alaska	M. L. Magnusson	M. L. Magnusson	1957	177
172	41⅛	41⅞	14⅛	14⅛	6⅝	6⅝	26⅝	26⅝	Wrangell Mts., Alaska	Carroll W. Gibbs	Carroll W. Gibbs	1957	177
172	41⅛	42	13⅝	13⅜	6⅜	6⅜	25⅜	25⅜	Sheep Mt., Yukon	Ray Hoffman III	Ray Hoffman III	1961	177

DALL'S SHEEP—Continued
Ovis dalli dalli and Ovis dalli kenaiensis

Score	Length of Horn R.	L.	Circumference of Base R.	L.	Circumference at Third Quarter R.	L.	Greatest Spread	Tip to Tip Spread	Locality Killed	By Whom Killed	Owner	Date Killed	Rank
172	36	39	15	15⅛	8	8	22⅝	20	Chugach Mts., Alaska	Ward Gay, Jr.	Ward Gay, Jr.	1962	177
172	41⅛	41⅛	14⅞	14⅞	6⅞	6⅞	22⅜	22⅜	Sekwi Mt., N.W.T.	J. D. Martin, Jr.	J. D. Martin, Jr.	1978	177
171⅞	45⅜	42⅞	13⅛	13⅛	6	6⅛	27⅞	27⅞	McCarthy, Alaska	Eugene E. Saxton	Eugene E. Saxton	1953	182
171⅞	43⅜	41⅛	13⅝	13⅜	6⅛	6⅛	25⅝	25⅝	Talkeetna Mts., Alaska	Paul S. Lawrence	Paul S. Lawrence	1960	182
171⅞	39⅜	38	15⅝	15⅞	6	6⅛	25⅝	25⅝	Wrangell Mts., Alaska	Kenneth Knudson	Kenneth Knudson	1963	182
171⅞	41⅛	40⅛	13⅜	13⅜	7⅛	7⅜	44⅞	44⅞	Chugach Mts., Alaska	Herb Klein	Herb Klein	1964	182
171⅛	41⅝	40⅜	14⅝	14⅜	6⅛	6⅛	22⅝	22⅝	Chugach Mts., Alaska	Frank Cook	Frank Cook	1965	182
171⅛	40⅜	40⅜	14⅛	14⅜	6⅜	6⅜	28⅜	28⅜	Wrangell Mts., Alaska	Brent R. Hanks	Brent R. Hanks	1983	188
171⅛	38⅜	42⅛	14	13⅞	6⅜	6⅛	28⅛	28⅛	Wrangell Mts., Alaska	Charles C. Parsons	Charles C. Parsons	1955	188
171⅛	42⅛	42⅜	13⅞	14	6⅛	6⅜	30⅜	30⅜	Wrangell Mts., Alaska	Ross Jardine	Ross Jardine	1960	188
171⅝	35⅜	42	14⅞	14⅞	6⅜	6⅜	24⅜	24⅜	Chugach Mts., Alaska	C. J. McElroy	C. J. McElroy	1969	188
171⅝	41⅜	41⅞	14⅜	14⅛	5⅞	6⅛	26⅜	26⅜	Chugach Mts., Alaska	Justin L. Smith	Justin L. Smith	1963	191
171⅝	40⅜	41	14⅜	14⅜	6⅝	6⅛	22⅛	22⅛	Nabesna Glacier, Alaska	John F. Saltz	John F. Saltz	1983	191
171⅝	40⅜	40⅜	13⅜	13⅜	6⅜	6⅜	23⅜	23⅜	Kenai Pen., Alaska	C. R. Wright	C. R. Wright	1936	193
171⅛	40⅜	39⅜	14⅛	15	6⅜	5⅞	28	28	Whitehorse, Yukon	Howard Creason	Howard Creason	1969	193
171⅛	41⅝	42⅜	13⅜	13⅝	6⅜	6⅝	26	26	Wrangell Mts., Alaska	Robert V. Walker	Robert V. Walker	1971	193
171⅜	44⅜	45⅜	12⅞	13	6⅜	5⅞	34⅜	34⅜	Wood River, Alaska	R. R. M. Carpenter	Acad. Nat. Sci., Phil.	1940	196
171⅜	39⅜	40⅛	13⅝	13⅜	7⅜	7⅞	27⅜	27⅜	Coal Creek, Alaska	W. W. Fultz	W. W. Fultz	1955	196
171⅜	41⅛	41⅜	14	14	6⅛	6⅜	30⅜	30⅜	Chugach Mts., Alaska	Perley Colbeth	Perley Colbeth	1958	196
171⅜	42	42⅜	13⅜	13⅜	7⅜	7⅜	29⅜	29⅜	Wrangell Mts., Alaska	Arthur R. Dubs	Arthur R. Dubs	1962	196
171⅜	36⅜	44	14⅛	14⅝	6⅜	6⅜	25⅛	25⅛	Wrangell Mts., Alaska	Doug McRae, Sr.	Doug McRae, Sr.	1972	196
171⅜	41⅛	42⅜	14	14	6	6⅛	26⅜	26⅜	Chugach Mts., Alaska	Michael J. Ebner	Michael J. Ebner	1977	196
171⅜	42⅜	42⅜	14	14	5⅝	5⅜	32⅜	32⅜	Carcajou River, N.W.T.	Colin J. Kure	Colin J. Kure	1980	196
171⅛	36⅜	38⅛	14⅜	14⅜	7⅞	7⅞	24⅜	24⅛	Wrangell Mts., Alaska	Gordon Madole	Gordon Madole	1956	203
171⅛	39⅜	40	12⅜	12⅛	9⅜	9⅜	21⅜	21⅛	Ruby Range, Yukon	Picked Up	William J. Joslin	1960	203
171⅛	39⅜	41⅜	14⅜	14⅜	6	6	24⅜	23⅜	Wrangell Mts., Alaska	Rudolpho Valladolid	Rudolpho Valladolid	1974	203
171⅛	45	44⅛	12⅜	12⅜	6⅜	6⅜	26⅜	26⅜	Wrangell Mts., Alaska	Picked Up	Dick Gunlogson	1968	206
171⅛	42	42⅜	13⅜	14	6⅛	6⅜	24	24	Kusawa Lake, Yukon	Maurice G. Katz	Maurice G. Katz	1970	206
171⅛	40⅜	40⅜	13⅜	14	6⅜	6⅜	22⅜	22⅜	Robertson River, Alaska	Beuron A. McKenzie	Beuron A. McKenzie	1971	206
171	42⅜	43⅜	13⅜	13⅜	5⅝	5⅜	30⅜	30⅜	Carcross, Yukon	Henry Brockhouse	Henry Brockhouse	1955	209
171	36⅜	39⅜	14	14	8	8⅜	20⅜	19⅜	Chugach Mts., Alaska	Raymond Capossela	Raymond Capossela	1961	209
171	42⅛	41⅛	14	13⅜	6⅛	6⅜	26⅜	26⅜	Alligator Lake, Yukon	D. Graham	D. Graham	1968	209

448

171	40⅝	41⅞	14	13⅞	6⅜	6⅜	26⅞	26⅞	Ruby Range, Yukon	Harry T. Scharfenberg	Harry T. Scharfenberg	1977
170⅞	41⅛	41⅛	14⅛	14⅛	5⅞	5⅝	26⅞	26⅞	Kenai Pen., Alaska	David Jones	David Jones	1963
170⅞	35⅝	39⅝	15⅝	15⅜	7⅛	7⅞	25⅞	25⅞	Wrangell Mts., Alaska	Richard Stingley	Richard Stingley	1965
170⅞	42	41⅛	14⅛	14	6⅜	6⅜	29⅞	29⅞	Wrangell Mts., Alaska	Thomas Sperstad	Thomas Sperstad	1969
170⅞	36	36⅝	14⅜	14⅜	9⅛	9⅛	25⅞	25⅞	Chugach Mts., Alaska	Gerald L. Warnock	Gerald L. Warnock	1970
170⅞	40⅝	40⅞	14⅛	14⅛	6	6	26⅞	26⅞	Trench Lake, N.W.T.	Wayne G. Myers	Wayne G. Myers	1974
170⅞	41⅝	41⅛	14⅛	14⅛	5⅞	6⅝	26⅞	26⅞	Wrangell Mts., Alaska	Joseph A. Tedesco	Joseph A. Tedesco	1959
170⅞	39⅞	39⅞	14⅜	14⅜	6⅞	6⅜	28⅞	28⅞	Wrangell Mts., Alaska	George Stelious	George Stelious	1962
170⅞	42⅛	42⅛	13⅞	13⅜	6⅛	6⅛	26⅞	26⅞	Wrangell Mts., Alaska	Robert V. Broadbent	Robert V. Broadbent	1965
170⅞	44	44	13⅜	13⅜	5⅝	5⅜	30⅞	30⅞	Teepee Mt., B.C.	Steve Snider	Jon K. Mahoney	1983
170⅞	41⅛	41⅞	14	14	6⅝	6⅛	30⅞	30⅞	Nabesna River, Alaska	J. S. Rutherford	J. S. Rutherford	1956
170⅞	42⅛	40⅝	12⅞	12⅞	7⅜	7⅝	21⅞	21⅞	Wrangell Mts., Alaska	W. A. Fisher	W. A. Fisher	1959
170⅞	41⅜	42⅜	13⅜	13⅜	6⅜	6⅜	25⅞	25⅞	Wrangell Mts., Alaska	Gene Sperstad	Gene Sperstad	1961
170⅞	43⅜	40⅞	14⅛	14⅛	5⅞	5⅞	25⅞	25⅞	Nutzotin Mts., Alaska	Dorothy Andersen	Larry Folger	1965
170⅞	41⅜	42⅛	14⅞	15	5⅜	5⅜	28	28	Chugach Mts., Alaska	Harry C. Heckendorn	Harry C. Heckendorn	1972
170⅞	44⅜	38	13⅞	13⅞	6⅜	6⅜	29⅞	29⅞	Wrangell Mts., Alaska	Harry L. Swank, Jr.	Mrs. Harry L. Swank, Jr.	1962
170⅞	40⅞	40⅝	14⅜	14⅜	6⅜	6⅜	21⅞	21⅞	Ruby Range, Yukon	Harold C. Casey	Harold C. Casey	1964
170⅞	41⅜	41⅞	14⅛	14⅛	6⅜	6⅜	23⅞	23⅞	Brooks Range, Alaska	Donald E. Harrell	Donald E. Harrell	1979
170⅞	40	40⅜	14⅜	14⅜	6⅜	6⅜	22	22	Kenai Pen., Alaska	Vance Corrigan	Vance Corrigan	1957
170⅞	39⅞	40⅝	14⅜	14⅜	6⅜	6⅜	28	28	Wrangell Mts., Alaska	J. A. Tadesco	J. A. Tadesco	1960
170⅞	42⅞	41⅞	13⅞	13⅞	5⅜	5⅛	31⅞	31⅞	Chugach Mts., Alaska	William H. Smith	William H. Smith	1961
170⅞	41⅝	39⅞	13⅜	13⅜	7⅜	7⅜	27⅞	27⅞	Wrangell Mts., Alaska	Willie Bogner, Sr.	Willie Bogner, Sr.	1961
170⅞	40⅝	41⅞	15⅜	15⅜	7	7	22⅞	22⅞	Kenai Pen., Alaska	C. R. Wright	C. R. Wright	1935
170⅞	39⅜	39⅞	13⅞	13⅞	6⅜	5⅜	25⅞	25⅞	Champagne, Yukon	Walter Butcher	Walter Butcher	1956
170⅞	39⅝	41⅝	14⅜	14⅜	6⅜	6⅜	23⅞	23⅞	Tonsina River, Alaska	R. J. Uhl	R. J. Uhl	1959
170⅞	38⅞	39⅝	13⅞	13⅞	6⅜	6⅛	19⅞	19⅞	Chugach Mts., Alaska	Donald Stroble	Donald Stroble	1961
170⅞	37⅞	38	14⅛	14	6⅜	7	20⅞	20⅞	Kenai Pen., Alaska	Lee Miller	Lee Miller	1963
170⅞	40⅜	40⅜	14⅞	14⅞	5⅜	6	27⅞	27⅞	Wrangell Mts., Alaska	C. Driskell	C. Driskell	1965
170⅞	41	40	14⅛	14⅜	8⅜	6⅜	28⅞	28⅞	Wrangell Mts., Alaska	Jim Babala	Jim Babala	1967
170⅞	41⅛	41⅞	13⅞	13⅞	6⅛	6⅜	25⅞	25⅞	Talkeetna Mts., Alaska	H. Albertas Hall	H. Albertas Hall	1971
170⅞	40	40	14⅛	14⅜	6⅛	6	26⅞	26⅞	Wrangell Mts., Alaska	Bernard J. Meinerz	Bernard J. Meinerz	1972
170⅞	40	40	14⅛	14⅜	7⅜	7	29⅞	29⅞	Snake River, Yukon	Norman M. Thachuk	Norman M. Thachuk	1982
170	42⅞	42⅞	13⅞	13⅜	6⅜	6⅜	28	28	Donjek, Yukon	Unknown	Acad. Nat. Sci., Phil.	1921
170	42	42	13⅜	13⅜	6⅜	6⅜	25⅞	25⅞	Mt. Arkell, Yukon	Ed Steiner	Ed Steiner	1955
170	40⅛	41	14⅜	14⅛	7⅝	6	22	22	Wrangell Mts., Alaska	Chester Beer	Chester Beer	1959
170	40⅜	40⅞	13⅜	14	6⅛	6⅜	24⅞	24⅞	Chugach Mts., Alaska	James A. Kirsch	James A. Kirsch	1961
170	41⅛	41⅛	14	14	6⅛	6⅛	20⅞	20⅞	Wrangell Mts., Alaska	W. T. Yoshimoto	W. T. Yoshimoto	1967
170	38	37⅞	13⅛	13⅛	6⅛	7⅜	30⅞	30⅞	Wrangell Mts., Alaska	Ralph Morava, Jr.	Ralph Morava, Jr.	1954
170	42	42⅜	13⅜	14⅜	6⅛	6	27⅞	27⅞	Nabesna River, Alaska	Raymond A. Talbott	Raymond A. Talbott	1958
170	40⅞	42⅛	14⅜	14⅛	8⅛	6	23⅞	23⅞	Kluane Lake, Yukon	Herb Graham	Herb Graham	1959
170	40⅞	39⅞	13⅜	13⅜	6⅛	6⅛	23⅞	23⅞	Wrangell Mts., Alaska	Mrs. Melvin Soder	Mrs. Melvin Soder	1961
170	41⅛	42⅜	13⅜	13⅜	6⅛	6⅝	23⅞	23⅞	Farewell Lake, Alaska	Frank G. Merz	Frank G. Merz	1983
170	41⅞	42⅞	14	13⅞	5⅞	5⅞	24⅞	24⅞	Haley Creek, Alaska	Larry C. Munn	Larry C. Munn	1985

DALL's SHEEP—*Continued*

Ovis dalli dalli and Ovis dalli kenaiensis

Score	Length of Horn R.	L.	Circumference of Base R.	L.	Circumference at Third Quarter R.	L.	Greatest Spread	Tip to Tip Spread	Locality Killed	By Whom Killed	Owner	Date Killed	Rank
187 1/8*	45 1/8	47 7/8	14 3/8	14 3/8	7 3/8	7 3/8	25 3/8	25 3/8	Jacksina Creek, Alaska	Sherwin N. Scott	Sherwin N. Scott	1984	
185 3/8*	46	45 7/8	15 7/8	15 7/8	6 3/8	6 3/8	29 3/8	29 3/8	Coast Mts., Yukon	David W. Young	David W. Young	1972	
178 4/8*	42 3/8	43 3/8	14 3/8	14 4/8	6 7/8	7 3/8	27 3/8	27 3/8	Nabesna Glacier, Alaska	Floyd Saltz, Jr.	Floyd Saltz, Jr.	1982	
176*	41 7/8	41 3/8	14 7/8	14 7/8	6	6 3/8	24 3/8	24 3/8	Nabesna Glacier, Alaska	Sandra T. Saltz	Sandra T. Saltz	1982	
175 6/8*	42	43 3/8	15	15	6	6	27 3/8	27 3/8	Mt. Ingram, Yukon	Steve Zimmerman	Steve Zimmerman	1979	
175 2/8*	39	39 7/8	15	15	7 7/8	7 7/8	26 3/8	26 3/8	Wrangell Mts., Alaska	Russell A. Reed	Russell A. Reed	1983	
173 3/8*	44	43 7/8	14 4/8	14 4/8	5 3/8	5 3/8	30 3/8	30 3/8	Cache Lake, N.W.T.	Lester Behrns	Lester Behrns	1980	

*Final Score subject to revision by additional verifying measurements

450

WORLD'S RECORD STONE'S SHEEP
SCORE: 196 6/8

Locality: Muskwa River, British Columbia Date: 1936
Hunter: L.S. Chadwick Owner: The B&C National Collection.
Many sportsmen consider this trophy the finest known from North America

Photograph by Ray Todd

NUMBER TWO STONE'S SHEEP
SCORE: 190
Locality: Sikanni Chief River, British Columbia Date: 1962
Hunter and owner: Norman Blank
Winner of the Sagamore Hill Medal, 1963

452

Stone's Sheep
Ovis dalli stonei

Minimum Score 170

Score	Length of Horn R.	L.	Circumference of Base R.	L.	Circumference at Third Quarter R.	L.	Greatest Spread	Tip to Tip Spread	Locality Killed	By Whom Killed	Owner	Date Killed	Rank
196⅝	50½	51½	14⅞	14⅞	6⅞	7	31	31	Muskwa River, B.C.	L. S. Chadwick	B&C National Collection	1936	1
190	46⅜	46⅜	15⅝	15⅛	6⅝	6⅞	30⅜	30⅜	Sikanni Chief River, B.C.	Norman Blank	Norman Blank	1962	2
189⅞	48⅜	46⅞	14⅞	14⅞	7⅞	7⅛	28	28	Blue Sheep Lake, B.C.	G. C. F. Dalziel	G. C. F. Dalziel	1965	3
187⅞	43	44	14⅞	14⅞	8⅜	8⅜	22	22	Ospika River, B.C.	Paul D. Weingart	Paul D. Weingart	1970	4
184⅞	43	43⅜	15⅝	15⅝	7	7⅛	28⅜	28⅜	Prophet River, B.C.	Joseph H. Shirk	Mrs. C. Barnaby	1948	5
184⅞	44⅜	45	15⅜	15⅜	6⅜	6⅜	26⅜	26⅜	Hudson Hope, B.C.	John W. Pitney	Am. Mus. Nat. Hist.	1936	6
184⅜	44⅜	46	14⅛	14⅜	8	7	28⅜	28⅜	Colt Lake, B.C.	Lloyd E. Hall	Lloyd E. Hall	1963	7
184⅞	42⅜	42⅜	16⅞	16⅜	7⅛	7⅛	24⅜	24⅜	Blue Sheep Lake, B.C.	G. C. F. Dalziel	G. C. F. Dalziel	1964	8
184⅞	47⅜	45⅜	14⅜	14	6⅞	6⅜	31⅜	31⅜	Colt Lake, B.C.	Herb Klein	Herb Klein	1965	8
184⅜	45⅞	42⅞	15	15	7⅜	7⅜	22⅜	22⅜	Kechika Range, B.C.	Arthur R. Dubs	Arthur R. Dubs	1966	8
183⅞	44⅜	45⅜	13⅞	13⅞	7	7⅜	23⅞	23⅞	Hudson Hope, B.C.	Picked Up	Bill Beattie	1961	11
183⅞	44⅜	44⅜	14⅜	14⅜	7	6⅞	20⅜	19	Dease Lake, B.C.	Otis Chandler	Otis Chandler	1966	12
183⅜	43⅜	43⅞	14⅞	14⅞	7⅛	7	25⅜	25⅛	Sikanni Chief River, B.C.	Picked Up	Bob & Don Beattie	1962	13
183⅜	44⅜	44⅛	15	15	6⅜	6⅜	26⅜	26⅛	Kechika Range, B.C.	John Caputo, Jr.	John Caputo, Jr.	1961	14
183⅜	49⅞	44⅞	13⅜	13⅜	6⅜	6⅜	25	25	Terminus Mt., B.C.	Picked Up	Herb Klein	1969	14
183⅜	44⅜	46⅜	14⅛	14⅛	6⅜	7	29⅜	29⅜	Cassiar Mts., B.C.	Robert S. Jackson	Robert S. Jackson	1968	16
183	45⅜	44⅜	14	14	7⅜	7⅜	25⅜	25⅜	Muskwa River, B.C.	T. E. Shillingburg	T. E. Shillingburg	1937	17
183	44	44⅜	14⅜	14⅜	7	7⅜	25⅜	25⅜	Kechika Range, B.C.	John Caputo, Sr.	John Caputo, Sr.	1966	17
183	45⅜	44⅜	14⅜	14⅜	6⅜	6⅜	27⅜	27⅜	Cassiar Mts., B.C.	Gordon Studer	Gordon Studer	1967	17
182⅝	46⅛	45⅜	14⅜	14⅜	6⅜	6⅜	26⅜	26⅜	Cassiar Mts., B.C.	Alex Cox	Alex Cox	1959	20
182⅝	43	42⅜	15⅛	15⅜	7⅛	7⅜	24⅜	24⅜	Redfern Lake, B.C.	James P. Winters	James P. Winters	1970	20
182⅞	43	44⅜	14⅜	14⅜	7	7	26⅜	26⅜	Kechika Range, B.C.	Hallett Ward, Jr.	Hallett Ward, Jr.	1967	22
182⅞	45⅛	45⅞	14⅜	14⅜	6⅜	6⅜	31⅜	31⅜	Telegraph Creek, B.C.	Mrs. John Crowe	Mrs. John Crowe	1967	22
182	41	42	15⅜	15⅜	8	8⅜	27	27	Prophet River, B.C.	John E. Hammett, Jr.	John E. Hammett, Jr.	1944	24
182	45⅜	45⅜	14⅜	14⅜	6⅜	7⅛	26⅜	26⅜	Sand Pile Lake, B.C.	Al Robbins	Al Robbins	1963	24
182	45⅛	44⅜	14⅜	14	6⅜	6⅜	26	26	Gataga River, B.C.	Gary Moore	Gary Moore	1965	24
181⅞	43⅜	43⅜	15	15	6⅜	6⅜	26⅜	26⅜	Cassiar Mts., B.C.	Norman Lougheed	Norman Lougheed	1965	27
181⅞	39	45⅜	13⅜	14⅜	7⅜	7⅜	23⅜	23⅜	Burnt Rose Lake, B.C.	Lloyd Zeman	Lloyd Zeman	1970	28
181⅜	44⅜	44⅜	15	14⅜	6⅜	6⅜	27⅜	27⅜	Toad River, B.C.	Jerry E. Dahl	Jerry E. Dahl	1971	29
181	44⅜	44⅜	14⅜	14⅜	6⅜	6⅜	30⅜	30⅜	Watson Lake, B.C.	C. W. Houle	C. W. Houle	1967	30

STONE'S SHEEP—*Continued*
Ovis dalli stonei

Score	Length of Horn R.	L.	Circumference of Base R.	L.	Circumference at Third Quarter R.	L.	Greatest Spread	Tip to Tip Spread	Locality Killed	By Whom Killed	Owner	Date Killed	Rank
180⅞	41⅛	42⅞	15	14⅞	7⅞	7⅞	26⅞	26⅞	Hudson Hope, B.C.	Don Beattie	Don Beattie	1945	31
180⅞	44	43⅛	14⅞	14⅞	6⅞	6⅞	26⅞	26⅞	Sand Pile Lake, B.C.	David S. Loos	David S. Loos	1967	31
180⅝	40⅜	43	14⅛	14⅜	7⅞	8	22⅞	22⅞	Hudson Hope, B.C.	David Slutker	David Slutker	1966	33
180⅝	38⅜	38⅜	15⅜	15⅛	9⅛	9⅜	23⅜	19	Prophet River, B.C.	Joseph Madonia	Joseph Madonia	1970	33
180⅜	44⅜	44⅜	14⅜	14⅜	6⅞	6⅞	23⅜	23⅜	Kechika Range, B.C.	Tucker Davis	Tucker Davis	1965	35
180⅜	45⅝	44⅝	14⅜	14⅜	6	6⅜	29	29	Telegraph Creek, B.C.	John B. Winsor	John B. Winsor	1966	36
180⅜	44⅛	44	14⅞	14⅛	7	6⅝	26⅜	26⅜	Burnt Rose Lake, B.C.	E. L. Cook	E. L. Cook	1970	37
180⅛	42⅞	42⅛	14⅝	14⅜	8	7⅞	24⅞	24⅞	Prophet River, B.C.	Bill Thomas	Bill Thomas	1963	38
179⅞	44	43⅜	14⅜	14⅛	7⅞	7⅝	0	28	Ice Mt., B.C.	J. E. Mason	J. E. Mason	1966	38
179⅞	39⅛	44⅛	13⅝	13⅞	8⅞	8⅝	21⅜	21⅜	Cassiar Mts., B.C.	Ralph W. Hull	Ralph W. Hull	1963	40
179⅜	45⅛	44⅞	14⅜	14⅜	6⅝	6⅜	24	24	Gathto Creek, B.C.	Gary J. Powell	Gary J. Powell	1970	41
179⅜	43⅞	39⅜	14⅞	14⅝	7⅜	7⅞	21⅜	21⅛	Pink Mt., B.C.	Gerald E. Howe	Gerald E. Howe	1970	41
179⅜	43⅜	44⅜	13⅞	13⅝	7⅞	6⅞	26⅜	26⅜	Toad River, B.C.	Dennis Callison	Dennis Callison	1957	43
179⅛	40⅜	40⅜	14⅜	14	8⅜	8⅜	22⅜	19⅜	Eydee Creek, B.C.	Jack McNeill	Jack McNeill	1967	44
178⅞	44⅜	45⅜	13⅜	14	6⅞	6⅜	28⅜	28⅜	Kechika River, B.C.	W. C. Waldron	W. C. Waldron	1967	45
178⅜	39⅜	48	13⅜	13⅜	7	7⅜	26	24⅛	Moody Lake, B.C.	J. Martin Benchoff	J. Martin Benchoff	1966	46
178⅜	43⅜	42⅜	14⅝	14⅜	6⅜	6⅛	27⅜	27⅞	Muskwa River, B.C.	Don S. Hopkins	Don S. Hopkins	1948	47
178⅜	43⅜	44⅜	14⅜	14⅜	6⅜	6⅜	24⅜	24⅜	Tuchodi Lakes, B.C.	Ross Peck	Ross Peck	1963	47
178⅞	40⅞	41⅛	14⅞	14⅞	7⅞	7⅜	24	24	Moody Lake, B.C.	Raymond G. Speer	Raymond G. Speer	1966	47
178⅛	43⅜	45	13⅞	14	6⅞	6⅞	26⅞	26⅞	Gataga Mts., B.C.	Dan Auld	Dan Auld	1960	50
178⅛	42⅞	43⅜	14⅜	14⅜	7⅛	7	27⅜	27⅜	Watson Lake, B.C.	James C. Maly	James C. Maly	1963	50
177⅞	41⅜	40⅜	14⅜	14⅜	8⅝	8⅞	24⅜	24⅜	Frog River, B.C.	Don Palmer	Don Palmer	1968	52
177⅞	44⅜	43⅜	15	15	5⅞	6	31	31	Skookum Mt., Yukon	Ira H. Kent	Ira H. Kent	1968	52
177⅞	44	44	13⅜	13⅜	6⅜	6⅜	28⅜	28⅜	Sikanni Chief River, B.C.	Steven L. Rose	Steven L. Rose	1961	54
177⅞	43⅜	44⅜	13⅝	14	6⅝	6⅞	27⅜	27⅜	Kechika Range, B.C.	John Caputo, Sr.	John Caputo, Sr.	1961	54
177⅞	39⅛	39⅜	14⅜	14⅝	9	9	22⅜	22⅜	Turnagain River, B.C.	Byron Dalziel	Byron Dalziel	1970	54
177⅜	43⅜	44	14⅜	14⅜	6⅝	6⅞	26⅜	26⅜	Telegraph Creek, B.C.	Paul O'Hollaren	Paul O'Hollaren	1967	57
177⅜	45⅜	44⅜	13⅜	13	7	6⅞	27⅜	27⅞	Toad River, B.C.	Dewey Rawlings	Dewey Rawlings	1969	57
177⅜	44⅜	42⅜	14⅜	14⅜	6⅝	6⅜	24⅜	24⅜	Watson Lake, Yukon	Edgar A. Robertson	Edgar A. Robertson	1968	59
177⅜	42⅜	42	13⅜	13⅜	8	8⅛	23⅜	23⅜	Toad River, B.C.	John Huml	John Huml	1969	60
177⅜	42⅜	42	14⅜	13⅜	7⅜	7⅝	22⅜	22⅜	Racing River, B.C.	Robert H. Kunzli	Robert H. Kunzli	1959	61

Score									Locality	Owner	Hunter	Rank	Year
177⅞	44⅜	44⅝	13⅜	13⅜	6⅞	6⅞	24⅞	24⅞	Atlin, B.C.	Delmar Aldrich	Delmar Aldrich	61	1964
177⅞	40⅜	42⅜	15⅜	15⅜	6⅝	6⅜	29⅞	29⅜	Ft. St. John, B.C.	Ted T. Dabrowski	Ted T. Dabrowski	61	1967
177⅞	38⅜	38⅝	14⅜	14⅜	9	8⅞	20⅛	20⅛	Watson Lake, Yukon	Keith Thompson	Keith Thompson	61	1969
177⅞	43⅜	42⅜	14⅜	14⅜	6⅛	6⅛	29⅜	29⅜	Cassiar Mts., B.C.	H. H. Kissinger	H. H. Kissinger	66	1970
177⅞	44	42⅜	15	15	6⅛	6	27⅜	27⅜	Redfern Lake, B.C.	National Collection	W. H. Kirk	66	1923
177⅞	40⅞	40⅞	14⅜	14⅜	7⅛	7⅛	23⅜	23⅜	Mt. Lady Laurier, B.C.	Chet Gifford	Chet Gifford	68	1963
177	42⅛	40⅞	14⅜	14⅜	6⅞	6⅞	25⅜	25⅜	Prophet River, B.C.	Wade Martin	Wade Martin	69	1960
176⅞	44⅝	40⅜	13⅜	14⅜	6⅝	6⅝	25⅜	25⅜	Dease Lake, B.C.	Thomas M. Dye	Thomas M. Dye	69	1966
176⅞	45⅜	45⅜	13½	13⅜	6⅞	6⅝	29	29	Rabbit River, B.C.	George H. Rhoads	George H. Rhoads	71	1971
176⅞	41⅞	39⅜	15½	15⅜	7⅛	7	25⅜	25⅜	Cassiar Mts., B.C.	Donald J. Robb	Donald J. Robb	72	1969
176⅞	43⅜	43⅜	14	14	6	6	24⅜	24⅜	Muskwa River, B.C.	T. E. Shillingburg	T. E. Shillingburg	73	1947
176⅞	40	43⅜	14⅜	14⅜	6⅞	7⅜	23	23	Prophet River, B.C.	Jim Caves	Jim Caves	73	1959
176⅞	42⅞	39⅜	13⅜	13⅜	8⅜	8⅜	21⅜	21⅜	Gataga River, B.C.	David C. Coleman	David C. Coleman	75	1980
176⅞	45⅜	44⅜	14⅜	14⅜	5⅜	5⅜	28⅜	28⅜	Cassiar Mts., B.C.	Gene Klineburger	Gene Klineburger	75	1965
176⅞	44	44⅜	14⅜	14⅜	6⅜	6⅜	28⅜	28⅜	Prophet River, B.C.	O. B. Kahn	O. B. Kahn	75	1965
176⅞	40⅞	40⅜	15⅜	15⅜	6⅜	6⅜	23⅜	23⅜	Nabesche River, B.C.	Kenneth W. Kleiman	Kenneth W. Kleiman	78	1973
176⅞	42⅞	43⅜	15	15	5⅜	5⅜	29⅜	29⅜	Prophet River, B.C.	W. A. Newmiller	W. A. Newmiller	79	1958
176⅞	41⅛	44	14⅜	14⅜	6⅜	6⅜	26⅜	26⅜	Richard Creek, B.C.	James Milito	James Milito	79	1967
176⅛	36⅜	39⅞	15	15	8⅜	7⅛	22⅜	22⅜	Pink Mt., B.C.	Roland Schroeder	Roland Schroeder	79	1968
176⅛	40⅞	36	15	15	7⅜	7⅜	21⅜	21⅜	Watson Lake, B.C.	Elgin T. Gates	Elgin T. Gates	82	1969
176	43⅜	43⅜	14⅜	14⅜	6⅜	6⅝	25⅜	25⅜	Cassiar Mts., B.C.	Walter O. Ford, Jr.	Walter O. Ford, Jr.	82	1967
176	45⅜	41⅜	13⅜	13⅜	6⅝	7	25⅜	25⅜	Gataga River, B.C.	William A. S. Heuer	William A. S. Heuer	84	1979
175⅞	39⅜	39⅜	15	15	7⅜	7⅜	20⅜	20⅜	Prophet River, B.C.	Jack O'Connor	Jack O'Connor	84	1946
175⅞	41⅜	39⅜	14⅜	14⅜	7⅜	7⅜	22⅜	22⅜	Terminus Mt., B.C.	Irvin Hart	Irvin Hart	84	1964
175⅞	40⅞	40⅜	13⅜	13⅜	8⅜	9	23⅜	23⅜	Turnagain River, B.C.	Lester C. Brewick	Lester C. Brewick	84	1967
175⅞	42⅜	37⅜	15⅜	15⅜	7	7⅛	21⅜	21⅜	Blue Sheep Lake, B.C.	John M. Griffith, Jr.	John M. Griffith, Jr.	88	1971
175⅞	43⅜	43⅜	14⅜	14⅜	6⅝	6⅝	29⅜	29⅞	Pelly Mts., Yukon	John Caputo	John Caputo	88	1953
175⅞	42⅝	42⅜	14⅜	14⅜	6⅝	6⅜	22	22	Top Lake, B.C.	Richard Buffington	Richard Buffington	88	1964
175⅞	42⅛	41⅜	14	14	6⅝	6⅜	21⅜	21⅜	Hudson Hope, B.C.	Jim Papst	Jim Papst	91	1966
175⅞	46⅜	43⅜	13⅜	13⅜	5⅜	5⅜	28	28	Kiniskan Lake, B.C.	Richard Stough	Richard Stough	91	1961
175⅞	46⅝	48	12⅜	12⅜	5⅜	5⅜	30⅜	30⅜	Frog River, B.C.	Robert McMurray	Robert McMurray	91	1968
175⅞	41⅞	41⅜	14	14	7⅜	7⅜	23⅜	23⅜	Colt Lake, B.C.	Marsh Dear	Marsh Dear	91	1970
175⅞	42	42	14⅜	14⅜	6⅜	6⅜	28⅜	28⅜	Prophet River, B.C.	Sam C. Arnett III	Sam C. Arnett III	91	1972
175	40⅜	36⅜	14⅜	14⅜	8	7⅜	22⅜	22⅜	Muskwa River, B.C.	Robert M. Case	Robert M. Case	91	1980
175	38⅜	38	15	15	8	8	23⅜	23⅜	Pelly Mts., Yukon	Pat S. McInturff	Pat S. McInturff	96	1962
175	43	42⅜	14⅜	14⅜	6⅜	6⅜	26	26	Hudson Hope, B.C.	Harry M. Haywood	Harry M. Haywood	97	1949
175	42⅜	41⅜	14⅜	14⅜	6⅜	6⅜	26⅜	26⅜	Cassiar, B.C.	John Sochor	John Sochor	97	1962
175	40⅜	41⅜	14⅜	14⅜	7⅛	7⅜	22	22	Cold Fish Lake, B.C.	Chris Reynolds	Chris Reynolds	97	1963
175	42⅜	42⅜	13⅜	13⅜	6⅜	6⅜	28⅜	28⅜	Colt Lake, B.C.	Warren Page	Warren Page	97	1965
175	42⅜	43⅜	14⅜	14⅜	6⅜	6⅜	24	24	Toad River, B.C.	William E. Butler	William E. Butler	97	1975
174⅞	41⅛	42⅜	14⅜	14⅜	8⅜	7⅜	22⅜	22⅜	Cassiar, B.C.	John W. Hull	John W. Hull	102	1962
174⅛	38⅜	38⅜	14⅜	14⅜	7⅜	8	21⅜	21⅜	Watson Lake, B.C.	Philip English	Philip English	103	1965

STONE'S SHEEP—Continued
Ovis dalli stonei

Score	Length of Horn R.	L.	Circumference of Base R.	L.	Circumference at Third Quarter R.	L.	Greatest Spread	Tip to Tip Spread	Locality Killed	By Whom Killed	Owner	Date Killed	Rank
174⅝	42⅛	41⅛	14⅝	14⅛	6⅛	6	30⅜	30⅜	Stikine River, B.C.	Hugh J. O'Dower	Hugh J. O'Dower	1952	104
174⅝	41⅛	41⅛	14⅛	14⅛	7⅜	6⅝	24⅜	24⅜	Sikanni Chief River, B.C.	Joseph W. Quarto	Joseph W. Quarto	1965	104
174⅜	40⅝	41⅜	15	14⅝	8	8⅜	27⅜	27⅜	Dease Lake, B.C.	Alice J. Landreth	Alice J. Landreth	1964	106
174⅜	42⅜	42	14⅜	14⅜	5⅝	6	24⅜	24⅜	Ram Lake, B.C.	Walter Smetaniuk	Walter Smetaniuk	1966	106
174⅜	41⅞	40⅛	13⅞	13⅝	7⅞	8	20⅜	20⅜	Racing River, B.C.	Lash Callison	Lash Callison	1959	108
174⅜	39⅞	41⅛	14⅞	14⅛	7⅞	6⅝	21⅞	21⅞	Top Lake, B.C.	W. E. Fisher	W. E. Fisher	1964	108
174⅜	37	38⅝	14⅞	14⅜	8⅞	8⅝	21	21	Cassiar Mts., B.C.	Gordon Studer	Gordon Studer	1966	111
174⅜	46⅝	46⅜	13⅜	13⅜	5⅝	5⅜	33	33	Watson Lake, B.C.	G. C. F. Dalziel	G. C. F. Dalziel	1962	111
174⅜	42⅜	42⅜	12⅝	12⅜	6⅝	6⅜	26⅜	26⅜	W. Toad River, B.C.	Unknown	N. B. Sorenson	PR1969	113
174⅜	42⅛	41⅜	14	14	7	7⅞	23	23	Cold Fish Lake, B.C.	Roberto De La Garza	Roberto De La Garza	1961	113
174⅛	43⅞	43⅜	14⅞	15⅜	5⅝	5⅞	25	25	Gold Bar, B.C.	Henry O. Carlson	Henry O. Carlson	1962	113
174⅛	41⅜	41⅜	14⅜	14⅛	6⅛	6⅞	25⅜	25⅜	Mt. Winston, B.C.	Norman A. Hill	Norman A. Hill	1967	113
174⅛	41⅜	41⅜	14⅛	14⅛	6⅝	6⅞	23⅜	23⅜	Muskwa River, B.C.	Gary Powell	Gary Powell	1974	117
174⅛	44⅛	41⅛	14	13⅝	6⅝	6⅞	22⅞	22⅞	Muskwa River, B.C.	Wade Martin	Wade Martin	1961	117
174	41⅛	40⅝	14⅜	14⅛	6⅝	6⅞	26⅜	26⅜	Cassiar Mts., B.C.	George H. Glass	George H. Glass	1966	117
174	44⅛	41⅛	14⅜	14⅛	6⅜	6⅛	27	27	Cassiar Mts., B.C.	Russell Castner	Russell Castner	1966	117
174	40	41	14⅜	14⅛	6⅝	6⅞	20⅜	19⅞	Muskwa Area, B.C.	W. R. Collie	W. R. Collie	1972	121
174	43⅝	43⅜	13⅜	13⅛	7	6⅞	27⅞	27⅞	Stikine River, B.C.	Vernon D. E. Smith	Vernon D. E. Smith	1960	121
173⅞	44⅜	44⅜	13⅜	13⅜	5⅞	6	29⅞	29⅞	Cassiar, B.C.	Fred F. Wells	Fred F. Wells	1961	121
173⅞	38⅞	38⅜	14⅜	13⅜	8⅞	9	25	25	Gataga River, B.C.	H. L. Hale	H. L. Hale	1968	125
173⅞	40⅛	40⅛	13⅜	13⅜	8⅜	8⅝	20⅜	16	Tetsa River, B.C.	Eugene P. LaSota	Eugene P. LaSota	1973	125
173⅞	47⅞	43⅞	13⅜	14	6⅜	5⅜	25⅜	25⅜	Halfway River, B.C.	Lynn Ross	Lynn Ross	1957	125
173⅞	43⅞	43⅝	13⅜	14⅜	6⅝	6⅞	28⅜	28⅜	Terminus Mt., B.C.	Chester A. Crago	Chester A. Crago	1962	125
173⅞	43⅝	43⅝	14	14	6⅝	7⅞	25⅜	25⅜	Muskwa River, B.C.	Wm. Michalsky	Wm. Michalsky	1965	129
173⅞	40⅞	40⅞	13⅜	14⅜	6⅜	6⅛	30⅜	30⅜	Kechika Range, B.C.	Russell C. Cutter	Russell C. Cutter	1965	129
173⅞	43	43	14	14	6⅝	6⅞	26⅜	26⅜	Peace River, B.C.	Melvin Shearer	National Collection	1933	129
173⅞	40⅛	41	13⅜	13⅜	6⅜	5⅞	23⅜	23⅜	Hudson Hope, B.C.	G. F. Moore	G. F. Moore	1963	132
173¾	45⅞	42	14⅜	14⅜	6⅝	6⅜	22⅜	22⅜	Rose Mt., Yukon	Karl Fritzsche	Karl Fritzsche	1972	132
173¾	42	42	13⅜	13⅜	8⅛	7⅞	20⅜	20⅜	Cassiar, B.C.	Charles F. Haas	Charles F. Haas	1960	132
173¾	41⅛	41⅞	14⅛	14⅛	6⅝	6⅞	28⅜	28⅜	Telegraph Creek, B.C.	L. Iverson	L. Iverson	1961	132
173¾	39	42	15	15	7⅞	6⅜	22⅜	22⅜	Dease Lake, B.C.	George I. Parker	George I. Parker	1963	132

Score									Locality	By whom killed	Owner	Date	Rank
173⅝	39⅝	41	14	14	8⅛	8	23	23	Watson Lake, Yukon	Harry S. Rinker	Harry S. Rinker	1964	132
173⅝	41	41⅛	14	14	9⅜	9	27	27	Dease Lake, B.C.	John T. Blackwell	John T. Blackwell	1964	132
173⅝	43⅜	44	13⅜	13⅜	6	6⅜	28	28	Toad River, B.C.	H. L. Vidricksen	H. L. Vidricksen	1960	137
173⅝	38⅜	38⅜	14⅜	14⅜	8⅜	8	20	19⅞	Tuchodi Lakes, B.C.	George S. Gayle III	George S. Gayle III	1972	137
173⅝	41⅛	41⅜	14⅜	14⅜	6⅞	6⅜	24	24⅜	Cassiar Mts., B.C.	John Caputo	John Caputo	1962	139
173⅝	44⅛	45	13⅜	13⅜	5⅜	5⅜	26	26⅜	Cassiar Mts., B.C.	William Warrick	William Warrick	1963	139
173⅝	40⅛	41⅛	14	14	7	6⅜	24	24⅜	Halfway River, B.C.	Frank H. Rogers	Frank H. Rogers	1962	141
173⅝	40⅜	41⅜	14⅜	14⅜	6	6⅜	27	27⅜	Cassiar Mts., B.C.	Charles F. Nadler	Charles F. Nadler	1967	141
173⅝	41⅜	40	14⅛	14⅜	7⅜	7⅜	21	21⅜	Summit Lake, B.C.	Henry L. Baddley	Henry L. Baddley	1979	141
173	39⅜	38	14⅜	14⅜	8	8	26	26	Muskwa River, B.C.	Elmer Keith	Elmer Keith	1937	144
173	34	45	15	15	7⅜	7⅜	24	24⅜	Gataga River, B.C.	Wilson Southwell	Wilson Southwell	1958	144
173	40⅜	41⅜	13⅜	13⅜	7⅜	7⅜	23	23⅜	Prophet River, B.C.	Merrimen M. Watkins	Merrimen M. Watkins	1965	144
173	42	42⅜	14⅜	14⅜	5⅜	5⅜	22	22⅜	Watson Lake, Yukon	E. P. Gray	E. P. Gray	1968	144
173	42	42⅜	13⅜	14	6⅜	6⅜	23	23⅜	Prophet River, B.C.	Robert E. Hammond	Robert E. Hammond	1969	144
173	42⅜	42⅜	14	14	5⅜	5⅜	27	27⅜	Cold Fish Lake, B.C.	A. H. Clise	A. H. Clise	1970	144
173	41⅜	42⅜	14⅜	13⅜	5⅜	5⅜	24	24	Mile 422, Alaska Hwy., B.C.	Garland N. Teich	Garland N. Teich	1971	144
172⅞	40⅜	39⅜	14⅜	14⅜	6⅜	6⅜	24⅜	24⅜	Prophet River, B.C.	Harry M. Haywood	Harry M. Haywood	1956	151
172⅞	40⅞	42⅜	14⅜	14⅜	5⅜	6	25⅜	25⅜	Summit Lake, B.C.	A. Tony Mathisen	A. Tony Mathisen	1958	151
172⅞	42⅜	42⅜	13⅜	13⅜	6⅜	6⅜	25⅛	25⅛	Cassiar Mts., B.C.	Wayne C. Eubank	Wayne C. Eubank	1963	151
172⅞	46⅜	35	14	14	6⅜	6⅜	21⅜	21⅜	Cassiar Mts., B.C.	Orval H. Ause	Orval H. Ause	1968	151
172⅞	37	37	15	14⅞	7⅜	7⅜	23	23	Cassiar Mts., B.C.	Greg Williams	Greg Williams	1976	151
172⅞	36⅜	37	14⅞	15	8⅜	8⅜	19⅞	19⅞	Sikami Chief River, B.C.	Mrs. Maitland Armstrong	Mrs. Maitland Armstrong	1962	156
172⅞	40⅜	41⅜	14⅜	14⅜	6⅜	7	22	22	Gataga River, B.C.	Basil C. Bradbury	Basil C. Bradbury	1968	156
172⅞	36⅜	36⅜	14⅞	15	8⅜	8⅜	21⅜	21⅜	Muskwa River, B.C.	Andrew A. Samuels, Jr.	Andrew A. Samuels, Jr.	1969	156
172⅞	42	41⅜	14⅜	14⅜	6⅜	6⅛	27⅜	27⅜	Dall Lake, B.C.	Robert J. Rood	Robert J. Rood	1971	156
172⅞	43⅜	43⅜	13⅜	13⅜	6⅜	6⅜	28⅜	28⅜	Cassiar Mts., B.C.	Kenneth Campbell	Kenneth Campbell	1959	161
172⅞	40⅜	40⅜	14⅜	14⅜	7⅜	7⅜	24⅜	24⅜	Liard River, B.C.	Jack N. Allen	Jack N. Allen	1958	162
172⅞	42	42	13⅜	13⅜	6⅛	5⅜	29⅜	29⅜	Halfway River, B.C.	Cecil V. Mumbert	Cecil V. Mumbert	1963	162
172⅞	40⅜	41⅜	14⅜	14⅜	6⅜	6⅜	25	25	Dease Lake, B.C.	John T. Blackwell	John T. Blackwell	1969	162
172⅞	37⅜	38	15⅜	15⅜	6⅜	6⅜	27⅜	27⅜	Prophet River, B.C.	William A. Miller	William A. Miller	1970	162
172⅞	39⅜	42	14⅜	14⅜	6⅜	6⅜	25⅜	25⅜	Watson Lake, B.C.	Julian Gutierrez	Julian Gutierrez	1971	162
172⅞	37⅜	41⅜	14⅜	14⅜	6⅜	7	23⅜	23⅜	Muskwa River, B.C.	L. A. Denson	L. A. Denson	1980	162
172⅞	41⅜	41⅜	15⅜	15⅜	6	6⅛	28⅜	28⅜	Mile Creek, B.C.	H. D. Miller	H. D. Miller	1957	168
172⅞	37⅜	38⅜	14⅜	14⅜	8⅜	8⅜	23⅜	23⅜	Sandbar Creek, B.C.	John La Rocca	John La Rocca	1960	168
172⅞	41⅜	42⅜	14⅜	14⅜	5⅜	5⅜	27⅜	27⅜	Pelly Mts., Yukon	Walter R. Michael	Walter R. Michael	1961	168
172⅞	45⅜	45⅜	13	13	5⅜	5⅜	28	28	Cold Fish Lake, B.C.	Juan Brittingham	Juan Brittingham	1964	168
172⅞	39⅜	39⅜	15⅜	15⅜	6	6	20⅜	20⅜	Ospika Drainage, B.C.	Mark Swenson	Mark Swenson	1965	168
172⅞	41⅜	41⅜	14⅜	14⅜	6⅛	6⅛	23⅜	23⅜	Dall Lake, B.C.	Paul M. Rothermel, Jr.	Paul M. Rothermel, Jr.	1985	168
172⅞	38⅜	38⅜	15⅜	15⅜	6⅜	6⅜	25⅜	25⅜	Muskwa River, B.C.	Ken W. Scheer	Ken W. Scheer	1961	174
172⅞	41⅜	41⅜	14⅜	14⅜	6	6	21⅜	21⅜	Prophet River, B.C.	George F. Crain	George F. Crain	1963	174
172⅞	40⅜	38⅜	14⅜	14⅜	6⅜	7	21⅜	21⅜	Muskwa River, B.C.	Arvid F. Benson	Arvid F. Benson	1963	174
172⅞	42⅜	42⅜	14⅜	14⅜	5⅜	5⅜	29	29	Prophet River, B.C.	S. E. Burrell	S. E. Burrell	1967	174

STONE'S SHEEP—Continued
Ovis dalli stonei

Score	Length of Horn R.	L.	Circumference of Base R.	L.	Circumference at Third Quarter R.	L.	Greatest Spread	Tip to Tip Spread	Locality Killed	By Whom Killed	Owner	Date Killed	Rank
172⅞	39⅞	42⅝	14	14⅝	7⅝	6⅝	26⅜	26⅜	Cassiar Mts., B.C.	Michaux Nash, Jr.	Michaux Nash, Jr.	1967	174
172⅞	41⅛	36⅞	14⅝	14⅛	7⅛	8	23⅜	23⅜	Sikanni Chief River, B.C.	John B. Collier IV	John B. Collier IV	1967	174
172⅞	41⅛	41⅛	14⅛	14⅛	6	6⅛	28⅛	28⅛	Akie River, B.C.	O. J. Baggenstoss	O. J. Baggenstoss	1968	174
172⅞	39	38⅛	14⅛	14⅛	7⅛	7⅛	20⅛	18⅛	Prophet River, B.C.	Larry Ciejka	Larry Ciejka	1977	174
172⅛	41⅛	41	13	13	9⅛	9⅛	30	30	Dease Lake, B.C.	W. M. Rudd	W. M. Rudd	1964	181
172⅛	39	40⅛	14⅛	14⅛	7⅛	6⅛	23⅜	23⅜	Alaska Hwy., B.C.	Robert Murdock	Robert Murdock	1968	181
172⅛	37⅛	34⅛	14	14⅛	9⅛	9⅛	23⅜	19	Cassiar Mts., B.C.	Keith M. Kissinger	Keith M. Kissinger	1968	181
172⅛	40⅛	38⅛	14⅛	14⅛	7⅛	7⅛	23⅜	21⅛	Burnt Rose Lake, B.C.	John K. De Broux	John K. De Broux	1970	181
172⅛	40⅛	41	14⅛	14⅛	6⅛	6⅛	20⅛	20⅛	Muskwa River, B.C.	Greg L. Stires	Greg L. Stires	1984	181
172	39⅛	40⅛	15	15	6⅛	6⅛	23⅜	23⅜	Hudson Hope, B.C.	Don Stewart	Don Stewart	1961	186
172	45⅛	43⅛	12⅞	13	6⅛	6	25⅞	25⅞	Atlin, B.C.	Thomas E. Francis	Thomas E. Francis	1964	186
172	40⅛	41⅛	14⅛	14⅛	6⅛	6	25⅛	25⅛	Pelly Creek, B.C.	Robert A. Lubeck	Robert A. Lubeck	1968	186
172	41⅛	41⅛	14⅛	14⅛	6⅛	6⅛	26⅛	26⅛	Denetiah Lake, B.C.	Michael G. Meeker	Michael G. Meeker	1969	186
172	40⅛	40	14⅛	14⅛	6⅛	6⅛	29	29	Prairie River, B.C.	C. J. McElroy	C. J. McElroy	1969	186
172	42⅛	42⅛	14	14	6⅛	6⅛	25⅛	25⅛	Toad River, B.C.	David G. Kidder	David G. Kidder	1975	186
171⅞	38⅛	38⅛	14⅛	14⅛	7⅛	7⅛	23⅜	20⅛	Akie River, B.C.	Henry K. Leworthy	Henry K. Leworthy	1966	192
171⅞	38⅛	39	13⅞	13⅞	8⅛	8⅛	20⅛	20⅛	Island Lake, B.C.	Martin Frank Wood	Martin Frank Wood	1970	192
171⅞	43⅛	41⅛	14⅛	14⅛	5⅛	5⅛	30⅛	30⅛	Cache Creek, B.C.	Kenneth A. Jeronimus	Kenneth A. Jeronimus	1974	192
171⅞	39⅛	41	13⅞	13⅞	8	8	27⅛	27⅛	Gataga River, B.C.	Dan Auld	Dan Auld	1958	195
171⅞	43⅛	43	14⅛	14⅛	5⅜	5⅛	27⅛	27⅛	Cassiar Mts., B.C.	John Caputo, Sr.	John Caputo, Sr.	1960	195
171⅞	40⅛	42⅛	14	14⅛	6⅛	7⅛	24⅛	24⅛	Trimble Lake, B.C.	Roy E. Stare	Roy E. Stare	1962	195
171⅞	36⅛	37	14⅛	14⅛	10⅛	8⅛	21⅛	13⅛	Muskwa River, B.C.	W. I. Spencer	W. I. Spencer	1963	195
171⅞	39⅛	41⅛	14⅛	14⅛	6	6⅛	23⅜	23⅜	Dease Lake, B.C.	Michaux Nash, Jr.	Michaux Nash, Jr.	1965	195
171⅞	37⅛	39⅞	16	16	6⅛	6⅛	21⅛	21⅛	Gataga River, B.C.	D. R. Seabaugh	D. R. Seabaugh	1971	195
171⅞	38⅛	38⅛	15⅛	15⅛	6⅛	6⅞	23⅜	24	Prophet River, B.C.	Don Haemmerlein	Don Haemmerlein	1977	195
171⅛	37⅛	37⅛	14	14	8⅛	8⅛	20⅜	20⅛	Tuchodi Lakes, B.C.	Win Condict	Win Condict	1951	202
171⅛	42⅛	42⅝	13⅛	13⅛	6⅛	6⅛	26⅛	26	Dease Lake, B.C.	C. E. Krieger	C. E. Krieger	1962	202
171⅛	44⅛	40	13⅛	13⅛	6⅛	6⅛	25⅛	25⅛	Muncho Lake, B.C.	H. W. Julien	H. W. Julien	1966	202
171⅛	38⅛	36⅛	14⅛	14⅛	8⅛	8⅛	20⅛	20⅛	Toad River, B.C.	H. W. Julien	H. W. Julien	1969	202
171⅛	37⅛	45⅝	14⅛	14⅛	6	6⅛	24	21⅛	Prophet River, B.C.	John Whitcombe	John Whitcombe	1981	202
171⅛	40⅛	40⅛	14⅛	14⅛	5⅛	6	22⅛	22⅛	Pink Mt., B.C.	Paul V. Palmer, Jr.	Paul V. Palmer, Jr.	1985	202

Score	Length of Horn R	Length of Horn L	Circ. of Base R	Circ. of Base L	Circ. Third Qtr. R	Circ. Third Qtr. L	Greatest Spread	Tip to Tip Spread	Locality	Hunter	Owner	Date	Rank
171 1/8	40 6/8	40 6/8	14 6/8	14 6/8	6 6/8	6 6/8	23 6/8	23 6/8	Prophet River, B.C.	L. A. Denson	L. A. Denson	1963	208
171 1/8	37	38 6/8	14 4/8	14 4/8	7 6/8	7	22 2/8	22 2/8	Trutch, B.C.	Charles F. Waterman	Charles F. Waterman	1964	208
171 1/8	42 6/8	43 6/8	13 6/8	13 6/8	6 6/8	5 6/8	29 6/8	29 6/8	Turnagain River, B.C.	Lewis M. Mull	Lewis M. Mull	1966	208
171 1/8	45	45	13 6/8	13 6/8	5 6/8	5 4/8	29 6/8	29 6/8	Turnagain River, B.C.	George H. Landreth	George H. Landreth	1966	208
171 1/8	38 6/8	39	14 6/8	14 6/8	7	7	23	23	Cassiar Mts., B.C.	Robert R. Bridges	Robert R. Bridges	1966	208
171 1/8	43 6/8	45	13 2/8	13 2/8	5 4/8	5 4/8	28 6/8	28 6/8	Cassiar Mts., B.C.	William A. Kelly	William A. Kelly	1969	208
171 1/8	34 6/8	39	15 6/8	15 6/8	7 6/8	7	25 6/8	25 6/8	Lower Besa River, B.C.	Peter Hochleitner	Peter Hochleitner	1977	208
171	43	42 6/8	13 6/8	14	6	6	30	30	Kechika Range, B.C.	H. I. H. Prince Abdorreza Pahlavi	H. I. H. Prince Abdorreza Pahlavi	1960	215
171	37	37 6/8	14	14 1/8	8	8	21 6/8	21 6/8	Horseshoe Lake, Yukon	Jack G. Giannola	Jack G. Giannola	1973	215
171	38 6/8	39 6/8	14 1/8	14	7	7	22 6/8	22 6/8	Besa River, B.C.	Dale Webber	Dale Webber	1984	215
170 7/8	42 6/8	42 6/8	13 6/8	13 6/8	6	6	24 6/8	24 6/8	Muskwa River, B.C.	Bernard J. Brown	Bernard J. Brown	1953	218
170 7/8	41	41 6/8	13 7/8	13 7/8	6	6	26	26	Pelly Mts., Yukon	Jack Tillotson	Jack Tillotson	1955	218
170 7/8	43	43	13 6/8	13 6/8	6 6/8	6 6/8	27 6/8	27 6/8	Cold Fish Lake, B.C.	Robert Brittingham	Robert Brittingham	1961	218
170 7/8	39 6/8	41	14 3/8	14 3/8	6 6/8	6 6/8	20	21	Cassiar Mts., B.C.	G. A. Treschow	G. A. Treschow	1966	218
170 7/8	43 6/8	43 6/8	12 7/8	12 7/8	5 6/8	5 6/8	27 6/8	27 6/8	Pelly Lake, B.C.	Robert M. Mallett	Robert M. Mallett	1966	218
170 7/8	40 6/8	40 6/8	15 3/8	15 3/8	6	6	25 6/8	25 6/8	Colt Lake, B.C.	Roscoe Hurd	Roscoe Hurd	1967	218
170 7/8	45 6/8	45 6/8	13	13 3/8	7 6/8	6 6/8	20	20	Telegraph Creek, B.C.	Picked Up	John Crowe	PR 1967	218
170 7/8	42	42	13 6/8	13 6/8	6	6	26 6/8	26 6/8	Cassiar, B.C.	Herb Parsons	Herb Parsons	1969	218
170 6/8	39 6/8	40 6/8	14 6/8	15	5 6/8	5 6/8	28 6/8	28 6/8	Cassiar, B.C.	Wilson Potter	Harvard Univ. Mus.	1906	226
170 6/8	40	40 4/8	14 6/8	14 6/8	6 6/8	6 6/8	25 6/8	25 6/8	Sandbar Creek, B.C.	John La Rocca	John La Rocca	1958	226
170 6/8	41 6/8	41 6/8	14	14	5 6/8	5 6/8	24 6/8	24 6/8	Halfway River, B.C.	S. J. Seidensticker	S. J. Seidensticker	1962	226
170 6/8	40 6/8	41 6/8	14	14	6 6/8	6 6/8	22 6/8	22 6/8	Cassiar Mts., B.C.	Sam Jaksick, Jr.	Sam Jaksick, Jr.	1967	226
170 6/8	35 6/8	38 6/8	14 6/8	14 6/8	7	6	27 4/8	27 4/8	Wrede Creek, B.C.	Jack Feightner	Jack Feightner	1972	226
170 6/8	41	44 6/8	13 6/8	13 6/8	6	6	27 6/8	27 6/8	Cassiar Mts., B.C.	Ed Stedman, Jr.	Ed Stedman, Jr.	1974	226
170 6/8	38 6/8	40 6/8	14 7/8	14 7/8	6	6	24 4/8	24 4/8	Ice Mt., B.C.	David P. Jacobson	David P. Jacobson	1974	226
170 6/8	39	40 6/8	14 7/8	14 7/8	6	6	18	18	Burnt Rose Lake, B.C.	John Drift	John Drift	1977	226
170 5/8	41 6/8	41 6/8	13 3/8	13 3/8	7 6/8	7	26 6/8	26 6/8	Watson Lake, B.C.	Ed Ball	Ed Ball	1960	234
170 5/8	44 6/8	44 6/8	13 3/8	13 3/8	6 6/8	6 6/8	28	28	Watson Lake, Yukon	Richard G. Peters	Richard G. Peters	1962	234
170 5/8	39	39 6/8	14	15	6 6/8	6 6/8	19 6/8	19 6/8	Prophet River, B.C.	John J. Lo Monaco	John J. Lo Monaco	1963	234
170 5/8	38	38 6/8	14 4/8	14 4/8	8	7 6/8	19	19	Prophet River, B.C.	Ted Howell	Ted Howell	1964	234
170 5/8	37 6/8	38 6/8	14 6/8	14 6/8	7 6/8	7	18 6/8	18 6/8	Tuchodi Lakes, B.C.	Robert C. Ries	Robert C. Ries	1965	234
170 5/8	39 6/8	41 6/8	14 6/8	14 6/8	6 6/8	6	28 4/8	28 4/8	Telegraph Creek, B.C.	R. B. England	R. B. England	1966	234
170 5/8	37 6/8	38 6/8	14 6/8	14 6/8	7 6/8	7 6/8	23	23	Cassiar Mts., B.C.	W. G. Rathmann	W. G. Rathmann	1971	234
170 4/8	42	41	14	13 7/8	6 4/8	6	24 4/8	24 4/8	Peace River, B.C.	C. A. Freese	C. A. Freese	1960	241
170 4/8	41	41	14	14	6	6	27 6/8	27 6/8	Gataga River, B.C.	Herb Klein	Herb Klein	1963	241
170 4/8	43	42 6/8	13 6/8	13 6/8	5 6/8	5 6/8	22 6/8	22 6/8	Pelly Creek, B.C.	Jon A. Jourdonnais	Jon A. Jourdonnais	1968	241
170 4/8	40 6/8	41	14 6/8	14 6/8	6 6/8	6 6/8	25 6/8	25 6/8	Kechika Range, B.C.	Ferdinand Stemann	Ferdinand Stemann	1970	241
170 3/8	43 6/8	43 6/8	13 6/8	13 6/8	6 4/8	6	29 6/8	29 6/8	Cassiar, B.C.	John W. Beban	John W. Beban	1956	245
170 3/8	40 6/8	40 6/8	14 6/8	14 6/8	6	6	29 6/8	29 6/8	Prophet River, B.C.	E. R. Wells	E. R. Wells	1967	245
170 3/8	39	39	14 6/8	14 6/8	6 6/8	6 6/8	21 6/8	21 6/8	Toad River, B.C.	Jay Stewart	Jay Stewart	1969	245
170 3/8	40 6/8	40 6/8	14	14	6 6/8	6 6/8	24 6/8	24 6/8	Prophet River, B.C.	Robert E. Speegle	Robert E. Speegle	1983	245

Score	Length of Horn R.	L.	Circumference of Base R.	L.	Circumference at Third Quarter R.	L.	Greatest Spread	Tip to Tip Spread	Locality Killed	By Whom Killed	Owner	Date Killed	Rank
170⅞	42⅞	42⅝	13⅝	13⅝	6	5⅞	33⅛	33⅛	Pelly Mts., Yukon	William Fisher	William Fisher	1957	249
170⅞	39⅝	40	14	14	7	6⅝	22	20⅞	Toad River, B.C.	Fred Sothmann	Fred Sothmann	1963	249
170⅞	42	42	13⅜	13⅜	6⅛	6⅛	26⅛	26⅝	Telegraph Creek, B.C.	Joseph T. Pelton	Joseph T. Pelton	1963	249
170⅞	40⅞	39⅜	14⅜	14⅜	6⅜	6⅜	21⅝	21⅛	Dease Lake, B.C.	Melvin A. Hetland	Melvin A. Hetland	1965	249
170⅞	41⅞	40	14⅜	14⅜	6⅝	6⅝	26⅛	26⅛	Pink Mt., B.C.	Rita Oney	Rita Oney	1966	249
170⅞	40	40⅞	14⅜	14⅜	6⅞	6⅞	21⅛	22⅞	Watson Lake, B.C.	W. Brandon Macomber	W. Brandon Macomber	1966	249
170⅞	32	41⅛	14⅜	14⅜	8	8⅜	22	24	Muskwa River, B.C.	Donald P. Eickhoff	E. C. Eickhoff	1968	249
170⅞	42⅝	40⅜	13⅜	13⅜	6⅜	6⅜	25⅝	25⅝	Mt. Edziza, B.C.	William J. Pollard	William J. Pollard	1974	249
170⅞	41⅜	40⅜	13⅞	13⅞	6⅜	6⅜	22⅜	22⅜	Sikanni, B.C.	W. A. K. Seale	W. A. K. Seale	1961	257
170⅜	39⅞	40⅞	14	14	6⅜	6⅜	28	28	Kechika Range, B.C.	Basil C. Bradbury	Basil C. Bradbury	1965	257
170⅜	37⅝	38⅜	14⅜	14⅜	6⅜	6⅜	22⅜	22⅜	Ospika Area, B.C.	Ray E. Bigler	Ray E. Bigler	1972	257
170⅝	40	43⅜	13⅜	13⅜	8⅜	6⅜	25⅜	25⅜	Beale Lake, B.C.	John Forester	John Forester	1963	260
170⅝	35	35⅝	14⅝	14⅝	8	8⅜	21⅛	19⅜	Richards Creek, B.C.	Herbert A. Leupold	Herbert A. Leupold	1965	260
170⅝	38⅝	39	15	14⅜	6⅝	6⅝	22⅝	22⅝	Halfway River, B.C.	Steven L. Rose	Steven L. Rose	1967	260
170⅝	41	41	14⅜	14⅜	6⅜	6⅜	26	26	Keohka River, B.C.	Fritz A. Nachant	Fritz A. Nachant	1970	260
170⅝	39⅜	39⅝	14⅝	14⅜	6⅜	6	21⅜	21⅞	Muskwa River, B.C.	James S. Griffin	James S. Griffin	1972	260
170⅝	38⅜	43⅜	14⅛	14⅛	6⅜	6⅜	23⅜	23⅜	Turnagain River, B.C.	Jerald T. Waite	Jerald T. Waite	1976	260
170⅝	36⅜	37	14⅜	14⅜	8⅜	8	20⅜	19⅜	Townsley Creek, B.C.	Robert L. Williamson	Robert L. Williamson	1981	260
170⅜	41	39⅜	14⅜	14⅜	6⅜	6⅜	24⅜	24⅜	Racing River, B.C.	Bill Stevenson	Bill Stevenson	1983	260
170⅜	40⅜	39⅜	14⅜	14⅜	6⅜	6⅜	25⅜	25⅜	Prophet River, B.C.	Steve J. Polich	Steve J. Polich	1984	260
170⅛	43⅜	42⅝	13⅜	13⅜	6	6	30⅜	30⅜	Rabbit River, B.C.	George W. Young	George W. Young	1965	269
170⅛	39⅜	38⅜	14⅜	14⅜	6	6⅜	24⅜	24⅜	Ram Creek, B.C.	Kim Cox	Kim Cox	1966	269
170⅛	39⅜	43⅜	13⅜	13⅜	6⅛	6⅜	21⅜	21⅜	Needham Creek, B.C.	Roy Fukunaga	Roy Fukunaga	1974	269
170⅛	43⅜	42⅜	12⅜	12⅜	6⅜	6⅜	27⅜	27⅜	Cassiar Mts., B.C.	James H. Duke, Jr.	James H. Duke, Jr.	1976	269
170	42⅜	38⅜	14⅜	14⅜	6	6	24⅜	24⅜	Prophet River, B.C.	Walter B. McClurkan	Walter B. McClurkan	1945	273
170	39⅜	43⅜	13⅜	13⅜	6⅜	6	25	25	Cold Fish Lake, B.C.	Howard Boazman	Howard Boazman	1962	273
170	42	37	14⅜	14⅜	6⅜	6⅜	22⅜	22⅜	Alaska Hwy., B.C.	Arthur Gordon	Arthur Gordon	1965	273
170	39⅜	39⅜	14⅜	14⅜	6⅜	6⅜	27⅜	27⅜	Cassiar Mts., B.C.	Neil Castner	Neil Castner	1966	273
170	39⅜	40⅛	14⅜	14⅜	6⅜	6⅜	21⅜	21⅜	Cassiar Mts., B.C.	Glen E. Park	Glen E. Park	1967	273
170	38⅜	39⅜	13⅞	13⅞	7⅜	7⅜	21	16⅜	Tetsa River, B.C.	Owen R. Walker	Owen R. Walker	1967	273
170	41	41	14	14	6⅜	6⅜	20⅜	20⅜	Prophet River, B.C.	Jim Nystrom	Jim Nystrom	1968	273

170	42⅜	43⅞	13⅞	13⅞	6	6⅛	29⅞	29⅞	Gataga River, B.C.	Paul L. C. Snider	Paul L. C. Snider	1970	273
170	40	39⅞	15⅞	15⅞	5⅞	5⅞	22⅞	22⅞	Muskwa River, B.C.	W. J. Boynton III	W. J. Boynton III	1970	273
186⅝*	44⅛	44	16⅛	16	6⅛	6⅞	26⅞	26⅞	Watson Lake, B.C.	Keith Brown		1971	
185⅝*	47⅞	49⅞	13⅜	13⅞	6⅛	7⅞	29	29	Ice Mt., B.C.	Bruce Creyke	Picked Up	1977	
185⅜*	45⅞	44⅜	15⅞	15⅞	6⅛	5⅞	29⅞	29⅞	Prophet River, B.C.	Felipe Palau	Felipe Palau	1970	
181⅝*	40⅞	41⅞	14⅞	14⅞	9	8⅞	24⅞	24⅞	Tuchodi Lakes, B.C.	Romeo Leduc	Romeo Leduc	1981	
178⅞*	42⅞	43⅞	15	15⅞	5⅞	5⅞	25⅞	25⅞	Racing River, B.C.	Dick Sullivan	Dick Sullivan	1982	
174*	40⅞	40⅞	15⅞	15⅞	6⅜	6⅛	25⅛	24⅞	Muskwa River, B.C.	R. L. Gearhart	R. L. Gearhart	1983	
173*	41⅞	42⅞	13⅞	13⅞	6⅞	7	24	23⅞	Rapid River, B.C.	Bill Silveira	Bill Silveira	1983	

*Final Score subject to revision by additional verifying measurements

461

Score Charts
of the
Official Scoring System
for
North American
Big Game Trophies

Records of North American
Big Game

BOONE AND CROCKETT CLUB

P.O. Box 547
Dumfries, VA 22026

Minimum Score:	Awards	All-time
Alaska brown	26	28
black	20	21
grizzly	23	24
polar	27	27

BEAR

Kind of Bear ___ black

Sex ___ unknown

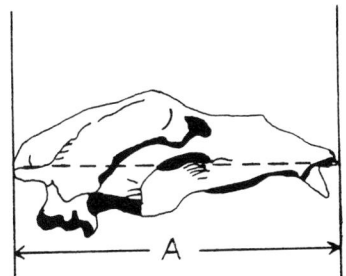

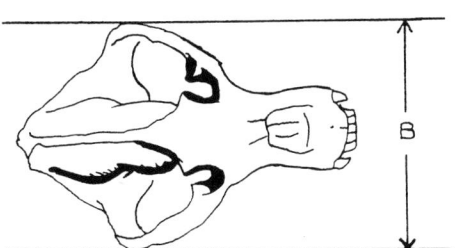

SEE OTHER SIDE FOR INSTRUCTIONS	Measurements
A. Greatest Length Without Lower Jaw	14 12/16
B. Greatest Width	8 14/16
FINAL SCORE	23 10/16

Exact Locality Where Killed: 7 miles east of Ephraim, San Pete Co., Utah

Date Killed: 7/1/75 By Whom Killed: Picked Up

Present Owner: Alma R. Lund and Merrill Daniels

Address:

Guide Name and Address:

Remarks: (Mention Any Abnormalities or Unique Qualities)

I certify that I have measured the above trophy on ___ 9 January ___ 19 76

at (Address) ___ 1596 W. N. Temple ___ (City) Salt Lake City (State) Utah

and that these measurements and data are, to the best of my knowledge and belief, made in accordance with the

instructions given.

Witness: ___ Harold Boyack ___ Signature: ___ Rudy Drobnick ___

B&C OFFICIAL MEASURER

I.D. Number

INSTRUCTIONS FOR MEASURING BEAR

Measurements are taken with calipers or by using parallel perpendiculars, to the nearest one-sixteenth of an inch, without reduction of fractions. Official measurement cannot be taken until skull has dried for at least sixty days after the animal was killed. All adhering flesh, membrane and cartilage must be completely removed before official measurements are taken.

A. Greatest Length is measured between perpendiculars parallel to the long axis of the skull, without the lower jaw and excluding malformations.

B. Greatest Width is measured between perpendiculars at right angles to the long axis.

* * * * * * * * * * * * * * * *

FAIR CHASE STATEMENT FOR ALL HUNTER-TAKEN TROPHIES

To make use of the following methods shall be deemed as UNFAIR CHASE and unsportsmanlike, and any trophy obtained by use of such means is disqualified from entry.

 I. Spotting or herding game from the air, followed by landing in its vicinity for pursuit;

 II. Herding or pursuing game with motor-powered vehicles;

 III. Use of electronic communications for attracting, locating or observing game, or guiding the hunter to such game;

 IV. Hunting game confined by artificial barriers, including escape-proof fencing; or hunting game transplanted solely for the purpose of commercial shooting.

* * * * * * * * * * * * * * * *

I certify that the trophy scored on this chart was not taken in UNFAIR CHASE as defined above by the Boone and Crockett Club. I further certify that it was taken in full compliance with local game laws of the state, province, or territory.

Date: _____ Signature of Hunter: _____

(Have Signature Notarized by a Notary Public)

Records of North American
Big Game

BOONE AND CROCKETT CLUB

P.O. Box 547
Dumfries, VA 22026

Minimum Score:	Awards	All-time
cougar	14-8/16	15
jaguar	14-8/16	14-8/16

COUGAR AND JAGUAR

Kind of Cat __cougar__

Sex __male__

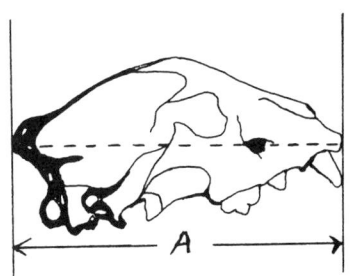

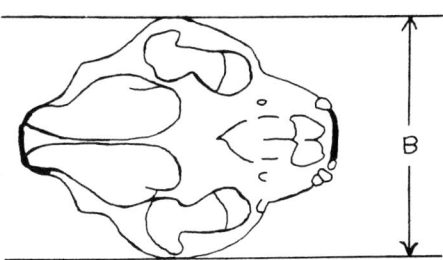

SEE OTHER SIDE FOR INSTRUCTIONS	Measurements
A. Greatest Length Without Lower Jaw	8 13/16
B. Greatest Width	6 10/16
FINAL SCORE	15 7/16

Exact Locality Where Killed: Cranbrook, B.C.

Date Killed: 12/28/81 By Whom Killed: Donovan W. Ellis

Present Owner: Donovan W. Ellis

Address:

Guide Name and Address:

Remarks: (Mention Any Abnormalities or Unique Qualities)

I certify that I have measured the above trophy on __22 June__ 19 __83__

at (Address) __Dallas Museum of Natural History__ (City) __Dallas__ (State) __Texas__

and that these measurements and data are, to the best of my knowledge and belief, made in accordance with the

instructions given.

Witness: __Frank Cook__   Signature: __Steve Kubasek__

B&C OFFICIAL MEASURER

I.D. Number

466

INSTRUCTIONS FOR MEASURING COUGAR AND JAGUAR

Measurements are taken with calipers or by using parallel perpendiculars, to the nearest one-sixteenth of an inch, without reduction of fractions. Official measurements cannot be taken until the skull has dried for at least sixty days after the animal was killed. All adhering flesh, membrane and cartilage must be completely removed before official measurements are taken.

A. Greatest Length is measured between perpendiculars parallel to the long axis of the skull, without the lower jaw and excluding malformations.

B. Greatest Width is measured between perpendiculars at right angles to the long axis.

* * * * * * * * * * * * * * * *

FAIR CHASE STATEMENT FOR ALL HUNTER-TAKEN TROPHIES

To make use of the following methods shall be deemed as UNFAIR CHASE and unsportsmanlike, and any trophy obtained by use of such means is disqualified from entry.

I. Spotting or herding game from the air, followed by landing in its vicinity for pursuit;

II. Herding or pursuing game with motor-powered vehicles;

III. Use of electronic communications for attracting, locating or observing game, or guiding the hunter to such game;

IV. Hunting game confined by artificial barriers, including escape-proof fencing; or hunting game transplanted solely for the purpose of commercial shooting.

* * * * * * * * * * * * * * * *

I certify that the trophy scored on this chart was not taken in UNFAIR CHASE as defined above by the Boone and Crockett Club. I further certify that it was taken in full compliance with local game laws of the state, province, or territory.

Date: _____ Signature of Hunter: _____

(Have Signature Notarized by a Notary Public)

Records of North American
Big Game

BOONE AND CROCKETT CLUB

P.O. Box 547
Dumfries, VA 22026

Minimum Score:	Awards	All-time
Atlantic	95	95
Pacific	100	100

WALRUS

Kind of Walrus __Pacific__

Sex __male__

SEE OTHER SIDE FOR INSTRUCTIONS	Column 1	Column 2	Column 3
A. Greatest Spread	unknown	Right Tusk	Left Tusk	Difference
B. Tip to Tip Spread	unknown			
C. Entire Length of Loose Tusk		32 2/8	32 1/8	1/8
D-1. Circumference of Base		12 2/8	13	6/8
D-2. Circumference at First Quarter		11 6/8	12 2/8	4/8
D-3. Circumference at Second Quarter		9 5/8	9 5/8	--
D-4. Circumference at Third Quarter		7 2/8	7 1/8	1/8
TOTALS		73 1/8	74 1/8	1 4/8

Enter Total of Columns 1 and 2	147 2/8	Exact Locality Where Killed:	Chukchi Sea off Point Hope, Alaska
Subtract Column 3	1 4/8	Date Killed: Spring '57 By Whom Killed:	Eskimo
FINAL SCORE	145 6/8	Present Owner:	Jonas Brothers of Seattle
		Guide Name and Address:	
		Remarks:	skull missing - both tusks slightly chipd.

I certify that I have measured the above trophy on __18 February__ 19 __58__

at (Address) __American Museum of Natural History__ (City) __New York__ (State) __NY__

and that these measurements and data are, to the best of my knowledge and belief, made in accordance with the

instructions given.

Witness: _____   Signature: __Grancel Fitz__

B&C OFFICIAL MEASURER

I.D. Number

468

INSTRUCTIONS FOR MEASURING WALRUS

All measurements must be made with a 1/4-inch, flexible steel tape to the nearest one-eighth of an inch. Wherever it is necessary to change direction of measurement, mark a control point and swing tape at this point. Enter fractional figures in eighths, without reduction. Tusks must be removed from mounted specimens for measuring. Official measurement cannot be taken until tusks have dried for at least sixty days after the animal was killed.

A. Greatest Spread is measured between perpendiculars at a right angle to the center line of the skull.

B. Tip to Tip Spread is measured between tips of tusks.

C. Entire Length of Loose Tusk is measured over outer curve from base to a point in line with tip.

D-1 Circumference of Base is measured at a right angle to axis of tusk. Do not follow edge of contact between tusk and skull.

D. 2-3-4 Divide measurement C of longer tusk by four. Starting at base, mark both tusks at these quarters (even though the other tusk is shorter) and measure circumferences at these marks.

* * * * * * * * * * * * * * * * * *

FAIR CHASE STATEMENT FOR ALL HUNTER-TAKEN TROPHIES

To make use of the following methods shall be deemed as UNFAIR CHASE and unsportsmanlike, and any trophy obtained by use of such means is disqualified from entry.

  I. Spotting or herding game from the air, followed by landing in its vicinity for pursuit;

  II. Herding or pursuing game with motor-powered vehicles;

  III. Use of electronic communications for attracting, locating or observing game, or guiding the hunter to such game;

  IV. Hunting game confined by artificial barriers, including escape-proof fencing; or hunting game transplanted solely for the purpose of commercial shooting.

* * * * * * * * * * * * * * * * * *

I certify that the trophy scored on this chart was not taken in UNFAIR CHASE as defined above by the Boone and Crockett Club. I further certify that it was taken in full compliance with local game laws of the state, province, or territory.

Date: _____ Signature of Hunter: _____

(Have Signature Notarized by a Notary Public)

Records of North American
Big Game

BOONE AND CROCKETT CLUB

P.O. Box 547
Dumfries, VA 22026

Minimum Score: Awards All-time
360   375

TYPICAL
AMERICAN ELK (WAPITI)

DETAIL OF POINT
MEASUREMENT

Abnormal Points	
Right Antler	Left Antler
2 5/8	

E. Total of Lengths of Abnormal Points	2 5/8

SEE OTHER SIDE FOR INSTRUCTIONS				Column 1	Column 2	Column 3	Column 4
				Spread Credit	Right Antler	Left Antler	Difference
A. No. Points on Right Antler	8	No. Points on Left Antler	7				
B. Tip to Tip Spread	39 6/8	C. Greatest Spread	51 6/8				
D. Inside Spread of Main Beams	45 4/8	(Credit May Equal But Not Exceed Longer Antler)		45 4/8			
F. Length of Main Beam					55 5/8	59 5/8	4
G-1. Length of First Point					20 5/8	20 5/8	--
G-2. Length of Second Point					27 3/8	25 5/8	1 6/8
G-3. Length of Third Point					20	18 5/8	1 3/8
G-4. Length of Fourth (Royal) Point					22 4/8	21 5/8	7/8
G-5. Length of Fifth Point					15 7/8	15 4/8	3/8
G-6. Length of Sixth Point, If Present					11 7/8	7 3/8	4 4/8
G-7. Length of Seventh Point, If Present							
H-1. Circumference at Smallest Place Between First and Second Points					12 1/8	11 2/8	7/8
H-2. Circumference at Smallest Place Between Second and Third Points					7 5/8	7 5/8	--
H-3. Circumference at Smallest Place Between Third and Fourth Points					7 7/8	8	1/8
H-4. Circumference at Smallest Place Between Fourth and Fifth Points					8	9	1
TOTALS				45 4/8	209 4/8	204 7/8	17 4/8

Enter Total of Columns 1, 2, and 3	459 7/8	Exact Locality Where Killed:	Dark Canyon, Colorado	
Subtract Column 4	14 7/8	Date Killed: 1899	By Whom Killed:	John Plute
Subtotal	445	Present Owner:	Ed Rozman	
Subtract (E) Total of Lengths of Abn. Points	2 5/8	Guide Name and Address:		
FINAL SCORE	442 3/8	Remarks:		

470

I certify that I have measured the above trophy on ___8 February___ 19 62

at (address) __American Museum of Natural History__ City __New York__ State __NY__
and that these measurements and data are, to the best of my knowledge and belief, made in accordance with the
instructions given.

Witness: _____ Signature __Elmer M. Rusten__

<table>
<tr><td>B&C OFFICIAL MEASURER</td><td>| | | | |</td></tr>
<tr><td></td><td>I.D. Number</td></tr>
</table>

INSTRUCTIONS FOR MEASURING TYPICAL AMERICAN ELK (WAPITI)

All measurements must be made with a 1/4-inch flexible steel tape to the nearest one-eighth of an inch. Wherever
it is necessary to change direction of measurement, mark a control point and swing tape at this point. (Note: a
flexible steel cable can be used to measure points and main beams only.) Enter fractional figures in eighths,
without reduction. Official measurements cannot be taken until the antlers have dried for at least 60 days after
the animal was killed.

A. Number of Points on Each Antler: to be counted a point, the projection must be at least one inch long, with
length exceeding width at one inch or more of length. All points are measured from tip of point to nearest edge
of beam as illustrated. Beam tip is counted as a point but not measured as a point.

B. Tip to Tip Spread is measured between tips of main beams.

C. Greatest Spread is measured between perpendiculars at a right angle to the center line of the skull at widest
part, whether across main beams or points.

D. Inside Spread of Main Beams is measured at a right angle to the center line of the skull at widest point
between main beams. Enter this measurement again as Spread Credit if it is less than or equal to the length of
longer antler; if longer, enter longer antler length for Spread Credit.

E. Total of Lengths of all Abnormal Points: Abnormal Points are those non-typical in location (such as points
originating from a point or from bottom or sides of main beam) or pattern (extra points, not generally paired).
Measure in usual manner and record in appropriate blanks.

F. Length of Main Beam is measured from lowest outside edge of burr over outer curve to the most distant point of
what is, or appears to be, the main beam. The point of beginning is that point on the burr where the center line
along the outer curve of the beam intersects the burr, then following generally the line of the illustration.

G. 1-2-3-4-5-6-7 Length of Normal Points: Normal points project from the top or front of the main beam in the
general pattern illustrated. They are measured from nearest edge of main beam over outer curve to tip. Lay the
tape along the outer curve of the beam so that the top edge of the tape coincides with the top edge of the beam
on both sides of point to determine the baseline for point measurement. Record point length in appropriate
blanks.

H. 1-2-3-4 Circumferences are taken as detailed for each measurement.

* * * * * * * * * * * * * * * * * *

FAIR CHASE STATEMENT FOR ALL HUNTER-TAKEN TROPHIES

To make use of the following methods shall be deemed as UNFAIR CHASE and unsportsmanlike, and any trophy
obtained by use of such means is disqualified from entry.

    I. Spotting or herding game from the air, followed by landing in its vicinity for pursuit;

    II. Herding or pursuing game with motor-powered vehicles;

    III. Use of electronic communications for attracting, locating or observing game, or guiding the
        hunter to such game;

    IV. Hunting game confined by artificial barriers, including escape-proof fencing; or hunting game
        transplanted solely for the purpose of commercial shooting.

* * * * * * * * * * * * * * * * * *

I certify that the trophy scored on this chart was not taken in UNFAIR CHASE as defined above by the Boone
and Crockett Club. I further certify that it was taken in full compliance with local game laws of the
state, province, or territory.

Date _____ Signature of Hunter _____

(Have signature notarized by a Notary Public)

Records of North American
Big Game

BOONE AND CROCKETT CLUB

P.Q. Box 547
Dumfries, VA 22026

Minimum Score: Awards All-time
385   385

NON-TYPICAL
AMERICAN ELK (WAPITI)

Abnormal Points	
Right Antler	Left Antler
1 3/8	14
8 7/8	11 3/8
	10 1/8
	1 4/8

E. Total of Lengths of Abnormal Points	47 2/8

SEE OTHER SIDE FOR INSTRUCTIONS			Column 1	Column 2	Column 3	Column 4
			Spread Credit	Right Antler	Left Antler	Difference
A. No. Points on Right Antler	8	No. Points on Left Antler 10				
B. Tip to Tip Spread	30	C. Greatest Spread 55 6/8				
D. Inside Spread of Main Beams	39 5/8	(Credit May Equal But Not Exceed Longer Antler)	39 5/8			
F. Length of Main Beam				53 6/8	52 1/8	1 5/8
G-1. Length of First Point				15 6/8	16 3/8	5/8
G-2. Length of Second Point				17 7/8	17 6/8	1/8
G-3. Length of Third Point				17 2/8	17 2/8	--
G-4. Length of Fourth (Royal) Point				19 6/8	23 3/8	3 5/8
G-5. Length of Fifth Point				20 5/8	17 3/8	3 2/8
G-6. Length of Sixth Point, If Present						
G-7. Length of Seventh Point, If Present						
H-1. Circumference at Smallest Place Between First and Second Points				8 2/8	8 6/8	4/8
H-2. Circumference at Smallest Place Between Second and Third Points				6 5/8	7	3/8
H-3. Circumference at Smallest Place Between Third and Fourth Points				6 6/8	7 1/8	3/8
H-4. Circumference at Smallest Place Between Fourth and Fifth Points				7 3/8	7 4/8	1/8
TOTALS			39 5/8	174	174 5/8	10 5/8

Enter Total of Columns 1, 2, and 3	388 2/8	Exact Locality Where Killed: Kaibab Nat. For., Coconino Co., AZ
Subtract Column 4	10 5/8	Date Killed: 9/14/85 By Whom Killed: James L. Ludvigson
Subtotal	377 5/8	Present Owner: James L. Ludvigson
Add (E) Total of Lengths of Abnormal Points	47 2/8	Guide Name and Address:
FINAL SCORE	424 7/8	Remarks:

472

I certify that I have measured the above trophy on ___January 16___ 19 87

at (address) __5242 West Cheryl Drive__ City __Glendale__ State __AZ__
and that these measurements and data are, to the best of my knowledge and belief, made in accordance with the instructions given.

Witness: __Hilde Cupell__ Signature __Michael C. Cupell__

INSTRUCTIONS FOR MEASURING NON-TYPICAL AMERICAN ELK (WAPITI)

All measurements must be made with a 1/4-inch flexible steel tape to the nearest one-eighth of an inch. Wherever it is necessary to change direction of measurement, mark a control point and swing tape at this point. (Note: a flexible steel cable can be used to measure points and main beams only.) Enter fractional figures in eighths, without reduction. Official measurements cannot be taken until the antlers have dried for at least 60 days after the animal was killed.

A. Number of Points on Each Antler: to be counted a point, the projection must be at least one inch long, with length exceeding width at one inch or more of length. All points are measured from tip of point to nearest edge of beam as illustrated. Beam tip is counted as a point but not measured as a point.

B. Tip to Tip Spread is measured between tips of main beams.

C. Greatest Spread is measured between perpendiculars at a right angle to the center line of the skull at widest part, whether across main beams or points.

D. Inside Spread of Main Beams is measured at a right angle to the center line of the skull at widest point between main beams. Enter this measurement again as the Spread Credit if it is less than or equal to the length of longer antler; if longer, enter longer antler length for Spread Credit.

E. Total of Lengths of all Abnormal Points: Abnormal Points are those non-typical in location (such as points originating from a point or from bottom or sides of main beam) or pattern (extra points, not generally paired). Measure in usual manner and record in appropriate blanks.

F. Length of Main Beam is measured from lowest outside edge of burr over outer curve to the most distant point of what is, or appears to be, the main beam. The point of beginning is that point on the burr where the center line along the outer curve of the beam intersects the burr, then following generally the line of the illustration.

G. 1-2-3-4-5-6-7 Length of Normal Points: Normal points project from the top or front of the main beam in the general pattern illustrated. They are measured from nearest edge of main beam over outer curve to tip. Lay the tape along the outer curve of the beam so that the top edge of the tape coincides with the top edge of the beam on both sides of point to determine the baseline for point measurement. Record point length in appropriate blanks.

H. 1-2-3-4 Circumferences are taken as detailed for each measurement.

* * * * * * * * * * * * * * * * * *

FAIR CHASE STATEMENT FOR ALL HUNTER-TAKEN TROPHIES

To make use of the following methods shall be deemed as UNFAIR CHASE and unsportsmanlike, and any trophy obtained by use of such means is disqualified from entry.

   I. Spotting or herding game from the air, followed by landing in its vicinity for pursuit;
   II. Herding or pursuing game with motor-powered vehicles;
   III. Use of electronic communications for attracting, locating or observing game, or guiding the hunter to such game;
   IV. Hunting game confined by artificial barriers, including escape-proof fencing; or hunting game transplanted solely for the purpose of commercial shooting.

* * * * * * * * * * * * * * * * * *

I certify that the trophy scored on this chart was not taken in UNFAIR CHASE as defined above by the Boone and Crockett Club. I further certify that it was taken in full compliance with local game laws of the state, province, or territory.

Date _____ Signature of Hunter _____

(Have signature notarized by a Notary Public)

Records of North American
Big Game

BOONE AND CROCKETT CLUB

P.O. Box 547
Dumfries, VA 22026

Minimum Score: Awards   All-time
275   290

ROOSEVELT'S ELK

Crown Points	
Right Antler	Left Antler
10 6/8	11

I. Add to Total	21 6/8

Abnormal Points	
Right Antler	Left Antler

DETAIL OF POINT MEASUREMENT

E. Total of Lengths of Abnormal Points

SEE OTHER SIDE FOR INSTRUCTIONS				Column 1	Column 2	Column 3	Column 4
A. No. Points on Right Antler	9	No. Points on Left Antler	8	Spread Credit	Right Antler	Left Antler	Difference
B. Tip to Tip Spread	40 3/8	C. Greatest Spread	49 1/8				
D. Inside Spread of Main Beams	41 1/8	(Credit May Equal But Not Exceed Longer Antler)		41 1/8			
F. Length of Main Beam					48 4/8	49	4/8
G-1. Length of First Point					14	14 5/8	5/8
G-2. Length of Second Point					15 1/8	14	1 1/8
G-3. Length of Third Point					14 7/8	14 4/8	3/8
G-4. Length of Fourth (Royal) Point					19 5/8	17 4/8	2 1/8
G-5. Length of Fifth Point					13 6/8	12 1/8	
G-6. Length of Sixth Point, If Present					1 7/8	6 6/8	
G-7. Length of Seventh Point, If Present					2 4/8		
H-1. Circumference at Smallest Place Between First and Second Points					8 7/8	9 4/8	5/8
H-2. Circumference at Smallest Place Between Second and Third Points					7 4/8	8	4/8
H-3. Circumference at Smallest Place Between Third and Fourth Points					8 2/8	8	2/8
H-4. Circumference at Smallest Place Between Fourth and Fifth Points					9 3/8	10 1/8	6/8
TOTALS				41 1/8	164 2/8	164 1/8	6 7/8

Enter Total of Columns 1, 2, 3 and (I)	391 2/8	Exact Locality Where Killed:	Saddle Mt. Unit, Oregon
SUBTRACT Column 4	6 7/8	Date Killed: 1949 By Whom Killed:	Bob Sharp
Subtotal	384 3/8	Present Owner:	Harold Stepp
SUBTRACT (E) Abn. Pts.		Guide Name and Address:	
FINAL SCORE	384 3/8	Remarks:	

I certify that I have measured the above trophy on ___13 May_____ 19 _86___

at (address) __Nevada State Museum_____ City __Las Vegas__ State __NV___
and that these measurements and data are, to the best of my knowledge and belief, made in accordance with the
instructions given.

Witness: __Glenn St. Charles_____ Signature __C. Randall Byers_____

B&C OFFICIAL MEASURER

I.D. Number

INSTRUCTIONS FOR MEASURING ROOSEVELT'S ELK

All measurements must be made with a 1/4-inch flexible steel tape to the nearest one-eighth of an inch. Wherever
it is necessary to change direction of measurement, mark a control point and swing tape at this point. (Note: a
flexible steel cable can be used to measure points and main beams only.) Enter fractional figures in eighths,
without reduction. Official measurements cannot be taken until the antlers have dried for at least 60 days after
the animal was killed.

A. Number of Points on Each Antler: to be counted a point, the projection must be at least one inch long, with
length exceeding width at one inch or more of length. All points are measured from tip of point to nearest edge
of beam as illustrated. Beam tip is counted as a point but not measured as a point.

B. Tip to Tip Spread is measured between tips of main beams.

C. Greatest Spread is measured between perpendiculars at a right angle to the center line of the skull at widest
part, whether across main beams or points.

D. Inside Spread of Main Beams is measured at a right angle to the center line of the skull at widest point
between main beams. Enter this measurement again as the Spread Credit if it is less than or equal to the length
of longer antler; if longer, enter longer antler length for Spread Credit.

E. Total of Lengths of all Abnormal Points: Abnormal Points are those non-typical in location (such as points
originating from a point or from bottom or sides of main beam) or pattern (extra points, not generally paired).
Measure in usual manner and record in appropriate blanks. **Note: do not confuse with Crown Point that may occur
at base of Royal.**

F. Length of Main Beam is measured from lowest outside edge of burr over outer curve to the most distant point of
what is, or appears to be, the main beam. The point of beginning is that point on the burr where the center line
along the outer curve of the beam intersects the burr, then following generally the line of the illustration.

G. 1-2-3-4-5-6-7 Length of Normal Points: Normal points project from the top or front of the main beam in the
general pattern illustrated. They are measured from nearest edge of main beam over outer curve to tip. Lay the
tape along the outer curve of the beam so that the top edge of the tape coincides with the top edge of the beam
on both sides of point to determine the baseline for point measurement. Record point length in appropriate
blanks.

H. 1-2-3-4 Circumferences are taken as detailed for each measurement.

I. Crown Points: From the well-defined Royal on out to end of beam, all points other than the normal points in
their typical locations are Crown Points. This includes points occurring on the Royal, on other normal points,
and on Crown Points. Measure and record in appropriate blanks provided and add to score below.

* * * * * * * * * * * * * * * * *

FAIR CHASE STATEMENT FOR ALL HUNTER-TAKEN TROPHIES

To make use of the following methods shall be deemed as UNFAIR CHASE and unsportsmanlike, and any trophy
obtained by use of such means is disqualified from entry.

    I. Spotting or herding game from the air, followed by landing in its vicinity for pursuit;

   II. Herding or pursuing game with motor-powered vehicles;

  III. Use of electronic communications for attracting, locating or observing game, or guiding the
        hunter to such game;

   IV. Hunting game confined by artificial barriers, including escape-proof fencing; or hunting game
        transplanted solely for the purpose of commercial shooting.

* * * * * * * * * * * * * * * * *

I certify that the trophy scored on this chart was not taken in UNFAIR CHASE as defined above by the Boone
and Crockett Club. I further certify that it was taken in full compliance with local game laws of the
state, province, or territory.

Date _____ Signature of Hunter _____

(Have signature notarized by a Notary Public)

Copyright © 1988 by Boone and Crockett Club
(Reproduction strictly forbidden without express, written consent)

475

OFFICIAL SCORING SYSTEM FOR NORTH AMERICAN BIG GAME TROPHIES

Records of North American
Big Game

BOONE AND CROCKETT CLUB

P.Q. Box 547
Dumfries, VA 22026

Minimum Score:	Awards	All-time
mule	185	195
Columbia	120	130
Sitka	100	108

TYPICAL
MULE AND BLACKTAIL DEER

Kind of Deer _mule_

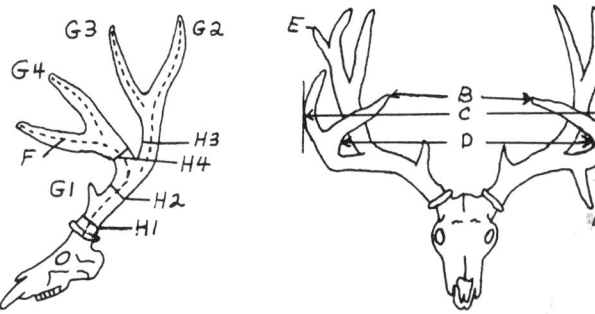

DETAIL OF POINT
MEASUREMENT

	Abnormal Points	
	Right Antler	Left Antler
	2 5/8	
E. Total of Lengths of Abnormal Points	2 5/8	

SEE OTHER SIDE FOR INSTRUCTIONS				Column 1	Column 2	Column 3	Column 4
				Spread Credit	Right Antler	Left Antler	Difference
A. No. Points on Right Antler	6	No. Points on Left Antler	5				
B. Tip to Tip Spread	28 5/8	C. Greatest Spread	33 2/8				
D. Inside Spread of Main Beams	30 7/8	(Credit May Equal But Not Exceed Longer Antler)		30 1/8			
F. Length of Main Beam					30 1/8	28 6/8	1 3/8
G-1. Length of First Point, If Present					2 3/8	2 6/8	3/8
G-2. Length of Second Point					22 4/8	22 3/8	1/8
G-3. Length of Third Point, If Present					14 2/8	14 3/8	1/8
G-4. Length of Fourth Point, If Present					14 6/8	13 6/8	1
H-1. Circumference at Smallest Place Between Burr and First Point					5 2/8	5 3/8	1/8
H-2. Circumference at Smallest Place Between First and Second Points					4 4/8	4 4/8	--
H-3. Circumference at Smallest Place Between Main Beam and Third Point					4	4 1/8	1/8
H-4. Circumference at Smallest Place Between Second and Fourth Points					4 2/8	4 4/8	2/8
TOTALS				30 1/8	102	100 4/8	6 7/8

Enter Total of Columns 1, 2, and 3	232 5/8	Exact Locality Where Killed:	Cortez, Colorado
Subtract Column 4	4 2/8	Date Killed: 10/19/72 By Whom Killed:	Doug Burris, Jr.
Subtotal	228 3/8	Present Owner:	Doug Burris, Jr.
Subtract (E) Total of Lengths of Abn. Points	2 5/8	Guide Name and Address:	
FINAL SCORE	225 6/8	Remarks:	

476

I certify that I have measured the above trophy on ___27 February_____ 19 _74___

at (address) ___Grash-Tucker Inc._____ City __Atlanta____ State __GA__
and that these measurements and data are, to the best of my knowledge and belief, made in accordance with the instructions given.

Witness: ___B. A. Fashingbauer_____ Signature: ___Arnold O. Haugen_____

B&C OFFICIAL MEASURER

INSTRUCTIONS FOR MEASURING TYPICAL MULE AND BLACKTAIL DEER

I.D. Number

All measurements must be made with a 1/4-inch flexible steel tape to the nearest one-eighth of an inch. Wherever it is necessary to change direction of measurement, mark a control point and swing tape at this point. (Note: a flexible steel cable can be used to take point and beam length measurements only.) Enter fractional figures in eighths, without reduction. Official measurements cannot be taken until antlers have dried for at least 60 days after the animal was killed.

A. Number of Points on Each Antler: to be counted a point, the projection must be at least one inch long, with length exceeding width at one inch or more of length. All points are measured from tip of point to nearest edge of beam as illustrated. Beam tip is counted as a point but not measured as a point.

B. Tip to Tip Spread is measured between tips of main beams.

C. Greatest Spread is measured between perpendiculars at a right angle to the center line of the skull at widest part, whether across main beams or points.

D. Inside Spread of Main Beams is measured at a right angle to the center line of the skull at widest point between main beams. Enter this measurement again as Spread Credit if it is less than or equal to the length of longer antler; if longer, enter longer antler length for Spread Credit.

E. Total of Lengths of all Abnormal Points: Abnormal Points are those non-typical in location such as points originating from a point (exception: G-3 originates from G-2 in perfectly normal fashion) or from bottom or sides of main beam, or any points beyond the normal pattern of five (including beam tip) per antler. Measure each abnormal point in usual manner and enter in appropriate blanks.

F. Length of Main Beam is measured from lowest outside edge of burr over outer curve to the most distant point of what is, or appears to be, the Main Beam. The point of beginning is that point on the burr where the center line along the outer curve of the beam intersects the burr, then following generally the line of the illustration.

G. 1-2-3-4 Length of Normal Points: Normal points are the brow and the upper and lower forks as shown in the illustration. They are measured from nearest edge of beam over outer curve to tip. Lay the tape along the outer curve of the beam so that the top edge of the tape coincides with the top edge of the beam on both sides of point to determine the baseline for point measurement. Record point lengths in appropriate blanks.

H. 1-2-3-4 Circumferences are taken as detailed for each measurement. If brow point is missing, take H-1 and H-2 at smallest place between burr and G-2. If G-3 is missing, take H-3 halfway between the base and tip of second point. If G-4 is missing, take H-4 halfway between second point and tip of main beam.

* * * * * * * * * * * * * * * * * *

FAIR CHASE STATEMENT FOR ALL HUNTER-TAKEN TROPHIES

To make use of the following methods shall be deemed as UNFAIR CHASE and unsportsmanlike, and any trophy obtained by use of such means is disqualified from entry.

    I. Spotting or herding game from the air, followed by landing in its vicinity for pursuit;

    II. Herding or pursuing game with motor-powered vehicles;

    III. Use of electronic communications for attracting, locating or observing game, or guiding the hunter to such game;

    IV. Hunting game confined by artificial barriers, including escape-proof fencing; or hunting game transplanted solely for the purpose of commercial shooting.

* * * * * * * * * * * * * * * * * *

I certify that the trophy scored on this chart was not taken in UNFAIR CHASE as defined above by the Boone and Crockett Club. I further certify that it was taken in full compliance with local game laws of the state, province, or territory.

Date: _____ Signature of Hunter: _____

(Have signature notarized by a Notary Public)

Copyright © 1988 by Boone and Crockett Club
(Reproduction strictly forbidden without express, written consent)

Records of North American
Big Game

BOONE AND CROCKETT CLUB

P.O. Box 547
Dumfries, VA 22026

Minimum Score: Awards All-time
225   240

NON-TYPICAL
MULE DEER

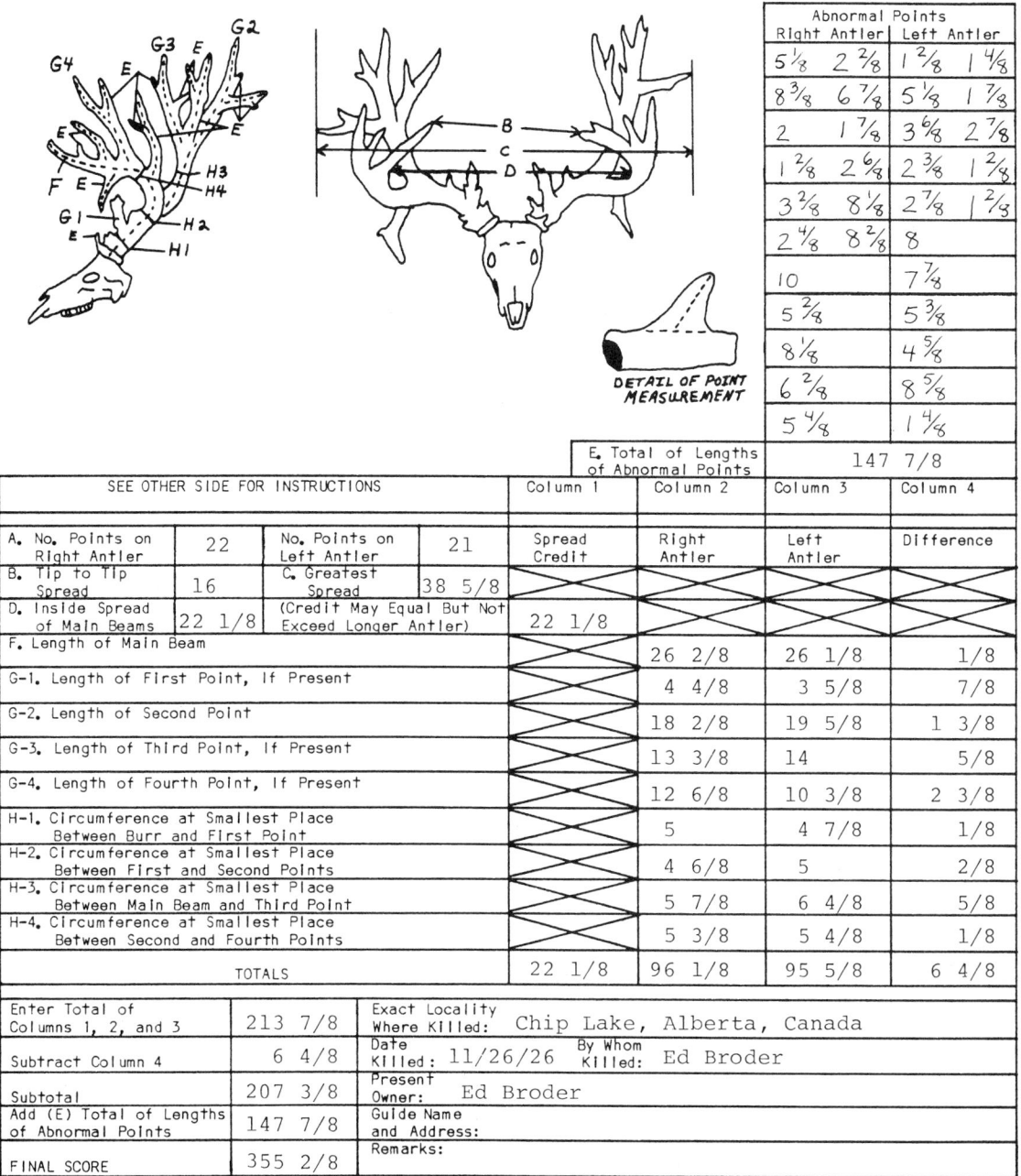

Abnormal Points			
Right Antler		Left Antler	
$5\frac{1}{8}$	$2\frac{2}{8}$	$1\frac{2}{8}$	$1\frac{4}{8}$
$8\frac{3}{8}$	$6\frac{7}{8}$	$5\frac{1}{8}$	$1\frac{7}{8}$
2	$1\frac{7}{8}$	$3\frac{6}{8}$	$2\frac{7}{8}$
$1\frac{2}{8}$	$2\frac{6}{8}$	$2\frac{3}{8}$	$1\frac{2}{8}$
$3\frac{2}{8}$	$8\frac{1}{8}$	$2\frac{7}{8}$	$1\frac{2}{8}$
$2\frac{4}{8}$	$8\frac{2}{8}$	8	
10		$7\frac{7}{8}$	
$5\frac{2}{8}$		$5\frac{3}{8}$	
$8\frac{1}{8}$		$4\frac{5}{8}$	
$6\frac{2}{8}$		$8\frac{5}{8}$	
$5\frac{4}{8}$		$1\frac{4}{8}$	

E. Total of Lengths of Abnormal Points	147 7/8

SEE OTHER SIDE FOR INSTRUCTIONS				Column 1	Column 2	Column 3	Column 4
A. No. Points on Right Antler	22	No. Points on Left Antler	21	Spread Credit	Right Antler	Left Antler	Difference
B. Tip to Tip Spread	16	C. Greatest Spread	38 5/8				
D. Inside Spread of Main Beams	22 1/8	(Credit May Equal But Not Exceed Longer Antler)		22 1/8			
F. Length of Main Beam					26 2/8	26 1/8	1/8
G-1. Length of First Point, If Present					4 4/8	3 5/8	7/8
G-2. Length of Second Point					18 2/8	19 5/8	1 3/8
G-3. Length of Third Point, If Present					13 3/8	14	5/8
G-4. Length of Fourth Point, If Present					12 6/8	10 3/8	2 3/8
H-1. Circumference at Smallest Place Between Burr and First Point					5	4 7/8	1/8
H-2. Circumference at Smallest Place Between First and Second Points					4 6/8	5	2/8
H-3. Circumference at Smallest Place Between Main Beam and Third Point					5 7/8	6 4/8	5/8
H-4. Circumference at Smallest Place Between Second and Fourth Points					5 3/8	5 4/8	1/8
TOTALS				22 1/8	96 1/8	95 5/8	6 4/8

Enter Total of Columns 1, 2, and 3	213 7/8	Exact Locality Where Killed:	Chip Lake, Alberta, Canada
Subtract Column 4	6 4/8	Date Killed: 11/26/26	By Whom Killed: Ed Broder
Subtotal	207 3/8	Present Owner:	Ed Broder
Add (E) Total of Lengths of Abnormal Points	147 7/8	Guide Name and Address:	
FINAL SCORE	355 2/8	Remarks:	

I certify that I have measured the above trophy on _____24 February_____ 19 62

at (address) _American Museum of Natural History_ City _New York_ State _NY_
and that these measurements and data are, to the best of my knowledge and belief, made in accordance with the
instructions given.

Witness: _Grancel Fitz_ Signature: _John E. Hammett_

B&C OFFICIAL MEASURER

I.D. Number

INSTRUCTIONS FOR MEASURING NON-TYPICAL MULE DEER

All measurements must be made with a 1/4-inch flexible steel tape to the nearest one-eighth of an inch. Wherever it is necessary to change direction of measurement, mark a control point and swing tape at this point. (Note: a flexible steel cable can be used to measure points and main beams only.) Enter fractional figures in eighths, without reduction. Official measurements cannot be taken until antlers have dried for at least 60 days after the animal was killed.

A. Number of Points on Each Antler: to be counted a point, the projection must be at least one inch long, with the length exceeding width at one inch or more of length. All points are measured from tip of point to nearest edge of beam as illustrated. Beam tip is counted as a point but is not measured as a point.

B. Tip to Tip Spread is measured between tips of main beams.

C. Greatest Spread is measured between perpendiculars at a right angle to the center line of the skull at widest part, whether across main beams or points.

D. Inside Spread of Main Beams is measured at a right angle to the center line of the skull at widest point between main beams. Enter this measurement again as the Spread Credit if it is less than or equal to the length of longer antler; if longer, enter longer antler length for Spread Credit.

E. Total of Lengths of all Abnormal Points: Abnormal Points are those non-typical in location such as points originating from a point (exception: G-3 originates from G-2 in perfectly normal fashion) or from bottom or sides of main beam, or any points beyond the normal pattern of five (including beam tip) per antler. Measure each abnormal point in usual manner and enter in appropriate blanks.

F. Length of Main Beam is measured from lowest outside edge of burr over outer curve to the most distant point of what is, or appears to be, the main beam. The point of beginning is that point on the burr where the center line along the outer curve of the beam intersects the burr, then following generally the line of the illustration.

G. 1-2-3-4 Length of Normal Points: Normal points are the brow and the upper and lower forks, as shown in the illustration. They are measured from nearest edge of main beam over outer curve to tip. Lay the tape along the outer curve of the beam so that the top edge of the tape coincides with the top edge of the beam on both sides of point to determine the baseline for point measurement. Record point lengths in appropriate blanks.

H. 1-2-3-4 Circumferences are taken as detailed for each measurement. If brow point is missing, take H-1 and H-2 at smallest place between burr and G-2. If G-3 is missing, take H-3 halfway between the base and tip of second point. If G-4 is missing, take H-4 halfway between second point and tip of main beam.

* * * * * * * * * * * * * * * * *

FAIR CHASE STATEMENT FOR ALL HUNTER-TAKEN TROPHIES

To make use of the following methods shall be deemed as UNFAIR CHASE and unsportsmanlike, and any trophy obtained by use of such means is disqualified from entry.

    I.   Spotting or herding game from the air, followed by landing in its vicinity for pursuit;

    II. Herding or pursuing game with motor-powered vehicles;

    III. Use of electronic communications for attracting, locating or observing game, or guiding the
         hunter to such game;

    IV. Hunting game confined by artificial barriers, including escape-proof fencing; or hunting game
         transplanted solely for the purpose of commercial shooting.

* * * * * * * * * * * * * * * * *

I certify that the trophy scored on this chart was not taken in UNFAIR CHASE as defined above by the Boone and Crockett Club. I further certify that it was taken in full compliance with local game laws of the state, province, or territory.

Date: _____ Signature of Hunter: _____

(Have signature notarized by a Notary Public)

Records of North American Big Game	BOONE AND CROCKETT CLUB	P.O. Box 547 Dumfries, VA 22026

Minimum Score: Awards All-time
whitetail 160 170
Coues' 100 110

TYPICAL
WHITETAIL AND COUES' DEER

Kind of Deer __whitetail__

DETAIL OF POINT MEASUREMENT

	Abnormal Points	
	Right Antler	Left Antler
E. Total of Lengths of Abnormal Points		

SEE OTHER SIDE FOR INSTRUCTIONS				Column 1	Column 2	Column 3	Column 4
				Spread Credit	Right Antler	Left Antler	Difference
A. No. Points on Right Antler	5	No. Points on Left Antler	5				
B. Tip to Tip Spread	7 5/8	C. Greatest Spread	23 6/8				
D. Inside Spread of Main Beams	20 1/8	(Credit May Equal But Not Exceed Longer Antler)		20 1/8			
F. Length of Main Beam					30	30	--
G-1. Length of First Point, If Present					7 6/8	7 3/8	3/8
G-2. Length of Second Point					13	13 1/8	1/8
G-3. Length of Third Point					10	10 4/8	4/8
G-4. Length of Fourth Point, If Present					6	7 5/8	1 5/8
G-5. Length of Fifth Point, If Present							
G-6. Length of Sixth Point, If Present							
G-7. Length of Seventh Point, If Present							
H-1. Circumference at Smallest Place Between Burr and First Point					6 2/8	6 1/8	1/8
H-2. Circumference at Smallest Place Between First and Second Points					6 2/8	6 4/8	2/8
H-3. Circumference at Smallest Place Between Second and Third Points					7 3/8	7 4/8	1/8
H-4. Circumference at Smallest Place Between Third and Fourth Points					7	6 7/8	1/8
TOTALS				20 1/8	93 5/8	95 5/8	3 2/8

Enter Total of Columns 1, 2, and 3	209 3/8	Exact Locality Where Killed:	Burnett Co., Wisconsin
Subtract Column 4	3 2/8	Date Killed: 1914	By Whom Killed: James Jordan
Subtotal	206 1/8	Present Owner:	Charles T. Arnold
Subtract (E) Total of Lengths of Abn. Points		Guide Name and Address:	
FINAL SCORE	206 1/8	Remarks:	

480

I certify that I have measured the above trophy on ___28 February_____ 19 66___

at (address) _Carnegie Museum_____ City _Pittsburgh__ State _PA___
and that these measurements and data are, to the best of my knowledge and belief, made in accordance with the
instructions given.

Witness: _George P. Morris_____ Signature: _George T. Church, Jr.___

B&C OFFICIAL MEASURER

I.D. Number

INSTRUCTIONS FOR MEASURING TYPICAL WHITETAIL AND COUES' DEER

All measurements must be made with a 1/4-inch flexible steel tape to the nearest one-eighth of an inch. Wherever it is necessary to change direction of measurement, mark a control point and swing tape at this point. (Note: a flexible steel cable can be used to measure points and main beams only.) Enter fractional figures in eighths, without reduction. Official measurements cannot be taken until antlers have dried for at least 60 days after the animal was killed.

A. Number of Points on Each Antler: to be counted a point, the projection must be at least one inch long, with the length exceeding width at one inch or more of length. All points are measured from tip of point to nearest edge of beam as illustrated. Beam tip is counted as a point but not measured as a point.

B. Tip to Tip Spread is measured between tips of main beams.

C. Greatest Spread is measured between perpendiculars at a right angle to the center line of the skull at widest part, whether across main beams or points.

D. Inside Spread of Main Beams is measured at a right angle to the center line of the skull at widest point between main beams. Enter this measurement again as the Spread Credit if it is less than or equal to the length of longer antler; if longer, enter longer antler length for Spread Credit.

E. Total of Lengths of all Abnormal Points: Abnormal Points are those non-typical in location (such as points originating from a point or from bottom or sides of main beam) or extra points beyond the normal pattern of points. Measure in usual manner and enter in appropriate blanks.

F. Length of Main Beam is measured from lowest outside edge of burr over outer curve to the most distant point of what is, or appears to be, the main beam. The point of beginning is that point on the burr where the center line along the outer curve of the beam intersects the burr, then following generally the line of the illustration.

G. 1-2-3-4-5-6-7 Length of Normal Points: Normal points project from the top of the main beam. They are measured from nearest edge of main beam over outer curve to tip. Lay the tape along the outer curve of the beam so that the top edge of the tape coincides with the top edge of the beam on both sides of the point to determine the baseline for point measurements. Record point lengths in appropriate blanks.

H. 1-2-3-4 Circumferences are taken as detailed for each measurement. If brow point is missing, take H-1 and H-2 at smallest place between burr and G-2. If G-4 is missing, take H-4 halfway between G-3 and tip of main beam.

* * * * * * * * * * * * * * * * * *

FAIR CHASE STATEMENT FOR ALL HUNTER-TAKEN TROPHIES

To make use of the following methods shall be deemed as UNFAIR CHASE and unsportsmanlike, and any trophy obtained by use of such means is disqualified from entry.

    I. Spotting or herding game from the air, followed by landing in its vicinity for pursuit;

    II. Herding or pursuing game with motor-powered vehicles;

    III. Use of electronic communications for attracting, locating or observing game, or guiding the hunter to such game;

    IV. Hunting game confined by artificial barriers, including escape-proof fencing; or hunting game transplanted solely for the purpose of commercial shooting.

* * * * * * * * * * * * * * * * * *

I certify that the trophy scored on this chart was not taken in UNFAIR CHASE as defined above by the Boone and Crockett Club. I further certify that it was taken in full compliance with local game laws of the state, province, or territory.

Date: _____ Signature of Hunter: _____

(Have signature notarized by a Notary Public)

Records of North American
Big Game

BOONE AND CROCKETT CLUB

P.O. Box 547
Dumfries, VA 22026

Minimum Score:	Awards	All-time
whitetail	185	195
Coues'	105	120

NON-TYPICAL
WHITETAIL AND COUES' DEER

Kind of Deer __whitetail__

Abnormal Points			
Right Antler		Left Antler	
3 1/8	5 3/8	1 3/8	1 4/8
5 5/8	6	1	2 1/8
4 3/8	8	1 1/8	4 7/8
2 4/8	7	2 1/8	1 1/8
5 4/8	7	9 4/8	2 7/8
12 5/8		2 6/8	7 7/8
11 3/8		7 3/8	9 4/8
4 6/8		1 6/8	4
3 2/8	10		3
7 6/8		5 4/8	4 6/8

E. Total of Lengths of Abnormal Points	184	6 2/8

DETAIL OF POINT MEASUREMENT

SEE OTHER SIDE FOR INSTRUCTIONS				Column 1	Column 2	Column 3	Column 4
				Spread Credit	Right Antler	Left Antler	Difference
A. No. Points on Right Antler	19	No. Points on Left Antler	25				
B. Tip to Tip Spread	27	C. Greatest Spread	33 3/8				
D. Inside Spread of Main Beams	23 3/8	(Credit May Equal But Not Exceed Longer Antler)	23 3/8				
F. Length of Main Beam					24 1/8	23 3/8	6/8
G-1. Length of First Point, If Present					8 1/8	7	1 1/8
G-2. Length of Second Point					7 1/8	8 1/8	1
G-3. Length of Third Point					6 3/8	7 6/8	1 3/8
G-4. Length of Fourth Point, If Present							
G-5. Length of Fifth Point, If Present							
G-6. Length of Sixth Point, If Present							
G-7. Length of Seventh Point, If Present							
H-1. Circumference at Smallest Place Between Burr and First Point					5 1/8	5 1/8	--
H-2. Circumference at Smallest Place Between First and Second Points					4 4/8	4 4/8	--
H-3. Circumference at Smallest Place Between Second and Third Points					7 6/8	6 5/8	1 1/8
H-4. Circumference at Smallest Place Between Third and Fourth Points					3 1/8	3 7/8	6/8
TOTALS				23 3/8	66 2/8	66 3/8	6 1/8

Enter Total of Columns 1, 2, and 3	156	Exact Locality Where Killed:	St. Louis Co., Missouri	
Subtract Column 4	6 1/8	Date Killed: 11/15/81	By Whom Killed:	Picked Up
Subtotal	149 7/8	Present Owner:	Missouri Dept. of Conservation	
Add (E) Total of Lengths of Abnormal Points	184	Guide Name and Address:		
FINAL SCORE	333 7/8	Remarks:		

482

I certify that I have measured the above trophy on ___22 June_____ 19 _83_

at (address) ___Dallas Museum of Natural History___ City ___Dallas___ State ___TX___
and that these measurements and data are, to the best of my knowledge and belief, made in accordance with the
instructions given.

Witness: ___George Tsukamoto___ Signature: ___Glen C. Sanderson___

B&C OFFICIAL MEASURER

INSTRUCTIONS FOR MEASURING NON-TYPICAL WHITETAIL AND COUES' DEER

I.D. Number

All measurements must be made with a 1/4-inch flexible steel tape to the nearest one-eighth of an inch. Wherever
it is necessary to change direction of measurement, mark a control point and swing tape at this point. (Note: a
flexible steel cable can be used to measure points and main beams only.) Enter fractional figures in eighths,
without reduction. Official measurements cannot be taken until antlers have dried for at least 60 days after the
animal was killed.

A. Number of Points on Each Antler: to be counted a point, the projection must be at least one inch long, with
the length exceeding width at one inch or more of length. All points are measured from tip of point to nearest
edge of beam as illustrated. Beam tip is counted as a point but not measured as a point.

B. Tip to Tip Spread is measured between tips of main beams.

C. Greatest Spread is measured between perpendiculars at a right angle to the center line of the skull at widest
part, whether across main beams or points.

D. Inside Spread of Main Beams is measured at a right angle to the center line of the skull at widest point
between main beams. Enter this measurement again as the Spread Credit if it is less than or equal to the length
of longer antler; if longer, enter longer antler length for Spread Credit.

E. Total of Lengths of all Abnormal Points: Abnormal Points are those non-typical in location (such as points
originating from a point or from bottom or sides of main beam) or extra points beyond the normal pattern of
points. Measure in usual manner and enter in appropriate blanks.

F. Length of Main Beam is measured from lowest outside edge of burr over outer curve to the most distant point of
what is, or appears to be, the main beam. The point of beginning is that point on the burr where the center line
along the outer curve of the beam intersects the burr, then following generally the line of the illustration.

G. 1-2-3-4-5-6-7 Length of Normal Points: Normal points project from the top of the main beam. They are
measured from nearest edge of main beam over outer curve to tip. Lay the tape along the outer curve of the beam
so that the top edge of the tape coincides with the top edge of the beam on both sides of the point to determine
the baseline for point measurement. Record point lengths in appropriate blanks.

H. 1-2-3-4 Circumferences are taken as detailed for each measurement. If brow point is missing, take H-1 and
H-2 at smallest place between burr and G-2. If G-4 is missing, take H-4 halfway between G-3 and tip of main
beam.

* * * * * * * * * * * * * * * * * *

FAIR CHASE STATEMENT FOR ALL HUNTER-TAKEN TROPHIES

To make use of the following methods shall be deemed as UNFAIR CHASE and unsportsmanlike, and any trophy obtained
by use of such means is disqualified from entry.

   I. Spotting or herding game from the air, followed by landing in its vicinity for pursuit;

   II. Herding or pursuing game with motor-powered vehicles;

   III. Use of electronic communications for attracting, locating or observing game, or guiding the
      hunter to such game;

   IV. Hunting game confined by artificial barriers, including escape-proof fencing; or hunting game
      transplanted solely for the purpose of commercial shooting.

* * * * * * * * * * * * * * * * * *

I certify that the trophy scored on this chart was not taken in UNFAIR CHASE as defined above by the Boone and
Crockett Club. I further certify that it was taken in full compliance with local game laws of the state,
province, or territory.

Date: _____ Signature of Hunter: _____

(Have signature notarized by a Notary Public)

Records of North American
Big Game

BOONE AND CROCKETT CLUB

P.O. Box 547
Dumfries, VA 22026

Minimum Score:	Awards	All-time	
Alaska-Yukon	210	224	
Canada	185	195	
Wyoming	140	155	

MOOSE

Kind of Moose __Alaska-Yukon__

DETAIL OF POINT MEASUREMENT

SEE OTHER SIDE FOR INSTRUCTIONS	Column 1	Column 2	Column 3	Column 4
A. Greatest Spread	77	Right Antler	Left Antler	Difference
B. Number of Abnormal Points on Both Antlers				
C. Number of Normal Points		18	16	2
D. Width of Palm		20 6/8	15 6/8	5
E. Length of Palm Including Brow Palm		49 5/8	49 6/8	1/8
F. Circumference of Beam at Smallest Place		7 7/8	7 5/8	2/8
TOTALS	77	96 2/8	89 1/8	7 3/8

Enter Total of Columns 1, 2, and 3	262 3/8	Exact Locality Where Killed:	McGrath, Alaska
Subtract Column 4	7 3/8	Date Killed: 9/9/78 By Whom Killed:	Kenneth Best
FINAL SCORE	255	Present Owner:	Kenneth Best
		Guide Name and Address:	
		Remarks:	

I certify that I have measured the above trophy on ___13 March___ 19 80

at (Address) __Missouri Dept. of Conservation__ (City) __Jeff. City__ (State) __MO__

and that these measurements and data are, to the best of my knowledge and belief, made in accordance with the

instructions given.

Witness: ___B. A. Fashingbauer___   Signature: ___Glen C. Sanderson___

B&C OFFICIAL MEASURER

I.D. Number

All measurements must be made with a 1/4-inch flexible steel tape to the nearest one-eighth of an inch. Enter fractional figures in eighths, without reduction. Official measurements cannot be taken until antlers have dried for at least sixty days after animal was killed.

A. Greatest Spread is measured between perpendiculars in a straight line at a right angle to the center line of the skull.

B. Number of Abnormal Points on Both Antlers: Abnormal points are those projections originating from normal points or from the upper or lower palm surface, or from the inner edge of palm (see illustration). Abnormal points must be at least one inch long, with length exceeding width at one inch or more of length.

C. Number of Normal Points: Normal points originate from the outer edge of palm. To be counted a point, a projection must be at least one inch long, with the length exceeding width at one inch or more of length.

D. Width of Palm is taken in contact with the under surface of palm, at a right angle to the length of palm measurement line. The line of measurement should begin and end at the midpoint of the palm edge, which gives credit for the desirable character of palm thickness.

E. Length of Palm Including Brow Palm is taken in contact with the surface along the underside of the palm, parallel to the inner edge, from dips between points at the top to dips between points (if present) at the bottom. If a bay is present, measure across the open bay if the proper line of measurement, parallel to inner edge, follows this path. The line of measurement should begin and end at the midpoint of the palm edge, which gives credit for the desirable character of palm thickness.

F. Circumference of Beam at Smallest Place is taken as illustrated.

* * * * * * * * * * * * * * * * *

FAIR CHASE STATEMENT FOR ALL HUNTER-TAKEN TROPHIES

To make use of the following methods shall be deemed as UNFAIR CHASE and unsportsmanlike, and any trophy obtained by use of such means is disqualified from entry.

   I. Spotting or herding game from the air, followed by landing in its vicinity for pursuit;

  II. Herding or pursuing game with motor-powered vehicles;

 III. Use of electronic communications for attracting, locating or observing game, or guiding the hunter to such game;

  IV. Hunting game confined by artificial barriers, including escape-proof fencing; or hunting game transplanted solely for the purpose of commercial shooting.

* * * * * * * * * * * * * * * * *

I certify that the trophy scored on this chart was not taken in UNFAIR CHASE as defined above by the Boone and Crockett Club. I further certify that it was taken in full compliance with local game laws of the state, province, or territory.

Date: _____ Signature of Hunter: _____

(Have Signature Notarized by a Notary Public)

Records of North American
Big Game

BOONE AND CROCKETT CLUB

P.Q. Box 547
Dumfries, VA 22026

Minimum Score:	Awards	All-time
barren ground	375	400
mountain	360	390
Quebec-Labrador	365	375
woodland	265	295
Central Canada barren ground	330	345

CARIBOU

Kind of Caribou __mountain__

DETAIL OF POINT MEASUREMENT

SEE OTHER SIDE FOR INSTRUCTIONS			Column 1	Column 2	Column 3	Column 4
A. Tip to Tip Spread	27 1/8		Spread Credit	Right Antler	Left Antler	Difference
B. Greatest Spread	33 3/8					
C. Inside Spread of Main Beams	30 3/8	(Credit May Equal But Not Exceed Longer Antler)	30 3/8			
D. Number of Points on Each Antler Excluding Brows				18	15	3
Number of Points on Each Brow				4	4	
E. Length of Main Beam				43 1/8	42 2/8	7/8
F-1. Length of Brow Palm or First Point				16 4/8	16 1/8	
F-2. Length of Bez or Second Point				20 4/8	20 5/8	1/8
F-3. Length of Rear Point, If Present				6 4/8	8	1 4/8
F-4. Length of Second Longest Top Point				22	23 2/8	1 2/8
F-5. Length of Longest Top Point				22 5/8	23 4/8	7/8
G-1. Width of Brow Palm				11 2/8	5	
G-2. Width of Top Palm				16 4/8	15 6/8	6/8
H-1. Circumference at Smallest Place Between Brow and Bez Points				7 3/8	7 5/8	2/8
H-2. Circumference at Smallest Place Between Bez and Rear Point, If Present				6 6/8	6 4/8	2/8
H-3. Circumference at Smallest Place Before First Top Point				6 1/8	6 1/8	--
H-4. Circumference at Smallest Place Between Two Longest Top Palm Points				17 6/8	26 4/8	8 6/8
TOTALS			30 3/8	219	220 2/8	17 5/8

Enter Total of Columns 1, 2, and 3	469 5/8	Exact Locality Where Killed:	Turnagain River, B.C.
Subtract Column 4	17 5/8	Date Killed: 9/15/76	By Whom Killed: Gary Beaubien
FINAL SCORE	452	Present Owner:	Gary Beaubien
		Guide Name and Address:	
		Remarks:	

486

I certify that I have measured the above trophy on _____7 June_____ 19 77 _____

at (address) __6060 Broadway_____ City __Denver_____ State __CO_____
and that these measurements and data are, to the best of my knowledge and belief, made in accordance with the
instructions given.

Witness: __John G. Stelfox_____ Signature _____Frank Cook_____

<table>
<tr><td>B&C OFFICIAL MEASURER</td><td></td><td></td><td></td><td></td></tr>
</table>

I.D. Number

INSTRUCTIONS FOR MEASURING CARIBOU

All measurements must be made with a 1/4-inch flexible steel tape to the nearest one-eighth of an inch. Wherever
it is necessary to change direction of measurement, mark a control point and swing tape at this point. (Note: a
flexible steel cable can be used to measure points and main beams only.) Enter fractional figures in eighths,
without reduction. Official measurements cannot be taken until antlers have dried for at least 60 days after the
animal was killed.

A. Tip to Tip Spread is measured between tips of main beams.
B. Greatest Spread is measured between perpendiculars at a right angle to the center line of the skull at widest
part, whether across main beams or points.
C. Inside Spread of Main Beams is measured at a right angle to the center line of the skull at widest point
between main beams. Enter this measurement again as Spread Credit if it is less than or equal to the length of
longer antler; if longer, enter longer antler length for Spread Credit.
D. Number of Points on Each Antler: To be counted a point, a projection must be at least one-half inch long,
with length exceeding width at the point of measurement. Beam tip is counted as a point but not measured as a
point. There are no "abnormal" points in caribou.
E. Length of Main Beam is measured from lowest outside edge of burr over outer curve to the most distant point of
what is, or appears to be, the main beam. The point of beginning is that point on the burr where the center line
along the outer curve of the beam intersects the burr.
F. 1-2-3 Length of Points are measured from nearest edge of beam on the shortest line over outer curve to tip.
Lay the tape along the outer curve of the beam so that the top edge of the tape coincides with the top edge of
the beam on both sides of point to determine the baseline for point measurement. Record point lengths in
appropriate blanks.
F. 4-5 Length of Points are measured from the tip of the point to the top of the beam, then at a right angle to
the lower edge of beam. The Second Longest Top Point cannot be a point branch of the Longest Top Point.
G-1 Width of Brow is measured in a straight line from top edge to lower edge, as illustrated, with measurement
line at a right angle to main axis of brow.
G-2 Width of Top Palm is measured from midpoint of lower rear edge of main beam to midpoint of a dip between
points, at widest part of palm. The line of measurement begins and ends at midpoints of palm edges, which gives
credit for palm thickness.
H. 1-2-3-4 Circumferences are taken as described for measurements. If brow point is missing, take H-1 at
smallest point between burr and bez point. If rear point is missing, take H-2 and H-3 measurements at smallest
place between bez and first top point. Do not depress the tape into any dips of the palm or main beam.

* * * * * * * * * * * * * * * * *

FAIR CHASE STATEMENT FOR ALL HUNTER-TAKEN TROPHIES

To make use of the following methods shall be deemed as UNFAIR CHASE and unsportsmanlike, and any trophy
obtained by use of such means is disqualified from entry.

   I. Spotting or herding game from the air, followed by landing in its vicinity for pursuit;

  II. Herding or pursuing game with motor-powered vehicles;

 III. Use of electronic communications for attracting, locating or observing game, or guiding the
      hunter to such game;

 IV. Hunting game confined by artificial barriers, including escape-proof fencing; or hunting game
      transplanted solely for the purpose of commercial shooting.

* * * * * * * * * * * * * * * * *

I certify that the trophy scored on this chart was not taken in UNFAIR CHASE as defined above by the Boone
and Crockett Club. I further certify that it was taken in full compliance with local game laws of the
state, province, or territory.

Date _____ Signature of Hunter _____

(Have signature notarized by a Notary Public)

Records of North American
Big Game

BOONE AND CROCKETT CLUB

P.O. Box 547
Dumfries, VA 22026

Minimum Score: Awards All-time
80   82

PRONGHORN

SEE OTHER SIDE FOR INSTRUCTIONS		Column 1	Column 2	Column 3
A. Tip to Tip Spread	8 1/8	Right Horn	Left Horn	Difference
B. Inside Spread of Main Beams	12 5/8			
IF Inside Spread Exceeds Longer Horn, Enter Difference				
C. Length of Horn		17 6/8	17 4/8	2/8
D-1. Circumference of Base		6 7/8	7	1/8
D-2. Circumference at First Quarter		6 7/8	7 2/8	3/8
D-3. Circumference at Second Quarter		4 3/8	4 4/8	1/8
D-4. Circumference at Third Quarter		3 1/8	3 2/8	1/8
E. Length of Prong		8	8 2/8	2/8
TOTALS		47	47 6/8	1 2/8

Enter Total of Columns 1 and 2	94 6/8	Exact Locality Where Killed:	Coconino Co., Arizona
Subtract Column 3	1 2/8	Date Killed: 9/20/85 By Whom Killed:	Michael J. O'Haco, Jr.
FINAL SCORE	93 4/8	Present Owner:	Michael J. O'Haco, Jr.
		Guide Name and Address:	
		Remarks:	

I certify that I have measured the above trophy on ___13 May___ 19 86

at (Address) ___Nevada State Museum___ (City) ___Las Vegas___ (State) ___NV___

and that these measurements and data are, to the best of my knowledge and belief, made in accordance with the

Instructions given.

Witness: ___George Tsukamoto___ Signature: ___Walter H. White___

B&C OFFICIAL MEASURER

I.D. Number

488

INSTRUCTIONS FOR MEASURING PRONGHORN

All measurements must be made with a 1/4-inch, flexible steel tape to the nearest one-eighth of an inch. Wherever it is necessary to change direction of measurement, mark a control point and swing tape at this point. Enter fractional figures in eighths, without reduction. Official measurement cannot be taken until horns have dried for at least sixty days after the animal was killed.

A. Tip to Tip Spread is measured between tips of horns.

B. Inside Spread of Main Beams is measured at a right angle to the center line of the skull, at widest point between main beams.

C. Length of Horn is measured on the outside curve on the general line illustrated. The line taken will vary with different heads, depending on the direction of their curvature. Measure along the center of the outer curve from tip of horn to a point in line with the lowest edge of the base, using a straight edge to establish the line end.

D-1 Measure around base of horn at a right angle to long axis. Tape must be in contact with the lowest circumference of the horn in which there are no serrations.

D. 2-3-4 Divide measurement C of longer horn by four. Starting at base, mark both horns at these quarters (even though the other horn is shorter) and measure circumferences at these marks. If the prong interferes with D-2, move the measurement down to just below the swelling of the prong. If the prong interferes with D-3, move the measurement up to just above the swelling of the prong.

E. Length of Prong: Measure from the tip of the prong along the upper edge of the outer curve to the horn; then continue around the horn to a point at the rear of the horn where a straight edge across the back of both horns touches the horn, with the latter part being at a right angle to the long axis of horn.

* * * * * * * * * * * * * * * * *

FAIR CHASE STATEMENT FOR ALL HUNTER-TAKEN TROPHIES

To make use of the following methods shall be deemed as UNFAIR CHASE and unsportsmanlike, and any trophy obtained by use of such means is disqualified from entry.

   I. Spotting or herding game from the air, followed by landing in its vicinity for pursuit;

  II. Herding or pursuing game with motor-powered vehicles;

 III. Use of electronic communications for attracting, locating or observing game, or guiding the hunter to such game;

  IV. Hunting game confined by artificial barriers, including escape-proof fencing; or hunting game transplanted solely for the purpose of commercial shooting.

* * * * * * * * * * * * * * * * *

I certify that the trophy scored on this chart was not taken in UNFAIR CHASE as defined above by the Boone and Crockett Club. I further certify that it was taken in full compliance with local game laws of the state, province, or territory.

Date: _____   Signature of Hunter: _____

(Have Signature Notarized by a Notary Public)

Records of North American Big Game	BOONE AND CROCKETT CLUB	P.Q. Box 547 Dumfries, VA 22026

Minimum Score: Awards All-time
           115   115

BISON

Sex ___male___

SEE OTHER SIDE FOR INSTRUCTIONS		Column 1	Column 2	Column 3
A. Greatest Spread	35 3/8	Right Horn	Left Horn	Difference
B. Tip to Tip Spread	27			
C. Length of Horn		21 2/8	23 2/8	2
D-1. Circumference of Base		16	15	1
D-2. Circumference at First Quarter		13 4/8	13	4/8
D-3. Circumference at Second Quarter		11 4/8	11	4/8
D-4. Circumference at Third Quarter		8 2/8	8	2/8
TOTALS		70 4/8	70 2/8	4 2/8

Enter Total of Columns 1 and 2	140 6/8	Exact Locality Where Killed:	Yellowstone Natl. Park, Wyoming
Subtract Column 3	4 2/8	Date Killed: 1925 By Whom Killed:	S. Woodring
FINAL SCORE	136 4/8	Present Owner:	Fishing Bridge Museum
		Guide Name and Address:	
		Remarks:	

I certify that I have measured the above trophy on ___24 September___ 19 _51_

at (Address) ___Yellowstone National Park___ (City) _____ (State) _WY_

and that these measurements and data are, to the best of my knowledge and belief, made in accordance with the

instructions given.

Witness: _____ Signature: ___Grancel Fitz___

                                    B&C OFFICIAL MEASURER

                                     I.D. Number

All measurements must be made with a 1/4-inch, flexible steel tape to the nearest one-eighth of an inch. Wherever it is necessary to change direction of measurement, mark a control point and swing tape at this point. Enter fractional figures in eighths, without reduction. Official measurement cannot be taken until horns have dried for at least sixty days after the animal was killed.

A. Greatest Spread is measured between perpendiculars at a right angle to the center line of the skull.

B. Tip to Tip Spread is measured between tips of horns.

C. Length of Horn is measured from the lowest point on underside over outer curve to a point in line with tip. Use a straight edge, perpendicular to horn axis, to end the measurement, if necessary.

D-1 Circumference of Base is measured at a right angle to axis of horn. Do not follow the irregular edge of horn; the line of measurement must be entirely on horn material, not the jagged edge often noted.

D. 2-3-4 Divide measurement C of longer horn by four. Starting at base, mark both horns at these quarters (even though the other horn is shorter) and measure circumferences at these marks, with measurements taken at right angles to horn axis.

* * * * * * * * * * * * * * * *

FAIR CHASE STATEMENT FOR ALL HUNTER-TAKEN TROPHIES

To make use of the following methods shall be deemed as UNFAIR CHASE and unsportsmanlike, and any trophy obtained by use of such means is disqualified from entry.

    I. Spotting or herding game from the air, followed by landing in its vicinity for pursuit;

    II. Herding or pursuing game with motor-powered vehicles;

    III. Use of electronic communications for attracting, locating or observing game, or guiding the hunter to such game;

    IV. Hunting game confined by artificial barriers, including escape-proof fencing; or hunting game transplanted solely for the purpose of commercial shooting.

* * * * * * * * * * * * * * * *

I certify that the trophy scored on this chart was not taken in UNFAIR CHASE as defined above by the Boone and Crockett Club. I further certify that it was taken in full compliance with local game laws of the state, province, or territory.

Date: _____ Signature of Hunter: _____

(Have Signature Notarized by a Notary Public)

Records of North American
Big Game

BOONE AND CROCKETT CLUB

P.O. Box 547
Dumfries, VA 22026

Minimum Score: Awards All-time
47   50

ROCKY MOUNTAIN GOAT

Sex ___male___

SEE OTHER SIDE FOR INSTRUCTIONS		Column 1	Column 2	Column 3
A. Greatest Spread	9 2/8	Right Horn	Left Horn	Difference
B. Tip to Tip Spread	9			
C. Length of Horn		12	12	--
D-1. Circumference of Base		6 4/8	6 4/8	--
D-2. Circumference at First Quarter		4 7/8	4 6/8	1/8
D-3. Circumference at Second Quarter		3 2/8	3 1/8	1/8
D-4. Circumference at Third Quarter		2	2	--
TOTALS		28 5/8	28 5/8	2/8

Enter Total of Columns 1 and 2	57	Exact Locality Where Killed:	Babine Mountains, B.C.
Subtract Column 3	2/8	Date Killed: 1949 By Whom Killed:	E. C. Haase
FINAL SCORE	56 6/8	Present Owner:	B & C National Collection
		Guide Name and Address:	Allen Fletchers
		Remarks:	

I certify that I have measured the above trophy on ___28 January___ 19 50 ___

at (Address) __American Museum of Natural History__ (City) __New York__ (State) NY

and that these measurements and data are, to the best of my knowledge and belief, made in accordance with the instructions given.

Witness: ___Samuel B. Webb___   Signature: ___Grancel Fitz___

B&C OFFICIAL MEASURER

I.D. Number

INSTRUCTIONS FOR MEASURING ROCKY MOUNTAIN GOAT

All measurements must be made with a 1/4-inch, flexible steel tape to the nearest one-eighth of an inch. Wherever it is necessary to change direction of measurement, mark a control point and swing tape at this point. Enter fractional figures in eighths, without reduction. Official measurement cannot be taken until horns have dried for at least sixty days after the animal was killed.

A. Greatest Spread is measured between perpendiculars at a right angle to the center line of the skull.

B. Tip to Tip Spread is measured between tips of horns.

C. Length of Horn is measured from the lowest point in front over outer curve to a point in line with tip.

D-1 Circumference of Base is measured at a right angle to axis of horn. Do not follow irregular edge of horn.

D. 2-3-4 Divide measurement C of longer horn by four. Starting at base, mark both horns at these quarters (even though the other horn is shorter) and measure circumferences at these marks.

* * * * * * * * * * * * * * * * *

FAIR CHASE STATEMENT FOR ALL HUNTER-TAKEN TROPHIES

To make use of the following methods shall be deemed as UNFAIR CHASE and unsportsmanlike, and any trophy obtained by use of such means is disqualified from entry.

   I. Spotting or herding game from the air, followed by landing in its vicinity for pursuit;

   II. Herding or pursuing game with motor-powered vehicles;

   III. Use of electronic communications for attracting, locating or observing game, or guiding the hunter to such game;

   IV. Hunting game confined by artificial barriers, including escape-proof fencing; or hunting game transplanted solely for the purpose of commercial shooting.

* * * * * * * * * * * * * * * * *

I certify that the trophy scored on this chart was not taken in UNFAIR CHASE as defined above by the Boone and Crockett Club. I further certify that it was taken in full compliance with local game laws of the state, province, or territory.

Date: _____ Signature of Hunter: _____

(Have Signature Notarized by a Notary Public)

Records of North American
Big Game

P.O. Box 547
Dumfries, VA 22026

BOONE AND CROCKETT CLUB

Minimum Score: Awards All-time
105   105

MUSKOX

Sex male

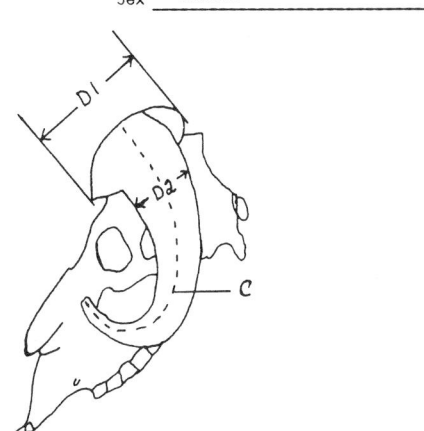

SEE OTHER SIDE FOR INSTRUCTIONS		Column 1	Column 2	Column 3
A. Greatest Spread	30 5/8	Right Horn	Left Horn	Difference
B. Tip to Tip Spread	30 3/8			
C. Length of Horn		29	28 1/8	7/8
D-1. Width of Boss		10	9 7/8	1/8
D-2. Width at First Quarter		7	6 3/8	5/8
D-3. Circumference at Second Quarter		12 1/8	10 6/8	1 3/8
D-4. Circumference at Third Quarter		6 5/8	5 7/8	6/8
TOTALS		64 6/8	61	3 6/8

Enter Total of Columns 1 and 2	125 6/8	Exact Locality Where Killed:	Perry River, N.W.T., Canada
Subtract Column 3	3 6/8	Date Killed: 1979	By Whom Killed: Picked Up
FINAL SCORE	122	Present Owner:	Robert J. Decker
		Guide Name and Address:	
		Remarks:	

I certify that I have measured the above trophy on __12 March__ 19 80

at (Address) __Missouri Dept. of Conservation__ (City) __Jeff. City__ (State) __MO__

and that these measurements and data are, to the best of my knowledge and belief, made in accordance with the

instructions given.

Witness: __Philip L. Wright__   Signature: __Frank Cook__

B&C OFFICIAL MEASURER

I.D. Number

494

INSTRUCTIONS FOR MEASURING MUSKOX

All measurements must be made with a 1/4-inch, flexible steel tape and adjustable calipers to the nearest one-eighth of an inch. Wherever it is necessary to change direction of measurement, mark a control point and swing tape at this point. Enter fractional figures in eighths, without reduction. Official measurement cannot be taken until horns have dried for at least sixty days after the animal was killed.

A. Greatest Spread is measured between perpendiculars at a right angle to the center line of the skull.

B. Tip to Tip Spread is measured between tips of horns by using large calipers, which are then read against a yardstick.

C. Length of Horn is measured along center of upper horn surface, staying within curve of horn as illustrated, to a point in line with tip. Attempt to free the connective tissue between the horns at the center of the boss to determine the lowest point of horn material on each side, near the top center of the skull. Hook the tape under the lowest point of the horn and measure the length of horn, with the measurement line maintained in the center of the upper surface of horn following the converging lines to the horn tip.

D-1 Width of Boss is measured with calipers at greatest width of base, with measurement line forming a right angle with horn axis. It is often helpful to measure D-1 before C, marking the midpoint of the boss as the correct path of C.

D. 2-3-4 Divide measurement C of longer horn by four. Starting at base, mark both horns at these quarters (even though the other horn is shorter). Then, using calipers, measure width of boss at D-2, making sure the measurement is at a right angle to horn axis and in line with the D-2 mark. Circumferences are then measured at D-3 and D-4, with measurements being taken at right angles to horn axis.

* * * * * * * * * * * * * * * * *

FAIR CHASE STATEMENT FOR ALL HUNTER-TAKEN TROPHIES

To make use of the following methods shall be deemed as UNFAIR CHASE and unsportsmanlike, and any trophy obtained by use of such means is disqualified from entry.

I. Spotting or herding game from the air, followed by landing in its vicinity for pursuit;

II. Herding or pursuing game with motor-powered vehicles;

III. Use of electronic communications for attracting, locating or observing game, or guiding the hunter to such game;

IV. Hunting game confined by artificial barriers, including escape-proof fencing; or hunting game transplanted solely for the purpose of commercial shooting.

* * * * * * * * * * * * * * * * *

I certify that the trophy scored on this chart was not taken in UNFAIR CHASE as defined above by the Boone and Crockett Club. I further certify that it was taken in full compliance with local game laws of the state, province, or territory.

Date: _____ Signature of Hunter: _____

(Have Signature Notarized by a Notary Public)

Records of North American
Big Game

BOONE AND CROCKETT CLUB

P.O. Box 547
Dumfries, VA 22026

Minimum Score:	Awards	All-time		Kind of Sheep	Stone's
bighorn	175	180	SHEEP		
desert	165	168			
Dall's	165	170			
Stone's	165	170			

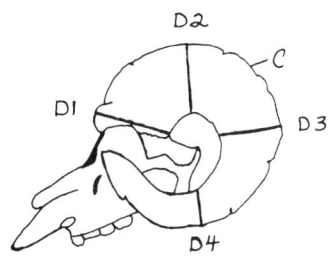

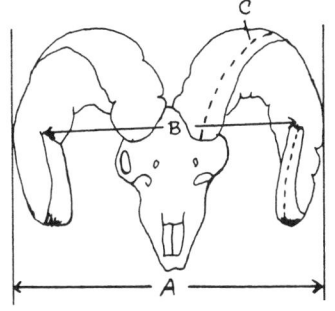

MEASURE TO
A POINT IN
LINE WITH
HORN TIP

SEE OTHER SIDE FOR INSTRUCTIONS		Column 1	Column 2	Column 3
A. Greatest Spread (Is Often Tip to Tip Spread)	31	Right Horn	Left Horn	Difference
B. Tip to Tip Spread	31			
C. Length of Horn		50 1/8	51 5/8	
D-1. Circumference of Base		14 6/8	14 6/8	--
D-2. Circumference at First Quarter		14 1/8	14 2/8	1/8
D-3. Circumference at Second Quarter		11 7/8	12 1/8	2/8
D-4. Circumference at Third Quarter		6 6/8	7	2/8
TOTALS		97 5/8	99 6/8	5/8

Enter Total of Columns 1 and 2	197 3/8	Exact Locality Where Killed:	Muskwa River, B.C.	
Subtract Column 3	5/8	Date Killed: 1936	By Whom Killed:	L. S. Chadwick
FINAL SCORE	196 6/8	Present Owner:	B & C National Collection	
		Guide Name and Address:		
		Remarks:		

I certify that I have measured the above trophy on _____ 10 April _____ 19 51

at (Address) __American Museum of Natural History__ (City) __New York__ (State) __NY__

and that these measurements and data are, to the best of my knowledge and belief, made in accordance with the

Instructions given.

Witness: __Samuel B. Webb__   Signature: __Grancel Fitz__

B&C OFFICIAL MEASURER

I.D. Number

<u>INSTRUCTIONS FOR MEASURING SHEEP</u>

All measurements must be made with a 1/4-inch, flexible steel tape to the nearest one-eighth of an inch. Wherever it is necessary to change direction of measurement, mark a control point and swing tape at this point. Enter fractional figures in <u>eighths</u>, without reduction. Official measurement cannot be taken until horns have dried for at least sixty days after the animal was killed.

A. Greatest Spread is measured between perpendiculars at a right angle to the center line of the skull.

B. Tip to Tip Spread is measured between tips of horns.

C. Length of Horn is measured from the lowest point in front on outer curve to a point in line with tip. <u>Do not</u> press tape into depressions. The low point of the outer curve of the horn is considered to be the low point of the frontal portion of the horn, situated above and slightly medial to the eye socket (not the outside edge). Use a straight edge, perpendicular to horn axis, to end measurement on "broomed" horns.

D-1 Circumference of Base is measured at a right angle to axis of horn. <u>Do not</u> follow irregular edge of horn; the line of measurement must be entirely on horn material, not the jagged edge often noted.

D. 2-3-4 Divide measurement C of longer horn by four. Starting at base, mark <u>both</u> horns at these quarters (even though the other horn is shorter) and measure circumferences at these marks, with measurements taken at right angles to horn axis.

* * * * * * * * * * * * * * * * * *

FAIR CHASE STATEMENT FOR ALL HUNTER-TAKEN TROPHIES

To make use of the following methods shall be deemed as UNFAIR CHASE and unsportsmanlike, and any trophy obtained by use of such means is disqualified from entry.

I. Spotting or herding game from the air, followed by landing in its vicinity for pursuit;

II. Herding or pursuing game with motor-powered vehicles;

III. Use of electronic communications for attracting, locating or observing game, or guiding the hunter to such game;

IV. Hunting game confined by artificial barriers, including escape-proof fencing; or hunting game transplanted solely for the purpose of commercial shooting.

* * * * * * * * * * * * * * * * * *

I certify that the trophy scored on this chart was not taken in UNFAIR CHASE as defined above by the Boone and Crockett Club. I further certify that it was taken in full compliance with local game laws of the state, province, or territory.

Date: _____ Signature of Hunter: _____

(Have Signature Notarized by a Notary Public)

This book was:

Compiled with able assistance of:

Lise Boorse Capobianco
Carol D. Eads
Carol A. Palmerino

Book design and layout by: Wm. H. Nesbitt

Typeset by: Graphic Composition, Inc.
Athens, GA

Printed and bound by: Arcadia Graphics/Hawkins
Church Hill, TN